D1368033

America's Best Bed & Breakfasts

Delightful Places to Stay

Great Things to Do When You Get There

3rd Edition

FODOR'S TRAVEL PUBLICATIONS, INC.

NEW YORK • TORONTO • LONDON • SYDNEY • AUCKLAND

AMERICA'S BEST BED & BREAKFASTS

Editor: Caroline Haberfeld

Editorial Production: Stacey Kulig

Creative Director: Fabrizio La Rocca

Design: Guido Caroti

Production/Manufacturing: Mike Costa

Cover Photograph: Chris Mead

Third Edition

ISBN 0–679–00181–6

SPECIAL SALES

Fodor's Travel Publications are available at special discounts for bulk purchases for sales promotions or premiums. Special editions, including personalized covers, excerpts of existing guides, and corporate imprints, can be created in large quantities for special needs. For more information contact your local bookseller or write to Special Markets, Fodor's Travel Publications, 201 East 50th Street, New York, NY 10022. Inquiries from Canada should be directed to your local Canadian bookseller or sent to Random House of Canada, Ltd., Marketing Department, 1265 Aerowood Drive, Mississauga, Ontario L4W 1B9. Inquiries from the United Kingdom should be sent to Fodor's Travel Publications, 20 Vauxhall Bridge Road, London, England SW1V 2SA.

PRINTED IN THE UNITED STATES OF AMERICA

10 9 8 7 6 5 4 3 2 1

CONTENTS

FOREWORD

Although every care has been taken to ensure the accuracy of the information in this guide, the passage of time will always bring change, and consequently, the publisher cannot accept responsibility for errors that may occur.

All prices and listings are based on information supplied to us at press time. Details may change, however, and the prudent traveler will avoid inconvenience by calling ahead.

Fodor's wants to hear about your travel experiences, both pleasant and unpleasant. When an inn or B&B fails to live up to its billing, let us know and we will investigate the complaint and revise our entries where the facts warrant it.

Send us your thoughts via e-mail at editors@fodors.com (specifying the name of the book on the subject line) or on paper in care of the America's Best B&Bs editor at Fodor's Travel Publications, 201 East 50th Street, New York, NY 10022.

INTRODUCTION

You'll find bed-and-breakfasts in big houses with turrets and little houses with decks, in mansions by the water and cabins in the forest, not to mention structures of many sizes and shapes in between. B&Bs are run by people who were once lawyers and writers, homemakers and artists, nurses and architects, singers and businesspeople. Some B&Bs are just a room or two in a hospitable local's home; others are more like small inns. So there's an element of serendipity to every stay in an inn or B&B. But although that's part of the pleasure of visiting these establishments, it's also an excellent reason to plan your travels with a good B&B guide. The one you hold in your hands serves the purpose neatly. We think it's the best of its kind.

To create this guide, we've handpicked a team of professional writers who are confirmed B&B lovers: people who love the many manifestations of the Victorian era; who go wild over wicker and brass beds, four-posters and fireplaces; and who know a well-run operation when they see it and are only too eager to communicate their knowledge to you. We've instructed them to inspect the premises and check out every corner of the premier inns and B&Bs in the areas they cover and to report critically on only the best. They've returned from their travels with comprehensive reports on the very best B&Bs—establishments that promise c unique experience, a distinctive sense of time and place. All are destinations in themselves: not just places to put your head at night, but an integral part of a weekend escape. In our writers' evaluations you'll learn what's good, what's bad, and what could be better; what they liked and what you might not like. We also include names and addresses of B&B reservations services, just in case you're inspired to search out additional properties on your own.

Reviews are organized by state and then by region. At the beginning of every review is the address and telephone, with a mailing address in parentheses if there is one. A double room is for two people, regardless of the size or type of beds it contains. Unless otherwise noted, rooms don't have phones or TVs. Note that even the most stunning homes, farmhouses and mansions alike, may not provide a private bathroom for each individual. We list the number of rooms in the establishment that do have them en suite. Rates are for two, excluding tax, in high season, and include breakfast unless otherwise noted.

What we call a restaurant serves meals other than breakfast and is usually open to the general public. At inns listed as operating on the Modified American Plan (MAP), rates include two meals, generally breakfast and dinner.

The following credit card abbreviations are used throughout this guide: AE, American Express; DC, Diner's Club; D, Discover; MC, MasterCard; V, Visa.

Although we abhor discrimination, we have conveyed information about innkeepers' restrictive practices so that you will be aware of the prevailing attitudes. Such discriminatory practices are most often applied to small children, traveling with their parents, who may not, in any case, feel comfortable having their offspring toddling amid breakable bric-a-brac and near precipitous stairways.

OUR BEST TIP

When traveling the B&B way, always call ahead. If you have mobility problems or are traveling with children or pets, if you prefer a private bath or a certain type of bed, or if you have specific dietary needs or any other concerns, discuss them with the innkeeper. If you're traveling to an inn because of a specific feature, make sure that it will be available when you get there and not closed for renovation. The same is true if you're making a special detour to take advantage of specific sights or attractions.

A POINT OF PRIDE

It's a sad commentary on other B&B guides today that we feel obliged to tell you that it is our writers, not the innkeepers, who wrote the reviews. No one paid a fee or promised to sell or promote the book in order to be included in it. (In fact, one of the most challenging parts of our writers' work is persuading the innkeepers and B&B owners that they need provide nothing more than a tour of the premises and the answers to a few questions!) Fodor's has no stake in anything but the truth.

So trust us the way you'd trust a knowledgeable, well-traveled friend. Let us hear from you about your travels, whether you found that the B&Bs you visited surpassed their descriptions or the other way around. And have a wonderful trip!

Karen Cure
Editorial Director

ALABAMA

North Alabama

LODGE ON GORHAM'S BLUFF 🕊
101 Gorham Dr. (Box 160), Pisgah 35765, tel. 256/451–3435, fax 256/451–7403

In the early 1990s, the McGriff family began to develop their land, 3 mi north of Pisgah, into a new town that will eventually have scores of homes, shops, an artists' workshop district, meetinghouse, town green, and post office. This new town, or neighborhood, is being built with a nod to tradition: Sidewalks and front porches, for instance, are common. The Lodge on Gorham's Bluff is the crown jewel of the endeavor.

The three-story, clapboard lodge has upstairs and downstairs porches across the front. It is strategically built with a view of the Tennessee River and passing barges. The McGriffs, with deep roots in nearby Sand Mountain, where Bill is a CPA and Clara is a former schoolteacher, have outfitted their lodge with thick robes, smooth cotton sheets, down-filled pillows and comforters, bath salts, and whirlpool tubs. Soft music plays throughout common areas and in bedrooms; guests have volume controls at bedside.

Third-floor rooms, ideal for honeymooners, have whirlpool tubs for two and fireplaces that open both into the bedroom and bath. Second-floor rooms have one-person jetted tubs, and balconies with rocking chairs and abundant planters. The glass-enclosed tower with a widow's walk is a good place to savor the view.

In the first-floor living area, guests have access to a VCR, a collection of videotapes, abundant books, and a small kitchen stocked with snacks and cold drinks. A 20-seat restaurant at the lodge serves Sunday lunch and candlelight dinner nightly. Reservations are required; lodge guests have priority.

The Overlook Pavilion is a good place to watch the river and spot soaring eagles. This new Appalachian town is a welcome respite from the bustle of big-city living. ♠ *6 double rooms with baths. Restaurant, air-conditioning, phone, whirlpool tub, robes, and fireplace in rooms, VCR in common area, fishing, kite flying, hiking. $110–$165; full breakfast, snack-filled kitchen. AE, MC, V. Some age restrictions for children.*

WOOD AVENUE INN 🕊
658 Northwood Ave., Florence 35630, tel. 256/766–8441

Square and octagonal towers rise high above the garden of this three-story Queen Anne house. On a tree-lined street in a college town, this inn, built in 1889, is pure Victorian, with 14-ft ceilings, nooks, crannies, and bay windows.

Owners Alvern and Gene Greeley have both worked in various fields, he as a clergyman turned auto-parts salesman, she as the dean of a Bible college and then as a real estate agent. With her radiant smile and enveloping warmth, Alvern makes innkeeping an art form. Since she likes to pamper people, she is doing what comes naturally in running a bed-and-breakfast and delights in making home-cooked delicacies. Her zucchini bread is unsurpassed.

The house has an inviting porch with green wicker furniture and begonias in flower boxes. The formal parlor opens off the wide central hall, which bisects the two lower floors. One drawing room has dark-green walls with gleaming white wood-work, a 150-year-old red velvet sofa, and a cabinet in a corner. Its rosewood shelves have held china for more than a century. But it's the bric-a-brac that sets the tone. Arranged among and around the furniture are enough figurines, artificial flowers, bows, wreaths, footstools, and ruffled cushions to stock a theatrical warehouse. Five minutes in that room and you know exactly how the well-to-do characters in a Dickens novel live.

Fireplaces are in every room, even the bathrooms, two of which have narrow claw-foot tubs. Beside the tub a table holds a bottle of sparkling cider and two sil-ver-wrapped chocolates. After a good soak, you climb into a huge bed, its pale rose-colored spread topped by matching pillows against the 19th-century-look wallpaper.

Outside the back door, wisteria climbs over an arbor, and a black carriage hand-made by the Amish stands under a protective roof. △ *6 double rooms and 2 singles with baths, 2 suites. Air-conditioning in rooms, cable TV in lounge; bad-minton, horseshoes. $62–$95; full breakfast. MC, V. No smoking.*

OTHER CHOICES

Capps Cove. 4126 County Hwy. 27, Oneonta 35121, tel. and fax 205/625–3039 or tel. 800/583–4750. 2 double rooms with baths, 2 cabins with baths. Air-conditioning; fireplace, refrigerator, and microwave in cabins; hiking trails, free home tour. $80–$150; full breakfast, soft drinks and snacks. MC, V. No smok-ing.

Mentone Inn. Rte. 117 (Box 290), Mentone 35984, tel. 256/634–4836 or 800/455–7470. 12 double rooms with baths. Air-conditioning, cable TV in living room. $70; full breakfast, afternoon refreshments. AE, MC, V. No smoking.

Raven Haven. 651 County Rd. 644, Mentone 35984, tel. and fax 256/634–4310. 4 double rooms with baths. TV in common area, VCR in library, fax. $70–$90; full breakfast, snacks. No credit cards. No smoking, children over 14 only, 2-night minimum Apr.–Oct.

Winston Place: An Antebellum Mansion. 353 Railroad St. (Box 165), Val-ley Head 35989, tel. 256/635–6381 or 888/494–6786. 3 double rooms with baths, 1 suite. Air-conditioning, cable TV, kitchen, free home tour. $125–$150; full breakfast. MC, V. No smoking.

Central Alabama

GRACE HALL ☜
506 Lauderdale St., Selma 36701, tel. 334/875–5744, fax 334/875–9967

Grace Hall, built in 1857, also is known as the Ware-Baker-Jones House, after the three families who lived here for more than 110 years. The mansion became run-down apartments and then a grungy boardinghouse but today is resplendent again, with many original antiques. The owners are Coy and Joey Dillon, he a former steel executive, she a semi-retired interior designer. Since the age of 16, when Joey bought her first antique (an oval mirror for $10), she has been interested in old buildings. She jumped at the chance to buy and restore Grace Hall. The Dillons drifted into B&B management when the mayor of Selma asked them to house a visiting dignitary.

The house, a certified restoration of an antebellum home, is stunning, with double parlors, a pressed-tin ceiling in the study, red stained glass, Romantic-period portraits in the hallway, heart-pine floors, and windows 10 ft tall. The dining room has its original mahogany pedestal table, seating 12, and a smaller room behind used for guests' three-course breakfast. Solid brass chandeliers light the house; on the south porch overlooking the manicured garden and its huge live oak is original wicker furniture.

The large bedrooms in the main house have marble fireplaces. Other features include oak desks, Oriental rugs, hand-painted enamel clocks, and antique, step-up carved rosewood beds. Wallpapers are copies of 19th-century designs; in one bedroom, the Brighton pattern fits perfectly with a four-poster bed flanked by brother-and-sister walnut chests. TV sets are concealed in cabinets. Leading off the back is a latticed, galleried wing, whose porches, facing the garden, provide open-air sitting space for three more smaller, but just as charming, bedrooms. Fitting the southern surroundings, an overhead fan turns lazily above a large bowl holding branches full of cotton bolls. The Dillons occasionally give tours to bus groups on weekdays during the day. ♿ *6 double rooms with baths. Air-conditioning, cable TV and phone in rooms, free home tour. $69–$99; full breakfast, evening refreshments. AE, D, MC, V. No smoking, pets by prior arrangement, children over 6 only.*

KENDALL MANOR INN 🐚
534 W. Broad St., Eufaula 36027, tel. 334/687–8847, fax 334/616–0678

Kendall Manor stands majestically on a hill in historic Eufaula, a town filled with the state's second most abundant collection of structures on the National Historic Register. Filled with moss-draped trees, Eufaula draws visitors to its spring Pilgrimages and fish-laden Lake Eufaula. Built in 1872, the inn offers weekend dining, by reservation, to the public.

Transplanted northerners, Timothy and Barbara Lubsen left the corporate world to live out their dream of owning a B&B. It was an ambition they harbored more than a decade while he worked as a consumer products researcher and she as a travel agent, tour director, and interior designer.

Ruby-etched glass panels accent 10-ft entrance doors that open to reveal spacious rooms with 16-ft ceilings and elaborate moldings. The parlor, with original furnishings, has detailed carvings in rosewood and walnut, windows topped with gold-leaf cornices, antiques, and Oriental rugs. A rosewood square grand piano and a sunroom are available for guests' use. There is an adult-size rocking horse in the upstairs sitting area.

Rooms upstairs have wood floors, Oriental-style rugs, 10-ft windows with Venetian blinds, and cloud shades. The Alabama Room, with yellow and black accents, includes a king rice bed (which has wood posts carved with a rice motif), antique armoire and chest, love seat, chair, and ottoman. Floral wallpaper is the backdrop in the Georgia Room. Flowers in rooms and goodies such as lemon bars or brownies are standard. Wine is by request.

Verandas extend around three sides of the home. A second-story sitting porch, with comfortable chairs, overlooks the front lawn's dogwood and magnolias. Chippendale railings surround the rear deck, which leads to a fountain, bench, and gardens where breakfast sometimes is served.

In the rooftop belvedere, earlier visitors have left their mark: Hundreds of signatures, some dating to the home's early years, have been scrawled on the walls. Overnight guests are invited to continue the tradition. *6 double rooms with baths. Air-conditioning, cable TV and phone in rooms, ceiling fans, fax, copier, free home tour, bikes, croquet. $89–$114; full breakfast, beverage, afternoon refreshments, dinner by request. AE, D, MC, V. No smoking, children over 14 only, minimum stay during special events.*

ORANGEVALE PLANTATION

1400 Whiting Rd., Talladega 35160, tel. 256/761–1827, fax 256/761–8794

Orangevale Plantation, on 150 acres 4 mi south of Talladega, once was the center of a 3,000-acre cotton plantation. Built in 1854, the main house is Greek Revival with six 25-ft-tall pillars and white exterior.

Orangevale is run by Billy Bliss and her husband, Richard, a physician who served in three branches of the U.S. military. With two married sons living nearby, the Blisses maintain cattle, sheep, horses, ducks, geese, an orchard, cornfields, fishponds, and a vineyard. Guests may stroll a nature trail lined with azaleas, dogwoods, and ferns.

The Blisses live downstairs in their antiques-filled home and leave the upstairs, which has its own living-room area, to guests. In typical antebellum fashion, the bedrooms open off a central hall, and, though these rooms have their own bathrooms, you have to tiptoe down the hall to reach them. Both bedrooms have fourposter beds with down comforters, Sheraton chests, brick fireplaces, and large windows.

There are three outbuildings. The farthest, which the innkeepers reach via golf cart, overlooks the orchard. Each of its two rooms, connected by a dogtrot, has a queen-size and single bed, a freestanding brick fireplace, a rocking chair, and walls and ceiling made of rough-hewn wood.

Behind the main house and within view of the tree-canopied brick patio are two units, both with exposed wood, kitchenettes, living areas, and baths. Cabin interiors, smelling of old pine logs, appear rustic but are exceptionally comfortable.

Guests find fresh fruit and produce and Billy's specialty—iced tea sweetened with mint sprigs from the grounds. Breakfast often is served at the kitchen's lazy Susan, where the Blisses' four children once gathered when growing up here. Orangevale gives a true taste of the Old South, and the Blisses, who welcome families, are well suited for their roles as caretakers of the past. *2 double rooms with baths, 1 cottage, 2 cabins. Air-conditioning, TV in common areas, kitchen, fax, copier, washer/dryer, free tour of house and grounds, nature trail, 2 fishing ponds. $95; full breakfast. No credit cards.*

ST. JAMES HOTEL

1200 Water Ave., Selma 36701, tel. 334/872–3234 or 888/264–6788, fax 334/872–0332

Outlaw Jesse James once was a guest in the St. James Hotel, which dates to the 1830s, when parlors bustled with wealthy cotton planters, merchants, and politicians. The completely restored St. James reopened in late 1997, almost 100 years after closing as a hotel. In intervening years, the riverfront structure housed various businesses. The hotel today is a private and public partnership owned by the City of Selma, which united government, community, and private investors in the $6 million restoration. A management company oversees the property with southern hospitality.

Outside, lacy ironwork trims balconies, just as it did when the hotel was in its glory days. The lobby has antiques, heart-pine floors, an original hotel mantel, and draperies made from antique French fabric.

Guests are served afternoon tea and lemonade on the hotel's front balcony, which has views of Lafayette Park, the Alabama River, Water Avenue, and the Edmund Pettus Bridge, best remembered as the setting for Bloody Sunday, when marchers, in 1965, headed to Montgomery, some 50 mi away, to seek voting rights for blacks.

Guest rooms are furnished with 19th-century plantation reproductions from the Vestiges collection of Lexington Furniture. Carpets, draperies, and bedspreads were designed and woven especially for the hotel. Bathroom tiles, clustered in mosaic designs, were created for the St. James. All guest rooms have private baths. The hotel's four suites, each with jetted tub and bidet, have fireplaces with gas logs, original oil paintings, four-poster beds, and walk-in closets. Suites, with some 800 square ft, open onto balconies with views of the river and nearby bridge.

Antique reproductions fill the Drinking Room, where French silk draperies of muted bronze-color reproduction fabric made in France puddle on floors. The quietly elegant, white tablecloth Troup House Restaurant, furnished with a mixture of antiques and reproductions, oversees a fountain-centered courtyard. △ *38 rooms with baths, 4 suites. Restaurant, air-conditioning, turndown service, cable TV in rooms, lounge, use of nearby fitness center, valet parking. $64–$128; Continental breakfast. Restaurant, lounge. AE, D, DC, MC, V. Restricted smoking.*

OTHER CHOICES

Jemison Inn. 212 Hwy. 191, Jemison 35085, tel. and fax 205/688–2055. 3 double rooms with baths. Air-conditioning, ceiling fans, cable TV/VCR in 2 common areas and guest rooms, fruit and flowers in room, turndown service with mints, champagne in room for honeymooners, in-room snacks, video library, fax, copier, free home tour, gardens, swimming pool. $75–$135; full breakfast, afternoon refreshments, pool-side snacks. AE, D, DC, MC, V. No smoking, children by prior arrangement.

Gulf Coast Delta

BAY BREEZE ☜
742 S. Mobile St. (Box 526), Fairhope 36533, tel. 334/928–8976, fax 334/928–0360

Not far from downtown Fairhope, a winding white-shell driveway leads through a landscaped camellia and azalea garden to a stucco-and-wood guest house built in the early 1930s. Owners Bill and Becky Jones, who have restored and enlarged her childhood home, live in their own wing, while guests enjoy the main house and nearby cottages, which offer privacy. The house fronts Mobile Bay, where, not far away, is the Yankee ironclad *Tecumseh*, which sank with 116 sailors. Stretching into the bay is a private 462-ft pier with a kitchen, where Bill often cooks Saturday breakfast or a seafood supper. Fortunate guests may find themselves here for Jubilee—a natural phenomenon that takes place only two places in the world when a lack of oxygen forces bottom dwellers—crab, shrimp, flounder—to shore.

A large front lawn has a stone fountain and pine benches. In the sunny living room are china and rare books in a cabinet next to a musket from the War of 1812. The Bay Room has white wicker chairs facing large French windows and the bay. A cozy sitting room hides an upright piano and brick fireplace. Breakfast is served in the dining room; a view of ducks and the bay enhances the meal.

The three bedrooms in the main house have wooden floors, brass queen beds, old family portraits, large windows, and antique furnishings. Cottage suites are light and spacious, decorated with antiques, Oriental and hooked rugs, brick floors, and white pine paneling. In one suite, the bedroom has a large queen brass bed, mini-kitchen, and comfortable sofa sleeper that increases accommodations to four.

Becky, a retired biology instructor, loves sitting at the end of the pier and weaving tales while guests revel in this casual escape on historic Mobile Bay. ♦ *3 double rooms with baths, 2 cottages. Air-conditioning, cable TV in rooms, games, VCR in game room, ceiling fans, fax, free home tour, bikes, pond, pier. $95–$105; full breakfast, refreshments on arrival. AE, MC, V. No smoking, pets and children by arrangement only, minimum stay during special events.*

BEACH HOUSE, A BED & BREAKFAST BY THE SEA ☙
9218 Dacus La., Gulf Shores 36542, tel. 334/540–7039 or 800/659–6004

Wrapped in porches and nestled among dunes, the Beach House is a tribute to owners Russ and Carol Shackelford, former therapists who know well how to promote relaxation. The couple designed their haven to showcase views of the beach and ocean. A favorite spot is the screened porch, a grand vantage point for spotting dolphins at play from "swing" chairs, which are suspended from the ceiling.

French doors open into a large living room where rough-hewn columns look like masts of an old sailing ship. (The look was not happenstance but by design.) Exposed beams and book-lined walls are bathed in the filtered light from tall windows draped in billowing gauze. An overstuffed sofa and deep club chairs are accented by an occasional wicker piece, while nautical knickknacks, a library table, and an antique armoire from Indonesia (laden with board games) add inviting touches.

The five guest rooms are uncluttered and breezy and let the ocean seem almost to come indoors. Pine floors are scattered with Oriental rugs, and walls are painted with soft colors. Each guest room has a waveless water bed covered with a plush feather bed. Cape May and Key West rooms share a second-floor porch with a hammock, swing chairs, and a skywalk that leads to an open deck with a hot tub. Third-floor suites have king-size beds, whirlpool tubs, private decks, and floor-to-ceiling windows offering gulf views.

Guests may choose to eat breakfast on the front porch or in the kitchen, where a refrigerator is stocked with snacks. Breakfasts include choices such as apple-puff pancakes drizzled with maple syrup and homemade biscuits topped with melted cheese and smothered in tomato-basil gravy.

A favorite pastime for many visitors is traipsing through nearby National Wildlife Refuge or running along the beach to catch salty breezes. ♦ *5 rooms with baths. Air-conditioning, TV in rooms by request, ceiling fans in rooms, snacks in guest* *refrigerator; kites. $130–$231; full breakfast, snacks. No credit cards. No smoking, 3-night minimum.*

OTHER CHOICES

Original Romar House. 23500 Perdido Beach Blvd., Orange Beach 36561, tel. 334/974–1625 or 800/487–6627, fax 334/974–1163. 4 double rooms and 1 single with baths, 1 suite, 1 cottage. Air-conditioning, cable TV in living room and bar, hot tub, hammock, bicycles. $79–$200; full breakfast, wine and cheese. AE, MC, V. No smoking, children over 12 only.

ALASKA

Anchorage

AURORA WINDS ☞
7501 Upper O'Malley Rd., Anchorage 99516, tel. 907/346–2533, fax 907/346–3192

Aurora Winds's facilities rival those of downtown hotels: four stone fireplaces, big-screen TV, hot tub, sauna, and work-out area with four-station Nautilus, stair climber, and treadmill. For outdoor recreation, the entrance to Chugach State Park is just up the road.

This contemporary home is an eclectic mix of styles, from neoclassical to high-tech, art deco to Oriental. Exposed-beam ceilings enclose 5,200 square ft of space, all of which is open to guests. The formal living room showcases a white baby grand piano and Oriental screens, while the den downstairs has a slot machine, billiard table, 52-inch projection-screen TV, 150-gallon aquarium, and fireplace.

The Garden Room is the brightest of the five large suites, each of which has its own bathroom, sitting area, phone, TV, and VCR. This upper-story room has a queen-size bed, leather recliner, and a Murphy bed. Down the hall, the Mountain View room is classically decorated and masculine in feel, with a wood armoire and mule bed, and a four-poster bed. The Southern Comfort room is contemporary in design, with black wrought iron, ceramics, and flowing fabrics. A small kitchenette sets the Copper Room apart from the others. The grandest of the rooms is the 1,000-square-ft McKinley Suite, which, in addition to the standard queen bed, also has a queen-size hide-a-bed, fireplace, walk-in closet with ironing board and robes, and a small office hidden behind the mirrored door. The work space is complete with computer, printer, and fax. The spacious bath has a built-in habitat environmental chamber (when it's working, lie down and experience wind, rain, steam, sun, and music), double Jacuzzi, and double vanity.

Your host in all this is James Montgomery, who sets out a Continental breakfast for those with early morning departures. But you really don't want to miss his full breakfast, which often includes French toast with Grand Marnier syrup. ☖ *2 double rooms, 2 triple rooms and 1 quad room, all with private baths. Cable TV/VCRs, dataports, 4 fireplaces, 52-inch projection-screen cable TV in den, exercise equipment, billiard table, slot machine, hot tub. $95–$195; full or Continental breakfast. AE, D, MC, V.*

THE OSCAR GILL HOUSE ☞
1344 W. 10th Ave., Anchorage 99501, tel. 907/258–1717, fax 907/258–6613

Innkeepers Mark and Susan Lutz bought this historic, two-story clapboard house in 1993 for $1, moved it to its current site across from the Denaley Park Strip downtown, and spent the next year converting it into their home and three-bedroom

B&B. The Lutzes have done a wonderful job breathing new life into the home, which was built around 1913 by Oscar Gill, an Iditarod mail carrier, lighterage businessman, and speaker of Alaska's Territorial House. Historic photos hang in the entryway, including a photo of Gill himself. The house is full of interesting knickknacks yet does not feel cluttered; an old leather suitcase holds magazines, while glass cabinets upstairs display political pins. A woodstove, antique tables, and comfortable chairs with reading lamps make the small living room inviting; family photos, scattered books, and a child's rocker give it a homey feel. The dining room, also small, has a nice view of the park strip, which is approximately 12 blocks long and 1 block wide and which has a rose garden. The dining room chairs arrived in Seward, Alaska, in 1914 as a wedding present for a now anonymous pioneer bride; much of the rest of the home's furnishings have come from second-hand stores and yard sales.

All the guest rooms are upstairs and have light-colored walls and simple, light-colored furniture. A front bedroom has a double bed, rocker, and dresser, while a back room has twin beds and a writing desk. A shared bath has a claw-foot tub. The third room is larger, with a queen bed as well as a single. On a clear night you can see Mt. McKinley from the room's large window. The private bathroom has a whirlpool bath. Each guest room has down comforters and guest robes, and bathrooms provide Body Shop amenities.

Popular breakfast items include omelets, pancakes, fresh fruit, and old-fashioned oatmeal. The nearby coastal trail is the ideal setting for a ride, ski, or after-dinner stroll. ♨ *2 double rooms with shared bath, 1 triple. Whirlpool tub in 1 room, complimentary bikes and skis, phones, laundry facilities, TV, crib, freezer space. $55–$95; full breakfast. AE, MC, V.*

OTHER CHOICES
Swan House Bed and Breakfast. 6840 Crooked Tree Dr., Anchorage 99516, tel. 907/346–3033 or 800/921–1900, fax 907/346–3535. This house is swan shaped with 127 windows. 3 double rooms with baths. Cable TV, phone, toiletries, hair dryer, robes, slippers, feather beds in rooms, Corian fireplace in common room. $159–$179; full breakfast. AE, D, MC, V. 2-night.
Yukon Don's Bed and Breakfast Inn. 2221 Yukon Circle, Wasilla 99654, tel. 800/478–7472, fax 907/376–7470. 4 quad rooms with shared baths, 3 suites, 1 cabin. Phones, cable TV/VCR in 1 suite; no electricity, phone or water in cabin; kitchen in 2 suites, common room with pool table, glass-enclosed rooftop viewing room, guided adventure tours arranged. $75–$125; Continental breakfast. AE, D, MC, V.

Healy

ROCK CREEK COUNTRY INN ☞
Mile 261 of the Parks Highway, 20 mi north of Denali National Park (HC1 Box 3450), Healy 99743, tel. 907/683–2676

Driving up to Wayne and Lolita Valcq's B&B is like arriving on the set of a made-for-TV movie about life on the last frontier. Manicured grounds have interesting Alaskan touches such as a collection of antlers out front, totems, and old traps and snowshoes mounted on outside walls.

Since they moved to Alaska in 1978, the Valcqs have built a spacious log home, three guest cabins with running water, a workshop with a two-bedroom suite above it, and an outdoor shower house on this site overlooking the Nenana River. There's even a two-seater outhouse complete with curtains and crocheted seat covers.

In the main house, the two rooms upstairs have twin beds; guests use a shared bath downstairs. A spacious room in the finished basement has a queen bed and two twins and a large, private bath across the hall. The cabins, which are in the woods behind the house just yards from the river, offer a variety of sleeping arrangements. The largest has a double bed, two twin beds, and a double hide-a-bed.

Lolita has decorated each clean but simple accommodation with homemade quilts, original wildlife paintings, and other Alaskan touches. The cozy sitting room and dining area in the main house contains trophy birds and mammals, many of which Lolita has stuffed. There's also a snowshoe and antler chandelier and a table lamp crafted from moose hooves.

In addition to running the B&B year-round, the Valcqs mush sled dogs and house 29 huskies in the lot next to the house. Wayne has competed twice in the Yukon Quest, a grueling race from Fairbanks, Alaska, to Whitehorse, Yukon Territory.

Because of the wooded setting there's a strict no-smoking policy and mosquitoes can be pesky. △ *1 room with queen bed, 2 singles and private bath; 2 rooms with twin beds and shared bath; 1 2-bedroom suite with 2 queen beds and a single, plus a private bath; 3 private cabins with private baths. Outdoor log shower house, common sitting area with TV. $75–$110; full breakfast, Continental breakfast for those with early morning departures. MC, V accepted if reservations are made through Alaska Private Lodgings/Stay with a Friend (Box 200047, Anchorage 99520–0047, 907/258–1717, fax 907/258–6613).*

Fairbanks

FORGET-ME-NOT LODGE/THE AURORA EXPRESS ☙
Box 80128, Fairbanks 99708, 907/474–0949, fax 907/474–8173

The guest rooms here are spotless, the floral decor bright and cheerful, and the views of the Tanana River expansive. But it is the opportunity to stay in one of the refurbished Alaska Railroad sleeper cars that makes this B&B unique.

Mike and Susan Wilson have done a wonderful job turning American Standard and 1956 Pullman train cars into comfortable guest quarters. Their attention to detail takes you back to a time long forgotten. The sleeping compartments of the National Domain car have themes: a richly appointed bordello, can-can room, gold mine, and chapel. These rooms, as well as a large room in a caboose, have private entries; beautifully painted, arched 10-ft ceilings; crystal chandeliers; and gilded bath fixtures in addition to queen beds and private baths with showers. The chapel compartment, modeled after Fairbanks's historic Immaculate Conception church, has a stained-glass window, altar chairs, and prayer bench. The Arlene car, a good choice for families, has two bedrooms, a small kitchen, a living room, and is decorated in navy and yellow—the colors of the Alaskan Railroad.

Guests staying in the National Emblem car have the run of an entire car. Up to five guests can stay here, each tucked into a tiny room with a single bed. There are two toilets and sinks at the front of the car, two showers at the rear, and a sitting area decorated with rich green drapes and pillows. A private two-person car is the Golden Nellie caboose.

In the main house, a full breakfast of fresh fruit, pastries, pancakes, salmon quiche, or omelets is served in the glassed-in dining room. ⌂ *Lodge: 2 doubles share bath, 1 suite. National Domain: 4 doubles with baths and private entrances. National Emblem: large sleeper car with bath and private entrance can accommodate up to 5 people. Caboose: double with bath and private entrance. Arlene: 2-bedroom suite with bath and private entrance, kitchenette, and living room that can accommodate up to 4 people. Large common dining and sitting areas in main lodge. Lodging available May–Oct. $85–$250. MC, V.*

Homer and Seldovia

ISLAND WATCH BED & BREAKFAST 🐾
Box 1394, Homer 99603, tel. 907/235–2265

One mile up scenic West Hill Road and five minutes from downtown Homer, this rambling, secluded B&B is a perfect place to relax. Guest rooms in the spruce log cabin and main house are casually comfortable with queen beds, modern facilities, and private baths. The great views of Kachemak Bay and the Kenai Mountains set this B&B apart.

Eileen Mullen grew up along the Kenai River and for several years she fished commercially. As it became harder and harder to make a living off the sea, this gracious, soft-spoken woman moved to Homer and in 1991 opened her home to guests. The two-bedroom suite on the lower level of Eileen's home is perfect for families with small children: One bedroom has two single beds, the other a queen-size bed, and a built-in bench provides sleeping space for a fifth person. A place for sitting, along with a dining and kitchen area, allows guests to be comfortable and self-sufficient. A spacious third-floor room sleeps three, with a private bath across the hall. Outside there's a large yard and picnic table.

The spruce cabin, which Eileen built, has two queen beds (one in a sleeping loft reached by a spiral staircase), a day bed, a small kitchen, a radio, tape player, and board games. The floors are carpeted and the interior walls are sheetrocked. But again, it's the view that makes this place special—a deck with a swing chair facilitates your enjoyment of the scenery. Another choice, more recently added, is a cozy, private cabin for two, also with a kitchen.

A roomy unit for three has a private entrance and is wheelchair accessible. From here there are lovely views of Eileen's horse pasture and Kachemak Bay.

Eileen serves a large, heart-healthy breakfast from 5:30 to 8:30 AM (to accommodate those going fishing) that often features buckwheat hotcakes with garden-fresh rhubarb-strawberry sauce. ⌂ *2 cabins with kitchen, private bath, and deck; 1 2-bedroom suite (sleeps 4) with bath and kitchen; 1 triple with bath (wheelchair accessible). (Cabins available May 1–Oct. 1. $80–$110 (extra person); full breakfast. D, MC, V.*

OTHER CHOICES

Swan House South. Box 11, Seldovia 99663, tel. 907/346–3033 or 800/921–1900, fax 907/346–3535. 2 rooms with baths, 2 suites. Toiletries, hair dryers, robes, slippers in rooms; VCR, video library, in-room coffee and tea in suites; gazebo, hot tub, sunroom, 50-ft dock, hiking, kayaking, fishing charters, transportation arranged (fee). $129–169; full breakfast. AE, D, MC, V. No smoking. Closed after Labor Day weekend–Memorial Day.

Juneau

Pearson's Pond. 4541 Sawa Circle, Juneau 99801-8723, tel. 907/789–3772 or 888/6JUNEAU, fax 907/789–6722. 3 double rooms with baths. Kitchenette, private entrances, deck, robes, slippers, hair dryers, toiletries, CD player, TV/VCR, phone, dataports in rooms, computer with Internet access, cellular phone, video camera, sitting room with fireplace, 2 hot tubs, barbecue pit, garden, hiking/biking/skiing trails, pond, dock, bikes, rowboats, fishing poles, travel/tour services. $229; Continental-plus breakfast. AE, D, DC, MC, V.

ARIZONA

Northern Arizona,
Including the Grand Canyon,
Sedona, Flagstaff,
and Indian Country

BOOTS AND SADDLES 🖋

2900 Hopi Dr., Sedona 86336, tel. 520/282–1944 or 800/201–1944, fax 520/204–2230

This intimate bed-and-breakfast owned by John and Linda Steele is an economical alternative to Sedona's expensive B&Bs. Although three of the guest rooms have been enlarged to accommodate such amenities as hot tubs, gas fireplaces, and private decks, the rustic mountain feel of this cedar A-frame cabin makes it a healthy choice.

Guest rooms have been individually decorated in the western tradition. Upstairs, the Bunk House Room was built using Kansas barnwood; rusted-iron wall lamps with Western-style motif cutouts glow over each side of the bed. The downstairs Wrangler Room is filled with furniture made from old corral fencing; horseshoe racks and barbed wire line the bathroom's walls. The Lariat Room has a queen-size bed and chairs of lodgepole pine and a cathedral window with sweeping views of the Mongollan rim.

Come morning, Southwest enchiladas with blue-corn muffins, cowboy beans, and fruit tacos are among the items that may be laid out in the common room for breakfast. Afterwards, you can relax in the small sitting room, which has a fireplace and board games, or take a hike from the property's edge. ⚃ *4 double rooms with baths. Hot tub, fireplace, and private balcony in 3 rooms; TVs, phones, and outdoor hot tub. $100–$185, full breakfast, afternoon refreshments. AE, D, MC, V. No smoking.*

BRIAR PATCH INN 🖋

HC 30, 3190 N. Hwy. 89A, Sedona 86336, tel. 520/282–2342 or 888/809–3030, fax 520/282–2399

Shaded by a canopy of sycamore, juniper, canyon oak, pine, elm, and cottonwood trees, 17 individual log cabins nestle on the floor of Oak Creek Canyon, just north of Sedona. The murmur of the spring-fed creek blends with the rustle of the leaves and chirping of the birds to create a relaxing, peaceful ambience on this wooded, 9-acre property. It isn't hard to believe that the Briar Patch Inn has been called a "healing, magical oasis."

In the early 1880s, this was the site of a goat barn, and there's still a resident goat, along with a friendly sheep and some chickens. The cabins were built during the 1940s to provide a summer getaway from the heat of urban Phoenix; at an elevation of 4,484 ft, this area is always temperate. The place became a bed-and-breakfast in 1983.

June through September, guests enjoy the quiet strains of a violinist and classical guitarist who play by the creek during breakfast. Some Sunday afternoons bring outdoor chamber music concerts on the lawn. The library is stocked with volumes on Native American culture and the history and geography of the Southwest. Innkeeper Rob Olson also likes to schedule small workshops on the creative arts here: Navajo weaving, Native American arts, painting, photography, philosophy, self-healing, and more. Events usually take place in the meetinghouse, which can accommodate up to 50 people, or it can sleep 7 if rented as a private cottage.

The cabins are rustic cozy, with log walls, beam or plank ceilings, southwestern furnishings, and private patios or decks. All except the three on the creek—Deck House, Creekside, and Kingfisher—have fireplaces, and a supply of aromatic, shaggy-bark cedar firewood is stacked outside the front door. One of the newest cabins, Eagle, has a Native American theme, featuring a lodgepole-pine bed, table, and chairs; polished clear-pine floors; and an armoire, paneling, and bath done in knotty pine. One windowed wall faces the tree-shaded creek. Blue Jay, the oldest cabin on the property, has the smallest windows.

Iced tea, coffee, and cookies are always available in the main building. In the morning, a heart-healthy buffet breakfast includes home-baked seven-grain bread or muffins, granola, yogurt, fresh eggs, hot apple sauce from local apples, and seasonal juices and fruits. Guests can take a tray to their room, dine at private tables in the main building, or eat at tree-shaded picnic tables overlooking the creek.

   △ *13 2-person cabins, 4 4-person cabins, 1 7-person cottage. Air-conditioning, kitchens in 12 cabins, masseuse available, yoga (weekends), meeting house. $149–$295, full buffet breakfast. AE, MC, V. No smoking indoors. 2-night minimum Mar.–Nov.*

CANYON VILLA BED & BREAKFAST INN 🐚
125 Canyon Circle Dr., Sedona 86351, tel. 520/284–1226 or 800/453–1166, fax 520/284–2114

Opened in 1992, Canyon Villa combines the personal comforts of a traditional inn with the amenities of a first-class resort. Innkeepers Chuck and Marion Yadon researched the business for 18 months, visiting B&Bs from New England to California, before distilling their knowledge into this elegant two-story accommodation.

The site at the edge of the Coconino National Forest has uninterrupted views of Sedona's main attractions: the red sandstone cliffs of Castle Rock, Bell Rock, and Courthouse Butte. This is prime property, and staying at Canyon Villa is very much like visiting the mansion of a wealthy Arizona rancher. Guests' spaces include a well-stocked library: a beam-ceiling, skylit modern living room with a glass-enclosed fireplace; and a 32-ft heated swimming pool in the garden. Snacks and beverages are set out each afternoon in the dining room.

A broad stairway covered with thick carpeting leads to the five upstairs guest rooms, all with large windows and glass French doors to capitalize on the breathtaking scenery; the less expensive room on the ground floor has less stunning views. All the rooms are named after the flowering cacti and shrubs found in the Sedona area and have private baths, balconies or patios, wall-to-wall carpeting, individual heating and cooling units, telephones, cable TV, 10-ft ceilings with fans, and eclectic decor; the larger ones also have double sinks and fireplaces.

Santa Fe–themed Ocotillo has a wrought-iron four-poster bed and a fireplace. The bed in Manzanita, done in blue, is also a four-poster. The corner Strawberry Cactus Room, with white wicker furniture and a blue carpet, has views from two sides and a bath with a stained-glass window. The Spanish Bayonet is perfect for honeymooners, with its private balcony, fireplace, and bathtub two steps from the king-size bed.

Two long tables, each with eight purple-accented place settings, fill the huge, carpeted dining room, where Marion's catering background is revealed at breakfast time. Marion, Chuck, and hired help (there is a staff of 11) serve a nutritious breakfast of fruit, just-baked bread, and an entrée such as chili-cheese quiche, pumpkin pancakes, or sour cream waffles; a drawback for people traveling alone is that they may be assigned to a seat for the meal. ⚘ *11 double rooms with baths. Cable TV, CD player, whirlpool tub, robes, and pool towels in rooms. $145–$225; full breakfast, afternoon snacks. AE, MC, V. No smoking. 2-night minimum weekends, 3-night minimum some holidays.*

GRAHAM B&B INN ⚘
150 Canyon Circle Dr., Sedona 86351, tel. 520/284–1425 or 800/228–1425, fax 520/284–0767

Carol and Roger Redenbaugh view their bed-and-breakfast as original art—a chance to create a mood by offering their guests uniquely themed rooms and warm, personalized service in an enchanting setting. This may well be Sedona's best inn, and it claims to have the highest annual occupancy of any B&B in the country.

Spacious accommodations in the main inn feature antiques, original artwork, fresh flowers, and thick robes, as well as modern amenities like TVs, VCRs, and video libraries. Every item in the room matches the theme; for example, seashells are sprinkled throughout the soft blue and peach San Francisco Room, where a hot-air balloon floats over the chaise, a cable car and crystal dolphin rest on the California dresser, and a birdhouse shaped like a lighthouse sways gently over the private balcony.

Next to the main inn, the Adobe Village houses the Graham's most distinctive suites. The four lavish casitas range in style from elegant to rustic, artsy to adventurous—yet each is intensely romantic. The owners spared no expense in endearing them with full-size Jacuzzis, waterfall showers, two fireplaces each, entertainment centers with VCRs and CD-stereos, and private decks (all have magnificent views of the surrounding red-rock landscape). The elegant Sunset Casita, decorated in light clay colors, has floor-to-ceiling windows, a massive fireplace, and some striking Indian sculpture. Its iron bed holds up 9-ft posts that branch out like wild trees. The cowboy-themed Lonesome Dove, with its hardwood floors, red-rock fireplace, barnwood cabinetry, and high-poster bed, sends you back to a simpler time. The lone cactus has a country guitar as its only friend, and an old saloon door opens to an immense lantern-lit bathroom that glows over the four-person Jacuzzi. Upon arrival, you'll be greeted by the smell of freshly baked bread and the melancholic songs of Randy Travis.

Breakfast may be savored in the dining room, outside on the deck, or in your casita. Popular entrées include German pancakes, maple bread pudding, and *huevos rancheros.* In the morning, Carol also gives newly arrived guests an orientation on the area. Some of the best assets of this contemporary, two-story inn are outside: a heated pool and spa; a walled, landscaped lawn and garden; and a broad deck for outdoor dining. ♙ *5 double rooms with baths, 1 suite, 4 casitas. TV/VCR, phones, kitchenettes and Jacuzzis in casitas, pool, bicycles. $119–$369; full breakfast, afternoon refreshments. AE, D, MC, V. No smoking indoors, 2-night minimum weekends.*

INN AT FOUR TEN ☞
410 N. Leroux St., Flagstaff 86001, tel. 520/774–0088 or 800/774–2008, fax 520/774–6354

Now a friendly bed-and-breakfast, the Inn at Four Ten was built in 1907 by Tom E. Pollock, a wealthy banker and cattle rancher, as the manor house of his grand estate; its extensive grounds included a stable and separate quarters for the grooms. After Pollock died, the property was split up, and some years later the main building became a fraternity house.

After completing extensive renovations, including the installation of an all-white commercial kitchen, the Inn at Four Ten opened for business in 1991. Howard and Sally Krueger, who bought the inn in 1993, upgraded the rooms, making them some of the most luxurious in Flagstaff. Guests step from a broad front porch to an open living room with polished-oak floors, bookcases, door frames, ceiling beams, and a tile fireplace. South-facing windows in the adjoining dining room let in the soft morning light, while a small courtyard and garden beckon guests to relax outside.

A great deal of detail went into the decoration of the guest rooms. The elegant Tea Room, with hunter green and rose carpeting, has a floor-to-ceiling mahogany bookcase, a wrought-iron king-size bed, and a 7-ft walnut burl armoire; polished-oak doors lead directly into the living room. Also downstairs, the Southwest Room is Santa Fe style all the way with a Saltillo-tile floor, kiva fireplace, and lodgepole-pine bed imported from New Mexico.

Upstairs, the Conservatory resembles Beethoven's private studio; a bust of the great composer rests on a mahogany secretary, white sheet music doubles for wallpaper, and an antique music stand waits patiently near the fireplace. The two rooms of the Dakota suite are dressed in cowboy decor, with log beds and barnwood walls.

You can eat breakfast in the sunny dining room or under the gazebo in the garden. Sally's cooking has been praised in a national B&B recipe contest; favorites include fresh fruit with cinnamon and honey followed by stuffed French toast with cream cheese and orange marmalade. ♙ *9 double rooms with baths. Coffeemaker and mini-refrigerator in rooms, whirlpool in 3 rooms, fireplace in 7 rooms. $125–$175; full breakfast, afternoon tea and snacks. MC, V. No smoking. 2-night minimum weekends, 3-night minimum some holiday weekends.*

INN ON OAK CREEK ☞
556 Hwy. 179, Sedona 86336, tel. 520/282–7896 or 800/499–7896, fax 520/282–0696

One of Sedona's newest and most luxurious B&Bs, the Inn on Oak Creek opened in late 1996. The young energetic owners, Rick Morris and Pam Harrison, left the corporate world behind to create their dream inn, and great attention to detail has brought them to their goal.

Of the 11 carefully designed rooms, 7 have private decks that face Oak Creek; all have fireplaces, cotton waffle-weave robes, marble bathrooms, and whirlpool tubs. The Rested Rooster Room, dressed in country French fabrics, has roosters everywhere: on the pillow shams and on the mantle top, posing in wall paintings and hopping along the wallpaper. An adjoining "Hen House" with a trundle bed can be added to make it a suite. Likewise, the Golf on the Rocks Room, decorated with Scottish plaid, attaches to the Pro Shop—it's a golfer's dream suite. The Hollywood Out West Room commemorates the 43 Westerns filmed in Sedona with items such as original playbills, a star-patterned antique reproduction quilt, a Winchester ammunition box and lariat, and John Wayne and Maureen O'Hara director's chairs. The inn's most romantic room must be the Rose Arbor Room, with soft floral prints and panoramic views of Sedona's red mountains.

Rick and Pam serve gourmet breakfasts in the dining room, which has pine tables and fresh flowers; or, in summer, you can eat on the outdoor deck. Professionals bake the pastries and main dishes—like French toast with a fresh berry sauce, kiwis, and bacon—leaving the owners free to chat with guests. Come evening, tasty hors d'oeuvres are set out in the intimate sitting room with a red-rock fireplace. You can wander the parklike grounds, which extend to a creek that flows from springs in the canyon. Here you can fish or wade by the water's edge. You might also select a film from the video library before retiring for a peaceful Arizona night. ⚠ *11 double rooms with baths. TV/VCR and phone in rooms, trout fishing with permit. $160–$245; full breakfast. D, MC, V. No smoking, 2-night minimum weekends.*

OTHER CHOICES

Apple Orchard Inn. 656 Jordan Rd., Sedona 86336, tel. 520/282–5328 or 800/663–6968, fax 520/204–0044. 7 double rooms with baths. TVs/VCR, phone, refrigerator in rooms, whirlpool tub in 6 rooms, fireplace in 2 rooms, hiking. $135–$195; full breakfast. MC, V. No smoking.

Birch Tree Inn. 824 W. Birch Ave., Flagstaff 86001, tel. 520/774–1042 or 888/774–1042, fax 502/774–8462. 3 double rooms with baths, 2 doubles share bath. TV in living room. $55–$109; full breakfast, afternoon refreshments. AE, D, MC, V. No smoking indoors.

Jeanette's Bed-and-Breakfast. 3380 E. Lockett Rd., Flagstaff 86004, tel. 520/527–1912 or 800/752–1912. 4 double rooms with baths. Fireplace in 2 rooms. $95–125, full breakfast, afternoon refreshments. AE, D, MC, V. No smoking indoors.

Territorial House. 65 Piki Dr., Sedona 86336, tel. 520/204–2737 or 800/801–2737, fax 520/204–2230. 4 double rooms with baths. TV/VCR in 3 rooms and in living room, hot tub, bicycles. $115–$165; full breakfast, afternoon snacks. AE, D, MC, V. No smoking indoors, 2-night minimum weekends.

RESERVATIONS SERVICES

Arizona Association of Bed & Breakfast Inns (Box 7186, Phoenix 85011, tel. 800/284–2589). **Arizona Trails Bed and Breakfast Reservation Service** (Box 18998, Fountain Hills 85269, tel. 602/837–4284 or 888/799–4284, fax 602/816–4224). **Mi Casa Su Casa B&B Reservation Service** (Box 950, Tempe 85280, tel. 602/990–0682, 800/456–0682 reservations only, fax 602/990–3390).

Central Arizona, Including Phoenix, Prescott, and the White Mountains

GREER LODGE 🖙

Box 244, Greer 85927, tel. 520/735—7216 or 888/475–6343, fax 520/735–7720

An alpine lodge that could have come straight from the drafting board of a Hollywood set designer, this 1948 building in the White Mountains is made entirely of polished logs, exposed inside and out. The spacious lobby is replete with deer antlers, a black bearskin, wagon-wheel chandeliers, lodgepole-pine furniture, and plank floors. A stone fireplace crackles with juniper logs.

The backdrop—pine-studded Greer Valley, at an elevation of 8,500 ft, with deer and elk grazing in the meadows—is equally picture perfect. The Little Colorado River, stocked with trout and dammed here and there by beaver colonies, meanders through the grounds.

The rooms pick up the rustic theme, with knotty pine or polished log walls, oak or pine plank floors, and cheerful chintz curtains and bedspreads; each has a private bath and individual electric heat controls. First choice are the corner rooms, such as Nos. 2, 4, and 5, which have views of both the valley and the wooded mountains. On the third floor, under the peaked roof, is a romantic pine-paneled room with a clear view to the south. In addition to the accommodations in the lodge, there are similarly furnished rooms in the Little Lodge, a four-bedroom log cabin with a kitchen and a deck overlooking the river; and rooms in a variety of smaller cabins, some with kitchens and fireplaces.

Breakfast, lunch, and dinner are served in the skylit solar-heated dining room, open to the public. It's surrounded by glass, and every table overlooks the creek, three ponds, an expansive lawn populated with ducks, and the wooded hills beyond. Breakfast possibilities include Belgian waffles with strawberries, biscuits and gravy, and blueberry pancakes. At lunchtime, salads, burgers, and hot and cold sandwiches are available.

No license is required to fish in the Lodge's two fishing ponds, but there is a fee. If you catch something in the larger fly-fishing pond, you have to throw it back, but you can keep whatever bites in the smaller bait-fishing pond. **⌂** *7 double rooms with baths, 2 suites in Lodge, 2 1-bedroom cabins, 5 2-bedroom cabins, 1 4-bedroom cabin. Fruit basket upon arrival, cable TV in lounge, bar, restaurant, fly-fishing classes Apr.–Oct. $75—280; meals extra. AE, D, MC, V. 2-night minimum weekends, 3-night minimum holidays.*

LYNX CREEK FARM 🖙

Box 4301, Prescott 86302, tel. 520/778—9573 or 888/778–9573

There are more than 200 fruit trees, including seven varieties of apple, at this 25-acre property on a hilltop east of Prescott. The farm overlooks Lonesome Valley and the Blue Hills; in addition, there's a menagerie of chickens, pigs, parrots, goats, cats, and dogs on the property. At the bottom of the hill, Lynx Creek meanders through a shady grove of tall cottonwood trees. This idyllic setting is equally suited to honeymooners and families, offering privacy as well as plenty of space and activities for restless children.

Built in the early 1980s, the farm was bought by Greg and Wendy Temple in 1985 and turned into a bed-and-breakfast. Across the driveway from the main house, where Greg and Wendy live, is a guest house with two rooms; each has a wood-burning stove and there's a shared hot tub on the viewside deck. The cozy pine-paneled Sharlot Hall Room, named for a Prescott pioneer woman, is filled with antiques, books, and memorabilia. One of the room's two king-size beds is set in a low-ceiling loft reached by ladder—an ideal space to stow the kids. The White Wicker Room next door is light, lacy, and romantic, with wicker furniture and a queen-size bed with a striking gauze canopy.

In 1992 Greg added a handsome log cabin with four inviting rooms. All have wall-to-wall Berber carpets, king-size beds, and private hot tubs on outdoor decks with valley views. The Old West–style Chaparral Room is decorated with beat-up saddles, antlers, and a hand-stitched quilt, while the more romantic Country Garden Room features lots of plants and whitewashed log-beam ceilings. A living room with a kitchenette can be connected to any of the rooms to create a two-room suite; two daybed couches open up into four single beds for extra family members.

Mornings bring guests to the breakfast room of the main house, decorated with blue ribbons that the Temples were awarded for their apples, or to the wide deck overlooking the creek below. Large breakfasts usually feature organically homegrown fruits, quiches, homemade yogurt, fresh-baked muffins, breads, and coffee cakes. On request, a Continental breakfast-in-a-basket will be delivered to your door. △ *4 double rooms with baths, 2 suites. Terry-cloth robes and coffeemaker in rooms, playground, basketball, volleyball, horseshoes, hiking. $75–$145; full breakfast, afternoon refreshments. AE, D, MC, V. No smoking indoors.*

MARICOPA MANOR BED AND BREAKFAST INN ❦
15 W. Pasadena Ave., Phoenix 85013, tel. 602/274–6302 or 800/292–6403, fax 602/266–3904

Business travelers appreciate this all-suite facility, centrally located near downtown Phoenix and just minutes from the Heard Museum, the Herberger Theatre, and the America West Arena. Innkeepers Paul and Mary Ellen Kelley raised 12 children in this 1928 residence, on a quiet, palm-shaded street, before turning it into an elegant executive retreat.

The immaculate Spanish colonial–style home is decorated with fine art and stocked with countless books. Visitors have the run of the high-ceiling family room, living room, dining room, and outdoor patio. Stressed guests can let off steam by soaking in the hot tub in the gazebo out back or floating in the heated pool with Mexican fountains.

The accommodations have every amenity offered by the posh Phoenix resorts—fresh flowers, expensive toiletries—and even some they don't have: an array of paperbacks in each room and rubber duckies in the bathtub.

The Victoria Suite is in the main house. Set off the family room, it is done in satin, lace, and antiques; the private bath is across the hall. The other accommodations are arrayed outside in adjoining buildings. A private entrance leads to the Library Suite, with volumes of leather-bound books, a desk, and a canopied king-size bed.

In an adjoining guest house with its own carport and a gated driveway are two more spacious suites. Reflections Past has a fireplace, antique mirrors, and king-size bed with a tapestry canopy. Reflections Future, done in black and white with a

Chinese flavor, has a living room, a full kitchen with breakfast area, and a small study with a desk and phone.

A Franklin stove sets the tone for the traditional American decor in the Palo Verde Suite, which has two bedrooms and an enclosed sunporch. The large Master Suite features a three-sided fireplace that separates the living room from the mahogany-furnished bedroom; there's also a double whirlpool bath.

Breakfast—orange juice, hot coffee, a fresh fruit plate, homemade bread or pastries, and a hot cheese miniquiche—is delivered to your door, at the hour you specify, in a wicker picnic basket. ♨ *5 1-bedroom suites (1 with private bath across the hall), 1 2-bedroom suite. Double whirlpool and fireplace in 3 rooms; bathrobes, cable TV, and phone in rooms; hot tub, pool. $89–$229, full breakfast. AE, D, MC, V.*

RED SETTER INN ☞
Box 133, Greer 85927, tel. 520/735—7441 or 888/99–GREER, fax 520/735–7425

Ken Conant and Jim Sankey packed their corporate suitcases and kissed Los Angeles goodbye in order to open this widely acclaimed '40s-style lodge in Arizona's White Mountains. Antiques fill every nook and cranny of this three-level inn, built with hand-peeled lodgepole pine. A marvelous toy collection is displayed in the high-ceiling Gathering Room, and you'll find wood-cased radios in many guest quarters. Downstairs, there's an antique Bally's mini–bowling alley and old pinball machine in the game room, which always has popcorn and sodas waiting for the inn's adults-only guests. There's a formal living room near the entrance with a fireplace and overstuffed lodge couches. Because of the Red Setter's size—there are many common areas—it feels roomy and comfortable even when there's a full house.

Nine individually decorated rooms promise one thing in common: a figurine or book about a red setter stemming from Jim's love for the breed. Beyond that, some rooms have views of the Little Colorado River, and some have fireplaces and whirlpool tubs. The four downstairs rooms lead to a common deck from which you step down to the river, just 25 ft away. On the main floor, a room equipped for people with disabilities has a Western-style queen-size bed, dormer window, and private deck with a telescope leading to the front of the house. Upstairs, spacious Room 9 has two double beds with country quilts separated by a room divider. In Room 4, a queen-size sleigh bed, whirlpool tub, fireplace, vaulted ceilings, and private deck make for a romantic escape. Across the river is a newly purchased housekeeping cottage for eight, or three more private guest rooms. Two rooms have fireplaces, and all have VCRs and coffeemakers. You'll want to cross the bridge and wander the gardens regardless of which side of the river you choose.

A considerable breakfast of pancakes and sausage, egg frittatas, quiche, or eggs Benedict is served in the lodge's skylit dining room. Guests who stay two or more nights are entitled to a sack lunch with deli sandwiches and cookies, which they can take to explore the beautiful surrounding area. When they return, afternoon refreshments will welcome them back to their home-away-from-home. ♨ *12 double rooms with baths, or 9 rooms and housekeeping cottage for 8. Ceiling fan and private balcony in rooms. $130–$195; full breakfast, refreshments. AE, MC, V. No smoking, 2-night minimum weekends.*

OTHER CHOICES

Hillside Hideaway Bed and Breakfast. 621 Hillside La. (HC 66 Box 2695), Pinetop 85935, tel. 520/367–0212. 2 double rooms with baths. TVs, phones, refrigerators, TV/VCR in living room, library in loft. $85–$95; full breakfast, evening snacks. No credit cards. No smoking indoors.

Log Cabin Bed-and-Breakfast. 3155 N. Hwy. 89, Prescott 86301, tel. and fax 520/778–0442 or tel. 888/778–0442. 4 double rooms with baths. TV/VCR in common room, hot tub. $85–$125; full breakfast. MC, V. No smoking, some pets welcome by arrangement.

Marks House. 203 E. Union St., Prescott 86303-3813, tel. 520/778—4632 or 800/370–MARK. 2 double rooms with baths (1 adjoining), 1 1-bedroom suite, 1 2-bedroom suite. Welcome mineral water in rooms, gift shop. $75–$135; full breakfast, afternoon hors d'oeuvres. D, MC, V. No smoking indoors, 2-night minimum some holidays.

Paisley Corner Bed & Breakfast. Box 458, Springerville 85938, or 287 N. Main St., Eagar 85925, tel. 520/333–4665. 3 double rooms with baths, 1 2-bedroom suite. Welcome basket, TV in living room, spa in gazebo. $65–$95; full breakfast. No credit cards. No smoking indoors.

RESERVATIONS SERVICES

Arizona Association of Bed & Breakfast Inns (Box 7186, Phoenix 85011, tel. 800/284–2589). **Arizona Trails Bed and Breakfast Reservation Service** (Box 18998, Fountain Hills 85269, tel. 602/837–4284 or 888/799–4284, fax 602/816–4224). **Mi Casa Su Casa B&B Reservation Service** (Box 950, Tempe 85280, tel. 602/990–0682, 800/456–0682 reservations only, fax 602/990–3390).

Tucson and Environs

CACTUS QUAIL ☜
14000 N. Dust Devil Dr., Tucson 85739, tel. 520/825–6767

About 9 mi north of Tucson, in a residential enclave, the Cactus Quail has one of the most impressive vistas you could hope to find. The contemporary Southwest-style bed-and-breakfast looks out over the Sonoran Desert and directly at the Santa Catalina Mountains, larger than life and pasted against an endless sky. Best of all, the view will never be obstructed because the land belongs to Catalina State Park. In the foreground, large-eared rabbits and other desert creatures keep guests entertained, as do the horses, dogs, and cats that belong to the inn's proprietors, Marty and Sue Higbee.

On the walls of the smallish Pueblo Room, Tucson artist D. Lawrence West painted ancient Native American cliff dwellings that he saw first in a dream; he designed the Hacienda Room, which shares a bath with Pueblo, to resemble a Mexican village. The Bunkhouse, with a private bath and an upstairs sleeping loft, has a more unadorned Western theme. All are luxurious, with not only beautiful, high-quality furnishings but also plush robes and cable TV with VCR. △
1 room with bath, 2 rooms share bath. VCR library, fireplace in living room, arrangements made for horseback riding and Jeep tours. $95–$110; full breakfast. MC, V. No smoking.

CATALINA PARK INN ☞
309 E. 1st St., Tucson 85705, tel. 520/792–4541 or 800/792–4885

Some people are perpetual tinkerers, always aiming at perfection. Mark Hall and Paul Richard, who moved from San Francisco to Tucson in 1994 so that they could afford to open up an inn that met their high standards, fit this profile to a tee. Although their bed-and-breakfast appears completely and beautifully finished, they're constantly on the lookout for ways to improve it. Right now, for example, a pool with a small bathhouse is in the works.

Mark and Paul had a wonderful base from which to begin: a centrally located two-story residence graced with neoclassic symmetry. Because the place had only been in three other hands since it was built in 1927, many of the original details were left intact. These include the extensive wood trim made from amapa, a blond mahogany brought in from the interior of Mexico, and the Art Nouveau lotus-pattern tiles used as borders in many of baths. An overhang on the second floor and French doors in the upstairs rooms, where most of the guest quarters are located, were designed so that the house could stay relatively cool, even in pre-air-conditioned Tucson summers.

To the upper-level rooms in the main house, Mark and Paul added a downstairs unit, converted from a family game room. You can still see the shallow closets that used to hold pool cues, as well as the scored concrete floor, very much in vogue again in the Southwest. A huge closet made from a Kentucky cedar closet was the perfect spot to install a raised whirlpool tub. The last project, transforming the old garage, introduced two more rooms, one with a wood-burning fireplace, and both with private entrances. All the accommodations are decorated in a distinctive style that makes extensive use of antiques but is never overly fussy. There is a nice contrast in the Oak Room, for example, between its ornate four-poster bed and plush tapestry chairs and a rough-hewn wood desk.

Breakfast is as gracious as you might expect, served on fine china in either a cozy separate nook or, for the more social, in a larger dining room. Fresh fruit, yogurt, muesli, and home-baked goods supplement such entrées as stuffed French toast or delicate, raspberry-topped pancakes. △ *6 rooms with baths. TV, telephone, robes, hair dryer, iron and board in rooms, fireplace in 1 room, private balcony in 2 rooms, fireplace in living room, gardens. $95–$115; full breakfast. D, MC, V. No smoking indoors, minimum stay some holidays and special events.*

HACIENDA DEL DESIERTO ☞
11770 Rambling Trail, Tucson 85747, tel. 520/298–1764 or 800/982–1795, fax 520/722–4558

It's a family affair here. The distinctive, high-ceiling home that Rosemary and David Brown built grew, as the Brown children grew, into a little desert complex. Because the additions to the house were designed to provide privacy as well as space, Hacienda del Desierto is the perfect place to bring *your* family, too.

The house is an amalgam of local history, incorporating wood from a renovated Tucson hospital, timbers from abandoned telephone poles, and ceramic roof tiles from Mexico, but the result couldn't look more unified. As you walk through tall, rough-hewn wooden doors into a Spanish-style courtyard, you almost feel as though you're entering a religious retreat. Abundant ivy, hanging plants, and mature trees help create a serene atmosphere, as do shaded wraparound porches.

Which is not to suggest there's no action here. Although the Browns no longer keep pigs, horses, and chickens, you'll be entertained by several friendly cats and a herd of visiting javelinas. (Sticks are provided in order to keep these somewhat stinky wild pigs from poking their noses into your business.) The inn's 16-acre spread is less than a mile from Saguaro National Park East, so hiking and desert biking are also options.

Lovebirds will like the romantic Rose Room, with its fluffy pillows and appropriately reddish-hued decor, but a pull-down Murphy bed means there's always room for one (or two) more. The Patio Suite has a double hide-a-bed in its separate living room, along with a lovely view of the courtyard. Largest of all, the two-bedroom Casita features a hot tub looking out on the Santa Rita mountains. All the units are equipped with kitchen facilities (full-size in the case of the Casita), TV, VCR, and a gas or wood-burning stove; all have carpeting and private entrances, too. Exposed adobe brick walls and Mexican tile are among the many touches that lend Southwest character.

A buffet of fruit, yogurt, cold cereals, baked goods, and hard boiled eggs is laid out in the courtyard, cozy dining area, or great room, depending on the weather and guests' inclinations. ♨ *1 room with bath, 1 suite, 1 casita. Kitchenettes, TV/VCRs, film library, hot tub. $95–$150; Continental breakfast. MC, V. No smoking indoors, 2 night-minimum in casita. Closed July–Aug.*

MI GATITA ♟
14085 Avenida Haley S. (HCR 70, Box 304A), Sahuarita 85629, tel. 520/648–6129

You never know what to expect at this bed-and-breakfast in Sahuarita, some 25 minutes south of Tucson. Ron White, cowboy poet and the world's last mule skinner, may come riding up on Yaqui, his dancing horse. Ron is a local celebrity who appeared on the Johnny Carson show, but he hasn't let it go to his head; if you ask nicely, he'll get Yaqui to do a little two-step (or is that four-step?) for you.

One of Rusty's two-legged pals is Bill Lambert, who built the house Mi Gatita now occupies on land that used to be part of the Navarro Ranch, deeded to its owner by the King of Spain. In keeping with the Hispanic spirit of the place, Lambert designed the former ranch house along Mexican lines, with lots of niches, courtyards, and gardens, as well as private entrances. Among the many interesting items he acquired during his travels—he finally sold the place in order to indulge his wanderlust—are the carved Tarahumara columns that buttress the portico.

Current owners Jean and Bentley Pace have added their own character, not only by adopting three desert cats—one of whom, Jean claims, gave them the original tour of the house—but also with their creative furnishings. The San Blas room has a carved wooden bed (from which there's a wonderful view of Tucson), as well as an antique hatstand and Mexican equipale (pigskin) furniture. The more casual two-bedroom San Carlos/Cozumel Suite also has Mexican touches, including a piñata that none of the guests has smashed (yet). In both rooms you'll find books and games, fresh flowers, terry robes, and Sees candy.

The chocolate is but a hint of the culinary delights to come. Chile relleno puffs or oat waffles with hot ginger peach topping are among Jean's delicious, elaborate breakfast entrées. Bentley makes a mean cup of coffee, but it's his tour-guiding skills that especially endear him to guests. He's an expert on the San Xavier Mission, only 10 minutes away, and familiar with all the natural attractions in the area. ♨ *1 room with bath, 1 suite. Fireplace in 1 guest room and in common room. $85; full breakfast, afternoon snack. No credit cards. No smoking indoors or in common outdoor areas.*

PEPPERTREES BED AND BREAKFAST INN 🐾
724 E. University Blvd., Tucson 85719, tel. and fax 520/622–7167 or tel. 800/348–5763

Early settlers who came to the Arizona Territory at the turn of the century tried to create pockets of civilization in what was then a dusty desert outpost. Some 80 years later, perhaps in a similar spirit, Marjorie Martin brought antiques from her family home in the English Cotswolds to furnish her 1905 redbrick Victorian. After a careful restoration, she opened the Peppertrees in 1988. The classic residence is two blocks from the main gate of the University of Arizona and near the Fourth Avenue shopping district.

To check into the inn, guests enter the main house. Rooms with 12-ft-high ceilings and pine floors covered with Oriental carpets highlight Marjorie's furnishings, most of which date back to the last century. The mahogany-and-glass bookcase in the living room contains the family's Royal Doulton china.

Penelope's Room has windows on three sides; the one to the south looks out on a mature pomegranate tree and landscaped patio. It's decorated in Victorian style, with a white wrought-iron bed, a frilly rose-patterned comforter, and a 150-year-old mirrored mahogany dresser.

Adjacent to the main house is a 1917 Bungalow-style home with a large, comfortable living room and two bedrooms decorated with mahogany furniture, frilly patterned comforters, and lace curtains. Behind the main house, across a cozy garden with a splashing Mexican-tile fountain, are two fully equipped guest houses. Each duplex unit, furnished in contemporary style, has two bedrooms upstairs with a shared bath. Downstairs are a half-bath, living room, dining area, full kitchen, and private patio. A studio apartment decorated in a Mexican casita style has recently been added, which accommodates two comfortably and has a kitchenette.

A gourmet cook, Marjorie published her *Recipes from Peppertrees Bed and Breakfast Inn.* Breakfast is served buffet-style in the dining room or, on those perfect southern Arizona mornings, outdoors on the patio. There is always fresh fruit and home-baked breads or scones and a main dish such as blue-corn pancakes or savory French toast filled with cream cheese and orange. Special diets can be accommodated with advance notice, and picnic baskets may be ordered for day excursions. ♨ *3 double rooms with baths, 2 2-bedroom duplex guest houses, 1 studio apartment. TV, phone, washer/dryer in guest houses. $78–$175; full breakfast. D, MC, V. No smoking, 2-night minimum holiday weekends.*

RANCHO QUIETO 🐾
12051 W. Fort Lowell Rd., Tucson 85743, tel. 520/883–3300

When watercolorist Corinne Still bought Rancho Quieto (pronounced Kay-*et*-o) in 1990, she had in mind an artist's retreat. As it turned out, the Southern Arizona Watercolor Guild sometimes has its "paint outs" here, but the less artistically talented portion of the populace also has the chance to stay at this unique 40-acre bed-and-breakfast, only a few minutes from Saguaro National Park West.

It was designed in 1970 by local landscape architect Mervin Larson, best known in Tucson for the real-looking boulders he made for the Arizona-Sonora Desert Museum (which adjoins this property). To the mature desert foliage he added fruit trees—orange, tangerine, lemon, lime, grapefruit, tangelo, and fig—six types of palms, and ironwoods, and he even imported a stand of bamboo from the San Diego Zoo. The centerpiece of this little portion of paradise is the swimming pool, which resembles a natural rock grotto; it's fed by a waterfall created by pumped and recirculated well water. A gently bubbling outdoor spa looks enough like a genuine hot spring to make Mother Nature do a double take.

The house, which draws from a variety of Southwest and Mexican styles, is as dramatic as the setting; a saguaro rib ceiling and beams made of redwood collected from old railroad bridges and trestles are among its interesting details. Decorating the tremendous sunken living room was one of Corinne's many artistic outlets, and she's demonstrated that she's no slouch, either, when it comes to creating illusions: Because she couldn't afford a Navajo rug large enough to fit the large space above her fireplace, she simply painted one on the wall. Her country-hearty breakfasts are served in the adjacent dining room.

You might be tempted to settle in here for a while. The three split-level suites in the main house and the separate guest house all have full kitchens, wet bars, and fireplaces; Suite II also features a Jacuzzi tub for two in a paradisiacal plant-filled bathroom. Individually chosen by Corinne, the contemporary Southwest furnishings have an artistic flair. And you'll never tire of watching the sunset from your private patio or deck. △ *3 suites, 1 guest house. Guest phone, kitchens, fireplaces, TV, piano in living room, barbecue grills, horseshoes, pool. $125–$150; full breakfast. No credit cards. Closed June–mid-Sept.*

OTHER CHOICES

Adobe Rose Inn. 940 N. Olsen Ave., Tucson 85719, tel. 520/318–4644 or 800/328–4122, fax 520/325–0055. 3 rooms with bath, 1 cottage, 1 suite. TV in rooms, pool. $65–$115; full breakfast. AE, D, MC, V. No smoking indoors.
Bienestar. 10490 E. Escalante Rd., Tucson 85730, tel. 520/290–1048, fax 520/290–1367. 1 room with bath, 1 suite, 1 casita. TV and phone in suite and casita, hot tub, library with piano, gift shop, pool. $85–$125; full breakfast, afternoon high tea. D, MC, V. No smoking, horses allowed (trailer space available), 2-night minimum weekends during high season.
El Presidio Bed & Breakfast Inn. 297 N. Main Ave., Tucson 85701, tel. 520/623–6151 or 800/349–6151, fax 520/623–3860. 3 suites. TV, phone, and bathrobes in rooms, kitchen in 2 suites stocked with beverages and fruit, TV in sitting room. $95–$115; full breakfast. No credit cards. No smoking indoors.
Jeremiah Inn. 10921 E. Synder Rd., Tucson 85749, tel. 520/749–3072. 3 rooms with baths. TV and phone in rooms, TV/VCR in living room, guest refrigerator, pool. $70–$100; full breakfast, afternoon snack. MC, V. No smoking indoors or in outdoor public areas.

RESERVATIONS SERVICES

Arizona Association of Bed & Breakfast Inns (Box 7186, Phoenix 85011, tel. 800/284–2589). **Bed & Breakfast Southwest** (2916 N. 70th St., Scottsdale 85251, tel. 602/995–2831 or 800/762–9704, fax 602/874–1316). **Mi Casa Su Casa B&B Reservation Service** (Box 950, Tempe 85280, tel. 602/990–0682, 800/456–0682 reservations only, fax 602/990–3390). **Old Pueblo Home-Stays RSO** (Box 13603, Tucson 85732, tel. and fax 520/790–2399 or 800/333–9776). **Premiere Bed & Breakfast Inns of Tucson** (316 E. Speedway Blvd., 85705, tel. 520/628–1800 or 800/628–5654, fax 520/792–1880).

Southern Arizona

CASA DE SAN PEDRO

8933 S. Yell La., Hereford 85615, tel. 520/366–1300 or 800/588–6468,
fax 520/366–9701

Everything's up-to-date in Hereford, a sleepy town near Sierra Vista—or at least it is at the Casa de San Pedro. Everything seems like new at the hacienda-style inn built adjacent to the San Pedro Riparian National Conservation area in 1995. Even the bird-watching is high-tech: A computer with Robert Tory Peterson software in the high-ceiling common room lets avian admirers check their daily sightings against the lists of the departed master.

Guest quarters, arranged around a tiled central courtyard, are bright and modern, too, with handcrafted wooden furnishings from northern Mexico lending local character. Each room is individually decorated. In one there's a bed with a saguaro rib headboard, for example, while another has a cheerful Western-pattern bedspread and curtains.

Because the place is so new, the surrounding landscape is still a bit sparse, but hiking trails just beyond the house lead directly into the lush nature preserve. Breakfasts are designed to be as healthy or indulgent as you like; they're light on cheese and eggs, and meat is served on the side. ♨ *10 rooms with baths. Guest services area with house phone, refrigerator, and microwave; library, gift shop, barbecue grill, guest laundry for longer stays. $115; full breakfast. D, MC, V. No smoking indoors, minimum stay some holiday weekends.*

DUQUESNE HOUSE BED AND BREAKFAST ⚘

357 Duquesne St., Box 772, Patagonia 85624, tel. 520/394–2732

Don't be startled when you enter this unusual, tree-shaded Eden in tiny Patagonia and see a 21-ft-long snake. Innkeeper Regina Medley is an artist who works with textiles; her reptile and other soft sculptures and artwork enliven various parts of her tin-roofed adobe inn, as do the creations of other local artists.

Buttresses and plastered Santa Fe benches have been added to the B&B, built as a boardinghouse for miners more than 90 years ago, and burned adobe bricks replaced the original wood floors, but the 17-inch-thick adobe walls, narrow doors, and lintels are all original. The Western period furniture throughout the house was collected in the Patagonia area. Each of its four high-ceiling guest units has its own private street entrance. The rooms are not luxurious, but creative-minded visitors find that such details as hand-painted scrollwork and colorful tiles compensate. Two rooms have a wood-burning stove.

Regina's breakfasts, served buffet style, may be enjoyed in your room, on the flower-filled screen porch, or at the hostess's table in the dining room, part of a Santa Fe–style great room. ♨ *3 suites, 1 efficiency apartment. Radio and ceiling fan in rooms, kitchenette and TV in apartment, common area with TV and house phone. $70–$85; full breakfast. No credit cards. No smoking.*

GUEST HOUSE INN ⚘

700 Guesthouse Rd., Ajo 85321, tel. 520/387–6133

Like virtually every other building in Ajo, this one was built by the Phelps Dodge Corporation; it was designed in high style in 1925 to accommodate executives visiting the copper mine. Abandoned when the mine closed in 1985, the inn was purchased three years later by Norma Walker, who used to work here as a housekeeper.

The four original VIP guest rooms, now beautifully remodeled, all have different themes. The Ajo Room features Santa Fe–style decor, while the Old Pueblo Room emphasizes Ajo's Spanish-colonial heritage. The Bisbee Room has twin brass beds and Victorian furnishings, and the Prescott Room boasts a four-poster bed and fittings reminiscent of Arizona's Territorial days.

The B&B's pride is the stately dining room with its formal, 20-ft carved walnut table where breakfast is served; specialties include pecan waffles with berries and cream, and blueberry French toast. A longtime Ajo resident, Norma can direct you to all the best places for bird-watching in the area. ♠ *4 double rooms with baths. Individual heating/air-conditioning controls in rooms, fireplace and TV in common room. $69–$79; full breakfast. DC, MC, V. No smoking.*

HIGH DESERT INN ♥
Box 145, 8 Naco Rd., Bisbee 85603, tel. 520/432–1442 or 800/281–0510

Bisbee is nothing if not adaptable. The little hillside town looked like it might go under in 1975, when Phelps Dodge shut down the copper mine, but many miners liked the place well enough to hang around. They were soon joined by hippies, who opened crafts shops and started an annual poetry festival. Now there's a new wave of urban refugees, who enjoy Bisbee's tranquillity but also want a bit of the consumerist good life.

Count Margaret Hartnett in the latter category. The Cordon Bleu–trained chef, who had been cooking for some major political movers and shakers in New York City, was on a trip out West when, as she puts it, "I got off I–10 in New Mexico and found myself in Bisbee an hour later." It was love at first sight. She bought a house within a week, and then convinced her other love (now husband), actor Darrell Dixon, to come out and open up a restaurant and inn with her.

Using a lot of elbow grease and imagination, the couple set to work on restoring the 1908 county jail, little more than four walls and a lot of turn-of-the-century electricity when they acquired it in 1992. It took them 10 months to gut and restore the neoclassic-style building, but the metamorphosis was little short of amazing: The inn that opened in 1994 at the edge of Bisbee's historic district offers the most up-to-date and stylish accommodations in town—not to mention some of the best food.

No attention to detail was spared: All five rooms feature handmade wrought-iron beds imported from Paris, covered by 200-count cotton sheets. Craftsman-style end tables were handcrafted in Bisbee to match the beds' higher-than-standard-size frames. Modern amenities include data-compatible phones with built-in answering machines, not available anywhere else in town; the rooms also have cable TV. The chic Continental restaurant, which doubles as an art gallery, is only open for dinner Thursday through Saturday; seasonally changing dishes might include baked Brie and goat cheese followed by French-trimmed pork chops. ♠ *5 double rooms with baths. Coffee bar in lobby. $65–$90; breakfast not included. D, MC, V. No smoking. Closed 1st 3 wks in June.*

MINE MANAGER'S HOUSE INN ♥
1 Greenway Dr., Ajo 85321, tel. 520/387–6505, fax 520/387–6508

The imposing, 5,000-square-ft mansion that once belonged to the superintendent of the Phelps Dodge copper mine overlooks the entire town from its site atop the highest hill in Ajo. The public areas include a library-sunroom, a spacious living room, and a formal dining room with a view out over the town. A hot tub in the back is wonderful for soaking tired muscles after a day of desert travel.

Each of the five individually decorated rooms has high ceilings and ceiling fans. The Greenway Suite, also called the "honeymoon suite," is the largest one and boasts a marble bathtub and vanity, and pretty floral drapes. The Nautical Room has two queen-size brass beds and a 180-degree view out over the town; parts of an old schooner, including the steering wheel, are worked into the decor.

Breakfasts are served on linens and fine china in the superintendent's light-filled formal dining room. The meal may feature eggs Benedict or waffles, in addition to coffee, fresh juices, and seasonal fruits. ♠ *2 double rooms with baths, 3 suites. TV/VCR in living room, library, guest coin laundry, outdoor hot tub, barbecue grill, off-street parking. $72–$105; full breakfast. MC, V. No smoking indoors, off-site pet boarding.*

OLNEY HOUSE BED & BREAKFAST ☜
1104 Central Ave., Safford 85546, tel. 520/428–5118 or 800/814–5118

George Olney was a sheriff of Graham County in the Wild West days of the 1870s. Unable to budget a salary, the county fathers agreed to pay him $2.50 for every arrest. Within two years he had amassed $30,000. Much of these earnings were spent on this classic, two-story example of Western Colonial Revival, completed in 1890. From the bay windows on the second floor, with a 180-degree view of Safford and the verdant Gila River valley, Sheriff Olney could look for local desperados.

In 1988 the National Park Service announced that 20 Safford buildings had qualified for listing in the National Register of Historic Places: the 1920 Arizona Bank, the 1920 Southern Pacific Railroad Depot, a 1915 schoolhouse, a 1920 hotel, and 16 private residences. The oldest of these was the Olney House.

Innkeepers Patrick and Carole Mahoney, from San Francisco, spent four years renovating the redbrick, 14-room mansion. In 1992 they opened it as Graham County's first B&B. The home boasts 12-ft ceilings (now with circulating fans); five fireplaces with unusual, ceramic-tile detailing; polished oak and maple floors; and lots of elegant wood paneling. The bright corner dining room fills with morning light from three wide, 7-ft windows. Many of the furnishings are treasures brought back by the Mahoneys from travels in Southeast Asia. Upstairs there are three corner bedrooms.

A huge pecan tree shades two cottages in the back. Other trees on the landscaped corner lot include willows, cottonwood, Italian and Arizona cyprus, native pine, ash, and paloverdes. Each year the Mahoneys harvest fresh fruit from their apple, plum, and peach trees to make jams.

The breakfast coffee beans, ground fresh daily, are from Graffeo in San Francisco. The dill and cilantro in the omelets and potatoes are picked from the garden. Guests have a choice of muesli with yogurt, honey, and fruit; oatmeal with pecans, wheat germ, honey, and fruit; or a cheese omelet spiced with roasted New Mexico chilies (mild, medium, or hot). ♠ *3 double rooms share bath, 2 cottages. TV, cable, fireplace in living room, spa. $70; full breakfast. MC, V. No smoking indoors.*

RAMSEY CANYON INN ☜
31 Ramsey Canyon Rd., Hereford 85615, tel. 520/378–3010

When guests talk turkey around the breakfast table at the Ramsey Canyon Inn, you can take that literally: Wild toms often strut their stuff in full view of the visitors. But it's the hummingbirds—all 14 species that visit the Nature Conservancy's Mile Hi/Ramsey Canyon preserve, adjacent to the inn—who are the stars. Some true devotees also come to see the elegant Trogon, a rare species that has successfully nested in the area.

But this scenic, tree-filled gorge in the Huachuca Mountains, 10 mi south of Sierra Vista, is not only a haven for bird-watchers; at 5,400 ft, it's also one of the most temperate spots in the nation, with an annual average high of 75°F and average low of 50°F. You can walk the shaded paths of the preserve and see all kinds of wildlife—coatimundi, deer, and the endangered Ramsey Canyon frog.

The inn is almost as interesting as its setting. The front section, built of native stone and wood in 1963, incorporates local Arizona history with planks from the old post office at Fort Huachuca, the train station at Fairbank, and the Lavender Pit Mine in Bisbee. The 1988 addition at the back of the house includes the six guest rooms, named by owner Shirlene DeSantis after her favorite hummingbirds. These accommodations, furnished in country Victorian style, enjoy the soothing ripple of a year-round stream, as do two separate housekeeping cottages (those who stay there don't get breakfast but have their own kitchens).

Not only the rooms, but every area of the house is filled with fascinating collectibles. On the staircase leading up to the guest rooms you can see antique tobacco artifacts, including an ad for Lucky Strikes featuring Ronald Reagan. In the kitchen the focus is naturally on food-related items, and the old jars and containers often fascinate guests who remember them from their childhood.

If your fortifying breakfast—perhaps stuffed French toast or blue-corn pancakes served with jam from the inn's own orchard—doesn't hold you through the afternoon, there are always two fresh-baked pies waiting for you in the kitchen. **⌂** *6 double rooms with baths, 8 cottages. Fireplace in living room, gift shop. $90–$105 rooms, full breakfast; cottages, accommodating up to 4 people, $95– $135, no breakfast. No credit cards. Smoking on patio only.*

SAN PEDRO RIVER INN ☙
8326 S. Hereford Rd., Hereford 85615, tel. 520/366–5532

Walter Kolbe is proof that you *can* go home again. When, after 25 years of living in Illinois, he decided he wanted to return to the ranch country of southern Arizona where he grew up, he was hard pressed to figure out how he and his wife, May, could make the move financially feasible. Enter Walt's sister, Beth, who works for the Nature Conservancy in Tucson. The story goes that the nonprofit group needed to sell off 20 acres of land adjoining the San Pedro Riparian National Conservation area, and they were hoping to find someone who would turn the former dairy farm into a low-impact business—say, a bed-and-breakfast. Walt and May jumped at the chance, and the rest is hospitality history.

The inn's four separate guest houses are perfect for a variety of visitors. Proximity to the preserve makes this place ideal for groups of bird-watchers—a banding seminar was once offered here—while families appreciate the full kitchens and barbecue grills of each house, as well as the on-site laundry facilities. There are even jungle gyms and swings. This is a spot where you'll want to settle in and relax for a spell, maybe fish from the shores of one of the two ponds or picnic under a spreading willow tree. You can even bring your pets, if you're willing to leave them outdoors in the large, coyote-proof pen that a former owner built for his Barbados sheep.

Furnishings in the houses are low-key and country comfortable; you don't come here for glitz but for peace and quiet (although the media-addicted can tune into noncable TV). With the fully supplied kitchen—baked goods, fresh fruit, and juice—you can keep pretty much to yourself if you like, but then you'd miss the sing-alongs May sometimes leads in the main house, as well as Walt's colorful ranch stories. Ask him about the time his father came home with a Gila monster. *△ 1 1-bedroom cottage, 2 2-bedroom cottages, 1 3-bedroom cottage. Conference center, piano lounge, fireplace in 2 cottages. $95 for 2 guests in a cottage ($135 for 4 guests, $210 for 6 guests). Continental breakfast. No credit cards. Pets accepted in outdoor pen, corrals available for horses.*

SCHOOL HOUSE INN BED & BREAKFAST ☙
Box 32, 818 Tombstone Canyon, Bisbee 85603, tel. 520/432–2996 or 800/537–4333

The two-story brick Garfield School, in the Tombstone Canyon neighborhood on Bisbee's west side, was built in 1918 to educate children in grades 1 through 4. The original four large classrooms, one for each grade, were divided into apartments in the 1930s and used as a nursing home in the 1970s. Abandoned by 1981, the building was refurbished and converted to a B&B in 1989.

The innkeepers took the built-in schoolhouse theme and ran with it. Depending on how you feel about your school days, the guest rooms, all on the second floor, may strike horror into your heart or fill you with fond memories. Here's your chance to sleep, with impunity, in the Principal's Office, the Library, the Music Room, or the History Room, among others; just pick the subject you found the most soporific.

The spacious accommodations are country comfortable, with flowery quilted comforters, dark-wood furniture, lace curtains, and stenciled wall borders. Those at the front of the building provide views of upper Tombstone Canyon and the Mule Mountains. Children are not welcome here. *△ 6 double rooms with baths, 3 2-bedroom suites. Library, barbecue grill, off-street parking. $55–$80; full breakfast. AE, D, DC, MC, V. No smoking.*

SKYWATCHER'S INN ☙
420 South Essex La., Tucson 85711 (directions to the inn, outside Benson, are complicated), tel. and fax 520/745–2390

Astronomers keep strange hours, not much different from those of rock stars. So don't be surprised if you learn that some of your fellow guests are taking late-afternoon naps when you check into this unique bed-and-breakfast, which has its own astronomical observatory. Or perhaps it's more accurate to say the Vega-Bray Observatory, just outside of Benson, has its own bed-and-breakfast: Dr. Ed Vega, a longtime amateur astronomer, built a stargazing facility that proved so popular that he ended up adding a place where visitors could bed down after a long night of looking into the skies.

Six professional telescopes, ranging 6–20 inches, are available to guests on two bases: Those sufficiently familiar with the equipment can rent it (except for the 20-incher) for $35. Others can pay $85 (per group) for basic instruction and guided viewing; more advanced supervision, including lessons in using the CCD imaging camera, can cost up to $150.

This is a great place for an educational family vacation. During the daytime, guests can browse through a classroom with fossils, meteorites, and a variety of interactive projects; the room also includes an impressive science library. Those whose sights are not quite as high in the sky can sit out on one of two porches with impressive vistas and look at birds through mounted binoculars. And when Kartchner Caverns State Park opens nearby, there'll be a lot of attention paid to below-ground wonders.

The four guest rooms all offer comfortable contemporary furnishings in science-oriented settings. One room, with a domed ceiling, can function as a planetarium, another reveals the night sky above when you switch on a black light, and the third lets you turn on the lamps over your bed simply by touching the headboard. The newly remodeled Egyptian Room is entirely accessible to wheelchairs.

For obvious reasons, breakfast tends to be served on the late side (between 9 and 10). However, a stocked refrigerator lets early risers prepare their own morning meals. ♨ *4 rooms with baths. Kitchenette in 1 room, Jacuzzi in 1 room, TV/VCR with astronomy videos in living room–science studio, dark room, crib available. $65–$99; full breakfast. MC, V. No smoking indoors, pets accepted with advance permission.*

OTHER CHOICES

Amado Territory Inn. Box 81, 3001 E. Frontage Rd., Amado 85645, tel. 520/398–8684 or 888/398–8684, fax 520/398–8186. 9 double rooms with baths. TV lounge, restaurant next door. $90–$250; full breakfast. AE, D, MC, V. No smoking indoors.

Victoria's. Box 37, 211 Toughnut St., Tombstone 85638, tel. 520/457–3677 or 800/952–8216, fax 520/457–2450. 3 double rooms with baths. TVs. $55–$75; full breakfast. MC, V. No smoking indoors.

Vineyard Bed-and-Breakfast. 92 Los Encinos Rd., Sonoita 85637, tel. 520/455–4749. 3 rooms with baths, 1 casita. Player piano, Jacuzzi, pool. $85– $95; full breakfast. No credit cards. No smoking indoors.

Yee Ha Ranch. Box 888, Sonoita 85637, tel. 520/455–9285. 3 rooms with baths. Wood-burning stoves, TV/VCRs. $85; Continental-plus breakfast. AE, MC, V. No smoking indoors.

RESERVATIONS SERVICES

Arizona Association of Bed and Breakfast Inns (Box 7186, Phoenix 85011, tel. 800/284–2589). **Bed & Breakfast Southwest** (2916 N. 70th St., Scottsdale 85251, tel. 602/995–2831 or 800/762–9704, fax 602/874–1316). **Mi Casa Su Casa B&B Reservation Service** (Box 950, Tempe 85280, tel. 602/990–0682, 800/456–0682 reservations, fax 602/990–3390).

ARKANSAS

The Ozarks

ARKANSAS HOUSE BED AND BREAKFAST ☙
Box 325, Jasper 72641, tel. 501/446–5900 or 888/274–6873

People still stop in the middle of the road just to chat in the quaint historic town of Jasper, nestled among the Ozark Mountains along the Buffalo National River. While the town seems sleepy, the area does offer many attractions. Guided hiking and floating along the Buffalo are very popular, with spectacular scenery like majestic 500-ft bluffs and 200-ft waterfalls.

Built during the 1940s, this unique rambling structure has a bottom floor that is made from individual stone casings and that once served as the Newton County Jail. Complimentary refreshments are available in the spacious common area, which has a stone fireplace, working antique pump organ, piano, and, for more modern tastes, a stereo, video library, and satellite big-screen TV.

One of the most notable attractions at Arkansas House is the resident pet, Coco, a 5-year-old 600-pound black bear who arm wrestles, gives kisses, and eats 40 to 50 pounds of food each day. Coco, of course, stays outside in his air-conditioned den, but guests are welcome to visit him.

The Visnoskys moved here from Texas in 1994 and bought the restaurant adjacent to what is now Arkansas House. A short time later they purchased the rest of the property, remodeled it, and opened the Arkansas House in 1996. Larry Visnosky is retired from the military and his wife, Karen, taught English and drama. She now lends her dramatic touches to the guest rooms, filling them with old books, antiques, and memorabilia. Though each room is individually decorated, Old English style predominates, with four-poster beds and antiques in every room.

Breakfast begins under skylights in the plant-filled Cedar Room with Karen's specialty, Slovakian bread, as well as fresh fruit, coffee, tea, and juice. Two more courses of homemade offerings follow. Room service is available, as are morning newspapers, for those who are in no rush to start their day. ♙ *2 double rooms with baths, 3 suites, 1 guest house (sleeps 6) with kitchen. Air-conditioning, cable TV/VCRs, phones, ceiling fans, coffeemakers, whirlpool bath in 2 suites, kitchenette in suites, restaurant, washer/dryer off common area, off-street parking. $65–$125; full breakfast, evening dessert. AE, MC, V.*

BRIDGEFORD HOUSE ☙
263 Spring St., Eureka Springs 72632, tel. 501/253–7853 or 888/567–2422

This humble 1884 Victorian, a former residence of a Civil War captain, is centrally located for exploring downtown Eureka Springs. A fashionable spa at the turn of the century, this Ozark town attracted everyone from Carry Nation to Diamond Lil. Today, it's a thriving arts-and-crafts colony, with residents from around the globe lending a cosmopolitan air.

In a town where crooked staircases and terraced gardens career down steep hills, and hiking trails vanish into thick foliage, owners Linda and Henry Thorton oversee one of the extravagant and carefully maintained Victorians interspersed among rough-hewn limestone buildings. In fact, strict laws in Eureka Springs ensure that the Bridgeford House (on the National Register of Historic Places) and buildings downtown (a National Historic District) conform to their original look.

As a result, the building's sole embellishments are a gable roof, a lone bay window, and a painted exterior not unlike cotton candy—predominantly peach and apricot with accents of maroon and blue. But its simplicity is deceptive: Like many other buildings in this hilly, "crazy quilt" town, it has entrances on several levels. Welcome modern luxuries such as cable TVs, coffeemakers, and mini-refrigerators in each room cohabit with such traditional country English antiques as iron and walnut beds and cherry armoires.

Formerly a student of New Orleans School of Cooking, Linda has an obvious expertise. Breakfasts are carefully prepared, some dishes with a cajun spark, and are served on fine, antique china with silver. A fruit cup, orange juice, and coffee may begin the meal to be followed by eggs Benedict, strawberry-stuffed French toast, or artichoke frittata served with New Orleans-style hash browns or garlic roasted potatoes.

Guests of Bridgeford House are often newlyweds and their families and friends, as two to three weddings a month are held here. Low rock walls, old trees, and a large stone fountain in the flower garden provide a romantic atmosphere for the ceremony, while the suite with a fireplace and Jacuzzi is a satisfying place to retreat afterward. △ *3 double rooms with baths, 1 suite. Air-conditioning, cable TV, coffeemaker, mini-refrigerator in rooms, fireplace in 1 room and suite, Jacuzzi in 1 room and suite. $85–$145; full breakfast, refreshments. AE, D, MC, V.*

HEARTSTONE INN ☞
35 Kingshighway, Eureka Springs 72632, tel. 501/253–8916 or 800/494–4921

A white picket fence and an inviting pink-and-cobalt patio spilling over with Boston ferns and potted geraniums greet visitors to this sprawling 1903 late-Victorian inn on Eureka Springs's historic loop. This gabled two-story home might have been used as the set of *It's a Wonderful Life*; innkeepers Iris and Bill Simantel complete the picture of small-town warmth and hospitality.

The Simantels opened the main house as an inn in 1985 and gradually renovated the carriage house and two dollhouse cottages to receive guests. Bill was in the construction business, so he is constantly renovating and making improvements. Iris hails from London, and her tasteful touch is evident throughout. Most notable is her superlative collection of antique English pottery: Handsome royal blue–glazed Torquay pots and humorous Toby mugs adorn both the parlor (which doubles as an informal gallery) and the cheerful breakfast room, where Iris serves chocolate-chip muffins made from scratch, crepes, frittatas, German apple pancakes, and all the not-so-trim trimmings like bacon and sausages. Often, classical musicians play softly on the deck, or in the gazebo on weekend mornings in the summer.

All rooms have English-country antiques, including brass or four-poster beds; many also have rocking chairs and intricate tracery. Each is individually decorated, Laura Ashley–style, according to a floral theme. The Devon Wildflower room—its large bay window overlooking the garden—has delicate hues of teal, pink, and ecru and displays framed pressed flowers; the Rose Arbor room is fittingly garnished with a profusion of roses and lace. The English Garden suite suggests a conservatory, with an ivy-covered white trellis, neoclassical garden statues, floral wallpaper, and plush, forest-green carpeting. Tucked away in the garden, the cozy Country Cottage is ideal for honeymooners, with floral decor, a private deck (including a porch swing and a barbecue), and modern conveniences like cable TV and a full kitchen. The 1882 Victoria House cottage is crammed with antiques and has polished oak and pine floors under lofty 10-ft ceilings, a working fireplace in the master bedroom, and its own porch and terraced garden.

Both Iris and Bill are extremely knowledgeable about the area and can provide information about such local activities as walking tours of the Victorian homes, spa makeovers, and the famed Great Passion Play. ♠ *8 double rooms with baths, 4 suites, 1 1-bedroom cottage, 1 2-bedroom cottage. Air-conditioning, cable TV, ceiling fan, radio, refrigerator, and coffeemaker in suites, kitchenette and fireplace in cottages, wet bar in 1 suite, Jacuzzi in 2 suites, gift shop, off-street parking, massage therapy available. $71–$130; full breakfast. AE, D, MC, V. Closed late-Dec.–late-Feb.*

WILDFLOWER BED AND BREAKFAST 🐦
Courthouse Sq. (Box 72), Mountain View 72560, tel. 870/269–4383 or 800/591–4879

The Wildflower Inn sits on the northeast corner of Courthouse Square in the sleepy town of Mountain View. Visitors are often drawn to the popular Ozark Folk Center, which is dedicated to preserving local culture by offering daily crafts demonstrations, storytelling hours, cooking classes, and musicals. Local musicians still congregate in the square each warm Saturday evening for "pickin' and grinnin'," the sweet zing of their fiddles and dulcimers filling the air.

Come for the almost vanished tradition of hospitality that is pure old-time Ozark; an opportunity to enjoy the community's unique musical heritage; and the gentle scenery of rolling hills, thickly wooded hollows, lakes, and streams. Almost a legacy of Ozarks musical inheritance, the Wildflower Inn has its own string band who performs on weekend evenings on the inn's wraparound portico or in the parlor. Originally opened in 1918 as the Commercial Hotel, the inn has since been renovated by LouAnne Rhodes, to bring modern comforts to guests.

The rooms are furnished plainly in old-fashioned Ozark style, with most of the original handcrafted dressers and iron bedsteads, along with hand-sewn curtains and dust ruffles, and more modern solid-color quilts. Some feature an "Ozark closet," walls with embellished 2½-ft wrought-iron rods forged by local blacksmiths. Each room is named for a local wildflower, with colors to match. Dogwood, for example, is a delicate whitish pink; an artist's painting of the blossoms hangs on the wall. Columbine's hue is a soothing rust. The Jonquil, in bright yellow, is ideal for families, with its kitchenette and bunk nook for kids.

There's no TV on the premises, but no one seems to mind, as there's often live entertainment. People rock on the porch, listening to crickets and to the musicians that stop by nearly every afternoon and evening. Kids play games on the courthouse lawn or swim à la Huck Finn and Tom Sawyer in one of the many nearby streams.

Guests gather for a large breakfast buffet, supplied by the on-site bakery (under different ownership), featuring delectable pastries, muffins, breads, fresh fruit, and homemade jams. ♠ *3 double rooms with baths, 2 doubles share bath, 4 suites. Air-conditioning, bakery, book shop. $50–$85; Continental breakfast. D, MC, V. Closed Jan.–Feb.*

OTHER CHOICES

Arsenic & Old Lace. 60 Hillside Avenue, Eureka Springs 72632, tel. 501/253-5454 or 800/243-5223. 5 double rooms with baths. Cable TV/VCRs, robes, whirlpool tubs, fireplace in 3 rooms, book and video library. $125–$160; full breakfast, snacks, and refreshments. AE, D, MC, V.

Brambly Hedge Cottage Bed & Breakfast. HCR 31 (Box 39), Jasper 72641, tel. 870/446–5849 or 800/272–6259. 3 double rooms with baths. TV, CD/tape player in 1 room, tape player in 2 rooms, massage therapy available. $75–$125; full breakfast, evening dessert. No credit cards. No smoking, 2-night minimum.

Brownstone Inn. 75 Hillside St., Eureka Springs 72632, tel. 501/253–7505, or 800/973–7505. 2 double rooms with baths, 2 suites. Air-conditioning, ceiling fans, cable TVs, off-street parking. $90–$110; full breakfast, snacks, and refreshments. D, MC, V.

1881 Crescent Cottage Inn. 211 Spring St., Eureka Springs 72632, tel. 501/253–6022 or 800/223–3246. 4 double rooms with baths. Cable TV/VCRs, whirlpool tubs, fireplace in 2 rooms, video library. $97–$139; full breakfast, refreshments, dinner packages available. D, MC, V.

Inn at Mountain View. W. Washington St. (Box 812), Mountain View 72560, tel. 870/269–4200 or 800/535–1301. 10 double rooms with baths. Air-conditioning; TV, fireplace, piano in common room. $62–$72; full breakfast. D, MC, V.

Olde Stonehouse Inn. 511 Main St., Hardy 72542, tel. 870/856–2983, fax 870/856–4036. 6 double rooms with baths, 3 suites in cottage. Air-conditioning, ceiling fans, radios, whirlpool tubs and fireplace in 2 suites, kitchenette in suites. $65–110; full breakfast. D, MC, V. 2-night minimum for suites on weekends.

Piedmont House. 165 Spring St., Eureka Springs 72632, tel. 501/253–9258 or 800/253–9258. 6 double rooms with baths, 1 suite. Air-conditioning, ceiling fans, whirlpool tub in suite, off-street parking. $79–$129; full breakfast. AE, D, MC, V.

Ridgeway House. 28 Ridgeway St., Eureka Springs 72632, tel. 501/253–6618 or 800/477–6618. 3 double rooms with baths, 2 suites. Air-conditioning, robes, cable TV/VCR, whirlpool tubs and kitchenettes in suites. $89–$149; full breakfast, evening desserts, refreshments. D, MC, V.

RESERVATIONS SERVICES

Arkansas Ozarks Bed & Breakfast Reservation Services (HC 79, Box 330A, Calico Rock 72519, tel. 501/297–4197 or 800/233–2777). **Bed and Breakfast Association of Eureka Springs** (7 Kings Hwy., Eureka Springs 73632, tel. 800/401–4667). **Eureka Springs Chamber of Commerce** (Box 551, Eureka Springs 72632, tel. 501/253–8737 or 800/638–7352).

Central Arkansas:
From Hot Springs to Helena

THE EMPRESS OF LITTLE ROCK ☜
2120 Louisiana, Little Rock 72206, tel. 501/374–7966, fax 501/375–4537

The music of *Gone With the Wind* dips and swells as Rhett and Scarlett greet you upon entering this magnificent Gothic Queen Anne mansion in Little Rock's Quapaw Quarter Historic District. It is your imagination, but if the ambience alone doesn't remind you of the mansion Rhett built for Scarlett, then its history will.

James Hornibrook moved from Canada to Little Rock where he opened a saloon and became very wealthy during the Civil War occupation, as did many "carpetbaggers." Although he quickly became one of the wealthiest men in Little Rock and the state of Arkansas, like Rhett Butler, he was shunned by the town's upper crust. He got his revenge by building the grandest, most elaborate house in town, Hornibrook Mansion, for his wife, Margaret, at a then-exorbitant cost of $20,000.

Perhaps the most stunning features of the mansion are the double walnut-and-chestnut staircase and 64-square-ft stained-glass skylight. Many of the rooms are octagonal, including the corner tower room where legend says Hornibrook carried on illegal high-stakes poker games while paying young boys to act as lookouts from the tower windows. The five guest rooms are beautifully decorated in the Victorian style with many authentic antiques and large floral Aubusson rugs.

Sharon Welch-Blair, a financial services consultant for New York Life, and her husband, Bob, who is in upper-level management at Southwestern Bell, bought the Hornibrook mansion in 1993, restored and renamed it the Empress, and opened their doors in late 1995. When Sharon is asked about the house, her eyes take on a sparkle, making her love for the mansion and its history obvious. She is in her element, sometimes even wearing period costumes when she leads tours through the Empress.

Sharon serves a full candlelit breakfast on china in the graceful dining room. A few of her favorites dishes are ham and asparagus roll-ups with hollandaise sauce, croissants à l'orange, and Russian raspberry soup. She feels an elegant breakfast is part of the whole experience at the Empress. "You can go anywhere for just bacon and eggs," says Sharon. ♧ *5 double rooms with baths. Air-conditioning, cable TV, phones, radios, robes, fax and copier. $115–$175; full breakfast. AE, MC, V.*

STITT HOUSE BED & BREAKFAST INN ℘
824 Park Ave., Hot Springs 71901, tel. 501/623–2704

Everyone from Hernando de Soto (in 1541) to Al Capone took the cure at Hot Springs, Arkansas. At the turn of the last century, it was one of the country's leading spas; in the Roaring Twenties, the city was a hotbed for bathtub gin, gambling, and flappers. The elegant buildings and fragrant magnolias of Hot Springs, boyhood home of President Bill Clinton, have withstood the years gracefully, and its waters still draw people from all over the country. Today the springs are administered as part of the Hot Springs National Park; the spectacular Spanish Renaissance Revival–style Fordyce Bathhouse serves as the park's visitor center.

The Stitt House, an 1875 pre-Victorian restored mansion and the oldest dwelling still standing in Hot Springs, specializes in service. Gourmet breakfasts, which may include eggs Benedict, baked berry French toast, quiche, and fresh fruit, is served in bed, in the formal dining room, or on the open front veranda. Complimentary fruit and refreshments are provided for weary sightseers, and a heated outdoor swimming pool is open April through September.

Horst and Linda Fischer purchased the Stitt House in 1983, and Linda applied her expertise in gourmet food to open the Stitt House Restaurant in the mansion. She later moved her business, naming it Grady's Grill Restaurant, to the Majestic Hotel at one end of Hot Springs' historic Bathhouse Row. Horst is general manager of the Arlington and Majestic hotels. In February 1995 the Fischers opened the 6,000-square-ft Stitt House as a bed-and-breakfast inn, providing many of the amenities one expects at a luxury hotel.

Because the property had stayed in the Stitt family until the Fischers purchased it, the mansion remains much as it was originally built. The hand-carved oak staircase in the entry hall is breathtaking, while the four guest rooms are accented by antiques and interesting European artifacts.

The extensive grounds viewed from the front veranda are meticulously landscaped and include exotic trees and foliage. In response to a comment on the beauty of the grounds, a good friend of the Fischers, and native of Hot Springs, Mary Jo Rogers, exclaimed, "Oh yes, it's a wonderful yard. We'd all come here to play as kids. In fact, Bill Clinton lived right up the street, too, and we would all gather in this front yard for hide-and-seek and tag." One shouldn't neglect the landscaped yard behind the inn, however, which is now the site of a waterfall and fish pond.

🛆 *3 double rooms with baths, 1 suite. Air-conditioning, TVs, robes, turndown service, whirlpool tub in 1 room, pool, off-street parking. $100–$120; full breakfast. AE, D, MC, V.*

OTHER CHOICES

Edwardian Inn. 317 S. Biscoe St., Helena 72342, tel. 870/338–9155. 7 double rooms with baths, 5 suites. Air-conditioning, cable TV, phones, radios, minibars. $65–$75; full breakfast. AE, D, DC, MC, V.

Gables Inn. 318 Quapaw Ave., Hot Springs 71901, tel. 501/623–7576. 4 double rooms. Air-conditioning, ceiling fans, TV/VCRs, phones, clock radios. $69–$89; full breakfast, afternoon dessert. AE, MC, V.

Hotze House. 1619 Louisiana, Little Rock 72206, tel. 501/376–6563. 5 double rooms with baths. Desks, phones with dataports, gas fireplaces, cable TVs, party/meeting facilities. $80–$100; full breakfast, complimentary snack bar. AE, MC, V.

Pinnacle Vista Lodge. 7510 Ark. 300, Little Rock 72212, tel. 501/868-8905. 2 double rooms with baths, 1 suite. Cable TVs, kitchenette in suite; whirlpool, pool table, pinball and jukebox in common area; hiking, fishing, horseback riding. $89–$115; full breakfast, evening refreshments. MC, V.

Wildwood 1884 Bed & Breakfast. 808 Park Ave., Hot Springs National Park 71901, tel. 501/624–4267. 5 double rooms with baths. 3 rooms. Wedding/party packages available. $85–$95; full breakfast. D, MC, V.

RESERVATIONS SERVICES

Dr. Witt's House State Bed and Breakfast Referral Service (tel. 501/376–6873; referrals over phone only). **Hot Springs Convention and Visitors Bureau** (134 Convention Blvd., Box K, Hot Springs 71902, tel. 800/772–2489; call for brochure only). **Phillips County Chamber of Commerce** (Box 447, Helena 72342, tel. 501/338–8327; listings in Helena only).

CALIFORNIA

San Diego County

HERITAGE PARK BED & BREAKFAST INN 🐚
2470 Heritage Park Row, San Diego 92110, tel. 619/299–6832 or 800/995–2470, fax 619/299–9465

This turreted Victorian in a historic park is the ideal headquarters for touring San Diego's Old Town, a shopping-restaurant complex across the street. It's also convenient for exploring San Diego's other attractions via the San Diego Trolley, which can take you from Old Town to nearly all area sights.

The inn consists of two adjacent historic buildings. The main one is a beautiful 1889 Queen Anne. It has a wraparound veranda decorated with spindle work, a variety of chimneys, stained-glass windows, and ornate millwork on its banisters and wainscoting. Furnishings include an unusual double Eastlake panel bed with carved sunflowers, four-poster canopy beds, an antique fainting couch, and antique quilts. The second, smaller building has two rooms on the ground floor and an expansive two-bedroom family suite on the second floor.

Rooms range from smallish to ample; most are bright and cheery. Some rooms in the main house have detached private baths. Upstairs rooms have views of the park and Mission Bay beyond. One of the most popular rooms is the Turret, which has a sitting room in the inn's two-story tower that offers city and park views. From Queen Anne, a spacious room on the second floor, you can gaze out to the water through a squared bay window. Downstairs, the Garden Room, which looks out on the sunny Victorian garden, is another guest favorite.

Longtime San Diegans Charles and Nancy Helsper can make arrangements for gondola rides on the bay and balloon excursions. They've produced a walking and jogging map that guides guests through one of San Diego's most lovely residential neighborhoods.

Breakfast is served in a formal dining room, where tables are set for two to six guests. There's candlelight, flowers, and even place cards for each guest. Nancy, formerly director of catering at a San Diego resort, offers a varied menu that includes entrées such as French toast with apple cider syrup and eggs Florentine. She also presents an elaborate tea each afternoon. ♨ *12 double rooms with baths, 1 suite. Phone in rooms, TV in 2 rooms, fireplace in 3 rooms, whirlpool tub in 3 rooms. Off-street parking. $90–$250; full breakfast. AE, D, DC, MC, V. No smoking, 2-night minimum on weekends in July–Aug.*

JULIAN WHITE HOUSE ☙

3024 Blue Jay Dr. (Box 824), Julian 92036, tel.760/765–1764 or 800/948–4687,
fax 760/765–1764

Alan and Mary Marvin fell in love with Julian the way most folks do. They visited on a day outing, tasted some apple pie, marveled at the beautiful countryside—and then decided to move there. They found a house that looked out of place among the rustic cabins and oak-studded hills; it's a miniature antebellum mansion complete with Greek Revival columns. The previous owner called it the White House.

There's nothing pretentious about this homey inn, where guests like to spend time in the parlor "doing nothing." Or if the weather is fine, they can find a sunny spot in the rose garden and curl up with a good book. Bicycles are available for exploring the Julian countryside.

Guest rooms offer a bit of whimsy. The French Quarter, tucked into a corner on the first floor, boasts a collection of New Orleans feather masks and a Louis XVI bed. Upstairs via a spiral staircase, the Honeymoon room reveals great treetop views, has a bathroom with stained-glass windows and a corner fireplace; the East room is bright and sunny with a two-person shower.

Alan and Mary make an occasion of serving breakfast, setting the dining table with fine china and candlelight. Typically they offer eggs Benedict or a frittata, pancakes, or vegetarian entrées along with fresh fruit. ♦ *4 double rooms with baths. Fireplace in 2 rooms. Guest refrigerator, outdoor hot tub. $90–$145; full breakfast. MC, V. No smoking.*

LOMA VISTA BED AND BREAKFAST ☙

33350 La Serena Way, Temecula 92591, tel. 909/676–7047, fax 909/676–0077

The first bed-and-breakfast accommodations in California were the 21 missions built during the 18th century by the Spanish padres, providing lodging and food along El Camino Real. The missions are also the inspiration for the design—and the hospitality—of the Loma Vista Bed and Breakfast.

The inn sits like a terra-cotta crown atop a hill in the Temecula wine country, about an hour's drive north of San Diego. The look is more like a hacienda than a mission. Carefully tended rose gardens border red-tiled patios. Hummingbirds poke their long beaks into the hearts of fragrant flowers.

Inside, the inn is cool and inviting, with ceiling beams and other oak details. Large picture windows in the common rooms reveal gardens and vineyard-covered hillsides. The views from the bedrooms upstairs are more dramatic, unfolding in a broad panorama of citrus groves, distant mountains, and even the Mt. Palomar observatory.

The guest rooms are named for varietal wines, but the connection ceases there. Zinfandel is swathed in green and peach, with Colonial reproductions that include a handsome Chippendale-style secretary bookcase with bonnet top. Chardonnay is furnished in oak and has a Laura Ashley look. Art Deco describes Champagne, with a black lacquer bed, tubular steel chairs, and photographs of Marilyn Monroe and Fred Astaire on the walls. Each room is stocked with fresh fruit and sherry. Weeping wisteria frames the edges of balconies of four rooms.

Sheila and Walt Kuczynski recently acquired the inn, vowing not to make any changes. Champagne at breakfast, served family-style in the inn's large dining room, is a festive meal that includes Canadian bacon and eggs, and ham and chicken crepes. And you can count on tasting some tangy grapefruit juice freshly squeezed from the trees just beyond the front door. ♨ *6 double rooms with baths. Air-conditioning in rooms. Outdoor hot tub, fire pit. $100–$150; full breakfast. MC, V. No smoking, 2-night minimum on weekends.*

ORCHARD HILL COUNTRY INN ❦

Washington St. (Box 425), Julian 92036, tel. 760/765–1700, fax 760/765–0290

Orchard Hill Country Inn offers a level of luxury and service not usually expected in rustic, gold rush–era Julian. Owners Darrell and Pat Straube reconstructed four cottages from the foundation up and added a massive Craftsman-style lodge, with soaring two-story-high windows, open beam ceilings, a great stone fireplace, and patios tucked under overhangs.

Guest rooms in both the lodge and the cottages are spotted on a hillside overlooking town. Cottages contain three beautifully appointed guest rooms surrounded by a broad veranda furnished with big green wicker chairs. They have private entrances, whirlpool tubs, see-through fireplaces visible from both bedroom and sitting room, wet bars, and window seats. One of the nicest is the large McIntosh. It's decorated with green plaid wallpaper and contains a bathroom accessible to guests with disabilities. The Black Gilflower is also a charmer, with pillow-ticking-style wallpaper and an oversize whirlpool in the bathroom.

Rooms in the lodge are smaller and less luxurious, but with an attractive "Grandma's attic" feel to them. They feature skylights over the bathtubs, small desks, overstuffed chairs, handmade quilts, down comforters, and the best views of the town and surrounding mountains.

Orchard Hill sits on 4 hillside acres, which are planted with a profusion of native plants including deep-blue ceanothus, golden poppies, and fragrant white locust trees. In spring, guests can explore paths that meander through fields of yellow and purple iris, sit in a secluded corner and admire the roses and peonies, or doze in a hammock strung between trees.

A full breakfast served in the bright dining room might include Gruyère egg puff, blintzes, seasonal fresh fruit, baked goods, and cereal. A prix-fixe four-course dinner, served to guests two nights a week, features seafood, pasta, or steak, depending on the season. ♨ *22 double rooms with baths. Air-conditioning, TV/VCR, and refrigerator in rooms, fireplace in 11 rooms, wet bar in 12 rooms, whirlpool bath in 8 rooms. Meeting facilities. $155–$225; full breakfast. AE, MC, V. No smoking, 2-night minimum on weekends.*

WIKIUP BED & BREAKFAST ❦

1645 Whispering Pines Dr. (Box 2363), Julian 92036, tel. 760/765–1890 or 800/526–2725, fax 760/765–1515

"You've got to love animals to want to stay at this inn," laughs Linda Stanley, who operates the Wikiup along with her husband, Lee. Linda isn't kidding. She counts 16 llamas, three dogs, eight cats, a donkey, sheep, two goats, and two birds among her pets. You'll get to meet them all if you stay at her inn, a rustic contemporary cedar-and-brick lodge located just outside the historic town of Julian. And guests are welcome to bring their own pets here as well.

The lodge, set among 3 wooded acres and surrounded by animal pens, has a distinctive '70s look. There are high open-beam ceilings with skylights, cedar paneling, a common room encompassing living and dining, lots of Danish modern furnishings, and stacks of books and magazines everywhere. Rooms located on the main floor and tucked into a slope beneath the house have different themes. Rose's Secret is a Victorian floral fantasy with skylights in the bathroom. Pueblo

Dreamcatcher is southwestern with redwood floors, a kiva-style fireplace and a view of the woods outside. Willow Warren has a handmade canopy bed fashioned out of willow branches.

The inn is well configured for families. One room has an extra bed. There's a play area with swing and teeter-totter, and of course, there are the animals. The real stars of this inn are the llamas, which you can pet, feed, or take on guided treks through Julian. Such treks include wooded trails, apple orchards, a winery for tasting, and historic gold mines.

Guests gather for breakfast in the inn's dining room, where the fare is Continental midweek and hearty on the weekends, when the menu might feature a soufflé, omelet, or baked-egg casserole. △ *3 double rooms with baths. Fireplace, whirlpool tub, refrigerator, and microwave in 2 rooms. Outdoor hot tub. $105–$140; Continental midweek, full breakfast weekends. MC, V. 2-night minimum on weekends.*

OTHER CHOICES

Brookside Farm. 1373 Marron Valley Rd., Dulzura 91917, tel. 935/468–3043, fax 935/468–9145. 8 double rooms with baths, 2 suites. Air-conditioning, fireplace in 6 rooms, refrigerator in 4 rooms. Library, guest refrigerator, outdoor hot tub, badminton, horseshoes, croquet. $80–$115; full breakfast, informal dinner Sun.–Thurs. included, dinner ($15 per person) Fri.–Sat. AE, MC, V. No smoking, 2-night minimum on weekends.

Rancho Valencia Resort. 5921 Valencia Circle (Box 9126), Rancho Santa Fe 92067, tel. 858/756–1123 or 800/548–3664, fax 858/756–0165. 43 suites. Air-conditioning, TV/VCR, phone, fireplace, stocked minibar, safe, and coffeemaker in room; 24-hr room service, children's programs, conference facilities, 2 pools, 2 outside Jacuzzis, tennis, golf, fitness facilities, spa. $395–$900; breakfast not included. AE, DC, MC, V. Smoking suites available, 2-night minimum on weekends, 3-night minimum on holiday weekends.

RESERVATIONS AND REFERRAL SERVICES

Bed and Breakfast California (Box 282910, San Francisco 94128, tel. 650/696–1690 or 800/872–4500, fax 650/696–1699). **Bed and Breakfast Guild of San Diego** (tel. 619/523–1300). **Eye Openers Bed and Breakfast Reservations** (Box 694, Altadena 91003, tel. 626/398–0525 or 800/458–1221, fax 626/296–0183).

The Desert and the San Bernardino Mountains from Palm Springs to Lake Arrowhead

❖⊰✿⊱❖

BRACKEN FERN MANOR 🖋

815 Arrowhead Villas Rd. (Box 1006), Lake Arrowhead 92352, tel. 909/337–8557, fax 909/337–3323

This is an inn with a sordid past, some of which is still apparent to guests. Built by members of the Mob during Prohibition, it was both a hideout and a brothel. Water from a spring in the wine cellar produced some of the best bathtub gin in California; it was delivered to a speakeasy across the street through underground tunnels.

The Mob was long gone when Cheryl Weaver found the three-story Tudor-style building and gutted and renovated it into an inn that preserves some of the flavor of that earlier era. (The tunnels, for example, still exist.) Rooms named for the "girls," aspiring actresses who frequented the place, are small and simply furnished with brass beds and cat decorations. There are many beautiful windows, including stained-glass transoms identifying each guest room; others are etched, beveled, and leaded. Cheryl preserved the basement, where the gin was distilled, transforming it into a wine cellar used for tastings.

The inn has several outdoor decks and patios, where one can sit and admire the scenic surroundings, which are particularly beautiful in spring when the mountain dogwoods are in bloom.

Some of the breakfast offerings Cheryl serves are orange stuffed French toast and egg casserole, with bacon or sausage. She also offers wine, cider, or lemonade along with light appetizers in the afternoon. △ *8 double rooms with baths, 2 doubles share 1 bath. Sauna, outdoor whirlpool bath. $65–$185; full breakfast. MC, V. No smoking, 2-night minimum on weekends.*

INGLESIDE INN 🐾
200 W. Ramon Rd., Palm Springs 92264, tel. 760/325–0046 or 800/772–6655, fax 760/325–0710

Garbo slept here—so did Elizabeth Taylor, Marlon Brando, and diva Lily Pons. Ingleside Inn has been a Palm Springs hideaway for celebrities, Hollywood and otherwise, since the 1930s. The reasons become obvious when you step inside this unpretentious hacienda-style inn. On a quiet street just a few blocks from Palm Canyon Drive, the inn is a tranquil and private enclave surrounded by verdant gardens and a high adobe wall.

Individually and elegantly decorated villas and cottages are scattered around the property. All rooms have whirlpool tubs and steam showers. Some are furnished with valuable antiques; the suite occupied by Pons for 13 years features her Louis XV bedroom set.

An official Palm Springs historic site, the inn was originally built in 1925 as the Humphrey Birge estate (the family who owned the Pierce Arrow Car Company). The property became lodging in the 1930s and is now owned by gregarious Mel Haber, who purchased it on a whim in 1975. Haber caters to guests in an old-fashioned way, table-hopping at his restaurant and bar, Melvyn's (where stars old and new occasionally drop by), and glad-handing guests lounging poolside. △ *30 double rooms with baths. Air-conditioning, TV/VCR, phone, stocked refrigerator, and whirlpool bath in rooms, fireplace in 13 rooms. Restaurant, lounge, meeting facilities, pool and outdoor whirlpool, limousine pickup at local airport. $95–$600; Continental breakfast. AE, D, DC, MC, V. 2-night minimum on weekends Oct.–May.*

ROUGHLEY MANOR 🐾
74744 Joe Davis Dr., Twentynine Palms 92277, tel. 760/367–3238, fax 760/367–1690

This inn is a strikingly elegant contrast to the rustic nature that describes most of Twentynine Palms. The house, situated on 25 acres planted with native Washingtonia palms, was built of native stone by Pennsylvania craftsmen for the pioneering Campbell family. Shortly after homesteading here, the Campbells inherited a fortune, which accounts for the manor's elegant features: a 50-ft-long great room with Vermont maple planked floors and great stone fireplace, leaded and stained-glass windows, extraordinarily detailed carpentry on walls, and original blue, yellow, and green bathroom tile and fixtures.

Gary and Jan Peters purchased the property in 1994 when he retired from the Marine Corps and transformed it from its function as a space for weddings and corporate meetings to a bed-and-breakfast. The five bedrooms in the main house are furnished with antiques including poster and canopied beds, marble-topped dressers and nightstands, and a cherrywood hutch. Two rooms have fireplaces. Two more rooms lie in outbuildings: the Cottage has a separate sitting room and bathroom furnished with antique claw-foot tub; the Farmhouse can accommodate four guests and has a kitchenette.

The inn's colorful gardens contrast markedly from the surrounding desertscape. Roses bloom in profusion. Towering Washingtonia palms offer welcome shade. Fountains gurgle quietly while guests lounge in a hammock or curl up with a book in an overstuffed sofa.

Guests gather outdoors in the expansive gardens under the palm trees, the gazebo, or in the formal dining room for breakfast, which usually features a fruit appetizer such as pears stuffed with granola or fruit salad with sorbet, followed by potato quiche or stuffed twice-baked potato topped with scrambled eggs. Evening refreshments and dessert are also offered. ♦ *2 double rooms with baths, 5 doubles share 2 baths. Air-conditioning in rooms. Outdoor hot tub. $75–$125; full breakfast. AE, MC, V. No smoking.*

TRES PALMAS BED AND BREAKFAST ⚘
73135 Tumbleweed La. (Box 2115), Palm Desert 92261, tel. 760/773–9858 or 800/770–9858

This bed-and-breakfast in posh Palm Desert provides an affordable glimpse into the lifestyle that lures thousands of wealthy vacationers to this resort town each winter. On a residential street just a block from El Paseo shops and galleries, this is a typical sand-color, stucco desert home with red-tile roof and deep covered porches. Landscaped gardens include a gurgling fountain, succulents, cactus, and lemon and grapefruit trees. An azure swimming pool dominates the backyard.

The house itself is spacious and bright, its design highlighted by enormous windows, high open-beam ceilings, whitewashed wood, and textured peach tile floors. Southwestern decor in common areas and guest rooms includes fine old Navajo rugs from the collection of innkeepers Terry and Karen Bennett. Rooms are functional rather than luxurious. A lodgepole-pine bed is the centerpiece of the Coyote. Kokopelli has a pencil-point bed, a Navajo rug on the wall, and French doors leading to a small private patio.

Many guests spend their afternoons lounging around the inn's pool, sipping cool lemonade that's always available. In the afternoon, Karen puts out an hors d'oeuvre spread. A simple Continental breakfast offers fresh muffins daily.

If you're a member of the shop-till-you-drop brigade, the location of this inn, just steps from El Paseo, can't be beat. You can browse through hundreds of boutiques, shops, and galleries that are tucked into the courtyards that line this chic district. ♦ *4 double rooms with baths. Air-conditioning and TV in rooms. Pool, outdoor hot tub. $110–$185; Continental breakfast. AE, MC, V. No smoking, 2-night minimum on weekends Oct.–June.*

TWO ANGELS INN ❦

*78–120 Caleo Bay, La Quinta 92253, tel. 760/564–7332 or 888/226–4546,
fax 760/564–6356*

The two angels here are Hap and Holly Harris, who have created a heavenly inn in a serene lakeside setting in the fast-growing desert community of La Quinta. The inn, dark and cool, is reminiscent of an old French chateau with contemporary luxurious ambience.

Rooms, located on the first and second floors of the chateau and in an adjacent boathouse, have lake or mountain views. Some have skylights or strategically placed windows that reveal a star-studded night sky. Many have opulent bathrooms with double sinks, walk-in showers, and whirlpool tubs. All are elegantly appointed. La Mancha, done in deep reds and rich golds, has a Spanish theme. Bouquet Français features a four-poster bed dripping in pastel florals and golds. Plaid and natural pine mark St. Andrews.

The two boathouse rooms feature nautical and Oriental themes; each has a private patio with an outdoor hot tub. Antiques and memorabilia, much collected by Hap's family, abound. Common areas include the inn's grand salon, which opens to gardens and lake La Quinta, a cool meditation room, where Holly conducts meditation and yoga classes, and an expansive dining room with a 140-inch-long glass table.

The innkeepers offer a generous breakfast, which guests may enjoy at tables set up on the patio. Typical menus feature chilled fruit soup or frappe, spiced pumpkin pancakes, zucchini frittata, and sweet corn-and-green-onion pancakes. The hosts also invite guests to join them each afternoon for wine and hors d'oeuvres. ♨ *11 double rooms with baths. Air-conditioning, TV, phone, fireplace, and guest refrigerator in rooms. Pool, outdoor whirlpool, lake access. $185–$350; full breakfast. AE, D, MC, V. No smoking, 2-night minimum on weekends.*

WILLOWS HISTORIC PALM SPRINGS INN ❦

*412 W. Tahquitz Canyon Way, Palm Springs 92262, tel. 760/320–0771,
fax 760/320–0780*

Einstein slept in this Mediterranean villa located on a hillside in the heart of old Palm Springs. The scientist vacationed here as the guest of former U.S. Secretary of the Treasury Samuel Untermyer, who built the house in 1927 as his winter retreat. "When we saw that, we just had to own the villa," explained Tracy Conrad, who along with her partner, Paul Marut, purchased the home, renovated it, and opened the Willows in 1996.

The renovation, supervised by Tracy, preserved the villa's most elegant features: natural hardwood and slate floors, stone fireplaces, frescoed ceilings, hand-painted tiles, iron balconies, a veranda, fossilized stone walkways winding through a hillside garden, and a stunning 50-ft waterfall that splashes into a pool outside the dining room.

Each of the rooms, spread among the three levels of the villa, resembles a bedroom seen in the movies of Hollywood's golden era. There are antique beds, upholstered sofas and chairs, and opulent floor-to-ceiling window treatments. Bathrooms are exceptional. One contains a shower that splashes onto a boulder that the room was built around. Another bathroom, the size of a small bedroom, is furnished with a chaise longue and a two-person claw-foot tub lit by a silver chandelier.

Einstein is said to have loved to walk through the Zen-like gardens surrounding the villa, which the innkeepers have re-created. Just after sunrise he could take in a sweeping view of the desert awash in shades of pink, orange, and gold. Guests here can still enjoy Einstein's vista, or curl up in one of the chairs tucked into several secluded corners of the garden.

The innkeepers, both busy emergency-room physicians, have an efficient young staff who serve a full breakfast in the waterfall dining room. The menu includes entrées such as rolled cilantro omelet with salsa fresca and asparagus, or puffed German pancakes. In the afternoons the innkeepers offer wine and hors d'oeuvres such as empanadas, tortas, baked Brie, or stuffed mushrooms. ▲ *8 double rooms with baths. Air-conditioning, TV, phone, and stocked refrigerator in rooms, fireplace in 2 rooms. Pool, outdoor whirlpool. $250–$500; full breakfast. AE, D, DC, MC, V. No smoking, 2-night minimum on weekends.*

WINDY POINT INN 🐾

39015 North Shore Rd. (Box 375), Fawnskin 92333, tel. 909/866–2746, fax 909/866–1593

With its sweeping mountain and lake views, rooms providing all the privacy you could want, and accommodating innkeepers, Windy Point Inn offers the ultimate in romance. The inn sits on a rocky spit of land surrounded on three sides by water, occupying one of the most scenic spots on Big Bear Lake's north shore.

The decor is sleek and bright, dominated by vaulted ceilings, white walls, and skylights to show off innkeepers Val and Kent Kessler's eclectic art collection— Old West saddles, contemporary graphics, and folk art, to name just a few.

The best room is the Peaks, a master suite with plate-glass windows on three sides. It has a wraparound sofa by the fireplace, his and hers vanities, a two-person steam shower, and a deck with a partially enclosed glass wind screen. You can watch the sun rise while lying in bed in the Pines, and hear the water lap against the shore from your bed in the Sands. The Shores and the Cove are set up so you can see the fireplace from the bed or double whirlpool tub.

Breakfast may be served in the privacy of a guest's room or enjoyed outside on one of the inn's decks. Each meal is prepared to order; Val's repertoire includes baked crepes accompanied by poached eggs and ginger pancakes. Each afternoon Val also presents a selection of hors d'oeuvres and beverages. ▲ *5 double rooms with baths. Fireplace, stocked refrigerator, and wet bar in rooms, whirlpool bath in 4 rooms, TV/VCR on request. Ski storage; private beach on lake. $125–$245; full breakfast. AE, D, MC, V. No smoking, 2-night minimum on weekends.*

OTHER CHOICES

The Carriage House. 472 Emerald Dr., Box 982, Lake Arrowhead 92352, tel. 909/336–1400. 3 double rooms with baths. TV/VCR in 1 room. $95–$140; full breakfast. AE, D, MC, V. 2-night minimum on weekends, 3-night minimum on some holidays.

Villa Royale. 1620 Indian Trail, Palm Springs 92264, tel. 760/327–2314 or 800/245–2314, fax 760/322–3794. 33 double rooms with baths, 12 suites. Air-conditioning, TV, and phone in rooms, fireplace in 14 rooms, whirlpool bath in 7 rooms, kitchen in 14 rooms. Restaurant, cocktail lounge, in-room massage and facial available, room service during restaurant hours, 2 swimming pools, hot tub. $95–$295; Continental breakfast. AE, D, DC, MC, V. 2-night minimum on weekends, 3-night minimum on holidays.

RESERVATIONS SERVICES
Bed and Breakfast California (Box 282910, San Francisco 94128, tel. 650/696–1690 or 800/872–4500, fax 650/696–1699). **Eye Openers Bed and Breakfast Reservations** (Box 694, Altadena 91003, tel. 626/398–0525 or 800/458–1221, fax 626/296–0183).

Los Angeles
with Orange County

BLUE LANTERN INN 🕊

34343 St. of the Blue Lantern, Dana Point 92629, tel. 949/661–1304 or 800/950–1236, fax 949/496–1483

This contemporary Cape Cod–style hotel is perched on a bluff above the Dana Point Marina in southern Orange County. One of the few small inns around, it offers sweeping marina and ocean views from almost every room.

The Blue Lantern is operated by the Four Sisters Inns group, which owns a number of inns and small hotels, mostly in northern California. Each guest room contains an unusually spacious bathroom; most have double sinks, showers, and whirlpool baths. The decor is bright and beachlike; some rooms have French country accents. Tall mahogany four-poster beds are focal points in the Tower suites; other rooms have brass or sleigh beds. Wing chairs, small boudoir chairs, and Queen Anne–style desks can be found in nearly every room, as well as armoires that conceal TV sets, and refrigerators stocked with complimentary soft drinks.

The lobby is set up with tables for two and four for the ample buffet-style breakfast featuring entrées such as hobo breakfast (a potato-and-cheese casserole), quiches, and French bread soufflé. (Breakfast in bed is available in the Tower suites.) French doors lead to an outdoor sitting area, where many visitors take coffee and the morning paper. The library, which contains a small collection of books you might actually want to read, is where guests gather in the afternoons for wine and hors d'oeuvres.

Bicycles are available for exploring the many trails that crisscross the surrounding hills. The innkeepers will make arrangements for sail- or powerboat charters or whale-watching excursions in season. They will also prepare a picnic basket for guests to enjoy at one of the two parks within walking distance of the inn. In addition, guests can visit the mission and the chic boutiques, art galleries, and antiques stores at San Juan Capistrano, just a 10-minute drive away. ⚠
29 double rooms with baths. Air-conditioning, whirlpool bath, refrigerator, TV, and phone in rooms, telescope in Tower rooms. Fitness center, conference facilities. $140–$500; full breakfast. AE, MC, V. No smoking.

CHANNEL ROAD INN 🕊

219 Channel Rd., Santa Monica 90402, tel. 310/459–1920, fax 310/454–9920

Originally the home of Thomas McCall, a pioneering Santa Monica businessman, this house was moved from a hilltop site to its current location tucked in a hillside of Santa Monica Canyon, one block from the beach. With the help of the local historical society, innkeeper Susan Zolla saved the Colonial Revival building from demolition and turned it into a gracious inn.

The house is sheathed in blue shingles, a rarity in Los Angeles and for a Colonial Revival house. The architectural details are pure Craftsman. Windows are very large and abundant, to take advantage of cool ocean breezes and bright sunlight. The honey-color woodwork in the living room is unusually elegant, with moldings and baseboards carefully milled.

Beds are the focal point in the rooms: four-poster beds, pencil-post canopy beds, and sleigh beds. Special attention has been paid to the needs of guests, particularly business travelers who require phones or writing surfaces. Several rooms have access to balconies or decks with views of the flowering hillside and a glimpse of the ocean.

The inn serves a generous breakfast in the bright dining room, including healthy items such as cereal, yogurt, and fresh fruit, plus a tasty egg dish.

The broad white-sand beach is just across Pacific Coast Highway; it's bordered on one side by a 30-mi-long bicycle path that stretches north to Malibu and south to Venice Beach. The Venice portion of the path is a colorful carnival on weekends as crazily clad street musicians beat out tunes, vendors sell everything from food to art, and skaters zip by. The new Getty Center, with its lovely gardens and superb art collection, is a short drive away. ♠ *12 double rooms with baths, 2 suites. Cable TV and phone in rooms, refrigerator in 4 rooms, Jacuzzi in 2 rooms, fireplace in 2 rooms, VCR in 8 rooms. Outdoor hot tub, bicycles, off-street parking. $125–$285; full breakfast. AE, MC, V. No smoking.*

CHRISTMAS HOUSE ☞
9240 Archibald Ave., Rancho Cucamonga 91730, tel. 909/980–6450, fax 909/980–6450

Built by wealthy ranchers in 1904, this late Queen Anne mansion was known locally as the Christmas House because of the many lavish holiday parties thrown here. Set amid an acre of grapefruit and tangerine trees, this inviting house has turrets, gables, stained-glass windows, sweeping verandas, seven working fireplaces, dark wood wainscoting, and a grand staircase leading to the second floor. Colors are cool deep greens and burgundies. Among the inn's fine group of antiques are a 150-year-old brass bed and a family collection of framed handkerchiefs.

Guest rooms are on the first and second floors of the main house and in a carriage house behind. Decorated with an English floral theme, Elizabeth has a private rose-garden entry, a black iron bed, and green wicker furnishings; French doors lead to a romantic tropical plant-filled grotto containing a massive outdoor shower. The adjacent Carriage Room has a more masculine feel, with its fireplace, burgundy sofa, and dark antiques, including a sleigh bed. This room has a private garden with a whirlpool tub set into a gazebo.

In the main house, one ground-floor room has a private courtyard with its own hot tub. Upstairs, the Celebration Suite, a huge double room with bedchamber and parlor divided by an enormous pocket door, is a popular choice of honeymooners. It has fireplaces in the corners of both rooms; a dining table set up in front of one fireplace, where breakfast is served; and a lace-draped antique canopy bed.

Breakfast is served in the dining room and may include sausage–apple–cheddar-cheese quiche and blueberry custard crepes with a red-wine sauce. Guests will also find a plate of cookies and a bowl of fresh fruit in their rooms upon check-in. ♠ *3 double rooms with baths, 2 doubles share 1 bath, 1 suite. Air-conditioning in rooms, fireplace in 4 rooms, TV/VCR in 1 room, hot tub in 2 rooms. $80–$180; full breakfast. AE, D, MC, V. No smoking.*

INN AT PLAYA DEL REY ☜
435 Culver Blvd., Playa del Rey 90293, tel. 310/574–1920, fax 310/574–9920

This luxury inn is close enough to Los Angeles International Airport to serve as an overnight stop for an ongoing traveler but remote enough to have a 350-acre bird sanctuary in its backyard, and the main channel of Marina del Rey behind that. Such is the human sanctuary created by owner Susan Zolla (who also owns the Channel Road Inn) and her staff.

This three-story, gray-and-white clapboard Cape Cod–style inn offers several levels of luxury: from glamorous suites with sweeping wetland and marina views to small but well-equipped rooms designed for a budget traveler. The most spacious suite, filling a third-floor corner, is decorated in tan and white; it has a large living room with a fireplace, two bathrooms, a whirlpool tub, and a view of the wetlands and sailboats from beyond the deck. More modest rooms have see-through fireplaces and double whirlpool baths. But even the least expensive rooms have work spaces and unexpected windows or balconies. The decor is contemporary but comfortable, with many hand-painted beds and armoires, canopied beds draped with gauze curtains, and quilts and fresh flowers.

As lovely as the rooms are, guests will also want to linger in the inn's spacious living room and savor a fresh ocean breeze from the wraparound deck (no doubt while sipping a glass of icy lemonade and munching on some homemade cookies). There's also a very private garden with hot tub for lounging. For interested birders, the innkeepers will provide a guide to the more than 90 species that inhabit the sanctuary.

Susan, mindful of her guests' occasional need to catch early flights, puts coffee out at 5 AM, and a buffet breakfast appears in the dining room at a more civilized hour. Selections include home-baked breads, cereal, fresh fruit with yogurt, and an egg dish such as chili cheese puff or artichoke soufflé. ⚘ *19 rooms with baths, 2 suites. Air-conditioning, TV/VCR, phone, voice mail, and dataport in rooms, fireplace and whirlpool bath in 8 rooms. Bicycles, exercise room, underground parking, conference facilities. $145–$275; full breakfast. AE, MC, V. No smoking.*

INN ON MT. ADA ☜
398 Wrigley Rd. (Box 2560), Avalon 90704, tel. 310/510–2030 or 800/608–7669, fax 310/510–2237

Chewing-gum magnate William Wrigley Jr. built this impressive Georgian Colonial mansion in 1921 as his Catalina Island summer retreat. Occupying a 5-acre hilltop site, it has a stunning view of Avalon Harbor, the coastline, and the mountains beyond from nearly every room.

Though the home is grand, Wrigley furnished it as a less-formal (for his times) idyll for his family and guests, who included U.S. presidents Calvin Coolidge and Herbert Hoover, and the Duke of Windsor. But you don't have to be royalty to enjoy the millionaire's mansion that Susie Griffin and Marlene McAdam transformed into an inn.

From the moment the innkeepers pick you up at the boat terminal (or helipad, if you prefer) you'll feel pampered here: a guided tour of Avalon on the way to the inn, an invitation to lunch even before you check into your room, and instruction in use of the golf cart provided to each guest for island transportation. You'll be tempted to collapse into a chair on the expansive veranda and admire the view of jewel-like Avalon harbor. Or you may want to select a book or magazine from the inn's library, spy on the town through the telescope that's set up in the solarium window, or sample the cookies that are always out.

Furnishings are comfortable rather than elegant: overstuffed sofas and wing chairs in the living room, natural wicker in the downstairs den. The rooms range from spacious to small, but all offer a sea view and they come with little touches such as a ladies' dressing table in Ada Wrigley's suite. Not surprisingly, the standout room is Wrigley's own suite, which occupies a second-floor corner; it has a large living room that opens onto a very private deck.

Meals at the Inn on Mt. Ada include a full breakfast, a buffet-style lunch, a three-course dinner, evening wine and hors d'oeuvres, and beverages. The menu changes seasonally; breakfast might include mushroom omelet or eggs Florentine. Dinner, also seasonal, usually includes rack of lamb, prime rib, and seafood.
△ *4 double rooms with baths, 2 suites. TV in rooms, fireplace in 4 rooms. Conference facilities. $250–$620; all meals. MC, V. No smoking, 2-night minimum on weekends and holidays.*

OTHER CHOICES

Casa Tropicana. 610 Avenida Victoria, San Clemente 92672, tel. 949/492–1234 or 800/492–1245, fax 714/492–2423. 9 double rooms with baths. TV, refrigerator, and phone in rooms, air-conditioning in 3 rooms, double whirlpool bath in 8 rooms, fireplace in 8 rooms. Room service after 4. $85–$350; full breakfast. AE, D, DC, MC, V. No smoking, 2-night minimum on weekends.

Inn at 657. 657 W. 23rd St., Los Angeles 90007, tel. 213/741–2200 or 800/347–7512. 6 suites. Air-conditioning, TV/VCR, phone, and kitchen in rooms. Outdoor spa, off-street parking. $110–$135; full breakfast. No credit cards. No smoking.

Lord Mayor's Inn. 435 Cedar Ave., Long Beach 90802, tel. 562/436–0324, fax 562/436–0324. 11 double rooms with baths, 2 doubles share 1 bath. Phone in rooms. Computer available, off-street parking. $85–$125; full breakfast. AE, D, MC, V. Smoking on porches and balconies only.

Malibu Beach Inn. 22878 Pacific Coast Hwy., Malibu 90265, tel. 310/456–6444 or 800/255–1007, fax 310/456–1499. 47 double rooms with baths. Air-conditioning, TV /VCR, phone, refrigerator, honor bar, wet bar, and coffeemaker in rooms, fireplace in 42 rooms, hot tub in 7 rooms. Room service, off-street parking. $169–$299; Continental breakfast. AE, DC, MC, V. 2-night minimum on weekends and holidays.

Seal Beach Inn and Gardens. 212 5th St., Seal Beach 90740, tel. 562/493–2416 or 800/443–3292, fax 562/799–0483. 9 double rooms with baths, 14 suites. Air-conditioning, TV, phone, robe, and refrigerator in rooms, fireplace in 13 rooms, whirlpool bath in 5 rooms. Pool, beach towels, picnic baskets, library, gift shop. $155–$325; full breakfast. AE, D, DC, MC, V. No smoking.

RESERVATIONS AND REFERRAL SERVICES

Bed and Breakfast California (Box 282910, San Francisco 94128–2910, tel. 650/696–1690 or 800/872–4500, fax 650/696–1699). **Eye Openers Bed and Breakfast Reservations** (Box 694, Altadena 91003, tel. 626/398–0525 or 800/458–1221, fax 626/296–0183).

Central Coast from Santa Barbara to San Simeon

THE BLUE WHALE INN 🐚
6736 Moonstone Beach Dr., Cambria 93428, tel. and fax 805/927–4647

Like many southern Californians, Fred Ushijima had been visiting the town of Cambria regularly for years, attracted by the laid-back beachfront atmosphere, good restaurants, and the shops and galleries of a growing artists' colony. Cambria's proximity to the Hearst Castle at San Simeon has always meant large numbers of visitors, but the village hasn't become touristy or overdeveloped.

Fred decided to sink roots in Cambria, and he found the perfect location on a triangular point of land jutting out to the sea along Moonstone Beach Drive. A visual delight, the Blue Whale consists of six guest rooms stepped back from the ocean at such an angle that each captures a bit of the view (the best views, surprisingly, are from the rooms farthest back). At the front of the inn is a spacious living room furnished with overstuffed sofas and chairs and a wood-burning stove; it adjoins the dining area, and the two together create a great room with a wall of windows revealing the ever-changing ocean vista.

A tiny Japanese-style garden separates the guest rooms from the parking lot. Planted with a colorful selection of native —including lupine, coreopsis, and thyme—the garden is punctuated by a series of stepping-stones that lead from the parking area to the decks in front of the guest rooms.

In sharp contrast to the expansive views of sea and sky outside, the inn's interior is a riot of wallpapers and flowered fabrics, mostly in shades of blue; white-washed pine is the wood of choice. Appointments are comfortable: step-up canopy beds, love seats, desks, a coffee table, and a side chair in each room. Skylights punctuate each vaulted ceiling. Bathrooms, also skylit, have adjacent dressing areas complete with a sink set into a long vanity.

Although Fred is often at the inn, gardening and sharing his dining suggestions, Karleen and Bob Hathcock are the day-to-day innkeepers. Karleen is the breakfast chef, known for her croissant French toast with strawberry sauce. △ *6 double rooms with baths. Fireplace, refrigerator, cable TV, and phone in rooms. $165–$195; full breakfast. MC, V. No smoking, 2-night minimum on weekends and holidays.*

THE CHESHIRE CAT 🐚
36 W. Valerio St., Santa Barbara 93101, tel. 805/569–1610, fax 805/682–1876

Two words sum up these adjacent gray-and-white Victorian-era houses linked by a brick patio: "Laura" and "Ashley." If you like the late designer's delicate floral fabrics, bedding, and wallpapers, then you'll be in heaven here. Owner Christine Dunstan, who once owned and ran a B&B in Scotland, gave her American inn a thoroughly British look, from the picket-fenced flower gardens to the formal entry and fireplace-warmed sitting area. Some masculine English antiques offset the frilly prettiness of the public rooms, most notably the huge refectory-style table and weighty sideboard in the dining room.

Dunstan has the help of a manager, Amy Taylor, and a small crew of friendly folks to cook the substantial full breakfast and tend to the guests and the property. There's a fair amount to tend to: the main house, all Victorian turrets and bays;

the neighboring house, a Georgian-style box with shutters and bay windows; the Tweedledum & Tweedledee house, a simple clapboard cottage, in back; and three new cottages, complete with ultramodern kitchens. There's also a gazebo-covered whirlpool spa and a large brick patio where a first-rate breakfast is served, including quiche (sometimes made with artichoke hearts, other times with hash browns), fresh-squeezed juices, cereal, and fresh fruit in summer, cooked fruit in winter.

Larger and more upscale than most other B&Bs in town, the Cheshire Cat is popular with small groups for retreats or meetings, but most of its customers are couples seeking romance. They generally find it, particularly if they splurge on the Eberle Suite, which has a brick fireplace and a sunken whirlpool tub, surrounded by plush carpeting and delicately tiled walls, for two; the White Rabbit Suite, whose private patio overlooks the gardens; or the swank Tweedledum Suite in the newer back house, complete with living room, dining room, kitchenette, fireplace, TV, king-size bed, and whirlpool tub.

The west-facing rooms in the main house can be a bit noisy, since they're the closest to busy Chapala Street. On the plus side, the inn is a short walk from the shops and restaurants of State Street. ♨ *7 double rooms with baths, 7 suites, 3 cottages. Phone in rooms, fireplace in 7 rooms, whirlpool bath in 4 rooms, TV in 9 rooms. Meeting room, spa. $140–$300; full breakfast. MC, V. No smoking, 2-night minimum on weekends.*

CRYSTAL ROSE INN ☙
789 Valley Rd., Arroyo Grande 93420, tel. 805/481–1854 or 800/767–3466, fax 805/481–9541

It's hard to miss the Crystal Rose Inn, a three-story, pinker-than-pink Queen Anne–style house whose spindles, porches, and tower loom over Valley Road in Arroyo Grande. Built in 1890, the house was a walnut farm for many years, evolving in 1957 into a restaurant and residence; it became an inn in 1981.

Proprietors Dona Nolan and Bonnie Royster bought the big pink house in 1994 and developed its rose-theme rooms, rose hues, and abundance of crystal chandeliers. They have carefully preserved the ornate Victorian style, using antiques, period reproductions, and Waverly wall coverings, and they have decorated each room around a favorite rose. The roses themselves grow in the 1½-acre garden, whose gazebo is frequently used for weddings. Guests looking for a romantic hideaway can climb the narrow staircase to the third-floor Queen Elizabeth Tower Suite, whose sitting room overlooks the Oceano sand dunes. Those seeking privacy may try one of the rooms in the carriage house in back; alternatively, children are welcome in these rooms.

Among the most romantic rooms is the First Kiss room, with a back door opening onto the Secret Garden. A room off this garden also serves as a wine-tasting spot.

Breakfast includes cheese blintzes, pastries, and gourmet omelets. Afternoon high teas are served in the tea room, a large room with lace-covered tables and a collection of tea pots, silver sugar bowls, and tea strainers. A Mediterranean gourmet dinner is also served here, with specialties including cockles Marseilles and Majorca paella. ♨ *8 double rooms with baths. Restaurant, bicycles. $95–$185; full breakfast. AE, D, MC, V. No smoking.*

GILLIE ARCHER INN 🐦

1433 Oak St., Paso Robles 93446, tel. 805/238–0879, fax 805/238–2516

Fans of the serenity and architectural purity of Craftsman houses will like this soft-spoken five-room B&B on a quiet residential street in the heart of suburban Paso Robles. The large common rooms flow together, built-ins abound, and as befits this style of house, there's lots of woodwork, from the maple floors in the living and dining rooms to the clear cedar wainscoting in the dining room. Original Arts and Crafts fixtures are much in evidence, even in the garden, where a gazebo looks over the expanse of lawn. Furnishings, however, jump from era to era: a pine sleigh bed here, an Early American Windsor chair there, polished mahogany in the dining room.

The rooms themselves are somewhat simple, some with floor rugs, others with black and white tiles underfoot. Frilly drapes and flowery bedcovers lend an old-time feel to the place, and bucolic watercolors on the walls add a gentle touch.

Kathleen Stratton-Haas is a hands-on innkeeper who cooks the buffet breakfast (strudels, streusels, and scones, with plenty of fruit from the local farmers' market), prepares the afternoon tea, and steers guests to the best wineries and most worthy antiques shops in the area, often described as what Napa Valley was 25 years ago. ⌂ *3 double rooms with baths, 2 doubles share 1 bath. Air-conditioning and cable TV/VCR in rooms, fireplace in 1 room. $85–$125; full breakfast. AE, D, MC, V. No smoking.*

HOUSE OF ANOTHER TYME 🐦

227 Le Point St., Arroyo Grande 93420, tel. 805/489–6313

In 1997 retired local couple Jack and Judy Tiedemann realized a long-time dream and converted an old wooden house into this lovely little B&B in the hills on the outskirts of Arroyo Grande. The rambling garden has a small goldfish pond and a birdhouse full of finches. Totally lacking in pretensions, the blue cottage, built in 1916, was overhauled by the couple, who put in a vaulted pine ceiling and touched up the old redwood walls.

Jack is a former engineer, his wife an ex-teacher and a current real estate saleswoman. They are both friendly and take a lively interest in their guests.

The two rooms each have a modern bathroom and come complete with antique furnishings. The parlor contains a fireplace, a piano, and an old clock collection (the name of the inn refers to both the clocks and the thyme that grows in the yard). If you want to break up your coastal drive and don't want to spend a fortune, this is a good bet.

Full country breakfasts always include a gourmet quiche and fresh-fruit smoothies. ⌂ *2 double rooms with baths. $95; full breakfast. AE, D, MC, V. No smoking.*

SIMPSON HOUSE INN 🐦

121 E. Arrellaga St., Santa Barbara 93101, tel. 805/963–7067 or 800/676–1280, fax 805/564–4811

Although red-tile roofs are the norm in Santa Barbara, Victoriana runs rife as well, since so many Brits settled here in the late 1800s. One such emigrant was Robert Simpson, the Scotsman who built this Eastlake-style house in 1874. It is now one of the finest B&Bs in the Central Coast.

Set on a quiet, exquisitely landscaped acre in the heart of town, the Simpson House Inn offers something for almost everyone. Traditional B&B fans should stay in the main house, where larger-than-average rooms are paeans to Victorian style, color, and elegance. One room pays tribute to famed Victorian designer Christopher Dresser; several display custom hand-printed wallpaper, produced by Bradbury & Bradbury, famous for its period designs. Oriental rugs, English lace curtains, wicker, and claw-foot tubs add to the atmosphere.

Those put off by Victorian primness and the occasional discomforts of 100-year-old bathrooms should consider the newest additions to the property: three cottages and a restored 100-year-old barn. The cottages have a private courtyard (with bubbling fountain), queen feather bed, love seat set beside a wood-burning fireplace, teak floors, in-room whirlpool, superb shower, hidden TV/VCR, and plenty of privacy. Though a bit less dreamy, the four large barn suites are exceptional. Oriental rugs rest on antique pine floors, French doors open to private decks, king-size beds wear high-quality linens, English pine armoires hide TVs and VCRs, showers are modern and roomy, and fireplaces burn real wood, not those ubiquitous metal logs.

The substantial breakfast ranges from savory eggs to lemon curd and baked pears, which can be taken on the veranda, in the garden, or in one's suite. But it is the early evening that is most memorable, when guests toast the balmy Santa Barbara twilight with local wines and elegant hors d'oeuvres while knocking around croquet balls, stoking the fireplace, or sitting for a spell on a wicker sofa in the gardens. **△** *6 double rooms with baths, 3 cottages, 4 suites. Air-conditioning and fireplace in rooms, TV/VCR on request. Bicycles, croquet, beach chairs, towels, picnics. $160–$400; full breakfast. AE, D, MC, V. No smoking, 2-night minimum on weekends.*

UNION HOTEL/VICTORIAN MANSION ☙
362 Bell St. (Box 616), Los Alamos 93440, tel. 805/344–2744 or 800/230–2744, fax 805/344–3125

In the tiny Old West outpost of Los Alamos, some 50 mi north of Santa Barbara, these two inns present a study in fantasy fulfillment. The Union Hotel, a one-time Wells Fargo stagecoach station dating from 1880, was turned into one of the first bed-and-breakfasts in California and is currently owned by Christine Williams, a long-time owner of a veterinarian clinic in Orange County looking for a new chapter in her life. The whimsical Old West atmosphere, which begins with the honky-tonk wooden facade, straight out of a Hollywood western, continues with a lobby peopled with mannequins costumed in frontier finery, and a saloon decorated with mahogany Ping-Pong table supported by marble statues, and comes to a stop in the bedrooms with their French and patriotic wallpapers.

In the neighboring yellow three-story 1864 mansion, mere whimsy gives way to flat-out fantasy. The Egyptian Room is designed to make a couple feel like Antony and Cleopatra camping out in the desert. A step-up white bed, canopied with gauze, stands in the middle of the room facing a wall-size mural of a desert. Walls are draped with Near East–motif fabrics, and there's a step-up hot tub and a marble-faced fireplace flanked by floor cushions. The bathroom door is a life-size statue of King Tut, opened by tugging his beard, and the bathroom itself resembles the inside of a pyramid. Desert robes, backgammon, computer-controlled background music, and videotapes such as film classics *Lawrence of Arabia* and *The Wind and the Lion* round out the fantasy.

Other rooms are equally fantastic: Roman, Gypsy, Pirate, '50s Drive-In (complete with a 1956 Cadillac convertible, its interior converted into a luxury bed)—

each with fitting murals, bed, theme robes, music, movies, games, and menus. Breakfast is delivered to the theme rooms through lockers concealed in the walls.

Among the grounds' distinguishing features are the largest hedge maze west of the Mississippi and a 67-ft yawl that once belonged to the King of Denmark. ♦ *4 double rooms with baths, 10 doubles with sinks share 2 baths in hotel; 6 double rooms with baths in mansion. Air-conditioning in mansion. TV/VCR, phone, hot tub, fireplace, robe, and refrigerator in mansion rooms. Restaurant, saloon, shuffleboard, Ping-Pong, pool, spa in gazebo. $88–$242; full breakfast. AE, D, MC, V.*

THE VINEYARD COUNTRY INN ☜
7840 Vineyard Dr., Paso Robles 93446, tel. 805/239–4678, fax 805/238–6355

The newest B&B in the region, this low-lying creamy adobe with red-tile roof was opened in the spring of 1998. Run by retirees Ken and Miriam Dibert, who had lived in the hacienda for a decade before deciding to rent the rooms out, the Vineyard is a nice, friendly place to stay.

The three rooms—the Vineyard, Sir George's (named after the owners' son), and Miss Victoria's (named after their daughter)—make up in size and coziness what they lack in uniqueness. The rooms have large armchairs and beds topped with colorful comforters; glass walls provide ample views of the rolling hills.

Cooked-to order breakfasts (guests can choose among pancakes, eggs, bacon, and other standard breakfast fare) are served in a huge dining room.

This is a good place to stay if you're driving through the wine region and aren't looking to spend a fortune. ♦ *3 double rooms with baths. Air-conditioning and TV in rooms, fireplace in 1 room. Pool, tennis. $90–$250; full breakfast. MC, V.*

OTHER CHOICES

Ballard Inn. 2436 Baseline Ave., Ballard 93463, tel. 805/688–7770 or 800/638–2466, fax 805/688–9560. 15 double rooms with baths. Air-conditioning in rooms, fireplace in 7 rooms. Carriage rides. $170–$250; full breakfast. AE, MC, V. No smoking, 2-night minimum on weekends.

The Beach House. 6360 Moonstone Beach Dr., Cambria 93428, tel. 805/927–3136. 7 double rooms with baths. Cable TV in rooms, fireplace in 2 rooms. Mountain bikes. $125–$155; full breakfast. MC, V. No smoking.

Just Inn. 11680 Chimney Rock Rd., Paso Robles 93446, tel. 805/238–6932 or 800/726–0049, fax 805/237–4109. 3 suites. Air-conditioning, fireplace, whirlpool bath, and phone in rooms, TV/VCR in 1 room. Restaurant, pool, and spa. $225–$275; full breakfast. AE, D, MC, V. 2-night minimum on weekends and holidays.

Los Olivos Grand Hotel. 2860 Grand Ave., Los Olivos 93441, tel. 805/688–7788 or 800/446–2455, fax 805/688–1942. 21 suites. Air-conditioning, fireplace, phone, cable TV, wet bar, and refrigerator in rooms, whirlpool bath in 5 rooms. Restaurant, lounge, meeting and banquet rooms, room service, swimming pool, spa, bicycles, picnics. $175–$340; full breakfast. AE, D, DC, MC, V. 2-night minimum on weekends.

The Mary May Inn. 111 W. Valerio St., Santa Barbara 93101, tel. and fax 805/569–3398. 12 double rooms with baths. Fireplace and whirlpool bath in 4 rooms, TV in 8 rooms. Croquet. $150–$180; full breakfast. No smoking, 2-night minimum on weekends.

Old Yacht Club Inn. 431 Corona del Mar Dr., Santa Barbara 93103, tel. 805/962–1277 or 800/676–1676, fax 805/962–3989. 12 double rooms with baths. Phone in rooms, whirlpool bath in 5 rooms. Bicycles. $105–$185; full breakfast. AE, D, MC, V. No smoking, 2-night minimum on weekends.

The Parsonage. 1600 Olive St., Santa Barbara 93101, tel. 805/962–9336 or 800/775–0352, fax 805/962–2285. 5 double rooms with baths, 1 suite. Fireplace in 2 rooms, whirlpool bath in 2 rooms. $115–$265; full breakfast. AE, D, MC, V. No smoking, 2-night minimum on weekends, 3-night minimum on holidays.

Secret Garden Inn and Cottages. 1908 Bath St., Santa Barbara 93101, tel. 805/687–2300 or 800/676–1622, fax 805/687–4576. 6 double rooms with baths, 5 suites. Fireplace in 1 suite, hot tub in 2 rooms and 2 suites, TV in 3 rooms. Bicycles. $110–$180; full breakfast. AE, D, DC, MC, V. No smoking, 2-night minimum on weekends.

Theodore Woolsey House. 1484 E. Ojai Ave., Ojai 93023, tel. 805/646–9779, fax 805/646–4414. 5 double rooms with baths. Air-conditioning in rooms, fireplace in 2 rooms, TV and phone in 3 rooms. Pool, outdoor whirlpool bath, volleyball court, croquet, horseshoes. $85–$125; Continental breakfast. No credit cards. No smoking, 2-night minimum on weekends.

RESERVATIONS AND REFERRAL SERVICES

Bed & Breakfast Santa Barbara (tel. 805/898–1905 or 800/557–7898). **Santa Barbara Bed & Breakfast Innkeepers Guild** (Box 90734, Santa Barbara 93190, tel. 800/776–9176).

Monterey Bay, Including Santa Cruz and Carmel

BABBLING BROOK INN 🐚

1025 Laurel St., Santa Cruz 95060, tel. 831/427–2437 or 800/866–1131, fax 831/427–2457

This inn, the oldest and largest bed-and-breakfast in Santa Cruz, offers a combination of romantic setting, California history, and a convenient location for business travelers. Though in the heart of the city, the inn's "babbling brook," wooded grounds, and flower gardens help to make guests feel worlds away.

Now owned by the same partners (Suzie Lankes and Dan Floyd) who run the stellar Inn at Depot Hill in nearby Capitola and the Bayview Hotel in Aptos (*see below*), the Babbling Brook combines four cedar-shingle-sided buildings set on different levels of the hillside property. Portions of the main house's stone foundation date from 1796, when the mission fathers built a gristmill for grinding corn. In 1981, when it became a bed-and-breakfast inn, three cottages were added. After a seven-decade absence, the historic waterwheel has been returned to its original pond setting in front of the building.

The rooms are decorated in French-country style: soft colors, floral-print curtains, and iron beds covered with floral spreads. The most charming are in the main house, especially the romantic Honeymoon Suite, which offers couples seclusion (breakfast in bed is available to guests staying here) as well as a private deck overlooking a waterfall. The expansive Garden has a wood-burning stove and a great garden view. The Contessa, the largest room, has two queen-size beds and a fireplace.

A buffet-style breakfast of frittatas or other egg dishes, pancakes, and fresh muffins and croissants with jam is set out in the living room, although guests can go either into the adjacent dining room or outside to enjoy their meals in the shade of the redwood trees. In the afternoon, the innkeepers serve tea and freshly baked cookies; later, a congenial wine hour takes place in front of the fire in the comfortable living room. ♙ *12 double rooms with baths. Cable TV and phone in rooms, fireplace in 10 rooms, whirlpool bath in 4 rooms. Picnic baskets available. $145–$195; full breakfast. AE, D, MC, V. No smoking, 2-night minimum on weekends.*

COBBLESTONE INN ✹

8th and Junipero Aves. (Box 3185), Carmel 93921, tel. 831/625–5222 or 800/833–8836, fax 831/625–0478

Stones gathered from the Carmel River cover the lower level of this two-story inn that belongs to the Four Sisters Inn group, which also runs bed-and-breakfasts in Pacific Grove and elsewhere in California.

Opened in 1984, the Cobblestone maintains an English-country theme, both in its outdoor gardens and its room decor. Outside, the inn surrounds the gardens on three sides like a horseshoe; a slate courtyard contains tables for warm-weather dining. In the rooms, expect thick quilts, English antiques (genuine and reproductions), and stone fireplaces (again, with stones taken from the Carmel River); the public parlor also has a large stone fireplace. The largest room—the Honeymoon Suite—has a four-poster bed with draped canopy, a window seat, sitting area, and a large bath. Families traveling with small children should ask the innkeepers about appropriate rooms.

An expanded Continental buffet breakfast—fruit, pastries, and breads—is served in the dining room or on the patio; guests may also request breakfast in bed. English-style tea and wine and hors d'oeuvres are served in the afternoon. The inn's location is just far enough off the most heavily beaten paths in Carmel to provide some quiet, yet it's within easy walking distance of shops and restaurants. ♙ *22 double rooms with baths, 2 suites. Phone, cable TV, fireplace, and refrigerator in rooms. $95–$180; Continental-plus breakfast. AE, DC, MC, V. No smoking.*

GREEN GABLES INN ✹

104 5th St., Pacific Grove 93950, tel. 831/375–2095 or 800/722–1774, fax 831/375–5437

The Green Gables Inn, a striking landmark along the oceanfront of Pacific Grove, dates from 1888, when Los Angeles businessman (and amateur architect) William Lacy built the two-story, half-timbered and gabled Queen Anne for his lady friend.

This elegant white-and-green mansion, in which nearly every room has a three-sided bay window, offers sweeping views of the Monterey Bay shoreline. Framed entirely of redwood, it has solid maple floors; countless angles, slopes, and nooks; exposed ceiling beams; intricate moldings, woodwork, and arches; and even stained-glass windows framing the fireplace. The windows, fixtures, and woodwork are all original.

Roger and Sally Post bought the house as a family home for their four daughters in 1970. The Posts began renting out rooms to summer visitors, and in 1983 the Green Gables became a full-time inn (and the cornerstone of the Four Sisters Inns group).

Guest rooms in the recently renovated carriage house, perched on a hill out back, are larger than those in the main house and have more privacy as well as views of the ocean. They also offer more modern amenities, but the rooms in the main house, with their intricately detailed molding and woodwork, have more charm. The Lacy Suite on the main floor, doubtless a converted parlor and library, has a fireplace, built-in bookshelves, and a claw-foot tub in the bathroom. Upstairs in the Gable Room, a window seat under leaded-glass windows overlooks the ocean. The Balcony Room is like a sleeping porch, and the Chapel Room actually resembles a church, with a vaulted ceiling and a pew-like window seat stretching across the front of the room. Four rooms in the main house do share baths, however. If you're traveling with children, ask the innkeepers which rooms might be appropriate.

The food, always fresh, is served family-style. The ample buffet breakfast includes selections such as frittatas, a fruit plate, an assortment of breads and scones, and apple pancakes. Afternoon refreshments include wine and hors d'oeuvres. The staff is gracious and can offer assistance with dinner reservations and sightseeing information. ♠ *6 double rooms with baths, 4 doubles share 2 baths, 1 suite. Fireplace in 6 rooms. Picnic baskets available, bicycles, limited parking. $110–$180; full breakfast. AE, MC, V. No smoking.*

INN AT DEPOT HILL ☞
250 Monterey Ave. (Box 1934), Capitola by the Sea 95010, tel. 831/462–3376 or 800/572–2632, fax 831/462–3697

Innkeepers Suzie Lankes and Dan Floyd have created one of the most beautiful B&Bs in California. And they provide exquisite pampering to complement the splendid surroundings.

Once a historic railroad station in the beachside village of Capitola, the Inn at Depot Hill is now a vision of turn-of-the-century European-style luxury. Most rooms have a Continental theme: Delft, a corner suite, includes a big blue-and-white sitting room, a bedroom with a huge feather bed draped in Belgian cutwork lace and linen, a private patio filled with tulips and irises, an outdoor whirlpool tub, and a gray-marble bathroom with double shower. Portofino captures a sunny Italian mood, with a vine-and-leaf-decorated feather bed and a private Mediterranean garden planted with orange and lemon trees. Departing from the European motif, the Railroad Baron room honors local history. This accommodation, resembling a posh railroad car, has deep red brocade upholstery, a red-and-gold sitting room, and a circular lit dome over the bed.

The inn has now expanded with three more rooms and suites in a rear house, including the stunning Kyoto room, whose Japanese theme (modified for Western habits) sports an indoor soaking tub and glassed-in garden shower.

The food here is ample and well prepared. For breakfast there are fresh fruit, croissants, and pastries laid out buffet-style, followed by a hot entrée (such as buckwheat pancakes with fresh strawberries) served at elegantly set tables in the dining room. When the weather is nice, breakfast may be served outside in the brick courtyard. The chef puts together a late-afternoon hors d'oeuvre buffet with local wines, a canapé tray, and crudités and dip. A homemade dessert and port and sherry welcome guests returning from dinner. ♠ *6 double rooms with baths, 6 suites. Fireplace, cable TV/VCR, and phone with fax or modem connection in rooms, hot tub in 9 rooms. $190–$275; full breakfast. AE, MC, V. No smoking, 2-night minimum on weekends.*

MARTINE INN 🐚
255 Ocean View Blvd., Pacific Grove 93950, tel. 831/373–3388 or 800/852–5588, fax 831/373–3896

Elegance, grace, and service are the keys to the Martine Inn, a nearly 100-year-old mansion perched above the cove-pocked Pacific Grove shoreline. Originally a Queen Anne with turrets and towers, the home was later remodeled in Mediterranean style. Don Martine's family acquired the house in 1972; by 1984 he and wife Marion had opened it as an inn.

Don and Marion have assembled an extensive antiques collection, mostly American pieces dating from 1840 through 1890: an Eastlake suite used by publisher C. K. McClatchy; a mahogany suite exhibited at the 1893 Chicago World's Fair; Academy Award–winning costume designer Edith Head's bedroom suite; and an 1860 Chippendale Revival four-poster bed. There are two pianos in the main house, one a music-reproducing baby grand that plays itself during the complimentary wine and hors d'oeuvres hour.

Guest rooms are on the ground and second floors of the main house; some have stunning views of the water through arched front windows. Other rooms are in what was once the carriage house off the courtyard and in a recently purchased separate house next door. An abundance of antique mirrors brightens many rooms by reflecting the ever-changing light of the bay. Original fixtures grace most of the large bathrooms.

The parlor, which occupies the glassed-in front of the house's main floor, lures guests to savor the sea vistas. A small library contains a personal collection of books and magazines, and two small solarium sitting rooms adjoin guest rooms on the ground and second floor (these can be rented to form suites as well). A games room contains an 1870 oak slate pool table, a 1917 nickelodeon, and a slot machine from the 1930s.

In the dining room, the chef serves up a lavish breakfast spread, including fruit, granola, a baked item, an egg or other hot entrée, and fresh orange juice. Guests eat at large lace-clad tables set with Sheffield silver, Victorian-style china, and crystal. △ *25 double rooms with baths. Phone and refrigerator in rooms, fireplace in 11 rooms. Conference facilities, picnic baskets available. $135–$245; full breakfast. AE, D, MC, V. Restricted smoking, 2-night minimum on weekends, 3-night minimum on holidays.*

OLD MONTEREY INN 🐚
500 Martin St., Monterey 93940, tel. 831/375–8284 or 800/350–2344, fax 831/375–6730

When Gene Swett was transferred to Monterey from the Bay Area in 1968, the family needed a house that was big enough for eight. Although the house they found, an English Tudor–style home built in 1929 by Carmel Martin, then the mayor of Monterey, was run down, the Swetts purchased it, renovated it, and by 1978 had created one of the loveliest inns in California.

In the Old Monterey Inn, Ann and Gene Swett have elevated the business of innkeeping to a high art, offering their guests quietly elegant accommodations in a historic home—and the type of pampering that "fulfills our guests' needs before they know what they are," as Ann puts it. The bathrooms, for example, come stocked with 20 different amenities.

Outside, Gene made an oasis of year-round color. Inside was Ann's domain. She searched for antiques and contemporary furnishings to suit the ever-changing themes and color schemes of the rooms. The Serengeti room evokes a turn-of-the-century African safari, with mosquito netting over the bed, rattan chairs, pith helmets, a table made from antique leather hatboxes, and a brass-elephant birdcage stand. In the Library Room, floor-to-ceiling bookshelves contain volumes of nostalgic children's literature; a private sundeck overlooks the garden and a massive 300-year-old oak. The Ashford Suite, once the house's master bedroom, is the only room that can accommodate three people. All the rooms have feather beds and down comforters.

Guests have the option of having breakfast in bed or being served in front of the fireplace in the formal dining room, at a table set for 14 with exquisite Oriental china; weather permitting, it may be served in the Rose Garden. Guests dine on fruit, breads, and quiche, served course by course. Gene is the consummate host, mingling and getting to know each guest before recommending romantic picnic spots, local galleries and shops, and restaurants. The inn doesn't encourage young children; ages 14 and older are fine. ⚲ *8 double rooms with baths, 1 suite, 1 cottage suite. Fireplace in 9 rooms, whirlpool bath in 3 rooms, TV/VCR by request. Picnic baskets available, fitness center passes. $200–$350; full breakfast. MC, V. No smoking, 2-night minimum on weekends, 3-night minimum on holidays. Closed Christmas Day.*

OTHER CHOICES

Inn at Manresa Beach. 1258 San Andreas Rd., La Selva Beach 95076, tel. 831/728–1000 or 888/523–2244, fax 831/728–8294. 9 double rooms with baths. Phone, cable TV/VCR, and fireplace in rooms. 2 tennis courts, croquet, volleyball. $150–$195; full breakfast. AE, D, MC, V. No smoking.

The Jabberwock. 598 Laine St., Monterey 93940, tel. 831/372–4777, fax 831/655–2946. 5 double rooms with baths, 2 doubles share 1 bath. Off-street parking. $105–$195; full breakfast. MC, V. No smoking, 2-night minimum on weekends, 3-night minimum on holidays.

Mangels House. 570 Aptos Creek Rd. (Box 302), Aptos 95001, tel. 831/688–7982 or 800/320–7401. 6 double rooms with baths. Fireplace in 1 room. $120–$160; full breakfast. AE, MC, V. No smoking, 2-night minimum on weekends.

Post Ranch Inn. Hwy. 1 (Box 219), Big Sur 93920, tel. 831/667–2200 or 800/527–2200, fax 831/667–2824. 29 double rooms with baths, 1 suite. Fireplace, whirlpool bath, massage table, and coffeemaker in rooms. 2 pools, guided walks/stargazing, yoga/exercise classes, picnic lunches, massage, aromatherapy, facials, tarot readings, gift shop, limousine service (fee) from Monterey, restaurant. $365–$900; Continental-plus breakfast. AE, MC, V. No smoking, 2-night minimum on weekends, 3-night minimum on holidays.

Stonepine—An Estate Resort. 150 E. Carmel Valley Rd., Carmel Valley 93924, tel. 831/659–2245, fax 831/659–5160. 8 double rooms with baths, 4 suites, 2 two-bedroom cottages. TV/VCR, fireplace, whirlpool bath, and phone in rooms. Restaurant, room service, honor bar, picnic baskets, 2 tennis courts, 2 pools, croquet, archery, health club, hiking and riding trails, bicycles, equestrian center. $275–$750; full breakfast. AE, MC, V. No smoking, 2-night minimum on weekends and holidays.

RESERVATIONS AND REFERRAL SERVICES

Carmel Innkeepers Association (Box 1362, Carmel 93921). **Santa Cruz County Bed and Breakfast Referral Service** (Box 464, Santa Cruz 95061, tel. 831/425–8212). for all accommodations on the Monterey Peninsula, call the **Tourist Information Room Finders** (tel. 831/624–1711 or 800/847–8066).

San Francisco from North Beach to the Sunset District

ARCHBISHOPS MANSION 🐚

1000 Fulton St., San Francisco 94117, tel. 415/563–7872 or 800/543–5820, fax 415/885–3193

The Archbishops Mansion is an elegant European manor reborn in San Francisco. The Second Empire–style residence, built in 1904 for Archbishop Patrick Riordan, faces Alamo Square and its "postcard row" of restored Victorians. In the early 1980s, designers Jonathan Shannon and Jeffrey Ross spent three years restoring the home, now managed by Joie de Vivre Hotels, to that era of opulence. Ornate Belle Epoque furnishings and reproductions, such as the crystal chandelier that hung in Scarlett O'Hara's beloved Tara in *Gone With the Wind*, fill the public areas and rooms. Everything about the mansion—the scale, the ornamentation, the Napoléon III antiques—is extravagant.

A three-story redwood staircase rises majestically from the coffered foyer. Above, sunlight filters through a 16-ft-wide, oval leaded-glass dome that survived the 1906 earthquake. While you sip your evening wine in the front parlor, which is dominated by a massive redwood fireplace with fluted Corinthian columns, you'll be serenaded from the hall by a 1904 ebony Bechstein piano once owned by Noel Coward.

Guest rooms, named for operas, are unabashedly romantic. The gold-hued Don Giovanni Suite conveys a Renaissance formality and, appropriately, has an impressive bed. The zebrawood canopy four-poster bed found in a castle in southern France was masterfully carved during the Napoleonic period. The bath is simply huge. The Carmen Suite also has a stunning bathroom: a claw-foot tub rests in front of a fireplace to enhance your soaking pleasure. A second fireplace warms the bedroom, where the 1885 settee has its original horsehair covering. Billowing draperies, canopied beds, and ceramic-tile fireplaces are routine here.

A breakfast of pastries, fresh fruit, and orange juice and hot beverages is brought to your room on a silver tray, or you can join the other guests in the formal dining room. Complimentary wine and hors d'oeuvres are offered in the early evening in the parlor. △ *10 double rooms with baths, 5 suites. Phone and cable TV/VCR in rooms, fireplace in 11 rooms, whirlpool bath in 2 rooms. Elevator, laundry service, limited room service, concierge service, conference facilities, limited off-street parking. $139–$399; Continental breakfast. AE, DC, MC, V. Smoking in dining room only, 2-night minimum on weekends.*

CHATEAU TIVOLI 🐚

1057 Steiner St., San Francisco 94115, tel. 415/776–5462 or 800/228–1647, fax 415/776–0505

A stay in this ornate fin-de-siècle château in the historic Alamo Square district may forever alter your decorating sensibilities. Built in 1892, this historic painted lady wears no fewer than 22 colors, from raisin brown to turquoise, with ornamentation picked out in gold leaf.

The château's past is as colorful as its exterior. The house once belonged to lumber baron Daniel Jackson and later to Ernestine Kreling, owner of San Francisco's Tivoli Opera House. Subsequently, the mansion was a Hebrew Cultural Center, a rooming house, and an ashram. The building was extensively restored and opened as a bed-and-breakfast in 1989. Current owners Dr. Stephen Shohet and his wife, Geraldine, purchased it in 1996.

The flamboyant appearance of the exterior extends to the interior. Every room, hallway, and wall is packed with antique furnishings and art, housewares, knickknacks, and a somewhat haunting taxidermy collection. Competing for attention are the cornices and carved oak paneling of the entrance hall, double parlor, and staircase.

The riotous, museumlike quality of the château's busy public areas is carried over into the guest rooms. A sultan and his elephant could both stay comfortably in the glorious Mark Twain suite; its Renaissance Revival–style parlor alone is 500 square ft. Romantics relish the Luisa Tettrazini suite's huge French Renaissance canopy bed, frescoed ceilings, and marble bath with double shower head. Although all rooms here are spacious, two of them share baths. Another drawback may be the neighborhood, which can be a tad dicey at night and is sometimes noisy. Rollaways are available to accommodate families, and pets can be boarded across the street.

An expanded Continental breakfast of homemade pastries and breads, cereals, juices, and fresh fruit is served weekdays at a grand dining room table that seats eight, with a more intimate table for two nearby. A champagne brunch with hot entrées is served on weekends. ♣ *3 double rooms with baths, 2 doubles share 1 bath, 4 suites. Phone in rooms, fireplace in 1 room and 1 suite. $99–$225; Continental-plus breakfast weekdays, full breakfast weekends. MC, V. No smoking.*

HOTEL DAVID BED AND BREAKFAST ☜

480 Geary St., San Francisco 94102, tel. 415/771–1600 or 800/524–1888, fax 415/931–5442

Just two blocks west of Union Square, in the heart of the Theatre District, Hotel David claims "the best location in San Francisco"—or so says its owner and innkeeper of nearly a half-century, who goes simply by the name David (he won't say if it's first, last, or both.) "Across the street," David says, referring to the Four Seasons Clift Hotel, "you pay four times as much and have to look at the Hotel David. If you stay here you get a view of the Four Seasons."

Even many longtime San Franciscans aren't aware that right next door to David's Delicatessen, a longtime dining fixture along Geary Street, this unprepossessing, moderately priced European-style bed-and-breakfast hotel lures guests partially on the promise of a bounteous cooked-to-order morning meal at the restaurant. Guests can choose anything off the menu—from juices, fresh fruit, baked-on-the-premises pastries, omelets, and pancakes to house specialties like cheese blintzes or kosher corned beef croquettes with poached eggs. (And how about a half-pound meat ball or some marinated herring on the side?)

Don't come here if you're looking for a grand lobby to lounge in. You'll be lucky to find room to stand while David checks you in (in one of the nine languages he speaks; the hotel is well known among European visitors). Don't look for antiques—unless you count the tiny elevator. Rooms here are modestly sized and sparely furnished. Decor is contemporary and attractive: white walls, bright bedspreads, and sleek maple headboards, chairs, tables, and nightstands. Everything is immaculately clean (David awards free T-shirts to anyone who finds a spot of dirt); bathrooms are tiled in white and contain heated towel racks. Each room has cable TV, a phone, a radio, and either one or two beds. Extras include free airport transportation for guests staying at least two nights, discounts on other meals at David's Delicatessen, and David's own comic charm. ♣ *50 double rooms with baths. Phone and cable TV in rooms. Valet parking ($15). $99–$169; full breakfast. AE, D, MC, V.*

THE MANSIONS HOTEL 🖝

2220 Sacramento St., San Francisco 94115, tel. 415/929–9444 or 800/826–9398, fax 415/567–9391

If inns were awarded prizes for showmanship, the Mansions Hotel would win top honors. Where else can you see the innkeeper, clad in sequined dinner jacket, play the saw? And then there's Merlin's Magic Music Box, an indoor snowstorm, and other illusions. They're all part of the live "magic extravaganzas" held every night at the Mansions, which are free to overnight guests. (Zany innkeeper Bob Pritikin, an adman and author, does his saw-concert on weekends only.) The cabaret also draws diners (who pay a cover charge) from the highly praised hotel restaurant. The restaurant is a wonder of floor-to-ceiling stained glass.

The Mansions, which consists of two adjacent Queen Anne Victorians a short walk from the chic boutiques and eateries of Pacific Heights, is as visually flamboyant as its entertainment. In the public areas no surface has been left unembellished. Objects, wall murals, curios (a selection of ugly ties, for example), and sculptures, many by Beniamino Bufano, are everywhere. The porcine theme in the room known as the International Pig Museum is tough to miss, surrounded as you are by an old wooden carousel pig and wall painting depicting a swine-filled picnic in progress.

All of the east-wing guest rooms have murals that portray the famous San Francisco personage for whom the room is named. The authentic Victorian reproduction decor might include a rolltop desk, four-poster canopy bed, and Tiffany-style lamp. Most west-wing rooms are suites that have fireplaces and decks; some have parlors and two baths. Particularly lavish is the French-themed Louis IV (or Josephine) room, where Barbra Streisand and other celebrity guests have enjoyed the immense gold-leaf half-tester bed and wardrobe, Venetian chandeliers, and private redwood deck.

A full breakfast of fresh fruit and juice, cereal, eggs cooked to order, and potatoes can be delivered to your room. Guests also receive a "care package" of snacks upon check-in. The Mansions is dog-friendly and family-friendly as well, though it's primarily a special-occasion spot. △ *13 double rooms with baths, 8 suites. Phone in rooms, fireplace in 6 suites, whirlpool bath in 1 room. Restaurant, limited room service, laundry service. $139–$350; full breakfast. AE, D, DC, MC, V. Dogs allowed.*

THE QUEEN ANNE 🖝

1590 Sutter St., San Francisco 94109, tel. 415/441–2828 or 800/227–3970, fax 415/775–5212

This majestic, four-story Victorian ranks among the loveliest of San Francisco's classic painted ladies. Its rose and green gables and distinctive corner turret rise proudly above a neighborhood of vivid Victorians in lower Pacific Heights. Japantown with its restaurants and the Fillmore shopping area are just around the corner.

The building's roots as a luxurious boarding school for girls (not to mention its later incarnations as a bordello and a private men's club), constructed by silver mogul and Senator James G. Fair in 1890, still show in its rich cedar and oak paneling and the lofty staircase winding four flights up to an antique skylight. (An elevator equipped with chandelier and settee provides an alternate route up.) A sprawling lobby full of Victoriana—from brocade chairs to crimson walls— encompasses most of the ground floor. Guests can curl up with coffee or sherry before a crackling fire or partake of the breakfast buffet set out in the adjoining salon each morning (many prefer to take a tray back to their room). Among the offerings at breakfast are English coffee cake, raspberry and blueberry scones, and a variety of fruit juices and hot beverages.

The hotel's spacious public area, which fans into adjoining conference chambers, makes it ideal for weddings and business meetings. The front-desk staff is adept at attending to guests' faxing, computing, secretarial, and copying needs.

All the rooms and suites are different, blending contemporary comforts, historic accents, and occasional tacky touches such as TV tables. Carpeting is plush, bedspreads are mostly modern, and baths are equipped with phones and hair dryers. Fireplaces warm many quarters; one enormous room has two brick hearths at either end. The accommodations, generally large for a small hotel, range from a two-bedroom, two-bath, split-level town house with a private deck to a snug top-story room with slanted ceilings. △ *45 double rooms with baths, 3 suites, 1 suite. Phone, cable TV, and hair dryer in rooms, fireplace in 9 rooms. Conference and reception facilities, concierge-secretarial service, laundry service, complimentary limousine shuttle within San Francisco, off-street parking ($12). $120–$195; Continental breakfast. AE, D, DC, MC, V.*

VICTORIAN INN ON THE PARK 🕊

301 Lyon St., San Francisco 94117, tel. 415/931–1830 or 800/435–1967, fax 415/931–1830

Overlooking Golden Gate Park's Panhandle (a spot to avoid at night), this lime-green Queen Anne Victorian is a riot of gables, finials, and cornices. Renowned San Francisco architect William Curlett designed the mansion in 1897; also known as the Clunie House, it's a registered historic landmark. In 1980, Paul and Shirley Weber purchased the building; their daughter, attorney Lisa Benau, and her husband, William, soon helped transform it into one of San Francisco's first bed-and-breakfasts. They now live next door and provide close supervision.

If you've ever wanted to experience the more luxurious aspects of life in the Gay '90s, this is the place to do it. Step across the threshold to a grand entrance of rubbed mahogany paneling and oak parquet floors; they look even more burnished when a fire is lit in the immense brick fireplace framed by a sculpted wood mantel. The parlor is rather formal, with a graceful Rococo Revival fainting couch in floral brocade and a velvet settee. Wine is served here in the evening by the white-tile and painted-wood hearth. Light filters through period fringed and embroidered lamp shades. A breakfast of seasonal fruit, cheeses, juices, croissants, and breads is served in the oak-paneled dining room.

Guest rooms occupy three floors and are decorated with Rococo Revival and Eastlake antiques and peppered with modern reproductions. The striking wallpapers, which combine different floral motifs in rich blues, purples, greens, and gold, were meticulously hand silk-screened by Bradbury & Bradbury, a local firm. Piles of pillows, marble bathroom counters, Victorian-era prints and photos, and a decanter of sherry in every room are other special touches. The most unusual architectural feature is the open belvedere in a cupola, one of only two existing in the city; it's a private retreat for guests in the upstairs Belvedere Room. The delightfully asymmetrical Iris Suite, with a small alcove, skylight, and TV, is ideal for families with small children. The rooms on the street level are quiet and removed but a bit dark. △ *12 double rooms with baths, 1 suite, 1 double suite with 2 baths. Phone in rooms, fireplace in 2 rooms, TV on request. Meeting facilities, parking ($15). $124–$345; Continental-plus breakfast. AE, D, DC, MC, V. No smoking in rooms, 2-night minimum on weekends, 3-night minimum on holiday weekends.*

WHITE SWAN INN ☞

845 Bush St., San Francisco 94108, tel. 415/775–1755 or 800/999–9570, fax 415/775–5717

Fireplaces in every room (with hard-cover books on the mantels), romantic furnishings, delicious food, top-notch amenities, and a location just four blocks from Union Square make the White Swan Inn one of the premier bed-and-breakfasts in San Francisco. This circa-1908 building has the look of a London town house, and the decoration is studiously English. The fireplace-warmed library seems the epitome of an exclusive gentleman's club, with tufted wing chairs; rich, dark wood; sparkling brass fixtures and hardware; hunting scenes on the pillows; and a red tartan couch. Afternoon hors d'oeuvres—vegetables with curry dip, stuffed grape leaves, specialty cheeses, and lemon cake, accompanied by wine, sherry, and other drinks—are served here.

The guest rooms, predominantly green and burgundy with touches of yellow and rose, have a more informal look than the public rooms. All are similarly furnished with reproduction Edwardian pieces in cherry and other dark woods. Four-poster beds, wing-back or barrel chairs, TVs enclosed in an armoire or a cabinet, and Laura Ashley–style floral wallpaper are standard in most rooms. Four rooms have bay windows. Two "romance suites" have canopy beds, VCRs, and in-room champagne and chocolates.

The hotel has been one of the Four Sisters Inns group since 1986 and is on the same block as the Petite Auberge (*see below*), another Four Sisters property. The group's trademark teddy bears cuddle in the reception area, peeking through banisters and perched on the mantel over the perpetually lit fire. A plush bear also adorns each guest room.

Typical breakfast fare, served in your room or buffet-style downstairs, may include Mexican quiche, soda-bread toast, Swiss oatmeal, fresh fruit, granola, and doughnuts. Everything is homemade. △ *23 double rooms with baths, 3 suites. Phone with voice mail and dataport, TV, fireplace, wet bar, refrigerator, and hair dryer in rooms, VCR in 2 rooms. Laundry service, conference and catering facilities, valet parking ($19). $150–$250; full breakfast. AE, DC, MC, V. No smoking.*

OTHER CHOICES

Dolores Park Inn. 3641 17th St., San Francisco 94114, tel. and fax 415/621–0482. 2 double rooms and 1 single share 3 baths, 1 suite, carriage house. Air-conditioning and cable TV in rooms, fireplace in 2 rooms. On- and off-street parking. $89–$325; Continental-plus breakfast. MC, V. No smoking, 2-night minimum (3-night minimum for carriage house).

Inn at the Opera. 333 Fulton St., San Francisco 94102, tel. 415/863–8400 or 800/325–2708, fax 415/861–0821. 30 double rooms with baths, 17 suites. 2-line phone with voice mail and dataport, cable TV/VCR, wet bar, microwave, refrigerator, and hair dryers in rooms. Limited room service, business-secretarial service, laundry service, valet parking ($19). $165–$280; Continental breakfast. AE, D, DC, MC, V. 4 no-smoking floors.

Inn 1890. 1890 Page St., San Francisco 94117, tel. 415/386–0486 or 888/466–1890, fax 415/386–3626. 7 double rooms with bath, 2 doubles share 1 bath. Phone with voice mail, TV, microwave oven, and refrigerator in rooms, fireplace in 3 rooms. Health club privileges, limited off-street parking ($5). $79–$119; Continental-plus breakfast. MC, V. No smoking.

Inn San Francisco. 943 South Van Ness Ave., San Francisco 94110, tel. 415/641–0188 or 800/359–0913, fax 415/641–1701. 18 double rooms with baths,

2 doubles share 1 bath, 1 housekeeping suite. Phone, TV, and refrigerator in rooms, whirlpool bath in 5 rooms, fireplace in 4 rooms, hot tub in 1 room. Limited off-street parking ($12). $85–$235; full breakfast. AE, D, DC, MC, V. No smoking in parlor.

Jackson Court. 2198 Jackson St., San Francisco 94115, tel. 415/929–7670, fax 415/929–1405. 10 double rooms with baths. Phone and TV in rooms, fireplace in 2 rooms. Off-street parking ($10). $139–$195; Continental-plus breakfast. AE, MC, V. No smoking.

Petite Auberge. 863 Bush St., San Francisco 94108, tel. 415/928–6000 or 800/365–3004, fax 415/775–5717. 26 double rooms with baths. Phone and TV in rooms, fireplace in 13 rooms, whirlpool bath in 1 room. Laundry service, valet parking ($19). $110–$225; full breakfast. AE, DC, MC, V. No smoking.

Spencer House. 1080 Haight St., San Francisco 94117, tel. 415/626–9205, fax 415/626–9230. 6 double rooms with baths. Phone in rooms, TV on request. Limited off-street parking ($6). $120–$170; full breakfast. AE, MC, V. No smoking, 2-night minimum on weekends, 3-night minimum on holiday weekends.

Union Street Inn. 2229 Union St., San Francisco 94123, tel. 415/346–0424, fax 415/922–8046. 6 double rooms with baths. Phone, cable TV, and hair dryers in rooms, whirlpool bath in 3 rooms. Guest fax, limited off-street parking ($12). $135–$245; full breakfast. AE, MC, V. Smoking in garden only, 2-night minimum on weekends.

Washington Square Inn. 1660 Stockton St., San Francisco 94133, tel. 415/981–4220 or 800/388–0220, fax 415/397–7242. 15 double rooms with baths. Phone in rooms, TV on request. Laundry service, limited room service, valet parking ($20). $120–200; Continental breakfast. AE, D, DC, MC, V. No smoking.

RESERVATIONS AND REFERRAL SERVICES

Bed & Breakfast California (Box 282910, San Francisco 94128, tel. 650/696–1690 or 800/872–4500, fax 650/696–1699). **Bed & Breakfast San Francisco** (Box 420009, San Francisco 94142, tel. 415/479–1913, fax 415/921–2273).

Bay Area: Marin, East Bay, and the Peninsula

CAPTAIN WALSH HOUSE 🐚
235 E. L St., Benicia 94510, tel. 707/747–5653, fax 707/747–6265

Reed and Steve Robbins didn't intend to be innkeepers. But once Reed, an architectural designer, and Steve, a former IBM salesman, began remodeling the 1849 Captain Walsh House, they realized the historic home was too much for just the two of them. After two years of renovations—almost all by themselves—they opened their bed-and-breakfast in 1991; Reed and Steve now live in the carriage house behind it. The result is an inn where every square foot reflects the owners' personalities and creativity.

The house was built as a wedding gift for Epiphania, a daughter of Gen. Mariano G. Vallejo. It was later purchased by Capt. John Walsh, a retired sea captain, and his wife, Eleanor, whose spirit is rumored to visit on occasion.

Although no two rooms are alike, certain unusual themes and elements repeat: gargoyles, Gothic shapes, and quirky collections. Epiphania's Room, which has a view of the Carquinez Strait, is decorated in rich ivory fabrics that engulf the canopied four-poster bed set. To one side is a classic claw-foot tub—with 24-karat gold claws! The Harvest Room is dominated by a walnut Gothic armoire and matching bed and a fireplace made of white brick. Regency furniture adorns the Salon guest room, which has a marble fireplace offset by gilt-edge Gothic wall panels. The Library (another guest room) has vaulted ceilings, dark-green walls, shelves lined with books, and a private reading loft that resembles an elaborate crow's nest. A private deck overlooks the garden, and a secret passageway connects to the Captain's Den, which is furnished in English oak antiques and contains a striking model ship.

Breakfast is lavish in quantity and presentation and includes a fresh fruit platter and hot dishes such as apple pancakes or crab cake Benedict; orange juice is fresh-squeezed from the trees on the inn's property. △ *5 double rooms with baths. Air-conditioning and TV in rooms, phone in 2 rooms. Business services. $125–$150; full breakfast. AE, MC, V. No smoking.*

CASA DEL MAR ⚐
37 Belvedere Ave. (Box 238), Stinson Beach 94970, tel. 415/868–2124 or 800/552–2124, fax 415/868–2305

This three-story, pale stucco Mediterranean-style villa perches at the top of a landscaped knoll overlooking the Pacific Ocean in the village of Stinson Beach. It was purchased in 1987 by Rick Klein, a local lawyer and sometime builder. Klein soon found that making it an inn was the best way to support his passion for restoring the cascading gardens, a riot of flowering bulbs, citrus trees, and other Mediterranean-style vegetation that date from the 1930s. The gardens are an integral part of this inn; guests may follow winding paths through them, fresh flowers adorn each room, and herbs flavor breakfast dishes.

Inside, the decor is crisp and brightened by seascapes and other local artwork. The entry level has an open-space floor plan, with a breakfast room at one end flanked on two sides by large windows and warmed by sunlight or heat from a dark-blue tile wood-burning stove. Here guests are served the morning meal: typically yogurt, granola, fresh fruit salad with garden blossoms, fresh baked goods, and a main dish such as Granny's French toast (with poached pears and cream cheese) or the Mexican-accented Casserole del Mar (sourdough bread, sausage, mushrooms, and salsa). The Mexican paver floor extends to the parlor area, which has its own built-in fireplace and attractive rattan furniture. Evening hors d'oeuvres and homemade cookies are served here.

The rooms themselves are fairly small but made to seem larger by the use of pale painted walls, lots of windows, and simple furnishings. Several rooms derive their names from the motifs (shell, passionflower, etc.) painted on the tile work within each shower stall. All rooms have balconies or a patio. Two face the ocean; two, forested Mt. Tamalpais, which towers behind (hiking trails lead up the mountain from behind the inn. The best views—of both ocean and mountain—are from the penthouse suite, which has slanted ceilings, skylights, and a huge European soaking tub. The downstairs Garden Room, which has a private patio (guests may have breakfast here), is a good one for families. △ *5 double rooms with baths, 1 suite. $125–$225; full breakfast. AE, MC, V. No smoking, 2-night minimum on weekends, 3-night minimum on holiday weekends.*

CASA MADRONA HOTEL ✿

801 Bridgeway, Sausalito 94965, tel. 415/332–0502 or 800/567–9524, fax 415/332–2537

Occupying a hillside in the heart of Sausalito, Casa Madrona is several inns in one. There are 100-year-old rooms, cozy cottages, and contemporary accommodations—all at different levels above the main street, Bridgeway, which runs along Richardson Bay.

Though today it's a striking Sausalito landmark, Casa Madrona was a decaying 1885 Victorian mansion until owner John Mays renovated and reopened it as a hotel in the late 1970s. The New Casa, a multilevel addition, drops in steps down to the street below like an Italian hill town.

The New Casa's 17 guest rooms share a magnificent view of the marina, Belvedere and Angel islands, and the forested hills of Tiburon beyond. Many rooms have private balconies, and each room has a distinct personality. The Renoir Room, hung with prints of the artist's work, has a window seat, large deck, fireplace, and a claw-foot tub surrounded by an impressionistic mural of a flower garden. In the Artist's Loft, an easel and watercolor paints await your talents. Kathmandu has cushions for lounging and exotic alcoves. The 12 guest rooms in the original Victorian building are decorated in period style and have high ceilings and four-poster or brass beds. Rooms facing east or south have views. There are also five cottages. The management will recommend several rooms that are good for families.

The New Casa's outdoor deck and the Victorian's parlor and balcony are the only common areas. In the evening, wine and cheese are served in the parlor, and guests can relax in the antique settees or in the balcony's wicker chairs.

A buffet-style breakfast—such as fresh fruit and juice, scones, English muffins, scrambled eggs, and bacon—is served in the Mikayla Restaurant, attached to an upper level of the New Casa. The restaurant has a dining terrace with retractable roof and sliding glass walls. △ *26 double rooms with baths, 3 suites, 5 cottages. Phone, TV, and minibar in rooms, fireplace in 18 rooms. Room service during restaurant hours, laundry service, in-room massage, conference facilities, concierge, business and secretarial services, outdoor hot tub, valet parking ($7). $138–$260; full breakfast. AE, MC, V. No smoking, 2-night minimum on weekends.*

JENNER INN AND COTTAGES ✿

Hwy. 1 (Box 69), Jenner 95450, tel. 707/865–2377 or 800/732–2377, fax 707/865–0829

This bed-and-breakfast inn occupies an enviable spot—or spots—in the hamlet of Jenner, which is perched dramatically overlooking the mouth of the Russian River as it flows into the Pacific on the Sonoma County coast. With several different houses and cottages just off coastal Highway 1, Jenner Inn has locked up some of the prime views for its guests.

Owner Richard Murphy, a longtime local resident, keeps expanding by buying up new properties; there are now four large houses—divided into a combination of suites and standard rooms—and four smaller "hideaway" cottages. Some units are intimate and ideal for couples in search of romance. Others are well suited to families. Captain Will's Room, for instance, comes with a bedroom, a sitting room, a sleeping loft for the kids, a kitchen, vaulted ceiling, and wood-burning stove.

All the accommodations have private baths and entrances; most have private decks with water views. Several have fireplaces, kitchens, or whirlpool tubs. Decor is eclectic, ranging from antiques to wicker, and at times a bit eccentric, reflecting Richard's tastes. The Rosewater Cottage, which has knockout views of the estuary, a bird sanctuary, and Goat Rock Beach, combines Victorian and California beach-house styles. It has a full kitchen, a big stone fireplace with sitting area, a bedroom with beach view, and an outdoor hot tub that it shares with neighboring Rosebud Cottage.

Breakfast is laid out buffet-style in the lodge parlor, where the woodstove, antiques, vaulted ceiling, and windows looking out toward the sea seem particularly appealing on foggy days. Fare includes fresh fruit, juices, baked goods, and a hot dish such as quiche or frittata (although not made on the premises, they are made especially for the inn). In the afternoon, wine and tea are served here. The attached Jenner By the Sea Restaurant specializes in seafood lunches and dinners. ⚱ *9 double rooms with baths, 3 suites, 4 cottages. Fireplace in 7 rooms, whirlpool tub in 6 rooms, outdoor hot tub for 2 rooms, kitchen in 7 rooms. Conference room, restaurant, off-street parking. $75–$215; full breakfast. AE, MC, V. No smoking, 2-night minimum on weekends, 3-night minimum on holidays.*

THE MILL ROSE INN 🌾
615 Mill St., Half Moon Bay 94019, tel. 415/726–8750 or 800/900–7673, fax 415/726–3031

Set amid a lush flower garden, the Mill Rose Inn is one of the most indulgent, romantic hostelries in northern California. The word *pampered* takes on new meaning here—guests are provided virtually everything they need for a carefree stay. Innkeepers Eve and Terry Baldwin, who purchased the home in 1978 and have run it as an inn since 1981, pay attention to every detail.

The inn is 30 mi south of San Francisco, in the historic district of the oceanside hamlet of Half Moon Bay, and a short drive from Pacific Coast beaches. Eve and Terry both hold degrees in horticulture and take full advantage of the gentle climate. The front garden is an explosion of color, with more than 200 varieties of roses, lilies, irises, daisies, and other flowers, all framed by the inn's crisp white exterior.

Virtually no corner of the guest rooms has gone undecorated. Each is done in rich, deep tones with floral-patterned wall coverings, burgundy carpeting, custom-made brass chandeliers and wall sconces, and watercolor paintings. All have private entrances opening to a balcony that faces the back courtyard, with its hanging potted flowers, brick patio, and whirlpool hot tub secluded in an old-fashioned gazebo (guests can reserve times for private use).

Most rooms have Eastlake and other antique furnishings, brass feather beds, down comforters, billowing draperies, and fireplaces framed with hand-painted tiles. Some have claw-foot tubs or whirlpool baths. All come equipped with a refrigerator stocked with beverages, fruit and nut basket, candies, coffeemaker and sherry and brandy.

Sinfully rich desserts are always available in the parlor, and you'll wake to a sumptuous champagne breakfast, which most guests have in their rooms. Courses might include orange-banana frappé, fresh fruit, raspberry crème fraîche soufflé, crisp bacon, enormous croissants, local champagne, and Mexican hot chocolate. If you eat at the breakfast table, bouquets on each table and a fire in the hearth set the stage. ⚱ *4 double rooms with baths, 2 suites. Phone, cable TV/VCR, refrigerator, and hair dryer in rooms, fireplace in 5 rooms. Conference facility. $165–$285; full breakfast. AE, D, MC, V. No smoking, 2-night minimum on weekends.*

THE PELICAN INN 🦤
Star Rte. (Hwy. 1), Muir Beach 94965, tel. 415/383–6000, fax 415/383–3424

Upon first seeing the Pelican Inn, you may think you've taken a wrong turn and somehow stumbled into the English countryside. Just off Highway 1 in Marin County, the inn is fronted by a formal English garden and set in an expanse of lush lawn. This whitewashed Tudor with black timbers is a replica of a 16th-century British inn, built by transplanted Englishman Charles Felix in 1977.

Now run by owner Katrinka McKay, the hostelry is a favorite stopping place for visitors to nearby Muir Woods or Muir Beach. Guests are often drawn to the Pelican's pub. Amiable bartenders, a dart board, and an assortment of beers, ales, and wines create a convivial setting. The aptly named Snug is a parlor set aside for registered guests only. English-country antiques, old books, prints, and curiosities, as well as a comfortable sitting area by the wood-burning fireplace make this an ideal sanctuary.

The inn's restaurant is right out of Merry Olde England, with heavy wooden tables and a dark, time-worn atmosphere, enhanced by foxhunt prints and an immense walk-in hearth with cast-iron fittings. During breakfast and dinner, the room is lit only by the fireplace, the tall red tapers on each table, and cut-tin lanterns on the walls. Lunch and dinner items include bangers and mash, shepherd's pie, and fish-and-chips. A hearty English breakfast, served here or in your room, includes eggs cooked to order, breakfast meats, and toasted breads. In the backyard beer garden, sunlight filters through a greenery-entwined trellis, and a brick fireplace keeps things cozy.

Planked doors with latches open to the guest rooms, some of which are decorated with antiques from different periods. Each room has leaded, multipane windows, Oriental scatter rugs, English prints, heavy velvet draperies, hanging tapestries, and half-tester beds. Don't expect light and airy; most rooms can get dark indeed. (Room 1 may be the lightest and includes views of stables and rolling hills.) The bathrooms are equipped with Victorian-style hardware and hand-painted tiles in the shower. ⚓ *6 double rooms with baths, 1 suite. Restaurant, off-street parking. $174–$198; full breakfast. MC, V. Closed Dec. 24–25.*

THE ROSE GARDEN INN 🦤
2740 Telegraph Ave., Berkeley 94705, tel. 510/549–2145, fax 510/549–1085

A 10-minute walk from the University of California Berkeley campus, the Rose Garden Inn (formerly Gramma's) combines two turn-of-the-century mansions and three newer, smaller buildings behind them. The two mansions are the 1903 shingle Fay House and the Main House, an 1899 half-timber; both were built by the Marshall brothers, who made a fortune paving Berkeley sidewalks. The inn takes its name from the gardens showcasing hundreds of roses, along with foxgloves, geraniums, and daisies.

Inside, the inn is a blend of well-worn comfort and more upscale luxury. The common rooms, in the Main House, have a lived-in feel. The parlor's rose-colored wing chairs and floral-print overstuffed sofas face the fireplace. The sunny, skylight-topped breakfast room, called the Greenhouse, opens to the patio and the garden beyond, which are dotted by fountains and umbrella tables. An expanded Continental breakfast of fresh fruit, hot and cold cereals, English muffins, bagels, and quiche is served here, as are afternoon tea, coffee, and cookies.

All the public rooms and guest rooms were recently refurbished. The newer buildings are somewhat quieter than the older ones, which sit on a corner of busy Telegraph Avenue. Rooms in the Garden House are sunlit, with modern bleached-wood furnishings, tile fireplaces, brass beds, and private entrances. The Carriage House rooms all have fireplaces but lack the character of the older buildings. The Cottage House offers larger rooms, all with fireplaces, desks, and sitting areas. Many rooms throughout have balconies overlooking the gardens, Berkeley, or San Francisco Bay. ⚓ *40 double rooms with baths. Phone with dataport and cable TV in rooms, fireplace in 20 rooms. Off-street parking. $99–$225; Continental-plus breakfast. AE, D, DC, MC, V. No smoking.*

OTHER CHOICES

Blackthorne Inn. 266 Vallejo Ave. (Box 712), Inverness Park 94937, tel. 415/663–8621, fax 415/663–8635. 3 double rooms with baths, 2 doubles share 1 bath. Guest refrigerator, outdoor hot tub, off-street parking. $175–$250; full breakfast. MC, V. No smoking, 2-night minimum on weekends.

Cypress Inn. 407 Mirada Rd., Half Moon Bay 94019, tel. 415/726–6075 or 800/832–3224, fax 415/458–2490. 12 double rooms with baths. Phone and fireplace in rooms, TV/VCR, stereo, and whirlpool bath in 4 rooms. In-room massage, off-street parking. $170–$275; full breakfast. AE, MC, V. No smoking.

East Brother Light Station. 117 Park Pl., Point Richmond 94801, tel. 510/233–2385, fax 510/232–5325. 2 double rooms with baths, 2 doubles share a bath. Fireplace in 1 room. $235–$325; full breakfast, dinner. AE, MC, V. No smoking. Closed Mon.–Wed.

Gerstle Park Inn. 34 Grove St., San Rafael 94901, tel. 415/721–7611 or 800/726–7611, fax 415/721–7600. 8 suites, 2 apartments, 2 cottages. Dual-line phone with voice mail and dataport, cable TV/VCR, and hair dryer in rooms, whirlpool or steam bath in 5 rooms. Conference room. $139–$199; full breakfast. AE, MC, V. No smoking, 2-night minimum on weekends, 3-night minimum on holidays.

The Inn Above Tide. 30 El Portal, Sausalito 94965, tel. 415/332–9535 or 800/893–8433, fax 415/332–6714. 28 double rooms with baths, 2 suites. Phone and TV in rooms, fireplace in 22 rooms. Room service, in-room massage, concierge service, valet parking ($8). $195–$445; Continental breakfast. AE, DC, MC, V. No smoking, 2-night minimum on weekends and holidays.

Pillar Point Inn. 380 Capistrano Rd. (Box 388), Princeton-by-the-Sea 94018, tel. 650/728–7377 or 800/400–8281, fax 650/728–8345. 11 double rooms with baths. Phone, TV/ VCR, radio, mini-refrigerator, and fireplace in rooms. Conference room, off-street parking. $140–$185; full breakfast. AE, MC, V. No smoking.

RESERVATIONS AND REFERRAL SERVICES

Bed & Breakfast California (Box 282910, San Francisco 94128, tel. 650/696–1690 or 800/872–4500, fax 650/696–1699). **Bed & Breakfast San Francisco** (Box 420009, San Francisco 94142, tel. 415/479–1913 or 800/452–8249, fax 415/921–2273). **Coastal Lodging of West Marin** (Box 1162, Point Reyes Station 94956, tel. 415/663–1351). **Inns of Marin** (Box 547, Point Reyes Station 94956, tel. 415/663–2000). **Inns of Point Reyes** (Box 145, Inverness 94937, tel. 415/663–1420). **Point Reyes Lodging** (Box 878, Point Reyes Station 94956, tel. 415/663–1872).

Wine Country, Including Napa, Sonoma, Southern Mendocino Counties

APPLEWOOD INN ☜

13555 Hwy. 116, Guerneville 95446, tel. 707/869–9093, fax 707/869–9170

Nestled amid the redwoods in Pocket Canyon just south of the Russian River resort town of Guerneville, Applewood is surrounded by 6 acres of land, including apple and pear orchards and flower and herb gardens. The inn combines two salmon-colored Mission Revival–style villas, both with stucco walls and red-tile roofs. Owners Jim Caron and Darryl Notter, who bought the property in 1985, view the inn as a romantic retreat and, from breakfast to evening turn-down service, do their best to make it just that.

Belden House, the original villa built in 1922, has nine double rooms; Piccola Casa, added in 1996, has seven suites. Furnishings are French country (some antique, some reproductions), with queen-size beds topped by down comforters and pillows and Egyptian linens. Rooms are individually decorated in deep greens and other rich earth tones. Several open onto covered verandas, courtyards, or private terraces. The newer accommodations are generally larger and more elaborate—all have fireplaces and either couple's showers or two-person whirlpool baths. Particularly noteworthy are the Honeymoon Penthouse, which has a rooftop deck and cathedral ceiling, and the Slavianka Suite, with whirlpool tub and private terrace with terra-cotta fountain.

Guests receive a full cooked-to-order breakfast, served at small tables in a sunny dining room overlooking the redwoods; it includes fresh fruit and juices as well as hot dishes such as eggs Florentine, pancakes, or French toast. Wine is served in late afternoons. The inn also has a fine restaurant, which serves dinner five nights a week (Tuesdays through Saturdays); chef David Frakes specializes in "Wine Country Rustic"—a combination of Mediterranean, French country, and California cuisines. **&** *9 double rooms with bath, 7 suites. TV and phone in rooms. Pool, outdoor hot tub, restaurant, off-street parking. $125–$250; full breakfast. AE, D, MC, V. No smoking.*

FOOTHILL HOUSE ☜

3037 Foothill Blvd., Calistoga 94515, tel. 707/942–6933 or 800/942–6933, fax 707/942–5692

This small, family-run bed-and-breakfast is surprisingly quiet, considering its location just off Highway 128 on the western edges of Calistoga. Beautifully landscaped—with an herb garden, rose garden, little waterfalls, and gazebo with views of Mt. St. Helena—the property comprises three rooms in the main house, all on one level, and a separate cottage up the hillside behind the inn. All have private entrances.

Owners Doris and Gus Becker, who bought Foothill House in 1991 (the inn was originally opened in 1982), take immense pride in getting the details right. All rooms are done in Laura Ashley signature style and have fireplaces or wood-burning stoves, oak and pine country antiques, small refrigerators, irons and ironing boards, and decks or patios; a laundry room is available. The most private—and regularly booked up—accommodation is the spacious cottage, known as the Quail's

Roost. High ceilings and skylights make the 1,000-square-ft hideaway feel even larger than it is. (Many San Francisco apartments are less well equipped: the Quail's Roost has a full kitchen, wet bar, fireplace, and a washer and dryer.) A glass-enclosed two-person whirlpool tub and adjacent shower give the illusion of bathing outdoors—they look out onto a mini-waterfall on the hillside. In the main house, the Evergreen Suite has a four-poster bed, a small whirlpool tub, and a private deck with view of Mt. St. Helena.

With a chef trained at the San Francisco Culinary Academy, Foothill House serves up innovative breakfast fare such as fruit soup (made with seasonal berries), French toast soufflé, or eggs mornay with chicken-artichoke sausage. Guests may eat either in the main-house common room, in their rooms, or on their decks. Afternoon appetizers may include provolone torta or smoked salmon with little bagels. The Beckers are glad to suggest local restaurants and sightseeing activities. ♨ *3 double rooms with baths, 1 suite. Fireplace or woodstove in rooms, whirlpool bath and TV/VCR in 3 rooms. $150–$300; full breakfast. AE, D, MC, V. No smoking.*

HONOR MANSION ☙
14891 Grove St., Healdsburg 95448, tel. 707/433–4277 or 800/554–4667, fax 707/431–7173

From its white-picket fence and immaculate grounds shaded by century-old magnolias and oaks to its impeccably furnished bedrooms and formally set dining table, the Honor Mansion is a study in how to pamper guests. Owner Cathi Fowler, who bought the historic but neglected 1883 Victorian in 1994 and transformed it into an elegant inn, knows how to attend to details.

Most of the inn's furnishings are genuine antiques, and the beds are a focal point of each room. All are raised feather beds with down comforters, sit-up pillows, double sheeting, and luxurious linens. The main house has five rooms, each named for a tree or flowering bush found just outside. Of these rooms, the Rose Room has the most amenities: a fireplace, TV, spacious bathroom, and a private deck with wicker chairs. The Magnolia Room, whose centerpiece is a carved four-poster bed, has a shower in a transformed closet complete with hand-painted grapevine tiles. Several rooms have trompe-l'oeil murals commissioned from a local artist. Those seeking more privacy can opt for the Squires Cottage, a short walk from the main house past a little waterfall and a koi pond—many guests like to feed the "kissing" koi. Besides its four-poster bed, the cottage has a gas fireplace with sofa, TV with VCR and tapes, a stereo, a claw-foot tub with separate shower, vaulted ceiling, and private deck.

For breakfast, which is served on china, silver, and crystal at a large dining table downstairs (or by the koi pond in warm weather), expect high quality rather than huge portions: a baked pear, perhaps, followed by eggs Benedict or broccoli frittata and accompanied by fresh-squeezed orange juice and strong coffee. Fresh-baked cookies are always waiting; there's a 24-hour cappuccino machine, and sherry in the rooms. ♨ *5 double rooms with bath, 1 cottage. TV in 2 rooms (with VCR in 1). Pool. $130–$250; full breakfast. D, MC, V. No smoking, 2-night minimum on weekends, 3-night minimum some holiday weekends.*

KENWOOD INN ☙
10400 Sonoma Hwy., Kenwood 95452, tel. 707/833–1293 or 800/353–6966, fax 707/833–1247

Terry and Roseann Grimm deserve an award for transforming a ramshackle antiques shop into a romantic Italian-style retreat facing the vineyards that lie on the hillsides across Highway 12, ½ mi south of Kenwood. Although the highway is well traveled, a stone wall and parking area separate the inn from the road, and there's little traffic noise after dark anyway. If there's one drawback, it's for traveling families: although this may be a place for making babies, the innkeepers frown on bringing them.

The extensive grounds are landscaped with dozens of rose bushes, as well as persimmon, fig, apple, and olive trees. A swimming pool and a large stone deck shaded by trellises and grapevines are flanked by several Tuscan-style villas. A full-service spa is also on the premises; guests can book an outdoor massage overlooking the pool.

Rooms are adorned with rich fabrics in colors such as ocher and gold, and all contain genuine antiques, not reproductions. Though each is decorated differently, they all contain one queen-size feather bed and a fireplace. The Tuscany Suite, upstairs over the dining room, claims the most privacy and the best vineyard view.

The owners have paid lavish attention to detail, from the down comforters covered with Egyptian cotton sheets to the aromatic sprigs of fresh-from-the-garden herbs used to garnish the inventive breakfast dishes. The latter might include home fries with golden beets, salmon, olive tapenade, and poached egg; or an oatmeal soufflé, accompanied by fresh-baked scones or muffins and fresh fruit. Complimentary wine waits in every room upon check-in. The chef will also prepare private dinners for guests with advance notice. ⌂ *11 double rooms with baths, 1 suite. Fireplace in rooms. Pool, sauna, steam bath, off-street parking, conference room. $255–$395; full breakfast. AE, MC, V. No smoking, 2-night minimum on weekends.*

MADRONA MANOR 🐚
1001 Westside Rd., Healdsburg 95448, tel. 707/433–4231 or 800/258–4003, fax 707/433–0703

Entering the grounds to Madrona Manor is like stepping into a genteel Merchant-Ivory film set. A fraction of its original size, this European-style estate dates from 1881, when San Franciscan John Paxton commissioned a mansion to be built on 240 acres in the Dry Creek Valley on the outskirts of Healdsburg. To the Eastlake-style architecture he added gingerbread flourishes, steeply pitched dormers, gables, a mansard roof, and a wraparound porch. He filled it with massive furniture; many pieces, including a rosewood square grand piano, are still in use.

Today the estate comprises an 8-acre wooded knoll. In 1981 it was bought by Carol and John Muir, who remain the innkeepers. After redecorating the Carpenter Gothic carriage house, they added four third-floor guest rooms in the main house for a total of nine. The five rooms on the first two floors contain original antiques and double beds, and the four on the third floor have antique reproductions and queen beds. All have fireplaces and plenty of space.

The accommodations in the outbuildings lack the elegance of the original rooms; in some cases, you may even feel you've entered the servants' quarters. The Meadow Wood complex, with its very private bedroom and deck, is deemed suitable for travelers with children and pets. The Garden Suite, set in a secluded spot beyond the garden, is decorated with rattan furniture, a marble fireplace, and sunken tub. The Carriage House, with its massive Nepalese hand-carved rosewood door, houses eight rooms, mostly with contemporary furnishings and queen- or king-size beds.

Herbs and some vegetables from the inn's extensive gardens find their way to the dinner menu at Madrona Manor, where the Muirs' son Todd is executive chef. Local fish, poultry, and game are often smoked on the premises. Typical breakfasts are substantial: seasonal fruits, fresh juice, granola, sliced meats and cheeses, soft-boiled eggs, fresh-baked breads with homemade jams, and perhaps a vegetable frittata with fresh salsa. △ *18 double rooms with baths, 3 suites. Phone and air-conditioning in rooms, fireplace in 18 rooms. Restaurant, pool. $155–$255; full breakfast. AE, D, MC, V. No smoking.*

WINE COUNTRY INN 🖙

1152 Lodi La., St. Helena 94574, tel. 707/963–7077, fax 707/963–9018

The Wine Country Inn enjoys one of the select spots along or near the Napa Valley's busy Highway 29 corridor—it's off the highway a bit, down a quiet lane north of St. Helena and perched on a hill overlooking mountains and vineyards. The inn blends in well with its surroundings—with an exterior of stone and wood and distinctive mansard roof, it could be a winery itself.

From the beginning, the inn has been a three-generation Smith family project. Current innkeeper Jim Smith and siblings helped their parents build the original three-story house in 1975; Jim was the stonemason, his brother was the contractor, his mother and sister the decorators, his grandmother the stitcher and quilter, his late father the fund-raiser. Additional buildings were added in 1979. Although every room is decorated differently, they're all spacious and done in country casual style, with iron beds, homemade quilts, walls of muted natural colors, and a mix of antiques (some reproductions) and more contemporary furnishings.

Fifteen rooms have fireplaces, and 19 have balconies or patios. Three rooms have exterior hot tubs and one, No. 24, has an interior whirlpool bath. A year-round outdoor heated pool and hot tub lie just down the slope from the main house.

A buffet-style breakfast is served in the fireplace-warmed Common Room and the adjoining breakfast room, which has both small and large tables; guests can also eat out on the deck. A typical breakfast includes fresh fruit and juices, fresh-baked muffins and pecan rolls, and a frittata or other hot egg-based dish, often a family recipe. (Don't count on low-cal: one is called "Death by Cheese.") An afternoon wine tasting includes vintages from a different local winery each day, accompanied by freshly made appetizers. The Wine Country Inn is a romantic hideaway—there are no TVs, for instance—and doesn't encourage small children. △ *24 double rooms with baths. Fireplace in 15 rooms, hot tubs in 4 rooms. Pool, outside hot tub. $140–$258; full breakfast. MC, V. No smoking.*

OTHER CHOICES

The Boonville Hotel. Hwy. 128 and Lambert La. (Box 326), Boonville 95415, tel. and fax 707/895–2210. 6 double rooms with baths, 4 suites. Restaurant, off-street parking. $75–$200; Continental-plus breakfast. MC, V. No smoking.
Gaige House Inn. 13540 Arnold Dr., Glen Ellen 95442, tel. 707/935–0237 or 800/935–0237, fax 707/935–6411. 13 double rooms with baths. Phone in rooms, fireplace in 3 rooms. Pool, off-street parking. $155–$275; full breakfast. AE, D, MC, V. No smoking, 2-night minimum on weekends and holidays.
Maison Fleurie. 6529 Yount St. (Drawer M), Yountville 94599, tel. 707/944–2056, fax 707/944–9342. 13 double rooms with baths. Air-conditioning, fireplace in 6 rooms. Wine cellar, pool, hot tub, bicycles. $110–$230; full breakfast. AE, MC, V. No smoking.

RESERVATIONS AND REFERRAL SERVICE

Wine Country Inns of Sonoma County (tel. 707/433–4667 or 800/946—3268).

North Coast and Redwood Country, Including Mendocino and Eureka

ABIGAIL'S ELEGANT VICTORIAN MANSION 🐚
1406 C St., Eureka 95501, tel. 707/444–3144, fax 707/442–5594

This 1888 Stick-style Eastlake mansion stands on a quiet street several blocks from downtown Eureka. Its Victorian exterior only begins to hint at the labor of love that has transformed the interior into one of the great reconstructed turn-of-the-century houses in America.

Hosts Doug and Lily Vieyra are likely to welcome their guests wearing turn-of-the-century costumes. Doug may invite you for a spin in one of his antique Fords or start a croquet match on a lawn surrounded by flowers popular in Victorian-era gardens. He will certainly indulge his passion for living history and explain to you where the decor comes from, what styles the fantastic wallpapering is in, why the lights are dim (the original lamps only held 15-watt bulbs), and who the jazz singer is whose voice is coming off the antique phonograph.

The four rooms upstairs are comfortably furnished with antiques; the Senator, for example, contains a bedroom set that Lily used as a child in her native Belgium. Many also have original artwork, by, among others, Salvador Dali. Common areas include an enormous double parlor furnished with family heirlooms, a games room–library, and a family room with TV, VCR, and stereo, with the floors carpeted with William Morris designs specially re-created in England for the inn. The house also boasts a glorious collection of silent movies and golden-age jazz classics.

Lily, whose cooking has gained an excellent reputation locally, serves a breakfast that features French specialties in the formal dining room. This is one of the most quixotic, and unexpected, pleasures on the North Coast. **�†** *3 double rooms share 3 baths, 1 suite. Swedish massage, Finnish sauna, laundry service, bicycles. $85–$185; full breakfast. MC, V. No smoking.*

ELK COVE INN 🐚
6300 S. Hwy. 1 (Box 367), Elk 95432, tel. 707/877–3321 or 800/275–2967, fax 707/877–1808

A night spent in one of the cottages on the bluff at Elk Cove is the closest thing around to sleeping right on the beach. No matter where you stay at this inn, which boasts an oceanfront location in a hidden cul-de-sac off the Coast Highway, you can drift off to sleep to the sounds of the surf and awaken to birdsong. Some visitors insist on staying in the main house (an 1883 Victorian)—usually, says the innkeeper, East Coast guests nervous about earthquakes—while others demand one of the cottage rooms time and time again, lulled by the siren song of the sea and the beauty of the rocky cove outside the window.

The inn is run by affable Alabama-born Elaine Bryant. Guest rooms on the second floor of the main house share a parlor, with French doors leading to a roof deck overlooking the ocean. There are long window seats for reading, gazing at the sunset, and admiring the raised beds where Elaine grows herbs and flowers. Two sitting rooms are on the second floor; one inside, the other on a protected deck. The decor throughout is simple: old-fashioned floral wallpaper, Victorian-style light fixtures, antique furnishings, and plenty of bare wood.

The four cheek-by-jowl cabins offer more privacy; two have high-beam ceilings, woodstoves, and white-paneled walls. Five new cottages, designed in the Arts and Crafts style, come equipped with microwaves, stereos, whirlpool baths, and wet bars. Outside, benches and a Victorian-style gazebo are perched on the edge of the bluff. The beach is accessible by a steep wooden staircase.

Elaine prides herself on her ability to serve guests a different breakfast for as long as two weeks, with always at least one southern-type dish such as a creamy corn pudding or peach-pineapple bread pudding with a rum-ginger sauce. Dinner is available midweek. △ *10 double rooms with baths, 5 cottages. $108–$218; full breakfast. AE, MC, V. No smoking, 2-night minimum on weekends, 3-night minimum on holiday weekends.*

GINGERBREAD MANSION ❧

400 Berding St. (Box 40), Ferndale 95536, tel. 707/786–4000 or 800/952–4136, fax 707/786–4381

The Gingerbread Mansion has long been a tourist attraction in and of itself; visitors are constantly making the detour from U.S. 101 to the Victorian village of Ferndale so they can take a picture of its bright-orange-and-yellow exterior and its flower-filled English gardens. The 1899 Gingerbread, with its spindle roof ridges and icicle eaves, its bay windows and shingled turret, must be one of the most-photographed buildings in California. Pity those who never get inside to enjoy the whimsical fantasy rooms and the warm hospitality of innkeeper Ken Torbert and his staff.

The inn is full of surprises—pleasant ones, such as rooms with mirrors for people of all heights, and a pair of claw-foot tubs set toe to toe on a white-fenced platform. In 1995, Torbert transformed the top floor into a Roman fantasy full of fine marble, gleaming brass fixtures, a mammoth glassed-in shower, several seating areas and an antique claw-foot tub.

The bathrooms are a special delight. The Fountain Suite bath has side-by-side claw-foot tubs facing a mirrored wall in which the flames in the newly added tiled fireplaces can be seen flickering. The claw-foot tub on a platform in the Rose Suite bathroom is surrounded by floral wallpaper under a mirrored ceiling; bathing there gives one the feeling of being in a garden.

Rooms are straightened, and the lamps and shades are adjusted at turndown each evening. Umbrellas are propped for protection when it rains. Morning coffee is prepared to order for each guest before breakfast, which is served at two large tables in the dining room. This is the time for conversation over a variety of home-baked breads, a selection of unusual local cheeses, and fruit. △ *9 double rooms with baths, 2 suites. Fireplace in 4 rooms. Guest refrigerator, bicycles. $140–$350; full breakfast. AE, MC, V. No smoking, 2-night minimum on weekends and holidays.*

JOSHUA GRINDLE INN ❧

44800 Little Lake Rd. (Box 647), Mendocino 95460, tel. 707/937–4143 or 800/474–6353

Like many other buildings in Mendocino, the Joshua Grindle Inn looks as if it were imported directly from New England and plunked down on the California coast. And in a way it was. Joshua Grindle, like many of the area's other settlers, hailed from Maine. A raftsman for the Mendocino Lumber Company, he built the two-story redwood farmhouse for his bride in 1879; it stayed in the family until 1967.

The inn displays many of Mendocino's best qualities: functional New England architecture, a respect for the land, and a casual, relaxing ambience. The original farmhouse has five guest rooms, a parlor, and a dining room. Three bedrooms upstairs are bright and airy, with either ocean or treetop views. The small, cozy Library guest room has its own seating area, a four-poster queen-size bed, and floor-to-ceiling bookcases flanking a fireplace decorated with hand-painted tiles depicting Aesop's fables. In the late afternoon guests converge in the farmhouse parlor, reading or playing backgammon, sipping sherry, or fingering the antique pump organ.

There are several outbuildings for guests. The weathered redwood Watertower has three rooms, including one on the second level with windows on four sides and, naturally, a splendid view of the ocean and town as well as the mountains to the east. The Cottage, which has two rooms, is shaded by cypress trees that Joshua Grindle planted 100 years ago. Furnishings throughout the inn are simple but comfortable American antiques: Salem rockers, wing chairs, steamer-trunk tables, painted pine beds. There is also a newly built guest house, down the road at the Russian Gulch, a creek flowing down from the hills. Intended for longer-staying guests, this modern house, with a simple wooden interior, complete with a sunken living room and a large fireplace, is self-sufficient, with a state-of-the-art kitchen.

At breakfast, which may include quiche, frittata, and a warm fruit compote, guests gather around a long, 1830 pine harvest table. They then frequently take the short walk into town to shop for antiques or explore the art galleries. ♙ *10 double rooms with baths. Fireplace in 6 rooms. Guest refrigerator. $100–$195; full breakfast. MC, V. No smoking, 2-night minimum on weekends, 3-night minimum on holidays.*

LIGHTHOUSE COVE BED AND BREAKFAST 🐾
215 S. A St., Crescent City 95531, tel. 707/465–6565

Perched on the edge of a shallow cliff, overlooking a wild rocky inlet, this tiny cedarwood inn, with just one guest room, offers one of the best views along the coast. At low tide, guests can clamber out to the Crescent City Lighthouse, atop one of the larger rocks. Strong winds blow off the ocean here, just 15 mi south of the Oregon border, and standing on the deck outside the inn, guests could be forgiven for thinking they were on the rugged Cornish coast in southern England.

The innkeepers are Barbara and Clarence Bowman, a couple from Cambria who migrated northward in search of the perfect view. They opened the inn in 1996 and often rent their room out to long-staying guests, who want to explore the region from one base over the course of a few weeks.

The guest room itself is spacious, though fairly simple. "No antiques!" Barbara explains. "Ocean view is what we sell." The living room for this suite, with a large glass wall, is perched on the Pacific's edge.

Breakfasts may include Barbara's homemade waffles and orange liqueur–flavored French toast and are served either in the common room or in the bedroom. ♙ *1 double room with bath. TV/VCR and phone in room. $100; full breakfast. AE, MC, V. No smoking. Closed Dec.–May.*

MENDOCINO FARMHOUSE 🐾
Box 247, Mendocino 95460, tel. 707/937–0241 or 800/475–1536

Hidden in the redwood forests a few miles inland from Mendocino, this is one of the region's more inspiring surprises. The wooden houses, a main building and a tree-surrounded cedar cabin, are set amidst a verdant English country garden, in which wild chickens strut and ducks swim on the pond. Unlike on the coast, the fog rarely reaches this spot, and when it feels like fall on the coast, it's still summertime in the hills. And after a few days of hugging the coast, it's somewhat liberating to head inland to spend a night in this farmhouse.

The rustic-style rooms are fairly small, but the space is used wisely. Thick wooden floors, large fireplaces, and somewhat low ceilings generate an authentic old-time ambience. The sloped-ceiling rooms in the main building are named after the owners Margie and Bud Camb's now-grown children. All the windows look onto the forests, providing a rather humbling view when one wakes up in the morning.

Although near the main house, the cabin is surrounded by tall evergreen trees and feels exceptionally private. For those who appreciate the earthy smell of the redwoods, this inn makes a good romantic hideaway.

Eggs with pesto, baked pancakes, and other specialties are served in a parlor, next to a lovely old piano. △ *5 double rooms with baths. Fireplace in 4 rooms. $85–$130; full breakfast. MC, V.*

MYERS COUNTRY INN ❦
Box 173, Myers Flat 95554, tel. 707/943–3259

A modest, dark wooden English cottage, this inn is of interest for its location rather than for its amenities. Located along the stunning 33-mi Avenue of the Giants, in the town of Myers Flat, the inn is minutes away from the finest redwood groves in the world and is also close to the pristine aquamarine South Eel River. The inn is also worthy from a historic standpoint: Ulysses S. Grant stayed here back in the days when it was a stagecoach resting point.

The inn is owned by Rod Moschetti, whose family roots in this part of the country go back nearly a century. The inn's 10 rooms, recently refurbished and freshly painted, are cluttered with family antiques. Rod plans to upgrade one as Grant's presidential suite.

Hearty lumberjack breakfasts, served in the lobby, prepare visitors for a day of walking among the great trees. Rod also takes guests on guided powerboat tours of the South Eel River.

With the scarcity of upscale Redwood Country accommodations, an intrepid traveler might well be willing to sacrifice a bit of luxury for a night here among the giants. △ *10 double rooms with baths. $80–$100; full breakfast. AE, MC, V.*

OLD MILANO HOTEL ❦
38300 Hwy. 1, Gualala 95445, tel. 707/884–3256, fax 707/884–4249

Just north of Gualala, this historic 1905 building, furbished in frilly Victorian elegance, offers up some of the best ocean views around. Located directly above a rocky cove, this deceptively modest set of cottages, centered on a main building on 3 acres of lawn, is a rewarding, though pricey, place to stay. In front of the main lawn a two-pronged rock soars out of the ocean toward the sky, and guests can sit in deck chairs watching the surf.

The inn is owned by Leslie Lenscheid, an ex-CEO at Macy's, who has run the inn since 1983. The six cottages provide seclusion and space amid verdant gardens. The Vine Cottage includes a reading loft and a large woodstove. The rooms in the main building, though charming, are somewhat on the small side, with functional, but not fancy, bathrooms. Antique roll-top desks add a touch of class to some of these rooms, as do the antique telephones atop the desks. The best option here is the suite, with a separate living room, antique rocking chairs, and a glass wall overlooking the ocean.

A full country breakfast, with an emphasis on bacon and eggs, is served in a large dining room, with a fireplace to keep the guests warm. The Old Milano restaurant is also known for its fine fresh fish at dinner. ♠ *4 double rooms with baths, 1 suite, 6 cottages. Phone in rooms. Restaurant. $115–$210; full breakfast. MC, V.*

WAGON CREEK INN ☞
1239 Woodland Park Dr., Mount Shasta 96067, tel. 530/926–0838

Just outside the town of Mount Shasta, this is probably the most atmospheric place to stay in the immediate Mount Shasta vicinity. A faux-old log cabin, built in 1984 and converted into a B&B in 1997, it is run by a bohemian young woman named Kim Smith, who wanted a change from the big city and convinced a friend to sell her the cabin. In winter, this is a good base for a skiing holiday; other times of the year, the region provides rich hiking, fishing, and rafting opportunities.

The inside walls are hung with Latin American rugs, masks, and art work. Kim boasts a huge collection of classic film videos and a fairly decent collection of 1960s psychedelic Grateful Dead posters. This is definitely one of the more eclectic places in the region.

The three rooms are lit up by large, sloped skylights, and elegant lounge chairs complement the spacious beds. All three have their own refrigerator; request the skylighted room, from which you can see the great redwoods heading straight up into the sky. This room also has a deck looking into the woods.

Kim serves up big buffet breakfasts of eggs, cereals, and fruits designed to give vacationers energy to hike, fish, and study nature in this near-pristine wilderness. The inexpensive rates here make this one of the best deals in northern California. ♠ *1 double room with bath, 2 doubles share 1 bath. Volleyball, croquet, hammocks, bicycles. $65–$85; full breakfast. AE, D, DC, MC, V.*

OTHER CHOICES

Shaw House. 703 Main St., Ferndale 95536, tel. and fax 707/786–9958 or 800/557–7429. 7 double rooms with baths. Horseshoes, hammocks. $75–$145; full breakfast. MC, V.

The Stanford Inn by the Sea. Coast Hwy. and Comptche-Ukiah Rd. (Box 487), Mendocino 95460, tel. 707/937–5615 or 800/331–8884, fax 707/937–0305. 23 double rooms with baths, 10 suites. Fireplace, refrigerator, phone, TV/VCR, and CD player in rooms. Indoor pool, exercise room, canoes and bicycles available. $215–$700; full breakfast. AE, D, DC, MC, V. No smoking, 2-night minimum on weekends, 3-night minimum on holidays.

The Whale Watch Inn by the Sea. 35100 Hwy. 1, Gualala 95445, tel. 707/884–3667 or 800/942–5342, fax 707/884–4815. 11 double rooms with baths, 7 suites. Fireplace in rooms, whirlpool bath in 12 rooms, kitchen in 5 rooms. Private beach access. $170–$270; full breakfast. AE, MC, V. No smoking, 2-night minimum on weekends, 3-night minimum on holiday weekends.

RESERVATIONS AND REFERRAL SERVICES

Bed and Breakfast International (Box 282910, San Francisco 94128, tel. 800/872–4500, 415/696–1690 outside the U.S.). **Mendocino Coast Accommodations** (tel. 707/937–1913). **Mendocino Coast Innkeepers Association** (Box 1141, Mendocino 95460, tel. 707/964–0640 or 800/382–7244). For information about the various inns along the Avenue of the Giants, in the heart of Redwood Country, phone **Humboldt Redwoods Visitors Center** (tel. 707/946–2263).

Sacramento and the Central Valley, Including the Sierra Foothills

ABIGAIL'S 🐚

2120 G St., Sacramento 95816, tel. 916/441–5007 or 800/858–1568, fax 916/441–0621

There may be no Abigail, but Susanne Ventura, who owns this light-filled 1912 Colonial Revival house with her husband, Ken, is as warm and welcoming as a favorite aunt. She leaves her guests homemade cookies on a carved wooden sideboard at night, and the dining-room breakfast table is set with silver flatware and draped with a lacy cloth.

Susanne first visited Abigail's as a paying guest in 1985. A year later, she quit her job with an insurance company and bought the place, situated on a tree-lined street in what was once one of Sacramento's toniest neighborhoods. By the 1960s, many of the area's big, boxy mansions had become run-down; Abigail's, renovated in the early 1980s, was one of the first gentrified houses in this now eclectic community, a few blocks from corner coffeehouses, antiques shops, and art galleries.

Abigail's rooms, named for Susanne's and Ken's relatives, include Margaret, with a queen-size verdigris bed and an ever-changing canopy: winter white, springtime roses, hearts and flowers for Valentine's Day. Keeping a watchful eye over the proceedings is Ken's Aunt Margaret, depicted in all her flapperish glory in a large photograph on the wall. Breezy Aunt Rose is feminine with a gauzy wall canopy above the headboard of the queen-size brass bed, flowered yellow wallpaper, and an appealing green wing chair.

Abigail's has two big welcoming parlors. The more formal has two sofas and a wing chair facing a cheery fireplace. The sitting room across the hall reflects Susanne's interest in the arts; it contains an upright piano and a bulletin board listing the latest gallery openings and who's playing at the concert hall.

A fine cook whose recipes have been published widely and have won prizes, Susanne continues to innovate in the kitchen, serving such delights as zucchini waffles, potato-crust quiche, and sour-cream pancakes. ♨ *5 double rooms with baths. Air-conditioning, TV, phone, and radio in rooms, whirlpool tub in 1 room, VCR in 1 room. Garden hot tub, off-street parking. $115–$185; full breakfast. AE, D, DC, MC, V. No smoking, 2- to 3-night minimum on holiday weekends.*

AMBER HOUSE 🐚

1315 22nd St., Sacramento 95816, tel. 916/444–8085 or 800/755–6526, fax 916/552–6529

Michael Richardson admits that running a bed-and-breakfast inn has its challenges. "It's like having your mother-in-law for Christmas dinner every day of the year," he says. Still, Michael and his wife, Jane Ramey, former southern California residents, have no regrets about their decision to move to Sacramento in 1986 to become proprietors of Amber House, an inn consisting of three homes situated not far from the State Capitol.

Jane, a former merchandise manager for Marriott hotels, redecorated the original 1905 Arts and Crafts house's five guest rooms, haunting estate sales for antiques and fashioning each room around a poet. Michael, formerly in real estate, set about buying and restoring the 1913 Mediterranean-style house next door, which now hosts an enormous sitting room with a fireplace and four guest rooms, all under the spell of French Impressionist color schemes. In addition, the recently added 1895 Dutch Colonial Revival Musician's Manor has five rooms named after famous composers. All three homes are on the city's historic preservation list.

Amber House is atmospheric, with lots of nooks and crannies. The main sitting room with its boxed-beamed ceiling has plenty of comfortable chairs. In the late afternoons, guests snack here on cookies, coffee, and mineral water, or retreat to the smaller, front sitting room, with glass-fronted bookshelves and a window seat. Classical music wafts through all the public rooms.

The 14 guest rooms are floral and romantic, most with unusually luxurious bathrooms. They range from snug (Chaucer) to gloriously spacious (Renoir). The latter has leaded-glass windows, a king-size bed, a sofa, and a bathtub built for two. Emily Dickinson, occupying a former sleeping porch, is bright and airy, with a fireplace separating the sleeping area from the bathroom where there's a whirlpool bath with waterfall faucet and skylights that open. The sunny yellow Van Gogh is arguably the most glamorous; it's dominated by a sybaritic greenhouse bathroom with a corner heart-shape whirlpool for two and white wicker chaise longue.

Breakfast is served at a large antique Duncan Phyfe table in the dining room, in the garden, or at little tables in each guest room. The time and place are chosen by guests when they check in. Since guests often stay more than one night, the menu is never the same two days in a row. The first course is always a seasonal fruit dish with a special sauce, followed by a hot dish and fresh-baked item. Quiche and potatoes with bell peppers is an Amber House specialty, as are waffles and strawberries. As a prelude to the meal, Michael sets early morning coffee or tea on a tiny table outside each room. ♨ *14 double rooms with baths. Air-conditioning, phone, and cable TV in rooms, whirlpool bath in 11 rooms. Bicycles. $119–$249; full breakfast. AE, D, DC, MC, V. No smoking.*

THE ESPLANADE ☙
620 The Esplanade, Chico 95926, tel. 530/345–8084

This cheerful, homey inn is ideally located directly across the street from the historic Bidwell Mansion, where Chico's founder resided at the turn of the century, and just steps from the state university and downtown Chico.

The sunny yellow-shingled 1915 Craftsman house, with broad white columns and a large covered front porch, sits on the tree-lined Esplanade next door to a Mormon church. A burbling fountain and big "Welcome" sign greet arriving guests, who then meet the innkeepers, Lois Kloss and George Fish. A self-professed "happy, loving couple," Lois and George prefer innkeeping to running the motel Lois owned while raising her five children. The couple encourage their guests to feel at home, even to invite their friends in if they wish. Cocktails, juice, and home-baked cookies are served on request in the homey parlor or outside on the front porch.

The house is furnished eclectically with pieces chosen by Lois with comfort as the supreme goal. The living room features a cozy fireplace, and though the inn is on a relatively busy street, it is well insulated and quiet, as are the guest rooms. Natalie's, in lavender, has bay windows and custom stained-glass windows overlooking the Esplanade. Susan's, upstairs, has a queen-size poster bed and a view of Bidwell Mansion, while Kelsey's, in the rear of the house, is flooded with light from wraparound windows with southeast exposure, and a bath featuring hand-painted double sinks and gilded mirrors.

The ample breakfast includes fresh fruit, egg dishes such as eggs Benedict or various omelets, strawberry waffles, French toast, and plenty of home-baked muffins. Guests are welcome to second (and third!) helpings if they so desire. *△ 5 double rooms with baths. Air conditioning and cable TV in rooms, whirlpool bath in 1 room. $65–$85; full breakfast. MC, V. Closed July. No smoking.*

HARTLEY HOUSE BED & BREAKFAST INN ☙
700 22nd St., Sacramento 95816, tel. 916/447–7829 or 800/831–5806, fax 916/447–1820

Boulevard Park is one of Sacramento's less-heralded historic treasures. Not far from the State Capitol, the area boasts several blocks of magnificent turn-of-the-century houses. The six little parks in the middle of 21st and 22nd streets form the district's centerpiece; each is a large, grassy, tree-shaded oval, remnants of a former racetrack. Later, Boulevard Park became Sacramento's first residential subdivision, where houses cost $3,700 and no livestock was permitted. Such gentility disappeared at the end of World War II, and by the 1950s, Boulevard Park had become boardinghouse row.

A fourth-generation Sacramentan, innkeeper Randy Hartley purchased this onetime boardinghouse in 1987 and brought new life into it. He restored the hardwood floors and stained-glass windows in the public rooms to their former glory and outfitted the five guest rooms with a cozy, chintz-free mix of antiques and amenities that evoke the relaxed, sophisticated ambience of an Edwardian town house. Guests may read or chat before the cozy fireplace in the parlor. A collection of antique clocks, original brass and crystal gas light fixtures converted to electricity, and the hitching posts that remain at curbside serve as reminders of the earlier era.

Brighton, set in what was once the sunporch, is arguably the prettiest and certainly the lightest guest room, with three walls of windows, a white wrought-iron bed, a ceiling fan, and a small TV. Dover flaunts the house's original bathroom fixtures, including a claw-foot tub.

Breakfast—with offerings such as omelets, blintzes, Belgian waffles, and eggs Benedict, as well as freshly baked muffins or date pecan scones (or lower fat items if you prefer)—is ordered from a menu and served in the spacious dining room at small tables or, in good weather, in the flower-filled courtyard. Guests sometimes sit on the expansive front porch in the afternoon, often on the big porch swing, and sip fresh lemonade or other beverages while nibbling on home-baked cookies. *△ 5 double rooms with baths. Air-conditioning, multiline phone, modem port, voice mail, and satellite TV in rooms. Garden courtyard with whirlpool spa. $110–$160; full breakfast. AE, D, DC, MC, V. No smoking.*

WINE & ROSES COUNTRY INN ☙
2505 W. Turner Rd., Lodi 95242, tel. 209/334–6988, fax 209/334–6570

Located on 5 acres of rich farmland in Lodi, a grape-growing, wine-making community half an hour south of Sacramento, Wine & Roses is an unexpected romantic surprise. A historic white farmhouse that's nearly 100 years old, the inn is prim and pretty and surrounded by acres of fragrant gardens and towering century-old deodar fir trees. The largest and oldest rose bush in the county (a 1935 Lady Banks that's 30 ft high and 100 ft long) is bigger than the barn it grows over and produces hundreds of thousands of blossoms in early spring.

The inn, very much a family affair, is the creation of former realtor Kris Cromwell, her son Del Smith, and his wife, Sherri, whom he met when she was hired as the inn's chef. Sherri, now a mother of two and the executive chef, supervises the inn's food service.

Comfort, coziness, and strong colors dominate the guest rooms. Edelweiss, which overlooks the garden, boasts deep green walls, pale mauve carpeting, and a green floral-print duvet on the big brass bed. The bathroom has a claw-foot tub with a shower. Moonlight and Roses is a melody in mauve and pink, with bouquets of roses adorning the walls and floral drapes framing the claw-foot tub; there's a small comfortable sitting area by the room's bay window. Victorian touches abound: pots of potpourri, pink bows on the bathroom tissue, fresh flowers. Brides love the attic suite with its cathedral ceilings, French doors, rooftop deck, and sitting room furnished with two velvet wing chairs. All travelers appreciate the homelike ambience of the sitting room, which is set up with overstuffed sofas and chairs, a crackling fire in winter, and plenty of reading material filling library shelves.

Breakfast, Sunday brunch, lunch (Tuesday–Friday), and dinner (Wednesday–Saturday) are served in the mauve dining room, overlooking the rosebushes, or on the terrace in season. Meals emphasize local valley ingredients; fresh herbs and hand-picked flowers grace each plate. ♣ *9 double rooms with baths, 1 suite. Air-conditioning, cable TV, phone, and dataport in rooms. Restaurant, conference facilities, croquet, badminton, horseshoes, free use of health club off-site. $89–$165; full breakfast. AE, D, DC, MC, V. No smoking.*

OTHER CHOICES

Johnson's Country Inn. 3935 Morehead Ave., Chico 95928, tel. and fax 530/345–7829. 4 double rooms with baths. Air-conditioning and phone in rooms, whirlpool bath and fireplace in 1 room. Horseshoes, lawn games. $80–$125; full breakfast. MC, V. No smoking, 2-night minimum on holiday weekends and for CSU/Chico graduation.

RESERVATIONS AND REFERRAL SERVICES

B&B International (Box 282910, San Francisco 94128, tel. 650/696–1690 or 800/872–4500, fax 650/696–1699). **California Association of B&B Inns** (2715 Porter St., Soquel 95073, tel. 408/464–8159, fax 408/462–0402). **Eye Openers B&B Reservations** (Box 694, Altadena 91003, tel. 626/398–0528, fax 626/296–0183).

Gold Country:
Along Highway 49

CITY HOTEL ☞

Main St., Columbia State Historic Park (Box 1870), Columbia 95310, tel. 209/532–1479 or 800/532–1479, fax 209/532–7027

In 1856, when Columbia was all ablaze with gold fever, George Morgan built the City Hotel in the heart of town (now inside Columbia State Historic Park). Intended as a lodging for gentlemen, this two-story brick storefront was refurbished by the state in 1975 and now, of course, welcomes all.

The restoration and furnishings accurately reflect the gold-rush era, with only a nod to contemporary conveniences. All rooms contain massive carved wooden beds, marble-topped dressers, Oriental rugs, and Victorian-style floral wallpapers. Each room has a half-bath equipped with a wicker basket of "necessary items"—robe, disposable slippers, and towels—for the walk to the shower down the hall. A central sitting parlor scattered with Oriental rugs has a felt-topped poker table, books, magazines, and games.

The hotel routinely schedules Victorian-theme special events. Most popular is the annual Victorian Christmas Pageant and Feast, a typical holiday celebration of the 1860s, complete with costumed revelers. Other events include mystery weekends, a Victorian Easter Parade, a fireman's muster, and a re-creation of the argonauts at work in the mines.

The clubby restaurant at the City Hotel has long been considered among the best in the Gold Country. The à la carte menu includes an array of classic French and California selections, and the wine list represents a who's who of California wine makers. The What Cheer Saloon next door may look like a knock-off of a western movie set, but as with everything else about Columbia, it's an accurate reflection of gold-rush-era watering holes.

(Under the same management, and just two blocks away, is the elegant Victorian Fallon Hotel, with many original antiques and furnishings.) △ *10 double rooms with half-baths share 2 showers. Air-conditioning in rooms. Restaurant, saloon, theater-dinner packages, off-street parking. $85–$105; full breakfast. AE, D, MC, V. No smoking, closed first 2 wks Jan.*

DOWNEY HOUSE ☙
517 W. Broad St., Nevada City 95959, tel. 530/265–2815 or 800/258–2815

This inn is an anachronism in Nevada City. It's Victorian on the outside and contemporary with a southwestern flavor on the inside. An Eastlake Victorian that was built in 1869, it's a standout on Broad Street atop Nabob Hill (one of seven hills in the city), surrounded by beautiful gardens complete with a koi pond and within easy walking distance of everything in town.

The parlor has some Victorian antiques including a lovely buffet. Rooms, located on the first and second floors, are very quiet and painted the light pinks and blues one associates with the desert. Although most of the bedrooms are quite small, the bathrooms are larger than you might expect. Decorated identically in most respects, room furnishings include platform beds, small white lacquer nightstands, a pair of easy chairs, and oversize Chinese ginger jars that serve as coffee tables. There's also a tiny aquarium with live fish in each room, with a light that guests can turn on or off.

Innkeeper Miriam Wright has been catering to guests since the inn opened in 1988. She pampers them with delicious homemade breakfasts served in the kitchen, parlor, sunroom, or outside on the terrace, veranda, or in the garden. There's always a platter of fresh fruit and an interesting hot dish like Dutch babies (a baked and fruit-filled pancake), served on Santa Fe Railroad signature dinnerware. Wine is served in the afternoon. △ *6 double rooms with baths. Air-conditioning in rooms. $75–$100; full breakfast. MC, V. No smoking, 2-night minimum on weekends.*

EMMA NEVADA HOUSE ☙
528 E. Broad St., Nevada City 95959, tel. 530/265–4415 or 800/916–3662, fax 530/265–4416

When innkeeper Ruth Ann Riese acquired the 1856 Victorian cottage that was the childhood home of opera singer Emma Nevada, most of the restoration had already been completed. A local contractor saved the original gaslights, doors, hardware, and beveled-glass windows. Ruth Ann simply added the touches, like exquisite linens and an impressive tea cup collection, that brought Emma's childhood home back to life, and then invited guests to share the living antique that she created.

Guest rooms on the first and second floors are unusually spacious, bright, and airy and are furnished with tasteful antiques. The two best are the Nightingale's Bower, once the front parlor, which contains a lovely bay window and a woodstove dating to the 1860s, and Empress's Chamber, a symphony in ivory and burgundy with a bay-window sitting area that's favored by honeymooners. Emma's Hideaway, tucked into an upstairs dormer, is another cozy retreat.

The common rooms are particularly inviting. A cozy game room–library is stocked floor-to-ceiling with books, games, and an antique slot machine; the sitting room has overstuffed furnishings set fireside. A bright circular sunroom, one of the places breakfast is served, has windows all around.

The tree-shaded garden includes a meandering creek, paths, and secluded sitting areas. The property was a cherry orchard in 1856, and cherry trees still pop up through holes cut out in the back deck, furnishing fresh fruit for Ruth Ann's homemade cherry cobbler. Breakfast may be orange French toast and sausages, garden quiche with scones, oven-roasted apples, or mountain berry cobbler. Afternoon tea is served with home-baked cookies. ♨ *6 double rooms with baths. Air-conditioning and phone in rooms, TV in 3 rooms, whirlpool bath in 2 rooms, fireplace in 1 room, woodstove in 1 room. $100–$160; full breakfast. AE, DC, MC, V. No smoking, 2-night minimum on weekends Apr.–Dec. and holidays.*

THE FOXES BED AND BREAKFAST INN ☙

77 Main St., Sutter Creek 95685, tel. 209/267–5882 or 800/987–3344, fax 209/267–0712

The simple pale gray two-story Foxes Bed and Breakfast Inn in Sutter Creek was built during the gold rush; although its 19th-century origins are certainly intriguing, this elegant seven-room inn owes its chief appeal to the late-20th-century pampering of its guests. Min Fox, who has owned the inn with her husband, Pete, since 1980, sits down with guests each evening and discusses the next day's breakfast. (There's an airy French toast made with apple juice and egg white for the cholesterol-conscious.) Breakfast is served in guests' rooms on an antique wooden table or at a private table in the shaded garden. An ornate silver pot holds coffee or tea. The place mats are crocheted, as are the little doilies that are slipped over the bases of the stemmed orange-juice glasses.

The big Blue Room, with ice-blue floral-print wallpaper, has a large bed with a carved headboard. A wooden half-tester canopy with pale blue curtains is suspended overhead. A print of a red fox in winter repose hangs on one wall. (Every room here has a foxy touch, whether in pillow or print.) Appealing in a different way, the Anniversary Room in the front of the main house is tucked into a gable with light-filled windows on three sides; it has an elaborately carved 10-ft-tall armoire facing the bed. The bathrooms are a treat, too; three of them have clawfoot tubs, some have pull-chain toilets, and one is 16 ft long with a separate shower, claw-foot tub, and a crystal chandelier over the tub!

The house has a peach-color front parlor, with a spool-based table and a couple of sofas for curling up with a good book. Or guests may sit in the gazebo out back and admire the lush garden, particularly enticing in the spring when the big pink dogwood is in bloom. ♨ *5 double rooms with baths, 2 suites. Air-conditioning in rooms, fireplace in 4 rooms, cable TV in 3 rooms. Off-street parking.*

*$130–$180; full breakfast. D, MC, V. No smoking, 2-night minimum on week-
ends and holidays.*

GROVELAND HOTEL ☞

*18767 Main St., Groveland 95331, tel. 209/962–4000 or 800/273–3314,
fax 209/962–6674*

When Peggy Mosley discovered that the Groveland Hotel, an adobe built in 1849,
and an adjacent 1914 Queen Anne Victorian were for sale and slated for demolition in 1990, she bought them and began the renovations that would make
both buildings inviting to 20th-century guests without compromising their 19th-
century history. Thus the adobe still displays its original facade, wraparound
verandas, casement windows, and a central staircase. Likewise the Victorian
has gingerbread and bay windows. Peggy looked to the past in decorating by
installing floral wallpapers, antique French beds, wicker furnishings, and English armoires.

Operating the Groveland Hotel is a new career for Peggy, a spunky woman who
spent more than 40 years in the aerospace industry and pilots her own airplane.
Highlights of her life, she says, include knowing Elvis Presley and flying in the
Powder Puff Derby.

The three suites are the nicest accommodations; each occupies a pair of the
original hotel rooms. Lillie Langtry on the first floor, a popular choice with honeymooners, is the prettiest of the suites, with soft pink sponge-painted walls
surrounding a brass cannonball bed. There's a sofa opposite the fireplace and
a spa tub in the bathroom. Two of the four upstairs rooms in the original adobe have
stenciled decorations on the walls and French doors providing direct access to the
veranda; they all open onto the guest lounge, where there's a TV and a selection of books, magazines, and games.

The restaurant at the Groveland Hotel, open for dinner and Sunday brunch, has
a classic menu (prime rib, roast duck, surf and turf), casual ambience, and good
service. The inn is a short drive from Yosemite National Park. ⬥ *14 double
rooms with baths, 3 suites. Air-conditioning and phone in rooms, fireplace and whirlpool bath in suites. Limited room service, restaurant, saloon. $115–$195; Continental breakfast. AE, D, DC, MC, V. No smoking.*

THE SEASONS ☞

2934 Bedford Ave., Placerville 95667, tel. 530/626–4420

Located one block north of downtown Placerville, and a short walk from Gold
Bug Park and Mine, is the former Ollis-Plumando house, an 1859 pre-Victorian
structure. Now know as the Seasons, it has a wraparound wood porch, a first floor
built of placerite stone (formed from ancient alluvial or glacial deposits, and often
containing precious metals), and upper floors made of red brick. The builder (Henry
Ollis), once employed Henry Studebaker before he made his fortune in wheelbarrows
and wagons. Catalina and Eric McElwain purchased the house in 1994, performed prize-winning renovation work, and opened it as a B&B in 1996. They
have furnished and decorated the inn in a sophisticated, eclectic manner, with many
unusual, original works of art throughout.

The main entry is into the parlor, with its large stone fireplace and baby grand
piano, and the dining room, with a chandelier made from an antique weather vane,
designed as is the wood-and-wrought iron dining table, by local artists Leslie
and Dennis Stokes. There are also several pine antiques from Romania and
Hungary, including a hand-painted Hungarian day bed in the upstairs guest suite.

The spacious Palladian Suite, which takes up the entire third floor of the house, has a sitting room and bath with pedestal sink and stained-glass windows.

The two other guest rooms are located in cottages nestled within the wonderful gardens, with a seasonal creek providing the sounds of rushing water November through May. Cottage has its own picket fence–enclosed mini-garden, an antique brass bed, sitting area, and kitchen area with refrigerator. The Dreamer Room features a claw-foot tub and French doors leading onto a little porch. The main garden has several delightful areas: a wrought-iron gazebo, central stone fountain, and rock waterfall off in one corner. A Victorian lightning rod is one of many surprises to be found as one explores the gardens.

The Seasons emphasizes privacy for guests; all rooms have individual entrances, and guests may have as much or as little interaction with the innkeepers and other guests as they choose. Breakfast, served in the dining room or the gardens, may include an omelet with potatoes or corn cakes; French toast or waffles; and baked apples, fruit compote, or fresh fruit with fresh baked coffee cake or sweet bread. Afternoon refreshments, including cookies and a complimentary bottle of local wine, are served in the rooms. ♠ *3 double rooms with baths, 1 suite. Air-conditioning in rooms, woodstove in 1 room, cable TV in 2 rooms, refrigerator in 1 room. $95–$125; full breakfast, MC, V. No smoking.*

SHADOWRIDGE RANCH & RESORT ☙
3500 Fort Jim Rd., Placerville 95667, tel. 530/295–1000 or 800/644–3498; fax 530/626–5613

Four miles southeast of Placerville, up in the wooded hills where the wind whispers through the trees, Carlotta and Jim Davies have created a bit of rustic heaven. They've transformed the homestead that Carlotta's father literally carved out of the forest into a showplace lodge that mixes '30s Adirondack and gold-rush trappings and down-home comfort with some of the concierge services of a fine hotel. The ranch complex consists of beautifully restored hand-hewn log buildings with flooring, windows, and doors salvaged from the 1915 San Francisco Panama Exposition (World's Fair) and brought here by horse-drawn wagon.

Each suite is loaded with antique artifacts of ranch and lodge life, including saddles, garden tools, hunting, fishing and sporting gear, and even some dramatic taxidermic specimens such as a crouching mountain lion and a young grizzly bear. Three suites have river-rock hearths and wood-burning stoves. All suites have refrigerators stocked with beverages and cupboards filled with snacks and a wide variety of thoughtful personal amenities. Baths are all modern and well appointed, with matching maroon or black fixtures. Each suite has its own patio area with chairs and tables, which affords guests privacy as the main patio plays host to public lunches on weekends. Each evening, the Davieses' young son Spencer delivers baskets filled with fresh cowgirl cookies (described by Carlotta as "thigh-quiveringly, sinfully delicious chocolate bar cookies") to each suite.

Two of the suites sit atop a 137-year-old stone wine cellar where guests can taste the resident vintages and snack on a huge platter of afternoon appetizers that Carlotta presents, consisting of a wheel of baked Brie, stuffed artichokes, fresh fruits, salamis, and other cheeses. Hikers will enjoy exploring the ridge roads and trails on and adjacent to the property, and the lodge itself has beautifully kept grounds with vast lawns and thousands of flowers that serve as a colorful setting for the weddings that take place here.

Breakfast is incredibly generous, consisting of an assortment of fresh-baked muffins and breads, fruit, two juices and fresh-roasted coffee, ham, bacon, and sausage, fresh eggs from a neighbor's ranch, Shadowridge potatoes, and an English muffin with butter and jam. △ *4 suites with baths. Air-conditioning in suites. Gift shop. $120–$160; full breakfast. AE, MC, V. No smoking, 2-night minimum on weekends, 3-night minimum on holiday weekends. Closed Jan.–Mar.*

WEDGEWOOD INN ☞

11941 Narcissus Rd., Jackson 95642, tel. 209/296–4300 or 800/933–4393, fax 209/296–4301

Innkeepers Vic and Jeannine Beltz have created a brand-new Victorian with the most modern of creature comforts. But the inn also contains enough family memorabilia to satisfy the demands of the most dedicated antiques-hound. Vic was an engineer with IBM before getting into innkeeping and gold prospecting, and Jeannine, who has been perfecting her skills as a homemaker within the family for many years, now considers innkeeping yet another level of hospitable service to others. The Beltzes have turned two of the downstairs rooms into retail spaces: one offers a variety of gift items, and the other is a gallery of paintings produced by an art studio headquartered in Placerville.

All the rooms here are filled with memorabilia from four generations of the Beltz family. Granny's Attic, tucked into a gable on the third floor, is the most charming of the rooms, with a skylight over the bed, a long window seat that's just right for curling up with a good book, and a collection of antique nightclothes on display. The wooden cradle used by all the Beltz children stands in a corner of Country Pine. Wedgewood Cameo, a bright morning room, displays a wedding dress worn by one of the Beltz daughters.

The gardens are laid out English country-style, with a rose arbor, gurgling fountains, and a Victorian gazebo. Guests can play croquet and horseshoes on the lawn. In a little outbuilding, a restored 1921 Ford named Henry is on display.

Guests are requested to gather promptly at 9 AM for breakfast, which is preceded by a Christian blessing. Jeannine prepares an ample meal, such as poppy seed–almond cake, a turkey-sausage blintz, and raspberry sorbet, served on fine china by candlelight. △ *5 double rooms with baths, 1 suite. Air-conditioning in rooms, TV and phone in suite, woodstove in 4 rooms, whirlpool bath in suite. Gift shop, stocked guest refrigerator, microwave. $100–$165; full breakfast. AE, D, MC, V. No smoking, 2-night minimum on holiday weekends.*

OTHER CHOICES

The Coloma Country Inn. 345 High St. (Box 502), Coloma 95613, tel. 530/622–6919, fax 530/622–1795. 3 double rooms with baths, 2 doubles share 1 bath, 1 suite, 1 double suite. Air-conditioning in rooms, kitchen in suites. Canoe, hot-air-balloon and white-water-rafting packages. $95–$185; full breakfast. No credit cards. No smoking, 2-night minimum on holiday weekends.

Murphy's Inn. 318 Neal St., Grass Valley 95945, tel. 530/273–6873 or 800/895–2488, fax 530/273–5157. 5 double rooms with baths, 3 suites. Air-conditioning, cable TV/VCR, and phone in rooms. $100–$160; full breakfast. AE, MC, V. No smoking, 2-night minimum on weekends June–Dec.

RESERVATIONS AND REFERRAL SERVICES

Amador County Innkeepers Association (Box 1347, Sutter Creek 95685, tel. 209/267–1710 or 800/726–4667). **B&B International** (Box 282910, San

Francisco 94128, tel. 650/696–1690 or 800/872–4500, fax 650/696–1699). **California Association of B&B Inns** (2715 Porter St., Soquel 95073, tel. 408/464–8159, fax 408/462–0402). **Eye Openers B&B Reservations** (Box 694, Altadena 91003, tel. 626/398–0528 or 800/458–1221, fax 626/296–0183). **Gold Country Inns of Tuolumne County** (Box 462, Sonora 95370, tel. 209/533–1845 or 888/465–1849).

High Sierra, Including Yosemite, Lake Tahoe, and the Eastern Sierra

THE CAIN HOUSE 🐾

340 Main St. (Box 454), Bridgeport 93517, tel. 760/932–7040 or 800/433–2246, fax 760/932–7419

Innkeeping is in Marachal Gohlich's blood. In 1972, when she was 10, her family fled the Orange County smog to open the Walker River Lodge in Bridgeport, a town of 500 residents in the Eastern Sierra. In 1989, she returned to Bridgeport from southern California, where she had worked as a hotel operations director, and bought the Cain House, which she and her husband, Chris, converted to a B&B.

In the late 1920s the descendants of James Stuart Cain, the principal landowner in what was once the nearby boomtown (now ghost town) of Bodie, built this two-story brown-shingle house just two doors from Bridgeport's landmark 1880 courthouse. The house is surrounded by a lush green lawn and bordered by a white picket fence; a swing chair on the porch completes the picture of small-town America.

Guest rooms occupy both floors. Roomy Aurora, all peaches and pinks, is furnished in whitewashed pine. Silverado's pale greens are a cool complement to its white wicker bedroom set; it's a peaceful room, reminiscent of a quiet summer day in the shade. The J. S. Cain Room is arresting, with its four-poster cherrywood bed frame and dark red-and-green paisley wallpaper and quilt. Guests in this room, which has a private entrance and deck off the rear lawn, can enjoy breakfast outside. The only really discordant note is struck in the Candelaria Room, which is entered via the bathroom, an oddity left over from the original house plan.

The dining room is decorated with Swiss posters, a woodstove, and a large built-in china cabinet; French doors lead to the side porch. Guests can sit at one of several tables and savor such delights as raspberry-stuffed French toast with bacon or sausage, or for lighter eaters—Marachal always offers a choice—fresh fruit and juice, yogurt, and muffins. ⚑ *7 double rooms with baths. Cable TV and phone in rooms, air-conditioning in 6 rooms, refrigerator in 2 rooms. Off-street parking. $80–$135; full breakfast. AE, D, DC, MC, V. No smoking, 2-night minimum last weekend in June and 4th of July weekend. Closed late Oct.–mid-Apr.*

CHANEY HOUSE ☞

4725 W. Lake Blvd. (Box 7852), Tahoe City 96145, tel. 530/525–7333, fax 530/525–4413

This castle-like stone house is one of the top bed-and-breakfasts at Lake Tahoe. Resting amid pines just past the hamlet of Tahoe Pines on the lake's scenic western shore, Chaney House is one of Tahoe's few remaining all-stone houses (Emerald Bay's Vikingsholm is another). Built by Oakland's Cutting family as a vacation home in the 1920s, the house has all its original stonework, including exterior walls that are 18 inches thick. Innkeepers Lori and Gary Chaney have called it home since 1974 and have run it as a B&B since 1989.

Lori, a former nurse, and Gary, a boat salesman, are friendly hosts. Lori, who loves to cook, fixes big buffet breakfasts that start with fresh fruit or a fruit dish such as berry parfait, bananas Bombay, or baked peaches, followed by an entrée such as eggs with artichokes or stuffed French toast with hot blackberry sauce. Guests eat at the dining room table in winter, or, in summer, on the outside patio, where there are lovely views of the lake across the road. (The inn has a private pier on the lake as well.) Afternoon refreshments are also served.

The four guest rooms, all of which have private baths, are decorated country-style with floral wallpapers or pine-paneled walls; some have beamed ceilings or slanted roofs. The upstairs Master Suite comes with a king-size bed, a roomy sitting area, a dressing room, a two-person shower, and a forest view. Guests in Russell's Room, which is reached by a circular staircase, can lie in bed and view the lake. Jeanine's Room, the smallest, still comes with a queen-size antique brass bed, a roomy closet, and a big glass shower in the bath. Out back over the garage is the Honeymoon Hideaway, outfitted with gas fireplace, wet bar, TV with VCR, dressing area, feather bed, and granite whirlpool tub; unless they wish to, guests need seldom emerge. △ *2 double rooms with baths, 2 suites. TV/VCR and whirlpool tub in 1 suite. $110–$195; full breakfast. MC, V. No smoking, 2-night minimum on weekends, 3-night minimum on holidays.*

LE CHÂTEAU DU SUREAU ☞

48688 Victoria La. (Box 577), Oakhurst 93644, tel. 209/683–6860, fax 209/683–0800

Nestled in the Sierra Nevada foothills on 7 acres of wooded grounds and manicured gardens just outside the town of Oakhurst is the exquisite inn Le Château du Sureau (Estate by the Elderberries). Viennese owner Erna Kubin modeled the château after those in southern France, evoking childhood memories of her visits to the houses of her well-to-do relatives.

To provide authenticity wherever possible, Erna incorporated centuries-old tapestries, antique French furniture, and 15th-century tile into a structure built in 1991. With a bit of ingenuity, even the new became old: The carpenter who created the château's 40 wooden doors beat them with chains, and after the limestone floors were laid, they were cracked and chipped.

Each of the 10 bedrooms is named for a plant or an herb; all have a fireplace, a view of the Sierra, Provençal fabric, and an enormous bathroom with a deep tub. The Rosehip Room has an Empire-style queen-size bed and a 10-ft-high armoire. Elderberry is set in blue-and-white toile. The Napoleonic-era Saffron Room contains ebony furnishings inlaid with ivory; the Lavender Room is a castle nook with a panoramic mountain view.

The aroma of fresh breads, baked on the premises, is a wake-up call to innovative breakfasts that may include corn cakes with fresh kernels, layered with lox and basil sauce, fresh fruit with homemade yogurt, and fresh-squeezed juice. Guests may eat in the dining room or the garden, among the flowers and a fountain. Dinner is also served on the premises at Erna's Elderberry House, just a short walk from the château along a winding path; exceptional prix-fixe meals change nightly. ♦ *10 double rooms with baths. Wood-burning fireplace and CD sound system in rooms. Restaurant, pool, off-street parking. $285–$485; full breakfast. AE, MC, V. No smoking, 2-night minimum on weekends, 3-night minimum on holiday weekends.*

THE FEATHER BED ☙
542 Jackson St. (Box 3200), Quincy 95971, tel. 530/283–0102 or 800/696–8624, fax 530/283–1067

Bob and Jan Janowski escaped the corporate world of the San Francisco Bay Area and took over the Feather Bed in 1992. Their 1893 Queen Anne–style house, with such Greek Revival touches as Corinthian columns, is a pale peach charmer with turquoise and brick-red trim. Across from the historic courthouse in downtown Quincy, the inn is within walking distance of Main Street dining, shopping, and entertainment.

The inn's formal Victorian gardens, spectacular in spring, surround a stone fountain. The large front porch of the main house, lined with chairs and settees made from willow branches, is a quiet setting for reading, relaxing, or conversing (guests often find themselves chatting with the gregarious innkeepers).

The pleasant atmosphere continues in the dining room, where the Janowskis serve up enticing breakfasts that start with the inn's trademark smoothie, made from homegrown blackberries and raspberries. These are followed by home-baked muffins or coffee cake, and then a hot entrée such as quiche or pancakes with smoked sausage. Dining on the flower-bedecked front porch in summer is a real treat.

The spacious rooms are decorated with vintage wallpapers, a few well-chosen Victorian antiques, and a variety of teddy bears. (One thing you won't find here, however, are feather beds.) The Morning Room on the second floor gets lots of morning sun and overlooks the courthouse, and Jennie's Sewing Room has a clawfoot tub and a view of the garden. Behind the house, the secluded Sweetheart Cottage, as romantic as its name, has a brass and white-iron bed, delicate floral wallpaper, gas fireplace, and a claw-foot tub in the carpeted bathroom; French doors open onto a private garden. The Guest House next to the main house combines elegance and ruggedness with its gas fireplace and rustic pheasant borders; it holds up to four people and is good for a family. It's also accessible for guests with disabilities. ♦ *4 double rooms with baths, 1 suite, 2 guest houses. Phone and radio in rooms, air-conditioning in 5 rooms. Bicycles, airport pickup, off-street parking. $80–$130; full breakfast. AE, D, DC, MC, V. No smoking.*

MAYFIELD HOUSE BED & BREAKFAST ☙
236 Grove St., Tahoe City 96145, tel. 530/583–1001

If Stan Scott hadn't broken his leg in 1997 while skiing at Kirkwood, a resort south of Lake Tahoe, he and his wife, Colleen McDevitt, who both lived in Chicago at the time, might never have become the new innkeepers at the Mayfield House. Stan, a computer salesman, decided to spend the rest of his vacation scouting out possible properties to open as a B&B. He found Mayfield House (a B&B for two decades) up for sale, and he and Colleen took over in 1998.

Mayfield House, a English Tudor–style house that dates from 1932, is situated just a block from the often-crowded North Lake Boulevard in Tahoe City, but it's far enough away from the traffic that the location is relatively quiet. Amid the mostly modern jumble of architecture in Tahoe City, the half-stone, half-brown-shingle residence with the stone chimney, green lawn, and surrounding tall pines seems lifted from an earlier era.

Inside, guests may lounge in the comfortable sitting room with its overstuffed blue sofas, fireplace, and beamed ceilings. The six guest rooms, which display an intriguing variety of alcoves, nooks, and slanted ceilings, have been freshened under Colleen and Stan's ownership. Fabrics now include lots of bright colors, gingham, plaids, and stripes, and the house has a more rustic, cabinlike feel. The Guest Room, off by itself upstairs and with a view of the yard, offers privacy with one exception—its bath, though exclusive to the room, is downstairs. Julia's Room, named for architect Julia Morgan (who once stayed here), and the spacious Mayfield Room both have king-size beds. The latter also comes with a sitting area, a big bath with whirlpool tub, and a futon suitable for a child to sleep on (ages 12 or older are preferred here).

A breakfast of fresh fruit followed by items such as French toast or bacon and eggs can be eaten in your room, in the small dining nook, or, in warm weather, on the patio out back. △ *6 double rooms with baths. TV in 2 rooms, whirlpool bath in 1 room. $95–$200; full breakfast. MC, V. No smoking, 2-night minimum on weekends, 3-night minimum on holiday weekends.*

RICHARDSON HOUSE ℗

10154 High St. (Box 2011), Truckee 96160, tel. 530/587–5388 or 888/229–0365, fax 530/587–0927

This striking green-and-gold gingerbread Victorian, which dates from the 1880s, is perched on hill overlooking downtown Truckee. Built as a private residence by the Warren Richardson family, later turned into a bed-and-breakfast but allowed to fall into a state of disrepair, it was recently renovated and restored to turn-of-the-century elegance by owner James Beck, who lives in the Bay Area.

The result is something of a Victorian showplace, with antiques, vintage fixtures, plush carpeting and drapery, and plenty of period lace, fringe, and brocade. (Modern amenities aren't overlooked, either: near the parlor's old-fashioned player piano are a cable TV with VCR and a CD player.) A full breakfast is served in the formal dining room, where the table is covered with lace and brightened by a huge floral bouquet. After starting with granola and yogurt or other cereals, plus fresh-squeezed orange juice and fruit, guests may have bagels with salmon cream cheese and an oven omelet. No afternoon refreshments are served, but guests have 24-hour access to complimentary beverages, and the rooms contain decanters of sherry.

The eight guest rooms are replete with antiques such as carved headboards, four-poster canopy beds with step stools, brocade settees, oak rocking chairs, and claw-foot tubs, accented by lace curtains, fringed lampshades, and floral wallpapers. Feather beds supply comfort, and slanted roofs add character to several rooms. Two adjoining rooms—the smallish Warren's Woods Room and Maggie's Garden Room—share a bath and can be rented together to form a family-size suite. Children ages 10 and older are welcome.

Richardson House has an inviting front porch, where guests can sit and look out at the Sierra peaks or at the Victorian gardens in the front yard, as well as down to the Old West–flavored town of Truckee. A gazebo in the side yard is popular for weddings. △ *6 double rooms with baths, 2 doubles share 1 bath. $100–$180; full breakfast. AE, MC, V. No smoking, 2-night minimum on weekends.*

SHORE HOUSE ☞

7170 N. Lake Blvd. (Box 343), Tahoe Vista 96148, tel. 530/546–7270 or 800/207–5160, fax 530/546–7130

Located at a sharp curve in the road on Lake Tahoe's North Shore, this gem is easy to miss. But, starting with its prime lakeside setting, it's well worth looking for. The deep greens of private gardens and lawn commingle with the startling blue of the lake and an adjoining sandy public beach. (Guests also have use of the Shore House pier for boat launches.) Each floor of the main house is surrounded by balconies and decks offering a view of the grounds, the lake, and the surrounding mountains. Several rooms offer exceptional lake views as well.

The personable owners, Marty and Barb Cohen and their teenage son, Jake, are longtime Tahoe residents and live on site. Marty, who's active in Tahoe tourism, and Barb, who used to own an outdoors shop in Tahoe City and led adventure tours for women, are happy to share their expertise with guests.

Though each of the seven guest rooms and two private cottages is individually decorated, all contain knotty-pine walls, custom-built log furniture, down comforters and feather beds, gas fireplaces, and a private entrance and bath. Some rooms have hand-painted bathroom tiles; other room walls are decorated with original art—produced by guests themselves. A room called the Studio contains an easel and art supplies that guests are invited to use; some have turned out wonderful work, most often scenic lake views. Since the Shore House is designed as a romantic hideaway, and only one room contains two beds, call first for advice on bringing children.

The breakfast room, with log furniture and a river-rock fireplace, has a shimmering lake view. A typical breakfast might include poached pears or baked apples, home-baked scones or blueberry muffins, and eggs Benedict with potatoes or stuffed French toast with chicken-apple sausage. In nice weather, guests can eat out on the glass-top tables that dot the lawn. △ *7 double rooms with baths, 2 cottages with baths. Fireplace and refrigerator in rooms, kitchen in 2 rooms, whirlpool bath in 1 room. Outdoor hot tub, off-street parking. $130–$190; full breakfast. D, MC, V. No smoking, 2-night minimum weekends, 3-night minimum holiday weekends.*

SORENSEN'S ☞

14255 Hwy. 88, Hope Valley 96120, tel. 530/694–2203 or 800/423–9949

Those seeking a bona fide High Sierra atmosphere in rustic surroundings amid Douglas fir, piñon, and ponderosa can find it at this historic mountain resort alongside the Carson River. Sorensen's, just east of Carson Pass and about 25 mi south of Lake Tahoe, is open year-round. It offers access to 600 square mi of public land. Hiking, fishing, cross-country skiing, stargazing, fly-fishing classes—you name it, you'll find it here.

The inn provides comfortable accommodations, ranging from the rudimentary to the classy, in bed-and-breakfast units and housekeeping cabins connected by a network of trails. One of the latter is a replica of a 13th-century Norwegian summer home shipped to Hope Valley piece by piece by Sorensen's former owner. Another, the Chapel, is a honeymooners' favorite. The log cabin has a steeple, church doors, vaulted ceilings, and a spiral staircase to heaven—well, to the bedroom, anyway.

Some of the cabins date from the turn of the century, when Martin Sorensen, an immigrant Danish shepherd, and his wife, Irene, began camping here. The

Sorensen family ran the inn for more than 50 years; when they sold it in 1970, it went into a decade of decline and came to be known locally as the "Last Resort."

Then John and Patty Brissenden, from Santa Cruz, purchased it and set about renovating some cabins and building new ones. Most of the cabins have kitchens; many have sitting areas and lofts. All cabins are offered on a housekeeping basis (breakfast not included), but three small, simply furnished bed-and-breakfast rooms are available as well. Guests select breakfast from the menu at the Country Café, housed in a log cabin and open for all three meals; choices include quiche of the day, scrambled eggs with ham, and buttermilk waffles.

Just down the road from Sorensen's along the West Fork Carson River is a sister property, the Hope Valley Resort. It includes a three-bedroom house, campgrounds, a convenience store, and a prime fishing location. *1 double room with bath, 2 doubles share bath, 24 housekeeping cabins, 3 houses accommodating 2–6 persons each. Wood-burning stove in 18 rooms. Restaurant, convenience store, sauna, trout pond, picnic tables, barbecues, children's play area, off-street parking. $70–$400; full breakfast (for B&B guests). MC, V. No smoking, 2-night minimum on weekends, 3- or 4-night minimum on holidays.*

WHITE SULPHUR SPRINGS ✒
Hwy. 89 (Box 136), Clio 96106, tel. 530/836–2387 or 800/854–1797, fax 530/836–4457

This big white farmhouse has welcomed travelers since the 1850s, when it was built as an overnight lodge for the Quincy Mohawk Stage Line. Though a tranquil charm surrounds the inn now, thousands of prospectors once ranged over these tree-covered hillsides and gentle valleys.

White Sulphur Springs has been a B&B since 1984; owner-innkeeper Don Miller inherited it from his great-aunt in 1993. But the home has been in his family for more than a century, and the ambience remains much as it was when it was a stagecoach stop. Many of the furnishings are original to the inn: a pump organ in the parlor that came via Cape Horn, an antique piano that guests can play, a 200-year-old walnut dining-room table, and a pine bedroom set handcrafted by the inn's original owner. One bathroom contains the original woodstove after which the town of Clio (previously Boozetown) was named. The attic has been converted to a museum where visitors can view collectibles from the stagecoach days.

There are six guest rooms in the main house (five of which share two baths) and two cottages, the Dairy House and the Hen House (the original chicken coop). The latter has two bedrooms, a fireplace, and full kitchen. All have views of meadows and mountains; a balcony across the front of the main house extends the view for guests on the second floor. The Victorian furnishings include brocade-covered settees, a fainting couch, antique washstands, dry sinks, and rocking chairs.

Guests are served an elaborate ranch-style breakfast in the formal dining room or in the cottages. Breakfast is likely to consist of items such as sausage-spinach frittata or strawberry crepes, accompanied by home-style potatoes, homemade bread, and fruit. The inn's warm (78°F year-round), spring-fed Olympic-size swimming pool is used mainly in summer, though heartier souls can jump into the steamy waters during other seasons. *1 double room with bath, 5 doubles share 2 baths, 2 housekeeping cottages. Pool, picnic area, barbecue, off-street parking. $85–$140; full breakfast. D, MC, V. No smoking, 2-night minimum on summer and holiday weekends.*

OTHER CHOICES

Busch and Heringlake Country Inn. Main St. (Box 68), Sierra City 96125, tel. and fax 530/862–1501. 5 double rooms with baths. Whirlpool bath in 3 rooms, fireplace in 2 rooms. Restaurant and bar (seasonal). $90–$130; full breakfast. D, MC, V. No smoking.

Chalfant House. 213 Academy St., Bishop 93514, tel. 760/872–1790. 5 double rooms with baths, 3 suites. Air-conditioning in rooms, TV in suites. Off-street parking, airport pickup. $60–$100; full breakfast. AE, D, MC, V. No smoking.

The Matlick House. 1313 Rowan La., Bishop 93514, tel. 760/873–3133 or 800/898–3133. 5 double rooms with baths. Air-conditioning in rooms. Off-street parking. $75–$85; full breakfast. AE, D, MC, V. No smoking.

Rainbow Tarns. Rainbow Tarns Rd. (off Crowley Lake Dr., Rte. 1, Box 1053), Crowley Lake 93546, tel. and fax 760/935–4556 or tel. 888/588–6269. 3 double rooms with baths. Whirlpool bath in 2 rooms. $75–$140; full breakfast. No credit cards. No smoking, 2-night minimum on weekends, 3-night minimum on holiday weekends. Closed Dec. 24–25 and Mar.

White Horse Inn. 2180 Old Mammoth Rd. (Box 2326), Mammoth Lakes 93546, tel. 760/924–3656 or 800/982–5657. 4 double rooms with baths. Laundry facilities, pool table, fireplace, outdoor hot tub, ski storage area. $85–$135; Continental-plus breakfast weekdays, full breakfast weekends. D, MC, V. No smoking.

The Yosemite Peregrine. 7509 Henness Circle, Yosemite West 95389, tel. 209/372–8517 or 800/396–3639, fax 209/372–4241. 3 double rooms with baths. Fireplace, refrigerator, and coffeemaker in rooms, TV in 1 room, whirlpool bath in 1 room. Outdoor hot tub, off-street parking. $120–$170; full breakfast. MC, V. No smoking. Closed last 2 wks of Dec.

Yosemite West High Sierra. 7460 Henness Ridge Rd., Yosemite West 95389, tel. 209/372–4808. 3 double rooms with baths. Whirlpool bath in 1 room. $130–$190; full breakfast. MC, V. No smoking.

RESERVATIONS AND REFERRAL SERVICES

Bed and Breakfast California (Box 282910, San Francisco 94128, tel. 650/696–1690 or 800/872–4500, fax 650/696–1699). **Tahoe Bed and Breakfast Association** (tel. 800/562–1292).

COLORADO

Denver

QUEEN ANNE INN 🐚
2147 Tremont Pl., Denver 80205, tel. 303/296–6666 or 800/432–4667,
fax 303/296–2151

The Queen Anne Inn, part of the nationally registered Clements Historic District, is just five minutes' walk from the attractions of downtown Denver, whose skyscrapers loom like the Rockies from the front porch. A walking tour might include various excellent art museums, the ornate State Capitol and U.S. Mint, the huge Tabor Center mall, and the chic shops and restaurants of LoDo (Lower Downtown), a converted warehouse district.

Two adjoining houses form the inn: one is an 1886 High Victorian with a magnificent open 35-ft turret; the other is an 1879 Queen Anne mansion. Owner Tom King converted the former, which had served as the innkeeper's residence, into two-room guest suites and added the sweeping Victorian-style porch. The Queen Anne was built for Edwin Pierce, the brother of Augusta Tabor, whose husband, Horace, was a flamboyant mining magnate. Both houses are fitted with handsome oak wainscoting and balustrades, vaulted 10-ft ceilings, bay windows, and period furnishings such as wrought iron, brass, and four-poster canopy beds, cherry or pine armoires, oak rocking chairs, and elaborate cherry mantel-top mirrors. Many of the exquisite, creatively decorated rooms and suites have soothing views of Benedict Fountain Park.

Each of the four High Victorian gallery suites is dedicated to a famous artist—Remington, Audubon, Rockwell, and Calder; all have exposed brick walls and reproductions of the artists' representative works. The Calder Suite has a jetted tub and gas fireplace, the Remington Suite has a hot tub on a small porch that opens onto the garden, and the Rockwell Suite has a 5-ft stained-glass window and a casement opening onto the turret. The decor of the bedrooms in the Queen Anne section is even more unusual. The most spectacular touches are the mural of the home in the Tabor Room, set during a typical garden party in 1894, and a hand-painted aspen grove snaking around the turret of the Aspen Room.

After leaving his post as a promotion and advertising executive for Braniff Airlines, Tom King opened the highly rated Babbling Brook Inn in Santa Cruz, California. He sold the Babbling Brook to work as a consultant, advising clients who were searching for that perfect inn. He spotted the Denver Queen Anne while scouting for a client and bought it; he has since acquired another irresistible property in Denver, which he also oversees, called the Capitol Hill Mansion. Tom's guests appreciate his professionalism and expertise. He's always available during the evening beverage and cheese hour, which often includes tastings of the little-known but excellent Colorado wines (plus hot spiced cider in winter).

Breakfast is served either in bed or in the spacious dining room. Each morning, the buffet includes heart-healthy selections like all-natural granola, fresh fruits and juices, Tom's own blend of coffee (a Venezuelan–Costa Rican–Colombian mix), muffins, scones, croissants, oatmeal, and a hot entrée, possibly quiche, cheese strudel, or an omelet. ⚠ *10 double rooms with baths, 4 suites. Air-conditioning, phone, hair dryer, iron and ironing board, cable TV in suites, whirlpool bath or outdoor hot tub in some rooms, off-street parking. $75–$175; full breakfast, evening wine. AE, D, DC, MC, V.*

OTHER CHOICES

Castle Marne. 1572 Race St., Denver 80206, tel. 303/331–0621 or 800/926–2763, fax 303/331–0623. 7 double rooms with baths, 2 suites. Air-conditioning, phones, ceiling fans; fireplace and whirlpool tub in suites; croquet; off-street parking. $85–$220; full breakfast, Victorian Tea ($28), 6-course Romantic Dinner ($120 for two). AE, D, DC, MC, V.

The Capitol Hill Mansion. 1207 Pennsylvania St., Denver 80203, tel. 303/839–5221 or 800/839–9329, fax 303/839–9046. 5 double rooms with baths, 3 suites. Air-conditioning, phones; private balcony and whirlpool tub in 3 rooms; fireplace in 2 rooms; fresh flowers; tours and carriage rides arranged (fee), off-street parking. $95–$175; buffet breakfast, evening refreshments. No smoking indoors.

RESERVATIONS SERVICE

Bed & Breakfasts Innkeepers of Colorado (Box 38416, Dept. S-95, Colorado Springs 80937-8416, tel. 800/265–7696).

The High Rockies

BED AND BREAKFASTS ON NORTH MAIN STREET 🐦
303 N. Main St., Breckenridge 80424, tel. 970/453–2975

Innkeepers Fred Kinat and Diane Jaynes spent a year restoring an intimate 1885 miner's cottage and named it the Williams House. Until a year ago Williams and Willoughby House, a circa 1880 "Victorian dollhouse" cottage for two, housed guests with more than enough comfort and privacy. Most recently, Barn Above the River, furnished with new country reproductions and antiques, was added, to take advantage of the willow-lined Blue River and wildflower garden that it overlooks.

The inns are perfectly situated for a walking tour of Breckenridge—one of Colorado's largest National Historic Districts and the oldest continuously occupied town (founded 1859) on the western slope of the Continental Divide. The town's lovingly restored and repainted structures include log cabins, false-fronts, and Victorian gingerbreads.

Williams House has a cream, chartreuse, and forest-green facade, framed by vaulting snowcapped peaks. The Williams House is a dream B&B, with a cozy front parlor, done in pink and ultramarine, and exquisitely detailed accommodations. The rooms are romantically decorated, with chintz or lace curtains, Laura Ashley and Ralph Lauren linens, mahogany beds, walnut wardrobes or cherry armoires, Oriental rugs, old framed magazine covers, hand-blown globe lamps, fresh flowers and sachets, and footed tubs. All rooms have a private deck or patio. Quilts, rockers, and two-person showers are present in the newer Barn Above the River, where most rooms also have fireplaces and mountain views.

The yellow-and-white–trim Willoughby Cottage next door has scalloped lace curtains, intricately carved Victorian doors and balustrades, elaborate mantel with hand-painted tiles, gas fireplace, whirlpool bath for two, kitchenette, and rustic antique fixtures and furnishings, including a graceful mirror and a cherry love seat. In other words, it's ideal for a honeymoon or for a peaceful, undisturbed getaway.

Best of all are the affable hosts, who moved to the mountains from Houston in the 1980s. Avid skiers, they warn guests to expect cold cereal on powder days—a pity since Diane's muffins, quiches, kugel, and frittatas are addictive. Summit County is a year-round sports paradise, particularly noted for skiing: Breckenridge, Copper Mountain, Keystone, and Arapahoe Basin are all within minutes of one another, with Vail only a bit farther. In the summer, Fred and Diane take guests on hikes. ⚱ *9 double rooms with baths, 1 suite, 1 cottage. Ceiling fan, tub for two, fireplace in 1 suite; TV, phone, fireplace in 4 rooms; outdoor hot tub. $169–$285; full breakfast except on "powder days." AE, D, MC, V.*

IRWIN LODGE ☜
Box 457, Crested Butte 81224, tel. 970/349–9800 or 888/464–7946

The Irwin touts itself as the "best-kept secret in the Rockies," and it's no idle boast. Talk about seclusion: In winter you must take a thrilling snowmobile ride around several switchbacks to reach this aerie, nearly 1,000 ft above (and 8 mi from) Crested Butte. The lodge sits 10,700 ft above sea level on a remote ridge overlooking Lake Irwin and the Sangre de Cristo range. Built in 1976, this cedar-log structure has several cozy lounge areas, which circle a magnificent fieldstone fireplace in the expansive and recently renovated lobby. Here, guests mingle throughout the day, exchanging anecdotes about their adventures, playing pool, darts, and Foosball, or watching videos on the big-screen TV. Hot tubs are also popular with guests who want to ease their tired, over-skied bodies.

The smallish, charmingly rustic rooms have pine walls and are tastefully appointed with mahogany furnishings. Due to its isolated nature, rates usually include all meals—a hearty breakfast and a fine Continental lunch and dinner, served family style—although breakfast-only rates are also available. The predominantly repeat clientele knows this is the premier place in America for powder skiing, as the surrounding area gets an average of 500 inches of fluffy white stuff a year. A Snowcat will take you up to 12,000 ft, accessing a 2,000-ft vertical drop, for guided skiing and snowboarding. Summer activities include mountain biking as well as fishing and canoeing on Lake Irwin.

With no phones, just a shortwave radio to civilization, the Irwin represents the ultimate in total isolation. If you crave a little shopping or want to experience the nightlife, you can always make arrangements to head into Crested Butte, a carefully preserved Victorian mining town that is a National Historic District (chartreuse, hot pink, and powder-blue facades attest to the locals' warmth and whimsy). There's also the modern mountain village of Mt. Crested Butte, about 3 mi away, which sprouted around the increasingly popular ski-area of the same name. It's considered the quintessential ski bum town: friendly and reasonably priced, with great bars, top galleries, and impressive restaurants for a town its size. ⚱ *24 double rooms with baths, 1 suite. 2 hot tubs, downhill and cross-country skiing, snowmobiling, snowboarding, fishing, canoeing. $230–$330 per person (all-inclusive); lunch and dinner available for nonguests. MC, V. 3-night minimum weekends Nov.–Apr., 2-night minimum weekdays Nov.–Apr.*

SARDY HOUSE 🦟

128 E. Main St., Aspen 81611, tel. 970/920–2525 or 800/321–3457, fax 303/920–4478

The Sardy is a classic 1892 red sandstone-brick Queen Anne in downtown Aspen. One of the world's fabled resorts, Aspen is synonymous with glitz, glamour, and glorious skiing (the hiking, fishing, and mountain biking are equally superb from spring through fall). An exquisitely preserved Victorian mining town, it has gracious mansions and lacy pastel-color gingerbreads that today house one gourmet restaurant and stylish shop after another—an eye-popping display of conspicuous consumption.

The inn's two buildings are connected by an enclosed gallery: The original mansion has turrets, gables, and a striking black linseed roof; the carriage house was built in 1985 to duplicate the authentic Victorian attributes of the original house.

The tiny reception area gives little hint of the sumptuous interior. It opens onto an inviting parlor with bay windows that drip with lace and chintz. A narrow, winding staircase with a magnificent oak balustrade leads to the winsome bedrooms, individually decorated in aubergine, mauve, and rose, with Axeminster carpets from Belfast, cherry armoires and beds, wicker furniture, and such welcome touches as Laura Ashley bed linens, heated towel racks, and whirlpool tubs; many have stellar views of the ski slopes.

The Sardy (as well as the equally posh Hotel Lenado; *see below*) has been smoothly run for the last decade by co-owner Daniel Delano and general-manager Jayne Poss, who have crafted elegant yet homey surroundings. The staff's professional demeanor—friendly without being familiar—results in an ambience that is slightly more formal than at other similar B&Bs. Guests linger over breakfasts that are served in the cozy dining room in winter and by the outdoor pool in summer. The fluffy blueberry pancakes are justly famous; other standouts include eggs Benedict, Brie omelets, and home-baked fruit breads. In the evenings the dining room doubles as Jack's, one of Aspen's more select restaurants, emphasizing fresh indigenous ingredients such as Colorado rack of lamb and flaky Rocky Mountain trout meunière. △ *14 double rooms with baths, 6 suites. Ceiling fans, cable TVs, phones, whirlpool tubs, heated towel racks; VCR, stereo, dry or wet bar in suites; restaurant, pool, hot tub, sauna. $165–$450 (summer), $85–$195 (spring and fall), $265–$650 (winter), $365–$750 (Christmas week); full breakfast. AE, DC, MC, V.*

OTHER CHOICES

Apple Blossom Inn. 120 W. 4th St., Leadville 80461, tel. 719/486–2141. 3 double rooms with baths, 4 doubles share 2 baths, 1 suite. Alarm clocks, robes; fireplace in 1 room; pass to Lake County Recreation center, with gym and pool. $59–$118; full breakfast. AE, MC, V.

Hardy House Inn. 605 Brownell St., Georgetown 80444, tel. 303/569–3388 or 800/490–4802. 3 double rooms with baths, 1 2-bedroom suite. TV/VCRs, outdoor hot tub. $80–$125; full breakfast. MC, V.

Hotel Lenado. 200 S. Aspen St., Aspen 81611, tel. 303/925–6246 or 800/321–3457, fax 303/925–3840. 19 double rooms with baths. Ceiling fans, cable TVs, phones, outdoor hot tub. $95–$440; Continental breakfast. AE, DC, MC, V.

Mary Lawrence Inn. 601 N. Taylor St., Gunnison 81230, tel. 970/641–3343. 3 double rooms with baths, 2 suites. Fans, radios; TV in suites. $69–$89; full breakfast. MC, V.

Ski Tip Lodge. Keystone Resort, Box 38, Keystone 80435, tel. 970/496–4950 or 800/222–0188, fax 970/468–4343. 9 double rooms with baths, 2 doubles share bath. Restaurant, ski shuttle. $79–$200; full breakfast. AE, DC, MC, V.

RESERVATIONS SERVICE

Bed & Breakfasts Innkeepers of Colorado (Box 38416, Dept. S-95, Colorado Springs 80937-8416, tel. 800/265–7696).

North Central Colorado: Rocky Mountain National Park

BOULDER VICTORIA 🐚
1305 Pine St., Boulder 80302, tel. 303/938–1300

The Victoria sits in the heart of downtown, just off the Pearl Street Mall, an eye-catching array of trendy restaurants and boutiques where all Boulder hangs out. Owners Matthew Dyrofs and Jeff White, noted for their renovations of several historic Boulder homes, set out to create a model B&B when they restored this 1876 Classical Revival beauty, painted in muted blue, mauve, and beige. When it was redesigned in 1889, in addition to building a second floor, architects added unusual features for the time—bay and leaded-glass windows, most of which descend from ceiling to floor, allowing light to stream in throughout the house. French doors open onto the formal Victorian gardens: Trumpet honeysuckles climb the entire west side of the building, rose bowers and banks of poppies and columbine adorn the walkways, and wisteria welcomes guests to the front porch.

The rooms, each named for a previous or present owner of the house, are individually decorated in similarly tasteful styles. Most have the Laura Ashley–English-country-home look, with brass beds, down comforters, lace curtains, dried flowers, rocking chairs, and other period antiques. Terry cloth robes and TVs, discreetly placed in armoires, bring the picture up-to-date. Some rooms, such as the Nicholson, also offer stunning views of the Flatiron Mountains that ring the town.

Meredith Lederer is the capable innkeeper (the owners aren't involved in day-to-day operations but often stop by to chat). She splits her time between the Boulder Victoria and the owners' new property down the street, the Earl House (*see below*). The Boulder Victoria also oversees several downtown apartments in an historic building, which are as tastefully decorated as the inn and are available short or long term.

At Boulder Victoria, breakfast is served in the small, dainty breakfast room. Featured are lemon-blueberry bread, spiced dried fruit compote, homemade muesli, and maple pecan granola. Cookies (ask for the sublime ginger snaps) and scones with lemon curd dress the informal afternoon tea; evening port in the parlor is another complimentary treat.

Boulder is one of the country's most progressive cities, a town of cyclists and recyclers obsessed with environmental concerns and physical fitness: A local joke is "Even the dogs jog." There are more bikes than cars in this uncommonly beautiful and beautifully uncommon city. To the northeast of town is the alpine wonderland of Rocky Mountain National Park, which was sculpted by violent volcanic uplifts and receding glaciers. Its three distinct ecosystems, verdant subalpine (towering Ponderosa pines), alpine (silvery streams, turquoise lakes, emerald meadows woven with wildflowers), and harsh tundra (wind-whipped trees growing at right angles and microscopic versions of familiar plants), provide varied hiking experiences. The park teems with wildlife—beavers, bighorn sheep, majestic elk, soaring bald eagles. △ *6 double rooms, 1 suite. Air-conditioning, cable TVs, phones. $109–$189; full breakfast. AE, MC, V.*

OTHER CHOICES

Briar Rose. 2151 Arapahoe Ave., Boulder 80302, tel. 303/442–3007. 9 double rooms with baths. Clock radios; air-conditioning and ceiling fan in 4 rooms; fireplace in 2 rooms; patio or balcony off 4 rooms; TV in common room. $124–$149; Continental-plus breakfast, afternoon tea. AE, DC, MC, V.

Earl House. 1305 Pearl St., Boulder 80302, tel. 303/938–1400. 6 double rooms with baths, 2 carriage houses with 3 bedrooms. Air-conditioning, cable TV, phone, kitchen in carriage houses. $109–$179 with 2-night minimum on weekends (carriage houses $90–$350 with 3-night minimum); full breakfast and afternoon refreshments (except in carriage houses). AE, MC, V.

Coburn House. 2040 16th St., Boulder 80302, tel. 303/545–5200 or 800/858–5811. 12 double rooms with baths. Air-conditioning, ceiling fans, cable TV, phones, off-street parking. $135–$167; Continental breakfast, afternoon refreshments. AE, D, MC, V. No smoking.

Pearl Street Inn. 1820 Pearl St., Boulder 80302, tel. 303/444–5584 or 800/232–5949. 7 double rooms with baths, 1 suite. Air-conditioning, cable TV, phone, fireplaces. $95–$145; full breakfast, afternoon refreshments. AE, MC, V.

RESERVATIONS SERVICE

Bed & Breakfasts Innkeepers of Colorado (Box 38416, Dept. S-95, Colorado Springs 80937–8416, tel. 800/265–7696).

South Central Colorado Along I–25

HOLDEN HOUSE ☜
1102 W. Pikes Peak Ave., Colorado Springs 80904, tel. 719/471–3980

Holden House has three separate buildings: The main house is a 1902 Colonial Revival Victorian in robin's-egg blue with off-white and burgundy trim; it has a porch with round pillars, a turret, and a steep roof. The carriage house is more High Victorian in style, with dual column pillars. Also a Colonial Revival, the third house is painted a light grayish mauve with burgundy trim and has intricate fish-scale gingerbread adorning the main pillars.

Owners Sallie and Welling Clark took their new careers as innkeepers seriously, enrolling in hotel management courses while they lived off Welling's navy pension. In the more than a decade since they purchased the house (and spent a solid year renovating it), they've become bona fide B&B mavens, enthusiastically joining state and national associations, contributing to B&B cookbooks, and corresponding with fellow innkeepers throughout the world. That they love their work is evident. Among the little extras they provide is a 24-hour coffee, tea, and cookie bar. Sallie serves gourmet three-course breakfasts on a Queen Anne-style dining table that seats 10, in the antique- and heirloom-filled parlor. Her specialties include Holden House eggs goldenrod (puff pastry shell filled with eggs hollandaise) and Southwest eggs fiesta (a tortilla shell wrapped to form a hood on the back of a soufflé cup, then filled with eggs, cheese, bacon, salsa, and sour cream). Don't be deceived, however—Holden House is really run by house cats Ming Toy (a black beauty with gleaming gold eyes) and Muffin (part Siamese). They've been written up in the Lifestyle section of *Cats* magazine but, swears Sallie, "fame hasn't gone to their heads—they were already spoiled."

Some rooms have period decor while others are furnished in a frillier style; many include heirloom quilts pieced by Sallie's great-grandmother. A homey atmosphere prevails, with old family photos and keepsakes placed throughout. The Aspen Suite has an open-beam turret, see-through fireplace made of clear materials, and mountain views. The Goldfield has a 4-ft skylight above the bed, a marble tub, exposed brick walls, an oak fireplace, and antique waterfall furniture courtesy of Sallie's grandmother. The Silverton Suite is awash in Victorian elegance, with a mahogany four-poster bed, a Mission oak fireplace, and a marble tub for two.

Holden House is in downtown Colorado Springs, the state's second-largest city. Attractions include historic areas like Manitou Springs and Old Colorado City, the Pro Rodeo Hall of Fame and Museum of the American Cowboy, and the jutting spires and sensuously abstract red-rock monoliths of the Garden of the Gods and the famed craggy Pikes Peak. △ *5 suites. Air-conditioning, phones, fireplaces, oversize tubs. $105–$115; full breakfast. AE, D, DC, MC, V.*

OTHER CHOICES

Abriendo Inn. 300 W. Abriendo Ave., Pueblo 81004, tel. 719/544–2703, fax 719/542–1806. 10 double rooms with baths. Air-conditioning, TVs, phones, off-street parking. $59–$110; full breakfast. AE, DC, MC, V.

Adobe Inn. 303 N. Hwy. 24, Buena Vista 81211, tel. 719/395–6340. 5 double rooms with baths. Ceiling fans, cable TVs; fireplace in 1 room; restaurant, hot tub. $55–$89; full breakfast. MC, V.

Cottonwood Inn. 123 San Juan Ave., Alamosa 81101, tel. 719/589–3882 or 800/955–2623. 3 double rooms with baths, 2 doubles share bath, 4 suites. Phones; TV in suites; gallery; gift shop; massage (fee); golf, horseback riding, and hot-springs packages available; art and cooking workshops. $64–$98; full breakfast. AE, D, MC, V.

RESERVATIONS SERVICE

Bed & Breakfasts Innkeepers of Colorado (Box 38416, Dept. S-95, Colorado Springs 80937–8416, tel. 800/265–7696).

Southwest Colorado:
The San Juan Mountains
and the Four Corners

SAN SOPHIA B&B 🌱
330 W. Pacific St., Telluride 81435, tel. 970/728–3001 or 800/537–4781

This "contemporary Victorian," built in 1988 in downtown Telluride, has a handsome cream-color paint job with jade trim, whimsical gables, turrets, bay windows, and oddly angled nooks and crannies that personalize the interior. Owners Alicia Bixby and Keith Hampton also run an advertising and promotion firm in town, put on the annual Wine Festival, and raise two young children, but they still manage to spend time mingling with guests.

Pristine mountain light streams into every room, each one warmly accented with whitewashed oak woodwork. Each cozy bedroom has contemporary brass beds with handmade quilts, elegant pine armoires, tables and nightstands handcrafted by Colorado artisans, skylights in their tiled bathrooms, and stained-glass windows over the oversize tubs. Color schemes favor desert pastels—terra cotta with teal accents, mint or purple with blue trim. Thoughtful extras include plush terry cloth robes, ideal for heading downstairs to the six-person hot tub in the gazebo. The San Sophia Mercantile sells items such as fanny packs, water bottles, and signature sweatshirts.

The San Sophia embodies the concept of a room with a view: Vistas include the magnificent San Sophia ridge, gushing creeks and waterfalls, and spectacular sunrises over Telluride Peak. The third-story octagonal observatory offers smashing 360-degree panoramas. Hanging throughout the inn are fine photographs of the region, bringing the views indoors. There's also a newly added restaurant with creative, new American meat and fish specialties.

The atmosphere here is wonderfully convivial: Guests mingle in the hot tub, in the observatory, and over breakfast and complimentary afternoon wine and hors d'oeuvres. Breakfast is served in the dining room, whose two-story picture windows look east over the San Juan Mountains. Vaulting floral arrangements and crisp apricot napery grace the tables. The menu for the bountiful breakfast buffet changes daily but always includes yogurt, fresh fruit salads, cereals, muffins, and such treats as cream cheese and dill johnnycakes with smoked salmon and almond apple pan puff. Afternoon cocktails are offered, as are late-night ports and single-malt scotches.

Telluride, a valley caught between azure sky and gunmetal mountains, was once so inaccessible that it was a favorite hideout for desperadoes like Butch Cassidy, who robbed his first bank here in 1889. Some locals claim that it is named not for the mineral tellurium but for the saying "To Hell You Ride." Today the savage but beautiful terrain attracts mountain people of a different sort—alpinists, telemarkers, snowboarders, freestylers, mountain bikers, and freewheeling four-wheelers—who attack any incline with consummate abandon. One local quips, "The Wild Bunch is alive and well."

Gorgeously preserved, Telluride is full of cotton-candy-colored Victorian gingerbreads and frontier trading posts. Every corner yields stunning prospects of the San Juan Mountains, which loom menacingly or protectively, depending on the lighting. Telluride deserves a prize for most annual festivals: wine, hot-air ballooning, and mushrooms are celebrated, in addition to film and music, both of which attract high-profile international industry folk. ⚑ *16 double rooms with baths. Cable TVs, phones, fans, restaurant, concierge, hot tub, ski lockers, underground parking. $114–$295; full breakfast. AE, MC, V.*

OTHER CHOICES

Pennington's Mountain Village Inn. 100 Pennington Ct., Telluride 81435, tel. 970/728–5337 or 800/543–1437. 9 double rooms with baths, 3 suites. Minirefrigerators, cable TVs, phones, billiard room, hot tub, laundry, steam room. $140–$300; full breakfast, afternoon wine and hors d'oeuvres. AE, MC, V. No smoking.

St. Elmo Hotel. 426 Main St., Ouray 81427, tel. 970/325–4951. 7 double rooms with baths, 2 suites. Clock radios, restaurant, TV in parlor, sauna, outdoor hot tub. $75–$110; buffet breakfast. AE, D, DC, MC, V.

 RESERVATIONS SERVICE

Bed & Breakfasts Innkeepers of Colorado (Box 38416, Dept. S-95, Colorado Springs 80937–8416, tel. 800/265–7696).

CONNECTICUT

The Southwestern Coast

COTSWOLD INN ☞
76 Myrtle Ave., Westport 06880, tel. 203/226–3766, fax 203/221–0098

For years honeymooners have been known to nest at the Cotswold Inn, a charming gray-cedar-shake cottage with a proliferation of gables and skylights. Nowadays you're also likely to encounter Europeans touring the Connecticut shoreline and New Yorkers looking for a short break from urbanity (Manhattan is just 50 mi away).

Though the steep gables, stone porches, and neatly manicured hedges and flower gardens recall England's Cotswold region, rooms capture the essence of 18th-century Connecticut, with reproduction Chippendale and Queen Anne furnishings—highboys, mule chests, wing chairs. Two rooms have canopy beds, the suite has a fireplace, and all are spruced up daily with fresh flowers. A common living room is made welcoming with about a dozen dried-flower arrangements and soft classical music. Here a Continental breakfast of fresh muffins, fruit, yogurt, and gourmet coffees is laid out; wine, cordials, and snacks are set out here early each evening. More museumlike than it is homey (and not a place to bring young children), the Cotswold is perfect if you're looking for the efficiency and privacy of a small hotel *and* the intimacy of a B&B. ♨ *3 double rooms with baths, 1 suite. Air-conditioning, cable TV, phone, terry cloth robes, hair dryers in rooms. $175–$245; Continental breakfast. AE, MC, V.*

INN AT NATIONAL HALL ☞
2 Post Rd. W, Westport 06880, tel. 203/221–1351 or 800/628–4255, fax 203/221–0276

The self-important name belies the whimsical, exotic interior of this towering red-brick Italianate on the downtown banks of the Saugatuck River. Built by Lee Tauck, the owner of the renowned tour company, Tauck Tours, the Inn opened in 1993, becoming the second truly world-class luxury hotel in Connecticut—after the equally sumptuous Mayflower Inn, in Washington, Connecticut, which opened in 1992.

Each of the rooms here is a study in innovative restoration, wall stenciling, and decorative design. The trompe l'oeil touches are evident from the moment you enter the lobby elevator, whose walls are painted to look like tome-filled bookshelves. A tour of the lounge and lobby reveals an exquisite furniture collection. Note the 300-year-old Swedish grandfather clock by the reception desk and also the chandelier, which once hung in London's Savoy Hotel, over the table in the small, elegant, conference room. Downstairs is a classic snooker table, imported from England. The hallways feature fine hand stenciling and delicate wood paneling.

Rooms and suites are magnificent—four of them have sleeping lofts, and several have 12-ft-high windows. All have opulent four-poster beds adorned with corollas or canopies and have limestone bathrooms with sleek marble baths, heated towel bars, hair dryers, and plush Turkish-cotton bathrobes. All rooms are also completely soundproof and have modem and fax lines.

The Turkistan Suite is probably the largest, with a two-story floor-to-ceiling bookcase, 12-ft-high windows overlooking the river below, and, behind the loft's bowfront balcony, an ornate king-size four-poster with an Egyptian-print canopy and painted valance. The Equestrian Suite (its walls are covered with horse stenciling) has an armoire fitted with a custom-made kitchenette, its own Jacuzzi, an enormous bathroom, and a remote-controlled gas fireplace. A smaller suite, the Saugatuck, offers expansive river views as well as French doors that separate the bedroom from the living area—perfect for entertaining. The Acorn Room is one of the smallest, but it's still larger than what you'd find in a typical first-rate hotel.

With its Corinthian columns and tasseled curtain swags, the Restaurant at National Hall, on the lushly decorated ground floor, is being renovated and will reopen in late 1998. ♣ *8 double rooms with baths, 7 suites. Restaurant; airconditioning, cable TV/VCR, phone, refrigerator in rooms; kitchenette, fireplace in 1 suite; 24-hr room service, meeting facilities. $195–$525; Continental breakfast. AE, DC, MC, V. No smoking.*

MAPLES INN 🐚
179 Oenoke Ridge, New Canaan 06840, tel. 203/966–2927, fax 203/966–5003

From its location on Oenoke Ridge, just a short drive from New Canaan's downtown, the vast, white-trimmed, yellow-clapboard Maples Inn reveals only a few of its 13 gables. Its many windows (too many to count) blink invitingly at night and have been welcoming guests since Cynthia T. Haas took over as owner in early 1982.

Cynthia, a longtime New Canaan resident, had always wanted to run an inn. When her chance came, she made sweeping changes, rearranging rooms, bathrooms, closets, even walls. Her efforts have created a subdued but elegant, warm, and romantic atmosphere.

Most of the guest rooms have canopied, four-poster, queen-size beds and numerous antiques from Cynthia's own collection. The presence of such modern equipment as phones and TVs is never intrusive. Mahogany chests, gilt frames, and brass lamps all gleam, and the imaginative use of light floral fabrics and paper fans is an education in design. The fully equipped four-bedroom cottage displays the same sensitivity to beauty and comfort.

You can help yourself to breakfast in the Mural Room, with its three chandeliers and walls painted with striking images of New Canaan during each season. French doors open onto a wicker-filled wraparound porch—an ideal dining spot in warm weather—that overlooks a deep lawn with venerable maples.

The small apartments and the cottage seem to encourage long-term stays by families, and youngsters, generally respectful of the premises, are made to feel at home in the friendly, informal atmosphere. The Maples Inn is that kind of place. ♣ *7 double rooms with baths, 4 suites, 10 apartments. Air-conditioning, cable TV, phone in rooms; mini-refrigerator in most rooms; fireplace in 2 apartments. $135–$250; Continental breakfast. AE, MC, V.*

SILVERMINE TAVERN ☙
194 Perry Ave., Norwalk 06850, tel. 203/847–4558, fax 203/847–9171

Silvermine is a pre-Revolutionary town that lies within the borders of Norwalk, New Canaan, and Wilton. The Tavern (part of which dates from 1642), the Country Store, the Coach House, and the Old Mill are all clustered at the intersection of Silvermine and Perry avenues in Norwalk, just north of the Merritt Parkway.

If he has a moment to spare in his busy schedule, innkeeper Frank Whitman Jr. can fill you in on local history. His family has been running things here since 1955, and he grew up within the solid post-and-beam walls of the Colonial building at the heart of the present-day Tavern. Frank's eyes never seem to rest because he never lets up on the high standards he sets for the food and accommodations.

Though best known for its romantic restaurant, which overlooks the Silvermine River and the millpond, the inn also has wonderful guest rooms in the main building and across the road above the Country Store. (Note to collectors: they carry Mary Hadley Pottery here.) The Tavern's common areas and multiple dining rooms have unusual displays of primitive paintings, store signs, prints, and Early American tools and utensils. The guest rooms, with their own complement of antique furnishings, have an equally pleasant atmosphere. The configuration of these rooms has evolved over the ages, and the odd shapes only add to the charm. Room T-8 is entered through the bathroom but is particularly cozy once you're inside. Three rooms have tubs but no showers because of the slanted ceilings. Wide-plank floors have hooked rugs to bridge the cracks of age, and starched white curtains grace the small, multipaned windows.

Be sure to eat at least one meal here (and try the Tavern's signature honey buns). Traditional New England favorites are given some new slants: The duckling is semiboneless and served with rhubarb and dried cherry chutney, and the preparation of the filet mignon and salmon change seasonally. Sunday brunch on the tree-shaded outdoor deck is a local tradition. The Whitmans have mapped out a 2-mi walking tour of Silvermine that's ideal for an after-dinner stroll. ♠ *10 double rooms with baths. Restaurant, air-conditioning. $99–$125; Continental breakfast. AE, DC, MC, V. Closed Tues.*

THREE CHIMNEYS INN ☙
1201 Chapel St., New Haven 06511, tel. 203/789–1201, fax 203/776–7363

Running along the New Haven Green and into the heart of the Yale University campus, Chapel Street seems an infinite stretch of shops, old hotels, bookstores, and restaurants until you come to a surprise: Behind a neatly kept garden stands a freshly painted green, white, and pink Victorian mansion, complete with gingerbread trim and a carpeted stairway flanked by potted geraniums. It's amazing that this 1870 structure never fell to the wrecker's ball as its neighbors undoubtedly did; it's equally mind-boggling that someone had the vision to restore it and convert it into a thriving, much-needed lodging in this vibrant college town.

When the owners took over this establishment, formerly the Inn at Chapel West, they were determined to create a small hotel of uncommon luxury that would be ideal both for couples seeking a romantic retreat and for businesspeople. They have succeeded. Each room has been completely renovated and has posh Georgian and Federal furnishings, grand mahogany four-poster beds, oversize armoires, Chippendale-style desks, and Asian rugs whose colors are reflected in the rich, warm tones of the decor. A basket of homemade cookies (chocolate chip, if you're lucky) and tea is the perfect welcoming touch.

The inn also offers complete conference facilities for groups of up to 30 (depending on the function), with catered meals—so a whiff of something appetizing wafting through its doors at mealtimes is to be expected. You can lounge in both the breakfast room and the library; each has double fireplaces. Sherry is best enjoyed in the library and the inn's full gourmet breakfast in the breakfast room.

The staff here is delighted to recommend restaurants in New Haven or make arrangements for theater tickets and a university tour. Such personal attention makes the inn an urban oasis. ⚜ *10 double rooms with baths. Air-conditioning, cable TV, phone in rooms, free parking. $160; full breakfast. AE, D, MC, V. No smoking.*

OTHER CHOICES

Harbor House Inn. 165 Shore Rd., Old Greenwich 06870, tel. 203/637–0145, fax 203/698–0943. 17 double rooms with baths, 6 doubles share 2 baths. Air-conditioning, TV/VCR, mini-refrigerator, coffeemaker, phone in rooms; laundry facilities, video library, bicycles. $99–$169; Continental breakfast. AE, DC, MC, V. No smoking.

Stanton House Inn. 76 Maple Ave., Greenwich 06830, tel. 203/869–2110, fax 203/629–2116. 19 double rooms with baths, 2 doubles share bath, 1 suite. Air-conditioning, cable TV, phone, hair dryer in rooms; wet bar in 7 rooms; small conference room, outdoor pool. $95–$175; Continental breakfast. AE, D, DC, MC, V. No smoking. 2-night minimum weekends.

RESERVATIONS SERVICES

Bed & Breakfast, Ltd. (Box 216, New Haven 06513, tel. 203/469–3260). **Covered Bridge Bed & Breakfast Reservation Service** (Box 447, Norfolk 06058, tel. 860/542–5944). **Nutmeg Bed & Breakfast Agency** (Box 1117, West Hartford 06127, tel. 860/236–6698 or 800/727–7592).

Litchfield County South and Ridgefield

BOULDERS INN ☙
E. Shore Rd. (Rte. 45), New Preston 06777, tel. 860/868–0541 or 800/552–6853, fax 860/868–1925

Built in 1895 as a private house, the stone and shingle Boulders inn, with its carriage house and four guest houses, sits on a gentle slope with panoramic views of Lake Waramaug. The innkeepers, Kees and Ulla Adema, came from Holland and Germany, respectively, in the '60s, and now that their children are grown and away at school, they're able to devote themselves exclusively to the running of the inn. A bit of European charm seems appropriate to this hillside retreat.

The guest rooms are a curious—though luxurious—mixture, with picture windows, Asian rugs, antique Victorian furniture and bric-a-brac, as well as reproduction and overstuffed pieces. The eight rooms in the guest houses up the hill have private decks and working fireplaces. The carriage house has three well-furnished rooms with private entrances and fireplaces.

In the main inn building, the sumptuous living room and adjoining TV library both overlook the lake and welcome you for relaxed reading, conversation with other guests, and spectacular sunsets. A recreation room in the basement has a pool table, an antique pinball machine, darts, and an assortment of games. Across the road the inn has a private stretch of waterfront suitable for swimming and a beach house with a hanging wicker swing for passing peaceful moments. The more adventurous may set forth in a canoe or a paddleboat, both provided free.

At dinner in the glass-enclosed Lake Room, you can choose from among several outstanding dishes, which may include roasted free-range chicken with tarragon, lemon essence, carrot chips, and vegetable fricassee or pan-seared Chilean sea bass with Swiss chard, leeks, diced potato, saffron, and aioli with red-wine fumet. The menu changes often, so be prepared for some imaginative specials.

Running the inn is a full-time job, but Kees and Ulla squeeze in time for their hobbies. He is an avid stamp collector who exhibits internationally, and Ulla's specialty can be seen in the meticulously cut lamp shades used throughout the inn. ▲ *15 double rooms with baths, 2 suites. Restaurant; air-conditioning, hair dryer in rooms; double Jacuzzi in 4 guest-house rooms; mini-refrigerator, coffeemaker in carriage house and guest houses; lake swimming, boating, tennis court; bicycles and helmets, hiking trail. $250–$300; full breakfast. AE, MC, V. No smoking. Children under 12 by special arrangement, 2-night minimum weekends.*

HOPKINS INN ☞
22 Hopkins Rd., New Preston 06777, tel. 860/868–7295, fax 860/868–7464

This grand, yellow and white, 1847 Victorian on a hill overlooking Lake Waramaug has grown from a 19th-century summer boardinghouse to a delightful 20th-century country inn. As you drive up the short street that leads to both the inn and the Hopkins Winery (this is possibly the only inn in Connecticut with vineyards and a winery at its doorstep), note the flag flying over the front entry; the countless mullioned windows flanked by shutters; and all the gables, awnings, roofs, and porches. But presiding serenely over everything, the present-day innkeepers Franz and Beth Schober are the picture of efficiency.

At the inn, where dining has become celebrated, Franz is usually found in the kitchen, whence come the Austrian and Swiss dishes that form the centerpiece of the menu. His insistence on fresh ingredients extends to the maintenance of a fish tank stocked with trout, and he is also responsible for the extensive selection of wine that is carefully stored in the inn's cellar.

Beth's touch is seen just about everywhere else. She was a university librarian before taking over the inn in 1977, and her organizational skills show up in its smooth operation.

Each guest room has a unique shape and decor, though Colonial-print wallpapers and fabrics and light florals are used extensively throughout. Furniture runs the gamut of country styles, with emphasis on crisp, ruffled bed linens; sturdy, comfortable brass beds; good chairs for reading; and a variety of antique decorative pieces scattered about. A two-bedroom apartment has been added in the annex.

You can relax by the fireplace in the cozy, Victorian-style living room on chilly days, or you can sit or dine under the shade of the trees and awnings on warmer ones. Anywhere you wander, it's hard to top the spectacular views of the lake below.

The Schobers have maintained the friendly, informal atmosphere that guests have relied on since the inn's inception. Glancing through the guest book, you'll discover many names reappearing year after year—one indication of their success. ▲ *8 double rooms with baths, 2 doubles share bath, 1 double with hall bath, 2 apartments. Restaurant; phone, cable TV in 1 apartment; private lake beach. $65–$140; breakfast extra. AE, MC, V. 2-night minimum weekends. Closed Jan.–late Mar.*

HOUSE ON THE HILL 🐚
92 Woodlawn Terr., Waterbury 06710, tel. 203/757–9901

"Rus en urbe" ("city and country") is owner-innkeeper Marianne Vandenburgh's motto for her House on the Hill. The Latin phrase is an apt description of this fanciful B&B, which is surrounded by lush gardens in Waterbury's historic Hillside neighborhood.

The three-story, 20-room Victorian has a glorious exterior color scheme of teal, sage green, red, and ivory. It was built in 1888 by the Camp family—brass barons of this industrial Brass City—and Marianne is its third owner. The curved central staircase, the hand-carved paneling and fireplace surrounds, the built-in cabinetry, the intricate moldings, and the wainscoting are testaments to all three owners' respect for craftsmanship. Today, as more than a century ago, the library—with its rich mahogany, its fireplace, and its cinnamon-colored walls—is a favorite gathering spot. In warm weather the hammock on the west porch is *the* place to lounge.

When Marianne isn't outside tending to her gardens, she's inside tending to your creature comforts. An ample supply of tea, coffee, and cocoa in each room and sherry in the library are among her considerate touches. She has infused welcoming comfort in the four guest suites, which are furnished with a carefully chosen mix of antiques and memorabilia. The suite in the turret at the tip-top of the house is a favorite. Its spacious bedroom and sitting room are separated by sliding pocket doors made of the same rich oak used for the moldings, the mantel, and the floor. The fern green walls pick up the colors of the stained-glass window over the fireplace, and light pours in through windows in the eastern, western, and southern walls.

Although Waterbury's attractions (a museum, a theater, a symphony, and a ballet) and the charms of Litchfield are nearby, guests are never in a hurry to rush out each morning. They prefer to linger in the antiques-filled kitchen watching Marianne do her stuff. Breakfast may consist of fluffy pancakes made with cornmeal ground at Marianne's parents' Ohio farm, lemon French toast, or green eggs (scrambled with cheese and fresh herbs) and ham. The food, like the rest of the inn, is memorable. ⚓ *4 suites. Air-conditioning in 1 suite; cable TV, phone in suites; VCR in 2 suites. $100–$150; full breakfast. No credit cards, no smoking, 2-night minimum weekends. Closed Dec. 15–Jan. 15.*

MAYFLOWER INN 🐚
118 Woodbury Rd. (Rte. 47), Washington 06793, tel. 860/868–9466, fax 860/868–1497

Oh, to live every day as they do at the Mayflower. This picture-perfect country inn—a three-story clapboard-and-shingle beauty—is in Washington, an ever-so-perfect country village perched atop a mound of old New England money. Perfection, however, comes with a price: Certain suites here will set you back $580 a night. Nevertheless, weekends have been booked solid since Adriana and Robert Mnuchin opened the inn in March 1992. On any given Saturday afternoon you'll find the parking lot bumper to bumper with limos and BMWs.

If you can stand that the Reynolds portrait in the parlor is a tad livelier than many of the guests (note that this is not a place for children), this opulent, if self-conscious, country inn is worth a splurge. The 28 impeccably groomed acres are replete with streams, stone walls, century-old rhododendrons, rare specimen trees, and hiking trails, not to mention a fitness center better suited to an NFL football team than a gaggle of bon vivants. And each of the 17 rooms and 8 suites, spread among the main inn, the Standish House, and the Speedwell, is decorated with fine 19th-century English and French antiques and four-poster canopy beds (with Frette linen sheets and lush feather beds); the walls are hung with noteworthy prints and paintings and papered in Regency stripes. Sherry is, of course, always waiting on the sideboard, and the colossal mahogany-wainscoted bathrooms are marble throughout, with brass and Limoges fittings and handmade Belgian tapestries set importantly upon the floors.

If all that doesn't entice you, the mouthwatering cuisine of renowned chef Thomas Moran probably will. Although the menu changes daily, you may be tempted by such an appetizer as smoked salmon with a potato, caper, and crème fraîche salad and such an entrée as roasted duck breast on a barley, wheat-berry, and vegetable risotto. If nothing else, come just to stare at this imposing compound. ⌂ *17 double rooms with baths, 8 suites. Restaurant; air-conditioning, cable TV, phone, minibar in rooms; fireplace in 14 rooms; massage, fitness center, yoga, game room, boutique, meeting rooms, tennis, pool. $260–$680; breakfast extra. AE, MC, V. No smoking, 2-night minimum weekends, 3-night minimum holiday weekends.*

OTHER CHOICES

Curtis House. 506 Main St. (Rte. 6), Woodbury 06798, tel. 203/263–2101. 12 doubles with bath, 6 doubles share bath. Restaurant; air-conditioning, cable TV in some rooms. $40–$123; Continental breakfast extra. D, MC, V. 2-night minimum weekends.

Elms Inn. 500 Main St., Ridgefield 06877, tel. and fax 203/438–2541. 815 double rooms with baths, 5 suites. Restaurant; air-conditioning, cable TV, phone in rooms. $120–$175; Continental breakfast. AE, DC, MC, V. No smoking.

Stonehenge. Box 667, Ridgefield 06877, tel. 203/438–6511, fax 203/438–2478. 12 double rooms with baths, 4 suites. Restaurant; room service, air-conditioning, cable TV, phone in rooms; mini-refrigerator in suites. $75–$200; Continental breakfast. AE, MC, V.

West Lane Inn. 22 West La., Ridgefield 06877, tel. 203/438–7323, fax 203/438–7325. 18 double rooms with baths. Air-conditioning, cable TV, phone, modem in rooms; kitchenette in some rooms; laundry and dry cleaning available, meeting room. $125–$165; Continental breakfast, full breakfast extra. AE, DC, MC, V. 2-night minimum holiday weekends.

RESERVATIONS SERVICES

Bed & Breakfast, Ltd. (Box 216, New Haven 06513, tel. 203/469–3260). **Covered Bridge Bed & Breakfast Reservation Service** (Box 447, Norfolk 06058, tel. 860/542–5944). **Nutmeg Bed & Breakfast Agency** (Box 1117, West Hartford 06127, tel. 860/236–6698 or 800/727–7592).

The Southeastern Coast

ANTIQUES & ACCOMMODATIONS ☜
32 Main St., North Stonington 06359, tel. 860/535–1736 or 800/554–7829, fax 860/535–2613

The British accent of this 1861 Victorian B&B in the center of North Stonington is no accident. Owner-managers Thomas and Ann Gray are avowed Anglophiles who travel twice yearly to England to buy things for the house. Their background as appraisers and liquidators of antiques has stood them in good stead; the place is teeming with them.

And here's good news for guests: Some of what you see is for sale. The Grays decided to combine their multiple interests by running a small, elegantly decorated hostelry that doubles as an antiques shop. Do you like that pair of Ponty Pool sconces with the unusual George III seals? That painted-pine 19th-century corner cupboard? How about the Massachusetts Sheraton four-poster in Timothy's Room? It could be yours . . . for a price.

The rooms are furnished, it should be noted, with *livable* antiques. In the ground-floor Jeni's Room there are a small library, a working fireplace, and an antique chandelier over the bed. The bridal suite is called Susan's Room after one of the first brides to nest here. All the rooms are filled with bright Victorian touches with fresh as well as dried flower arrangements and gently scented candles everywhere. A multicourse candlelight breakfast using sterling silver, crystal, and bone china is served to those who stay in the main-house guest rooms or the suites in the adjacent 1820 Colonial. Dishes might include crabmeat Benedict, a salmon and aquavit omelet, or cantaloupe and honeydew soup, all garnished with fresh flowers in season.

The front parlor is a pleasant place to relax and have tea; in warm weather, however, you might prefer the stone terrace out front, shaded by a flowering crabapple tree. You might also stroll through the fragrant English and herb gardens. As you amble in the early morning sun, you may savor the memory of breakfast, or let your thoughts drift to the turned-down bedclothes and the decanter of cream sherry awaiting you at the end of the day. △ *3 double rooms with baths, 2 suites. Air-conditioning, cable TV in rooms; canoes, bicycles, box lunches available. $169–$225; full breakfast. D, MC, V. No smoking.*

BEE & THISTLE INN 🦜
100 Old Lyme St., Old Lyme 06371, tel. 860/434–1667 or 800/622–4946, fax 860/434–3402

On a long, wide avenue in the Old Lyme historic district, behind a weathered stone wall, is a two-story 1756 Colonial house that has evolved gracefully into the Bee & Thistle Inn. Set on 5½ acres along the Lieutenant River, which joins the Connecticut to flow into Long Island Sound, the inn's broad lawns, towering trees, formal flower garden, and herbaceous borders will charm you.

In the 14 years since Penny and Bob Nelson left behind the corporate world and academia in New York, they have realized a family dream here. A complete turnaround in their lifestyle occurred when they decided to become innkeepers while their two children were in the last years of school. But so successful were they and such was the lure of this special place that both kids now work here: son Jeff (a former line chef at Boston's Ritz-Carlton) in the kitchen and daughter Lori out front greeting, seating, and helping guests settle in. (Given the inn's romantic appeal, however, it's best to leave *your* children at home.)

Restoration has taken priority over renovation—which they have done only when comfort was at stake—and the result is the re-creation of a Colonial ambience in the best sense. The rooms vary in size, but all are inviting, with fireplaces in the downstairs parlors and dining rooms and light and airy curtains at the multipaned guest-room windows. Almost all rooms have canopy or four-poster beds, with old quilts and afghans providing warmth when needed. Little touches change with the seasons—hanging on each door might be tiny ribboned straw hats or sprigs of evergreen or holly. No slave to Colonial New England style, Penny brings to the rooms touches of Williamsburg and even Victoriana, with such oddities as a wing chair our Puritan forebears surely wouldn't recognize.

Breakfast can be brought to your room before or after a morning soak in an herbal bath (scented soap provided). And downstairs you might encounter a harpist one evening or take high tea late some winter afternoon. In the restaurant a romantic atmosphere is created by working fireplaces and candlelight that, coupled with high-class cuisine, make for a memorable evening. △ *11 double rooms with baths, cottage. Restaurant; air-conditioning, phone in rooms; cable TV in cottage. $75–$210; breakfast extra. AE, D, DC, MC, V. No smoking. Closed 2 wks in Jan.*

STEAMBOAT INN ℣

73 Steamboat Wharf, Mystic 06355, tel. 860/536–8300, fax 860/536–9528

Location, location, location—it's hard to top that of this posh inn settled dockside just a foot from the Mystic River in the heart of downtown Mystic. Each of the rooms in the yellow clapboard built in the early 1800s is named after a famous Mystic ship from the long-ago-and-faraway days of schooners: *Annie Wilcox, Ariadne, Marie Gilbert, Early Dawn*—their photos can be seen around the inn. Furnished with fine antiques and reproductions, all but one of the spacious rooms have superb water views. Peek your head outside the second-story window of *Summer Girl,* and you have a fine view of not only the Mystic drawbridge but the *Argia* cruise ship docked beneath your window. *Harmony* has a king-size bed whose headboard is fashioned from antique church doors, a wet bar, and a *double* whirlpool tub. Before you head out for a busy day downtown, a spread of homemade muffins, fresh fruits, bagels, and granola is laid out for your pleasure in the crisp black-and-white-tiled common room. It is here, too, that you may partake of a touch of sherry late in the afternoon. △ *10 double rooms with baths. Air-conditioning, cable TV, phone, whirlpool bath in rooms; fireplace in 6 rooms; wet bar, mini-refrigerator in 4 rooms. $160–$275; Continental-plus breakfast. AE, D, MC, V. No smoking, 2-night minimum weekends.*

OTHER CHOICES

Captain Stannard House. 138 S. Main St., Westbrook 06498, tel. 860/399–4634. 6 double rooms with baths. Air-conditioning, common refrigerator, bicycles, croquet set. $95; full breakfast. MC, V. No smoking, 2-night minimum weekends. Closed Jan.–Mar.

Harbour Inne & Cottage. 15 Edgemont St., Mystic 06355, tel. 860/572–9253. 5 double rooms with baths, cottage. Air-conditioning, cable TV in rooms; gazebo by water, gas grill, picnic facilities. $95–$250; no breakfast. No credit cards. 2-night minimum weekends Memorial Day–late Oct.

Old Lyme Inn. Box 787, 85 Lyme St., Old Lyme 06371, tel. 860/434–2600, fax 860/434–5352. 5 double rooms with baths, 8 suites. Restaurant; air-conditioning, cable TV, phone in rooms; cable TV, working fireplace in library. $99–$150; Continental breakfast. AE, D, DC, MC, V.

Randall's Ordinary. Rte. 2, Box 243, North Stonington 06359, tel. 860/599–4540, fax 860/599–3308. 14 double rooms with baths, 1 suite. Air-conditioning, whirlpool bath in rooms; cable TV, phone in barn rooms. $95–$195; Continental breakfast. AE, MC, V. 2-night minimum holiday weekends.

Stonecroft. 515 Pumpkin Hill Rd., Ledyard 06339, tel. 860/572–0771, fax 860/572–9161. 4 double rooms with baths. Air-conditioning in rooms; bicycles, horseshoes, darts, massages on request. $130–$170; full breakfast. AE, MC, V. No smoking, 2-night minimum weekends.

Tidewater Inn. 949 Boston Post Rd., Madison 06443, tel. 203/245–8457, fax 203/318–0265. 9 double rooms with baths. Air-conditioning, cable TV, phone in rooms; TV/VCR in 3 rooms. $90–$160; full breakfast. AE, MC, V. No smoking. 2-night minimum weekends July–Aug. and holidays.

Connecticut River Valley

COPPER BEECH INN 🐚
46 Main St., Ivoryton 06442, tel. 860/767–0330, fax 860/767–7840

Picture a rambling Victorian country cottage—with a carriage barn and terraced gardens—set behind oak and beech trees on 7 acres near a river. You've just conjured up the Copper Beech Inn. Built in the 1880s as a residence for the ivory importer A. W. Comstock, the building is now a dining and lodging haven in the quintessential Connecticut River valley town of Ivoryton.

The current innkeepers, Eldon and Sally Senner, took over in 1988 and have made their mark. The four rooms in the main house have 19th-century artwork, antique furniture, and bric-a-brac that all contribute to the warm, traditional ambience. Spacious Room 1, which once belonged to the lady of the house, has two bay windows, a love seat, a chaise longue, and a king-size bed with a pale blue canopy.

The renovated carriage house has nine spacious guest rooms with cathedral ceilings and exposed beams. Although these rooms are essentially modern, the country theme of the main building is maintained in the furnishings, antique odds and ends, floral wall coverings, and botanical prints. The contemporary bathrooms here have large whirlpool tubs. With the combination of old and new, indoors and out, you truly feel as if you're in a country retreat.

At one time the ground floor of the main house was full of the endless reception rooms so beloved by the Victorians. The larger rooms have been converted to a series of dining areas that are elegant and romantic, particularly in the evening, when candlelight is reflected on sparkling crystal and gleaming silver. The hearty French country cuisine is complemented by a wine list with a stellar selection of French and American vintages. In 1993 a Victorian-style solarium was added to the main house—it's now the perfect spot to sip evening cocktails before the collection of neatly framed Audubon prints.

You won't find anything stressful here. The beautiful grounds, comfortable guest rooms, abundant lounge space, lack of young guests (children under 10 are best left home), and welcoming dining rooms may well make your quest for a quiet country inn end at the Copper Beech. **⌂** *13 double rooms with baths. Restaurant; air-conditioning, phone in rooms; cable TV, decks in carriage-house rooms. $105–$175; Continental breakfast buffet. AE, DC, MC, V. No smoking, 2-night minimum weekends.*

RIVERWIND 🐚
209 Main St., Deep River 06417, tel. 860/526–2014

As you approach busy downtown Deep River, you can't miss the rose-beige clapboard building with the ivory gingerbread trim. At the Riverwind, the innkeepers in residence, Barbara Barlow and Bob Bucknall, welcome you with a cup of something soothing. Barbara came north from Virginia, where she taught school for a number of years and fell in love with the Connecticut River valley. When she found this Victorian, fallen sadly into disrepair, her preservationist instincts sensed a challenge. The process involved Bob, a local builder, who saw a different challenge, which he met by wooing and winning her. Barbara, who's also a justice of the peace, has filled the house with dozens of romantic touches—it may be enough to inspire marriage or at least a renewal of vows.

New England charm and Southern hospitality make a stay here comfortable, indeed. Throughout the house you'll find countless carefully placed antiques and bibelots ("I have a collection of collections," says Barbara) and such thoughtful touches as a decanter of sherry (help yourself) in the parlor—one of eight inviting common rooms, four of which have fireplaces.

Each guest room has a theme, and all have antique furnishings, collectibles, and touches of stenciling. (Note that because of all the antiques, Riverwind is not suitable for children.) In one room you'll find a country pine bed and a painted headboard; in another there's a carved oak bed; and in still another, an 18th-century bird's-eye-maple four-poster with a canopy. The bathrooms have modern plumbing, but there's a beautiful Victorian claw-foot tub in the Barn Rose Room. In the spectacular Champagne and Roses Room, soft pinks, blues, and roses enhance a fabric-draped queen-size bed that's surrounded by a vanity desk, a carved armoire, and blush-color wing chairs. You might drink the champagne that comes with this room on its private balcony.

In the 18th-century-style keeping room that was added onto the original building just a few years ago, there's a huge stone cooking fireplace, where hot cider and rum are mulled all winter. Close by, Barbara serves a hearty country breakfast, featuring Smithfield ham, her own baked goods, and several casseroles. Freshly brewed tea and coffee and homemade cookies are always on hand, and in the front parlor a piano is ready for those inclined to play. Such touches lift Riverwind into the realm of the extraordinary. ⚙ *7 double rooms with baths (1 is hall bath), 1 suite. Air-conditioning and terry cloth robes in rooms. $105–$175; full breakfast. MC, V. 2-night minimum weekends Apr. 15–Jan. 2.*

SIMSBURY 1820 HOUSE 🐚

731 Hopmeadow St., Simsbury 06070, tel. 860/658–7658 or 800/879–1820, fax 860/651–0724

Perched on a hillside above the main road through Simsbury is a classic country inn—a two-story brick mansion built in 1820, with an 1890 addition on its west side. The property had ended up in the hands of the town, which didn't know what to do with it. In 1985 it was turned over to Simsbury House Associates, which rescued it from decay, restored it, and began to operate it as a country inn and restaurant.

In just a few years, the associates wrought a remarkable, wonderful change. The Brighenti family, which purchased the inn in 1997 and which owns three other area lodgings, is working hard to continue the associates' tradition of excellence. The restaurant has won praise from leading food critics; the romantic candlelight setting elicits almost as much applause as the victuals.

Guest rooms have a judicious mix of antiques and modern furnishings. Each of the 18 rooms and 2 junior suites in the main house has its special feature—a decorative fireplace or balcony, a patio, a wet bar, a dormer with a cozy window seat. The complementary use of rich colors—maroon, yellow, blue, green, and pink—and patterns creates a restful atmosphere.

Under the porte cochere and across the parking lot is the old carriage house, which now houses 11 rooms and the split-level Executive Suite, with its private patio and entrance and its Jacuzzi. The formal taupe and green decor of the rooms here is offset by touches of whimsy, including well-chosen horse prints on some bedcoverings and curtains. Most rooms have imported English four-poster beds, but in one, old barn doors are used as a combination room divider and king-size headboard. It works. *△ 29 double rooms with baths, 3 suites. Restaurant; air-conditioning, cable TV, phone in rooms. $119–$179; Continental breakfast. AE, D, DC, MC, V. Pets allowed in 1 room of carriage house.*

OTHER CHOICES

Barney House. 11 Mountain Spring Rd., Farmington 06032, tel. 860/674–2796, fax 860/677–7259. 7 double rooms with baths. Air-conditioning, cable TV, phone in rooms; meeting rooms; tennis court. $89; Continental breakfast. AE, MC, V. No smoking.

Chimney Crest Manor. 5 Founders Dr., Bristol 06010, tel. 860/582–4219, fax 860/584–5903. 2 double rooms with baths, 4 suites. Air-conditioning, cable TV, terry cloth robes, homemade cookies, fresh fruit, coffee/tea in rooms; turn-down service; hot-air ballooning. $80–$165; full breakfast. MC, V. No smoking, 2-night minimum Sept. 15–late Oct.

Griswold Inn. 36 Main St., Essex 06426, tel. 860/767–1776, fax 860/767–0481. 18 double rooms with baths, 12 suites. Restaurant. $90–$185; Continental breakfast. AE, MC, V. No smoking.

RESERVATIONS SERVICES

Bed & Breakfast, Ltd. (Box 216, New Haven 06513, tel. 203/469–3260). **Covered Bridge Bed & Breakfast Reservation Service** (Box 447, Norfolk 06058, tel. 860/542–5944). **Nutmeg Bed & Breakfast Agency** (Box 1117, West Hartford 06127, tel. 860/236–6698 or 800/727–7592).

The Northwest Corner

MANOR HOUSE ☞

69 Maple Ave., Norfolk 06058, tel. and fax 860/542–5690

A pleasant stroll up a side street off Norfolk's village green will bring you to a Bavarian Tudor residence that has been turned into a thriving B&B. After several years of working in Hartford's hectic insurance industry, owner-managers Diane and Henry Tremblay (who also own Covered Bridge Reservation Service) were both ready for a career change when they discovered an unusual house for sale. Designed and built in 1898 by Charles Spofford, the architect of London's subway system, the house has 20 stained-glass windows designed and given by Louis Tiffany, a full Victorian complement of reception rooms, and extensive bedrooms.

The Tremblays took over in 1985 and have gradually refurnished the inn and restored the Victorian atmosphere with a light touch. Henry devotes himself to the surrounding 5 acres of gardens, with beehives and a raspberry patch, whose yields find their way to the breakfast table.

The bedrooms are all furnished with antique and reproduction beds, Louis Nicole wallpapers, well-chosen bibelots, prints, ancestral photographs, mirrors, and carpets. In winter flannel sheets and down comforters add to the warmth. The vast Spofford Room has windows on three sides, a king-size canopy bed with a cheery fireplace opposite, and a balcony. The intimate Lincoln Room has an antique

French queen bed, a white fainting couch, and a working fireplace—along with the best view of the neighboring landscape. But the Balcony Room has the most remarkable feature—a private, operational, wood-paneled elevator (added in 1939). It also has a private deck.

In the roomy living room, with its mammoth raised fireplace, music lovers who have come to Norfolk for the annual Chamber Music Festival (within easy walking distance) may choose from the large collection of compact discs. You may tickle the keys of the grand piano or, if you're in a quiet mood, seek the seclusion of the library and choose from its numerous volumes. (Note that this inn is not suitable for preteens.) ▲ *8 double rooms with baths, 1 2-bedroom suite. Fireplace in 3 rooms, Jacuzzi in 4 rooms, cable TV, house phone in common area. $115–$225; full breakfast. AE, MC, V. No smoking, 2-night minimum weekends, 3-night minimum holidays.*

UNDER MOUNTAIN INN ☞

482 Undermountain Rd., Salisbury 06068, tel. 860/435–0242, fax 860/435–2379

Driving north on Route 41 from Salisbury's Main Street, you cut through sweeping fields where horses graze and silos rise in the distance. After about 4 mi, a stone's throw from the Massachusetts border, stands the Under Mountain Inn— a white clapboard farmhouse built in the early 1700s.

The owners, Marged and Peter Higginson, bill themselves as innkeepers and chefs, since the inn is also a popular restaurant. Their personal stamp—a part of which is defined by Peter's British origins—is found all over, from the decor of the intimate dining rooms (each with a working fireplace) to the VCR and extensive collection of British videos in Arabella's Lounge (named after Marged's grandmother and adorned with her prized antique china). In the back of the house is the pub, a faithful replica of a typical English taproom, whose paneling was found, during a restoration, beneath the attic floorboards. Since Colonial law awarded such choice lumber to the king of England, Peter reclaimed it in the name of the Crown.

Upstairs, the rooms are furnished in English country style. All have spectacular mountain views. Room names recall favorite London haunts: The spacious Downing Street has a queen-size bed; Buckingham Gate has one fit for a king; Drury Lane has a private entrance and a romantic canopy bed hung with mosquito netting. A decanter of sherry is found in each room, and Marged serves English tea and shortbread daily at 4 PM. With such pristine surroundings, parents traveling with young children should think twice about staying here.

Three surrounding acres boast birch, fir, maples, and a thorned locust tree, which is rumored to be the state's oldest. Across the road is Fisher Pond; you can use the 2-mi path around the pond for a bracing stroll—the form of exercise favored by the English.

For dinner, which along with a full breakfast is included in the cost, Peter prepares such specialties as steak-and-kidney pie, roast goose, or bangers and mash (sausage and mashed potatoes to the uninitiated). Save room for the English trifle—dessert par excellence. ▲ *7 double rooms with baths. Restaurant, air-conditioning in rooms. $170–$195; MAP, 7% service charge. MC, V. No smoking, 2-night minimum weekends.*

WHITE HART ☞

The Village Green, Box 545, Salisbury 06068, tel. 860/435–0030, fax 860/435–0040

With its fresh coat of white paint and its broad front porch, the White Hart really stands out on Salisbury's village green. This venerable country inn, which has welcomed travelers since the 1860s, fell on hard times in the 1980s. Before reopening in February 1990 owner-manager Juliet Moore renovated the place—inside and out. Her efforts show a respect for tradition and an appreciation of fine contemporary materials.

The green and rose carpeting in the lobby continues along the upstairs hallways, which also have champagne-striped wallpaper and white woodwork. Guest rooms and suites have excellent Colonial-reproduction furniture, good reading lamps, and modern bathrooms. Upholstery, bedspreads, and curtains are done in contrasting colors and patterns—a lively stripe here, a floral splash there, and maybe a colorful ribbon to tie it all together. Instead of tearing down walls to eliminate quirky room configurations, the quirks have been accommodated with pleasing results. Several rooms on the east side have private entrances, and a few steps away in the 1815 Gideon Smith House, similar rooms and suites are available on two levels.

In winter guests gather in the snug Hunt Room, with its wood paneling, roaring fireplace, and gleaming hardwood floors. In warmer weather the front porch, with its pink and white wicker love seats, colorful chintz, and trailing morning glory vines, is unbeatable. Dining in any of the White Hart's three restaurants—the bright and sunny Garden Room with its wall of French doors, the tavern-like Tap Room, or the elegant American Grill—is a pleasure. ♙ *23 double rooms with bath (1 is hall bath), 3 suites. 3 restaurants; air-conditioning, cable TV, phone in rooms; meeting rooms. $115–$195; breakfast extra. AE, DC, MC, V. 2-night minimum weekends Apr. 12–Nov. 14, 3-night minimum holiday weekends.*

OTHER CHOICES

Country Goose. Kent-Cornwall Rd. (Rte. 7), Kent 06757, tel. 860/927–4746. 3 double rooms and 1 single share 2 baths. Hiking (Appalachian Trail) nearby. $90; Continental breakfast. No credit cards. No smoking, 2-night minimum weekends. Closed Mar.–Apr. 10.

Greenwoods Gate. 105 Greenwoods Rd. E (Rte. 44), Norfolk 06058, tel. 860/542–5439, fax 860/542–5897. 3 suites, 1 2-bedroom suite. Air-conditioning in rooms, whirlpool spa in 1 suite, cable TV/VCR in common room. $175–$245; full breakfast. No credit cards. No smoking, 2-night minimum weekends.

Old Riverton Inn. Rte. 20, Riverton 06065, tel. 860/379–8678 or 800/378–1796, fax 860/379–1006. 11 double rooms with baths, 1 suite. Restaurant; air-conditioning, cable TV in rooms; tubing, fishing, swimming nearby. $85–$175; full breakfast. AE, D, DC, MC, V. Pets allowed with prior approval, 2-night minimum holiday weekends.

Tollgate Hill Inn & Restaurant. Rte. 202 (Tollgate Hill Rd.), Litchfield 06759, tel. 860/567–4545 or 800/445–3903, fax 860/567–8397. 15 double rooms with baths, 5 suites. Restaurant; air-conditioning, cable TV, phone in rooms; bar, mini-refrigerator, TV/VCR in suites. $110–$175; Continental breakfast. AE, D, DC, MC, V. 2-night minimum weekends.

RESERVATIONS SERVICES

Bed & Breakfast, Ltd. (Box 216, New Haven 06513, tel. 203/469–3260). **Covered Bridge Bed & Breakfast Reservation Service** (Box 447, Norfolk 06058, tel. 860/542–5944). **Nutmeg Bed & Breakfast Agency** (Box 1117, West Hartford 06127, tel. 860/236–6698 or 800/727–7592).

DELAWARE

Wilmington and Northern Delaware

WILLIAM PENN GUEST HOUSE 🐚
206 Delaware St., New Castle 19720, tel. 302/328–7736

A historic marker stands on the streets of New Castle, a block from the banks of the Delaware River: "Near here October 27, 1682, William Penn first stepped on American soil. . . ." In the same year that Penn strode onto the shores of the New World, and on the same streets that he first trod, the William Penn Guest House appeared on the map, though perhaps not with quite the same historic significance. But Penn knew a good thing when he saw it; ask Irma Burwell, who runs the place now, and she will tell you how the founder of Pennsylvania would sometimes bed down here.

Irma will also tell you what she and her husband, Dick, charged when they started their bed-and-breakfast operation in 1956: $8 a night. Rates are still surprisingly reasonable, and they're not likely to rise in the near future, since the hosts like the sensibilities and spending habits of their longtime clientele (repeat visitors account for two-thirds of their business). The Burwells welcome an international set of diverse ages and tastes—senior ambassadors who snooze and dewy-cheeked naturalists who cycle—all of whom appreciate a quiet, civilized atmosphere that doesn't cost them an unearthly sum.

The William Penn is a handsomely restored, impressively maintained Colonial structure that is modest in its air and amenities. Soft, wide-board Delaware-pine floors, a claw-foot tub, and an 18th-century chandelier in the dining room take guests back to an earlier era. The bedrooms—one with king-size bed, another with one set of twins, and two with doubles—are carpeted blandly and furnished with pine antiques. If air-conditioning turns you off, there are ceiling fans to keep both second-floor units cool and ventilated in the summer.

You'll find the William Penn a perfect jumping-off point for touring Longwood Gardens, the Brandywine River Museum, Winterthur, the Hagley Museum, and Nemours Mansion. Cyclists in particular will delight in the area: The house borders Battery Park, which runs right along the river and has a 2-mi biking path and promenade, as well as benches, picnic tables, tennis courts, and play areas for children. **⚲** *4 double rooms with 2 baths (can be shared or private). Air-conditioning, TV in 3 rooms. $60–$85; Continental breakfast. No credit cards. No smoking indoors.*

OTHER CHOICES

Boulevard Bed & Breakfast. 1909 Baynard Blvd., Wilmington 19802, tel. 302/656–9700, fax 302/656–9701. 3 double rooms with baths, 1 double and 1 single share bath, 1 suite. Air-conditioning, cable TV, phone in rooms, fireplace in library and parlor, whirlpool in suite, off-street parking. $60–$80; full breakfast. AE, MC, V. No smoking indoors.

Cantwell House. 107 High St., Odessa 19730, tel. 302/378–4179. 2 double rooms share bath, 1 suite. Air-conditioning in suite and 2nd-floor canopy bedroom, TV in suite, fireplace in one bedroom and in living room, dining room, and kitchen. $60–$85 (inquire about rates for the cottage); Continental-plus breakfast. No credit cards. No smoking.

RESERVATIONS SERVICE

Bed & Breakfast of Delaware (2701 Landon Dr., Suite 200, Wilmington 19810, tel. 302/479–9500).

The Beaches

ELI'S COUNTRY INN 🐦

Rte. 36 Greenwood–Milford Rd., Greenwood 19950-0779, tel. 302/349–4265 or 800/594–0048, fax 302/349–9340

The seven Shrock sisters grew up on a 160-acre family farm midway between (and a half hour from) Dover and Delaware's Atlantic beaches in the Mennonite community of Greenwood. In 1992 they converted the family farmhouse into Eli's, an eight-bedroom B&B, and began farming 70 acres, planting hay meadows and corn and soybean fields. Although you're just 8 mi from the wealthy town of Milford, you can "hear the quiet" while relaxing on the house's large wraparound front porch, while strolling the nature paths that surround the property, or while watching the sunsets from the garden.

The sisters can provide a country dinner (by reservation) in the informal dining room. Ask about a hot-air balloon flight after breakfast with a launch from the front lawn.

Eli's is a good place for children, because the large lawn is well suited for badminton, volleyball, and horseshoes. The inn is also one of three stops packaged in the Biking Inn to Inn Delaware (tel. 800/845–9939) program. ⏃ *8 double rooms with baths. Air-conditioning, TV room. $65–$75; Continental breakfast. D, MC, V. No smoking.*

INN AT CANAL SQUARE 🐦

122 Market St., Lewes 19958, tel. 302/645–8499 or 800/222–7902, fax 302/645–7083

This decidedly upscale inn is a relatively new addition to the lodging scene in Lewes, a small, historic town that serves as both a gateway to the Atlantic beaches and a peaceful retreat for travelers along the Atlantic seaboard. This inn is special because of its waterfront location and unusual accommodation choices. Aside from 19 conventional rooms in the main building, travelers here can also opt for the *Legend of Lewes,* a houseboat with modern galley, two bedrooms, and two baths that floats peacefully at dockside (this arrangement is not recommended for families with children under 14). The inn is conveniently situated in a meandering complex of shops and a restaurant. Design purists may protest the stylistic mélange;

the exterior of the inn looks like a developer's reproduction of a Nantucket village, yet the decor in the lobby resembles the interior of a typical Malibu hideaway.

In the four-story main building, the rooms are large and furnished with Federal reproductions. The honeymoon suite (Room 305) has Palladian windows and a private balcony. It is not terribly spacious, but it's cozy, enjoys the best view in the inn, and has a queen-size bed. King-size-bed advocates have their pick of three rooms on the top floor.

The simple Continental breakfast can be eaten downstairs or taken back to the bedrooms on trays. Innkeeper Lonnie Brown recommends Gilligan's, the restaurant next door, open daily in season, from 11 AM to 1 AM, or the Buttery.

Besides Lewes's Zwaanendael Museum and historic district, there are the beaches of Cape Henlopen State Park to keep you occupied; or you can try your hand at hooking a shark from a chartered fishing boat. If you're a shopper, you'll enjoy the no-sales-tax outlet stores. △ *17 double rooms with baths, 2 suites, 1 houseboat. Air-conditioning, cable TV and phone in rooms, conference room. $145–$165; Continental breakfast; houseboat $225 ($1,300 a wk). AE, D, DC, MC, V. 2-day minimum. Closed Oct.–May.*

NEW DEVON INN ☞

142 2nd St., Lewes 19958, tel. 302/645–6466 or 800/824–8754, fax 302/645–7196

This hotel, with its striped awnings and lobby-level stores, opened in 1989 in the heart of Lewes's historic district. It has fine views of St. Peter's Episcopal Church and historic cemetery. Built in 1926, it received a complete makeover beginning in 1986 at the hands of its owners, Dale Jenkins and Bernard Nash. Little remains of its past except the lustrous heart-pine floors.

The guest rooms are furnished with antiques, Oriental carpets, and beds swaddled in designer linens. They are relatively small but warmly appointed, immaculately clean, and quite comfortable. The corner rooms (108, for example) are the ones most requested. Room 101, with a double bed, receives buckets of early morning sunlight. There is turndown service, candy, and cordials in the rooms, and morning coffee served in delicate antique cups. Silver service, crystal, and china make the Continental breakfast special. The Buttery, a top regional restaurant, is also on the premises.

Of late the New Devon Inn has become known as a politician's hideout—Senators Simon and Biden have both stayed here to escape media frenzy—and business travelers can rely on a highly professional staff. △ *22 double rooms with baths, 2 single rooms with baths, 2 suites. Air-conditioning, phone in rooms. $85–$170; Continental breakfast. AE, D, MC, V.*

SPRING GARDEN BED & BREAKFAST INN ☞

R.D. 5, Box 283A, Delaware Ave. Extended, Laurel 19956, tel. 302/875–7015

This inn reveals its character slowly and subtly. It's an abundantly lived-in place that is deeply appreciated by its owner, Gwen North. She was raised by her parents in this half-Colonial, half-Victorian farmhouse on the outskirts of Laurel before she flew the coop for New York. During that absence she came to realize that her heart lay back at home. Says Gwen, "When you stay in the same place all your life, you stop seeing what's there."

What's here is a red-shutter country house that stands beside a creek lined with daylilies in spring. As pleasant as its exterior is, the inside is even better. The Colonial section, built between 1760 and 1780 by a Captain Lewis of Bethel, remained in the Lewis family for 100 years. Its front parlor and back kitchen have wood-plank floors and the snug, slightly off-kilter feeling of a boat. Breakfast, highlighted by Scotch eggs and homegrown fruit, is served beside a woodburning stove.

A steep, narrow staircase takes guests to the inn's two Colonial rooms; the one called Naomi (for Gwen's mother) has a fireplace, a lace-canopy double bed, and a walnut rocker. Three bedrooms in the Victorian section, added in the late 1800s, have views of the garden and are filled with a soothing collection of antique furnishings, including a Victorian spool bed and Belgian cathedral chairs.

The Atlantic beaches are about 20 mi from the inn, but Gwen is quick to point out the other diversions to be found in this landlocked region of Delaware, such as canoeing and fishing at Trap Pond State Park and exploring the historic districts of Bethel and Laurel. An antiques dealer, Gwen sells collected pieces in a barn next to the inn.

Tops among the activities here is bicycling, a pastime Gwen has encouraged by organizing the Biking Inn to Inn Delaware program (tel. 800/845–9939), a three-day tour that includes stays at Spring Garden, the New Devon Inn, and Eli's Country Inn. The route takes bikers along the flat back roads of the Eastern Shore and offers opportunities for crabbing, bird-watching, and swimming. △ *4 double rooms with baths, 2 doubles share bath. Air-conditioning, TV in sitting room, 3 fireplaces. $65–$85; full breakfast. No credit cards. Smoking in designated areas.*

THE TOWERS ☜
101 N.W. Front St., Milford 19963, tel. 302/422–3814; 800/366–3814 outside DE

Edgar Allan Poe's friend and fellow poet John Lofland lived at the Towers, which was once the Milford home of Lofland's stepfather, Dr. John Wallace. Lofland was an opium addict and Poe an alcoholic, but in their wildest hallucinations neither could have dreamed up a house like the Towers, a Steamboat Gothic palace adorned with 10 varieties of gingerbread painted in 12 colors. Here flamboyant Victoriana radiates from the cherry, mahogany, and walnut finishings. Inside, the music room has a coffered sycamore ceiling and an 1899 Knabe grand piano. You're likely to find a record—perhaps Gene Autry's rendition of "Rudolph the Red-Nosed Reindeer"—spinning on the Victrola. The parlor is decorated with French antiques, and the dining room provides views of the gazebo, pool deck, and garden in back.

The warm but unobtrusive custodians of this 200-year-old marvel (it's on the National Register of Historic Places) are Rhonda and Daniel Bond, who bought it in January 1992 and now live on the premises in the old servants' quarters. They couldn't resist the ubiquitous stained glass, the carved garlands on the fireplaces, and the gold leaf peeking from behind the plywood walls. Rhonda can tell you about the Italian architect commissioned in the 1890s to transform the structure into the Victorian extravaganza you see today; it is said that between $30,000 and $40,000 was spent on that renovation.

The Tower room on the second floor is a favorite, with a turret niche and lots of rosy stained glass. The third floor's two suites are a bit more modern in character but still whimsically wonderful. All four doubles have their own bathrooms, but guests occupying the second-floor rooms must walk through a common area to enter theirs, and the third-floor facilities have showers only.

Rhonda fortifies her guests for a day of exploring or antiquing with a full breakfast—often ricotta pancakes, served with fresh fruit or raspberry purée and ham. The inn is across the street from one of Delaware's premier eating establishments, the Banking House, which is also an 18th-century-inspired bed-and-breakfast. Dinner at the Banking House and a stay at the Towers is a perfect combination.

△ 4 double rooms with baths. Air-conditioning, gas-log fireplace in music room and dining room, pool. $95–$125; full breakfast. AE, MC, V. No smoking.

WILD SWAN INN ☙
525 Kings Hwy., Lewes 19958, tel. and fax 302/645–8550

There's a pink Victorian house across from the library in Lewes where you can be serenaded with music from a 1912 player piano, an original 1908 Edison phonograph, or a mahogany pre–World War I Victrola. The 1900s house was built and originally occupied by Capt. Arthur Hudson, who ran the Fenwick Island Lightship. Inside the classic Queen Anne Victorian-style home are high ceilings, delicately carved scrollwork, lavish wallpaper, antique furnishings, lots of eclectic collectibles, and typical Victorian detail in pattern and color.

During their six years as innkeepers, Hope and Mike Tyler have attracted lots of media attention: his asparagus pie won a national cooking contest, and the recipe for their signature honey-banana-raisin bread has appeared in more than one cookbook. Guests are treated to even more than that: a deliciously memorable breakfast in the dining room under brass "gasolier" chandeliers. At the end of a busy day you may look forward to a cool glass of sun tea or a cordial on the porch gazebo or in the privacy of the poolside patio garden. There's plenty of fine, fun dining in Lewes, just a walk away. When you return to your room at night, you'll find it's been freshened and a plate of cookies will be waiting at your bedside.

△ 3 rooms with baths. Air-conditioning, bikes, gazebo, pool. $85–$135; full breakfast. No credit cards. No smoking, 2-night minimum weekends and July–Aug.

OTHER CHOICES

Pleasant Inn. 31 Olive Ave., Rehoboth Beach 19971, tel. 302/227–7311. 10 double rooms with baths, 2 1-bedroom apartments, 1-bedroom carriage house. Air-conditioning, limited off-street parking. $95–$150; no breakfast. No smoking, 3-day minimum holidays.

RESERVATIONS SERVICE

Bed & Breakfast of Delaware (2701 Landon Dr., Suite 200, Wilmington 19810, tel. 302/479–9500).

FLORIDA

St. Augustine

CASABLANCA INN

24 Avenida Menendez, St. Augustine 32084, tel. 904/829–0928 or 800/826–2626, fax 904/826–1892

Overlooking scenic Matanzas Bay, the Casablanca Inn is a charming base from which to explore the nooks and crannies of America's oldest city. Like nearly every other structure in St. Augustine, the Casablanca has stories to tell. Built in 1914 in the Mediterranean Revival style favored by architects of that era, the Casablanca was originally a residence hotel called the Matanzas. During Prohibition, the building's ideal location inspired rum-runners to use it as a signal house for contraband cargo. Eventually the building fell onto hard times, and then it remained unoccupied for decades.

Today, the only interior remnant of its colorful history is the word MATANZAS spelled out in the pale-green-and-white entryway tiles, which were an inspiration for the celery-color, deep-pile carpet covering the floors and stairway. Rooms are gracefully furnished with antiques and reproductions. The Casablanca's Celebration Suite, with its private sundeck and double hammock overlooking Matanzas Bay, is a loafer's delight. An oversize whirlpool (terry cloth robes are thoughtfully provided) will sooth tired muscles.

Innkeepers Anthony and Brenda Bushell serve the morning meal in either the sunny breakfast room or on the stately grand porch, a soothing spot to sip your coffee. At any time of the day, you can relax in one of the rocking chairs and drink in the sweeping view of the bay. Cooled by slowly rotating ceiling fans and ocean breezes, you'll enjoy watching the boats and tourists pass by. *△ 18 suites; 2 rooms accessible for people who use wheelchairs and equipped for people who are hearing-impaired. Air-conditioning, whirlpool bath in 7 rooms, bicycles available. $89–$199; full breakfast, champagne and chocolates for weekend and holiday arrivals, beverages. AE, D, MC, V.*

OTHER CHOICES

Carriage Way. 70 Cuna St., St. Augustine 32084, tel. 904/829–2467 or 800/908–9832, fax 904/826–1461. 9 double rooms with baths. Air-conditioning, fireplace in 1 room, cable TV in parlor. $69–$125; full breakfast, afternoon desserts. AE, D, MC, V.
Casa de la Paz. 22 Avenida Menendez, St. Augustine 32084, tel. 904/829–2915 or 800/929–2915, fax 904/824–6269. 4 double rooms with baths, 2 suites. Air-conditioning, cable TV, fireplace in 1 room. $95–$195; full breakfast; D, MC, V.
Kenwood Inn. 38 Marine St., St. Augustine 32084, tel. 904/824–2116, fax 904/824–1689. 10 double rooms with baths, 4 suites. Air-conditioning, cable

TV in some rooms, pool. $85–135; Continental breakfast, afternoon cookies and beverages. D, MC, V.

Old Powder House Inn. 38 Cordova St., St. Augustine 32084, tel. 904/824–4149 or 800/447–4149, fax 904/825–0143. 8 double rooms with baths, 1 suite. Air-conditioning, whirlpool bath in 1 suite, outdoor whirlpool bath. $79–$169; full breakfast, afternoon tea, evening wine and hors d'oeuvres. D, MC, V.

Secret Garden Inn. 56½ Charlotte St., St. Augustine 32084, tel. 904/829–3678. 3 suites. Air-conditioning, cable TV, coffeemakers, kitchenette in suites. $89–$109; Continental breakfast. MC, V.

Southern Wind. 18 Cordova St., St. Augustine 32084, tel. 904/825–3623, fax 904/825–0360. 9 double rooms with baths, 1 suite. Air-conditioning, cable TV, whirlpool bath in 4 rooms. $75–$135; full breakfast. AE, D, MC, V.

Amelia Island
❖❖❖

HOYT HOUSE ❦
804 Atlantic Ave., Amelia Island 32034, tel. 904/277–4300 or 800/432–2085, fax 904/277–9626

Once inside Hoyt House, a 1905 Queen Anne residence, you'll find it hard to leave, despite its central location between the town of Fernandina Beach and the beaches of Amelia Island. Innkeepers John and Rita Kovatchavitch have re-created a gracious, turn-of-the-century Victorian home, successfully mixing fine period furniture with kitschy, one-of-a-kind accent pieces, such as the 5-ft-tall ceramic giraffe from Key West that stands guard near an emerald-green tile fireplace in one of three sitting rooms. An enormous wraparound porch, complete with wicker porch swing and rocking chairs, encourages relaxation. The formal parlor, decorated mostly in soft pinks, houses many of Rita's Lladro figurines and bone-china collectibles. Breakfast is served in the formal dining room, which has warm purple walls, an elegant crystal chandelier, and many fine antiques.

Each of the nine guest rooms is tastefully appointed and individually decorated, with an eye to comfort as well as style. In a pale lavender room, for example, silver-framed photographs of a World War II–era couple rest on an étagère. While most rooms have a decidedly Victorian bent, one has a thoroughly modern flair, including an overstuffed black leather chair and a Tizio lamp. John and Rita named each room after the color of its walls: Blueberry, Sweet Lavender, Fire Coral, and Sea Foam Green, among others.

While the upstairs rooms invite guests to linger, patrons find themselves sooner or later in the Kovatchavitch's sleek, modern kitchen. It's here that Rita prepares not only the daily breakfast but an assortment of cookies and other goodies that brings guests downstairs like a magnet. "It's just like our house back in Connecticut," John says. "Everyone used to congregate in the kitchen to watch Rita bake." ♦ *9 double rooms with baths (4 wheelchair accessible). Air-conditioning, cable TV in rooms. $104–$144; full breakfast, afternoon cookies and beverages. AE, D, MC, V.*

OTHER CHOICES

Elizabeth Pointe Lodge. 98 S. Fletcher Ave. (S.R. A1A), Amelia Island 32034, tel. 904/277–4851 or 800/772–3359, fax 904/277–6500. 24 double rooms with baths (1 wheelchair accessible), 1 suite. Air-conditioning, cable TV, FM radios, mini-refrigerator and microwave in 2 rooms, whirlpool bath in 11 rooms. $115–$225; full breakfast, evening wine and hors d'oeuvres. AE, D, MC, V.

Florida House Inn. 20–22 S. 3rd St., Amelia Island 32034, tel. 904/261–3300 or 800/258–3301, fax 904/277–3831. 15 double rooms with baths, 1 suite. Air-conditioning, cable TV, fireplace in 10 rooms, whirlpool bath in 6 rooms, restaurant, pub. $70–$145; full breakfast. AE, MC, V.

1735 House. 584 S. Fletcher Ave. (S.R. A1A), Amelia Island 32034, tel. 904/261–4148 or 800/872–8531, fax 904/261–9200. 5 suites. Air-conditioning, cable TV/VCR, mini-refrigerators, coffeemakers, microwaves. $100–$160; Continental breakfast. AE, D, MC, V.

Williams House. 103 S. 9th St., Amelia Island 32034, tel. 904/277–2328 or 800/414–9257, fax 904/321–1325. 6 rooms, 2 suites. Air-conditioning, cable TV/VCR, paddle fans, fireplace in 5 rooms. $135–$200; full breakfast, private catered dinners by prior arrangement. MC, V.

Northwest Florida and the Panhandle

JOSEPHINE'S FRENCH COUNTRY INN ☞
101 Seaside Ave., Seaside 32459, tel. 850/231–1940 or 800/848–1840, fax 850/231–2446

With six stately columns supporting the front of its whitewashed facade, Josephine's has the air of a gracious antebellum plantation. Its location in the heart of Seaside—the carefully planned, award-winning, architectural gem of a beachfront community in the heart of Florida's Panhandle—makes it appealing at first glance. And after guests walk through the front gate of Josephine's white picket fence, cross the broad front porch with its comfortable wooden rocking chairs, and step into the parlor, they want to linger for a good while.

Guests stay in either the main house or in one of two separate buildings, each containing two suites. Rooms are individually decorated with antiques, balloon curtains, and a variety of guest-room furnishings, including four-poster and sleigh beds. Many have Battenburg lace–embellished comforters. All rooms have tub/shower combinations with extra-long tubs designed for luxuriant soaking. Kitchenettes in each room include mini-refrigerators, wet bars, and microwaves and are stocked with the fixings for making coffee.

A full breakfast is served daily in the richly appointed Josephine's Dining Room. Over the fireplace, softly lit by crystal sconces, hang tasteful reproductions of Redouté flower prints originally commissioned by Napoleon's empress, the Josephine for whom the inn is named. The intimate restaurant also serves lunch and dinner Wednesday through Sunday with an eclectic menu of meats, poultry, and fish. Crab cakes are a house specialty.

With its overstuffed chairs and sofa, the parlor invites guests to stay awhile with a good book. But it's the lure of the sea and its breezes that brings most visitors to Seaside, and Josephine's guests can take advantage of the rocking chairs on either the downstairs porch or upstairs veranda. A true bonus for guests is to climb up to the inn's roof, where deck chairs are available for sunning, although most guests simply take in the superb view of Seaside's pastel cottages, emerald waters, and white-sand beaches along the Gulf of Mexico. ☆ *11 double rooms with baths, 4 suites. Air-conditioning, cable TV/VCR, clock radios, fireplace in most rooms, kitchenettes, bicycles available; use of Seaside amenities, including community pool, tennis courts, croquet lawn, and shuffleboard courts ($5 daily fee). $130–$220; full breakfast. AE, MC, V.*

OTHER CHOICES

Dolphin Inn. 107 Savannah St., Seaside 32459, tel. 850/231–5477 or 800/443–3146. 2 double rooms with baths. Air-conditioning, TV/VCR, fireplace in living room, mini-refrigerators, bicycles available, use of Seaside community amenities, including pool and tennis courts ($5 daily fee). $98; Continental breakfast. MC, V.

Henderson Park Inn. 2700 Hwy. 98, Destin 32541, tel. 850/837–4853 or 800/336–4853. 18 double rooms with baths, 2 suites. Restaurant, air-conditioning, cable TV, fireplace in some rooms; refrigerator, microwave, coffeemaker, whirlpool bath in most rooms; beachfront, pool. $89–$239; full breakfast. AE, D, MC, V.

Sugar Beach Inn. 3501 Scenic Hwy. 30A, Seagrove Beach 32459, tel. 850/231–1577, fax 850/231–5456. 4 double rooms with baths. Air-conditioning, fireplace in 2 rooms. $100–$150; full breakfast. MC, V.

North Central Florida
◆❁❁❁◆

MAGNOLIA PLANTATION BED & BREAKFAST INN ☙
309 S.E. 7th St., Gainesville 32601, tel. 352/375–6653 or 800/201–2379, fax 352/338–0303

Right in the middle of one of Gainesville's Southeast historic districts, Magnolia Plantation is the result of a painstaking restoration undertaken by owners Joe and Cindy Montalto. The house, one of the South's few remaining examples of French Second Empire architecture, was built in 1886 by Emmet Baird, a local businessman. According to legend, Baird built the mansion with profits from a pirate treasure that he uncovered on the Suwannee River. Rumors of the remaining treasure still persist, but when Joe and Cindy gutted the house, the only "booty" they found were a few old coins (one penny dates to the mid-1840s) that probably fell from the pockets of the mansion's original builders.

The tall Italianate windows, mansard roof, and decorative moldings of the home pay tribute to a bygone era. Its focal point, a tall tower with decorative rooftop cresting, is a photographer's delight. Film buffs may notice a resemblance to the infamous house featured in *Psycho*, and Joe is quick to point out that the French Empire style is, in fact, characteristic of both structures; here, however, the similarities end. Painted in an inviting Covington blue, with dark red trim, Magnolia Plantation's enchanting exterior is a mere prelude to its interior delights.

The public rooms, which include both a "Gentlemen's" and "Ladies' " parlor, are liberally decorated with antiques and numerous photographs from Joe and Cindy's family albums. Leading to the second floor is a graceful mahogany staircase, accented with a garland of silk magnolia blossoms and tiny silver ornaments.

"My Christmas decorations," says Cindy. "I liked the way they looked, so I've never taken them down."

Guest rooms, named after species of flowers, are individually decorated in a variety of styles. Gardenia, the bridal suite, has lace curtains brought to America from Germany by Joe's aunt. The mid-18th-century Eastlake bed has a 6-ft-high headboard. The shower "curtain" around the in-room claw-foot tub is delicate white tulle. Jasmine, or the "Baby Room" is delightfully decorated with memorabilia from Joe and Cindy's childhoods, such as her christening gown and his lederhosen. (Remember that crocheting German grandmother?) There's even a child's rocking chair, which was Cindy's mother's. A close look at the photos reveal baby Joe and baby Cindy, as well as other family members.

The Magnolia Plantation bears all the earmarks of a family operation. Cindy's mother, who lives in the carriage house behind the mansion, helps manage the inn. It was she who needlepointed the nameplates for each guest room. Joe's father, a landscape architect, helped design and install the delightful backyard garden, which has a pond, waterfall, and a gazebo that invites guests to sit a spell. Together, Cindy and her mother hand-painted the rose-tone floral accents that frame the windows of the Azalea Room.

On the back of each guest-room door is an information card that expresses Joe and Cindy's philosophy as hosts: "You are here to relax, so relax. You do not have to pick up after yourself or make your bed." After a few days of that kind of pampering, it will be very hard to check out. ⬥ *5 double rooms with baths, 2 2-bedroom cottages. Air-conditioning, clock radio, fireplace, and cassette player in rooms, cable TV in parlor and 2 rooms, whirlpool in 1 cottage, tandem bikes available. $85–$150; full breakfast; beverages, wine, and snacks served in evenings. AE, MC, V. 2-night minimum in cottage.*

OTHER CHOICES

Clauser's Bed & Breakfast. 201 E. Kicklighter Rd., Lake Helen 32744, tel. 904/228–0310 or 800/220–0310, fax 904/228–2337. 8 double rooms with baths. Air-conditioning, whirlpool tub in 2 rooms, terry cloth robes, outdoor hot tub and nature trail. $75–$120; full breakfast, port wine and sherry. AE, D, MC, V.
Herlong Mansion. 402 N.E. Cholokka Blvd., Micanopy 32667, tel. 352/466–3322 or 800/437–5664, fax 352/466–3322. 5 double rooms with baths, 4 suites, 2 cottages. Air-conditioning, clock radios, whirlpool bath in 2 suites, cable TV in music room, kitchen; bicycles. $70–$175; full breakfast. MC, V.
Lakeside Inn. 100 N. Alexander St., Mount Dora 32757, tel. 352/383–4101 or 800/556–5016, fax 352/735–2642. 60 double rooms with baths, 16 parlor rooms, 11 lake-view rooms, 1 suite. Air-conditioning, cable TV, terry cloth robes, mini-refrigerator in some rooms, restaurant, bar, pool, tennis courts; boats available for rent. $105–$210; Continental breakfast. AE, D, MC, V.
Seven Sisters Inn. 820 S.E. Ft. King St., Ocala 34471, tel. 352/867–1170, fax 352/867–5266. 8 double rooms with baths. Air-conditioning, cable TV in 3 rooms, fireplace in 4 rooms, whirlpool bath in 1 room. $105–$165; full breakfast. AE, D, MC, V.
Shady Oak Bed & Breakfast. 203 Cholokka Blvd., Micanopy 32667, tel. 352/466–3476. 7 double rooms with baths. Air-conditioning, cable TV, whirlpool bath in 1 room. $75–$150; full breakfast, catered dinners on request. AE, D, MC, V.

Central and East Central Florida

LIVE OAK INN & RESTAURANT ☞

444–448 S. Beach St., Daytona Beach 32114, tel. 904/252–4667 or 800/881–4667, fax 904/239–0068

Set across the street from Halifax Harbor (guests with their own boats can use one of its slips), in the heart of the historic section of Daytona Beach, the Live Oak Inn & Restaurant seems worlds away from the gaudy glitz of the beach-front scene. Guests at the Live Oak travel through time to the early days of Daytona Beach's history. The two houses that compose the inn date from 1871 and 1881, respectively, long before anyone in Daytona ever thought about a Speed-way or driving on the beach. The historic air that permeates the inn is the mark of innkeepers Jessie and Del Glock, retired missionaries who spent a number of years in Japan. Many of the wall hangings in the guest rooms reflect the time they spent in the Far East.

The exterior of the inn is dominated by a wonderfully twisted century-old oak tree from which the inn takes its name. Gracefully draped with Spanish moss, the tree recalls a bygone era when genteel young women and their suitors courted beneath its branches. Diners seated by the front windows in the inn's candlelit restaurant get a view of the tree up close, as well as of the busy harbor across the street.

Each of the guest rooms is named after a prominent Floridian or a figure who was central to Daytona Beach history. Composer Stephen Foster is the inspira-tion for the Foster Room, painted a delicate shade of blue. In the peach-tone Audubon Room, guests will find an elaborate wicker birdcage on the dresser. Not all the rooms are named for famous people from the past, however. The Harley Room is decorated with motorcycle photographs and memorabilia. The Disney Room—with a stuffed Mickey and Minnie on the bed—is a tribute not only to Walt but to the Glocks' status as ministers at Disney World's Wedding Pavilion. As a result of their missionary work in Japan, both are fluent in Japanese; many of the couples who tie the knot at Disney are from the Land of the Rising Sun, and the Glocks conduct the ceremony in Japanese.

Others thinking about getting hitched in Daytona can do so right at the inn. Del Glock will officiate, and the sweeping staircase in the 1871 house provides a dramatic entrance for any bride. Guests can stay at the inn, of course, and the reception can be held in either the restaurant or a lovely private room with carved wooden walls in the 1881 house or the sunny breakfast room in the 1871 house.

The Glocks have taken great pains to re-create the furnishings of the period. Rather than decorate each room solely with antiques, they carefully mixed old and new pieces to create a look that reflects the heyday of Daytona's pioneers. Many set-tlers could bring only a few precious heirlooms on the difficult trek to central Florida; they then made up for the lack of their "northern"-style furnishings by adding pieces produced by local artisans. Thus, in the Foster Room, guests will find a delicate oak antique secretary, as well as white wicker end tables; in the Audubon Room, a massive mahogany bed, more than 150 years old, and mahogany chest are complemented by a wicker chaise longue.

While the inn's furnishings reflect the Glocks' commitment to historic preservation, its amenities are thankfully late-20th century. Many rooms have tiled baths with whirlpools, and terry cloth robes are thoughtfully provided. Should guests want to get away from it all, they have the option of using their in-room video-cassette players. (Tapes are available.) However, those who want to forget about the present can lose themselves in one of the fine books available from a tea cart in the upstairs hallway. With most of the rooms having private porches, there's no finer way to experience old Florida. △ *15 double rooms with baths. Air-conditioning, cable TV, video and audio cassette players, clock radio, whirlpool bath in 6 rooms, restaurant, bar. $75–$200; Continental-plus breakfast. No credit cards.*

OTHER CHOICES

Coquina Inn Bed & Breakfast. 544 S. Palmetto Ave., Daytona Beach 32114, tel. 904/254–4969 or 800/805–7533, fax 904/254–4969. 4 double rooms with baths. Air-conditioning, fireplace in 1 room, outdoor whirlpool; bicycles. $80–$175; full breakfast. AE, MC, V.

Courtyard at Lake Lucerne. 211 N. Lucerne Circle E, Orlando 32801, tel. 407/648–5188 or 800/444–5289, fax 407/246–1368. 6 double rooms with baths in Norment-Parry Inn, 3 doubles in I. W. Phillips House, 15 suites in Wellborn Suites. Air-conditioning, cable TV, fireplace in some rooms, kitchenette in suites, whirlpool bath in 2 suites, bar. $89–$165; Continental-plus breakfast. AE, DC, MC, V.

Inn at Cocoa Beach. 4300 Ocean Beach Blvd., Cocoa Beach 32931, tel. 407/799–3460 or 800/343–5307, fax 407/784–8632. 41 double rooms with baths, 9 junior suites. Air-conditioning, cable TV, whirlpool bath in 5 rooms, pool, bar. $99–$195; Continental breakfast, wine-and-cheese hour. AE, D, MC, V.

Night Swan Intracoastal Bed & Breakfast. 512 S. Riverside Dr., New Smyrna Beach 32168, tel. 904/423–4940 or 800/465–4261, fax 904/427–2814. 4 double rooms with baths, 4 suites. Air-conditioning, TVs, guest refrigerator. $80–$150; full breakfast. AE, D, MC, V.

PerriHouse Bed & Breakfast Inn. 10417 Centurion Ct., Lake Buena Vista 32830, tel. 407/876-4830 or 800/876–4830, fax 407/876–0241. 8 double rooms with baths (1 room can sleep 4). Air-conditioning, TVs, phone, private entrances, pool, outdoor spa. $99; Continental breakfast. Minimum stay required on weekends and holidays. AE, MC, V.

Key West

GARDENS HOTEL ☜
526 Angela St., Key West 33040, tel. 305/294–2661 or 800/526–2664, fax 305/292–1007

Although only one short block from the throngs of tourists on Duval Street—Key West's main drag—the Gardens Hotel is, quite literally, a tropical oasis. The hotel's main building, which dates from the 1870s, is one of Key West's oldest Bahama-style homes. The home and surrounding property were purchased in 1930 by Peggy Mills and her first husband. Mrs. Mills then spent the remainder of her life carefully cultivating the land, creating magnificent tropical gardens whose beauty guests can enjoy as they swim in the pool or take a leisurely walk around the grounds.

The gardens are filled with bromeliads, mango, balsa, breadfruit trees, and giant crotons. Flowering plants include lilies, hibiscus, bougainvillea, orange jasmine, and magnolia. Wrought-iron benches are strategically placed throughout the plantings, allowing for a contemplative stop. The garden's pathways are lined with 87,000 red bricks, which Mrs. Mills had imported from Cuba, Honduras, and England. Also interspersed with the flora and fauna are four enormous earthenware jars, or *tinajones,* used by Spanish settlers to catch rainwater for drinking. Mrs. Mills found them in Cuba about 1950 and persuaded then-president Batista to allow her to bring the 18th-century artifacts back to the United States.

After Mrs. Mills died in 1979, the property and buildings went through several owners and periods of great neglect. In 1992, Bill and Corinna Hettinger purchased the property and, after a 14-month, multimillion-dollar restoration, the Gardens Hotel welcomed its first guests.

There are two historic guest rooms upstairs in the main house; additional accommodations in the Gardens and Courtyard buildings are a short, delightful walk away. In addition, there are the Eyebrow Cottage, Carriage House, and Master Suite. All rooms are elegantly decorated with an eye for the telling detail: soft, floral prints in the bedspreads and matching curtains; gleaming hardwood floors; 12-ft ceilings with 10-inch moldings; pristine white marble baths with double sinks and whirlpool tubs. Each room contains an original impressionist painting by New Zealand artist Peter Williams, whose style perfectly captures the island spirit.

Under the dining room's elaborate tin ceiling, the breakfast table is spread with fresh fruits, cheeses, chocolate croissants, and Key-lime pastries, a repast guests can enjoy in the nearby sunroom. An antique grandfather clock stands watch in the hallway, its hands permanently set at 11:20. (Since it's Key West, nobody cares what time it really is, anyway.) Guests can also dine on the patio, where they will be entertained by Peggy, a very friendly macaw who will eat from guests' hands, if given the slightest encouragement.

With its pale blue walls, overstuffed striped couch, fireplace, and built-in bookcases, the living room invites guests to linger, whether over morning coffee or afternoon drinks. An inlaid-wood backgammon and checkers table is thoughtfully provided. But as Key West's tropical air circulates, guests find themselves drawn to the swimming pool with its mirrored bar, or to the fountains in the gardens and the courtyard. △ *15 double rooms with baths, 2 suites. Air-conditioning, cable TV, whirlpool baths, minibar in 13 rooms, pool. $245–$675; Continental-plus breakfast. AE, MC, V.*

OTHER CHOICES

Curry Mansion Inn. 511 Caroline St., Key West 33040, tel. 305/294–5349 or 800/253–3466, fax 305/294–4093. 24 double rooms with baths, 4 suites. Air-conditioning, cable TV, mini-refrigerators, whirlpool bath in some rooms, beach privileges at Marriott's Casa Marina and at Pier House, pool. $160–$275; Continental-plus breakfast, evening cocktails. AE, D, DC, MC, V.

Heron House. 512 Simonton St., Key West 33040, tel. 305/294–9227 or 800/294–1644, fax 305/294–5692. 23 double rooms with baths. Air-conditioning, cable TV, phones, mini-refrigerators and wet bars, whirlpool bath in 1 room, weight room, pool. $189–$289; Continental-plus breakfast. AE, DC, MC, V.

La Mer Hotel. 506 South St., Key West 33040, tel. 305/296–5611 or 800/354–4455, fax 305/294–8272. 7 double rooms with baths, 4 doubles with baths. Air-conditioning, cable TV, kitchenette in 5 rooms, bicycles, pool (at sister hotel next door). $190–$300 ($25 extra person); Continental-plus breakfast, afternoon tea. AE, MC, V.

Merlinn Guest House. 811 Simonton St., Key West 33040, tel. 305/296–3336, fax 305/296–3524. 9 double rooms with baths (1 wheelchair accessible), 1 single with bath. Air-conditioning in most rooms, cable TV, mini-refrigerator in some rooms, pool. $70–$160; Continental-plus breakfast. AE, D, MC, V.

Simonton Court. 320 Simonton St., Key West 33040, tel. 305/294–6386 or 800/944–2687, fax 305/293–8446. 9 double rooms in inn, 2 suites in manor house, 6 cottages, 6 double rooms in mansion. Air-conditioning, cable TV/VCR in some rooms, mini-refrigerators, kitchen in some rooms, 4 pools, outdoor hot tub. $145–$325; Continental breakfast. AE, D, MC, V.

Watson House. 525 Simonton St., Key West 33040, tel. 305/294–6712 or 800/621–9405, fax 305/294–7501. 2 suites in main house, 1 cabana. Air-conditioning, kitchen in 2 suites, cable TV, outdoor whirlpool, pool, coffeemakers. $125–$370; Continental breakfast. AE, MC, V.

Southwest Florida

BANYAN HOUSE ☙
519 S. Harbor Dr., Venice 34285, tel. 941/484–1385, fax 941/484–8032

If you know the lyrics to "Don't Sit Under the Apple Tree with Anyone Else But Me," you'll feel right at home at the Banyan House. Just change the type of tree from apple to banyan and you will have captured the flavor of the only bed-and-breakfast in Venice, a small but delightful Gulf Coast beach town.

Constructed in 1926 by railroad builders, the Banyan House has served as a museum, tearoom, USO Headquarters, and day nursery. Since 1986 it has been a bed-and-breakfast. Owners Chuck and Susan McCormick are eager to accommodate their guests, offering a welcoming drink and conversation.

Accommodations in the main house are three one-bedroom efficiency apartments with balconies. Continental breakfast and full maid service are included. Five additional apartments, with no maid service, are in two additional buildings on the property. Rooms in all buildings are spacious and elegantly appointed in bright, airy Florida pastels. A common area downstairs has games and books available at no charge, along with tourist brochures. The Spanish-themed backyard patio area has a lovely pool and hot tub, which appropriately sits under the spreading branches of the banyan tree.

The Banyan House is very conveniently located within walking distance of the historic Venice shopping district. The beautiful Venice beach is just a short ride away; bikes are available at no charge. Sarasota is just 20 minutes away by car; the Banyan House's location also makes it easily accessible to major Central Florida attractions, such as Busch Gardens and Walt Disney World. ⚘ *3 1-bedroom efficiencies, 5 1-bedroom apartments, 1 double room with bath. Air-conditioning, cable TV, pool, outdoor hot tub, bicycles. $89–$119 daily, $575–$695 weekly; Continental breakfast and maid service for efficiencies only. MC, V. No smoking.*

MANSION HOUSE BED & BREAKFAST ☙
105 5th Ave. NE, St. Petersburg 33701, tel. and fax 727/821–9391 or 800/274–7520

Just a few minutes' walk from the St. Petersburg waterfront on Tampa Bay, the Mansion House is a delightful hostelry in the city's historic district. Innkeepers Rosie and Robert Ray are the hosts, and they'll do just about anything to make you feel at home.

The two houses date to 1904 and 1912 and are decorated with an eclectic mix of Rob and Rosie's family heirlooms and lots of white wicker accented with peach and minty-green cushions. Photos of the Rays' children—now college students—are much in evidence. A whimsical decorating touch in the dining room is the copper double boiler filled with Cabbage Patch dolls. A centerpiece of the parlor is the gleaming hardwood floor staircase, which leads to four upstairs guest rooms. (A fifth bedroom is downstairs, and there's also a separate carriage house behind the main house.) Guest rooms are cozily furnished with the same mix of antiques and wicker as the public rooms.

A sitting room upstairs has a large TV, antique writing desk, and lots of paperbacks and board games. It's a cozy spot to while away a few hours. A well-stocked mini-refrigerator is also here; guests are welcome to help themselves to its contents.

A unique advantage of the Mansion House is Rob's status as licensed boat captain. Guests can charter the 23-ft sport cruiser *Aussie Spirit* for a customized charter on the Gulf of Mexico that can range from an hour to a full day.

A highlight of a stay here is the morning meal, cooked by Rosie and served with charm and grace. Two popular items are her blueberry pancakes and orange French toast. If you want the recipe, it's yours, but Rosie does request that you provide her with a recipe in return. "But it's not a house rule," she emphasizes. ⚐ *10 double rooms with baths, including carriage house. Air-conditioning, cable TV, terry cloth robes, toiletries, pool, outdoor spa. $110–$165; full breakfast; wine, cheese, snacks, coffee, tea, and soft drinks. AE, MC, V.*

OTHER CHOICES

Bayboro House Bed & Breakfast on Old Tampa Bay. 1719 Beach Drive SE, St. Petersburg 33701, tel. and fax 727/823–4955. 4 rooms with baths, 1 suite. Air-conditioning, kitchen in suite, TV/VCRs, pool, off-street parking; beach towels and beach chairs available. $85–$145; Continental-plus breakfast. MC, V.

Bay Gables Bed & Breakfast, Garden & Tea Room. 136 4th Ave. NE, St. Petersburg 33701, tel. 727/822–8855 or 800/822–8803, fax 727/824–7223. 5 rooms with baths (1 wheelchair accessible), 4 suites. Air-conditioning, whirlpool bath in 1 room, kitchenette in 4 rooms. $85–$135; Continental breakfast. AE, MC, V.

Gilchrist Bed & Breakfast. 115 Gilchrist St., Punta Gorda 33950, tel. 941/575–4129, fax 941/575–9666. 2 double rooms with baths. Air-conditioning, cable TV in common area, outdoor hot tub, grill, bicycles. $85–$95; Continental breakfast. D, MC, V.

Inn by the Sea. 287 11th Ave. S, Naples 34102, tel. 941/649–4124 or 800/584–1268, fax 941/434–2842. 3 double rooms with baths, 2 suites, 1 cottage. Air-conditioning, cable TV in living room. $149–$189; Continental breakfast. AE, MC, V.

Inn on the Beach. 1401 Gulfway, St. Petersburg Beach 33706, tel. 813/360–8844. 12 double rooms with baths. Air-conditioning, cable TV, phones. $70–$150; Continental breakfast weekends. AE, D, MC, V.

Sanibel's Song of the Sea. 863 E. Gulf Dr., Sanibel 33957, tel. 941/434–2842 or 800/231–1045, fax 941/472–8569. 22 rooms, 8 suites. Air-conditioning, cable TV, phones, wine and flowers upon arrival, pool and outdoor hot tub, books and movies, shared recreational facilities with Sanibel Inn next door. $310–$370; Continental breakfast. AE, D, DC, MC, V.

GEORGIA

North Georgia and Atlanta

BRASSTOWN VALLEY RESORT 🏕

6321 U.S. Hwy. 76, Young Harris 30582, tel. 706/379–9900 or 800/201–3205, fax 706/279–9999

The Blue Ridge Mountains shelter one of Georgia's and the South's most encompassing resorts, Brasstown Valley, a cooperative venture between state and private entities. Opened in 1995, Brasstown Valley is an ecologically sensitive design, with a lodge whose sweeping 72-ft fieldstone fireplace and floor-to-ceiling windows seem perfectly suited to the surrounding lush canopy of hardwoods and pines. Massive chandeliers made from shed deer antlers make the soaring ceilings glow with warm light.

The lodge itself contains 120 generously configured rooms, 33 with working fireplaces. Eight adjacent log cottages each hold four guest rooms and a grand parlor with a wood-burning fireplace, kitchenette, and veranda. Color schemes are forest green, burgundy, and navy, and furnishings suggest Early American twig furniture. Decorative elements showcase the work of local artisans, supporting the culture of this mountain environment.

With its Dennis Griffiths–designed par-72 Scottish links golf course and a well-equipped conference center, Brasstown Valley is ideal for business meetings. Mountain South Outfitters, which is on site, is a good place to acquire last-minute fishing and hiking items. They lead white-water rafting, trout fishing, hiking, biking, and lake and river kayaking trips. Nearby Brasstown Bald, the highest point in Georgia, offers a challenging hike to its peak. Reserve a 25-gear mountain bike for the day to explore the terrain, or get serious at the Unicoi World Championship Course, a 6-mi Olympic test for mountain bikers.

Off-site, guests will find plenty of antiques shops, art galleries featuring local crafts, cultural activities (mountain music at Georgia Mountain Fair in nearby Hiawasee and theater at Young Harris College), and natural attractions.

The resort does both bed-and-breakfast packages throughout the week and golf packages (Sunday through Thursday only), with prices varying according to the season. Off-season prices are excellent values. *♨ 129 rooms with baths, 5 suites. 2 restaurants; air-conditioning, cable TV, desk, and phone in rooms; fireplace and kitchenette in cabins; conference center. $149–$174; breakfast not included (packages including breakfast are available). AE, D, DC, MC, V. Restricted smoking.*

GLEN-ELLA SPRINGS COUNTRY INN & CONFERENCE CENTER ☞

Bear Gap Rd. (Rte. 3, Box 3304), 8½ mi north of Clarkesville 30523, tel. 706/754–7295 or 888/455–8891, fax 706/754–7295

Just outside of Clarkesville, the Glen-Ella Springs Country Inn, a hideaway more than a century old, was lovingly renovated in 1987 by Barrie and Bobby Aycock. The small hotel, listed on the National Register of Historic Places, sits by a gravel road on 17 acres of meadows and gardens.

At first glance the Glen-Ella, with its heart-pine floors, walls, and ceilings, appears down-home, but its uptown flair soon becomes evident. The front lobby, filled with chintz and antiques, serves as a parlor, and fires are lit here against the cool night air. From welcoming porches furnished with country-style rocking chairs, you enter the guest rooms, where quilts, chintzes, original art work, painted reproduction antiques, and Oriental and area rugs convey an English country feeling within naturally finished and painted pine-paneled interiors.

The hotel's dining room, which has a fireplace, is the realization of Barrie's original dream: to own her own restaurant. Her kitchen is the source of the sweet baked goods—blueberry-granola pancakes and oat scones—served at breakfast and regional southern cuisine served at dinner. The food here has so enhanced the inn's reputation that it has become a culinary hot spot for Atlantans, who will drive the two hours for the sumptuous meals.

Those not involved in special occurrences such as mystery weekends and herb-gardening conferences may relax by the pool on the large sundeck surrounded by flower gardens. Sports lovers will find excellent hiking at nearby Tallulah Falls. Golf (as well as tennis) is found at the Orchard, a championship course within a few miles of the inn. Kayaking and white-water rafting on the Chattooga River also are popular, and the inn arranges horseback riding.

During the week, the conference center is frequently booked by Fortune 100 companies. △ *14 double rooms with baths, 2 suites. Air-conditioning, phone with voice mail in rooms; fireplace and whirlpool tub in suites; satellite TV in lobby; pool; conference center. $100–$180; full breakfast. AE, MC, V. No smoking.*

SHELLMONT BED & BREAKFAST ☞

821 Piedmont Ave., Atlanta 30306, tel. 404/872–9290, fax 404/872–5379

Atlanta's Midtown, lying between Piedmont Park and Downtown, developed in the late 19th and early 20th centuries. The neighborhood's spacious, ornate Victorian homes exhibit a wealth of period detail. This fine example of Victorian-era classical eclecticism, listed on the National Register of Historic Places and a City of Atlanta Landmark, reflects that taste for detail. It was designed in 1891 by the Massachusetts-born, Atlanta-reared architect Walter T. Downing for Dr. William Perrin Nicholson. The exterior proudly displays classical architectural elements, including heavily carved woodwork, columns with shell-adorned capitals, and finely detailed stained-glass windows. One is particularly dramatic: The magnificent, huge window behind the staircase in the reception space casts a warm light throughout.

The urban pocket garden is filled with Carolina jasmine, azaleas, and hostas. An herb garden supplies fragrant additions to breakfast, especially herbed mint tea. A fern-design-filled wrought-iron bench, a reproduction 19th-century Charleston bench, invites contemplative moments.

Owners and resident innkeepers Debbie and Ed McCord established the Shellmont in Nicholson House in 1983. Coming to hospitality from pharmaceutical marketing (Debbie) and real estate development (Ed), the McCords have established a following among business visitors to the city. Desks and phones with dataports have been added to the rooms.

Besides restoring the stained-glass window with painstaking care, the couple has reproduced another Victorian detail: most of the house's original stenciling, above sponge-painted walls. Upstairs bedrooms have reproduction period wallcoverings and lace panels at the windows. The Eastlake Room has an antique bed with an 8-ft-high headboard and matching marble-topped dresser. Curved windows fitted with curved glass in that room are an original architectural feature.

In a green, yellow, and burgundy color scheme, the carriage house has white plantation shutters and an antique reproduction four-poster bed. Recessed lighting warms the spaces and hardwood floors gleam under Oriental rugs. There's a kitchen, a bath with a ceramic tile and marble steam shower/bath, a sleigh bed, two TV/VCRs, and two phones.

Breakfast varies; some favorites are Belgian waffles and frittatas. Always on hand are gourmet coffee, fresh juice, and homemade breads (pumpkin, blueberry, pear and nutmeg, banana), scones, or cinnamon rolls. ♠ *2 double rooms, 2 suites, 1 carriage house. Air-conditioning, TV and phone in rooms, kitchen and 2 TV/VCRs in carriage house. $90–$169; full breakfast, turndown service with gourmet chocolates. AE, DC, MC, V. No smoking.*

OTHER CHOICES

Mountain Memories. 285 Chancey Dr., Hiawasee 30546, tel. 706/896–8439 or 800/335–8439. 6 rooms with baths. Air-conditioning, cable TV/VCR, and whirlpool tub in rooms; 400-film tape library; lounge. $100–$145; full breakfast, complimentary dessert buffet. D, MC, V. No smoking.

Nicholson House. 6295 Jefferson Rd., Athens 30607, tel. 706/353–2200, fax 706/353–7799. 9 double rooms with baths. Air-conditioning, cable TV, and phone in rooms. $75–$95; Continental breakfast. AE, D, MC, V. No smoking.

Serenbe. 10950 Hutcherson Ferry Rd., Palmetto 30268, tel. 770/463–2610, fax 770/463–4472. 4 double rooms with baths, 1 cottage. Whirlpool bath in 1 room, common area with satellite TV/VCR and video library, fireplace, pool and hot tub, canoeing, hiking, fishing, lake. $115–$150; full breakfast. No credit cards. No smoking.

Skelton House. 97 Benson St., Hartwell 30643, tel. 706/376–7969, fax 706/856–3139. 7 rooms with baths. Air-conditioning, cable TV, and phone in rooms. $85–$100; full breakfast. AE, D, DC, MC, V. No smoking.

RESERVATIONS SERVICES

Bed & Breakfast Atlanta (1608 Briarcliff Rd., Suite 5, Atlanta 30306, tel. 404/875–0525 or 800/967–3224, fax 404/875–8198). **R.S.V.P. Grits** (541 Londonberry Rd., Atlanta 30327, 404/843–3933 or 800/823–7787).

Middle Georgia

HENDERSON VILLAGE ☞

125 S. Langston Cir., Perry (1 mi west of Exit 41, I–75), tel. 912/988–9009 or 888/615–9722, fax 912/988–9009

About 20 years ago, German electronics entrepreneur Bernhard Schneider bought an 8,000-acre ostrich and cattle operation in middle Georgia. He had wanted a farm in the southeastern U.S. anywhere he could reach on a nonstop flight from Munich. Schneider's offices, at the intersection of GA 26 and U.S. 41, were in a neighborhood whose aesthetic character he found less than appealing. While he was looking for a way to enhance it, one of the owners of a nearby early 20th-century residence asked him to buy the property, and he was on his way to developing one of the state's most exquisite lodging-and-dining resorts.

On pristine, rolling farmland, Henderson Village is a cluster of buildings, three original to the site; the others Schneider acquired and moved to the complex. He plans to find, acquire, move, and restore more, creating ultimately a study in area vernacular architecture. Within the transformed residences, some of them formerly simple farm homes, are sumptuously decorated interiors. One of the original-to-the-site structures, an 1838 Greek Revival house, is the Langston House 1838, the village's restaurant. Here, French-American chef François de Melogue has developed a superior menu, with such entrées as squab with foie gras, grilled diver scallops on minced asparagus, extraordinary desserts, and a fine collection of wines, including some German ones in deference to the owner. Breakfast includes fresh juices, house-baked breads, stone-ground grits, and egg dishes that take advantage of local ingredients like country ham and Vidalia onions.

♨ *24 rooms, 4 suites. Air-conditioning, gas-log fireplace, robes in rooms; whirlpool tubs in suites; restaurant, pool. $145–$205; full breakfast. AE, MC, V.*

OTHER CHOICES

1842 Inn. 353 College St., Macon 31201, tel. 912/741–1842 or 800/336–1842, fax 912/741–1842. 12 double rooms with baths in house, 9 doubles with baths in cottage. Air-conditioning, cable TV and phone in rooms; fireplace in 6 rooms; whirlpool bath in 4 rooms. $115–$185; Continental breakfast (full breakfast is extra), afternoon refreshments, turndown service with chocolates. AE, MC, V.
Grand Hotel. 303 E. Main St., Hogansville 30230, tel. 706/637–8828 or 800/ 324–7625, fax 706/637–4522. 5 double rooms, 5 suites. Air-conditioning, cable TV and phone in rooms; conference and banquet facilities. $75–$150; Continental breakfast, afternoon cocktails and hors d'oeuvres. AE, MC, V. No smoking.

Coastal Georgia

THE GASTONIAN ☞

220 E. Gaston St., Savannah 31401, tel. 912/232–2869 or 800/322–6603, fax 912/232–0710

Two blocks from Savannah's Forsyth Park and 12 from River Street stands the Gastonian. Hinting of the comforts within, a pineapple, symbolic of hospitality, is engraved on the brass sign at the entry. The two Regency Italianate mansions that compose the inn had been constructed for two prosperous merchants after the Civil War. In October 1996 Ann Landers (not the advice columnist) bought and redecorated much of the inn.

Authentic Georgian- and Regency-period antiques set the 19th-century ambience. In the front parlor and formal dining room, the antiques have the patina that comes from being well loved and much-polished. Guests are encouraged to lounge in the coral upholstered wing chairs on either side of the drawing-room fireplace or pick out tunes on the antique baby grand piano in the front parlor. Scalamandré's Savannah-collection wallpapers adorn the hallways. One guest room has rustic country decor, ladder-back cane chairs, and antique trunks; another recalls Colonial America, with crewel draperies and bedspreads. Most have rice poster or Charleston canopy beds. Romance seekers should ask about the Caracalla Suite, with its huge bedside hot tub.

A sumptuous southern breakfast is served in the large country kitchen or the dining room. Dishes feature such specialties as ginger pancakes. Late risers may opt for a Continental breakfast delivered bedside on a silver tray along with the local paper. An elevated sundeck with chaise longues, a wisteria- and jasmine-draped pergola, and a large hot tub are pleasant spots to laze away the afternoon. The concierge has plenty of suggestions for terrific restaurants and will arrange for transport by horse-drawn carriage. March, April, May, September, and October are the inn's busiest times, so call well in advance. △ *14 double rooms with baths, 3 suites. Air-conditioning, cable TV, phone, and gas fireplace in rooms; off-street parking. $150–$350; full breakfast, turndown service, evening cordials. AE, D, MC, V. No smoking.*

GREYFIELD INN ☙
Cumberland Island (Box 900, Fernandina Beach, FL 32035), tel. 904/261–6408 (reservations and information), fax 904/321–0666

Greyfield Inn is accessible only by boat (passage on the inn's *Lucy R. Ferguson* is free to guests) or by private plane, landing only by prior arrangement on a grass strip.

The imposing house with wide colonnade porches was the setting for John F. Kennedy's 1996 wedding to Carolyn Bessette. It was built in 1901 by tycoon Thomas Carnegie for his daughter, Margaret. Operated by Mitty Ferguson, Carnegie's great-great-grandson, and his wife, Mary Jo, the inn contains family photographs, tabletop collections of seashore memorabilia, and antique rugs. A resident innkeeper, Brycea Merrill, takes care of day-to-day details.

Dark, heavy, late-19th-century furniture, some of it original to the house, appoints the inn's rooms. Bathrooms have antique tubs, and an enclosed backyard shower house is another full bath. Downstairs, the library bedroom has its own bath. The top floor holds two suites with king-size beds and private baths. Two cottages each contain two bedrooms with private baths and a common living area. All guest rooms were air-conditioned in 1998. By 1999, half baths will be added to those guest rooms that share baths.

Rates include all meals. Breakfast is informal but substantial. Hors d'oeuvres start the cocktail hour; then a bell rings to announce the formal gourmet evening meal. Dressing for dinner (jackets for gentlemen and dressy casual attire for women) transforms the nightly ritual into a festive occasion, but the atmosphere still is relaxed.

The best times to visit are in spring and early autumn, when the insect population and humidity level remain low. △ *7 double rooms with baths, 7 doubles* *and 1 suite share 3 baths, outdoor shower house. Air-conditioning, shuttle to ferry, bikes, guided nature tours. $275–$395; AP, afternoon refreshments. MC, V. No smoking.*

JEKYLL ISLAND CLUB HOTEL ☞
371 Riverview Dr., Jekyll Island 31527, tel. 912/635–2600 or 800/535–9547, fax 912/635–2818

Originally settled by Guale Indians, Jekyll Island was colonized first by Spanish missionaries, then by William Horton, one of Gen. James Edward Oglethorpe's most trusted officers. Oglethorpe had named the island for a friend, Sir Joseph Jekyll. Horton developed a thriving plantation, and the remains of his second home still stand, begging for restoration.

The island was developed in the late 19th century as a private hunting club for New York's most wealthy. For its 100 members, the island became a vacation home. Its elite members included William Rockefeller, J. P. Morgan, Joseph Pulitzer, and William Vanderbilt. The centerpiece of this development was the dramatic Victorian clubhouse designed by architect Charles A. Alexander and built in 1887. With its Queen Anne–style turret, wraparound porch, and sweeping landscape, the club became famous for its fine dining and exquisite service. In 1896 a syndicate of selected wealthy members constructed the Sans Souci apartments, where J. P. Morgan resided. Finally, in 1901, an annex containing eight privately owned apartments was built at the end of the clubhouse.

These buildings, abandoned when the club ceased to function after World War II, form the nucleus of this unique resort. Custom-decorated guest accommodations in both the restored clubhouse and the Sans Souci apartments have warm color schemes, mahogany beds, luxurious baths, and some fireplaces. A croquet lawn, 22 mi of bicycle trails, tennis, golf, beaches, and swimming are among the amenities that recall the opulence of the club era. Bed-and-breakfast packages are available Sundays through Thursdays for $59 to $69 per person, depending on the season. The main dining room remains a culinary destination. ⚑ *117 rooms, 17 suites. 2 restaurants, air-conditioning, concierge, meeting and banquet rooms; off-street parking, pool, 9 tennis courts, croquet, bicycles. $119–$169; full breakfast with bed-and-breakfast package only. AE, D, DC, MC, V.*

LODGING AT LITTLE ST. SIMONS ISLAND ☞
Box 21078, St. Simons Island 31522, tel. 912/638–7472 or 888/733–5774, fax 912/634–1811

To describe this island retreat as unique does it little justice. Nowhere in Georgia is a sunset more glorious than over the marshes that ring this still privately owned island. Most likely, you will be exhausted after a day exploring its 7 mi of pristine beaches. Trails crisscross the island and are excellent for hiking or bicycling. More than 200 different species of birds have been observed here. Canoe the island's waterways, or maybe go fly fishing under the direction of an Orvis-endorsed guide. Ride horses along the trails. You'll hear armadillos thrash through the underbrush and cranes call and spot alligators snoozing in the sun.

Family programs educate and entertain the smaller guests, who learn about the environment in a natural classroom. Parents and children may go on safari with an island naturalist or conduct a scavenger hunt.

Romance seekers will enjoy the privacy of a freestanding cottage, Michael's Cottage, which has a living room and kitchenette (no oven). The River Lodge and Cedar House are simply but comfortably furnished, with four bedrooms, each with its bath and deck. The bedrooms are arranged around a common living room with fireplace and screened-in porch across the back. The very rustic original lodge, now air-conditioned, has two bedrooms. The 1929 Helen House, made of traditional tabby (a shell-and-mortar material), has two baths, a living room, fireplace, and screened porch.

Rates include all three meals, prepared by a staff headed by chef Charles Bostick. His emphasis is on regional cuisine, so dishes include peach pecan pancakes for breakfast, fried chicken, blue crab cakes, crispy flounder with ginger peach sauce, and prickly pear sorbet. Lunch may be served in the dining room or packed in picnic baskets. ♙ *15 rooms with baths. Air-conditioning, hiking, bicycling, horseback riding, birding, canoeing, fly fishing. $350–$550; AP. MC, V. No smoking.*

OTHER CHOICES

Bed and Breakfast Inn. 117 W. Gordon St., Savannah 31401, tel. 912/238–0518, fax 912/233–2537. 12 rooms, 1 suite, 2 cottages with kitchens (1 with oven). Air-conditioning, cable TV, and phone in rooms. $85–$110; full breakfast. AE, MC, V. No smoking.

Foley House. 14 W. Hull St., Savannah 31401, tel. 912/232–6622 or 800/647–3708, fax 912/231–1218. 19 rooms with baths. Air-conditioning, robes, cable TV/VCR and phone in rooms; fireplace in 15 rooms; oversize whirlpool in 5 rooms; film library. $135–$250; Continental breakfast. AE, DC, MC, V. No smoking.

Perrin Guest House Inn. 208 Lafayette Dr., Augusta 30909, tel. 706/731–0920 or 800/668–8930. 10 double rooms with baths. Fireplace in rooms, whirlpool tub in 6 rooms, gazebo. $100–$150; Continental breakfast. AE, MC, V. No smoking.

President's Quarters. 225 E. President St., Savannah 31401, tel. 912/233–1600 or 800/233–1776, fax 912/238–0849. 8 double rooms with baths, 11 suites. Air-conditioning, cable TV and phone in rooms; whirlpool bath in 7 suites; gazebo; off-street parking. $137–$215; Continental breakfast. AE, D, DC, MC, V. Restricted smoking.

RESERVATIONS SERVICE

Savannah Historic Inns (147 Bull St., Savannah 31401, tel. 912/233–7660 or 800/262–4667).

Southwest Georgia

MELHANA PLANTATION ☙
301 Showboat La., Thomasville 31792, tel. 912/226–2290 or 888/920—3030, fax 912/226–4585

Wealthy from oil money and industrial enterprises, Howard Melville Hanna of Cleveland, Ohio, represents just one of many monied northern families who bought plantations in southwest Georgia in the late-19th and early 20th centuries. He purchased this plantation, originally built in the 1820s and known as Melrose, in the late-19th century. Nearby Pebble Hill was a Hanna-owned plantation, and another daughter owned yet a third plantation.

Charlie and Fran Lewis purchased a piece of the plantation land and shared their home, Owl's Nest, on that parcel with their two sons Zachary and Nick. In 1997, the couple purchased the adjacent Pink House, the heart of the original 3,000-acre plantation, and some 40 acres to develop a luxury resort property. Listed on the National Register of Historic Places, the Pink House, the former Hanna family residence, now contains 11 sumptuously furnished guest rooms, many with whirlpool tubs and fireplaces. Lewis family businesses include insurance brokerage and marketing for Charlie, who also manages investments, and jewelry design for Fran. But most of their energies these days are devoted to developing the resort.

To enjoy Melhana, explore the exquisite gardens, which are being carefully restored and reinvigorated. Relax on the porch with a book, or ride a horse from nearby stables down an easy trail. The theater on the site is thought to have been used for a first screening of *Gone With the Wind*, as neighbor Jock Whitney was one of the film's investors.

Breakfast might include fresh fruit and juices, baked egg dishes or omelets, and homemade breads. The menu in the restaurant changes weekly, but look out for fried green tomatoes with Vidalia onion relish, rosemary-skewered shrimp, and game when the region's hunting season is in full swing. ⚘ *33 rooms with baths. Air-conditioning, robes in rooms, whirlpool tub in 16 rooms, restaurant, conference center, theater. $250–$550; full breakfast. AE, D, DC, MC, V.*

WINDSOR HOTEL ☙
125 W. Lamar St., Americus 31709, tel. 912/924–1555 or 888/297–9565, fax 912/928–0533

Among Georgia's and America's most intriguing historic hotels is the Windsor Hotel, a seeming maze of redbrick turrets and Romanesque arcades by Swedish-born (1846) Atlanta architect Gottfried L. Norrman. Norrman's work was all over this small (population 18,000) southwest Georgia town, as well as across the entire Southeast. Built in 1892, and named for John Windsor, one of its developers, the Richardsonian Romanesque eclectic hotel is on the National Register of Historic Places and is one of the National Trust's Historic Hotels of America.

Time was not kind to the hotel, which had disintegrated by the 1960s and was threatened with demolition. But Americus's citizens rose up to reclaim their grande old dame before she could be leveled for, yes, a parking lot. The original 100 rooms were reduced to 53 rooms and suites, and all were given private baths. Today, there is a small meeting room and a fine dining room.

Entering the hotel, one is amazed by its lobby, a study in neo-Moorish design. Norrman was influenced to some extent by the Hotel Alcázar in St. Augustine, Florida. Moorish-style arches sweep to the second story, and the entrance floor tiles, made of Georgia marble and oak and installed in 1912, were laid in a complex geometric pattern reminiscent of floors in southern Spain.

Reproduction gold oak furnishings, deeply carved, appoint the rooms. One of the suites served as home to Hume Cronin and Jessica Tandy while she was filming *Fried Green Tomatoes*. Amenities include a Ladies Tea Parlor, a pub, and a fine gifts gallery. Street-level retail shops include an antiques shop.

Special events at the hotel include holiday madrigal dinners with singing by faculty and students from nearby Georgia Southwestern University. ⚘ *51 double rooms with baths, 2 suites. Air-conditioning, cable TV and phone in rooms, hair dryers; in-room coffee and tea. $80–$195; breakfast not included. AE, D, MC, V.*

OTHER CHOICES

1870 Rothschild-Pound House. 201 7th St., Columbus 31901, tel. 706/322–4075 or 800/585–4075. 7 double rooms with baths. Air-conditioning, cable TV/VCR and phone in rooms; whirlpool bath in 2 rooms; kitchenette in 3 rooms; living room; garden; in-room coffee and tea. $85–$140; full breakfast, evening hors d'oeuvres and wine. AE, D, MC, V. No smoking.

HAWAII

Big Island of Hawaii

HALE MALUHIA 🐚

76–770 Hualalai Rd., Kailua-Kona 96740, tel. 808/329–1123 or 800/559–6627, fax 808/326–5487

Although the bed-and-breakfast is a business, Ken and Sue Smith, owners of Hale Maluhia (House of Peace) treat guests as if they are old friends come to visit. With an abundance of space, they opened their Swiss Family Robinson–style home to guests in 1992. The various levels of the property, which is set among the lush banyan and monkeypod trees, gives you the feeling of living in a luxurious tree house. The landscaping and placement of the rooms also afford privacy.

The arrangement of the rooms fosters privacy, too. The Maile and Pikaki rooms each have their own bath. The kitchenette in Pikaki can make these two rooms into the stand-alone retreat called the Gate House. The Main House contains the Makua and Malia rooms, each with a private bath plus easy access to the dining room, living room, and breakfast lanai. The main house also has cable TV, a stereo, a pool table, and a piano. Away from those enclaves, the 800-square-ft Banyan Cottage looks out over the Kona Coast. Its king-size bed dominates a bay-windowed alcove, and stained-glass windows surround a private marble whirlpool that has a spectacular view of the mountainside.

Inside and out, the sprawling house is surrounded by unique alcoves and lush flora. The eclectic mix of wicker and Victorian heirlooms—here an Oriental rug, there an antique cheval mirror—has the unmatched but loved look of the furnishings of *ohana* (extended-family) homes. Banana, mango, papaya, breadfruit, and banyan trees shade the compound, which is punctuated with streams, koi ponds, and waterfalls.

All guests have access to a Japanese stone-tiled spa with massage jets—as well as the game room and library, which are well stocked with books, videos, and games. Arts and crafts supplies are on hand as well, and the Smiths may direct guests in search of inspiration to the nearby artists' colony of Holualoa, a little farther up Hualalai Mountain.

For all its seclusion, Hale Maluhia is only minutes from the shops and beaches of Kailua-Kona. The ski slopes of Mauna Kea are less than an hour away. These slopes are not for beginners, but Sue can tell you where to get a "Ski the Volcano" T-shirt in Kailua-Kona even if you miss out on the slopes. ⌂ *4 double rooms with baths, 1 cottage that sleeps 6. TV/VCRs, kitchenettes, library, game room, massage spa, office facilities; barbecues and beach/snorkeling equipment available. $75–$145; full breakfast. AE, D, MC, V.*

HALE OHIA 🐚

*11–3968 Hale Ohia Rd. (Box 758), Volcano Village 96785, tel. 808/967–7986 or
800/455–3803, fax 808/967–8610*

Calm beauty and old-fashioned character will fill your senses as you come upon
Hale Ohia. This is the house you wish your grandparents had lived in and left
you alone to play in: a minifortress of stone and cedar shakes, with red-shingle
roof, hexagonal rooms, secluded spaces—and a turret! Your more mature tastes
will fancy the leaded-glass windows and stone fireplace. The gardens are for
connoisseurs of beauty—and who isn't?

In fact, says owner Michael Tuttle, the house did remind him of his grandmother's place, back in Kentucky, but what he really fell in love with was the landscape—"so lush, so green"—which is actually part of a rain forest. The house was
built in 1931 by a Scottish sea captain who had come to the Big Island to manage Ohelo plantation, near Hilo. It was sold 10 years later to the Hawaiian
Dredging Company and became the summer estate of the Dillingham family. It
had been built for "living in a rain forest," says Michael, and loving care and
diligence through the years have helped it stand up to the climate.

Four buildings on the Hale Ohia property have guest accommodations. The Dillingham Suite, in the main house, has its own entrance. Three more suites, one of which
has a kitchen, are in a second building. Two cottages each have a fireplace, kitchen,
and covered lanais filled with tropical plants. In the three-bedroom Ohia cottage, the decor and placement of the rooms suggest a turn-of-the-century lighthouse. (The feel of all the interiors reflects the builder's nautical tastes.) A
curved stairway leads to the top two bedrooms, passing a bathroom on the stair
landing, across from a stained-glass window. Other windows in Ohia cottage
are of leaded glass. The focal point of the second-floor living room is a game
table.

The real star at Hale Ohia—the house (*hale*) is named for the ohia trees in the area—
is the grounds. Tended for many years by the same landscape caretaker who had earlier laid out Hilo's beautiful Liliuokalani Gardens, these grounds include giant topiary,
cymbidium orchids, kahili ginger, hydrangea, and five kinds of camellias, which provide a year-round show. Stone-lined walkways tempt guests to linger in the spectacular gardens even though one of nature's most spectacular shows is only a mile
away: Volcanoes National Park. ♨ *5 suites, 2 cottages. Mini-refrigerators, Japanese* furo *(soaking) tub. $65–$125; Continental breakfast. MC, V.*

KILAUEA LODGE 🐚

*On Old Volcano Rd. (Box 116), Volcano Village 96785, tel. 808/967–7366,
fax 808/967–7367*

Ballyhooed by food critics and quietly hailed by local residents (who would like
to keep it a secret), the Kilauea Lodge Restaurant will make you wish you had
booked an extra week's stay. While dinner is open to the public, only those staying at the lodge have access to the full breakfast, which includes fresh island fruits
and the most popular item, sweet-bread French toast.

Owners Albert and Lorna Jeyte discovered this former YMCA camp when they
honeymooned in 1986 at Volcanoes National Park. Two years later, the former
Magnum, P.I. makeup artist and his wife turned the main building into a restaurant and the old bunkhouse into Hale Makua—four fireplace-warmed double
rooms beautifully furnished with the light woods and snuggle-up fabrics that
typify this Hawaiian mountain region as well as large skylights in the bathrooms. Tutu's Cottage, on a separate part of the property, has its own wide porch,

a gas stove, and large yard. In 1991 the Jeytes added the seven guest rooms of Hale Aloha, which are centered on a sitting room warmed by a fireplace. (Guests from the cottage and Hale Makua are also welcome to relax in the deep-cushioned comfort of the Hale Aloha sitting room, and it is spacious enough to accommodate all the guests at once.) Additional amenities include towel warmers in every bath, in-room coffee and tea servers, books, and sightseeing videos.

The Jeytes love this part of the Big Island and are happy to share their knowledge of local lore and geography with their guests. Visitors who know his TV background press Albert for stories about the famous "faces" he has made up or ask whether celebrities ever stay at the lodge. (They do, and their privacy is respected, as is every guest's.)

Kilauea Lodge still has the air of a mountain summer camp—or enough of it, at least, to bring back youthful fantasies, such as afternoon dips and midnight trysts. There are, as well, hiking opportunities aplenty, either in the rain forest that surrounds the lodge or in the national park just five minutes away. These need be only as arduous as you wish; Devastation Trail and some other park "hikes" are actually on boardwalks, and the lodge is encircled by forests of tree ferns with well-marked paths suitable for easy strolling. △ *11 double rooms with baths (1 room wheelchair-accessible), 2 cottages. Restaurant (dinner only; chair-lift can bring mobility-impaired guests to and from the restaurant), library, central heating. $110–$145; full breakfast. MC, V.*

OTHER CHOICES

Suds' Acres. Box 277, Paauilo 96776, tel. and fax 808/776–1611. 1 double room with bath, 1 suite, 1 cottage. $55 ($10 per extra person); Continental breakfast. MC, V.

Maui

KULA LODGE ☙

On Haleakala Hwy., just past 5-mi mark on Rte. 377, ¾ mi from Crater Rd.; R.R. 1 (Box 475), Kula, Maui 96790, tel. 808/878–1535 or 800/233–1535, fax 808/878–2518

A Swiss-style chalet 20 minutes from Kahului Airport may sound improbable, but Kula Lodge, surrounded by farms and protea fields, sits 3,200 ft up on the side of Mount Haleakala, where the roads are winding and the terrain laced with hiking trails and bridle paths. Of course, once you spot the fine view of the island's west coast and, on a clear day, Lanai and Kahoolawe islands sitting across the channel, you'll know you're nowhere else but on Maui.

This is not the Maui with steamy tropical waterfalls or the one with crescents of white-sand beach or the one with paper umbrellas in improbably. This is Upcountry Maui, land of real cowboys, working farms and ranches, and mountain air—and less than an hour from the beaches of Wailea or the quirky whaling town turned arts center of Lahaina. Kula is a year-round home to many and a great place to meet locals.

The lodge was built as a private home in the 1940s and has operated as a small inn since the 1960s. The current owner, Fred Romanchak, looks after business in the restaurant, the gift shop, the art gallery, and the guest rooms and lives just up the street.

The lodge's restaurant—which offers unparalleled views from wraparound windows—serves hearty breakfasts, lunches, and dinners to sightseers heading to or from Haleakala's 10,000-ft summit. And the dining room's huge stone fireplace is a welcome sight to returning climbers who never dreamed it could be so cold on a volcano.

The mountain atmosphere extends to the lodge's wood-paneled sleeping quarters as well. The two largest units share a building to the right of the main lodge. Each has a queen-size bed, a sitting room, a gas fireplace, and a loft with twin beds; the private decks look northwest, along the coast toward Lahaina. Another building has two units with queen-size beds, private baths, and smaller sleeping lofts (the twin-size futons are just right for kids who are old enough to enjoy the adventure of loft-sleeping, with Mom and Dad not too far away downstairs); the private decks here look southwest, toward the Wailea coastline. A fifth unit, dubbed a studio, is downstairs from the restaurant; it has a private bath and deck, but the owners don't brag about this view (it is not as spectacular as the one from upstairs). Space heaters are available when it gets chilly in the rooms without fireplaces. ⌂ *3 double rooms with baths, 2 suites. Coffeemakers, restaurant. $110–$165; breakfast not included. AE, MC, V.*

OTHER CHOICES

Kamuela Inn B&B. Box 1994, Kamuela 96743, tel. 808/885–4243 or 800/555–8968, fax 808/885–8857. 31 rooms with baths, 3 suites. Kitchen in suites, lanai in 1 suite. $59–$185; Continental breakfast. AE, D, DC, MC, V.
Waimea Gardens Cottage B&B. Box 563, Kamuela 96743, tel. 808/885–4550 or 800/262–9912, fax 808/885–0559. 2 cottages. $110–$135; fully stocked kitchen with breakfast items. No credit cards.

RESERVATIONS SERVICES

Affordable Paradise B&Bs (226 Pouli Rd., Kailua 96734, tel. 800/925–9065). **All Islands B&Bs** (823 Kainui Dr., Kailai 96734, tel. 800/542–0344). **B&B Hawaii** (Box 449, Kapaa 96746, tel. 800/733–1632). **B&B Honolulu** (3242 Kaohinani Dr. 96817, tel. 800/288–4666). **Bed & Breakfast Maui-Style** (Box 98, Kihei 96784, tel. 808/870–7865; Maui only). **Hawaii's Best B&Bs** (Box 563, Kamuela 96743, tel. 808/885–4550). **Volcano Accommodations** (Box 28, Volcano 96785, tel. 808/967–8662; volcanoes region only). **Volcano Reservations** (Box 998, Volcano 96785, tel. 808/967–7244; volcanoes region only).

Oahu

MANOA VALLEY INN ❧
2001 Vancouver Dr., Honolulu 96822, tel. 808/947–6019 or 800/634–5115, fax 808/946–6168

Thoughtfully and authentically restored in 1982 and listed on the National Register of Historic Places, Manoa Valley Inn is a find for anyone who wants to enjoy nearby Waikiki without trying to sleep amid its bright lights and bustle. Located in Manoa Valley, one of Honolulu's finest residential neighborhoods, the inn is just a short walk from the University of Hawaii's main campus and from the bus to Waikiki (2 mi away), downtown Honolulu (4 mi), or Ala Moana beach-side park and shopping center (2 mi). There is free parking (a rarity in Honolulu) for guests' cars.

Built in 1919, the house has many links to Hawaiian history. Guest rooms are named after such legendary families as Dole, Dillingham, Alexander, and Baldwin—and innkeeper Herb Fukushima shares tales of earlier times with interested visitors.

Inside and out, the house is for time-travelers. Walls are papered with rose and Oriental-inspired florals; fringed apricot-silk lamp shades hover over reading chairs set around the living room's big stone fireplace; white crocheted doilies, table runners, and antimacassars are everywhere, from the billiard room's sideboard to the sunroom's card table: 20th-century accoutrements like color TV (in the living room) and in-room telephones are tucked out of sight when not in use.

A wicker-furnished lanai runs the entire length of the house and looks out across the back lawn to the high-rises of Waikiki. The Continental breakfast buffet and a late-afternoon fruit-and-cheese tray are served here, and it's a popular spot for guests at any hour.

A suite and six double rooms are all upstairs, outfitted with exquisite beds made of antique iron or inlaid island woods, marble-top tables, and cut-glass lamps. The attention to authenticity banishes television for the most part (except in the suite and the cottage, which do have sets). The cottage—a double room with private bath in a separate building—offers the greatest privacy, but because it is built on ground slightly lower than the main house, it does not enjoy the mountain or ocean views that the upstairs guest rooms have. Still, the inn's own garden, full of croton, dracaena, delphinium, and plumeria, is just outside the cottage door. ▲ *3 double rooms with baths, 3 doubles share bath, 1 suite, 1 cottage. Ceiling fan, phone, terry cloth robes, safe in rooms, TV in suite and cottage; piano, croquet. $99–$190; Continental breakfast. AE, DC, MC, V.*

IDAHO

Northern Panhandle

CLARK HOUSE ON HAYDEN LAKE 🐚

E. 4550 S. Hayden Lake Rd., Hayden Lake 83835, tel. 208/772–3470 or 800/765–4593, fax 208/772–6899

If you visit the Clark House on Idaho's Hayden Lake, a 40-minute drive from Spokane, Washington, you will become immersed in the inn's history and mystery. The reclusive mining millionaire F. Lewis Clark had the home built as a replica of a summer palace of Kaiser Wilhelm II of Germany. Construction on the 33 rooms and 10 fireplaces began in 1895 but wasn't completed until 1910. Clark and his wife, Winifred, lived in the house for four years; then he and all of his money disappeared mysteriously. Winifred waited patiently for her husband's return but was forced to sell off the land, furnishings, and eventually the house to pay back taxes.

In 1989 innkeeper Monty Danner and his son Mark bought and restored the mansion, now on the National Register of Historic Places, after it sat empty for 20 years. Monty and his partner, Rod Palmer, masterfully decorated the house; the result is a sumptuously comfortable country inn, set on a secluded 13-acre estate. In the long second-floor gallery, light filters through grand Palladian windows at both ends and murals brighten the walls. The walls of the smaller downstairs dining room are also covered by a mural, this one depicting the house's history. The downstairs library offers a variety of diversions, including a scrapbook chronicling the disappearance of F. Lewis Clark.

The furnishings are both elegant and understated, and even the occasional spectacular decorative flourishes, such as the intricately carved walnut buffet crafted in Connecticut during the 1870s, blend in effortlessly with the overall scheme. Guest rooms are individually decorated and quietly luxurious. Mrs. Clark's Room, done in a tea-rose motif, has a white-and-gold-trimmed Louis XIV–style writing table and high chest. The F. Lewis Clark Room, with its canopied bed, and the Cedar Suite, done in burgundy and deep green, have a masculine, Ralph Lauren look. The Hayden Lake Room, with cream and white brocade and natural wicker furniture, has the best view of the lake. French doors are in every room, some leading outdoors to deck and terrace areas, a lush lawn overlooking Hayden Lake, and a wildflower-filled garden. ♨ *10 double rooms with baths. TVs (on request), robes, fireplace in 4 rooms, guest refrigerator, hot tub, conference facilities, nature trails, marina, skiing nearby. $100–$200; full breakfast, 6-course gourmet dinner by reservation 5 nights a week, wine and beer available. AE, D, DC, MC, V. No smoking, 2-night minimum Memorial Day–Labor Day.*

CRICKET ON THE HEARTH BED AND BREAKFAST INN 🐦
1521 Lakeside Ave., Coeur d'Alene 83814, tel. 208/664–6926

Those who are turned on by theater and theme rooms will have their fantasies fueled at the Cricket on the Hearth Bed and Breakfast Inn, 10 minutes from downtown Coeur d'Alene. Actors and hosts Tom and Julie Nash, who met while doing summer stock in 1972 (he played Harold Hill in *The Music Man*, and she was in the orchestra pit), draw on their extensive theatrical background to create a whimsical bed-and-breakfast experience. These ardent thespians have decorated the guest rooms in their 1920 stucco Craftsman cottage with musical-comedy themes ranging from *Cats* to *Carousel* to *The Unsinkable Molly Brown*. Each of these rooms features original posters from the Broadway productions and remains true to its chosen theme with various props. The Carousel Room has a painted carousel horse, and the Kabuki Room is filled with authentic Japanese prints, wall hangings, and artifacts.

You can relax in the game room, which opens onto a deck equipped for barbecuing. Tom and Julie serve generous breakfasts of fresh fruit, breads or muffins, and a main dish such as a casserole, French toast, or waffles, in the dining room or on the deck in good weather. ♣ *3 double rooms with baths, 2 doubles share bath. Guest refrigerator, hot tub, ski packages. $55–$85; full breakfast. No credit cards. No smoking.*

GREGORY'S MCFARLAND HOUSE 🐦
601 Foster Ave., Coeur d'Alene 83814, tel. 208/667–1232

At Gregory's McFarland House in Coeur d'Alene, a spacious Classical Revival–Italianate structure, old meets new flawlessly. Built in 1905 for Idaho's second attorney general, the house is a blend of treasures and elegant family heirlooms from other eras and modern comforts and conveniences.

Innkeepers Winifred, Stephen, and Carol Gregory share with guests a home full of family history; many of their 19th-century antiques came from Winifred's ancestral home in England. The carved claw-foot table in the dining room, which once made a journey around Cape Horn, sits on one of several Chinese rugs scattered throughout the house's gleaming bird's-eye maple floors. In one of the common areas, interested guests may play a game of pool on the 1920 regulation Brunswick table.

The guest rooms are large and bright, with rose and pink accents, hand-crocheted bedspreads, and curtains of German lace. One room features an inlaid-wood bedroom suite from the 1860s, with a marble-top table and low dresser. Several rooms have four-poster beds. Breakfast is served in a bright, glassed-in conservatory overlooking the English garden. On a quiet tree-lined street, Gregory's McFarland House provides a soothing atmosphere only six blocks from downtown. ♣ *5 double rooms with baths. Air-conditioning. $85–$125; full breakfast, afternoon refreshments. MC, V. No smoking, 2-night minimum mid-May–mid-Oct., mid-Nov.–early Jan., and holidays.*

HISTORIC JAMESON 🐦
304 6th St., Wallace 83873, tel. 208/556–1554

The historic community of Wallace is midway between Spokane, Washington, and Missoula, Montana, in northern Idaho's Silver Valley—the world's largest silver mining district. Due to its colorful past and the preservation of many original buildings, the entire town is listed on the National Register of Historic Places. On a downtown street corner is a three-story redbrick building opened as the

Theodore Jameson Steak and Billiard Hall in 1889. Today, the Historic Jameson houses a saloon and restaurant on the first floor, conference space on the second floor, and bed-and-breakfast accommodations on the third floor.

The Jameson's rooms are small yet charming. Furnishings include high-post beds, old-fashioned ceiling fans and luggage racks, side chairs, armoires, miniature dressers, and vanity tables with mirrors. Small brass reading lamps on doilies sit on petite bedside tables; vintage photographs and prints hang on the walls; and simple white woven bedspreads offset dark oak and walnut headboards. The late-Victorian decor, in warm hues of brown, tan, and cream, is complemented by dainty floral wallpaper.

Maggie has been the Jameson's resident ghost since the 1930s. Manager Rick Shaffer says, "Legend has it that either she died here or thought it was such a nice place that she didn't want to leave." Fortunately, she has a playful spirit. Among her favorite ploys are hiding guests' keys, turning on ceiling fans, and turning off hot water as guests shower.

A Continental breakfast of juice, croissants, and coffee is served in guests' rooms or in the parlor. The restaurant also has an extensive breakfast menu if heartier fare is preferred. Serving classic American cuisine, the Jameson Restaurant is best known for its homemade bread and Irish coffee, made with the establishment's own brand of Irish whiskey. Ceiling fans, bentwood chairs, polished brass chandeliers, and a massive mirrored antique bar reveal its past as a fancy turn-of-the-century, Old West saloon. *6 double rooms share 1 bath. Restaurant, indoor pool, sauna, hot tub nearby. $68; Continental breakfast included, full breakfast available. AE, MC, V.*

OTHER CHOICES

Berry Patch Inn. 1150 N. Four Winds Rd., Coeur d'Alene 83814, tel. 208/765–4994. 3 doubles with baths. Satellite TV/VCR, stereo, and stone fireplace in common area; 1 room with private entrance. $115–$135; full breakfast. MC, V.

Blackwell House. 820 Sherman Ave., Coeur d'Alene, ID, tel. 208/664–0656. 3 double rooms with baths, 2 doubles share 1 bath, 3 suites. Air-conditioning in 4 bedrooms; cable TV in music room; fireplace in living room, morning room, and 1 suite. $75–$140; full breakfast. AE, D, MC, V.

RESERVATIONS SERVICE

Idaho Department of Commerce (Box 83720, Boise 83720, tel. 800/635–7820; listings only—call for brochure).

Central Rockies

IDAHO COUNTRY INN 🐦
134 Latigo La. (Box 2355), Sun Valley 83353, tel. 208/727–4000 or 800/250–8341, fax 208/726–5718

Railroad mogul William Averell Harriman dispatched Austrian count Felix Schaffgotsch to find a site for a destination ski resort in the west "of the same character as the Swiss and Austrian Alps." What he came up with was Sun Valley, the grande dame of ski resorts in the central Idaho Rockies, which has been luring seekers of plentiful sun and snow with its Old World charm and western hospitality since 1936.

The inn's site on a sun-washed saddle affords spectacular views of the nearby ski mountain and the Wood River valley. Its location—midway between Ketchum and Sun Valley village—is convenient, yet removed and quiet.

It was ice and snow that attracted Terry and Julie Heneghan, proprietors of the Idaho Country Inn, to Sun Valley. Terry, from Massachusetts, and Julie, from Arizona, were inspired to build an inn that would reflect Idaho's lore while providing first-class accommodations. Because this is a newer inn (built in 1990), it has a fresh, shiny look.

Here, rustic simplicity blends with contemporary sophistication. Peeled timber and smooth river rock from the area were used throughout, and local artisans built most of the furniture. Log beams, whitewashed walls, and a river-rock fireplace in the high-ceiling living room create a warm setting. In the afternoon, the Heneghan's two big Newfoundland dogs often amble in, hoping for attention from guests.

Terry, a longtime fly-fishing guide, decorated the inn with a fish motif: Wall hangings include mounted trout and salmon; the tiles on the library's fireplace are decorated with fish; and a hand-painted headboard depicting central Idaho's famed fly-fishing hole, Silver Creek, is in the Angler Room. Terry's own artful fly-tying handiwork is also on display.

Natural twig furniture and a willow-and-wood poster bed set a romantic tone in the Willow Room. The Wagon Days Room pays tribute to the valley's mining heyday with a giant wagon wheel at the head of a heavy pine bed. Most of the rooms have patios or balconies.

For breakfast, Julie always makes something decadent and something healthy. Guests gather in the sunroom adjoining the living room to dine on chokecherry corn cakes with ham, potato crepes with Basque filling (red and green peppers, yellow onions, tomatoes, and artichoke hearts), and piping-hot muffins. In the afternoon, Julie serves hot appetizers and homemade cookies fireside. △ *11 double rooms with baths. Air-conditioning in 5 rooms, phone, cable TV, 2 fireplaces in common rooms, hot tub, winter packages available. $132–$205; full breakfast and afternoon snacks. AE, D, MC, V.*

OTHER CHOICES

Idaho Rocky Mountain Ranch. HC 64, Box 9934, Stanley 83278, tel. 208/774–3544, fax 208/774–3477. 4 double rooms with baths, 8 duplex cabins, 1 honeymoon cabin. Fireplace in cabins, lodge, and dining room; outdoor hot-springs, pool, hiking, cross-country skiing, horseback riding, white-water rafting, mountain biking nearby. June–Sept., $180; full breakfast and dinner. Nov.–Apr., $105–$125 (2 cabins only); full breakfast.

Knob Hill Inn. 960 N. Main St. (Box 800), Ketchum 83340, tel. 208/726–8010, fax 208/726–2712. 20 double rooms with baths, 4 suites. Cable TV, phones; minibar and VCR in suites; fireplace in 4 rooms and 4 suites; café and restaurant, indoor lap pool, hot tub, fitness room, sauna, ski lockers, transportation from municipal airport, masseuse available, downhill and cross-country skiing, nature trail nearby. $185–$375; full breakfast, peak season afternoon refreshments. AE, MC, V.

Boise Valley

IDAHO HERITAGE INN

109 W. Idaho St., Boise 83702, tel. 208/342–8066, fax 208/343–2325

This stately home in a historic residential district of Idaho's capital was built by Henry Falk in 1904. Roughly 40 years later, then-governor Chase A. Clark acquired it and later passed it to his daughter and son-in-law, Frank Church, a senator and presidential candidate. The Churches used it as their Idaho residence until 1987, when Tom and Phyllis Lupher turned it into a gracious bed-and-breakfast inn.

Having renovated several historic properties and owned an antiques mall in Boise, the Luphers were well equipped to take on this inn, listed on the National Register of Historic Places. Period wall coverings, antique fixtures and furniture, diamond-pane glass windows, and Oriental rugs are found throughout. The dining room, beyond the large entryway, has a built-in walnut china cabinet with leaded-glass doors. The sunroom (with TV and VCR) combines with the living room to create a spacious common area with ample seating.

The Luphers have paid homage to the house's history by following a political theme in naming its rooms. Upstairs, the sunny Governor's Suite has mementos from Chase Clark's tenure as governor. Its color scheme is dark green and rose; white woodwork blends with the antique oak sleigh bed and dresser. Adding to its allure, the suite has a roomy bath with an art-deco, tiled walk-in shower and separate tub, and French doors that open to an enclosed sun porch with white wicker rockers. The extra-large Judge's Chambers has Victorian walnut furnishings and a covered veranda; and the Carriage House has a wet bar, microwave, refrigerator, and privacy. In keeping with the political-history theme, the inn was proud to host former First Lady Barbara Bush, who stayed here in 1993.

Because it's in the Warm Springs district of Boise, this inn enjoys the luxury of never running out of hot water. Endless gallons of geothermal spring water in the bathrooms can be a spa-like experience.

Typical breakfast fare includes fresh-squeezed juice, fruit, baked German pancakes, apricot cream-cheese–stuffed French toast, and apple skillet cake. △ *3 double rooms, 2 suites, carriage house. Air-conditioning; cable TV in suites and carriage house, cable TV/VCR in sunroom, fireplace in living room, fax service, mountain bike rental. $60–$95; full breakfast, wine in the evening. AE, D, MC, V.*

OTHER CHOICES

Idaho City Hotel. 215 Montgomery St. (Box 70), Idaho City 83631, tel. 208/392–4290, fax 208/392–4505. 5 double rooms with baths. Cable TV, phone, clock radio, year-round natural hot-water pool nearby. $39; breakfast packages available ($12 for two persons). AE, D, DC, MC, V.

RESERVATIONS SERVICE

Idaho Department of Commerce (Box 83720, Boise 83720, tel. 800/635–7820; listings only—call for brochure).

ILLINOIS

Galena

FELT MANOR 🐚
125 S. Prospect St., Galena 61036, tel. 815/777–9093 or 800/383–2830

On a weekday afternoon in historic Galena, time passes slowly on its quiet Victorian-era streets. The scene changes, however, when thousands of visitors descend on this charming and best-preserved old river town of the Upper Mississippi region. In this world of here-today-and-gone-tomorrows, travelers cherish the locale as a picturesque getaway and historic center (the site of Ulysses S. Grant's home, among other attractions). With streets that are museums of mid-19th-century architecture—ranging from early Federal cottages to *Gone With the Wind*-style mansions—it's little wonder that Galena has become a B&B haven.

"Is it 1893 or 1993?" a visitor once wrote in the guest book of Felt Manor. "After 15 minutes and a glass of sherry, it's hard for a harried Chicagoan to tell. Here in the parlor, there is no noise but the ticking of the clock." At Laura and Dan Balocca's B&B, guests often feel transported back to the golden era of 19th-century America, and no more so than during one of Laura's afternoon teas, highlighted perhaps by artichoke puffs and new potatoes stuffed with sour cream and caviar. Other old-time elements, such as gilt-framed Victorian lithographs, music on the square-box grand piano, and soft lighting from silk-fringed lamps combine to make guests feel, as one eloquently put it, "enfolded within the inn's Victorian skirts."

Built atop Quality Hill, the town's tallest bluff, Felt Manor is a four-story, orange brick, Second Empire Victorian mansion with teal shutters: It sits next door to Ulysses S. Grant's first Galena home. The house was constructed in 1848 by dry-goods entrepreneur Lucius Felt, who became a millionaire despite an offer from Marshall Field's to merge companies. The inn has several entrances, but try climbing the imposing limestone staircase built into the steep slope leading up to the house: Listed with the Library of Congress as a national landmark, the 1850 staircase was then known as "Felt's Folly" because of its $40,000 cost.

There is also an underground ice house and a brick coach house. The inn's terraced grounds are being returned to the Victorian-era layout by a gardener from the Chicago Botanic Society. Once it's finished, masses of tea-rose, black-night nasturtium, phlox, and foxglove will surround the veranda, which offers a panoramic view of the storybook town below.

Upstairs, five guest rooms are each furnished in period style. The Lucius Felt Room has a double window view of the Galena Valley, dark wood antiques and reproductions, and an original marble sink in a small wood-paneled wall recess. Also, at press time (winter 1998), two rooms with shared baths were being converted into luxury suites with whirlpool baths and fireplaces to be completed by late spring. In the meantime, guests may want to consider one of the customized packages (starting at $175), which include overnight accommodations and dining or entertainment.

Mornings bring gourmet breakfasts, which, like the afternoon teas, are filled with irrefutably delicious offerings, as Laura worked as a sous-chef to two renowned chefs in Naperville. At sunset, the town below becomes a sea of twinkling lights, and guests can often enjoy the free entertainment provided by the Northern Lights in the sky above. ♨ *3 double rooms with baths, 2 double rooms with shared bath. 7 fireplaces, original marble sinks, CD player in 1 room, TV in game room. $105–$160; full breakfast and Saturday afternoon tea. AE, D, MC, V.*

HELLMAN GUEST HOUSE ❦
315 Hill St., Galena 61036, tel. 815/777–3638

A fortuitous concentration of elaborate 19th-century mansions whose original owners had amassed fortunes from merchandising, mining, and steamboating operations, Galena features a wide range of houses built in the Greek and Italian Revival styles popular in the 1840s and 1850s. As a town stocked with the type of houses that seem to inspire people to lay claim to and restore them, it has, not surprisingly, become a B&B boom town. Evelyn and Roger Bird discovered the lovely Queen Anne Victorian that is now the Hellman Guest House and acquired it in the fall of 1998. Like the guest house's previous owner, who did much to help save and restore this charming bit of history, the Birds are also interested in preserving the touches, tastes, and architectural details of the Victorian mid-century throughout the inn.

Updating an historic home while preserving its original character is apparently not an easy task. The original paint schemes had to be researched, new plumbing and electrical systems installed, bathrooms were refurbished, and the bedrooms remodeled. To determine the exact appearance of the original wraparound porch and the second-story porch over the entry, vintage photographs and newspaper articles were unearthed. Today, guests can enjoy the fruits of these arduous efforts. The carefully refurbished sumptuous oak and pine woodwork in the five guest rooms, the colorful ceramic tiles—reminiscent of those of 19th-century lavatories—that ornament the bathrooms, the hand-carved newel posts accenting the grand staircase, and the eye-catching turret room all testify to an age no more. An inviting parlor beckons with the best seat in the house—a lovely 19th-century wingback chair positioned by the picture window and an antique telescope focused on the craggy bluffs surrounding the town.

As to the four guest rooms, the Master Bedroom has a queen-size brass bed, a fireplace, and tower alcove, while the others—named Pauline, Irene, and Eleanor, after the daughters of John V. Hellman, the original owner of the house—are cozy cocoons decorated with antique beds and wicker rocking chairs. Breakfast served by Evelyn and Roger might include just-out-of-the-oven quiche, pancakes and fruit, and fresh juices. ♨ *4 double rooms with baths. Air-conditioning, fireplace in common rooms and Master Bedroom. $119–149; full breakfast. D, MC, V.*

INN AT IRISH HOLLOW ❦
2800 S. Irish Hollow Rd., Galena 61036, tel. 815/777–2010 or 815/777–6000, fax 815/777–6100

A turn onto Irish Hollow Road makes it immediately clear why 19th-century Irish settlers gave this charming countryside nook—five minutes outside the town of Galena—its name. Lushly green, with a winding stream and a misty haze that lingers through the morning, it resembles the idealized image many people have of Ireland. Once active in the 19th century as Galena's hub of the Great Western Railway (city fathers, many of whose fortunes were based on steamboating, fought against allowing the train to enter directly into the town), the Irish Hollow dell attracted various services, one of which was a general store. Today, the store, exquisitely renovated, serves as a novel entrance for the Inn at Irish Hollow, which B&B connoisseurs now regard as one of the more unique inns of the Midwest.

In 1989, Bill Barrick and Tony Kemp purchased the general store, its attached shopkeeper's house, and a nearby storybook cottage and, after extensive renovations to the property, began to welcome their first guests. The word quickly spread about the inn's gourmet kitchen, the luxurious modern amenities, and the charming parlor rooms, accented with antiques such as an old Steinway grand piano, a grandfather clock, and tapestry-covered chairs.

Acclaimed by *Glamour* magazine as one of the premier romantic getaways in the country, the French Maid Cottage—the legend is that it was built in the 1880s by a neighboring landowner as a discreet hideaway for his ladylove, a maid he had brought over from France—is very popular with honeymooners. This delightful cottage-for-two has a large whirlpool bath, a two-sided fireplace, a four-poster bed, and a sitting porch.

The inn is noted for its weekend packages (two-night affairs, complete with candlelit dinner); its picture-book Christmas festivities; and its renovated general store, which has an antique coffee grinder, wooden scales, and old postal boxes. After feasting on stuffed French toast drizzled with the inn's fresh apple-orchard syrup, guests may choose to set off for Galena or nearby Chestnut Mountain Ski Resort, or simply to curl up in the inn's library to enjoy the comforting and warm haven that is the Inn at Irish Hollow. ▲ *5 double rooms with baths, 1 cottage. Restaurant, air-conditioning; balcony in 2 rooms; CD player, double whirlpool bath, wet bar, microwave, mini-refrigerator in cottage. $110–$175 weekday; $325–$475 weekend packages, with dinner; $325–$585 holiday packages (including Thanksgiving, Christmas, and Valentine's Day); full breakfast. D, DC, MC, V. 2-night minimum weekends.*

OTHER CHOICES

Pine Hollow Inn. 4700 N. Council Hill Rd., Galena 61036, tel. 815/777–1071. 5 double rooms with baths Fireplace in rooms, whirlpool bath in 2 rooms. $75–$125; breakfast not included. D, MC, V.

Central Illinois
❦❦❦

OLD CHURCH HOUSE INN BED & BREAKFAST ☙
1416 E. Mossville Rd., Mossville 61552, tel. 309/579–2300, fax 309/691–1834

"Sleeping in church is encouraged here," says Holly Ramseyer, innkeeper of the Old Church House Inn Bed & Breakfast. No need to ponder Holly's sense of good behavior, as she is the proud chatelaine of a hostelry converted from an 1869 Colonial-style Presbyterian church. After purchasing the structure—which had already been renovated into a private home—in 1988, Holly and husband

Dean set about creating a bit of B&B heaven in Mossville, a quaint old river village on the north edge of Peoria.

Originally part of the church sanctuary, the formal living and dining rooms have tall, arched windows and 18-ft-high tongue-and-groove wood ceilings. The eye is caught by an aerie-level balcony-library, entered by means of a nearby ladder, which adds to the effect of the room's great height. The decor is a felicitous blend of eras—mixing classic heirloom pieces with reproductions—but a pulpit, altar table, and authentic vintage photographs and church bulletins attest to the fact that, as Holly puts it, "traveling pastors once led scores of souls to the Lord here."

Guests have a choice of two distinctive accommodations. Most noticeable upon entering the one called the Bedchamber is an 1860s carved-walnut bedstead whose handmade log cabin–motif quilt coordinates with the room's hunter-green and bordeaux-red color scheme. By contrast, the Garden Room is a lace-festooned boudoir: A sheer white canopy cascades over a white-iron and brass bed, and traceries of roses and peonies adorn the papered walls. Feather-bed mattresses provide nights of pleasant dreams. The inn's top rate, called the Sweetheart rate, offers its guests a private bath and the run of the entire inn.

At breakfast, a scattering of violets and nasturtiums over a fresh fruit medley is a delightful surprise, followed by Dean's made-from-scratch frosted cinnamon rolls and a delicious porridge that would please even Goldilocks. After spending a day on the nearby Rock Island Bike Trail, you'll enjoy returning to the Old Church House Inn for afternoon tea and a batch of Holly's chunky chocolate-chip cookies. ♙ *2 double rooms with shared bath. Fireplace in 1 room, TV/VCR (upon request), turndown service with Swiss chocolates. $75–$119; Continental breakfast. D, MC, V.*

Southern Illinois

MAGNOLIA PLACE BED AND BREAKFAST 🕊

317 S. Main St., Red Bud 62278, tel. 618/282–4141

South of the state capitol of Springfield, Illinois takes on a flavor far removed from that of much of the rest of the state. Called "Little Egypt" for its location between the valleys of the Ohio and Mississippi rivers, southern Illinois has some of the most remarkable scenery in the country.

Along the Great River Road of Illinois Route 3, just 40 mi southeast of St. Louis, the quiet German farming community of Red Bud offers a peaceful retreat in a prosperous rural area. This is the town where Dolly Krallman was born and raised and where she opened Red Bud's first B&B, in 1993. In the town's historic district, Magnolia Place is a stately three-story mansion designed by an English architect in the 1850s.

Dolly's love of all things blooming is apparent not only in the name of her inn and her four exquisite guest rooms but also in the beautiful gardens. The gardens and the antebellum gazebo are often the site of weddings and, when weather permits, breakfast for overnight guests.

Guest rooms bear the names of Dolly's favorite flowers: Magnolia, Rose, Wisteria, and Gardenia. The Grand Magnolia Suite has an oversize whirlpool bath, big-screen TV/VCR, and movie library. Pocket doors, fireplaces, and curved-glass windows are highlights of the other three rooms.

Breakfast is an elaborate buffet featuring pastries, muffins, breakfast meats, and egg dishes. ⚐ *2 double room with baths, 2 suites. Air-conditioning, whirlpool and TV/VCR in 1 suite, fireplace in 1 suite, off-street parking. $60–$140; full breakfast. AE, D, MC, V.*

OTHER CHOICES

Isle View Bed and Breakfast. 205 Metropolis St., Metropolis 62960, tel. 618/524–5838 or 800/566–7491. 3 rooms with baths. 2 suites. Cable TVs, phones, fireplace and whirlpool bath in suites. $42.50–$125; full breakfast, romantic dinner or champagne packages. AE, D, DC, MC, V.

Olde Squat Inn. Rte. 7 (Box 247), Marion 62959, tel. 618/982–2916. 12 cabins with baths. Fireplace in 3 cabins, hot tub, deck, horseshoes, walking trails. $59; full breakfast. No credit cards.

RESERVATIONS SERVICE

Illinois Bed and Breakfast Association (Box 82, Port Bryon 61275, tel. 309/523–2406).

INDIANA

Southern Hills

ARTISTS COLONY INN ✒

Van Buren and Franklin Sts. (Box 1099), Nashville 47448, tel. 812/988–0600 or 800/737–0255, fax 812/988–9023

Fifty miles south of Indianapolis, the landscape swells and dips, spared by an ancient glacier that flattened much of northern Indiana. Amid this landscape of sweeping vistas, log cabins, and dense woodlands, a colony of impressionist artists found the perfect subject matter for their canvases in the early 1900s.

Ever since the hamlet of Nashville in Brown County hosted the Hoosier School of Artists, arts and crafts have thrived here. Today, with more than 300 shops and 50 full-time crafters, Nashville bulges year-round with tourists.

Jay and Ellen Carter built this rectangular, three-story wood-frame building off downtown Nashville's busy main street in 1992 and surrounded it with gardens and trees. A redbrick walkway leads to a wide front porch that, weather permitting, hosts alfresco dining. Inside, the palette is dominated by deep blue, green, burgundy, and cream; and the simple Early American furnishings draw from the Carter's own collection. Reproduction cherrywood and painted furniture, Windsor-style chairs, and woven coverlets furnish the spare yet comfortable rooms. Shaker-style peg boards and tables and graceful wrought-iron floor lamps further denote Colonial simplicity. Many of the furnishings, including the scatter rugs and runners that cover the stained pine floors, were made by local artisans. A long-time friend and furniture maker crafted the pencil-post beds, tables, cupboards, and all 224 of the chairs. The boulders in the massive stone fireplace were salvaged from local 19th-century homes.

Although they rely on a professional manager to oversee operations, the Carters are often on hand to greet guests, seat diners, and share a little history of the artists' colony. Ellen's father, Frederick W. Rigley, is the last living original art colony member. The large, airy dining room with beamed ceiling doubles as a gallery showcasing much of the couple's extensive collection of Hoosier School art. Each bedroom is named for one of the early artists and has both a photographic portrait and a short biography of the artist, in addition to a reproduction of one of his or her works.

In a town buzzing with tourists, this inn has a genial setting that complements the country-style food served for breakfast, lunch, and dinner (meals not included). **♨** *20 double rooms with baths. Air-conditioning, cable TV, phones, restaurant, outdoor hot tub. $140–$170; breakfast not included. AE, MC, V.*

OTHER CHOICES

Allison House Inn. 90 S. Jefferson St. (Box 1625), Nashville 47448, tel. 812/988–0814. 5 double rooms with baths. Air-conditioning, TV in lounge, fireplace in library. $95; full breakfast. No credit cards. No smoking, 2-night minimum.

Columbus Inn. 445 5th St., Columbus 47501, tel. 812/378–4289. 29 double rooms with baths, 5 suites. Restaurant, air-conditioning, TVs, phones, clock radios, kitchenette in 3 suites, TV/VCR in game room, conference facilities, off-street parking. $96–$190; full buffet breakfast. AE, D, DC, MC, V.

5th Generation Farm. Bear Wallow Rd. (R.R. 4, Box 90-A), Nashville 47448, tel. 812/988–7553 or 800/437–8152. 2 double rooms with baths, 3 suites. Air-conditioning, TV in suites and common area, fireplace, hot tub. $85–$125; full breakfast. D, MC, V.

Grant Street Inn. 310 N. Grant St., Bloomington 47408, tel. 812/334–2353 or 800/328–4350, fax 812/331–8673. 22 double rooms with baths, 2 suites. Air-conditioning, cable TV, phone, clock radio, fireplace in 10 rooms and suites, whirlpool bath in suites. $90–$160; full breakfast. AE, D, MC, V. 2-night minimum stay weekends Sept.–late Nov. and during special events.

Ohio River Valley

MAIN STREET BED AND BREAKFAST ⬚
739 W. Main St., Madison 47250, tel. 812/265–3539 or 800/362–6246

Of all the Indiana towns born along the bustling water highway of the mighty Ohio River, perhaps the most notable is Madison. Roughly 60 mi downstream from Cincinnati, Madison is distinguished by a staggering array of architectural styles: ornate Steamboat Gothic, stately Federal, imposing Greek Revival, and gingerbread-perfect Victorian. Dubbed the "Williamsburg of the Midwest," Madison has more than 133 blocks listed on the National Register of Historic Places.

Main Street Bed and Breakfast, on a deep and narrow lot behind a wrought-iron fence and under a leafy canopy, is a short walk from the city's main historic district. The inn, built in 1843, was once the home of Madison's Civil War hero Col. Alois Bachman. Dark-green shuttered windows, a white-painted brick facade with Italianate details, and a modest front portico face Main Street. The building's understated presence belies its spaciousness: This Greek Revival–style home has 5,000 square ft of living space.

Owners-innkeepers Mark and Mary Balph, natives of the Ohio River valley, lived and traveled all over the world, returning to their hometown in 1992. Their experiences are reflected in a delightful mix of old and new traditional furnishings—English country antiques, Oriental rugs, comfortable wingback chairs, and light wall coverings. The most unusual piece, an 8-ft-tall stuffed giraffe, a remnant from the Balphs' days in the retail toy business, presides over the guest rooms in the second-floor hallway.

The McIntyre Room, named for the building's architect, overlooks Main Street and is full of soft colors, including floral Laura Ashley wallpaper; there are also a love seat, wingback chair, built-in bookcase, and shuttered windows. Pale-yellow walls with white trim create a gentle backdrop for the bleached English pine furniture and rose comforter and wingback chairs in the Hennessey Room, named for longtime owners of the home. A daybed and twin bed tucked away in an adjoining room, reached only through the spacious bath, is perfect for children or singles traveling together.

The Lockridge Room, named for Mary's grandparents, has white walls trimmed in Wedgwood blue and a blue mottled rug covering the poplar floor. Two cozy wing chairs and a Queen Anne–style coffee table decorate its small sitting area. A fourth, slightly smaller room that joins the Lockridge has wall-to-wall wheat-color carpeting and Wedgwood-blue woodwork. Although each room has a fireplace, none are operational. Environmentally conscious, Mark and Mary discreetly placed tasteful recycling baskets in each room.

Morning coffee is served in the privacy of your room, but breakfast is a social event in the airy main-floor dining room. Mark is the breakfast chef and will prepare anything according to your tastes and personal needs. The full breakfast always includes fresh fruit from local growers and homemade cream cheese–filled raspberry muffins. Be sure to smile before you leave. Mark and Mary fill photo albums of all their guests at Main Street B&B. △ *4 double rooms. Air-conditioning. $89; full breakfast. MC, V.*

OTHER CHOICES

Cliff House. 122 Fairmount Dr., Madison 47250, tel. 812/265–5272. 6 double rooms with baths. Air-conditioning, cable TV/VCR in common area, mints, chocolate-chip cookies, fresh fruit. $96.25; hearty Continental breakfast. AE, D, MC, V.

Crescent House. 617 W. Main St., Madison 47250, tel. 812/265–4251. 1 suite. Fresh cut flowers, bath robes, toiletries, TV/VCR, refrigerator, in-room coffeemaker, telephone, private entrance in rooms. $110; Continental breakfast. MC, V.

Jelley House Country Inn. 222 S. Walnut St., Rising Sun 47040, tel. 812/438–2319. 1 double room with bath, 2 doubles share 1 bath, 1 housekeeping suite. Air-conditioning, TVs, clock radios, cable TV/VCR, fireplace in living room, picnic lunches, fishing expeditions, boat rentals. $45–$65; full breakfast. V.

Kintner House Inn. N. Capitol and Chestnut Sts., Corydon 47112, tel. 812/738–2020. 15 double rooms with baths. Air-conditioning, cable TV/VCR, phone, fireplace in 5 rooms. $49–$99; full breakfast, evening refreshments. AE, MC, V.

River Belle Bed & Breakfast. State Rd. 66 (Box 669), Grandview 47615, tel. 812/649–2500 or 800/877–5165, fax 812/649–2500. 1 double room with bath, 4 doubles share 2 baths, 1 cottage. Air-conditioning, TV, fireplace in common areas. $65–$75; Continental breakfast. MC, V.

Indianapolis

Frederick Talbott Inn. 13805 Allisonville Rd., Fishers 46038, tel 317/578–3600 or 800/556–BEDS. 10 rooms with baths. TV, phones, whirlpool in 1 room, fireplace in 1 room, meeting room, refreshments. $99–$179; full breakfast. AE, D, MC, V. No smoking.

Amish Country

PATCHWORK QUILT COUNTRY INN ☙

11748 County Rd. 2, Middlebury 46540, tel. 219/825–2417, fax 219/825–5172

Just north of the toll road linking Illinois, Indiana, and Ohio, in the middle of 18 acres of corn and soybeans, is the matriarch of northern Indiana's legion of country inns. For more than a quarter of its existence, this century-old farmhouse has been welcoming guests for farm vacations. Although the heart of northern Indiana's Amish country now has more than 50 country inns, the Patchwork Quilt, under the watchful eyes of Ray and Rosetta Miller, still sets the standard begun more than 25 years ago.

True country comforts, such as patchwork quilts and stick-to-your-ribs cooking, are offered within an immaculate, uncluttered setting. Throughout the inn, quilts adorn the beds, sofas, and walls. Mostly stitched by local Amish and Mennonite women, the brightly colored pieces of handiwork come in a variety of patterns like Lone Star, Wedding Band, and Flower Basket. The Cherry Basket pattern, the inn's logo, is replicated on linens, stationery, and wall hangings.

Inside the front door is a small parlor with a sofa, easy chairs, and piano. In the main dining room (the Keeping Room), a large quilt hangs for sale opposite a massive brick hearth. When it is purchased, another original piece takes its place. A larger selection of locally made wall hangings and quilts are also sold in the small shop next door.

The bedrooms, painted shades of blue, yellow, green, and red, have light-stained-pine and yellow-oak poster beds and bedside tables with low lamps. Just a few touches, like stenciled borders and woven rugs, dress them up.

The good-eating tradition associated with the Amish holds true here. Dinner is served buffet-style and always includes the inn's award-winning crunchy buttermilk pecan chicken along with a dozen or so homemade salads. Other entrée selections change nightly and include Amish wedding steak, baked ham, BBQ ribs, beef "porcupine" balls, and baked cod on Fridays. The mashed potatoes and dessert pies are particularly incomparable.

Within a 150-mi radius is the nation's third largest concentration of Amish and Mennonites. Few Amish families allow the English, as outsiders are known, to experience their lifestyle and culture first-hand. A tour guide tailors outings to guests' interests: quilts, crafts, farming, or harness and buggy making. ⌂ *15 double rooms with baths, 3 doubles share 1 bath, 1 suite. Restaurant, air-conditioning, restaurant, TV, whirlpool bath in 2 rooms and suite, guided tours. $70–$100; full breakfast. MC, V.*

VICTORIAN GUEST HOUSE ☙

302 E. Market St., Nappanee 46550, tel. 219/773–4383

In the heart of northern Indiana's "plain and simple" Amish country, the Victorian Guest House stands out like a polished gemstone. This gabled and turreted mansion, two blocks from Nappanee's historic town square, stands resplendent in its Victorian charm.

Listed on the National Register of Historic Places, this 1887 Queen Anne–style masterpiece was built for the Coppes family. Frank Coppes, whose company manufactured free-standing kitchen cabinets, insisted on expert craftsmanship, down to every exquisite detail: extensive wood paneling, stained-glass windows, brass hardware. Many locals were involved in the original construction of the house, and almost all of Nappanee had something to do with its transformation into an inn in 1986.

The etched-glass entryway leads through beveled-glass pocket doors into an expansive living room with polished hardwood floors and tall ceilings. Recently restored were the room's crown moldings, from which the Victorians hung pictures, and an original fireplace. Graceful Victorian upholstered chairs and tufted footstools are present here and throughout the building. A wide doorway opens to the dining room, where period wallpaper softens rich wood paneling. The massive 11-ft dining-room table, with a servant buzzer hidden on the underside, is an original piece. Stained-glass windows made by Nappanee's renowned Lamb Brothers, whose work rivals that of Louis B. Tiffany, line the dining room and the cross-cut golden oak staircase that leads to the bedrooms upstairs.

The Coppes Suite—originally the master bedroom—is paneled in light oak. Its bath has a large stained glass window with a sinuous rose design set against a cobalt blue background and a vintage bathtub made to comfortably accommodate its original occupant, who stood at 6 feet 3 inches: Fifty gallons of water are required for a soak. Catherine's Room—named for Coppes's wife, who was the epitome of elegance—is furnished with a brass bed and a rocking chair, among other vintage Victorian pieces. Although it's the smallest, the Sewing Room has a private rooftop balcony. Offering the most privacy, the Maid's Chambers, on the third floor, is an intimate space with an antique bathtub and pedestal sink.

Owners-innkeepers Vickie and Bruce Hunsberger had never stayed in a B&B when they happened on a for-sale sign in front of "The Old Coppes House" in 1992. However, their sensibilities about gracious accommodations, modern amenities, and personal service are evident. Guests are treated to an evening tray of assorted teas, hot chocolate, and cookies in their rooms. Breakfast, in the dining room, is an elegant affair, served on depression-era glass dinnerware with crystal goblets and crisp cloth napkins. ♠ *6 double rooms with baths. Air-conditioning, cable TV, phone in rooms on request, turndown service, airport transportation. $139; full breakfast. D, MC, V.*

OTHER CHOICES

Beiger Mansion Inn. 317 Lincolnway E, Mishawaka 46544, tel. 219/256–0365 or 800/437–0131, fax 219/259–2622. 6 double rooms with baths, 1 suite. Air-conditioning, cable TV, clocks, phones, fireplaces in 2 rooms and common areas, gourmet restaurant with bakery, conference facilities. $75–90, $195 suite; full breakfast. AE, D, DC, MC, V.

Checkerberry Inn. 62644 County Rd. 37, Goshen 46526, tel. 219/642–4445, fax 219/642–4445. 11 double rooms with baths, 2 suites. Restaurant, air-conditioning, phones, TVs, pool, tennis courts, croquet. $155–$375; Continental breakfast. AE, MC, V.

Market Street Guest House. 253 E. Market St., Nappanee 46550, tel. 219/773–2261 or 800/497–3791. 4 double rooms with baths, 2 double rooms share 1 bath. Air conditioning, TVs, fireplace in living room. $65–$75; full breakfast. D, MC, V.

1898 Varns-Kimes Guest House. 205 S. Main St., Middlebury 46540, tel. 219/825–9666 or 800/398–5424, fax 219/825–5839. 5 double rooms with baths. Air-conditioning, clock radios, whirlpool bath in 1 room, cable TV in den, fireplace in living room, turndown service and chocolates. $85; full breakfast. MC, V.

North Coast

HUTCHINSON MANSION INN ❦
220 W. 10th St., Michigan City 46360, tel. 219/879–1700

Built in 1876 by William Hutchinson—a lumber baron, world traveler, and former mayor of Michigan City—this stately, redbrick inn takes up an entire city block. Less than 1 mi from both the sandy stretches of Lake Michigan and the 18,000-acre Indiana Dunes National Lakeshore, this elegant Queen Anne–style mansion presides over the town's historic residential and commercial district.

History and antique buffs, the DuVals—Ben (a retired law professor) and Mary (a former teacher and realtor)—acquired, restored, and redecorated the mansion in 1991. The home's charm and warmth reflect their roots. Both native Virginians, the DuVals are delighted to share the mansion's history and to treat guests to their brand of southern hospitality—fresh flowers, chocolates, and friendly conversation.

Although Queen Anne decor usually consists of dark interiors with heavy drapes, the DuVals have kept their inn surprisingly airy. The home is distinguished by stained-glass windows, tall beamed-and-molded ceilings, and dark-wood paneling; many of the massive antique pieces are family heirlooms. There are many whimsical architectural details—private terraces, alcoves and nooks, and even a secret door hidden in the dining room's wood paneling. Oriental rugs cover polished hardwood floors. Above the wood paneling in the dining room is period wallpaper with a subtle rose motif; a pair of tall candlesticks and a cut-glass punch bowl sit on a dark-wood sideboard, and a wide, matching mirror is hung above.

A massive 8-ft antique Renaissance Revival bed with inlaid burled wood is the focal point of the Hutchinson Room. A decorative marble fireplace, ceiling friezes, long lace curtains, and period light-colored wallpaper complete the refined setting. The Patterson Room has an 1820 museum-quality four-poster Southern Plantation bed with a canopy; high off the floor, it is reached by steps. In a corner overlooking the gardens and carriage house, the Jenny Lind Room has an unusual four-poster Jenny Lind bed with undulating spindles; it dates from the mid-1800s. The subdued Servant's Quarters has a white-and-gold iron bed, private porch, and turn-of-the-century original bath. The redbrick carriage house, topped with a cupola and weather vane, has three luxurious suites with whirlpool baths and one with an extralarge soaking tub. One suite has a sitting room, garden room, and private terrace; another has a sitting room and a private porch with a two-seat swing.

In the library, filled with tall wood bookcases full of Ben's books, refreshments are served in the evening. A full breakfast might be served by candlelight (on dark or dreary mornings) on fine china and crystal with hand-crocheted place mats. ⚠ *5 double rooms with baths, 5 suites. Air-conditioning, phone with modem hookup in rooms, croquet, sunroom. $85–$140; full breakfast. AE, MC, V.*

OTHER CHOICES

Creekwood Inn. U.S. 20/35 at I–94, Michigan City 46360, tel. 219/872–8357, fax 219/872–8357. 12 double rooms with baths, 1 suite. Restaurant, coffee bar, air-conditioning, TVs, phones, clock radios, turndown service, conference facilities, horseshoes, paddleboat and bikes available, boat rentals, conservatory, exercise equipment, outdoor whirlpool, tennis courts and horseback riding nearby. $118–$173; Continental-plus breakfast AE, DC, MC, V.

Gray Goose Inn. 350 Indian Boundary Rd., Chesterton 46304, tel. 219/926–5781 or 800/521–5127, 219/926–4845. 5 double rooms with baths, 3 suites. Air-conditioning, phones, TVs, fireplace in 3 suites, Jacuzzi in 1 suite, paddleboats, train station transportation. $80–165; full breakfast. AE, D, MC, V.

RESERVATIONS SERVICE

Indiana Tourism Division, Department of Commerce (1 N. Capitol St., Suite 700, Indianapolis 46204–2288, tel. 317/232–8860).

IOWA

The Amana Colonies

DIE HEIMAT COUNTRY INN 🐚
Amana Colonies, Homestead, tel. 319/622–3937

The Amana Colonies region of east-central Iowa is known for its simple beauty and the old-world culture of the Swiss and German immigrants who moved here. In 1855, members of the Amana Church Society settled on 26,000 acres of what is now just north of I–80, about an hour east of Des Moines. Seven small "colonies," or villages, display the history, culture, and religion of the Amana Church Society, often confused with the Amish.

Built in 1858, Die Heimat Country Inn personifies the region and is on the National Register of Historic Places and in the heart of Main Amana. It has served the colonies as a stagecoach stop, a communal kitchen, a meeting room, and now as one of the most popular bed-and-breakfast inns in the state. Owners Jackie and Warren Lock purchased the property in 1993 and have made only minor changes. The small guest rooms have walnut and cherry furniture made by local artisans. Each bed is queen-size and is covered with wool blankets made at the Amana Woolen Mill, and Jackie's own handmade quilts and hand-loomed rugs. Original samplers, calligraphy, and century-old photos throughout the inn provide a glimpse into the history and culture of both the building and the community.

Jackie serves a full farm-style breakfast of scrambled eggs, homemade biscuits, French toast, and hot maple syrup. Because breakfast is served buffet style, guests can eat in the privacy of their rooms, on picnic tables outdoors, or in the large yet comfortable dining room. The mismatched pieces of antique china were brought back from antiques stores around the world: The variety of serving pieces and patterns often spurs conversation as guests remember similar patterns at their own family homes.

Although Warren and Jackie are not members of the Amana Church Society, many of their employees are and are pleased to explain the history of the society and its culture. In January and February the inn hosts murder-mystery weekends. University of Iowa sporting events, Cedar Rapids, and the Amish community of Kalona are all less than an hour away. ♙ *19 double rooms with baths. Air-conditioning, TVs, large meeting facilities, picnic facilities. $50–$70; full breakfast. D, MC, V.*

OTHER CHOICES

Lucille's Bett Und Breakfast. 2835 225th St., Williamsburg 52361, tel. 319/668–1185. 2 double rooms with 1½ baths. Fireplace, TV, and piano in common room, croquet and lawn sports. $55; full breakfast, snacks upon arrival. No credit cards.

Rawson House Bed and Breakfast. Box 118, Homestead 52236, tel. 319/622–6035 or 800/637–6035. 2 double rooms with baths, 4 suites. Air-conditioning, TV in rooms, whirlpool in suites, communal kitchen. $55–$95; full breakfast. MC, V.

Mississippi River

HANCOCK HOUSE BED AND BREAKFAST ❦
1105 Grove Terr., Dubuque 52001-4644, tel. 319/557–8989, fax 319/583–0813

The majesty and grandeur of the mighty Mississippi River–bluff region of northeastern Iowa befits the Victorian elegance of Dubuque's Hancock House Bed and Breakfast. Built in 1891 and now on the National Register of Historic Places, the Hancock House demonstrates Queen Anne architecture at its finest.

Meticulous renovations, begun in 1985, turned a poorly maintained apartment building into one of the Midwest's premiere B&Bs. After driving up the circular carriage drive and facing the inn's flower-lined birdbath and portico, guests are greeted with genuine enthusiasm by owners-innkeepers Chuck and Susan Huntley.

Each of Hancock House's nine guest rooms is furnished with feather ticks (mattress bolsters) and named after a member of the Hancock family, the Midwest's largest grocer-distributor at the turn of the century. Amenities to choose from include fireplaces and potbellied stoves, whirlpools and claw-foot bathtubs, iron and canopy beds, stained-glass windows, and skylights. Rooms in the back look right out onto a bluff; the front rooms face the meeting point of Iowa, Wisconsin, Illinois, and the Mississippi River valley.

An 1850s brick miner's cottage, renovated in 1998, is adjacent to the inn. With three bedrooms and private dining, it's ideal for families.

Breakfast, served in the formal Victorian dining room on Victorian china, varies seasonally in order to feature local produce: An omelet may include Wisconsin Brie cheese and Iowa-grown apples. Coffee is roasted especially for the Hancock House in neighboring Galena, Illinois, and beer, stocked in the refrigerator, is brewed right in Dubuque.

The Dubuque area has skiing, bicycle trails, river boat cruises, carriage rides, and great antiques shops. ♨ *9 double rooms with baths, 3-bedroom cottage. Individual heating/cooling controls, cable TV, clock radios, whirlpool in 4 rooms. $75–$165; full breakfast, beverages, snacks. D, MC, V.*

OTHER CHOICES

Bishop's House Inn of St. Ambrose University. 1527 Brady St., Davenport 52803, tel. 319/322–8303. 5 double rooms with baths, 1 suite. Air-conditioning, ceiling fans, fireplace and whirlpool in suite, meeting facilities, library, laundry room. $65–$140; full breakfast. MC, V.

Fulton's Landing Bed and Breakfast. 1206. E. River Dr., Davenport, 52803, tel. 319/322–4069. 5 double rooms with baths. Air-conditioning, phones, TVs, meeting rooms. $60–$125; full breakfast. AE, MC, V.

North Central Iowa

MRS. B'S BED AND BREAKFAST 🐚
920 Division St., Garner 50438, tel. 515/923–2390

A trip to the British Isles inspired Pat Buntenbach to return to her Colonial home in rural north-central Iowa and open a B&B she thinks is just as good as or better than what the British have to offer. Inspired by the beautiful English gardens, Pat and her husband, Red, turned much of their 4 acres into a garden: They converted an old stone barbecue grill to a fountain surrounded by English tea roses, foxglove, and other "old-time" flowers. The large back porch and gazebo, where Pat serves a full country breakfast of eggs, ham, homemade breads, and juice, have a view of the garden.

When Pat and her husband built their dream home more than 30 years ago, they selected green limestone from western Pennsylvania for the exterior. The massive fireplace that dominates much of the common room and kitchen, however, is made of clinker Dutch brick. That Pat and Red worked for years in the cattle business is reflected in what Pat calls the Cowboy and Indian Room. Photos and other items from century-old cattle drives they acquired and restored are displayed with their sons' old cowboy boots and hats and with Native American memorabilia from their frequent trips to reservations.

The other two guest rooms upstairs have more delicate decor: One room done in blue has family-heirloom quilts and samplers; the peach room with green accents, designed for guests staying more than a few nights—like the traveling professors who visit the nearby community college—includes a desk, telephone outlet, and a cozy reading area.

Some guests come for all-night quilting sessions at nearby Country Threads Quilt Shop, while others enjoy the local gift shop, old-fashioned dry goods store, and the "Surf" Ballroom Dance Hall. ⌂ *3 double rooms with baths. Cable TV, ceiling fans, fireplace in common room, bicycles. $60–$70; full breakfast. No credit cards.*

OTHER CHOICES

Antique City Inn. 400 Antique City Dr., Walnut 51577, tel. 712/784–3722. 5 double rooms with baths, 1 suite. TV and phone in 3 rooms, whirlpool bath in suite. $45–$55; full breakfast, dinner available. AE, D, MC, V.

Larch Pine Inn. 401 N. 3rd St., Clear Lake 50428, tel. 515/357–7854. 3 double rooms with baths. Kitchenette, TV in parlor, bicycles and Burley cart available, off-street parking. $75; full breakfast. AE, D, MC, V.

KANSAS

Eastern Kansas

LYONS' VICTORIAN MANSION 🐚

742 S. National St., Fort Scott 66701, tel. 316/223–0779 or 800/784–8378

Just 90 minutes south of Kansas City, Fort Scott offers visitors tours of the 1840s military post and the Victorian buildings downtown.

Innkeeper Pat Lyons came to the Fort Scott area from the East Coast and, much like original female pioneers, brings a feminine touch to the rugged prairie. The home's north parlor is used for such Victorian pastimes as needlepoint and knitting: Pat encourages her guests to bring along their needlework and join her in the parlor for conversation and handwork. Pat's favorite threads are silk, wool, and angora, and the results of her work, plus her collection of spinning wheels, can be found throughout the inn.

Original chandeliers, hardwood floors, and a massive, native black-walnut staircase greet you as you enter the foyer. Parlors decorated in dark green with soft pink ceilings grace each side of the foyer and join the formal dining room through alcoves. Lyons' Victorian Mansion has four guest rooms with baths, sitting rooms, televisions, and fireplaces (only two fireplaces are in working order).

Southern breakfasts feature such treats as biscuits and gravy, broiled or fried green tomatoes, and ham, sausage, and bacon. Formal afternoon tea is served in the south parlor.

Pat's 1876 Victorian home is the focal point of many Fort Scott social events, especially around Christmas. Long before Thanksgiving, the house is elegantly trimmed for a Victorian holiday and the "Evening of Victorian Elegance," a nine-course dinner followed by historic vignettes reliving events in Fort Scott's history during the three weeks between Thanksgiving and Christmas. Lyons' Victorian Mansion also hosts mystery evenings, tea parties, weddings, and other social occasions limited only by the imagination. ♙ *4 double rooms with baths, 1 2-bedroom suite. Air-conditioning, phones, TVs, dataports, library, laundry. $85; full breakfast, afternoon tea. AE, D, MC, V.*

OTHER CHOICES

Almeda's Inn. 220 S. Main St., Tonganoxie 66086-0113, tel. 913/845–2295. 1 double room with bath, 2 doubles share bath, 1 suite. Air-conditioning, fireplace and TV in gathering room. $25–$65; Continental breakfast. No credit cards.
Bednobs and Biscuits Bed & Breakfast. 15202 Parallel Ave., Basehor 66007, tel. 913/724–540. 3 double rooms share bath. Air-conditioning, cable TV/VCR in gathering room. $65–$70; full breakfast, fresh-baked cookies upon arrival. No credit cards.

Bennington House. 123 Crescent Dr., Fort Scott 66701, tel. 316/223–1837. 1 double room with bath, 2 doubles share bath. Alarm clocks; air-conditioning, cable TV/VCR in family room; gift shop. $45; full breakfast. MC, V.

Chenault Mansion. 820 S. National St., Fort Scott 66701, tel. 316/223–6800. 3 double rooms with baths, 2 suites. 4 fireplaces, air-conditioning, TVs, cribs, off-street parking. $80–$90; full breakfast. AE, D, MC, V.

Elderberry House. 1035 S.W. Fillmore St., Topeka 66604, tel. 785/235–6309. 2 suites. Air-conditioning; TV/VCR, fireplace; off-street parking. $45–$55; full or Continental breakfast, evening snacks. No credit cards.

Halcyon House Bed and Breakfast. 1000 Ohio St., Lawrence 66044, tel. 785/841–0314 or 888/441–0314. 4 double rooms share 2 baths, 4 suites. Air-conditioning, phones, cable TV in suites, fireplace in 1 suite and in common room. $50–$85; full breakfast. AE, MC, V.

Hedgeapple Acres. 4430 U.S. Hwy. 54, Moran 66755-0247, tel. 316/237–4646. 6 rooms with baths. Whirlpool bath in 1 room, family room with cable TV/VCR, 2 fireplaces, 2 fishing ponds. $75; full breakfast, supper. AE, D, MC, V.

The Pickering House. 507 W. Park St., Olathe 66061, tel. 913/829–7800. 2 double rooms with baths, 1 suite. Air-conditioning, phones, restaurant, sauna, exercise room. $105–$115; full breakfast. AE, MC, V.

The Plumb House. 628 Exchange St., Emporia 66801, tel. 316/342–6881 or 800/288–6198. 4 double rooms with baths, 2 suites. Bathrobes; TV, refrigerator, and microwave in 1 suite; off-street parking. $65–$80; full breakfast. AE, D, MC, V.

The Sherman House. Box 15, Elk Falls 67345, tel. 316/329—4425. Guest house with 1½ baths. Air-conditioning, TV/VCR, phones, lounge, dining room. $40–$50; full breakfast. No credit cards.

Central Kansas

SWEDISH COUNTRY INN 🐦

112 W. Lincoln St., Lindsborg 67456, tel. 785/227–2985 or 800/231–0266, fax 785/227–3268.

Central Kansas is an unlikely place to experience the European hospitality of a place like the Swedish Country Inn. A remote community of 3,000 Swedish-Americans, the town of Lindsborg is known throughout the Midwest as "Little Sweden on the Plains."

Built during the 1920s, the Swedish Country Inn became a hotel in the 1930s and a bed-and-breakfast in the 1970s. The spacious lobby has Swedish pine furniture, game tables, television, and a fire burning in the fireplace no matter the temperature outside. An adjoining gift shop sells many of the unique Swedish gift items made in the community, such as music boxes, linens, and the ever-present Dala Horse, a symbol of Swedish heritage. Swedish is spoken throughout the community and by several staff members at the Swedish Inn. Innkeeper Becky Anderson, a native of the area, knows a little Swedish and does her best to keep up with guests and others fluent in the language.

The inn's spacious rooms and suites are all furnished with Swedish pine and accented with handmade quilts and bold Scandinavian blues, greens, and yellows softened by Swedish lace curtains. Flower stenciling, native to the culture, is in most rooms.

A delightful Scandinavian buffet breakfast features Swedish tea rings, pickled herring, meats, cheeses, and Swedish meatballs. Imported coffees and teas round out a breakfast not found at any other B&B in the state of Kansas. If that didn't fill you up, an in-house bakery offers baked goods to go.

To burn off a few of the calories consumed at breakfast, guests are welcome to borrow bicycles for a leisurely ride around town. Although this part of Kansas has no hills to speak of, any sore muscles can be pampered in the inn's private sauna.

In keeping with the Swedish culture, Lindsborg is the site of a much-celebrated Holy Week festival at Easter, the Svensh Hyllningsfest in October, and the St. Lucia Festival in December. Reservations are highly recommended at the Swedish Country Inn during these periods. △ *19 double rooms with baths, 1 family suite, 1 bridal suite. Air-conditioning, TV, phones, sauna, gift shop, bicycles. Handicapped accessible. $50–$80; full breakfast. AE, D, MC, V.*

OTHER CHOICES

Balfours' House Bed and Breakfast. 940 1900 Ave., Abilene 67410-6330, tel. 785/263–4262. 2 double rooms with baths, 2 suites. Bathrobes, fireplace in living area, piano, stereo, cable TV/VCR, indoor pool, spa. $55–$150; full breakfast. AE, MC, V.

Ravenwood Mission Creek Lodge. 10147 S.W. 61st St., Topeka 66610, tel. 785/256–6444 or 800/656–2454, fax 785/256–6888. 8 rooms. Air-conditioning, dining room, conference facilities, hunting and fishing. $130; full breakfast. MC, V.

KENTUCKY

Louisville/Bluegrass West

INN AT THE PARK 🐦
1332 S. 4th St., Louisville 40208, tel. 502/637–6930 or 800/700–7275

The Inn at the Park is a splendid example of Richardsonian Romanesque architecture, with a turreted window bay, Dutch-style chimney, and onion-dome ornament. Depending on your taste, its rusticated stonework exterior might strike you as quirky or charming. The house makes a whimsical impression in a neighborhood dominated by staid Victorians.

Built in 1886, Inn at the Park was originally the home of Russell Houston, a well-known attorney and a co-founder of the Louisville & Nashville Railroad. The 7,500-square-ft stone mansion was restored to its original elegance in 1985 and opened as a bed-and-breakfast in December 1993. Innkeepers John and Sandra Mullins, who bought the property in early 1995, are native Louisvillians.

Modern-day Scarletts will love sweeping down the grand and graceful staircase of the entry foyer. Other period touches are rich hardwood floors, 14-ft ceilings, eight marble fireplaces, crown moldings, and second- and third-floor stone balconies overlooking the city's Central Park. The inn is furnished throughout with Victorian antiques and reproductions. Its largest and most elegant quarters, the Durrant Suite, has a four-poster bed and fireplaces in both bedroom and bath, along with a beautiful view of the park, a vista also seen from several other guest rooms.

Guests share several common areas, including living and dining rooms with magnificent carved fireplaces, a library, and a refreshment room where beer, wine, and soft drinks are offered without charge. Sandra also puts out wine and cheese for guests most evenings. In the morning, there's very little chance of going hungry: breakfasts—which can be taken in either the elegant dining room or in your own room—include banana-walnut pancakes, grilled-ham omelets, and Belgian waffles. ♨ *4 double rooms with baths, 2 doubles share bath, 1 suite. Cable TVs, fireplaces. $79–$119; full breakfast. AE, MC, V.*

OLD LOUISVILLE INN BED & BREAKFAST 🐦
1359 S. 3rd St., Louisville 40208, tel. 502/635–1574, fax 502/637–5892

After passing a welcoming five-globe lamppost out front, a guest entering the lobby of the Old Louisville Inn is apt to be struck, if not overwhelmed, by the heroic scale of the place, dramatized by a massive set of ornately carved mahogany columns. That's exactly the reaction John Armstrong desired in 1901 when he built the handsome Victorian structure as his private home; nothing less would do for the then-president of the Louisville Home Telephone Company. The 10,000-square-ft mansion was used as office space for several decades until a renovation in the early 1970s restored it to the splendor it had enjoyed as a monument to Armstrong's success as a business Titan.

The inn is tastefully decorated with furnishings bought from antiques shops or at local estate auctions. The breakfast room, which seats 20, has an original etched-glass chandelier and a built-in elaborately carved buffet. In the parlor is a fireplace and an eclectic lending library, as well as a collection of menus from nearby restaurants to help guests decide where to dine. The game room offers board games, including chess, backgammon, and a 1946 version of Monopoly. The most eye-catching features of the decor are the murals that adorn the inn's 12-ft ceilings; innkeeper Marianne Lesher will happily elaborate on the stories the murals tell.

Five of the guest rooms have marble baths with original fixtures, modernized to include showers; all guests sleep under antique quilts. Bay windows in some second-floor bedrooms have picturesque views of one of Louisville's best-preserved historic neighborhoods.

Old Louisville Inn is a hostelry suffused with romance. The third-floor Celebration Suite has a king-size arched-canopy bed, a sitting area, a fireplace, and a modern bath with whirlpool. If requested, Marianne will cater a private candlelit tête-à-tête dinner in your room. Your wake-up call the next morning will be the mouthwatering aromas of her muffins and popovers and of the inn's signature blend of coffee. ♙ *8 double rooms with baths, 3 doubles share bath. Air-conditioning, whirlpool bath in suite, exercise room, TV/VCR with video library in game room. $95–$195; full breakfast. MC, V.*

ROSE BLOSSOM BED & BREAKFAST ☙
1353 S. 4th St., Louisville 40208, tel. 502/636–0295 or 502/969–3923

Old Louisville, just south of downtown, is the most elegant of this city's neighborhoods. Many streets are fascinating architectural smorgasbords: Richardsonian Romanesque, Queen Anne, Châteauesque, and Beaux Arts are just a few of the styles. One of the homes built in the Victorian Italianate manner is the Rose Blossom—an 18-room, three-story house listed on the National Register of Historic Places. It was built in 1884 as the residence of Vernon D. Price, who achieved fame as president of the *Saturday Evening Post.* When Mary Ohlmann purchased the property more than a century later, it was in need of total renovation. By 1992, she had completed a pumpkin-to-carriage transformation.

Mrs. Ohlmann went to great lengths to preserve the original appearance of the house: she cleaned and polished the hammered-brass hardware piece by piece; installed period-style windows and transoms to coordinate with the leaded-glass panes in the entrance hall and stairwell; restored the beautiful oak stairwell and the rear stairway to the original construction. Modern lighting systems now brighten what was probably a gloomy interior in the early days of gaslight. And in place of a dank cellar, the tireless chatelaine—mother of nine children—has opened a small but charming gift shop.

The house's 14-ft ceilings have been enhanced with crown moldings and medallions. The light fixtures, many of crystal and brass, are in keeping with the era and recapture the elegant feeling of the late-19th century, when this neighborhood was the most prestigious in Louisville.

The parlor rooms of the Rose Blossom have Victorian-era antiques and reproductions. Throughout the house, 10 original working fireplaces have carved mantels and ornate tile or metal decorations. The seven guest rooms share 4½ bathrooms.

A sunroom and solarium added at the rear offer quiet retreats. There are also a large, well-lighted breakfast room and a Victorian-style front porch—complete with a rare reversed-paint-on-glass ceiling—for guests who want to relax and look over the beautiful gardens.

The Rose Blossom is directly across the street from Central Park, part of a city park system designed by Frederick Law Olmsted, a co-designer of New York City's Central Park. Louisville's version is small and serene and is a happy haven for squirrels; here you can play tennis, take an evening stroll, or, in the summer, watch Shakespeare in the Park.

A full family-style breakfast is served by Mary herself with near-maternal devotion. Coffee, juice, and conversation are always available to guests. △ *7 double rooms share baths. Air-conditioning, cable TV, several fireplaces. $85; full breakfast. AE, D, MC, V.*

OTHER CHOICES

Bruntwood Inn. 714 N. 3rd St., Bardstown 40004, tel. 502/348–8218. 4 double rooms with baths, 2 rooms share bath. Air-conditioning. $65–$85; full breakfast. No credit cards.

Glenmar Plantation Bed & Breakfast. 2444 Valley Hill Rd., Springfield 40069, tel. 606/284–7791 or 800/828–3330, fax 606/284–7791. 5 double rooms with baths, 2 doubles with share bath, 1 suite, 1 cottage (sleeps six). Air-conditioning, meeting room, fishing pond. $85–$200; full breakfast, evening dessert. AE, MC, V.

Honeymoon Mansion. 1014 E. Main St., New Albany, IN 47150, tel. 812/945-0312. 6 suites. 3 whirlpool baths, fireplace. $70–$140; full breakfast. MC, V.

Linden Hill Bed & Breakfast. 1607 Frankfort Ave., Louisville 40206, tel. 502/583–1400. 8 double rooms with baths. Air-conditioning, 10 working fireplaces. $75. No credit cards.

Mansion Bed & Breakfast. 1003 N. 3rd St., Bardstown 40004, tel. 502/348-2586 or 800/399–2586, fax 502/349–6098. 8 double rooms with baths. Air-conditioning. $85; Continental breakfast. AE, D, MC, V.

Myrtledene. 370 N. Spalding Ave., Lebanon 40033, tel. 502/692–2223 or 800/391–1721. 4 double rooms share baths. $65; full breakfast. MC, V.

Talbott Tavern/McLean House. Court Square, Bardstown 40004, tel. 502/348–3494, fax 502/348–0673. 8 double rooms with baths, 2 doubles with shared bath. Air-conditioning, restaurant. $50–$89; Continental breakfast. MC, V.

Yellow Cottage. 400 N. Central Ave., Campbellsville 42718, tel. 502/789–2669. 2 double rooms with baths. Air-conditioning. $40–$50; Continental breakfast. No credit cards.

RESERVATIONS SERVICE

Kentucky Homes Bed & Breakfast (1219 S. 4th St., Louisville 40203, tel. 502/635-7341) has about 40 properties scattered throughout Kentucky, most in the Louisville metro area.

Lexington/Bluegrass East

BOONE TAVERN HOTEL
Main St. at Prospect St. (Box 2345), Berea 40404, tel. 606/986–9358 or
800/366–9358, fax 606/986–7711

Boone Tavern is a grand country inn managed and operated by students of a unique educational institution—Berea College—which charges no tuition, admits only low-income students, limits enrollment to 1,500, and requires all students to work in college jobs.

Berea, one of the first interracial colleges in the South, was founded in 1855 by John G. Fee and Cassius M. Clay to provide the needy youth of Southern Appalachia a high-quality liberal-arts education within the context of the Christian faith. For many years, enrollment was about half white and half black; African-American enrollment is now around 10 percent. Berea alumni include Harriette Simpson Arnow, author of *The Dollmaker*; former New York Yankee Earle Combs (1924–35), the first Kentuckian inducted into the Baseball Hall of Fame; country-music songwriter Billy Edd Wheeler; and Juanita Kreps, Secretary of Commerce under President Jimmy Carter.

Boone Tavern was built at the suggestion of Nellie Frost, the wife of Berea's president, who, in 1908, understandably felt put-upon after providing lodging and meals at her home for about 300 summer guests. The stately, white-columned, three-story guest house that is now the Boone Tavern Hotel was begun the following year, and it has been renovated several times since. Inside, guests will find a traditional decor, with antique furniture reproductions (crafted by student woodworkers), bouquets of seasonal cut flowers, and a portrait of Daniel Boone greeting them in the main salon.

Service at the inn (where no alcoholic beverages are served, despite the word "Tavern" in its name; Berea is in dry Madison County) is provided largely by the students, many of them hotel-management majors. Since Boone Tavern opened, its dining room has become renowned for its Kentucky farm cuisine, notably its spoon bread (a cornbread soufflé) and corn sticks. Other specialties include chicken flakes in a bird's nest and cinnamon kites. Guests can take in the college's convocation series, music program, and art exhibits, which are open to the public. ♠ *59 double rooms with baths. Air-conditioning, restaurant. $63–$87; breakfast not included. AE, D, DC, MC, V.*

SHAKER VILLAGE OF PLEASANT HILL
3501 Lexington Rd., Harrodsburg 40330, tel. 606/734–5411,
reservations 800/734–5611, fax 606/734–5411

Considerably before Mies van der Rohe uttered the modernist rallying cry of "less is more," the Shakers perfected a style built from necessity: spare rooms, simple natural fabrics, plain wood furniture. Observers may think these are hardly the ingredients that constitute an extraordinary hostelry. But as many visitors to Pleasant Hill—the largest restored historic Shaker village in the United States—discover, the 80 guest quarters of this museum-like settlement offer the unique experience of living amid Shaker-style furnishings. In doing so, many guests come to truly appreciate the Shakers' timeless world of subtle and quiet beauty.

The Shakers were a utopian religious sect that flourished during the 19th century in villages in the eastern and midwestern United States, stretching from Maine to Indiana. They believed that "true Gospel simplicity . . . naturally leads to plainness in all things." Today, the Shaker belief that "utility is beauty" strikes a chord with visitors at Pleasant Hill, who marvel at Shaker architecture, furniture, and textiles. The settlement was founded in 1805 by hardworking farmers, first- or second-generation descendants of the pioneers who settled the Kentucky River frontier in the early 1800s. Within 20 years there were nearly 500 members living on 4,500 acres. Over time, the Shakers built a total of 270 structures at Pleasant Hill—utilitarian buildings with little adornment but with classical lines, a sense of proportion, and a breathtaking simplicity.

Visitors have the choice of staying in rooms in 15 of the 33 original buildings, including the Old Stone Shop, the Old Ministers' Workshop, the Tan Yard House, and the Farm Deacon's Shop. Rooms (often on the second floors) are decorated in the best Shaker style, with reproduction drop-leaf tables, rockers, candle stands, ladder-back chairs, and pegboards offering distinctive touches. Modern-day comforts are not forgotten. Bathrooms have replaced water closets, and king-size beds offer spacious comfort (in lieu of the single beds celibate Shakers used). TVs in each room remind guests they haven't completely forsaken the 20th century. Outside, however, the clock has been magically turned back to 1850. When Pleasant Hill's historic restoration began in 1961, all utilities were buried, walks were repaired or replaced, U.S. 68 was rerouted around the village, and the village road was restored to its 19th-century condition.

Pleasant Hill offers six visitor services: touring, dining, lodging, meeting facilities, shopping, and riverboat excursions. The self-guided village tour includes 13 buildings. Costumed interpreters describe Shaker history and the Shaker way of life while working at 19th-century crafts, such as broom making and spinning. For meals, guests congregate in the old inn once used by Shakers to entertain "the world's people." Here, Kentucky's regional cuisine is served family-style; don't miss the justly-famous Shaker lemon pie. After breakfast (which is not included in the room rate), you can shop for a wide variety of Kentucky crafts and handmade items. And if you're staying at Pleasant Hill from late April through October, riverboat excursions on the Kentucky River are available aboard *The Dixie Belle*. ♠ *80 double rooms with baths. TVs, crafts shops. $50–$115; breakfast not included. MC, V.*

OTHER CHOICES

Canaan Land. 4355 Lexington Rd., Harrodsburg 40330, tel. 606/734–3984. 7 double rooms with baths. Air-conditioning, hot tub, pool. $75–$105; full breakfast. No credit cards.

Cherry Knoll Farm Bed & Breakfast. 3975 Lemons Mill Rd., Lexington 40511, tel. 606/253–9800. 2 double rooms with baths. Air-conditioning, restaurant. $75; full breakfast. AE, D, MC, V.

Gratz Park Inn. 120 W. 2nd St., Lexington 40507, tel. 606/231–1777 or 800/227–4362, fax 606/233–7593. 38 double rooms with baths, 6 suites. Air-conditioning, cable TV, fax, copy machine, fitness center available. $120–$199; Continental breakfast. AE, D, DC, MC, V.

Rosehill Inn. 233 Rose Hill, Versailles 40383, tel. 606/873–5957. 4 double rooms with baths. Air-conditioning, whirlpool bath in 1 room. $69–$89; full breakfast. AE, MC, V.

Sandusky House. 1626 Delaney Ferry Rd., Nicholasville 40356, tel. 606/223–4730. 3 double rooms with baths, log home (1820s) with 2 double rooms. Air-conditioning, fireplace and whirlpool tub in log cabin. $75–$95; full breakfast. MC, V.

RESERVATIONS SERVICE

Bluegrass Bed & Breakfast (2964 McCracken Pike, Versailles 40383, tel. 606/ 873–3208) has 18 properties in central Kentucky, ranging from cozy cottages to big Victorian homes in urban settings to manor houses on horse farms.

Northern Kentucky

Carneal House Inn. 405 E. 2nd St., Covington 41011, tel. 606/431–6130, fax 606/581–6041. 6 double rooms with baths. Air-conditioning, private balconies. $80–$120; full breakfast. AE, MC, V.

Gateway Bed & Breakfast. 326 E. 6th St., Newport 41071, tel. 606/581– 6447. 1 double room with bath, 2 doubles share a bath. Air-conditioning. $75– $85; full breakfast. AE, MC, V.

Ghent House. 411 Main St. (Box 478), Ghent 41045, tel. 502/347–5807. 3 double rooms with baths. Fireplaces, whirlpool bath in 1 room, outdoor hot tub. $60–$90; full breakfast. AE, MC, V.

Lamplighter Inn. 103 W. 2nd St., Augusta 41002, tel. 606/756–2603. 9 double rooms with baths. Restaurant, tennis courts, pool, murder-mystery weekends. $65–$80; Continental breakfast. MC, V.

Eastern Kentucky

Blair's Country Living. Hwys. 80 and 421 (R.R. 3, Box 865-B), Manchester 40962, tel. 606/598–2854. 2 double rooms with baths. Air-conditioning, cable TV. $50–$65; Continental breakfast. No credit cards.

Charlene's Country Inn Bed & Breakfast. Hwys. 7 and 32 (HC 75, Box 265), Sandy Hook 41171, tel. 606/738–5712, fax 606/738–4640. 3 double rooms with baths, 3 doubles share bath. $65–$75; full breakfast. No credit cards.

Western Kentucky

Log House. 3239 Franklin Rd., Russellville 42276, tel. 502/726–8483, fax 502/ 726–2270. 4 double rooms with baths. Air-conditioning, hot tub. $75–$85; Continental breakfast. AE, D, MC, V.

Round Oak Inn. U.S. 68 W (Box 1331), Cadiz 42211, tel. 502/924–5850. 6 double rooms with baths. $45–$55; full breakfast. AE, D, MC, V.

Silver Cliff Inn. 1980 Lake Barkley Dr., Old Kuttawa 42055, tel. 502/388–5858. 2 rooms with baths, 2 rooms share bath (can be rented as a 2-bedroom suite). Air-conditioning, 7 fireplaces, swimming nearby. $70–$85; full breakfast. No credit cards.

LOUISIANA

Greater New Orleans

CLAIBORNE MANSION ☙
*2111 Dauphine St., New Orleans 70116, tel. 504/949–7327 or 800/449–7327,
fax 504/949–0388*

Faubourg Marigny, adjacent to the French Quarter, was one of New Orleans's first suburbs (*faubourg* is French for suburb). In the 1850s, the son of William C. C. Claiborne, Louisiana's first American governor, built this Greek Revival mansion for his family. Claiborne's descendants lived here until 1905; it was an apartment house when Cleo Pelleteri bought and restored it.

Cleo has created an elegant, secluded haven favored by some celebrities. In contrast to those in the area's Victorian B&Bs, the Claiborne's furnishings and objets d'art are contemporary. Crystal chandeliers hang from high ceilings, shining on polished hardwood floors and vases of fresh flowers. The sun-filled rooms and marble baths are spacious.

There are three suites and a room in the main house. Each suite has a large parlor and bedroom. One has a huge four-poster, curtained in an elegant white fabric. The room in the rear, overlooking the courtyard, has a canopy bed in delicious rose and white colors. The ground-floor room of the slave quarters, near the pool in the landscaped courtyard, has a wheelchair ramp; its bedroom–sitting room has slate floors, and twin red leather armchairs flank a fireplace. The two rooms above it, with whitewashed brick walls and white slip-covered sofas and chairs, can be combined for a suite.

For breakfast, Cleo does anything from croissants to waffles, depending on guests' individual preferences. In pleasant weather, guests like to eat beside the pool, but she says they often perch on stools in the kitchen.

A fax machine is available for guests, and there's a rack of videos in the hall. Pets are welcome with advance notice. ❧ *1 double room with bath and 3 suites in main house; 1 double with bath and 1 suite in slave quarters. Air-conditioning, phone with voice mail and cable TV/VCR in rooms, afternoon cocktails; pool, off-street parking. $150–$350; full breakfast. AE, D, MC, V. No smoking.*

DEGAS HOUSE ☙
*2306 Esplanade Ave., New Orleans 70119, tel. 504/821—5009 or 800/755–6730,
fax 504/821–0870*

On an 1872 visit to New Orleans, French Impressionist painter Edgar Degas stayed with relatives in this double-galleried Greek Revival house near City Park. Here, in a sun-filled studio, he produced 17 paintings. It is now operated by the Degas Foundation as an art gallery–cum–B&B.

This historic home, built in 1852, has been carefully restored, following original floor plans and original, gorgeous colors, which include pale peach, celadon, and golden mustard. Second-floor rooms are spacious and have floor-length windows with white lace curtains, antique claw-foot tubs, and chandeliers that hang from 14-ft ceilings: one room has a whirlpool bath; another, which has both a four-poster and a white-iron daybed, has exclusive use of an upper gallery, complete with rocking chairs, that stretches across the front of the house. Fresh flowers, antique hand-painted porcelain washbasins, and heavy wooden wardrobes commingle in rooms with modern-day conveniences such as TVs, clock radios, and individual temperature controls.

Third-floor garret rooms are small, have sloping ceilings and no windows, but are decorated with Degas's works and are less expensive. Parlors on the first floor have the artist's prints (more than 60 can be seen in the house) and can be visited by nonguests (call for specific dates and times). Overnighters may enjoy breakfast on a small private rear courtyard, where there is a garden with period flora. △ *7 rooms with baths. Air-conditioning, clock radio, phone, and cable TV in rooms. $125–$200; Continental breakfast. AE, MC, V. No smoking, 2-night minimum stay weekends, 4-night minimum for Jazz Fest and Mardi Gras.*

HOUSE ON BAYOU ROAD ☞
2275 Bayou Rd., New Orleans 70119, tel. 504/945–0992 or 800/882–2968, fax 504/945–0993

In New Orleans, near City Park, Cynthia Reeve's 1798 West Indies–style home and its cottages provide a quiet, elegant retreat. At various times, Brad Pitt, Dan Aykroyd, Alfre Woodard, and Fran Drescher have been guests.

The property sits on 2 landscaped acres; in pleasant weather, guests can enjoy the gourmet breakfast beside the pool and large hot tub, which sits in a tin-roofed gazebo.

The house and cottages are furnished with early Louisiana antiques; family heirlooms and oil portraits are displayed throughout. The house has hardwood floors, Oriental rugs, old brick fireplaces, screened porches, and large windows that afford a light, airy ambience.

Rooms and suites, each with a feather bed and a private entrance, are in the main house as well as in the cottages. The Kumquat, a large Victorian cottage to the rear, has four suites, one with a handsome antique sleigh bed, another with a big four-poster and a double whirlpool tub. A real treasure is the private Creole cottage, with a skylight over its four-poster, a wet bar, and stained-glass window in the bathroom, which has a hot tub. Both cottages have porches with rocking chairs and tinkling wind chimes. Among the main-house suites, one has a fireplace, shelves filled with books, and a polo motif, reflected in framed prints.

Guests may use the fax machine; a modem is also available. A year-round cooking school is conducted here (ask about packages). Limousine service from the airport is provided at an extra charge.

A full breakfast is served every morning, but on Saturday and Sunday, Cynthia prepares a champagne mimosa breakfast that may include eggs Benedict or a soufflé Florentine. △ *4 double rooms with baths in main house, 4 suites in cottage, 1 cottage. Air-conditioning, cable TV, minibars, robes, complimentary sherry, and phone in rooms. $145–$250; full breakfast. AE, D, DC, MC, V. No smoking, 5-night minimum for Mardi Gras and Jazz Fest.*

SALMEN-FRITCHIE HOUSE ☞
127 Cleveland Ave., Slidell 70458, tel. 504/643–1405 or 800/235–4168,
fax 504/643–2251

The little town of Slidell, on the Pearl River, about 35 minutes from downtown New Orleans, is home to one of the state's showplace B&Bs. Owners Sharon and Homer Fritchie live upstairs, and all 12 rooms on the main floor, as well as the restored carriage house, are for overnighters. The 1895 white mansion, which has a high-pitched roof, broad front porch, porte cochere, and beveled-glass door, basks on a spacious lawn. Immediately upon stepping inside the central hall, you'll notice a white Italian-marble sculpture on a table and an elaborate burgundy jardiniere, both original to the house. Nearby stands an 18th-century Chippendale long-case clock. A tour of the mansion and its priceless antiques is included.

The mansion has 12-ft ceilings, wood-burning fireplaces with ornate mantelpieces, cypress paneling, and a central hall that measures 85 ft by 25 ft. Within that ample space are a sitting area (with a TV/VCR) and a grand piano, which displays miniature family photographs. The twin Queen Anne sofas flanking the fireplace in the library came from Linden in Natchez, Mississippi; the bookcase holds contemporary novels and volumes of the *Encyclopaedia Britannica*.

Each of the guest rooms is furnished in period style. The Mallard Bedroom, for example, features the hand-carved work of Prudent Mallard, a well-known 19th-century New Orleans furniture maker. Three of the guest rooms have wood-burning fireplaces, and two can be combined to create a suite. Baths are spacious and modern. The carriage house, with contemporary furnishings, full kitchen, huge four-poster, and double whirlpool bath, has a large screened porch surrounded by greenery.

Breakfast, served at a long table in a many-windowed breakfast room, may take the form of pecan waffles, French toast stuffed with fruit; or cheese, chive, and mushroom omelets with bacon. ▲ *5 double rooms with baths, 1 cottage. Air-conditioning, clock radio, Corell toiletries, phone and cable TV in rooms, TV/VCR in one room. $85–$150; full breakfast. AE, D, MC, V. No smoking.*

OTHER CHOICES

B&W Courtyards. 2425 Chartres St., New Orleans 70117, tel. 504/945–9418 or 800/585–5731, fax 504/949–3483. 4 rooms with baths, 1 suite. Air-conditioning, phone and cable TV in rooms. $105–$125; Continental breakfast. AE, D, MC, V. 3-night minimum stay weekends Sept.–July, 5-night minimum stay for Mardi Gras and 2nd wk of Jazz Fest, 4-night minimum 1st weekend of Jazz Fest.

Lanaux Mansion. 547 Esplanade Ave., New Orleans 70116, tel. 504/488–4640 or 800/729–4640, fax 504/488–4639. 3 suites, 1 cottage. Air-conditioning, cable TV, and phone with answering machine in rooms. $102–$252; Continental breakfast. AE, D, MC, V. No smoking.

RESERVATIONS SERVICES

Bed & Breakfast, Inc. (1021 Moss St., Box 52257, New Orleans 70152–2257, tel. 504/488–4640 or 800/749–4640). **New Orleans Bed & Breakfast** (Box 8163, New Orleans 70182, tel. 504/838–0071, fax 504/838–0140).

Plantation Country

COTTAGE PLANTATION ☞

10528 Cottage La., St. Francisville 70775, tel. 504/635–3674

The country road to Cottage Plantation ambles across a wooden bridge and through a splendid wooded area thick with moss-covered live oaks, as well as dogwood, mimosa, and crepe myrtle trees. The plantation nestles in 400 such idyllic acres, far from traffic noises and other 20th-century distractions.

Built between 1795 and 1850, Cottage is one of only a handful of antebellum plantations that still have their original outbuildings. The office and one-room schoolhouse, kitchen, tiny milk house, barns, slave quarters, and other dependencies that made up the working plantation are intact, though weathered. One outbuilding is now a rustic restaurant called Mattie's House (open for dinner only); another is an antiques shop.

The well-maintained main building is a long, low yellow-frame structure; green shutters outline the gallery and dormer windows. The sloping roof is punctuated with chimneys and dormers from which window air-conditioning units jut anachronistically. A variety of dogs and cats nap or amble around the grounds.

Angling off from the main house is a similar structure—also original to the plantation—which houses the guest rooms. Downstairs rooms open onto the porch and get more light than those upstairs. All have four-posters and baths with modern plumbing and fixtures.

A tap on the door in the morning signals the arrival of a demitasse of coffee, accompanied by a flower. A serious breakfast is later served in the formal dining room, which, like the rest of the house (including guest rooms), is furnished with antebellum Louisiana pieces that might have been in the house when Gen. Andrew Jackson called on the original owners after the 1815 Battle of New Orleans.

The plantation has been in the Brown family since 1951; Harvey and Mary Brown, the present owners, moved to St. Francisville from Miami to take charge in 1984. One of Mary's hobbies is apparent when you see the flower gardens that decorate the grounds near the main building. **⌂** *5 double rooms with baths. Restaurant, air-conditioning, TV in rooms, pool. $95; full breakfast. MC, V. No smoking. Closed Dec. 24–25.*

MADEWOOD PLANTATION ☞

4250 Rte. 308, Napoleonville 70390, tel. 504/369–7151 or 800/375–7151, fax 504/369–9848

In a lush country setting about equidistant from New Orleans and Baton Rouge, this handsome 21-room Greek Revival mansion offers a nostalgic glimpse of 19th-century life. Built in 1846 for Col. Thomas Pugh, the house was bought and restored in 1964 by the Harold K. Marshall family of New Orleans. It is now owned by the Marshalls' son Keith and his wife, Millie. The Marshalls sometimes spend weekends at Madewood, but the resident managers are Janet Ledet and Michael Hawkins, who preside at the informal wine-and-cheese gatherings and candlelit southern dinners served to guests in the main mansion. Thelma Parker, the cook and housekeeper, who's been at Madewood for more than 25 years, makes a mean pumpkin casserole.

Madewood has spacious rooms with high ceilings, hardwood floors, handsome carved moldings, Oriental rugs, and sparkling crystal chandeliers. In addition to 18th- and 19th-century Louisiana antiques in the mansion and in Charlet House, there are English antiques collected by Keith when he was a Rhodes scholar.

There are four bedrooms upstairs and one downstairs; the latter has a handsome half-tester bed. Though all baths are private, those for the two back bedrooms upstairs can only be reached through the hall. Originally dressing rooms, these baths are much more spacious than those that were squeezed in when indoor plumbing became all the rage. The master bedroom, upstairs, has a large canopied four-poster; across the hall is a guest room decorated with antique children's toys. In addition, there are three suites in Charlet House, an outbuilding on the property. Its Honeymoon Suite has a working fireplace and a large screened porch. The house has served as a set for films, among them *A Woman Called Moses,* starring Cicely Tyson. ⚘ *5 double rooms with baths, 3 suites. Air-conditioning, turndown service, free tour of house and grounds. $215; MAP. AE, D, MC, V. No smoking. Closed Thanksgiving Eve and Day, Dec. 24–25, Dec. 31–Jan. 1; rooms must be vacated for tours 10 AM–5 PM in the main mansion and noon–3 PM in Charlet House.*

TEZCUCO PLANTATION ⚘
3138 Rte. 44, Darrow 70725, tel. 504/562–3929, fax 504/562–3923

While vacationing in Louisiana, Annette Harland fell in love with the area—and with this historic 1855 plantation. (Tezcuco is an Aztec word meaning "place of rest.") She eventually purchased it and made it her home. On the River Road between New Orleans and Baton Rouge, it's an ideal base for sightseeing in this section of Plantation Country.

The extensive grounds are decorated with gazebos, flowering plants, a honey-suckle-covered wishing well, and a tiered cast-iron fountain, all shaded by moss-draped oaks. One of the outbuildings houses the African-American Museum, which traces the history of blacks on the River Road.

There are three rooms for overnighters in the main mansion; all other guest rooms are in 19th-century cottages. Of brick-between-post construction, with exposed beams and hardwood floor, each cottage has a kitchen; all but two have wood-burning fireplaces. Most have front porches with rocking chairs. Rooms are furnished in period antiques: brass or white-iron beds, four-posters, or sunburst testers. Shelves are filled with books, and there are plenty of magazines to read.

Breakfast—sausage, scrambled eggs, biscuits, and grits—is brought to each cottage on a silver tray. Guests who stay in the main mansion have breakfast in the full-service restaurant on the property. ⚘ *3 rooms in mansion, 17 cottages. Restaurant, air-conditioning, TV, clock radio, kitchen, tea- and coffeemaker in cottages, free home tour, free parking, antiques-gift shop, Civil War museum. $65–$165; full breakfast, welcome glass of wine. AE, D, MC, V. No smoking in main mansion. Closed Thanksgiving Day, Dec. 25, and Jan. 1.*

OTHER CHOICES

Butler Greenwood. 8345 U.S. 61, St. Francisville 70775, tel. 504/635–6312, fax 504/635–6370. 6 cottages. Air-conditioning, cable TV and clock radio in cottages; pool, guided nature/bird-watching walks. $100–$110; Continental breakfast. AE, MC, V. No smoking.

Garden Gate Manor. 204 Poydras St., New Roads 70760, tel. and fax 504/638–3890 or 800/487–3890. 4 double rooms with baths, 1 suite. Air-conditioning, cable TV/VCR in suite, cable TV in parlor, off-street parking. $90–$140; full breakfast, afternoon tea. AE, MC, V. No smoking indoors.

RESERVATIONS SERVICE
Bed & Breakfast Travel (8211 Goodwood Blvd., Suite F, Baton Rouge 70806, tel. 504/923–2337 or 800/926–4320, fax 504/923–23744) has B&B listings for Louisiana and other southern states.

Cajun Country

CHRÉTIEN POINT PLANTATION ☞
665 Chrétien Point Rd., Sunset 70584, tel. 318/233–7050 or 800/880–7050, fax 318/662–5876

In the early 1930s, a local photographer took pictures of this house and sent them to Hollywood. As a result, the stairway and the window above it were used as a model for those in Scarlett O'Hara's Tara. Then, too, there's the tale of the long-ago lady of Chrétien Point who shot a man on the steps. Owners Jeanne and Louis Cornay will point out where the man was standing when he was killed.

Of solid brick construction, with six white columns and double front galleries, the two-story house was built in 1831 for Hypolite Chrétien II and his wife, Félicité. During the Civil War, the house figured in a major battle. There is still a bullet hole in one of the front doors. The last Chrétiens lost the house a few years after the war, and it began to fall into a sorry state.

Louis found the deteriorated mansion while looking for a barn in which to keep his son's horse. Hay was stored in it; chickens, cows, and pigs roamed through it. The Cornays bought the house and restored it to its former grandeur.

The colors used in the house are those of nature's sunsets. Silk wall coverings are in vivid scarlets and pinks; one of the ceilings is painted a cool blue. There are six working fireplaces with imported French Empire marble mantels. The 19th-century Louisiana antiques include a carved armoire and four-poster by Mallard.

Three rooms have full-tester beds, and the others canopy and spread in rich fabrics and bold colors. A downstairs room, formerly the wine cellar, has red-brick floors, blue velvet chairs, a New Orleans armoire, and a hand-carved bed. The bins that once held wine are now filled with books.

Guests get acquainted over afternoon mint juleps and the big plantation breakfast, served in the formal dining room. ⚐ *5 double rooms with baths. Air-conditioning, free mansion tour, meeting room, pool, tennis court. $110–$225; full breakfast. AE, MC, V. No smoking.*

COOK'S COTTAGE AT RIP VAN WINKLE GARDENS ☞
5505 Rip Van Winkle Rd., New Iberia 70560, tel. 318/365–3332 or 800/375–3332, fax 318/365–3354

In the late 19th century, American actor Joseph Jefferson toured the country portraying Washington Irving's Rip Van Winkle. On a hunting trip to South Louisiana, Jefferson fell in love with the area and purchased several thousand acres on which he built an elaborate winter home. Twenty-five acres of that property now compose the Rip Van Winkle Gardens, a showcase of landscaped gardens that sit adjacent to Lake Peigneur.

Within the lovely gardens, the three-room former cook's cottage for the estate has been transformed into a modern and private guest house. It is furnished with a blend of antique and reproduction early French Louisiana pieces, including a handmade mahogany four-poster bed with down pillows. The bath is stunning, with a big whirlpool tub and shower, a large mirror, as well as a lighted magnified makeup mirror, a spacious vanity, a line-up of aromatherapy soaps and sundry lotions, and a hair dryer. An ironing board and iron are tucked in the closet.

For entertainment, there is a stereo and a CD player, and TV/VCR. In the small kitchenette area, where there is a wet bar, microwave, toaster oven, and coffeemaker, the fridge is stocked with the makings of a do-it-yourself Continental breakfast, including fresh fruits and gourmet coffees. There are always fresh flowers from the gardens placed around the cottage.

Guests have unlimited access to the gardens and are given a complimentary tour of the Jefferson House, which is a wonderful Gothic house with Moorish flourishes. There is a restaurant overlooking the lake, and boat tours on the lake are conducted daily (at a reduced rate for B&B guests). ♨ *1 cottage. Restaurant, air-conditioning, cable TV/VCR, stereo, CD player, wet bar, microwave, refrigerator, phone in rooms; complimentary house tour. $145–$175; Continental breakfast. No smoking.*

LA MAISON DE CAMPAGNE ☜
825 Kidder Rd., Carencro 70520, 318/896–6529 or 800/895–0235, fax 318/896–1494

Fred and Joeann McLemore's home is a gabled and galleried Acadian house, built in about 1871. It sits in a quiet country setting in a suburb about 15 minutes north of Lafayette. The drawing room is elegantly furnished with Victorian antiques: velvet and brocade-upholstered settees and chairs, marble-top tables, and white lace curtains. Frilly old-fashioned ladies' hats are perched here and there on gilded mirrors.

The Magnolia Room, downstairs, is the honeymoon suite: a spacious room with 13½-ft ceilings, heart-of-cedar floors, a reproduction canopy bed and armoire, and an 1890 marble-top dresser. Its bath has the original claw-foot tub and matching water closet, and a shower with a frilly white curtain. The Country Room, peopled with stuffed dolls, has turn-of-the-century Cajun furnishings, including a white-iron bed draped with a diaphanous canopy. A matching antique 1890 bedroom set is in the French Room, where German porcelain lamps are on the night stands. Attention to detail is evident in touches such as the wallpaper border that matches the golden oak finish of the furniture. Baths in this and the Country Room have walk-in closets.

In addition to rooms in the main house, there is the Sharecropper's Cottage, which was moved from a nearby plantation and restored with century-old cypress lumber—the same material used for the king-size bed and an entertainment center complete with TV/VCR and refrigerator. This cottage, suitable for families with children, has a full kitchen with microwave, dishwasher, and washer/dryer, rocking chairs, patchwork quilts, and a collection of German dolls.

The author of the cookbook *Lache Pas La Patate* (Don't Drop the Potato), Joeann takes pride in gourmet breakfasts that may include scrumptious seafood sauces, egg dishes, and homemade breads. ♨ *3 double rooms with baths, 1 cottage. Air-conditioning, pool. $95–$145; full breakfast. D, MC, V. 2-night minimum* *for Mardi Gras, Festival International, Festival Acadien, and Crawfish Festival. No smoking, no alcoholic beverages on premises.*

OTHER CHOICES

Estorge House. 427 Market St., Opelousas 70570, tel. 318/942–8151. 2 double rooms with baths. Air-conditioning, turndown service, free mansion tour, outdoor hot tub. $75–125; full breakfast. No credit cards. No smoking.

RESERVATIONS SERVICE

Bed & Breakfast Travel (8211 Goodwood Blvd., Suite F, Baton Rouge 70806, tel. 504/923–2337 or 800/926–4320 outside Louisiana, fax 504/923–2374, www.bnbtravel.com) has B&B listings for Louisiana and parts of East Texas, Mississippi, Alabama, and the Gulf Coast.

North-Central Louisiana

BEAU FORT PLANTATION 🦜
4078 Rte. 494, Bermuda (Box 2300), Natchitoches 71457, tel. 318/352–5340 or 318/352–9580

On the banks of the Cane River Lake, 10 mi south of Natchitoches, the home of Ann and Jack Brittain is a 265-acre working cotton and corn plantation. Built in 1790, the house, with its 84-ft gallery, is approached via a long alley of oaks. Louisiana Empire and European antiques, including stunning tester beds, sit among scores of other heirlooms and objets d'art that include Tsinge Dynasty lamp bases, original Audubon and Clementine Hunter paintings, and fascinating 19th-century artifacts. The house is famed in these parts for the punkah (pronounced *poon*-kah; or shoo-fly) fan that hangs over the dining-room table. Suites, each with a private entrance, are unusually large—the master suite is 28 by 26 ft—as are the modern tile baths, which were originally screened porches. Displays of antique clothing, patchwork quilts, dolls, and family pictures are abundant. 🛏 *3 suites. Air-conditioning, satellite TV in master suite, phone in 2 suites, free home tour. $125–145; full breakfast. DC, MC. No smoking.*

CLOUTIER TOWNHOUSE AND PETIT TARN 🦜
416 Jefferson St., Natchitoches 71457, tel. and fax 318/352–5242 or 800/351–7666

In 1998 Conna Cloutier sold her town house on Front Street (also called the Cloutier Townhouse) and opened two bed-and-breakfasts in restored houses. Her present home is a 12-room turn-of-the-century house just a half block from Front Street's shops and restaurants. She is also the proprietor of the Petit Tarn, a restored 1950s cottage that sits in the hills on Natchitoches's east bank, a stroll across the downtown bridge away from Front Street attractions.

The high-ceiling Townhouse is furnished with a collection of antiques, dating mostly from the Louisiana Empire and Victorian periods. Conna's purchase of two beds that had been in the old St. Mary's Convent in Natchitoches inspired her to create a convent suite. The four-posters, draped in mosquito netting, date from the early 19th century. Conna has decorated this suite with religious artifacts, including an old-fashioned nun's habit that hangs from a wooden peg. The master suite has a full tester bed, with embroidered spread, wing chairs, an upholstered settee, TV/VCR, and a whirlpool bath.

Conna's other bed-and-breakfast—the Petit Tarn—is named for the French town that was the ancestral home of Irma Sompayrac Willard, the noted Natchitoches artist and historian who built the house. In a garden setting, this house is filled with her artwork and family memorabilia. Each of the three stories is a suite: the top-floor Treehouse Suite, with two balconies, has a massive Empire bed; below it, the balconied Library Suite has an Eastlake Victorian half-tester. The ground-floor River Suite has a water view, as well as a full kitchen. All three suites have whirlpool baths.

In the Townhouse, breakfasts that include homemade breads and mini-meat pies are served; in the Petit Tarn, the makings for a do-it-yourself Continental breakfast are provided. ▲ *2 suites in Cloutier Townhouse, 3 suites in the Petit Tarn. Air-conditioning; whirlpool bath in 4 suites; TV/VCR in 1 suite; full kitchen in 1 suite; refrigerator, microwave, and coffeemaker in 2 suites. $95–$110. AE, MC, V. No smoking, 2-night minimum Thanksgiving–Jan. 1.*

LEVY-EAST HOUSE ☞
358 Jefferson St., Natchitoches 71457, tel. 318/352–0662 or 800/840–0662

The home of Avery and Judy East, a galleried 1838 house with lacy ironwork, gabled roof, and twin brick chimneys is just a block and a half from Front Street shops and restaurants. Furnished with Victorian antiques and heirlooms, the elegant house has heart-pine floors, six fireplaces, baths with beaded-wood wainscoting, and luscious mauve and green colors. Upstairs guest rooms, which flank a common room that opens onto a back porch with rocking chairs and a view of a century-old magnolia tree, have enlarged antique beds and armoires in which TVs and phones are tucked. Each room has a volume-control speaker that plays romantic CDs. Guests are given keys to a private entrance. A formal dining room, with handsome silver candelabra and fresh flowers, is the setting for a breakfast that may be a fruit-topped French toast sundae or baked eggs served in heart-shaped dishes. ▲ *4 double rooms with baths. Air-conditioning, coffeemaker, cable TV/VCR, phone, whirlpool tub, and terry cloth robes in rooms, turndown service with candy, off-street free parking. $115–$195; full breakfast, sherry, complimentary champagne for guests celebrating their honeymoon or anniversary. MC, V. No smoking, 2-night minimum for Christmas Festival.*

LOYD HALL ☞
292 Loyd Bridge Rd., Cheneyville (5119 Masonic Dr., Alexandria 71301), tel. 318/776–5641 or 800/240–8135, fax 318/776–5886

Loyd Hall is a 640-acre working plantation that grows cotton, corn, and soybeans. Frank Fitzgerald's father bought the land in 1949, unaware that a deteriorated 19th-century mansion was buried beneath a tangle of trees and bushes. Frank and his wife, Anne, now live in the restored house. Frank is a veterinarian, and in addition to sundry farm critters, a small army of cats and dogs calls Loyd Hall home.

Several of the plantation's original outbuildings have been restored and contain modern guest accommodations. There are two suites in the 1800s carriage house; the others are in one- or two-bedroom cottages. All are furnished with 19th-century Louisiana, such as tester and four-poster beds, and some have wood-burning fireplaces. Each has a kitchen with modern appliances, including microwave, toaster, and coffeemaker. Two cottages have washer/dryers, and one of them—the McCullough House—has a two-person hot tub in its garden. Kitchens are stocked with ingredients for a Continental breakfast, which guests prepare at their leisure and enjoy in privacy, wrapped in the cushy terry cloth robes provided.

This is an excellent place for families; there is no charge for children under six.

The plantation is in a quiet country setting, 16 mi south of Alexandria near the intersection of U.S. 167 and 71. *4 cottages, 2 suites. Air-conditioning, TV/VCR in cottage and suites, washer/dryer in 2 cottages; pool, bicycles, fishing rods, tour of mansion. $95–$145; Continental breakfast, complimentary wine on arrival. AE, MC, V. No smoking.*

MAGNOLIA PLANTATION ☞
5487 Rte. 119, Natchez 71456, tel. 318/379–2221

More than 20 cats, several peacocks, and a variety of other critters are at home on this 2,400-acre working plantation, the grounds of which are lavish with live oaks, greenery, and flowering plants. A barn houses the only cotton press in the country still in its original location.

With its broad porches, pitched roof, dormers, and chimneys, this raised cottage epitomizes early Louisiana plantation houses. One of only two National Bicentennial Farms west of the Mississippi River, Magnolia has been in the same family since a 1753 French land grant. The original Big House was severely damaged by fire during the Civil War. Restored in 1896, using the original brick foundation and 18-inch-thick brick walls, it is now the home of Mrs. Matthew Hertzog and her daughter Betty.

Upstairs and downstairs rooms open onto central hallways. The front door opens to a handsome crystal chandelier that shines over red velvet Victorian settees; every room in the 27-room house, except the hall, has an open, non-working fireplace. Walls are lined with family portraits; glass cases display fine china and crystal. There is a marvelous back porch, with a punkah fan, wind chimes, and a big Victorian oak hat rack. In a wing off the back porch there is a chapel, in which services are still held.

Throughout the house are the Hertzog family's collection of Southern Empire furniture, such as a cherry early Louisiana bed and matching armoire in a guest room. One guest room has a sunburst tester, while another has an early Victorian mahogany bed and a cherry armoire. All three rooms are exceptionally large, and have antique washbasins as well as terry cloth robes. The upstairs hall has a cable TV/VCR, a fridge, and coffeemaker, but a full breakfast is served in the formal dining room beneath a splendid brass chandelier. *3 double rooms with baths. Air-conditioning, cable TV/VCR, refrigerator, coffeemaker, complimentary tour of the house. D, MC, V; full breakfast. No smoking.*

OTHER CHOICES

Tante Huppé House. 424 Jefferson St., Natchitoches 71457, tel. 318/352–5342 or 800/482–4276. 3 suites. Air-conditioning, kitchen, coffeemaker, phone with 2 private lines, 2 cable TVs/VCRs and videos of locally made movies in each suite; bottle of wine on check-in; free home tour. $95; full breakfast. AE, MC, V. No smoking.

RESERVATIONS SERVICE

Bed & Breakfast Travel (8211 Goodwood Blvd., Suite F, Baton Rouge 70806, tel. 504/923–2337 or 800/926–4320 outside Louisiana, fax 504/923–2374, www.bnbtravel.com) has B&B listings for Louisiana and parts of East Texas, Mississippi, Alabama, and the Gulf Coast.

MAINE

The Southern Coast:
Kittery to Portland

CAPTAIN LORD MANSION ⚘
Pleasant and Green Sts. (Box 800), Kennebunkport 04046, tel. 207/967–3141,
fax 207/967–3172

Of the mansions in Kennebunkport's historic district that have been tastefully converted to inns, the 1812 vintage Captain Lord Mansion is hands down the most stately and sumptuously appointed. The three-story, pale-yellow house sits in the middle of a manicured lawn in the historic district. The inn has an air of formal—but never stiff—propriety, seen to best advantage in the refined Gathering Room, which looks like a period room (Chippendale) in a museum, except for the guests lounging before the hearth.

Innkeepers Bev Davis and Rick Litchfield, former advertising executives, are far more laid-back than the house they meticulously restored. They chat and joke with you over family-style breakfasts served informally at the two harvest tables in their cheerful country kitchen.

Bev and Rick rescued the Captain Lord Mansion from its Victorian gloom and refurbished it with crisp, authentic Federal decor. Guest rooms, which are named after old clipper ships, are large and stately. Ship Lincoln, to many minds the finest room in the house, with a step-up four-poster bed and damask-covered walls, is also the room in which the inn's benign resident ghost appears (only women have ever seen her). Bark Hesper, on the third floor, is a whimsical country-style room, quainter and smaller than the downstairs rooms, with green dot-and-flower wallpaper and leafy views out the windows.

Bev and Rick seem always a step ahead of other area inns, and in 1997 they added the Captain's Suite, which is a monument to hedonism. From the king-size lace canopy bed you can watch flames dance in the gas fireplace. You step from the hydro-massage shower onto heated marble floors. In the spa room you and your loved one can unwind in the two-person whirlpool tub in front of another fireplace or ride the exercise bicycle and watch TV. It's all decorated in deep reds with gold accents, including a chandelier in the spa.

The Captain Lord is a pleasing base from which to venture forth on forays to Kennebunkport's architectural treasures, the shops of Dock Square, or the sand beaches lining the chill Atlantic. ⚱ *16 doubles with bath. Air-conditioning and phone in rooms, fireplace in most rooms, gift shop, TV room. $159–$399; full breakfast, afternoon tea. D, MC, V. No smoking. 2-night minimum weekends, 3-night minimum holiday weekends.*

ROCKMERE LODGE ☞
40 Stearns Rd. (Box 278), Ogunquit 03907, tel. 207/646–2985

With a location midway along Ogunquit's famed Marginal Way and views that seem to go as far as England, the Rockmere Lodge is an ideal retreat from the hustle and bustle of Perkins Cove or the shops and restaurants of downtown Ogunquit, both just a ½ mi away. Partners Andy Antoniuk and Bob Brown rescued the 1899 Victorian shingle-style cottage, which had been turned into apartments, and completely renovated it. The skills Andy had amassed from owning a gift-basket business and store in Connecticut and also designing sets for theater productions came in handy when the two retired here in 1992. Andy has redone some rooms no fewer than four times in six years: "I like guests to be surprised," he says, adding that Bob tries to keep him out of wallpaper stores.

The house faces the sea, and it's difficult to drag yourself away from the wraparound porch with its white wicker furniture and hanging baskets of flowers. Inside the front door the mood changes abruptly to high Victorian. Forest green, navy blue, and rich burgundy mix in the striped wallpaper, Oriental rugs, and upholstery. Bob and Andy have furnished the living room with family antiques, such as the Victorian sofa, and pieces they've purchased over the years, including a desk from New York's Plaza Hotel, three carved straight-back chairs that once graced a church altar, and a grandfather clock with a Waterford crystal pendulum. The nutcrackers that guard the Italian tile fireplace are holdovers from Andy's shop. At Christmas they're joined by others, and the house is decorated with a special tree in every room. (Note that given all the antiques and delicate pieces, this inn is not suitable for children.)

Guest rooms all have prized corner locations and are large and airy; all but one have excellent water views. Room 7 has hand-painted decoration on the door and the window frames that matches the mirror frames and dressers. Room 6 has the best views and brings the outdoors in with an arbor motif in green, white, and purple and a green iron bedstead with ivy strewn through the frame. The Lookout sitting area on the third floor is a wonderful retreat, with views to Kennebunkport. △ *8 double rooms with baths. Ceiling fan and cable TV in rooms, beach within walking distance. $100–$150; Continental breakfast. AE, D, MC, V. No smoking, 2-night minimum weekends and holidays.*

OTHER CHOICES

Captain's Hideaway. 12 Pleasant St. (Box 2746), Kennebunkport 04046, tel. 207/967–5711, fax 207/967–3843. 1 double room with bath, 1 suite. Cable TV/VCR, phone, and refrigerator with beverages in rooms; beach chairs, towels, picnic lunches available. $229–$279; full breakfast. MC, V. 2-night minimum weekends.

Edward's Harborside Inn. Stage Neck Rd. (Box 866), York Harbor 03911, tel. 207/363–3037 or 800/273–2686, fax 207/363–1544. 3 double rooms with baths, 4 doubles share 2 baths, 3 suites. Air-conditioning, cable TV, phone in rooms. $70–$220; Continental breakfast. MC, V. No smoking.

RESERVATIONS SERVICE
B&B of Maine (377 Gray Rd., Falmouth 04105, tel. 207/797–5540).

Mid-Coast: Freeport
to Port Clyde
❦❦❦

EAST WIND INN & MEETING HOUSE ☞
Mechanic St. (Box 149), Tenants Harbor 04860, tel. 207/372–6366 or
800/241–8439, fax 207/372–6320

If you've read *The Country of the Pointed Firs,* Sarah Orne Jewett's charming
sketches of coastal Maine, you may have an eerie sense of déjà vu as you drive
the 10 mi down Route 131 into Tenants Harbor. Not much has changed since Jewett wrote here at the turn of the century: the neat little white-clapboard houses
set in tangles of tall grass and beach roses, the narrow harbor from which the nearly
black evergreens rise like sawteeth, the distant glimpse of islands and open water.

Set on a little knob of land overlooking the harbor and islands, the three-story, white-
clapboard East Wind Inn has, in the course of its 130 years, served as a sail loft
and mason's hall. Today it's hard to imagine it as anything other than the perfect rustic inn, complete with wraparound porch. Innkeeper Tim Watts gave up his work
as an accountant to buy the East Wind in 1974, and in his yearlong renovation,
he was careful to leave its innocence and simplicity very much intact.

You stay either in the inn or the meetinghouse, a converted ship captain's house
just up the hill. The inn's front rooms command a view of sunrise over the islands. The bedrooms are furnished with a hodgepodge of simple Early American–
style brass bedsteads and pine chests; oak and mahogany furnishings give the
meetinghouse rooms more of a Victorian air. All the rooms are appealingly plain,
as is the inn's living room, with its baby grand piano, nautical charts, and comfortable sofas and easy chairs. The three apartments in the Ginny Wheeler Cottage, added in 1996, are fancier and have private decks and fabulous views.
Two have fireplaces, and all have kitchens.

The East Wind's restaurant overlooks the harbor, and the menu fittingly emphasizes fresh fish. From the inn you can drive (or bike) to Port Clyde for a picnic at the Marshall Point Lighthouse. Other options include a day trip to Monhegan
or an afternoon with the Wyeths at the Farnsworth Art Museum, in Rockland.
⚓ *5 double rooms with baths, 7 doubles share 4 baths, 1 suite in inn; 8 doubles with
bath, 2 suites, 1 apartment in meetinghouse; 3 apartments in Wheeler Cottage.
Restaurant; TV in suites, apartment, and living room; phone in rooms; conference room, store. $90–$275; full breakfast. AE, D, MC, V. No smoking in restaurant. Closed Dec.–Apr.*

NEWCASTLE INN ☞
60 River Rd., Newcastle 04553, tel. 207/563–5685 or 800/832–8669, fax 207/563–6877

Like so many other innkeepers, Howard and Rebecca Levitan decided to break
with their previous careers—his as a lawyer, hers in sales—to find a better lifestyle.
Both had ties to Maine, and in 1995 they purchased the Newcastle Inn. They've
redecorated in a French country style, enlarging and adding whirlpool baths
and gas fireplaces to some rooms and beautifying the grounds, which slope down
to the Damariscotta River. For two weeks in June, lupines bloom here, and they
have become the inn's theme.

Rooms are named after lighthouses along the Maine coast. Both Matinicus Rock,
which has a two-person whirlpool tub, and Tenants Harbor have quiet, back-
of-the-house locations, gas fireplaces, and river views. Floral wallpapers offset

the Oriental rugs for a comforting yet elegant atmosphere. Pemaquid Point offers the best view in the house from its queen-size canopy bed; it also has a gas fireplace and two-person whirlpool tub. Monhegan is the grandest in the house: It has a four-poster, king-size rice bed (its posts are carved to look like sheaves of rice); a large gas fireplace; and burgundy-and-navy paisley wallpaper that complements the room's Oriental rug. (Owing to all the carefully selected and meticulously arranged furnishings, you should leave your wee ones at home.)

The front living room is an inviting place to rest or plan a day's adventure, but the rear sitting room is even more delightful: It's cozy and has a fireplace and a river view. The small adjacent pub, with its vibrant red walls, teal accents, and Southwestern artwork, should seem out of place here, but somehow it blends well.

In fine weather breakfast—perhaps eggs Benedict or cinnamon-raisin French toast stuffed with ricotta cheese—is served on the deck overlooking the river. The inn also offers four-course prix-fixe dinners in its dining rooms; you will need to make reservations.

Newcastle is a town with more charm than action; but the inn makes a convenient base for forays to Boothbay Harbor or Pemaquid Point or for a quiet afternoon of canoeing on the river. In summer the inn's sunporch, with white wicker furniture and ice-cream-parlor chairs, makes a particularly appealing spot to contemplate the Damariscotta River and congratulate yourself for having found such a special place. △ *13 double rooms with baths, 2 suites. Restaurant, pub, air-conditioning and fireplace in 6 rooms, TV in den, whirlpool tub in 2 suites, turn-down service. $110–$210; full breakfast. AE, MC, V. No smoking, 2-night minimum peak holiday weekends.*

POPHAM BEACH BED & BREAKFAST ❦
Beach Rd. (HC 31, Box 430), Phippsburg 04562, tel. 207/389–2409

Peggy Johanessen calls the B&B she's created in a former Coast Guard station a work in progress. If you're willing to overlook peeling paint and a few unfinished rooms, it's a gem. How can it miss with a waterfront location on Popham, one of Maine's prettiest beaches?

The red-roofed building topped with a watchtower was constructed in 1883 as a U.S. Lifesaving Station; it was taken over by the Coast Guard in 1935 and decommissioned in 1971. Guest rooms in the front of the house have marvelous views: the Library Room, with hardwood floors and natural wicker furniture, is where boats were once stored; the Bunk Room, with marine-blue carpeting and plenty of white wicker, is the largest in the house. You can relax in the airy living room, furnished with a hodgepodge of pieces and a woodstove that provides warmth when needed.

The quiet location allows you to hear the waves breaking on the shore and a bell buoy clanging at sea. It's a short walk to Civil War–era Ft. Popham or to Spinney's, a casual beach restaurant that serves lobster. △ *3 double rooms with baths, 1 double shares bath, 1 suite. $80–$145; full breakfast. MC, V. 2-night minimum weekends July–Aug. Closed Nov.–Apr.*

SQUIRE TARBOX INN ❦
Rte. 144 (R.R. 2, Box 620), Wiscasset 04578, tel. 207/882–7693, fax 207/882–7107

As you drive the 8½ mi from Route 1 down Route 144 and onto Westport Island, you may wonder if you made a wrong turn as the signs of civilization peter out into lush rolling hills, woods, and a sprinkling of farmhouses. Then the reassuring champagne-yellow clapboard front of the Squire Tarbox looms into view, and you know just where you are: deep in the country at one of Maine's most serene inns.

"This is a really nourishing place," says innkeeper Karen Mitman with a soft smile while in a rocking chair next to the fireplace, beside the grandfather clock. "People come here to reflect, to walk in the woods, to look at the birds." They also come to watch Karen and her husband, Bill, milk their goats and to sample their delicious goat cheese, served each night. For the Squire Tarbox is not only an inn, and on the National Register of Historic Places, but it's also a working farm, with a small herd of goats, a horse, laying hens, and a few donkeys. "We are goat missionaries who rent rooms," Karen says.

Karen and Bill had hotel experience in Boston, but none as goat farmers, when they bought the inn in 1981. Yet somehow they seem to have been in the rambling Federal house forever. Some of it dates from 1763 and some from 1820, and among the downstairs public rooms are a rustic dining room—where dinner is served fireside beneath old ships' beams—and a music room with a player piano.

Of the bedrooms, Room 1, in the main part of the house, is choice—a huge room with king-size bed, braided rugs on pumpkin-pine floors, fireplaces, and an antique footlocker. The attached barn has four rooms that are more rustic in feel and smaller than the inn rooms, but also more private. Room 11 is the best for privacy, with gray-green woodwork, more space than the other barn rooms, and a view of the pasture.

When you tire of strolling around the property and bird-watching from the deck, ask the Mitmans to direct you to the shops of Wiscasset, the Maritime Museum at Bath, the lobster pier and scenic back roads of Five Islands (good for biking), and the beach at Reid State Park. Of course, if you're really weary, you could just rest in front of a fireplace in one of the common rooms. **△** *11 double rooms with baths. Rowboat, farm animals. $164–$225; MAP. AE, D, MC, V. No smoking. Closed late Oct.–mid-May.*

OTHER CHOICES

Flying Cloud. River Rd. (Box 549), Newcastle 04553, tel. 207/563–2484. 4 double rooms with baths, 1 suite. TV/VCR in sitting room. $75–$95; full breakfast, afternoon refreshments. AE, D, MC, V. No smoking, 2-night minimum holiday weekends.
Marston House. Main St. (Box 517), Wiscasset 04578, tel. 207/882–6010 or 800/852–4137, fax 207/882–6965. 2 double rooms with baths. Terry cloth robes $90; Continental breakfast. AE, MC, V. No smoking. Closed Nov.–Apr.
1774 Inn. Parker Head Rd., Phippsburg Center 04562, tel. 207/389–1774. 4 double rooms with baths. TV/VCR in den. $85–$125; full breakfast. No credit cards. No smoking.

RESERVATIONS SERVICE

B&B of Maine (377 Gray Rd., Falmouth 04105, tel. 207/797–5540).

Around Penobscot Bay: Rockland to Blue Hill

CASTINE INN 🖋

Main St. (Box 41), Castine 04421, tel. 207/326–4365, fax 207/326–4570

The well-respected Castine Inn acquired new owners in 1997, and the young energetic couple haven't missed a beat. Amy and Tom Gutrow wanted to escape

New York City, where she was a lawyer and he a chef. Both grew up in rural areas, Amy in Vermont and Tom in Michigan, and both wanted to return to a simpler lifestyle. Amy wanted New England, Tom wanted water, and both wanted an existing inn. The Castine Inn fit the bill.

The stately yellow-clapboard inn celebrates its 100th anniversary in 1998. The living room is warm and welcoming, with a curio cabinet filled with beachcombing finds as well as comfortable chairs and a fire burning in the Count Rumford fireplace on cool evenings. It's the kind of place in which you can let out a huge sigh and relax. Off the lobby there's a snug little pub, the perfect spot for an evening rendezvous.

Rooms are simply furnished, some with Colonial reproductions. Those on the third floor are the biggest and command the finest views. From one side you see the harbor over the inn's formal garden; from the other you overlook the town and more gardens.

If you wonder what the view looks like in entirety, head to the spacious dining room, where there's a wraparound mural of the town and harbor. Tom, who trained with top chefs in New York and Paris, has added his own touches to the inn's most popular dishes (such as the crabmeat cake with mustard sauce appetizer). For his entrées he uses fresh local foods, so the menu changes regularly. At breakfast you have a choice of such dishes as apple-bread French toast and a herbed goat cheese omelet.

Castine is a perfect New England small town that invites you to linger, stroll along Main Street down to the harbor, or out along Perkins Street, past Federal, Greek Revival, and shingle-style houses to the lighthouse. The sea air and exercise will make the return to the Castine Inn and its hearty dinners all the more enjoyable. **⌂** *15 double rooms with baths, 2 doubles with detached bath, 3 suites. Restaurant, pub, sauna. $85–$135; full breakfast. MC, V. No smoking in dining room. 2-night minimum July–Aug. Closed Nov.–Apr.*

EGGEMOGGIN REACH BED AND BREAKFAST ☙

Herrick Rd. (R.R. 1, Box 33A), Brooksville 04617, tel. 207/359–5073, fax 207/359–5074

Approached by a long, wooded drive, Eggemoggin Reach Bed and Breakfast stands on a point behind which shimmer the waters of Eggemoggin Reach. After summering in the area for years, Michael and Susie Canon built the post-and-beam Maine farmhouse in 1988 as a family retreat. They furnished it with an assortment of antiques, Oriental rugs, and such simple decorative pieces as duck decoys and ginger jars. In 1993 they opened their home to guests. The house has an open plan, and every room overlooks the water. The living room's large brick fireplace keeps the chill off on cool evenings; the smaller den, with its woodstove, is the perfect place to escape the gloom of a rainy afternoon.

Breakfast is served buffet style in the living-dining room. It includes juices, muffins, and a hot entrée such as oven-baked apple pancakes, Charleston House French toast, or sour-cream breakfast cake. On warm days most guests choose to breakfast outside on the large covered deck, part of which is screened in. The lovely view here and from the upstairs suite is over the Reach to Little Deer Isle and Pumpkin Island Lighthouse.

The third-floor Wheelhouse Suite is spacious and elegant, with white walls and off-white carpeting. There's a king-size bed in the bedroom, and the large, comfortable living room has a sofa bed and an extra single bed.

The inn's two one-room cottages, Port Watch and Starboard Watch, face Deadman's Cove. Both have efficiency kitchens, woodstoves, bathrooms with cedar showers, and private screened porches. Each also has a king-size bed and a small sitting area with a love seat, a table, and chairs.

Similar in design, but larger and with a better view, are the six rooms, two per floor, in the gambrel-roof annex called the Bay Lodge. Two have woodstoves, and on the upper floors the rooms can be connected through common sitting areas, a popular option for couples traveling together.

The Canons love to entertain, and if six or more couples desire, they will arrange for a shorefront picnic, with lobster delivered right to the dock. There's plenty to explore nearby, including Deer Isle, Blue Hill, and Castine. △ *6 double rooms with baths, 1 suite, 2 cottages, 1 apartment. TV/VCR in living room, rowboat, canoe, dock, mooring. $140–$165; full breakfast. MC, V. No smoking, 2-night minimum weekends June 15–Labor Day. Closed mid-Oct.–mid-May.*

GOOSE COVE LODGE ☜

Goose Cove Rd. (Box 40), Sunset 04683, tel. 207/348–2508 or 800/728–1963, fax 207/348–2624

When life seems too complicated, you can always head to the Goose Cove Lodge in the quiet community of Sunset, just outside Deer Isle. With its private location at the end of a dirt road overlooking Penobscot Bay and abutting nature conservancy lands, it's the kind of place where you can forget that the rest of the world exists.

Owners Dom and Joanne Parisi preside over a talented, service-oriented staff. Dom was president of an energy conservation management company in western Massachusetts, where Joanne operated a restaurant and worked as a caterer. They decided to improve the quality of their lives and began a search for a simple, rustic natural resort with '90s-era amenities—including fine dining. They found it here.

The main lodge, built as a nature camp in the 1940s, is rustic and homey, with a big fieldstone fireplace, a library, and a small bar on one level and the dining area a few steps down. What takes center stage here is the sweeping view of Penobscot Bay and the islands: no signs of development, just towering pines, rocky shores, a narrow beach, and boats. Guests rooms in the lodge and at the front of the attached wing all have this view as do most of the cottages, which are nestled in the pines throughout the inn's 21 acres. Cottages are simply furnished with country pieces, collectibles, and reproductions—perhaps a braided rug, a rocking chair, or a lobster-trap table—and have woodstoves or fireplaces that are prepared each day by the staff. Some have kitchenettes, and all have decks or granite ledge patios.

Guests truly appreciate the quiet and the natural environment. Dom leads weekly nature walks, and the lodge provides maps for trails on its property and the nature conservancy's adjacent 50 acres, where at low tide you can walk out to an island via a sandbar.

The inn is renowned for its dining room (rates include breakfast and dinner from May through October), which serves creative renditions of classic fare using Maine ingredients. With the exception of the weekly lobster bake on the beach, young children, infants to age 12, eat dinner separately from their parents, entertained by the lodge's staff from 5:30 to 8. Teenagers eat together in the adult dining room. △ *2 double rooms, 2 singles with baths; 8 suites; 13 cottages. Restaurant, children's program, beach, bicycles, canoes, hiking trails, sea* kayaks, 24' sloop (available for rent). $170–$260; full breakfast, hors d'oeuvres, 4-course dinner. AE, D, MC, V. 2-night minimum off-season, 3-person minimum for cottages July–Aug. Closed mid-Oct.–mid-May.

JOHN PETERS INN 🐚
Peters Point (Box 916), Blue Hill 04614, tel. 207/374–2116

When you turn down the narrow lane and catch your first glimpse of this country inn, you may wonder whether your car has slipped into some bizarre wrinkle in the time–space continuum. The John Peters, with its four colossal Doric pillars and its views over green fields to the head of Blue Hill Bay, looks like something out of Tidewater, Virginia.

On closer inspection you will see that it is actually a classic brick Federal mansion, built in 1810, to which the columned porch was added in the 1930s. No matter. The John Peters is unsurpassed for its privacy, its tastefully decorated guest rooms, and the whimsical informality of its innkeepers, Barbara and Rick Seeger. Rick gladly left an engineering job in Massachusetts for what the Seegers describe as their "fantasy utopia" just outside the town of Blue Hill.

More often than not, you will be greeted excitedly by the resident Welsh terrier, DOC (for disobedient canine), before Barbara or Rick escorts you into the living room with its two fireplaces, books and games, baby grand piano, and traditional furniture. Oriental rugs, which the Seegers collect, are everywhere. (Given the furnishings, this inn is not suitable for children.) Huge breakfasts in the light, airy dining rooms include the famous lobster omelet, served with lobster-claw shells as decoration. After breakfast you can lope down the hill to your boat or stroll into Blue Hill for a morning of browsing in the pottery and crafts shops.

The Surry Room, a standout guest room (though all are lovely), has a king-size bed, a fireplace, a maple chest, a gilt mirror, and six windows with delicate lace curtains. The Blue Hill Room is immense and has a wet bar and mini-refrigerator, an Empire sofa, a four-poster bed, a deck, and a view of Blue Hill Bay. In this room you can have breakfast served to you in bed. The large rooms in the carriage house, a stone's throw down the hill from the inn, have dining areas, cherrywood floors and woodwork, wicker and brass accents, and a contemporary feel. Four have decks, kitchens, and fireplaces—real pluses. But at the John Peters, nothing is a minus, except having to say good-bye. ⚓ *7 double rooms with baths, 1 suite in inn; 6 doubles with bath in carriage house. Phone in 4 carriage-house rooms, pool, rowboat, canoe, sailboat, pond, 2 moorings. $105–$165; full breakfast. MC, V. No smoking. Closed Nov.–Apr.*

WHITEHALL INN 🐚
Rte. 1 (Box 558), Camden 04843, tel. 207/236–3391 or 800/789–6565, fax 207/236–4427 in season

Camden's best-known inn was built in 1834 as a ship captain's home. At the turn of the century it began its life as an inn, and another wing was then added. You'll sense the long history of civilized comfort as you cross the wide, cheery porch and walk through the decorous lobby on the soft, time-faded Oriental rugs. The location is ideal: midway between the shops, restaurants, and windjammers of Camden and the trails of Camden Hills State Park. Penobscot Bay opens up across the road.

Siblings J.C., Chip, and Heidi Dewing grew up at the inn, and now—along with J.C.'s wife and their uncle, Don Chambers—manage it. "What we try to do here is preserve what the inn has always been," J.C. says, adding that there have only been four innkeepers since Ruth Barrett Ordway opened it in 1901.

The Whitehall is dear to the hearts of literary folk: Edna St. Vincent Millay, a Rockland girl, came here in the summer of 1912 to recite her poem "Renascence" and launch her literary career. The Millay Room, just off the lobby, contains Millay memorabilia.

The inn's loyal adherents cherish its high-toned literary aura and the fact that everything looks the same year after year—right down to the old-fashioned phones connected to an ancient switchboard with plugs. Still, newcomers may be disappointed by the small, sparsely furnished rooms, with their old dark-wood bedsteads, Currier and Ives prints, claw-foot bathtubs, and not much else in the way of style.

Though the Whitehall has a countrified stateliness, you'll hear the traffic on Route 1 unless you get a garden-facing room in the rear wing. The rooms in the Victorian annexes, the Maine and the Wicker house across Route 1, offer more seclusion; their quiet back rooms face the water. The dining room is open for breakfast and dinner, and the menu is heavy on home-baked goods and local fish and produce. △ *35 double rooms and 5 singles with baths, 4 doubles share 2 baths. Restaurant, cable TV in public room, phones in rooms, meeting rooms, tennis court, shuffleboard, golf privileges. $135–$175; full breakfast, dinner. AE, MC, V. Closed mid-Oct.–mid-May.*

YOUNGTOWN INN ☞

Rte. 52 and Youngtown Rd., Lincolnville 04849, tel. 207/763–4078 or 800/291–8438, fax 207/763–4078

Manuel and MaryAnn Mercier have turned the Youngtown Inn, a white Colonial farmhouse built in 1910, into a French-inspired country retreat that's off the beaten track yet just 10 minutes from Camden. Manuel, a chef, was born in Paris and has trained in Cannes, in New York, and on cruise ships. He met MaryAnn, a stockbroker, in Copenhagen.

Upstairs the guest rooms are simple and airy and are furnished with pieces such as a painted armoire, a sleigh bed, and a green-metal canopy bed. The suites have fireplaces, and all rooms open onto decks with views of the rolling countryside.

The well-respected restaurant, which takes up the first floor, serves classic cuisine. Breakfast is a treat—perhaps crepes with farmer cheese and blueberries, French toast stuffed with apples, or potato pancakes with smoked salmon and scrambled eggs, and of course croissants. Dinner entrées may include rack of lamb with fresh thyme or pan-seared pheasant breast with foie gras mousse. Also downstairs is a cozy pub. After dinner you can retreat to the upstairs sitting room, with its fireplace and TV.

Lake Megunticook, Fernald's Neck Nature Preserve, and Camden Hills State Park are all nearby. △ *5 double rooms with baths, 1 suite. Restaurant, air-conditioning in rooms, fireplace in suite and 1 room, TV in sitting area and 2 rooms. $99–$140; full breakfast. AE, MC, V.*

OTHER CHOICES

Buck's Harbor Inn. Rte. 176 (Box 268), South Brooksville 04617, tel. 207/326–8660, fax 207/326–0730. 6 double rooms share 2½ baths. $65–$75; full breakfast, dinner available Sat. in winter. MC, V. No smoking, no pets in summer.

Keeper's House. Box 26, Isle au Haut 04645, tel. 207/367–2261. 4 doubles share 2 baths in main house, 1 double shares bath in woodshed, 1 double with cold-water spigot, outdoor shower, outhouse, bicycles. $250–$285; full breakfast, lunch, dinner. No credit cards. 2-night minimum July–Aug.

Pilgrim's Inn. Main St., Deer Isle 04627, tel. 207/348–6615, fax 207/348–7769. 10 double rooms with baths, 2 doubles and 1 single share bath, 2 cottages. Restaurant, TV in cottages, gift shop. $150–$205; full breakfast, dinner. MC, V. No smoking in rooms, pets allowed in cottage. Closed mid-Oct.–mid-May.

Victorian Inn. Sea View Dr. (Box 258), Lincolnville 04849, tel. 207/236–3785 or 800/382–9817. 4 double rooms with baths, 2 suites. Air-conditioning on 3rd floor; phone, hair dryer, toiletries, robes in rooms; turndown service on request; safe available. $135–$245; full breakfast. AE, MC, V. No smoking, 2-night minimum mid-June–mid-Oct. weekends.

RESERVATIONS SERVICES

B&B of Maine (377 Gray Rd., Falmouth 04105, tel. 207/797–5540), **Camden Accommodations** (77 Elm St., Camden 04843, tel. 207/236–6090).

Down East: Deer Isle and Mount Desert Island

CLAREMONT HOTEL 🐦
Claremont Rd. (Box 137), Southwest Harbor 04679, tel. 207/244–5036 or 800/244–5036, fax 207/244–3512

A stay at the four-story, yellow-clapboard Claremont evokes the long, slow vacations of bygone days. It was built as an inn in 1884, and today John Madeira, Jr., who manages it for the McCue family, welcomes guests as they've always been welcomed; in summer he is joined by a large, youthful staff. This complex of a main house, two guest houses, and 12 cottages is at the end of a quiet road yet just a short stroll from bustling Southwest Harbor. In warmer months you can play croquet on the lawn (the August tournament is a highlight) or partake of cocktails at the boathouse. Year-round, you'll enjoy spectacular views of Somes Sound.

The main hotel was completely renovated several years ago, but traditionalists will be hard pressed to notice any changes (it was pieced back together under the direction of a historic preservationist). Although some public rooms seem underfurnished, the stone fireplaces and the wicker and straight-back chairs in the library and sitting room are in keeping with Southwest Harbor's rugged, fishing village character. Light streams through the picture windows in the large, rather formal dining room (open to the public for dinner), making it a fine place to plan a day of hiking in the national park, biking on the network of carriage paths, or sailing on Somes Sound.

Guest rooms are painted in mottled pastels but retain their simplicity. The views through gauzy white curtains are unforgettable—there's nothing like the sight of the silvery sound at dawn. Some of the rustic guest houses and cottages have the same view. ⌂ *24 double rooms with baths in main house, 6 doubles with bath in Phillips House, 1 suite in Clark House, 12 cottages. Restaurant, air-conditioning in dining room, cable TV in parlor, phone in rooms, tennis court, croquet, bikes, dock, rowboats, moorings. $120–$155; full breakfast (MAP rates* *only mid June–mid-Sept.). No credit cards. No smoking in rooms. Hotel and dining room closed mid-Oct.–mid-June, cottages closed late Oct.–mid-May.*

INN AT BAY LEDGE ❦
1385 Sand Point Rd., Bar Harbor 04609, tel. 207/288–4204, fax 207/288–5573

Jeani and Jack Ochtera, corporate refugees from Massachusetts, operated another inn in Bar Harbor before purchasing the Bay Ledge in 1993. Originally built as a minister's house in the early 1900s, it became an inn in the 1940s and was famous for its cliff-top location. "It's five minutes from town but feels 100 mi away," Jeani says. You'll see what she means as you descend the 76 steps to the rocky beach and its Cathedral Rock and cavelike Ovens formations (given the cliffside site, this inn isn't appropriate for young children). With such a peaceful location, no wonder it was once a spa (be sure to take a dip in the oceanfront pool and whirlpool or spend time in the sauna or the steam room).

The Ochteras have filled the house with antiques, paintings and prints by local artists, Oriental rugs, and Jeani's collection of baskets. Guest rooms in the main house have four-poster or canopy beds, feather beds, and down comforters; three have whirlpool baths, and most have dreamy ocean views. The pine-paneled living room has a brick fireplace and a rustic lodge feel. It opens into the sunroom, which has wicker furniture and yet another fireplace and is where a multicourse breakfast (homemade granola, muffins, fruit, and such entrées as French toast stuffed with peaches and cream) is served. Hidden in the evergreens across the street from the main inn are three cottages; two have fireplaces. △ *7 double rooms with baths, 3 cottages. TV/VCR in upstairs common room, steam room, sauna, pool and outdoor whirlpool, private beach. $85–$250; full breakfast, afternoon refreshments. MC, V. No smoking, 2-night minimum mid-June–Oct. Closed mid-Oct.–mid-May.*

LE DOMAINE ❦
Rte. 1 (Box 496), Hancock 04640, tel. 207/422–3395 or 800/554–8495

Nine miles east of Ellsworth, on a rural stretch of Route 1, you'll find a little slice of French dining and lodging sophistication that's as welcome as it is improbable. Owner-chef Nicole L. Purslow trained at the Cordon Bleu and apprenticed in Switzerland. Here, in the Maine countryside, she whips up classic haute cuisine dishes, the perfect accompaniments to which are bound to be hiding amid the more than 40,000 bottles of French vintage in the wine cellar. Meals are served in an elegant dining room whose white walls and dark-wood accents are evocative of a French château. A massive brick fireplace dominates one end of the room, and family coats-of-arms, posters of France, and shiny copper pots are displayed throughout.

Although Le Domaine is known primarily for its restaurant, the small, French country–style guest rooms are just as inviting. All have chintz fabrics, wicker furnishings, and simple desks and sofas near the windows; four have balconies or porches over the gardens. The inn owns 100 acres situated halfway between Mount Desert Isle and Schoodic Point. With so much space, the great outdoors will surely beckon you for a walk along the inn's paths or for a game of badminton on the lawn. △ *7 double rooms with baths. Restaurant, air-conditioning in 4 rooms, radio and fruit in rooms. $200; MAP. AE, D, MC, V. Closed late-Oct.–mid-May.*

THE TIDES ☙
119 West St., Bar Harbor 04609, tel. 207/288–4968, fax 207/288–2997

The trouble with staying here is that you're tempted never to leave the grounds despite all the attractions of Bar Harbor and Acadia National Park. The oceanfront, 16-room, Greek Revival–style "cottage," built in 1887, is in Bar Harbor's historic district and is listed on the National Register of Historic Places. Joe and Judy Losquadro purchased the Tides in 1996, after running another inn in town. Prior to that they were in Washington, D.C., where Joe entered the corporate world after a 20-year naval career.

The back veranda, more an outdoor living room than a porch, hints at the house's grandeur. Henry Link wicker furniture is grouped in front of an outdoor fireplace that has a painting hanging over its mantel. Beyond the semicircular porch's vine-covered columns and rails, a landscaped lawn slopes down to the water. Breakfast, perhaps Acadian buckwheat blueberry pancakes, is served here in fine weather. On chilly days you may prefer to eat in the formal dining room, with its fireplace and its long, cushioned seat built into a curved wall of windows that overlook the bay. The formal living room, decorated in blue and white, opens onto the veranda and shares the same views.

The suites are grand both in size and amenities: All have cable TV; CD players; and such details as patterned, lead-glass interior shutters in the windows. The Master Suite and the Ocean Suite have ocean views, sitting areas, and gas fireplaces. The third-floor Captain's Suite lacks a fireplace but has the best views over Frenchman's Bay. In the informal upstairs living room, you can curl up by the fire with a book, set up a jigsaw puzzle, or examine Judy's collection of nutcrackers.

△ *1 double room with bath, 3 suites. Ceiling fans on 3rd floor, guest refrigerator in dining room. $150–$275; full breakfast. D, MC, V. No smoking.*

ULLIKANA ☙
16 The Field, Bar Harbor 04609, tel. 207/288–9552

The Ullikana is an oasis of calm and quiet in busy downtown Bar Harbor. In the garden of this traditional timber, stone, and stucco cottage is a piece of modern sculpture. This unusual blend of traditional and modern continues inside, where the decor juxtaposes traditional antiques with more contemporary country pieces, abstract art with folk art, and vibrant color with French country wallpapers. The result, says co-owner Roy Kasindorf, "is like a marriage. It's a reflection of Hélène and I." The contrasts are shocking, but they work.

Roy and Hélène are a vibrant couple who have breathed new life into this 1885 estate. She ran the French program at the United Nations School in New York, and he worked in commercial photography. On a visit to the Maine coast, they stumbled upon the Ullikana. "I thought it was a disaster," he recalls, but "Hélène fell in love with it."

Room 3 mixes dark woodwork and a teal floor with pink floral-and-striped wallpaper and a pink sofa. It's a spacious room with a fireplace, a water view, and a large bath with claw-foot tub. Audrey's Room is a private retreat decorated in lilac-blue florals, and it has an exposed-beam cathedral ceiling, a tin king-size bed with a cameo of cherub angels, and a fainting sofa. From the claw-foot tub in the oversize bathroom, you look out to the islands. Room 5 is done in a French country motif, with rose toile de Jouy wallpaper and drapes and a fireplace. French doors open to a covered deck that overlooks the water. (Owing to all the antiques and artwork, this inn is not suitable for children.)

Breakfast—perhaps poached pears in red wine sauce followed by puffed pancakes with raspberries and blueberries—is served in the dining room, where deep red walls are set off by a teal-green floor and bright pastel dishes, or on the patio. On cool mornings a fire in the hearth takes away the chill. In the afternoon refreshments are served in front of the living room fireplace (you'll also find fireplaces in the foyer and two other guest rooms). ⚱ *10 double rooms with baths. $120–$205; full breakfast, afternoon refreshments. MC, V. No smoking. Closed Nov.–May.*

WESTON HOUSE 🦢
26 Boynton St., Eastport 04631, tel. 207/853–2907 or 800/853–2907

Jett and John Peterson offer comfortable, elegant lodgings in Eastport, one of the first towns in the country to see the sun rise. The couple came here from California in 1985 and purchased this 1810 Federal-style home, filling it with antiques and turning it into a gracious B&B. The Petersons' two dogs, a West Highland terrier and a Scottish terrier, will greet you enthusiastically, adding to the feeling of welcome.

Throughout the house are antique clocks, including a grandfather in the hall and a half-dozen or so others that John winds daily. Jett is a marvelous cook who makes excellent use of herbs from her garden and other local produce. Breakfast is served in the formal dining room, and it's accompanied by classical music. The meal begins with fresh fruit or juice and may include blueberry bread and an entrée such as eggs with locally smoked salmon or pancakes with apricot syrup. With advance notice, Jett will prepare box lunches or serve an elegant four-course dinner. Port and sherry are always available in the parlor as are games and magazines. The family room, with a fireplace and a TV, is a casual place to plan the day's activities.

Upstairs, five guest rooms share 2½ baths. The nicest are the Audubon Room and the Weston Room, both of which are in the front of the house and overlook the gardens, the town of Eastport, and the Passamaquoddy Bay. The Weston Room, done in soft pastels, has a working fireplace, a king-size four-poster bed, an antique rocker, a love seat, and cable TV. The Audubon Room is named for its most famous guest, John J. Audubon, who stayed here in 1833.

The Weston House is centrally located for day trips to Campobello or St. Andrews-by-the-Sea. There are a number of walking trails, and the Moosehorn National Wildlife Refuge is nearby. Eastport offers the easternmost Mexican restaurant in the country and salmon—it's worth coming for the annual Salmon Festival in early September. You can purchase authentic sweet-grass baskets at the Indian reservation on Pleasant Point. ⚱ *4 double rooms and 1 single share 2½ baths. TV/VCR in family room, terry cloth robes in rooms. $60–$75; full breakfast. No credit cards. No smoking.*

OTHER CHOICES

Crocker House Inn. Hancock Point Rd., Hancock 04640, tel. 207/422–6806, fax 207/422–3105. 9 double rooms with baths in main house; 1 double, 1 quintuple with bath in carriage house. Restaurant, TV room, phone in rooms, Jacuzzi, bicycles, kayaks. $90–$130; full breakfast. AE, D, MC, V.

Island View Inn. Rte. 1 (HCR 32, Box 24), Sullivan Harbor 04664, tel. 207/422–3031. 6 double rooms with baths. Fans in rooms, beach access, canoe, dinghy, 18′ sloop (rental). $60–$90; full breakfast. D, MC, V. Restricted smoking. Closed mid-Oct.–late May.

Oceanside Meadows. Rte. 195 (Box 90), Prospect Harbor 04669, tel. 207/963–5557. 12 double rooms with baths, 2 suite. $105–$125; full breakfast. AE, MC, V. No smoking. Closed Nov.–Apr.

RESERVATIONS SERVICE
Bed & Breakfast of Maine (377 Gray Rd., Falmouth 04105, tel. 207/797–5540).

The Western Lakes
and Mountains
❖❖❖❖

LAKE HOUSE ☞
Rtes. 35 and 37 (Box 82), Waterford 04088, tel. 207/583–4182 or 800/223–4182, fax 207/583–6078

Though not actually on a lake, the Lake House is near several (Keoka Lake is a stone's throw away, and Long Lake is 5 mi south), and it's right in the middle of the tiny, picturesque town of Waterford. The most Victorian in style of the area inns, the Lake House has a Carpenter Gothic front with a pleasant screened porch and guest rooms that some may find a touch cluttered.

The inn's long history includes stints as a private home; periods as an inn (Mickey Rooney, Claudette Colbert, and Judy Garland have stayed here); and, in the mid 19th-century, service as the Maine Hygienic Institute for Ladies. Today, Michael Uhl-Myers operates the inn and restaurant, which is open to the public for dinner and serves entrées such as roast duckling in a romantic setting (best to leave your children at home).

The spacious, bright Grand Ballroom Suite has a four-poster bed, a stained pine floor, and a bathtub that's in the center of the room. Those who seek privacy might ask for the one-room cottage behind the inn. ⚱ *4 double rooms with baths, 1 cottage. Restaurant, coffeemaker in rooms, fireplace in sitting room. $84–$130; full breakfast. MC, V. No smoking. Closed Apr. and Nov.*

NOBLE HOUSE ☞
Highland Rd. (Box 180), Bridgton 04009, tel. 207/647–3733

Set on a hill crest amid massive white pines, this grand but utterly unpretentious house was built on a quiet residential street near town by a Maine state senator in 1903. Jane Starets runs the inn with her husband, Dick (when he isn't at work as a commercial pilot), and the summertime help of their four children.

You cross the wide porch to enter a simply appointed parlor with a comfortable sofa, wing chairs, and a grand piano. Behind the parlor is the formal dining room, where an abundant breakfast buffet (fruit, eggs, pancakes, baked goods) is usually served.

The guest rooms don't quite measure up to the elegance of the public rooms: Most are small and a bit spartan in their furnishings. The Honeymoon Room, however, has a good lake view, a whirlpool bath (as do three other rooms), white wicker furniture, and fresh flowers.

A real asset is the dock across the street on Highland Lake, with chairs and a hammock and the view of Mt. Washington and the Presidential Range rising in the distance. ⚱ *6 double rooms with baths, 3 doubles share bath. TV/VCR in lounge,* *floating dock for swimming, croquet, canoe, paddleboat. $78–$125; full breakfast. AE, MC, V. 2-night minimum weekends. Open only with reservations mid-Oct.–mid-June.*

OXFORD HOUSE ☞

105 Main St., Fryeburg 04037, tel. 207/935–3442 or 800/261–7206, fax 207/935–7046

The Edwardian-style Oxford House was built as a private home in 1913 on part of the foundation of the Oxford Hotel, a summer resort that burned in 1906. John and Phyllis Morris purchased the house in 1985 and turned it into an inn. The two previously ran an inn in nearby North Conway, New Hampshire, but sought a quieter location to raise their two children, Bennett and Garvin.

Magnificent cypress woodwork and floral wallpapers decorate both the public rooms and the bedrooms. From both Room 3 and the Sewing Room you can watch the sun set behind the Saco River valley and the Presidential Range of the White Mountains; Room 1 is spacious but lacks this view. All are decorated with country pieces. Breakfast is served in the glassed-in dining room, which has the same view. The well-respected restaurant is open to the public for dinner year-round and for lunch in the summer. There's also a pub in the basement with a full bar and a pool table. ⌂ *4 double rooms with baths, 1 double with bath across hall. Restaurant, pub, TV in rooms. $75–$125; full breakfast. AE, D, DC, MC, V. No smoking. Closed 2 wks in Nov.*

QUISIANA ☞

Pleasant Point Rd., Center Lovell 04016, tel. 207/925–3500, fax 207/925–1004

Music lovers will think they've found heaven on earth at this delightful but rustic lakeside resort, which is staffed by students and graduates of some of the finest music schools in the country. Every evening a performance is staged in the lakeside music hall; shows run the gamut from Broadway revues to piano recitals to operas. And on Tuesday evening the chamber ensemble plays during the weekly cocktail party on the point. But the music isn't the only reason to come. You'll also enjoy the clean air and the crystal clear waters of 10-mi-long Kezar Lake. The lake is mostly undeveloped, and across it you can see the Presidential Range of New Hampshire's White Mountains.

This old-fashioned family retreat has been in existence since around 1915 and has been operated by Jane Orans and her son, Sam, since 1984. It's the kind of place families come to year after year, always staying in the same lodgings. Legend has it that one couple waited years for their turn until another couple passed away, enabling them to move up to a shorefront cottage.

You choose from 2 lodges and 32 cottages, some nestled in the pines and others perched on the lake's edge. Each cottage is simply decorated with wicker and maple pieces accented with Waverly fabrics, and some have fireplaces. Of the guests who return, "90 percent request the same cottage," Jane says. "They think theirs is the perfect one." There are two large sand beaches to enjoy as well as a variety of watercraft and three clay tennis courts. Use of most facilities as well as three meals daily are included in the rates. ⌂ *11 double rooms with baths in 2 lodges, 32 cottages. Nightly musical performances; 3 clay tennis courts; 2 beaches; no charge for canoes, sailboats, rowboats, lake kayaks, Windsurfers; charge for fishing guides, waterskiing, lake tours, boat motors. $110–$160 per person; breakfast, lunch, dinner. No credit cards. 1-wk minimum in high season. Closed Sept.–mid-June.*

WATERFORD INNE 🐚

Chadbourne Rd. (Box 149), Waterford 04088, tel. and fax 207/583–4037

The tiny white-clapboard and green-shuttered villages known as the Waterfords have fine country inns, but the Waterford Inne stands out for its breezy hilltop location and for its warmly convivial owners, Rosalie and Barbara Vanderzanden, a mother-and-daughter innkeeping team.

Back in the mid-1970s Barbara and Rosalie were schoolteachers in New Jersey and avid world travelers, when they decided they wanted a change of lifestyle and geography. As Barbara tells it, they had been looking all over Maine when a real estate agent showed them what was to become the Waterford Inne. They made an offer on the spot. "It was the feeling of the house that settled it," Barbara reminisces. She has preserved the secluded feeling of the house by purchasing adjacent property as it becomes available. "When people ask me what I'm going to do with it," she says, "I tell them 'nothing.' "

The property was a dairy farm in the 1820s, and 40 years later a prominent lumber family bought it. With open fields all around, huge pine trees fringing the fields, an orchard out back, and a big red barn off to the side, the place retains vestiges of its farming heritage and its decades serving as a wealthy family's hideaway.

Barbara and Rosalie have done a superb job renovating the gold-painted, curry-yellow-trimmed house. The sitting room is cozy, with dried flowers hanging from exposed beams, a sofa facing the woodstove, and barn-board walls.

The bedrooms have lots of nooks and crannies. Nicest are the Nantucket Room, which has whale-motif wallpaper and a harpoon, and the Chesapeake Room, with a private porch; a woodstove; pumpkin-pine floors; a king-size bed; and ducks, ducks, ducks. A converted woodshed has five additional rooms, and though they have slightly less character than the inn rooms, four of them have sunny decks.

The Vanderzandens enjoy trading travel tips with their guests and directing them to area lakes, ski trails, and antiques shops. They will prepare elaborate dinners by prior arrangement. Pets are welcome, but there is an extra charge. △ *6 double rooms with baths, 3 doubles share bath, 1 suite. TV in common room, apple picking, antiques shop, cross-country ski trails, ice-skating pond, badminton. $74– $99; full breakfast. AE. No smoking in dining room. Closed Apr.*

OTHER CHOICES

Augustus Bove House. Corner of Rtes. 302 and 114, Naples 04055, tel. 207/ 693–6365. 2 double rooms with baths, 4 doubles share 2 baths. Air-conditioning, TV in rooms; hot tub; gas fireplace in living room; beach access; shop. $79– $89; full breakfast. D, MC, V. No smoking.

Bridgton House. 2 Main St., Bridgton 04009, tel. 207/647–0979. 3 double rooms with baths, 3 doubles share 2 baths. Cable TV, ceiling fan in rooms, fireplace in living room, beach access. $85–$90; full breakfast. No credit cards. Closed Nov.–Apr.

RESERVATIONS SERVICE

B&B of Maine (377 Gray Rd., Falmouth 04105, tel. 207/797–5540).

The Great North Woods

CHESUNCOOK LAKE HOUSE 🐚

Rte. 76 (Box 656), Chesuncook Village, Greenville 04441, tel. 207/745–5330 or 207/695–2821 for Folsom's Air Service

Chesuncook Lake House gives meaning to the Maine adage "You can't get there from here." This remote, rustic inn has been an outpost of civilization in the otherwise rugged wilderness since 1864. You can travel here by boat, an 18-mi journey; by floatplane from Greenville or Bangor; or on foot—it's a 5-mi hike over a rough woods road.

Chesuncook Village was formed around 1820 and hit its heyday in the 1860s, when it boasted a population of around 200, most of whom worked in the woods. Chesuncook Lake House was built as part of a farm where food and hay were grown to feed timber workers and their animals. When roads began to replace river drives, the village began to die. Today Chesuncook Village is on the national register as a historic site.

Paris-born Maggie McBurnie came here in the early 1950s after marrying Bert, who grew up here. She took to it immediately and decided to remain even after Bert passed away in 1997. A small but strong woman, she provides three full meals daily—solid New England fare with a French accent, and many of the ingredients come from her gardens.

The living room is furnished with a jumble of comfortable but worn chairs and sofas, an upright piano, and a large woodstove that keeps everything cozy on cooler nights. The walls and ceiling here, as in the dining room, are tin. Upstairs are four small, simply furnished guest rooms that share two baths. Although all have lake views, from the two front rooms you can gaze down the lake at Mt. Katahdin.

The remote location means no electricity and no phones. You must entertain yourself, but given the wilderness playground out back and the lake out front, that's easy to do. It may take you a few days just to adjust to the quiet and learn to relax. "Relaxing is an art," Maggie says. "You have to work at it." For such work, Chesuncook Lake House is the place to be. 🛏 *4 double rooms share 2 baths. Boats, motors (rental). $90; breakfast, lunch, dinner. No credit cards. Smoking on porch only. Closed mid-Oct.–May.*

LODGE AT MOOSEHEAD LAKE 🐚

Lily Bay Rd. (Box 1167), Greenville 04441, tel. 207/695–4400, fax 207/695–2281

Just outside Greenville on a hill overlooking Moosehead Lake, this inn is a final vestige of civilization before the wilderness. After a day of hiking, boating, skiing, or white-water rafting, it's a welcome retreat. Jennifer and Roger Cauchi had careers in hotel and event management in Pennsylvania but wanted a change. "We couldn't explain what we wanted," Jennifer says, "but we knew it when we saw it, and this was it."

The inn, a former summer estate built in 1917, brings the outside in, with decorations that include antlers, small evergreens, pinecones, and branches. Nearly every room has a patterned twig border or other accent that Jennifer painstakingly created by hand. This is not, however, a rustic retreat: off-white carpeting, Oriental rugs, and soothing earth tones make it luxurious and welcoming.

All rooms have air-conditioning; whirlpool spas; fireplaces; TV/VCRs; and hand-carved, four-poster, queen-size beds that depict the animal or theme for which the room is named (Totem, Loon, Bear, Moose, and Trout). Although Moose and Totem are the largest rooms, Bear has a private deck. Four rooms have water views—the sunsets over Moosehead Lake are spectacular. Three new suites, added in the carriage house in 1997, offer such touches as a swinging bed and glass doors that open to a patio and gardens. Guest rooms also have such thoughtful amenities as coffeemakers, wineglasses, ice-filled coolers, makeup mirrors, hair dryers, scales—even pillows for the hot tub.

The Cauchis serve a full gourmet breakfast in the expansive, light-filled dining room overlooking Moosehead Lake. In the evening you can sit on the deck (which also has a lake view) in front of the great room's massive stone fireplace or in adjacent Toby Room, with its English Toby mug collection. Downstairs is a game room with a pool table. ♨ *5 double rooms with baths, 3 suites. Air-conditioning, coffeemaker, hair dryer, whirlpool bath in rooms. $250–$350; full breakfast, afternoon hors d'oeuvres, dinner (in off-season). D, MC, V. No smoking.*

SKY LODGE ☜
Rte. 201, Moose River 04945, tel. 207/668–2171, fax 207/668–9471

In the 1940s planes landed on the Sky Lodge's 1,750-ft runway while guests watched from a rooftop gallery. The massive log cabin, built in 1929 as a private home for a New York multimillionaire, was reputed to have secret closets and tunnels to hide bootleg liquor. And some say that Al Capone stayed here. You can sense the excitement and intrigue of those bygone days in the great room, which has soaring fieldstone fireplaces at either end; two mirror-image, curving staircases leading to a balcony that rims the second floor; and a beamed cathedral ceiling. The soft glow of polished wood is everywhere; bear skins, a moosehead, a wooden canoe, and snowshoe furniture complete the decor.

Guest rooms in the lodge aren't as splendid as the great room (indeed, they need a little sprucing up). Nevertheless, some, such as spacious Room 1, have fireplaces and are welcoming in their simplicity. The Sutro Suite has two fireplaces: one in its sitting room and one in its bathroom—right next to a big old-fashioned tub.

A Continental breakfast buffet is served by the fireplace in the restaurant, which is also open to the public for dinner. Breaking your fast on the dining-room porch, with its views of the rolling countryside, is a great way to start the day. ♨ *5 double rooms and 2 triples with baths, 2 suites. Restaurant. $99–$125; Continental breakfast. AE, D, MC, V. Closed Oct.–June.*

RESERVATIONS SERVICE
B&B of Maine (377 Gray Rd., Falmouth 04105, tel. 207/797–5540).

MARYLAND

Oxford/Easton/Eastern Shore

ASHBY 1663 ☙
27448 Ashby Dr. (Box 45), Easton 21601, tel. 410/822–4235

This is a manor house *magnifico,* or a Colonial estate with Italian dressing. The original foundation was laid in 1663 for a wealthy merchant family by the name of Goldsborough, who engaged the services of some 20-odd servants. The Italian influence entered the picture in the mid-19th century, when the villalike structure arose. If the setting looks familiar to you, it's because Ashby is a star—some scenes in the movie *Silent Fall,* starring Richard Dreyfuss, were filmed here, and *Country Inn* magazine named the inn one of the top 12 in the country in 1996.

Jeanie Wagner and Cliff Meredith, both Eastern Shore natives, purchased Ashby in 1986 and transformed it from ramshackle to technologized high-gloss. Cliff, who once presided over his own contracting company, engineered all the wiring, heating, air-conditioning, and plumbing. Under his direction, small, divided spaces were demolished and opened up. No sign of the former kitchen exists, for Cliff created (from scratch) a wall-to-wall, white, custom-equipped design, which has since appeared on the cover of a popular builders' magazine. Composing Ashby is Manor House, the George Goldsborough House, and Miles River Cottage.

The pièce de résistance, however, is the Goldsborough Suite on the second floor. If you've never seen a fireplace in a bathroom, now's your chance: The room is exceedingly large and sumptuous, with marble surfaces, brass railings, a bidet, a whirlpool-rigged bath, and a two-headed shower separate from the honeymooners' tub. The sleeping chamber is dominated by a four-poster canopy bed (king-size, of course) adorned with garden-print ruffles, but its best feature is its walls of glass.

The list of perks here is endless. Warm, soft-spoken Jeanie will guide you through the downstairs fitness and tanning center, outdoors around the heated pool (with a river view) and lighted tennis courts, and back in to the screen porch. Some bed-and-breakfasts claim "full" morning meals and slap an egg on your plate. Not Jeanie. Request the California eggs with salsa and sour cream, or the Belgian waffles: Both presentation and quality are superior. ⌂ *12 double rooms with baths. Air-conditioning, TV and phone in manor-house rooms, kitchen in cottage and carriage house, library, exercise room, tanning bed, pool tablepool, boat dock, paddleboat, canoe, lighted tennis court. $215–$595; full breakfast, evening cocktails. AE, MC, V. No smoking indoors, 2-night minimum with Sat. reservation.*

ATLANTIC HOTEL ✵

2 N. Main St., Berlin 21811, tel. 410/641–3589 or 800/814–7672, fax 410/641–4928

The historic district in Berlin, Maryland, got a significant boost when a group of local investors renovated and opened the town's Victorian centerpiece, the Atlantic Hotel, built in 1895. This three-story, bracketed brick inn, just 8 mi from Assateague National Seashore and Ocean City, offers a quiet, quaint spot for a beach escape. The 16 guest rooms lining a wide central corridor are decorated with Oriental and floral-patterned rugs, tasseled draperies, Tiffany-style lamps, and antique double beds. Rooms 10 and 14, on the north and south ends, are notable for their spaciousness and Main Street views. Downstairs, at the Drummer's Cafe, there's piano entertainment on Friday and Saturday evenings and a four-star restaurant that will satisfy your sophisticated palate.

If you're looking for something else to do one evening, discover the town's most recent addition: the restored, Spanish Mission–style Old Globe movie house with live entertainment, or the interesting mix of old and new shops. ♨ *16 double rooms with baths. Restaurant, air-conditioning, phone in rooms. $65–$150; full breakfast. AE, MC, V. No smoking in rooms, 2-night minimum in summer with Sat.-night stay.*

BISHOP'S HOUSE ✵

214 Goldsborough St. (Box 2217), Easton 21601, tel. and fax 410/820–7290; 800/223–7290 outside MD

This handsome Victorian home (circa 1880) was built for former Maryland governor Philip Frances Thomas and his wife. After the governor's death in 1892, the house was sold to the Episcopal Diocese and served as the Bishop's home, hence the name. Conveniently located near the heart of historic Easton, the Bishop's House features large first-floor rooms with a 14-ft ceiling and large plaster medallions. The first floor is centrally air-conditioned and offers facilities for social functions and business meetings. Second-floor guest rooms have 12-ft ceilings and are decorated in romantic 19th-century oak, walnut, and mahogany; three guest rooms have working fireplaces and two have whirlpool baths. For socializing or for people-watching there's a wonderful wraparound front porch.

Golf packages, cycling tours, and sightseeing excursions are available to guests, and since the present owners are members of Biking-Inn-to-Inn on the Eastern Shore, they can assist with arrangements for staying at other member properties. Owner Diane Laird-Ippolito is proud of the inn's hot sumptuous breakfasts and knows Easton's restaurants well. She carefully matches her guests with what will be an appropriate dining experience.

Easton is centrally located in the heart of James Michener's *Chesapeake* country. It's just 10 mi to either Oxford or St. Michael's, both popular tourist villages on Maryland's Eastern Shore. The land is flat and ideal for bicyclists, because most of the country roads offer wide shoulder lanes exclusively for bicycles. With so much water nearby, in autumn you'll hear and see large numbers of Canada and snow geese overhead and in the nearby fields. ♨ *4 rooms with baths, 2 rooms share bath. Air-conditioning in rooms, fireplace in 3 bedrooms and 2 common rooms, TV/VCR in common room, off-street parking, bicycle rentals and storage. $75–$85 Sun.–Thurs., $110–$120 weekends and holidays; full breakfast. No credit cards. No smoking indoors, 2-night minimum.*

BRAMPTON 🐚

25227 Chestertown Rd., Chestertown 21620, tel. 410/778–1860, fax 410/778–1805

Brampton's charming character derives from both its house and its grounds. The inn is set in the fields south of Chestertown, framed by two towering, 120-year-old spruce trees at the end of a long drive. It's a three-story brick building with a white columned porch and 14 front windows, the perfect gentleman-farmer's country seat. The house is listed on the National Register of Historic Places, as are 4 of its surrounding 35 acres (the site of some famous experiments in crop rotation). Enter and pass through the airy foyer into a bookcase-lined living room, or climb the solid-walnut staircase. This front section of Brampton was built around 1860 by Henry Ward Carville as a wedding present to his wife.

Upstairs in the seven guest rooms the present owners' excellent taste becomes apparent. Michael Hanscom spent 10 years in San Francisco renovating old homes before moving here. His Swiss wife, Danielle, is responsible for the European atmosphere in the guest rooms. The bed linen and towels look and smell as if they've been dried on a line in the Alps. Eight rooms have working fireplaces. The ceilings on the second floor are 11 ft high. The Yellow Room at the front of the house is a favorite, a sunny paradise with a canopy above the bed. The two third-floor rooms are decorated in country style with locally crafted chairs and have trundle beds.

The Hanscoms have operated Brampton for more than 10 years, and they've made many additions: a mammoth Vulcan commercial stove that enables them to offer guests a choice of breakfast entrées; a TV room downstairs; and the Rose Room, outfitted with a king-size bed and a large private bath (but reached by a staircase so narrow that Danielle advises no one over 6 ft to book this unit).

Danielle and Michael can suggest walks on the Brampton grounds to a pond or to the east fork of Langford Creek. There is something Old World about these unassuming hosts, both of whom are dedicated to perfecting every detail. △ *8 double rooms with baths, 2 suites. Air-conditioning, TV in 1 suite. $95–$155; full breakfast, afternoon tea. AE, MC, V. No smoking, 2-night minimum on weekends.*

CHANCEFORD HALL 🐚

209 W. Federal St., Snow Hill 21863, tel. 410/632–2231

What is a spruce little town like Snow Hill, Maryland, doing in among the chicken farms of the DelMarVa peninsula? For the answer, look to the narrow but deep Pocomoke River, which in the 17th and 18th centuries made Snow Hill a bustling port, frequented by tall-masted schooners sailing in from the Chesapeake. Today, you can stay at Chanceford Hall, a bed-and-breakfast inn that would have pleased any visiting Colonial dignitary. The mansion was constructed in three stages, beginning with the Georgian front section in 1759.

Some 230 years later a pair of old-house restorers, Thelma and Michael Driscoll, moved in and turned Chanceford Hall into a showplace. The Federal-style mantels, painted in cool Williamsburg greens and blues, match the moldings, and there are merino-wool mattress pads and down comforters on the lace-canopy beds. The house has 10 working fireplaces and reproduction furniture crafted by Michael himself. Thelma welcomes guests with wine and hors d'oeuvres on silver trays and will lend bikes or explain where to rent canoes for river exploring. △ *4 double rooms with baths, 1 suite. Air-conditioning, TV with VCR in sunroom, lap pool, bicycles. $125–$150; full breakfast. No credit cards.*

INN AT PERRY CABIN

308 Watkins La., St. Michael's 21663, tel. 410/745–2200 or 800/722–2949, fax 410/745–3348

This grand white frame house, much enlarged from the original farmhouse, sits serenely at the edge of the Miles River, as it has since 1810. Much of the decor of the Inn at Perry Cabin is pure Laura Ashley, which is only fitting, since this, the first Ashley Inn, is owned by Sir Bernard Ashley, husband of the late designer.

The reception rooms have been done à la English country-house hotel, and from time to time Sir Bernard and Lady Ashley would swoop down on St. Michael's, bringing new furniture and decorations (not really new, of course, but brought from their house in the Bahamas or from the antiques emporiums of the world). Every object has been chosen with care, and most of them are antique—from the Colonial American chests of drawers, highboys, and bedside tables that came with the house to the mirrors, lamps, pictures, and the Oriental rugs spread everywhere you look. All of the bedrooms are done in antiques, and all are completely Laura Ashley—fabrics, wallpapers, sprig-decorated tables, and beds with spiral posts.

The main dining room, a soaring chamber two stories high, has an open wood-burning fireplace at one end. The food is excellent, and the silent, unobtrusive service lives up to the British tone of the place. Boat owners would find it a welcome change from galley fare and marina dining. The employees run the inn impeccably. The only conceivable drawback is the unfortunately situated residential development across the harbor, but that's hardly reason for second thoughts. Service, from the moment you enter the reception hall, is exemplary. General manager Stephen Creese sees to it that mineral water, ice, a plate of fresh fruit, and homemade cookies await guests in their rooms; the rate includes a daily newspaper, full English breakfast, and afternoon tea. The addition of swimming and exercise facilities, a traditional English snooker room, and a conservatory has extended the house's pleasures, and nearby recreations are plentiful: The inn arranges outings for everything from golf, fishing, and sailing to helicopter tours and riding lessons. It's worth noting, for business travelers, that the management accommodates any and all conference and meeting requirements. *35 double rooms with baths, 6 suites. Restaurant, air-conditioning, cable TV and phone in rooms, indoor pool, steam room, sauna, exercise room, snooker room, conservatory, library, room service, croquet, short-term docking facilities, free bikes. Sun.–Thurs. $195–$595, Fri.–Sat. $295–$695; full breakfast, afternoon tea. AE, DC, MC, V. No smoking in dining room.*

ROBERT MORRIS INN

314 North Morris St. (Box 70), Oxford 21654, tel. 410/226–5111, fax 410/226–5744

Although the town of Oxford and its historic inn came vividly into the public eye around the time of the American bicentennial celebration, the Robert Morris has managed to avoid being spoiled by success. Built by Robert Morris, Sr., as a residence in 1710 and run as an inn since the 1940s, it was bought by Ken and Wendy Gibson in 1975 and is just what a country inn should be.

The 18th-century section of the inn is on Oxford's Morris Street, facing the ferry dock, where there's always a line of tourists waiting to board the tiny Tred Avon Ferry, which tools between Oxford and Bellevue. You might also find a line at the Robert Morris restaurant, which occupies most of the inn's first floor. Its Hitchcock chairs and murals (actually 140-year-old hand-printed wallpaper samples) make it an attractive place to eat; crab cakes and Oxford coolers head the rather predictable menu. The slate-floor tavern beyond the dining room has a working fireplace and is reputedly where James Michener wrote the outline for *Chesapeake.*

Staying at the Robert Morris may prove more difficult than simply supping here. The Gibsons begin taking reservations on January 10 of each year and won't book a room more than a year in advance. Historic-minded souls should be adamant about claiming rooms in the 1710 section, where there's a rare, enclosed Elizabethan staircase and white-pine floors fastened with hand-hewn pegs. Top choices among the four guest rooms here are 2 and 15, the latter with a step-up poster bed and hand-stenciled borders on the walls. You might also request the room once occupied by Robert Morris, Jr., a signer of the Declaration of Independence, or that of his father (who met a lamentable fate when he was hit by a cannon fired in his honor).

The Gibsons know that some people are willing to dispense with history altogether in favor of luxurious quietude. To that end they've restored a roomy 1875 Victorian home, surrounded by mimosa and weeping copper-beech trees, just steps from the main house. Almost all the rooms in Sandaway feature screen porches, pine paneling, and immense claw-foot tubs (ask for 203, which has a chandelier over the bath; for 303, with its own staircase; or for one of the romantic River Rooms overlooking the Tred Avon). ♠ *33 double rooms with baths, 2 efficiencies. Restaurant, air-conditioning, TV in efficiencies. $90–$240; Continental breakfast included midweek, breakfast extra other days. MC, V. No smoking.*

WADES POINT INN ☞
Wade's Point Rd. (Box 7), St. Michael's 21663, tel. 410/745–2500, fax 410/745–3443

Aside from a chartered yacht, there's no better place from which to appreciate the blue sweep of the Chesapeake than the Wades Point Inn. Halfway between St. Michael's and Tilghman Island, this rambling bed-and-breakfast on 120 acres is surrounded on three sides by the bay.

The oldest section of the inn was built in 1819 by shipwright Thomas Kemp, whose sleek Baltimore clippers were credited with winning the War of 1812. On the land side, this glowing white Georgian house has porches on two floors and chimneys at either end; an observation nook attached to one chimney was Thomas Kemp's lookout and is reached through a trapdoor in one of three rooms in the old portion of the house.

In 1890 Kemp built an addition to the house on the bay side and opened the place as an inn. The present owners, Betsy and John Feiler, call this addition the Bay Room and have put it to use as a common area; it's large enough to hold a cotillion and is lined with windows and furnished with white wicker. Above the Bay Room is the Summer Wing, which holds six small chambers. These aren't air-conditioned, but given their proximity to the water and multitude of windows, they don't need it. There are washbasins in all of the Summer Wing rooms, as well as pastel prints and dancing white curtains that catch the rejuvenating breeze. Maybe that's why Mildred Kemp, the last of the family to occupy Wades Point, looked so hearty at age 90, when Betsy Feiler met her. "If living at Wades Point made her look like that," Betsy says, "I wanted to buy the place."

Building additions seems to be something of a tradition with the owners of Wades Point. There's a four-room summer cottage, and in 1989 Betsy and John completed a 12-room guest house about 200 yards from the main inn. These modern rooms have water views, private porches, and balconies, and the two queen-size beds and kitchenette in three of the rooms make them a good choice for families. If you're looking for bona fide old Chesapeake Bay atmosphere, however, opt for a room in the main house. ♤ *15 double rooms with baths, 9 doubles share 5 baths. Air-conditioning in new guest house, TV and fireplaces in common rooms, pond, private crabbing and fishing dock, walking and jogging trail, public boat ramp nearby. $80–$195; Continental breakfast. MC, V. Smoking on porches only, 2-day minimum on weekends. Closed Jan.–Feb.*

OTHER CHOICES

White Swan Tavern. 231 High St., Chestertown 21620, tel. 410/778–2300, fax 410/778–4543. 4 double rooms with baths, 2 suites. Tearoom, air-conditioning, cable TV in sitting room. $100–$150; Continental breakfast. MC, V.

RESERVATIONS SERVICES

Amanda's Bed & Breakfast Reservation Service (1428 Park Ave., Baltimore 21217, tel. 410/225–0001 for information, 800/899–7533 for reservations, fax 410/728–8957). **Bed & Breakfast of Maryland/The Traveller in Maryland** (Box 2277, Annapolis 21404, tel. 410/269–6232, fax 410/263–4841). **Inns of the Eastern Shore** (1500 Hambrooks Blvd., Cambridge 21613, tel. 410/228–0575 for information, 888/373–7890 for reservations).

Annapolis/Western Shore/ Southern Maryland

WILLIAM PAGE INN ☙
8 Martin St., Annapolis 21401, tel. 410/626–1506 or 800/364–4160, fax 410/263–4841

If your travels take you to Annapolis for Commissioning Week at the Naval Academy, for the December Parade of Lights, or simply for strolls around the city's walkable historic district, there's rest for the weary explorer at the William Page Inn. Built in 1908, this brown-shingle Victorian is a youngster by Annapolis standards, but one with an accommodating style. Its wraparound porch offers deep Adirondack chairs, and the boxwood in the William Paca House gardens perfumes the air. Somewhere over the high white wall at the end of Martin Street you might hear Naval Academy "middies" drilling, and four blocks away, at eateries around City Dock, crabs are being devoured, but on the William Page porch such distractions seem light-years away.

The genial innkeeper is Rob Zuchelli, a designer of theatrical lighting. He took very early retirement to refurbish the inn, which had served as the First Ward Democratic Clubhouse for 50 years. He aired out the smoke-filled rooms; stripped 11 coats of paint from the massive staircase, to reveal oak, mahogany, and cherrywood; and filled the inn with Queen Anne and Chippendale reproductions. He also turned the third floor into one smashing suite, with a sleigh bed, skylight, window seats, and balloon shades that lift to reveal views of the Annapolis rooftops. Guests might take the presence of a whirlpool bath in the suite in stride, but they are likely to be surprised by the one attached to the little blue room on the second floor.

There's a wet bar stocked with setups, a working fireplace in the carpeted downstairs common room, and a discreet dog named Chancellor, who is always happy to accompany guests on walks. Breakfast, served from the sideboard in the common room, consists of freshly baked muffins and breads, fruit-and-cheese trays, and perhaps an egg casserole or crepes, depending on chef Rob's mood. ⏁ *2 double rooms with baths, 2 double rooms share bath, 1 suite. Air-conditioning, cable TV in suite, wet bar, 2 whirlpool baths, robes for guests using shared bath, off-street parking. $105–$200; full breakfast. MC, V. No smoking, 2-day minimum peak-season weekends and during special events, 5-day minimum during Boat Show and Commissioning Week.*

OTHER CHOICES

Back Creek Inn. Alexander and Calvert Sts., Solomons 20688, tel. 410/326–2022, fax 410/326–2946. 4 rooms with baths, 2 suites, 1 cottage. Air-conditioning, cable TV, access to nearby swimming pool, bicycles, dock with 2 deep-water slips. $65–$145; both full and Continental breakfast (full breakfast served later in morning). AE, MC, V. Smoking in common rooms only, 2-day minimum holiday weekends, closed mid-Dec.–Jan.

RESERVATIONS SERVICES

Amanda's Bed & Breakfast Reservation Service (1428 Park Ave., Baltimore 21217, tel. 410/225–0001). **Annapolis Association of Licensed Bed & Breakfast Owners** (Box 744, Annapolis 21404). **Bed & Breakfast of Maryland/ The Traveller in Maryland** (Box 2277, Annapolis 21404, tel. 410/269–6232).

Baltimore
◆━◆◆◆━◆

MR. MOLE ☞
1601 Bolton St., Baltimore 21217, tel. 410/728–1179, fax 410/728–3379

How did such an elegant town house in Baltimore's exclusive Bolton Hill neighborhood get such a name? It all goes back to the children's book *The Wind in the Willows*, where Mole exclaims "Oh My" each time he encounters exceptional hospitality and accommodations. Mr. Mole is ideally situated for guests who want the convenience of a city inn and the comfort usually associated with large suburban properties. In downtown Baltimore's Bolton Hill, a onetime suburb of the wealthy, Mr. Mole is within walking distance of Baltimore's "Cultural Corridor" (including the Lyric Opera House, Myerhoff Symphony Hall, and Howard Street's Antique Row).

Co-owners and hosts Paul Bragaw and Collin Clarke have spared no effort to make their accommodations unique and comfortable. The first floor consists of a dining room with a large, lovely bay window and two sitting rooms full of color and elegant clutter. Guests can eat at individual tables or in the adjoining rooms. Typically, the Dutch-style breakfast consists of fresh fruits, Amish cheeses and meats, homemade breads, and coffee cake.

Each of the five guest suites has a private white bath, fresh flowers, a direct-dial phone, a clock radio, and a garage. The second-floor Explorer Suite feels like a tented en-suite camp for African adventurers. Also on this floor is the Print Room, filled with prints and engravings, which is actually part of a two-bedroom suite with a marble fireplace, chairs and sofas, and loads of books on the shelves. A plant-filled sunroom on the third floor is probably the most romantic suite. ⏁ *5 rooms with baths. Air-conditioning, private-line direct dial phones and voice mail, fax, fresh flowers, Caswell-Massey toiletries. $105–$165; Continental-plus breakfast. AE, DC, D, MC, V. No smoking, 2-night minimum on weekends.*

OTHER CHOICES

Admiral Fell Inn. 888 S. Broadway, Baltimore 21231, tel. 410/522–7377 or 800/292–4667, fax 410/522–0707. 80 double rooms with baths (55 no-smoking). 3 restaurants, air-conditioning, TV and phone in rooms, conference room, room service, parking, free van service in city 7 AM–10:30 PM. $145–$350; Continental breakfast. AE, DC, MC, V.

RESERVATIONS SERVICES

Amanda's Bed & Breakfast Reservation Service (1428 Park Ave., Baltimore 21217, tel. 410/225–0001). **Bed & Breakfast of Maryland/The Traveller in Maryland** (Box 2277, Annapolis 21404, tel. 410/269–6232).

Frederick and Environs

CATOCTIN INN 📷

MD Rte. 85, 3613 Buckeystown Pike (Box 243), Buckeystown 21717, tel. 301/874–5555 or 800/730–5550, fax 301/874–2026

Just south of Frederick, in the historic village of Buckeystown, you'll find the Catoctin Inn right on the picturesque main street. Get there before Hollywood discovers this beautifully restored stretch of 18th-century structures. You couldn't want a more central location for touring Maryland's Civil War sites and memorials, and it's within a short drive of Harpers Ferry, Antietam, the Monocacy Battlefield, Frederick, the C&O Canal, Sugarloaf Mountain, the Appalachian Trail, New Market (Maryland's antiques capital), and the world-famous Lilypons Aquatic Gardens (tel. 800/999–5459). In summer, you might enjoy a visit to Frederick to watch the Keys, a Baltimore Oriole farm team.

The inn, circa 1780, shares 4 acres with a 1890s carriage house, now used as a conference center. All guest rooms have queen- or king-size beds, cable TV, phones, and private baths; 12 rooms feature whirlpool tubs and working fireplaces. A full hearty breakfast is served in the dining room or on the sunporch. Businesspeople will find the inn well suited for their traveling needs; the large lawn and wraparound veranda are ideal for special functions and events, and the conference center can accommodate 130 people. 🛏 *4 rooms with baths, 1 suite, 11 cottages. Air-conditioning, TV, phones, fireplaces, robes, hair dryers, whirlpool baths in cottages; cable TV and phone in rooms; whirlpool tub and fireplace in 12 rooms. $65–$150. AE, D, DC, MC, V. Smoking in 1 bedroom only.*

INN AT ANTIETAM 📷
220 E. Main St. (Box 119), Sharpsburg 21782, tel. 301/432–6601, fax 301/432–5981

Anyone who's ever visited a Civil War battlefield knows how haunting the site is, how the dawns seem to echo with the sound of bugles and gunfire, how at night the voices of soldiers rise like mist from the glades. Antietam, which surrounds the dusty little town of Sharpsburg, is surely one of the most stirring of such places, for it was here in September 1862 that one of the worst battles of the Civil War claimed more than 23,000 lives in a single bloody day.

Just north of town there's a national cemetery, with a statue by Daniel Chester French (who sculpted the statue of President Lincoln at Washington's Lincoln Memorial), called "The Private Soldier," which serves as the headstone for

5,000 Union dead. Adjoining the graveyard on a hillock facing the hazy Blue Ridge is the Inn at Antietam, a 1908 Queen Anne cottage with a wraparound porch, shaded by a giant silver maple and set amid fields. Owners Cal and Betty Fairbourn have restored the place in the style of turn-of-the-century Victorian, filling the parlor with Rococo Revival walnut furniture, the porch with rockers, and guest rooms with Eastlake dressers and beds.

The Fairbourns, who had restored another house in the area before moving into this one in 1983, enlisted the aid of a decorator here, which resulted in beautifully finished guest rooms. The converted smokehouse at the rear has a large brick fireplace, a sitting room lined with beaded paneling, and a loft bed. The master suite, another favorite, has an 1880s four-poster bed; matching spread, curtains, and wallpaper; and Battenberg lace.

After breakfast, served in the formal dining room on Royal Copenhagen china, Cal and Betty can offer tips on how best to see the battlefield—on foot, by bicycle, or even on cross-country skis. The surrounding area is also surprisingly rich in good restaurants, such as the Yellow Brick Bank, in nearby Shepherdstown, West Virginia, and Old South Mountain Inn in Boonsboro. During the first weekend in December, the Valley Craft Network runs an annual Holiday Studio Tour; pottery, quilts, furniture, and natural fiberwear make ideal Christmas gifts. Shutterbugs should ask Cal about local photo opportunities. **⌂** *4 suites. Air-conditioning, TV in smokehouse suite. $95–$115; full breakfast. AE. No smoking, 2-night minimum on weekends and holidays. Closed Dec. 22–Feb. 1.*

SPRING BANK 🐚
7945 Worman's Mill Rd., Frederick 21701, tel. 301/694–0440, fax 301/694–5926 (call first)

When you ask Beverly and Ray Compton why they bought their cavernous, 100-year-old farmhouse just north of Frederick in 1980, Beverly has a disarming answer: "We bought it to live in and be happy in." And indeed it seems this warm couple is happy here, though the road to inhabiting the house was paved with hard work interspersed with joyful architectural surprises. While restoring the Italianate and Gothic Revival structure, the Comptons found details that seemed too good to be true: engraved designs in the glass of the front door, random-width hardwood floors, faux-marble mantels, antique William Morris wallpaper, and a wet-plaster fresco on the ceiling of the old billiard room—now a first-floor guest room. Some of these design points had been damaged over the years, but after a thorough cleaning, they stand as witnesses to another time and lifestyle. Ray is the son of a Chadd's Ford, Pennsylvania, antiques dealer, and perhaps Ray's penchant for restoration is in his blood; in 1990 he received an award from the Historical Society of Frederick for the work he's done here. Beverly haunts local auctions and flea markets, and during the week she commutes to a federal job in Rockville.

The brick house is built in textbook-perfect telescoping style, with porches stretching across the front and along two stories on the side. The backyard gives way to farmland; the 20th century rarely intrudes at Spring Bank, despite its proximity to Highway 15. Choose your room upon arrival; the converted billiard parlor and the Sleigh Bedroom on the second floor are favorites, both sparely decorated with Eastlake-style antiques. In keeping with the 19th-century ethos the baths have not been extensively modernized—no whirlpool tubs or French magnifying mirrors here.

For breakfast, the Comptons serve homemade breads with local jams and plenty of information on nearby auctions, held almost every day. One note of advice: If you have fears about booking a room with a shared bath, you should put them to rest. No one has to wait in line here, and if you were to pass up Spring Bank for this reason, you'd be missing out on one of the handsomest, best-run establishments in western Maryland. ▲ *1 double room with bath, 4 doubles share 2½ baths. Air-conditioning, cable TV in parlor. $65–$95; Continental breakfast. AE, D, MC, V. No smoking, 2-night minimum on holiday weekends and weekends Apr.–mid-June and mid-Sept.–mid-Nov.*

OTHER CHOICES

Tyler-Spite Inn. 112 W. Church St., Frederick 21701, tel. 301/831–4455, fax 301/662–4185. 6 rooms with shared baths, 4 suites with baths. Air-conditioning in rooms, fireplace in 8 bedrooms and 3 common rooms, pool. $100–$250; full breakfast, high tea weekends. AE, MC, V. No smoking.

RESERVATIONS SERVICES

Bed & Breakfast Accommodations of Frederick and Western Maryland (7945 Worman's Mill Rd., Frederick 21701, tel. 301/694–5926). **Bed & Breakfast of Maryland/The Traveller in Maryland** (Box 2277, Annapolis 21404, tel. 410/269–6232).

MASSACHUSETTS

Southeastern Massachusetts

LIZZIE BORDEN BED AND BREAKFAST 🖋
92 2nd St., Fall River 02721, tel. and fax 508/675–7333

Here you can get 40 winks while dreaming about the 40 whacks Lizzie Borden (supposedly) gave her father and stepmother back on August 4, 1892. The Greek Revival house—erected in 1845 and until 1996 a private residence—has been turned into the city's most quixotic sightseeing spot. Borden buffs, true-crime fans, and the curious flock here to sleep, snoop, and have their photos taken in the exact spots where the bodies were found.

The six rooms are small but cozy and have double beds; four rooms share baths. Each has been faithfully restored to look the same way it did on that fateful August day, and all but the three attic rooms are named for a Borden family member. The rooms all have Borden family-member portraits, Borden memorabilia, and a diary in which guests leave thoughts. (Young children may not appreciate the theme or the museum-like atmosphere here.)

The Lizzie and Emma Suite (formerly Lizzie and Emma's bedrooms) has the green silk dress that actress Elizabeth Montgomery wore when she played Lizzie in a TV movie. It doesn't take a detective to figure out that the most popular room is the John Morse Guest Room, named for Lizzie's uncle and the one in which step-mom Abby was found hacked to death. (Those wanting to spend August 4 in this room should reserve early; it's usually booked a year in advance.) Breakfast—bananas, johnnycakes, sugar cookies, and coffee—is similar to the last one the Bordens ate. And don't forget to check out the framed hatchet hanging on the kitchen wall; it was found in a closet during a 1948 renovation; police investigations have determined it was not the murder weapon.

If you'd rather not spend the night, you can just take one of the nine daily tours led by knowledgeable guides in Victorian garb. They begin in the first-floor sitting room, where Andrew was murdered. (Those dying for more morbidity should check out the grisly crime-scene photo on the wall.) The sitting room has a video and book lending library and sundry souvenirs for sale. So did Lizzie—who was tried and acquitted of the crimes—do it? Says B&B co-owner Ron Evans with a smile: "We let the guests make up their own minds." ⌂ *2 double rooms with baths, 4 doubles share bath, 1 suite. Air-conditioning. $150–$200; full breakfast, tour. AE, D, MC, V. No smoking.*

ONSET POINTE INN 🖋
9 Eagle Way (Box 1450), Onset 02558, tel. 508/295–8442 or 800/356–6738, fax 508/295–5241

Looking for a seaside resort with all the charm (and romance) of Cape Cod that's off the beaten track? Look no farther. Situated on Pointe Independence, a spit of land in Buzzards Bay near the entrance to the Cape Cod Canal, this Victorian mansion (circa 1880) offers a prized proximity: the marina and private beach are just a few footprints in the sand away.

The seven main-house rooms are furnished in a typical, yet tasteful, seaside resort way: wicker and chintz, and lots of it. Two second-floor rooms have private balconies; the largest room, Bay View, is on the turreted third floor and offers panoramic water views of Onset Marina and Buzzards Bay and spectacular sunsets. In addition to the main house, you'll also find a guest house with five quarters (two suites that have kitchens and three rooms that sleep at least three people); a carriage house with two suites (one with a kitchen and one without); and one fully furnished apartment. (Families traveling with children should be sure to book a room in the guest house or the carriage house—where everyone will be most comfortable.)

The sun-drenched, glass-walled common room is replete with TV, stereo, fireplace, and myriad puzzles and games. It's also easy to while away your time in an Adirondack chair on one of the inn's many porches. Breakfast is served in the equally stunning, flagstone, ivy-trimmed sunporch. ❧ *7 double rooms with baths, 3 triples with bath, 4 suites, 1 apartment. Phones, beach access, volleyball. $100–$200; Continental-plus breakfast for main-building guests. AE, D, MC, V. No smoking. 2-night minimum weekends and 3-night minimum holidays in peak season.*

SALT MARSH FARM 🐚
322 Smith Neck Rd., South Dartmouth 02748, tel. 508/992–0980

Located on the historic Isaac Howland homestead farm at the quiet end of a harborside road in South Dartmouth, this two-story, mint-condition Georgian farmhouse (circa 1770) is run by Sally and Larry Brownell and has been in Sally's family since World War II. In the back of the house lie 90 acres of grounds, where nature trails lead to maples, oaks, and hollies; a 30-acre salt marsh; and the sparkling waters of Little River.

The Brownells have turned over the front of their home to guests, who may lounge by the fireplace in the living room filled with books on local nature lore and history. A large gallery-type family room, where you'll probably see jigsaw puzzles laid out, runs the length of the house. The building is full of choice antiques—virtually all passed down through Sally's or Larry's families. Some of the pieces date back generations, such as the massive mahogany sideboard in the intimate dining room, where portraits of four of Sally's Colonial ancestors gaze down on the scene.

Each of the two guest rooms has its own hall and stairway; one has twin four-poster beds and the other a double bed. Handmade quilts cover the beds, and freshly picked flowers decorate the rooms. On the wall in the Rocking Horse Room is an unusual picture of a parrot made entirely of feathers. One of the bathrooms has an oversize, claw-foot tub and a tub-height window with a view of the grounds.

Sally is an accomplished cook who makes good use of her organic herb and vegetable gardens. Her breakfast repertoire includes five-grain pancakes, fresh eggs (from the Brownell's henhouse) prepared in a number of ways, prize-winning blueberry muffins, and double-dipped French toast that's sometimes served with a special orange sauce and what Sally calls "mystery" syrup—made from rhubarb.

The town beach is within biking distance, and New Bedford is about 6 mi away. Padanaram, the name of the local harbor village, is used on many signposts. ❧

2 double rooms with baths. TV and phone in common area, bicycles (including one built for 2), nature trails. $85–$95; full breakfast, afternoon tea. MC, V. No smoking, children allowed but only if a separate room is rented for them. 2-night minimum weekends in peak season and holidays.

THE SALTWORKS ☞
115 Elm St., South Dartmouth 02748, tel. 508/991–5491, fax 508/979–8470

On what was once the grounds of an 1840 saltworks now sits a posh—but hardly pretentious—B&B, tucked away inside a private gated community. David Hall, a boat restorer, and his wife, Sandra, opened the Saltworks in 1995, mixing new and old with unsurpassed finesse.

There are only two rooms, each a suite with private bath and a working fireplace. The South Suite has a stunning 1895 Simmons brass bed that will offer you the best sleep you've had in years (best to leave the kids at home); the bath has an original claw-foot tub, a marble sink, and pine-plank floors that are painted red.

The large, airy common room has a TV, a fireplace, and enough reading material to keep a bibliophile busy for days—grab your favorite prose and cozy up in the window seat. The wraparound porch—crammed with nautical touches such as a lobster-trap-cum-table—offers panoramic views of Padanaram Harbor. A short walk will take you to Padanaram Village—that is, *if* you want to leave. ⌂
2 suites. TV in common room, beach access. $95; Continental-plus breakfast. AE, MC, V. No smoking, 2-night minimum weekends and holidays in peak season. Closed mid-Dec.–mid-Jan.

SCONEHEDGE ☞
280 Sandwich St., Plymouth 02360, tel. 508/746–1847, fax 508/746–3736

At first glance this large, cedar-shingle, 1910 mansion (no other word will do) is unpretentious and plain. Then the massive oak doors open and . . . well, think back to when Dorothy landed in Oz, and everything turned from sepia to Technicolor. But remember: This is real—not reel—life.

With its formal, dark poplar-beamed entrance hall (covered in muted, moss-green, swan-motif wallpaper), its ornate staircase, its diamond-pane windows, and its whimsical pierced-copper-and-glass light fixtures made by owner David Berman, Sconehedge seems to have been decorated—at least in part—by Charles Addams *and* Edward Gorey . . . perhaps even Norman Bates. Berman—who bought the dilapidated house in 1994 and spent 10 months restoring it—is an expert on the English designer-architect Charles Voysey, and every room is enriched with faithful reproductions of Voysey's designs, from wallpaper to clocks to curtains. This is a house where Victorian and Edwardian meld with Arts and Crafts, Gothic, even a little Berman. How else could you explain the odd pieces of taxidermy here and there?

There are three rooms and one suite, all with hand-painted furniture (yet another of Berman's talents) that seem plucked from the pages of turn-of-the-century fairy tales, four-poster or antique brass beds, private baths, and fireplaces. The second-floor suite, which has a sunporch that overlooks the gardens, is perhaps the most spectacular. It is connected to the Alice in Wonderland Room, so named because its wallpaper features Lewis Carroll's characters.

Why Sconehedge? Friends came up with the name because of Berman's love for baking classic English scones. You'll find out at breakfast just how good they are; *almost* as delicious as the house itself. ▲ *3 double rooms with baths, 1 suite. Air-conditioning, TV in common area, croquet. $95–$165; full breakfast. MC, V. No smoking, 2-night minimum weekends, 3-night minimum holidays.*

OTHER CHOICES

Edgewater Bed and Breakfast. 2 Oxford St., Fairhaven 02719, tel. 508/997–5512, fax 508/997–5784. 4 double rooms with baths, 1 suite, 1 efficiency. TV and phone in rooms. $65–$85; Continental-plus breakfast. AE, D, MC, V. No smoking in common area, 2-night minimum weekends and holidays in peak season.
Jackson-Russell-Whitfield House. 26 North St., Plymouth 02360, tel. 508/746–5289, fax 508/747–2722. 2 double rooms share bath in summer (another double, which shares bath, is available in winter). Air-conditioning. $80–140; Continental-plus breakfast. MC, V. No smoking, 2-night minimum weekends and holidays in peak season.
Windsor House. 390 Washington St., Duxbury 02332, tel. 781/934–0991 or 800/934–0993, fax 781/934–5955. 3 double rooms with baths. 2 restaurants, pub. $95–$135, $25 additional for each extra adult, $10 additional for each child under 16; full breakfast. AE, D, MC, V. No smoking.

RESERVATIONS SERVICE

New England Hospitality Network (Box 3291, Newport, RI 02840, tel. 401/849–1298 or 800/828–0000).

Cape Cod

BEACH HOUSE INN 🐦

61 Uncle Stephen's Way (Box 494), West Dennis 02670, tel. 508/398–4575 or 617/489–4144 off-season

If the Beach House Inn were any closer to the water, you'd be sleeping with the fish. Here Nantucket Sound is your backyard: Shingles are weathered gray from salt air; you're surrounded by white wicker and natural oak furniture that's practical yet comfortable; and walls of glass frame the beauty—and, sometimes, the ferocity—of the Cape.

There are seven rooms on two floors, and all have decks and are decorated in the same plain maple and wicker flavors (but let's face it—you probably didn't come here for the furniture). Some rooms have brass or four-poster beds, ceiling fans, and views of the front yard. Room 2 has a second-story deck with a staircase down to the private beach.

The common room has a TV and wide assortment of hit movies on video. You can use the barbecue grills or the fully equipped kitchen—if that fresh cup of coffee doesn't wake you up, then the sight of the crashing waves just beyond the sliding glass doors certainly will. There's also a private, fenced-in playground for when the young (and young-at-heart) no longer want to frolic in the water or build sand castles. ▲ *7 double rooms with baths. TV in rooms, ceiling fan in some rooms, private beach, playground, shuffleboard. $75–$105; Continental-plus breakfast. No credit cards. No smoking, 2-night minimum weekends and holidays in peak season.*

BRASS KEY ☙
9 Court St., Provincetown 02657, tel. 508/487–9005 or 800/842–9858, fax 508/487–9020

On a quiet side street just a block from the center of town, this 1828 sea captain's home is fast becoming a premier guest house. The entire property has been completely and luxuriously restored, and it now includes several buildings as well as the original house.

Owner Michael MacIntyre, a Ritz-Carlton alum, and his partner, Bob Anderson, have balanced modern convenience with rustic charm. The rooms are cozy and have exquisitely papered and/or stenciled interiors and wall-to-wall carpeting. They're furnished with simple country-style antiques such as pencil-post, sleigh, and canopy beds; carved wood armoires; and slant-top writing desks. One of the more spacious rooms is done in rich hues of burgundy and gold and has a queen-size bed with a headboard made from a fireplace mantel. Amenities here go beyond the usual creature comforts: Bose stereos, Caswell-Massey toiletries, hair dryers, and bathrobes. Deluxe rooms have gas fireplaces, whirlpool tubs, and private decks. Two rooms are cottages in an enclosed brick courtyard.

A heated outdoor pool provides a freshwater alternative to the beach. Little umbrella tables are set about for those who prefer the shade. There are also common decks, including a widow's walk roof deck with spectacular views of Cape Cod bay. In season complimentary Cape Codders (vodka and cranberry juice) are served in the courtyard beside the huge, hot-spa dip pool. In winter wine is served beside a roaring fire in the sitting-dining area, which has wide-board floors, original beams and wainscoting, and a beautiful antique table that was once used for kneading dough. Each morning you can help yourself at a buffet.

The Brass Key attracts a large gay clientele, especially in summer. The attentive staff makes everyone welcome and comfortable and offers tips about not-to-be-missed events in town. △ *34 double rooms with baths. Air-conditioning, cable TV/VCR, phone, mini-refrigerator, hair dryer, bathrobes in rooms; video library, turndown service, heated spa pool, heated outdoor pool. $185–$335; Continental breakfast. AE, MC, V. No smoking in common and some guest rooms. Minimum stay required in season, on holidays, and during special events (number of nights varies).*

CAPTAIN FARRIS HOUSE ☙
308 Old Main St., South Yarmouth 02664, tel. 508/760–2818 or 800/350–9477, fax 508/398–1262

Steps from the Bass River Bridge, which divides South Yarmouth and West Dennis, and a short way from congested Route 28 sits this 1845 Greek Revival home that was built by the sea captain for whom it is named. In 1996 innkeepers Stephen and Patty Bronstein took over the newly refurbished and restored home, turning it into a first-class B&B—enriching its look while maintaining its hold on the past.

Your eye cannot possibly take it all in at once: Tasteful reproductions of priceless artwork hang everywhere, and nooks and crannies are crammed with collectibles, coveted treasures, and sculptures. The French salon–style living room has a 1920s baby grand that you can play if you're so inclined. The dining room walls are painted to look as if they're covered with wallpaper, and the room has art and antiques that would be the envy of even the most jaded collector (the many antiques make this inn inappropriate for children). And don't forget to investigate the unique dining table . . . can you figure out its secret?

Guest rooms are large and comfortable with antique or canopy beds; extra pillows; plush comforters; and tiled sunken baths that have a Jacuzzi, a hair dryer, and imported toiletries. Two have fireplaces and sundecks. The Honeymoon Suite has both a sundeck and a two-person Jacuzzi. In each room fancy drapes fill the windows; fancier antiques and quality reproductions fill the rest of the space.

Breakfast is served in the dining room or in the brick courtyard—a slice of Tuscany right on the Mid-Cape. △ *8 double rooms with baths, 4 suites. Air-conditioning in 3 rooms; TV, phone, Jacuzzi, hair dryer in rooms. $95–$185; full breakfast. AE, MC, V. No smoking, 2-night minimum weekends, 3-night minimum holidays.*

CHATHAM BARS INN ☞
Shore Rd., Chatham 02633, tel. 508/945–0096 or 800/527–4884, fax 508/945–5491

Atop a rise that overlooks Pleasant Bay, just a stroll from the shops of Chatham, is this old-style oceanfront resort. Built as a hunting lodge in 1914 and once used as an exclusive club, Chatham Bars remains a classy place. The crescent-shape main building and 26 one- to eight-bedroom cottages (either in woods near the main inn or across the street on the bluff above the beach) are set on 20 landscaped acres. You're surrounded by elegance here, so feel free to dress in your best during peak season (no jeans or T-shirts in common areas after 6 PM).

Most rooms have decks, and all the cottages have common rooms, some with fireplaces. Throughout, rooms are carpeted in shades of sand and sea and are attractively appointed with traditional pine pieces, more modern upholstered pieces, Queen Anne reproductions, gilt-framed art, and Laura Ashley touches.

Off the grand entry hall is the South Lounge, which has Victorian-style overstuffed chairs and comfortable couches in burgundy and beige, pots of eucalyptus, and an enormous fireplace; a brick terrace with views of the bay and the famous sandbars; and a year-round casual restaurant-bar. The elegant main dining room has a wall of windows with sea views and a crisp decor with a deep green rug offset by white accents. The lavish breakfast buffet is served here and includes fresh fruits, sliced meats, smoked fish, and finger pastries; hot dishes are also available. At dinner expect creative takes on traditional New England fare. The beach house grill has lighter meals and clambakes in summer, and the tavern offers upscale pub grub year-round. △ *136 double rooms with baths, 22 suites. 3 restaurants; phone, cable TV in rooms; common mini-refrigerator in cottages; lending library, movies, exercise room, cocktail parties, children's program (July–Aug.), complimentary newspapers, baby-sitting services, private beach, 4 tennis courts, putting green, heated outdoor pool, volleyball, harbor cruises, launch service. $170–$1,000; breakfast not included. AE, DC, MC, V.*

HEAVEN ON HIGH ☞
70 High St., West Barnstable 02668, tel. 508/362–4441 or 800/362–4044, fax 508/362–4465

This 11-year-old B&B is, indeed, heaven, nestled as it is high on a hill—and on one of the Cape's oldest roads—overlooking dunes, the Great Salt Marsh, and the Bay at Sandy Neck. Opened in 1996 by displaced Connecticutites Deanna and Gib Katten, it is a feast for the spirit. The fantasy begins before you step inside: Deanna is an award-winning horticulturist, and the grounds demonstrate her talents. The garden motif spills into the house. The walls of the main foyer are a jungle of hand-stenciled and hand-painted sunflowers, ivy, and hummingbirds. (Look up: The ceilings have billowing clouds.)

Throughout, the decor is a mixture of California beach house and Cape Cod comfort—light, airy, and breezy. Deanna is also a collector; you'll find her treasures—one-of-a-kind miniature dressers, autographs (Al Jolson, Eleanor Roosevelt, Groucho Marx), priceless Tiffany silver—grouped here, there, and everywhere (such bits and bobs make this inn unsuitable for children). The Great Room has overstuffed chairs and couches, a fireplace, a TV, natural oak flooring, and a classical CD collection. Sliding glass doors lead to a peaceful living room and a deck that runs the length of the house. From here you have unobstructed views of sand and surf.

Three immense, immaculate guest rooms are filled with enviable antiques, walk-in closets, and unsurpassed decorative details (each room is named for the collection that it houses). The luxurious Silhouettes and Mirrors Room extends the width of the house and is fully carpeted. It has a queen-size bed, a fireplace, a tiled bath with two vanity sinks, a large deck, and, of course, silhouettes and mirrors of all types. Each room has a vintage handkerchief collection, and you are encouraged to take one as a memento. There's also an extensive audio-book collection for the long trip home; Deanna and Gib trust you to send the tapes back.

At breakfast the table is set with fine china and Tiffany silverware (Deanna smiles when she boasts that she can set the table for a whole month and not duplicate a place setting). The food is just as fine, featuring such culinary concoctions as tiramisu French toast, pear pancakes, and pineapple-walnut-raisin muffins—just one more reason to try to get to Heaven. ⚱ *3 double rooms with baths. Air-conditioning, mini-refrigerator in rooms, TV in living room, putting green. $130–$145; full breakfast. MC, V. No smoking, 2-night minimum weekends, 3-night minimum holidays in peak season.*

INN ON THE SOUND ☙
313 Grand Ave., Falmouth Heights 02540, tel. 508/457–9666 or 800/564–9668, fax 508/457–9631

Despite being smack dab on busy Grand Avenue, this inn is very tranquil. You see, it's also on a bluff that overlooks Vineyard Sound and offers glimpses of the island itself. All the rooms, from the living room—with its enormous boulder fireplace, oversized windows, and overstuffed chairs—to each of the 10 guest rooms (all named for various Falmouth area landmarks), face the water.

David Ross owns the inn with his sister, Renee, an interior decorator who knows her stuff. (The atmosphere here is perfect for couples or families with teenagers; this inn is not suitable for small children.) Nobska Light, the only guest room with a fireplace, has a minimalist white-on-white color scheme that plays brilliantly off the sweeping views of the sound. Every room has a queen-size bed and simple, contemporary furnishings: natural oak tables, unbleached cottons, and ceiling fans—the last really unnecessary owing to the sea breezes.

Common areas include an art-filled living room, a bistrolike breakfast room (try the French toast stuffed with cream cheese), and a 40-ft deck. Go ahead and dawdle. ⚱ *10 double rooms with baths. TV in room on request, beach access, beach chairs and towels. $95–$155; full breakfast. AE, D, MC, V. No smoking, 2-night minimum weekends, 3-night minimum holidays.*

MOSES NICKERSON HOUSE 🕊

364 Old Harbor Rd., Chatham 02633, tel. 508/945–5859 or 800/628–6972, fax 508/945–7087

Linda and George Watts are proof of the magical romantic influence of the Moses Nickerson House. When the company Linda worked for moved its operations to New York City in 1995, Linda quit the corporate world and came back to her roots on the Cape. She'd enjoyed managing a B&B in college, and when she came across this 1839 former whaling captain's home—a white Greek Revival with gray-blue shutters and a large fan ornament—she bought the place. The inn had only been open for a week or so when George drove in from Canada late one afternoon looking for a place to stay. The rest is history. They were married that Thanksgiving and have run the inn together ever since.

Fine antiques, attention to detail, and warm hospitality are the hallmarks here. Breakfast is served on gleaming crystal in the glass sunroom, which has garden views, or in the formal dining room when the weather turns cold. Linda prepares delectable dishes such as egg and cheese casseroles or fruit pizza (a pastry crust topped with cream cheese and a variety of fruit). In the afternoon homemade lemonade is served in the parlor. Here you'll find a fireplace, an Aubusson rug, a lyre-base Duncan Phyfe table, Cape Cod cranberry glass, and a hand-carved Mexican horse inlaid with agates.

Guest rooms have wide-board pine floors and firm queen-size beds with comforters, color-coordinated linens, and lots of pillows; most rooms have pedestal sinks, and several have gas-log fireplaces. Special touches include stenciling, scented drawer liners, padded clothes hangers, and dimmer switches on reading lamps.

Room 7 is clubby and masculine, with Ralph Lauren fabrics, dark leathers and woods, and a fireplace; on the walls hang hunting hats and horns. In Room 4 you need a stool to climb into the canopy bed; a wooden rack displays antique laces and linens, and a Nantucket hand-hooked rug complements the stenciled and whitewashed walls. Off the parlor is Room 1, with a romantic antique four-poster bed and armoire that are hand-painted with roses and a blue velvet Belgian settee before the fireplace. ▲ _7 double rooms with baths. Turndown service in season. $129–$169; full breakfast, afternoon lemonade. AE, MC, V. No smoking, 2-night minimum summer weekends, 3-night minimum holidays._

TRURO VINEYARDS AND INN 🕊

Rte. 6A (Shore Rd., Box 165), North Truro 02652, tel. 508/487–6200, fax 508/487–4248

When innkeepers Judy Wimer and Kathy Gregrow, both with plant science backgrounds, bought the historic Hughes-Rich farmstead, they had a grand plan: transform one of the Cape's last working farms, on 5 rolling acres, into a vineyard. Once they had established the French _vinefera_ vines, they then concentrated on turning the rundown 1836 Federal-style house into a romantic guest house.

The vineyard theme continues inside, with a decor of deep greens and burgundies and antique casks and presses tucked into corners. Rooms are elegant and have names relating to the vineyard. All have country antiques, rich carpets, four-poster king- or queen-size beds, and modern tiled baths (most with tub and shower). The Vintage Suite has exposed beams and period furnishings, a king-size four-poster bed, and a large bath with a two-person Jacuzzi.

A full breakfast, often garnished with garden-grown berries, is served in the sunroom or on the patio. A large common sundeck offers a sweeping view of the vineyard and is a perfect place to relax with a book. ♨ *5 double rooms with baths. $89–$129. No smoking. MC, V. Closed Jan.–Apr.*

WILDFLOWER INN 🦜
167 Palmer Ave., Falmouth 02540, tel. and fax 508/548–9524 or tel. 800/294–5459

The Wildflower Inn first bloomed in 1995, when owners Phil and Donna Stone decided to become innkeepers. They call their decorating style "old made new again": Tables are constructed from early 1900s pedal sewing machine bases; in a former life the living room–breakfast area's sideboard server was a 1920s Hotpoint electric stove; and the antique Hoosier now holds beverages and snacks.

The Stone's innovative decor (and infectious sense of humor) continues in the guest rooms. The Jasmine Room has a safari theme, with soft gold walls, animal wood carvings that have burlap and bamboo accents, and an antique iron four-poster bed with a mosquito-netting canopy. In the skylighted, third-floor, Moonflower Room—where everything is coming up . . . well, sunflowers—the bed is tucked into the eaves so you can count stars instead of sheep. In the attached town house (formerly a stable) the fully furnished Loft Cottage has a spiral staircase that winds up to a bedroom. (Note that although this inn is full of whimsy and humor, it is not suitable for families with young children.)

Donna whips up edible delights using the wildflowers she grows out back. The wraparound porch serves as the summer's breakfast nook; one morning the five-course breakfast might include sunflower crepes or calendula corn muffins—floral feasts that have been featured on the PBS series *Country Inn Cooking*. ♨ *5 double rooms with baths, 1 cottage. Air-conditioning, TV in common room, whirlpool bath in 2 rooms, bicycles. $115–$175; full breakfast. AE, MC, V. No smoking, 2-night minimum weekends and holidays.*

WINGSCORTON FARM 🦜
11 Wing Blvd., East Sandwich 02537, tel. 508/888–0534

This working farm is also an enchanting oasis where you can commune with nature when you're not busy talking (literally) to the animals. A long, winding driveway—sheep on the left, metal pig sculpture on the right, and groves of trees and pastures all around—brings you past a two-bedroom cottage (rented by the week) to the main house, which was built in 1763 and was once a stop on the Underground Railroad.

The dining room has one of the largest fireplaces in New England—the hearth alone is 9 ft long. (When a major snowstorm surprised the Cape back in 1996, owners Sheila Weyers and Richard Loring kept their guests comfy, cozy, and warm!) A richly paneled communal library-den has Oriental rugs, wing-back chairs, bestsellers and magazines, and a TV. Each of the four main-house guest suites has a fireplace, braided rugs atop wide-plank floors, wainscoting, and an adjoining smaller bedroom—formerly the birthing rooms. (Today, they hold twin beds and mini-refrigerators.)

For privacy (Sheila assures that "only a goat or sheep could spy on you"), request the detached stone carriage house. This honeymooner's haven has a fully equipped kitchen, a living room with a sofa bed and a wood-burning stove, a spiral staircase that leads to a loft bedroom, and a large sundeck. The cottage is fully equipped—perfect for family reunions.

While roaming the 13 acres, expect to run into lots of four-legged critters: the two house dogs, ducks, Genevieve the donkey, chickens (yes, you can help gather eggs), the pair of llamas that occasionally make their presence known, and the various "well-trained" pets brought by guests. The beach is a five-minute walk away. Another favorite feature: the traditional clambakes prepared year-round by visiting members of Martha's Vineyard's Wampanoag tribe. △ *4 suites, carriage house, 2-bedroom cottage. TV in library-den, mini-refrigerators, private beach. $115–$200; full breakfast. AE, MC, V. 2-night minimum weekends and holidays.*

OTHER CHOICES

Captain Freeman Inn. 15 Breakwater Rd., Brewster 02631, tel. 508/896–7481 or 800/843–4664, fax 508/896–5618. 7 double rooms with baths, 5 suites. Common refrigerator and ice maker, mini-refrigerator in some rooms, movie library, pool, croquet, badminton, bicycles. $135–$225; full breakfast. AE, MC, V. No smoking, 2-night minimum peak season and weekends.

Captain's House Inn. 371 Old Harbor Rd., Chatham 02633, tel. 508/945–0127, fax 508/945–0866. 14 double rooms with baths, 5 suites. Air-conditioning in rooms; TV/VCR, refrigerator, coffeemaker, whirlpool bath in some rooms; croquet, bicycles. $135–$325; full breakfast, afternoon tea. AE, D, MC, V. No smoking.

Four Chimneys Inn. 946 Main St. (Rte. 6A), Dennis 02638, tel. 508/385–6317 or 800/874–5502, fax 508/385–6285. 7 double rooms with baths, 1 suite. Ceiling fan, TV in 6 rooms and common room. $85–$125; Continental-plus breakfast. AE, D, MC, V. Restricted smoking. 2-night minimum weekends, 3-night minimum holidays. Closed late Oct.–late Apr.

Inn at Sandwich Center. 118 Tupper Rd., Sandwich 02563, tel. 508/888–6958 or 800/249–6949. 5 double rooms with baths. Terry cloth robes in rooms. $85–$110; Continental-plus breakfast. AE, D, MC, V. No smoking, 2-night minimum weekends and holidays.

Isaiah Clark House. 1187 Rte. 6A (Box 169), Brewster 02631, tel. 508/896–2223 or 800/822–4001, fax 508/896–2138. 7 double rooms with baths. Air-conditioning, cable TV in rooms, turndown service, games, beach chairs and towels, airport or train-station pickup. $98–$125; full breakfast, afternoon tea, evening cookies and milk on request. AE, D, MC, V. No smoking, 2-night minimum weekends in peak season.

Isaiah Hall B&B Inn. 152 Whig St. (Box 1007), Dennis 02638, tel. 508/385–9928 or 800/736–0160, fax 508/385–5879. 9 double rooms with baths, 1 suite. Air-conditioning in rooms, mini-refrigerator in suite, badminton, croquet. $85–$142; Continental-plus breakfast. AE, MC, V. No smoking, 3-night minimum weekends and holidays in season. Closed mid-Oct.–mid-Apr.

Penny House Inn. 4885 County Rd. (Rte. 6), North Eastham 02651, tel. 508/255–6632 or 800/554–1751, fax 508/255–4893. 11 double rooms with baths. Air-conditioning, phone, mini-refrigerator in some rooms; TV in common room. $115–$180; full breakfast, afternoon tea. AE, D, MC, V. No smoking.

Ruddy Turnstone. 463 Rte. 6A, Brewster 02631, tel. 508/385–9871 or 800/654–1995, fax 508/385–5696. 5 double rooms with baths. Guest refrigerator, TV in parlor, croquet, badminton, horseshoes. $95–$150; full breakfast. MC, V. No smoking. Closed Jan.–Feb.

Wood Duck Inn. 1050 County Rd., Cataumet 02534, tel. 508/564–6404. 3 suites, 1 cottage. Air-conditioning in 2 suites; TV, mini-refrigerator in suites; nature trails, ice-skating. $85–$95; Continental-plus breakfast. No credit cards. Smoking in 1 suite, 2-night minimum weekends and holidays in season.

RESERVATIONS SERVICES

Bed and Breakfast Cape Cod (Box 341, West Hyannis Port 02672-0341, tel. 508/775–2772 or 800/686–5252). **House Guests Cape Cod and the Islands** (Box 1881, Orleans 02653, tel. 800/666–4678). **Orleans Bed & Breakfast Associates** (Box 1312, Orleans 02653, tel. 508/255–3824 or 800/541–6226; covers Lower Cape, Harwich to Truro). **Provincetown Reservations System** (293 Commercial St., Provincetown 02657, tel. 508/487–2400 or 800/648–0364; also shows, restaurants, and more).

Martha's Vineyard

CHARLOTTE INN 🌱

27 S. Summer St., Edgartown 02539, tel. 508/627–4751, fax 508/627–4652

On a quiet street in the center of well-groomed Edgartown is an inn that stands out like a polished gem. Gery Conover, owner for more than 20 years, and his wife, Paula, oversee every detail with meticulous care and obvious pride. From the original structure, an 1860 white-clapboard home that belonged to a whaling-company owner, the Charlotte has grown into a five-building complex connected by lawns and a courtyard. Ivy-bordered brick walkways lead past pockets of garden to flower-filled nooks perfect for reading or reflection. Across the street is the early 18th-century Garden House; one gorgeous room has French doors that open to a terrace that looks onto a large English garden.

True Anglophiles, the Conovers have furnished the inn through antiquing trips to England—and continue to do so, since each room is redone completely every five years. Guest rooms feature mahogany furniture; brass lamps; original art; richly colored wallpapers; lush fabrics; and down-filled pillows, comforters, and chair cushions. One room in the veranda-wrapped 1850 Summer House has a fireplace and a baby grand piano.

The most exquisite accommodations on the island are here, in the Coach House. Set above a re-created estate garage lined with gleaming natural wood walls, the suite has cathedral ceilings, a Palladian window, French doors, a green marble fireplace, and sumptuous furnishings. Everywhere you look there's something wonderful: sterling silver lamps, Minton bone china, white cutwork bed linens.

The main inn's ground floor is spacious and elegant, with sporting and marine art and contemporary works displayed throughout. The mahogany-paneled common room with a fireplace draws guests for afternoon tea and cocktails. In winter breakfast is served there on white-cloth-covered tables. (Note that the atmosphere here is not conducive to the patter of little feet.)

The fine restaurant L'étoile, set in a glassed-in summerhouse, is open for dinner and Sunday brunch. It mixes luxuriant greenery, spotlighted oil paintings, and surprising antique accents, such as leather-bound books perched on the rafters. The contemporary French menu highlights local seafood and game. ♦ *23 double rooms with baths, 2 suites. Restaurant (closed Jan.–mid-Feb.), air-conditioning, TV in some rooms, phone in rooms. $295–$695; Continental breakfast, afternoon tea. AE, MC, V. 2-night minimum weekends, 3-night minimum holidays.*

LAMBERT'S COVE COUNTRY INN 🦜

*Lambert's Cove Rd. (R.R. 1, Box 422), West Tisbury 02575, tel. 508/693–2298,
fax 508/693–7890*

Approached via a narrow, winding road through pine woods, this secluded retreat is everything a country inn should be. The 1790 farmhouse is set amid an apple orchard, a large English garden bordered by lilac bushes, and woods that hide a tennis court. In spring an ancient tree is draped in blossoms from 20-ft wisteria vines (a popular photo spot for the many weddings held here); in fall a Concord grape arbor scents the air.

The inn's common areas are elegant yet welcoming, with rich woodwork and large flower arrangements. In the large, airy gentleman's library, part of the additions made in the 1920s, you'll find book-lined white walls, a fireside grouping of upholstered wing chairs, rich red Oriental carpets on a polished wood floor, and French doors that open to the orchard. A cozier reading area on the second-floor landing offers a sofa and shelves of books and magazines.

The guest rooms are in the main house and in two adjacent buildings. Most main-house rooms have a soft, soothing country look framed by Laura Ashley wallpapers; two at the back can be converted to a suite with a connecting sitting room that has a sofa bed and sliders opening onto a backyard deck. Rooms in the other houses are more rustic. Two rooms upstairs in the Barn have exposed beams; downstairs one large room with a sofa bed has sliders out to a deck. The Carriage House has camp-style decks and screened porches. Comfort is the focus, meaning unfussy furnishings; firm beds with country quilts; and bright, cheerful baths with plush towels.

Fine dining is part of the experience, and the romantic restaurant serves unpretentious Continental cuisine in an intimate atmosphere of soft lighting and music. The innkeepers since 1996 are Louis and Katherine Costabel; he is an awarding-winning Cordon Bleu chef. ⌂ *15 double rooms with baths. Restaurant (dinner and Sun. brunch; off-season, weekends only), air-conditioning in some rooms, TV in common room, beach passes, tennis court. $125–$175; Continental breakfast. AE, MC, V. No smoking in common areas, 3-night minimum July–Aug.*

OAK HOUSE 🦜

Sea View Ave. (Box 299), Oak Bluffs 02557, tel. 508/693–4187, fax 508/696–7385

Among the summer homes along the coast road just outside Oak Bluffs center stands the Oak House B&B. Built in 1872 and enlarged and lavishly refurbished in the early 1900s, this wonderful Victorian beach house features a playful gingerbread-trimmed pastel facade and a wraparound veranda with much-used rockers and even a swing or two.

Inside, the reason for the inn's name becomes clear: Everywhere you look, you see richly patinated oak: in ceilings, wall paneling, wainscoting, and furnishings. The two bedrooms that constitute the Captain's Room are fitted out like ship cabins and have oak wainscoted walls and ceilings. The best of the rooms with balconies (large enough for two chairs) is the Governor Claflin Room; its French doors open wide to let in a broad expanse of sea and sky. Unfortunately, cars whiz past on the road below, which some people may find distracting.

When the Convery family bought the Oak House in 1988, they created several tiny bathrooms out of existing closets. One spacious hall bath, with peach-painted pressed-tin walls and ceiling, a dressing table, and the inn's only tub, was turned into a private bath for the very feminine Tivoli Room.

Alison Convery's island antiques shops provided much of the inn's superb furniture, brass lamps, sea chests, and such. The entrance hall evokes an elegant Victorian home, with high ceilings, a baby grand piano, a hand-cranked organ, potted palms, and an impressive central staircase lined with sumptuous red Oriental carpeting. The sunporch has lots of white wicker, plants, floral print pillows, and original stained-glass window accents. (With so many antiques here, it's best to leave the wee ones at home.)

In the afternoon guests wander back from the beach (across the street) to chat. Homemade lemonade and iced tea, along with elegant tea cakes and cookies, are provided by Alison's daughter, Betsi Convery-Luce, the warm and open innkeeper and a Cordon Bleu–trained pastry chef. △ *8 double rooms with baths, 2 suites. Air-conditioning in 4 rooms; TV in common room, some rooms, and both suites; beach access. $130–$225; Continental breakfast, afternoon tea. AE, D, MC, V. 3-night minimum weekends and holidays in season. Closed mid-Oct.–early May.*

OUTERMOST INN ☞
Lighthouse Rd. (R.R. 1, Box 171), Gay Head 02535, tel. 508/645–3511, fax 508/645–3514

In 1990 Hugh and Jeanne Taylor (he's singing James's brother) finished converting the sprawling, gray-shingle home they built 20 years ago—and are raising their two children in—into a B&B. Hugh's redesign takes full advantage of the superb location, at the sparsely populated westernmost end of the island. Standing alone on acres of wide-open moorland, the two-story house is wrapped with picture windows that reveal breathtaking views; to the north are the Elizabeth Islands and, beyond, mainland Cape Cod. The sweeping red and white beams of the Gay Head Lighthouse, just over the moors on the Gay Head Cliffs, add a touch of romance at night. (Indeed, the atmosphere here is more suited to couples than to families with young children.)

White walls and polished light-wood floors of ash, cherry, beech, oak, and hickory create a bright, clean setting for simple contemporary-style furnishings and local art. Fabrics used throughout the inn are all natural—in the dhurrie rugs, the down-filled cotton comforters, and the all-cotton sheets. Several corner rooms offer window walls on two sides. The Lighthouse Suite has a private entrance, a skylighted bath, and a separate living room with a butcher-block dining table. The Oak Room has French doors that open onto a deck with a great view.

The porch, set with hammocks and rocking chairs, is ideal for relaxing and watching birds and deer. Breakfast is served there or in the dining room, which has a fireplace and window wall. In the afternoon complimentary hors d'oeuvres and setups for drinks are provided on request. During peak season the inn operates a restaurant (by reservation only) that offers a mix of gourmet and home cooking prepared by a Culinary Institute–trained chef—another excuse for you not to wander far from the nest.

When you are ready to venture out, the owners are happy to help with arrangements for all kinds of activities. Hugh has sailed the local waters since childhood, and he will charter out his 50-ft catamaran for excursions to Cuttyhunk Island. There's a privately accessed beach just a five-minute walk away. △ *6 double rooms with baths, 1 suite. Restaurant (in season), phones, beach passes. $240–$320; full breakfast. AE, MC, V. Smoking only on porch, 2-night minimum weekends.*

THORNCROFT INN ☞

460 Main St. (Box 1022), Vineyard Haven 02568, tel. 508/693–3333
or 800/332–1236, fax 508/693–5419

Set amid 3½ wooded acres about a mile from town and the Vineyard Haven ferry, the Thorncroft seems a piece of English countryside. Beyond a manicured lawn bordered in neat boxwood hedges and flowering shrubs is the tidy Craftsman bungalow—gray-green with white shutters and a dormered second story—that was built in 1918 as the guest house of a large estate.

Since they bought the place in 1981, Karl and Lynn Buder have renovated it from top to bottom, furnishing it beautifully with a mix of antiques and reproductions to create an environment that is elegant yet soothing. In addition, they built a Carriage House that has five double rooms geared for romance, with large whirlpool baths (backed with mirrored alcoves) and fireplaces. Two other irresistible rooms have private hot-tub rooms with screens just under the roof that let in fresh air for an alpine effect.

Considering Lynn's master's degree in business administration and Karl's in public administration, it is not surprising that the Thorncroft—now their only business—is run so efficiently. The fine Colonial and richly carved Renaissance Revival antiques are meticulously maintained. Beds are firm, floors thickly carpeted, tiled bathrooms modern and well lighted. Room fireplaces are piled with logs and kindling each day, ready for the touch of a match. Ice buckets, wine glasses, and corkscrews are provided in each guest room, as is a notebook of information on the area. The bedrooms are wired for computer modems—for those who just *can't* leave work behind. And for those who can, there's a bookcase full of magazines on an amazing range of subjects. There's also a wicker sunporch in which to read them, if you like.

You can have a Continental breakfast delivered to your room and set up elegantly on table-height trays, or you can sign up for one of two seatings the night before. A bell calls you to the table, where you can exchange touring tips with other guests over such entrées as almond French toast and Belgian waffles. △ *14 double rooms with baths. Mini-refrigerator in some rooms; air-conditioning, bathrobes, hair dryer, iron, cable TV, phone in rooms; whirlpool bath in 5 rooms; hot tub in 2 rooms; complimentary morning newspaper. $260–$450; full breakfast, afternoon tea. AE, D, DC, MC, V. No smoking.*

OTHER CHOICES

Crocker House Inn. 12 Crocker Ave., Vineyard Haven 02568 tel. 508/693–1151 or 800/772–0206, fax 508/693–1123. 8 double rooms with baths. Air-conditioning, mini-refrigerator in 1 room and common area, beach access, free parking (first-come, first-served basis). $85–$160; Continental breakfast. AE, MC, V. No smoking.

Duck Inn. State Rd. (Box 160), Gay Head 02535, tel. 508/645–9018. 4 double rooms share 3 baths, 1 suite. TV in suite and common room, phone in rooms, hot tub, beach access. $95–$175; full breakfast. MC, V. No smoking in common room.

Greenwood House. 40 Greenwood Ave., Vineyard Haven 02568, tel. 508/693–6150 or 800/525–9466, fax 508/696–8113. 1 double room with bath, 3 suites. Air-conditioning, cable TV, phone, mini-refrigerator, hair dryer in rooms; croquet. $159–$239; Continental-plus breakfast. AE, DC, MC, V. No smoking, children allowed only in 1 room, 3-night minimum weekends and holidays.

Victorian Inn. 24 S. Water St., Edgartown 02539, tel. 508/627–4784. 14 double rooms with baths. $110–$225; full breakfast, afternoon tea. AE, MC, V. No smoking, 2-night minimum weekends, 3-night minimum holidays.

RESERVATIONS SERVICES

Any Day Reservations (tel. 508/696–9990 or 888/633–3700 in MA or CT). **House Guests Cape Cod and the Islands** (Box 1881, Orleans 02653, tel. 508/896–7053 or 800/666–4678). **Martha's Vineyard and Nantucket Reservations** (Box 1322, Vineyard Haven 02568, tel. 508/693–7200 or 800/649–5671 in MA).

Nantucket

CENTERBOARD GUEST HOUSE ☞
8 Chester St. (Box 456), Nantucket 02554, tel. 508/228–9696

The look of this inn, a few blocks from the center of town, is unique on the island. In the high-ceilinged guest rooms, white walls (some with murals of moors and sky in soft pastels), blond-wood floors, white or natural wood furniture, white slatted shutters, and natural woodwork with a light wash of mauve tint create a cool, spare, dreamy atmosphere. There's more white, still, in the lacy linens and fluffy comforters on the feather beds, each mounded with four pillows. Restrained touches of color are added by small stained-glass lamps, antique quilts, dishes of pink crystals, and fresh flowers.

The large Room 4 has a queen-size bed, a sofa, and an oversize shower; Room 2 has two antique brass and white-painted iron double beds. The small but pleasant studio apartment is suggestive of a cabin on a ship, with a galley kitchen, two double beds in a berthlike alcove, a separate twin bed in its own cubbyhole (fun for a child), a dining area, and a private entrance.

The first-floor suite is a stunner. Its large living room evokes the house's Victorian origins, with an 11-ft ceiling, the original parquet floor, a working fireplace topped by an elaborately carved oak mantel, and antique accents (a carved duck, a tapestry fire screen, lighting fixtures, and books). A nice modern touch is the wet bar. A lush hunter-green and rose Oriental carpet, a sofa bed, and upholstered chairs nicely complement the eggplant-color walls and the richness of the wood. Off the small separate bedroom, with a custom-built, cherry, four-poster bed topped by a high fishnet canopy, is a well-appointed bath with a whirlpool tub and highly polished dark-wood cabinetry set off by a rich green marble floor.

Manager Kim Gloth, an Ohio native, is enthusiastic about living on Nantucket, and her enthusiasm is evident in the way she tends to the needs of her guests. Unobtrusive yet available to remedy any problem, she has a cheerful disposition that sets the mood here. Each morning she puts out cold cereals, fruit, muffins, Portuguese bread, teas, and coffees in the sunny dining room amid such artistic touches as a sand-and-shell assemblage under glass and an 18th-century corner cupboard spilling antique blue and purple dried hydrangeas. ♧ *4 double rooms with baths, 1 studio apartment, 1 suite. Air-conditioning, TV, phone, minirefrigerator in rooms; beach towels. $165–$285; Continental breakfast. AE, MC, V. No smoking, 2-night minimum weekends.*

JARED COFFIN HOUSE ☞

29 Broad St., Nantucket 02554, tel. 508/228–2400 or 800/248–2405, fax 508/228–8549

Amid the shops, restaurants, and activity of downtown stands this perennial favorite—loved because of its location, dependability, conveniences, and class. It consists of six structures dating from the 18th century to the 20th, and all are well maintained and landscaped.

The landmark main inn is the most impressive. In 1845 Jared Coffin, a wealthy shipowner, built this glorious three-story redbrick Greek Revival with a portico, a parapet, a hip roof, and a cupola (ask for a key to go up in it and check out the panoramic view). In 1847 it became a stopover for travelers, in 1961 the Nantucket Historical Trust restored it, and today it is watched over by Phil and Margaret Read—owners since 1976.

The first-floor public rooms are elegant yet welcoming—with Oriental rugs and antique Sheraton and Chippendale furniture, portraits, clocks, and lace curtains. In cool weather you can sit by the fire sipping drinks brought to you from the downstairs bar and restaurant, the Tap Room. Breakfast and dinner are served in the formal restaurant, Jared's, a lovely, high-ceilinged room with pale-green swag draperies, Federal-period antiques, and chandeliers with frosted-glass globes.

The main house's 11 guest rooms have Oriental carpets and a blend of 19th-century antiques and reproductions, including gilt-wood mirrors, upholstered chairs, and carved four-poster pineapple beds. The second-floor corner rooms are the largest (they have sitting areas), and the front corner rooms have more windows. The inexpensive single rooms—a rare commodity on the island—are small but tastefully done. The small, clean, and comfortable rooms of the Ethan Allen Wing, all with private baths and TVs, also cost less than other rooms.

The Harrison Gray House, an 1842 Greek Revival across Centre Street, is the most popular part of the inn, offering bigger rooms—many with sitting areas and large baths—as well as a common living room and a sunporch. Both this and the 1821 Henry Coffin House have queen-size canopy beds. The Daniel Webster House, built in 1964, with uninspired decor by Ethan Allen, is adjacent to the outdoor café and has a second-floor lobby and a small deck at the back, where you can relax and have a drink or read the paper. ♨ *52 double rooms with baths, 8 singles with bath. 2 restaurants; TV, phone in rooms; mini-refrigerator in some rooms. $90–$210; full breakfast. AE, D, DC, MC, V.*

TEN LYON STREET INN ☞

10 Lyon St., Nantucket 02554, tel. 508/228–5040

In 1986 Ann Marie and Barry Foster opened this B&B on a quiet street about a five-minute walk from the town center. Barry completely rebuilt the three-story Colonial-style house from its foundations; Ann Marie used her decorating skills—from upholstery to antiques restoration—to make this an eye-pleasing place. Inside the gate, exotic bulbs, lilacs, and other perennials curve around the lawn and pink and peach roses climb the trellises against the house's weathered gray shingles.

Barry, an electrical contractor, wanted the house to have a historical feel, so to the smooth white-plaster walls and ceilings and light-wood moldings he added golden-pine floors in planks of varying widths, salvaged Colonial-era mantels, and hefty antiqued-red oak ceiling beams.

Guest rooms have a spare, uncluttered look yet are warmed by details. The white walls create pristine surroundings for exquisite antique Oriental rugs in deep colors and such choice antiques as an English-pine sleigh bed or a tobacco-leaf four-poster. Chairs are upholstered in English florals, and there are bits of lace as well. The beds have hand-stitched quilts, down comforters, and all-cotton sheets (which Ann Marie actually *irons*). Bathrooms are large, white, and well appointed, with maize-and-white-striped floor runners and delicate wall hangings from Ann Marie's native Austria. Several baths have deep claw-foot tubs with separate showers; all have antique porcelain pedestal sinks and brass fixtures.

Large, lush Room 1 has a 19th-century French-country tester bed romantically draped in gauzy white mosquito netting, stunning red Turkish carpets, potted palms, gilt mirrors, and little antique gilt-wood cupids on either side of the bed.

Ann Marie provides a healthful Continental breakfast that is served in the breakfast nook; the muffins are low in sugar and fat, the jellies low in sugar, yet all is delicious. Common areas include a small upstairs sitting room and a living room with a book-filled cabinet and an Oriental carpet. △ *7 double rooms with baths. $180–$235; Continental breakfast. MC, V. No smoking. Closed mid-Dec.–mid-Apr.*

WESTMOOR INN 🐚
Cliff Rd., Nantucket 02554, tel. 508/228–0877, fax 508/228–5763

At this yellow Federal mansion, you'll find a tradition of gracious entertaining that was established when the Vanderbilts built it as their summer house in 1917. The entry, with its sweeping staircase, conveys the imposing air of a manor house. Off the entry is the living room, in which you'll find a grand piano and a games table, and a sunporch with white-wicker chairs and a TV (for those inevitable rainy days).

Outside, the wide lawn has Adirondack chairs and a garden patio behind 11-ft hedges—the perfect place to lounge on a summer day. A mile from the shops and restaurants and just a short walk from an uncrowded ocean beach and the Madaket bike path, the inn is a good choice for those who want space and seclusion.

Guest rooms are bright and white and have eyelet comforters and pillows, framed botanicals, old prints, and some very nice antiques. Third-floor rooms have lots of dormers and angles, with stenciling on the white eaves. The second floor features highly polished wide-board pine floors. Most baths are modern, though a few need updating (old, metal shower units and tile floors)—specify if it matters to you. One first-floor suite has a giant bath with an extralarge Jacuzzi and French doors that open onto the lawn. The third-floor master bedroom, with its king-size bed and queen-size sofa bed, has a broad view of moors and the ocean beyond to the north; to the east it looks onto a neighbor's private baseball diamond.

Mornings you gather with other guests in a room that has a glass ceiling and walls for a buffet of yogurt, fruit salad, granola, croissants, home-baked scones or nut breads, juices, and more. Tables are set with white damask, flowers, and white china. There are also such thoughtful touches as ramekins of jams and butter, a bowl of ice around the milk pitcher on the buffet, daily newspapers, and soft classical music. After a day of exploring the island, you can gather with others yet again for a predinner wine-and-cheese reception. △ *14 double rooms, 3 apartments. Bicycles, beach towels. $155–$255; Continental breakfast, wine and cheese. AE, MC, V. No smoking, 3-night minimum mid-June–mid-Sept. Closed early Dec.–Mar.*

OTHER CHOICES

76 Main Street. 76 Main St., Nantucket 02554, tel. and fax 508/228–2533. 18 double rooms with baths. Cable TV, mini-refrigerator in annex rooms. $135–$155; Continental breakfast. AE, D, MC, V. No smoking.

The Wauwinet. Wauwinet Rd. (Box 2580), Nantucket 02584, tel. 508/228–0145 or 800/426–8718, fax 508/228–7135. 25 doubles with bath, 5 cottages. Restaurant, bar; air-conditioning, TV/VCRs in rooms; turndown service, room service, business services, concierge, video library, 2 tennis courts, sailboard and Sunfish rentals/lessons, croquet, mountain bikes, picnic cruises, Jeep tours, ferry pickup. $250–$500; full breakfast. AE, DC, MC, V. No smoking. 3-night minimum summer and holiday weekends. Closed Dec.–Mar.

White Elephant. Easton St. (Box 1139), Nantucket 02554, tel. 508/228–2500 or 800/475–2637, fax 508/325–1195. 48 doubles with bath, 32 1- to 3-bedroom cottages. Restaurant, lounge; cable TV, phone in rooms; air-conditioning, mini-refrigerator in some rooms; room service, concierge, pool, croquet court, putting green, boat slips. $245–$650; breakfast not included. AE, D, DC, MC, V. Closed Nov.–Apr.

RESERVATIONS SERVICES

DestINNations (tel. 800/333–4667). **House Guests Cape Cod and the Islands** (Box 1881, Orleans 02653, tel. 508/896–7053 or 800/666–4678). **Martha's Vineyard and Nantucket Reservations** (Box 1322, 73 Lagoon Pond Rd., Vineyard Haven 02568, tel. 508/693–7200 or 800/649–5671 in MA). **Nantucket Accommodations** (Box 217, Nantucket 02554, tel. 508/228–9559).

Boston

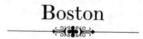

82 CHANDLER STREET ✎
82 Chandler St., Boston 02116, tel. 617/482–0408 or 888/482–0408

Located in Boston's recently revitalized South End—on a quiet, tree-lined street of tall, redbrick row houses—this B&B is just a 5-minute walk from the city center, a 10-minute taxi ride from the airport, and around the corner from Amtrak's Back Bay station. Constructed in 1863, the building sits on former tidal marshlands that were filled in to provide housing space for the city's growing middle class. Its mansard roof and brown stone are trademarks of 19th-century Boston homes.

Owners Denis Coté and Dominic Beraldi bought the house in 1978 and, after major renovation, turned it into apartments. In 1983, however, when one tenant moved out, they decided to try their hand at innkeeping. According to Denis, a social worker for 25 years, innkeeping is a positive kind of social work, "but more enjoyable, since you're helping people to have a good time, rather than to survive!"

A full breakfast, including pancakes, French toast, or crepes, is served family style in the big, sunny penthouse kitchen, which has exposed-brick walls, plants, skylights, and windows that overlook the city's rooftops. The bedroom across the stairwell is the Room with a View: Its wide bay window looks out on downtown Boston and several landmark skyscrapers. The walls are exposed brick, the floors are polished pine with Oriental rugs, there's a working marble fireplace, and a skylight in the bathroom. Ask for this room first when making reservations (especially since all rooms cost the same).

The 82 Chandler Street inn is very much an "up and down" house: all other guest rooms open off the staircase and are color coded with green, red, blue, or yellow schemes. Front rooms have large bay windows, and two have working fireplaces; all are spacious and sunny, with white enamel and brass headboards, pedestal sinks, Oriental rugs, and a kitchen area with refrigerator.

Ever devoted to his guests' well-being, Denis provides a wealth of tourist information, directions, and advice on the best sights to see. Although you can use two nearby parking lots (costing $16–$18 per day), parking is problematic throughout Boston, and you're better off without a car. △ *3 double rooms with baths, 2 studios for short-term rental. Air-conditioning, phone, kitchen area in rooms. $95–$160; full breakfast. No credit cards. No smoking, 2-night minimum Apr.–Nov.*

MARY PRENTISS INN 🗬
6 Prentiss St., Cambridge 02140, tel. 617/661–2929, fax 617/661–5989

Originally built in 1843 as a country estate for Cambridge resident William Augustus and his new wife, Mary Prentiss, this yellow Greek Revival house sits on what is now a narrow residential street just off busy Massachusetts Avenue. Innkeeper Charlotte Forsythe and her architect husband, Gerald, opened the inn in 1992 after extensive renovations that included adding a new wing and a spacious oasis of a deck. Some rooms have wide-board pumpkin-pine floors, antique armoires, original wooden shutters, Oriental rugs, and either four-poster or cannonball beds. Charlotte collects old photographs of young children, which are displayed throughout the inn.

A full breakfast—which may include fresh fruits, blintzes with strawberry sauce, quiche, or fresh-baked muffins—and afternoon tea are served in front of the fireplace in the breakfast room, or in mild weather, on the deck. Located ½ mi north of Harvard Square and a four-block walk from the Porter Square subway station (15 minutes to downtown Boston), the inn is just steps from the neighborhood's many eclectic restaurants, clothing stores, and one-of-a-kind gift shops. △ *14 double rooms with baths, 6 suites. Air-conditioning, cable TV, phone in rooms; wet bars in some rooms; limited free parking. $99–$179; full breakfast. AE, MC, V. No smoking, 2-night minimum some weekends, 3-night minimum holidays and college commencement weekends.*

NEWBURY GUEST HOUSE 🗬
261 Newbury St., Boston 02116, tel. 617/437–7666 or 800/437–7668, fax 617/262–4243

This trio of elegant redbrick and brownstone row houses was built in 1882 as private homes in Boston's fashionable Back Bay, still *the* place to live in Boston. A father-and-son team, Nubar and Mark Hagopian, bought the first four-story house in 1990 and, after extensive restoration and renovation, opened it as a B&B in January 1991. Not surprisingly (considering the location, the price, and the quality of the inn), business went well, and in 1994 the Hagopians expanded into the two neighboring buildings.

The location of this inn is perfect: Newbury Street—famous for its gas streetlamps, broad sidewalks, leaded windows, and neat front gardens—is the city's smartest shopping street, home to a wide selection of clothing stores, antiques shops, art galleries, hair salons, sidewalk cafés, restaurants, and trendy bars. It's also a short walk to the Public Garden, Boston Common, Copley Square, and many other attractions.

The first-floor lobby features an arched stained-glass window, hand-painted in the 1880s by an artist from Tiffany's. Stained-glass panels also adorn the entryway doors. Guest rooms open off the beautifully carved oak staircases of these tall, narrow houses. Several rooms have cherry four-poster or sleigh beds, nonworking fireplaces, and intricately cut plaster moldings; all feature reproduction Victorian furnishings, dark-stained pine or oak floors and rugs, queen-size beds, and prints from the Boston Museum of Fine Arts.

Throughout the house, "bay" guest rooms have couches and oriel windows that overlook Newbury Street; less expensive traditional rooms have wing chairs and are smaller.

A Continental breakfast of breads and pastries is served in the dining room with its Victorian furnishings; in summer guests can eat outside on the brick patio.

There's metered street parking just outside, and the inn offers a limited number of spaces to guests for $15 per night. You don't need a car here, but if you will have one, reserve a space in advance. △ *32 double rooms with baths. Air-conditioning, cable TV, phone in rooms; limited parking (fee). $100–$140; Continental breakfast. AE, MC, V. 2-night minimum weekends.*

OTHER CHOICES

A Cambridge House Bed-and-Breakfast. 2218 Massachusetts Ave., Cambridge 02140, tel. 617/491–6300 or 800/232–9989, fax 617/868–2848. 12 double rooms with baths, 1 single with bath, 3 doubles share 2 baths. Air-conditioning, cable TV, and phone in rooms; free parking. $109–$260; buffet breakfast, hors d'oeuvres, soft drinks. AE, D, DC, MC, V. No smoking, 2-night minimum weekends.

Beacon Hill Bed and Breakfast. 27 Brimmer St., Boston 02108, tel. 617/523–7376. 3 double rooms with baths. Air-conditioning, TV in rooms; elevator for luggage. $200–$225; full breakfast. No credit cards. No smoking.

RESERVATIONS SERVICES

Bed & Breakfast Agency of Boston (47 Commercial Wharf, Boston 02110, tel. 617/720–3540 or 800/248–9262, fax 617/523–5761). **Bed & Breakfast Associates Bay Colony Ltd.** (Box 57166, Babson Park Branch, Boston 02157, tel. 617/449–5302 or 800/347–5088, fax 617/449–5958). **Bed and Breakfast Cambridge and Greater Boston** (Box 1344, Cambridge 02238, tel. 617/262–1155 or 800/888–0178, fax 617/227–0021). **Bed and Breakfast Reservations: North Shore, Greater Boston, Cape Cod** (Box 35, Newtonville 02160, tel. 617/964–1606 or 800/832–2632, fax 617/332–8572). **Greater Boston Hospitality- A Bed and Breakfast Reservations Service** (Box 1142, Brookline 02146, tel. 617/277–5430). **New England Bed and Breakfast, Inc.** (1753 Massachusetts Ave., Cambridge 02138, tel. 617/498–9819).

North Shore

ADDISON CHOATE INN 🐦
49 Broadway, Rockport 01966, tel. 978/546–7543 or 800/245–7543, fax 978/546–7638

Rockport offers an excellent selection of inns, and the Addison Choate is one of the best. Shirley Johnson, an interior designer, bought the inn in 1992 with her husband, Knox, a landscape architect, and together they set about enhancing the historical character of an already attractive property.

Made of white clapboard, the long, narrow, two-story house, built in 1851, is rumored to be the site of Rockport's first bathtub. The living room has a Greek Revival mantel, cozy reading nooks, and classical antique furnishings. A Continental breakfast with home-baked goods is served in the dining room; in summer you can sit on the porch and gaze at the inn's perennial garden.

Spacious rooms in the main inn have big, tiled bathrooms. The navy and white Captain's Room has a dark-wood, four-poster canopy bed; polished pine floors; handmade quilts; New England rag rugs; and paintings of ships. The Chimney Room has a white brick chimney, wide-board floors, a Victorian maple bureau with a mirror, and a rocking chair with a hand-woven seat. Other rooms contain Hitchcock rockers and headboards, spool beds, quilts, local paintings, and wooden antiques. The third-floor Celebration Suite was converted from a loft, and its two huge windows have sea views over the rooftops. The bedroom has wide-plank pine floors, patterned fabrics, white wicker furniture, a TV, and a refrigerator.

Beyond the main building, the former stable house contains two one-bedroom apartments, and still farther back is a fenced-in swimming pool. The large apartments offer first-floor living space and kitchens; one contains an iron spiral staircase leading to a bedroom with cathedral ceilings, wooden beams, and a skylight; the other has a loft bedroom, stained-glass windows, and a patio.

Knox's hobby since childhood has been bird-watching, and he offers guided birding tours in the greater Rockport area. The inn, which is not suitable for young children, is a minute's walk from the town center and two blocks from the Rockport–Boston railway station. △ *5 double rooms with baths, 1 suite, 2 1-bedroom apartments. Air-conditioning in inn rooms, pool, free parking. $110–$140; Continental breakfast. D, MC, V. No smoking. 2-night minimum weekends, 3-night minimum July 4 weekend.*

CLARK CURRIER INN 🐦
45 Green St., Newburyport 01950, tel. 978/465–8363

Built by shipping merchant Thomas March Clark in 1803, this three-story clapboard mansion is a typical example of the Federal architecture for which Newburyport is famous. The interior has been completely renovated to reveal many period splendors, such as polished wide-plank floors, window seats, original Colonial-style shutters, woodstoves, and a Federal "good morning" staircase—so called because two small staircases join at the head of a large one, permitting family members to greet one another on their way down to breakfast.

Guest rooms, named after former owners or residents of the house, are all spacious and carefully decorated in period style and with Federal antiques. Some feature pencil-post beds, and one contains a sleigh bed dating from the late-19th century. Many of the rooms have fireplaces with carved-wood surrounds, but these are not in use. Typical of the Federal home, ceilings become lower as you reach the upper stories, so in first-floor rooms the ceilings are 11 ft high but only 7 ft on the third floor, where guest bedrooms are converted from former servants' quarters; upstairs, the ambience is less formal but still authentic.

Bob Nolan, an international banker and currency trader in New York City, and his wife, Mary, a political science teacher at Rutgers University in New Jersey, stepped out of their high-stress jobs back in 1990 to take on the Clark Currier. They wanted a more family-oriented lifestyle for themselves and their daughter, Melissa. Since taking over, they've opened up the ground floor to create a large living room with a working fireplace, antique desks couches, and bookcases. A second-floor library has books and writing desks and a display of antique toys on the landing outside. The inn offers a buffet-style breakfast of breads and muffins, afternoon tea, complimentary sherry in the evening, and such in-room extras as candy dishes—restocked daily by Melissa. In summer you can eat in the garden with its rocking chairs and gazebo. ⌂ *8 double rooms with baths. Air-conditioning, TV in garden room, free parking. $85–$155; Continental breakfast. AE, D, MC, V. No smoking.*

EDEN PINES INN ☞
48 Eden Rd., Rockport 01966, tel. 978/546–2505, fax 978/546–1157

Built in 1900 as a private summer cottage, Eden Pines stands so close to the ocean that the whole place seems about ready to sail off to sea—in fact, two of the wood decks already did, which prompted owner-managers Inge and John Sullivan to build a stormproof brick deck that has survived for years. The house looks out to the twin lights of Thatcher's Island; below the deck lie rocks and the raging (or lapping) waves. The Sullivans bought the inn nearly 30 years ago, and they use its location to the utmost. The large bedrooms have great ocean views, and six out of seven have secluded balconies. Rooms are eclectically furnished with a mixture of modern rattan or wicker, some canopy beds, and a few older pieces picked up at antiques shops. A fresh look predominates, however, with pastel blue, green, or yellow walls; modern floral fabrics; bright white moldings; and pastel-tone carpets. One room has a nonworking white brick fireplace. Most of the large bathrooms offer marble baths or vanities and brass fixtures.

Downstairs, the living room has a stone fireplace with a stone surround and dark-stained, pine-paneled, and white papered walls. The breakfast room, with its white trellises and wood-plank walls, opens onto the oceanside deck; the room's huge windows provide excellent sea views.

For even better ocean vistas, take a look at the Sullivans' other property just down the street, the four-bedroom Eden Point House, which they rent by the week. It stands on a rock, surrounded by the sea on three sides, and is done in a contemporary, open-plan design, with a semicircular living room; a stone, floor-to-ceiling fireplace surround; a high cathedral ceiling; and a large, modern kitchen.

Eden Pines Inn and Eden Point House are a five-minute drive from Rockport center and two minutes by car from the nearest beach. ⌂ *7 double rooms with baths. Air-conditioning, cable TV in rooms, croquet. $100–$165; Continental breakfast. MC, V. No smoking, 3-night minimum holiday weekends. Closed mid-Nov.–mid-May.*

HARBOR LIGHT INN 🐚
58 Washington St., Marblehead 01945, tel. 781/631–2186, fax 781/631–2216

On a bustling narrow street at the heart of Marblehead's historic district, this Federal-style inn competes with the Clark Currier Inn in Newburyport as one of the classiest, most relaxing, and most authentic inns on the whole of the North Shore. If you take the Harbor Light Room and stand on tiptoe, you can see the lighthouse in the harbor; otherwise you'll only have an occasional glimpse of the sea. Nevertheless, you're bound to be impressed with the building's interior— wide-board floors, chintz chairs, silver ice buckets and candy bowls, original shutters that fold into the wall, and Chinese rugs. As for the beds, you can choose between a pencil-post bed and a hand-carved mahogany four-poster bed with a floral canopy. Bathrooms have huge mirrors and skylights, and some contain whirlpool baths as well.

The old building dates from the early 1700s, with one wing constructed in the 19th century. When innkeepers Peter and Suzanne Conway bought the place in a state of disrepair in 1986, they opened up the third floor and added a completely new section to the back of the house. They're veteran, energetic innkeepers, whose hard work and attention to detail have resulted in a luxurious inn with excellent amenities but undisturbed original features. The character of the rooms varies tremendously—those in the earlier structure have more original features, such as arched doorways, working fireplaces, and wide-board floors. On the third floor, however, rooms have skylights, exposed brick, cathedral ceilings, and wooden beams. In the new addition, rooms are modern in concept and in decor, and some have decks.

In 1992 the innkeepers bought the building next door and over the next year expanded the inn, adding seven more big, beautiful bedrooms with working fireplaces, four-poster beds, and painted wood paneling. One room has an old-fashioned bathroom with a claw-foot tub; the top-floor rooms have exposed beams and large, modern bathrooms. The inn has two parlors with Chippendale furniture, wing chairs, and open fireplaces; Continental breakfast is served in the dining room. Sophisticated, older children may enjoy the elegant atmosphere, but it's best to leave the littlest ones at home. ♙ *20 double rooms with baths, 1 suite. Air-conditioning, cable TV in rooms, meeting room, pool. $95–$245; Continental breakfast. AE, MC, V. No smoking in public rooms, 2-night minimum weekends, 3-night minimum holiday weekends.*

YANKEE CLIPPER INN 🐚
96 Granite St. (Box 2399), Rockport 01966, tel. 978/546–3407 or 800/545–3699, fax 978/546–9730

The white Georgian mansion that forms the main part of this imposing, perfectly located Cape Ann establishment stands surrounded by gardens, challenging the waves from a rocky headland. Constructed as a private home in the 1930s, this three-story oblong building with big square windows has been managed as an inn by one family for more than 50 years. Guest rooms in the mansion vary in size, but they're generally large; because the sea is on three sides, most rooms have fabulous views. Many also offer weatherized porches, such as the one that wraps around the enormous suite where John and Jacqueline Kennedy stayed when the late president was still a Massachusetts senator. Furnished with Queen Anne– and Victorian-style reproductions, the rooms contain four-poster or canopy beds, chaise longues, and wicker porch furniture.

Across the lawns in a newer structure called the Quarterdeck, picture windows in all the rooms provide impressive ocean views. Modern and stylish, the spacious (some are huge), well-designed rooms have floral wallpaper, seascape paintings, large bathrooms, and sitting areas with wing chairs and modern couches.

On the other side of the street from the main inn is the Bullfinch House, an 1840 Greek Revival home, appointed with dark wood antiques, floral wallpapers, lacy curtains, and pineapple four-poster beds.

Guests dine at the main inn on a sunny porch with wrought-iron chairs, again overlooking the sea. Just behind the porch, the lounge has a huge fireplace with a mahogany surround and large floral stencils at either side. Dusky pink tones, pink velvet couches, and heavy-framed painted portraits re-create a Victorian atmosphere. Below the lounge a conference center caters to business clientele. The well-managed inn has a friendly staff, and careful touches abound—the outdoor swimming pool, for example, is attractively landscaped and virtually invisible from the road. The Yankee Clipper is more than 1 mi north of Rockport, so guests will need transport in and out of town. ☖ *21 double rooms with baths, 5 suites. Restaurant, air-conditioning, phone in rooms; TV in some rooms; whirlpool baths, pool. $109–$269; full breakfast in peak season, Continental breakfast off-season. AE, D, MC, V. No. Closed mid–Dec.–Feb.*

OTHER CHOICES

Inn on Cove Hill. 37 Mt. Pleasant St., Rockport 01966, tel. 978/546–2701 or 888/546–2701. 9 double rooms with baths, 2 doubles share bath. Air-conditioning, fans, TV in rooms. $48–$113; Continental breakfast. MC, V. No smoking, 2-night minimum July–Aug. and weekends May–June and Sept.–Oct. Closed mid-Oct.–mid-Apr.

Miles River Country Inn. 823 Bay Rd. (Box 149), Hamilton 01936, tel. 978/468–7206. 5 double rooms (1 can be rented with an adjacent area that has a single bed) with baths, 2 doubles share bath. Air-conditioning, TV in sitting room. $84–$195; full breakfast. AE, MC, V. No smoking, 2-night minimum weekends June–Sept. Closed Christmas week.

Tuck Inn. 17 High St., Rockport 01966, tel. 978/546–7260 or 800/789–7260. 10 double rooms with baths, 2 suites, 1 apartment. Air-conditioning, cable TV in rooms, pool, free parking. $75–$95; Continental breakfast. MC, V. No smoking, 2-night minimum weekends May–Oct.

RESERVATIONS SERVICES

Bed and Breakfast Associates Bay Colony Ltd. (Box 57166, Babson Park Branch, Boston 02157, tel. 617/449–5302 or 800/347–5088, fax 617/449–5958).
Bed and Breakfast Reservations: North Shore, Greater Boston, Cape Cod (Box 35, Newtonville 02160, tel. 617/964–1606 or 800/832–2632, fax 617/332–8572).

The Pioneer Valley

ALLEN HOUSE VICTORIAN INN ☙

599 Main St., Amherst 01002, tel. 413/253–5000

Dozens of bed-and-breakfast inns fall under the general term of "country-style"— and a few do have good antiques and interesting decor. But inns that are restored with historic precision and attention to every last detail are rare indeed: The Allen House, honored with a Historic Preservation Award from the Amherst Historical Commission in 1991, is one of them.

Alan Zieminski, a former biochemist at the University of Massachusetts, has lived in the 1886 Queen Anne stick-style house since the late '60s. He bought it in 1988, and once he and his wife, Ann, began to put their vague ideas of restoration into practice, the project took on a life of its own. Along with Alan's brother, Jonas, the family soon became experts in the Aesthetic period—a Victorian movement heavily influenced by trade with Japan.

Guest rooms are museumlike representations of the Aesthetic era. They have impressive period wallpapers, and sunflowers, the Aesthetics' emblem, are everywhere. Furnishings include some original Charles Eastlake pieces, such as the matching burled-walnut headboard and dresser in the upstairs Eastlake room; other rooms have Eastlake reproductions, wicker "steamship" chairs (replicas of those used aboard steamships of this era), pedestal sinks, screens, carved golden oak or brass beds, goose-down comforters, painted wood floors, and claw-foot tubs. Public areas are just as impressive: The breakfast room has Anglo-Japanese reproduction wallpapers and an intricately carved fireplace; its floor is covered with grass reed matting imported from Japan. The sitting room floor also has reed matting, which is topped by an 1880s Oriental hand-stitched rug.

When the Zieminskis bought the house, it was a kind of time capsule of original, if faded, relics. The upstairs hallway is lined with pictures found stashed away in a locked room. Modern advantages are tourist information, poetry books, afternoon tea, a hearty cooked breakfast, and free pickup service from the nearby train and bus stations. The inn is a short walk from the center of Amherst, rates are reasonable, and the hosts—who seem a little overwhelmed by what they've achieved—are extremely pleasant company. ♧ *7 double rooms with baths. Air-conditioning, phone in rooms, free parking. $45–$135; full breakfast, afternoon tea. D, MC, V. Smoking on veranda only, 2-night minimum in summer, 3-night minimum foliage and special college-events weekends.*

DEERFIELD INN ☙

81 Old Main St., Deerfield 01342, tel. 413/774–5587 or 800/926–3865, fax 413/773–8712

Perfectly situated on a street that's lined with museums, the peaceful Deerfield Inn, with its columned facade and white-clapboard exterior, harks back to a gentler era. Built in 1884, it was substantially modernized after a fire in 1981, which explains the square, spacious guest rooms—reminiscent of more modern hotels. The style and grace of the light, airy interior owe much to the flair and imagination of the young, enthusiastic innkeepers, Karl Sabo and his English wife, Jane, who bought the place in 1987, leaving their fast-track lives in New York's Greenwich Village for "something different."

The couple has worked hard on redecoration; for example, they've had reproduction period wallpapers custom designed for the reception room, tavern, and many of the bedrooms. Guest rooms have light floral themes and are furnished with sofas, bureaus, eclectic Federal-style antiques, and replicas of Queen Anne beds and Chippendale chairs. Some rooms have four-poster or canopy beds. Green, quilted "TV cozies" hide the televisions when you don't want the modern world to intrude.

The large, sunny, first-floor dining room is elegantly decorated with Federal-style chairs and antique side tables and is graced with candlelight in the evening. The contemporary American cuisine is first-rate, giving the inn a well-deserved reputation for dining. Specialties change with the seasons, but they may include Atlantic salmon served over spinach-studded angel hair pasta or maple-glazed boneless pork loin. A cheerful café that opens onto the terrace serves inexpensive sandwiches and salads during the day.

The inn is formal enough to make your stay a special event but friendly enough to create a relaxed and welcoming atmosphere. Just down the road are the dozen 17th- and early 18th-century house museums of Historic Deerfield which provide year-round lectures and tours. The Barnard Tavern has a ballroom with a fiddlers' gallery and several hands-on displays: You can climb into the rope bed and write on the slates. The Memorial Hall Museum has displays about the Native American Pocumtuck as well as relics from the village's history. ♠ *23 double rooms with baths (2 rooms wheelchair accessible). Restaurant, café, lounge; air-conditioning, TV, phone in rooms. $169–$241; full breakfast. AE, DC, MC, V. No smoking. Closed Dec. 24–26.*

STURBRIDGE COUNTRY INN ☞
530 Main St. (Box 60), Sturbridge 01566, tel. 508/347–5503, fax 508/347–5319

This white 1840s building has a Greek Revival facade more evocative of a grand municipal edifice than the farmhouse that this once was. Guest rooms, all of which have working fireplaces, are furnished with Colonial reproductions that blend with the modern design. And every room has a whirlpool bath.

Upstairs, Rooms 7 and 8 are good choices. One has wicker furnishings, the other brass; both have a sunporch, exposed hand-hewn beams, and steps that lead down from the whirlpool bath to a large bedroom. The suite occupies the entire third floor and has cathedral ceilings, a large whirlpool bath in the living room, a wet bar, and big windows. Try to avoid the one very small first-floor room; the plumbing gurgles, and whirlpool tubs upstairs tend to reverberate downstairs.

Innkeeper Patricia MacConnell, whose brother owns the establishment, has a light Continental breakfast set up for you in the first-floor lounge. Here you'll also find an open fireplace and Colonial-style furnishings and decor that blend remarkably well with the open, 20th-century floor plan and cathedral ceilings. The innkeepers try to maintain a romantic atmosphere that is not suitable for young children. In summer you can relax—despite the street noise—in the garden gazebo, and Old Sturbridge Village is just a short walk away. Next door, the Stageloft Repertory Theatre performs year round. ♠ *6 double rooms with baths, 3 suite. Air-conditioning, cable TV, fireplace, whirlpool bath in rooms; TV/VCR in some rooms. $69–$159; Continental breakfast. AE, D, MC, V. No smoking in rooms.*

OTHER CHOICES

Brandt House. 29 Highland Ave., Greenfield 01301, tel. 413/774–3329 or 800/235–3329, fax 413/772–2908. 6 double rooms with baths, 2 doubles share bath. Air-conditioning, cable TV, and phone in rooms; TV/VCR in some rooms; tennis court. $90–$165; Continental breakfast weekdays, full breakfast weekends. AE, D, MC, V. No smoking.

Publick House and Colonel Ebenezer Crafts Inn. Rte. 131, On-the-Common, Sturbridge 01566, tel. 508/347–3313 or 800/782–5425, fax 508/347–5073. 17 double rooms with baths (Publick House); 8 doubles with bath (Crafts Inn). 3 restaurants, bar, air-conditioning, meeting rooms, tennis court, outdoor pool, shuffleboard, playground (Publick House); air-conditioning, outdoor pool (Crafts Inn). $59–$155; Continental breakfast (Crafts Inn). AE, DC, MC, V.

Yankee Pedlar Inn. 1866 Northampton St. (Box 6206), Holyoke 01040-6206, tel. 413/532–9494, fax 413/536–8877. 18 double rooms with baths, 10 suites. Restaurant, bar; air-conditioning, cable TV in rooms; 8 banquet rooms. $65–$125; Continental breakfast. AE, D, DC, MC, V. Closed Dec. 25.

RESERVATIONS SERVICE

Berkshire Bed and Breakfast Homes (Main St., Box 211, Williamsburg 01096, tel. 413/268–7244, fax 413/268–7243).

The Berkshires

APPLE TREE INN ☙
10 Richmond Mountain Rd., Lenox 01240, tel. 413/637–1477, fax 413/637–2528

This country inn has a fantastic setting on a gently sloping hillside with marvelous views over the Stockbridge Bowl and Laurel Lake. It's also across the street from Tanglewood's main gates. In fact, you're so close to the music festival that you don't even need a ticket—you can listen to concerts from the inn's own gardens amid 450 varieties of roses and surrounded by 22 acres of apple orchards.

The main building, constructed in 1885, has public areas that are furnished with Victorian antiques, including a massive wooden bench. You enter through the parlor, with its arches, Persian rugs, open fireplace, velvet couches, and grand piano. In the tavern oak-paneled walls support a collection of old tools and a water-buffalo head that stares out over the fireplace. The main restaurant, a circular 1960s addition, has a marqueelike ceiling with spokes of lightbulbs. Picture windows afford excellent views of the lawns and orchards.

Upstairs, guest rooms are furnished with antiques, including four-poster and brass beds, Victorian washstands, and wicker pieces. Four rooms have working fireplaces, and several have window seats with fabulous views. The generally spacious rooms have unusual shapes that add to their character; this is particularly true of rooms on the top floor, which have eaves, gables, and skylights. It's best to avoid some of the smaller rooms, especially Room 5 (Woodside), which is over the kitchen and can be hot and noisy. The nearby lodge has 21 motel-like rooms.

The Apple Tree Inn has an interesting past and once belonged to Alice of the Arlo Guthrie song "Alice's Restaurant"—though she catered primarily to diners, not guests. Owners Joel Catalano and Sharon Walker relocated from New York City when they bought the inn in 1996. ♣ *10 double rooms with baths, 2 doubles share bath, 2 suites (inn); 21 doubles with bath (lodge). Restaurant, tavern, air-conditioning in rooms, cable TV in suites and lodge rooms, pool, tennis court. $130–$300; Continental breakfast. AE, D, DC, MC, V. 3-night minimum weekends July–Aug.*

BLANTYRE ☙

16 Blantyre Rd. (off Rte. 20), Lenox 01240, tel. 413/637–3556, fax 413/637–4282

Surrounded by 100 magnificent acres, the palatial Blantyre was built in 1901 and has a Tudor style that is unique to the region (its design is based on an ancestral Scottish home). Senator John Fitzpatrick and his family, who also own the Inn in Stockbridge, acquired the estate in 1980 and with it the mammoth task of restoration. Some of the furnishings in the great hall are original, as are the plaster relief ceilings, the intricately carved oak paneling, and the leather-backed wallpaper.

Although the hall, with its heavy wooden furnishings (including a rocking horse in full heraldic gear), appears imposingly solemn, the long, cream-tone music room next door evokes a lighter mood, with inlaid chess tables, an antique Steinway grand piano, a harp, antique Dutch and Italian cabinets, and exquisite chairs and couches. Doors open onto a terrace set with tables overlooking two large, perfectly manicured croquet lawns.

Staying at Blantyre is an expensive proposition, so make the most of it by reserving one of the five largest rooms in the main house (and by leaving the children at home). Although the entire property is stylishly finished, rooms in the carriage house and cottages don't quite compare with these spacious accommodations, which have hand-carved four-poster beds, bay windows, high ceilings, working fireplaces, chintz chairs, overstuffed chaise longues, boudoirs, walk-in closets, and Victorian bathrooms. The huge Paterson Suite has two bathrooms; a sitting room with a fireplace; a pineapple four-poster bed; and pale green wallpaper, linens, and draperies. If the larger main-house rooms are booked, the smaller Ashley Suite or the carriage house's split-level suites beside the pool are next best.

The first-rate service rests in the hands of Scottish manager Roderick Anderson. The many extras include bathrobes, toiletries, newspapers, turndown service, and mineral water, cheese, and fruit. ♣ *13 double rooms with baths, 10 suites. Restaurant; air-conditioning, cable TV, phone in rooms; room service, pool, whirlpool bath, sauna, 4 tennis courts, 2 croquet lawns, walking trails. $285–$675; Continental breakfast. AE, DC, MC, V. 2-night minimum Oct. and weekends. Closed early Nov.–mid-May.*

FIELD FARM ☙

554 Sloan Rd. (off Rte. 43), Williamstown 01267, tel. and fax 413/458–3135

Neither your average B&B nor your typical Berkshire cottage estate, this former home of art collector Lawrence H. Bloedel has been owned by the Trustees of Reservations since 1984 and is now managed by innkeepers Sean and Jean Cowhig. The stark geometric exterior of this modern (1948) structure, with its cedar shingles painted beige, contrasts unromantically with the region's profusion of period homes. But consider its advantages: 296 acres of private, wooded grounds containing a pond, a pool, a tennis court, and trails for hiking or cross-country skiing. The place is not yet well known, and because it has only five guest rooms, staying here is like living on your own country estate.

The interior is unashamedly square in shape, and the house, designed as a sort of display case for Bloedel's art collection (which went to the Williams College museum after his death), feels a bit like a modern museum. In 1994 the college returned eight pieces on long-term loan, and they are now displayed in the public areas. Most of the oak, cherry, and walnut furniture was handmade by Bloedel, and others are 1950s Scandinavian-modern pieces he collected—even the plastic doorknobs were custom made, quite a coup in the 1940s. Modern sculptures decorate the gardens. The first-floor guest room and upstairs master bedroom are huge, and all bedrooms have modern furnishings and big picture windows with views over the grounds toward distant hills. Three bedrooms have private decks, and two have working fireplaces surrounded by custom-made tiles depicting animals, birds, and butterflies.

Downstairs in the large public sitting room, you'll discover another working fireplace and more modern art. You can use the pantry, which has a refrigerator, toaster, and wineglasses, to make your own lunch, snacks, or cocktails; the veranda is a good place to enjoy a breakfast of fresh breads with homemade jams, granola, eggs, or French toast or to sip an afternoon drink. ⬧ *5 double rooms with baths. Pool, pond (fishing poles available), tennis, cross-country skiing. $100–$125; full breakfast. D, MC, V. Smoking on decks and verandas only.*

MERRELL INN ℘
1565 Pleasant St. (Rte. 102), South Lee/Stockbridge 01260, tel. 413/243–1794 or 800/243–1794, fax 413/243–2669

Believe it or not, this Federal-style red-clapboard building with a columned facade remained uninhabited for almost 100 years. When the present owners bought it in 1981, they restored the building and installed heat, running water, and electricity. In the process they created one of the most authentic inns in the Berkshires—one that's on the National Register of Historic Places. Owners Charles and Faith Reynolds are retired schoolteachers who were honored with a Preservation Award from the Massachusetts Historical Commission in 1982.

Built about 1794 and turned into a stagecoach inn in 1817, the lodging is blessed with some good-size guest rooms. They have polished wide-board floors, area rugs, painted-plaster walls, iron door latches, and mellow wood antiques. Most beds are pencil four-posters, and some have simple white canopies. Three rooms contain working, Count Rumford–style, wood-burning fireplaces. The necessity of abiding by a 500-year covenant that protects the building's historic status means small (but beautifully decorated) bathrooms—on the third floor, where rooms were built in the shell of the old ballroom, some bathrooms are housed in the former drovers' sleeping quarters.

The original keeping room, now the guest parlor, has a beehive oven as well as a large cooking fireplace with a Franklin stove. A breakfast of pancakes, French toast, or omelets is served in the original tavern room, which contains an open fireplace and the only complete "birdcage" Colonial bar in America. Look for the 19th-century detail: The wood grain on the bar and the doors is hand-painted, not natural; the pulley wheels on the ceiling were used to raise and lower the original candle chandelier (now in a Boston museum). The inn is about a mile east of Stockbridge, beside busy Route 102, but it's well back from the road. Behind the building, 2 acres of landscaped gardens with a gazebo descend gently to the Housatonic River. A grand suite has recently been added, with a private balcony overlooking the river. ⬧ *9 double rooms with baths, 1 suite. Air-conditioning, TV room, phone in rooms. $75–$250; full breakfast. MC, V. No smoking. 3-night* *minimum summer and holiday weekends, 2-night minimum other weekends. Closed Dec. 24–25.*

RIVER BEND FARM 🐚
643 Simonds Rd., Williamstown 01267, tel. 413/458–5504 or 413/458–3121

One of the oldest buildings in the Berkshires, this property was constructed in 1770 by Col. Benjamin Simonds, a founder of Williamstown and a commissioned officer of the Berkshire militia during the American Revolution. The restoration of River Bend Farm is totally authentic, and it is listed on the National Register of Historic Places. A stay here transports you to another era.

You enter through the kitchen (called the keeping room) and are greeted by an open-range stove and an oven hung with dried herbs. Chairs hang on pegs on the walls Shaker-style, and the room is filled with 18th- and 19th-century country antiques, from wooden washtubs and spoon racks to flatirons and cooking implements. Also downstairs is a small formal sitting room with a fireplace, but "formal" only means the walls are plastered—upstairs it's another story. Bedroom walls consist of wide wood panels, some of them painted in their original colors (owners Dave and Judy Loomis, who restored the building, scraped their way through layers of paper and paint to discover them). Others are whitewashed or made of simple, scrubbed wide planks, as are the floors and doors. Window treatments are tab curtains (no hooks, just cloth loops) of unbleached muslin. Accurate Colonial-style reproductions of candle chandeliers hang from the ceilings, and sconces with candles are fixed to the walls. Some rooms have brick (nonworking) fireplaces and antique four-poster or canopy beds. Other antique pieces include a spinning wheel here, a wing chair or a chamber pot there.

Speaking of chamber pots . . . the farm's only disadvantage is that four guest rooms share two bathrooms, one of which is on the ground floor. The first-floor bathroom is an absolute Aladdin's cave of utilitarian antiques, including washbowls, jugs, lamps, butter tubs, and hanging herbs.

Outdoors you have access to the river for canoeing, and you can visit a warm spring pool, ¼ mi upriver. Williamstown is about an eight-minute drive away. 🜂 *4 double rooms share 2 baths. $80–$100; Continental breakfast. No credit cards. No smoking, 2-night minimum during college-events weekends. Closed late Oct.–Mar.*

WHISTLER'S INN 🐚
5 Greenwood St., Lenox 01240, tel. 413/637–0975, fax 413/637–2190

Elegant, ornate, and somehow exotic, Whistler's Inn stands apart from its nearby competitors, with lavish Louis XVI antiques in the parlor; heavy, dark wood furniture in the baronial dining hall; and African artifacts in the office. Innkeepers Joan and Richard Mears, with their easy style, maintain an extraordinary ambience at this English Tudor mansion, built in 1820 by railroad tycoon Ross Wynans Whistler.

The Mearses, who have owned Whistler's since 1978, are widely traveled hosts and great conversationalists. Richard, a published novelist, and Joan, formerly a teacher of art and English, continue to work on new writing projects.

Public rooms are impressive, with Chippendale furniture, ornate antiques (including Louis XVI palace mirrors, candelabra, clocks, and love seats), chandeliers, original artwork, Persian rugs, and marble fireplaces. A Steinway grand piano graces the music room–parlor, and next door is a well-stocked library, where you can partake of complimentary sherry, port, or afternoon tea. The dining room or the sunporch provides a restful setting for breakfast. Be sure to peek at the Mearses' first-floor office—it features many souvenirs brought back from their travels, including African pieces and a large wooden elephant puppet from a maharaja's palace.

Guest rooms are attractively decorated with designer draperies and bedspreads. They vary in size from the large master bedroom to two small chambers beneath the eaves. All are furnished with antiques (one has a Chippendale armoire), and some have working fireplaces. Most rooms have superb views across the small valley that includes 7 acres of private gardens, a croquet lawn, and a badminton court. This peaceful place is only a short walk from the center of Lenox. ♠ *14 double rooms with baths. Dining room, air-conditioning in most rooms, phone in rooms, croquet, badminton. $90–$225; full breakfast, afternoon tea. AE, D, MC, V. No smoking, 3-night minimum weekends July–Aug. and Oct.*

OTHER CHOICES

Candlelight Inn. 35 Walker St., Lenox 01240, tel. 413/637–1555 or 800/428–0580. 8 double rooms with baths. Restaurant, bar, air-conditioning, TV in sitting room. $95–$175; Continental breakfast. AE, MC, V. 3-night minimum weekends July–Aug. Inn and restaurant closed Tues. in winter.

Gables Inn. 81 Walker St., Lenox 01240, tel. 413/637–3416 or 800/382–9401. 14 double rooms with baths, 4 suites. Air-conditioning, cable TV in rooms, TV/VCR in suites. $80–$210; full breakfast. D, MC, V. No smoking in guest rooms or breakfast room, 3-night minimum during Tanglewood, 2-night minimum fall and holiday weekends.

Gateways Inn. 51 Walker St., Lenox 01240, tel. 413/637–2532 or 888/492–9466, fax 413/637–1423. 11 double rooms with baths, 1 suite. Restaurant, air-conditioning, cable TV, and phone in rooms; restaurant. $105–$325; Continental breakfast. AE, D, DC, MC, V. Smoking on porch only.

The Orchards. 222 Adams Rd. (Rte. 2), Williamstown 01267, tel. 413/458–9611 or 800/225–1517, fax 413/458–3273. 49 double rooms with baths. Restaurant, tavern; air-conditioning, cable TV/VCR in rooms; room service, pool, exercise room with sauna and whirlpool. $165–$230; breakfast not included, afternoon tea. AE, DC, MC, V. 2-night minimum weekends July–Oct., 3-night minimum college commencement weekends.

Turning Point Inn. 3 Lake Buel Rd. (R.D. 2, Box 140), Great Barrington 01230, tel. 413/528–4777. 4 double rooms with baths, 2 doubles share bath, 1 cottage. Fans in rooms, TV in lounge, cross-country ski trail. $80–$115 (full breakfast), cottage $220 (breakfast extra). AE, MC, V. No smoking, 3-night minimum weekends July–Aug.

Wheatleigh. Hawthorne Rd., Lenox 01240, tel. 413/637–0610, fax 413/637–4507. 17 double rooms with baths. Restaurant, air-conditioning, TV/VCR and phone in rooms, room service; tennis, pool, fitness room, massage room. $175–$625; breakfast not included. AE, DC, MC, V. 3-night minimum during Tanglewood and holiday weekends.

Windflower Inn. 684 S. Egremont Rd., Great Barrington 01230, tel. 413/528–2720 or 800/992–1993, fax 413/528–5147. 13 double rooms with baths. Air-conditioning, TV in rooms, pool. $100–$180; full breakfast, afternoon tea. AE. Smoking in living room only, 3-night minimum summer weekends and holidays, 2-night minimum other weekends in foliage season.

RESERVATIONS SERVICES

American Country Collection of B&B (1353 Union St., Schenectady, NY 12308, tel. 518/370–4948 or 800/810–4948, fax 518/393–1634). **Berkshire Bed and Breakfast Homes** (Main St., Box 211, Williamsburg 01096, tel. 413/268–7244, fax 413/268–7243). **New England Hospitality Network** (Box 3291, Newport, RI 02840, tel. 401/849–1298 or 800/828–0000, fax 401/849–1306). **Nutmeg B&B Agency** (Box 1117, West Hartford, CT 06127, tel. 860/236–6698 or 800/727–7592, fax 860/232–7680).

MICHIGAN

Southeastern Michigan, Including Ann Arbor and Detroit

MONTAGUE INN

1581 S. Washington Ave., Saginaw 48601, tel. 517/752–3939, fax 517/752–3159

Robert Montague was a respected businessman and civic leader when he built his 12,000-square-ft Georgian house—all of handmade brick—in 1929 in Saginaw's historic Grove District. To help preserve important landmarks of the district—once an enclave of stunning residences—the city bought Montague's home in the early 1960s and demolished several of the more rickety surrounding properties. Then a group of five entrepreneurial-minded couples bought it from the city in 1985. Eight months later, they reopened the restored mansion and the adjacent carriage house as the Montague Inn. Not only has the three-story brick mansion been named to the State Register of Historic Places, but it is also considered one of Michigan's best inns, a designation that's hard to dispute.

The inn's location on 8 gently rolling acres overlooking Lake Linton is a mixed blessing. There is usually a lot of activity on the grounds, and on days when the city park across the water is staging a concert or a raft race, there can be a large volume of traffic in the area. Caveat noted, the inn is still a champion. A winding staircase connects the three floors of guest rooms. The Georgian-style quarters typically contain four-poster beds and wing chairs and are tastefully decorated in subtle hues and patterns. The most compelling—and at $160 per night, the most expensive—is the elegant two-room Montague Suite, which features a fireplace, green Pewabic tile, and great views of the impeccably landscaped grounds. Other interesting accommodations are in the former chauffeur's quarters and the cleverly renovated five-car garage.

Guests enjoy a Continental breakfast of oatmeal, cereals, juice, and baked goods in the dining room. Lunches and candlelight dinners are first-class affairs, too, with an expansive (and expensive) menu and wine list. After meals—everything from asparagus ravioli to honey-marinated quail—logs are lighted in the fireplace of the main-floor library, and guests can look for the hidden cabinets inside the library walls, where Montague stashed his expensive liquor during Prohibition (by special request, you can even dine in a secret alcove behind a bookcase). Other guests choose to wander in the extensive herb and flower garden, participate in one of the inn's exciting events (Independence Day picnic, black-tie New Year's Eve dinner, or summer herb-garden luncheons), or just pen a postcard at the antique writing desk. Those who scrawl "Wish you were here" know what they're talking about. ♙ *16 double rooms with baths, 2 doubles share bath,*

1 suite. Restaurant, air-conditioning, phone and TV in rooms. $65–$160; Continental breakfast. AE, MC, V. No smoking.

RAYMOND HOUSE INN ☙
111 S. Ridge St., Port Sanilac 48469, tel. 810/622–8800 or 800/622–7229

As the inn's owners, Shirley and Ray Denison, enjoy pointing out, there is no McDonald's in Port Sanilac. The retired couple do what they can to keep the golden arches at bay by heading a movement to have this old port village declared a Historic Maritime District, thereby limiting commercial development.

Port Sanilac sits halfway up the eastern edge of the Thumb region on Route 25, about 30 mi north of Port Huron and less than two hours from Detroit. It was one of Lake Huron's first ports of call during the heyday of steamship lines. Its colorful history includes lumberjacks, lake storms, rum-running, and forest fires that more than once destroyed the town. The port's history is honored in the newly opened shipwreck and maritime center.

The background of this comfortable, impressive Victorian house, which is listed on the State Register of Historic Places, is a little calmer but nevertheless significant. In 1850, Uri Raymond, the original owner, opened what is reputed to be the first hardware store in the state (Raymond Hardware, just a block down the road, is still in business). Raymond built his three-story brick residence in 1871, adorning it with classic Victorian touches: elaborate moldings and a winding oak staircase inside and a gingerbread facade with dripping white icicle trim outside. It stayed in the family for the next 112 years until Ray and Shirley— he's a retired Washington lobbyist for the AFL-CIO, she's an artist and conservation expert who in 1976 reframed the Constitution for the Bicentennial—bought it in 1983 and moved here from Washington, D.C.

The house, set on an acre planted with trees and gardens of wildflowers, was in good condition and is now full of family heirlooms, antiques, and numerous examples of Shirley's considerable artistic and restorative skills. She has recaned the chairs, restored the frames that hold a collection of old family photos in an upstairs hallway, and designed the clock in the dining room (she also designs and crafts artistic dolls). The upstairs quarters are authentically furnished, down to crocheted lacework on the window shades, handmade quilts, and hand-crocheted rugs. Lake Huron, 500 ft away, can be spied from upstairs. ♟ *7 double rooms with baths. Air-conditioning, cable TV and phone in rooms, fireplace in parlor. $65–$115; full breakfast. AE, D, MC, V. No smoking. Closed Dec.–Apr.*

STACY MANSION ☙
710 W. Chicago Blvd., Tecumseh 49286, tel. 517/423–6979

The story of one of the state's grandest homes can be gleaned from a quick look inside its first-floor library. On a desktop, the 1874 *Historical Atlas of Lenawee County* is opened to a sketch of the four-story brick mansion as it looked when Judge C. A. Stacy owned it. Directly above the open book hangs a buffalo head, provided by the current owners, Sonny and Joyce Lauber, who, among their other business interests, run one of the few bison farms in the country.

Stacy, newspaper publisher, businessman, and the first probate judge in the county, built the 8,000-square-ft house in the mid-1850s in anticipation of using it as the governor's residence. He lost the gubernatorial election but held on to the house, which has fine examples of 19th-century craftsmanship such as a foyer with marbled wood and a rare cantilevered staircase.

"Sonny drove past the house for 25 years and always talked about buying it," says Joyce. When the badly neglected building on the outskirts of Tecumseh came on the market in 1988, the Laubers didn't think twice. The house had been stripped of nearly everything—from the furnishings to the brass doorknobs and gingerbread trim—so restoration has been a slow, expensive process. To their credit, they have taken time to research—and have spent the money necessary to recall—its 19th-century ambience. They tore out the carpeting, restored the floors and woodwork, and replicated the plasterwork. They also researched historical wallpapers and were even able to buy back some of the furniture from former owners and area real-estate agents. All told, the house "is about 95% antiques," says Joyce. One bedroom has a double-mirrored wardrobe, another an 8½-ft-high, ornately carved walnut headboard. The only incongruous item is the water-filled mattress in the master bedroom. "We couldn't find a mattress that would fit the odd-sized mahogany full-tester bed," she explains.

During your stay, a morning "wake-up" tray of tea, coffee, juice, and homemade coffee cake is brought to your door, followed later by a full gourmet breakfast in the formal dining room.

The 1¼-acre site is expertly landscaped. Judge Stacy, who owned a local brickyard, would certainly approve of the 45,000 bricks the Laubers used to create the paths that wind through the yards and gardens. A 150-year-old pine tree shades a formal garden often abloom with annuals and perennials and accented with wrought-iron garden furniture, while old-fashioned street lamps and red maple trees flank the circular drive and help to make the outdoors an appealing retreat in itself. △ *5 double rooms with baths. Air-conditioning, phone in sitting room. $85–$120; full breakfast. MC, V. No smoking indoors.*

VICTORIAN INN ☜
1229 7th St., Port Huron 48060, tel. 810/984–1437

This inn, once one of Port Huron's most magnificent houses, the old James A. Davidson residence, is now safely in the hands of Marvin and Susan Burke, onetime guests who couldn't resist buying the place in 1997. Davidson, founder of a large furniture and dry goods company that bore his name, had built the elaborate Queen Anne house in 1896 and lived in it until his death in 1911. In 1983 the place was totally renovated, per the original architectural plans and spec sheets. Halfway through the project, the house was placed on the State Register of Historic Places. The result is a harmonious combination of luxurious lodging and fine dining in a neighborhood of well-maintained Victorian-era buildings that has become a travel destination in itself.

The common rooms are warm and comfortable, with green and rose-patterned carpets and coordinated cabbage-rose wallpapers and trims. The living room has a gray-brick fireplace and lush lilac settee and is popular for weddings. The second-floor guest rooms are similar blends of antique furnishings and little flourishes: a needlepoint headboard, a papier-mâché picture frame. Two rooms have modern private baths, one with a whirlpool tub, and the Devonshire and Burkshire rooms share a pedestal sink, claw-foot tub (no shower), and pull-chain toilet.

Guests can eat breakfast in the main-floor restaurant, where 24 wingback chairs and green linen-covered tables with white starched squares give the place an elegant, crisp atmosphere. The tradition of a new menu every month is adhered to, and as a special treat the Burkes offer guests English toffee after the meal.

The inn is just a couple of blocks from the St. Clair River, which carries freighter traffic and cool breezes. The Museum of Arts and History is one block over, on

Court Street, and houses one of the finest collections of marine lore in the state. Travel the dozen or so blocks to the Fort Gratiot Lighthouse, the first one on the Great Lakes, and return to the inn and wet your whistle at the stone-walled Pierpont Pub. Originally a cellar, it features an old red oak bar that used to be a dry goods counter. ⚠ *2 double rooms with baths, 2 doubles share bath, 1 suite. Restaurant, pub, air-conditioning, room service, whirlpool bath in 1 room, fireplace in parlor, gift shop. $85–$160; Continental breakfast. AE, D, MC, V.*

WILLIAM CLEMENTS INN 🐚
1712 Center Ave., Bay City 48708, tel. 517/894–4600, fax 517/895–8535

This gray Queen Anne–style mansion in Bay City is what eccentric Great-Aunt Emily's house always looked like, at least in the movies: Ornately carved staircases and ceilings, heavy oak furniture, and voluminous velveteen drapes establish the look. The house was built in 1886 for William Clements, a local lumber baron and a collector of rare books who donated his impressive collection to the University of Michigan library in 1920.

Today, his love of books is still felt in the inn, where each suite is named after a writer or fictional character—from Louisa May Alcott and Emily Brontë to Henry David Thoreau and Charles Dickens. This is just one of the lovely touches the owners, Brian and Karen Hepp—a local couple with a great appreciation of history—brought to the inn when they purchased it in 1994. The two most lavish accommodations are the Ernest Hemingway Suite, a two-room whirlpool suite with a working fireplace, sitting area, French doors, a king-size bed, and an in-room shower for two, and the Alfred Lord Tennyson Suite, which is actually the 1,200-square-ft former ballroom, now outfitted with a kitchen, living room, dining room, and queen-size bed. Second-floor guest rooms are spacious and filled with period furnishings, including iron or brass beds, marble-top tables, and oak armoires. One bathroom is particularly gracious, featuring china tiles bordered with hand-painted morning glories.

As the quintessential 19th-century man of industry and culture, Clements also exhibited a respect for music, equipping the music room with a magnificent Steinway grand piano. But Clements's true passion was books, and a few volumes from his former collection remain in the richly paneled main-floor library. Guests, however, are more likely to be found in the screened-in back porch, shaded by a 200-year-old beech tree. There they play cards and talk of the sea captains and lumber barons who built the other grand mansions that fill this historic district. ⚠ *4 double rooms with baths, 3 suites. Air-conditioning, TV, phone, and toiletries in rooms; fireplace in 4 rooms; whirlpool bath in suites. $70–$175; Continental breakfast by candlelight, evening refreshments. AE, D, MC, V. No smoking.*

OTHER CHOICES

Blanche House Inn and the Castle. 506 Parkview Dr., Detroit 48214, tel. 313/822–7090. 13 double rooms with baths, 1 suite. Air-conditioning, cable TV, and phone in rooms, hot tub in 4 rooms. $60–$125; full breakfast. AE, D, DC, MC, V. No smoking.

Botsford Inn. 28000 Grand River, Farmington Hills 48336, tel. 248/474–4800, fax 248/474–7669. 13 double rooms, 10 rooms with bath. Restaurant, air-conditioning, cable TV, phone in rooms. $65–$75; full breakfast. AE, D, DC, MC, V.

Chicago Street Inn. 219 Chicago St., Brooklyn 49230, tel. 517/592–3888, fax 517/592–9025. 2 double rooms with baths, 4 suites. Air-conditioning, cable

TV in rooms, phone in entranceway, fireplace in sitting room. $75–$165; full breakfast. MC, V. No smoking.

Corktown Inn B&B. 1705 6th St., Detroit 48226, tel. 313/963–6688, fax 313/964–3883. 4 double rooms with baths. Air-conditioning, TV, VCR, and phone in rooms, video library, exercise room in basement. $135; full breakfast. AE, MC, V. No smoking.

Dundee Guest House. 522 Tecumseh St., Dundee 48131, tel. 734/529–5706 or 800/501–4455. 1 double room with bath, 1 suite. Air-conditioning. Croquet and gazebo in backyard. $55–$95; Continental breakfast. MC, V. No smoking.

Southwestern Michigan, Including Battle Creek, Grand Rapids, Kalamazoo, and Saugatuck

CHICAGO PIKE INN ☞
215 E. Chicago St., Coldwater 49036, tel. 517/279–8744, fax 517/278–8597

Parental love is the simple story behind this large yellow inn, which sits on U.S. 12 halfway between Detroit and Chicago. Looking to lure their daughter Becky back to Michigan, Harold and Jane Schultz dangled a carrot: They would buy one of Coldwater's most elegant mansions and convert it into a B&B if she would come home to run it. Becky, who had studied hotel management in college and was working at a plush Florida resort at the time, immediately agreed.

The 7,500-square-ft mansion was built in 1903 by local mercantilist Morris G. Clarke, who hired Asbury Buckley to design it. The Chicago architect was responsible for many of the fine homes built on Mackinac Island in the 1890s. Although the mansion was being used as a boardinghouse when the Schultzes bought it, it was still in remarkably fine condition. Today, such elegant touches as the built-in mirrored buffet in the cherry-paneled dining room, the double-mantel fireplace in the reception room, and the oak parquet floors can make you feel almost guilty about showing up in jeans and a T-shirt.

Guest rooms in the main house are appointed with period wall coverings and Victorian antiques such as marble-top tables. All but one are on the second floor; the exception is the Clarkes' Own Room (as it was labeled on the original architectural drawings). Off the library—a restful refuge with a marble fireplace and century-old tea table—this room is furnished with an ornately carved, lace-covered canopy bed. At the top of the stairs is Miss Sophia's Suite, the inn's most popular room, which has a yellow-tile fireplace with an oak mantel and a private balcony. A gambrel-roofed, two-story carriage house contains the two newest rooms. Decorated in the same style as the main house, these lodgings also include air-conditioning, whirlpool baths, refrigerators, and private balconies. All rooms reveal the innkeepers' attention to detail and include nice touches such as individual thermostats and four pillows—two hard, two soft.

The antiques centers of Allen and Marshall are nearby, and northern Indiana—home to the famous Shipshewana auctions and a thriving Amish community—is just a half hour's drive away. Or you can hop on one of the inn's bicycles and explore Coldwater, a drowsy town filled with 19th-century statuary and Victorian-era homes. △ *5 double rooms with baths, 3 suites. Air-conditioning in 2 rooms, cable TV and phone in rooms, refrigerator and whirlpool bath in 2 rooms, fireplace in common area, bicycles. $90–$180; full breakfast, afternoon refreshments. AE, MC, V. Smoking in common areas only.*

KINGSLEY HOUSE ⊮
626 W. Main St., Fennville 49408, tel. 616/561–6425, fax 616/561–2593

In 1995 Gary and Kari King bought this impressive Queen Anne house in tiny Fennville, which is "as American as apple pie." It was built in 1886 by Harvey Kingsley, who introduced fruit trees to this area around Lake Michigan. Tipping their caps to Kingsley, the Kings have placed his picture in the living room (guests say he bears an uncanny likeness to Gary) and named each of the guest rooms after a variety of apple. An oak stairway leads to six second-story chambers, two of which are dubbed McIntosh and Golden Delicious. The most interesting is the Jonathan Room, formerly a stable boy's quarters, with a century-old bed and an 1850s platform rocker. Nestled in the tower is the Dutchess Room, which, with five windows, is the brightest and is regally decorated in cranberry-hued wallpaper and antique lace. Immediately above it is Northern Spy, a honeymoon suite, which features an electric fireplace, a whirlpool bath, and a tower sitting room, with a calming view of miles of rolling countryside.

The household is run with smooth efficiency and simple elegance. The guest rooms and common areas are spacious and immaculately clean. The furnishings are a tasteful blend of oak and cherry antiques and the Kings' collections, including china, beaded purses, and vintage clothing.

A Continental breakfast is served during the week. On weekends, breakfast is served family style and could include honey-glazed pecan French toast or a zucchini-tomato-basil frittata, served on linens and Royal Doulton china in the formal cherrywood dining room. The Delftware and silver are typical of the elegant touches throughout the house.

With busy Route 89 close at hand, traffic noise can be a problem in the front rooms. To escape, hop on one of the four 18-speed bikes that are provided and pedal 8 mi south to the Allegan State Game Area, famous as a rest stop for geese and other migrating waterfowl. Once there, you can hike, canoe, swim, cross-country ski, or pick wild blueberries, strawberries, and other fruit. △ *1 king-size room, 1 queen-size room, four double rooms, all with baths, 3 suites. Air-conditioning, TV, phone, fireplace, and whirlpool tub in suites, 2 phones in common areas, TV/VCR available in rooms, movie library. $65–$145; full breakfast on weekends, buffet breakfast weekdays, refreshments all day. AE, D, MC, V. No smoking.*

NATIONAL HOUSE INN ⊮
102 S. Parkview St., Marshall 49068, tel. 616/781–7374, fax 616/781–4510

More than a smooth-running and magnificently preserved hostel from another period, the National House Inn is a centerpiece of what many consider the finest cross section of 19th-century architecture in the country. The oldest inn in the state opened as a stagecoach stop in 1835, two years before Michigan was admitted to the Union. For many years it served double duty as one of the final stops on the Underground Railroad, which spirited escaped slaves to Canada, 120 mi to the east. In 1878, it was converted into a wagon and windmill factory. The inn was drawing its final breath as an apartment house when a consortium of local businesspeople bought and restored it for the nation's Bicentennial.

For the past 14 years, innkeeper Barbara Bradley has watched a parade of tourists, business travelers, and honeymooners pass through the rustic entryway, which is warmed by a massive beam-and-brick open-hearth fireplace. The rough-hewn ceiling beams and aged plank floors are the framework for the particular selection of country antiques found in each room. There are punched-tin chandeliers; Windsor, ladderback, and herringbone wing chairs in the living room; spindle-leg tables and hurricane lamps in the dining room; and gilt-framed oil portraits throughout. Thanks to a unique fireplace set into handcrafted paneled cabinets, the upstairs lounge is comfortable and inviting, although in warmer weather guests prefer moving to the back porch and gardens.

Guest rooms are attractively wallpapered and carpeted, with the decor ranging from country style to the Victorian-era design of the Ketchum Suite, which overlooks a handsome garden and the village circle. There's plenty of elbow room in the dining room, where a Continental breakfast of boiled eggs, bowls of fruit, wheat bread, coffee, and a wide variety of fruit juices and teas is served.

Marshall is right off I–94, 10 mi east of Battle Creek. In 1991, the village—frequently referred to as "the Williamsburg of the Midwest"—was designated a National Historic Landmark District. The district encompasses some 850 structures (and nearly 50 historical markers), including striking examples of Queen Anne, Italianate, and Gothic Revival architecture. **&** *16 double rooms with baths. Air-conditioning, cable TV, and phone in rooms. $66–$120; Continental breakfast. AE, MC, V. No-smoking rooms available.*

PEBBLE HOUSE ☙
15093 Lakeshore Rd., Lakeside 49116, tel. 616/469–1416, fax 616/469–0455

"Serenity is our goal," says Jean Lawrence, who, along with her husband, Ed, owns the relaxing Pebble House. Chicago expatriates, Jean was an art therapist and Ed a real estate investment analyst when they fell in love with the 1912 concrete-block and river-rock house on the shores of Lake Michigan. The Lawrences decided to furnish the inn in mission-style furniture because it seemed to fit, and at the time, it was still relatively inexpensive. Today, the Pebble House is one of the few B&Bs faithful to the revolutionary early 1900s style that preached a return to handcraftsmanship. The Lawrences have meticulously furnished all the guest rooms and public areas with distinctive, clean-lined mission-style furniture and accessories, including hand-hammered copper bowls and green lead-glass lamps. Even Jean's Scandinavian-style breakfasts of baked Finnish pancakes and homemade coffee cakes are served on Roycroft Revival china.

The Lawrences work hard to make this a true retreat: There are no phones in the guest rooms, and as an alternate pleasure to the electronic age, more than 2,000 books, including volumes of fiction, travel, and design, are tucked all about. Needless to say, their collection of books on the Arts and Crafts movement is a connoisseur's delight. If you're looking to explore the area's bountiful antiquing, you're in luck: Ed's even written a guidebook to the region's shops. For those who prefer more active relaxation, a beach also beckons. **&** *3 double rooms with baths, 3-bedroom Coach House with bath, 2-bedroom Blueberry House with 2 baths. Air-conditioning, TV in rooms, phone in main lounge, kitchenette and wood-burning stove in Blueberry House. $110–$250; full breakfast, refreshments. D, MC, V. No smoking indoors. Closed Dec. 24.*

SOUTH CLIFF INN ☞
1900 Lakeshore Dr., St. Joseph 49085, tel. 616/983–4881, fax 616/983–7391

Seven years ago, Bill Swisher left behind a decade-long career as director of the Cassopolis, Michigan, Probate Court and opened the South Cliff Inn. "I grew up in the area, and I suppose I was always looking for an excuse to come back," he says.

In the pre-air-conditioning days of the early 1900s, St. Joseph (or St. Joe, it's sometimes called) and its sister city, Benton Harbor, were among the Midwest's most popular lakefront summer resorts. The collapse of the area's manufacturing base led to a decline of its fortunes in the 1970s, especially in Benton Harbor, always the more blue-collar of the two. South Cliff Inn, a salmon-color brick English cottage, is a small but important representative of an economic renaissance that once again is capitalizing on the therapeutic breezes of Lake Michigan.

The 82-year-old inn is perched on a bluff, giving three of the guest rooms superb views of the water. The Sunset Suite is perhaps the most popular. The queen-size bed, sofa, and wing chair are dressed in complementary English chintz fabrics; the private bath features a custom-designed marble tub. In the Harbour Room, guests can lie back in a bubbling whirlpool bath and watch the sun melt into the lake in the evening. Two rooms now have balconies overlooking the lake. The entire place is decorated in English country style (not surprisingly, a perennial garden was added), with plenty of bold prints, chintz fabrics, and a large number of antiques. One of the guest rooms houses an imposing 150-year-old oak armoire that is so large it had to be hoisted through the windows.

The trouble was worth it: The inn is comfortable, sun-filled, commendably unhurried. The Continental breakfast includes juice, homemade bread, muffins, coffee cakes and—after all, this is orchard country—plenty of fresh fruit. That's enough carbohydrates to fuel a short walk to the downtown of this pleasant harbor town, whose turn-of-the-century storefronts and monuments, landscaped brick streets, and Lake Michigan backdrop combine to make it perhaps the most picturesque in the entire state. ⚱ *7 double rooms with baths. Air-conditioning, cable TV in den, fireplace in 2 rooms, whirlpool bath in 2 rooms. $75–$165; Continental breakfast, refreshments all day. AE, D, MC, V. No smoking, 2-night minimum weekends, 3-night minimum holidays.*

WICKWOOD COUNTRY INN ☞
510 Butler St. (Box 1019), Saugatuck 49453, tel. 616/857–1097, fax 616/857–4168

Guests at Saugatuck's oldest bed-and-breakfast are in for a treat, both figuratively and literally. The owner, Julee Rosso-Miller, is the coauthor of *The Silver Palate Cookbook*. With 2 million copies of her gourmet masterpiece sold, only *Joy of Cooking* has kept it from being the best-selling cookbook of all time.

Julee came to her new career as innkeeper in much the same way she became a well-known gourmet writer: serendipity. Her mother's heart attack in 1986 forced Julee to reappraise her own hectic lifestyle as co-owner of one of the first-ever gourmet take-out shops in the country, New York's Silver Palate. She moved to Saugatuck and fell in love with the sunsets over Lake Michigan—and with Ray Miller, a local builder. They married, then persuaded their neighbors to sell what has long been regarded as the best B&B in town. Of course, the location doesn't hurt: It's two blocks from downtown's many fine shops and restaurants and a short walk from the beach and other lakefront attractions.

With its brick floors, cedar walls, and vaulted ceilings, the circa-1940 inn resembles one of those small toasty hotels that dot the English countryside. The main-floor rooms, filled with overstuffed chairs, French and English antiques, fresh flowers, and original art, surround a courtyard blooming with perennials, roses, and herbs. The guest rooms have individual themes but are uniformly captivating, with plenty of antique lace, Ralph Lauren and Laura Ashley fabrics, and cabbage-rose patterns on the walls and beds.

Guests are pampered from daybreak to dusk. A buffet breakfast is served and a newspaper supplied weekday mornings on the old English pine buffet table in the dining area, which is filled with antique toy trains, boats, and trucks. On weekends, a hearty brunch is prepared. Hors d'oeuvres, which might include a light salmon mousse, bruschetta, Chinese ribs, and crudités with low-fat dip, are put out at 6 PM. As if this weren't enough, candies and jars of spiced nuts are placed in each room. Calorie counters can relax, though: most items are selections from Julee's recent low-fat cookbook, *Great Good Food.* ☘ *11 double rooms with baths, 2 suites. Air-conditioning, fireplace in 1 suite, cable TV in library, phone in common room. $140–$190; full breakfast, evening refreshments. MC, V. 2-night minimum weekends. Closed Dec. 24–25.*

OTHER CHOICES

Fairchild House. 606 Butler St., Saugatuck 49453, tel. 616/857–5985. 3 double rooms with baths. Air-conditioning; phone, TV, and fireplace in parlor. $125; Continental breakfast. No credit cards. No smoking, 2-night minimum weekends.

Greencrest Manor. 6174 Halbert Rd., Battle Creek 49017, tel. 616/962–8633, fax 616/962–7254. 6 double rooms with baths, 2 double rooms with shared bath, 4 suites. Air-conditioning, cable TV, phone in rooms, whirlpool bath in suites. $75–$200; Continental breakfast. AE, MC, V. No smoking.

Inn at Union Pier. 9708 Berrien St. (Box 222), Union Pier 49129, tel. 616/469–4700, fax 616/469–4720. 16 double rooms with baths. Air-conditioning, cable TV and phone in Great House, fireplace in 12 rooms, hot tub, sauna, beach towels. $125–$195; full breakfast, afternoon and evening refreshments. D, MC, V. No smoking, 2-night minimum weekends, 3-night minimum holidays.

Maplewood Hotel. 428 Butler St. (Box 1059), Saugatuck 49453, tel. 616/857–1771 or 800/650–9790, fax 616/857–1773. 15 double rooms with baths. Air-conditioning, cable TV, phone in rooms, fireplace in 5 rooms, whirlpool bath in 5 rooms, lap pool. $115–$175; full breakfast. AE, MC, V. No smoking, 2-night minimum weekends, 3-night minimum holidays. Closed for 3 days at bo'h Thanksgiving and Christmas.

McCarthy's Bear Creek Inn. 15230 C. Dr. N, Marshall 49068, tel. 616/781–8383. 14 rooms with bath. Air-conditioning, TV on request, phone in common area. $65–$98; breakfast buffet. AE, M, V.

Mendon Country Inn. 440 W. Main St., Mendon 49072, tel. 616/496–8132, tel. 616/244–9022. 9 double rooms with baths, 9 suites. Air-conditioning, sauna, rooftop garden, picnic area, bikes, canoes available. $69–$159; Continental breakfast. AE, D, MC, V. No smoking.

Parsonage 1908. 6 E. 24th St., Holland 49423, tel. 616/396–1316. 1 double room with bath, 2 doubles share 1 bath. Air-conditioning, TV in sitting room, portable phone in hallway. $90–$100; full breakfast, refreshments. No credit cards. No smoking. Closed last wk in Feb.

Pine Garth Inn. 15790 Lakeshore Rd. (Box 347), Union Pier 49129, tel. 616/469–1642, fax 615/469–0418. 7 double rooms with baths, 5 2-bedroom cottages. Air-conditioning, TV and VCR in rooms, phone in library and upstairs, hot tub and fireplace in cottages. $125–$250; full breakfast, afternoon refreshments (inn only). AE, MC, V. No smoking, 2-night minimum weekends, 3-night minimum holidays.

Stuart Avenue Inn. 229 Stuart Ave., Kalamazoo 49007, tel. 616/342–0230. 15 double rooms with bath, 4 suites. Air-conditioning, TV and phone in rooms. $59–$150; Continental breakfast. AE, D, DC, MC, V. No smoking, 5-day cancellation policy.

Twin Oaks Inn. 227 Griffith St. (Box 867), Saugatuck 49453, tel. 616/857–1600. 8 double rooms with bath, 3 suites, cottage. Air-conditioning, cable TV/VCR in rooms, phones. $65–$95; Continental breakfast weekdays, full breakfast weekends. D, MC, V. No smoking.

Victorian Villa Inn. 601 North Broadway St., Union City 49094, tel. 517/741–7383 or 800/34–VILLA, fax 517/741–4002. 5 double rooms with baths, 5 suites. Restaurant, air-conditioning in most rooms, fireplace in 2 suites, phone in common area, bicycles built for 2 available. $75–$145; full breakfast, afternoon tea, dinner in adjacent restaurant available. D, MC, V. No smoking indoors.

Yelton Manor. 140 N. Shore Dr., South Haven 49090, tel. 616/637–5220, fax 616/637–4957. 17 double rooms with baths. Air-conditioning, cable TV in rooms, fireplace in 7 rooms, whirlpool bath in 11 rooms, 6 guest phones in common areas. $125–$250; full or Continental breakfast, refreshments. AE, MC, V. No smoking indoors.

Upper Peninsula

LAURIUM MANOR INN ☙
320 Tamarack, Laurium 49913, tel. 906/337-2549

Dave and Julie Sprenger were working as engineers in San Jose, California, when, as Julie describes it, they "decided to commit corporate suicide" and trade the Golden State's laid-back charms for the ruggedly isolated Keweenaw Peninsula. They shared a dream of owning a mansion they had visited in Laurium, a former copper boomtown. In 1989, they bought the vacant three-story neoclassical house and, after three years of restoration work, reopened its heavy oak doors as a bed-and-breakfast.

The Upper Peninsula's largest (13,000 square ft!) and most opulent mansion was built in 1908 by Capt. Thomas H. Hoatson, owner of the Calumet & Arizona Mining Company. At a time when miners were toiling 6,000 ft underground for 25 ¢ an hour, Hoatson spent $50,000 constructing the 40-room mansion and an additional $35,000 furnishing it. The copper magnate had impeccable taste, as lodgers and afternoon tour groups ($3 a head) quickly learn.

Every room is a marvel. Silver-leaf overlay draws your eye to the ceiling of the music parlor. The dining room boasts stained-glass windows and gilded elephant-hide wall coverings, and the kitchen includes a built-in icebox covering an entire wall and made of marble, tile, and oak.

While all the bedrooms were built on an extralarge scale, the Laurium Suite exhausts all superlatives; it covers a majestic 680 square ft and has a hand-carved oak fireplace and private balcony. All the guest quarters feature queen- or king-size beds, handmade flannel quilts, and period antiques.

The National Park Service named the inn a "cooperating site" of the new Keweenaw National Historical Park, recognizing its significance in the area's mining heritage. Plan day trips to some of the national park's other historic sites, including the Calumet Theatre (where Sarah Bernhardt, Lillian Russell, and Douglas Fairbanks Jr. performed) or to one of the ghost towns sprinkled throughout the copper region. Lake Superior is just 4 mi away; Fort Wilkins State Park, a mid-19th-century army post on the northernmost tip of Keweenaw, is a short drive up U.S. 41. ⚑ *8 double rooms with baths, 2 doubles share bath, 2 suites. Phone and cable TV in 10 rooms, fireplace in 5 rooms. $55–$119; full breakfast. D, MC, V. No smoking.*

OTHER CHOICES

Big Bay Point Lighthouse. 3 Lighthouse Rd., Big Bay 49808, tel. 906/345–9957, fax 906/345–9418. 7 double rooms with baths. Sauna. $115–$175 May–Oct., $85–$145 Nov.–Apr.; full breakfast. No credit cards. No smoking.

Celibeth House. Blaney Park Rd., M-77 (Rte. 1, Box 58A), Blaney Park 49836, tel. 906/283–3409. 6 double rooms with baths, 1 quad. Phone in hallway. $50–$55 (4% discount if paid by cash or check); Continental breakfast. MC, V. No smoking.

Pinewood Lodge. Rte. 28 (Box 176), Au Train 49806, tel. 906/892–8300, fax 906/892–8510. 3 double rooms with baths, 3 suites. Sauna. $95–$125; full breakfast. D, MC, V. No smoking indoors.

Sand Hills Lighthouse Inn. Five Mile Point Rd. (Box 414), Ahmeek 49901, tel. 906/337–1744. 7 double rooms with baths (1 room includes additional single daybed). Portable phone available for guest use, fireplace in 1 room and common room. $115–$175; full breakfast. No credit cards. No smoking.

Thunder Bay Inn. Box 286, Big Bay 49808, tel. 906/345–9376, fax 906/345–9392. 2 double rooms with baths, 5 doubles with half baths and shared showers, 5 suites. TV and pay phone on 1st floor, gift shop. $70–$105; Continental breakfast. D, MC, V. No smoking on 2nd floor.

Water Street Inn. 140 E. Water St., Sault Ste. Marie 49783, tel. 906/632–1900 or 800/236–1904. 4 double rooms with baths. No air-conditioning, shared phone. $75–$105; full breakfast. D, MC, V. No smoking indoors.

Mackinac Island

BAY VIEW AT MACKINAC ☙

Summer: Main St. (Box 448), Mackinac Island 49757, tel. 906/847—3295

Owner Doug Yoder's great-great-grandfather, Dr. John R. Bailey, a surgeon at Ft. Mackinac, would be pleased. Doug, who works in the music industry in Nashville during the winter, has painstakingly restored this 1890s house, which has been in his family for more than 100 years. The two-year renovation, which cost half a million dollars, has made the most of the home's elegance.

The sitting room's tin ceiling and fireplace and the refinished wood moldings throughout the house have kept their charm. The wraparound porch is decked out in green and white with skirted glass-top tables. Panoramic views of the water and abundant bright begonias and geraniums make this a perfect place to enjoy late-afternoon refreshments.

Guest rooms feel more modern than Victorian as a result of the renovation, but bright new fabrics, skirted tables, and flower-garden wallpaper borders mixed with authentic period pieces, such as an antique inlaid-mahogany headboard, create a nice blend of old and new. Marble floors and ceramic tile in the bathrooms add a classic touch. All the curtains and bedspreads have been handmade for the inn, as was the carpeting in all the hallways and on all the stairs. Three different designs were cut and laid together to create a beautiful rose-colored and flowered carpet.

Newlyweds and chronic romantics will especially enjoy Doug's final additions— three suites, each luxuriously furnished with a whirlpool bath, a television, a CD and video library, a wet bar, and a private balcony overlooking the harbor. There have already been several weddings on those balconies.

Upon arrival you'll discover a sampling of fudge in your room in true Mackinac Island tradition. In the morning you'll awaken to the aroma of Doug's Bay View Blend Coffee and home-baked pastries. Take your breakfast up to the second-floor balcony and start your day off right—with a spectacular view of the Straits of Mackinac. △ *17 double rooms with baths, 3 suites. Whirlpool bath, TV/VCR, CD and video library, wet bar, and balcony in suites, ceiling fan in rooms, TV in sitting room on request, conference room, gallery and marine supply store, short-term docking facilities. $95–$285; Continental breakfast. MC, V. 2-night minimum weekends. Closed Oct.–Apr.*

HAAN'S 1830 INN 🐚
Summer: Huron St. (Box 123), Mackinac Island 49757, tel. 906/847–6244.
Winter: 3418 Oakwood Ave., Island Lake, IL 60042, tel. 847/526–2662

The charm of Haan's 1830 Inn is not just in its appearance but in the owners themselves. Vernon and Joy Haan share business responsibilities at the inn with their son Nicholas and his wife, Nancy. Even their grandchildren lend a hand by folding napkins before breakfast at the 12-ft harvest table.

The house was built around the foundations of a log cabin that had been dragged over the ice from the mainland during the Revolutionary War. In the mid-1800s, it was the home of Ft. Mackinac officer and onetime island mayor Colonel Preston. The white columns in front give evidence the inn is the oldest Greek Revival home in what was the Northwest Territory; it was also the first B&B on Mackinac Island.

The Haans have turned what could have seemed old and shabby into someplace warm and inviting. Guest rooms are named after figures from the island's past and are tastefully decorated with a variety of antiques, including an elegant burled-walnut headboard. Taller guests should avoid the Reverend William Ferry and Pere Marquette rooms, since the ceilings in that part of the house are unusually low, probably to retain heat in the winter.

A fascinating centerpiece in the sitting room is a large black safe originally used by one of fur trader John Jacob Astor's agents. Original 1830 prints hang on the wall, and there is a large, dark cherrywood desk that was built and used in Ft. Mackinac. The second-story porch, tucked under the trees, is a great place to hide out and absorb the island's atmosphere; for those looking for more excitement, the island's downtown is a mere three blocks away.

The Haans clearly enjoy running the inn. The marble-top breakfast buffet brims with delicious coffee cakes, muffins, and jams to be enjoyed at your leisure in front of a crackling fire in the dining room. Vernon is a history buff with a special talent for bringing history to life. In fact, you won't need to spend money on any of the island tours; Vernon is far more interesting and lively. The *Haan* in the inn's name, like the *1830*, is clearly not just for effect. △ *4 double rooms with baths, 2 doubles share bath, 1 housekeeping suite. Ceiling fans and chocolates* *in rooms, vouchers for cocktails at local restaurants. $80–$140; Continental break-fast. No credit cards. No smoking indoors. Closed mid-Oct.–mid-May.*

INN ON MACKINAC ☞

Summer: Main St., Mackinac Island 49757, tel. 906/847–6348 or 800/462–2546.
Winter: Box 7706, Ann Arbor 48107, tel. 313/665–5750

Trying to find all 13 colors on the inn's exterior, beyond the easier-to-identify hues of purple, pink, green, and peach, is a favorite pastime of guests. Assistant general manager Kelly Irby says most people can only identify five or six. The bright colors, inspired by Victorian homes like the so-called painted ladies of San Francisco, make the Inn on Mackinac one of the more eye-catching houses on the island.

Built in 1867, with the back section added later, the house used to be called the Chateau Beaumont in memory of the fort's famous army surgeon, William Beaumont. In 1988, the inn was remodeled to emphasize its quaint Victorian charm yet still provide a number of modern amenities.

The larger and more expensive rooms are in the front, which is the older section; they are charmingly furnished with cherrywood armoires, white shutters in the windows overlooking the street, and white lace swags over the beds. Although rooms in the back section are comfortable and also redecorated, they don't have as good a view and are smaller. Request a room with a bay window (found in both sections) since they add a sense of spaciousness to the room.

Although you are unlikely to meet up with owners Pat and Alice Pulte (they also own the Murray Hotel; *see below*), a complete staff is on hand to answer any questions about the island or the inn. Because of its size, the inn may lack some intimacy found at other B&Bs, but it makes up for that in style and convenience. Although not right in the center of town, it is certainly close.

A sense of camaraderie is evident as soon as you step onto the expansive, second-floor wraparound porch, where guests gather throughout the day. In fact, the outdoor areas at the inn are as enjoyable as the rooms. At street level, a lattice-covered arch leads to a charming brick patio surrounded by gardens. This level, which includes the lobby and dining room, was created during the remodeling by digging out the home's basement and adding French doors all the way around. You can eat breakfast inside or on the patio or sample some of the Pultes' home-made fudge, made fresh daily and sold in the lobby. △ *44 double rooms with baths. Air-conditioning, TV in rooms, wheelchair accessible. $99–$250; Continental breakfast. MC, V. No smoking. Closed Oct. 12–Apr.*

METIVIER INN ☞

Summer: Market St. (Box 285), Mackinac Island 49757, tel. 906/847–6234,
fax 906/847—0370

You can't miss the Metivier Inn, on a quiet section of Market Street one block from the hustle and bustle of Main Street. Beautiful landscaping and a white picket fence along the front sidewalk make this inn a standout.

The house, built in 1877, was a single-family home until 1984, when it opened as a B&B. Originally it had only 13 guest rooms, but recent renovations have added more on the third floor. One of the new rooms boasts a Jacuzzi and a small deck overlooking the magnificent Grand Hotel and its golf course. A side porch, accessible from four rooms on the second floor, is perfect for a group of people looking for some shared privacy. The front porch runs the full width of the house and is nicely furnished with the owners' personal collection of antique white wicker.

In fact, soft colors and antique-style furniture throughout give the inn a simple, clean, and tasteful look.

Various names from Mackinac Island's past adorn the doors to each guest room. Because of its larger size and unique view, the John Jacob Astor Room, in the turret at the front of the house, is one of the nicest. An antique sleigh bed adorns one of the main-floor rooms, or for a romantic night, try one of the four rooms outfitted with a four-poster canopy bed.

A Continental breakfast, brought from a local bakery each morning, is served in the lobby, which is somewhat sparse but comfortable; it is furnished with couches, chairs, and a wood-burning stove that adds atmosphere when stoked up on cooler days or in the evenings.

Metivier is efficiently run and quiet, but it lacks some of the personal touches that can make for a unique stay. Although it is owned by two couples, Ken and Diane Neyer and Mike and Jane Bacon, the inn is professionally managed by George and Angela Leonard, who live on the premises and seem very responsive yet not intrusive to their guests' needs.

Guests can also enjoy a visit to Biddle House, a restored turn-of-the century home right next door. △ *20 double rooms with baths, 1 suite. Jacuzzi in 1 room, cable TV in conference room, wood-burning stove in sitting room. $115–$255; Continental breakfast. AE, D, MC, V. No smoking. Closed Nov.–Apr.*

OTHER CHOICES

Bogan Lane Inn. Bogan La. (Box 482), Mackinac Island 49757, tel. 906/847–3439. 4 double rooms share 2 baths. Ceiling fan in rooms. $55–$65; Continental breakfast. No credit cards. No smoking indoors.

Cloghaun Bed & Breakfast. Summer: Market St. (Box 203), Mackinac Island 49757, tel. 906/847–3885 or 888/442–5929, fax 906/847—4064. 8 double rooms with baths, 2 doubles share bath. $90–$140; Continental breakfast. No credit cards. No smoking indoors. Closed Oct. 31–May 15.

Murray Hotel. Summer: Main St. (Box 476), Mackinac Island 49757, tel. 906/847–3361 or 800/462–2546, fax 906/847–6110. Winter: Box 7706, Ann Arbor 48107, tel. 313/665–5750. 69 double rooms with baths. Air-conditioning and TV in rooms, whirlpool bath in 2 rooms. $89–$225; Continental breakfast. MC, V. No smoking. Closed Oct. 15–Apr.

Market Street Inn. Market St. (Box 315), Mackinac Island 49757, tel. 906/847–3811, fax 906/847–0902. 7 double rooms with baths. Ceiling fan, cable TV in rooms, wheelchair accessible. $90–$185; Continental breakfast. MC, V. No smoking, 3-night minimum during boat races. Closed Nov.–Apr.

Grand Traverse Region, Including Traverse City

CENTENNIAL INN 🐚
7251 E. Alpers Rd., Lake Leelanau 49653, tel. 616/271–6460

The Centennial Inn, in the heart of Leelanau County's rolling farmland, was designated a Michigan Centennial Farm by the state's Historical Commission.

In the same family for more than 100 years, the farm got its first new owners when Karl and JoAnne Smith bought it eight years ago.

The Smiths have carefully restored the two-story clapboard farmhouse, built in 1865. The original barn and two outbuildings are still in excellent condition. The smaller one has been turned into a gift shop, featuring antiques and folk art created by local artisans, as well as JoAnne's baskets and Karl's reproduction furniture. Since the inn is about 6 mi from the small town of Lake Leelanau, guests will need to drive a short way to find restaurants and shops.

As you approach the house, you'll come across a glistening sundial. The lettering around it reads, "Grow old along with me, the best is yet to be." The Centennial Inn is proof that what is old can also be very good. On the front porch, pots of red-blossomed geraniums are placed around a white bench, creating a colorful frame for the entrance.

The Smiths have decorated the farm in Shaker style, yet their loving attention makes what could seem sparse feel warm and inviting. A scattering of Oriental rugs complements the glow of the refinished, original hardwood floors. A candle chandelier hangs over the rough-hewn pine table in the dining room, and an elaborate pewter collection is displayed above the buffet. The parlor, one of the coziest spots, is perfect for reading, watching TV, or just enjoying the country fireplace.

The guest rooms continue the Shaker theme. The front room downstairs has a four-poster bed with a white lace canopy and homemade white quilt. Every detail harmonizes, down to the blue-and-white checkered curtains in the window and the old crockery on the tables.

A deluxe full breakfast is more than enough to fill you up. In the cooler months, breakfast can be enjoyed in the cozy dining room, but during the summer, either of two outside areas makes a perfect eating spot: The deck on the west side overlooks a big birch tree and apple orchards, and, on the east side, there's a redbrick patio with twig furniture. A swing in the back overlooks acres of unspoiled rolling land: The peaceful sight can take you back 100 years. ⌂ *3 doubles share bath. Nordic ski trails, bicycling trails. $70; full breakfast. No credit cards. No smoking.*

LINDEN LEA ☙
279 S. Long Lake Rd., Traverse City 49684, tel. 616/943–9182

A small and enchanting spot on the shore of a crystal-clear inland lake, Linden Lea is, as one of its owners describes it, reminiscent of scenes in the movie *On Golden Pond.* Country roads wind their way to the bed-and-breakfast, and, once you've found it, you won't want to leave.

In 1979, Jim and Vicky McDonnell bought a small summer cottage built around the turn of the century by three Civil War veterans. Vicky remembers, "The original cottage was a mess—rotting floors and everything—but I just kept looking at the view and saying, 'This is it. This is the place.'" Since then, Jim, a former teacher, has skillfully renovated the building and tacked on an addition; nine years ago the couple opened their multilevel, contemporary home as a B&B.

The living room, complete with a marble and cherrywood fireplace from the late 1800s, expansive picture windows, high ceilings, and a large, comfortable leather sofa and love seat, is an inviting place to unwind and enjoy the view. With that in mind, the guest rooms have cushioned window seats that overlook the lake. The rooms, separate from the family quarters, also offer a measure of privacy.

The mix of antiques and treasures creates a warm, eclectic atmosphere. Jim began collecting unusual paperweights on a trip to Scotland, and now more than 60 of the colorful glass pieces adorn a table near the stairway. The handmade dolls and the decorative plates scattered throughout the house are gifts Vicky's mother received while serving as an army nurse.

The McDonnells and their children, Audrey and Wyatt, are a congenial family. They've been known to offer baby-sitting services and to invite guests to join the family for dinner on cold winter nights when the prospect of curling up in front of the fireplace seems more appealing than braving the elements to find a restaurant.

The breakfast menu varies, and guests may be treated to such delights as quiches, freshly baked peach puffs, chocolate-chip banana muffins, and stuffed French toast. After breakfast, guests can take the rowboat or paddleboat to explore one of Long Lake's many islands. **△** *2 double rooms with baths. Air-conditioning, TV and VCR in living room, private sand beach, rowboat and paddleboat available. $85–$100; full breakfast. No credit cards. No smoking, 2-night minimum weekends May–Oct.*

OTHER CHOICES

Aspen House. 1353 N. Manitou Trail W (Box 722), Leland 49654, tel. 616/256–9724 or 800/762–7736, fax 616/256–2777. 3 double rooms with baths. Terry cloth robes, TV/VCR in living room, computer in small office. $100–$135; full breakfast. MC. V. No smoking indoors.

Bowers Harbor Bed & Breakfast. 13972 Peninsula Dr., Traverse City 49684, tel. 616/223–7869, fax 616/223–7872. 3 double rooms with baths. Air-conditioning, off-street parking. $110–$140; full breakfast. No credit cards. No smoking, 2-night minimum weekends July–Sept. 15, 3-night minimum holidays.

Brookside Inn. 115 N. Michigan Ave., Beulah 49617, tel. 616/882–7271, fax 616/882–4600. 20 double rooms with baths. Air-conditioning, sauna, steam bath, and tanning solarium in some rooms. $210–$265; full breakfast and dinner for 2. AE, D, DC, MC, V.

Chateau Chantal. 15900 Rue de Vin, Traverse City 49684, tel. and fax 616/223–4110. 1 double room with bath, 2 suites. Air-conditioning, TV, phone, individual heat and air controls in rooms, winery tours and wine tastings. $95–$125; full breakfast. MC, V. No smoking indoors, 2-night minimum June 15–Oct.

Cherry Knoll Farm. 2856 Hammond Rd. E, Traverse City 49684, tel. 616/947–9806 or 800/847–9806. 3 double rooms share 2 baths. Air-conditioning, restricted-diet breakfasts on request. $65–$70; full breakfast. MC, V. No smoking indoors. Closed Nov.–May.

Lee Point Inn. 2885 S. Lee Point La. (Rte. 2, Box 374B), Suttons Bay 49682, tel. 616/271–6770. 1 double room with bath, 2 doubles share bath. Ceiling fan in rooms; picnic table, canoe. $95–$125; full breakfast. MC, V. No smoking indoors.

Leelanau Country Inn. 149 E. Harbor Hwy., Maple City 49664, tel. 616/228–5060, fax 616/228–5013. 5 single and 1 double rooms share 2 baths. Off-street parking. $45–$55; Continental breakfast. MC, V. Smoking in restaurant only, no dogs. Open weekends only Nov.–Apr., closed Mar.

Neahtawanta Inn. 1308 Neahtawanta Rd., Traverse City 49684, tel. 616/223–7315. 4 double rooms share bath, 1 double room with bath. Sauna, private beach. $70–$120; Continental breakfast. MC, V. No smoking.

Old Mill Pond Inn. 202 W. 3rd St., Northport 49670, tel. 616/386–7341. 5 double rooms share 2½ baths. $90–$120; full breakfast. MC, V. No smoking. Closed Nov.–May.

Omena Shores Bed and Breakfast. 13140 Isthmus Rd. (Box 154), Omena 49674, tel. 616/386–7313. 3 double rooms with baths, 1 double shares bath. Ceiling fan in rooms, TV/VCR in living room, terry cloth robes, croquet set outdoors. $70–$95; full breakfast. No credit cards. No smoking indoors, 2-night minimum weekends May–Oct.

Open Windows Bed & Breakfast. 613 St. Mary's Ave. (Box 698), Suttons Bay 49682, tel. and fax 616/271–4300 or 800/520–3722. 3 double rooms with baths. Air-conditioning in 1 room, ceiling fan in 2 rooms, TV/VCR in common room, croquet set. $110–$110; full breakfast. No credit cards. No smoking indoors, 2-night minimum holidays and weekends May–Oct.

Snowbird Inn. 473 N. Manitou Trail W (Box 1124), Leland 49654, tel. 616/256–9773, fax 616/256–7068. 2 double rooms with bath, 2 doubles share 1½ baths. Ceiling fan in rooms, fireplace in dining room. $85–$125; full breakfast. No credit cards. Smoking on porch only, 2-night minimum weekends Memorial Day–Oct.

Victoriana 1898. 622 Washington St., Traverse City 49684, tel. 616/929–1009, fax 616/929–2966. 2 double rooms with baths, 1 suite. Air-conditioning, fireplace in parlor. $65–$90; full breakfast, evening refreshments. No credit cards. Smoking on porch only.

Little Traverse Bay Region

MONTGOMERY PLACE 🐾
618 E. Lake St., Petoskey 49770, tel. 616/347–1338, fax 616/348–8311

As former executives in the field of assisted-living facilities in Detroit, Ruth Bellissimo and Diane Gillette know something about looking after people. As hosts they go out of their way to help you enjoy your stay by providing area restaurant menus, a travel planner, and chocolates in each guest room.

Set in a quiet, tree-filled neighborhood in Petoskey, Montgomery Place has an enviable location. As the locals tell it, when it opened in 1879 as the Ozark Hotel, people were aghast that anyone would put such an establishment so far from downtown. Nowadays, however, guests are only a few blocks' walk from the shopping and entertainment of the Gaslight District and minutes by car from first-class golf and skiing, but they still feel—what bliss!—miles away.

The two-story wood-frame house has been thoroughly renovated to provide modern amenities while still retaining elements of its Victorian history: high ceilings, wood moldings, pocket doors, old gas fixtures, floral prints, hardwood floors, and area rugs. The spacious guest rooms have individual themes, from the cathedral ceiling, dark wood, and fruitwood hand-carved Peruvian bed of the Grand Master Suite to the white wicker and original wooden water closet in the bathroom of the Wicker Room.

Adjacent to the large living room is a game room, complete with an elegant parquet floor, entertainment center, backgammon and cribbage boards, puzzles, books, and a cozy couch, where the Bensons say they often discover guests relaxing and taking a short nap.

The most popular gathering spot is the 80-ft veranda, which wraps around two sides of the house and overlooks Little Traverse Bay. Furnished with white wicker and ablaze with colorful hanging plants, it is the perfect place to enjoy Diane's hearty breakfasts during the warmer months. Her menu varies and includes a ham-asparagus quiche and Finnish pancakes with raspberry sauce. And, after a long day of shopping or relaxing, you can return to the veranda, where the Bensons' afternoon hors d'oeuvres quell those hunger pangs and make you feel at home once again. ♨ *4 double rooms with baths. Fireplace in living room. $95–$135; full breakfast. D, MC, V. No smoking indoors, 2-night minimum weekends in summer, 3-night minimum holidays.*

HOUSE ON THE HILL 🐦

9661 Lake St. (Box 206), Ellsworth 49729, tel. 616/588–6304

As part of their early retirement plan, lifelong Texans Buster and Julie Arnim considered opening an art gallery in the Southwest, but after a tour of New England bed-and-breakfasts, they decided to open their own. Selling their Houston suitcase business in 1984, the Arnims moved north to see the turn-of-the-century farmhouse they had purchased, sight unseen, after an eight-state hunt for the perfect rural setting. A real-estate ad stated it was "near a gourmet restaurant"; Julie was convinced their B&B would be a success if good food was at hand. Indeed, two of northern Michigan's finest restaurants, Tapawingo and the Rowe Inn, are within two blocks.

After some hard work during the renovation process, the Arnims have made their House on the Hill a successful and elegant B&B. The carefully restored gray-and-white Victorian (including an addition used as their private quarters) sits on a hill near the little village of Ellsworth, overlooking 53 acres of countryside and the St. Clair Lake. Guests are free to hike or ski cross-country around the property and even borrow the boat docked at the lake. A spacious veranda wraps around the house and is filled with white wicker furniture and rocking chairs.

Inside, a curved staircase leads to the guest rooms upstairs. They are all spacious, immaculate, and pleasantly decorated. Each has its own thermostat, fresh flowers, candy, ice water, and bedside lights. A favorite is the Pine Room, with its cathedral ceiling, custom-built four-poster bed draped in white lace, and peaceful view of the woods behind the house. Antiques and such touches as a 200-year-old hand-carved ebony Oriental desk, Julie's rose-colored glass collection, and Japanese-style porcelain could make you nervous about kicking back and really relaxing, but the Arnims make you feel at home with a perfect blend of friendliness and reserve.

Julie and Buster serve a marvelous hearty breakfast on their large oak table, complete with fine china and silver. A culinary whiz, Julie rotates 65 different breakfast menus; for early risers, she puts out a basket filled with home-baked muffins, juice, and coffee, which goes beyond yum to yum-yum. ♨ *7 double rooms with baths. Ceiling fan in rooms, cable TV in parlor. $115–$125; full breakfast. MC, V. Smoking on porch only.*

KIMBERLY COUNTRY ESTATE 🐦

2287 Bester Rd., Harbor Springs 49740, tel. 616/526–7646

The Greek Revival architecture and the gracious hospitality of the Kimberly Country Estate recall the genteel era of the Old South, but the interior is an elegant re-creation of an English country estate. Regardless of either impression, it's a treat to discover this 8,000-square-ft house in the heart of northern Michigan.

Owners Billie and Ronn Serba spent more than a year carefully remodeling this 30-year-old home in an effort to enhance its architecture while adding some modern conveniences. They put in new fireplaces, an updated kitchen, recessed lighting, and traditional mullion-style windows to take the place of the modern casements. In the living room, they replaced the sliding glass doors leading to the terrace with more graceful French doors. This attention to detail is evident throughout the house.

The Serbas moved from the Detroit area to Harbor Springs in the early 1980s, after owning a flower shop as well as restoring and decorating three homes together. Once in Harbor Springs, they first opened the shop Kimberly's Nest; the bed-and-breakfast followed in 1989. Throughout their 40-year marriage, they have been avid antiques collectors, acquiring such treasures as a Dutch pin armoire, a cast-iron chandelier, four-poster beds, and numerous chairs and accessories.

Floral chintz mixed with stripes and plaids creates a warm, romantic look, as do the fresh flowers, overstuffed sofas and chairs, Oriental rugs, and Battenburg lace bedspreads in the guest rooms. The B&B has become a very popular place for weddings; the entire house is often rented out on these occasions (or for the occasional executive retreat).

All the guest rooms are very spacious. The two largest rooms are the Lexington, with a fireplace, sitting area, and separate study, and the Verandah, which opens to a private terrace and has a fireplace and whirlpool bath. Guests are free to use the main-floor library; with its North Carolina black walnut paneling, fireplace, English-style armchairs, and paisley fabric–covered ceiling, it has the feeling of an old club—an old club founded on the grounds of a stately southern plantation. ⌂ *5 double rooms with baths, 1 suite. Baby grand piano in living room, pool. $135–$250; Continental breakfast, afternoon tea. MC, V. No smoking, 2-night minimum weekends, 3-night minimum holidays. Closed Apr.*

STAFFORD'S BAY VIEW INN ☙

613 Woodland Ave. (U.S. 31), Petoskey 49770, tel. 616/347–2771 or 800/456–1917

It's hard to miss Stafford's Bay View Inn, set just off the main road running through Petoskey's historic Bay View District. A popular dining spot for both tourists and residents as well as a bustling inn, the imposing three-story Victorian was built in 1886; it served as lodging for summer visitors coming north via the now-defunct railroad to enjoy Bay View's cultural programs.

Owners Stafford and Janice Smith met and fell in love while working at the inn for the previous owner. They purchased it during the early 1960s and have now been joined in running the inn by their son and daughter-in-law, Reg and Lori, who are the day-to-day innkeepers. Over time, they have redecorated and added onto the inn—including five new suites—while retaining its comfortable charm. Furnishings in the second- and third-floor guest rooms include canopy and four-poster beds, richly colored wallpapers, antique dressers, wicker furniture, and such details as handmade eyelet and ribbon pillows.

The Smiths renovated the third floor in 1987, including adding a sitting room. Ever mindful of maintaining the house as a haven for young families, they provided this room so parents could enjoy stepping out without venturing too far from sleeping young ones. Children can often be seen happily romping in the first-floor common areas while parents finish their meal at a leisurely pace.

What the Bay View Inn may sometimes lack in quiet it makes up for in its delicious food and the unending hospitality of its hosts. Open and airy, the main dining room is decorated with chandeliers, draped tables with fan-back chairs, fresh flowers and plants, and white lattice dividers between booths. Sometimes it may feel as though the restaurant crowd has taken over the inn, but a trip to the third floor or a stroll down to the water offers a good escape for overnight guests. The menus include such specialties as steaming bread pudding with raisins and cream. A splendid buffet awaits guests for Sunday brunch; selections may include ham, turkey, whitefish, chicken, biscuits, and scrumptious desserts. Although the inn does not serve alcoholic beverages, guests are invited to bring their own wine to dinner. ⌂ *17 double rooms with baths, 14 suites. Air-conditioning, gas fireplace and whirlpool bath in 5 suites, cable TV in sunroom and library. $79–$195; full breakfast. AE, MC, V. No smoking in 3rd-floor guest rooms.*

OTHER CHOICES

Bridge Street Inn. 113 Michigan Ave., Charlevoix 49720, tel. 616/547–6606, fax 616/547–1812. 3 double rooms with baths, 6 doubles share 3 baths. Ceiling fan in rooms, baby grand piano in common area. $85–$140; full breakfast. MC, V. No smoking 2-night minimum weekends July–mid-Oct.

Gingerbread House. 205 Bluff St. (Box 1273), Bay View 49770, tel. 616/347–3538. 3 double rooms with baths, 1 housekeeping double with bath, 1 housekeeping suite. Private outside entrances to guest rooms. $55–$100; Continental breakfast. MC, V. No smoking. Closed Nov.–Apr.

Torch Lake Bed & Breakfast. 10601 Coy St., Alden 49612, tel. 616/331–6424. 1 double room with bath, 2 doubles share bath. No Ceiling fan in rooms. $65–$85; full breakfast. No credit cards. No smoking indoors. Closed mid-Sept.–Memorial Day weekend.

Veranda at Harbor Springs. 403 E. Main St., Harbor Springs 48740, tel. 616/526–7782. 4 double rooms with baths, 1 suite. TV and phone in rooms, fireplace in sitting room, refrigerator and ice machine for guests. $95–$175; full breakfast. MC, V. Smoking on guest balconies only.

Walloon Lake Inn. 4178 West Rd. (Box 85), Walloon Lake Village 49796, tel. 616/535–2999. 5 double rooms with baths. Restaurant, beach and dock access on lake. $50–$70; Continental breakfast. MC, V.

MINNESOTA

Twin Cities Area

ANN BEAN HOUSE 🐚
319 W. Pine St., Stillwater 55082, tel. 651/430–0355 or 800/933–0355

Their 1880 Victorian stick-style house is a graceful one, with many bay windows and towers and turrets of varying heights. The interior is filled with woodwork that reflects Minnesota's lumbering past, including a beautiful carved oak banister and cherry, oak, and walnut parquet flooring in the vestibule. The abundance of large windows makes the house light and airy. Ken and Kim Jadwin bought the place in spring 1998.

Two of the five bedrooms, the Guest Room and Ann and Albert's Room, measure a luxurious 400 square ft. The Guest Room has a brass sleigh bed, an enormous bay window, and a working fireplace with a carved oak mantel. Ann and Albert's Room has a north-facing bay window, as well as a bath with a tempting whirlpool that fits into the shorter of the building's towers. Cynthia's Room has a whirlpool 6 ft in diameter and a fireplace embedded with teal-colored marble tiles.

Even more impressive, perhaps, is the whimsical pink Tower Room, with a slanted ceiling and a white cast-iron bed. A few stairs up, you'll find a delightful white wicker table for two, perfect for morning coffee or wine in the evening. Up another flight of stairs at the top of the tower is the star attraction—a spacious aerie with windows on four sides offering spectacular views of hilly Stillwater and the St. Croix River. On its way to becoming the most popular room, however, is the newest addition, Jacob's Room, with its carved-mahogany furniture and sunny window seat.

The house's charm is accentuated by the Jadwins' hospitality, especially Victoria's cooking. Breakfast is an elegant four-course affair with fruits, bread, and even dessert. After breakfast, your hosts can tell you about paddle-boat trips, hot-air ballooning, and antiques hunting in the area. ▲ *5 double rooms with baths. Air-conditioning, fireplace in 3 rooms, whirlpool tub in 4 rooms. $79–$129 weekdays, $99–$159 weekends; full breakfast, afternoon refreshments. AE, D, MC, V. No.*

ASA PARKER HOUSE 🐚
17500 St. Croix Trail N, Marine on St. Croix 55047, tel. 612/433–5248 or 888/857–9969

On a rainy day, the Asa Parker House, in the tiny historic village of Marine on St. Croix, looks like something out of a British TV miniseries. Extensive grounds, elaborate flower gardens, a tennis court, and a gazebo make the setting of this Greek Revival B&B one of the finest in Minnesota. The house, built in 1856 by lumber-industry pioneer Asa Parker, was distinctive enough to tempt owners Connie and Chuck Weiss to venture into the B&B business, with the hope of providing a "romantic respite for people in love."

The public and guest rooms are all airy, bright, and predominately floral. The two downstairs parlors are done in a most attractive pink, with stylish accents of white wicker and chintz. The "receiving" music room has dried-flower wreaths, delicate furniture, and an organ, while the adjacent Gentlemen's Parlor offers plush leather reading chairs and a wooden chessboard.

If you can get past the frills, the guest rooms can be quite lovely—especially those bouquets of fragrant flowers. Truly luxurious is the rose-and-dusty-green Isabella Parker Room, with white wicker furniture, a claw-foot tub, and spectacular river-valley views from its corner spot. The Alice O'Brien Suite, tucked under the eaves, has gabled windows, a large bath with a whirlpool tub, and a private deck with white Adirondack chairs and views of the flowering lawns—perfect for a reclusive weekend of romance or solitude. A screened porch downstairs overlooks a rock garden and fountain.

Connie uses the freshest fruits (her husband is in the produce business) to top off her hearty breakfasts, which include such favorites as baked peach pancakes and Grand Marnier French toast. She'll also encourage guests to reserve the screened gazebo for a private afternoon barbecue or to enjoy a hike in William O'Brien State Park, just down the road. The park has miles of hiking, biking, and cross-country ski paths. There's also a marina a couple of blocks away, where you can rent canoes. But the sweeping views of the St. Croix River are so beautiful—particularly once the leaves begin to fall—that guests may just want to relax on the lawn. △ *3 double rooms with baths, 1 suite. Air-conditioning, whirlpool bath in suite, stove in 1 room, tennis court, screened gazebo. $99–$159; full breakfast, afternoon refreshments. D, MC, V. No smoking.*

COVINGTON INN ☞

Pier One, Harriet Island, St. Paul 55107, tel. 612/292–1411

On Harriet Island across from downtown St. Paul, this may be the only B&B with a true view of the Mississippi River. In fact, the inn is a towboat on the river itself. Wanting to provide people with an opportunity to experience life on the Mississippi, owners Tom Welna and Ann Reeves opened the No Wake Cafe on the boat in 1987. The success of the restaurant led to renovating the remaining portions of the towboat into an elegant B&B. The result might please even Mark Twain.

Originally named the *Codrington*, the boat has a unique engine that set the standard for the transport of liquid cargo, still in effect today. However, little remains of its industrial past. Anne and Tom dry-docked the boat to restore the hull and gutted the interior before artfully rebuilding it using mostly recycled materials. The result is an elegant yet nautical B&B with pine wainscoting and unusual portholelike wall lamps.

The one common space is a bright salon on the main level of the boat. The salon's furniture is a mixture of antiques and clever touches, such as paddle-wheel ashtrays and boat-shaped cribbage boards. Plush couches and chairs surround a fireplace below a huge clear-story skylight. Guests can also stroll along the many outer decks, weather permitting.

The guest rooms are all creatively designed, with TV/VCRs hidden away in decorative wall cabinets and small—remember, this *is* a boat—but efficient bathrooms. The two-level Pilot House Suite is the most spectacular. It has a bedroom with a corner fireplace made from hand-painted Portuguese tiles. A short climb up a private narrow staircase leads you to the original pilothouse, now the suite's comfortable sitting room. Completely encircled with windows, it has soft futon sofas and a large brass helm, which once controlled the rudders and engines. From here, or out on a private fir-wood deck, the entire St. Paul skyline can be seen aglow on a starry night. The bright and airy Master's Quarters also has a private deck, a fireplace, and pine and cedar woodwork.

A warm breakfast of fruit, coffee cake, an egg dish, and coffee is served in the salon, or you can have it brought to your room. Ann and Tom want their guests to feel like part of the crew—a boating etiquette manual can be found in each room—but there is no swabbing of the deck to be done here. Guests can just relax and enjoy the views and the gentle swaying of the mighty Mississippi. △ *2 double rooms with baths, 3 suites. Air-conditioning, phone in 3 rooms, fireplace in 2 rooms, off-street parking. $105–$165 Oct.–Apr., $135–$195 May–Oct.; full breakfast. MC, V. Smoking on decks only.*

ELEPHANT WALK 🐾
801 W. Pine St., Stillwater 55082, tel. 651/430–0359 or 888/430–0359, fax 651/351–9080

Don't be surprised if you are summoned for breakfast at this delightful B&B by a gong—one that is attached no less to a beautiful and elaborately carved teak-wood dragon embedded with glass and mica. From that first morning call, you'll know that Rita Graybill's Elephant Walk provides a refreshing alternative to the standard Victorian B&B. On the outside, one sees a stick-style pale-yellow-and-salmon Victorian home, complete with a cozy porch swing on a wrap-around porch. One step inside, however, and you could almost believe you've made a detour to the Raffles Hotel in Singapore.

Rita spent 20 years traveling with her husband—he worked for the navy—mostly in Asian countries, and collected hundreds of spectacular and exotic items that now decorate the downstairs and guest rooms. In fact, the B&B's name comes from Rita's realization while unpacking boxes that the majority of her treasures were elephant keepsakes of various sizes and materials. She arranged them tastefully throughout the house, proceeded to add three bathrooms, three fireplaces, and four whirlpool baths, and opened for business in 1993.

Elephants are not the sole decor emphasis. There are other intriguing artifacts to discover, and better yet, there is an interesting story behind each and every one. Each of the bedrooms highlights a different country or region, and all are luxuriously fitted with whirlpool tubs and fireplaces. The Rangoon Room, done in cinnamon-and-gold tones, has mosquito netting over the four-poster teakwood bed, a hand-forged copper sink—formerly a candy kettle from Spain—and ornate Balinese masks. The Raffles Room has a unique whirlpool tub with an ivy trellis; the water trickles into the tub from the surrounding stone wall—reminiscent of a natural hot spring.

Most spectacular is the two-room Cadiz Suite, named for the city in Spain where Columbus set off to discover the new world. The spacious and bright window-lined suite is decorated with centuries-old hand-carved cathedral doors from Cadiz, a double-sided gas fireplace, a whirlpool surrounded by lush plants and hanging orchids, and an Indian rosewood sitting bench, which has hand-carved elephant armrests—of course. The suite leads to a private sundeck overlooking Rita's fish- and lily-filled water gardens.

Topping off this memorable experience are Rita's ample breakfasts and consistent hospitality. This B&B is as elegant as the more traditional Victorian fare but will fill you with dreams of travels to come. △ *3 double rooms with baths, 1 suite. Air-conditioning, gas fireplace, whirlpool bath, ceiling fan, refrigerators, and radio-stereo in rooms. $149–$219; full breakfast. MC, V. Smoking on porch only.*

LE BLANC HOUSE ☙

302 University Ave. NE, Minneapolis 55413, tel. 612/379–2570

Le Blanc House is an elegant piece of the 19th century tucked into a modest and modern Minneapolis neighborhood. The 1896 Queen Anne is a striking structure with a delicate lavender exterior. In summer, its banks of petunias and walls of morning glories and nasturtiums are famous in the neighborhood. Add sparkling stained-glass windows and inviting front and back porches—the latter with the traditional swing—and you could be back in the days when the original owner, William Le Blanc, returned home each evening from the grain mills along the Mississippi.

Current owners Barb Zahasky and Bob Shulstad now run the inn full time and have kept the decor faithful to the inn's period and named the three guest rooms after the daughters of its former owners. Both Zofi's and Amelia's rooms have great views of the city skyline. Zofi's Room, a corner room with a bay window and a private bath—perfect for weekday business travelers—is furnished with a 19th-century high-topped walnut bed and matching marble-top dresser. Marissa's Room, the smallest of the three, is invitingly cozy. It has an antique brass bed, oak furnishings, handmade quilts and linens, and an unusual porthole window. All rooms have colorfully patterned Victorian reproduction wallpaper.

You'll awaken to the aroma of Bob's homemade breakfasts wafting from the dining room. Dishes include "heavenly" Belgian waffles, spinach-pistachio quiche, French toast stuffed with jelly and cream cheese, and filled crepes. Barb's sister owns a St. Paul bakery, and many mornings she brings over fresh muffins and pastries.

Le Blanc House is just blocks from the many attractions of the Minneapolis riverfront, where you'll find the restaurants St. Anthony Main and Riverplace, as well as Boom Island Park, which offers paddleboat cruises, the River City Trolley, and an extensive riverfront walk. The area is quite culturally diverse, so you'll also find a wide variety of restaurants—Japanese, Italian, Lebanese, and Polish—within walking distance. △ *1 double room with bath, 2 doubles share bath. Air-conditioning, TV available, off-street parking. $85–$105; full breakfast. AE, MC, V. Smoking on front porch only. 2-night minimum on summer weekends.*

RIVERTOWN INN ☙

306 Olive St. W, Stillwater 55082, tel. 651/430–2955 or 800/562–3632, fax 651/430–0034

In 1882, wealthy Stillwater lumber baron John O'Brien built what is now the elegant Rivertown Inn. In 1987, Chuck and Judy Dougherty were searching for a change. They considered opening a restaurant, but after seeing this imposing Queen Anne Victorian, they realized they had found their calling. Although the mansion was designed as a stylish home for the O'Brien family, the Doughertys thought its wraparound porch and its site—on a hill near the St. Croix River—would be perfect for a B&B. After major renovations—seven bathrooms were added—the Rivertown Inn opened for business.

The downstairs has kept its turn-of-the-century character, with four-wood parquet floors, stained-glass windows, and ball-and-stick wooded archways. There are many impressive antiques, as well as smaller knickknacks reminiscent of the Victorian love for detail. The most notable of the larger furnishings, a matching dining-room table and buffet, came all the way from a castle in England. There is also an ornate Ben Franklin stove, which serves as the centerpiece of the parlor. In the summer, guests can relax in the gazebo or on a screened porch with a wicker swing.

The guest rooms are named after former residents. Julie's Room, done in blues, has a high walnut bed and dresser and once the leaves have fallen, a lovely view of the river. Faith's Room, in peach and blue, has an enormous black-walnut half-tester bed, a fireplace, and a double whirlpool bath. The rooms on the third floor are smaller, some under dormered eaves, but pleasantly cozy nonetheless. All floors have sitting areas with books, games, and plush reading couches.

Breakfast, either served downstairs or brought up to the rooms, consists of an assortment of homemade pastries, flans, an egg dish, and sometimes even champagne. The Doughertys now also run the Cover Park Manor across town, which offers more modern accommodations. △ *8 double rooms with baths (1 bath is non-adjoining). Ceiling fan and whirlpool bath in 5 rooms. $69–$169; full breakfast, afternoon wine, hors d'oeuvres. AE, D, MC, V. No smoking, 2-night minimum fall and holiday weekends.*

WILLIAM SAUNTRY MANSION ☞
626 N. 4th St., Stillwater 55082, tel. 651/430–2653 or 800/828–2653, 651/351–7872

The William Sauntry Mansion is a meticulous restoration of an enormous 1890 Queen Anne home. The work done in the parlor—which was re-created down to the wall beading and corner ornaments—was so accurate that a visiting former resident remarked to owners Art and Elaine Halbardier on how well the wallpaper had held up. Some things *are* original: the parquet flooring laid in four woods and the parlor's oil-on-canvas ceiling, as well as light fixtures, fireplaces, and special stained-glass windows.

The Halbardiers bought the place in 1997. The previous owners found the 25-room mansion converted to apartments and deteriorating. In 1991, after a two-year restoration in which the second floor was stripped down to the studs, they opened it as a bed-and-breakfast.

Aiming to remain true to the period not only in architecture and design but in mood as well, they maintain authentic touches as harpsichord playing in the parlor during the afternoon social hour. The bedrooms, which have large windows and fireplaces, are also done in a Victorian style, with Oriental and floral motifs and the richly hued paints favored by 19th-century builders.

Beltram's Room, with its south-facing tower bay window overlooking the gardens, green-tiled fireplace, spoon-carved cherry bedroom set, and private bath, is especially pleasant. For a Japanese ambience, try William's Room, which has crown dentil molding and is papered in an exotic pattern of gold, blue, and rust.

Sauntry, an Irish immigrant turned lumber baron, had maverick ideas about home construction: He sent his architects as far as the Alhambra Palace in Spain to gather details. Behind his home he built a recreation facility complete with ballroom, bowling alley, and swimming pool, and connected it to the house with Minnesota's first skywalk. The skywalk is gone, and the building is owned by another family, but Sauntry's spirit lives on in his enormous house. △ *6 dou-*

ble rooms with baths (2 nonadjoining). Air-conditioning, fireplace in all rooms, double whirlpool in 5 rooms, bathrobes. $109–$189; full breakfast, early morning coffee, afternoon refreshments. D, DC, MC, V. No smoking.

OTHER CHOICES

Afton House Inn. 3291 St. Croix Trail S (Box 326), Afton 55001, tel. 612/436–8883, fax 612/436–6859. 15 double rooms with baths, 1 guest cottage with 2 bedrooms. Restaurant, bar, air-conditioning, TV and phone in rooms, gas fireplace in 8 rooms, double whirlpool bath in 10 rooms, private balcony in 4 rooms. $60–$140; Continental breakfast. AE, D, MC, V. No smoking in some rooms.

Bluff Creek Inn. 1161 Bluff Creek Dr., Chaska 55318, tel. 612/445–2735 or 800/307–0019. 5 double rooms with baths. Air-conditioning, whirlpool bath in 3 rooms, fireplace in 1 room. $75–$130 weekdays, $85–$150 weekends; full breakfast, afternoon wine and hors d'oeuvres. AE, D, MC, V. No smoking.

Chatsworth B&B. 984 Ashland Ave., St. Paul 55104, tel. 651/227–4288, fax 651/225–8217. 3 double rooms with baths, 2 doubles share bath. Air-conditioning, whirlpool tub in 2 rooms, private deck in 1 room, NordicTrack, exercise bike. $65–$125; Continental breakfast on weekdays; full breakfast on weekends. D, MC, V. No smoking.

Elmwood House. 1 E. Elmwood Pl., Minneapolis 55419, tel. 612/822–4558. 2 doubles share 1 bath, 1 suite. Air-conditioning, TV/VCR in rooms, refrigerator, laundry facilities. $55–$85; Continental breakfast. AE, MC, V. Smoking on front porch only, 2-night minimum weekends June–Aug.

Evelo's Bed & Breakfast. 2301 Bryant Ave. S, Minneapolis 55405, tel. 612/374–9656. 3 double rooms share bath. Clock radio in rooms, refrigerator, coffeemaker, and phone on 3rd-floor landing, additional single bed in 2 rooms. $50; full breakfast. AE, D, DC, MC, V. Smoking on porch only.

Garden Gate Bed and Breakfast. 925 Goodrich Ave., St. Paul 55105, tel. 651/227–8430 or 800/967–2703, fax 651/225–9791. 3 double rooms and 1 suite share bath. Air-conditioning. $55–$75; Continental breakfast. AE, D, MC, V. Smoking on porch only.

Harvest Restaurant and Inn. 114 E. Chestnut St., Stillwater 55082, tel. 651/430–8111. 3 double rooms with baths. Air-conditioning, double whirlpool, and fireplace in rooms. $129–$139; full breakfast. AE, D, MC, V. No smoking.

James A. Mulvey Residence Inn. 622 W. Churchill St., Stillwater 55082, tel. 651/430–8008 or 800/820–8008, fax 651/430–2801. 7 double rooms with baths. Air-conditioning, fireplace, and whirlpool bath in rooms. $99–$179; full breakfast, afternoon refreshments, picnic lunches available. AE, D, MC, V. Smoking on porch only.

Laurel Street Inn. 210 E. Laurel St., Stillwater 55082, tel. 612/351–0031 or 888/351–0031, fax 612/439–0903. 3 double rooms with baths. Air-conditioning, whirlpool bath and gas fireplace in 2 rooms. $105–$125 Nov.–Apr., $155–$175 May–Oct.; full breakfast. AE, D, MC, V. Smoking on porch only.

Lumber Baron's Hotel. 101 Water St. S, Stillwater 55082, tel. 612/439–6000, fax 612/430–9393. 18 double rooms with baths, 20 suites. Restaurant, pub, air-conditioning, TV, phone, double whirlpool bath, and gas fireplace in rooms, 5 conference rooms. $89–$159 weekdays; $129–$199 weekends; full breakfast. AE, D, DC, MC, V. Designated smoking rooms.

1900 Dupont. 1900 Dupont Ave. S, Minneapolis 55403, tel. 612/374–1973. 4 double rooms with baths. Air-conditioning, TV available upon request. $85–$119; Continental breakfast. No credit cards. No smoking.

Mississippi River Valley and Bluff Country

JAILHOUSE INN ☙

109 Houston NW (Box 422), Preston 55965, tel. 507/765–2181, fax 507/765–2558

Law-abiding citizens of the past century hurried past this 1869 Italianate redbrick building, which served as the Fillmore County Jail for more than 100 years. After then sitting empty for 15 years, the jail and the adjacent sheriff's quarters and offices were turned into a 13-room inn, after a renovation so extensive it is almost impossible to guess the structure's original use. Almost. One room provides an unforgettable reminder: The Cell Block Room still has its bars. Otherwise, it is much more comfortable than any inmate could have dreamed. Two queen-size beds with tufted bedspreads occupy separate cells, which are fitted with rag rugs, a whirlpool bath big enough for two, a sitting area, and the original toilet and basin.

Rest assured you won't feel the least bit incarcerated in the other bedrooms, all with beautiful pine or oak floors and many decorated with Eastlake furniture. The blue-and-rose Master Bedroom has a wood-burning fireplace, large windows, and a huge, old 1,000-pound china tub. The Oriental Room has a purple-and-black marble fireplace and a large, comfortable bathroom with a claw-foot tub. The pine-floored, maroon-and-rust Detention Room has access to the south-facing second-floor porch. The newest room, once the drunk tank, has the original oversize sheriff's tub. Even some of the JailHouse's smaller rooms—such as the bright yellow-and-white Sun Room or the blue-and-white Amish Room—are just as light and clean as the larger rooms.

There are plenty of public spaces, including the front parlor, which has a pine floor, marble fireplace, and grandfather clock; the larger and brighter oak-floored kitchen; and the first- and second-floor porches. Breakfast is served in a sunny, spacious basement dining area.

Owners Jeanne and Marc Sather, former restaurant designers from San Francisco, are accomplished cooks and veteran hosts, happy to lend their premises and their talents to special events or even to make impromptu trout dinners if you should find yourself lucky enough to catch one in the nearby Root River. ♲ *11 double rooms with baths, 1 2-bedroom suite. Air-conditioning, fireplace in 4 rooms, whirlpool bath in 3 rooms, breakfast room and parlor, meeting room, audio-visual equipment; near Root River trailhead. $42–$115 weekdays, $69–$149 weekends; full breakfast, afternoon refreshments. D, MC, V. No smoking.*

MRS. B'S HISTORIC LANESBORO INN ☙

101 Parkway Ave. (Box 411), Lanesboro 55949, tel. 507/467–2154 or 800/657–4710

A cheery, four-story 1872 limestone structure on the Root River in downtown Lanesboro, this inn spent part of its 125-year history as a combination retail furniture company and funeral home. No vestige of its former use can be found today: Mrs. B's is bright, light, and bursting with the energy of the outdoorsy people who make up much of its clientele.

Lanesboro is a picturesque small town in the heart of the bluffs. The 45-mi asphalt recreation trail for hiking, biking, and cross-country skiing that follows the Root River runs right by Mrs. B's. You can rent bikes and canoes just down the street, or enjoy the view of the river from the two side decks or the backyard garden patio that faces it.

Inside, Mrs. B's is cozy if not historically significant. Before opening as an inn in 1984, it was essentially gutted—and rooms and baths added. The bathrooms are jarringly modern, but the guest rooms are much more creatively decorated, with most of the furniture (including sleigh and cupboard-style beds) locally made, some of it reflecting the Scandinavian heritage of the town's residents. The nicest rooms are the two back corner ones, which have river views. Also desirable are the three rooms with direct access to the inn's wooden side decks, furnished with large, comfortable wooden rocking chairs.

The inn's only common area is a rather small but comfortable lobby, equipped with a piano, warmed by a fireplace, and brightened by huge arched windows facing the street. In summer, guests can use the two-story side porch and the riverfront patio.

"Our goal is to make guests comfortable," says owner Bill Sermeus, who along with his wife, Mimi Abell, bought the inn in early 1991. "We don't have antiques, but we do have good beds, soft chairs, and good food."

Indeed, Mrs. B's is well known for its dinners, which are five-course table d'hôte affairs that take advantage of local products. Dinners are available by reservation only and include such specialties as wildflower salad, corn and wild-rice chowder, and wild-berry sorbet. ♙ *10 double rooms with baths. Restaurant, air-conditioning, gas fireplace in 2 rooms. $58–$75 weekdays, $85–$95 weekends; full breakfast, afternoon tea on weekends. No credit cards. Smoking on porches only. Closed Dec. 24–26.*

PRATT-TABER INN ☞
706 W. 4th St., Red Wing 55066, tel. 612/388–5945

If you're interested in antiques, there are few better choices in this region than the Pratt-Taber Inn. Owners Jim and Karen Kleinfeldt fell in love with this house, not only for its location in historic Red Wing away from the bustle of big city life but also for its potential as a historically authentic backdrop for their extensive antiques collection. The sturdy, white-trimmed brick Italianate Victorian inn is named after A. W. Pratt, a banker who built the house for his family in 1876, and his son-in-law, Robert Taber, who bought it in 1905. Ninety years later, it has become the Kleinfeldts' home, passion, and profession. Along with their gracious hospitality, they offer some of the best B&B breakfasts around.

The house, which is listed in the National Register of Historic Places, was restored in 1984. Old photographs guided much of the exterior work, including the replacement of the porches; one of them is embellished with a detailed star pattern honoring the United States' Centennial in 1876, the year the inn was built. Inside there are parquet floors, butternut and walnut woodwork, glass chandeliers, feather-painted slate fireplaces, and, in the dining room, a large bay window. Throughout the house you'll find early Renaissance Revival and country Victorian antique furniture that dates from the late 1700s to the late 1800s, including a 112-year-old Murphy bed housed in a Victorian buffet and a stereopticon with a rare and complete *Tour the World* collection.

Three of the four upstairs rooms are corner rooms, and all are large and filled with impressive antiques. Polly's Room is particularly nice, with its queen-size brass bed, soft blue-and-ecru decor, black marble fireplace, and inviting clawfoot tub. Mary Lu's Room has views of Barns Bluff, and Beatrice's Room has an

1860s burled walnut Victorian dresser topped with Limoges china items, lending an aura of a time gone by.

Breakfasts—specialties include eggs Benedict with asparagus on homemade sourdough bread or cinnamon-orange French toast—are served in the dining room, on the porches, or in the guest bedrooms, all of which contain tables for two (Jim and Karen will serve from their collection of 1870 Limoges china upon request).

Being a bit of a town booster, Jim is also glad to provide guests with information on local activities, especially the summer trolley tours, which stop right at the inn's front door. △ *2 double rooms with baths, 4 doubles share 2 baths. Air-conditioning, clock radio in rooms, fireplace in 1 room, storage for bicycles, pickup service at airport, dock, or train station. $89–$110; full breakfast, afternoon refreshments. No credit cards. No smoking.*

THORWOOD HISTORIC INNS ☞
315 Pine St., Hastings 55033, tel. 651/437–3297 or 888/TORWOOD, fax 651/437–4129

If you want a luxurious bed-and-breakfast visit, as so many of the repeat guests do, the Thorwood Historic Inns—the 1880 Queen Anne Rosewood and the 1880 Second Empire–style Thorwood—are for you.

Pam and Dick Thorsen, a down-to-earth and friendly couple, fell in love with the river town of Hastings, 20 mi south of St. Paul, and opened Thorwood in 1983. The 6,600-square-ft house was built by a local lumber baron, William Thompson, and his wife, Sara, as their family home. Then, in 1989, the Thorsens opened the 10,000-square-ft Rosewood, six blocks away.

Interestingly, both inns had been hospitals, and occasionally people born in the buildings come back as guests to celebrate their birthdays.

Thorwood and Rosewood are not cozy, family-style bed-and-breakfasts. Thorwood has retained more of its original rooms and fixtures and, because the Thorsens live there, is the homier of the two inns. It has a bay window and a fireplace in its main parlor, an interesting square bay in the front parlor, and maple-and-cherry floors throughout.

Rosewood has a grand piano, a large fireplace, large ornate public rooms, and several bay windows big enough to park a Volkswagen in. Dark-green-and-rose wallpapers and carpets and white-and-oak woodwork, along with the building's great size, make Rosewood's parlors almost overwhelmingly formal.

Remodeling has given fireplaces and whirlpool baths to both inns' guest rooms. The largest and most ornate is a 900-square-ft suite called Mississippi Under the Stars, which has five skylights, a fireplace, a teakwood double whirlpool tub under a skylight, a round shower, a copper soaking tub, and a queen-size bed.

Thorwood's most elaborate rooms are the Oh Promise Me Suite, a lavender-and-white three-level arrangement, with a skylight over the bed, a double whirlpool tub, and the best view; and the Beautiful Dreamer Room, with a built-in whirlpool bath set right into the steeple and a glass-domed fireplace dividing the bath area from the bedroom. Any of the other third-floor rooms at either inn are also bound both to intrigue and spoil even the hardest-to-please of people.

The Thorsens have taken to offering breakfast either in the public rooms or in baskets at your door. △ *11 double rooms with baths, 4 suites. Air-conditioning, TV/VCRs available, fireplace in 13 rooms, whirlpool bath in 11 rooms, gift shop. $97–$257; full breakfast, afternoon refreshments, dinners available. AE, D, MC, V. No smoking.*

VICTORIAN BED & BREAKFAST 🐦

620 S. High St., Lake City 55041, tel. 612/345-2167

Wonderful views of Lake Pepin from each guest room make Lake City's Victorian Bed & Breakfast special. The lake, which many people claim is the most beautiful spot on the Mississippi, also dominates the perspective from the large windows in the downstairs public rooms.

Owners Ione and Bernie Link—originally from Wichita, Kansas—traveled far to settle in Lake City. One look at the grand view from the porch, and they decided on the spot to buy the inn.

The building, although an 1896 stick-style Victorian, has a refreshing simplicity inside. Butternut wood on the staircase banisters and elsewhere is carved, but not elaborately so; small and simple stained-glass windows in rose, amber, and blue are set atop larger plain-glass windows.

Decorated with antiques and modern sofas, the Victorian is eclectic and comfortable, but not overstuffed. The most interesting items are the oak pump organ, made in 1905, and the many delicate glass lamps, some of which are handcrafted by Bernie himself.

The Redbud Room is best, with sweeping lake views from the huge bay window, a king-size bed, a private bath with a wide-plank pine floor, an oversize footed tub, and a rare antique pillbox toilet. The chaise longue provides an excellent opportunity for getting lost in a book.

The sunny Magnolia Room is a large corner room at the front of the house with wonderful lake views, a canopy bed topped with a feather mattress, and an antique claw-foot tub with brass fixtures. The Dogwood Room has carved oak furniture, a reading desk, and a unique stereopticon, but its bathroom is downstairs off the den.

Breakfast is served either in the sunny dining room, which also overlooks the lake, or in guest rooms. Wherever you partake of your wake-up meal, you'll probably love Ione's baked apple pancakes, often made with just-picked apples from local orchards. ♨ *3 double rooms with bath (1 nonadjoining). Air-conditioning, TV/VCR in den, ceiling fan, down comforters, and feather beds in rooms. $65–$85; full breakfast, afternoon refreshments. No credit cards. Smoking on porch only.*

OTHER CHOICES

Archer House. 212 Division St., Northfield 55057, tel. 507/645–5661 or 800/247–2235, fax 507/645–4295. 17 double rooms with baths, 19 suites with whirlpool baths. Restaurants, air-conditioning, cable TV and phone in rooms, ice and soft-drink machines, shops, 3 conference rooms. $45–$140; breakfast not included. AE, D, MC, V.

Bridgewaters Bed and Breakfast. 136 Bridge Ave., Wabasha 55981, tel. 612/565–4208. 2 double rooms with baths, 3 doubles share 2 baths. Air-conditioning, stereo with CD player in common area. $68–$145; full breakfast on weekends, Continental breakfast on weekdays. MC, V. Smoking on porches only.

Candle Light Inn. 818 W. 3rd St., Red Wing 55066, tel. 612/388–8034. 4 double rooms with baths, 1 suite. Air-conditioning, fireplace in 2 rooms, whirlpool bath in 3 rooms. $85–$145; full breakfast, afternoon refreshments. MC, V. No smoking.

Carriage House Bed & Breakfast. 420 Main St., Winona 55987, tel. 507/452–8256, fax 507/452–0939. 4 double rooms with baths. Air-conditioning, fire-

In case you want to see the world.

At American Express, we're here to make your journey a smooth one. So we have over 1,700 travel service locations in over 120 countries ready to help. What else would you expect from the world's largest travel agency?

do more ®

http://www.americanexpress.com/travel

In case you want to be welcomed there.

We're here to see that you're always welcomed at establishments everywhere. That's why millions of people carry the American Express® Card — for peace of mind, confidence, and security, around the world or just around the corner.

do more ®

Cards

In case you're running low.

We're here to help with more than 118,000 Express Cash locations around the world. In order to enroll, just call American Express before you start your vacation.

do more ®

AMERICAN EXPRESS

Express Cash

And just in case.

We're here with American Express® Travelers Cheques and Cheques *for Two*.® They're the safest way to carry money on your vacation and the surest way to get a refund, practically anywhere, anytime.
Another way we help you...

do more ®

AMERICAN EXPRESS

Travelers Cheques

place in 2 rooms, free bicycles, shuttle service from boat docks or train station. $70–$110; Continental-plus breakfast. D, MC, V. No smoking.

Carrolton Country Inn. R.R. 2 (Box 139), Lanesboro 55949, tel. 507/467–2257. 2 double rooms with baths, 2 doubles share bath. Air-conditioning, clock radio in rooms, phone in 2 rooms, fireplace in 1 room, piano, TV/VCR in parlor, picnic table. $65–$100; full breakfast. MC, V. No smoking.

Historic Scanlan House. 708 Parkway Ave. S, Lanesboro 55949, tel. 507/467–2158 or 800/944–2158. 5 double rooms with baths. Air-conditioning, cable TV, chocolates, and minibottle of champagne in rooms, whirlpool bath in 4 rooms, bicycle and cross-country ski rentals, tubing, off-street parking. $65–$135; full breakfast, afternoon refreshments. AE, D, MC, V. Smoking on porch only.

Hungry Point Inn. 1 Old Deerfield Rd., Welch 55089, tel. 612/437–3660 or 612/388–7857. 4 double rooms share 1½ baths, 1 2-bedroom log cabin with bath. Air-conditioning, fireplace in 2 rooms and cabin, whirlpool bath in cabin. $73–$135; full breakfast, afternoon herbal tea and cookies. MC, V. No smoking.

Martin Oaks. 107 1st St., Box 207, Dundas 55019, tel. 507/645–4644. 2 double rooms and 1 single share 1½ baths. Air-conditioning, ceiling fan in 2 rooms, grand piano in living room. $55–$69; full breakfast, evening dessert. MC, V. No smoking.

Quill & Quilt. 615 W. Hoffman St., Cannon Falls 55009, tel. 507/263–5507 or 800/488–3849, fax 507/263–4066. 3 double rooms with baths (2 nonadjoining), 1 suite. Air-conditioning, coffeemaker and clock radio in rooms, whirlpool bath in suite, biking, hiking, cross-country skiing on nearby Cannon Valley Trail. $60–$130; full breakfast. MC, V. No smoking.

Red Gables Inn. 403 N. High St., Lake City 55041, tel. 612/345–2605. 5 double rooms with baths. Air-conditioning, ceiling fan in rooms, bicycles. $85–$95; full breakfast, all-season picnic boxes, mystery evenings. D, MC, V. Smoking on porch only.

Duluth and the North Shore

BEARSKIN LODGE 🐾
Box 275, Grand Marais 55604, tel. 218/388–2292 or 800/338–4170, fax 218/388–4410

Dave Tuttle worked at Bearskin Lodge Resort when it was just an old lodge and several cabins 25 mi down the Gunflint Trail from Grand Marais and Lake Superior. Then in 1973, while still a senior in college, he bought it.

Today it remains low-key and woodsy but a bit more ambitious. Since it's adjacent to the Boundary Waters Canoe area, you'll find hiking and cross-country ski trails; boat, ski, and mountain-bike rentals; and a naturalist program. There's even a masseuse. The new lodge, built in 1980, has four large town houses; there are also 11 new or spruced-up log or log-frame cabins. The multilevel town houses, though within a wing of the lodge, feel secluded, and each has a private deck. Some of the seven older cabins, built in the '20s, '30s, and '50s, have been remodeled to include room-brightening skylights above the beds. All are pleasant and have two or three bedrooms, woodstoves, and large, well-equipped kitchens. In addition, several have screened porches—critical during the buggy north-woods summers.

Rooms in both the town houses and the cabins are simple and comfortable, with chenille bedspreads and pine furniture. Each of the five two- or three-bedroom log cabins is charming, though cabins 9 and 10, built in 1990 of Engelmann spruce, are especially lovely. These cabins, although they're a bit far from the lake, have birch hardwood floors, braided rugs, renovated kitchens as well outfitted as any home's, and big, screened porches. The new pinewood cabin is wheelchair accessible.

One of the resort's most popular spots is the Hot Tub Hus, which guests sign up for in advance for private use. Its walls, benches, and ceiling are of pine, and it has a large deck and separate men's and women's changing rooms and showers.

Originally a summer-only resort, Bearskin now draws kudos from winter-sports lovers for its ice rink and 55 mi of cross-country ski trails (1 mi of which is lighted). Lodge-to-lodge skiing packages are available. ♠ *11 2- to 3-bedroom cabins and 4 1- to 3-bedroom lodge town houses. Woodstove in cabins, kettle grill outside cabins; full meal service available in lodge dining room, wine and beer for sale, sauna, masseuse, spa house, baby-sitting, children's program, sand beach, boat and mountain-bike rental, 55 mi of hiking/cross-country ski trails, ski school, ski rental, ice-skating rink, broomball rink, naturalist program. $110–$231 with spring and late-fall specials; breakfast not included. D, MC, V. No smoking in public areas of lodge.*

ELLERY HOUSE 🐚
28 S. 21st Ave. E, Duluth 55812, tel. 218/724–7639 or 800/355–3794

If it's a comfortable family place you're looking for, Jim and Joan Halquist's beautiful 1890 Queen Anne is the place to stay. The house is on a fairly busy street yet feels rather removed because of its ¾-acre lot, hilltop location, and backyard ravine with creek.

The large, sunny rooms, lighted by large picture windows that face in three directions, are decorated in a trim, moderate Victorian style. The large bay window in the living room has a lake view that's best in winter (shade trees partially obscure the view in summer). In the adjoining dining room, a collection of turn-of-the-century tables and cabinets surrounds the dark oak dining table.

Breakfast is served in the dining room or in three of the four guest rooms. All are delightful. The Ellery Suite, at the front of the house, has a small private balcony and a 1920s-style bathroom. The Sunporch, a three-room suite, is composed of a cozy, floral-wallpapered bedroom with a brass bed; a large bath with oversize claw-foot tub; and a sunny, plant-filled porch with a wood-burning stove and treetop views. The Thomas Wahl Room is particularly nice, with a tiny table for two tucked into a large lake-view bay window; it also has an 1890s gas fireplace in the corner, a double marble shower, maple floors, and a cabbage rose–motif hooked rug.

Joan, a violinist with the Duluth-Superior Symphony Orchestra, encourages duets on the parlor's baby grand piano. Jim, whose background is in hotels, makes a point of offering comfort and relaxation to tired and stressed-out guests. The popular lake walk is just 2½ blocks from the inn, and the Halquists, both active, outdoorsy folks, can also recommend their favorite bike and cross-country ski trails; they even have a storage shed for any equipment you may bring. In addition, with two small children themselves, the Halquists don't mind accommodating the families of others. Their congeniality make the Ellery House very homey indeed. ♠ *2 double rooms with baths, 2 suites. Ceiling fan and fresh flowers in rooms, fireplace in 2 rooms, balcony in 1 room, off-street parking. $69–$98 winter, $85–$125 summer; full breakfast. AE, MC, V. Smoking on porches only.*

FINNISH HERITAGE HOMESTEAD 🐿

4776 Waisanen Rd., Embarrass 55732, tel. and fax 218/984–3318 or 800/863–6545

About 1891, Finnish immigrant John Kangas nearly froze to death for lack of shelter in the wilds of northern Minnesota—the state's Mesabi Iron Range region. As a blizzard moved in, Kangas shot a moose and—so the legend goes—cut the animal open to crawl inside as protection against the elements. Having survived a night there, he decided this had to be the place the heavenly powers wanted him to build his family's home. Almost 100 years after John began building his Embarrass, Minnesota, homestead, the area remains pretty wild, but the accommodations have improved considerably—thanks to Kangas's hard work and Finnish craftsmanship. He built nearly half a dozen log structures, including a rare 2½-story log building that served as a Finnish *poikatalo*, or boardinghouse, for loggers, miners, and railroad workers. Today, some of these buildings survive and can be explored, along with the fields and woods of the 32-acre farm.

In 1991, Buzz Schultz and his wife, Elaine Braginton, left the sweltering heat of Arizona to be closer to their beloved Boundary Waters Canoe Area (just a half hour away from Embarrass). The new owners of the Kangas homestead learned Embarrass townfolk frequently advised visiting dignitaries to "go stay with Buzz and Elaine. They've got room." So it seemed natural to convert the multiple-dwelling grounds of the farm into what the Finnish immigrants called a *matka koit*—a house to stay in while on a journey. The B&B offers five cozy, though somewhat small, upstairs rooms laid out in simple, comfortable farm style, with comforters on the beds and a few Norman Rockwell porcelain plates, photos, and memorabilia as wall hangings. All rooms share a bath, but guests are provided with terry cloth robes and, in winter, warm footies. The bathroom is almost as large as a guest room: One wall offers a bookcase stocked with everything from Garrison Keiller to guides on log-house restoration, and there's even an ironing board.

Short jaunts around the "neighborhood" can lead to skiing resorts in the winter or nifty places for fishing, swimming, canoeing, golfing, or hiking during warm weather. In Embarrass itself (the name derives from the term French voyagers gave the region's difficult-to-navigate rivers), townsfolk have revived the Finnish immigrant heritage with a gift shop, a heritage park, and the Heritage Pioneer Homestead Tour that, needless to say, includes the Kangas farm. ♙ *5 double rooms with shared bath. TV/VCR in parlor, wood-fired sauna. $68–$95 with special block rates to rent entire upstairs; full breakfast, bag lunch available for hikers, dinners available for extended-stay guests. MC, V. Smoking in designated areas only.*

MANSION BED & BREAKFAST INN 🐿

3600 London Rd., Duluth 55804, tel. 218/724–0739

Though imposing from the front, this 1928 rubble-stone and half-timbered Tudor mansion is really oriented toward its backyard. And what a backyard it is: Five hundred feet of Lake Superior shore provides the house with incredible views from almost every room. Who can resist sitting on the ample lawn in summer or fall to watch the many ships go by?

Built for mining executive Harry C. Dudley and his wife, Marjorie Congdon Dudley, daughter of Duluth lumber baron Chester Congdon, the Mansion is an inviting combination of grandeur and comfort. The main floor has a sunny dining room with a terrazzo floor, a wood-paneled library with a large fireplace and antique books, a large gallery with four window seats and three sets of French doors leading to a lakefront stone terrace, and a huge living room that opens onto a screened porch, a favorite spot for guests.

Sunny, lined with bear and wolf skins and moose heads, guarded by a suit of armor, and fitted with a huge lake-view window seat, the third-floor Trophy Room is the inn's designated quiet room. Guests use it for reading and dreaming and "fall asleep here all the time," says proprietor Sue Monson, who, along with her husband, Warren, bought the building in 1983. Warren is a busy physician, so Sue, who likes to cater to the guests, runs the Mansion herself with some help from her daughter and a small part-time staff.

The bedrooms that belonged to members of the Dudley family, such as the Anniversary Suite and the Master Suite, are the largest, but the coziest are the former maids' quarters, now called the Peach, Yellow, and Beige rooms. The Master Suite can expand to an additional bedroom, while the carriage house offers one-, two-, or three-bedroom accommodations. Some of the bedrooms, all of which are carpeted and contain antiques and reproductions, do pale in comparison to the absolute splendor of the Mansion itself, but as one of the guests said, "I can't imagine anyone coming here and not being completely impressed and comfortable."

The 7-acre grounds are given over to lawns, gardens, and a forest of northern hardwoods, pine, and cedar; there's also a private beach, where guests often build bonfires on summer evenings. △ *6 double rooms with baths, 4 doubles share 2 baths, 1-bedroom carriage-house suite. Large-screen TV/VCR in living room, kitchenette in carriage house, private beach, off-street parking. $115–$245, $185 for carriage house; full breakfast. MC, V. Smoking on screened porch only.*

OLCOTT HOUSE ☞
2316 E. 1st St., Duluth 55812, tel. 218/728–1339 or 800/715–1339

At the turn of the century, William Olcott, president of Oliver Mining and onetime employee of John D. Rockefeller, and his wife, Fannie, traveled around the country, sketchbook in hand to record their favorite houses. In 1904, their dreams and sketches came together to create an impressive Georgian Colonial mansion, the Olcott House. The white-columned mansion set on emerald green lawns was built with hospitality in mind—as visitors will note when they discover its small basement ballroom. Today, that tradition continues, since the Olcott is now a hostelry that fits comfortably into Duluth's East End, just four blocks from Lake Superior and minutes to Canal Park and downtown. Since 1994 the Olcott has been the cherished possession of Barb and Don Trueman, and they've appropriately furnished the 12,000 square ft of the house, plus a carriage house, for its new life as a B&B.

Their choices make the house lush but not cluttered. People who had lived, worked, or studied in the house during its incarnations as a family home and later as a school of music for the University of Minnesota-Duluth made contributions to the house collection, such as the photographs of the Olcott family that now grace several walls or the chapter about life in the house from an Olcott daughter's biography—charmingly copied for guests to peruse.

The Truemans revel in their historic dwelling and give interested guests a tour of the home on their first evening. The entryway is suitably elegant, with dentil work and a gracefully curved staircase. The music room, to the left of the entry, was built with coved corners for acoustic quality and now sports a baby grand piano. The side-by-side dining rooms, where breakfast is served, have tables set with all the crystal and china trimmings and matched-pattern mahogany sliding doors, wainscoting, and beams. Upstairs, the house has five suites and one double room, each with a special offering, such as the three-season porch and bay window with lake and harbor view from the Lake Superior Suite, or the charm of the blue-and-white Summer Suite with its inlaid-tile fireplace.

The separate carriage house has a small, equipped kitchen, a large living room with a fireplace, arched paladium windows, and a queen-size bed beneath an overhead fan, along with white wicker furniture. △ *1 double room, 5 suites, carriage house. Air-conditioning in 3 suites, cable TV, telephone, and stereo in carriage house, TV in rooms on request, fireplace in suites. $85–$155 June–Oct, $75–$145 Nov.–May; full breakfast. D, MC, V. Smoking on porch only, 2-night minimum weekends June–Oct.*

STONE HEARTH INN BED & BREAKFAST ℝ

1118 Hwy. 61 E, Little Marais 55614, tel. 218/226–3020 or 888/206–3020, fax 218/226–3466

In 1989, when Charlie Michels came to Little Marais, he wanted to buy some land on Lake Superior. Two years later he had a five-bedroom, 70-year-old inn, and a wife, Susan, who'd been one of his first guests.

The Stone Hearth Inn was the original homestead of the Benjamin Fenstad family. Benjamin built a log cabin on the site in 1893 and, in 1924, built the home that Charlie owns today. An accomplished Twin Cities carpenter and contractor, Charlie did most of the renovation work himself. He made 10 rooms into 6, stripped the narrow-plank maple floors, added beams and molding downstairs, and collected stones from the shores of Lake Superior to use in the construction of the large living-room fireplace.

Just 80 ft from the lake, the house has a wonderful long porch furnished with Adirondack chairs, perfect for relaxing in these serene surroundings. French doors open onto it from both the simple dining room, whose large handmade pine table sits in the center, and from the living room, where soft chairs and sofas flank the giant hearth and guests take turns playing the piano.

In all seven guest rooms, you can fall asleep to the comforting sounds of the lake, but you'll get the best views from Rooms 2, 3, and 4. Room 2, a corner room in blue and white with a four-poster canopy bed, has a lake view even from its pink-and-white ceramic-tile bathroom.

An old boathouse just 30 ft from the lake was renovated in 1992 and rebuilt as a two-unit cottage. One unit is a suite with a bedroom, bathroom, living room with sofa bed, and kitchenette. Both are upstairs and have gas fireplaces, whirlpool baths, and especially dramatic views from their picture windows. On the drawing board are two more double units with whirlpool baths and gas fireplaces, to be constructed in the carriage house.

Blueberry–wild rice pancakes, Austrian apple pancakes, lake trout sausage, and vanilla poached pears are perfect examples of Susan and Charlie's innovative cooking. On most clear nights, there is a bonfire down by the lake, with s'mores provided by the Micheles and, if you're lucky, northern lights provided by Mother Nature. △ *6 double rooms with baths, 1 suite. Gas fireplace, coffeemaker, and whirlpool bath in 2 rooms and suite, kitchenette in suite, trail lunches available, bonfire, lodge-to-lodge hiking program. $84–$139; full breakfast in inn, Continental breakfast in boathouse double room. AE, D, MC, V. No smoking.*

OTHER CHOICES

Fitger's Inn. 600 E. Superior St., Duluth 55802, tel. 218/722–8826 or 800/726–2982 or 888/FITGERS, fax 318/722–8826. 42 double rooms with baths,

18 suites. Air-conditioning, phone, cable TV, and clock radio in rooms, room service, conference facilities, 160-seat theater, off-street and free valet parking, adjoining shopping and restaurant complex, fitness center. $92–$250; Continental breakfast. AE, D, DC, MC, V.

Lindgren's Bed & Breakfast. 5552 County Rd. 35 (Box 56), Lutsen 55612-0056, tel. and fax 218/663–7450. 3 double rooms with baths, 1 room with 10 beds. TV in rooms, phone in 2 rooms, whirlpool bath in 1 room, fireplace in 1 room, Finnish sauna, bonfire pit, horseshoe pit, lodge-to-lodge ski and hiking program. $85–$125; full breakfast, trail lunch available. MC, V. No smoking.

Mathew S. Burrows 1890 Inn. 1632 E. 1st St., Duluth 55812, tel. and fax 218/724–4991 or 800/789–1890. 2 double rooms with baths, 3 suites. Alarm clock, radio/tape player, fireplace, and marble shower in 1 suite, off-street parking. $95–$118; full breakfast. AE, D, DC, MC, V. No smoking, 2-night minimum summer weekends. Closed Dec. 24–25.

Superior Overlook B&B. U.S. 61, Milepost 112 (Box 963), Grand Marais 55604-0963, tel. 218/387–1571 or 800/858–7622, fax 218/387–1899. 1 double room with nonadjoining bath, 1 suite. TV/VCR, phone, and wood-burning stove in living room, kitchenette in suite, sauna. $95–$130; full breakfast. AE, D, MC, V. No smoking.

The Northwest and the Cuyana Iron Range, Including Brainerd and Detroit Lakes

ELM ST. INN ☞

422 Elm St., Crookston, tel. 218/281–2343 or 800/568–4467, fax 218/281–1756

In the prairie town of Crookston, Minnesota, historic buildings are not a rarity: Thirty-five buildings in its business district alone are listed in the National Register of Historic Places. The architect of several of those buildings also designed this charming Arts & Crafts–era house in 1910. From lawyer to doctor to banker, the house served as a presentable, livable home for the town's professional families until it fell to the Crookston School Board, which had plans to demolish it. John and Sheryl Winters, both involved in a local law firm, saved it from that fate in 1976. By 1992, their children had left home, and the Winterses decided it was time to open their home to guests rather than ramble around in the suddenly all-too-ample space.

Downstairs, the small Grandmother's Room has a hunter-green iron bed from the family's heirlooms as well as a maple antique vanity dresser with an hourglass-shaped mirror. Upstairs, the maple-floored rooms "blossom." The Prairie Rose Room's sponge-painted walls are done in dusty rose and peach. A white wrought-iron bed with eyelet comforter and ruffles is accented with a hand-painted pillow, while a restored oak rocker cradles a teddy bear. The Morning Glory Room, done in pink-and-blue floral patterns, has a handmade "quilter's quilt" on the high queen-size bed (a wooden step is stowed below the bed for those needing a boost).

The passionate purples of the Lilac Room have become a favorite with guests, according to the Winterses. Pinks and purples dominate just about everything—

even the hangars are purple. A hand-tied quilt covers the Pennsylvania cherrywood antique bed. The private bath next door is another reason so many guests lay claim to this room. Its delicate floral patterns of faded greens and peaches, a stained-glass window of greens and lavenders, and an assortment of bubble baths and an oversize claw-foot tub (big enough for two) make long soaks a luxurious temptation. For more aquatic relaxation, you can opt for a pass to the township's enclosed pool, just across the lawn from the inn.

Breakfast is served—charmingly by candlelight—on stylish china in the dining room, and guests benefit from John's upbringing in the family bakery. Wild rice–buttermilk pancakes with sunflower seeds top the favored fare. A music room; a library room with a TV, a well-stocked bookcase, and a couch; and an airy upstairs screened porch with white wicker furnishings and a beguiling assortment of wind chimes—all conspire to make the inn a hard place to leave. ♙ *4 double rooms with baths. Air-conditioning in some rooms, alarm clock in rooms, TV/VCR in living room. $55–$65; full breakfast. AE, D, MC, V. No smoking indoors.*

HOSPITAL BAY B&B 🐦
620 Lake St. NE, Warroad 56763, tel. 218/386–2627 or 800/568–6028

You'd think the name of this hostelry would be inspired by the neighboring bay; in fact, it's the other way around—the bay in Warroad, Minnesota, got its moniker from this turn-of-the-century house, which spent a spell as the region's hospital. Its heyday was during the Midwest's logging and commercial-fishing boom from the 1920s through the 1940s. Today, however, the area still boasts one of the lowest unemployment rates in the Midwest, with the nearby Marvins Windows and Polaris factories employing all comers in this sparsely populated region.

The house was built in 1906 by local merchant Carl Carlquist for his family and at one time featured a magnificent turret (now removed). Happily, the picturesque horseshoe arches remain over the outside windows. The original interior of the house has been altered several times, particularly when the structure was a hospital ward. Its current owners, Harvey and Mary Corneliusen, purchased this one-time sanctuary of healing in 1985, when ill health forced them to leave their nearby farm and settle down to a less rigorous way of life. Together, they've made it airy and bright, with white walls and white lace curtains as a tranquilizing backdrop. Two special spots invite guests to relax and mellow out: a charming paisley-print love seat and matching armchair in the living room, and the sitting room—a comfy cocoon with brick fireplace and built-in bookcases. Many eyes remain focused on the views out the windows: Warroad is on the state's Wildflower Route and offers some of the best bird-watching around, with several migration routes traversing directly around the site.

Just off the sitting room is the Parkside Room, done in pale rose-colored floral wallpaper, with a four-poster Broyhill bed covered simply with a white spread. Here you'll find one of the many porcelain lamps scattered through the house—in this case, a lovely blue-and-pink number that complements the room's palette. An antique accent is a turn-of-the-century oak washstand with an inset of birds'-eye maple. Upstairs beyond the dining room is Lisa's Room, named after the Corneliusens' daughter, who actually designed the room—which has a river view—from its compelling dark pink hue to its wallpaper border of an undersea motif. The white wrought-iron bed is a pleasing touch to this homey chamber. Next door, the room's small private bath has an enclosed claw-foot tub.

All in all, this is a pleasant and relaxing B&B—its ambience all the more welcome, for this is as far north as a B&B gets in rugged Minnesota. ♙ *3 double rooms* with private baths. Air-conditioning in 2 rooms, TV/VCR in living room, fireplace in sitting room, free docking on river for guests with boats. $45–$60; full breakfast. MC, V. No smoking.

PARK STREET INN ☙
620 Lake St. NE, Warroad 56763, tel. 218/386–2627 or 800/568–6028

This little jewel box sits on a little street in a little town you'd miss if you drove too fast. Nevis, once a prosperous logging town, now makes a bid for tourism with the nearby Heartland Bike Trail and Lake Belle Taine. The Park Street Inn represents this newer Nevis, although it is also rooted in the town's history.

Built in 1912 by Justin Halvorson, a well-to-do banker and local land developer, the house is more of a bungalow than a mansion, but it was done up in style—or more accurately, all kinds of styles, for Halvorson apparently was no purist. The compact oak stairway and banister were constructed out of state and brought to town by train. Other midwestern craftsmen contributed a beveled-glass fan window and exquisite entry arches of carved oak in a French Empire style, with acanthus-topped fluted columns and flower-basket bas-reliefs. In contrast, an oak mantel sports the clean, simple lines of mission-style design.

Halvorson lost his money in the depression and moved to California. Given that Nevis, too, was declining, it's surprising so many of the original treasures in the house remained. Irene and Len Hall bought the place in 1996 after it had already been a B&B for several years. Many of the house furnishings are original, but the Halls added their own personal touches to the rooms so tactfully that returning guests felt sure several new pieces had been there all along.

In the living room and dining area, subdued wallpaper and matching valances complement lace-curtained windows. The Halls decided to make a major statement in the living room; they adorned it with a bubbling fountain, and dominating one corner is a striking backlit stained-glass window whose original home was a Methodist church.

The upstairs is a bit less restrained but still interesting. The largest guest room, which has a wicker-furnished sleeping porch facing Lake Belle Taine, also features a two-person whirlpool whose oak arch came from a Lutheran church altar—a nice ecumenical touch given the stained-glass window below, Len likes to note. Each room has its own wallpaper pattern and quilt—a handmade double wedding-ring quilt in one bedroom, a bright star pattern in another. The Halls also restocked the numerous built-in bookshelves (with both new and antique vintage editions) and added many more, making the house a sort of B&B—Bed, Book, and Breakfast. ⌂ *Rte. 3 (Box 554), Nevis 56467, tel. 218/652–4500 or 800/797–1778. 3 double rooms with baths, 1 suite. TV in sitting room. $70–$125; full breakfast, evening refreshments. MC, V. Smoking in designated area only.*

PETERS' SUNSET BEACH ☙
2500 S. Lakeshore Dr., Glenwood 56334, tel. 320/634–4501 or 800/356–8654 in MN

One look inside the main lodge's dining room gives you the flavor of this classic lakeside resort: knotty-pine paneling, fish trophies, paintings of scenes from a Hiawatha-like Native American legend, light fixtures done up like painted drums, and a broad porch overlooking Lake Minnewaska.

The lodge, a gorgeous example of Craftsman-style design, is one of the resort's three buildings on the National Register of Historic Places. The place has changed a bit since train conductor Henry Peters jumped off the Soo Line in Glenwood and opened his summer hotel in 1915. It has grown from a small hostelry to a resort, complete with its own 18-hole golf course, accommodating up to 175 guests in a variety of up-to-date rooms, cottages, and luxury town houses. But it's still run by the Peters family, and they have restored the historic 1923 Annex to its old-fashioned appearance—making it, in the words of Henry's grandson Bill Peters, "our country inn."

From the outside, the Annex looks a lot like the main lodge, almost like a wing that detached itself and settled several steps away.

The Peterses have installed antique bedsteads, tables, and dressers, many of them from the turn of the century, to fit in with the refinished original woodwork. Quilts, made by a local artisan, grace each bed; the wallpaper is quietly floral. The whole building has an agreeable, unpretentious air about it, although there are some discordant touches left over from the Annex's prerestoration interim years.

Still, the Annex has a certain charm, and there are other compensations: The restaurant serves some of the best food in the area. The nearby town of Glenwood is pretty, the resort's grounds are gracious, and Lake Minnewaska itself is lovely. You can certainly see why Henry Peters made this the end of his line.

⚱ *20 double rooms (12 in Court Bldg., 8 in Annex) with baths; 3 suites in Main Lodge, 10 town houses sleep 4–9 people; 2 1-bedroom cottages, 5 2-bedroom cottages, 3 3-bedroom cottages, 1 4-bedroom cottage; 1 7-bedroom housekeeping cottage. Restaurant, snack bar, air-conditioning, cable TV in all units, meeting room, beach, boat rentals, tennis, golf, racquetball. $65–$250; full breakfast and dinner. MC, V. 2- to 4-night minimum. Closed Oct.–Apr.*

SPICER CASTLE ☙
11600 Indian Beach Rd. (Box 307), Spicer 56288, tel. 320/796–5870 or 800/821–6675, fax 320/796–4076

If you somehow missed the opportunity to live in an old country mansion circa 1913, here's your chance. This imposing house, now on the National Register of Historic Places, was built in 1895 by farm developer John Spicer, one of the founders of Minnesota's branch of the Democratic Party. According to current owner Allen Latham, Spicer's grandson, the last renovations on the house were done in 1913, shortly after it was wired for electricity, and the building hasn't been changed since. Set on the wooded shores of Green Lake, the Tudor-style half-timbered house was originally called Medayto Cottage, but in the 1930s fishermen on the lake started referring to it as "the Castle," perhaps because of its crenellated tower. Though it's otherwise not particularly castlelike, the name stuck.

However beautiful its exterior, it's the interior that makes the Castle distinctive. The furnishings, rugs, china, and Craftsman-style lamps and clocks are all antiques and have been in place since the 1913 redecoration. Walking across the gleaming maple floors, through the living and dining rooms, the well-stocked library, and the grand porch overlooking the lake, you get the sense you are not just viewing the past but actually participating in it.

The first floor, with dark furniture and burlap wall coverings (a typical period Craftsman touch), might seem dark, but it's not oppressive—rather, it encourages quiet reflection and talk. In winter, it becomes downright cozy, as the fireplaces throw their flickering light on the ceiling beams.

Upstairs, it's almost like a different house. White beaded paneling and large windows give the place the bright air of a Nantucket summer cottage. Some renovation has been done up here, primarily in the bathrooms, but Allen and his wife, Marti, have kept to the period, with pedestal sinks and claw-foot tubs (some in the rooms themselves). The bedsteads and dressers are in various styles, but all belonged to the Lathams' forebears. Two equally well preserved cottages offer more privacy.

Breakfast is served in the dining room in cool months, on the lakeside porch in summer. There are no TVs, telephones, or air-conditioning. This is pure 1913—they won't be missed. ⚘ *8 double rooms with baths, 2 cottages. Ceiling fan in rooms, whirlpool bath in 1 bedroom and 1 cottage. $75–$140; full breakfast, afternoon tea. AE, D, MC, V. No smoking. Closed weekdays Sept.–Apr.*

OTHER CHOICES

Carrington House. 4974 Interlochen Dr., Alexandria 56308, tel. 320/846–7400 or 800/806–3899. 4 double rooms with baths, 1 cottage. Air-conditioning, cable TV on porch, ceiling fans in commons area, whirlpool bath in cottage and 1 room. $100–$150; full breakfast. MC, V. No smoking.

Heartland Trail Inn. Rte. 3 (Box 39), Park Rapids 56470, tel. 218/732–5305. 6 double rooms share 3 baths. Air-conditioning, ceiling fans in some rooms. $45–$60; full breakfast. MC, V. No smoking.

Log House on Spirit Lake and Homestead. Ottertail Rte. 4 (Box 130), Vergas 56587, tel. 218/342– or 800/342–2318, fax 218/342–3294. 5 double rooms with baths. Air-conditioning, terry cloth robes and fresh flowers, fireplace and whirlpool bath in 3 rooms. $95–$165; full breakfast, welcome tray. D, MC, V. No smoking.

Nims' Bakketopp Hus. R.R. 2 (Box 187A), Fergus Falls 56537, tel. 218/739–2915 or 800/739–2915. 3 double rooms with baths. Air-conditioning, cable TV on request, phone in rooms, whirlpool bath in 1 room. $65–$95; full breakfast, evening refreshments. D, MC, V. No smoking.

Prairie View Estate. Rte. 2 (Box 443), Pelican Rapids 56572, tel. 218/863–4321 or 800/298–8058. 3 double rooms with bath. Air-conditioning, TV in parlor. $55–$70; full breakfast, evening refreshments. D, MC, V. No smoking.

Whistle Stop Inn. Rte. 1 (Box 85), New York Mills 56567, tel. 218/385–2223 or 800/328–6315. 2 double rooms with baths, 1 suite, 1 caboose, 1 Pullman car. Air-conditioning in Pullman car; whirlpool in caboose and Pullman car; cable TV in suite, Pullman car, and 1 bedroom; ceiling fans, sauna. $49–$125; full breakfast, evening refreshments upon request. AE, D, MC, V. Smoking on porch only.

The Southwestern Prairie

SOD HOUSE ON THE PRAIRIE ☙
1259 Magnolia Ave., Sanborn 56083, tel. 507/723–5138

When Stan McCone was growing up, older relatives told him tales of his forebears—sodbusting white settlers of the Great Plains, just like those that Willa Cather and Laura Ingalls Wilder wrote about. Since few trees sprouted on the grasslands, pioneers built their houses out of the earth. These sod houses, made of blocks of cut turf, were held together by the dense root systems of the prairie grass.

McCone dreamed of re-creating this lost type of architecture. After working for several years as a cattle buyer, he got a chance to make his dream come true when he learned one of his neighbors in rural Sanborn had a patch of virgin prairie on his land. Soon Stan set to work, with the same kind of grit and sweat as his pioneer ancestors, cutting massive blocks of sod (he describes the sound as "the ripping of a giant canvas"). The result is two buildings set amid acres of (reseeded) prairie grass: a rudimentary "poor man's dugout" and a larger "rich man's soddy," both open to the public as a museum. For those who want a full dose of pioneer experience, the larger is a snug, rustic bed-and-breakfast. Just recently, the McCones renovated an authentic 19th-century log cabin, which guests delight in touring.

The house's furnishings—antique bedsteads and buffets, kitchen and farm implements hanging on the walls and beams—are practical and sturdily beautiful. The only piece that could be considered at all fancy is the leather fainting couch that doubles as a bed, across which is spread a heavy, shaggy horse-hide robe.

Authenticity is the key word here. There are no wires or pipes running through the soddy's turf walls—heating comes from a potbellied stove, air-conditioning from open windows, light from oil lamps. The bathroom is a two-seat outhouse steps away; to wash, guests must pour water from a jug into the 100-year-old pitcher and bowl.

Virginia and Stan McCone provide a simple, hearty country breakfast incorporating high-quality meats, which is Stan's other line of business. In winter, if you want to cook your other meals, throw some logs into the mighty Monarch stove. One family spent a prairie Christmas here, cooking up a feast on the Monarch, with the soddy so snug the kids padded about in shorts. Though few of us today would want to live day to day with the rigors of pioneer life, we can still savor a sample of it, thanks to the McCones. Needless to say, Laura Ingalls Wilder fans welcome! △ *1 house with 2 double beds and outhouse. No air-conditioning, wood-burning stove. $100–$160; full breakfast. No credit cards.*

FERING'S GUEST HOUSE ☞
708 N. Main St., Blue Earth 56013, tel. 507/526–5054, fax 507/526–7004

Charles and Phyllis Fering freely admit that Blue Earth, while attractive, isn't a tourist hot spot, despite its attractive courthouse, many antiques shops, and lovely woods. The same can be said of this large, frame Victorian house, built in 1889, where the Ferings have lived for more than 20 years. Rather than a renovated showplace, it looks like the ideal small-town home, all porch and tall windows with a lush, shady yard. Original oak woodwork exists alongside more recent birch paneling and country-style wallpaper; family knickknacks are scattered about. When the Ferings opened their bed-and-breakfast in 1990, after most of their kids had grown and gone, they expected to attract folks who were just looking for a good night's lodging.

Still, the Ferings' guests often send them Christmas cards, bottles of wine, invitations to visit. Why? "We're like family," says Charles. They're affable, open-minded, and flexible—for example, although they usually serve only Continental breakfasts, once when guests were stranded by a sudden snowstorm, they whipped up three square meals a day until the snow cleared. That's small-town America for you. △ *1 double room with bath, 2 doubles share bath. Air-conditioning, cable TV in rooms. $36–$45; Continental breakfast. No credit cards. No smoking.*

PRAIRIE HOUSE ON ROUND LAKE ☞
R.R. 1 (Box 105), Round Lake 56167, tel. 507/945–8934

In 1879, Chicago commodity trader Owen Roche built this grand American Bracket–style house, nicknamed "Roche's Roost" and surrounded by a 2,500-acre estate on Round Lake. It's smaller than it used to be, having been truncated to save money during the depression (in an odd twist, the bottom floor rather than the top was removed); the estate has shrunk to 44 acres, but it still remains a good place to escape urban stress.

Now owned by horse breeders Ralph and Virginia Schenck, the house is set amid horse barns and wildlife preserves. Inside, there are some antiques (claw-foot tubs, some fine old tables) and beamed ceilings, but the wall-to-wall carpets, modern bathroom fixtures, and other furnishings suggest the interior of a suburban home more than a country inn. Fresh flowers from the Schencks' greenhouse and the whinnying of their American paint horses help remind you of your rural surroundings. Canada geese, white pelicans, and other waterfowl thrive in peace here. Except for outdoor recreation, there isn't much to do here—but that's enough. △ *1 double room with bath, 1 double with half-bath, 2 doubles share bath. Air-conditioning, lakeside beach, tennis court. $55; full breakfast. No credit cards. No smoking.*

MISSISSIPPI

North Mississippi Hill Country

BARKSDALE-ISOM HOUSE ☙
1003 Jefferson Ave., Oxford 38655, tel. 601/236–5600

From its humble beginnings in 1838 as a three-room office for local physician Dr. T. D. Isom, the Barksdale-Isom House has become an upmarket southern planter-style B&B filled with fine French antiques and its own chef, who serves a sumptuous gourmet buffet each morning.

The original builder would be amazed at the Continental rebirth of the structure he built of hand-planed native timber. According to local legend, as Dr. Isom's practice grew, so did his office-home, and it took on the planter style of the era. Owner Susan Barksdale renovated the house a few years back and gave it its new lease on life, and new names for each room. The Rose Room is so named because of a rumored connection with Oxford native William Faulkner's "A Rose for Emily." The owners have used a rose motif, and the room has a working fireplace and mid-18th-century French furniture. The Barksdale Room, done entirely in red, from the wallpaper to the canopy and bedspread, is notable for three sets of French doors. The Worthy Room has two double beds and a wisteria motif. The dark-gray and green Saunders Room contains a king-size canopy bed. The Weems Room is yellow and white, and the golden-beige Miss Sallie Room has a private kitchen and entrance. All bedrooms have a number of antiques.

Guests are pampered here: Massages are available with advance reservations, and for the gourmand, the chef may share a recipe or two. The breakfast buffet includes two choices of cereals, breakfast breads, fruit, cheese grits, juice, and coffee. The hosts serve hors d'oeuvres in the afternoon and tea on weekends. ♨ *5 double rooms with baths. Air-conditioning, TV, phones in rooms. $120–$150; full breakfast. AE, MC, V. No smoking.*

HIGHLAND HOUSE ☙
810 Highland Circle, Columbus 39701, tel. and fax 601/327–5577

Once known by locals as the Lindamood House, this imposing Greek Revival mansion has dominated Highland Circle in Columbus since the early 1900s, when it was rebuilt after a disgruntled housekeeper purportedly set fire to the original 1862 wood structure. Now Jim Holzhauer, a physician, and his wife, Celeta, are the proud owners-innkeepers of this 9,000-square-ft showplace B&B. The house boasts a widow's walk, 78 windows, 13 working fireplaces, 14-ft ceilings, two parlors, and three dens.

Downstairs to the left, two parlors are separated by faux marble columns. To the right are two festively decorated dining rooms, with a huge brick fireplace directly ahead. The fireplace is a replica of a brick kiln once used by brick-maker Mr. Lindamood. Above it all is a hand-painted ceiling that took two years to complete. Jim's chess-set collection is displayed throughout the house.

One guest room is downstairs, near the wide staircase behind the fireplace that winds up to the second story, where three more guest rooms await. Antiques and Oriental pieces are used in the colorful guest rooms, giving them an eclectic, interesting feel. Even amid the architectural excellence and expensive furnishings, the Highland House is quite comfortable, and guests are made to feel as though they've "come home." Upon arrival, Celeta offers a wonderful minted lemonade and a tour of the house. She's from a small town in Alabama and is a soft-spoken southern belle who gives guests her undivided attention.

Other nice touches include various exotic birds, a pool, a hot tub, and a video library of 3,000 movies, plus mint juleps on the veranda, Bailey's and coffee in the evening, and a breakfast extravaganza with menu items that might include orange-poached pears with white chocolate and raspberries, baked apples, home-made breads, jams, and casseroles. △ *4 double rooms with baths. Fireplace, phone, TV/VCR in rooms; pool, exercise room, tanning bed. $100–$160; full breakfast, champagne brunch on Sunday. AE, MC, V. No smoking.*

MOCKINGBIRD INN 🐦

305 N. Gloster St., Tupelo 38801, tel. 601/841–0286, fax 601/840–4158

Jim and Sandy Gilmer decided to leave the corporate world and strike out on their own. So in addition to starting a recycling business, they transformed a spacious old two-story home on a shady street corner into a B&B. In researching the home's history, the Gilmers found that the original builders from 1925 loved to entertain and had theme parties relating to various countries. The globe-trekking Gilmers named their B&B the Mockingbird Inn, after the state bird—a symbol of hospitality. It's only fitting that a mockingbird appears at the porch windows periodically.

It's also only fitting that people who have seven favorite places in the world and seven rooms to decorate should re-create those places in the decor of the rooms and the bathrooms. You can almost hear gondolas gliding across a canal in the Venice Room, where rich Venetian tapestry and old lace make it more authentic. The Mackinac Island Room resembles a wonderful whitewashed lakeside cottage, light and airy, with pickled wood. A pewter wedding canopy bed and chaise longue are two of many elements that leave no doubt as to the inspiration for the Paris Room. The large Athens Room has Greek columns and an L-shape whirlpool for two. Even Isak Dinesen would feel at home in the Africa Room, where faux jungle-animal skins and mosquito netting around the bed set the scene. Pastels and seashells make the Sanibel Island Room as authentic as possible; add the verdigris iron bed and wicker furniture, and it's Florida revisited. Finally, in the Bavaria Room, lots of knotty pine, a sleigh bed, antique skis, and typical lace-trimmed windows bring southern Germany to northern Mississippi.

Guests linger on the indoor porch, with its wicker furniture and coffee and tea makings. The inn is popular with businesspeople who attend one of the two Tupelo furniture markets and with tourists of the rock-and-roll persuasion, who like to look across at the school where Elvis Presley attended sixth and seventh grades. △ *7 double rooms with baths. Air-conditioning, cable TV and phone in rooms; fireplace in 1 room, whirlpool bath in 1 room. $75–$125; full breakfast, afternoon refreshments. D, MC, V. No smoking.*

SPAHN HOUSE 🐚
401 College St., Senatobia 38668, tel. 601/562–9853 or 800/400–9853

Senatobia, just 30 minutes south of Memphis, is a pretty-as-a-picturebook small town, where you'll find what's quickly becoming one of the state's most popular B&Bs: the Spahn House. The owners are Joe and Daughn Spahn. He's a building contractor, and she's a former partner in a brokerage firm who came "back home" to the Magnolia State via Chicago, New York City, and Miami after she married Joe. Their 15-room southern mansion, built in 1904, is on a tree-canopied street in a quiet, historic neighborhood.

The grand old house was a true Victorian until its renovation in 1948, which left it bearing a slight resemblance to the Greek Revival style. When the Spahns bought the house in 1994, they transformed it into a B&B. The parlor's recessed arches give the first inkling that this is no ordinary house. High ceilings, original pine floors, and rich woods add to the turn-of-the-century ambience. Throughout the house, window treatment may be lace left over from a wedding or vines carefully crafted as valances. A wide staircase leads to the second-story common area, which connects to all the guest rooms. Antiques were purchased in Memphis and New Orleans and "all in between," according to Daughn. Each room has a different theme, including the Gentlemen's Room, where antique clothing and hats are casually displayed. Quaint old chests have been converted to vanities; this utilitarian use of odd pieces of furniture adds to this B&B's appeal.

Daughn is now a caterer with a full staff, and guests can arrange a private gourmet dinner. Breakfasts are elegant: Expect a soufflé that may be filled with ham and cheese, strawberries and whipped cream, fresh fruits, and an assortment of other gourmet offerings, all served with panache. Also on-site is a business office for the use of guests. ♠ *4 double rooms with baths. Whirlpool bath in 2 rooms, TV in common area. Private candlelight dinner available with advance reservation. $75–$110; full breakfast. AE, MC, V. No smoking.*

SASSAFRAS INN 🐚
785 Hwy. 51, (Box 612), Hernando 38632, tel. 601/429–5864 or 800/882–1897, fax 601/429–4591

Just south of Memphis, in a town depicted in one of John Grisham's novels, this English Tudor home is almost hidden by trees and landscaping. As guests arrive, owners Dennis and Frances McClanahan extend a hospitable southern welcome. Dennis, a builder, and Frances, a floral designer, have a home with architectural extras such as skylights in one of the bedrooms and eight stained-glass windows in the indoor pool area. Amenities include a climate-controlled indoor pool, hot tub, and a recreation room with Ping-Pong and pool tables. There's a cottage on the grounds where honeymooners—or anyone else who appreciates romantic settings—can enjoy absolute privacy.

The guest-room decor is lacy Victorian. All bedrooms have queen-size beds, CD players, sound machines (you can listen to the ocean, for example), and bathrobes. The Victorian Room contains cherrywood furniture from that period, including a four-poster bed, and delicate lace and satin drapings. The Magnolia Room combines oak furniture with a bedspread and wallpaper in a magnolia motif. Ivy-pattern decor contributes to the cheeriness of the Skylight Room.

Business travelers will enjoy the inn's technological amenities: A computer, copier, and fax are all available. Guests can choose from a choice of breakfast locations: poolside table, formal dining room, or room service. ♠ *3 double rooms with baths, 1 cottage suite. Microwave and mini-refrigerator in cottage suite, TV* *and phone in rooms; indoor pool, hot tub, business facilities. $85–$225; full breakfast. AE, D, MC, V. No smoking.*

OTHER CHOICES

Alexander House. Anderson and Green Sts. (Box 187), West 39192, tel. 601/967–2266 or 800/350–8034. 3 double rooms with baths, 2 doubles share bath. TV in two rooms and upstairs common area. $85; full breakfast. D, MC, V. No smoking.

Arbor House. 518 College St., Columbus 39701, tel. 601/241–5596. 4 double rooms with baths. Air-conditioning, cable TV, phone in rooms. $95–$135; full breakfast. MC, V.

Backstrom B&B. 4567 Hwy. 182 E (Box 2311), Columbus 39704, tel. 601/328–0222 or 800/698–3983. 3 double rooms with baths. Air-conditioning, TV/VCR, and phone in rooms. $75; full breakfast. MC, V. No smoking.

Caragen House. 1108 Hwy. 82 W, Starkville 39759, tel. 601/323–0340. 5 double rooms with baths. Air-conditioning, cable TV, wet bar in rooms. $100; full breakfast. AE, MC, V. No smoking.

Rambling Rose. 621 10th St. N, Columbus 39701, tel. 601/327–2952. 2 double rooms with baths, 1 double shares a bath. Air-conditioning, cable TV/VCR in common room, hot tub. $70; full breakfast. MC, V.

RESERVATIONS SERVICES

Greater Golden Triangle Welcome Center (300 Main St., Columbus 39701, tel. 601/328–0222 or 800/689–3983). **Lincoln, Ltd. Bed & Breakfast Mississippi Reservation Service** (Box 3479, Meridian 39303, tel. 601/482–5483 or 800/633–6477).

Near the Natchez Trace

BAILEY HOUSE ☞
400 S. Commerce, Natchez 39120, tel. 601/442–9974, fax 601/442–9939

The personality of owner Lisa Brunetti is etched onto the walls of the Bailey House (circa 1897), with its murals and fanciful paintings of kudzu or wisteria sometimes cleverly disguising a crack in the plaster. A watercolor artist and art teacher, Lisa has applied her fine sense of line and aesthetics to this centrally located Natchez Garden District property, where her paintings are displayed throughout.

Rooms are uncomplicated and bright. Don't look for a lot of fussy antiques, just tasteful things old and new that keep the clean, allergen-free atmosphere informal and breezy. One of the most striking elements of the Victorian Colonial Revival–style house is a large, expressive stained-glass window over the landing (the 1870 painting it was derived from is hanging in the front parlor). "I saw it and felt sorry for the house," says Lisa, who was originally looking for an art studio when she bought Bailey House with her husband, Mike, a Louisiana farmer.

Bedrooms overlook picturesque Natchez street scenes that include an Episcopal church and a synagogue, as well as the home's courtyard, with its camellias, wisteria, old sweet-olive tree, and bubbling fountain with goldfish pond. Two second-story bedrooms share a veranda reachable through the large windows. (One small drawback to the house, where sound carries, is the somewhat-too-intimate proximity of one guest bathroom to an upstairs common area.)

Guests have commented on the warmth of the atmosphere and their quick rapport with both Lisa and her cook, Margaret, who lays out a breakfast that, like the rest of the house, is a work of art (butter served with cut violets is a particularly sweet touch). ♠ *5 double rooms with baths. Air-conditioning, cable TV in rooms. $125–$145; full breakfast. MC, V. No smoking.*

BALFOUR HOUSE ℘
1002 Crawford St. (Box 781), Vicksburg 39181, tel. 601/638–7113 or 800/294–7113, fax 601/638–8484

Civil War historians will surely be familiar with the Balfour House (circa 1835), for it was the home of diarist Emma Balfour, who kept a daily account of the Siege of Vicksburg in 1863. The diary is now part of the Emma Balfour Collection of the Mississippi Department of Archives and History. After the fall of Vicksburg, the Union army used the house, an outstanding example of the Greek Revival, as its local headquarters.

The Balfour House was the scene of a Christmas ball in 1862, where Confederate officers and their ladies had come for holiday festivities. The dance, however, was interrupted when a Confederate courier rushed into the ballroom to announce that Yankee gunboats had been sighted on the nearby Mississippi River. The festivities quickly ended as the men dashed out the door to defend the Confederacy. Each year, the Reenactment of the 1862 Christmas Ball at the Balfour House is a much-anticipated event in Vicksburg.

The house was meticulously restored in the early 1980s, won the 1984 Award of Merit from the Mississippi State Historical Society, is listed on the National Register of Historic Places, is featured at the Smithsonian, and is a designated Mississippi Landmark.

Period purists will be pleased to know that owner Sharon Humble has remained as authentic to the era of the house as possible. The graceful, elegant redbrick structure, with bold white trim, has a rare, three-story elliptical spiral staircase. In the three guest suites, the antique—predominantly Empire—furnishings reflect the age and style of the house. Guest-room colors range from dark green to mauve and pale green to pale pink, each with matching color schemes in the adjoining bath.

Breakfast menus vary, but guests can expect fare such as quiche Lorraine and fruit or an egg-and-cheese casserole with fruit and bread. ♠ *3 suites. Air-conditioning, TV and phone in rooms. $85–$150; full breakfast. AE, D, MC, V. No smoking.*

CANEMOUNT PLANTATION ℘
Hwy. 552 W (Rte. 2, Box 45), Lorman 39096, tel. 601/877–3784 or 800/423–0684

This 6,000-acre working plantation near Port Gibson, just off the Natchez Trace, is nestled quietly among vast forests and fields, flowing streams, and hills, welcoming guests to an idyllic escape. Canemount was built in 1855 in the Italianate Revival style. The house is almost unchanged, except that the butler's pantry has been converted to a small kitchen for the owners, Ray John and Rachel Forrest, and their son John. When it was built, the kitchen was out of doors, as is today's cozy, wood-paneled kitchen with a brick fireplace, where guests gather for breakfast.

Canemount, in all its Spanish moss–draped glory, is a haven for wildlife. The Forrests, formerly of Morganza, Louisiana, purchased it in 1981 as a hunting retreat, but according to Rachel, they "fell in love with the place and decided to stay permanently." White-tailed deer are so plentiful that Canemount was selected for a Mississippi State University study of their life span. Meandering paths and trails offer opportunities to see deer, Russian boar, and wild turkey. Certain areas are designated for wildlife photography, and a guided Jeep wildlife safari is offered every afternoon.

Guests are invited to have dinner with the Forrests at no extra charge and to tour the antiques-filled main house. Accommodations are in nearby, private, restored antebellum structures: Rick's Cottage, with brick walls, original wood floors, and a tester bed; Grey Cottage, which has a whirlpool bath; and Pond House, with a whirlpool tub. In addition, a restored 1829 carriage house has six guest rooms. Each cottage is furnished with antiques and contemporary pieces and is wonderfully quiet and undisturbed except for the sounds of birds and an occasional deer.

The plantation acreage includes the historic Windsor Plantation, where the haunting ruins—23 towering Greek columns—still stand, though the massive house was destroyed by fire in 1890. The Persnickety Pig dining area, also on the plantation, is in a converted dairy. It's where festive Cajun pig roasts are held, as well as catered parties and group dinners, by reservation. ♠ *6 double rooms with baths, 3 cottage suites. Air-conditioning, TV in some rooms and common area; pool, ponds. $165–$195; full breakfast, cocktails, hors d'oeuvres, dinner. AE, MC, V. No smoking.*

DUNLEITH ☞
84 Homochitto St., Natchez 39120, tel. 601/446–8500 or 800/433–2445

Dunleith is one of the South's most beautiful houses, from the colonnaded galleries that encircle it to the superior antiques within and the 40 acres of landscaped grounds, wooded bayous, and green pastures without. It is constantly photographed, often written about, and occasionally appears in films. Dunleith is also a National Historic Landmark on the National Register of Historic Places.

The palatial mansion (circa 1856) is owned by William Heins III of Natchez. A resident manager and staff run the business of daily tours and lodging, and it is, quite noticeably, a business. Fortunately, the magnificence of Dunleith's architecture and interiors neutralizes the regimented recitations of the staff, and the grandeur of the place prevails.

Among the elegant furnishings are the dining room's French Zuber wallpaper, printed from woodblocks circa 1855 that were hidden in a cave in France during World War I. The V'Soske carpet in the front parlor determined the color scheme for the room's walls, draperies, and upholstery; the greenish-gold walls and draperies perfectly complement the peachy pinks and gold tones in the carpet. A Louis XV ormolu-mounted mahogany Linke table is in a prominent place in the front parlor.

Three of the guest rooms at Dunleith are in the main house, and eight are in the former servants' wing, built in 1856. The rooms are quiet and private and are well decorated in mid-19th-century style, with a mixture of reproductions and antiques. A Victorian color scheme with peaches, blues, and pastels is used throughout. Each guest room has a working fireplace, original from the era of construction.

Another nice feature: The grounds are subtly lighted at night so that guests can stroll in the "moonlight" or enjoy the romantic views from wicker rockers on the galleries.

Old brick and warm woods set the stage for the big plantation breakfast served in the former poultry house. Exposed beams, lots of windows, and wooden floors add a homey touch that guests may have pined for in the elaborate, museum-like main house. ♨ *11 double rooms with baths. Air-conditioning, TV, phone, fire-places in rooms. $95–$140; full breakfast. D, MC, V. No smoking.*

MOLLY'S ☙
214 S. Bolivar Ave., Cleveland 38732, tel. 601/843–9913

Postmodern art and sculpture lovers will enjoy the *Pee-Wee's Playhouse* atmosphere of Molly's, which is not only a bed-and-breakfast but also a working sculpture studio and gallery.

Everywhere you turn is the playful, colorful, and surreal sensibility of nationally known artist Floyd Shaman. He and wife Molly have blended Victorian, Art Deco, and Art Nouveau furnishings with his figurative, laminated wood sculpture and other art work, most of which is for sale, to fun and frolicky effect. Floyd, who has mounted one-man shows in New York and around the country, will take guests on a studio tour upon request.

Once a genteel boarding house, Molly's now has rooms painted with western-motif murals, reflecting Floyd's Wyoming roots; a hall lined with hundreds of soda and beer bottles and cans; and a living room arranged around a giant wooden roller skate.

Molly's draws the Delta Blues Festival crowd in September, as it does those coming to Cleveland year-round to eat at renowned KC's restaurant, nearby. Breakfast, including Molly's famous muffins, is served on a porch in the shade of Chinese umbrella trees and overlooking a pleasant courtyard out back. Guests have access to a common TV and phone. ♨ *3 double rooms with baths. Air-conditioning, TV in common room. $55–$65; full breakfast. MC, V. No smoking.*

MONMOUTH ☙
36 Melrose Ave., Natchez 39120, tel. 601/442–5852 or 800/828–4531, fax 601/446–7762

The massive Monmouth (circa 1818) is not only one of Mississippi's best-known B&Bs, it's also the state's unofficial Hollywood connection. Monmouth appears to be the choice of the movie industry, according to reports from members of the Hollywood press corps who often accompany filmmakers to this most photogenic part of the sunny South. Actors and crew stayed here while in Natchez filming John Grisham's *A Time to Kill.*

Owners Ron and Lani Riches live in Los Angeles but stay at Monmouth as much as possible. The Richeses (he's a land developer) bought Monmouth about 20 years ago and have worked hard at restoring the grand old house. Monmouth's Greek Revival portico was added in 1853, at which time the original brick was covered with eggshell stucco and scored. The grounds, all 26 acres, are immaculate, and there's always something in bloom.

The interior mood is formal, with the blue-silk-covered Rococo Revival furniture in the double parlor made even prettier by the glow of a Waterford crystal chandelier. The windows are done with fanciful swags, valances, fringes, and lace.

The bedrooms in the main house are a decorator's dream. The peach bedroom, a favorite, has peach walls and fabrics made into magnificent draperies on the windows and the canopy bed. Other grand accommodations include the four garden cottages, the carriage house, the former servants' quarters, and the six Plantation Suites. The suites have fireplaces, whirlpool baths, and period furnishings. The Quitman Retreat is richly decorated in blues and creams and is the most exquisite of all. There's also a conference center to accommodate up to 120 for meetings. Those suites farthest away from the main house are the most elaborate in style.

Monmouth is the only property in Mississippi that's a National Trust–designated Historic Hotel of America, and it is a National Historic Landmark.

During the cocktail hour, complimentary hors d'oeuvres are served. In the morning, the full southern breakfast takes on a special elegance: It's served on fine china in a formal setting. ◬ *6 double rooms with baths and 1 suite in main house, 11 doubles with baths and 7 suites in outbuildings. Restaurant (dinner only, 1 seating nightly), air-conditioning, TV and phone in rooms, robes and luxury bath products in rooms; croquet course, fishing pond, walking trails. $135–$275; full breakfast, hors d'oeuvres during cocktail hour. AE, D, MC, V. No smoking.*

OTHER CHOICES

The Burn. 712 N. Union St., Natchez 39120, tel. 601/442–1344 or 800/654–8859, fax 601/445–0606. 4 double rooms with baths, 3 suites. Air-conditioning, fireplaces, and cable TV in rooms; pool. $125–$200; full breakfast. AE, MC, V. No smoking.

Cedars Plantation. Rte. 2 (Box 298), Church Hill 39120, tel. 601/445–2203, fax 601/445–2372. 3 double rooms with baths, 1 3-room suite. Mini-refrigerator, icemaker, robes, and phone in rooms. $150–$200; full breakfast, complimentary beverage. AE, MC, V. No smoking.

Fairview. 734 Fairview St., Jackson 39202, tel. 601/948–3429, fax 601/948–1203. 3 double rooms with baths, 5 suites. Air-conditioning, TV and phone in rooms, whirlpool tub in 2 rooms. $100–$150; full breakfast. AE, D, MC, V. No smoking.

Millsaps Buie House. 628 N. State St., Jackson 39202, tel. 601/352–0221 or 800/784–0221, fax 601/352–0221. 11 double rooms with baths. Air-conditioning, cable TV and phone with dataport in rooms. $100–$170; full breakfast. AE, D, DC, MC, V. No smoking.

Wensel House. 206 Washington St., Natchez 39120, tel. 601/445——8577 or 888/775–8577, fax 601/442–2525. 3 double rooms with baths. Phone and TV in rooms. $75; full breakfast. No smoking.

RESERVATIONS SERVICES

Lincoln, Ltd. Bed & Breakfast Mississippi Reservation Service (Box 3479, Meridian 39303, tel. 601/482–5483 or 800/633–6477). **Natchez Pilgrimage Tours Bed & Breakfast Reservations** (Box 347, Natchez 39121, tel. 601/446–6631 or 800/647–6742).

Mississippi Gulf Coast Region

INN AT THE PASS ☞
125 E. Scenic Dr., Pass Christian 39571, tel. 228/452–0333 or 800/217–2588

The Inn at the Pass has an enviable Pass Christian (pronounced *Christy*-Ann) address. The lovely little seacoast town is Mississippi's answer to Newport, Rhode Island, and is gaining a reputation as one of the South's best places.

The house was built in 1885 and was the home of the Emile Adam family for more than 75 years. The current proprietors, Brenda and Vernon Harrison, came to the Gulf Coast from Houston, where he practiced law and she was a psychologist. They have been instrumental in forming a Bed and Breakfast Association for Mississippi.

The Harrisons have turned the house they bought into Inn at the Pass, a pleasant, quiet B&B with Eastlake influences. The wide front porch with its wicker furniture offers a grand view of the Mississippi Sound, and inside, the furnishings complement each room's name. The Rose Room is Victorian; the Hunt Room is masculine in color and design elements, which include hunting trophies and plaid fabric. The Magnolia Room has bent-willow furniture and original art depicting beach scenes and landscapes. There is also a cottage that accommodates up to six.

A full breakfast, always delicious, is served. △ *4 double rooms with baths, 1 cottage. Air-conditioning, TV and phone in rooms, kitchenette in cottage. $75–$125; full breakfast. AE, D, MC, V. No smoking, kennel available for small pets.*

WHO'S INN?

623 Washington Ave., Ocean Springs 39564, tel. 228/875–3251 or after 5 PM and Sundays, 228/875–2900, fax 228/875–3251

In the heart of Ocean Springs, a quaint and artsy coastal town, Who's Inn? is for those who want cafés, boutiques, and antiques shops right outside their door. The tiny inn, run by botanical sculptor Trailer McQuilkin and his wife, Sharon, has a fairy-tale charm, as does the entire Ocean Springs historic district. The inn also serves as a gallery specializing in local and southern contemporary artists.

The two guest rooms open onto a pleasant porch with chairs and tables under ceiling fans. Each of the comfortable, modern rooms has a coffeemaker and a refrigerator stocked with sodas and bottled water, and bicycles are available for guests. One room has an ornate headboard made from an Indonesian wedding bed (which has, according to Sharon, fostered the fertility of at least one guest).

Breakfast is included, but you have to stroll across the street to a French bakery, where you are likely to meet locals eager to talk about their town and how it has maintained its character in the face of rapidly changing Gulf Coast life. On-site gallery director Bill Myers is friendly and knowledgeable about Ocean Springs and the local art scene. △ *2 double rooms with baths. Air-conditioning, cable TV, and phone with dataport in rooms; bicycles. $85–$95; Continental breakfast served in French bakery across the street. AE, MC, V. No smoking.*

OTHER CHOICES

Green Oaks. 580 Beach Blvd., Biloxi 39530, tel. 228/436—6257 or 888/436–6257, fax 228/436-6225. 5 double rooms with baths, 2 doubles and 1 suite in cottage. Air-conditioning, cable TV and phone with dataport in rooms; turndown service with chocolates. $125–$150; full breakfast, afternoon tea. AE, D, MC, V. No smoking, 2-night minimum on holiday weekends.

Shadowlawn. 112A Shearwater Dr., Ocean Springs 39564, tel. 228/875–6945, fax 228/875–6595. 4 double rooms. Air-conditioning, cable TV/VCR in rooms. $110–$135; full breakfast. MC, V. No smoking.

RESERVATIONS SERVICE

Lincoln, Ltd. Bed & Breakfast Service (Box 3479, Meridian 39303, tel. 601/482–5483 or 800/633–6477).

MISSOURI

Branson

BRANSON HOTEL 🍃
214 W. Main St., Branson 65616, tel. 417/335–6104

From the white-painted antique wicker rockers and Adirondack chairs on the shady front porch to the glass-walled dining room overlooking the yard's perennials and birdbath, the Branson Hotel seems miles away from the hustle and bustle of Branson's famed "strip." Teri Murguia and husband Jim renovated this 1903 hotel in 1991, with help from Teri's mother, Opal Kelly, who runs the nearby Branson House Bed and Breakfast. The whole family is into providing peaceful getaways from the cookie-cutter hotels and motels of this music boomtown. But the gridlock of tourists (and their exhaust-spitting cars and buses) begins on the street below.

Peach walls, blue-and-peach floral carpeting, and soft classical music greet guests inside the front door, where Teri offers sherry, tea or coffee, and butter cookies and English shortbread. Fresh flowers from the garden—peonies in spring—add to the relaxing ambience. Teri keeps ice and soda in a hall refrigerator near the unusual back-to-back staircases.

Rooms have a mix of reproduction antiques—for instance, new queen- and king-size iron, brass, and oak beds—and antique accents, such as Victorian prints and Tiffany-style reading lamps. Teri's favorite is the Honeymoon Suite, dressed in romantic pinks and blues and decorated with an oak four-poster bed with New England–style fishnet canopy, wing chairs, and an antique walnut dresser. The Wicker Room's white iron bed is matched up with antique white wicker chairs and soothing white and lavender linens. More masculine are the Duck Club and the Fox's Den, the latter designed around a large fox print Teri found in a gallery near her part-time home in Kansas City, where she formerly worked in the construction and engineering fields.

Guests gather around a large harvest table for breakfasts that may include banana-walnut pancakes and cheddar-cheese muffins or blueberry-stuffed French toast and sourdough bread. 🛆 *9 double rooms with baths. Air-conditioning, cable TV, phone and clock radio in rooms; off-street parking. $95–$105; full breakfast, afternoon refreshments. AE, MC, V.*

OTHER CHOICES

Cameron's Crag. 738 Acacia Club Rd. (Box 295), Branson 65616, tel. 417/335–8134 or 800/933–8529, fax 417/336–2238. 2 double rooms with baths, 1 suite. Air-conditioning, indoor hot tub and refrigerator in 1 room, outdoor hot tub on deck adjoining 1 room, whirlpool and kitchen in suite, phones and cable TV/VCR, private entrances. $75–$95; full breakfast. D, MC, V.

Emory Creek Bed and Breakfast. 143 Arizona Dr., Branson 65616, tel. 417/334–3805 or 800/362–7404, fax 417/337–7045. 6 double rooms with baths. Air-conditioning, clock radio, Jacuzzi, and TV in rooms, TV/VCR in sitting room; nature trails. $85–$125; full breakfast. MC, V.

Kansas City

SOUTHMORELAND ON THE PLAZA 🖙

116 E. 46th St., Kansas City 64112, tel. 816/531–7979, fax 816/531–2407

Within walking distance of the Country Club Plaza shopping mecca, this 1913 Colonial Revival mansion is set back from the street in the Southmoreland neighborhood of apartment buildings and condominiums. Penni Johnson, a lawyer, and Susan Moehl, a former executive at Kansas City–based Hallmark Cards, have transformed this gray-stucco mansion into the city's most popular B&B.

The innkeepers' attention to detail is evident in the fresh flowers, apples, sherry, and chocolates placed in each of the 12 guest rooms, many of which have fireplaces or decks. Each room is named for and decorated according to a Kansas City notable. For example, the Leroy "Satchel" Paige room, named for the Kansas City baseball legend, is paneled in knotty pine and made to look like a tiny northern-woods fishing cabin. Baseball memorabilia, antique skis, and snowshoes grace the walls, and a queen-size log bed is the centerpiece. The living room, decorated in rich Colonial colors (as are a number of the bedrooms), is stocked with books, jigsaw puzzles, and 162 "happy ending" movies for watching on the TV/VCR tucked into the 1865 Austrian armoire.

Chalkboard menus are updated each day in the dining room, where guests delve into gourmet breakfast fare like French toast stuffed with brown sugar–cured ham and Lorraine Swiss, batter fried and topped with slivers of toasted almonds. Guests dine either at the 1800s pine harvest table or on the side veranda, overlooking the shady lawn where Baby, the cat, sometimes lounges. A deck with views of the waterfall and goldfish pond has a gas grill that Susan sometimes uses for unusual breakfast creations.

Off the dining room is the solarium, decorated with cool white wicker and blue and white pillows. The innkeepers keep plenty of newspapers, including the *Wall Street Journal,* for business travelers or vacationers who don't want to get away from quite everything. ♠ *12 double rooms with baths. Air-conditioning, phone in rooms, fireplace in 3 rooms, Jacuzzi in 2 rooms, off-street parking, business services including fax and copier, airport shuttle, sports and dining privileges at nearby private club. $115–$165; full breakfast, wine and cheese. AE, MC, V.*

OTHER CHOICES

Behm's Plaza Carriage House. 4320 Oak St., Kansas City 64111, tel. 816/753–4434 or 888/832–6000, fax 816/756–3665. 5 double rooms with baths. Air-conditioning, Jacuzzi in 1 room, hot tub on private deck attached to 1 room, fireplace in 1 room, TV/VCR in living room, off-street parking. $112–$155; full breakfast, wine and cheese. AE, D, MC, V.

Benner House Bed and Breakfast. 645 Main St., Weston 64098, tel. 816/640–2616. 4 double rooms share 2 baths. Air-conditioning, fireplace, hot tub, off-street parking. Ski packages available. $85–$155; full breakfast. MC, V.

Doanleigh Wallagh Inn. 217 E. 37th St., Kansas City 64111, tel. 816/753–2667, fax 816/531–5185. 5 double rooms with baths. Air-conditioning, phone, computer modem access, cable TV/VCR, fireplace, Jacuzzi, and refrigerator in 3 rooms, fax and copier, off-street parking, park and tennis courts across the street. $95–$155; full breakfast, afternoon snacks. AE, D, MC, V.

St. Louis and Environs

BOONE'S LICK TRAIL INN ✒

1000 S. Main St., St. Charles 63301, tel. 314/947–7000

Historic old St. Charles, the state's first permanent settlement on the Missouri River, retains the leisurely charm of an 1800s river town just 25 minutes west of downtown St. Louis. Here was the last outpost of civilization, where Lewis and Clark launched their 1804 expedition and the state of Missouri assembled its first legislature, in 1821. Visitors stroll along cobblestone Main Street with its gaslights and restored brick buildings housing dozens of restaurants, cafés, and antiques and crafts shops. Others come for the hiking and biking along Missouri's Katy Trail, which begins here and travels west along an abandoned railroad right-of-way.

The Boone's Lick Trail Inn, which dates to around 1850, sits at the edge of this commotion behind a hedge of pink Simplicity roses. Through the years it has served as a rooming house, a private home, a hippie commune, and a health-food store. V'Anne and Paul Mydler purchased it in 1981 and renovated the brick, three-story Federal-style building, salvaging some of the original windows and pine plank flooring.

The attic room has sloping ceilings and a tiny walk-out balcony with a view of the Missouri River and the *Goldenrod Showboat* docked there. There's a double bird's-eye maple bed and an 1840s slave bed that can be pulled out to make a double. The large bathroom has a modern shower, old marble sink, a small makeup table, and plenty of thirsty towels.

Four smaller rooms, in a wing at the back of the house, have private entrances. The two upstairs open onto a porch that overlooks a historic gristmill and Boonslick Road—named, as was the inn, for an old trail Daniel Boone's sons used to take to a natural salt lick. Rooms have a mix of Early American antiques and family heirlooms, lace curtains, folk-art stenciling, and dried flowers from V'Anne's gardens.

V'Anne collects antiques, such as the 8-ft-long oak and walnut "textile table" from an old general store, on which she now sets her simple but filling buffet breakfasts. A hot dish, such as cheese-stuffed French toast or a baked egg casserole, is served with fresh fruit and pastries or muffins, with locally made jams and jellies. Paul has taken over the baking of a guest favorite—lemon "sandbag" biscuits. The "sandbag" was added during the Great Flood of 1993, when much of downtown St. Charles was sandbagged against the rising river, which stopped short of the inn by about 60 ft. ⌂ *5 double rooms with baths. Air-conditioning, phones, TV in 2 rooms, off-street parking. $85–$175; full breakfast. AE, D, DC, MC, V.*

THE INN ST. GEMME BEAUVAIS ☞
78 N. Main St., St. Genevieve 63670, tel. 573/883–5744 or 800/818–5744

With amenities like an outdoor hot tub and an on-call certified massage therapist, it's no wonder that the Inn St. Gemme Beauvais is known as a romantic hideaway. Constructed in 1848, this magnificent home with a brick facade and two-story white columns is in a quaint French community about 50 mi south of St. Louis. The original building is on the National Register of Historic Places, but a carriage house, added in 1998, could easily have been built 150 years earlier.

Just three blocks from the mighty Mississippi River, the three-story Inn St. Gemme Beauvais has an elegant dining room with marble fireplace and a banquet room among its common rooms. Innkeeper and co-owner Janet Joggerst, a lifelong native of St. Genevieve, will prepare your breakfast to order, taking special consideration for any dietetic needs. However, her specialty is a French recipe for pancakes that includes oats and apples.

The guest rooms are filled with period antiques and handmade quilts and are updated with modern conveniences: In the Governor's room, the television is tastefully hidden in the cabinet of an old Victrola. Each room, some with canopy beds or Murphy beds, has its own theme. The Memories room is filled with antique toys, dolls, and children's books.

After a day exploring the countryside in and around St. Genevieve or riding the Mississippi River ferry to Illinois and back, guests relax in the outdoor dining area for wine and hors d'oeuvres or high tea. ⚱ *3 double rooms with baths, 9 suites. Air conditioning, lounge and dining area, cable TV, banquet facilities, off-street parking. $89–$179; full breakfast; complimentary high tea, wine, and hors d'oeuvres. D, MC, V. No smoking.*

OTHER CHOICES

Eastlake Inn. 703 N. Kirkwood Rd., Kirkwood 63122, tel. 314/965–0066. 3 double rooms with baths. Air-conditioning, TV and fireplace in living room, turndown service, off-street parking. $65–$85; full breakfast. MC, V.

Winter House. 3522 Arsenal St., St. Louis 63118, tel. 314/664–4399. 2 double rooms with baths. Air-conditioning, clock radios, off-street parking. $80–$105; full breakfast, afternoon refreshments. AE, D, DC, MC, V.

RESERVATIONS SERVICES

B&B Inns of Missouri (Box 775294, St. Louis 63177, tel. 800/213–5642). **B&B–Kansas City** (Box 14781, Lenexa 66285, tel. 913/888–3636).

MONTANA

Gold West Country

BARRISTER BED & BREAKFAST 🦜
416 N. Ewing St., Helena 59601, tel. 406/443–7330 or 800/823–1148,
fax 406/442–7964

Across the street from lovely St. Helena's Cathedral stands the Barrister, a Queen Anne house built between 1874 and 1880. The Barrister once served as the rectory for the Helena diocese; today, innkeeper Nick Jacques displays a photo of himself as a young altar boy who once served Mass at the cathedral. "The first time I saw the inside of the house," Nick confesses, "was when I was being scolded by the Monsignor."

The former altar boy, a fifth-generation Montanan, is also a former public defender: The B&B's name is about the only reminder of Nick's former life. In 1993, when the house opened as a B&B, it was placed on the National Register of Historic Places.

The Barrister has an unusually large amount of public space: The parlor, formal dining room, den, TV room, library, office, and enclosed sun porch are all available for guests to use and enjoy. Incorporating six ornate fireplaces, four original leaded stained-glass windows, high ceilings, and carved staircases, the Barrister provides guests with an elegant return to the gracious living of the late-19th century.

Guest rooms are spacious, with queen-size beds, and reflect a variety of moods. The very masculine Captain's Quarters is decidedly nautical; a deep red carpet and paisley bedspread complement the theme. The Lilac Room has a clearly more feminine air, with frilly hats and a purse displayed on the wall. The Barrister Suite, the most elegant of all the rooms, has an elaborate armoire, lace curtains, and large bathroom. ⚓ *2 double rooms with baths, 3 rooms with private baths across the hall. Air-conditioning, rooms with baths across the hall have terry cloth robes, business center with computer dataports. $85–$100; full breakfast, evening social at 5:30 with wine and hors d'oeuvres. AE, MC, V.*

GOLDSMITH'S BED & BREAKFAST INN 🦜
809 E. Front St., Missoula 59802, tel. 406/721–6732, fax 406/543–0045

Goldsmith's Bed & Breakfast Inn welcomes travelers with a unique brand of hospitality. Unlike most other bed-and-breakfasts, in which the morning meal is served in a common dining room, Goldsmith's serves its guests next door at Goldsmith's Ice Cream Parlor and Restaurant, which is a favorite with university students and other local diners. Guests can choose from any item on the extensive breakfast menu.

Upon crossing the front porch (where breakfast may also be served), guests enter Goldsmith's B&B and find a startling photograph that shows the early 20th-century house up on blocks and rolling down one of Missoula's main streets. Owners Jeana and Richard Goldsmith moved the house from its original location to its present one on the banks of the Clark Fork River, across a footbridge from the University of Montana. A riverside walking path for leisurely strolling passes by the inn. The house, a 1911 brick jewel, was formerly the residence of Clyde Duniway, the university's second president. The Common Room has a lovely bay window that overlooks the river. Fresh flowers, a fireplace, a library, and maple and oak hardwood floors add to the ambience.

Guest rooms have Oriental carpets and period antiques and reproductions, including some sleigh beds. Bathrooms are hand-tiled and have oversize bath towels. Three of the rooms (Room 1, the Parlor Room; Room 4, the Red River Room; and Room 7, the Greenough Suite) have delightful views overlooking the Clark Fork River. But even without a river view, guests will find themselves happily ensconced in the comfort and privacy of this homey inn. △ *3 double rooms with baths, 4 suites. Air-conditioning, phone in rooms, hot tub in 1 room, cable TV in suites and common room, nook with library. $69–$129; full breakfast served next door at Goldsmith's Ice Cream Parlor and Restaurant. AE, D, DC, MC, V.*

SANDERS-HELENA'S BED & BREAKFAST ☜

328 N. Ewing St., Helena 59601, tel. 406/442–3309, fax 406/443–2361

In the heart of Helena's historic district, just a few short blocks from the Old Governor's Mansion is the Sanders, an 1875 home that was one of the first houses in what is now Montana's capital city. Set on a tree-lined street just three blocks from the lovely cathedral of St. Helena, the Sanders provides its guests with a gracious return to the days of the Montana Territory.

The house was built as a home for Wilbur and Harriet Sanders, who arrived in Montana in 1863 with the Sidney Edgerton wagon train. (Edgerton, the first governor of the Montana Territory, was Sanders's uncle.) Sanders, who in 1889 became one of Montana's first two senators when statehood was granted, was a founder of the Montana Historical Society and put much of his extensive mineral collection on display in the vestibule of his home. Glass-fronted cases show a large number of the rocks Sanders uncovered in his mines. Many are dated, including a jar with stones collected during the summer of 1863 by young Harriet Sanders during her crossing of the Great Plains with the Edgerton wagon train from Omaha, Nebraska, to Bannack, Montana. Not surprisingly, this B&B attracts many geologists.

Hosts Bobbi Uecker and Rock Ringling have preserved much of the Sanders's historic past. Various pieces of the furniture in the guest rooms are original, including several antique beds and bureaus. The public rooms are delightfully decorated with items such as an upright piano and a built-in buffet of warm, golden crosscut oak and beveled glass. Guests staying on the upper floors might be startled by the sight of "Chili Bean," a star bovine on the rodeo circuit who died of natural causes. Mounted above the staircase, Chili Bean gazes down upon all who pass under her. It's hard to take her terribly seriously, however, since her considerably large horns are adorned with a variety of unusual hats.

Guest rooms, named after members of Bobbi and Rock's families, are filled with delightful touches such as a mimeographed "Sanders Quiz" that guests can take at their leisure. Because of the Sanders's location in Montana's capital city, it receives its fair share of business as well as leisure travelers. Several rooms have been designed with corporate guests in mind. There are alarm clocks in every room; radios are thoughtfully labeled with stations and their formats; and in Teddy's Buckaroo, the 8-ft ceilings allow an roomy stall shower. Beth's Room, painted a cheerful yellow, has a stunning view of the Continental Divide. Althea's Room is perhaps the most historically accurate; almost all of its furniture is original to the house. Although its private bathroom isn't attached to the sleeping area, a terry cloth robe is provided for the short walk down the hall. ♠ *6 double rooms with baths, 1 room with bath down the hall. Air-conditioning, TV, 2 rooms with VCR, phones, modems, radios, guest refrigerator, hair dryers. $85–$105; full breakfast, afternoon homemade cookies, sherry, fruit, and beverages. AE, D, DC, MC, V.*

Yellowstone Country

GALLATIN GATEWAY INN 🐾

Rte. 191 (Box 376), Gallatin Gateway 59730, tel. 406/763–4672 or 800/676–3522, fax 406/763–4672, ext. 313

Opened in 1927 by the Chicago, Milwaukee, and St. Paul Railroad as one of the grand railroad hotels of the Rocky Mountain West, the 42,000-square-ft Gallatin Gateway Inn has high arched windows, Spanish-style corbels, and carved beams. The original railroad clock in the high-ceiling lobby still keeps accurate time, and the checkerboard-square tile floor and gleaming Polynesian mahogany woodwork look exactly as they did during the heyday of railroad travel.

The glorious Spanish Peaks form a picture-postcard-perfect backdrop to the inn's outdoor pool and tennis court. Its location 12 mi south of Bozeman and 80 mi north of Yellowstone National Park makes it an ideal stopping point for travelers. Fly fishermen take note: The Gallatin River is a five-minute walk away. In addition, there's a casting pond on the inn's property, giving folks an opportunity to practice before heading out to the real thing.

The inn's superb dining room is an experience in itself. Knowing locals from Bozeman head here on weekends, so reservations—even for inn guests—are essential. The extensive menu features a fresh catch of the day, of course, but there are also tempting beef, venison, lamb, roasted Boston haddock, salmon, and chicken entrées with unique presentations. For lighter fare, such as sandwiches, nachos, and fish-and-chips, guests may visit the Baggage Room Bar and Grill.

Although guests may want to curl up with a good book in front of the massive fireplace in the lobby, there are plenty of activities in and around the inn in both winter and summer. Gallatin Gateway is close to two of Montana's premier ski areas: Bridger Bowl and Big Sky. In the summer, horseback rides through the Lee Metcalf wilderness area in the Spanish Peaks can be arranged. ♠ *35 double rooms, 3 suites. Restaurant, pub, air-conditioning, cable TV, phone, coffeemaker, mini-refrigerator in suites, outdoor pool, hot tub, tennis court, casting pond; fly fishing, white water rafting, horseback riding, and snowmobiling adventures arranged; massages by appointment. $105–$175; Continental breakfast. AE, D, MC, V.*

OTHER CHOICES

Lindley House. 202 Lindley Place, Bozeman 59715, tel. 406/587–8403 or 800/787–8404, fax 406/582–8112. 3 double rooms with baths, 3 suites. Terry cloth robes, hair dryer, amenity basket, coffeemaker, cable TV/VCR in suites and 1 room, phone in suites, balcony, fireplace, and two-person bathtub in 1 suite, full kitchen and washer/dryer, outdoor hot tub, enclosed English Garden, deck in Penthouse Suite. $65–$250; full breakfast. MC, D, V.

Sacajawea Inn. 5 N. Main St. (Box 648), Three Forks 59752, tel. 406/285–6515 or 800/821–7326, fax 406/285–4210. 31 double rooms with baths. Restaurant, bar, cable TV, phone, air-conditioning in some rooms, billiard room, conference facilities. $59–$99; breakfast not included. AE, D, MC, V.

Sportsman's High Bed & Breakfast. 750 Deer St., West Yellowstone 59758, tel. 406/646–7865. 5 double rooms with baths. Hair dryer and toiletries in rooms, satellite TV in common area. $95–$115; full breakfast. AE, D, MC, V. No smoking. Closed Oct. 15–May.

Torch & Toes Bed & Breakfast. 309 S. 3rd Ave., Bozeman 59715, tel. 406/586–7285 or 800/446–2138. 2 double rooms with baths, 1 double room with private bath across hall, 1 suite (carriage house). $70–$90; full breakfast. AE, MC, V.

Voss Inn. 319 S. Willson St., Bozeman 59715, tel. 406/587–0982, fax 406/585–2964. 6 double rooms with baths. Phones, cable TV in parlor. $85–$95; full breakfast, afternoon English-style tea. AE, MC, V.

Glacier Country

EMILY A. BED & BREAKFAST ☞
Box 350, Seeley Lake 59868 (Mile Marker 20, 5 mi north of Seeley Lake on Montana Rte. 83), tel. 406/677–3474 or 800/977–4639, fax 406/677–3474

In the heart of the scenic Seeley-Swan Valley, one of Montana's premier outdoor recreation areas, lies the Emily A. Bed & Breakfast. On 160 acres of the Circle Arrow Ranch, as well as an 8-acre lake and the Clearwater River, the Emily A. offers a spectacular outdoor setting and an equally commanding interior. Built of locally harvested larch logs from the nearby hills that provide the lodge with a warm, soft golden glow, the Emily A. provides its guests with a true western experience with all the modern amenities.

The B&B is the brainchild of Marilyn and Keith Peterson. Keith, the retired team doctor for baseball's Seattle Mariners, has baseball memorabilia (including original wool jerseys worn by Pete Rose and Johnny Bench) on display in one of the downstairs common rooms. Marilyn, who handles the day-to-day operations of the inn, is a registered dietitian. The Emily A. represents the realization of their dream to share the Montana hospitality and lifestyle they know and love with their guests.

The Emily A. is named for Marilyn's grandmother Emily Alvis Stinson Shope, who came to Montana in 1893 to help found the Boulder School for the Deaf Mute. When her husband died, the young widow supported her seven children by running one of Missoula's first board and rooming houses. That family tradition of hospitality lives on today, as her granddaughter hosts guests from near and far.

There is plenty for guests to see and do in and around the Emily A. The headwaters of the Columbia River are close at hand, so both canoeing and fishing are popular pastimes. Or, you might want to spend some quality time on the back porch with binoculars: Ospreys, eagles, loons, ducks, geese, deer, and other wildlife contribute to an ever-changing view. Guests also come here to enjoy such winter sports as cross-country skiing and snowmobiling through the inn's pasture.

Evenings at the Emily A. are ideal for gathering around the huge two-story, 25-ft fireplace. As Marilyn says, "The stones of our two-story fireplace have their own stories to tell. They are geological specimens gathered by the Peterson family over several lifetimes." The Peterson family is evident in just about every room of the house, public or private. Cozy guest rooms are named after the Petersons' children; there's a Grandparents' Room as well. Family photographs are throughout the house, as well as keepsakes and other family heirlooms. △ *2 double rooms with baths, 3 double rooms with shared baths, 2-bedroom suite. Kitchen in suite, cable TV in upstairs common area, fishing, sled-dog rides, and horseback riding by arrangement. $115–$150; full or Continental breakfast. D, MC, V.*

OTHER CHOICES

Bad Rock Country B&B. 480 Bad Rock Dr., Columbia Falls 59912, tel. 406/892–2829 or 800/422–3666, fax 406/892–2930. 3 double rooms with baths in main house, 4 doubles with baths in 2 cottages. Gas-log fireplace in cottages, hot tub. $120–169; full breakfast. AE, D, DC, MC, V. No smoking.

Burggraf's Countrylane Bed 'n Breakfast. Rainbow Dr. on Swan Lake, Bigfork 59911, tel. 406/837–4608 or 800/525–3314, fax 406/837–2468. 5 double rooms with baths. Whirlpool bath in 1 room, free canoes, rental boats, croquet court. $85–$100; full breakfast. No credit cards.

Garden Wall Inn. 504 Spokane Ave., Whitefish 59937, tel. 406/862–3440 or 888/530–1700. 3 double rooms with baths, 1 suite. Crabtree & Evelyn toiletries, fresh flowers, evening turndown service with Dilettante chocolates, complimentary morning newspaper, morning coffee served in rooms. $85–$125; full breakfast, afternoon hors d'oeuvres and beverages. AE, D, MC, V.

Good Medicine Lodge. 537 Wisconsin Ave., Whitefish 59937, tel. 406/862–5488 or 800/860–5488, fax 406/862–5489. 9 double rooms with baths. Air-conditioning, phones, balcony in 5 rooms, cable TV in common room, outdoor spa, laundry service. $95–145; full breakfast. AE, D, MC, V. No smoking. Closed Apr. 12–May 14 and Nov. 1–Dec. 18.

Mountain Timbers Lodge & Cross Country Ski Area. 5385 Rabe Rd. (Box 94), Columbia Falls 59912, tel. 406/387–5830, fax 406/387–5835. 7 double rooms with shared baths. Whirlpool, croquet. $55–$125; full breakfast. MC, V.

O'Duach'ain Country Inn. 675 Ferndale Dr., Bigfork 59911, tel. 406/837–6851 or 800/837–7460, fax 406/837–4390. 4 suites, 1 2-bedroom suite. Private deck in 2 suites, hot tub. $95–180; full breakfast. AE, D, MC, V.

Plum Creek House. 985 Vans Ave., Columbia Falls 59912, tel. 406/892–1816 or 800/682–1429, fax 406/892–1876. 5 double rooms with baths, 1 suite. Cable TV/VCRs, phones, robes, slippers, coffee service, video library, barbecues, fire pit, heated pool, Jacuzzi. $105–$115; full breakfast, catered gourmet dinners available. AE, D, DC, MC, V.

NEBRASKA

Elgin

PLANTATION HOUSE 🌾
401 Plantation St., Elgin 68636, tel. 402/843–2287 or 888/446–2287

"Returning to the comfort of home" is how innkeeper Deb Warren describes her philosophy at the Plantation House, the landmark of tiny Elgin. A native of this Nebraska farm community, Deb and her husband, Kyle, lived in Colorado for several years before "returning to the comfort of home" to raise their two children. And there's plenty of room for the Warrens and guests in this 28-room Greek Revival–style mansion, which resembles a classic southern plantation.

The house was originally built in the 1880s by a Nebraska banker, with four cypress-wood columns added in 1916. Although the original estate was less than 700 acres, locals began calling the house "The Plantation." The inn was first remodeled for guests in 1989 and spruced up again in 1998 by former owners and friends of the Warrens, Merland and Barbara Clark.

All rooms and the guest cottage now have private baths, but the original architectural charm of the home has been retained and enhanced with many antiques and local craft work. Mrs. Butler's Room is a suite of turn-of-the-century Empire-style furniture, and the Old Guest Room has attractive rose-strewn wallpaper; both are accented with designer cloth dolls made by a local artist. The Stained Glass Room speaks for itself. In winter, guests enjoy the warmth of the cozy wood-burning stove in the family room or the five working fireplaces throughout the public areas of the house. The second-floor salon has a TV/VCR, phone, board games, computers, and whirlpool.

Out back stands an antique gazebo and one of the original workers' houses, now used as a guest cottage. All-white trim, pink shutters, and white wrought-iron furniture, the cottage is favored as a nuptial-night hideaway. Breakfast is served family-style in the formal dining room, where French toast with locally cured bacon is often on the menu.

Directly across the street, the Elgin City Park has an outdoor swimming pool, tennis, and volleyball courts. You can take a day trip to Ashfall State Park, where the prehistoric remains of three-toed horses and rhinos have been excavated from volcanic ash. △ *5 double rooms with baths, cottage. Air-conditioning, TV/VCR in common area. $50–$75; full breakfast. No credit cards.*

Hastings

GRANDMA'S VICTORIAN INN ℡

1826 W. 3rd St., Hastings 68901, tel. 402/462–2013

In the 1880s, railroad executive George H. Lamont's house in the heart of the famed Sandhill Crane region was featured in a handbill to entice Easterners "out West" to south-central Nebraska. More than 100 years later, the Kreuger family was also enticed by the then long-neglected house. After two years of renovation in the early 1990s, the family brought out once again its Victorian charm with the added insight of the Kreugers' heritage. The inn, a tribute to innkeeper Robin Sassman's great-grandmother, displays photos of five generations of Kreuger women, which greet guests in the lobby and throughout the two-story Victorian home.

Much of the original woodwork was saved during the renovation of the house, including a carved-wood and stained-glass front door. Gleaming wainscotting, trim, floors, and pocket doors to the dining room create touches of warmth. Robin's mother meticulously researched for period wallpaper and other furnishings for the home.

Antiques and handcrafted Battenberg-lace coverlets ornament the five spacious guest rooms, three of which commemorate Grandma Kreuger's given name— Margret Henrietta Selma. All have queen-size beds and family rocking chairs. A lavender fainting couch in Margret's room and an heirloom wedding gown hanging inside Henrietta's Victorian-period armoire create a unique personality for those rooms. The Heritage Room is notable because even with antique furnishings it (and its bath) complies with the American Disabilities Act for accessibility. The other four baths have period claw-foot tubs and raised tank toilets.

A path of brick from former local brickyards leads to an ornate cream-color exterior with green and cranberry latticework trim. White wicker furniture on the covered porch and the ice-cream-parlor table and chairs on the second-floor balcony encourage you to unwind.

Breakfast may be served in bed upon your request. However, the aroma of Belgian waffles, French toast, and homemade muffins will probably draw you to the sunny bay windows and glistening china of the dining room. Cozy tables for two are all the more pleasurable because of the nearby warmth of a working potbellied stove and flower-and-candle–laden buffet.

One-half mile from the many antiques shops of downtown Hastings, Grandma's Victorian Inn is in a comfortable residential area. A growing community of 25,000, Hastings is the home of the National Square Dance Festival each September, a pioneer museum, and an IMAX theater. ♿ *5 rooms with baths. Air-conditioning, dining room, off-street parking. $60; full breakfast. D, MC, V.*

Southeast Nebraska

THE HEART OF DANNEBROG BED AND BREAKFAST ℡

121 E. Elm St., Dannebrog 68831, tel. 308/226–2303

The warmth of candles glowing in each window and a cheery hello from innkeeper René Simdorn welcome you to the Heart of Dannebrog Bed and Breakfast. Of-

BONUS MILES MAKE
GREAT SOUVENIRS.

Earn Miles With Your MCI Card.

Take the MCI Card along on this trip and start earning miles for the next one. You'll earn frequent flyer miles on all your calls and save with the low rates you've come to expect from MCI. Before you know it, you'll be on your way to some other international destination.

Sign up for MCI by calling 1-800-FLY-FREE

Is this a great time, or what? :-)

Earn Frequent Flyer Miles.

With guidebooks for every kind of travel—from weekend getaways to island hopping to adventures abroad—it's easy to understand why smart travelers go with **Fodor's**.

At bookstores everywhere.
www.fodors.com

Smart travelers go with **Fodor's**™

ficially registered as the Danish Capital of Nebraska, the small town of 300 residents is also made famous as the focus of many "Postcards from Nebraska," a regular feature by Dannebrog writer Roger Welsch on *CBS Sunday Morning*.

A lifelong resident of the Dannebrog area, René grew up next door to the house she turned into the town's first bed-and-breakfast. Built in 1905, the house sat empty for several years before René and her family renovated it in 1994. During the renovation, René and her family took pains to save all the original woodwork in the house, and photo albums in the living area show the stages of their progress.

Guests are invited to play the family piano in the parlor or watch television in the living room. University of Nebraska football memorabilia are on display here, a tribute to René's son's career as a Cornhusker defensive back.

Three guest rooms atop the stairs share a bath and a cozy reading area. The larger of the rooms, the Spring Room, has Battenberg-lace tablecloths, a white rocking chair, and airy window coverings dappled with pansies. Across the hall, the Autumn Room has a comfortable double iron bed with an inviting green-and-rust comforter and matching pillows tucked into the eave. The Antique Room has an iron bed, school desk, and doll buggy.

Breakfast is a unique Danish treat. Just a few blocks from René's home is Harriett's Danish Café, where guests are treated to Danish pancakes, eggs, coffee, and Medisterp lse, a Danish pork sausage made just across the street at the Steakmaster. Much of the charm at Harriett's is from the locals who walk in, pick up their own coffee cup, serve themselves, and chat.

Dannebrog is small-town America at its best. Whether you're swinging on René's front porch swing or walking or biking the trail just two blocks away, the residents of Dannebrog greet you with a hearty wave and sincere hello. Just 20 minutes north of Grand Island, the town hosts a popular Grundlovs Fest the first weekend in June and a Danish Christmas the first weekend in December. △ *3 rooms share bath. Air-conditioning, cable TV/VCR. $40–$45. No credit cards.*

THE KIRSCHKE HOUSE BED AND BREAKFAST 🐦
1124 W. 3rd St., Grand Island 68801, tel. 308/381–6851 or 800/381–6851

Many bed-and-breakfast guests fall in love with the experience, but Dennis and Diane Gebers took the romance one step further and purchased the Kirschke House after honeymooning at the inn in 1997. Today, the Roses Room remains their personal favorite of the four double rooms.

The two-story, vine-covered brick home in Grand Island's residential area was built in 1902 by Otto Kirschke, a prominent contractor. The house features a windowed cupola, turret, and stained-glass windows over an open oak staircase. Diane's decorating style leans more to the country than Victorian, with a good number of family antiques and photos throughout the home, as well as craft works by local artists that are all for sale. Artwork by her own children is also on display, but it isn't for sale at any price, Diane says.

Just a few steps out the back door through a lovely country garden is the renovated brick carriage house, includes a whirlpool, fireplace, four-poster bed, and double-brick shower. Needless to say, the carriage house is popular with honeymooners and those celebrating special occasions. If guests make advance arrangements, Dennis and Diane will prepare a candlelight dinner of their choice, including a private violinist.

Preparations for breakfast begin the previous evening as Diane makes her own fluted quiche cups, which she freezes and fills the next morning with a variety of meats, cheeses, and eggs. Fresh breads and hand-ground coffee complete a filling breakfast. △ *4 double rooms share 2 baths, 1 suite. Air-conditioning, whirlpool in suite, TV/VCR and fireplace in parlor. $55–$145; full breakfast. AE, D, MC, V.*

OTHER CHOICES

Carriage House. Rte. 1 (Box 136B), Beatrice 68310, tel. 402/228–0356. 1 double room with bath, 5 doubles share 3 baths. Air-conditioning, phone, TV/VCR in living room, fireplace in parlor. $50–$65; full breakfast. MC, V.

Crow's Nest. 503 Grant St., Holdrege 68949, tel. 308/995–5440, fax 308/995–9380. 3 double rooms share bath. Air-conditioning, phone, TV/VCR, and fireplace in common area, hot tub. $40–$50; full breakfast. MC, V.

Home Comfort. 1523 N. Brown St., Minden 68959, tel. 308/832–0533. 5 double rooms with baths, 1 guest house (accessible for persons with disabilities). Air-conditioning and TV in common room. $50–$60; full breakfast. No credit cards.

J. C. Robinson House. 102 E. Lincoln, Waterloo 68069, tel. 402/779–2704 or 800/779–2705, fax 402/779–3232. 1 double room with bath, 3 doubles share bath. Air-conditioning, clock radio in rooms; cable TV/VCR, CD player in 2 common areas; 4 fireplaces. $50–$75; full breakfast. No credit cards.

Offutt House. 140 N. 39th St., Omaha 68131, tel. 402/553–0951. 5 double rooms with baths, 2 suites. Air-conditioning, phones, clock radios, TVs, 5 fireplaces, library, small bar. $65–$105; full breakfast. AE, D, MC, V.

Parson's House Bed & Breakfast. 638 Forest Ave., Crete 68333, tel. 402/826–2634. 2 double rooms share bath. Air-conditioning, cable TV/VCR, whirlpool tub, phone in den, fireplace in living room. $45; full breakfast. No credit cards.

Whispering Pines Bed & Breakfast. 21st St. and 6th Ave., Nebraska City 68410, tel. 402/873–5850. 2 double rooms with baths, 3 doubles share bath. Air-conditioning, phone in 2 rooms, cable TV/VCR, whirlpool tub. $50–$75; full breakfast. D, MC, V.

RESERVATIONS SERVICES

Nebraska Association of B&Bs (R.R. 2, Box 17, Elgin 68636, tel. 402/843–2287). **Nebraska Division of Travel & Tourism** (Box 94666, Lincoln 68509, tel. 402/471–3794; listings only).

NEVADA

Carson City and Environs

DEER RUN RANCH ☙
5440 Eastlake Blvd., Washoe Valley, Carson City 89704, tel. 702/882–3643

After an extended search for the perfect spot to build their bed-and-breakfast, David and Muffy Vhay ended up building right on the Washoe Valley ranch where Muffy grew up. Deer Run, opened in 1984, is a working alfalfa ranch in the Virginia Ranger permeated by the pungent smell of wild sage. The idyllic location at the southern end of the Quarter Circle J. P. Ranch has a small pond and large cottonwoods. The eastern escarpment of the Sierra Nevada mountains and Washoe Lake—in all its shimmering glory (after disappearing for several years due to drought)—are also in view.

That David Vhay is an architect is reflected not only in the house—which is bermed on two sides to compensate for the climate extremes of the high desert—but also in the layout of the grounds. Site and structure form a perfect union, creating a spacious, secluded, and sensuous B&B experience.

Both guest rooms have handmade quilts, wall-to-wall window seats with built-in magazine racks, and western decor. The two baths, across the hall from the rooms, have handmade pottery sinks and polished cedar vanities. In the common sitting room are a fireplace, mini-refrigerator, and crammed bookshelves. In the winter, guests skate on the pond and fly down the long sled run (equipment provided); in warmer weather, splashing in an 18-ft aboveground pool and bird-watching round out the recreation. There's also a potter's studio where Muffy turns out all the plates and containers (and even a couple of sinks!) used on the premises. The eponymous deer graze in the fields.

A large garden and small orchard feed the guests year-round. In addition to seasonal fruits, vegetables, and pancakes (such as pumpkin), breakfast, served in the sitting room, consists of frittatas, Dutch babies, and home-baked bread. ♨ *2 double rooms with baths. TV/VCR, fireplace, and mini-refrigerator in sitting room, pool. $85–$105; full breakfast, welcome basket of fruit, wine, and snacks. AE, D, MC, V.*

GENOA HOUSE INN ☙
180 Nixon St. (Box 141), Genoa 89411, tel. 702/782–7075

Genoa is the oldest town in Nevada, its location chosen by Latter-day Saint settlers in 1851 for its scenery and its agricultural and commercial potential. Today, commerce and agriculture have moved to neighboring communities, leaving the scenery and, of course, the history. Within walking distance of the Genoa House Inn, at the bottom edge of the sheer eastern escarpment of the Sierra Nevada mountains, are the rebuilt Mormon stockade and Nevada's oldest bar; on the B&B grounds is a giant oak, believed to be the oldest oak in the state.

The inn was built in 1872 and is listed on the National Register of Historic Places. It's a compact, two-story Victorian, which has withstood almost continual renovation for the last decade. One of the previous owners remodeled the second floor into a cross-gable two-bedroom addition, full of unusual angles, corners, nooks, and crannies. One of the two rooms has mahogany antiques and a private whirlpool bath; the other has antique Gothic stained-glass windows from New Zealand, an antique Turkish fainting couch, and a bilevel tile shower. Both have balconies.

The latest reconstruction was designed by Deer Run Ranch architect David Vhay and engineered by the current owners, Linda and Bob Sanfilippo. A third-generation Tahoan and a former business traveler, Linda stayed in her first B&B in the early 1970s and immediately became a hotel refugee. She and Bob, the town's maintenance man, bought the Genoa House in 1986 and furnished it with antiques, converted the garage into their quarters, and added a third guest room, downstairs, with a private entrance and bath (with a 1906 Wolf tank toilet).

A coffee tray at the door greets guests in the morning, and breakfast is usually coddled eggs, homemade cinnamon rolls, and fresh fruit. △ *3 rooms with baths. Fitness facilities nearby. $115–$150; full breakfast, refreshments served on arrival. D, MC, V.*

GOLD HILL HOTEL 🐾
1540 S. Main St. (Hwy. 341), Gold Hill 89440, tel. 702/847–0111, fax 702/847–0604

Gold was discovered on Gold Hill in 1859, when what was soon to become western Nevada was still the far western edge of Utah. Although its sister town, Virginia City, is far more famous, Gold Hill predates it. The Gold Hill Hotel harks all the way back to the first days of the Comstock Lode—making it the oldest operating inn, and one of the oldest buildings, in Nevada.

The hotel is just below Greiner's Bend, a steep and narrow S-curve in the 1-mi stretch of road that connects Virginia City with Gold Hill. The steepness is reflected in a noticeable tilt to the floors in the original wing, lending its foundation authenticity. The Great Room on the main floor (now the lounge) has a wood plank floor and fireplace, stucco walls with exposed brick, period furniture, and an antique piano and organ. The cozy bar was added in 1960, built to look original, with a stone floor; the Crown Point Restaurant, serving dinner and Sunday brunch year-round and also lunch in summer, was added in 1987 and is decorated with black-and-white photographs of the area's mining heyday.

The four guest rooms in the original building are small; two of the four share a bathroom, which has brick walls, wood fixtures, and a high-sided porcelain tub. Of the seven rooms in the new wing, built in 1987, all have air-conditioning. Four are spacious and have stone fireplaces, wet bars, TVs, balconies, and large modern baths. The all-wood Guest House across the road from the inn has two one-bedroom suites with full kitchens and sofa beds in the living room.

Proprietors Bill and Carol Fain have owned the Gold Hill Hotel for 10 years, and in keeping with the historical status of the inn, they present lectures on a variety of aspects of the Comstock experience every Tuesday evening. Adjoining the hotel is Western Books, a big specialty bookstore with a good selection of titles on the Comstock, Nevada, western explorers, railroads, and Native Americans. △ *10 double rooms with baths, 2 rooms share bath, 2 1-bedroom suites. Restaurant, TVs and phones in newer wing, fireplace in 4 rooms, clock radios. $40–$140; Continental breakfast. MC, V.*

HAUS BAVARIA ☙

593 N. Dyer Circle (Box 9079), Incline Village 89452, tel. 702/831–6122 or 800/731–6222, fax 702/831–1238

Built by a German couple in 1980 as a bed-and-breakfast, this alpine stucco-and-wood chalet was designed to be conducive to comfort, quiet, and privacy. One mile from Lake Tahoe and the only bed-and-breakfast on the Nevada side of the lake's north shore, Haus Bavaria sits at 6,300 ft with a view of the ski runs at Diamond Peak. It is a welcome alternative to the impersonal condos and cacophonous casinos of the resort towns on the east side of the lake.

The two-level inn has five guest rooms upstairs with Danish-style dressers and headboards, heavy quilts, and sliding glass doors that open onto wraparound balconies. Also upstairs is a large sitting room with leather sofas, sling chairs, a wood-burning stove, and maps and photographs of the lake.

A full breakfast is prepared by proprietor Bick Hewitt, a transplanted San Diegan who acquired Haus Bavaria in 1990. The day's first meal might consist of eggs, French toast, cornmeal pancakes (from his Texan grandmother's recipe), or waffles, along with fruit, muffins, and fresh-ground coffee. The dining room is paneled with tongue-in-groove knotty pine and decorated with a collection of German mugs and teapots. A swinging door and louvered shutters connect to the kitchen, where guests can sit in an Art Deco chair at the kitchen work top that Bick calls the "newspaper nook." Doors open onto a comfortable patio.

Guests are provided with passes to Incline Village's private beaches and recreation center; also nearby are two golf courses, tennis courts, downhill and cross-country skiing, hiking, and casino nightlife. ♣ *5 double rooms with baths. TV in sitting room, ski closet, beaches and skiing nearby. $110–$175; full breakfast. AE, D, MC, V.*

NENZEL MANSION ☙

1431 Ezell St., Gardnerville 89410, tel. 702/782–7644

This three-story, 8,000-square-ft mansion built in 1910 is surrounded by ranch land on three sides and faces downtown Gardnerville and the Sierra Nevada beyond. Its exterior would be reminiscent of a southern Colonial plantation big house if it weren't for New England–style dormers on the upper floors and a Nantucket-type widow's walk at the top.

The mansion's strength is in its details: The large foyer has four archways; its original wallpaper has been lovingly preserved; and its custom rounded double doors have the original mortise lock hardware. The Great Room is just that: 40 ft long and 18 ft wide, with contemporary couches and easy chairs, marble (gas) fireplace, and antique player piano. It seats 100 comfortably for wedding ceremonies or 40 for sit-down dinners. Twelve-foot ceilings enhance the house's already open, airy feel.

The four guest rooms are up 21 stairs. Two share a bath, which has an antique porcelain tub. The suite has honeymoon decor in white and blue florals, a sitting area, a walk-in closet, and an unusual bathroom with raspberry-color tiles and a bidet. The other rooms have wicker, brass, and antiques, with feather comforters, wooden rockers, and armoires.

The centerpiece of the formal dining room is the 19-bulb crystal and cut-glass chandelier: The mansion's other chandeliers have all been fabricated to match it. Soufflés, breakfast meats, Texas toast, biscuits, and fruit are served by your hosts, local administrators Chris and Virginia Nenzel and whichever of their four grown children and large extended family happen to be on the scene. ♨ *1 double room with bath, 2 doubles share bath, 1 suite. Laundry facilities. $80– $110; full breakfast. MC, V.*

WILD ROSE INN 🐚
2332 Main St. (Box 256), Genoa 89411, tel. 702/782–5697

The Wild Rose Inn is a three-story, 4,000-square-ft Queen Anne Victorian built by Sandi and Joe Antonucci in 1989. The Wild Rose is as modern as the Genoa House down the street is historic, and spacious as the Genoa House is cozy. With its wraparound porch, cupola tower, and bay windows, there's not a square room in the house.

The guest room on the first floor below the cupola has five windows, hand-stenciled walls, and an antique trunk. The second floor has three rooms in a unique circular floor plan: None of the bedrooms share a common wall and all are thus utterly private; interior-wall insulation further ensures the quiet. The bright room with floral wallpaper in the top of the cupola has a sweeping panorama of the valley and mountains, an iron bed, and antique oak furnishings. Another room's bath has a separate dressing room with built-in wardrobe and vanity.

The third floor contains the Wild Rose's suite, a sprawling affair that sleeps four, with an iron bed in the main room, a twin bed in the dormer alcove, and a trundle bed in the anteroom. The suite also has two skylights; cream with lace-trim sheets, bedspreads, and curtains; a wet bar with a mini-refrigerator in the sitting room; and a large bathroom with his-and-her shell-shape pedestal sinks and an oversize tub.

Breakfast is served buffet-style in the guest parlor on the ground floor: eggs, cereals, fruit, scones, French toast, plentiful cinnamon rolls, muffins, coffee. As at the Genoa House (*see above*), rates include admission to Walley's Hot Springs. Within walking distance of the Wild Rose are two dinner houses, a historic bar, and an old-fashioned country store. ♨ *4 rooms with baths, 1 suite. Air-conditioning, use of Walley's Hot Springs. $95–$130; full breakfast, afternoon wine. AE, MC, V.*

RESERVATIONS SERVICE

Nevada Commission on Tourism (Capitol Complex, Carson City 89710, tel. 800/638–2328; listings only; call for brochure).

NEW HAMPSHIRE

The Seacoast

ROCK LEDGE MANOR
1413 Ocean Blvd. (Rte. 1A), Rye 03870, tel. 603/431–1413

Built between 1840 and 1880 as part of a major seaside resort colony, Rock Ledge Manor is pure Victorian gingerbread. The white, gambrel-roof house with black shutters overlooks the Atlantic just south of Wallis Sands State Beach. In the distance you can see the Isles of Shoals.

The previous owners turned their oceanfront home into a B&B in 1982 and then sold the established business to Stan and Sandi Smith in 1997. "I've always loved B&Bs and the ocean," says Sandi, "so this is a dream come true."

In the breakfast room, with a view of the sea, the table is set formally with china and linens—the way the morning meal was served a century ago. Off the breakfast room, a delightfully old-fashioned sunroom full of plants is just the place to retire to with the morning papers. Or you might prefer to let the breeze ruffle your pages on the wide wraparound porch.

Two bedrooms are on the ground floor and two on the second, all with ocean views. Marble-top sinks and dressers are part of the authentic Victoriana, as are the brass-and-iron beds and the languidly turning paddles of the ceiling fans.

You may have to reserve well in advance in summer, when many returning guests come for a week or more, but Rock Ledge Manor is open year-round, and the seacoast is gloriously uncrowded in the spring and fall. You are only 5 mi from historic Portsmouth, with its museums, galleries, restaurants, and year-round schedule of special events. ♦ *2 double rooms with baths, 2 doubles with ½ baths, shared shower. $80–$90; full breakfast. No credit cards. No smoking, 2-night minimum holidays and weekends.*

OTHER CHOICES

Exeter Inn. 90 Front St., Exeter 03833, tel. 603/772–5901 or 800/782–8444, fax 603/778–8757. 48 double rooms with baths, 1 suite. Restaurant; air-conditioning, cable TV, phones in rooms; meeting rooms. $79–$190. AE, D, DC, MC, V. 2-night minimum Parents' Weekend (late Oct.).

Moody Parsonage Bed and Breakfast. 15 Ash Swamp Rd., Newmarket 03857, tel. 603/659–6675. 1 double room with bath, 3 doubles share bath. Air-conditioning. $60–$70; Continental breakfast. No credit cards. No smoking.

Sise Inn. 40 Court St., Portsmouth 03801, tel. 603/433–1200 or 800/267–0525 (reservations only), fax 603/433–1200. 26 double rooms with baths, 8 suites. Air-conditioning, cable TV/VCR, phone in rooms; whirlpool bath, fireplace, stereo in some rooms; meeting rooms, free parking. $135–$195; Continental breakfast. AE, DC, MC, V. No smoking in some rooms.

The Lakes Region

MANOR ON GOLDEN POND 🐦
Rte. 3 and Shepard Hill Rd. (Box T), Holderness 03245, tel. 603/968–3348
or 800/545–2141, fax 603/968–2116

Built between 1903 and 1907 by Isaac Van Horn, a developer from Florida, this yellow manor house is nestled among the trees on Shepard Hill overlooking Squam Lake. It has welcomed guests since the 1930s when it was owned by Harold Fowler, a renowned *Life* magazine photographer, who made it into a vacation colony for others of his ilk. Many guest rooms in the main house have lake views, as do the cottages (best for families) and the carriage-house rooms.

The wealth of polished dark wood and large fireplaces in the common areas, antiques from Great Britain, and rooms named for the likes of Wellington, Churchill, and Victoria all contribute to the English-manor ambience. Thirteen acres, three on the water, provide plenty of space to enjoy the serenity of Squam Lake—the very serenity that led this lake to be used as the setting for the 1981 film *On Golden Pond*.

Owners David and Bambi Arnold like to pamper their guests, so all the rooms have special touches like hair dryers, magnifying mirrors, padded hangers, Godiva chocolates, and Crabtree & Evelyn toiletries. Some rooms, like Savoy Court, have private decks and fireplaces. Four rooms have oversize whirlpool tubs, too.

Guests can enjoy a before-dinner drink in the Three Cocks Pub, a cozy bar with copper-top tables and a rooster motif. Five-course dinners are served either in the manor's dining room or the former billiards room, and the menu changes nightly. A typical meal might feature grilled herb-crusted rabbit in phyllo with a merlot demiglace sauce or roasted Statler chicken breast stuffed with mushroom duxelles and served with purple passion rice pilaf. The desserts are equally decadent: caramel-and-apple napoleon with vanilla-bean ice cream or a chocolate sampler with chocolate-raspberry truffle cake, chocolate turnover, and chocolate crème brûlée. ♦ *25 double rooms with baths in main house, 22-bedroom cottages. Restaurant, pub; air-conditioning, cable TV in rooms; pool, tennis courts, canoes, paddleboats, fishing, cross-country skiing. $210–$325; full breakfast, afternoon tea. AE, MC, V. No smoking. Cottages and carriage house closed mid-Oct.–July.*

TAMWORTH INN 🐦
Main St. (mailing address: 15 Cleveland Hill Rd.), Tamworth 03886, tel. 603/323–7721
or 800/642–7352, fax 603/323–2026

Tamworth village is synonymous with the Barnstormers Playhouse, summer-night entertainment no one—visitor or resident—would think of missing. Just down the street, the tower of the venerable Tamworth Inn is nearly as well known.

Phil and Kathy Bender, who bought the rambling 1830s Victorian in 1988, have achieved a rare balance. This haven for rest and refreshment since stagecoach days is now where townspeople come for a wedding in the gazebo, new American cuisine in the dining room, or a casual evening in the pub.

Behind the inn, gardens and lawn taper to Swift River. Here Kathy has put her former profession of landscape architect to work, making the most of the romantic gazebo setting with plants and flowers indigenous to New England. Phil, a former banker, manages and cohosts the inn.

The Benders have reduced the total number of rooms in favor of all private baths and more suites. All are furnished with a mixture of 19th-century country antiques and early 20th-century pieces.

In winter fires crackle on the hearths of the dining room, library, and living room, and pots of potpourri in water sit over warming candles. In the pub regulars swap ice-fishing stories around the Franklin stove. In summer you can hang out with the theater cast and crew at the 20- by 40-ft outdoor swimming pool. You can also carry a good book down to the hammock by the river and forget the world completely.

Morning coffee will be brought to your bedroom, if you like. When you amble at leisure to the cheery corner breakfast room you can help yourself to juice, cereal, home-baked breads and muffins, Kathy's special eggs, or French toast. △ *9 double rooms with baths, 7 suites. Restaurant, pub, TV/VCR in library and pub, pool, fly-fishing. $95–$130, full breakfast; $120–$160; MAP. MC, V. No smoking, 2-night minimum holidays.*

WAKEFIELD INN ☞
2723 Wakefield Rd., Wakefield 03872, tel. 603/522–8272 or 800/245–0841

When you turn off Route 16 and drive east to the historic district of Wakefield, time and traffic vanish. A New England miracle? Well, no, but the Wakefield Inn is listed on the National Register of Historic Places for good reason. This Federal-style building is as square and substantial as a fully rigged ship—precisely what its seagoing builder demanded. He also insisted it be an unconventional three stories high, so he could have the tallest house in the village, and he originally built two houses side by side. Soon the two were joined, and later, a wraparound porch was added.

All this and more you learn from Harry Sisson, who shares innkeeping and ownership with his wife, Lou. The Sissons came to New Hampshire from Connecticut. "We moved in, and the first thing I had to do was cater a wedding reception," Lou recalls. Wedding receptions are numerous here (the village church is across the street). Two doors away is the Museum of Childhood. Inn guests receive free passes.

Inside the inn there are surprises: a three-sided fireplace in the dining room and a freestanding spiral staircase (no supporting center pole) that is one of the few in the United States. The Indian shutters and wide-plank pine floors are also typical of the late-Colonial era. Upstairs, the guest rooms are named after important 19th-century visitors, such as poet John Greenleaf Whittier or local notables. Throughout the inn are framed tintypes of unsmiling New Englanders. Some pictures the Sissons found in the attic; some are the gifts of inn guests. Many of the subjects are unknown, the "instant ancestors" of the flea market.

All the bedrooms are large—several have an extra bed and are ideal for families—with views of the mountains and countryside or of the historic village. Forget your toothbrush? No matter. Baskets of "most likely to be forgotten" items sit on hall stands, inviting you to help yourself.

Lou's handmade quilts provide the decorative center for the bedrooms. She also holds special quilting weekends at the inn, assuring guests they will return home with completed (or nearly so) quilts of their own. △ *5 double rooms with baths, 2 suites. TV/VCR in living room. $55–$75; full breakfast. MC, V. No smoking in rooms, 2-night minimum holidays.*

WOLFEBORO INN 🐚

90 N. Main St. (Box 1270), Wolfeboro 03894, tel. 603/569–3016 or 800/451–2389, fax 603/569–5375

A landmark lakeside inn with the amenities of a complete resort, the Wolfeboro is a short stroll from the galleries, shops, and sights of the historic village. The original white-clapboard house with green shutters faces Main Street, but extensions overlook Wolfeboro Bay.

Structural additions have been made since the inn's beginnings in 1812: Rooms in the newest wing are a tad brighter, and many have balconies or decks. The oldest part of the inn includes some original bedrooms with fireplaces (decorative), as well as the venerable Wolfe's Tavern. The main dining room has Windsor chairs, a working fireplace, and paneling from the 1760s. In the old tavern there is an oven fireplace, and the serving staff can offer 40 brands of beer from all over the world.

Many guests are lake regulars (and remember coming here as children). Everything is available for a prolonged lake holiday, from the inn's excursion boat (no charge to guests for boat trips or any other amenity) to many other sports facilities. In winter you can try cross-country skiing, skating, ice fishing, and iceboating.
△ *41 double rooms with baths, 3 suites, 1 1-bedroom apartment. Restaurant, tavern; air-conditioning, cable TV, phone in rooms; elevator, room service 11 AM– 10 PM, private lake beach, excursion boat, fishing, conference facilities in inn or on boat. $119–$249; Continental breakfast. AE, MC, V.*

OTHER CHOICES

Blanchard House. 55 Main St. (Box 389), Center Sandwich 03227, tel. 603/284–6540. 2 double rooms share bath. Fireplaces in common areas, access to lake beach. $87.50; full breakfast. MC, V. No smoking.

Inn on Newfound Lake. Rte. 3A (1030 Mayhew Turnpike), Bridgewater 03222, tel. 603/744–9111 or 800/745–7990, fax 603/744–3894. 22 double rooms with baths, 84 doubles share 2 baths, 2 suites. Restaurant, cable TV/VCR in living room, game room, whirlpool bath, exercise room, swimming. $55–$215; Continental breakfast. AE, D, MC, V. No smoking except in restaurant or on porch, 2-night minimum weekends June–Oct.

The White Mountains
◆❖◆

INN AT THORN HILL 🐚

Thorn Hill Rd. (Box A), Jackson 03846, tel. 603/383–4242 or 800/289–8990, fax 603/383–8062

Romantic is a word you hear a lot at Thorn Hill, the mansion designed by Stanford White, the Gilded Age's most famous architect. Although the inn may feel like your own isolated and special place (the view of Mt. Washington is superb), staying here puts you within walking distance of shops, galleries, and many outdoor activities.

Jim and Ibby Cooper, owners and proprietors, came to Thorn Hill from hospitality and education careers in California, Texas, and Florida. Their older children— excited to be involved—fit right in with a lifestyle that seems less a business than a constant round of entertaining good friends. Yet the elegant past is never far away. A suite in the main house features a mannequin wearing an 1870s wedding dress. In one bedroom a blue velvet fainting couch is an invitation to swoon; spectacular Oriental rugs and electrified Victorian oil lamps are everywhere.

The rooms in the carriage house have a Victorian country-style decor. The open fireplace and overstuffed sofas of the Great Room encourage you to sprawl, and rather than the formality of the Steinway baby grand piano in the main-house drawing room, the carriage house offers an outdoor hot tub. Three cottages—beloved by honeymooners—have fireplaces, whirlpool baths, and other romantic touches.

Thorn Hill is a year-round retreat. In spring, summer, and autumn there are wildflowers and pine forests as well as swimming, hiking, and fishing. In winter you can step directly from the inn's waxing room onto the 150-km (93-mi) Jackson Ski-Touring cross-country trail network or ski downhill at five major areas nearby. You can toboggan on the property, or, if you prefer, have a horse-drawn sleigh pick you up at the door.

Thorn Hill's dining room is known throughout the valley for its contemporary New England cuisine and its wine list—as well as the candlelight. ♨ *14 double rooms with baths, 2 suites, 3 cottages. Restaurant, pub, air-conditioning, terry cloth robes, turndown service, cable TV/VCR in parlor, meeting room, badminton, shuffleboard, pool, croquet, horseshoes, cross-country ski trails, sleigh rides, tobogganing. $130–$230, full breakfast; $160–$260, MAP. AE, D, DC, MC, V. No smoking, 2-night minimum foliage, Christmas, and winter weekends; B&B only mid-wk in Apr.*

NOTCHLAND INN ☙
Rte. 302, Hart's Location, Bartlett 03812, tel. 603/374–6131 or 800/866–6131, fax 603/374–6168

There are llamas in the barn at Notchland Inn, and these unique animals are just one of the surprises that await you here. This mountain-lodge estate overlooks the Saco River valley at the entrance to Crawford Notch. It was built in 1852 by Samuel Beamis, a Boston dentist, and is constructed of locally quarried granite and native timbers. Beamis, a lifelong bachelor, bequeathed it to his loyal caretaker, whose children began to take in summer guests. Notchland became a year-round inn in 1983.

Subsequent renovations have added a new wing with a gourmet restaurant and a gazebo by the duck pond. An old schoolhouse has become a two-suite guest house with working fireplaces; early photographs of the surrounding mountains hang on the walls. The main house retains high ceilings, wood floors, fireplaces, and other 19th-century touches. The bedrooms have armoires, wing chairs, antiques, and fireplaces.

Les Schoof and Ed Butler, the current owners, bought the inn in 1993 when they moved here from Manhattan. They have brought their own touches, such as the award-winning perennial gardens and Cocoa, a lovable Bernese mountain dog.

Watching the seasons unfold from this mountainside vantage point is irresistible despite the fact that the house has a sad history—Samuel Beamis built it to soothe a broken heart; a marker in the living room tells of Nancy Barton, who in 1788 DIED IN A SNOWSTORM IN PURSUIT OF HER FAITHLESS LOVER on the edge of the property. You can try white-water canoeing in springtime, hiking and trout fishing in summer. There are ice-skating on the inn pond in winter and miles of trails for cross-country skiing. ♨ *7 double rooms with baths, 5 suites. Outdoor hot tub, river swimming, hiking. $170–$225, full breakfast; $210–$265, MAP. AE, D, MC, V. No smoking, 2-night minimum with Sat. night.*

OTHER CHOICES

Franconia Inn. 1300 Easton Rd., Franconia 03580, tel. 603/823–5542 or 800/473–5299, fax 603/823–8078. 31 double rooms with baths, 3 suites. Restaurant, cable TV/VCR in lounge, movie room, game room, hot tub, pool, 4 tennis courts, sleigh rides, cross-country skiing (instruction and equipment rentals), bicycles, croquet, horseback riding (fee), snowshoeing (equipment rentals), ice-skating rink, soaring center, privileges at nearby 9-hole golf course. $98–$158, full breakfast; $145–$205, MAP. AE, MC, V. No smoking. Closed Apr.–mid-May.
Snowvillage Inn. Stuart Rd. (off Rt. 153, south of Conway), Snowville 03849, tel. 603/447–2818 or 800/447–4345, fax 603/447–5268. 18 double rooms with baths. Restaurant, meeting rooms, resident privileges at lake, tennis court, volleyball, horseshoes, hiking trails, sauna, cross-country skiing (equipment rental/lessons), snowshoeing (equipment rental). $99–169; full breakfast. AE, D, DC, MC, V. No smoking.
Sunset Hill House. Sunset Hill Rd., Sugar Hill 03585, tel. 603/823–5522 or 800/786–4455, fax 603/823–5738. 27 double rooms with baths, 3 suites. Restaurant, tavern, phone and ceiling fan in rooms, cable TV/VCR in common area, heated pool, 9-hole golf course, cross-country ski trails, snowshoeing. $80–$160, full breakfast; $137–$232 MAP. AE, D, MC, V. No smoking, 2-night minimum during foliage season and holiday weekends.

RESERVATIONS SERVICES

Jackson Resort Association (tel. 800/866–3334). **Mt. Washington Valley Central Reservation Service** (tel. 800/367–3364). **Mt. Washington Valley Chamber of Commerce Travel & Lodging Bureau** (tel. 603/356–5701 or 800/223-7669). **Reservation Service of the Country Inns in the White Mountains** (tel. 603/356–9460 or 800/562–1300). For referrals (not direct reservations) in communities around Berlin, contact the **Northern White Mountains Chamber of Commerce** (tel. 800/992–7480).

Western and Central New Hampshire

BENJAMIN PRESCOTT INN 🐾
Rte. 124, 433 Turnpike Rd., Jaffrey 03452, tel. and fax 603/532–6637

A working dairy farm surrounds this 1853 Colonial farmhouse, making guests feel like they are miles out in the country rather than just minutes from the center of historic Jaffrey Village. The landscape here is so appealing that novelist Willa Cather, who spent many summers in Jaffrey, chose the Old Burying Ground as her final resting place.

Innkeeper Jan Miller is an award-winning quilt maker, and you'll find samples of her work throughout the inn, along with husband Barry's ship models. Jan is also an accomplished candy maker, and guests will find her homemade chocolates waiting for them each evening. The third-floor suite has a king-size four-poster canopy bed, double beds built into alcoves under the eaves, a bathroom with pocket doors, and a balcony that overlooks the farm. Despite the farmlike setting and the large rooms, this B&B is not appropriate for families with preteens.

You can prepare for a day of antiquing or climbing Mt. Monadnock with a full breakfast featuring Welsh miner's cakes, baked French toast with apples or peaches, or an egg-and-sausage casserole. △ *6 double rooms with baths, 4 suites. Air-conditioning in 2 rooms, cross-country skiing, hiking, snowshoeing. $75–$140; full breakfast. AE, MC, V. No smoking in rooms.*

CHASE HOUSE ☙

Rte. 12A (R.R. 2, Box 909), Cornish 03745, tel. 603/675–5391 or 800/401–9455, fax 603/675–5010

Salmon P. Chase, Lincoln's secretary of the treasury and then chief justice of the Supreme Court, was born in this 1775 Federal-style house on the banks of the Connecticut River. A National Historic Landmark, the house has been meticulously restored, and a 30- by 40-ft gathering room with a fieldstone fireplace and a minstrel loft has been added by salvaging the attic of an 1810 garrison house. Perennial gardens and a fruit orchard complete the bucolic setting.

Innkeeper Barbara Lewis bought the Chase House in 1991 and finished the addition in 1992. With her partner, Ted Doyle, Barbara enjoys introducing guests to the Connecticut River valley and sharing the history of the house and its celebrated early occupant.

The common areas provide plenty of homey touches: A nook holds a mini-refrigerator stocked with soft drinks, a countertop has the makings for coffee or tea (if it's not already made for you), and a cookie jar invites you to indulge a sweet tooth. The gathering room, with exposed beams, a hardwood floor, and a huge fireplace, has a TV and VCR as well as a variety of games. A small office for guests provides a private place to work or make phone calls. You can even keep up your fitness regime using the aerobics equipment in the exercise room.

Guest rooms have Oriental rugs, antique armoires, quilts on the beds, and high ceilings. All except the Kate Chase Room are named after Lincoln's cabinet members—including the bridal suite, which is named for Edwin Stanton, Lincoln's secretary of war. The Gideon Welles Suite offers a queen-size pineapple-post bed, a walk-in closet, and a settee under windows that provide a view of the fruit trees.

Breakfast is served in one of two dining rooms—both with fireplaces—or on the patio, depending on the weather and the number of guests. The Amish friendship bread pancakes and the popovers are especially popular. △ *5 double rooms with baths, 3 suites. Air-conditioning in rooms, cable TV/VCR in common rooms, exercise room, river swimming, canoeing, snowshoeing (equipment available). $105–$150; full breakfast. MC, V. No smoking. Closed Nov.*

HANCOCK INN ☙

33 Main St. (Box 96), Hancock 03449, tel. 603/525–3318, fax 603/525–9301

Hancock, north of Peterborough on Route 202, has been called one of New England's prettiest villages—and for good reason. Every house on Main Street is listed on the National Register of Historic Places, including the gray-clapboard, mansard-roof Hancock Inn. Although it has had several names over the years, the Hancock Inn began as a tavern in 1789, making it New Hampshire's oldest continuously operating inn.

The former tavern room is now a common room with a fireplace, an antique checkerboard, braided rugs, and period murals. Named for a stencil artist who lived in Hancock in the 1820s and whose work once graced the inn, the Moses Eaton Room was stenciled by innkeeper Linda Johnston using one of Eaton's original designs. In the Rufus Porter Room, an 1825 Porter mural depicts rural New England. Some guests have remarked that the village of red and white houses depicted in the mural is not unlike Hancock itself. In addition, the room has a cheery, gas fireplace stove; an antique trunk; and a four-poster bed. All the rooms have handmade quilts, antiques, and other period appointments. TVs are hidden under cozies with small signs that say, CAUTION: DO NOT REMOVE UNLESS YOU WISH TO RETURN TO THE 20TH CENTURY.

After retiring from nearly 20 years of innkeeping in North Conway, Linda and her husband, Joe, gave up retirement in 1991 to take over the Hancock. They truly appreciate the inn's history and are happy to share it with guests. Because that history permeates even the walls, the Johnstons believe that children under 12 would find the atmosphere restricting.

The chef also keeps history in mind via a menu that includes such updated New England fare as Shaker cranberry pot roast with garlic mashed potatoes, Down East Maine crab cakes served on julienne vegetables, and corn-crusted rainbow trout with herbed Parmesan couscous.

Guests come to the Hancock Inn to enjoy an area that might well be more rural than it was 200 years ago. Opportunities for hiking, cross-country skiing, and swimming are all close. Or you might prefer to just sit on the wide porch and listen as the Paul Revere bell in the nearby meetinghouse chimes the hour. ♠ *11 double rooms with baths. Restaurant (dinner only); air-conditioning, cable TV, phone in rooms; swimming, boating, fishing, and tennis within walking distance. $106–$172; full breakfast. AE, D, DC, MC, V. No smoking.*

INN AT MAPLEWOOD FARM ☙

447 Center Rd. (Box 1478), Hillsborough 03244, tel. 603/464–4242 or 800/644–6695, fax 603/464–5401

This white-clapboard 1794 farmhouse looks nearly as perfect on the side of Peaked Hill today as it did 200 years ago. From the moment you set foot on the Inn at Maplewood Farm's 14 acres—tucked away on a quiet country road—you feel transported back in time. White wicker chairs on the columned front porch invite you to sit, enjoy the afternoon, and watch the cows graze in a nearby pasture.

Inside, you'll think you've returned to the glory days of radio broadcasting—rather than the Colonial era—when you see the Simoeses' collection of antique radios. All the radios in the parlor work, as do the ones in the bedrooms. Every evening and any time by request, innkeepers Laura and Jayme Simoes start up their own 100-watt transmitter and treat guests to favorite old-time radio shows, from *Fibber McGee and Molly* to *The Shadow* with Orson Welles.

Rooms combine a mix of antiques and quilts with modern bathrooms and blissful peace and quiet. Three rooms have fireplaces. In the Garden Suite, a queen-size canopy bed, a fireplace, a skylight over the bathtub, and a sitting area with flowered cushions on wicker furniture make the room almost too inviting to leave.

The Inn at Maplewood Farm has won several awards for its innovative Continental breakfast, which uses local bread and fruits.

The pastimes are mostly rural in nature: hiking, swimming in the local pond, fishing, cross-country skiing, searching out the covered bridges, and picking apples, blueberries, or strawberries in season. But the Franklin Pierce Homestead, Canterbury Shaker Village, and the Mt. Kearsarge Indian Museum are all within easy driving distance as well. ♠ *3 double rooms with baths, 1 suite.*

TV/VCR in common area, guest area with refrigerator and coffeemaker. $75–$125; Continental breakfast. AE, D, DC, MC, V. No smoking. Closed mid-Nov–Apr.

ROSEWOOD COUNTRY INN ✹

67 Pleasant View Rd., Bradford 03221, tel. and fax 603/938–5253

In 1991 when Leslie and Richard Marquis found the former summer resort that is now the Rosewood Country Inn, the long-abandoned building had been gutted and was filled with debris. In pursuing their dream of owning an inn, they hadn't intended to take on such a drastic renovation project, but they were quick to see the 12-acre property's potential. Today the Victorian country house glistens with fresh beige paint, and rose-color shutters adorn each of the 126 new windows.

Inside, a formal living room in dove gray, rose, and white sets an elegant tone, as do the three-course breakfasts served in the dining room with china, crystal, and candlelight. In the slightly more casual Tavern Room you can indulge in tea and homemade treats in the afternoon, and there are complimentary sherry and chocolates in each guest room as well. You'll find Leslie's stenciling—in a variety of patterns—throughout. In the Bridal Suite, a wicker settee beckons from a bay window nook, and silk flowers woven into the canopy make the bed into a true bridal bower. Antiques, such as the bed warmer in the Williamsburg Room, make interesting accent pieces. ♠ *11 double rooms with baths, 1 suite. Cable TV/VCR in common area, lake, cross-country skiing, snowshoeing, downhill skiing nearby. $69–$140; full breakfast. AE, MC, V. No smoking.*

ZAHN'S ALPINE GUEST HOUSE ✹

Rte. 13, Mont Vernon (mailing address: Box 75, Milford 03055), tel. 603/673–2334, fax 603/673–8415

Tucked into a wooded area on Route 13 between the towns of Milford and Mont Vernon is a little bit of Austria in the form of Zahn's Alpine Guest House. Flowers trail from boxes that line the second-floor balcony, which circles the chalet and is protected by the overhanging roof. Inside, a blue-tiled *Kachelofen* (tile oven), built by a local Bavarian master builder, warms not only the breakfast room but also the rest of the inn.

Bud and Anne Zahn often led bike and ski groups through Bavaria during Bud's years as an importer of Bavarian goods. After retirement they missed meeting new people, so they built the inn on a secluded section of their dairy farm. They've used their knowledge of southern Germany and Austria to find antique farm furniture such as the carved wood and green glass armoire in Room 2 as well as the Alpine carpets and other accessories used to decorate other rooms. Even the dishes in the breakfast room are made by an Austrian potter and decorated with Alpine flowers. Rooms have double beds or European-style oversize twin beds that can be combined to make a king-size bed. ♠ *8 double rooms with baths. TV and phone in rooms, mini-refrigerator and coffeemaker in common area. $65; Continental breakfast. AE, D, MC, V. No smoking in rooms.*

OTHER CHOICES

Birchwood Inn. Rte. 45 (Box 197), Temple 03084, tel. 603/878–3285, fax 603/878–2159. 5 double rooms with baths, 2 doubles share bath. Restaurant (no lunch), TV in common area. $60–$70; full breakfast. No credit cards. No smoking. Closed 1 wk in Apr. and 1 wk in Nov.

Candlelite Inn. 5 Greenhouse La., just off Rte. 114, Bradford 03221, tel. 603/938–5571 or 888/812–5571, fax 603/938–2564. 6 double rooms with baths. Swimming, boating, fishing, cross-country and downhill skiing nearby. $70–$100; full breakfast. AE, D, MC, V. No smoking.

Colby Hill Inn. 3 The Oaks (Box 779), Henniker 03242, tel. 603/428–3281 or 800/531–0330, fax 603/428–9218. 16 double rooms with baths. Restaurant (dinner only), phone in rooms, cable TV/VCR in common areas, pool, fishing, tennis courts (across street), snowshoeing, cross-country skiing (not groomed). $85–$175; full breakfast. AE, D, DC, MC, V. No smoking.

RESERVATIONS SERVICE

Lake Sunapee Business Association (Box 400, Sunapee 03782, tel. 603/763–2495 or 800/258–3530).

NEW JERSEY

The Delaware and Its Surroundings

HUNTERDON HOUSE 🐚

12 Bridge St., Frenchtown 08825, tel. 908/996–3632 or 800/382–0942, fax 908/996–2921 (call first)

The exterior of this 1864 Italianate Victorian mansion is striking. Sitting in a beautifully landscaped garden, the taupe house with plum-and-beige trim is crowned with a belvedere, where guests can sit and look down on the river town. The interior is just as striking. High ceilings, tall shuttered windows, and period antiques make words like *formal* and *grand* seem insufficient when describing the blue parlor. Here guests can help themselves to cream sherry, coffee or tea, and baked goods. Guest rooms, named for members of the Apgar family, who lived here for 96 years, are dominated by huge, carved, mixed-wood Victorian bedroom sets.

Clark and Karen Johnson bought the bed-and-breakfast in 1992 and with the help of historic preservationists have restored it inside and out. The third-floor garret suite has slanting ceilings and a Leonardo da Vinci–design circular window—the Hunterdon House trademark.

The inn is half a block from the river, across the street from the highly rated Frenchtown Inn restaurant, and a short walk from the crafts, antiques, and specialty shops that line Bridge Street. Lambertville and New Hope are a 12-mi drive; public transportation is nearby. ⚐ *6 double rooms with baths, 1 suite. Air-conditioning in rooms; fireplace in 1 room, parlor, and dining room; onsite parking. $85–$160; full breakfast. AE, D, MC, V. Smoking on porch only, 2-night minimum weekends.*

INN AT MILLRACE POND 🐚

313 Johnsonburg Rd. (Rte. 519, Box 359), Hope 07844, tel. 908/459–4884, fax 908/459–5276

In the historic Moravian village of Hope, an old millrace leaves a small millpond and flows through a chasm of slate toward a 1769 stone gristmill, which once supplied flour to Washington's troops and is now an inn. When you enter its gorgeous foyer, you can look down a story and a half at the skeleton of the old wheel and walk downstairs between stone walls to see where the millrace once ran (in summer, a little water still flows in the channel). The spot now serves as the inn's wine cellar. Though the inn complex also includes two other Colonial buildings used for lodging, as well as antiques and gift shops, the focus is on the gristmill with its guest rooms, tavern, and gourmet restaurant. The architecture is stunning, from the bottom-floor tavern, with its huge walk-in fireplace, cage bar, and flour chute, to the top floor's bedrooms, where cathedral ceilings reveal the enormous timbers of the roof. The building's beams and wide-board floors have been preserved throughout.

The gristmill bedrooms have Shaker reproductions; elsewhere there are regional antiques made in New York, Pennsylvania, and New Jersey. The six-bedroom Millrace House, a frame building that was the miller's dwelling, has more formal furnishings and a parlor with a fireplace. Its bedrooms and the two in the Stone Cottage have collections of Queen Anne, Chippendale, and Sheraton pieces. Each of the Stone Cottage bedrooms (one upstairs and one down) has its own entrance, and they are prized for romantic seclusion. Previous inn guests have included Nick Nolte, Barbra Streisand, Dustin Hoffman, and Michael Feinstein.

Innkeepers Cordie and Charles Puttkammer took over in 1994 and have been sprucing up the place since. She is a professor of childhood development, and he runs the inn from a table in the dining room—that is, when he isn't collecting things or seeing to the property. They are currently completing renovations to a building moved to the site to serve as a center for business meetings. ♙ *16 double rooms with baths, 1 suite. Restaurant, tavern, air-conditioning; cable TV in 10 rooms and parlor; phone in rooms; fireplace in 1 room, parlor, and tavern; tennis; on-site parking. $85–$165; Continental breakfast. AE, D, DC, MC, V. No smoking in rooms, 2-night minimum with Sat. reservation.*

STEWART INN ☙
708 S. Main St. (Box 6), Stewartsville 08886, tel. 908/479–6060, fax 908/479–4211

Owner and innkeeper Lynne McGarry, an antiques collector and needlework-kit manufacturer, presides over this rambling 1770 fieldstone manor house. It was originally built for the owner of Stewartsville's gristmill, which ground flour to feed George Washington's troops during the Revolutionary War. Between 1800 and 1967, countless additions were made and it passed between many owners, among them Broadway producer Harry Bannister and his wife, actress Ann Harding, whose friends in the entertainment industry—among them Clark Gable—used the house as a retreat. Although the stars left nothing behind, the inn has retained a dramatic atmosphere.

About a 25-minute drive from the many fine restaurants of Lambertville, Stewart Inn has 16 acres of lawns, formal perennial gardens, a stocked trout stream, and a meandering pasture that leads to a working farm with ducks, sheep, goats, and peacocks. The eggs served at breakfast are provided by the farm's chickens. Lynne has a wild-game license, and it's not unusual for there to be a wounded animal in residence that she's nursing back to health. More animals, in the form of knickknacks, make their home in the common areas downstairs.

The best times to visit the inn are summer, when the swimming pool offers a respite from the heat, and fall, when the maple and apple trees show off their bright colors. (Unfortunately, the hum from nearby I–78 mars the otherwise bucolic setting.) In the winter, the house is filled with plants brought in from the outside.

Inside, off-white walls bring out the richness of the dark cherry and mahogany furnishings and the colorful tapestries and rugs. Many rooms have antique jam cupboards, and all have brass oil lamps on night tables beside the beds. Needlework is displayed throughout the house, and Lynne sells kits for those who are inspired. Long-term guests, often businesspeople in transit, frequently stay at the inn, taking breakfast in the cozy kitchen. Short-term visitors eat at individual tables in the dining room and enjoy such standbys as Jack's Flaps, named for a former longtime guest who loved to cook pancakes. ♙ *3 double rooms with* *baths, 4 suites. Air-conditioning, cable TV and phone in rooms, fireplace in 3 rooms and 3 common areas, badminton, on-site parking. $95–$125; full breakfast. AE, D, MC, V. Smoking on porch only, 2-night minimum weekends May–Oct.*

STOCKTON INN ☞

1 Main St. (Box C), Stockton 08559, tel. 609/397–1250, fax 609/397–8948

In 1934 Richard Rodgers and Lorenz Hart escaped from Manhattan to this inn, which inspired their 1936 musical, *On Your Toes,* and its song "There's a Small Hotel with a Wishing Well." Even today people call to ask if the wishing well is still there. It is, in the terraced garden with waterfalls and a trout pond.

Built as a private home in 1710, the inn became a stagecoach stop in 1796 and a hotel in 1832. Rooms are furnished with simple, tasteful Colonial-style reproductions and some antiques, and two suites share a balcony overlooking the small town of Stockton. Historic touches remain—eight bedrooms and the five dining rooms have working fireplaces—but the mood is more that of the famous "small hotel," with modern conveniences like cable TV and in-room phones scheduled to be added by 1998. The inn comprises four buildings: the inn itself, two carriage houses, and a house across the street. All have similar rooms. A good restaurant serving contemporary American and Continental food keeps the place bustling. △ *3 double rooms with baths, 8 suites. Restaurant, air-conditioning and TV in rooms, mini-refrigerator in 2 rooms, on-site parking. $65–$170; Continental breakfast. AE, D, MC, V. 2-night minimum weekends, 3-night minimum holiday weekends.*

OTHER CHOICES

Chimney Hill Bed and Breakfast. 207 Goat Hill Rd., Lambertville 08530, tel. 609/397–1516, fax 609/397–9353. 8 double rooms with baths. Air-conditioning in rooms, fireplace in 4 rooms and 3 public areas, on-site parking, balloon trips from inn arranged. $89–$250; Continental breakfast on weekdays, full breakfast weekends. AE, MC, V. No smoking indoors, 2-night minimum weekends in season and holiday weekends.

Holly Thorn House. 143 Readington Rd., Whitehouse Station 08889, tel. 908/534–1616, fax 908/534–9017. 4 double rooms with baths, 1 suite. Air-conditioning in rooms, mini-refrigerator in gathering and billiard rooms, pool, cabana, on-site parking. $115–$145; full breakfast. AE, D, MC, V. No smoking in rooms.

Isaac Hilliard House. 31 Hanover St., Pemberton 08068, tel. 609/894–0756 or 800/371–0756. 3 double rooms with baths, 1 suite. Air-conditioning, cable TV/VCR and fireplace in suite and parlor, mini-refrigerator in suite, pool, bicycles, on-site parking. $65–$140; full breakfast. AE, D, MC, V. No smoking indoors, 2-night minimum holiday weekends.

Wooden Duck. 140 Goodale Rd., Newton 07860, tel. 973/300–0395, fax 973/300–0395. 5 double rooms with baths, 2 suites. Air-conditioning, cable TV/VCR in rooms and game room, on-site parking. $100–$150; full breakfast. AE, D, MC, V. No smoking, 2-night minimum holiday weekends.

RESERVATIONS SERVICES

Amanda's Bed & Breakfast Reservation Service (21 S. Woodland Ave., East Brunswick 08816, tel. 732/249–4944, fax 732/246–1961). **Bed & Breakfast Adventures** (2310 Central Ave., Suite 132, North Wildwood 08260, tel. 609/522–4000 or 800/992–2632 for reservations, fax 609/522–6125). **Bed and Breakfast of Princeton** (Box 571, Princeton 08542, tel. 609/924–3189, fax 609/921–6271).

The Jersey Shore

GREEN GABLES INN ☞

212 Centre St., Beach Haven 08008, tel. 609/492–3553 or 800/492–0492, fax 609/492–2507

Like other Beach Haven inns, this 1880 green clapboard house with purple and yellow trim offers a romantic Victorian getaway a shell's throw from the beach. On the second and third stories, modest antiques are tucked into cozy rooms with old wide-plank floors, flowered wallpapers, and cheery paint, but what people really come here for is the exciting cuisine of the ground-floor restaurant.

You can sit in one of the comfortable Victorian dining salons or on the lattice-enclosed garden-side porch. There your dinner choices end. Owner-chef Adolfo DeMartino—who, along with lovely wife, Rita, hails from Italy by way of Manhattan—plans one five-course menu daily based on what's fresh at the market (be sure to mention any allergies or dislikes when you make your mandatory reservation). The less adventurous can take lunch or tea, though Green Gables's scrumptious tea pastries are an adventure in themselves. On Sunday, Russian gypsy card and tea-leaf readings are available.

Dinner/room packages enable guests to indulge in the culinary experience, collapse satisfied in a room upstairs, and awaken to home-baked goodies before a day at the beach. △ *2 double rooms with baths, 4 doubles share 2 baths. Beach tags. $90–$140; Continental breakfast. AE, MC, V. Smoking on porch only, 2-night minimum weekends, 3-night minimum holiday weekends mid-May–Sept.*

LA MAISON ☞

404 Jersey Ave., Spring Lake 07762, tel. 732/449–0969 or 800/276–2088, fax 732/449–4860

Unlike Spring Lake's other, mostly American- or British-inspired Victorian B&Bs, this 1870 inn has a French flair, and a visit here will have you exclaiming *"Vive la différence!"* Engaging Francophile Barbara Furdyna bought the mansard-roofed structure in 1982, when she worked for IBM, but she is now the full-time innkeeper. She has renovated and redecorated the sparkling rooms in country French style, transformed hall walls into a gallery of works (mostly watercolors) by La Maison's staff and larger "family," and imbued the house with easy European hospitality.

Mornings start with a decidedly un-Continental breakfast—perhaps crème brûlée French toast or a Provençal omelet with chèvre and herbes de Provence, always accompanied by baguettes, artfully arranged fresh fruit, fresh-squeezed orange juice or mimosas, and cappuccino or espresso on request. Return at happy hour for wine and cheese in front of the parlor's gas fireplace, and at night melt beneath fluffy duvets in the soft sheets of a sleigh bed. To dissolve further, take the room with a skylit whirlpool for two. Not surprisingly, the inn is a favorite of visitors from Europe and those who wish they were there. △ *5 double rooms with baths, 2 suites, housekeeping cottage. Air-conditioning, cable TV in rooms, VCR in 1 room, outbound-only phone in rooms, mini-refrigerator in dining room and hall, bicycles, outdoor shower, beach and saltwater-pool tags, beach chairs, fitness club passes, on- and off-site parking, transportation to and from train and bus. $145–$300; full breakfast, afternoon refreshments. AE, D, DC, MC, V. Smoking on porch only, small pets in cottage only, 2-night minimum weekends Sept.–*

June and weekdays July–Aug., 3-night minimum weekends July–Aug. and other
summer holiday weekends. Closed Jan.

NORMANDY INN 🦜
21 Tuttle Ave., Spring Lake 07762, tel. 732/449–7172 or 800/449–1888,
fax 732/449–1070

On the National Register of Historic Places, this huge Italianate villa with Queen Anne touches was built for the Audenreid family of Philadelphia around 1888 and became a guest house in 1909. It still had the feel of a guest house in 1982, when Michael and Susan Ingino, who had had an ice cream business in nearby Toms River, bought the inn and began to transform it into a textbook of museum-quality high-Victorian furnishings. Deliberately undercutting the formal atmosphere, the Inginos urge guests to relax. "To see a guest curl up on a sofa with a book is just what I want," Mike explains.

With the exception of rattan furniture in the casual enclosed side porch and a few necessities, such as a sleep sofa, there are no reproductions or modern pieces. Everything is genuine American Victorian. On the first floor are gasoliers, a wood-burning fireplace, and a Renaissance Revival parlor set with women's faces carved on the arms. Renaissance Revival predominates in the guest rooms, in addition to Rococo Revival and Eastlake.

Rooms are individually decorated down to the wallpaper and carpeting. Two are particularly spectacular, but for very different reasons. The drama in Room 102 is provided by 11-ft ceilings, rich green walls, and a very impressive four-piece burled-wood bedroom set. The less-formal, rose-color Tower Room has windows on four sides. Though its bathroom is down the stairs and down the hall (robes are provided), it's only a minor inconvenience when you consider the bright sunlight, cool breezes, and views over the rooftops to the ocean.

For families (well-behaved children are always welcome), there are two suites, one of which, above a 1930s garage, has a full kitchen and green marble bath with whirlpool for two. Period needle craft lends a country flair, but the suite is still dotted with turn-of-the-century antiques.

The newest rooms include one whose marble bath has a whirlpool tub and stained glass and whose gas fireplace is rimmed by an Eastlake mantel, typical of the period wood and marble mantels surrounding the five gas fireplaces in guest rooms. But though change is continual at the Normandy, four-course hot breakfasts remain a constant, enabling guests to skip lunch and spend the day at the beach, a two-minute walk away. △ *16 double rooms and 1 single with baths, 2 suites.*
Air-conditioning, cable TV on side porch and in rooms (on request), phone in rooms,
bicycles, beach towels and chairs, on-site parking for 9 rooms, transportation to and
from train and bus. $128–$300; full breakfast. AE, D, DC, MC, V. Smoking on
porches only, 2-night minimum weekdays July–Aug. and weekends Mar.–Nov.,
3-night minimum weekends July–Aug. and holiday weekends.

PIERRÓT BY THE SEA 🦜
101 Centre St., Beach Haven 08008, tel. 609/492–4424

Innkeepers Jane Loehwing and daughter Jennifer were living in North Jersey when, in 1994, in search of peace and quiet and the challenge of running a business, they bought this ivory-colored B&B on Long Beach Island.

The restoration of the 1865 inn is accurate to the high-Victorian era, with the exception of a 12-ft-tall mahogany reproduction of a bedroom set that a previous owner, a professional Victorian restorer, made to see how closely he could match the style. (He matched it perfectly.) There are intricately carved walnut bedroom sets, Oriental rugs, and multiple wallpapers in the bedrooms—but, oh, the stained glass.

A handful of original stained-glass windows remain, but the showstoppers all over the house were made by the previous owner. The front door has a beautiful palette of vibrant colors, the dining room has a stained-glass tree, and bedroom windows blend with each color scheme. One in a front bedroom glows at daybreak, and even the outside shower has its own stained glass.

Looking beyond the windows, you can see (and hear) the ocean from most rooms. (The inn is just a half block from the dune-backed beach.) Unfortunately, the modern motels across the street generate noise on Saturday nights in summer that, according to Jane, makes it seem like "42nd Street in a bathing suit." Air conditioners mask the sound.

A multicourse breakfast is served in the dining room in winter, while in warmer months guests and lighter fare move out to the wraparound veranda, where two rooms have private entrances. Other activities on your not-so-busy agenda might include walking, cycling, rollerblading, or taking the brick path to the gazebo for some serious seaside relaxation. △ *6 double rooms with baths, 3 doubles share bath. Air-conditioning in 4 rooms, fireplace in parlor, mini-refrigerator in dining room, bicycles, beach tags. $100–$175; Continental breakfast Mon.–Sat. and full breakfast Sun. Memorial Day–Labor Day, full breakfast Labor Day–Memorial Day. No credit cards. No smoking indoors, 2-night minimum weekends late June–Oct., 3-night minimum holiday weekends Memorial Day–Labor Day.*

OTHER CHOICES

Amber Street Inn. 118 Amber St., Beach Haven 08008, tel. 609/492–1611, fax 609/494–9165. 6 double rooms with baths. Air-conditioning, outbound-only phone in rooms, bicycles, outdoor shower, beach tags and chairs. $115–$165; Continental-plus breakfast Mon.–Sat. and full breakfast Sun. No smoking indoors, 2-night minimum on weekdays mid-June–mid-Sept. and weekends mid-June–July, 3-night minimum weekends in Aug., 3- or 4-night minimum holiday weekends. Closed mid-Nov.–mid-Feb.

Bayberry Barque. 117 Centre St., Beach Haven 08008, tel. 609/492–5216. 5 double rooms with baths, 3 doubles share bath. Air-conditioning in 2 rooms, cable TV in living room, mini-refrigerator in hall, outdoor shower, beach tags and chairs. $75–$160; Continental breakfast, Sat. afternoon wine-and-cheese parties in summer. MC, V. No smoking indoors, 2-night minimum weekends and 3-night minimum holiday weekends mid-June–mid-Sept. Closed Nov.–Apr.

Cashelmara. 22 Lakeside Ave., Avon-by-the-Sea 07717, tel. 732/776–8727 or 800/821–2976, fax 732/988–5819. 12 double rooms with baths, 2 suites. Air-conditioning, cable TV, and satellite TV in theater; gas fireplace in 7 units, dining room, foyer, and parlor; guest refrigerator, whirlpool in 2 suites; beach tags, towels, umbrellas, and chairs, on-site parking, transportation to and from train and bus. $79–$263; full breakfast. D, MC, V. Smoking on porch only, 2-night minimum weekends Labor Day–June, 3-night minimum weekends and 4-night minimum holiday weekends July–Labor Day.

Conover's Bay Head Inn. 646 Main Ave., Bay Head 08742, tel. 732/892–4664 or 800/956–9099, fax 732/892–8748. 12 double rooms with baths, 1 cottage. Air-conditioning, phone and TV/VCR in rooms, gas fireplace in 1 room, guest refrigerator, Jacuzzi, beach tags, towels, and chairs, on-site parking, transportation to and from train and bus. $135–$225; full breakfast, afternoon tea. AE, MC, V. No smoking indoors, 2-night minimum weekends mid-Sept.–mid-June, 3-night minimum weekends and 3- or 4-night minimum holiday weekends mid-June–mid-Sept.

SeaScape Manor. 3 Grand Tour, Highlands 07732, tel. 732/291–8467, fax 732/872–7932. 4 double rooms with baths. Air-conditioning and cable TV/VCR in rooms, fireplace in sitting room, mini-refrigerator in sitting room, bicycles, lawn games, barbecue grill, beach towels and chairs, recreation area passes, on-site parking, transportation to and from train, bus, and ferry. $90–$125; full breakfast. AE, MC, V. Smoking on decks only, 2-night minimum holiday weekends.

The Studio. 102 Cedar Ave., Island Heights 08732-0306, tel. 732/270–6058. 4 double rooms share 2 baths. Air-conditioning in rooms, cable TV in sunroom, fireplace in studio and library, bay and river beach tags, towels, and chairs, bicycles, transportation to and from bus. $85; full breakfast. AE. No cats.

RESERVATIONS SERVICES

Amanda's Bed & Breakfast Reservation Service (21 S. Woodland Ave., East Brunswick 08816, tel. 732/249–4944, fax 732/246–1961). **Bed & Breakfast Adventures** (2310 Central Ave., Suite 132, North Wildwood 08260, tel. 609/522–4000 or 800/992–2632 for reservations, fax 609/522–6125).

Cape May

THE ABBEY ℱ
34 Gurney St., at Columbia Ave., Cape May 08204, tel. 609/884–4506,
fax 609/884–2379

Built in 1869 as a summer home for Philadelphia coal baron John B. McCreary, the Abbey was named by current owners Jay and Marianne Schatz, who thought the Gothic Revival architecture resembled a house of worship.

Actually, the Abbey comprises two buildings. Jay and Marianne, both chemists before their love of old houses and antiques brought them to Cape May, opened the main house, the Villa, in 1979. In 1986 they renovated the adjacent 1873 Second Empire house, called the Cottage. Though each house has two parlors and bedrooms named for cities with Victorian architecture (many containing something from that city), the buildings have their own styles. The Villa, with its impressive 65-ft tower, is formal and dramatic, though some of its period antiques look a bit worn. The Newport Room's tower bath makes it an unusual guest quarter. In contrast, the Cottage, its parlor furnished in wicker, feels like a summer house.

Many B&Bs have a rack with vintage hats, but the very loquacious Jay, who admits he suffers from "achapeauphobia" (the fear of being hatless) doesn't stop there. He stashes a huge assortment of hats at the Abbey, but there's no sign of a cowl or wimple. ⚓ *12 double rooms with baths, 2 suites. Air-conditioning in 11 rooms, mini-refrigerator in rooms, beach tags and chairs, croquet, on- and off-site parking. $80–$275; full breakfast, afternoon refreshments. D, MC, V. Smoking on veranda only, 2-, 3-, or 4-night minimum weekends. Closed Jan.–Mar.*

JOHN F. CRAIG HOUSE ℱ
609 Columbia Ave., Cape May 08204, tel. 609/884–0100, fax 609/898–1307

Warm hosts and cool breezes are in store at this 1866 Carpenter Gothic inn. The focus is on "the positive aspects and beauty of the Victorian era," explain owners Connie and Frank Felicetti. "We don't want stuffy." And stuffy it is not.

There are plenty of places to curl up with a good book and plenty of books from which to choose. The library's collection ranges from heirloom to modern, and guests delight in antique volumes of Victorian poetry. You can relax in the parlor, warmed by a gas fireplace in winter and naturally cooled by floor-to-ceiling windows on late afternoons in summer, just as it was 100 years ago. Or follow the morning or afternoon sun to one of the porches enveloping the inn, where cats Heckle and Jeckle might be lolling on a leash.

For another excuse to leave the guest rooms, furnished with Eastlake and Renaissance Revival antiques and named for Craig family members, you can attend either of two breakfast seatings. Frank, an attorney turned avid chef, prepares varied menus that include pineapple ricotta muffins, ramekin eggs, Italian sausage with fennel, and nectarines with amaretto and orange—tasty sustenance for a relaxing day. △ *7 double rooms with baths, 1 suite. Air-conditioning in rooms, mini-refrigerator in 3rd-floor rooms and on porch, beach tags, towels, and chairs, on-site parking for those who won't use their car. $95–$175; full breakfast, afternoon tea. D, MC, V. Smoking on porch only, 2-night minimum weekends, 3-night minimum July–Labor Day. Closed Jan.–Feb.*

MAINSTAY INN ❦
635 Columbia Ave., Cape May 08204, tel. 609/884–8690

An 1872 men's social club formerly called Jackson's Clubhouse, the Mainstay is one of Cape May's best bed-and-breakfasts. Many a gambler whiled away the hours under these 14-ft ceilings and on the lofty veranda, which, more than 100 years later, is the city's most ostentatious spot for doing nothing.

In 1976 the property was purchased by Tom Carroll, who came to Cape May to serve at the nearby Coast Guard Training Center, and his wife, Sue, a collector of antiques. In renovating the building, they made it a focal point in the move to revive Victorian Cape May as a resort town. Included in the magnificent restoration are the house's original chandeliers as well as most of the original furniture.

The first hint of the Carrolls' astonishing attention to detail is found in the foyer, where a 13- by 7-ft rosewood-framed mirror, probably weighing 1,000 pounds (no one's ever taken it down to find out) hangs beneath a dramatic ceiling patterned with 17 different wallpapers. Guest rooms are named for famous Cape May visitors, such as the General Grant and Stonewall Jackson suites, which coexist as harmoniously as the elegant antiques, some of which are museum quality.

In addition to being active in Cape May historic preservation and the city's Victorian Week festivities, the Carrolls are enthusiastic fans of Victorian culture and games, the more whimsical the better. They socialize actively with guests, some of whom have been inspired to open B&Bs of their own, and turn breakfast and tea into friendly occasions. "We like guests to feel as if they're not just staying with us but that they're part of the Mainstay's atmosphere," says Tom.

For more privacy than the main-house drawing room and its inviting gas fireplace, gaming table, and 1886 piano afford, you can steal up to the cupola, which has a distant ocean view. Or you may choose to stay in the Officers' Quarters, the "new" building across the street. Built to house military personnel during World War I, it contains four one- or two-bedroom suites that offer the modern amenities lacking in the carefully preserved Mainstay and adjacent Cottage. Each suite here has its own cable TV with VCR, phone, whirlpool bath, gas fireplace, private porch, and snack bar; a Continental breakfast is delivered to each unit in a picnic basket. Despite the modern comforts, however, there are enough old touches, such as antique mantels in the sitting areas and back-lit stained glass in the bathrooms, to provide vintage Mainstay charm. ☚ *12 double rooms with baths, 4 suites. Air-conditioning in most rooms, microwave and mini-refrigerator in 4 suites, on-site parking for 14 rooms. $150–$275; Continental-plus breakfast June–Sept., full breakfast Oct.–May, afternoon tea. No credit cards. Smoking on veranda only, 2-night minimum weekends Oct.–May, 3-night minimum weekends June–Sept.*

SOUTHERN MANSION ☞
720 Washington St., Cape May 08204, tel. 609/884–7171, fax 609/898–0492

At this 1863 Samuel Sloan–designed home with 1997 wing, *B&B* might as well stand for "big and bold." But it's the scale, not the number of rooms, that's grand: Many of the 40,000-square-ft hotel's rooms are 400 square ft, ample space for the mostly king-size beds. First-floor rooms in the original building have 15½-ft ceilings, accommodating massive armoires (some 11 ft tall) and huge paintings of nudes, which hang on intensely hued walls.

Reclaiming the house from decades as a boardinghouse took 1½ years and 200 dumpsters. Antiques, most original to the house, are worth millions. The authentic restoration and the construction of the new wing, built in the style of the original and flanked by a pair of dramatic Honduran mahogany and purpleheart circular stairs, was overseen by Barbara Wilde and her family, who own the mansion.

The sumptuous surroundings lend themselves to romantic occasions. Two ballrooms at the mansion are available for weddings and other large events. For those not ready for a wedding, you can reserve the cupola for a romantic dinner and perhaps a proposal. And, for those with business on their minds, it is equally suitable for corporate retreats.

Modern amenities, facilities for business meetings, and a members/guests-only dining area are aimed at an exclusive clientele, and in time, management should gain the savvy and polish to match. ☚ *23 double rooms with baths, 2 suites. Air-conditioning, cable TV and phone in rooms, gas fireplace in ballrooms, beach tags, towels, and chairs, on-site parking. $195–$350; full breakfast, afternoon tea. AE, MC, V. No smoking, 2-night minimum weekends Oct.–May, 3-night minimum weekends July–Aug., 4-night minimum holiday weekends.*

OTHER CHOICES

Albert Stevens Inn. 127 Myrtle Ave., Cape May 08204, tel. 609/884–4717 or 800/890–2287, fax 609/884–8320. 7 double rooms with baths, 3 suites. Air-conditioning in rooms, TV in 2 suites, kitchen in 1 suite, gas fireplace in dining room and parlor, mini-refrigerator on enclosed porch, beach tags and towels, hot tub Oct.–Apr., on-site parking. $85–$165; full breakfast, afternoon tea. AE, D, MC, V. Smoking on front porch only, 2-night minimum weekends, 3-night minimum July–Aug. and holidays.

Inn at 22 Jackson. 22 Jackson St., Cape May 08204, tel. 609/884–2226 or 800/452–8177, fax 609/884–0055. 4 suites, cottage. Air-conditioning, gas fireplace in cottage and foyer, beach tags, towels, and chairs, bicycles, off-site parking. $195–$350; full breakfast, afternoon refreshments. AE, MC, V. Smoking on porches only, 2-night minimum weekends.

Manor House. 612 Hughes St., Cape May 08204, tel. 609/884–4710, fax 609/898–0471. 9 double rooms with baths, 1 suite. Air-conditioning in rooms, TV/VCR in 1 room, mini-refrigerator on side porch, whirlpool in suite, beach tags, towels, and chairs, outdoor shower, off-site parking. $100–$250; full breakfast, afternoon refreshments. D, MC, V. Smoking on porch and in garden only, 2-night minimum weekends, 3-night minimum July–Aug. Closed Jan.

Virginia Hotel. 25 Jackson St., Cape May 08204, tel. 609/884–5700 or 800/732–4236, fax 609/884–1236. 24 double rooms with baths. Restaurant, bar, air-conditioning, cable TV/VCR and phone in rooms, videotape rentals, beach tags, towels, and chairs, reduced-rate fitness club passes, valeted off-site parking. $180–$295; Continental breakfast. AE, D, DC, MC, V. No smoking in restaurant, 2-night minimum weekends off-season, 3-night minimum Memorial Day–Labor Day.

Wooden Rabbit. 609 Hughes St., Cape May 08204, tel. 609/884–7293, fax 609/898–0842. 2 double rooms with baths, 2 suites. Air-conditioning and TV in rooms, beach tags and chairs, on-site parking. $170–$200; full breakfast, afternoon tea. MC, V. No smoking, 2-night minimum weekends, 2-night minimum July–Aug.

RESERVATIONS SERVICES

Amanda's Bed & Breakfast Reservation Service (21 S. Woodland Ave., East Brunswick 08816, tel. 732/249–4944, fax 732/246–1961). **Bed & Breakfast Adventures** (2310 Central Ave., Suite 132, North Wildwood 08260, tel. 609/522–4000 or 800/992–2632 for reservations, fax 609/522–6125). **Cape May Reservation Service** (1382 Lafayette St., Cape May 08204, tel. 609/884–9396 or 800/729–7778).

NEW MEXICO

Santa Fe and Environs

DON GASPAR COMPOUND INN ☞
*623 Don Gaspar, Santa Fe 87501, tel. 505/986–8664 or 888/986–8664,
fax 505/986–0696*

Despite its proximity to Santa Fe's center, the Don Gaspar Compound feels worlds removed from urban life. Six spacious accommodations and a beautifully landscaped courtyard pamper guests within the property's adobe walls. Try to visit between May and October, when colorful flowers bloom along unhurried brick paths that weave between aspen, cottonwood, and fruit trees.

All guest rooms are individually decorated and have private entrances with pretty courtyard views, beds with down comforters, and kitchenettes.

The Southwest Suite, bathed in deep crimsons and sand colors, has a living room with a kiva fireplace and impressionist landscape prints on the walls. There's a separate room with a king bed and a fruitwood wardrobe. The Courtyard Casita, with a private garden, can sleep up to four. Like the inn's other casitas, it has French doors and a gas fireplace.

For larger parties, the Mission-style Main House, built in 1912 and listed on the State Historical Register, has two bedrooms, a dining room, living room, and full kitchen. There's another two-bedroom adobe home about 2 mi from the Compound in a quiet residential area.

As sleepy eyes give way to morning hunger, guests may enjoy a gourmet Continental breakfast in their rooms, in the dining room, or in the sun. If you opt for the courtyard, water trickles gently down a tiered fountain while fresh fruits and homemade breads, cereals, and regional specialties are laid out. Following breakfast, guests can easily walk to the Plaza where Santa Fe's best shops and sights await. ♙ *5 double rooms with baths, Main House accommodates up to 6 people. TV, phone, microwave, refrigerator in rooms. $85–$220; Continental-plus breakfast. AE, MC, V. No smoking.*

GRANT CORNER INN ☞
122 Grant Ave., Santa Fe 87501, tel. 505/983–6678

The only Colonial-style bed-and-breakfast in town, this is the place that innkeepers talk about when they get together over potluck dinners. It's one of the best-run and most successful in the state. Owner Louise Stewart, daughter of Jack Stewart, who founded the renowned Camelback Inn in Scottsdale, studied at the Cornell hotel school and worked as an interior designer before opening the Grant Corner Inn—and what a production it is.

Only two blocks from the Plaza in a small tree-filled lot, surrounded by a veranda and garden, the house originally belonged to the Winsor family, wealthy

New Mexican ranchers. The rooms and public areas are filled with antiques and treasures collected from around the world by Louise. Hand-stitched quilts, brass and four-poster beds, armoires, and artwork make each room unique. The undisputed star is Room No. 8, a visual treat with its white brass bed, love seat, quilted bedspread, Oriental rugs, and Old World touches. The downstairs public rooms also hark back to grander days, with lace curtains, antique oak tables, ceiling fans, crystal chandeliers, and a legion of bunnies.

The breakfast menu includes such treats as banana waffles, eggs Florentine, and green-chili-laden New Mexican soufflé, all accompanied by fresh-ground European coffee, fresh-squeezed juice, fruit, and homemade rolls and jellies. Small wonder the public comes clamoring on weekends when the dining room is open to one and all. Meals are served in front of a crackling fire in the dining room or, in summer, on the veranda. Guests get a complimentary glass of wine in the evening. Elaborately prepared picnic baskets are available, too.

The Grant Corner Inn also operates the Grant Corner Inn Hacienda, a southwestern-style condominium six blocks away; it's available for parties of up to four. Rates ($215–$255 per night) include breakfast at the inn. ♠ *7 double rooms with baths, 2 doubles share bath, 1 single. Cable TV and phone in rooms, in-house massages available; lounge with dining nook, microwave, and refrigerator; privileges at nearby tennis club. $70–$155; full breakfast. MC, V. No smoking.*

INN ON THE ALAMEDA 🐾
303 E. Alameda, Santa Fe 87501, tel. 505/984–2121 or 800/289–2122, fax 505/986–8325

Alameda means "tree-lined lane," befitting its location alongside the Santa Fe River, which gurgles virtually through the center of town. This setting, between the historic Santa Fe Plaza and gallery-filled Canyon Road, is both tranquil and convenient: Even without a car, guests have easy access to shops, museums, and restaurants.

Opened in 1986, this lodging was originally intended to be a bed-and-breakfast with resident managers. However, it soon blossomed into one of Santa Fe's most prestigious small hotels, combining the relaxed atmosphere of a New Mexico country inn with the amenities of a world-class hotel.

Rooms, in a contemporary adobe complex with a network of enclosed courtyards and portales are decorated in southwestern colors, down to the accessories, beds, wall hangings, and wood-frame mirrors. Many rooms have handmade armoires, oversize chairs, headboards, and colorful tiles exemplifying the best of local craftsmanship. Deluxe rooms contain private patios or balconies and refrigerators. Prints and posters by Amado Peña, R. C. Gorman, and other renowned local artists grace the walls. The inn's individually designed suites are appealing, some more opulent than others. Room 140, for example, features two kiva fireplaces, two TV sets, two phones, and a minibar. Here and there you'll find a bleached cattle skull mounted on the wall or over a door.

Although the inn has no full-service dining room, its complimentary breakfast buffet includes homemade muffins, bagels, creamy pastries, cinnamon rolls, fruit and fresh-squeezed fruit juices, teas, and coffee. Guests may eat at tables in the lobby's spacious library or in the Agoyo Room lounge; room service is also an option. A number of fine restaurants are nearby. The inn helps with tickets and reservations for evening entertainment and has a number of attractive package arrangements with spas, tours, and ski resorts. ♠ *59 double rooms with baths, 10 suites. Cable TV and robes in rooms, massage room, exercise center, guest*

laundry, 2 outdoor hot tubs, full bar. $147–$342; Continental-plus breakfast.
AE, D, DC, MC, V.

LA TIENDA ☙

*445 W. San Francisco St., Santa Fe 87501, tel. 505/989–8259 or 800/889–7611,
fax 505/820–6931*

Built as a *tienda*, or general store, in the 1930s, this salmon-color adobe with
turquoise trim is now a B&B; the building has been placed on the state historical register. Black-and-white photos of the Santa Fe community, taken at the
turn of the century, line the walls of the old-store common room, where overnighters
now take afternoon tea.

Three rooms occupy the main house, with another four in the adjacent, Territorial-style brick house. The Trujillo Room has Saltillo-tile floors and Southwest
pine furniture with teal, peach, and apricot glazes. Romero has hardwood floors,
a sunporch great for summer breakfasts, and reproduction Gustave Baumann
works of Old Santa Fe. The Montoya and Mascarell rooms can be combined to
make a two-bedroom suite. As there is no dining room, owners Leighton and
Barbara Watson deliver a Continental breakfast directly to guests' rooms in the
morning, with homemade pastries and warm breads, Blue Lake ranch jams, and
fresh fruit. In winter, guests sit by the fireplace in the living room to take tea.

⌂ *7 double rooms with baths. Cable TV, phone, private entrances, fireplace in 3
rooms, mini-refrigerator in 6 rooms. $90–$160; Continental-plus breakfast, afternoon tea. MC, V. No smoking indoors, -night minimum weekends, 3-night
minimum on some holidays.*

PRESTON HOUSE ☙

106 Faithway St., Santa Fe 87501, tel. and fax 505/982–3465

This 1886 blue-and-white Queen Anne Victorian house, the only one of its kind
in Santa Fe and with all of its angles and turrets intact, is the elegant restoration of noted artist-designer Signe Bergman, who moved from Santa Barbara to
Santa Fe in 1974 to pursue a painting career. It wasn't until she was commissioned
to do a large hotel mural in 1978 that she began to think of opening an inn of
her own. She purchased Preston House that year and set about restoring it, later
adding an adobe guest house and two Queen Anne–style garden cottages to the
property.

Preston House is tucked away in a quiet garden a few blocks from the Plaza. Its
guest house is just across the street and the cottages are in the back. The main
house is on the National Register of Historic Places.

The public rooms are open and sunny. Fruit bowls; original, fantastically futur-
istic stained glass; lace curtains; and fresh-cut flowers add to the appeal. Books
in the well-stocked library shed light on some of Preston House's former owners, among them three colorful characters: land speculator George Preston, who
operated with a band of other charlatans in divvying up the Southwest territo-
ries after the Civil War; a man who exposed the gigantic Peralta-Reavis land-grant
fraud; and a cure-all doctor.

Guest rooms in the main house are furnished in ornate late-19th-century fashion. Some have Edwardian fireplaces, ceiling fans, stained-glass windows, brass
beds, Queen Anne chairs, and fringed lace tablecloths. Room 1, off the dining
room, is for early risers. Rooms in the adobe guest house, in contrast, are done
in the traditional southwestern mode. Room 15, with a king and sofa bed, fireplace, and sitting room, has its own entrance opening up to an ivy-covered court-

yard. The Queen Anne–style garden cottages, with floral prints, queen beds, single-size window seats, and fireplaces, couldn't be cozier.

An elaborate Continental breakfast is served in both the main house and adobe guest house. Full afternoon tea and dessert are offered as well. The owner's paintings, which hang in galleries and private collections all over the country, are displayed throughout the house and may be purchased. ♦ *4 double rooms with baths, 2 doubles share bath in main house, 7 double rooms with baths in adobe guest house, 2 garden cottages. TV and phone in rooms. $75–$160; Continental-plus breakfast, afternoon tea. AE, MC, V. No smoking.*

RANCHO DE SAN JUAN 🌿
Box 4140, Espanola 87533, tel. 800/726–7121

Mountains, mesas, and the Ojo Caliente River valley make up the stunning vista from Rancho de San Juan, set beneath the petroglyph-dotted Black Mesa, 35 mi north of Santa Fe. Out in the middle of nowhere exists a stunning silence under a huge sky and this incredibly elegant Pueblo-style inn.

Conceived, owned, and run by David Heath and John Johnson, this enchanting B&B is their dream come true. David, formerly in real estate and retail—at Saks Fifth Avenue, among other fine stores—and John, a registered architect who worked extensively in the Far East, spent 10 years planning this career move. Searching for the perfect location, they stumbled upon this isolated valley and immediately knew they had found it. They bought a 225-acre tract.

When you enter the main building, an eye-dazzling painting of Navajo *yeis* (gods) greets you. To your left is the refined but relaxing living room, its 14-ft-high ceiling spanned by hand-peeled vigas centered by an immense fireplace. Oriental rugs, tile floors, wonderful southwestern and Native American art and artifacts, carved-wood corbels, and antique doors are indicative of meticulous attention to detail and finely honed design sensibilities.

To your right is the 16-seat dining room, open to the public Wednesday through Saturday nights, and to guests any night of the week with prior notice. Limoges china, silver, and linen create a graceful impression, highlighted by the antique wooden fireplace mantel. Here John serves up full breakfasts to guests and exquisite dinner delicacies, focusing on northern Italian and French cuisine, or local specialties. A more intimate dining room, seating up to 12, is off to one side.

The 12 accommodations cluster around a pretty courtyard. Each room has a different theme, but all are as finely finished and have Frette robes, oversize towels, and beds decked out in all-cotton linens that are starched and ironed. The San Juan room has a Victorian motif with a crocheted lace bedspread and plantation shutters. The Sierra Negra suite is located separately on the property, with a two-person spa, king-size bed, large sitting area, and kiva fireplace. The Black Mesa room contains a Territorial-style fireplace, a faux canopy bed, and a small flower garden. All rooms have ceiling fans.

Just a short walk from the inn is a series of sandstone caves created long ago by rushing waters. One of the caves has been carved into a shrine of vaulted ceilings, Gothic arches, and shell designs by artist Ra Paulette. Be sure to go take a look. ♦ *4 double rooms with baths, 8 suites. Restaurant, bar, ceiling fan in rooms, Jacuzzi in 7 rooms, outdoor hot tub, facials and herbal wraps by appointment, hiking paths. $175–$250; full breakfast. AE, D, MC, V. No smoking.*

TERRITORIAL INN ☞

215 Washington Ave., Santa Fe 87501, tel. 505/989–7737, fax 505/986–9212

The last of the private homes along tree-lined Washington Avenue in the heart of downtown Santa Fe—just off the Plaza—the Territorial Inn was built in the 1890s by Philadelphian George Shoch. A stylish blend of New Mexican stone and adobe architecture, this pitched-roof structure is surrounded by large cottonwoods, a front lawn, and a private rose garden.

In recent years, the building was occupied by a law firm. Legal secretary Lela McFerrin acquired the property in 1989, and she preserved or restored much of the century-old building. Now the inn has the gracious feel of the days when it was home to Levi A. Hughes, a well-known Santa Fe merchant who, with his wife, graciously entertained high society and visiting celebrities of the day.

The reception area and living room are large and comfortable, with overstuffed couches and chairs, fireplaces, a large bowl of candies, and a set of encyclopedias. An eye-catching turn-of-the-century brick stairway leads to the upstairs guest rooms.

The 10 bedrooms range from large and luxurious to cozy and quaint; all are individually furnished with period pieces; canopy, brass, or four-poster beds; handmade quilts; ceiling fans; and down comforters. Many of the ceilings have canopy linings, traditionally found in early adobe homes with viga beams. (They originally helped to keep dirt, twigs, and insects from falling into the soup; here, they cover the fluorescent lighting fixtures used in the legal offices of the former occupants.) The best rooms are No. 9, with its four-poster canopy bed and Victorian fireplace; spacious No. 10, with a brass bed, pine armoire, and ceramic pedestal sink; and No. 3, with a private patio.

Breakfast—fresh pastries, strawberries and cream or other fresh fruit, juice, and coffee—is delivered to the bedrooms or, in summer, served in the rose garden. There's afternoon tea or lemonade and cheese, and brandy turndowns with chocolates at night. ▲ *8 double rooms with baths, 2 doubles share bath. Air-conditioning, cable TV in rooms, fireplace in 2 rooms, gazebo-enclosed hot tub, off-street parking, laundry service available. $80–$160; Continental-plus breakfast. AE, DC, MC, V. No smoking.*

OTHER CHOICES

Adobe Abode. 202 Chapelle St., Santa Fe 87501, tel. 505/983–3133, fax 505/986–0972. 6 double rooms with baths. Cable TV, phone, coffeemaker, custom toiletries, and terry cloth robes in rooms. $110–$150; full breakfast, sherry and cookies always available. D, MC, V. No smoking in rooms.

Alexander's Inn. 529 E. Palace Ave., Santa Fe 87501, tel. 505/986–1431. 3 double rooms with baths, 2 doubles share bath, 2 cottages. TV in cottages and in common room, hot tub, health club membership and mountain bikes available free of charge. $75–$160; Continental-plus breakfast, afternoon snacks. MC, V. No smoking.

Dos Casas Viejas. 610 Agua Fria St., Santa Fe 87501, tel. 505/983–1636, fax 505/983–1749. 5 double rooms with baths, 2 minisuites, 1 suite. Cable TV, ceiling fan, mini-refrigerator, private entrance and patio, cotton robes, and fireplace in rooms, lap pool. $165–$245; Continental-plus breakfast. MC, V. No smoking.

Dunshee's. 986 Acequia Madre, Santa Fe 87501, tel. 505/982–0988. 1 2-bedroom casita, 1 1-bedroom suite. TV, stereo CD/tape player, microwave in suite. $110–$120; full breakfast with suite, Continental-plus in casita. MC, V.

Guadalupe Inn. 604 Agua Fria St., Santa Fe 87501, tel. 505/989–7422, fax 505/989–7422. 11 double rooms with baths, 1 suite. Cable TV, phone in 10 rooms, whirlpool tub in 4 rooms, gas fireplace in some rooms, covered parking. $125–$175; full breakfast. AE, D, MC, V. No smoking.

Hacienda Vargas. 1431 El Camino Real (Box 307), Santa Fe–Algodones 87001, tel. 505/867–9115 or 800/261–0006. 8 double rooms with baths. 5 kiva and 3 gas fireplaces throughout house, Jacuzzi in 4 rooms, private courtyard off 3 rooms, library, barbecue grill. $69–$139; full breakfast. MC, V. No smoking indoors.

Inn of the Animal Tracks. 707 Paseo de Peralta, Santa Fe 87504, tel. 505/988–1546. 5 double rooms with baths. Air-conditioning, cable TV in guest rooms, fireplace in 1 guest room and in common room. $90–$130; full breakfast, afternoon tea. AE, MC, V. No smoking indoors.

Inn on the Paseo. 630 Paseo de Peralta, Santa Fe 87501, tel. 505/984–8200 or 800/457–9045, fax 505/989–3979. 18 double rooms with baths, 1 2-bedroom suite, 1 loft suite. Air-conditioning, cable TV, phone in rooms, fax service, off-street parking. $80–$175; Continental breakfast. AE, DC, MC, V. No smoking, 2-night minimum weekends and some holidays and special events.

La Posada de Chimayo. 279 County Rd. 0101, Box 463, Chimayo 87522, tel. and fax 505/351–4605. 2 double rooms with baths, 2 suites. Fireplace in rooms, walking trails. $80–$125; full breakfast, afternoon wine. MC, V. No smoking indoors.

RESERVATIONS SERVICES

Bed and Breakfast of New Mexico (Box 2805, Santa Fe 87504, tel. 505/982–3332). **New Mexico Bed and Breakfast Association** (Box 2925, Santa Fe 87504, tel. 505/766–5380 or 800/661–6649).

Taos

AMERICAN GALLERY ARTISTS HOUSE ☞
132 Frontier Rd. (Box 584), Taos 87571, tel. 505/758–4446 or 800/532–2041, fax 505/758–0497

The 7-ft-tall, flat, black iron sculpture in front of the American Gallery Artists House isn't Kokopelli, whose flute-bearing image can be seen in every gift shop between San Diego and Santa Fe, but the *God of Bed and Breakfasts,* a special creation of artist Pozzi Franzetti. And it's not for sale—perhaps the only piece among the 500 or so works of art here that doesn't have a price tag. Although almost all B&Bs in northern New Mexico sell works by regional and nationally known artists—"It's a way to get paintings to hang on your walls without paying for them," says one wry innkeeper—this establishment is serious about its artistic endeavors. Owners LeAn and Charles Clamurro, who purchased the B&B in July 1994, have a passion for art, particularly that created by local artists. Charles especially is happy to discuss the array of art found in every room. The B&B frequently hosts art openings for featured artists; at other times, artists are invited to breakfast with the guests. Still, the B&B retains a relaxed atmosphere and, as Charles says, guests should "feel free to put their feet up on anything."

Another passion of the owners is their fine lodging. Charles is a graduate of the Cornell hotel program, and his experience includes a five-year stint running La Fonda Hotel in Santa Fe; LeAn has a similarly impressive background in hotel management and currently heads the Taos Bed & Breakfast Association's marketing committee. The inn is adjacent to a field where the Taos July 4 fireworks and the October Hot Air Balloon Festival take place, providing ringside seats for both.

Its seven rooms are spread throughout the adobe compound: three in the main house, two in an adjacent guest house, and the others in separate garden cottages. The relatively secluded Piñon Gallery Suite, or "honeymoon cottage," is decorated and furnished in southwestern style with an abundance of local art on display. All rooms have Carmen Velarde kiva fireplaces, colorful Mexican tiles in the bathrooms, Native American rugs covering tile or wooden floors, leather drum tables, and carved furniture. There are also three Jacuzzi suites in adobes with vega ceilings and Saltillo-tile floors.

Breakfast is served promptly at 8 AM around a large table in a glass-enclosed greenhouse-style dining area. One of 10 or so standard breakfast entrées—chili egg frittata, blue-corn pancakes with fresh blackberries, pecan-stuffed French toast—is accompanied by fresh fruits, home-baked breads, and fresh-brewed coffee or a variety of teas. △ *7 double rooms with bath, 3 suites. Jacuzzi in 3 rooms, outdoor hot tub. $75–$150; full breakfast, afternoon beverages and hors d'oeuvres. MC, V. No smoking, 2-night minimum weekends, 3-night minimum holidays.*

CASA EUROPA ☞
840 Upper Ranchitos Rd., Los Cardovas Route (HC 68, Box 3F), Taos 87571, tel. 505/758–9798 or 888/758–9798

There's a marvelous, ornate, 200-year-old brass bed in the French Room at the Casa Europa that must take an army of maids weeks to keep polished. But gleaming and polished it is, and you'll feel a little like Louis XIV or Catherine the Great as you drift off to sleep with sounds of crickets and field frogs wafting through the partially opened French windows above the courtyard of this 200-year-old hacienda. Casa Europa is run with care and precision by Marcia and Rudi Zwicker, the owner and chef of the popular Greenbriar Restaurant in Boulder, Colorado, for 16 years.

When they restored the inn in 1983, the couple left all its adobe bricks and wood viga ceiling beams intact. Among Casa Europa's many artistic treasures is the oldest door in Taos, discovered years ago in the basement of the Guadalupe Church and now decorating one of the B&B's hallways. The dining room, with its 3-ft-thick white adobe walls and hand-carved Spanish moldings, is also part of the original building.

An Austrian crystal chandelier hangs over the beautiful curved staircase that leads to the guest rooms. These rooms, whose whitewashed walls are splashed with sunlight, have been furnished with an eclectic collection of European antique and traditional southwestern pieces. Paintings, arranged gallery style, feature Native American and other contemporary artists; there are also three signed etchings by Salvador Dalí. Each of the rooms is based on a theme. The Spa Suite on the first floor has stained-glass windows, a steam shower and bath, and a skylit two-person jetted tub.

The astounding summer pastry selection includes chocolate mousse cake, truffles, fresh fruit tarts, and Black Forest tortes. Steaming coffee is served in individual decanters. △ *5 double rooms with baths, 2 suites. Phone, marble bath in rooms, fireplace in 6 rooms, cable TV in public rooms, Swedish sauna, hot tub. $80–$135; full breakfast, afternoon pastries in summer, hors d'oeuvres in ski season. MC, V. No smoking.*

HACIENDA DEL SOL 🦃

109 Mabel Dodge La. (Box 177), Taos 87571, tel. 505/758–0287, fax 505/751–0319

The Hacienda del Sol, which borders 95,000 acres of Pueblo land and overlooks some of the most spectacular scenery in northern New Mexico, was acquired in the 1920s by art patron Mabel Dodge Luhan. She and her fourth husband, Tony Luhan, a Taos Pueblo Indian, lived here while building their main house, Las Palomas de Taos, now the Mabel Dodge Luhan House (*see below*). They kept the Hacienda del Sol as a private retreat and a guest house.

Although it's only about a mile from the Plaza and just off a main roadway, the inn remains secluded. Innkeepers John and Marcine Landon, who bought the property in 1991, make sure everything runs like clockwork. The house, a model of adobe construction built in 1810, has viga ceilings, arched doorways with *ristras* (string of dried chili peppers) hanging from them, and large, quiet rooms.

Author Frank Waters was living in the Tony Luhan Room when he saw a young Taos Indian being arraigned by three police officials for killing a deer; the incident was the inspiration for his classic novel of Pueblo life, *The Man Who Killed the Deer*. Containing a kiva fireplace, sheepskin rug, and a bench under the window shaded by what's believed to be the oldest cottonwood tree in Taos, the room has undoubtedly changed little. The more contemporary Los Amantes Room adjoins a private room with a double-size black Jacuzzi on a mahogany platform, amid a jungle of potted plants; there's a skylight above, and the attached bathroom is a celebration of decadence with its jet-black sink, tub, shower, and toilet, all with gleaming silver hardware. In the bedroom bookcase are *Edge of Taos Desert*; *Taos, A Memory*; and *Winter in Taos*, all by Mabel Dodge Luhan; and, of course, *The Man Who Killed the Deer*. Most of the rooms feature kiva fireplaces, Spanish antiques, southwestern-style handcrafted furniture, and original artwork, much of it for sale. There's also an adobe casita with three guest rooms, two baths, and fireplaces, which can be rented as a suite.

Breakfast is served in front of the dining-room fireplace or, weather permitting, on the patio. Entrées might include a blintz soufflé or blue-corn pancakes with blueberry sauce, complemented by a robust house-blend coffee. ⌂ *9 double rooms with baths, 1 suite. Cable TV in public room, outdoor hot tub, gift shop. $70–$130; full breakfast, afternoon snacks. MC, V. No smoking.*

INN ON LA LOMA PLAZA 🦃

315 Ranchitos (Box 4159), Taos 87571, tel. 505/758–1717 or 800/530–3040, fax 505/751–0155

This upscale, historic inn is easily one of Taos's nicest. A beautifully restored estate with viga and latilla ceilings and thick adobe walls, some dating back to the 1800s, it's only three blocks from the Plaza in a quiet setting of trees, fountains, and mountains. Owners Peggy and Jerry Davis were married in their inn in 1992. She was the mayor of Vail, while he was mayor of Avon, Colorado.

The light-filled sunroom, decorated with plants and a gurgling fountain, is used for breakfasts and afternoon snacks. Next door, the sitting room is cozy with original artwork, a fireplace, overstuffed chairs and couches, and a book collection. The house was formerly owned by artist Carey Moore, whose studio is now the inn's premier suite. Also outstanding is the Happy Trails Room, complete with a bridle, chaps, and spurs, a horse-collar mirror, and an antique wooden rocking horse. All rooms are furnished with handcrafted pieces, pottery lamps, and Indian rugs. ⌂ *5 double rooms with baths, 2 4-person studios. Cable TV, phone*

in rooms; fireplace, kitchenette, robes, and hot tub in studios; outdoor hot tub.
$95–$195; full breakfast, afternoon refreshments. AE, MC, V. No smoking.

TAOS COUNTRY INN AT RANCHO RIO PUEBLO ☞

Upper Ranchitos and Karavas Rds. (Box 2331), Taos 87571, tel. 505/758–4900
or 800/866–6548, fax 505/758–0331

Yolanda Deveaux opened the Taos Country Inn after her children left for college, and in many ways the inn still feels like a family home. Yolanda resembles a hummingbird as she flits through spacious and well-lit rooms ensuring that guests' needs are met and adding thoughtful touches along the way, such as preparing fires in the rooms of guests returning from a day of skiing. In the morning, the aroma of strong coffee and good things cooking wafts through the rooms and hallways of this sprawling Spanish hacienda, parts of it built nearly two centuries ago. Yolanda is from an old-line Taos family that acquired the hacienda 20 years ago. Her father, Dr. Reynaldo Deveaux, "delivered half the people in Taos," she says.

The inn is on 22 acres of pastureland and cultivated orchards and gardens, 1 mi north of town adjoining the Rio Pueblo. Guests can wander about in the fields, marveling at the distant mountain horizons, still snowcapped in the spring; chat with a field hand burning off sections of grass; and photograph the horses and sheep in a neighbor's farmyard. In summer, local artists often set up their easels in the gardens.

The house reflects the talents of skilled local craftspeople—doors by Leroy Mondragon and Roberto Lavadi, abstract paintings in huge swatches of shocking red by James Mack, and fireplaces by Carmen Velarde, the Leonardo of fireplace makers. The public rooms, whose large windows bring the outdoors in, are filled with handcrafted furnishings, couches upholstered in textured desert tones, and glass-topped saguaro or cholla cactus-rib tables.

The guest rooms are spacious and sunny. All have stuccoed fireplaces, sitting areas, leather sofas, Native American artifacts, southwestern artwork, and king- or queen-size beds with fluffy down comforters and a mountain of pillows.

At breakfast—served at natural wood tables, one long and formidable, others smaller and more intimate—Yolanda unsuccessfully urges a second plate of Belgian waffles, piled high with whipped cream and strawberries, on a guest who could hardly manage the first. Her entrées might include cream cheese and salmon omelets or *huevos rancheros* or other regional specialties, all accompanied by a buffet of fruit dishes, yogurt, pastries, and breads. A small refrigerator contains juices and other soft drinks to which guests may help themselves at any time. △ *9 suites. Phone, fireplace, and cable TV in rooms, VCR units on request, massage available. $110–$150; full breakfast. MC, V. No smoking indoors.*

OTHER CHOICES:

Casa de las Chimeneas. 405 Cordoba Rd., Box 5303, Taos 87571, tel. 505/758–4777, fax 505/758–3976. 5 rooms with baths, 1 suite. Cable TV, phone, bar, mini-refrigerator in rooms, massage, fitness center, hot tub, sauna. $125–$155; full breakfast, afternoon hors d'oeuvres. AE, DC, MC, V. No smoking indoors.
Cottonwood Inn. 2 State Road 230 (HCR 74, Box 24609), El Prado-Taos 87529, tel. 505/776–5826 or 800/324–7120. 7 double rooms with baths. Balcony, steam shower, jetted bath, and fireplace in some rooms. $85–$160; full breakfast. MC, V. No smoking indoors.

Dream Catcher Bed and Breakfast. 416 La Lomita Rd. (Box 2069), Taos 87571, tel. 505/758–0613. 7 double rooms with baths. Mini-refrigerator, ceiling fan, fireplace, cassette player, and robes in rooms; outdoor hot tub. $79–$104; full breakfast, in-room coffee and snacks. AE, D, DC, MC, V. No smoking indoors, minimum-stay some weekends and holidays.

La Posada de Taos. 309 Juanita La. (Box 1118), Taos 87571, tel. 505/758–8164 or 800/645–4803, fax 505/751–3294. 5 double rooms with baths, 1 cottage. Fireplace in 5 rooms, whirlpool in 2 rooms, library, TV in common room. $85–$120; full breakfast. MC, V. No smoking.

Mabel Dodge Luhan House. 240 Morada La. (Box 558), Taos 87571, tel. 505/751–9686 or 800/846–2235, fax 505/737–0365. 14 double rooms with baths, 2 doubles share bath, 1 suite. Conference facilities. $75–$200; full breakfast. AE, MC, V. No.

Salsa del Salto. Hwy. 150 (Box 1468), El Prado 87529, tel. 505/776–2422 or 800/530–3097. 10 double rooms with baths. Pool, hot tub, tennis court. $85–$160; full breakfast, afternoon snacks. MC, V. No smoking.

RESERVATIONS SERVICES

Bed and Breakfast of New Mexico (Box 2805, Santa Fe 87504, tel. 505/982–3332). **New Mexico Bed and Breakfast Association** (Box 2925, Santa Fe 87504, tel. 505/766–5380 or 800/661–6649). **Taos Bed and Breakfast Association** (Box 2772, Taos 87571, tel. 800/876–7857). **Traditional Taos Inns** (137 Kit Carson Rd., Taos 87571, tel. 505/776–8840 or 800/939–2215).

Albuquerque

ADOBE GARDEN ☜

641 Chavez NW, Albuquerque 87107, tel. 505/345–1954

In 1993 owners Lee and Tricia Smith opened this bed-and-breakfast, set on 3 acres in a quiet neighborhood of Albuquerque. The common areas of the main house reflect the owners' worldwide travels, from the Bolivian and Lebanese artifacts in the hallways to the Korean rice chest, Chinese wall screen, and Japanese hibachi that decorate the sitting room.

There are three bedrooms in the main house; two have fireplaces. The upstairs room has a queen-size brass bed as well as a daybed, white wicker furniture, a wood-burning stove, and an impressive evening view of the city's lights. Next to the main house, a three-bedroom bunkhouse sleeps up to eight. This spacious building isn't glamorous (it was a stable in the 1940s), but families or large parties will appreciate the separate sitting room with an old woodstove, full kitchen with washer and dryer, phone, and television.

Each morning, fresh fruits, yogurts, breakfast breads, and cheeses are served in the main house. The dining room opens up to a portale, and in the courtyard you'll see tall cottonwood trees, a grape arbor, and a refreshing swimming pool.
　▲ *3 double rooms with baths, 7-person bunkhouse. Pool. $95–$125; Continental-plus breakfast. No credit cards. No smoking indoors.*

BOTTGËR MANSION 🕊

110 San Felipe NW, Albuquerque 87104, tel. and fax 505/243–3639 or 800/758–3639

This elegant, light blue Victorian-style B&B, built in 1912 by German-born Charles Bottgër, was once called "The Pride of Old Town." Under owners Patsy and Vince Garcia, who took control in 1992, it is returning to its former glory. With Old Town right out the door, the Albuquerque Country Club just a few blocks away, and the downtown area a 15-minute walk, one of the most appealing aspects of this B&B is its location.

Another is the character of the residence. Professional fixer-uppers, the Garcias acquired a real gem in this National Historic Landmark. Many interesting people have passed through its gate, among them Machine Gun Kelly and his cohorts. This and many other stories tumble from cheerful Patsy, who grew up in the area. Vince's family was one of the 12 families that founded Old Town in 1706, so the Garcias really know this intriguing section of Albuquerque.

All the rooms are named after family members. The Sofia Room has an ornate, delicately imprinted pressed-tin ceiling, a brass bed, and an adjoining sunroom with twin beds, tea table, and view of the courtyard. The Mercedes Room has a black marble jetted tub, wood shutters, and pink marble floors. Lola has a mural painted by one of the residence's former owners (George Gallegos), a ceiling frieze, a bathtub and shower flanked by marble columns, and a separate sitting room. Miquela, on the second floor, is decorated in ruby colors and has a four-poster mahogany bed with satin fabrics and lace drapes.

The living room has a striking marble fireplace, crystal chandelier, Tiffany-style lamps, and antique chairs and couches with ornately worked wood trim. Breakfast burritos smothered in green chili, Russian crepes, stuffed French toast, or whatever else is for breakfast is served in your room, outdoors in the courtyard, or in the sunny dining room with white wrought-iron tables and chairs. A refrigerator is well stocked with refreshments, and guests are welcome to it day or night. ▲ *5 double rooms with baths, 1 quad, 1 suite. Ceiling fan and radio in rooms, mobile phone, TV in living room. $89–$139; full breakfast, afternoon snacks. AE, D, DC, MC, V. No smoking.*

CASA DEL GRANJERO 🕊

414 C de Baca La. NW, Albuquerque 87114, tel. 505/897–4144 or 800/701–4144

Casa del Granjero means the "farmer's house," but don't start thinking rustic. It's the rare field hand who hangs his hat in a place that has a glass-enclosed hot-tub building and 52-inch stereo TV, business office with copier and fax, and plush white terry cloth robes. Some mighty sophisticated folks have stayed here, among them actor Mickey Rourke.

There *is* a rural quality to the inn's 3-acre North Valley property. But the B&B's Spanish appellation plays on the name of owners Butch and Victoria Farmer, who bought the Territorial-style adobe in 1987. More than 100 years old, the house was in rather sad shape when they acquired it. Butch, a contractor, converted the courtyard to a great room and added three baths, three sitting rooms, a portale, and an outbuilding.

The Farmers hadn't intended to operate a B&B, but when friends began urging them to open up their lovely home to guests, they decided to give it a go. It was such a success that Butch added a gazebo, bathhouse, hot tub, waterfall, built-in barbecue, and four more guest rooms in a separate ranch-style home across the street: the Bunk House.

Butch's construction skills can also be seen in many of the touches in the seven guest rooms: Santa Fe-style pine beds, carved wood corbels and beams, bright Mexican tiles inset into the kiva fireplaces. Victoria combs yard sales and auctions for treasures, coming up with an antique trastero or perhaps one of the colorful kilims or Navajo rugs scattered throughout the house. Even Butch's mother contributes to the cause, stitching pretty quilts for the rooms. The enormous Corte Grande Suite has a queen-size canopy willow bed with artificial ivy intertwined in the wood, two daybeds tucked in the adjacent room, and Tiffany-style lamps. Of all the accommodations, the Allegre Suite, with its lace-curtained canopy bed, is the most romantic.

Victoria, known as one of the best cooks in the community, prepares a serious breakfast feast—everything from Italian to New Mexican specialties; one morning you might be served a breakfast burrito with avocado, fresh fruit, and flan. You can indulge, with peer support, at the long, dark-wood table in the huge central dining room, or out on the portale with its willow patio furniture. △ *3 double rooms with baths, 4 suites. Desks and kiva fireplaces in all but 1 room, private entrances onto portale in suites, VCR and video library in common room. $79–$179; full breakfast. MC, V. No smoking.*

CASAS DE SUEÑOS ☙

310 Rio Grande SW, Albuquerque 87104, tel. 505/247–4560 or 800/242–8987, fax 505/842–8493

Houses rarely determine their own fate, but that's just one of the many ways in which Casas de Sueños (Houses of Dreams) is exceptional. In 1979, lawyer Robert Hanna commissioned Albuquerque architect Bart Prince to design an office above the entry to his low-slung adobe complex. So many people came by to gape at the result (the office looks like an enormous snail) that Hanna spent half his time inviting them in to look around. In 1990 he decided to turn this pleasant but distracting activity into a business—and thus a B&B was born.

The artistic inclinations of this inn, one block from Old Town, aren't limited to its recent addition. Casas de Sueños was designed as an artists' community in the 1930s by painter J. R. Willis; at the perimeter of his house and studio he built a group of rental cottages, which now house guests. Little inspirational paths and niches, some with bubbling streams, abound in the complex, and a profusion of blossoms climbs up walls and spills out onto a lush lawn. There are more than 50 rosebushes and a dozen varieties of grapevines on the acre of grounds.

In addition, the inn's dining room, where a gourmet hot and cold buffet is set out each morning, doubles as a gallery for local artists. With its French doors, lace tablecloths, viga ceilings, and kiva fireplace, the room is warm and cheerful. On nice days, you can head out to the lovely adjoining patio.

The guest rooms—or casitas—with private entrances to the courtyard, are decorated in different styles, each more attractive than the last. Most have fresh flowers and luxurious bedding; many have kitchens, fireplaces, Oriental rugs, and ornate wood furnishings acquired from the estate of a Spanish nobleman. The La Cascada suite lets out onto its own private waterfall; the Porter features a Willis mural and private patio with outdoor hot tub; Secret Garden has a four-person hot tub and a private massage room. If it's space you need, La Mirada is a two-bedroom suite with an enormous living room, vega ceilings, kiva fireplace, and Oriental artwork. △ *15 1-bedroom casitas with baths, 4 2-bedroom casitas with baths, 2 studios. Cable TV, voice-mail and phone in rooms; fireplace, mini-refrigerator,* *and hot tub in many rooms; library, off-street parking. $85–$240; full breakfast, evening hors d'oeuvres. AE, D, DC, MC, V. No smoking indoors.*

CASITA CHAMISA ❦
850 Chamisal Rd. NW, Albuquerque 87107, tel. 505/897–4644

The first B&B in Albuquerque, Casita Chamisa is also historic in other ways. Originally an adobe farmhouse dating back to 1850, it sits atop the ruins of five successive Pueblo and pre-Pueblo village sites, the oldest dating from around 720 BC! Jack Schaefer, previous owner of the home and author of *Shane*, used to find pottery shards from time to time (Shaefer used the present living room as his writing studio). The mother lode was hit when current owners Kit and Arnold Sargeant began construction of the B&B's 30-ft pool. Kit, an author and archaeologist, enlisted the help of the University of New Mexico to conduct a thorough excavation. More than 150,000 pottery shards and artifacts were eventually recovered. Some remain on view at the home in the basement.

Set in the pastoral North Valley, which was settled in the 1600s by the Spanish colonialists, this B&B has everything you associate with the region. It is shaded by massive river cottonwoods, which keep the place cool on even the hottest days. Chickens, roosters, beehives, herb and vegetable gardens, horses (not for riding), cats, fruit trees, and winding *acequias* (irrigation ditches) retain the former farm's character.

There are only two accommodations, so tranquillity is the order of the day. The six-person ivy-covered guest house has a small sitting room with a corner kiva fireplace, a queen bed, a private patio, and a greenhouse where you can sit and read or write. The kitchenette and a separate bedroom with twin beds covered with French knot bedspreads make this an ideal place for a small family. Animals, a sandbox, swing set, green house, and pool are real attractions for kids. The charming bedroom in the main house comes with a Mexican tin mirror and a hand-carved Mexican headboard; it also has a kiva fireplace and private entrance near the indoor pool and hot tub. Rich hibiscus and other tropical plants surround the pool.

The home contains a great library and a baby grand piano and is filled with wonderful arts and crafts from around the world, including a basket collection, Mexican textiles, and odds and ends gathered by Arnold during his worldwide travels with the U.S. Army.

A country Continental breakfast is served on a plant-filled, enclosed, glass-covered patio; in the dining room before a small fireplace; or out on the portale. It includes fruit, juices, coffee and tea, as well as coffee cakes and muffins, or another slice of history: some of Arnold's fresh sourdough bread, made from a 200-year-old Basque starter. ♙ *1 double room with bath, 1 2-bedroom casita. Fireplace in rooms, library, enclosed pool, hot tub, greenhouse, gardens. $95; Continental breakfast. AE, D, MC, V. No smoking indoors.*

ELAINE'S ❦
72 Snowline Estates (Box 444), Cedar Crest 87008, tel. 505/281–2467 or 800/821–3092

It might be hard to decide which you like better, Elaine O'Neil or her house, but then, the two are inextricably intertwined. One of the nicest building contractors you're ever likely to meet, Elaine supervised the construction of her rough-hewn stone-and-log cabin down to the last interesting detail—for example, the ornate iron braces that anchor the joints of the ceiling beams, which are at once decorative and functional.

A winding dirt road leads up to Elaine's, set in the heart of the Sandia Mountains in Cedar Crest, 15 mi east of Albuquerque on the historic Turquoise Trail to Santa Fe. But the bed-and-breakfast's rustic setting and structure belie its elegant interior. If the Victorians had slalomed, they doubtless would have headed to just such a retreat for après-ski sherries.

Although there are fine antiques all around the house, this is a cheerful, unpretentious place. Light from huge windows in the two-story-high cathedral ceiling streams into an upstairs common area, where an enormous stone fireplace is fronted by comfortable couches. Guests often just flop down on the plush hunter-green carpet and play one of the board games stocked in the rooms, read, or stare into the flames.

One of the second-level rooms has a whirlpool tub, while the third-level room has dramatic views of mountains and plains in three directions. Fresh flowers and soft, downy bedding help make all three accommodations, which mix sturdy wood furnishings and more delicate antiques, very appealing. One disadvantage: Because the romantic top-floor bedroom was built loft style, its occupants can overhear late-night revelers on the lower level—but it is still Elaine's most popular room.

Breakfast here, served in an airy, plant-filled breakfast room, is simple but hearty; large helpings of fresh fruit, pancakes or waffles, and sausage are standard, but guests can get pretty much what they like. Afterward, many find that the crisp mountain air inspires them to take a long walk. Charlie, a fat golden retriever who likes to laze on "his" front-porch bench, will happily accompany guests on a hike through the Cibola National Forest, abutting the inn's 4 acres. Eliot, part wolf, part German shepherd, disdains Charlie's friendly doggie ways but always condescends to come along for the exercise. ⚠ *3 double rooms with baths. Private balcony in top room, hiking trails on property, skiing and horseback riding nearby. $85–$99; full breakfast. AE, D, MC, V. No smoking.*

OTHER CHOICES:

Adobe and Roses. 1011 Ortega Rd. NW, Albuquerque 87114, tel. 505/898–0654. 1 double room with bath, 2 suites. TV, kitchenette, kiva fireplace in rooms, private entrances, laundry facilities available, barbecue grill, horse boarding. $55–$85; full breakfast. No credit cards. No smoking, 2-night minimum.

Britannia and W. E. Mauger Estate. 701 Roma Ave. NW, Albuquerque 87102, tel. 505/242–8755, fax 505/842–8835. 8 double rooms with baths. Cable TV, coffeemaker, hair dryer, iron, clock radio, and refrigerator in rooms, balcony in 1 room, fireplace and TV in sitting room, off-street parking. $79–$179; full breakfast, snacks, evening wine and cheese. AE, D, DC, MC, V. No smoking.

RESERVATIONS SERVICES

Albuquerque Bed & Breakfast Association (Box 10598, Albuquerque 87194, tel. 800/916–3322). **Bed and Breakfast of New Mexico** (Box 2805, Santa Fe 87504, tel. 505/982–3332). **New Mexico Bed and Breakfast Association** (Box 2925, Santa Fe 87504, tel. 505/766–5380 or 800/661–6649). **New Mexico Central Reservations** (121 Tijeras Ave. NE, Albuquerque 87125, tel. 800/466–7829).

Southern New Mexico

ELLIS STORE & CO. COUNTRY INN 🖋

*Hwy. 380, Mile Marker 98 (Box 15), Lincoln 88338, tel. 505/653–4609
or 800/653–6460, fax 505/653–4610*

This lodging's history dates back to 1850, when it was a modest, two-room adobe in territory where the Mescalero Indians still posed a threat to settlers. During the Lincoln County War, the building's thick walls provided refuge for members of the McSween faction, and Billy the Kid was kept here pending his trial. Today, the house looks out on a peaceful lawn where deer graze in the evening.

In 1993 David and Jinny Vigil ended their 10-year search for a B&B with this one. David, a former engineer whose family has been in New Mexico for nearly 300 years, has done a lot of work on the building, adding bathrooms and meticulously restoring the front portale to include its historic sag. Guests sit under it in the quiet of the morning while enjoying Jinny's gourmet cooking. In the evenings, her culinary skills draw people from as far away as Carlsbad. They come to enjoy such delicacies as rack of antelope or venison loin as part of a six-course meal served in the spacious depths of a dining room glowing with light from the fireplace.

Three of the guest rooms in the main house have wood-burning stoves, and each is named for a former resident of the house (though Billy the Kid only needed to stay a few days to get one named after him). Rooms, decorated with antiques, range from Old West style to Victorian. The Dr. James room attracts honeymooners with its king canopied bed, lace curtains, and fresh flowers. Behind the building sits the Mill House, which contains four more rooms sharing baths and a large gathering room with sofas and easy chairs. Three rooms have a wood-burning stove or fireplace.

However, it would be hard to imagine a guest staying indoors when there is so much to see in the surrounding area. David offers horseback hunting trips for ruggedly inclined guests, and there is fishing in the creek that runs through the property. Guests also have the option of hiking or taking a historical tour of Lincoln. ⚐ *3 double rooms with baths in main house, 1 double with bath and 3 doubles sharing 2 baths in Mill House. Fishing, hunting, hiking. $69–$129; full breakfast; 6-course dinner served by reservation. D, DC, MC, V. No smoking indoors.*

THE LODGE 🖋

1 Corona Pl. (Box 497), Cloudcroft 88317, tel. 505/682–2566 or 800/395–6343, fax 505/682–2715

Cloudcroft's Lodge embodies the yin and yang of late-Victorian design in a singularly appealing fashion. Built in 1899 by the Alamogordo and Sacramento Mountain railway to house its workers, this ornate but imposing structure has a lobby where any hunter would be proud to rest a gun: A stuffed bear stands snarling in the corner, and a long-horned eland stares down from over the copper fireplace at deep-maroon leather couches and chairs. But pink-floral carpets lead down the hallway to individually decorated rooms with chenille bedspreads, period antiques, pastel-flocked wallpaper, ceiling fans, and, in many cases, four-poster beds.

Some of the accommodations are rather small, but they're accordingly less expensive. And if you get one with a view, it'll open up the space immeasurably.

If you don't, you can always climb up to the hotel's copper-covered bell tower, which Judy Garland visited with Clark Gable. On a clear day, you can see White Sands National Monument in the distance. Those who really want to hide away with friends can rent the Retreat, a four-bedroom cottage with a kitchenette, located just across the front parking lot from the main building.

The pool on the lush back lawn is inviting in warm weather, but winter is as delightful as summer in this mountain retreat. A gently sloping, pine-shrouded golf course on the grounds becomes a playground for cross-country skiers; downhill runs at the Cloudcroft Ski Area are only 2 mi away; and snowmobiling and horse-drawn-sleigh rides can be arranged through the front desk.

Any time of year, it's a treat to visit Rebecca's, the Lodge's elegant American-southwestern dining room, named after the putative resident ghost. A full American breakfast is included in room rates for those who stay at the Pavilion, a bed-and-breakfast about ½ mi to the south of the main building that's still considered part of the Lodge. This single-level B&B is rustic in style—rooms have beamed ceilings, knotty-pine walls, and, in some cases, enormous stone fireplaces.

△ *10 single rooms with baths, 30 doubles with baths, 7 suites in hotel, 11 doubles with baths in B&B, 1 4-bedroom cottage. Phone and cable TV in rooms, sauna, spa, bar, gift shop, conference facilities. $65–$269; full breakfast included for those in suites or at the Pavilion B&B. AE, D, DC, MC, V.*

LUNDEEN INN OF THE ARTS 🐦

618 S. Alameda Blvd., Las Cruces 88005, tel. 505/526–3326 or 888/526–3326, fax 505/647–1334

You'll think you've died and gone to Santa Fe when you wake up at this arty, upscale bed-and-breakfast, but you'll be paying Las Cruces prices for the experience. Owned and designed by architect Gerald Lundeen and his wife, Linda, whose impressionist art gallery is on premises, the inn is designed to nurture aesthetic impulses in its visitors.

Gerald seamlessly joined two 1895 adobe houses, one Mexican colonial and the other Pueblo style, in order to create the B&B; what was once the patio between them became the 18-ft-high Marienda Room, where most of the inn's activity takes place. Guests attend art classes, conferences, and performances in this unusual space, which is decorated in an eclectic (and ecumenical) fashion: The ornate wood balustrade is from a synagogue in El Paso and the pressed-tin ceiling frieze is from a Methodist church in Lordsburg. Huge Palladian windows let in lots of light at breakfast, when guests enjoy elaborate meals here—at least one hot entrée as well as a tempting variety of baked goods.

Reading niches and comfortable sitting areas abound in both wings of the house. Guest rooms are named for western artists such as Georgia O'Keeffe and Frederic Remington. The one dedicated to Native American painter R. C. Gorman has a kiva fireplace, viga beams, and a curved seating nook with built-in bookcases. The connection between artist and decor is occasionally mysterious—one wonders, for example, how cowboy painter Gordon Snidow might feel about being represented by a room with a bidet in it—but never mind: All the accommodations are beautifully furnished with a whimsical mix of antiques and newer, handcrafted pieces. And, naturally, the walls are decked with art prints and reproductions. A restored adobe in the back of the inn adds three casitas with full baths to the rooms available. In fact, the Lundeen Inn offers long-term residence if you find you just can't separate yourself from Las Cruces. The summer (June–August) is a particularly good time to stay for a while, because rates are much lower ($65 double occupancy).

The inn offers courses in silversmithing, ceramics, coil pottery, and architecture, all of which are taught semiannually. Most of the classes last for five days, and people sign up months ahead for them, but guests can sign up for single classes. There is also a course on breadmaking, and to this end the Lundeens have installed an Indian *horno*, a lumpy adobe oven that can bake up to 18 loaves at a time.

⚠ *20 double rooms with baths, 8 suites. Phone and TV in rooms; fireplace, balcony, kitchenette in suites; off-street parking. $82–$125; full breakfast. AE, D, DC, MC, V. No smoking.*

OTHER CHOICES

Bear Mountain Guest Ranch. Box 1163, Silver City 88062, tel. 505/538–2538. 11 double rooms with baths, 2 3-room suites, 1 2-person cottage, 1 4-person cottage. Electric blankets, kitchenette in 2 cottages, outdoor ramada, nature classes available. $95–$105; breakfast, sack lunch, and small dinner included, weekly and "lodge & learn" rates available. No credit cards. No smoking in indoor common rooms.

Black Range Lodge. Star Rte. 2, Box 119, Kingston 88042, tel. 505/895–5652, fax 505/895–3326. 3 double rooms with baths, 4 suites, 1 4-person guest house. Private balcony in 2 rooms, piano, TV/VCR room, video library, Ping-Pong, Foosball, pool, greenhouse. $59 first night, $49 each additional night (except holidays), $89 guest house; full Continental breakfast. D, MC, V. Smoking outside or on balconies only.

Carter House. 101 N. Cooper St., Silver City 88061, tel. 505/388–5485. 4 double rooms with baths, 1 suite. Clock radio, ceiling fan in rooms, free local calls, library, TV room, off-street parking. $65—75; full breakfast. MC, V. No smoking.

Enchanted Villa. Box 456, Hillsboro 88042, tel. 505/895–5686. 5 double rooms with baths. Fireplace, TV/VCR room, video library, dog run. $70; full breakfast. No credit cards. No smoking in guest rooms.

Mesón de Mesilla. 1803 Avenida de Mesilla, Box 1212, Mesilla 88046, tel. 505/525–9212 or 800/732–6025, fax 505/527–4196. 8 double rooms with baths, 7 suites. In-room phone available, TV in rooms, kiva fireplace in king suites, pool, off-street parking, banquet room. $55–$135; full breakfast. AE, D, DC, MC, V.

RESERVATIONS SERVICES

Bed & Breakfast of New Mexico (Box 2805, Santa Fe 87504, tel. 505/982–3332). **New Mexico Bed and Breakfast Association** (Box 2925, Santa Fe 87504, tel. 505/766–5380 or 800/661–6649).

NEW YORK

The Adirondacks Region: Lake George to the High Peaks

BARK EATER INN 🐾
Alstead Hill Rd. (Box 139), Keene 12942, tel. 518/576–2221, fax 518/576–2071

In the 1800s, this farmhouse with a spectacular view of the High Peaks was a stagecoach stop on a line that ran between Lake Placid and Lake Champlain. Since then, the house has been expanded and altered; today it's a delightful inn with a horse stable. There are seven rooms in the main house and four in the newer Carriage House. In a hand-hewn log cottage a five-minute walk away, there are two additional three-room suites (individual rooms of the suites can be booked as well). Guest rooms have plain furniture, but that's okay: There's so much to do outside the inn, you probably won't spend much time in your room. When you do come indoors, you can get comfortable in front of the large stone fireplaces in the sitting and dining rooms.

Owner Joe-Pete Wilson is an avid rider and has more than 50 horses available for English- and Western-style riding; polo matches are often played in the neighboring field. Joe-Pete, a former Olympic bobsledder, is also an expert skier and will lead you to cross-country ski trails that connect with the extensive Jackrabbit Trail network. Right outside the inn's front door, these trails are also great for hiking.

Large and delicious breakfasts include a choice of several hot entrées. The inn's homemade granola is especially tasty. Dinner is available to both the inn's guests and outside diners if space permits. ⚕ *4 rooms with baths, 7 rooms share 2 baths, cottage with 2 suites. TV in sitting room, cross-country skiing, hiking, horseback riding, mountain biking. $98–136; full breakfast; MAP available. AE, MC, V.*

HOUSE ON THE HILL 🐾
Rte. 28 (Box 248), Warrensburg 12885, tel. 518/623–9390 or 800/221–9390

In 1990 Joe and Lynn Rubino moved from New Jersey and made their vacation home of 20 years a full-time labor of love—and between the setting, the house, and the hosts, it is a B&B experience you won't soon forget. The white, wooden circa-1750 house sits on a hill surrounded by 176 acres of meadows and forest, five minutes outside of Warrensburg. The common rooms are busy with all manner of antiques and knickknacks. Art and graphics fight for space on the crowded walls. Guest rooms are small but distinctive, combining a country decor with artistic touches; all have coffeemakers and café tables.

The Rubinos are active in local civic organizations—they know whom to contact for any area interest you want to pursue, from going on an airplane ride to exploring historical sites. Joe takes two Polaroids of every guest before departure, one as a memento to take home and one for the inn's photo album. △ *3 double rooms with baths, 1 double shares bath with owner. Air-conditioning. $89–$109; full breakfast. D, DC, MC, V. No smoking.*

INTERLAKEN INN ☞
15 Interlaken Ave., Lake Placid 12946, tel. 518/523–3180 or 800/428–4369

You won't have to look hard to find this fully restored 1906 Victorian inn, which stands high on a hill overlooking Mirror Lake. The Interlaken is three stories high, and its clapboard exterior is painted Colonial blue with cream trim. At night, tiny white lights outline the screened-in porch and roofline.

The large entryway is decorated with dried flowers, stuffed teddy bears, and an antique stroller filled with dolls. Also on the spacious first floor is a parlor room, newly renovated dining porch, and dining room, which is popular with locals as well as guests. On weekends, a five-course dinner is included with the price of your room. Dinner may start with lobster crepes and asparagus soup, followed by Caesar salad and sorbet, and that's only the halfway point—a breast of duck *au poivre* may be next and, to end, mocha tiramisu.

Each bedroom is a trove of antiques or reproductions: bird's-eye maple dressers, Lincoln rockers, and handmade quilts. Some rooms have four-poster canopy or brass beds; all except those on the third floor have ceiling fans. The inn is within walking distance of downtown Lake Placid. △ *11 rooms with baths. Restaurant. $140–$210; full breakfast, dinner included (dinner served Thurs.–Mon.), bed-and-breakfast-only rates available. AE, MC, V.*

LAKE PLACID LODGE ☞
Whiteface Inn Rd. (Box 550), Lake Placid 12946, tel. 518/523–2573, fax 518/523–1124

True Adirondack style permeates this property, from the twig and birch-bark furniture to the wood decks and stone fireplaces. Originally a rustic lodge built before the turn of the century, Lake Placid Lodge embodies the spirit of Lake Placid's past, but it cossets an international pool of guests with the comforts of modern-day, luxurious amenities. Kathryn Kincannon, managing director, and her ever-accommodating staff do everything possible to ensure that your stay is a memorable one.

Guest rooms, which are named for the region's high peaks and lakes, are in three buildings: the main lodge, Lakeside Lodge, and Cedar Lodge. There are also 16 studio and one- and two-bedroom lakefront cabins, although four more are soon to be added, with views of the lake and Whiteface Mountain. Although they vary in size, all the guest rooms are exquisite. All have Adirondack-style furnishings, log-beam trim, a large stone fireplace, a king-size bed, and a large soaking tub for two. Feather beds, terry cloth robes, Crabtree & Evelyn toiletries, fresh fruit, and warm cookies left at your bedside complete the experience.

If seclusion is what you're after, don't overlook the cabins, which were built in the 1930s and are only a short walk from the main lodge. They sit right on the shores of Lake Placid and have big picture windows and loads of privacy. All the cabins were renovated in 1997, and the attention paid to detail is remarkable, right down to the teas, coffees, and electric kettle placed in the room for early morning refreshment.

If you decide to pull yourself from your room or cabin (which can be difficult), you can walk down to the lake for a swim or canoe trip. A barge departs from the dock nightly for a sightseeing cruise on Lake Placid. If it's winter, you can head out on one of the many nearby cross-country ski trails. There's also a game room with a billiards table and an upright piano. And, if you decide to stay in your room after all, room service is available.

The restaurant serves new American cuisine, which is as good as—if not better than—many big-deal city restaurants. The innovative kitchen changes the menu seasonally; it may include grilled quail on rosemary branches with shiitake mushroom fritters or scallops with hickory-smoked mashed potatoes, grilled green onion, and oyster-spice vinaigrette. It's here in the dining room you'll also enjoy hearty Adirondack breakfasts, which include a cold buffet and hot entrée. *22 rooms with baths, 16 cabins with baths. Restaurant, bar, phone in rooms, mini-refrigerator in cabins, beach, bicycles, tennis, hiking, boating, golf, and Adirondack art and furniture gallery. $300–$650; full breakfast. AE, D, DC, MC, V.*

OTHER CHOICES

Country Road Lodge. HCR 1, No. 227 Hickory Hill Rd., Warrensburg 12885, tel. 518/623–2207, fax 518/623–4363. 2 double rooms with baths, 2 doubles share bath. Air-conditioning. $62; full breakfast. Lunch and dinner offered on winter weekends for extra cost. No credit cards. No smoking.

Friends Lake Inn. Friends Lake Rd., Chestertown 12817, tel. 518/494–4751, fax 518/494–4616. 17 rooms with baths. Restaurant, whirlpool tub in 7 rooms, wine bar, sauna, beach, cross-country skiing. $195–$285; full breakfast; MAP available. AE, DC, MC, V. Smoking in bar and lounge only.

Hilltop Cottage Bed and Breakfast. 4825 Lake Shore Dr. (Rte. 9N, Box 186), Bolton Landing 12814, tel. 518/644–2492. 2 double rooms with bath, 1-room cabin. TV and kitchenette in cabin. Piano and wood-burning stove in living room. $65–$80; full breakfast. MC, V. No smoking indoors, 2-night minimum on holiday weekends.

Lamplight Inn. 231 Lake Ave., Box 70, Lake Luzerne 12846, tel. 518/696–5294 or 800/262–4668. 17 double rooms with baths. Air-conditioning, TV in 7 rooms, fireplace in 12 rooms, whirlpool tub in 4 rooms, beach across street. $89–$165; full breakfast. AE, MC, V. No smoking in bedrooms, no pipes or cigars, 2-night minimum weekends, 3-night minimum holidays and during special events.

Sanford's Ridge Bed & Breakfast. 749 Ridge Rd., Queensbury 12804, tel. 518/793–4923. 3 double rooms with baths. Air-conditioning, TV in common room, pool. $75–$110; full breakfast. MC, V. No smoking, 2-night minimum holiday weekends.

Saratoga Rose. 4274 Rockwell St. (Box 238), Hadley 12835, tel. 518/696–2861 or 800/942–5025. 6 double rooms with baths. Restaurant, air-conditioning, pub, Jacuzzi in 3 rooms, fireplace in 1 room. $85–$175; full breakfast. D, MC, V. Smoking in pub only, 2-night minimum weekends.

RESERVATIONS SERVICES

Adirondack B&Bs Reservation Service (10 Park Place, Saranac Lake 12983, tel. 518/891–1632 or 800/552–2627). **American Country Collection** (1353 Union St., Schenectady 12308, tel. 518/370–4948 or 800/810–4948).

The Capital
and Saratoga Region

ADELPHI HOTEL 🐾
365 Broadway, Saratoga Springs 12866, tel. 518/587–4688

If Kublai Khan had decreed that his stately pleasure dome be built in late-19th-century Saratoga instead of in Xanadu, he might have come up with the Adelphi Hotel. This lodging is nothing like home, unless home is an Italianate-style palazzo, with the requisite piazza and ornamented by a maze of colorful fretwork. The opulent lobby with slowly rotating fans is done in a style so reminiscent of La Belle Epoque that one could picture the Divine Sarah Bernhardt holding court amid its splendor. It's hard to believe that not too long ago the Adelphi stood empty, evidence of fortune gone sour.

Saratogans shook their heads and laughed at what they took to be the foolhardiness of Gregg Siefker and Sheila Parkert when they bought the place in 1988, but no one's laughing anymore: The hotel is one of Saratoga's showpieces, its lobby bar and café a gathering place for natives and visitors alike (in July it's a favorite hangout of members of the New York City Ballet). Guests at the Adelphi have access to a parlor on the second floor, which has a grand porch overlooking Broadway. This is a great place for afternoon cocktails, especially during racing season, when it's fun to watch the buzz of activity on the street below. For a more quiet respite, the back courtyard has lots of flowering plants, Adirondack chairs, and an interestingly shaped pool that was designed by the owner.

No two rooms are the same: All the furnishings are eclectic—and recherché. If you seek accommodations that hark back to the Adirondack camps enjoyed by some of America's wealthiest families, ask for Room 16, the Adirondack Suite, with Mission-style furniture manufactured in Upstate New York, a twig settee, Papago Indian baskets on the wall, and a wood-paneled bathroom. If you yearn for the south of France but can't afford to go there, the Riviera Suite (Room 12) may lessen the pangs somewhat. Its sitting area, furnished with rattan, is graced with a Mediterranean mural; an amusing Casbah painting hangs on the bedroom wall; and the bathroom is decorated in apricot tones. Other rooms are furnished with Tiffany lampshades, brass-and-iron beds with crocheted bedspreads, wicker settees, and Victoriana. ⚐ *21 double rooms with baths, 18 suites. Café, air-conditioning, cable TV and phone in rooms, room service, pool. $95–$330; Continental breakfast. AE, MC, V. 2-night minimum weekends June–July, 3-night minimum Aug. closed Nov.–Apr.*

THE MANSION 🐾
Rte. 29 (Box 77), Rock City Falls 12863, tel. 518/885–1607

Rock City Falls, a 19th-century mill town 7 mi west of Saratoga Springs, seems an unlikely destination for travelers. The Kayaderosseras Creek still flows, but the mills and factories are quiet. Aside from a few antiques shops, there doesn't seem to be much that would draw visitors to this sleepy village . . . not much, that is, until one spots the Mansion, one of the most elegant and romantic bed-and-breakfasts you'll encounter anywhere. The Venetian villa–style residence was built in 1866 as a summer home for George West, a prominent industrialist and inventor of the folding paper bag. No expense was spared in the construction of the 23-room mansion; it has 12-ft etched-glass doors, marble fireplaces with inlaid mantels, copper and brass lighting fixtures, and Tiffany chandeliers.

It is a credit to proprietor Tom Clark and innkeeper Alan Churchill, who restored the mansion, that this bed-and-breakfast is both sumptuous and friendly. The art books stacked invitingly in the library are for browsing through, perhaps while sipping iced tea or Saratoga water on the side porch on a lazy summer afternoon. Classical music—anything from Bach to Berlioz—wafts through the house. The art, which Tom collects on his travels, invites close inspection. The antique parlor organ is there for playing. All the guest rooms are enticing, but the Four-Poster Room, with its queen-size carved bed, and the Queen Room, with garden views, are particularly handsome.

And there are the flowers. Baskets of fuchsia hang from the porches; roses, peonies, and delphiniums fill the gardens; and bouquets of fragrant Casablanca lilies and foxglove may greet you in the front hall or parlors. Throughout the year floral arrangements brighten every guest room. Alan of the green thumb even grows orchids: In one guest room the mauve of an orchid plant picks up the colors of the bedspread.

Alan nurtures his guests the way he nurtures his flowers—you are made to feel like a treasured friend in this hospitable house. Everything here—from the Victorian furnishings to the homemade fruit breads served with breakfast—is in excellent taste. As Alan says, "The house demands it. It's so special." ⌂ *4 double rooms with baths, 1 suite, 2-bedroom carriage house. Air-conditioning, pool. $95–$185; full breakfast. No credit cards. No smoking indoors, 2-night minimum Aug. and holiday weekends. Closed Thanksgiving and Dec. 25.*

SEDGWICK INN ☙
Rte. 22, Berlin 12022, tel. 518/658–2334, or 800/845–4886, fax 518/658–3998

The Sedgwick Inn, a rambling New England farmhouse with Victorian additions, was built in 1791 as a stagecoach stop. It sits on 12 verdant acres at the foot of the Berkshires, in Berlin; it was once a favorite getaway of New York politicos and their cronies and later became a popular tavern. It is said that Cole Porter once performed here. Today the inn combines all three of its earlier incarnations: It's a way station, where vacationers and second-home owners stop to refresh themselves on their journeys to points north; New York City residents come to get away from it all; and the inn's renowned restaurant (with live piano music on Friday and Saturday nights) draws visitors and locals alike.

Another major draw is innkeeper Edie Evans, a former psychiatric social worker. Sixteen years ago Edie and her late husband, Bob, bought the then-defunct inn and spent a year restoring it. You can sense her presence throughout the establishment, from her original sculptures in the living room to her blueberry muffins at breakfast.

Although the restaurant dominates a large part of the first floor, including a large screened porch with a brick floor and ceiling fans, you can be assured that there's still plenty of private space for the inn's guests, from the blue-and-white living room and more formal parlor to the spacious and homey bedrooms. The decor of each room varies: Room 9 has a four-poster bed and Oriental rug, Room 7 has a king-size brass bed, and Room 11 has an American Renaissance–style bed and book-lined shelves.

Edie is particularly proud of the inn's restaurant, which has an eclectic menu that changes weekly. It's not just the food and drink that soothe the soul here but also the innkeeper's attitude: "We only have one sitting a night for each table," she notes. "We don't want our guests to feel rushed."

Behind the inn there's a six-unit motel annex. The rooms there, decorated with Cushman Colonial furnishings, are less expensive than those in the main house. Edie has transformed an old carriage house behind the inn into a gift shop; there you can find antique jewelry, crafts, and one-of-a-kind items. △ *10 double rooms with baths, 1 suite (6 of these are in motel annex). Restaurant, TV/VCR in common room and in suite, limited room service, gift and gourmet shops. $75–$145; full breakfast. AE, D, DC, MC, V. Smoking in motel only, 2-night minimum holiday and summer weekends.*

OTHER CHOICES

Mansion Hill Inn. 115 Philip St., Albany 12202, tel. 518/465–2038, or 888/299–0455. 8 double rooms with baths. Restaurant, air-conditioning, cable TV in rooms, off-street parking. $105–$155; full breakfast. AE, D, DC, MC, V.

Saratoga Bed and Breakfast. Church St., Saratoga Springs 12866, tel. 518/584–0920. 8 double rooms with baths in farmhouse and 1850 House. Air-conditioning, TV in farmhouse common room, TV in 1850 House rooms, fireplace in 5 bedrooms. $65–$225; full breakfast. AE, D, MC, V. No smoking, 3-night minimum Aug. weekends.

Six Sisters. 149 Union Ave., Saratoga Springs 12866, tel. 518/583–1173, fax 518/587–2470. 5 double rooms with baths. Air-conditioning, whirlpool in 2 rooms, TV, mini-refrigerators. $70–$275; full breakfast. AE, MC, V. No smoking, 2-night minimum weekends Apr.–Nov., 4-night minimum Aug.

State House. 393 State St., Albany 12210, tel. 518/427–6063 or 888/427–6063, fax 518/465–8079. 4 double rooms with baths. Phone and modem line in rooms, library. $150–$210; Continental-plus breakfast. AE, D, MC, V.

The Catskills

ANTHONY DOBBINS STAGECOACH INN 🌿
268 Main St., Maplewood Terrace, Goshen 10924, tel. 914/294–5526

Since 1740, only three families have owned the Anthony Dobbins Stagecoach Inn. The present proprietor, Margo Hickock, takes pleasure in imagining what the original inn—complete with common room and bundling boards—must have been like. In its present incarnation as a bed-and-breakfast, the inn is no doubt a great deal more comfortable than its 18th-century predecessor. It even has an elevator.

The house is charmingly furnished with English antiques, some of which are family heirlooms. "Nothing matches, but everything fits," says Margo, whose family is descended from both Wild Bill Hickok and William Penn.

The William Penn Room, with flowered wallpaper and Williamsburg-blue trim, has an antique four-poster bed, fireplace, sundeck, and private bath; it can be transformed into a double suite with the Roosevelt Room next door. The Hickok Room has an antique brass bed and a fainting couch, and the Guggenheim Room has a small couch and two twin beds with high canopies.

You can breakfast on the terrace by the reflecting pool; in the sunroom by the fountain, with a pink flamingo; or at the Hepplewhite table with Windsor chairs in the formal dining room. A collection of Currier and Ives prints and paintings of horses adorns the inn's spacious entry hall, but for the real thing, visitors need only walk half a block to the racetrack. Goshen is known as the Cradle of the Trotters, and the harness track here is the nation's oldest. Tennis courts are also a short walk away, and hot-air-balloon rides can be arranged at a nearby airport. △ *4 double rooms with baths. Air-conditioning, cable TV in public room. $85– $150; Continental breakfast, afternoon tea. AE, MC, V. Smoking in sunroom only, 2-night minimum on weekends.*

AUDREY'S FARMHOUSE 🐾
2188 Brunswick Rd., Walkill 12589, tel. 914/895–3440, fax 914/895–8114

The Shawangunk mountain range rises dramatically behind this cedar-shingle farmhouse set on 135 acres of meadows in Walkill, a small hamlet about 20 minutes from New Paltz. With the "gunks" in its backyard, the activity quotient here is high. Owners Audrey and Don Leff have been hosting rock climbers, hikers, bikers, and cross-country skiers in their home for more than nine years. But if you're interested in less challenging feats, you can take a dip in the pool or hot tub. In summer, the yard is a great spot for lounging (try to snag the hammock if you can). There's also plenty of antiquing in nearby New Paltz.

The interior of the farmhouse is warm and inviting, with thickly plastered walls and dried flowers and baskets hanging from hand-hewn beams that cross the ceiling. In the smaller sitting room, you can see remnants of the original light blue milk paint that once decorated the floor.

The downstairs guest room has a magnificent view and a massive log bed (which dominates the small room) facing a window—it's just you, the bed, and the mountains. There's a private bath across the hall. The rooms upstairs are larger, especially the lofty Cathedral room, which has an angular beamed ceiling. Each room has a comfy down comforter, which is tied with ribbon and placed at the end of the bed.

A generous gourmet breakfast is served at a long rustic table in the larger sitting room. The menu might include homemade breads, potatoes, a fruit parfait, bacon or sausage, and California eggs with avocado, tomatoes, and string beans. Guests are welcome to use the kitchen throughout the day. △ *3 rooms with baths, 2 rooms share bath. Pool, hot tub, hiking trails. $90–$130; full breakfast. AE, MC, V. No smoking, 2-night minimum weekends, 3-night minimum holidays.*

BEAVERKILL VALLEY INN 🐾
Lew Beach 12753, tel. 914/439–4844

"I have laid aside business, and gone a-fishing," wrote Izaak Walton in *The Compleat Angler*; Walton would probably have loved the Beaverkill, America's most famous fly-fishing stream. Although the Beaverkill Valley Inn, built in 1893 as a boardinghouse at Lew Beach, never played host to Walton, Jimmy Carter, Robert Redford, Sigourney Weaver, Gary Trudeau, Jane Pauley, and assorted Kennedys have all been guests here. Owned and developed by Laurence Rockefeller and managed by able innkeeper Christina Jurgens, the inn caters to those who cherish privacy. Its surrounding forests and nearby fields, preserved as "forever wild," are protected from development.

This is not to say that accommodations are rustic at this wilderness retreat. The large house, which is on the National Register of Historic Places, sits proudly on an expanse of lawn that's met by the Catskill Mountains. The grounds, with an herb garden and pond, are immaculate, and a stretch of the Beaverkill River runs right through the property. Even the croquet court is outlined by small patches of flowers. White-painted rocking chairs line the wide porch, a welcoming fire warms the living room on frosty days, and the dining-room windows offer a panoramic view of the grounds. The card and billiard rooms, with their green-shade lamps, have a clubby, masculine atmosphere. Instead of card playing, however, you may see someone giving a lesson on how to tie a fly for tomorrow's catch. Fishing is definitely the draw here (the inn has a package arrangement with the Wulff Fly Fishing School nearby).

Guest rooms are simply furnished with brass-and-iron beds, comfortable chairs, handmade quilts, and good reading lamps. Many of the rooms have twin beds.

Dinner may include such offerings as poached Norwegian salmon with watercress sauce, and fillet of beef with blue-cheese sauce. All baked goods are made on the premises, and the inn uses homegrown herbs and salad greens.

For those not hooked on angling, there's certainly plenty else to do. A converted barn with a cathedral ceiling houses a heated swimming pool, a help-yourself ice cream parlor, a theater, and a children's playroom. Sports enthusiasts also have access to tennis courts, hiking, and cross-country ski trails and skating in winter. △ *13 double rooms with baths, 8 doubles share 5 baths. Restaurant, bar, conference facilities, game rooms, pool, stocked pond, Beaverkill fishing. $260–$330; breakfast, lunch, afternoon tea, dinner. AE, MC, V. No smoking indoors, 2-night minimum weekends, 3-night minimum holiday weekends.*

CAPTAIN SCHOONMAKER'S BED-AND-BREAKFAST 🐚
913 State Rte. 213 (Box 37), High Falls 12440, tel. 914/687–7946

You'll find it easy to lose yourself in the past in the meticulously restored 1760 Hudson Valley stone house where this inn's living room, dining room (where breakfast is served), library, solarium, and canopied decks are located. Americana is everywhere. The place at High Falls even claims its own Early American ghost, friendly Captain Fred.

And the new hosts, Judy and Bill Klock, are friendly, too. The inn's guest rooms are in the 1820 Carriage House, which is in front of the main stone house. The romantic rooms upstairs were once a hayloft, and the original beams have been left exposed. One downstairs room has a brass bed and a tree growing through the middle of a private deck. The upstairs rooms have private balconies.

Only the delicious breakfasts could tear guests away from their waterfall rooms: It's hard to ignore such culinary delights as lemon poppy-seed cake, poached pears in raspberry sauce, cheese soufflé, and blueberry strudel, served at an antique black-walnut table by the dining-room fireplace. Wines and cheeses are served in the afternoons as well. Nearby is the De Puy Canal House, a highly touted restaurant with a creative menu. △ *4 double rooms share 2 baths. Cable TV in library-den, fireplace in 3 public rooms, swimming and trout fishing in stream. $80–$90; full breakfast, afternoon snacks. No credit cards. Closed Christmas week.*

REDCOAT'S RETURN 🐚
Platte Cove (Dale La.), Elka Park 12427, tel. 518/589–9858

Up a twisting mountain road in the Catskill Game Preserve, you'll encounter a little bit of the spirit of England at the Redcoat's Return. Once the center of a potato-and-dairy farm, the 1860 home at Elka Park was later a summer boardinghouse. Now this lodging is known in the area for its English country hospitality.

Tom (the Redcoat) and Peg Wright have owned the inn since 1973; he was once a chef on the *Queen Mary* and she was an actress. The inn features extensive art and antiques collections that bring together mementos of trips abroad—

and there's a moose head, named Basil, over the fireplace. Tom, who has a quirky sense of humor, says that he plays golf in his spare time and that "Peg is interested in metaphysics." Both are practiced conversationalists. Tom is full of stories about his objets d'art, which include a cricket bat and a framed antique scarf commemorating the first boxing match between an Englishman and an American, in 1860. Zoe, the Wrights' Bernese mountain dog, can also be a charming hostess.

The Wrights have chosen to preserve the atmosphere of the old boardinghouse, so rooms are small but pleasantly cozy. Antique iron beds and oak dressers are part of the original decor. Third-floor bedrooms have eaved ceilings, and one large room offers two double beds. Rooms are supplied with bathrobes for guests.

Hikers should enjoy the numerous trails that lead from the inn onto nearby Overlook, Indian Head, Twin, and Hunter mountains. There are cross-country trails and three alpine ski areas close by. Spring anglers have access to a trout stream on the property, and golfers will find several fine courses a short drive away.

△ 7 double rooms with baths, 5 doubles share 3 baths. Restaurant. $70–$95; full breakfast. AE, D, MC, V. 2-night minimum July–Oct. and on Feb. weekends, 3-night minimum holiday weekends.

OTHER CHOICES

Albergo Allegria. Rte. 296, Windham 12496, tel. 518/734–5560 or 800/625–2374, fax 518/734–5570. 21 double rooms with baths. Air-conditioning in 7 rooms, TV/VCRs in rooms, fireplace in 8 rooms, whirlpool bath and CD/cassette player in 6 rooms, swimming hole, gift shop. $65–$225; full breakfast. MC, V. No smoking, 2-night minimum weekends, 3-night minimum holiday weekends.

Greenville Arms 1889 Inn. R.D. 1 (Box 2), Greenville 12083, tel. 518/966–5219, fax 518/966–8754. 12 double rooms with baths, 1 suite. Air-conditioning, restaurant, pool. $115–$150; full breakfast, afternoon tea. MC, V. No smoking, 2-night minimum holiday weekends.

Mountainview Inn of Shandelee. 913 Shandelee Rd., Livingston Manor 12758, tel. 914/439–5070. 8 double rooms with baths. Restaurant, tap room. $80–$87; full breakfast; MAP rates available. AE, D, DC, MC, V.

The Hudson River Valley

AUBERGINE ☞

Intersection of Rtes. 22 and 23, Hillsdale 12529, tel. 518/325–3412, fax 518/325–7089

This 1783 Dutch redbrick Colonial sits on one of the four corners at the traffic light in Hillsdale, a quiet town just a few miles from the Massachusetts border. David and Stacy Lawson took over the inn in 1994. (It was formerly the well-known L'hostellerie Bressane, established by Jean Morel in 1971.) The new owners have made changes to the decor and to the menu, but one thing has stayed the same: It's still "a restaurant with rooms," says David, the chef-owner. A native Minnesotan who studied under Albert Roux in London, David was the executive chef at Blantyre, in Lenox, Massachusetts.

The French-inspired country cooking is the main draw here. For starters, try the restaurant's signature dish: Maine scallop cakes with shiitakes, scallions, and bean sprouts in a warm ponzu vinaigrette. For your main course, the Atlantic salmon au poivre served over a fondue of leeks with rich red wine sauce is delectable, as is the pan-roasted skate with spinach, Thai chile, and lemon sauce. One of the most popular desserts is the moist chocolate hazelnut cake with pistachio sauce.

This inn is the perfect place for a gourmet getaway: You can leisurely eat a scrumptious meal and then toddle upstairs to your room. The rooms are simply furnished, and the two on the second floor have private baths, although they are down the hall. The two rooms on the third floor have attached baths. David loves to chat with his guests at breakfast, which is served in the bar area. With its shuttered windows and French country chandelier, the bar works very well as a breakfast room. **△** *4 double rooms. Restaurant (closed Mon.–Tues., no lunch), air-conditioning. MC, V. $85–$110; breakfast not included. Smoking in bar only.*

INN AT SHAKER MILL 🕊

Cherry La., off Rte. 22, Canaan 12029, tel. 518/794–9345 or 800/365–9345, fax 518/794–9344

The Inn at Shaker Mill, 10 mi from Tanglewood and from skiing at Jiminy Peak, is an unusual establishment for two reasons: its Shaker decor and its gregarious host, Ingram Paperny.

As befits a converted 1823 Shaker mill, the rooms are simply furnished in a comfortable but utilitarian style. Pegboards hang from the plaster walls, and in the Shaker tradition the common room has a barrel roof—though it also boasts a glass wall that looks out on the mill's picturesque brook and waterfalls.

After 25 years in the business, Mr. Paperny has been called the doyen of New England innkeepers. Staying at the inn is like spending time in the home of a fascinating new friend. As might be expected of a former consultant to the United Nations, Ingram is an internationalist; he speaks four languages and relishes playing host to an eclectic bunch of visitors. During summer he brings European hiking and cultural groups to the United States, acts as their tour leader and host, and encourages them to mix with the American guests at the inn. He is also a woodworker and is responsible for all the carpentry done in the building.

The inn is unique in another way: It charges per person, so singles who want to get away from the city can retreat to a place that doesn't put the emphasis on couples (which isn't to say that a room overlooking the waterfalls wouldn't serve as a romantic retreat for two). Also, several of the rooms are large enough to accommodate families: The stone-wall, wood-beam suites on the third floor can sleep six.

The inn's hospitality extends to meals as well. Breakfasts include juice, fresh fruit, cereals, yogurt, cheese, bagels, muffins, breads, and eggs. Dinners vary with the whim of the chef. On Saturday nights in summer there are outdoor barbecues. **△** *20 double rooms with baths. Restaurant, swimming pond, sauna. $80–$150; full breakfast and dinner. MC, V. No smoking in dining room.*

LE CHAMBORD 🕊

2075 Rte. 52, Hopewell Junction 12533, tel. 914/221–1941 or 800/274–1941, fax 914/221–1941

Although it is housed in an 1863 Georgian-style mansion one minute from the Taconic Parkway, Le Chambord could easily be the focal point of an antebellum southern plantation. In fact, Scarlett O'Hara would feel right at home on its pillared veranda. The mansion's involvement with things southern is more than skin-deep, however: The trap door under the inn's bar leads to a former stop on the Underground Railroad.

Miss O'Hara was not far from the mind of innkeeper Roy Benich when he named the latest additions to Le Chambord: Tara Hall, containing 16 rooms; and Butler Hall, which has corporate and banquet or wedding facilities for 300 people. Both structures are in keeping with the genteel traditions of the opulent dining and banquet rooms and the nine handsome bedrooms in the main building.

Roy, a former art-and-antiques dealer, has designed Le Chambord for aesthetic appeal and treats it as his home. "It's my wife and children," he says. He lives on the premises and laments that he works up to 19 hours a day on the inn and the restaurant. (You'll know that he's a bachelor as soon as you see him in one of the outrageous neckties for which he is renowned.) He chooses all the art and antiques for the inn, from the dining room's Chinese breakfront to the sofas and wing chairs covered in imported floral tapestries. No expense has been spared in selecting furniture and accessories—or food and wine, for that matter.

The owner's focus on visual delights is shared by his chef, Leonard Mott, a Culinary Institute of America graduate. For more than 10 years the two have collaborated on an elegant menu that satisfies both the palate and the eye.

Despite such luxuries, the inn is quite affordable. True, the wine list offers a 1929 Château Lafite Rothschild for $1,500—but there are also good wines in the $15 range. *⌂ 25 double rooms with baths. Restaurant, air-conditioning, cable TV in rooms, facilities (including fax) for corporate meetings, fitness room. $88–125; Continental breakfast. AE, DC, MC, V. No smoking.*

OLD CHATHAM SHEEPHERDING COMPANY INN ☞

99 Shaker Museum Rd., Old Chatham 12136, tel. 518/794–9774, fax 518/794–9779

As you approach, you'll probably hear a faint "baaaa" coming from the pastoral fields of this working sheep farm. In 1993 Tom and Nancy Clark purchased the 500-acre farm, and in October 1995, they opened the property's 1790 Georgian Manor House as a restaurant and inn. In the time it's been open, the restaurant has become a favorite with folks in the surrounding area. Sunday brunch is an especially active time, posing a problem for overnight guests, who have to compete for living-room couches with diners waiting to eat at the restaurant.

The guest rooms—spread throughout the main house and two neighboring buildings—are beautiful, and if you choose one with a private terrace, you may never want to leave it. Shrapshire, one of the smaller rooms in the main house, has a four-poster bed with down pillows and reading lamps on either side. The stunning bathroom has a sloping ceiling and large freestanding tub with wood banister handles. Amenities include terry cloth bathrobes embroidered with a sheep, lots of fluffy towels, and Neutrogena products. A few steps from the main house, past the 19th-century stone smokehouse, is a cottage with two rooms: Hampshire and Cotswold (all the rooms are named after breeds of sheep). Shades of periwinkle and yellow decorate Hampshire, and whimsical Peter Rabbit tiles border the bathroom. The bedroom has a twig bed and quilted chair, and there are two small yellow chairs in the entry hall. Two more rooms share the Carriage House with the company store, where you can buy the farm's delicious cheeses—try the Sheep's Milk Camembert—baked goods, and other sheep paraphernalia. In the works is the Barn, a new building that will house two suites, one of which will convert easily into a large meeting room; renovations are expected to be complete in late 1999.

The landscape—sweeping vistas of verdant sheep meadows dotted with large patches of woods—is remarkably reminiscent of the English countryside. Seemingly endless paths weave through the property for those interested in hiking or biking. There's a swimming hole for summer, and cross-country skiing in winter; golf, tennis, and horseback riding are nearby. Nancy and Tom don't live on the premises, but there's a full-time innkeeper. ▲ *5 rooms with baths in main house, 1 room with bath in Carriage House, 3 rooms with baths in cottage. Air-conditioning, phone in rooms, fireplace in 4 rooms. $195–$500; full breakfast. AE, MC, V. No smoking, 2-night minimum weekends, 3-night minimum holiday weekends.*

OLD DROVER'S INN 🖋

Off Rte. 22, Dover Plains 12522, tel. 914/832–9311

Although there are only four guest rooms at this inn, you're pampered as if it were a luxury hotel—not surprising, considering it has a staff of 22! Although these employees also run the award-winning restaurant, there is always someone to cosset you. Innkeepers Alice Pitcher and Kemper Peacock have undoubtedly created one of the state's most romantic hideaways. Old Drover's is one of only three Relais & Chateaux properties in Upstate New York.

One of the most wonderful things about the inn is its age: It's nearly 250 years old. It was opened by John and Ebenezer Preston in 1750 as the Clear Water Tavern, and it hosted many of the area's cattle drovers on their way to New York City. Since then, the deed has only changed hands three times, and the inn has always been open for business. You can absolutely *feel* the authenticity of the place. You may notice a slight rise and fall as you walk across the entryway's undulating floorboards, and if you're over 6-ft-1, you may have to duck when you're in the dining room.

The idiosyncratic charms of the house are matched by the great mix of furniture styles—a Louis XVI–style chair here, an American Chippendale there. There are plenty of places for lounging, from the library with down-filled couches and many, many books to the sitting room to the property's 12 acres.

Three of the guest rooms have working fireplaces, and all are stocked with terry cloth robes, soaps, bubble bath, shampoo, and conditioner. The largest room is the Meeting Room, with two double beds, a sitting area, and a high barrel-vault ceiling painted to look like parchment paper. It is also the only room with both a tub and shower (others have tubs only). Lovely botanical prints hang on the walls and built-in benches line the room, reflecting its original use as a hall for town meetings.

Everyone faces the center of the Federal dining room, which is lined with red banquettes. Murals, painted in 1941 by Edward Paine, cover three walls. The largest of the inn's nine working fireplaces is here. It's a dark, regal room where classical music quietly plays. Weekday Continental breakfasts include granolas, fruit, and homemade breads—the house specialty is an Amish Friendship bread. Weekend breakfasts are much more elaborate, with items such as Belgian malted waffles and southern-style grits.

Downstairs, where lunch and dinner are served, bartender Charlie has been serving his infamous double cocktails for 33 years. Copper pots hang from the dark-beamed ceiling, and empty bottles of impressive wines fill the shelves that line the room. The menu includes the inn's signature dishes—a silky-smooth cheddar cheese soup and browned turkey hash—along with other, more sophisticated entrées, perhaps seared mahimahi with ginger tomato sauce or roasted veal loin with shallot and truffle sauce. Don't pass up the lamb chops if they're offered.

The staff at the inn are happy to pick up passengers arriving by train; just let them know your travel plans when booking your accommodations. ♨ *4 double rooms with baths. Restaurant (no lunch Mon.–Thurs.), air-conditioning, fireplace in 3 rooms and 6 public areas, hiking. $150–$395; Continental-plus breakfast. MC, V. 2-night minimum weekends.*

TROUTBECK ☙

Leedsville Rd., Amenia 12501, tel. 914/373–9681, fax 914/373–7080

This Tudor-style manor house set amid 442 gracious acres outside the hamlet of Amenia figured prominently in American literary and political history. It was once home to Myron B. Benton, whose circle of friends included Emerson, Thoreau, and John Burroughs. The estate served as a gathering place for the likes of Sinclair Lewis, Teddy Roosevelt, and Lewis Mumford in the early 20th century, and black leaders formed the NAACP under its roof.

Today Troutbeck also serves the movers and shakers of the corporate world as a conference center during the week. On weekends, however, it is transformed into a country inn, the vision of genial innkeeper Jim Flaherty and his partner, Bob Skibsted. The atmosphere makes this a popular place for weddings, so beware—you may find yourself caught in the middle of someone else's romantic celebration.

The Troutbeck package includes three gourmet meals a day, an open bar, and access to all sorts of recreational activities, ranging from tennis, swimming (indoor and outdoor), fishing, and cross-country skiing to strolling through walled gardens and watching video movies or major sports events on cable TV.

Most of the guest rooms are charming, although the rooms in the main house seem more so. For the premium prices charged by Troutbeck, guests might prefer a room with a fireplace or sunporch in the manor house (with its leaded-glass windows, 12,000-book oak-panel library, and English country appointments) or the Garden House (overlooking the walled gardens) to the Americana offered in the neighboring Century Farmhouse rooms. Of course, guests in any of the buildings have access to all the inn's amenities.

If you can tear yourself away from the estate, the surrounding area is prime antiquing territory, and guests can take elegant prepared picnics with them on excursions. The inn will also arrange transportation to concerts at Tanglewood, dance performances at Jacob's Pillow, and Shakespeare at the Mount. ♨ *37 double rooms with private baths, 5 doubles share 3 baths. Restaurant, air-conditioning, fireplace in 9 rooms, banquet facilities, indoor and outdoor pools, tennis courts, fitness center. $375–$600; 3 meals, wines, and spirits. AE, DC, MC, V. No smoking in dining rooms.*

OTHER CHOICES

Hudson House. 2 Main St., Cold Spring 10516, tel. 914/265–9355, fax 914/265–4532. 12 double rooms with baths. Restaurant, air-conditioning. $150–$185; full breakfast. AE, MC, V. No smoking.

Plumbush Inn. Rte. 9D, Cold Spring 10516, tel. 914/265–3904. 2 double rooms with baths, 1 suite. Restaurant (closed Mon. and Tues.), air-conditioning, cable TV in sitting room. $95–$125; Continental breakfast. AE, MC, V. Smoking in one section of the restaurant area only.

Simmons Way Village Inn. 33 Main St., Millerton 12546, tel. 518/789–6235, fax 518/789–6235. 9 double rooms with baths. Restaurant, air-conditioning, cable TV in common room, banquet facilities, complimentary sherry. $145–$175; Continental breakfast, afternoon beverages. AE, DC, MC, V. Smoking in designated areas only, 2-night minimum weekends May 1–Nov. 1, 3-night minimum holiday weekends.

Veranda House. 82 Montgomery St., Rhinebeck 12572, tel. 914/876–4133. 4 rooms with baths. Air-conditioning, phones in rooms. $75–$150; full breakfast. No credit cards. No smoking in house.

RESERVATIONS SERVICE
American Country Collection (1353 Union St., Schenectady 12308, tel. 518/370–4948).

Eastern Long Island

J. HARPER POOR COTTAGE 🐦
181 Main St., East Hampton 11937, tel. 516/324–4081

Gary and Rita Reiswig have created the *definitive* East Hampton retreat, where you will be coddled as you should be in the Hamptons. More mansion than cottage, this inn dates back to the 1600s and has been expanded and renovated several times. It sits right on Main Street across from the village green.

In 1910 then-owner James Harper Poor hired architect Joseph Greenleaf Thorp to make renovations, mostly in the style of the English arts-and-crafts school. When the Reiswigs bought the property in July 1996, they hired architect Eric Woodward and interior designer Gary Paul to revive the very tired house. Today, exquisite William Morris papers cover the walls, and plush, overstuffed furniture graces the sitting rooms, which are filled with fresh flowers and a good collection of books. The spacious, airy public spaces are ever-so-genteel. You truly feel as if you're in an English country manor.

As you head upstairs, notice the portrait of Mrs. Poor hanging in the stairwell—it's on loan from her grandchildren. (The late Mrs. Poor was married in the house in 1915.) The guest rooms are stunning, with high-quality fabrics, serene colors, and tasteful furnishings. Each is stocked with terry cloth robes and Caswell-Massey products. Feather duvets and ceiling fans add to the ambience.

Formal English gardens grace the back of the property, and a 200-year-old white wisteria vine climbs the side of the house. If you decide to leave the shelter of the gardens, beach towels and beach parking passes are available. Large, extravagant breakfasts include an entrée, which might be pancakes, waffles, or eggs, plus a buffet of fresh fruit, juices, cakes, and muffins. ♣ *5 double rooms with baths. Air-conditioning, 2 phones per room with voice-mail, TV/VCR in rooms, in-room safes. $275–395; full breakfast. 3-night minimum summer weekends.*

RAM'S HEAD INN 🐦
108 Ram Island Dr., Shelter Island 11965, tel. 516/749–0811, fax 516/749–0059

Ospreys nest atop the telephone poles by this inn on Shelter Island. A yellow-and-white awning shelters the patio, and a beached rowboat sits in a children's play area on the wide front lawn. The voice of Billie Holiday is often heard in the dining room. The 1929 center-hall Colonial-style building is all weathered shakes, white trim, and green shutters. Guests can walk to a gazebo by the tennis courts, and a grassy path leads down to 800 ft of beachfront on Coecles Harbor. Summer guests are cooled by bay breezes.

Owners James and Linda Ecklund and innkeeper Jeanne LaMar collaborate in running the place, and each fills in wherever necessary to make sure guests are taken care of. In 1980 the Ecklunds bought the inn in a rather "decayed state," as they put it, and they have spent the intervening years restoring it.

The common rooms are often flooded with natural light. The lounge, decorated in a nautical theme, features ships' lanterns and a model sloop on the mantel. Green wicker couches have flowered cushions, and the library is the perfect spot for a rainy-day read. Here framed sheet music lines the walls, and a piano occupies an honored place. Every Sunday in summer from 7 to 11 PM, a local jazz group livens up the atmosphere. The dining-room menu stresses new American cuisine and includes fresh seafood creatively prepared and presented. You might choose from such specialties as shellfish bisque garnished with caviar and lobster, and braised red snapper accompanied by oyster mushrooms and artichokes.

Guest rooms are simple, bright, and airy; some have porches. Those with a water view are often requested, but in summer the harbor can be glimpsed only through the leaves of majestic oak trees. △ *5 double rooms with baths, 4 doubles share 2 baths, 4 suites. Restaurant, free use of tennis court and boats. $110–$230; Continental breakfast. AE, MC, V. No smoking, 3-night minimum holiday weekends, 2-night minimum other weekends.*

VILLAGE LATCH INN ✍

101 Hill St. (Box 3000), Southampton 11968, tel. 516/283–2160 or 800/545–2824

The theatrical air to the 5-acre compound that makes up the Village Latch Inn is no accident. Owner Marta White spent her life in the theater, and she revels in setting a stage. Her husband and fellow innkeeper, Martin, is a photographer who used to work in commercial films. The main house is "old Southampton, turn-of-the-century, Gatsby-style," says Marta. The circa-1900 building, once the annex to Southampton's most opulent hotel, may have been a Sanford White design. Near the main house are what Marta refers to as the "outbuildings," which were part of the old Merrill Lynch estate. These include the Terry Cottage, which features a comfortable living room with flowered wallpaper and Victorian dining room; the Potting Shed, where the first American locomotive was built and which is now used for corporate meetings; six modern duplexes with private decks; and two other large houses connected by a Victorian greenhouse. One of these houses has a distinguished collection of Mexican folk art.

The living room in the main house could be the set of a movie—perhaps *Around the World in 80 Days* with *Auntie Mame*. Plush leopard-print cushions and gold- and silver-threaded pillows are tossed artfully on the couches. Balinese marionettes hang from the walls. It's all eccentric, eclectic, and artsy—and it works.

No guest room resembles another, and Marta is always changing things. "If I'm not creating space, then it's boring," she comments. The rooms are decorated with a collection of antiques from different periods; many have fireplaces and private decks or balconies. Despite its lavishness, the inn is cozy—the sort of place where guests can help themselves to coffee or a cold drink any time of the day, even if the sign says KITCHEN CLOSED.

A number of the buildings can be rented to groups, and the facilities have been used for everything from fashion shoots to family reunions. The greenhouse is the perfect setting for an intimate wedding. The inn is a five-minute walk from town and a mile from the beach. ⚘ *50 double rooms with baths, 11 suites, 6 duplexes. Lunch catering on request, air-conditioning, cable TV, phones, pool, tennis courts, health club privileges. $125–$350; Continental breakfast. AE, D, DC, MC, V. 3-night minimum July–Aug. weekends, 2-night minimum other weekends.*

OTHER CHOICES

Huntting Inn. 94 Main St., East Hampton 11937, tel. 516/324–0410, fax 516/324–8751. 17 double rooms with baths, 2 single rooms with baths, 1 suite. Restaurant, air-conditioning, TV and phone in rooms. $225–$495; Continental breakfast. AE, DC, MC, V. No smoking, 2-night minimum weekends May–June and Sept.–Oct., 3-night minimum weekends July–Aug., 5-night minimum July 4 and Labor Day weekends.

Hill Guest House. 535 Hill St., Southampton 11968, tel. 516/283–9889 or 718/461–0014 (Nov.–Apr.). 1 double room with bath, 2 doubles share bath, 3 doubles share 2 hall baths. $70–$80; breakfast not included. No credit cards. 2-night minimum on weekends June and Sept., 3-night minimum weekends July–Aug. Closed Nov.–Apr.

Maidstone Arms. 207 Main St., East Hampton 11937, tel. 516/324–5006, fax 516/324–5037. 10 double rooms with baths, 6 suites, 3 cottages. Restaurant, air-conditioning, cable TV in rooms; car service from jitney, train, and East Hampton airport. $205–$355; Continental breakfast. AE, D, MC, V. Smoking in lounge only, 2-night minimum weekends, 3-night minimum weekends July–Aug.

Mill House Inn. 33 N. Main St., East Hampton 11937, tel. 516/324–9766. 8 double rooms with baths. Cable TV and phone in rooms, gas fireplace in 6 rooms, whirlpool tub in 4 rooms, beach passes. $200–$300; full breakfast, afternoon beverages. AE, MC, V. No smoking, 3-night minimum holiday weekends.

NORTH CAROLINA

The Carolina Coast

FIRST COLONY INN 🐚
6720 S. Virginia Dare Trail, Milepost 16, Nags Head 27959, tel. 252/441–2343 or 800/368–9390, fax 252/441–9234

The last of Nags Head's old shingle-style inns was scheduled for demolition when two generations of a Lexington family pooled their resources, mortgaged their homes, and bought the First Colony Inn in 1988. Richard and Camille Lawrence had two things going for them: a piece of land where the inn could be relocated and children with expertise, including a preservation architect, an engineer, an accountant, and a designer. The whole town lined the streets the night the inn (sawed into three pieces) was moved down the road, away from the ocean's grasping fingers.

Today the inn is listed on the National Register of Historic Places and is far more luxurious than it was in 1932, when it was first constructed. In all, nine of the Lawrences own and operate the inn, and they all helped to restore it with their own hands. The exterior has been returned to its original beauty, complete with two-story, continuous wraparound porches and a brown-shingled roof. The whole interior was reconfigured; now the 26 rooms have private baths and lots of extras, such as heated towel bars, English toiletries, irons and ironing boards, refrigerators, and microwaves. Luxury rooms also have wet bars or kitchenettes, as well as whirlpool baths and private screened porches. White walls give the inn a fresh feeling, and each room is furnished differently, with cherry beds and dressers, white wicker with floral-print cushions, or canopy beds with crocheted lace.

Breakfast, which includes a hot entrée, croissants, pastries, and fruit, is served in the first-floor dining room, which contains antique buffets, enormous old mirrors, and vintage photos of Nags Head. In the afternoon tea is served. The second-floor library is a cozy enclave where guests can read or play games. One of the most delightful bits of reading is a framed letter about a classic Nags Head vacation on letterhead stationery, circa 1934, when it was called LeRoy's Seaside Inn. There's a 55-ft pool with a roomy wooden deck in back, and the ocean is a short walk across the street.

The inn is also convenient to *The Lost Colony* outdoor drama in Manteo, hang gliding at Jockey's Ridge, first-flight history at the Wright Brothers National Memorial, and the many attractions of the Cape Hatteras National Seashore. ⚓ *26 double rooms with baths. Air-conditioning, cable TV and phone in rooms. $145–$275; full breakfast. AE, D, MC, V. No smoking, 2-night minimum weekends, 3-night minimum holidays.*

ISLAND INN 🐚

Lighthouse Rd. (Box 9), Ocracoke 27960, tel. 252/928–4351, fax 252/928–4352

This historic inn, the oldest one on the Outer Banks, has stood for nearly a century. It got its name because it sat on Ocracoke's highest point, with a creek on either side. Built in 1901 of old ship timbers, it served as an Odd Fellows Lodge, public school, and officers' club before becoming an inn in 1945. It may not be as polished as a modern hotel, but the inn has the character and atmosphere you won't find in a contemporary lodging. It even has a ghost, Mrs. Godfrey, the wife of a former innkeeper; she opens the kitchen door from time to time and leaves things out of place. People have such a good time here, they don't miss luxury; they do find good food and very caring, hospitable hosts. Bob and Cee Touhey, formerly of Winston-Salem, gave up careers in marketing and teaching, respectively, and are renovating the inn in stages. With basic improvements behind them, they've now added cosmetic touches such as blue-and-white striped awnings, interior doors, and carpeting.

The best rooms, with panoramic water views, are in the Crow's Nest, up some steep stairs. These rooms have light-gray natural-wood walls and ceilings, new bathrooms, and contemporary furnishings with a beach motif. The ocean breeze pours in from sliding glass doors on two sides. In the main inn, rooms have antique furnishings and vintage photographs and feel like Grandma's house. Families prefer the modern annex, where extralarge rooms open onto the heated pool. In June of 1998 villas were added. There are three 2-bedroom suites and one 1-bedroom suite, each with a kitchen, whirlpool bath, and private balcony.

The dining room, the oldest Outer Banks restaurant, has also gotten a face-lift, with fresh white walls, new windows, and new wood ceilings with track lighting. The prints on the walls—including one of the inn itself—were done by an Alabama artist who stays at the inn every summer. A no-smoking area is on the enclosed sun porch. Many cooks are children of people who cooked here decades ago; they use the same recipes for such trademark dishes as oyster omelets, crab cakes, clam chowder, and scrambled eggs with herring roe. A new chef has added dinner delights such as grilled shrimp with Aunt Annie's green chili cheese grits.

The village of Ocracoke is on the island of the same name, accessible only by ferry. The laid-back, casual atmosphere seems a little like that of Cape Cod. The pirate Blackbeard was killed close to where the Ocracoke Lighthouse is. At the British Cemetery, the Union Jack flies over the graves of British sailors killed offshore, and everyone loves Ocracoke's wild ponies. **△** *35 double rooms with baths, 4 suites. Air-conditioning, cable TV in most rooms, phone in annex rooms. $45–$150; full breakfast with room only in winter. D, MC, V. No smoking, 3-night minimum holidays.*

LANGDON HOUSE 🐚

135 Craven St., Beaufort 28516, tel. 252/728–5499, fax 252/728–1717

Langdon House, a block from the Beaufort waterfront and across the street from the Old Burying Ground, is just about as old as that historic cemetery. It's built of hand-hewn heart-pine timbers and put together with hand-forged nails, and owner Jimm Prest is fairly sure the ballast-stone foundation was laid in 1733. (The cemetery was deeded to the town in 1731.)

A Colonial–Federal-style house with a Bahamian roof line, Langdon House is painted white with dark green shutters and has upstairs and downstairs porches across the front. The floor plan is very simple—a central hall and stairway running down the middle, a parlor on the left side, a bedroom to the right (the largest and sunniest), and three to the rear. All the rooms have queen-size beds (with no headboards but with lots of comfy pillows) and are named for different guests. The dining room, upstairs over the parlor, resembles an 18th-century tavern; an Edwardian oak table takes up most of the room. The kitchen is also upstairs—an arrangement already in place when Prest renovated the house in 1985. Furnishings are an assortment of antiques, some on loan from local residents. The parlor contains an Estes pump organ, an 1840s Empire secretary, and other treasures—all furniture that is friendly and familiar, not museum pieces you wouldn't dare touch.

What really sets Langdon House apart is Prest himself. Having spent 365 days a year on the road for Coca-Cola before he became an innkeeper, he knows what it is to be a traveler, and he's accommodating to a remarkable degree. He'll arrange excursions, make sure guests are fishing with the right lure, and furnish beach baskets with towels and suntan lotion. Complimentary beverages are always available, as is just about anything a guest may have neglected to bring, from hip waders and clam rakes to Pepto-Bismol and Band-Aids. To top it off, he's just plain friendly, the kind of innkeeper who likes to share a glass of wine and good conversation with guests on the rocking-chair-dotted verandas.

Prest encourages his guests to sleep late and will cook a full breakfast for them anytime after 7:30 AM. He describes the food, such as too-pretty-to-eat orange-pecan waffles and omelets, as wholesome but not without sin. And he describes his business—aptly—not just as the renting of rooms but rather as the fine art of innkeeping. ♨ *4 double rooms with baths. Air-conditioning, bicycles, fishing rods, ice chests. $88–$120; full breakfast. No credit cards. No smoking, 2-night minimum summer weekends and holidays.*

PECAN TREE INN ♨
116 Queen St., Beaufort 28516, tel. 252/728–6733

On Joe and Susan Johnson's first visit to Beaufort, they sat in a waterfront restaurant and watched wild ponies graze on nearby Carrot Island. When dolphins swam up the river to complete the scene, the Johnsons took it as a sign they were where they belonged. Joe, who ran a chain of hardware stores, and Susan, who sold auto insurance, left New Jersey and bought a Victorian home less than a block from the waterfront. The home was built in 1856, and Victorian embellishments, including porches, turrets, and gingerbread trim, were added in the 1890s. Now restored to its original splendor, it's a charmer that lures 20–30 people a week just for a tour.

Rooms are bright and airy, with light floral wallpapers and bed covers. The furnishings are a mix of antiques and reproductions from different periods. The Blue Room, for example, has a queen-size pencil-post canopy bed in warm wood tones and antique tables and dresser. The Pine Room has a pine pencil-post canopy bed and an antique trunk. The Green Room was renamed the Wow Room for the response it inevitably provokes. Here, deep-green carpeting and fabrics provide a dramatic contrast to the white walls. The Bridal Suite is pure romance. The four-poster canopy bed is accented with a brocade coverlet, and the rose-and-white tile bath includes a two-person whirlpool.

A small library is outfitted with books, games, and a guest refrigerator stocked with complimentary beverages. Other favorite places for relaxing are the porches, where breakfast is often served in fair weather. The fare includes homemade muffins, cereals, fresh fruit, and, of course, pecan sticky buns.

Named for two ancient pecan trees that grow on the property, the inn is beautifully landscaped. There's a small yard in front and a huge garden in back, planted with more than 1,000 flowers, shrubs, and trees. (The local chefs also stroll back here to pluck some of Susan's herbs.) The city's best restaurants are all within walking distance, as are the historic district and the waterfront. ⚓ *7 double rooms with baths. Air-conditioning. $70–$135; Continental breakfast. MC, V. No smoking.*

ROANOKE ISLAND INN ☞

305 Fernando St., Manteo 27954, tel. 252/473–5511 or 877/473–5511, fax 252/473–1019

When he was five, John Wilson vowed that one day he'd own the waterfront house originally built for his great-great-grandmother in the 1860s. Today, he shares the home with summer visitors. Set on a large lot overlooking Shallowbag Bay, the house is surrounded by gardens.

It started as a simple island house, but each generation added on. The guest rooms, in a separate wing, are individually decorated, and some have massive beds created by seamlessly crafting additions onto smaller antiques. Each room has a private outside entrance, and all rooms access a large porch filled with rockers that overlooks the bay. The parlor is lined with books and decorated with explorer John White's original drawings of Roanoke. A guest kitchen provides soft drink and juice dispensers, coffeemaker, microwave, and separate refrigerators for milk and ice.

Though the busy Manteo waterfront shops and restaurants are only a block away, the inn is out of the hustle and bustle just enough to feel like a quiet retreat. ⚓ *6 double rooms with baths, 2 suites, 1 two-bedroom bungalow. Air-conditioning, cable TV and phone in rooms. $88–$128; Continental breakfast. AE, MC, V. Pets allowed (dogs must be leashed), 2-night minimum weekends.*

WHITE DOE INN ☞

319 Sir Walter Raleigh St., Manteo 27954, tel. 252/473–9851 or 800/473–6091, fax 252/473–4708

The white Victorian on the corner of Sir Walter Raleigh Street has been a Manteo icon for generations. The Meekins family of Rodanthe moved to the island and built the house in 1896 as a 1½-story frame structure. Years later, Rosa Meekins saw a picture in the Sears catalog and had her husband build an addition modeled on the Victorian home in 1910.

Bebe Woody grew up wondering what lay behind the lace curtains of the majestic Queen Anne. In 1993 she and husband Bob Woody bought the house, now on the National Register of Historic Places, and spent two years renovating the home into an inn. They were uniquely suited to the job: Bebe retired from 31 years with the National Park Service, specializing in historic preservation and restoration, and Bob still works in visitor services.

The study, tastefully furnished with antiques, has a fireplace with built-in bookcases on either side. A baby grand dominates the parlor, where chamber-music concerts are sometimes held. Breakfasts are three-course creations that include fruit, hot entrées, freshly baked breads, and gourmet coffees and teas. It's all served in the downstairs dining room or, weather permitting, on the veranda, where you can also enjoy afternoon refreshments.

The Garret Bedchamber, on the third floor, is one of the most unusual rooms. A two-way fireplace serves the bedroom and the bath, which has a whirlpool. The

Virginia Dare room is the most romantic, with a four-poster, queen-size rice bed and a bath with whirlpool. Light pours in through the windows of the Turret room, in the turret on the corner of the house. The Old Towne Bedchamber has two wicker double beds and a stained-glass window. The Scuppernong has 9-ft sloped ceilings and an antique cast-iron claw-foot tub.

The inn takes its name from an old Indian legend that Virginia Dare, the child who disappeared with the Lost Colony, was turned into a white doe that still roams the island today. △ *7 double rooms with baths. Air-conditioning, fireplace, ceiling fan, and phone in rooms, whirlpool tub in 2 rooms. $120–$190; full breakfast. AE, MC, V. No smoking, 2-night minimum on weekends Easter–Thanksgiving.*

WORTH HOUSE ☙
412 S. 3rd St., Wilmington 28401, tel. 910/762–8562 or 800/340–8559, fax 910/763–2173

This picture-perfect Queen Anne home stands out, even in a historic district full of beautiful homes. Its twin turrets, trimmed with shingles, their windows lined with lace curtains, promise an intriguing interior—and deliver. Built by merchant Charles Worth in 1893, it was a private home for many years before being converted to a boarding house during World War II, when shipbuilding boomed in the port city. Abandoned in the late 1970s and restored in the mid-'80s, it was purchased by Francie and John Miller in 1994.

Francie likes to say that while you might find more elegant accommodations, you won't find any more comfortable. The Worth House is, in fact, beautiful without being fussy or intimidating. It's furnished with antiques from the period, with the exception of a big-screen TV in one of the downstairs parlors. Mirrors, tables, and other pieces come from Baton Rouge, New Orleans, Atlanta, and Wilmington, North Carolina. There's a sitting room on each floor, as well as a garden with a decorative pond in back, and a porch on the second floor.

Guest rooms have antique wood beds, including four-posters. Favorite rooms include the Azalea and Rose suites, both of which have private glass-enclosed sun porches. The Azalea suite is inside the big turret and has two large bay windows. The third-floor bathrooms are not for tall people: conforming to the roof and turret lines, they have sloping ceilings and unusual shapes. But for some guests, that just adds to the charm.

Breakfast is served in one of three places: the formal dining room, the second-floor porch, or rooms. Francie will accommodate most any schedule. Special amenities include a modem line and a laundry room. △ *7 double rooms with baths. Air-conditioning, ceiling fan and phone in rooms, cable TV in library and third-floor lounge, fireplace in some rooms, laundry room. $80–$120; full breakfast. AE, MC, V. No smoking, 2-night minimum on holiday and special-event weekends.*

OTHER CHOICES

Cedars by the Sea. 305 Front St., Beaufort 28516, tel. 252/728–7036 or 800/732–7036, fax 252/728–1685. 10 double rooms with baths, 1 cottage. Air-conditioning and cable TV in rooms. $85–$165; full breakfast. MC, V. No smoking.
Granville Queen Inn. 108 S. Granville St., Edenton 27932, tel. 252/482–5296. 9 double rooms with baths. Air-conditioning, cable TV/VCR and phone in rooms. $95–$105; full breakfast, afternoon wine and cheese. No credit cards. No smoking.
Harmony House Inn. 215 Pollock St., New Bern 28560, tel. 252/636–3810 or 800/636–3113, fax 252/636–3810. 8 rooms with baths, 2 suites. Air-condi-

tioning, ceiling fan, cable TV, and phone in rooms. $89–$140; full breakfast. AE, D, DC, MC, V. No smoking.

King's Arms Inn. 212 Pollock St., New Bern 28560, tel. 252/638–4409 or 800/ 872–9306, fax 252/638–2191. 7 double rooms with baths, 1 suite. Air-conditioning, cable TV and phone in rooms. $100–$145; full breakfast. AE, MC, V. No smoking.

Tranquil House Inn. 405 Queen Elizabeth St. (Box 2045), Manteo 27954, tel. 252/473–1404 or 800/458–7069, fax 252/473–1526. 23 double rooms with baths, 2 suites. Air-conditioning, cable TV, and phone in rooms; bicycles. $129–$169; Continental breakfast. AE, D, MC, V. 2-night minimum summer weekends, 3-night minimum holiday weekends.

RESERVATIONS SERVICE

North Carolina Bed & Breakfast Association (Box 1077, Asheville 28802, tel. 800/849–5392).

The Piedmont

FEARRINGTON HOUSE ☞
Fearrington Village Center, U.S. 15–501, Pittsboro 27312, tel. 919/542–2121, fax 919/542–4202

If you didn't know better, you'd think a click of the heels had transported you to the Cotswolds of England. Actually, this bucolic setting is Fearrington Village, a 200-year-old farm remade into a residential community just off U.S. 15–501 between Chapel Hill and Pittsboro. The village is the creation of R. B. and Jenny Fitch, who studied inns and restaurants in Europe before they began the 1,100-acre project in 1974. It consists of the inn and private homes, a restaurant (in the former farmhouse), a bank, pharmacy, pottery, jewelry store, bookstore, garden shop, and market café.

The inn's guest rooms are clustered around a charming courtyard with a central fountain and look out over the gardens and the pasture, where Galloway cows graze. English pine furniture matches the flooring from a London workhouse; rooms also have floral-print fabrics and fresh flower arrangements. The luxurious bathrooms have towel warmers. The Fitch children now help run the business, from decorating the rooms to overseeing the restaurant and gardens.

Breakfast is served in the restaurant, which has several rooms decorated in the elegant country style that is Fearrington's hallmark. Green ivy stenciled on the walls provides a natural complement to the real vines and boughs that peek through the many windows overlooking the gardens. Dinner draws not only inn guests but diners from Chapel Hill and Durham. Entrées include sautéed halibut with roasted fennel; yellowfin tuna with white-wine ginger sauce and fried leeks; and grilled beef tenderloin on a Parmesan disk with peppercorn sauce. Most guests eat lunch in the Market Café or go for a picnic, which can be ordered from the deli. Then they gather for afternoon tea in the Garden Room.

One of the most pleasant things about the Fearrington is its low-key country atmosphere. You won't be subjected to a schedule here, but you might try a round of croquet or ride one of the bikes to the swimming pool and tennis courts. Of course, there are plenty of diversions nearby—the Morehead Planetarium at Chapel Hill, Duke Chapel, and the Duke Homestead. ♙ *17 double rooms with baths, 12 suites.*

Air-conditioning, TV and phone in rooms. $165–$275; full breakfast. AE, MC, V. Restricted smoking.

INN AT CELEBRITY DAIRY 🐾

2106 Mt. Vernon–Hickory Mountain Rd., Siler City 27344, tel. 919/742–5176, fax 919/742–1432

The Inn at Celebrity Dairy is one hour from Raleigh, one hour from Greensboro, and a world away from either of those urban centers. And that suits Fleming and Brit Pfann, their guests, and their goats just fine.

The couple—she a weaver of clothes and wall hangings, he an engineer—were weary of their transitory lifestyle. When Fleming inherited a 200-acre oak-shaded farm (circa 1820) from her father they decided to take the opportunity to return to her native state. They moved in 1987.

First came the goats, who were brought in to help clear the overgrown grounds. Goats begat more goats and eventually the Pfanns were licensed to run a dairy, where now a variety of award-winning goat cheeses are produced for gourmet grocers, restaurants, and farm markets. The animals, who are affectionate, intelligent, and docile, are named after celebrities such as Katharine Hepburn, Lauren Bacall, and Tina Louise—thus the name of the dairy and inn.

The second part of the plan, creating a bed-and-breakfast, took a bit longer, as the Pfanns designed and constructed the inn, which is actually two buildings. The heart of the inn, the Old House Suite, is the original settler's cabin. It has rough-hewn walls, heart-pine floors, stone fireplace, and hanging quilts made by local craftspeople. The new, three-story, Greek Revival–style farmhouse has wide porches. The rooms, named for goats past and present, are simply but comfortably and artfully decorated. All beds have feather padding atop firm mattresses. The uncarpeted ground-floor rooms with their extra-wide doorways are wheelchair accessible. Upstairs, Lauren's Room has a mirrored armoire and two-person whirlpool tub; Lynan's Room, with its four-poster bed, has walls of periwinkle blue stenciled with a lace-pattern border; and Benjamin's Room has teal tones and an ornate Victorian headboard.

Connecting the two buildings is a sunlight-filled atrium. This huge space, dominated at one end by a Jacobean chest, has hand-painted floors courtesy of Fleming. Breakfast, consisting of goat cheese (of course), freshly baked breads, and dishes made from the eggs of the chickens who roam the property, is eaten here. Guests are then invited to read in the inn's small library, hike in the nearby woods, try their hand at a spinning wheel or loom, or join in the chores and help with the milking of the goats. ♿ *5 double rooms with baths, 1 single with adjacent shower, 1 suite. Air-conditioning, ceiling fan in rooms, TV in common area, whirlpool tub in one room, therapeutic massage available by appointment. $60–$130; Continental breakfast weekdays, full breakfast on weekends. MC, V. No smoking.*

PILOT KNOB INN 🐾

Box 1280, Pilot Mountain 27041, tel. 336/325–2502

The two-story log tobacco barns that dot this rural landscape aren't usually the kind of places you'd consider spending the night. Here, however, they have become a one-of-a-kind B&B. The property adjoins Pilot Mountain State Park, and the knob that crowns the 1,500-ft mountain is within view. (If the names ring a bell, it's because they inspired the place names in Andy Griffith's mythical Mayberry.)

Five small barns and a slave cabin, all at least 100 years old, were moved to the 50-acre wooded site by innkeeper Jim Rouse, who enlarged the slave cabin and added decks and porches to the barns while keeping their rustic look. Jim's father, Don, who is also involved in the operation, can always find something that needs fixing or changing. Norman Ross, a silent business partner from Chicago, owns the collection of 6,000 records in the library. The barns have Oriental and dhurrie rugs and a mix of 18th-century reproductions, southern primitive, and country English antiques. Each has a whirlpool tub for two, a fireplace, bathrobes, hair dryers, fresh fruit, and flowers. Some of the barns have massive "Paul Bunyan" beds, handmade of juniper logs by a local craftsman. The common room, downstairs in the bilevel central barn—where guests gather to read and listen to music—has a 300-year-old Italian-marble fireplace, a William and Mary love seat, and a coffee table made of parquet flooring from Versailles (really!). There's a dry sauna and a pool, and a 6-acre lake and gazebo are ideal for fishing. A contemporary building overlooking the pool and the mountain beyond houses the office, kitchen, a conference room, and a gift shop, which sells community crafts. Guests can also while away the evening at a gazebo that has a ceiling fan and picnic tables.

Privacy and isolation are the main attractions at Pilot Knob. It's tucked away with no signs or billboards to point the way and is the perfect place to commune with nature, slow down, and rekindle romance. Guests usually get together at breakfast, which is served in the central barn. Prepared by Jim's mother, Pat, breakfast might be chocolate-chip sour-cream coffee cake, waffles and sausage, poached pears, or a peach and cream-cheese concoction called Peach Pilot—all served with fresh berries in season. ▲ *6 cabins. Air-conditioning, TV and phone in cabins. $110–$130; full breakfast. MC, V. 2-night minimum Oct. and holidays.*

WILLIAM THOMAS HOUSE BED & BREAKFAST ☞
530 N. Blount St., Raleigh 27604, tel. 919/755–9400 or 800/653–3466, fax 919/755–3966

Every day for eight years the Loftons would drive by the Victorian house on the edge of downtown Raleigh on their way to work: Sarah to the Executive Mansion where she served as the first lady's executive assistant, Jim to the state government complex where he was first the governor's chief of staff and then a member of his cabinet. When the governor decided to reenter private life, so did the Loftons—sort of. In June 1993 they bought the house, which for a decade had been functioning as an office building. By that December they had turned it into a home for themselves and a home away from home for visitors. The following year it was designated a Raleigh Historic Site.

The William Thomas House, named for the fathers of Jim and Sarah, is a spacious, stately place, stately but not stuffy. And it's quiet, thanks to the 7-inch-thick walls and double-paned windows. The richly hued common rooms, with their oversize windows and 12-ft ceilings, are filled with heirlooms: a grand piano from 1863, antique china, a refinished 1947 television serving as an end table. The library-media room, with original wainscoting, contains a TV/VCR, videos, compact disks, books, and periodicals, as well as bird-hunting trophies and menus from local restaurants.

Sleeping quarters are also named for Lofton family members, whose pictures are displayed throughout the house. The guests' rooms, with their muted tones, large beds, easy chairs, desks, ample but soft lighting, TVs, tapestries or framed art, Oriental rugs, and small but well-stocked refrigerators, are refuges. For the businessperson they can also double as an office. Front porches and a back deck with rocking chairs allow for down time and enjoyment of the afternoon wine and cheese. But if it's action you're after, the inn is within walking distance of shops, restaurants, and many state-run museums and historic sights, including the Queen Anne–style Executive Mansion. ♠ *4 double rooms with baths. Air-conditioning, ceiling fan, cable TV, mini-refrigerator and phone with fax hook-up in rooms, turndown service, off-street parking. $96–$135; full breakfast. AE, MC, V. No smoking.*

OTHER CHOICES

Arrowhead Inn. 106 Mason Rd., Durham 27712, tel. 919/477–8430 or 800/528–2207, fax 919/471–9538. 5 double rooms with baths, 3 suites, 1 cabin. Air-conditioning, phone, TV/VCR, coffeemaker, and ceiling fan in rooms; whirlpool bath in suites and cabin; guest refrigerator. $98–$195; full breakfast. AE, D, DC, MC, V. No smoking.

Henry F. Shaffner House. 150 S. Marshall St., Winston-Salem 27101, tel. 336/777–0052 or 800/952–2256, fax 336/777–1188. 6 double rooms with baths, 3 suites. Air-conditioning, cable TV, and phone in rooms; passes to nearby fitness center. $99–$219; Continental breakfast. AE, MC, V. No smoking.

The Homeplace. 5901 Sardis Rd., Charlotte 28270, tel. 704/365–1936, fax 704/366–2729. 2 double rooms with baths, 1 suite. Air-conditioning, ceiling fan, iron, and ironing board in rooms; cable TV in common areas and suite. $108–$135; full breakfast. AE, MC, V. No smoking; 2- or 3-night minimum holiday and special-event weekends.

RESERVATIONS SERVICE

North Carolina Bed & Breakfast Association (Box 1077, Asheville 28802, tel. 800/849–5392).

The Mountains

BALSAM MOUNTAIN INN ☙

Box 40, Balsam 28707, tel. 828/456–9488 or 800/224–9498, fax 828/456–9298

On spring nights, the moon rises perfectly placed between two mountain peaks, as if a painter set it there for the benefit of the folks sitting in rocking chairs at the Balsam Mountain Inn. Actually, it wasn't the moon but the inn that was strategically placed so that the sun, which warmed the porches in the morning, would leave them in shade during hot summer afternoons and so guests could watch the moonrise year-round.

At one time, the North Carolina mountains were full of rambling wood-frame inns like this one, but the Balsam Mountain Inn is one of only a handful remaining. Built at what was then the highest elevation of the Western North Carolina Railroad, it offered a cool escape from the summer heat when it opened in 1908 as the Balsam Mountain Springs Hotel. It operated into the 1980s but was boarded up and had 125 broken windows when Merrily Teasley bought it in 1990 and began restoration. Plumbing, wiring, and heat are all new, but the inn retains virtually all of its vintage charm. Bead-board paneling covers all the walls, and the heart-pine floors have a comforting creak.

A huge mansard roof with more than 100 dormer windows covers the inn, which is fronted by a two-story porch lined with rockers and hanging plants. Everything about this inn says "relax," from the library, stocked with 2,000 volumes, to the chairs gathered around the lobby fireplaces.

Some of the guest rooms have ornate iron beds, while others have "twig" beds—headboards fashioned from boughs and twisted vines by local craftspeople. Bathrooms have either showers or Victorian claw-foot tubs and corner-mounted sinks.

The large dining room is painted gray with lavender, green, and burgundy trim for a charming effect. The restaurant serves three meals on Sunday and two daily meals the rest of the week. Representative of the lavish breakfasts, included in room rates, is French toast with a caramelized syrup coating and topped with fresh fruit. There's help-yourself tea and hot chocolate in the lobby, and box lunches are available every day if ordered by 6 PM the day before. ♨ *42 double rooms with baths, 8 suites. Restaurant. $90–$160; full breakfast. D, MC, V. Restricted smoking, 2-night minimum some weekends and holidays.*

GREYSTONE INN ☞
Greystone La., Lake Toxaway 28747, tel. 828/966–4700 or 800/824–5766, fax 828/862–5689

In the early 1900s, wealthy folks arrived in their private railcars to vacation at secluded Lake Toxaway. Modern travelers head for the Greystone Inn, a Swiss-style mansion on the National Register of Historic Places that's at the edge of the lake. Built in 1915, the house was converted to an inn in 1985 by Tim Lovelace, a retired financial consultant, who later added Hillmont, a 12-room annex.

Guests can choose between staying in the historic house, which has casement windows, glass doorknobs, and antique beds, and enjoying the modern luxury of the Hillmont Annex, whose rooms contain fireplaces with gas logs, king-size beds, and private balconies overlooking the lake. These contemporary rooms are quite spacious. There are wing-back chairs by the fireplace and leather chairs by the window, and the huge bathrooms have large whirlpool baths and separate, free-standing glass showers. The Presidential Suite, the former library, is the most impressive of the mansion rooms, highlighted by soaring 25-ft ceilings, built-in oak bookcases, a huge floor-to-ceiling stone fireplace, and a bay window overlooking the lake. The Firestone Room, formerly the kitchen, still has a wood-burning stove, a stone fireplace, and exposed beams.

In the dining facility, a separate building that seats 80 and is open only to guests, vast windows frame the mountains and the lake. Chef Chris McDonald serves southern cuisine with a modern twist, such as trout Pontchartrain and delicate baby-corn fritters. The six-course gourmet dinner and lavish breakfast are included in the room rates.

Greystone guests can play tennis and golf at the adjoining Lake Toxaway Country Club and go swimming, waterskiing, windsurfing, sailing, and canoeing on the lake from the inn's private dock. Many guests enjoy hiking. There's Mills Creek Falls or Deep Ford Falls, ideal for a picnic, and an excellent trail runs along the Toxaway River. Rainy days are devoted to playing bridge and reading or pampering oneself at the spa.

After tea, a social highlight of the day, Tim conducts animated lake tours on the *Mountain Lily II*. Everyone gathers in the library lounge for hors d'oeuvres and cocktails before dinner. ♨ *30 double rooms, 3 suites. Air-conditioning, ceiling fan, cable TV/VCR, and phone in rooms, whirlpool baths in suites, turndown service, morning newspaper, airport transportation available. $265–$525; MAP. MC, V. 2-night minimum weekends, open weekends only Jan.–Mar.*

MAPLE LODGE BED & BREAKFAST 🐚
152 Sunset Dr. (Box 1236), Blowing Rock 28605, tel. 828/295–3331, fax 828/295–9986

Marilyn and David Bateman often visited the Maple Lodge Bed & Breakfast when vacationing from their own B&B in Annapolis. As luck would have it, the owner of Maple Lodge was ready to sell when the Batemans relocated to Blowing Rock in 1993.

The two-story Colonial-style inn was built in 1946. Today, with its white picket fence, Williamsburg gold exterior, and red shutters, it's a neighborhood standout. Pine paneling covers the walls of the foyer and twin parlors, and there are pine ceilings and woodwork throughout. The Bridal Wreath suite has eggshell-blue wallpaper and a four-poster rice bed draped with a hand-tied canopy. A few rooms are small, but most are big enough to hold comfortably a queen-size bed, antique dresser, small table with a decanter of cream sherry, and chair.

Breakfast is served in a large enclosed patio with a flagstone floor overlooking the wildflower garden. The granola and muesli cereals are homemade. Just off Main Street, it's convenient to the shops and restaurants of the quaint downtown. △ *10 double rooms with baths, 1 suite. Ceiling fan in rooms, cable TV in 4 rooms, and jacks for phones or modems in 2 rooms. $98–$150; full breakfast. AE, D, DC, MC, V. No smoking, 2-night minimum some weekends, closed Jan.–Feb.*

RICHMOND HILL INN 🐚
87 Richmond Hill Dr., Asheville 28806, tel. 828/252–7313 or 800/545–9238, fax 828/252–8726

As a young man, Thomas Wolfe used to look up at the Richmond Hill mansion and wonder what kind of people lived in such a glorious place. Years later he would meet members of the Pearson family and write that they were as grand as the house itself. The Queen Anne–style mansion was built in 1889 as the home of Richmond Pearson, a diplomat and statesman, and his wife, Gabrielle. It had long since fallen into disrepair when Jake and Marge Michel of Greensboro bought the home in 1987 and invested $3 million to restore it. The Richmond Hill Inn opened in 1989, and the Michels' daughter, Susan, is now the innkeeper.

The Michels retained not only the elegant architecture but also the gracious ways of the past, from valet service at the carriage entrance to afternoon games of croquet on the manicured lawn. Afternoon tea is served in the sweeping oak-paneled entry hall, where leather and tapestry-print Victorian chairs are grouped around the fireplace under the benevolent gaze of Gabrielle herself. The restored portrait is one of many Pearson family items that the Michels have recovered. Guests can relax on the porches or in a cozy oak-paneled library.

The 12 guest rooms in the mansion are named for historic figures of the era and North Carolina writers with Asheville ties and are furnished in antiques, such as canopy beds and claw-foot tubs. The most popular is the romantic Gabrielle Pearson Room, an eight-sided room that has lace curtains and a canopy bed draped in peach-colored fabric. The Chief Justice Suite has a whirlpool bath, wet bar, and fireplace with gas logs. In a more contemporary style, the nine rooms in the Croquet Cottages also have fireplaces with gas logs as well as pencil-post beds and private porches with rocking chairs. An addition includes 15 Garden Rooms, the most spacious rooms at the inn.

Gabrielle's, inside the mansion and one of Asheville's best restaurants, serves new American cuisine with southern regional influences. Breakfast, featuring fresh fruit crepes and exotic omelets, is served near the gardens. And just to make sure you really feel pampered, the turndown service includes chocolates and a gift to take home. ♨ *27 rooms with baths, 9 cottages. Air-conditioning, cable TV and phone in rooms. $135–$375; full breakfast. AE, MC, V. No smoking, 2-night minimum weekends, closed 2 wks in Jan.*

OTHER CHOICES

Cedar Crest Inn. 674 Biltmore Ave., Asheville 28803, tel. 828/252–1389 or 800/252–0310, fax 828/253–7667. 8 double rooms with baths, 1 suite, 1 cottage with 2 suites and common kitchen. Air-conditioning, cable TV in study and suites, phone in rooms. $120–$210; full breakfast. AE, D, DC, MC, V. No smoking, 2-night minimum weekends and holidays.

Inn at Taylor House. Rte. 194 (Box 713), Valle Crucis 28691, tel. 828/963–5581, fax 828/963–5818. 7 double rooms with baths, 3 suites. Air-conditioning on 3rd floor, ceiling fan in rooms, day spa with massage therapist. $135–$295; full breakfast. MC, V. No smoking, 2-night minimum weekends.

Mast Farm Inn. 2543 Broadstone Rd., Valle Crucis 28691, tel. 828/963–5857 or 888/963–5857, fax 828/963–6404. 9 rooms with baths, 4 cottages. Air-conditioning, ceiling fan in rooms. $96–$135; full breakfast. AE, MC, V. No smoking.

RESERVATIONS SERVICE

North Carolina Bed & Breakfast Association (Box 1077, Asheville 28802, tel. 800/849–5392).

NORTH DAKOTA

Eastern North Dakota

BEISEKER MANSION 🍃
1001 N.E. 2nd St. (Box 187), Fessenden 58438, tel. 701/547–3411

This imposing 15-room mansion stood vacant for a number of years and probably would have for many more if Paula and Jerry Tweton hadn't made a wrong turn in 1989 onto the residential street where it sits. The couple had already traveled to California, Illinois, and Wisconsin in their search for an inn to buy when Jerry, then a professor of history at the University of North Dakota, was asked to speak in the small community of Fessenden. Only 143 mi from their home in Grand Forks they found what they had been looking for all along. Shortly thereafter, they purchased the National Register–listed property and began restoring it.

The Queen Anne–style home was built in 1899 by T. L. Beiseker, a wealthy land speculator who owned 27 banks. He lived in the Victorian mansion until his death in 1942. From then until the mid-1970s it was used as a women's retirement home by the Order of the Eastern Star and then remained mostly vacant until the Twetons bought it.

Beiseker Mansion is one of only two Victorian homes in North Dakota with twin turrets. The cedarwood structure has a wraparound veranda of Pennsylvania sandstone, stained- and leaded-glass windows, golden oak wainscoting, and alabaster light fixtures. It is on several heavily treed acres within walking distance of most of the community. Hundreds of people pay a small fee to tour the home each year.

Four bedrooms on the mansion's second floor are available for guests. Furnished with antiques and twin-, double-, and queen-size beds, all rooms have cable TVs and VCRs. A third-floor special-occasion suite has Victorian-era Turkish decor, king-size bed, and whirlpool bath for two.

Guests often relax in wicker chairs on the veranda; join Jerry, a respected scholar, for an impromptu lesson on North Dakota history; or comb through the extensive library of books, magazines, and videocassettes.

The Twetons serve a full breakfast of freshly ground coffee, fruit, eggs, and other dishes made from scratch. Their family-recipe pancakes and special sausage are favorites with guests. Evening meals are also available at extra charge. The limited dinner can include a well-aged tenderloin steak Madeira, chicken in wine sauce, and a platter of Bohemian pot roast with all the trimmings. **△** *1 double room with bath, 3 doubles share 2 baths, 1 suite. Air-conditioning, TV/VCR, whirlpool bath in suite, fireplace in common area. $45–$95; full breakfast. MC, V.*

COUNTRY CHARM BED & BREAKFAST 🐦
R.R. 3 (Box 71), Jamestown 58401, tel. 701/251–1372 or 800/331–1372

This inn invites you to savor the bounty of its setting: the song of wild birds, great fields of wheat, the nearness of friendly hills, the sight of a chipmunk peering through the tall grass. Curious deer are frequent visitors to the 12 acres surrounding Tom and Ethel Oxtoby's country-farm bed-and-breakfast. Rabbits, squirrels, and other wildlife dot the beautifully manicured grounds, along with the occasional fox or coyote. And, since the farmstead is on one of America's busiest migratory flyways, numerous birds are attracted to the Oxtobys' feeders.

The 1897 farmstead sits on a gentle knoll just 1½ mi off Interstate 94. Pine, spruce, cottonwood, and fruit trees surround it on three sides while the prairie stretches as far as the eye can see to the south. The redwood deck and glassed-in sunporch—prettily stenciled with vine motifs—are the favored gathering spots and afford the pleasantest views. On clear nights, guests often gather on the front porch to watch the stars twinkle above the lights of Jamestown, 6 mi away. Or, they'll ask Tom to go for a ride along the country roads in his classic 1958 Ford Skyliner convertible (one of his five antique Ford vehicles); with its trademark hardtop down, it's a delightful way to go in search of the Big Dipper.

"Our inn is really peaceful," says Ethel Oxtoby. "That's why a lot of people come here. And if you want a quiet stay, visit during our North Dakota winters, which can last from Thanksgiving to early May. Twenty inches of snow, three-day blizzards, and hot-chocolate weather can really do the soul right." Ethel is a quilter (a big regional activity), and you'll find her "double wedding rings," "cathedral windows," and "fan patterns" throughout the guest rooms, which are also adorned with lace, country tins, hearts and sheep motifs, and North Dakota wheat wreaths and sculptures.

Full breakfasts with fresh orange juice and apple-raisin puffed pancakes are served on the round oak table in the dining area or on the walnut table on the sunporch. You can start the day counting the pheasants that fly past the window and trying to get a word in edgewise among the chattering bluejays. After a second cup of aromatic coffee or tea, head for the nearby Arrowwood Wildlife Center or historic Frontier Village. ⚠ *3 double rooms and 1 single share bath. Air-conditioning. $40–$50; full breakfast. No credit cards.*

Luverne

VOLDEN FARM 🐦
R.R. 2 (Box 50), Luverne 58056, tel. 701/769–2275, fax 701/769–2610

Forty-one miles north of Valley City and I–94, Volden Farm sits on a hilltop overlooking the Sheyenne River and the fertile farmland beyond. Natural stands of oak, virgin prairie, sparkling springs, and nature trails make this a wonderful place for outdoor lovers. The Wolds will even provide all the equipment for canoeing, cross-country skiing, and snowshoeing.

As the *Grand Forks Herald* charmingly put it, JoAnn and Jim Wold's inn is "the kind of place where guests can go to bed in Czarist Russia and wake up in Scandinavia—there are twin motifs at work." Icons and pre-revolutionary and dissident Russian art, acquired by the couple while Jim was a U.S. Air Force military attaché in Moscow, contrast with decorations reflecting the Wolds' Norwegian roots. Maple floors and furnishings add to the decidedly European look.

The original part of the house, built in 1926, includes the parlor, music room, library, and two guest bedrooms. The newer part was added in 1978 and is a light and airy space with a fireplace in the conversation pit. Redwood siding, which grays and weathers over time, was purposely chosen for the exterior for its ability to blend in with the surrounding trees, giving the home the look of a Russian dacha.

Furnishings in the guest bedrooms include family heirloom quilts, linens, and antiques from all over the world. A separate building that once served as Jim's law office is a short distance from the main house and has been transformed into a quaint guest cottage. In the main-floor bedroom, two Norwegian sleigh beds have been joined together and topped with a feather bed to make a king-size bed. Upstairs are twin beds, a built-in Swedish bed, and 1930s-style bed.

JoAnn serves a full Scandinavian breakfast beginning with fresh fruit juice, Swedish pancakes served with chokecherry-raspberry syrup, Norwegian cheese and flat bread, vegetables and fruits in season, and freshly ground coffee and herbal or Earl Grey tea. Other meals are available at an additional charge. ♤ *1 double room with bath, 2 doubles share bath. Bottled water in rooms, robes, toiletries. $60–$95; full breakfast, evening snack. No credit cards.*

OTHER CHOICES

Bohlig's Bed & Breakfast. 1418 3rd Ave. S, Fargo 58103, tel. 701/235–7867. 3 double rooms share 2 baths. Clock radio in rooms, TV in sitting room. $45–$55; full breakfast weekends, Continental breakfast weekdays. No credit cards.

511 Reeves Bed & Breakfast. 511 Reeves Dr., Grand Forks 58201, tel. 701/775–3585. 1 double room with bath, 2 doubles share bath. Air-conditioning, cable TV/VCR in library, fireplace in living room, fax available for business travelers. $65–$85; full breakfast. AE, MC, V.

House of 29. 215 7th St. S, Oakes 58474, tel. 701/742–2227. 1 double room with bath, 2 doubles share bath, 2 singles with baths. Air-conditioning, TV/VCR in common area. $40–$50; full breakfast. No credit cards.

Lord Byron's Bed & Breakfast Inn. 521 S. 5th St., Grand Forks 58201, tel. 701/775–0194. 2 double rooms share bath, 1 double with ½ bath. Air-conditioning. $75; full breakfast, evening snack. No credit cards.

Western North Dakota

Dakotah Rose Bed & Breakfast. 510 4th Ave. NW, Minot 58703, tel. 701/838–3548. 2 double rooms with baths, 3 doubles share bath, 2 suites. Air-conditioning in some rooms, TV/VCR, ballroom serves as common area for guests, tearoom open seasonally. $50–$75; full breakfast. MC, V.

Diamond Bar Bed and Breakfast. Box 554, Beulah 58523 (at entrance to the Theodore Roosevelt National Park), tel. 701/873–5117 or 701/623–4913. 3 double rooms share bath in log cabin. Camping, hunting, horseback riding, snowmobiling, cross-country skiing. $30–$40; full breakfast. No credit cards.

Farm Comfort Bed and Breakfast. 58200 394 Ave. NW, Kenmare 58746, tel. 701/848–2433. 2 double rooms share bath. Clock radio in rooms, phone, TV in living room and basement, snack kitchen in basement. $35–$40; full breakfast. No credit cards.

Historic Jacobson Mansion Bed and Breakfast. R.R. 2 (Box 15A), Scranton 58653, tel. 701/275–8291. 3 double rooms share 2 baths. Air-conditioning, phone in 1 room. $50–$60; full breakfast. No credit cards.

Logging Camp Ranch Bed & Breakfast. HC 3 (Box 27), Bowman 58623, tel. 701/279–5702. 2 double rooms share bath. Clock radio in rooms, phone, TV/VCR in living-dining area, hiking and horseback riding. $50; full breakfast. No credit cards.

The Villa Vallombrosa. 175 Pacific Ave., Medora 58645, tel. 701/623–4825. 3 suites. Kitchen and laundry facilities, private entrances, off-street parking. $100; full breakfast, AE, MC, V.

White Lace Bed & Breakfast. 807 N. 6th St., Bismarck 58501, tel. 701/258–6877. 2 doubles share bath. Air-conditioning, phone, TV. $75; full breakfast. AE, D, MC, V.

RESERVATIONS SERVICE

North Dakota Tourism Promotion Division (604 E. Blvd., Bismarck 58505, tel. 701/328–2525; listings only).

OHIO

Northern Ohio

BARICELLI INN ☙
2203 Cornell Rd., Cleveland 44106, tel. 216/791–6500, fax 216/791–9131

Nestled in Cleveland's Little Italy, a neighborhood of restaurants, bakeries, and art galleries, the Baricelli Inn offers European elegance in an urban American setting.

Four-poster Amish-built king- and queen-size beds dominate the inn's seven suites, where cable televisions are tucked away in authentic 1860s armoires of mahogany or oak. Rooms 3 and 6 are the most popular due to their spaciousness and views of the courtyards. Originally built in 1896, the inn was once the private residence of an academic and her physician husband.

The inn honors the memory of the Baricellis by serving fine European cuisine prepared by chef Paul Minnillo, Jr., who opened the inn and its restaurant in 1984 with his father. The chef is proud to tell visitors the inn's restaurant has no freezer: everything he serves is fresh. In addition to fine dining, the restaurant serves bistro fare on its shaded garden patio on summer evenings.

While Paul Jr. trolls Europe a couple of times a year for recipes and ideas for the kitchen, Paul Sr. collects bits and pieces of local history to decorate the five dining parlors and the bedrooms. His finds include brass-sill windows from an historic downtown Cleveland building that was demolished, stained-glass windows from an old church, and a statue of St. Thomas Aquinas that presides peacefully over an outdoor cocktail patio. This local color mixes well with the Villeroy and Boch china and silk-shaded crystal candleholders that adorn the dining tables in this turn-of-the-century brownstone.

Visitors to the inn find themselves within walking distance of a treasure trove of cultural and academic institutions, including Severance Hall, home to the celebrated Cleveland Orchestra; the world-renown Cleveland Museum of Art; Case Western Reserve University; the Museum of Natural History; Crawford Auto-Aviation Museum; and a host of others. The neighborhood, wedged into a hill leading to Cleveland Heights, is crisscrossed with redbrick streets and crammed with small houses, boutiques and a wide variety of restaurants—all Italian. ♨
7 rooms with baths. Phones, cable TVs. $125–$150; European breakfast. AE, DC, MC, V.

BOGART'S BED & BREAKFAST ☙
52 W. Main St., New Concord 43762, tel. 740/826–7439 or 740/872–3514

Jack and Sharon Bogart had their eyes on this exquisite 1830s landmark home for a while, and the minute it was available, they snapped it up and did most of the painstaking renovations themselves. Good thing, too: They were running out of room at their antiques store, 4 mi away. The Bogarts opened their B&B, on the quiet historic main street, in 1994. It is within walking distance of Muskingum College, shops, and restaurants.

The exquisitely decorated house has both a comfortable sitting room and dining room with fresh flowers in abundance. Outside there is a spacious, screened wraparound porch, ideal for relaxing with a book or eating breakfast.

The Bogarts's five guest rooms are named after people who have owned the house. Downstairs, off the kitchen and with private access to the porch, is a room that was added to the house in the 1930s. The wallpaper, an intricate design of small flowers, gives the room, which has twin beds, a homey feel. The front room has a double bed and an 1880s rosewood armoire. The rich color scheme (teal with wine trim) would make it an ideal choice in winter. The three upstairs rooms each have one double bed and a twin day bed. One has a sunflower motif and is a favorite among guests. Another has a country theme, with a beautiful tiger-maple bed and a matching chest of draws. The largest room is awash in lilacs and has a small kitchenette and eating area.

Guests can use the college gym, which is within easy walking distance. Also, golf courses, museums, and a state park are just a few miles away.

Sharon cooks breakfast to order each morning and is happy to fulfill special requests. △ *4 double rooms with baths. Air-conditioning, TV/VCR in sitting area. $65–$75; full breakfast, evening snacks. No smoking. MC, V.*

INN AT HONEY RUN 🐾
6920 Rte. 203, Millersburg 44654, tel. 330/674–0011 or 800/468–6639, fax 330/674–2623

If every B&B owner's dream is to have the perfect setting where the inn blends with its surroundings to create a pleasant ambience, then Marge Stock succeeded admirably. The design is modern, but the use of wood, especially oak, gives the impression that this inn is also part of nature's bounty.

Built in 1982, the inn consists of a main house with floor-to-ceiling windows, outside decks, and bird feeders everywhere; a guest house called the Honeycombs, an earth-sheltered building burrowed into a hillside with 12 guest rooms that, from the outside, does indeed look like a honeycomb; and two cabins each with two bedrooms, a small kitchen, a living room, and a private deck.

The inn is decorated simply, in deference to the plain-living Amish who reside in the area. At Christmastime, instead of lights, the inn hangs red-and-green-pattern quilts and scatters poinsettias throughout common areas. A Christmas tree, placed on a large outdoor deck off the inn's main floor, has decorations for the birds—literally. Carved-out gourds and halved grapefruits stocked with seeds hang from the branches, and strings of popcorn and cranberries draw brilliantly colored cardinals, along with a wide variety of other birds.

One wall of the inn has 43 planks of different kinds of wood culled from area trees; many of the inn's guests make a sport of trying to identify each one (a cheat sheet is kept on a nearby coffee table). Hickory rocking chairs and fireplaces make two common areas ideal spots for relaxed contemplation. In the inn's rooms, televisions and telephones are hidden in cabinets, and field guides for wildflowers and birds sit atop simple wooden end tables. Although several rooms are decorated in plain Shaker style, every room is different. About half of them have stunning views of the wooded hillside, and all have good light for reading.

The Honeycombs, set below the crest of a hill buried under a lush carpet of grass and wildflowers, appears cave-like and dark from the outside. Inside, however, glass-panel doors leading to stone-wall back patios look out on a series of rolling hills, where sheep and goats graze. The six rooms of the top floor have large sandstone fireplaces, and four of the Honeycomb rooms have secluded patios.

Simplicity reigns as well in the two guest houses, which are atop the hill. One is called Trillium, the other Cardinal, and the decor, from bedspreads to wall hangings, reflects these names. Each guest house has two bedrooms with double beds, along with a sofa bed and a bed hidden in the wall, making sleeping space for six in each. The houses are outfitted with microwave ovens, dishwashers, and washer-dryer units.

The Inn at Honey Run doesn't prohibit children, but it doesn't encourage parents to bring them, either. The relaxed pace and pastoral setting are engineered to please adults and don't offer much to active children. This is a place, says Marge, where people who lead stressful lives come to rest and recharge.

Meals are reflective of the inn—excellent, simple food. The menu changes daily and often features baked tenderloin of beef, pan-fried trout caught locally, and fresh, healthy, steamed vegetables. Out of respect for the Amish, the inn serves no alcohol and its restaurant is open only to inn guests on Sunday because the Amish disdain commercializing the Sabbath. Also, the resident pets, including Honey the cat and a few dogs, are very territorial; therefore, no other pets are allowed here.

Marge is building a large orchard, and she serves produce and preserves from the inn's property in the dining room. In fact, guests can watch the preserves being made at the Milkhouse Café. On the top of a hill, a short walk from the main inn, the café is a great place for visitors and guests to sample the preserves out on the deck (or by the fireplace) while drinking in the serene landscape.

Marge is constantly seeking guests' suggestions and criticism, and she seems to think of everything to make a stay here special—from leaving walking sticks outside all of the buildings to stocking shelves with books that guests can take home and send back when they finish reading them. ♠ *37 double rooms with baths, 2 cabins sleep 8. Air-conditioning, phones, TVs, radio-and-cassette alarm clocks, restaurant, café, exercise machines, meeting rooms. $79–$280; Continental breakfast. AE, MC, V. 2-night minimum in cabins.*

WHITE FENCE INN ❦
8842 Denman Rd., Lexington 44904, tel. 419/884–2356

When Bill and Ellen Hiser saw this breathtaking 73-acre farm 6 mi outside of Mansfield in 1987, their search for their dream inn was over. The Hisers left Phoenix, Arizona—where Bill had been teaching for 10 years—and threw themselves into the innkeeping business with a determination that has paid off. The setting is idyllic: woods, apple orchard, dairy barn, fishing pond with bass and blue-gill, and a full barn with chickens, cows, ducks, and turkeys, all set around a 107-year-old country farmhouse on 53 acres of tillable soil.

Inside the house, the seven guest rooms—four upstairs, two downstairs, and one in the basement—are decorated in different themes. Upstairs, the Amish room has authentic Amish oak furniture and chairs, shaker pegs with Amish clothes and hats hanging from them, and a high oak bed with an Amish handmade quilt. The Southwestern room is decorated with adobe items from Bill's days in Arizona: furniture and pottery, adobe-tile floor, Navajo rug, and southwestern wallpaper.

A third guest room is decorated in classic Victorian style; it has a sleigh bed with a tall cherry headboard, a cherry chest of drawers, and lots of blue and pink color to complement the Victorian wallpaper. The fourth room has a pre–Civil War brass bed and a stenciled wood floor in the traditional country style.

The most luxurious guest room in the inn is downstairs; it has a king-size four-poster bed, a cathedral wood ceiling, a sunken tub for two, a large fireplace, a private deck, a TV/VCR, and a refrigerator. The other downstairs room is smaller and is decorated in the turn-of-the-century Primitive style, with stenciled walls, a wood floor, and simple furniture.

Additionally, there is a large family room, with its own entrance, in the finished basement. This room has two double beds, a twin bed, and a Ben Franklin stovepipe fireplace. Also, the Hisers plan to convert the carriage house into a deluxe room.

Guests can relax by the fire in the comfortable sitting room that has a TV/VCR and a large bookshelf stacked with books and assorted reading material; or in the parlor, which also has a large fireplace and where there is a chest of drawers full of games. The large windows to the east allow for floods of light in the morning, as well as wonderful views of the farm and the surrounding countryside. And not to be missed is the secluded hot tub—just steps from the inn—in the converted chicken coop.

The White Fence is near the Amish country and there is an 18-mi bike trail close by. The Hisers can arrange for a pick-up truck to meet you at the end of the trail. There is also a playground on the premises, and children under six stay free. On summer weekends, the nearby Mid-Ohio Racetrack hosts race meets—rooms fill up fast, so book well in advance. ♦ *4 double rooms with baths, 2 doubles share bath, 1 family room (sleeps 5) with bath. Ceiling fans; TV/VCR and refrigerator in 1 room; TV/VCR in sitting room; games in parlor; fishing pond. $57–$104; full breakfast. Ground-floor rooms are wheelchair accessible. No credit cards. Closed Mar.*

WHITE OAK INN ☞
29683 Walhonding Rd. (Ohio Rte. 715), Danville 43014, tel. 740/599–6107

The White Oak Inn was built in 1915 from white oak trimmed on the property. It was converted into an inn in 1985 and was bought by current owners Yvonne and Ian Martin in 1992. Tired of the drill of corporate life in Toronto, the Martins threw themselves into their dream with gusto, and the result is an inn of great charm along a two-lane scenic route near Danville, 55 mi northeast of Columbus.

A beveled-glass front door leads into the house, where downstairs you will find a comfortable living room furnished in an eclectic—but thoroughly comfortable—style: sofas, rocking chairs, a large brick fireplace, a square grand piano, and an antique games table. As Yvonne says, "I want people to be able to sit down and relax with their feet on the coffee table." And guests do relax in here or, if the weather is clement, in a rocker or oak swing on the 50-ft-long front porch.

The 10 guest rooms are divided between the main house and a separate guest house. The seven guest rooms in the main inn are tastefully furnished with antique high beds covered with hand-sewn quilts from the nearby Amish community, ruffled curtains, and fresh flowers. Every room is named after the wood used in its design: the Ash Room, the Cherry Room, the Maple Room, the Oak Room, the White Oak Room, the Poplar Room, and the Walnut Room. The White Oak Room downstairs was once the family dining room and study; it is so big you could literally throw a party in the bathroom, so long as you move the single bed that the Martins have put into it to accommodate groups of three. Originally a chicken barn, the renovated guest-house has three comfortable guest rooms with oak-beam cathedral ceilings: Two have brick wood-burning fireplaces. All guest house rooms have oak antiques, and the headboards on the queen-size beds are reproductions of originals that were once in the main house.

Dinner in the inn's dining room, where guests sit at common tables, might include such entrées as apricot peppercorn pork loin, herb-stuffed chicken breast, and penne pasta with Italian sausage and chicken in a jalapeño sauce, followed by a dessert with an indulge-yourself name like Chocolate Decadence—a chocolate cake with chocolate chunks and chocolate, marshmallow, and pecan frosting, all covered with hot fudge sauce; or you could go for a less threatening peach cobbler.

The inn's environs contribute to a very relaxed atmosphere and easy pace. A walking trail on the property meanders through the acres of conservation land that surround the inn, and Amish country is close by as well. The Martins host special events throughout the year such as a Naturalists Weekend, a murder-mystery weekend, and a Big Band concert package. During the holidays, guests participate in dressing the Thanksgiving turkey or by enjoying the decorations and festivities of the inn's Charles Dickens' Christmas. ♦ *10 double rooms with baths. Air-conditioning, clock radios, fireplace in 3 rooms; bicycles; outdoor games; phones upon request. $75–$130; full breakfast, complimentary soft drinks, fresh-baked cookies. AE, D, MC, V. 2-night minimim during peak season.*

OTHER CHOICES

Michael Cahill Bed & Breakfast. 1106 Walnut Blvd., Ashtabula 44004, tel. 216/964–8449. 2 double rooms with baths, 2 doubles share 1½ baths. Air-conditioning, terry cloth robes in rooms, phone and TV in living room, tennis courts and beach within 2 blocks. $35–$55; full breakfast. No credit cards.

Mulberry Inn Bed and Breakfast. 53 N. 4th St., Martin's Ferry 43935, tel. 740/633–6058. 3 doubles share 2 baths. Air-conditioning, books, TV/VCR, fireplace in guest parlor. $55–$65; full breakfast. AE, D, MC, V. Closed Jan.–Feb.

Whitmore House. 3985 State Rte. 47 W, Bellefontaine 43311, tel. 937/592–4290. 2 doubles and 1 single room share bath. Air-conditioning, phone in 1 room, restaurant, library, garden, TV in library. $50; full breakfast, complimentary evening snacks. No credit cards.

OKLAHOMA

Northeastern Oklahoma

GRAHAM-CARROLL HOUSE ☙
501 N. 16th St., Muskogee 74401, tel. 918/683–0100 or 800/878–0167

Before Oklahoma was made a state, in 1906, Muskogee was far grander than "Tulsey Town" (Tulsa), 50 mi northwest. Muskogee was the center for commerce (cotton and oil) and the government policy headquarters for the five Native American tribes that were moved to Oklahoma from the southeastern United States 100 years previously. Today the old sandstone Agency building in Honor Heights Park houses the Five Civilized Tribes Museum, which exhibits artifacts and art from the Cherokee, Chickasaw, Choctaw, Seminole, and Creek tribes.

Sixteenth Street was once more commonly known as "Silk Stocking Avenue," where Muskogee's most fashionable and venerable citizens lived. Although paint now peels from some homes in this downtown neighborhood, the Graham-Carroll House, an 11-room mansion built with oil money, has been well maintained.

During the two years it took to build the house, the interior was thoroughly embellished. If a surface can be carved, polished, fluted, or scalloped, it is. Rooms with dark moldings and burnished hardwood floors hold carved mahogany furniture and plum upholstery. Innkeeper Linda Feickert makes a point, however, that she doesn't want guests to tiptoe around this ornate but sturdy 1935 Gothic Victorian.

Hand-cut marble fashions the foyer floor, and overhead, a chandelier sparkles with ropes of crystal. The Carroll Suite on the second floor is awash with '30s glamour, with green walls and a lavender bathroom; a 6-ft marble whirlpool tub set under stained-glass windows in the Honeymoon Suite overlooks roses and dahlias. Well-tended English gardens entice guests outdoors.

Linda serves breakfast in a glassed-in porch she calls the conservatory, where light shines in from the stained-glass windows she bought from the First Baptist Church. Her specialties are blueberry pancakes, omelets, and crepes. On weekends she prepares entrées such as Jamaican grilled shrimp, grilled salmon, and Chateaubriand. ♨ *6 suites. Air-conditioning, cable TVs, telephones; whirlpool bath in 5 suites; elevator. $80–$110; full breakfast. AE, D, DC, MC, V.*

INN AT WOODYARD FARMS ☙
Rte. 2 (Box 190), Pawhuska 74056, tel. 918/287–2699

The Tallgrass Prairie Preserve in Osage County is one of the largest remnants of the bluestem prairie that once stretched from the Gulf Coast through the Midwest. Cattle driven up the Chisholm Trail from Texas once grazed here; now bison nose through the wildflowers. The Inn at Woodyard Farms sits less than

6 mi away, on 75 acres of rolling hills dotted with yellow coreopsis, pale purple coneflowers, and cows ambling under the blackjack oaks. The agenda here, says Carol Maupin (who owns the inn with her sister, Nancy Woodyard), is to have no agenda other than watching the sun come up in a rocking chair on the porch, possibly visiting the sandstone Osage Tribal Museum, and then watching the sun go down from the porch's other side.

Carol can be a bit grand. Nothing ticks her off quite so much as to have someone assume that because she lives in rural Oklahoma she's a hick. "Honey," she says, "I've taken care of two presidents and a king." She also boasts of her culinary expertise: She was an apprentice to Helen Corbett, who in the 1950s and '60s reigned over the Zodiac Room at Neiman-Marcus in Dallas.

Like Helen, Carol makes food look and taste wonderful and pays no regard to fat and calories (unless requested to do so in advance). Breakfast may be ham steaks, eggs and green-chile grits, or eggs Benedict, and Carol's justly applauded biscuits.

The inn was built in vintage farmhouse style by a local high school carpentry class (Nancy is the school's superintendent) with wide-plank floors, a sandstone fireplace, and fanlight windows. The interior looks as if Carol refined not only her cooking but her decorating sense at Neiman-Marcus: The chairs are upholstered in lemony florals, the plaid sofas are deep, and the pumpkin-color breakfront holds a collection of Majolica tureens, platters, and bowls. The four bedrooms upstairs are fairly small, but everything is top drawer—silky sheets, bright floral bedspreads, antique armoires, and footed bowls holding chocolates. There are stacks of spy thrillers, novels, photography books, and everything Martha Stewart has touched. Only about an eighth of Carol's cookbook collection is on display in the baker's rack in the kitchen: Guests have been known to lug armfuls upstairs (followed by the inn's three cats) to read in bed like novels. A cautionary note: Summer can be searing in Oklahoma, especially on the prairie. △ *4 double rooms with baths. Air-conditioning, phones, cable TV/VCR in public area. $65; full breakfast. MC, V.*

OTHER CHOICES

Jarrett Farm Country Inn. 38009 US-75, Ramona 74061, tel. 918/371–1200. 11 suites. Wet bar and kitchenette in 2 suites, double whirlpool tub in 9 suites, fireplace in 9 suites, private patio off 4 suites, air-conditioning, TV/VCRs, restaurant, pool, outdoor hot tub, solarium. $145–$205; full breakfast. AE, MC, V.

RESERVATIONS SERVICE

Oklahoma Bed and Breakfast Association (766 DeBarr, Norman 73069, tel. 800/676-5522; listings only).

Central Oklahoma

THE MONTFORD INN ☞
322 West Tonhawa, Norman 73069, tel. 405/321–2200 or 800/321–8969, fax 405/321–8347

When Phyllis and Ron Murray built the Montford Inn in 1994, they intended the sprawling wooden house to have the feel of an early Oklahoma prairie-style farmhouse. But even Oklahoma Territory's most pampered residents didn't have switch-on gas fireplaces, jetted tubs, king-size beds, in-room coffee bars, or bathtubs with water jets.

The inn is named for Phyllis's ancestor Montford Johnson, a Chickasaw cattle rancher who was a chum of Jesse Chisholm. Family heirlooms are everywhere—Johnson's framed license to operate in Indian Territory hangs in the library and a Kiowa headdress, a gift to Johnson, hangs over the stairs. Much of the needlework was done by Ron's Danish grandmother.

Phyllis has a gift for imaginative juxtaposition: Upstairs, snowy curtains float from curtain rods made from elm and hackberry branches; and a collection of kachina dolls is displayed in a Victorian curio cabinet in the living room, where Oriental rugs mix with Navajo blankets, wingback chairs, and overstuffed sofas piled with pillows.

The inn's east wing has four eclectically furnished rooms, including two with private outdoor hot tubs and decks. Alma Mater pays homage to nearby University of Oklahoma, with a framed letter sweater, pennants, and vintage team photos; other rooms have sunny wicker and an 8-ft walnut headboard.

Upstairs, a Ponderosa-pine canopy bed, a lace-covered bonnet bed, and English hunting prints are among the varied furnishings. More secluded is the sole guest room on the west wing, which doesn't share a hallway with the other guest rooms; or the stand-alone, 1,000-square-ft cottage, Hidden Hollow. There are also two suites across the street that allow for privacy and slightly more independence. They have kitchenettes, living rooms, and two-person whirlpool baths. For mingling with other guests in the main house, the library off the main foyer has a woodburning fireplace and a collection of books and board games.

Breakfast is served around Phyllis's grandmother's walnut dining-room table or on tiny tables for two covered with garden-party cloths. Tonhawa Smoothies, a blend of yogurt, fruit, and juices, appear daily, along with such dishes as the Montford Sunrise, a savory blend of chiles, eggs, cheese, and grits, garnished with pansies. △ *10 rooms with baths, 5 suites. Air-conditioning, ceiling fans, phones, dataports, fireplaces, cable TV/VCR, clock radios, toiletries, irons and ironing boards; whirlpool tub in 8 rooms; outdoor hot tub and deck off 2 rooms; business facilities. $90–$195; full breakfast, morning coffee service, evening refreshments, freshly baked snacks. AE, D, MC, V.*

VICTORIAN ROSE ☞
415 E. Cleveland, Guthrie 73044, tel. 405/282-3928

To say that the Victorian Rose Bed and Breakfast in Guthrie is surrounded by history is no exaggeration: The 1894 Queen Anne-style house sits in the middle of 400 blocks of Victorian storefronts and residences (the largest urban area on the National Register of Historic Places).

The history of Guthrie is more aptly called a saga: The town became the territorial capital in 1889, when a land run opened the area to settlement. It was the most progressive city in the territory—the first to have lights and a Carnegie library—until statehood in 1910, when voters moved the state capital to Oklahoma City. For decades many local business owners and residents were too strapped for cash to remodel properly, so they simply covered things up—much to the delight of 1980s developers and preservationists, who found hundreds of stained-glass windows beneath plywood and original handblown light fixtures hanging above false ceilings.

The Victorian Rose, three blocks from the downtown business district, has its own treasures, like a working gas light fixture, polished oak floors and beveled windows. In the evenings, the inn literally glows—owner Foy Shahan makes Tiffany-style stained-glass lampshades and dozens of them light the inn, along with candles and oil lamps. Foy also makes the glass kaleidoscopes that rest on the marble-top table in the parlor.

All three of the inn's guest rooms are on the second floor. The most popular room, Victorian Dream, has a private balcony, a queen-size wrought-iron bed piled high with champagne-colored brocade bed coverings and pillows, and a huge rosy tiled bath with brass fixtures and a dressing table. Guests in the Victorian Promise room use a bath across the hall with a claw-foot tub. This room also has access to a private screened porch outfitted with a reading lamp and ceiling fan. Next door is the elegant 1920s Rose Bungalow, which is furnished in turn-of-the-century antiques and has a gas fireplace and whirlpool tub. The 1,400-square-ft, two-bedroom bungalow can sleep four, but it's also perfect for two who want to retreat. If the sequestered life suits you, breakfast can delivered to the bungalow in a basket.

Guests can usually be found relaxing on the patio in the side yard, where flowers and herbs bloom around a fountain, or on the wicker swing or rockers on the wraparound porch. As a foil to the carved mahogany and wicker found about the house are intriguing works of art, like a local artist's colored-pencil drawing of Cavalry soldiers and a Plains Indian scout.

But visual treats aren't the specialty of the house, according to Linda Shahan. "Guests come back for the breakfasts," she says. Linda once got a call from a bed-and-breakfast owner in Kentucky, who said one of her guests, who had stayed at the Victorian Rose, was craving Linda's banana crepes, and could she share the recipe. Also popular are gingerbread waffles, cheese muffins, and coddled eggs. Says Linda, "My guests leave here and go downtown to the antique stores to look for antique egg coddlers." △ *3 double rooms with baths, 1 bungalow (sleeps 4). Air-conditioning, TV/VCRS, turndown service; whirlpool and fireplace in bungalow. $69–$135; full breakfast. D, MC, V.*

OTHER CHOICES

Arcadian Inn Bed and Breakfast. 328 E. 1st St., Edmond 73034, tel. 405/348–6347 or 800/299–6347. 6 double rooms with baths, 2 suites. Air-conditioning; TV/VCR; whirlpool tubs for two; robes; chocolates; fireplace in 4 rooms. $75–$170; full breakfast, dinner and private candlelight breakfast available. AE, D, MC, V.

Cutting Garden Bed and Breakfast. 927 W. Boyd St., Norman 73069, tel. 405/329–4522. 3 double rooms with baths. Air-conditioning, cable TVs, phones. $75–$95; full breakfast. AE, D, MC, V.

Holmberg House. 766 Debarr St., Norman 73069, tel. 405/321–6221. 4 double rooms with baths. Air-conditioning, cable TV, whirlpool tub in 2 rooms. $65–$85; full breakfast. AE, D, MC, V.

RESERVATIONS SERVICE

Oklahoma Bed and Breakfast Association (766 DeBarr, Norman 73069, tel. 800/676-5522; listings only).

OREGON

South Coast

CHETCO RIVER INN ❦
21202 High Prairie Rd., Brookings 97415, tel. 541/670–1645 or 800/327–2688

Seventeen slow miles inland from Brookings, the Chetco River Inn lies beyond the reach of pavement and utility lines. Propane-generated electricity, gas lighting, and a cell phone provide the necessary modern comforts, and the contemporary design of the structure is anything but rough-and-ready. Long popular with fishermen—the crystal-clear Chetco, just outside the front door, is noted for its steelhead and Chinook salmon runs—the sublimely peaceful setting recommends itself to birders, hikers, and stressed city dwellers looking for a place to unwind.

Broad covered porches, cross-ventilating windows, and deep-green marble floors keep the inn cool during those occasional hot days of summer, when you can lounge in shaded hammocks or bob in the river in inner tubes. During the evenings, everyone gathers to talk in the airy, vaulted-ceiling common room furnished with Oriental carpets, leather couch, caned captain's chairs, and Chippendale dining ensemble.

Upstairs are tall shelves of books and games on the banistered landing outside the guest rooms. The rooms themselves, named after the most common of the many trees outside, are furnished with an eclectic mix of antiques, wicker, fishing creels, duck decoys, and reproduction brass and iron bedsteads. Myrtle and Oak look out onto the surrounding woods, and Alder and Willow overlook the river. An overflow room that opens onto a private bath can be used by families or a group of friends.

Your best dining option is Sandra's multicourse dinners, which are available by advance notice. Featuring fresh local ingredients, the menu might include smoked salmon pâté, orange-carrot soup with Grand Marnier, grilled game hen, and homemade ice cream. It's a good bet that you'll want to skip lunch after indulging in the ample breakfast (included in the tariff), but Sandra can also pack a lunch for your outing if you prefer. ⏳ *4 double rooms with baths. Portable phone, badminton, darts, horseshoes, swimming holes, nature trails, deep-sea charters or fishing guides by arrangement, fishing packages. $115–$135; full breakfast, afternoon refreshments, lunch and dinner available. MC, V. No smoking.*

CLIFF HOUSE ❦
Yaquina John Point, Adahi Rd. (Box 436), Waldport 97394, tel. 541/563–2506, fax 541/563–4393

This 1932 gable-on-hip-roof house, on Yaquina John Point in the coastal town of Waldport, is perhaps the closest you'll come on the Oregon coast to the Smithsonian's attic, with pieces by Steuben, Lalique, Tiffany, Dresden, and Rosenthal among the amazing abundance of objects here. Elaborate lead-glass chandeliers contrast—not unpleasantly—with knotty pine and cedar paneling, modern skylights, and an enormous river-rock fireplace. The setting is spectacular: the Alsea River winds from the graceful Alsea Bay Bridge to the Pacific just below the point, giving way to rolling green surf along endless white beaches.

Each of the four guest rooms reflects the romantic whims of owner Gabrielle Duvall. In the bedrooms, you will find potbellied wood-burning stoves; a profusion of fresh-cut flowers; trays of sherry and chocolates; fluffy down comforters; and mounds of pillows on brass, sleigh, or four-poster rice beds. The Bridal Suite, with a positively royal Louis XV gilt and ice-blue velvet bedroom set, and mirrored bathroom with two-person shower and whirlpool tub overlooking the ocean, is by far the most opulent chamber. In the Alsea, an extra-high bed gives a view of the water even when your head is on the pillow. Terry cloth robes and sandals are supplied for the short trip from your room to the large hot tub or sauna on the broad sundeck overlooking your ocean.

A run on the beach below or a vigorous game of croquet is a good way to work off the large morning meal, an elegant affair served at the black lacquer table on fine china with silver or gold flatware and plenty of fresh flowers. Gabby is happy to arrange a variety of romantic interludes—including catered dinners, sunset horseback rides, or champagne limousine drives into the nearby mountains. ♠ *4 double rooms with baths. Cable TV/VCR, individual heat control in rooms. Wood-burning stoves in some rooms, whirlpool in suite. Masseuse, hot tub, sauna. $120–$245; full breakfast, catered meals available. D, MC, V. No smoking, 2-night minimum on weekends, 3-night minimum on holidays. Closed Nov.–Jan.*

HECETA LIGHTHOUSE BED AND BREAKFAST ☙
92072 Hwy. 101 S, Yachats 97498, tel. 541/547–3696

Visitors to Heceta Head, a windswept cape south of Yachats, have a rare opportunity to encounter Pacific Northwest history face-to-face: Mike Korgan, who operates the Heceta Lighthouse Bed and Breakfast with his wife, Carol, is the former disc jockey who produced the Kingsmen's legendary "Louie, Louie." The two main attractions here, however, are the light station, one of the Oregon coast's most photogenic landmarks, and the inn, an 1893 Queen Anne that once housed the assistant keepers. Back when the light needed intensive maintenance and Florence, the nearest town, was a day's journey away, there was a small community living in two houses on the cape; one has since been torn down, and the other houses the Korgans and their three guest rooms.

The rooms, sparely and tastefully furnished with antiques, are quiet and well lit and have terrific views—but there is ample reason to spend as little time in them as possible. Trails lead over the cape and down to Devil's Elbow State Park on the water, and park volunteers give tours of the lighthouse. Guests can sit on the spacious, south-facing porch and watch storms and birds (including the half-dozen species of hummingbirds that visit the feeder) or just take in the unbeatable view. Nearby are abundant opportunities to explore tidal pools and observe sea lions and harbor seals.

Breakfast is a major event with up to nine courses, including exotic fruits, homemade bread, local salmon, fruit crepes, asparagus frittata, roasted garlic and artichoke sausages, and much more. For many years before they came to run the inn for the U.S. Forest Service, the Korgans, certified executive chefs, operated a popular Portland restaurant called the Strudel House, and they've brought its reputation for hearty and filling fare with them. At night, some say, a long-time guest comes calling: There have been many reports of a resident ghost, who goes by the name of Rue. ♨ *1 double room with bath, 2 doubles share bath. $115–$145; full breakfast. MC, V. No smoking.*

KITTIWAKE ☙
95368 Hwy. 101, Yachats 97498, tel. 541/547–4470

Joseph and Brigette Sweze swapped one coast for another when they moved from Miami to Yachats to build their contemporary oceanfront bed-and-break-fast in 1993. Brigette, a German-born former fashion designer, grew up in Europe and visited pensions when she traveled the countryside. Someday, she dreamt, she would own an inn of her own. When Joseph retired from the Air Force and from teaching business management, they resolved to fulfill her dream, and the pair were off and running.

This very sweet couple built their guest rooms with comfort and scenic views in mind, and they strive to accommodate both guests who want privacy and those who prefer to gather and chat at the picture windows in the airy common room. Firm beds with carved wooden headboards face windows and glazed doors that open onto decks overlooking the pounding surf; big bathrooms have whirlpool baths to further encourage relaxation. The 2½-acre grounds have been left in a natural state to attract deer, birds, and butterflies, and there are tidal pools to explore just below the bluff behind the house. Rubber boots, windbreakers, kites, beach chairs, coolers, and more are provided so that you can really enjoy the setting. Spectacular scenery aside, some guests have been known to return just for Brigette's ample German breakfasts. ♨ *3 double rooms with baths. Beach and rain gear, beach trail. $125–$140; full or Continental breakfast, complimentary coffee, tea, and cookies. AE, D, MC, V. No smoking, 2-night minimum on weekends and holidays.*

SEA QUEST ☙
95354 Hwy. 101, Yachats 97498, tel. 541/547–3782 or 800/341–4878, fax 541/547–3719

When Elaine Ireland and George Rozsa bought this contemporary cedar-shingle-and-glass home on a low coastal bluff outside Yachats, they remodeled it to create a romantic seaside retreat. They installed five guest rooms, a lounge, and a rounded entry on the ground floor, with a roomy kitchen open to the main living area above. A round gravel driveway was added to the property, but otherwise the grounds have been left in their natural state, preserving the habitat for the many birds in this area.

Elaine describes the decor as "eclectic, early garage sale," but her treasure trove of fine antique furniture and accent pieces would be the envy of any antiques hound. A pair of wooden skis and a weathered snowshoe hang over the drift-wood mantel of the massive fireplace, competing for attention with the intriguing geodes, coral, and polished stones used as accents in the brickwork.

Wall colors coordinate with valances, bed linens, and mounds of pillows on queen-size beds in the guest rooms, each equipped with a whirlpool bath and a private entrance. The hosts are friendly and cheerful. Their L-shape kitchen island becomes a buffet each morning, filled with platters of seasonal fruit, fresh-baked goods, hot entrées such as sautéed apples and sausages and fluffy quiches, and a large bowl of Elaine's homemade granola. You can dine out on the deck or at smartly set tables in the great room, protected from ocean breezes.

Both the deck and the large picture windows inside the house are excellent vantage points from which to experience one of this inn's special attractions: It's not at all unusual to see whales pass by fairly close to shore during their twice-yearly migrations between Baja California and Alaska. △ *4 double rooms with baths. $140–$175; full breakfast, evening snacks and beverages. D, MC, V. No smoking, 2-night minimum on weekends, 3-night minimum on holidays.*

TU TU TUN LODGE ✆

96550 N. Bank Rogue, Gold Beach 97444, tel. 541/247–6664 or 800/864–6357, fax 541/247–0672

Fine-dining options in the tiny coastal town of Gold Beach are few, but follow the Rogue River 7 mi inland and your culinary prayers will be answered at Tu Tu Tun (pronounced "too tootin") Lodge. Owners Dirk and Laurie Van Zante, two of Oregon's most gracious innkeepers, preside over cocktails and hors d'oeuvres as you relax on the piazza, enjoying the breathtaking river scenery. Then it's on to a multicourse, fixed-price dinner that often features barbecued Chinook salmon or prime rib accompanied by a superior selection of wines. During the busy high season (May–Oct.), there are only four spaces at the table for nonguests at breakfast and dinner (lunch is for guests only), so reservations are essential.

Named after the local riverbank-dwelling tribe, and surrounded by an abundance of wildlife dwelling in the old-growth timber and the rugged river, Tu Tu Tun is an ideal retreat. In the evenings, you might sit near the big stone fireplace in the modern, open-beam cedar inn watching for the pair of bald eagles that fly down over the river at sunset. At "O'dark hundred" (the Van Zantes' expression for daybreak), avid anglers are down at the dock seeking the Rogue's mighty steelhead and salmon.

The two-story wing of riverside guest rooms is motel-like in structure only. Named after favorite fishing holes on the Rogue River, each room features individual artwork and appointments; some have fireplaces, other have outdoor soaking tubs, and all have wonderful river views from a balcony or patio and thoughtful touches such as binoculars for wildlife viewing, fine toiletries, and fresh flowers. The cedar-lined, two-bedroom River House shares the great view and is equipped with a kitchen, as are the spacious suites in the main lodge and the charming, three-bedroom Garden House next to the orchard. △ *16 double rooms with baths, 2 housekeeping suites, 1 2-bedroom housekeeping unit, 1 3-bedroom housekeeping unit. Restaurant, bar, TV in suites, conference facilities, heated lap pool, 4-hole pitch-and-putt, horseshoe court, nature trails, jet-boat tour pickup from dock, guided fishing, complimentary use of fishing gear. $130–$310, with deeply discounted low-season rates; breakfast extra, dinner available May–Oct. MC, V. No smoking. Main lodge and restaurant closed last Sun. in Oct.–last Fri. in Apr.*

ZIGGURAT ✆

95330 Hwy. 101, Yachats 97498, tel. 541/547–3925

An ancient architectural form in a thoroughly modern incarnation, Ziggurat rises out of the tidal grasslands of the Siuslaw River 7 mi south of Yachats. This terraced, step-pyramid-shape inn, hand-built with native salt-silvered cedar siding, is without question the most unusual member of Oregon's B&B fraternity. Owner Mary Lou Cavendish soon realized that the interest the pyramid generated would bring a steady stream of visitors and that she and partner Irving Tebor had more than enough room to share, so she opened her amazing home as a bed-and-breakfast after construction was completed in 1987. Come here for the uniqueness of the structure, not for the company of the innkeepers, who prefer to leave guests to themselves.

Inside, an eclectic collection of original artwork—from Indonesian *wayang* puppets to Buddhist paintings from Nepal—and specially commissioned wooden furniture complement the house's sleek and ultramodern lines, stainless-steel trim, black carpeting, slatelike tiles, smooth white walls, and tinted triangular windows. On the ground floor, a narrow solarium surrounds two guest suites that share a living room–library, complete with microwave, sink, and refrigerator. The East Room has a modern canopy bed in elm and a sauna in the bathroom. The West Room has a 27-ft-long glass wall, slate tile floor, mirrored ceiling above the bed, and a glass-block shower separating the bedroom from the bathroom. A library nook, living room with grand piano and wood-burning stove, and dining room, kitchen, and bathroom with steam shower share space on the second floor.

A brisk walk to the beach below the house is a good follow-up to the large breakfast served on one of the two glass-enclosed sunporches. Ziggurat is within easy reach of the area's many coastal pleasures, including Cape Perpetua, Sea Lion Caves, Strawberry Hill Wayside, and the boutiques and restaurants of tiny Yachats.

▲ *1 double room with detached bath, 2 suites. Piano, library. $125–$140; full breakfast. No credit cards. No smoking, 2-night minimum on holidays.*

OTHER CHOICES

Coos Bay Manor. 955 S. 5th St., Coos Bay 97420, tel. 541/269–1224 or 800/269–1224. 3 double rooms with baths, 2 doubles share bath. Feather beds, robes, and coffeemaker in rooms. Bicycles. $75–$100; full breakfast. D, MC, V. No smoking. Well-behaved pets welcome.

Floras Lake House by the Sea. 92870 Boice Cope Rd., Langlois 97450, tel. and fax 541/348–2573. 4 double rooms with baths. Sauna, windsurfing classes and equipment, boats, bicycles. $100–$130; Continental-plus breakfast. D, MC, V. No smoking. Closed mid-Nov.–mid-Feb.

Home by the Sea. 444 Jackson, Box 606-F, Port Orford 97465, tel. 541/332–2855. 2 double rooms with baths. Cable TV. $85–$95; full breakfast. MC, V. No smoking.

Inn at Nesika Beach. 33026 Nesika Rd., Gold Beach 97444, tel. 541/247–6434. 4 double rooms with baths. Fireplace and whirlpool bath in 3 rooms. $100–$130; full breakfast. No credit cards. No smoking.

Johnson House. 216 Maple St., Florence 97439, tel. 541/997–8000 or 800/768–9488, fax 541/997–2364. 2 double rooms with baths, 3 doubles share 2 baths, 1 cottage suite. Individual heat control. Croquet, boccie. $95–$125; full breakfast. D, MC, V. No smoking.

The Lighthouse. 650 Jetty Rd. (Box 24), Bandon 97411, tel. 541/347–9316. 5 double rooms with baths. Cable TV in two rooms and common room, whirlpool bath in loft room. $90–$145; full breakfast. MC, V. No smoking. Closed July 4.

Serenity. 5985 Yachats River Rd., Yachats 97498, tel. 541/547–3813. 3 suites. Refrigerator in rooms. Nature trails. $99–$145; full breakfast. MC, V. No smoking.

RESERVATIONS SERVICE
Northwest Bed and Breakfast (1067 Hanover Court S, Salem 97302, tel. 503/370–9033, fax 503/316–9118).

Southern Oregon, Including Ashland

ANTIQUE ROSE INN 🐚
91 Gresham St., Ashland 97520, tel. 541/482–6285 or 888/282–6285

Listed on the National Historic Register, this three-story Queen Anne Victorian encrusted with gingerbread trim was a catalog home shipped by rail car from Philadelphia and constructed on a high hill in Ashland in 1888. Built by Henry Carter, who established the first electric company in the region, this dream house was one of the first homes in Ashland to have electric lights. Notice the original fixtures and switches, the amazing built-in hutch in the dining room, and the numerous stained-glass windows throughout.

Lovingly restored by native Oregonian Kathy Buffington, the home features three guest rooms furnished in period antiques and reproductions. Mahogany, named for its paneling, has an old tin ceiling and a claw-foot tub in the bathroom. Rose has a large four-poster bed, a fireplace, and a cozy balcony. Kathy recently refurbished a two-bedroom cottage next door, adding lots of romantic amenities (including a whirlpool bath, a fireplace, and a cedar sauna). All come with terry cloth robes, fresh flowers, and down comforters.

Hearty breakfasts often feature lemon puffs with raspberry sauce, gingerbread pancakes with lemon sauce, or asparagus crab quiche. But nothing beats Kathy's melt-in-your-mouth cinnamon rolls. △ *3 double rooms with baths, 1 2-bedroom housekeeping cottage. Fireplace in 1 room; kitchen, fireplace, whirlpool tub, and sauna in cottage. $117–$159; full breakfast, afternoon refreshments. AE, MC, V. No smoking, 2-night minimum weekends June–Sept. and holidays.*

LITHIA SPRINGS INN 🐚
2165 W. Jackson Rd., Ashland 97520, tel. 541/482–7128 or 800/482–7128, fax 541/488–1645

Off the first highway exit for Ashland, 1½ mi north of downtown, this sprawling, gray, Cape Cod–style inn offers an alternative to the froufrou, fancy B&Bs typical of this southern Oregon town. As the name suggests, the focus here is on the hot spring on the 8-acre property, which supplies the inn's water. The pungent, hot mineral water is piped into whirlpool baths in all but two of the large, comfortably furnished rooms.

Innkeeper Duane Smith's sense of humor is evident on the painted walls in the common areas; playful touches here and there suddenly appear to the eye and bring a smile and a laugh. These trompe l'oeil touches are echoed throughout the rooms, too.

The house, constructed in 1993, is still a work in progress, showing signs of newness and continued growth everywhere. Newly landscaped gardens, ponds, and meandering paths surround the inn. Twelve of the 14 rooms and suites have whirlpool baths, and several also include electric fireplaces. The Emperor's Room has one wall covered with an antique Chinese screen and a faux-finish bathroom called the Throne Room. One of the room's first guests interpreted the screen's story; Duane keeps a written copy in the room for other guests to enjoy.

Breakfast is served in the common room–dining room and features Starbucks coffee, papaya scones, fresh poppy seed bread, and a full country breakfast. △ *10 double rooms with baths, 4 suites. Mini-refrigerator, wet bar, CD player, fireplace, and whirlpool baths in suites and some rooms. Bicycle storage, bicycle trail. $85–$195; full breakfast. AE, D, MC, V. No smoking, 2-night minimum on weekends.*

PEERLESS HOTEL ☞
243 4th St., Ashland 97520, tel. 541/488–1082 or 800/460–8758

It took the creative eye of proprietress Crissy Barnett to envision a classic little hotel when looking at an abandoned brick boarding house in the heart of Ashland's railroad district. The rail workers who lived in the building at the turn of the century would be stunned by Crissy's extensive restoration and loving revitalization.

The building, "almost" condemned, had been vacant for years when Crissy bought it in 1991. After more than two years of restoration work, the structure was placed on the National Register of Historic Places.

Six intimate suites are filled with luxurious antiques, hand-painted murals, and rich bedding, draperies, and Oriental carpets. Stand-out rooms are Suite 7, draped in cotton damask and chenille and furnished with West Indies–style furniture, and Suite 3, with its Aesthetics Movement bedroom suit and his and hers clawfoot tubs in the oversize bathroom.

The full breakfast served in the parlor or in the back garden sometimes features such tasty dishes as marionberry crepes. Crissy recently opened the Peerless Restaurant, luring executive chef Daniel Durfort away from Michel's at the Colony Surf at Diamond Head in Honolulu. With all the wonderful things Crissy has done here, it's a safe bet that her incredible little hotel is fast becoming one of the ultimate addresses in Ashland. △ *4 double rooms with baths, 2 suites. Air-conditioning, phone, and TV (on request) in rooms, whirlpool bath in 3 rooms. Health club access. $95–$175; full breakfast, evening refreshments. AE, MC, V. No smoking.*

PINE MEADOW INN ☞
1000 Crow Rd., Merlin 97532, tel. and fax 541/471–6277 or tel. 800/554–0806

Picture a large midwestern farmhouse in a rural setting, far enough removed from the bustle of major towns in the Rogue Valley to promote an atmosphere of respite and renewal, and you see the charm of Pine Meadow Inn. Innkeepers Nancy and Maloy Murdock came to Oregon from the San Francisco Bay area in 1991 with the express desire of having their own bed-and-breakfast inn. Together they cleared the land and built Pine Meadow. The inn, the evident testimony of a true investment of heart and soul, opened in 1993.

The country-quaint rooms are furnished with turn-of-the-century antiques that are comfortable rather than formal. Homey, hand-stitched quilts and fresh flowers add a warm touch. Two rooms—Willow and Laurel—have cozy built-in window seats.

There are plenty of comfortable chairs on the wraparound porch and terraced garden deck, the perfect places to watch the shenanigans of bunnies, squirrels, deer, and birds parading through the property. There are also nature trails winding through the conifer forest, lovely gardens, and a koi pond to explore after enjoying a hearty breakfast featuring home-baked breads and the herbs, vegetables, and fruits the Murdocks grow themselves. △ *4 double rooms with baths. Air-conditioning and turndown service. $80–$110; full breakfast. D, MC, V. No smoking.*

WINCHESTER COUNTRY INN ☜
35 S. 2nd St., Ashland 97520, tel. 541/488–1113 or 800/972–4991, fax 541/488–4604

Of the many Victorian bed-and-breakfasts in Ashland, this 1886 Queen Anne is the only one with a restaurant, and it's the closest to the Shakespeare Festival theaters as well. Painstakingly renovated by Michael and Laurie Gibbs during the early 1980s and listed on the National Register of Historic Places, the Winchester has established a reputation as one of the finer dining spots in Ashland.

The decor of the guest rooms maintains the period style of the house without Victorian clutter. A mixture of American Colonial reproductions and antiques, as well as Rococo Revival and Eastlake reproductions, including tall-mirrored wardrobes and brass-and-iron or heavy, carved wooden bedsteads, adds distinction, while contemporary cushioned chairs and wall-to-wall carpeting make it comfortable. There are many nice touches in the main house, such as a hand-painted porcelain sink set into an antique dresser, which serves as a vanity in the bedrooms, and scented salts in the attached bathroom for luxurious soaking in the deep claw-foot tub. A crystal decanter of sherry and sinfully rich truffles on a tray on the dresser make a late-night snack irresistible.

Favorite rooms include the Sylvan Room, in sunny shades of peach, and the creamy-blue Garden Room, both of which have delightful bay sitting areas overlooking the terraced gardens. The Sunset Room has its own balcony view of the treetops of downtown Ashland. Rooms at the basement level have garden patios or small decks as compensation. The private cottage has two beautiful luxury suites, and the Victorian and its carriage house next door have a large guest library, four more suites, and five double rooms (one of which is accessible to wheelchair users), to add to Winchester's array of accommodations.

In winter and spring, the Gibbses offer a variety of special packages, from murder-mystery weekends to a popular Dickens Christmas Festival tie-in. △ *12 double rooms with baths, 6 suites. Air-conditioning in rooms, phone, TV/VCR, fireplace, whirlpool tub, and stereo in suites. Restaurant, library, gift shop. $95–$200; full breakfast. AE, D, MC, V. No smoking.*

OTHER CHOICES

Arden Forest Inn. 261 W. Hersey St., Ashland 97520, tel. 541/488–1496 or 800/460–3912. 4 double rooms with baths, 1 2-bedroom suite. Air-conditioning in rooms. Horseshoe court. $95–$130; full breakfast. AE, MC, V. No smoking.

Bayberry Inn Bed and Breakfast. 438 N. Main St., Ashland 97520, tel. 541/488–1252 or 800/795–1252. 3 double rooms with baths, 2 rooms with baths down the hall. Air-conditioning. $100; full breakfast, afternoon refreshments. MC, V. No smoking.

Chanticleer Inn. 120 Gresham St., Ashland 97520, tel. and fax 541/482–1919 or 800/898–1950. 6 double rooms with baths. Phone and climate control in rooms. Stocked refrigerator, TV. $85–$170; full breakfast, evening refreshments. AE, MC, V. No smoking, 2-night minimum on weekends June–Sept.

Country Willows Bed and Breakfast Inn. 1313 Clay St., Ashland 97520, tel. 541/488–1590 or 800/945–5697, fax 541/488–1611. 5 double rooms with baths, 3 housekeeping suites, 1 2-bedroom housekeeping cottage. Air-conditioning, phone, TV-VCR, and robes in rooms, fireplace in 2 rooms, whirlpool bath in 1 room. Pool, hot tub, mountain and road bicycles, video library, gift shop. $90–$175; full breakfast, evening refreshments. AE, MC, V. No smoking.

Flery Manor. 2000 Jumpoff Joe Creek Rd., Grants Pass 97526, tel. 541/476–3591, fax 541/371–2303. 2 double rooms with baths, 1 suite. Air-conditioning and robes in rooms. Nature trails, croquet, horseshoes. $75–$125; full breakfast, afternoon refreshments. MC, V. No smoking.

Jacksonville Inn. 175 E. California St. (Box 359), Jacksonville 97530, tel. 541/899–1900 or 800/321–9344, fax 541/899–1373. 8 double rooms with baths, 3 housekeeping cottages. Air-conditioning, mini-refrigerator, phone, and TV in rooms; whirlpool bath in 1 room; kitchenette, steam sauna, and whirlpool tub in cottages. Restaurant, bar, bicycles, wine shop, conference facilities. $115–$245; full breakfast. AE, D, DC, MC, V. No smoking.

Morical House Garden Inn. 668 N. Main St., Ashland 97520, tel. 541/482–2254 or 800/208–9869, fax 541/482–1775. 5 double rooms with baths, 2 housekeeping suites. Air-conditioning and phone in rooms. Badminton, croquet. $110–$160; full breakfast, afternoon refreshments. MC, V. No smoking, 2-night minimum on weekends Mar.–Oct.

Mt. Ashland Inn. 505 Mt. Ashland Rd., Ashland 97520, tel. and fax 541/482–8707 or tel. 800/830–8707. 2 double rooms with baths, 3 suites. Whirlpool tub and fireplace in 2 suites. TV/VCR and wet bar in meeting room, ski storage room, snowshoes, sleds, mountain bikes, cross-country skis. $99–$190; full breakfast. AE, D, MC, V. No smoking, 2-night minimum on weekends June–Oct. and holidays.

Romeo Inn. 295 Idaho St., Ashland 97520, tel. 541/488–0884 or 800/915–8899, fax 541/488–0817. 4 double rooms with baths, 1 suite, 1 housekeeping suite. Air-conditioning and phone in rooms. Library, pool, hot tub. $130–$180; full breakfast, afternoon refreshments, bedtime treats. MC, V. No smoking, 2-night minimum June–Oct. and weekends Mar.–Oct.

Touvelle House. 455 N. Oregon St. (Box 1891), Jacksonville 97530, tel. 541/899–8938 or 800/846–8422, fax 541/899–8938. 6 double rooms with baths. Cable TV in library, conference facilities, pool, hot tub, bicycles. $80–$155; full breakfast. AE, D, DC, MC, V. No smoking.

Woods House. 333 N. Main St., Ashland 97520, tel. 541/488–1598 or 800/435–8260, fax 541/482–8027. 6 double rooms with baths. Air-conditioning. $110–$120; full breakfast, afternoon refreshments. MC, V. No smoking, 2-night minimum June–Oct.

RESERVATIONS SERVICES

Ashland's B&B Clearinghouse (Box 1376, Ashland 97520, tel. 541/488–0338 or 800/588–0338). **Ashland's Bed and Breakfast Network** (Box 1051, Ashland 97520, tel. 800/944–0329). **Ashland/Jacksonville B&B Guild Reservations** (tel. 800/983–4667). **Bed & Breakfast Reservations, Oregon** (2321 N.E. 28th Ave., Portland 97212, tel. 503/287–4704 or 800/786–9476). **Northwest Bed and Breakfast** (1067 Hanover Court S, Salem 97302, tel. 503/370–9033, fax 503/316–9118).

Willamette Valley, Including Eugene

CAMPBELL HOUSE ✿
252 Pearl St., Eugene 97401, tel. 541/343–1119 or 800/264–2519, fax 541/343–2258

Innkeepers Myra and Roger Plant first saw this 8,000-square-ft 1892 Victorian mansion, one of the oldest buildings in Eugene, on a bike ride. Then vacant, it was almost totally obscured by shrubs, trees, and blackberry vines. After years of working to convince the heirs of the original owner to sell, they remade the place from the inside out, adding new oak floors, brass fittings, and turn-of-the-century–style moldings. The dining room and the library were refurbished and the corner sinks in bathrooms saved.

A long drive brings you past green grounds dotted with rhododendrons to the entrance, at the back of the house. The back patio and gazebo, where local wine is served in the afternoon, is lined with hanging, flowering plants. It's a lovely spot, although the scene deserves better than the white plastic lawn furniture provided. The guest rooms, though, make you quickly forget about lawn furniture. Each of the rooms is unique, although most have a vaguely English country look; some have views of the city and the Cascade Mountains. A new outbuilding, designed to match the style of the house, features luxury rooms and suites with fireplaces and whirlpool tubs.

One drawback of the Campbell House is its proximity to the train tracks, which are a few blocks downhill. Evenings can be a bit noisy, but the Plants provide earplugs.

Mornings begin with coffee on a tray outside your room and evolve into a full meal downstairs. Favorite entrées include Belgian waffles and crustless quiches. If possible, sit in the sunny library overlooking town. ⚴ *16 double rooms with baths, 2 suites. Phone, modem line, TV/VCR in rooms. Fax and photocopy service, conference facilities. $79–$379; full breakfast. AE, D, MC, V. No smoking.*

EXCELSIOR INN ✿
754 E. 13th Ave., Eugene 97401, tel. 541/342–6963 or 800/321–6963, fax 541/342–1417

Built in 1912, the Excelsior building spent most of this century as home to a campus fraternity, but its ambience these days is a far cry from *Animal House.* What was to become the Excelsior Inn began as a small café, which with increasing popularity gradually took over the entire ground floor. The upper floors followed in 1995, when they were changed from student housing into guest accommodations. Chef and innkeeper Maurizio Paparo cut no corners in outfitting the rooms along the lines of a sophisticated European inn; marble-and-tile bathrooms and cherry-wood doors, moldings, and furniture are throughout, and some rooms have hardwood floors, arched windows, and vaulted ceilings.

Guest rooms, named after European composers, range from the small, quiet Schumann, with a wood floor, shower, and queen bed, to Bach, a large corner room with high ceilings, sitting area, whirlpool bath, and courtyard view. All rooms are equipped to serve the visiting professor or businessperson as well as the casual traveler, with writing desks and modem lines.

The modest café that started it all is now one of Eugene's best dining establishments, with a full-scale restaurant and bar. The use of fresh local ingredients makes for seasonal changes in the menu, which is inflected with the forms and flavors of Paparo's native Italy: pastas, gnocchi, or grilled fish with *puttanesca* sauce (a spicy combination of tomatoes, onions, olives, capers, and oregano) are good choices. The wine list is excellent, and European-trained pastry chef Milka Babich prepares exquisite pastries and other desserts. When the rain abates in the spring, the front terrace allows for alfresco dining. ♨ *14 double rooms with baths. Phone, modem line, TV/VCR in rooms, whirlpool bath in 2 rooms. Conference facilities. $69–$180; full breakfast. AE, D, DC, MC, V. No smoking.*

HANSON COUNTRY INN ▧

795 S.W. Hanson St., Corvallis 97333, tel. 541/752–2919

In 1928 Jeff Hanson built this rotund Dutch Colonial on a high knoll overlooking the rolling Willamette Valley as the headquarters for his prospering poultry-breeding ranch. Here, in the egg house opposite the main house, he developed his world-famous strain of White Leghorn chickens. After Hanson died, the house stood empty for 13 years. In 1987 it was purchased by Patricia Covey, a friendly Californian looking for escape from the Bay area. With plenty of polish and elbow grease, Patricia was able to restore the grandeur of the house's unique features, including the carefully laid honeycomb tile work in the bathrooms and the spindle room divider and banister, both made of New Zealand gumwood carved by local craftsmen.

A baby grand piano, assorted sculptures, and a selection of Patricia's own paintings bring understated elegance to the great living room with its massive central fireplace. Sun pours through tall windowpanes, brightening the cozy reading nook where a plump easy chair sits beside floor-to-ceiling bookcases. The sunporch, with sparkling stained-glass windows and casual rattan furniture, looks onto a terraced garden with a stone fountain and a white vine arbor.

One suite has a lovingly polished four-poster bed, an attached sitting room, and a private veranda overlooking a gentle slope to the valley below. The largest room, a favorite of wedding couples for its romantic box-canopy bed, has a sitting alcove and windows on three sides—providing views of the valley, the terraced garden, and the quiet pasture behind the house. All rooms are appointed with 1920s American furniture and bed linens imported from England. The two-bedroom cottage with hardwood floors, iron bedsteads, and down comforters is perfect for families needing space and privacy.

Patricia reveals her cooking talent with her abundant breakfast, which starts out with teas and coffee, juice, fresh fruit, and freshly baked bite-size muffins. From there, move on to such treats as apple crepes, French toast, or "Elliott's pancakes," with cottage cheese and marionberry preserves, recently featured in *Bon Appétit*. ♨ *3 suites, 1 2-bedroom housekeeping cottage. Phone, cable TV in rooms. $75–$125; full breakfast. AE, D, DC, MC, V. No smoking.*

HARRISON HOUSE ▧

2310 N.W. Harrison Blvd., Corvallis 97330, tel. 541752–6248 or 800/233–6248

Maria and Charlie Tomlinson are refugees from Connecticut corporate culture who moved to Corvallis to take over the 1939 Dutch Colonial inn that for 50 years was home to noted geologist I. S. Allison and his family. The move was a good one, not only for them but also for their guests, as they have proven to be consummate innkeepers.

From the welcome announcement to the thank-you note that follows your stay, the Tomlinsons provide a rare level of hospitality and service. Amenities include fruit and snacks available throughout the day, tastings of local wines, stationery, a butler's basket of toiletries, morning newspapers, and evening turndown service. The immaculately clean house is furnished with Chippendale- and Williamsburg-style antiques, and the four guest rooms come with extra pillows, blankets, and towels. Breakfasts, which feature regional and seasonal ingredients, include a fruit dish and any one of a wide range of entrées, from French toast and Belgian waffles to frittatas and souflées.

Harrison House's location, just a few blocks from the Oregon State University campus, makes it a favorite with visiting parents and professors. Maria and Charlie provide bicycles for touring campus or downtown. Nearby attractions include wineries, Peavy Arboretum, and Mary's Peak, the highest mountain in the Coast Range and a favorite with day hikers. △ *2 doubles with bath, 2 doubles share bath. Phone, modem line in rooms. Piano, conference facilities, bicycles. $60–$80; full breakfast, afternoon refreshments. AE, D, MC, V. No smoking.*

OVAL DOOR BED AND BREAKFAST ☞
988 Lawrence St., Eugene 97401, tel. 541/683–3160 or 800/882–3160, fax 541/485–5339

This 2½-story, pitch-roof house with a wraparound porch was built in 1990 but matches the surrounding homes from the '20s and '30s in this centrally located, older neighborhood near the University of Oregon and the Hult Center for the Performing Arts in Eugene. A whimsical purple door hints at the unconventional things to come.

Inside is a collection of centuries-old antiques and comfortable, modern American furniture. The dining room has an 1860 Eastlake walnut dining table and floral prints filling one wall; another wall has glass doors that open onto a broad wraparound porch with cushioned chairs and a swing for resting beneath the rustling leaves of the shade trees.

Guest rooms are furnished with a mixture of antique pieces and reproductions; an open steamer trunk that serves as a dresser in one room is especially striking. Extra room touches include sparkling water and glasses on doily-covered trays, fresh and dried flower arrangements, candles and books of poetry, a choice of pillows (down, poly, or orthopedic), robes, and a selection of current paperbacks that you are free to take when you leave. The cozy, two-person whirlpool-tub room is adorned with candles, flower arrangements, mirrors, and a selection of scented bath salts and oils. The heated towel rack is a rare joy to find in the United States.

Hostess Judith McLane came to Eugene to run the inn after being downsized out of the California corporate fast lane. She uses a large tile set on the dining room buffet as a blackboard to announce the breakfast menu of the day, which always features fresh-baked bread; her specialties include Popeye's Morning (creamed spinach) and Idaho Sunrise (a twice-baked potato stuffed with a poached egg). △ *4 double rooms with baths. Phone, ceiling fan, individual heat control in rooms. $75–$110; full breakfast. AE, D, MC, V. No smoking.*

STEAMBOAT INN ☞
42705 N. Umpqua Hwy., Steamboat 97447, tel. 800/840–8825, fax 541/498–2411

Deep in the Umpqua National Forest, 38 winding mi east of Roseburg, this 1955 river-rock and pine lodge sits alongside the luminous blue North Umpqua River.

Fisherfolk from around the globe come here to test their skills against the elusive steelhead and trout. Owners Jim and Sharon Van Loan were themselves frequent visitors and worked as members of the inn's summer crew for three years before buying it in 1975.

While its fishing tradition is still much in evidence—rehabilitated fly-tying cabinets serving as the reception desk and fly shop—the Steamboat has seen a shift toward a more refined country inn. The rough edges of this fishing camp have been delicately hewn down with coordinated bedding, draperies, and carpets, as well as thoughtful decorative touches of dried flowers, botanical prints, and hand-quilted comforters in the refurbished riverside cabins. Knotty-pine paneling and rustic Americana furnishings in the guest rooms echo the decor of the main lodge.

Recent additions to the property include two detached suites along the river and five roomy, lofted chalets a ½ mi up the road, the latter perfect for families or small groups. The riverside suites offer intimate seclusion, with large wood-burning fireplaces, two-person Japanese-style soaking tubs, and large private decks over the river.

The Steamboat's famous candlelit evening dinner might include Northwest wines, salad spiced with roasted local nuts or garden-fresh herbs, fresh bread, a vegetable dish, and roasted lamb or fresh spring salmon. Wine-maker dinners, with guest chefs from the state's best restaurants, are the highlight of winter weekends.

Nonfishing activities in the area include hiking on the trails of the surrounding Umpqua National Forest, soaking in swimming holes, or making a day trip to cross-country ski at Diamond Lake or to admire the breathtaking, crystal-blue waters of Crater Lake. ⚠ *8 cabins with baths; 2 suites; 5 2-bedroom housekeeping cottages; 4 3-bedroom, 1-bath houses. Fireplace in cabins. Library, conference facilities, bicycles. $125–$235; breakfast not included, dinner available, limited midweek food service Mar.–May. MC, V. No smoking. Closed Jan.–Feb..*

WESTFIR LODGE 🐚
47365 1st St., Westfir 97492, tel. and fax 541/782–3103

Anchoring the tiny community of Westfir, just west of the crest of the Cascade Mountains, Westfir Lodge was long the hub of activity in the town, which had a population of several thousand in its heyday a half-century ago. You can't tell by looking at the two-story clapboard Arts and Crafts–style building, however, that it was formerly the main office of the Westfir Lumber Company.

Gerry Chamberlain and Ken Symons, who bought the building in 1990, added bathrooms to the building and converted the offices, which ring the first floor, into bedrooms. Over the years, four additional guest rooms were added on the second floor. The large central space became a living area, kitchen, and formal dining room. Antiques—some family heirlooms, others procured in Southeast Asia, and some purchased at local estate auctions—as well as heavy formal drapes on the windows and a wood-burning stove create a mixture of Oriental and English-country ambience in the common rooms.

Some rooms face a road traveled by logging trucks that often leave town before daylight, and the many trains that whistle past Westfir can be heard from here, but windows have recently been refitted with thicker glazing to cut down on the noise. The Willamette River is just across the road from the lodge, and if you're a sound sleeper, the river views and larger room size are inducements to opt for the accommodations on the east side of the building.

Ken, who is Australian, makes full English breakfasts featuring eggs, bangers with fried potatoes, and a broiled stuffed half-tomato. Accompaniments include scones and other breakfast breads, as well as fresh fruit. The garden offers a view of the 180-ft-long Office Bridge, the longest covered bridge in Oregon. A nearby kennel happily boards pet traveling companions. △ *7 double rooms with baths. Reception facilities. $70–$85; full breakfast. No credit cards. No smoking.*

OTHER CHOICES

Apple Inn Bed & Breakfast. 30697 Kenady La., Cottage Grove 97424, tel. 541/942–2393 or 800/942–2393, fax 541/767–0402. 2 double rooms with baths. TV in rooms, hot tub. RV parking. $65–$75; full breakfast, afternoon snacks. No credit cards. No smoking.

Beckley House. 338 S.E. 2nd St., Oakland 97462, tel. and fax 541/459–9320. 2 doubles with baths, adjoining twin room also available. $65–$85; full breakfast. AE, MC, V. No smoking.

House of Hunter. 813 S.E. Kane, Roseburg 97470, tel. 541/672–2335 or 800/540–7704. 2 double rooms with baths, 2 doubles with basins share bath, 1 2-bedroom suite. Air-conditioning in rooms. TV/VCR in living room, video library, laundry facilities. $50–$75; full breakfast. MC, V. No smoking.

McGillivray's Log Home Bed and Breakfast. 88680 Evers Rd., Elmira 97437, tel. 541/935–3564. 2 double rooms with baths. Air-conditioning in rooms. $70–$80; full breakfast. MC, V. No smoking.

RESERVATIONS SERVICE

Northwest Bed and Breakfast (1067 Hanover Court S, Salem 97302, tel. 503/370–9033, fax 503/316–9118).

Wine Country, Including Salem

FLYING M RANCH 🐾

23029 N.W. Flying M Rd., Yamhill 97148, tel. 503/662–3222, fax 503/662–3202

The mysterious red "M" signs begin in downtown Yamhill—a somnolent town of 700 or so in the very press of the wine country—and continue west for 10 mi into the Chehalem Valley, along the rugged foothills of the Coast Range. Following them alertly will bring you to the 625-acre Flying M Ranch, perched above the Yamhill River.

The centerpiece of this rough-and-ready, Wild West–flavored amalgam of motel, campground, dude ranch, timber camp, and working ranch is the great log lodge, decorated in a style best described as Paul Bunyan Eclectic and featuring a bar carved from a single 6-ton tree trunk. On weekends, this is *the* happening place; the adjoining restaurant serves thick steaks and prime rib, and there are even a few fish dishes on the menu now. Sensitive souls may notice the accusing eyes of dozens of taxidermic trophies watching while they eat.

You have a choice of eight secluded cabins and 28 motel units. The motel is modern and clean but lacks personality. The cabins, a better choice, are equipped with kitchens, living rooms, wood-burning stoves, and decks overlooking the river. The cozy Honeymoon Cabin has a huge stone-and-brick fireplace and a double whirlpool tub. The two-story Wortman Cabin sleeps up to 10 and has the newest furnishings.

A longtime Flying M specialty is the Steak Fry Ride. Participants ride a tractor-drawn hay wagon to the ranch's secluded creekside elk camp for a barbecued steak dinner with all the trimmings, including a crooning cowboy. There are also horseshoe pits, a big swimming hole, and good fly-fishing. As if this weren't enough, the wineries are a half-hour drive away over backcountry gravel roads. Be sure to make it back by dusk, because finding the Flying M in the dark can be a real challenge. *△ 24 double rooms with baths, 1 suite, 5 housekeeping cabins, 1 2-bedroom housekeeping cabin. TV in 2 cabins. Restaurant, bar, live entertainment, conference and catering facilities, swimming hole, tennis court, fishing, hiking trails, horseback riding, horseshoe pits, campsites, airfield. $75–$200; breakfast not included. AE, D, DC, MC, V. Limited service Nov.–Mar., closed Dec. 24–25.*

HOWELL HOUSE 🐾
212 N. Knox St., Monmouth 97361, tel. 800/368–2085

If Clint and Sandra Boylen hadn't happened along at just the right time, the 1891 Victorian known as Howell House would have ended up as a heap of scrap lumber. Built by carpenter and son of Oregon Trail pioneers John Wesley Howell, the house spent most of this century housing students at Western Oregon University (or the Oregon Normal School, as it was called at the turn of the century); it was, in fact, the oldest student rooming house in the state. Like off-campus housing everywhere, it suffered the ravages of a hard life and had been condemned when the Boylens bought it and began a 2½-year restoration. It is now on the National Register of Historic Places.

The period feel here goes beyond the house itself. Clint and Sandra collect vintage clothing and cars, and their antique furnishings have been accumulated over years of local estate-sale shopping. Even the musical entertainment is old; Sandra is a classical pianist who might sit down after breakfast at her antique parlor piano (in period dress, of course) and serve up some Chopin. The one concession to modernity is the backyard hot tub, tastefully housed in a Japanese-style enclosure. The rooms upstairs—the Seniors Guest Suite, Juniors Guest Room, and Alumni Parlor, which can be made into a guest room in a pinch—are filled with tasteful collegiate memorabilia and historical pieces and have 7-ft Victorian beds with matching marble dressers, lace curtains, and fluffy comforters. The House Mother's suite downstairs has its own entrance, and just outside is a flower-filled gazebo and the hot tub. Bathrooms have large clawfoot tubs and showers.

Breakfast, served on antique china, includes such dishes as blackberry pancakes, hazelnut Belgian waffles, omelets and frittatas, and homemade breads and muffins. In the evening you can sit outside and enjoy the fragrance of the 80 or so varieties of roses, some heirloom. *△ 1 suite with bath, 1 double and 1 suite share bath. $59–$89; full breakfast. MC, V. No smoking.*

MARQUEE HOUSE 🐾
333 Wyatt Ct. NE, Salem 97301, tel. 503/391–0837 or 800/949–0837, fax 503/391–1713

From the outside, this 1938 Colonial looks like a cross between George Washington's Mt. Vernon and *Gone With the Wind*'s Tara. Inside, amiable innkeeper Rickie Hart, who lived in Hollywood for years and developed a penchant there for collecting costumes and other theatrical memorabilia, has followed through on the movie theme, decorating and naming her five guest rooms after classic comedy films.

An inverted top hat serves as a planter in Topper, appointed with Early American barber stands, a straw boater, a bowler, and other vintage hats. More antique hats, hat stands, and a fox-hunting outfit are the highlights in Auntie Mame (the master bedroom of the house), while razor straps, an old sitz bathtub, and red long johns accent Blazing Saddles. Christmas in Connecticut, in a Christmas scheme, of course, has French Empire antiques and great views of the lovely creek and lawns behind the house.

Evenings bring movies, complete with popcorn and candy, screened in the living room, which follows the theme from *Harvey* (notice all the rabbits in the decor). Daytime entertainment is provided by live performers: the ducks that swim in Mill Creek, which winds along the backyard. Rickie's hearty breakfasts feature edible flowers, herbs, blackberries, and hazelnuts grown on the grounds. ♤ *3 doubles with baths, 2 double rooms share bath. TV/VCR and video collection in living room. $55–$90; full breakfast. D, MC, V. No smoking, 2-night minimum during holidays and university events.*

MATTEY HOUSE ☞
10221 N.E. Mattey La., McMinnville 97128, tel. 503/434–5058, fax 503/434–6667

Mattey House is a genteel Queen Anne mansion nestled behind its own little vineyard a few miles north of McMinnville. Its tasteful, distinctively western Victorian ambience and its experienced hosts make Mattey House the area's consummate B&B.

The house itself was built in 1892 by Joseph Mattey, a local butcher and cattle rancher. Jack and Denise Seed, originally from England, bought it in 1993 and have lavished great care on the guest rooms, public areas, and grounds. Their affable English sheepdog, Emma, is happy to show you around.

To wine-country visitors tuckered out by a long day's slurping, Mattey House is an oasis of welcoming warmth. Entering the living room, which is framed by Ionic columns and fretwork, you'll find a beckoning fire in the old carved-wood-and-tile hearth, reproduction William Morris wallpaper, and a cheerful mix of period furnishings and more informal modern pieces. There's a porch swing overlooking the vineyard, and 10 acres of grounds for those in a strolling mood.

The four guest rooms are named for locally grown grape varieties. The Chardonnay Room has tall windows and crisp white decor, and the Riesling Room is furnished with an antique pine dresser and a 6-ft-long claw-foot tub. A connecting door joins Chardonnay and Pinot Noir; you can reserve them as a two-couple suite. All bathrooms come with wine-glycerine soaps.

Breakfast features fresh local fruit, followed by fresh-baked scones and the house specialty, an Italian-style frittata, or Dutch apple pancakes. At the end of a day's wine touring, you are rewarded with hors d'oeuvres and one last cheering glass of the Oregonian grape. ♤ *3 double rooms with bath, 1 double with separate bath. Robes, clock in rooms. $85–$95; full breakfast, afternoon refreshments. MC, V. No smoking, 3-night minimum stay during Pinot Noir Festival (late July) and Linfield graduation, 2-night minimum on holiday weekends.*

YOUNGBERG HILL VINEYARD ☞

10660 Youngberg Hill Rd., McMinnville 97128, tel. 503/472–2727 or 888/657–8668, fax 503/472–1313

Like ghostly twilight sentinels, the deer come down to greet you at Youngberg Hill Farm. They have free run of this 700-acre estate, high in the hills west of McMinnville. Well, nearly free run—you must remember to close the gate of the deer fence that surrounds the house itself and its 10 acres of young Pinot Noir vines, a favorite midnight snack for these graceful thieves. This rural B&B, recently bought by silicon forest workers Kevin and Tasha Byrd, is a monster-size replica of a classic American farmhouse commanding breathtaking views over mountain and valley from atop a steep hill.

Youngberg Hill is a comfortable place with a proper, lived-in warmth. The common areas are spacious, modern, and high-ceilinged, with Victorian belly-band molding and bull's-eye corners. The furnishings are largely golden-oak period reproductions; the sitting room's deep sofa and settee, upholstered in an unusual grapevine-patterned chintz, are a welcoming touch, as are the suede-covered armchairs and wood-burning stove. Big windows make the most of the hilltop estate's romantic views. The five guest rooms are small to medium in size; furnished with golden oak and Victorian Cottage reproductions, they have a cozy modern ambience. Fresh flowers in the room and truffles on the pillow add a touch of romance.

The wine interest carries into the house from the vineyard: Rooms are named after clones of Pinot Noir, and among the inn's special attractions are a nicely stocked, reasonably priced wine cellar, including older vintages and small high-quality producers. Soon to join the cellar will be a winery, plans for which are just getting under way. Each morning, tea and fresh-brewed coffee can be enjoyed in your room or on the porch. Breakfast is served in a room with floor-to-ceiling windows and includes fresh fruit, homemade muffins, and a full country menu. △ *5 double rooms with baths. Air-conditioning in rooms, fireplace in 2 rooms. Conference and wedding facilities. $130–$150; full breakfast, afternoon refreshments. MC, V. No smoking, 2-night minimum holidays.*

OTHER CHOICES

Kelty Estate. 675 Hwy. 99 W, Lafayette 97127, tel. 503/864–3740 or 800/867–3740. 2 double rooms with baths. Cable TV in living room, billiards table, coin laundry. $70–$80; full breakfast. No credit cards. No smoking.

Main Street Bed & Breakfast. 1803 Main St., Forest Grove 97116, tel. 503/357–9812, fax 503/359–0860. 3 double rooms share bath. Phone in rooms. $55–$65; full breakfast, afternoon refreshments. AE, MC, V. No smoking.

Orchard View Inn. 16540 N.W. Orchard View Rd., McMinnville 97128, tel. 503/472–0165. 2 double rooms with baths, 2 doubles share bath. Laundry facilities. $70–$80; full breakfast. No credit cards. No smoking, 3-night minimum during Pinot Noir Celebration (late July).

Partridge Farm. 4300 E. Portland Rd., Newberg 97132, tel. 503/538–2050. 1 double room with bath, 2 suites. TV/VCR in library, nearby kennel for pets. $80–$110; full breakfast. MC, V. No smoking.

Springbrook Hazelnut Farm. 30295 N. Hwy. 99 W, Newberg 97132, tel. 503/538–4606 or 800/793–8528. 4 double rooms share 2 baths, carriage house. Kitchen in carriage house, TV in parlor. Library, tennis court, pool, trout pond. $90–$135; full breakfast. No credit cards. No smoking. Main inn closed Nov.–Apr.

State House. 2146 State St., Salem 97301, tel. 503/588–1340 or 800/800–6712, fax 503/585–8812. 2 double rooms share bath, 2 housekeeping suites. Air-conditioning and phone in rooms, TV in suites. TV in common room. $50–$70; full breakfast. D, MC, V. No smoking, 2-night minimum during university graduation in May.

Steiger Haus. 360 Wilson St., McMinnville 97128, tel. 503/472–0821 or 503/472–0238, fax 472–0100. 4 double rooms with baths, 1 suite. Fireplace in 1 room. Cable TV/VCR, bicycle storage, horseshoe pit. $70–$130; full breakfast. D, MC, V. No smoking, 2-night minimum during college-events and holiday weekends.

RESERVATIONS SERVICE

Northwest Bed and Breakfast (1067 Hanover Court S, Salem 97302, tel. 503/370–9033, fax 503/316–9118).

Portland
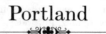

HERON HAUS ☞

2545 N.W. Westover Rd., Portland 97210, tel. 503/274–1846, fax 503/248–4055

A sense of luxurious seclusion is what sets Heron Haus apart. It's right in the heart of Nob Hill, northwest Portland's oldest and prettiest neighborhood, but occupies its own hilltop kingdom at the end of a secretive drive. From the driveway, a long flight of wooden stairs leads down not only to the mansion but to another hidden charm, a secluded orchard of pear, apple, cherry, and filbert trees.

Both urban and urbane, this is one of the most accomplished B&Bs in the Rose City. The house itself is a sturdy Tudor built in 1904 from stucco and Port of Portland ballast stone. It's convenient to the hiking trails and gigantic old-growth trees in Forest Park and the binge of shops, cafés, and restaurants lining Northwest 23rd Avenue. Julie Keppeler, the effervescent owner, worked in investment real estate, publishing, convention planning, and adult education before settling into the B&B business.

Keppeler renovated the 10,000-square-ft house in 1986 with taste, assurance, and charm. The modern touches, such as southwestern artwork and Scandinavian-flavor furnishings, subtly complement the house's existing features. There's an extralarge breakfast room with herringbone-pattern oak floors and fireplace; a warm, carpeted sunroom overlooking the backyard pool; and, in the mahogany-accented library, leaded-glass cabinets filled with everything from Isak Dinesen to Audubon.

The six guest suites on the second and third floors are extraordinarily large and impeccably furnished with a stylish blend of clean-lined modern pieces offset by one or two fine antiques. Each has a private bath, an enticing sitting area, a working fireplace, a phone, VCR, work desk, and a dataport. The most splendid of all is the Kulia Suite, with a roomy, romantic spa tub for bubbly, candlelit baths overlooking the downtown skyline. The Ko Room, just down the hall, is distinguished by its original 1904 seven-head shower and two sitting areas. (These two rooms can be converted into a $400-per-night suite.) At the top of the house, the Manu Room and the Mahina Room sprawl over a space so large that three average-size B&B rooms would easily fit into just one of them.

Breakfast is a Continental affair, with fresh fruits, croissants, pastries, and cereal. ♨ *6 suites. Air-conditioning, fireplace, phone, dataport, and cable TV/VCR in rooms. Pool. $95–$400; Continental-plus breakfast. MC, V. No smoking.*

LION AND THE ROSE ☙

1810 N.E. 15th Ave., Portland 97212, tel. 503/287–9245 or 800/955–1647, fax 503/287–9247

When it was built in 1906 for Portland brewing magnate Gustave Freiwald, this startlingly ornate, Queen Anne–style mansion was one of the city's showplaces. Its grounds, occupying nearly a full city block, featured parklike gardens, a stable for Freiwald's matched team of Clydesdale horses and, later, a garage for one of Portland's first horseless carriages.

By the time the house's current owners, Kay Peffer, Sharon Weil, and Kevin Spanier, took possession, Freiwald's showplace had been turned into a down-at-the-heels boarding house. The hard-working trio has since restored this neighborhood landmark, which now retains the splendor of its pre-Prohibition days.

Since its opening in 1993, the Lion and the Rose has been one of Portland's premier B&Bs. From the gleaming floors of oak inlaid with mahogany to the ornate period light fixtures (many original to the house) and the coffered dining-room ceiling, the Lion and the Rose has set a new standard of formal elegance among Portland inns.

The public areas offer an expanse of polished wood, antique silver, and delightful turn-of-the-century touches. The Freiwalds' original carved mahogany sofas share the front parlor with an 18th-century Miller pump organ and a 1909-vintage Bush & Lane walnut piano. The overall feel is substantial and ornate but just short of florid. The same attention to detail is evident throughout the six guest rooms. Lavonna, the nicest, features a round, sunny sitting area in the mansion's cupola, with an iron canopy bed and cheerful white wicker furniture. This room is also one of the most affordable because it shares a bath (across the hall) with an Eastlake dressing table and a deep claw-foot tub swathed in lace curtain.

A three-course breakfast as opulent as the surroundings is served in the dining room from 8 to 9:30; it starts with a fruit plate and muffins, continues with a pear pancake, crepe, or pumpkin waffle, and ends with a baked egg dish or omelet with bacon. Earlier risers can get a Continental breakfast at 7. Afternoon tea is also available. The inn is just a block from Northeast Broadway in an area filled with fine restaurants and shopping. ♨ *4 double rooms with baths, 2 doubles share bath. Air-conditioning, phone, robes, and TV/VCR (on request) in rooms. $99–$140; full breakfast. AE, MC, V. No smoking.*

MCMENAMINS EDGEFIELD ☙

2126 S.W. Halsey, Troutdale 97060, tel. 503/669–8610 or 800/669–8610, fax 503/665–4209

It takes a certain amount of chutzpah to turn a former county poor farm into an intriguing inn. But that's what Mike and Brian McMenamin have done with this property 15 minutes east of downtown Portland and 5 minutes west of the magnificent Columbia River Gorge National Scenic Area. The McMenamins have rescued several historic properties and converted them into brew pubs, but this was their first venture into innkeeping, and it's been a popular success since it opened in 1993.

The original residents of the Multnomah County Poor Farm, which operated from 1911 to 1947 and is now on the Register of National Historic Places, would still recognize the buildings, but little else. Today, this 25-acre estate has its own vineyard, winery and tasting room, brewery, bustling village pub, crafts shops, meeting facilities, fine-dining restaurant, movie theater, and beautifully landscaped gardens. The past is not ignored, but it's been transformed into a kind of funky, populist eccentricity.

Most of the guest rooms are in the complex's enormous four-story Colonial Revival centerpiece, Edgefield Manor. Historic photographs and artwork adorn the doors and hallways, softening the sense of institutional anonymity. A major renovation added 91 additional guest rooms to the original 14, as well as dormitory space for 24 guests (two single-sex rooms). The quietest double rooms are in the former administrator's Colonial-style house, set about 100 yards from the main building. The rooms all have scrubbed wood floors and are furnished with a few simple antiques; the ambience throughout is reminiscent of a comfortable, old-fashioned lodge. There are no telephones or TVs.

You are given vouchers for your breakfast of choice, chosen from the menu of the Black Rabbit Restaurant, also open for lunch and dinner. Choices include omelets, crunchy French toast, corned beef hash with poached eggs, fresh local fruit, and eggs Benedict. △ *100 double rooms share 55 baths, 3 suites, 2 hostel rooms. Restaurant, bar, brewery, pub, winery, outdoor beer garden (in summer), cinema, conference facilities. $50–$200; full breakfast. AE, D, MC, V. No smoking.*

PORTLAND GUEST HOUSE ❦
1720 N.E. 15th Ave., Portland 97212, tel. 503/282–1402

Northeast Portland's Irvington neighborhood used to be full of neatly kept working-class Victorians just like this one, with its flower-filled yard and window boxes. Most of them fell to the wrecking ball when the prosperous 'teens and '20s transformed Irvington into a neighborhood for the nouveau riche.

This house endured decades of neglect until longtime neighborhood residents Susan and Dean Gisvold brought it back to life in 1987. Now, with its exterior painted mocha and its interior rebuilt from the studs outward, the house breathes a quiet, comfortable sense of place and history. It's not as grand as the Lion and the Rose (*see above*), half a block away, or the nearby Portland's White House (*see below*), but it has a fresh, sunny authenticity all its own.

Each of the seven smallish, high-ceiling guest rooms has some special touch: an ornately carved walnut Eastlake bed or armoire, an immaculately enameled claw-foot tub, or a shady deck overlooking the back garden. A large, simply decorated suite in the sunlit basement is configured with families in mind. The tasteful mauve and gray walls of the downstairs living and dining rooms are finished with white bull's-eye molding; an Oriental carpet cushions the hardwood floor. The Eastlake living-room suite has been reupholstered in pretty rose satin.

Fifteenth Avenue, which runs by the etched-glass front door, can be busy in the mornings and afternoons, but this is barely noticeable in the soundproofed house. The conveniently central northeast Portland neighborhood is close to the MAX light-rail line and served by three major bus routes to downtown. Closer to home, the shops on Broadway offer Oregon wines and produce, imported cheeses, and fresh-baked breads for picnics in the landscaped yard.

The Gisvolds don't live on the premises, but Susan is around every day, and a full-time manager occupies a downstairs apartment. Breakfast—typically juice, coffee, fresh fruit, and a hot entrée such as quiche or homemade pumpkin waffles—is served in front of the cheerful dining room fireplace or alfresco on the back porch when it's nice out. △ *5 double rooms with baths, 2 doubles share*

bath. Air-conditioning and phone in rooms. Bicycle storage. $65–$95; full break-
fast. AE, MC, V. No smoking.

PORTLAND'S WHITE HOUSE ☙

1914 N.E. 22nd Ave., Portland 97212, tel. 503/287–7131 or 800/272–7131,
fax 503/249–1641

The splash of falling water provides a melodious welcome at this memorable north-east Portland B&B. Listed on the National Register of Historic Places, the house was built in 1912 in Southern Federal style. Except for the tile roof, it bears an un-canny resemblance to its District of Columbia namesake—a resemblance in-dicative of the chief-executive personality of its builder, timber tycoon Robert Lytle. Its circular driveway, carriage house, and Greek columns all speak of by-gone elegance.

Innkeepers Lanning Blanks, a hotel-restaurateur originally from South Car-olina, and Steve Holden, a former CPA, bought the Irvington mansion in 1997 and—with the help of Joanne Young, a third innkeeper—have lavished their time and attention on the sumptuous interior. The public areas gleam with hand-rubbed Honduran mahogany and ornately inlaid oak. The dramatic hand-carved stairway is lit by Pulvey stained-glass windows. Hand-painted scenic murals, commis-sioned in the '20s, line the walls of the foyer. Downstairs is a cavernous ball-room. Outside, Lanning and Steve have added sunny patios and courtyards with more fountains and are in the process of creating a large new garden from an adjoining lot.

The six spacious, high-ceiling guest rooms in the main house are furnished with a tasteful mix of antiques, period pieces, and reproductions. The Canopy and Baron's rooms feature ornate canopy beds and huge claw-foot soaking tubs. In the Garden Room, French doors open onto a private veranda. The Balcony Room has a tile Art Deco bathroom and a small balustrade balcony overlooking the court-yard fountain. In 1997, the former carriage house was converted into three smartly furnished new rooms; the Chauffeur's Quarters, on the first floor, has a four-poster bed and private whirlpool bath.

The breakfasts here, served in the formal dining room on heavy linen, are among the best in Portland. Native American French toast, one of the signature dishes, is black bread soaked in egg and heavy cream, slow-cooked to a custard, and covered with sautéed apples and oranges. The breakfast frittata, made with pears, apples, cheeses, and Portobello mushrooms, is served with pepper bacon. Af-ternoon tea is available. Groups often rent the entire house, so it's best to re-serve as far in advance as you can. ♙ *9 double rooms with baths. Air-conditioning, phone, and TV (on request) in rooms. $98–$159; full breakfast. AE, D, MC, V. No smoking.*

RIVERPLACE HOTEL ☙

1510 S.W. Harbor Way, Portland 97201, tel. 503/228–3233 or 800/227–1333,
fax 503/295–6161

The popular RiverPlace Hotel is the only downtown hotel sited directly on the banks of the Willamette River, which flows through the heart of downtown Port-land. The downtown skyline rears up behind the hotel, but it is the river—with its nearby yacht marina, floating restaurant, and pedestrian and bike trails—that makes RiverPlace special. Part of a 1985 development scheme that infused new life into downtown Portland's Waterfront Park, the hotel complex includes shops, restaurants, condominiums, and offices.

Inside, the RiverPlace has the feel of an intimate European hotel. The subtle luster of teak and green Italian marble is everywhere, and the staff provides a level of service seldom seen in this casual western city. (The 150 employees outnumber the guest rooms nearly two to one.) The lobby, bar, and restaurant are handsome spaces, luxuriously appointed with wood-burning fireplaces, rich fabrics, and Oriental carpets.

The 84 guest rooms overlook river, skyline, or, least desirable, a narrow courtyard. Thickly carpeted and well-soundproofed, they are painted a subtle yellow and furnished with modern, comfortable pieces that add blue to most of the color schemes. Junior suites have huge tile bathrooms and separate sitting areas. Fireplace suites are larger, with marble-top wet bars, king-size beds, small whirlpool baths, two color TVs, and tile, wood-burning fireplaces. You can reserve the hotel's whirlpool bath and sauna room for private use. Another nice feature is that you can get the complimentary Continental breakfast served in your room.

Dinner at the Esplanade Restaurant off the lobby is an experience to savor. The nightly menu varies according to what's in season but always includes fresh seafood. You might find grilled wild salmon with huckleberry honey, sautéed razor clams on wild greens dressed in lemon and lavender, seared halibut stuffed with Dungeness crab, or grilled steelhead. The Patio is open for outdoor riverside dining from Memorial to Labor Day. △ *39 double rooms with baths, 35 suites, 10 apartments. Air-conditioning, phone, cable TV, 24-hour room service, and voice mail in rooms. Restaurant, bar, sauna, valet parking. $210–$800; Continental breakfast. AE, D, DC, MC, V.*

TUDOR HOUSE ☜

2321 N.E. 28th Ave., Portland 97212, tel. 503/287–9478, fax 503/288–8363

Dolph Park, a four-block area on the edge of Irvington in northeast Portland, is notable for its gigantic houses set in park-size gardens. Back in the late 1920s, when the area was first being developed, exclusivity was maintained by restricting the number and size of the lots. Tudor House is a perfect example of that oversize planning. The 5,400-square-ft house, set on estate-size grounds rimmed by tall laurel bushes, hawthorn trees, and azaleas, was built to resemble a Tudor manor.

Milan Larsen, the sprightly owner and innkeeper, was an antiques dealer in San Francisco before she moved up to Portland. Not surprisingly, her B&B is loaded with fine pieces of antique furniture and paintings. Luckily, there's enough space—and then some—to accommodate all of it, but the overall effect may strike some as a bit ponderous.

Of the three guests rooms on the second floor, the Antique Suite is largest and best equipped. It has a fireplace, separate seating area, a large bathroom, and an adjacent snack room with refrigerator and microwave. The Blue Room, with windows on two sides, is furnished with a splendid turn-of-the-century French armoire and matching bed. Across from it is the Bordeaux Room, which has an Art Deco armoire and a small reading alcove. Larsen usually rents out only one of these rooms at a time, so guests have a private bathroom; couples or families renting both rooms and sharing the bath receive a discount. A large room on the lower level, suitable for families or friends traveling together, has its own bathroom and two beds.

Breakfast, served in the antiques-laden dining room, is a generous affair, which might include a spinach and bacon omelet, panfried potatoes, poached pears, and muffins. ⚖ *1 double room with bath, 2 doubles share bath, 1 suite. Phone and cable TV/VCR in rooms. $75–$100; full breakfast. AE, D, MC, V. No smoking.*

OTHER CHOICES

Clinkerbrick House. 2311 N.E. Schuyler St., Portland 97212, tel. 503/281–2533, fax 503/281–1281. 1 double room with shower, 2 doubles share bath. Kitchen, phone, and TV in common room. $55–$70; full breakfast. MC, V. No smoking.

General Hooker's B&B. 125 S.W. Hooker St., Portland 97201, tel. 503/222–4435 or 800/745–4135, fax 503/295–6410. 2 double rooms with baths, 2 doubles share bath. Air-conditioning, robes, cable TV/VCR, and dataport in rooms. ½-price YMCA passes. $75–$125; Continental-plus breakfast. AE, MC, V. No smoking, 2-night minimum Apr.–Oct.

Georgian House. 1828 N.E. Siskiyou St., Portland 97212, tel. 503/281–2250 or 888/282–2250, fax 503/281–3301. 1 double room with bath, 2 doubles share 1½ baths, 1 suite. Air-conditioning in 3 rooms, TV in 2 rooms, TV/VCR and phone in common room. $65–$100; full breakfast. MC, V. No smoking.

Hotel Vintage Plaza. 422 S.W. Broadway, Portland 97205, tel. 503/228–1212 or 800/243–0555, fax 503/228–3598. 82 double rooms with baths, 19 suites. 2 phone lines, TV, air-conditioning, 24-hour room service, voice mail, fax, and dataport in rooms, whirlpool tub in suites. Restaurant, piano lounge, concierge, valet parking. $170–$400; Continental breakfast. AE, D, DC, MC, V. No-smoking rooms.

MacMaster House. 1041 S.W. Vista Ave., Portland 97205, tel. 503/223–7362 or 800/774–9523. 5 double rooms share 2½ baths, 2 suites. Air-conditioning and cable TV in rooms. Bicycle storage. $80–$120; full breakfast. AE, D, DC, MC, V. No smoking.

RESERVATIONS SERVICE

A Northwest Bed & Breakfast Reservation Service (1067 Hanover Ct. S, Salem 97302, tel. 503/243–7616 in Portland, 503/370–9033 elsewhere, fax 503/316–9118).

North Coast

BENJAMIN YOUNG INN 🐚
3652 Duane St., Astoria 97103, tel. 503/325–6172 or 800/201–1286

This handsomely restored Queen Anne overlooking the Columbia River is on the National Register of Historic Places. The 5,500-square-ft inn surrounded by 100-year-old gardens underwent a name change when purchased by Carolyn and Ken Hammer in 1994 (people still come by looking for K. C.'s Mansion by the Sea). Ken works as a pastor across the river in Washington, while Carolyn runs the inn. In addition to seeing to the needs of bed-and-breakfast travelers, she also caters meetings, family reunions, and especially weddings, for which the Benjamin Young is a picture-perfect location.

The home itself, with its ornate period woodwork and fixtures, is the primary draw. Preservationists and old-house aficionados will marvel at the details: faux graining on frames and molding, shutter-blinds in windows, and Povey stained glass, all original. The living room has an imposing brick fireplace, large velvet Victorian couches, and the original, elaborate light fixtures hanging from the 12-ft-high ceiling. The house was in the same family for a century, and the Hammers have tracked down and bought back some of the old furnishings that were sold years ago but still remained in the area.

The four spacious guest rooms are simply furnished, with a mix of contemporary pieces and antiques, and offer views of the river through their tall windows. Roll-out beds and sofas expand the capacity of some rooms to five or six guests. The most popular is the Fireplace Suite, with a king-size bed, whirlpool bath, and (of course) a fireplace. ♙ *4 double rooms with baths, 1 2-bedroom suite. Fireplace and whirlpool bath in suite. $75–$135; full breakfast. AE, D, MC, V. No smoking, 2-night minimum on holiday weekends.*

GRANDVIEW BED & BREAKFAST ▧
1574 Grand Ave., Astoria 97103, tel. 503/325–0000 or 800/488–3250

Seen from a quiet residential street in Astoria, the Grandview Bed & Breakfast doesn't stand out. But once you're inside the nearly 100-year-old shingle-style house, you'll know what's special about it. Because the Grandview rises so precipitously from a hill that falls away steeply, the views from the inn are spectacular and the sensation of floating can be intense. Innkeeper Charlene Maxwell quickly brings you back to earth, however. She has steeped herself in local lore and shares it with you in an easygoing but authoritative manner.

The guest rooms upstairs are eccentrically decorated with a mixture of period furnishings and odd modern touches (for example, plastic patio furniture). A few rooms have canopy beds, and all are outfitted with faux fireplaces that heat the rooms. With unobstructed vistas of the Columbia River and the Coast Range of southern Washington, and of the dozens of church steeples of Old Astoria, you'll feel as if you're in an aerie. If you prefer to be earthbound, there is a very plain two-bedroom suite in the lower level of the house, with a separate entrance that's perfect for families. The arrangement of some of the guest rooms is flexible: Seven double rooms on the second and third floors can be divided into two suites or rented separately. Prices depend on whether you have a private bath. The entrance hall is cluttered with Charlene's work desk, which is only a few feet from the main door.

The dining area, however, is very inviting, positioned in a light-filled turret that offers views of the river and town. For more privacy, you might opt to dine in a smaller bullet turret on the other side of the kitchen, ideal for a twosome. Breakfast consists of five types of coffee, hot chocolate or cider, fresh fruits and juices, homemade muffins, and usually bagels and lox. ♙ *4 double rooms with baths (or 6 doubles share 2 baths, depending on bookings), 1 suite. $59–$159; Continental-plus breakfast. D, MC, V. No smoking, no alcohol on premises.*

NYE BEACH HOTEL ▧
219 N.W. Cliff St., Newport 97365, tel. 541/265–3334, fax 541/265–3622

Every so often, guests will insist that they remember the Nye Beach Hotel from way back when, maybe in the '50s, before it was restored. Innkeeper Crea Williams has to disagree politely, informing them that the building is less than 10 years old. She should know: She opened it with her husband David Baker, the architect who designed the 1992 structure to fit in with the turn-of-the-century style of its neighbors. Not that she can blame them; even a prominent guidebook to the region lists the Nye Beach as "a restored 1910s hotel."

The 18 guest rooms all have ocean views, private baths, fireplaces, and willow love seats; those on upper floors have balconies, and several are equipped with whirlpool tubs. The beds, covered with down comforters, were made in Holland, and they are so comfortable and cleanly designed that many guests inquire about where to buy them (unfortunately, they're not imported anymore). With pastel decor, potted tropical plants, and a macaw in the lobby, the hotel has a funky, distinctive personality that wouldn't be out of place in Key West.

A roomy café and full bar, with a grand piano and fireplace, occupies the beachfront portion of the bottom floor; one of Newport's better restaurants, Nye Beach Café, serves three meals a day and specializes in spicy seafood dishes. Heaters on the adjoining deck make it an ideal space to take in the surf, sunsets, and nearby Yaquina Head lighthouse, even on chilly evenings. △ *18 double rooms with baths. Down comforters, cable TV, fireplace in rooms, whirlpool tub in some rooms. $60– $125; breakfast not included. AE, D, MC, V. No-smoking rooms available.*

ST. BERNARDS ☞

3 E. Ocean Rd. (Box 102), Arch Cape 97102, tel. and fax 503/436–2800 or tel. 800/436–2848

Imagine having an extra million dollars and several years to travel the world collecting antiques and art that would one day fill your fantasy inn. After years spent visiting B&Bs and inns, the dream came true for gregarious innkeepers Don and Deanna Bernard. They built their enormous shingle castle, complete with turret and drive-through tunnel, on the scenic Oregon coast a few miles south of Cannon Beach.

Together, the Bernards designed and constructed the châteaulike structure, from the foundation to the scenes ingeniously depicted in the exterior shingles. Now they are content to stay at home, traveling vicariously through their many guests.

As one would expect of a fantasy castle, the guest rooms are quite grand. Decorated by Deanna with an artist's eye, they are appointed with every amenity for comfort and romance—down comforters on firm beds, plush robes, supersoft cotton sheets, large soaking tubs with ocean views, and gas fireplaces. A spacious workout room with sauna rounds out the well-thought-out amenities of this adult-oriented inn.

Ginger, appointed with ornate Austrian bedsteads dating from the 1860s, takes its palette from a collection of ginger jars. The walls of Gauguin employ the same muted pastels used by the painter, whose prints are hung on the walls. Tower, with its incredible Louis XIV Bombay bed, has an attached sitting room in the turret. Provence, on the garden level with a private patio overlooking the ocean, features terra-cotta floors, antique pine furniture, Pierre Deux fabrics in country French yellow and blue, and a two-person whirlpool bath.

Breakfast, served in the rounded dining room beneath the inn's cupola, is also a grand affair, with fresh juice, coffee cakes, seasonal fruits, and a hot entrée served on Deanna's fine collection of china and crystal. △ *6 double rooms with baths, 1 suite. Phone, TV/VCR, down comforters, robes, soaking tub, fireplace, and individual heating systems in rooms, whirlpool bath in 1 room. Sauna, exercise room. $129–$189; full breakfast, evening refreshments. AE, MC, V. No smoking.*

SANDLAKE COUNTRY INN ☞

8505 Galloway Rd., Cloverdale 97112, tel. 503/965–6745, fax 503/965–7425

On Christmas morning in 1890, the Norwegian schooner *Struan* was wrecked off Cape Lookout, leaving tons of heavy bridge timbers on their way to Australia strewn on the beach. Storm-weary homesteaders with few building materials hauled the timbers off and made sturdy homes. Only a few of these are still standing, the most notable of which is the weathered-shingle Sandlake Country Inn, where innkeepers Femke and Dave Durham preside.

The natural woodwork has been restored, and part of the dining-room ceiling was removed to reveal the old bridge timbers. The sitting room is a cozy creation, with velvet-covered Victorian settees, a stone fireplace, and views of flowering rosebushes outside. Upstairs is the honeymoon suite, taking up the entire floor and opening onto a deck that surveys the 2½-acre property; keep a lookout for deer and elk.

Just off the dining room is the Timbers, a wheelchair-accessible guest room with an outdoorsy feel, complete with a 1920s wicker fishing creel slung over the sturdy timber bedposts, a timber-framed fireplace, a deck in the garden, and a fragrant cedar-lined bathroom. There is also a charming cottage outside, about 100 ft from the main house: The interior is plush, with thick carpeting and huge throw pillows on the floor before a black marble fireplace. A large hot tub is strategically located between the bed and the deck. As in the suites, Arts and Crafts oak period pieces and reproductions predominate.

Homemade baked apple oatmeal is a breakfast staple, as are fruit parfaits and soufflés. The Durhams like to focus on providing a romantic retreat, so they see to it that you are treated to breakfast in bed: Every morning a tray with the multicourse repast elegantly presented on Royal Doulton china is delivered to your room. ⌂ *2 double rooms with baths, 1 suite, 1 housekeeping cottage. Radio/cassette player in rooms, TV/VCR in most rooms, fireplace and whirlpool bath in suite. Hot tub, bicycles. $90–$135; full breakfast. AE, D, MC, V. No smoking, 2-night minimum on weekends May–Oct. Closed Christmas wk.*

SYLVIA BEACH HOTEL ☞

267 N.W. Cliff St., Newport 97365, tel. 541/265–5428

Built in 1911, the Sylvia Beach Hotel was long known as a flophouse with a view until Portland restaurateur Goody Cable and Roseburg partner Sally Ford decided to make it a kind of literary lodging—or a library that sleeps 40. The Sylvia Beach in the name is not the sandy strip just outside (that would be Nye Beach) but rather the renowned patron of literary arts who in the 1920s and '30s ran the Shakespeare & Co. bookstore in Paris. Each room is dedicated to an author, with appropriate books and decorating scheme. The Hemingway Room, for example, is all the manly Papa could have hoped for: a bed made out of tree limbs under a mounted antelope head, and an old Royal typewriter in the corner.

Down the hall is the Oscar Wilde Room, a smallish place resembling a Victorian gentleman's lodgings. The view, which faces a roof from the other side of the hotel, is far from awe-inspiring. But the managers are way ahead of you. Right next to the window is a framed Wilde quote: "It's altogether immaterial, a view, except to the innkeeper who, of course, charges it in the bill. A gentleman never looks out the window."

The most popular rooms are the Poe Room, an eerie chamber in black and red, complete with raven and pendulum suspended over the bed, and the Colette Room, a sexy French suite with lace canopies, velvet window seat, and peach-color headboard. The upper reaches of the hotel are turned over to a large library (some 1,000 books), with plenty of nooks and crannies and comfortable armchairs for book lovers.

The food at the hotel's restaurant—Tables of Content—is excellent, an exception to the unwritten traveler's rule that one should sup and sleep in different places. That's not to say you should skip breakfast here, which starts with a buffet of juices, pastries, and fruits and moves on to a hot entrée such as quiche, French toast, or omelets. ◭ *20 double rooms with baths, 1 separate dormitory room with 8 bunks for women and 4 bunks for men. Fireplace in 3 rooms. Restaurant, library. $22–$152; full breakfast, evening refreshments. AE, MC, V. No smoking, 2-night minimum on weekends. Closed 1st wk in Dec.*

WHISKEY CREEK BED & BREAKFAST 𝕎
7500 Whiskey Creek Rd., Tillamook 97141, tel. 503/842–2408

Built in 1900 by the operator of a custom sawmill, the cedar-shingle Whiskey Creek Bed & Breakfast is paneled inside with rough-hewn spruce. Originally, the mill operator made spruce oars and used the odd pieces of leftover wood for the main floor. For years, the home and the mill were powered by a small hydroelectric turbine on Whiskey Creek, about 100 ft away at the southern boundary of the property.

The house is split into two guest rooms and an apartment with a private entrance; these can be rented nightly or weekly. Upstairs, the guest rooms are paneled with the original rough-hewn spruce and have terraces overlooking Netarts Bay; the cathedral-ceiling dining area is decorated with owner Allison Asbjornsen's rabbit objet d'art collection. A wood-burning stove keeps the smallish rooms warm and cozy when it's cold. Adorning the white walls of the one-bedroom downstairs apartment, which also offers a view of the bay and the lawn, are Allison's oil paintings, watercolors, collages, and sculptures. Both units have queen-size futon beds and overstuffed chairs, a living room, a bathroom, and a kitchen for cooking your own meals.

Allison will happily answer questions about the area and serve a full breakfast, perhaps involving omelets or oysters. Otherwise she leaves you alone to enjoy the beautiful natural surroundings, where bear, elk, and deer still roam. Blue herons are a common sight. Tillamook means "land of many waters," and there are streams everywhere for exploring. The inn is a retreat in winter, with yoga and shiatsu massage on site. ◭ *1 apartment, 2 double rooms with shared bath. $65–$90, additional cost for more than 2 people, weekly rates available; full breakfast. MC, V. No smoking.*

OTHER CHOICES
Anderson's Boarding House. 208 N. Holladay Dr., Seaside 97138, tel. 503/738–9055 or 800/995–4013. 5 double rooms with baths, 1 cottage. TVs, bicycle storage. $70–$115; full breakfast (guests in main house only). MC, V. 2-night minimum during July, Aug., and special events.

Astoria Inn. 3391 Irving Ave., Astoria 97103, tel. 503/325–8153. 4 double rooms with baths. Cable TV/VCR and karaoke machine in living room, bicycle storage. $70–$85; full breakfast, afternoon refreshments. D, MC, V. No smoking.

Channel House. 35 Ellingson St. (Box 56), Depoe Bay 97341, tel. 541/765–2140 or 800/447–2140, fax 541/765–2191. 5 double rooms with baths, 4 suites, 3 housekeeping suites. Cable TV and binoculars in rooms, kitchen in 3 rooms, whirlpool bath in most rooms. $60–$200; Continental breakfast. D, MC, V. No smoking.

Franklin St. Station. 1140 Franklin Ave., Astoria 97103, tel. 503/325–4314 or 800/448–1098, fax 503/325–2275. 3 double rooms with baths, 2 suites. Fireplace, cable TV/VCR, and stereo in 1 suite; wet bar in suites. $68–$120; full breakfast. MC, V. No smoking.

Hudson House. 37700 Hwy. 101 S, Cloverdale 97112, tel. 503/392–3533, fax 503/392–3533. 2 double rooms with baths, 2 suites. Coffee and tea in rooms. TV/VCR in library. $75–$85; full breakfast, refreshments throughout the day. MC, V. No smoking.

Inn at Manzanita. 67 Laneda St. (Box 243), Manzanita 97130, tel. 503/368–6754, fax 530/368–7656. 13 double rooms with baths. Wet bars, TV/VCR, and hot tub in rooms, kitchen in 2 rooms. Masseuse. $100–$145; no breakfast. MC, V. No smoking, 2-night minimum on weekends and July–Aug.

Stephanie Inn. 2740 S. Pacific Rd., Cannon Beach 97110, tel. 503/436–2221 or 800/633–3466, fax 503/436–9711. 42 double rooms with baths, 4 suites. Wet bar, phone, TV/VCR, fireplace, and whirlpool bath in rooms. Library, video library, masseuse. Free shuttle into town. $149–$399; full breakfast buffet, evening refreshments, dinners available. AE, D, DC, MC, V. No smoking, 2-night minimum in Aug., weekends, and holidays.

Tyee Lodge. 4925 N.W. Woody Way, Newport 97365, tel. 541/265–8953 or 888/553–8933. 5 double rooms with baths. Fireplace in 1 room. Bicycles, beach trail. $95–$120; full breakfast. AE, D, MC, V. No smoking.

RESERVATIONS SERVICE

Northwest Bed and Breakfast (1067 Hanover Court S, Salem 97302, tel. 503/370–9033, fax 503/316–9118).

Columbia River Gorge and Mt. Hood

BERYL HOUSE ☞
4079 Barrett Dr., Hood River 97031, tel. 541/386–5567

Before it became a popular spot for windsurfing, Hood River was best known for its fruit orchards. Even though Beryl House is run by a onetime windsurfer, its location amid apple and pear trees keeps you in touch with the town's roots.

John Lovell and Kim Pfautz found this 1910 house, a few miles out of Hood River, in 1994 and left their California occupations behind to renovate it. One of their favorite discoveries was a large pocket door entombed behind some molding. They now use it to block off the guest living room so that the wood-stove doesn't have to work as hard in winter.

John and Kim have created a remarkable place that feels like the well-kept old home of friends. Upstairs, the original old fir floors, accented by old-style braided rugs, lend the house a warm feeling. The decor is whimsical—a framed turn-of-the-century marriage license hung on the wall of the bridal suite, for example, and lodge-style furnishings in most of the rooms.

Breakfast may be served on the sundeck overlooking Asian pear trees, when weather permits. But even inside, blackberry cornmeal pancakes with local sausage—a cuisine John calls "Paul Bunyan meets Alice Waters"—always please.
△ *4 double rooms share 2 baths. Robes and slippers in rooms. TV/VCR, CD*

*player, and video and CD library in common room. Equipment storage. $60–
$70; full breakfast. MC, V. No smoking.*

BRIDAL VEIL LODGE 🐾
Box 87, Bridal Veil 97010, tel. 503/695–2333

In 1921, Virgil Amend hauled timbers from the mill down the hill to an empty spot
beside the Historic Columbia River Highway, in the tiny gorge community of Bridal
Veil. There, within the sound of delicate Bridal Veil Falls, he built a lodge.

After years of functioning as a lodge, years of being a family residence, and
years of being not much of anything, the old rustic Bridal Veil Lodge has re-
verted to its original purpose. Amend's great-granddaughter Laurel Slater and her
husband have created a country-style bed-and-breakfast within 20 minutes of
Portland's bustling waterfront.

But if Portland's lights are visible just to the west, it's what lies to the east that
makes Bridal Veil's location special. The log structure is on the edge of the Columbia River Gorge National Scenic Area, a 90-mi-long preserve of trails, dizzy-
ing waterfalls, rock formations, high cliffs, and wilderness. Trails going through
this region can be found within a mile of the lodge.

Inside, the inn is warm and the sense of family is unmistakable. Old photos
adorn the shelves in the dining area, which is dominated by a large, 1920s-vin-
tage harvest table and a huge wrought-iron cook stove. In the main common
area, a player piano holds sway beneath high, exposed fir beams. Quilts adorn
the walls of the two upstairs rooms. Grandpa's Room, with knotty-pine walls
and a hand-carved oak headboard and matching dresser, evokes the rough days
when the lodge was built. Grandma's Room, slightly bigger, has a feminine feel,
with table skirts, curtains, and plenty of light.

Perhaps the inn's greatest asset is Laurel Slater, who grew up in the house and
can answer questions about local history. Laurel's breakfasts tend to be healthy
and hearty, and often include German-style pancakes, fresh fruit, and plenty
of sausage and bacon as regular fare. ▲ *2 double rooms share 1½ baths. TV in common area. $62–$70; full breakfast. No credit cards. No smoking.*

BRIGHTWOOD GUEST HOUSE 🐾
*64725 E. Barlow Trail Rd. (Box 189), Brightwood 97011, tel. 503/622–5783
or 800/503–5783*

Innkeeper Jan Colgan has created a romantic Japanese-style guest house nestled in a garden of Asian plantings, situated on 2 acres of the historic Barlow Trail.
The house is surrounded by a clear mountain stream and tall firs and has its
own water garden. A footbridge and miniature koi pond complete the landscape.

The house is always filled with fresh flowers from the garden. The main level
offers a cozy sitting area and a small eating area with kitchenette. Herbs, spices,
and an exotic variety of teas—even microwave popcorn—fill the cupboards.
There's also a handy supply of bird seed and fish food for a little serene outdoor
entertainment by the koi pond. In the spacious bathroom, Jan provides an enticing
assortment of bath oils and salts and many personal items often forgotten from
home.

In the guest house, steps lead up to the sleeping loft and a heavenly feather bed
with views of the water garden. There are also several futons on the main level that
can be used as additional beds.

Jan, who once owned a bakery and managed a restaurant, has a particular appreciation for preparation and presentation. Breakfast can be vegetarian on request and may include a Hawaiian Treasure Fruit Plate. Otherwise, expect dishes such as waffles with freshly sliced berries or a roasted potatoes and onion omelet.
🔺 *1 guest house with sleeping loft. TV/VCR, videos, kimonos, and slippers in guest house. Bikes, newspapers. $125 for two, additional guests $15; full breakfast. No credit cards. No smoking.*

DOUBLEGATE INN 🐚
26711 E. Welches Rd., Welches tel. 503/622–4859

Tucked beneath towering cedars, the Doublegate Inn is a welcoming sight. Gaining its name from the double-gated, gray hand-chiseled wall in front, this big blue house is actually one of the area's most comfortable inns—especially if you like soaking in a tub.

Two of the four rooms have spa tubs, while a third has a luxurious soaking tub. Old-fashioned wainscoting surrounding the modern tubs adds to the get-away-from-it-all ambience. Each of the rooms has its own flair, from the warm cedar walls of the Bit O'Country to the happy bursts of color in the English Cottage room. The second-story deck, where breakfast is sometimes served in summer months, overlooks the calming Salmon River.

Innkeepers Gary and Charlene Poston maintain a friendly place where you can spend your evenings working on a giant jigsaw puzzle in front of a brick fireplace and munch on fresh-baked chocolate-chip cookies, a specialty of the inn. Both the Great Room and the Oregon Lodge Lounge are fitted with TV/VCRs, games, puzzles, books, and magazines.

The Postons serve a hearty, filling breakfast usually including fruit, fresh fruit juice, and a hot entrées such as stuffed French toast or baked oatmeal. The innkeepers prefer not to house kids under 14. 🔺 *2 double rooms with baths, 2 suites. Whirlpool bath in some rooms. TV/VCR in common rooms, video library, gift shop. $80–$115; full breakfast. AE, D, MC, V. No smoking.*

FALCON'S CREST INN 🐚
87287 Government Camp Loop Hwy. (Box 185), Government Camp 97028, tel. 503/272–3403 or 800/624–7384, fax 503/272–3454

Perched at the 4,000-ft level on the south flank of Mt. Hood, the chalet-style Falcon's Crest Inn, trimmed with warm woods and a mix of contemporary and traditional furniture, is just 44 mi from Portland. From its two-story glass-front living room and dining area, this intimate inn enjoys an expansive view of the Mt. Hood Skibowl recreational area. In the winter months, guests sitting in the upstairs common areas can watch night skiers make their way down the mountain while enjoying a jigsaw puzzle or card game or simply relaxing.

Each of the rooms and suites is decorated and furnished individually. Family heirlooms and keepsakes of innkeepers Bob and Melody Johnson are found throughout the house. Most of the rooms have mountain views, and all have in-room phones and private baths.

The Mexicali Suite on the first level of the inn, with a whirlpool tub for two, is decorated in the muted desert tones and vibrant colors of the Southwest. The trunk used as a coffee table in the spacious sitting room was used by Melody's grandfather to bring all his earthly possessions to America from Sweden. The Safari Suite on the main level is a guest favorite. Glass sliding doors open onto a deck overlooking the ski area below, which you can observe at night from the bamboo-cage bed beneath the room's own glowing star-studded ceiling. Rattan furniture and playful stuffed exotic animals complete the well-done theme.

Bob and Melody also operate an acclaimed fine-dining establishment at the inn and have a strong following. You enjoy multiple-course gourmet dinners at individual tables throughout the main common area (reservations required). In addition to containing a full breakfast for overnight guests, in-room morning trays are delivered with treats such as Falcon's Crest Magic Muffins with cranberry butter. △ *4 suites with private baths. Phone in rooms, soak tub on deck in 1 room, whirlpool bath in 1 room. TV/VCR, videos, games, restaurant. $100–$179; full breakfast, wine and beer available. AE, MC, V. No smoking.*

FERNWOOD AT ALDER CREEK 🐾
54850 Hwy. 26 E, Sandy 97055, tel. 503/622–3570

Nestled in the trees and ferns just off busy U.S. 26, this vintage log home feels miles away from anything noisy or modern. A huge, multipaned window set into one log wall seems vaguely Bavarian, but the atmosphere is purely Northwest. The highway's hum is washed away by Alder Creek, about 100 ft below the inn and in a major hurry to meet up with the Sandy River just beyond the highway bridge.

Inside, a warm and rustic feeling pervades with a collection of local handmade furniture and some antiques from the families of innkeeper Darrell Dempster and his wife, Margo. Part of the house is a bit dark, but the spacious dining room–library, with an immense supporting pole running vertically through it, is filled with natural light from a large window. Books and a collection of *Life* magazines dating back to the 1930s are displayed on the walls of this grand room, which has a loft that's perfect for reading or sleeping.

Both of the inn's two suites have decks and creek views. The Red Huckleberry Suite, downstairs, also features a private entrance and a small kitchen. It's easy to relax in the suite's knotty-pine bath, with its bucolic view of the creek and canyon. The Hallberg House, with its full kitchen and living room, is a good place for groups.

The Curly Willow Suite upstairs has a whirlpool tub. Its furnishings are more distinctive, especially the wrought-iron bed and the oak American Empire rocking chair. The view from the window seat is peaceful; it's not hard to imagine curling up with a good book here.

The hearty and creative family-style breakfasts served in the dining room on the main floor might include fresh fruit juice, a meat dish, and raspberry puffed pastries or blueberry waffles with homemade syrup. △ *2 suites, 1 cabin. Whirlpool bath in 1 suite, kitchen in 1 suite and in cabin. $75–$125; full breakfast. MC, V. No smoking.*

HOOD RIVER HOTEL 🐾
102 Oak St., Hood River 97031, tel. 541/386–1900, fax 541/386–6090

Although Hood River now bills itself as a kind of rustic Riviera for windsurfers, the Hood River Hotel is a reminder of the town's older character. True, Hood River's fresh identity as a recreational center is the reason the hotel was worth fixing up, but the hotel existed as a simple railroad stopover as early as 1910.

The 41-room brick-faced structure sits just off Main Street. At the front desk is innkeeper Pasquale Barone, a veteran of the European hospitality industry, who brings his Continental flair to Hood River. The rooms are furnished with Victorian reproductions; the beds add a much-needed touch of individuality, be they brass, four-poster, or canopy. In the hotel's two-story-high lobby—which flows into the restaurant and bar—there is a corner where children can find toys to pass the time.

The imposing wooden bar serves local beers and wines in a classy yet laid-back atmosphere. (Windsurfers are often big spenders, but they hang around in wet suits or Lycra shorts.) The bar and the dining room, which extends up to the mezzanine over the lobby, are immense, featuring the building's original pine woodwork.

The food continues the hotel's theme of being at once traditional and trendy. Dinners can get pricey, but the perfectly done seafood is worth it. Continental breakfasts are included as part of the room rate; full breakfasts are extra, but they are worth the money with specials such as chiles rellenos with home fries.

The hotel is close to Hood River's antiques shops and also near the town's liveliest nightspots. A few blocks away is the White Cap Brew Pub (tel. 541/386–2247), home of the Hood River Brewery, which serves its Full Sail Ale, one of the Northwest's most popular local ales. Closer to the hotel is the Brass Rail, a hopping dance club that features bands from the Portland and Seattle club scene. *41 double rooms with baths, 9 suites. Air-conditioning, room service, TV, and phone in rooms, kitchen in suites. Exercise room, sauna, whirlpool, full banquet room. $69–$145; Continental breakfast, full breakfast extra. AE, MC, V. No smoking.*

LAKECLIFF ESTATE BED & BREAKFAST 𝄞
3820 Westcliff Dr. (Box 1220), Hood River 97031, tel. 541/386–7000

From the front room of the stately Lakecliff Estate Bed & Breakfast, the Columbia River gorge is like a three-dimensional postcard. Framed by a window that stretches the width of the large, oak-beamed room, the river view is nothing short of transfixing. When the wind cooperates, legions of little specks with colorful sails—the gorge's latest fun seekers, windsurfers—dot the water.

The estate, now on the National Register of Historic Places, was designed by A. E. Doyle, a turn-of-the-century Portland architect who also designed the Multnomah Falls Lodge and several public buildings in Portland, as well as Portland's charming downtown drinking fountains. Originally built for a Portland merchant family as a country getaway, the large home is something of a grand bed-and-breakfast by Northwest standards. Three of the four guest rooms feature rugged fireplaces made with rocks found on the property when it was built in 1908. Three also have views of the gorge, while the fourth looks back on the woods between the estate and the highway. All are done in country-French style, with oak beams and down comforters on the beds.

Innkeepers Bruce and Judy Thesenga have created an impressive place to relax while taking in the sights of the gorge. In the dining area, Judy's collection of antique milk bottles rings an upper shelf. Bruce, who runs a horse ranch in the hills across the river from the Lakecliff, often takes a turn in the kitchen, where he produces Lakecliff bacon, a sweet, crunchy bacon served cold. Other breakfast mainstays are huckleberry pancakes, frittatas, Dutch babies, and oven-baked French toast. *2 double rooms with baths, 2 doubles share bath. Fireplace in 3 rooms. Shuffleboard court. $90–$110; full breakfast. No credit cards. No smoking. Closed Oct.–Apr.*

MAPLE RIVER ✾

20525 E. Mt. Country La. (Box 339), Brightwood 97011, tel. 503/622–6273

Maple River innkeepers Jim and Barbara Dybvig found the perfect location and, after much work, have remodeled an unassuming contemporary home into an attractive, spacious, and elegant bed-and-breakfast.

The property sits high above the rushing Salmon River, with decks overlooking the river offering peaceful refuge from the everyday world. In the front of the house, gardens, a pond, and a large lawn are surrounded by tall trees, giving the place a completely secluded feel. Inside, a large common room with a massive stone fireplace and vaulted ceilings invites guests to curl up on the deep, soft sofas and relax.

The inn has two suites, the St. Andrews and the Northwoods Room. At this writing, a small outbuilding was steadily being converted into a Honeymoon Suite. Both original suites have private entrances, fireplaces, river views, and pleasant environments. The St. Andrews Suite is tastefully golf themed, with plaid fabrics and memorabilia, while the Northwoods Room offers a more lodgelike feel. The private entrances open onto to a shared patio, and an outdoor hot tub is steps away.

Breakfast at Maple River is served family-style in the warm atmosphere of the country kitchen-dining area. Breakfast includes fruit, muffins, and a hot entrée such as Swedish pancakes, a pear soufflé, Dutch babies, or an egg dish. ♨ *2 suites with baths. Fireplace, robes, and sandals in rooms, TV/VCR and videos in 1 room. Hot tub. $90–$120; full breakfast, refreshments. MC, V. No smoking.*

OLD WELCHES INN ✾

26401 E. Welches Rd., Welches 97067, tel. 503/622–3754

During the days of the Oregon Trail, wagons frequently stopped in Welches on the Salmon River, well below the glaciers of Mt. Hood and its steep passes. Below spread the fertile Willamette Valley, the goal of the weary pioneers. By 1890 the valley had become civilized, and Welches Hotel lured the carriage trade from Portland with the promise of hiking, fishing, and relaxing.

A simple, white clapboard house is all that remains of the hotel. The new inn combines the atmosphere of a laid-back ski lodge and an old country estate. Bleached woodwork accentuates the sunny, airy feel of the place. Much of that feeling comes from Judi Mondun, who operates the inn with her husband, Ted.

The covered patio, with a floor of hand-fitted river stones and lattice walls, features an 8-ft-high stone fireplace that was originally part of the old hotel. Three upstairs rooms share two baths, and the newly added Forget-Me-Not room has a private bath. The largest, which overlooks Resort at the Mountain's 27-hole golf course and has views of Hunchback Mountain, has a sleigh bed, Georgian hunting scenes on the raw silk–covered walls, and a floral upholstered rocking chair. A second room lacks a dramatic view, but the rich cedar paneling and ornate iron bedstead more than compensate. The remaining room on that level has a cannonball-style headboard and is festooned with duck decoys.

An outlying cabin is even closer to the river and the golf course—it overlooks the first hole. The 1901 structure has its own kitchen, two bedrooms, and a river-rock fireplace. A full breakfast is served bright and early—from 7:30 to 9—in the dining room or on the patio; the favorite among guests is Grandma's Special Casserole, an herbed egg dish with sausage and cheese. ♨ *1 double room with bath, 3 double rooms share 2 baths, 1 2-bedroom cabin. TV in 1 room, kitchen* *and fireplace in cabin. $75–$175; full breakfast (except for cabin). AE, MC, V. No smoking, 2-night minimum on holiday weekends.*

OTHER CHOICES

Brookside Bed and Breakfast. 45232 S.E. Paha Loop, Box 1112, Sandy 97055, tel. 503/668–4766. 1 double room with bath, 2 double with shared bath. $35–$65; full breakfast. No credit cards. No smoking.

Chamberlain House. 36817 E. Crown Point Hwy., Corbett 97019, tel. 503/695–2200. 2 double rooms share bath. $50–$70; full or Continental breakfast, champagne splits in evening. No credit cards. No smoking.

Columbia Gorge Hotel. 4000 Westcliff Dr., Hood River 97031, tel. 541/386–5566 or 800/345–1921, fax 541/387–5414. 40 double rooms with baths. TV, phone, and turndown service in rooms, fireplace in 2 rooms. Restaurant, bar, lobby lounge, bikes, conference facilities. $150–$375; full breakfast, dinner and catering available. AE, D, MC, V. No smoking in restaurant.

Suite River Bed and Breakfast. 69437 E. Vine Maple Dr. (Box 530), Welches 97067, tel. 503/622–3547. 1 suite. TV/VCR, videos. $95; full or Continental breakfast. No credit cards. No smoking.

RESERVATIONS SERVICES

Bed & Breakfast Reservations—Oregon (2321 N.E. 28th Ave., Portland 97212, tel. 503/287–4704). **Northwest Bed and Breakfast** (610 S.W. Broadway, Portland 97205, tel. 503/243–7616). **The Bed & Breakfast Registry** (tel. 503/249–1997 or 800/249–1997).

Central and Eastern Oregon, Including Bend

ELLIOTT HOUSE ☞

305 W. 1st St., Prineville 97754, tel. 541/416–0423, fax 541/416–9368

Despite its rough-hewn reputation, Prineville has always been the most genteel town in central Oregon. Elliott House, a 1908 Queen Anne Victorian on the National Register of Historic Places, keeps that tradition of class in the outback alive. With its thick green lawns, wraparound porch, Tuscan columns, and bay windows, the house stands out like a well-groomed dowager in a quiet but otherwise undistinguished neighborhood. Re-creating the past has become a full-time occupation for the innkeepers, Andrew and Betty Wiechert. Once they found their "dream house," they moved up from the Bay Area and began carefully restoring it.

Fueled by their life-long passion for antiques, the Wiecherts have filled Elliott House with a marvelous collection of turn-of-the-century furnishings, most of it oak. There is an interesting piece wherever you look, including a working 1916 Wurlitzer nickelodeon in the parlor.

The two guest rooms on the second floor are also filled with vintage pieces and accessories. A 100-year-old mahogany side table and English oak commode with black marble grace one of them. In the second room, which has cabbage-rose wallpaper, there's a double cast-iron bed with a high mattress and an embroidered quilt that came by wagon train, as well as an 1890 oak "potty chair" (decorative, of course). The rooms share a large, sumptuous bathroom with floral-print wallpaper, original brass fixtures, and a marble-top sink.

Betty custom-designs breakfasts. Served by candlelight on antique china, the morning's repast might include a bowl of fresh fruit or homemade applesauce, Swedish waffles or crepes with raspberries, or eggs with sausage rolls. To accompany it all, she cranks up the Edison cylinder phonograph and fills the dining room with period music. The innkeepers ask that guests refrain from bringing children under 12. △ *2 double rooms share bath. Cable TV/VCR in attic lounge. Golf and fishing gear, bicycles. $70; full breakfast, afternoon refreshments. No credit cards. No smoking.*

FRENCHGLEN HOTEL ☜
Frenchglen 97736, tel. 541/493–2825, fax 541/493–2828

It's impossible to miss the Frenchglen Hotel—that is, once you *find* Frenchglen, a tiny spot on the map deep in the eastern Oregon desert. Built in 1920, still pioneer days in this remote region, the state-owned hotel resembles a simple prairie church, with a gabled roof visible from miles away as you approach from the north. Manager John Ross spent years as a cook on Alaskan fishing boats, so remoteness is nothing new to him. At least here, at the foot of Steens Mountain, he gets a fresh supply of faces every few days.

The hotel's interior is simple and rustic. A huge camp-type coffeepot is always on the hob in the combination lobby–dining room, where you can absorb local history and whet your appetite for touring with a collection of picture books. The two long pine dining tables serve as a gathering place for ranchers and visitors.

The food here has long been a standout. Every evening a large, hearty family-style dinner is served for overnight guests and the general public. A typical group might include a ranching couple who have driven 60 mi to celebrate their anniversary, a pair of bird-watchers, and a local mechanic. John whips up huge salads, rich casseroles, home-baked rolls, and a main meat dish for à la carte dining. Breakfast is also bountiful, although it's served individually from a menu and isn't included in the room rate.

Most of the people who stay at the hotel, which is on the National Register of Historic Places, are devoted bird-watchers who are drawn by the nearby Malheur National Wildlife Refuge. In the fall, however, Steens teems with hunters. The mix of hunters, ranchers, and conservationists can make for some lively conversations over breakfast. △ *8 double rooms share 2 baths. Restaurant. $53–$56; breakfast not included. D, MC, V. No smoking. Closed mid-Nov.–mid-Mar.*

GEISER GRAND HOTEL ☜
1996 Main St., Baker City 97814, tel. 541/523–1889 or 888/434–7374, fax 541/523–1800

You needn't ask for directions to the Geiser Grand; as you approach Baker City on the interstate, the brown highway signs that designate national parks and monuments lead the way. Few hotels get this kind of roadside publicity, but few hotels have undergone the kind of painstaking restoration that has made this remarkable Italian Renaissance Revival structure once again the jewel of eastern Oregon.

The wealth of the Geiser family's Bonanza gold mine, and the sophistication of Czechoslovakia-born, Chicago-trained architect John Benes, went into building the 1889 hotel. Its opulence, from the rich architectural detail and fine materials to the expansive scale of the rooms (10-ft windows and 18-ft ceilings), gave it a reputation as the finest hotel between Salt Lake City and Portland, and even now there are few that equal it in either city. It closed in 1968, however, and nearly fell to the wrecking ball after decades of disuse and decrepitude; it is thanks to the commitment and expertise of Barbara and Dwight Sidway that it stands today.

The Sidways have extensive experience in historic preservation, and their renovation of the Geiser Grand adhered to the strict guidelines of the National Park Service, down to laboratory analysis of paint flecks to determine and reproduce the original color scheme. The three-year, $6 million restoration earned the hotel National Historic Site status—hence the road signs.

Not only is the building itself a marvel, but the way the Sidways manage it is also highly professional and accommodating. Its ground-floor restaurant is Baker City's finest, with an accomplished menu and a respectable wine list, and tables arrayed underneath the largest stained-glass ceiling in the Northwest. △ *30 double rooms with baths. Room service. Restaurant, bar, exercise room, concierge, meeting rooms, library. $79–$199; breakfast not included. AE, D, DC, MC, V. No-smoking floors.*

LARA HOUSE ☞
640 N.W. Congress St., Bend 97701, tel. and fax 541/388–4064 or tel. 800/766–4064

Staying at Lara House, a cross-gabled Craftsman house built in 1910, gives you a glimpse of what life was like in Bend when it was a four-day trip to Portland instead of the present-day three-hour drive. Beside peaceful Drake Park on the Deschutes River near downtown, Lara House stands out; it's on a huge lot with a sloping lawn atop a retaining wall of native lava rocks.

The house's original woodwork can be seen in the trim and door frames and in the alderwood-coffered ceiling of the living room. There a massive, lodge-size fireplace dominates, to be enjoyed from two cream-and-blue patterned camelback love seats or from the ladder-back chairs about the gaming table. The walls here are heavily stuccoed. Walk through the double French doors and the atmosphere changes radically. Restored to its original style, the huge sunroom, with a glass table, overlooking the 11-acre riverside park is an airy, light-filled haven.

The large, carpeted guest rooms, all on the second floor, have seating areas and private bathrooms. The L-shape Drake Room, furnished in dark oak, has a duck theme: wallpaper borders swimming with them, framed prints of them, and a wall unit displaying knickknacks of these fine-feathered friends. The black clawfoot tub in the bathroom is the original. Softer and more romantic is the Shevlin Room, with its alcoved, lace-covered bed; Queen Anne–style couch and chair; and Cupid prints. A masculine tone predominates in the Cascade Room, which has handsome black-striped wallpaper.

There is a choice of venues for the full, home-style breakfast: the formal dining room, sunroom, or terraced redwood deck that surrounds the house. △ *6 double rooms with baths. Hot tub. $55–$110; full breakfast, afternoon and evening refreshments. D, MC, V. No smoking.*

SATHER HOUSE BED-AND-BREAKFAST ☞
7 N.W. Tumalo Ave., Bend 97701, tel. 541/388–1065 or 888/388–1065, fax 541/330–0591

Bend is booming, and its recent "discovery" has inevitably led to a great deal of undistinguished, fast-track development along its peripheries. Luckily, the charm and dignity of Bend's older neighborhoods can still be savored at the Sather

House, a spacious historic home on the northwest side of town, three blocks from the riverside Drake Park and walking distance from downtown.

Built in 1911 for the Sather family, who occupied it for 75 years, the house reveals characteristics of both Colonial Revival and Craftsman styles and is on the National Register. Owner Robbie Giamboi extensively renovated the house, and her meticulous taste is evident the moment you step inside. Period furnishings are used throughout, and the original Douglas-fir woodwork has been beautifully restored. Robbie sponged and rag-rolled the walls herself. The light-filled living room, with lace-curtained windows, has wingback chairs and a comfortable sofa gathered near a fireplace. Built-in benches in the parlor are used for a games area. There is also a big, airy kitchen and a butler's pantry, where you can get an early morning coffee.

Of the four guest rooms, all on the second floor, the largest and lightest is the Garden Room. It has a sofa and a rocking chair; Battenburg and lace are used for curtains and the comforter. The English Room is darker and more traditionally masculine. The Victorian Room, decorated in blues and pinks, has a 1910 claw-foot tub in the bath. Robbie says her goal is to "pamper the women and feed the men." Breakfast, served in the formal dining room, typically consists of French toast with raspberries and almonds or banana pancakes with lemon sauce. She serves fireside tea in winter and lemonade, iced tea, and cookies on the veranda in summer. ♦ *2 double rooms with baths, 2 doubles share bath. Cable TV in 1 room. TV, fireplace in common room. $75–$85; full breakfast, afternoon tea or refreshments. D, MC, V. No smoking.*

STANG MANOR ☜
1612 Walnut St., La Grande 97850, tel. 541/963–2400 or 888/286–9463

When Marjorie McClure was growing up during the late 1940s in La Grande, the Stang mansion, just a few blocks away, seemed a place of unattainable glamour. Owned by lumber baron August Stang, the richest man in the county, the 1926 Georgian Revival house on the western edge of this small college and ranching town was an obligatory stop for any political figure and celebrity passing through. It wasn't until 1992, when Marjorie and her husband, Pat, returned from California for her father's 100th birthday, that she finally got her chance to stay at the elegant manor. Three months later, the McClures had closed the deal to buy the place that Bing Crosby and Guy Kibbe had visited during Marjorie's childhood.

Stang Manor's interior is full of stylish details from the 1920s. You can enjoy the large Italian stone fireplace in the living room from a semicircular sectional couch upholstered in a rose-print tapestry fabric. Throw open the French doors of the Sun Room, complete with a working wall fountain of teal-color Italian tiles, and the years quickly melt away. Built-in benches line the perimeter of the window-filled room, affording views of the property. White rattan furniture adds to the Jay Gatsby aura of the room.

Extraordinary features are found in every room of this historic house, which has remained unmodified except for its wall coverings. The master suite boasts a turn-of-the-century mahogany four-poster bed and matching dresser with tilting mirror. The bathroom has its original "foot washer," fed with running water.

Breakfast is a lavish affair of fruit, homemade breads and muffins, and a hot dish served in the dining room under a pewter and crystal chandelier. Usually Pat and Marjorie will join you for breakfast, which might be considered an intrusion if they weren't so cordial, informative, and easygoing. ♦ *2 double rooms* *with baths, 2 2-bedroom suites. Cable TV and fireplace in 1 suite. $75–$90; full breakfast, afternoon tea. MC, V. No smoking.*

STEENS MOUNTAIN INN ☞

Hwy. 205, Frenchglen 97736, tel. 541/493–2738, fax 541/493–2835

In the 1920s, the home of the first schoolteacher in the tiny town of Frenchglen underwent an expansion, with the addition of a two-story dance hall hauled in from a ghost town not far away. The town hasn't grown much since then, but the recent conversion of the house into a quietly elegant inn by Lance and Missy Litchy has considerably increased its allure.

The Litchys are a young couple who traded in careers in Bend—hers as an art director, his working at the Mt. Bachelor ski area—to buy the 1876 Frenchglen Mercantile and the adjacent house. Careful craftsmanship, well-chosen art and antiques, and unsparing attention to detail have all gone into making the inn a standout destination in Oregon's desert country. The two upstairs guest rooms share a deck with an alder grove to one side and views of Steens Mountain to the other; white-tile private baths are just down the stairs. The Litchys' spare aesthetic is a sure antidote for bed-and-breakfast travelers who have overdosed on frills and Laura Ashley–style prints.

Next door, the Mercantile has also undergone a transformation, from a basic country store to a not-so-basic country store: Travelers' essentials such as maps, guidebooks, sunscreen, film, and cold drinks are available, as are Navajo rugs, Native American jewelry, and assorted antique accessories. The Litchys also run the adjacent Buckaroo Room, one of eastern Oregon's best restaurants, with a simple but sophisticated menu of filet mignon, pasta, roast chicken, and salads made from high-quality fresh produce. Breakfast choices vary daily; specialties include Black Forest ham and cheddar scrambled eggs with home-style red potatoes and *huevos rancheros.* △ *2 rooms with detached private baths. Guide service, room service, laundry. $75; full breakfast. AE, D, MC, V. No smoking.*

OTHER CHOICES

Bed-and-Breakfast by the River. HCR 77 (Box 790), Prairie City 97869, tel. 541/820–4470. 1 double room with bath, 2 doubles share bath. TV/VCR, pool table in games room. $40–$60; full breakfast. No credit cards. No smoking, no alcohol on premises.

Chandlers Bed, Bread & Trail Inn. 700 S. Main St., (Box 639), Joseph 97846, tel. 541/432–9765 or 800/452–3781. 3 double rooms with baths, 2 doubles share 1½ baths. TV/VCR in common area, computer available. Free shuttle to nearby trailheads. $50–$80; full breakfast. MC, V. No smoking.

Clear Creek Farm Bed-and-Breakfast. Rte. 1, Box 138, Halfway 97834, tel. 541/742–2238 or 800/742–4992, fax 541/742–5175. 4 double rooms share 3 baths, 3 cabin rooms with 3 detached baths. Hot tub, library, bicycles, conference facilities, horse lodging. $60–$66, $30 per person for parties of 2 or more; full breakfast. MC, V. No smoking. Bunkhouses closed Nov.–Apr.

Hotel Diamond. HC 72 (Box 10), Diamond 97722, tel. 541/493–1898, fax 541/493–2084. 3 double rooms with baths, 3 doubles share 2½ baths. TV, radio/CD player, and air-conditioning in rooms. Mountain bikes. $55–$90; Continental breakfast, dinner by reservation. MC, V.

Parker House Bed and Breakfast. 311 N. Main St., Pendleton 97801, tel. 800/700–8581. 5 rooms share 1 bath. Phone and TV in rooms. Fax and secretarial service on request, meeting room. $75–$85; full breakfast, afternoon refreshments. AE, MC, V. No smoking.

Pine Valley Lodge and Halfway Supper Club. 163 N. Main St., Halfway 97834, tel. 541/742–2027. 7 double rooms share baths, 2 suites share bath, dormitory-style accommodation sleeps up to 10. Restaurant, bicycles. $65–$140; full breakfast. No credit cards. No smoking.

Shaniko Hotel. 4th and E Sts., Shaniko 97057, tel. 541/489–3441 or 800/483–3441, fax 541/489–3441. 17 double rooms with baths, 1 suite. Whirlpool tub in suite. Restaurant. $56–$96; Continental or full breakfast. AE, D, MC, V. No smoking.

RESERVATIONS SERVICE

Northwest Bed and Breakfast (1067 Hanover Court S, Salem 97302, tel. 503/243–7616 or 503/370–9033, fax 503/316–9118).

PENNSYLVANIA

The Poconos

FRENCH MANOR ☙

Huckleberry Rd. (Box 39), off Rte. 191, South Sterling 18460, tel. 717/676–3244
or 800/523–8200, fax 717/676–9786

The 40-acre setting of this inn is aristocratic and the views exquisite. Rolling hills and mountain ranges reveal themselves periodically as you drive up the winding, wooded road toward the crest of Huckleberry Mountain to the fieldstone manor house with its slate roof, cooper-mullioned windows, and arched oak door.

Built between 1932 and 1937 as a summer residence for mining tycoon and art collector Joseph Hirschorn, the house was modeled after Hirschorn's château in southern France. After changing hands several times, it became an inn in 1985, and in 1990 it was bought by Ron and Mary Kay Logan, who own and manage the nearby Sterling Inn.

The 40-ft-high Great Room, with a vaulted cherrywood ceiling and a mammoth plastered-stone fireplace at each end, makes a spectacular restaurant. French doors with leaded glass open onto a slate terrace that has a sweeping view of the countryside. The guest rooms, named after European cities, have cypress and cedar walls and ceilings and are decorated in a mix of contemporary style and French antique reproductions. The Venice room has an ornate headboard on its king-size bed. Baths have old-fashioned tile with pedestal sinks. The carriage house has two suites each with fireplace and whirlpool bath and two rooms; it is furnished like the manor house but the rooms are smaller. Although it is secluded, the carriage house feels new, which makes it not nearly as nice as the larger house.

A full-service, no-smoking dining room with a full liquor license treats guests to an à la carte menu that changes about every two months and features highly touted French cuisine. A recent selection included grilled beef tenderloin nestled on a roasted garlic and tomato *concassée* cream; and fresh salmon baked in a sauce of champagne, white peppercorn, and asparagus.

With panoramic views as a backdrop, you can take peaceful walks or go cross-country skiing. Golf, horseback riding, and other recreations are nearby. The medieval atmosphere of the house creates a feeling of timelessness, and the thoughtful service of the Logans and their staff allows you to put your worries away.
△ *6 double rooms with baths, 3 suites. Restaurant (closed for dinner Mon., and Mon.–Thurs. Thanksgiving–Memorial Day), air-conditioning, TV in suites and lounge, Jacuzzi in 1 suite, fireplace in lounge, croquet. $130–$250; full breakfast. AE, D, MC, V. No smoking.*

INN AT MEADOWBROOK ☞
Cherry Lane Rd. E (R.D. 7, Box 7651), East Stroudsburg 18301, tel. 717/629–0296 or 800/249–6861, fax 717/620–1754

Guests who arrive at the Inn at Meadowbrook after dark are often relieved to find they aren't lost. On the long and winding 4½ wooded mi from Tannersville you may begin to think you've missed it, but suddenly, around a corner, there it is, blanketed by soft light and trees and chirping night sounds: a white clapboard manor house with green trim. And just across the road is a white mill house that's part of the inn. If you're going to get pleasantly lost anywhere in the Poconos, this is the place to do it.

For many years the 1867 house and its 43 acres were a horse farm, and in 1985 Kathy and Bob Overman bought the estate and turned it into a bed-and-breakfast. Kathy, an artist who loves to garden, has given each of the guest rooms a distinctive decor. Bob, the resident gourmet chef, has mastered the celebrated raspberry-cinnamon-raisin pudding recipe you may be lucky enough to sample for breakfast.

You can curl up with a book on the leather sofa in the light-flooded parlor or in wing chairs that face the fireplace, or you can simply gaze out the windows at the pond, gazebo, and mill house. The spacious hunter-green dining room, added in the '20s, is a setting out of *The Great Gatsby*, with 15-ft ceilings, arched columns, and tall Palladian windows on three sides framing the gardens, the rushing brook with footbridge, and a pond. French doors open onto the terrace for dining in warm months.

The guest rooms are furnished with English and American antiques and country pieces. There are patchwork quilts, lots of books, wicker chairs, and convenient reading lamps. Room 9, a favorite of guests, has rich burgundy paisley draperies, hunter-green walls, an antique brass bed, and a view of the stables. Room 10 overlooks the pond and has a white-birch four-poster bed that Bob built.

On the inn's grounds you can swim, fish, play tennis, ice-skate, and take leisurely walks with a picnic lunch. Bob and Kathy can arrange horseback riding and carriage and sleigh rides. The area also has its share of antiques shops and flea markets. ▲ *10 double rooms with baths, 6 doubles share 2 baths. Restaurant, TV/VCR in recreation room, pool, 2 tennis courts, shuffleboard, pond. $60–$95; full breakfast. AE, D, DC, MC, V. Smoking in common rooms only, 2-day minimum weekends.*

INN AT STARLIGHT LAKE ☞
Starlight (Box 27) 18461, tel. 717/798–2519 or 800/248–2519, fax 717/798–2672

The hamlet of Starlight, nestled in the foothills of the Moosic range, was once a railroad stop, and in 1909 this Adirondack-style lodge was built on the lake nearby to serve passengers. Today the sprawling white-and-green clapboard inn looks much as it did around the turn of the century, and it's just as peaceful. Jack and Judy McMahon have been innkeepers here since 1974. Before that they lived in New York City and worked in the theater, where they met while performing.

The rambling parlor, with its wood-burning stove, stone fireplace, and baby-grand piano, sets the homey, lodgelike mood. There's a comfortable mixture of antiques, Mission oak furniture, and well-lived-in pieces, with numerous Tiffany-style lamps for reading. In winter you might expect Bing Crosby to step out and warble "White Christmas."

Guest rooms on the second and third floors are simple and unpretentious, with framed prints on floral-papered walls, crocheted doilies, and lots of magazines. You'll find iron beds and marble-top dressers, but mostly a hodgepodge of old and not-so-old furniture. A row of recently renovated cottages is furnished with antique reproductions. The suite has a king-size bed and a whirlpool bath for two; above it is another charming room with an iron bed and a fieldstone fireplace.

Chef David Giles presides in the dining room. Everything served is made on the premises, including breads, pastas, ice cream, and pastries. You can work off a little of David's duck with orange sauce with a game of pool, Ping-Pong, or tabletop shuffleboard in the inn's game room.

No motors are allowed on the 45-acre lake, so it's quiet and crystal clean for swimming and fishing. On occasional murder-mystery weekends, whodunits are performed by the Starlight Players. In winter there's ice-skating, and the McMahons' son, a certified ski instructor, can take you down the property's slopes or show you the best trails for cross-country skiing. On crisp autumn mornings you are likely to see deer or flocks of wild turkeys through the early mist. ♨ *20 double rooms with baths, 2 doubles share bath, 1 suite, 3-bedroom family house. Restaurant, bar, TV/VCR in sunroom, baby-sitting arranged, bicycles, tennis court, canoes. $115–$200; full breakfast, dinner. MC, V. No smoking in dining room, 2-day minimum season, 3-day minimum holidays. Closed 1st 2 wks in Apr.*

SETTLERS INN ☞
4 Main Ave., Hawley 18428, tel. 717/226–2993 or 800/833–8527, fax 717/226–1874

This rambling Tudor-style grand hotel built in 1927 has been restored as a country inn. It's on a well-traveled bend of Route 6, five minutes from Lake Wallenpaupack, but once you enter the high-ceiling living room, with its chestnut beams and massive stone fireplace, you'll forget about the location. Antique marble-top tables and Victorian chairs and sofas evoke the atmosphere of an English country hotel. The rooms, furnished with "early attic" antiques, also have Early American memorabilia.

The popular dining room is the domain of Grant Genzlinger, who's not only chef-innkeeper but also a student of ancient Chinese languages. He and his wife, Jeanne, share innkeeping duties with their partner, Marcia Dunsmore, and distinguish themselves mightily in the kitchen arts. The flavorful, amply portioned dinners testify to the proprietors' assiduous search for locally grown ingredients as well as to their loyalty to regional specialties. Dishes reflect the joy of a year-round pursuit of the best and brightest in the Pennsylvania agricultural community. Witness the cheddar pasta supper dish, composed of fettuccine, leeks, and spinach tossed in a sauce of Up Country Pennsylvania sharp cheddar and Forest Home Dairy fresh cream; or the chicken schnitzel, a scallop of chicken dipped in a light lemon and thyme batter, scented with nutmeg, sautéed, and served with fettuccine and roasted zucchini, peppers, yellow squash, onions, and tomatoes. You'll dine sitting in one of the more than 100 Gothic, church-school chairs brought from the Bryn Athyn Cathedral near Philadelphia; and if you'd like, you may take your meal out on the terrace.

If you detect a sometimes whimsical, sometimes earnest voice in the menu descriptions, trust it for its very contradictions. The trio in charge does it all with a winning combination of dead seriousness and an insouciant aptitude for gustatory lucky strikes. Where else would you find garlic additions to an entrée honored on the menu as the "errant lily"?

The location is ideal for getting to winter or summer sports, and the town has enough antiques shops to keep you browsing for days. ♠ *16 double rooms with baths, 2 suites. Restaurant, air-conditioning, cable TV, 2 meeting rooms, large banquet room, gift shop. $83–$143; full breakfast. AE, D, MC, V. Smoking in lounge and bar only.*

STERLING INN ☞
South Sterling 18460, tel. 717/676–3311, 717/676–3338, or 800/523–8200

Ron Logan, owner of the Sterling Inn, has put together a 10-page document tracing the site's history, from its occupation by the Nini subtribe (a branch of the Leni–Lenape) all the way up to his and his wife's proprietorship. "There is little wonder why the Indians would choose this particular site for their village," he observes. "Mountains on either side, the Wallenpaupack Creek with an abundance of trout, level fertile land, bubbling springs, and plenty of deer, bear, and other game."

It's still lovely here today, and this in itself is testimony to Ron and Mary Kay Logan's talent, energy, and restraint. The inn consists of an inviting white clapboard main house with hunter-green rooftop, built in 1857, and a cluster of cottages. It all sits on the road, nestled in a forested valley traversed by nature trails and winding waterways. The couple provides once-a-week lectures and guided nature walks, conducted by local author John Serrao, so that guests can absorb more than a glimpse of the 105 surrounding acres of birch, hemlock, and American beech, not to mention the wildflowers and bird life.

A fresh, countrified air prevails inside the inn, notwithstanding a few modern embellishments—a heated indoor pool, a poolside bar, and a spa. The dining room, open to guests and nonguests alike, is dominated by a large stone fireplace and decorated with a delicate floral-patterned wallpaper, pink tablecloths and woodwork, and bright blue cotton curtains over broad window valances. Resident chef George Pelepko Filak, a graduate of the Culinary Institute of America, is happy to accommodate special diets, but each standard menu is lavished with entrées like medallions of veal lombardi; scampi with scallops, garlic, and wine; and steamed red snapper.

The rooms, accented by playful ruffles and flounces, echo the clean, bright-eyed ingenuousness of the downstairs dining room. They all have phones and private baths; fireplace suites and cottages are available. The Logans offer several discount package rates. Romance and privacy give visitors here a true escape. Winter delights include horse-drawn sleigh rides and cross-country skiing; in the summer diversions such as swimming, hiking, horseback riding, and fishing abound. ♠ *38 double rooms with baths, 27 suites. Phone in rooms, fireplace and Jacuzzi in 11 suites, indoor pool, spa, restaurant, gazebo, pond, cross-country ski trails, nature trails. $160–$260; full breakfast, dinner. AE, D, MC, V. No smoking in dining room.*

OTHER CHOICES

Brookview Manor. Rte. 447 (R.R. 1, Box 365), Canadensis 18325, tel. 717/595–2451 or 800/585–7974. 9 double rooms with baths, 1 suite. Whirlpool bath in 2 rooms, fireplace in 1 room, TV in den. $110–$150; full breakfast, afternoon tea. AE, DC, MC, V. No smoking indoors, 2-night minimum weekends Sept.–Oct and holidays.

Cliff Park Inn. Cliff Park Rd. (R.R. 4, Box 7200), Milford 18337, tel. 717/296–6491 or 800/225–6535, fax 717/296–3982. 19 double rooms with baths. Restaurant, air-conditioning, conference facilities, TV/VCR in meeting rooms, 9-hole golf course, pro shop, stable. $128–$205 (full breakfast and dinner); $110–$210 (breakfast only). AE, D, DC, MC, V. Closed Dec. 24–25.

Overlook Inn. Dutch Hill Rd. (Box 680), Canadensis 18325-9755, tel. 717/595–7519 or 800/590–3845. 18 double rooms with baths, 2 suites. Restaurant, air-conditioning, phone in rooms, TV in library, conference facilities, pool. $95–$115; breakfast, afternoon tea, dinner. AE, MC, V. No smoking in dining room or guest rooms.

New Hope, Bucks County, and Beyond

BARLEY SHEAF FARM ❧
Rte. 202 (Box 10), Holicong 18928, tel. 215/794–5104, fax 215/794–5332

Turn off well-traveled Route 202 10 minutes from New Hope, and you'll see sheep grazing in the pastures on either side of a sycamore-flanked lane. At the end is Barley Sheaf Farm, the 1740 mansard-roofed fieldstone house that in the '30s was the hideaway of playwright George S. Kaufman. Today this charming 30-acre farm, though just around the bend from the bustling antiques shops of Peddler's Village, manages to retain the quiet gentility that prevailed when Lillian Hellman, Alexander Woollcott, and Moss Hart visited here.

The swimming pool, a duck pond, and the bank barn add texture and a relaxed appeal to the house and grounds, which have been designated a National Historic Site. On a visit to the States in 1994, Peter and Veronika Suess, two businesspeople from Switzerland, saw Barley Sheaf and fell in love with it. They quit their jobs, bought the property via international fax, and arrived the first night to a full house of guests.

The house and adjacent cottage are furnished in a mixture of English and American antiques, with rich Oriental rugs scattered over the wide-plank floors. Guests gather in the common room by the fire for chess, checkers, and conversation.

The bedrooms on the second and third floors have elegant views. The rooms are decorated with floral prints and brass-and-iron beds. Peter and Veronika have brought with them from Switzerland furniture, antiques, and traditions, including breakfast *grittibaenz* (little men made of bread with raisin eyes).

The separate cottage is cozy, and in winter months there's always a crackling fire. The three bedrooms here are decorated with American folk art, both antique and reproduction. Each room has sloping eaves, hooked rugs, and antique pine furniture. Though the rooms are small, the cottage is perfect for families.

You should expect to hear noises in this rural setting—the noises of a working farm: the baaing of sheep, the buzzing of bees (which manufacture 300 pounds of honey annually), and the occasional rumble of a tractor. But that means you can count on the abundant breakfasts (which include eggs, bread, jams, and honey) to be farm fresh. � *7 double rooms with baths, 5 suites. Air-conditioning, Jacuzzi in 1 suite, TV in study, pool, badminton, croquet, meeting room in barn. $110–$235; full breakfast, afternoon tea. AE, MC, V. No smoking, 2-day minimum weekends, 3-day minimum holidays.*

EVERMAY-ON-THE-DELAWARE ✸
889 River Rd. (Box 60), Erwinna 18920, tel. 610/294–9100, fax 610/294–8249

Thirteen miles north of New Hope is Evermay-on-the-Delaware, a romantic country hotel with a carriage house and cottage set on 25 parklike acres between the river and the canal. Here Victorian elegance is still very much in fashion.

The mansion, which is on the National Register of Historic Places, was built in 1790 and had a third floor added in 1870. From 1871 through the early 1930s, it was a popular country hotel. It was the Stover family home for many years and was opened as an inn in 1982. Current innkeepers William and Danielle Moffly purchased the inn in 1996.

In the stately double parlor you can meet for afternoon tea or for an aperitif in the evening. The fireplace is inset with Mercer tiles, and there are crystal chandeliers, tapestry rugs, a Victorian grandfather clock, and brocade camelback settees. Breakfast is served in a conservatory off the back parlor. The bedrooms, carefully decorated with Victorian antiques and named after Bucks County notables, have wide-plank squeaky floors; some retain their original fireplaces. Carved walnut beds, massive headboards, marble-top dressers, Victorian wallpaper, and fresh fruit and flowers are everywhere. Ask for one of the six bedrooms in the main house that face the river. The carriage house may be preferable for groups traveling together. It has a two-bedroom suite with sitting room and bath on the second floor and two double rooms on the ground floor.

The inn's restaurant is open Friday, Saturday, and Sunday nights for one seating at 7:30 (6:30 on Sunday in winter). A six-course, fixed-price meal ($62 per person) is served, starting with a glass of champagne and hors d'oeuvres. There are two choices of entrée, which might include roast loin of venison.

Evermay is ideally located for enjoying the countryside in any season. If you venture out back into the meadows or into the old barn, you will run across sheep, chickens, and pheasants. ♠ *16 rooms with baths. Restaurant, air-conditioning and phone in bedrooms, hookups for modem. $135–$235; Continental-plus breakfast, afternoon tea. MC, V. No smoking, 2-day minimum with Sat. reservation, 3-day minimum holidays. Closed Dec. 24.*

GLASBERN ✸
2141 Pack House Rd., Fogelsville 18051-9743, tel. 610/285–4723, fax 610/285–2862

You will understand why Al and Beth Granger chose this name (which means "glass barn" in Old English) when you see their country inn. Glasbern is a 19th-century German bank barn, tucked into a quiet valley 10 mi west of Allentown, and the Grangers have reconstructed it of stone, wood, and lots of glass. The Great Room resembles a lofty stone sanctuary, with a fireplace and hand-hewn beams that crisscross through the high, open spaces. Guest rooms are decorated traditionally, with standard antique reproductions, and in contemporary style with glass tables and wicker. Brick walkways lead to a farmhouse and a carriage house, both renovated and similarly decorated—there's a certain sameness about the decor. All suites have whirlpool baths, and fireplaces, and some have kitchenettes and private entrances. Skiing, hiking, and antiquing are close by, but you may find you're content with just being on these 113 peaceful acres in the middle of nowhere. ♠ *14 double rooms with baths, 15 suites. Restaurant, air-conditioning, TV/VCR and phone in bedrooms, conference facilities, pool, fitness room, bicycles. $115–$355; full breakfast. AE, MC, V. 2-night minimum weekends Memorial Day–mid-Nov.*

INN AT FORDHOOK FARM 🐦
105 New Britain Rd., Doylestown 18901, tel. 215/345–1766, fax 215/345–1791

The Inn at Fordhook Farm, set on 60 acres a mile and a half from the center of Doylestown, is the Burpee family estate. There's a bank barn and a carriage house, surrounded by the fields and meadows where W. Atlee Burpee first tested seeds for his company before the turn of the century. The oldest part of the fieldstone-and-plaster house with a mansard roof dates from 1740. Through the years, additions were carefully made to blend architecturally with the original structure. Burpee's grandchild, Jonathan Burpee, grew up here. Thinking that a bed-and-breakfast would be a good way to preserve the family home, Jonathan and his wife, Carole, opened it to guests in 1985.

The house is furnished with English and American family antiques and photographs, grandfather clocks, and other Americana. In the dining room, the mantel is inlaid with Mercer tiles, and the long mahogany table is set with heirloom china each morning for breakfast. French doors open to a large terrace shaded by a 200-year-old linden tree, with a view of the broad, sweeping lawn. In the bedrooms, you will find floral prints, quilts, 19th-century four-poster beds, window seats, and family photographs and portraits.

The carriage house is a spacious two-bedroom suite not quite as carefully decorated as the main house but ideal for a family or for two couples. The chestnut-paneled Great Room there, once a study, has a vaulted ceiling and Palladian windows, and children's books, photographs, and other Burpee memorabilia everywhere.

The style at Fordhook Farm is a quiet, casual elegance. Carole serves an elaborate Saturday tea—by the fire during the winter, outdoors on the generous terrace in warm months. ♣ *5 double rooms with baths, 2 doubles share bath. Air-, conference room. $100–$300; full breakfast. AE, MC, V. No smoking, 2-day minimum weekends, 3-day minimum holidays.*

INN AT PHILLIPS MILL 🐦
2590 N. River Rd., New Hope 18938, tel. 215/862–2984

Perched at a bend in the road, in a tiny hamlet on the Delaware Canal near New Hope, is a 1750 stone inn that looks like an illustration from Grimm's Fairy Tales. There may be no country inn with a setting more romantic than the Inn at Phillips Mill. Built as a barn and a gristmill, it once stood next to the village piggery—a copper pig with a wreath around its neck now welcomes you from just above the deep-blue door.

For 70 years the gristmill has been the September home of the Phillips Mill Community Art Show. In the early 1970s, the main building and its walled garden caught the imagination of Brooks and Joyce Kaufman. Thinking it had the look of a European village, they bought it; Brooks, an architect, started the renovation, and Joyce began doing the interior. They opened in 1977.

The guest rooms are small, but they will enchant you. Some are tucked imaginatively into nooks and under eaves, and each is whimsically furnished. There are brass and iron and late-19th-century four-poster beds, and an eclectic mix of antiques, wicker, quilts, dried bouquets, hand-painted trays, embroidered cloths on night tables, Provençal fabrics, floral wallpapers, and oil paintings. The cottage, also decorated in a mix of French country and American antiques, has a bedroom, a bath, and a living room with a stone fireplace. If you wish, breakfast will be delivered to your bedroom door in a big basket. When you lift the blue-and-white checkered cloth, you will find muffins and a pot of coffee or tea.

Phillips Mill is famous for its restaurant, and rightly so. The candlelit tables in the three dining rooms are intimately nestled into nooks and crannies under low, rough-beamed ceilings. The menu is French and may feature garlic-encrusted sword-fish in a beurre blanc sauce, or smoked breast of mallard duck with herbed lentils. Two pastry chefs, Roz Schwartz and Thomas Millburn, prepare *les délices de la maison* (house delights).

The winding back roads are perfect for hiking, bicycling, or driving to see the fall foliage. ♣ *4 double rooms with baths, 1 suite, 1 cottage. Restaurant, air-conditioning, pool. $80–$125; Continental breakfast not included. No credit cards. BYOB, 3-night minimum holiday weekends. Closed early Jan.–early Feb.*

LONGSWAMP BED AND BREAKFAST ⚘

1605 State St., Mertztown 19539, tel. 610/682–6197

This white clapboard Federal manor house is in a rural village about 15 min-utes southwest of Allentown. Elsa and Dean Dimick restored the house, which was built in 1789, and opened it as a bed-and-breakfast in 1983. When they're not innkeeping, he's chief of medicine at the Lehigh Valley Hospital, and she's a professional chef. In the parlor, with its wood-pegged floors, deeply set windows, and settees before the fireplace, you can sit and enjoy the Dimicks' vast collec-tion of books and music. The large, sunny guest rooms are decorated in a mix of Pennsylvania and Victorian antiques, with Amish quilts and one-of-a-kind antique iron beds. The cottage at the side, used by the Underground Railroad, is much more haphazardly decorated, with antiques and family hand-me-downs. Golf, tennis, and horseback riding are nearby, and the Dimicks can help you map out drives down scenic back roads through farmland or to antiques shops for browsing. ♣ *4 double rooms with baths, 4 doubles share 2 baths, 2 suites. Air-conditioning, TV in summer kitchen and suites, hiking trails on 40 adjoin-ing acres. $78–$88; full breakfast, afternoon tea. AE, MC, V. No smoking.*

MANSION INN ⚘

9 S. Main St., New Hope 18938, tel. 215/862–1231, fax 215/862–0277

An atmosphere of romantic luxury and calm fills the Mansion Inn, just steps off bustling Main Street in New Hope. The pale yellow, 1865 Second Empire–style Victorian building, with a mansard roof and arched front door, is owned by Dr. Elio Filippo Bracco and Keith David, who opened the inn in 1995. They restored what had been a doctor's office, adding modern baths, some with whirlpool tubs. Innkeeper Diana Smith is on hand to offer suggestions for touring, shopping, and dining, but she also respects guests' privacy.

The two high-ceiling sitting areas are formal yet comfortably inviting. The buttery yellow drawing room is filled with floral-print furniture, some works by local artists, and Depression glass. The smaller drawing room, done in soothing beige tones, has books and games for adults. Besides the seven rooms in the house, the inn has two in a garden cottage. Each has a different color scheme, from the blue toile de Jouy print in Ashby to the rose chintz of Windsor. All rooms have antiques, such as settees, armoires, or trunks; some have four-poster canopy beds or fire-places. Egyptian cotton towels, starched and ironed sheets, and toiletries add lux-urious touches, and many rooms have TVs and blow dryers. Nightly turndown includes home-baked cookies and bottled spring water. You may hear some street noise on busy weekends in rooms facing Main Street.

Breakfast is served at white wicker tables and chairs in the green-and-white-wall-papered breakfast room. Early birds can have coffee and a newspaper delivered to their rooms. The hearty buffet of fresh-baked muffins, breads, fresh fruit, and granola is followed by a choice of a special French toast or an egg dish.

The English-style garden has a gazebo. A fenced-in swimming pool is just off the guests' parking area yet feels delightfully private—much like the inn itself. ♲ *5 rooms with baths, 4 suites. Air-conditioning, TV in most rooms, phone with dataport jacks, swimming pool. $160–$265; full breakfast. AE, MC, V. No smoking, 2-night minimum weekends, 3-night minimum holiday weekends.*

1740 HOUSE 🦜
River Rd., Lumberville 18933, tel. 215/297–5661

Travel 6½ mi north from New Hope on Route 32, one of the most scenic roads in Pennsylvania, and you will come to the 1740 House, an inn that takes full advantage of its picturesque location. The original 1740 two-story clapboard farmhouse, and its more recent attached additions, sits just off River Road and just a few feet from the Delaware Canal and the Delaware River. The guest rooms are decorated in beige and Wedgwood blue, many with wicker furniture and exposed beams. All have a balcony or terrace with an impressive view of the river. The suite has large windows on three sides and a four-poster bed. You'll have breakfast in the candlelit dining room, lined with plants and paintings and overlooking the river.

Innkeeper Robert John Vris has been connected to the inn since his grandfather Harry Nessler bought it in 1966; Bob took over in 1994 when Harry died. He will describe the walks you can take—up to 15 mi in either direction along the towpath, or across the river on a footbridge to a small state park. ♲ *23 double rooms with baths, 1 suite. Pool. $80–$118; Continental-plus breakfast. No credit cards. No smoking in dining room, 2-day minimum weekends Mar.–Nov.*

WEDGWOOD COLLECTION OF INNS 🦜
111 W. Bridge St., New Hope 18938, tel. 215/862–2570

You can't miss the Wedgwood Inn. This hip-gabled 1870 Victorian clapboard house on a tree-lined street is only two blocks from the center of New Hope, and it's painted bright Wedgwood blue. It has a large veranda loaded with pots of flowers and hanging ferns, a porte-cochere, and garden walks that wind around to a gazebo. The companion property next door, called Umplebey House, was built of plaster and stone about 1830 in the Classical Revival tradition. It has walls that are 26 inches thick, brick walkways through flowering gardens, and a carriage house in back. Across the street is another companion property, the Aaron Burr House, a six-bedroom Victorian with a maximum capacity of 18 guests, popular for business conferences.

Innkeeping seems a logical profession for owners Nadine Silnutzer and Carl Glassman, 14-year veterans of the B&B game. They like gardening, and they delight in finding antiques at auctions and flea markets. Carl, with his colleague Ripley Hotch, has published a book, *How to Start and Run Your Own Bed & Breakfast Inn* (Stackpole Books). He teaches innkeeping at New York University.

Wedgwood pottery, oil paintings, handmade quilts, and fresh flowers are everywhere in the sunny interior. The parlors in each house have coal-fed fireplaces and plush Victorian sofas and chairs. The windows are covered with lace swag curtains. Persian rugs lie on hardwood floors. Each house has bedrooms with bay windows, brass and four-poster beds, and Victorian antiques. Each room is decorated individually and hand-painted by a local artist. Private balconies have recently been added to three rooms, providing a treetop view. The circa-1890 carriage house has a small sitting room, a glass-enclosed porch, a kitchenette, and a four-poster bed in a loft overlooking a small deck. It's a private retreat that's ideal for reading a novel, or maybe writing one.

Days begin casually with a Continental-plus breakfast, served in the sunporch, the gazebo, or if you prefer, in bed. If you ask, Carl and Dinie will get you theater tickets, make dinner reservations, and arrange picnics, dinner in the gazebo, or a moonlight carriage ride. △ *16 double rooms with baths, 4 suites, 1 carriage house. Air-conditioning, TV in 4 rooms and in parlors, concierge services, swimming and tennis privileges for nominal fee at nearby club. $75–$210; Continental-plus breakfast, afternoon tea. AE, MC, V. No smoking indoors, 2-day minimum weekends, 3-day minimum holiday weekends.*

WHITEHALL INN ☙
1370 Pineville Rd., New Hope 18938, tel. 215/598–7945 or 888/379–4483

Ten minutes southwest of New Hope and five minutes from Peddler's Village is the Whitehall Inn, a white plaster-over-stone manor house, circa 1794, set on 12 rolling acres, with a huge white barn and stables at the side. It is one of the most peaceful and secluded inns in Bucks County.

Two transplanted Oklahomans, Mike and Suella Wass, are responsible for elevating the business of innkeeping to a fine art. No guest will feel neglected here; from the moment you cross the threshold, the Wasses convince you that your visit is important to them. They encourage your interest in the area, engage you in conversation, and ultimately earn your compliments. After years in their niche, the Wasses continue to stand above the rest.

Inside the house, past the sunroom, are high ceilings, Oriental rugs on wide-plank floors, and windows with deep sills. The parlor has a fireplace, a late-19th-century pedal organ, comfortable contemporary sofas with lots of Victorian lamps, and the soothing sounds of antique clocks ticking everywhere. The bedrooms (four with fireplaces) are furnished in a mixture of late Victorian and American country antiques. You will find a basket of apples, a bottle of mineral water, and Crabtree & Evelyn soaps, colognes, and shampoos. The linens are imported, and in winter you sleep between flannel sheets.

Heirloom china and ornate Victorian sterling flatware are used for breakfast, a sybaritic and beautifully orchestrated four-course feast, with lighted tapers on the table and sideboards. The Wasses keep your menu on file, so you'll never get a repeat unless you make a special request.

High tea is served at 4 each afternoon with crystal, china, and silver. In summer, you can relax by the pool, play tennis, or go horseback riding nearby. In October, you can walk in the gardens or fields, enjoy the foliage, and spend evenings by the fire in the candlelit parlor. Lovers of chocolate and/or chamber music should inquire about special-event weekends in the spring. △ *4 double rooms with baths, 2 doubles share bath. Air-conditioning, pool. $140–$200; full breakfast, afternoon tea. AE, D, MC, V. No smoking, 2-night minimum weekends, 3-night minimum holidays.*

OTHER CHOICES

Ash Mill Farm. Rte. 202 (Box 202), Holicong 18928, tel. 215/794–5373. 3 double rooms with baths, 2 suites. Air-conditioning. $100–$155; full breakfast, afternoon tea, complimentary brandy. No credit cards. Smoking on veranda only, 2-day minimum with Sat. reservation, 3-day minimum holiday weekends.

Bridgeton House. River Rd. (Box 167), Upper Black Eddy 18972, tel. 610/982–5856 or 888/982–2007, fax 610/982–5080. 8 double rooms with baths, 2 suites, penthouse. Air-conditioning, cable TV in 4 rooms; fireplace in dining room, suites, and penthouse. $119–$249; full breakfast, afternoon tea and sherry. MC, V. No smoking indoors, 2-day minimum weekends, 3-day minimum holiday weekends.
Bucksville House. 4501 Durham Rd. and Buck Dr., Kintnersville 18930, tel. 610/847–8948. 4 double rooms with baths, 1 suite. Air-conditioning, fireplace in 3 rooms, cable TV in den, water garden with waterfall, gazebo. $100–$130; full breakfast. AE, D, MC, V. No smoking.
Highland Farms. 70 East Rd., Doylestown 18901, tel. 215/340–1354. 4 double rooms with baths. Air-conditioning, cable TV with VCR in library, phone in library, pool, tennis court. $135–$195; full breakfast, sherry in evening. MC, V. No smoking, 2-day minimum weekends, 3-day minimum holidays.
Logan Inn. 10 W. Ferry St., New Hope 18938, tel. 215/862–2300. 16 double rooms with baths. Restaurant, tavern, air-conditioning, cable TV and phone in bedrooms, meeting room, free off-street parking. $95–$160; Continental-plus breakfast. AE, D, DC, MC, V. 2-day minimum weekends May–Dec., 3-day minimum holiday weekends.
Pinetree Farm. 2155 Lower State Rd., Doylestown 18901, tel. 215/348–0632. 3 double rooms with baths. Air-conditioning, cable TV in solarium, pool. $155–$185; full breakfast. No credit cards. No smoking, 2-day minimum weekends, 3-day minimum holiday weekends.

The Brandywine River Valley

DULING-KURTZ HOUSE & COUNTRY INN ☞
146 S. Whitford Rd., Exton 19341, tel. 610/524–1830, fax 610/524–6258

On a country road midway between Valley Forge and the Brandywine Battlefields is the Duling-Kurtz House & Country Inn. The driveway is lined with converted gas street lamps, and there are formal gardens, a Victorian-style gazebo, and a footbridge that crosses a stone-lined brook. The 1830s farmhouse and the adjacent barn, both white plaster over fieldstone, were elegantly restored and opened in 1983. Raymond Carr and David Knauer, who did the restoration, named the property after their mothers. The current owner, Michael Person—who hails from Vienna, Austria, and has a background in hotel management—has orchestrated a massive upgrading since taking over in 1992, and he is a decidedly hands-on operator. He staunchly defends the concept of fine dining and lodging at affordable prices, and he runs an intimate, service-oriented inn.

The guest rooms (in the barn) have been restored and furnished in Williamsburg period reproductions. You will find marble-top sinks; Oriental rugs; writing desks; and canopied, brass, and four-poster beds. One suite has its own courtyard. Rooms are named for historic figures: Honeymooners often request the George Washington Room, with its king-size, cherrywood canopy bed and step-down bathroom with claw-foot tub. A Continental breakfast is served on china in the parlor.

A sheltered brick walkway connects the barn and the farmhouse restaurant, which is also furnished with Colonial reproductions. Near the entrance you'll discover an unusual 18th-century beehive bread oven. Four of the dining rooms have stone fireplaces, and richly mullioned windows detail the dining areas. Under the direction of chef Michael Favacchio, the dinner menu features hickory-smoked buffalo fillet, duck confit with sweet potato ravioli, and a rich crepe stuffed with lobster and draped in brie sauce. The steaming, freshly baked popovers, served with tangy lemon curd, are legendary. Dinner entrées range from $18 to $30.

You can stroll through peaceful wooded areas adjoining the inn, and when it's warm you can enjoy tea in the gazebo. Museums and battlefields are not far away, and Michael and his staff will point you to the best antiquing and shopping. ▲ *15 double rooms with baths, 3 suites. Restaurant, air-conditioning, cable TV and phone in rooms, room service, 3 conference rooms with catering. $55–$120; Continental breakfast. AE, D, DC, MC, V. No smoking.*

FAIRVILLE INN ☞
Rte. 52 (Box 219), Fairville 19357, tel. 610/388–5900, fax 610/388–5902

In the heart of Andrew Wyeth country, on the road between Winterthur Museum and Longwood Gardens, this country-house inn is set on 5½ acres behind a split-rail fence. It is surrounded by estates, beautiful gardens, and miles of country roads. The hub of the inn is a pale yellow–colored 1826 Federal-style plaster-over-double-brick house with dark green shutters. There's a Victorian-style veranda across the front. In back are the Spring House and Carriage House, buildings that were constructed about 10 years ago but designed to match the character of the main house.

Swedish-born Ole Retlev and his wife, Patricia, both former ski instructors, owned two different inns in Mt. Snow, Vermont. But, as Ole explains, "there's more to draw travelers here on a year-round basis." So, in 1986, they moved to the Brandywine River valley and opened the Fairville Inn.

The rooms are bright and airy, appealingly furnished with Queen Anne and Chippendale reproductions. Before the fireplace in the living room are two blue settees, with a large copper-top coffee table between them. The flowered draperies and potted plants give the room an understated "relaxed formal feel," as Ole calls it. The bedrooms in the main house, all of quirky size and shape, are done in light, elegant country colors and are carpeted. You will also find four-poster beds, canopy beds, settees, writing desks, floral wallpapers—and fresh flowers. The four rooms in the Spring House are somewhat larger, and all have working gas fireplaces and private balconies. Siding from the old barn has been used for mantels and paneling, and some of the sinks have copper drain boards.

Private terraces, balconies that overlook a pond and rolling farmland, and gas fireplaces make the Carriage House rooms appealing. They are at the back of the property and away from traffic noise. With cathedral ceilings and old barn timbers for beams and mantels, two suites in the Carriage House are the most architecturally interesting.

Canoeing, hiking, antiquing, and museum-browsing are only some of the area's pastimes. Why not attend a polo match during one of the warmer months? ▲ *13 double rooms with baths, 2 suites. Air-conditioning, cable TV, and phone in rooms. $140–$195; Continental breakfast, afternoon tea. AE, D, MC, V. No smoking, 2-night minimum with Sat. reservation.*

HAMANASSETT ☞
Rte. 1 (Box 129), Lima 19037, tel. 610/459–3000

Meet Evelene Dohan, the proprietor of Hamanassett: She has taught English literature, run a catering business, and gone home a multiple champion from the Philadelphia Flower Show. Her gifts are evident both on the grounds and in the decor of this secluded estate.

The hilltop residence overlooks 48 acres of woods and meadow, shaded garden pathways, and stone-walled ponds. In April and May, approaching guests travel on a ½-mi driveway lined with ancient rhododendrons and well-established azaleas, blossoming in profusion all the way up to the ellipse that fronts the main house. Inside, the innkeeper's cut-flower arrangements grace each room; potted plants and hanging ferns flood the light-filled solarium. Mrs. Dohan, who came as a bride in 1950 and raised her children here, has appointed the rooms with four-poster canopied beds, Oriental rugs, and handsome antiques. And she single-handedly serves up delectable country breakfasts with homemade jams, compotes, and freshly baked confections.

Hamanassett was built in 1856 for Dr. Charles Meigs, a Philadelphia pioneer in obstetrics, but what you see today bears little resemblance to the doctor's summer retreat. As Mrs. Dohan will tell you, the little farmhouse then consisted of just "three rooms down, and three rooms up." But in 1870 her late husband's grandfather purchased the estate. His son—her father-in-law—didn't like the sensation of enclosure, and so he added onto and redefined the original structure (including the pumpkin pine flooring). He installed arched passageways instead of doors between rooms on the first floor, so the main body of the house feels united, allowing fluid movement from room to room and a less obstructed flow of light. Before ascending the main staircase, note the blue-and-white delft tile depiction of human history encased in the broad white arch to your right: The story begins with the expulsion from the Garden of Eden.

You may find yourself so seduced by the beauty this proficient innkeeper has created that you won't want to venture outside it. But if you do, all the most popular points of interest are only minutes away. Hamanassett sits just off well-traveled Route 1, but its acreage makes an ample buffer between the estate and the roadway. △ *7 rooms with baths, 1 suite. Air-conditioning in some rooms, TV in all, solarium. $90–$125; full breakfast. No credit cards. No smoking, 2-night minimum year-round.*

LENAPE SPRINGS FARM ☙
580 W. Creek Rd. (Box 176, Pocopson), West Chester 19366, tel. 610/793–2266 or 800/793–2234

You'll need directions to get to this out-of-the-way location in the Brandywine River valley, but that's what makes it so wonderful. Though only 4 mi north of Chadds Ford, Sharon and Bob Currie's 32-acre farm is down a dead-end country road that runs along a secluded section of the Brandywine River and is, as Bob says, "nicely isolated."

The three-story stone, Federal-style farmhouse was built in 1847 and is surrounded by hills, fields, arbors, gazebos, cows, and deer. The Curries bought the property in 1977 and spent 12 years renovating before opening their B&B.

Every view is a good one. From the glassed-in porch you can see the early 1800s, three-tiered bank barn. You can watch the horses from the windowed alcove while you eat breakfast or admire the sweeping lawn down to the Brandywine River as you unwind in the hot tub on the outdoor deck.

The house and its five bedrooms are filled with fun touches. The Bow Room has a collection of old bottles that were found on the property; the Doll Room has more than 60 dolls, many from Sharon's childhood; the quilt hanging on the wall was made by Sharon's great-grandmother.

There are plenty of leisurely things to do, including walking along the Brandywine, which may turn up an artifact, or easily twisting Bob's arm for a game of pool. ♨ *5 double rooms with baths. Air-conditioning, pool table. $70–$94; full breakfast. MC, V. Smoking in designated areas only.*

SCARLETT HOUSE ☙
503 W. State St., Kennett Square 19348, tel. 610/444–9592 or 800/820–9592

It's been around only since October 1990, but Scarlett House has risen quickly to the top with its comfort, beauty, and professionalism. The house sits right in the heart of Kennett Square's historic district. While the rough granite exterior may not seduce you, the minute you walk into the front door (flanked by leaded-glass panes and twin inglenooks) you'll pledge allegiance to this residence. It was built in 1910 by a prominent Quaker businessman for his son, Robert Scarlett, who lived here until the 1960s.

Innkeepers Sam and Jane Snyder are aficionados of adventure travel who have trekked the Himalayas and explored other exotic locations. He is a retired interior designer, she a former teacher. They have embellished the house with an eclectic collection of music boxes, spice canisters, miniatures, and teapots. Many of the furnishings were procured from house sales and auctions by the previous proprietor, Susan Lalli Ascosi, who had enough knowledge and decorative sense to take some license with Victorian tradition by manipulating color schemes. Where Victorians would have stayed with darker tones, Susan splashed pastels on the wooden walls of the bedchambers.

The second-floor master suite is decorated in high Victoriana. Its walls are pink, trimmed at the top with a light floral border. The ornate walnut bed is the room's decided cynosure. It's a stunner, with a huge Renaissance headboard looking down on all-cotton, hand-ironed sheets. Walnut reappears in a more ornately carved dresser with a framed full-length mirror; an exquisite plain-faced corner cupboard of the same wood, crafted by an Amish man in 1820, sits directly opposite.

Business travelers have closed deals in this place; women have completed theses; amorous young couples have basked in its charms. All guests eventually gravitate to the sitting room on the second floor: It faces south, so it's engulfed by light. This is a perfect place to leaf through all the local literature (including restaurant listings, with current menus) that the Snyders keep. You will also want to stroll through the English garden, with its arches, vines, and fish pond. ♨ *1 double room with bath, 2 doubles share bath, 1 suite. Air-conditioning, cable TV, fireplace and newspapers in downstairs parlor. $85–$135; full breakfast. AE, D, MC, V. No smoking indoors, 2-night minimum some weekends.*

SWEETWATER FARM ☙
50 Sweetwater Rd., Glen Mills 19342, tel. 610/459–4711, fax 610/358–4945

Fifteen minutes east of Chadds Ford, at the end of a circular driveway, is a stately 1734 Georgian fieldstone manor house with shutters the color of lemon custard. Sweetwater Farm once sheltered wounded Revolutionary War soldiers and the Marquis de Lafayette and was a refuge for slaves on the Underground Railroad.

In the fields around the 16-room house, Thoroughbreds and goats graze amid wildflowers. From each window there are views of majestic maples on the 15 lush acres, and of the 50 undeveloped acres beyond. Proprietors Grace Le Vine and Richard Hovespian were drawn to this bucolic charm. Le Vine, a niece of the late Princess

Grace of Monaco, has filled the living room with a marvelous display of vintage photos of her famous aunt.

Inside you will find tall, deep-set windows and a sweeping center-hall staircase. Almost every room has a wood-burning fireplace, random-width floors of oak and pine, and original paintings. Rustic Pennsylvania primitive pieces are mixed with 18th- and 19th-century antique furnishings and reproductions. The guest rooms have canopy beds and four-posters, with handmade quilts and fine linens, embroidered spreads, dried-flower wreaths, and hidden nooks containing odd collectibles.

There are a library with a fireplace and wall of books, a living room with a well-stocked humidor for cigar aficionados, and a sunroom with TV, which becomes a "boardroom" for small business meetings and luncheons. In warm weather, the broad back veranda overlooking the fields and the swimming pool is a favorite spot. With more than 20 horses residing on the property, guests can easily arrange for a ride through the countryside.

Breakfast, served in the dining room in front of the fireplace, features everything from sweet-potato waffles or puff pancakes with brown-sugar syrup to home-fried potatoes with sausage and bacon. Five cottages, also furnished in American antiques, are the ultimate romantic hideaways, with fireplaces, kitchens, and four-poster canopied beds. Museums, historic houses, and antiques shops are all nearby.

△ *7 double rooms with baths, 5 cottages. Air-conditioning, conference room, pool. $180–$275; full breakfast. AE, MC, V. No smoking.*

OTHER CHOICES

Bankhouse Bed and Breakfast. 875 Hillsdale Rd., West Chester 19382, tel. 610/344–7388. 2 double rooms share bath. Air-conditioning, ceiling fans. $70–$90; full breakfast. No credit cards. No smoking.

Bed and Breakfast at Walnut Hill. 541 Chandler's Mill Rd., Avondale 19311, tel. 610/444–3703. 2 double rooms share bath. Air-conditioning, TV in 1 room, 2 fireplaces and cable TV/VCR in family room, hot tub. $65–$80; full breakfast. No credit cards. Smoking in common room only.

Meadow Spring Farm. 201 E. Street Rd. (Rte. 926), Kennett Square 19348, tel. 610/444–3903. 5 double rooms with baths. Air-conditioning, TV in rooms, game room with pool table and table tennis, hot tub, kitchen privileges, pool, carriage rides. $75–$85; full breakfast, afternoon tea. No credit cards.

Pace One. Thornton and Glen Mills Rds. (Box 108), Thornton 19373, tel. 610/459–3702, fax 610/558–0825. 6 double rooms with baths. Restaurant, outdoor café, air-conditioning, phone in rooms, 3 conference rooms with catering. $75–$95; Continental breakfast. AE, DC, MC, V. Closed Dec. 25.

RESERVATIONS SERVICES

A Bed & Breakfast Connection/Bed & Breakfast of Philadelphia (Box 21, Devon 19333, tel. 610/687–3565 or 800/448–3619, fax 610/995–9524). **Association of B&Bs in Philadelphia, Valley Forge, and Brandywine** (Box 562, Valley Forge 19481-0562, tel. 610/783–7838 or 800/344–0123, fax 610/783–7783). **B&B of Chester County** (Box 825, Kennett Square 19348, tel. 610/444–1367).

Lancaster County/ Amish Country

CHURCHTOWN INN 🖋

Rte. 23, Churchtown (2100 Main St., Narvon 17555), tel. 717/445–7794, fax 717/445–0962

Across from the historic church in this tiny Pennsylvania Dutch village is the Churchtown Inn, a circa-1735 Georgian fieldstone inn and carriage house that are listed on the National Register of Historic Places. From 1804 to 1853 the inn was the home of Edward Davies, a member of the 25th Congress and a state legislator. Once you enter the restored mansion you will know it was built for the gentry.

To the right of the entryway are two parlors with Victorian antiques and original ornate mantels. Here each evening, innkeepers Jim Kent and Stuart and Hermine Smith entertain guests with music and conversation. Before opening their bed-and-breakfast in April 1987, the three stayed at 150 B&Bs in six states to pick up ideas. Back in New Jersey, Hermine was a health-food retailer, Stuart was a choral director whose choirs appeared at Lincoln Center and Carnegie Hall, and Jim was an accountant and ballroom-dancing teacher. (He'll gladly give you a quick lesson.) Stuart is known to delight guests with a concert on the grand piano, or he might wind up an antique music box from the inn's fine collection.

The 15-room center-hall mansion is decorated throughout with European and American antiques. The glassed-in garden room, where breakfast is served, overlooks farmland and a distant mountain range. A onetime summer kitchen with a walk-in fireplace has been converted into a den with a TV with VCR. Guest rooms have antique marble sinks, and brass, iron, sleigh, carved, or four-poster canopy beds. You'll find wardrobes, washstands, and TV cabinets handmade by an Amish craftsman. Each room has a sitting area. The dormer rooms on the third floor are comfortable but have low ceilings.

On many weekends special packages are offered that include scheduled events. These vary from Victorian balls, carriage rides, and murder mysteries to authentic Amish wedding feasts, barbecues with music, cabaret, classical string quartets, and festive holiday dinners. The inn is close to antiques and crafts markets, the Reading outlets, and Amish farms. You can bike, hike, fish, or cross-country ski in nearby French Creek State Park. **⚠** *7 double rooms with baths, 1 suite in carriage house. Air-conditioning and TV in rooms. $69–$135; full breakfast. D, MC, V. No smoking, 2-night minimum weekends, 3-night minimum holiday weekends.*

CLEARVIEW FARM BED AND BREAKFAST 🖋

355 Clearview Rd., Ephrata 17522, tel. 717/733–6333

Up a winding road along the base of a mountain ridge in northern Lancaster County is a beautifully restored three-story limestone farmhouse built in 1814. It sits on 200 acres of peaceful Pennsylvania farmland, and there's a huge bank barn nearby. There's also a pond out front that's the domain of two swans. The setting of Clearview Farm is elegantly pastoral; it's the kind of place you want to keep secret. Mildred and Glenn Wissler bought the house when they married nearly 40 years ago. Glenn is a farmer who also has a good eye for color, and Mildred is a talented decorator who grew up learning about her father's antiques business. After working together to choose the right furnishings and decorations, they opened the bed-and-breakfast in 1989.

Country antiques and collectibles are mixed with exquisite Victorian furnishings throughout. You'll find a fireplace in the den, and there are hooked rugs on the original random-width floors. Exposed beams and limestone walls give the kitchen a homey feel. Guest rooms are lushly textured with lots of colors and patterns. The Royal Room has an ornately carved walnut Victorian bed, a Victorian mirrored étagère displaying turn-of-the-century knickknacks, Victorian chairs, and marble-top tables. The Princess Room is lavished with lace and fitted with a canopy bed, a Victorian marble-top dresser, and a washstand. The French Room has a highly carved antique bed in a curtained alcove, a matching armoire, and French upholstered chairs. In the rooms on the third floor, hand-pegged rafters and limestone walls are exposed. Here you'll find homemade quilts, country antiques, and a doll collection.

Breakfast is served in the formal dining room, which overlooks the fields. The dining room has elegant draperies and Victorian-print wallpaper. Every morning Mildred prepares a full country breakfast.

The mountain ridge behind the house is great for hiking or taking quiet walks. In autumn, you can enjoy the fall foliage by car or by bike—just follow Clearview Road; it's one of those scenic back roads you always hear about. Nearby are Wahtney's Inn (an excellent restaurant), farmers' markets, and five antiques malls.

⚓ *5 double rooms with baths. Air-conditioning, TV in family room. $95–$130; full breakfast. D, MC, V. No smoking indoors, 2-night minimum weekends.*

LIMESTONE INN ❦
33 E. Main St., Strasburg 17579, tel. 717/687–8392 or 800/278–8392

In the very heart of the Amish country, in Strasburg's historic district, is the Limestone Inn. This elegant bed-and-breakfast, listed on the National Register of Historic Places, was built about 1786 as a merchant's residence. From 1839 to 1860 the principal of the noted Strasburg Academy boarded about 50 boys here. After the Civil War, the house served as an orphanage.

The 16-room house, based on a symmetrical five-bay Georgian plan, has a central hallway and some Germanic overtones. Details like the pent roof and decorative stonework (called tumbling) between the second-floor windows give the inn a distinctive architectural sense.

Innkeepers Jan and Dick Kennell are both natives of New Hampshire. Friends who ran a B&B gave them the idea of establishing their own, and they opened the Limestone in May 1985. Dick was with the Department of Agriculture and Forestry in Washington, D.C., for 30 years; and Jan, who is versed in Colonial history, was a tour guide in Annapolis.

Although antique clocks in the elegant rooms tick away, time stands still. The inn is furnished with Colonial and primitive family antiques and reproductions, and you'll find whitewashed walls, wide-planked wavy floors, and Williamsburg colors in every room. In the keeping room there are woven woolen rugs, lots of books and folk art, and settees in front of the fireplace. A spinning wheel stands in the corner. There are old family photographs and a player piano in the living room. Up the steep, narrow stairs you'll find the guest rooms, with old pegged doors, quilts, trunks, and complimentary chocolates. On the third floor, the original numbers on the doors indicate where boys from the academy once slept.

For the multicourse breakfast, served in the dining room at a long table set with a lace cloth, Dick, an excellent chef, may whip up his French toast or sourdough pancakes. He and Jan often serve their guests in period costumes.

The Limestone Inn is quiet and homey, and it's close to antiquing facilities. The Kennells have Amish friends nearby who have quilts for sale for less than you'd pay in commercial centers. With advance notice, they will set you up for dinner at an Amish home. ♙ *6 double rooms with baths. Air-conditioning. $75–$110; full breakfast. AE, V. No smoking, 2-night minimum holidays and weekends.*

SMITHTON COUNTRY INN ☙
900 W. Main St., Ephrata 17522, tel. 717/733–6094

Twelve miles north of Lancaster is one of the best inns in all of Pennsylvania Dutch country: the Smithton Country Inn, which began taking in lodgers in 1763. It was built by Henry and Susana Miller, who were householders of the Ephrata Community, an 18th-century Protestant monastic sect. Stone walls and flower gardens surround the fieldstone building on a hill overlooking the Ephrata Cloister. Innkeeper Dorothy Graybill is Pennsylvania Dutch. She bought Smithton in 1979, attentively restored it down to the most minute detail, and reopened it in 1982.

At dusk, lamps are lit in each window. The first floor has a Great Room and library to the right, and a dining room, where breakfast is served, to the left. Upstairs, guest rooms are individually decorated, but in each you'll find a working fireplace, antique or handmade reproduction furniture, handmade quilts, reading lamps, stenciling, mini-refrigerators, and chamber music. Feather beds are kept in trunks for guests who request them. Flannel nightshirts, coordinated to the color scheme of the room, hang on wooden pegs behind the doors. Many rooms have canopy beds; some have whirlpool baths.

The attached duplex suite has its own entrance. Inside there are a living room, a snack area, a queen-size bed, a twin cupboard bed, and a whirlpool bath. In 1992 Dorothy added a new unit, the Purple Room, on the second floor facing the back gardens. It includes hand-planed cherry woodwork and floors, an exposed-stone wall, a fireplace, a king-size canopied bed, an all-ceramic bathroom, and a whirlpool.

Numerous decorative influences come from the nearby Ephrata Cloister. The hand-hewn doors are pegged and have wooden hardware. Dorothy's partner, Allan Smith, hand-planed the old floorboards and made the clay tiles for the bathrooms and a Cloister-inspired buffet for the dining room.

Guests enjoy Smithton's breakfast, served by candlelight—usually a plate of fresh fruit, juice, Pennsylvania Dutch waffles, and pastry. Afterward, Dorothy gives tips on the proper etiquette when meeting the Plain People of Lancaster County. This is the place to find out how to avoid the tourist traps and spend your time at authentic preserves of the area's heritage. ♙ *7 double rooms with baths, 1 suite. Air-conditioning. $75–$175; full breakfast. AE, MC, V. No smoking, 2-night minimum with Sat. reservation and on holidays.*

 ## OTHER CHOICES

Adamstown Inn. 62 W. Main St., Adamstown 19501, tel. 717/484–0800 or 800/594–4808, fax 717/484–1384. 4 double rooms with baths. Air-conditioning, cable TV in 3 rooms, off-street parking. $70–$125; Continental-plus breakfast. MC, V. No smoking, 2-night minimum weekends Apr.–Dec.

Cameron Estate Inn. 1855 Mansion La., Mount Joy 17552, tel. 717/653–1773 or 888/722–6376, fax 717/653–1773. 16 double rooms with baths, 1 suite, conference center (up to 35 people). Air-conditioning, fireplace in 8 rooms. $130–$200; full breakfast, afternoon tea. AE, D, DC, MC, V. No smoking. Closed Thanksgiving and Dec. 24–25.

Inns at Doneckers. 318–324 N. State St., Ephrata 17522, tel. 717/738–9502, fax 717/738–9554. 32 double rooms with baths, 12 suites. Restaurant (closed Sun. and Wed.), air-conditioning, cable TV in common room. $65–$210; full breakfast. AE, D, DC, MC, V.

General Sutter Inn. 14 E. Main St., Lititz 17543, tel. 717/626–2115, fax 717/626–0992. 8 double rooms with baths, 3 suites. Restaurant, coffee shop, air-conditioning, TV and phone in rooms, library, 2 conference rooms can be combined. $79–$105. AE, D, MC, V. No smoking, 2-night minimum some holiday weekends.

King's Cottage. 1049 E. King St., Lancaster 17602, tel. 717/397–1017 or 800/747–8717, fax 717/397–3447. 9 double rooms with baths, 1 carriage-house suite. Air-conditioning, cable TV in library, off-street parking. $100–$175; full breakfast, afternoon tea. D, DC, MC, V. No smoking, 2-night minimum weekends, 3-night minimum holiday weekends.

Swiss Woods. 500 Blantz Rd., Lititz 17543, tel. 717/627–3358 or 800/594–8018, fax 717/627–3483. 6 double rooms with baths, 1 suite. Air-conditioning, TV in suite and in common room, whirlpool tubs, kitchenette for guest use. $88–$128; full breakfast. D, MC, V. No smoking, 2-night minimum weekends, 3-night minimum holidays.

RESERVATIONS SERVICE

Hershey Bed & Breakfast Reservation Service (Box 208, Hershey 17033, tel. 717/533–2928).

Gettysburg and York

BECHTEL VICTORIAN MANSION INN ☞
400 W. King St., East Berlin 17316, tel. 717/259–7760, or 800/579–1108

In 1897 the leading local businessman built this 28-room Queen Anne mansion in the center of East Berlin as a residence for his family. It's such a fanciful, through-the-looking-glass place that you'll know it at once. The yellow-brick-and-white-trim building has a high pointed turret, a long curved porch, and Victorian gardens.

Owners Charles and Mariam Bechtel live in Fairfax, Virginia, but every weekend they are resident hosts. Charles grew up on a nearby farm and will give you inside tips on touring the countryside. Innkeeper Ruth Spangler, who is always on hand, is knowledgeable about local history and customs.

The Bechtel, which became an inn in 1983, is furnished with American and European 19th-century antiques. It's on the National Register of Historic Places. Although some guests may find it a bit worn, those with a love of art and architecture will appreciate the intricate artisanship that went into the building and restoration of the house. The Victorian parlor has vertical shutters, sliding pocket doors, and a handsome mantel—all in elegant cherrywood. The dining room has etched-glass windows and a large window seat. The breakfast room was the original kitchen, and you'll find French windows in the chimney corner. Many rooms have original brass chandeliers, and handmade furniture, pottery, and paintings by local artists are distributed throughout the house.

Each bedroom is furnished in antiques, with handmade Pennsylvania quilts, lace curtains, and a brass chandelier. In many you will find built-in wardrobes with full-length mirrors, and two have private balconies. Bathrooms retain their ornate Victorian decor (though the plumbing is new). One of the most popular guest rooms is the Sara Leas Room, with its turret-shaped bay window and view of East Berlin's National Historic District.

You can easily spend a weekend exploring the Bechtel's nooks and crannies. Its location—almost equidistant from York, Gettysburg, and Hershey—makes it an ideal base for touring the area. ⚓ *7 double rooms with baths, 2 suites. Air-conditioning, cable TV in suites, gas fireplace in 1 suite, TV/VCR in 2 common areas, gift shop in carriage house. $85–$150; full breakfast. AE, D, MC, V. No smoking indoors, 2-night minimum holiday weekends and Oct. weekends.*

BEECHMONT INN ❦
315 Broadway, Hanover 17331, tel. 717/632–3013 or 800/553–7009

This 1834 Federal-style redbrick town house, with black shutters and window boxes overflowing with flowers, is on a tree-lined street in Hanover, about 13 mi south of Gettysburg and York. In 1994 William and Susan Day bought the Beechmont, after having worked here for three years. Bill was the handyman and Susan served the breakfast; now they live in the carriage house out back. The inn is furnished with elegant Federal-period antiques and replicas. In the library are 18th-century books and a collection of Civil War memorabilia. One suite has a marble fireplace, and one has a whirlpool. Up the winding staircase, guest rooms have four-poster beds, writing desks, and lace curtains. During warmer months you can relax in the old-fashioned glider in the landscaped courtyard. ⚓ *4 double rooms with baths, 3 suites. Air-conditioning, phone in rooms, off-street parking. $80–$135; full breakfast, afternoon tea. AE, D, MC, V. No smoking, 2-night minimum weekends for suites.*

BRAFFERTON INN ❦
44 York St., Gettysburg 17325, tel. 717/337–3423

A stay at the Brafferton Inn may be the most pleasant way to get a full sense of Gettysburg's historical richness. The 10-room stone house built in 1786, the first residence in town, faces a mid-19th-century street and has an adjacent six-room pre–Civil War clapboard addition. On the first day of the battle, a bullet shattered an upstairs window. It lodged in the mantel and is still there today. During the war, services were held here while the church was being used as a hospital. And just down the street is the house where Lincoln completed his Gettysburg Address.

In late summer 1998, Bill and Maggie Ward purchased the inn within two weeks of their wedding. Bill had always wanted to run an inn, and Maggie, who worked as a manager here under the previous owners for nearly two years, also had hopes of owning an inn some day. The two are devoted to the inn, which is listed on the National Register of Historic Places, and plan to furnish it with historical objects and Sam's family photos, further blending their own history with that of the inn.

The inn has high ceilings, oversize doors, and odd nooks, turns, steps up, and steps down that will constantly surprise you. It glows with Colonial colors. In the living room is the original fireplace, a 19th-century mantle clock, and an 18th-century sideboard. Guests breakfast in the dining room encircled by a folksy mural on four walls that depicts the area's historic buildings.

An atrium connects the stone house to the carriage house. This area, with brick floors and walls, is decorated with primitive pieces and pottery. Opened antique cupboards are filled with antique toys. Down a wooden walkway is a deck and a herb and perennial garden.

The guest rooms, with 18th-century stenciling on whitewashed walls, are furnished with country antiques and family pieces. You'll also find oil paintings, prints, and drawings. Maggie represents three nationally known artists whose authentic historical work decorates the walls. Also, a local potter made the basins for washstands and dressers that have been beautifully transformed into sinks.

After a candlelight breakfast set to classical music, you can relax in the atrium while you plan the day. The inn is an easy walk from the battlefield, shops, and restaurants. ♙ *11 double rooms with baths, 3 suites. Air-conditioning, off-street parking. $90–$135; full breakfast. AE, D, MC, V. No smoking indoors, 2-night minimum weekends Apr.–Nov.*

DOUBLEDAY INN ☙
104 Doubleday Ave., Gettysburg 17325, tel. 717/334–9119

You don't have to be a Gettysburg Battle buff to enjoy a stay at the Doubleday Inn, but if you are, you can't get any more "battlefieldy" than this. The Doubleday is the only B&B that is actually *on* the Gettysburg Battlefield. Situated upon Oak Ridge, with a view of the town of Gettysburg a half mile away, the inn nestles in a grove of trees on a monument-lined road, with the Railroad Cut, the Peace Light Memorial, and an observation platform all just a few steps from the door.

In 1994 Charles Wilcox, a financier in the futures industry, and his wife, Ruth Anne, a registered nurse, gave up their jobs and moved from Illinois to pursue their dream of owning and operating an inn. They bought the Doubleday, named after Abner Doubleday, the man who "invented" baseball and who also, as brigadier general, commanded the Union forces the first day of the battle on what is now the site of the inn.

Charles and Ruth Anne brought with them loads of Colonial country furniture and scoured Pennsylvania and Ohio for suitable period antiques. The recently redecorated bedrooms are a mix of four-posters, brass beds, iron beds, and an oak pineapple bed. Two rooms are what Ruth Anne calls "Grandma's rooms," with thick quilts and old-fashioned fabric prints. Another room has a Laura Ashley look. The third-floor attic room is more masculine, with dark greens and reds, bookcases, and both a double and a twin bed.

Every morning a full, hot breakfast is served by candlelight, on china and crystal. Civil War literature is available to read, and every Saturday night throughout the year and Wednesday nights during the busy season a licensed battlefield guide comes to lecture and answer questions about the battle. Breakfast discussions the following mornings are especially spirited. ♙ *5 double rooms with baths, 4 doubles share 2 baths. Air-conditioning. $89–$109; full breakfast, afternoon tea. D, MC, V. No smoking, 2-night minimum holiday weekends.*

MERCERSBURG INN ☜

405 S. Main St., Mercersburg 17236, tel. 717/328–5231, fax 717/328–3403

Mercersburg, at the foot of the Blue Ridge Mountains, is a historic village off I–81, an hour and a half from Washington, D.C. This country inn, on the outskirts of town, is an impressive Classical Revival redbrick structure with white trim, adorned with numerous porticoes, porches, and terraces.

It's the kind of place where you expect something romantic has either already happened or will. In the entrance hall, twin staircases wind dramatically to the second floor, and rose and green Scaglioli columns accent the chestnut wainscoting. The classic Arts and Crafts sunroom has a tiled floor and fireplace, high-beamed ceilings, and a wall of broad windows. It's done in peach and blue, with flowered upholstery and curtains. You can sit back on the deep window-seat cushions and admire the stately grounds.

Restored antiques and locally handmade pieces fill the spacious guest rooms. You will find four-poster, canopy, and king-size beds. Some rooms have fireplaces; others have private balconies with views of the mountains. Three rooms have tiled, high-ceiling bathrooms with antique needle showers, pedestal sinks, and freestanding tubs. Each bathroom has been meticulously restored to its turn-of-the-century grandeur.

In the formal mahogany-paneled dining room, there are a deep green marble fireplace, leaded-glass built-in cabinets, Tiffany stained-glass light fixtures, and parquet floors. Here the award-winning restaurant serves à la carte and five-course fixed-price dinners of regional new American cuisine.

A bit farther north is a pocket of Amish country that most tourists never hear about. Walter and Sandy Filkowski, who bought the property in June 1996 and took over as innkeepers, will fill you in on the area's touring, antiquing, fishing, and hiking opportunities. **△** *15 double rooms with baths. Restaurant (open Thurs.–Sat.), air-conditioning, phone in rooms, whirlpool bath in 1 room, TV/VCR in game room, conference room. $120–235; full breakfast. D, MC, V. No smoking indoors, 2-night minimum fall-foliage and ski-season weekends and holidays.*

OTHER CHOICES

Appleford Inn. 218 Carlisle St., Gettysburg 17325, tel. 717/337–1711 or 800/275–3373, fax 717/334–6228. 9 double rooms with baths, 1 suite. Air-conditioning, off-street parking. $85–$135; full breakfast, afternoon tea. AE, D, MC, V. No smoking, 2-night minimum weekends Apr.–Oct. and special-event weekends.

Emig Mansion. 3342 N. George St. (Box 486), Emigsville 17318, tel. 717/764–2226. 5 double rooms with baths, 4 doubles share 2 baths. Air-conditioning, off-street parking. $85–$110; full breakfast. MC, V. Smoking on balconies only.

Fairfield Inn. Main St., Fairfield 17320, tel. 717/642–5410. 2 double rooms share bath. Restaurant, air-conditioning, meeting room. $50–$75; Continental breakfast. AE, MC, V. No smoking in dining room. Closed Sun.–Mon., 1st wk of Feb., and 1st wk of Sept.

Historic Farnsworth House Inn. 401 Baltimore St., Gettysburg 17325, tel. 717/334–8838, fax 717/334–5862. 10 double rooms with baths. Restaurant, air-conditioning in bedrooms, whirlpool baths in 2 rooms, cable TV and fireplace in 4 rooms, TV in sunroom. $95–150; full breakfast. AE, D, MC, V. No smoking, 2-night minimum some weekends.

Tannery Bed and Breakfast. 449 Baltimore St., Gettysburg 17325, tel. 717/334–2454. 7 double rooms with baths, 2 suites. Air-conditioning, cable TV in

4 rooms and in sitting room, off-street parking. $85–$125; Continental-plus breakfast. MC, V. No smoking.

Pittsburgh and Environs

GLENDORN

1032 W. Corydon St., Bradford 16701, tel. 814/362–6511 or 800/843–8568, fax 814/368–9923

Tucked away on 1,280 acres in northwestern Pennsylvania near Allegheny National Forest, Glendorn was the summer retreat of the Dorns, who made their fortune in oil early in the century. Open to the public since 1995, it captures the spirit of rustic luxury. The lodge, a four-hour drive from Pittsburgh or Cleveland and 1½ hours from Buffalo, is for people who appreciate special places off the beaten path.

The magnificent all-redwood main lodge was begun in 1929. Up to 30 guests can stay in four rooms here and in nearby cabins. The Dorns (who still use some cabins) left many family items such as china and books, which enhance the feeling of being at the home of a wealthy friend. Managers Gene and Linda Spinner are unobtrusive hosts who care for guests' needs efficiently and pleasantly.

A two-story-high sandstone fireplace dominates the wood-beamed great hall where meals are served. You can relax on the sofas, have a snack from the butler's pantry, or try billiards in the game room. Lodge rooms include the Green Suite, with a tiled fireplace and chintz sofa. All six cabins have fireplaces. The one-bedroom Miller Cabin has chestnut paneling and overlooks a stream; the three-bedroom Roost has pecky cypress paneling and separate baths in the master bedroom.

The delicious meals (all included in the cost) are substantial. Fruit and a muffin or coffee cake precede eggs or pancakes. Dinner, for which men wear jackets and women wear dresses or nice pants, follows cocktails and appetizers. Chef Casey Fichte's American country cuisine includes seafood and game entrées.

Among the popular activities (included in the price) are skeet and trapshooting. Three small lakes are stocked with trout and bass, so bring your poles. Snowshoeing and cross-country skiing (use your own skis) are winter pleasures. For an extra cost, golf is nearby, and downhill skiing is a 45-minute drive away.
△ *2 rooms with baths, 2 suites, 5 1-bedroom cabins, 1 3-bedroom cabin, 1 4-bedroom cabin. Air-conditioning in 2 suites and 1 cabin; TV in rooms; phone, refrigerator, and coffeemaker in cabins; terry cloth robes and slippers, swimming pool, exercise room, hiking trails, bicycles, canoes, 3 tennis courts, conference facilities for 24. $425–$625; all meals included. AE, MC, V. 2-night minimum. Closed early Jan.–mid-Feb.*

OTHER CHOICES

Century Inn. Rte. 40, Scenery Hill 15360, tel. 724/945–6600. 5 double rooms with baths, 4 suites. Restaurant (closed Jan.–mid-Mar.) with conference facilities, air-conditioning, tennis court, croquet. $80–$140; full breakfast. MC, V.
The Priory. 614 Pressley St., Pittsburgh 15212, tel. 412/231–3338, fax 412/231–4838. 21 double rooms with baths, 3 suites. Air-conditioning, TV, and phone in rooms, weekday-morning transportation downtown. $98–$145; Continental-plus breakfast. AE, D, DC, MC, V.

RHODE ISLAND

Newport

CLIFFSIDE INN 🦜
2 Seaview Ave., 02840, tel. 401/847–1811 or 800/845–1811, fax 401/848–5850

This spellbinding Victorian B&B sits on a shady side street just up from Newport's Cliff Walk. The Cliffside Inn's charm does not necessarily stem from its remarkable amenities, refinements, and accolades; nor is it based in the well-mannered, expert services of innkeeper Stan Nicholas. Rather, the remarkable appeal of this inn radiates from the life story of a recluse whose paintings now adorn walls in all 15 rooms.

Maryland governor Thomas Swann built the home in 1880 as a retreat from his war-beleaguered state. In 1891 the home was sold to a Philadelphia cotton merchant whose 17-year-old daughter, Beatrice, was the love of his life. The fawning father had her removed from art school upon learning of her work with nude models. "Paint me a picture of yourself," he reportedly said.

After she died of malnutrition in 1948, townspeople discovered that Beatrice Turner—who lived for 35 years in a mansion painted black, had no friends, and dressed herself each day in Victorian clothing—had rendered 1,000 self-portraits in oil. Only 150 of her paintings survive. But thanks to the upgrades made by current owner Win Baker, the inn now has a sterling image, a polished repose that turns the eerie mystique of Beatrice Turner into outright charm.

Filled with cozy nooks and crannies and flooded with sunlight from its many bay windows and skylights, the Cliffside is a titillating place. Just off the large center hallway, with its original gleaming hardwood floor and double doors, is a spacious parlor that has a Victorian fireplace bedecked with an ornate antique mirror. (Note that this inn's wealth of knickknacks and antiques makes it inappropriate for children.)

The guest rooms are decorated with Victorian furniture and Laura Ashley fabrics, and each room has a name that recalls past residents or refers to its decor. The Governor's Suite has a king-size four-poster bed, a whirlpool bath, an antique birdcage shower, and an unusual two-sided fireplace (one side is in the bedroom, the other in the bathroom). Some rooms have fireplaces, and others have whirlpool baths (most have both). The new luxurious Cliff Suite has three fireplaces in four rooms.
△ *8 double rooms with baths, 7 suites. Air-conditioning, cable TV, phone in rooms. $195–$450; full breakfast, afternoon tea. AE, D, DC, MC, V. No smoking.*

ELM TREE COTTAGE 🦜
336 Gibbs Ave., 02840, tel. 401/849–1610 or 800/882–3356, fax 401/849–2084

In a quiet, tree-shaded neighborhood between Easton's Pond and Bellevue Avenue is the incomparable Elm Tree Cottage. The elegantly designed shingle-style house was built in 1882 by architect William Ralph Emerson (Ralph Waldo's cousin), who is best known for his stick-style Maine homes. Owners Priscilla and Thomas Malone—look for their stained-glass work throughout the home—bought the Elm Tree in 1989, when the city granted them special exception to run a B&B in a residential zone, a good-faith effort designed to save this architectural treasure from condominium plans.

Each massive room (often with a fireplace), furnished with French and English antiques and decorated by Priscilla, is an interior-design vignette. The Windsor Suite is more than 1,000 square ft and is fitted with a fireplace, a stereo, and a king-size bed with carved Louis XV headboard and canopy.

The spacious living room has two pianos and overlooks half an acre of gardens. You can help yourself to soft drinks or mix BYOB cocktails at the bar, which resembles the cabin of a yacht. (Although older children may enjoy the lawn and the common rooms, this inn is too upscale for little ones.)

Priscilla is also known for her creative, gourmet breakfasts. Homemade French-toast soufflé topped with whipped maple cream or a Florentine phyllo cup with a béarnaise sauce is served on white-linen tables and accompanied by a poem or a thought for the day. ⚠ *6 double rooms with baths. Air-conditioning. $175–$350; full breakfast. AE, MC, V. No smoking, 3-night minimum weekends. Closed Dec. 21–Feb. 1.*

FRANCIS MALBONE HOUSE ☞
392 Thames St., 02840, tel. 401/846–0392, fax 401/848–5956

This brick Colonial mansion on bustling Thames Street was built in 1760 by Col. Francis Malbone, a shipping magnate who, to avoid paying English taxes, ran a tunnel from the cellar to the pier where his ships landed. Ironically, the British used the adjacent "counting house"—which is now one of Newport's finest guest suites—as a gold storehouse during the Revolutionary War.

The home is listed on the National Register of Historic Places and is believed to have been designed by Peter Harrison (the architect responsible for the nearby Touro Synagogue and Redwood Library). The structure was immaculately restored from 1968 to 1974 and is now Newport's only Colonial mansion operating as an inn. It's only a 10-minute walk from Washington Square, a plus for visitors interested in historic Newport. However, the noise from tourist-thick Thames Street may induce light sleepers to opt for a room at the back.

In 1996, at a cost of $1 million, a 10-room addition was built; at the same time, a formal dining room with a domed ceiling, recessed lighting, and dental molding was added. All the new rooms have four-poster king-size beds, Jacuzzi baths, and fireplaces. The colonnade, which opens onto a courtyard and extends to the new wing, has 12 beautiful blue-on-white Portuguese baroque tiles. These "greeting figure" tiles were a popularly traded commodity during the time the Frances Malbone House was built.

All three public rooms are tastefully furnished with Colonial reproduction pieces and antiques. The original kitchen has an authentic Colonial brick fireplace with a beehive oven; tea and snacks are served here every afternoon. The full gourmet breakfast includes a main dish made-to-order; cereal and pastries are available at a buffet table.

Young innkeepers Mary Frances Mahaffey, Stephanie Walmsey, and Will Dewey are warm and welcoming. Repeat guests rave about the highly professional service and the elegant, gracious atmosphere (one that young children may not appreciate). ♨ *18 double rooms with baths. Whirlpool bath in 10 rooms, fireplace in 15 rooms, free parking. $165–$325; full breakfast. AE, MC, V. No smoking.*

INN AT CASTLE HILL 🐚
Ocean Dr., 02840, tel. 401/849–3800, fax 401/849–3838

The Inn at Castle Hill is perched in jaunty isolation on a 40-acre peninsula with its own private beach. Built as a summer home for scientist and explorer Alexander Agassiz, the inn is a rambling shingled structure, with curves, gingerbread woodwork, turrets, and jutting porches imitating the chalets of Dr. Agassiz's native Switzerland. Outbuildings dot the grounds, including Agassiz's former laboratory (which may be rented as a suite), a series of beach cottages (rented by the week), and the six Harbor Houses, where Grace Kelly lived while filming *High Society*.

Inside, many original furnishings reflect Agassiz's fondness for Chinese and Japanese art, particularly bronzes and porcelain (owing to all the fine pieces, it's best to leave children at home). The lounge, with Oriental rugs, has two small sofas nestled next to an unusual hand-carved fireplace—its design reminiscent of a stained-glass rose window in a Gothic cathedral. Three water-view dining rooms include the professor's original study, the Sunset Room, and the original dining room. The superb restaurant is particularly popular for Sunday brunch; on summer Sunday afternoons the inn holds a barbecue with music that has become de rigueur.

The seven spacious oceanside rooms in the main house, which must be booked months in advance, are furnished with Victorian antiques and comfortable chairs, decorated with bright floral fabrics, and have enormous bathrooms. Room 6, with a large bay window, was built for Mrs. Agassiz; Room 7, Dr. Agassiz's bedroom, has walls and a ceiling of inlaid oak and pine; Room 8 features an old claw-foot tub and a view of the bay and the Newport Bridge; Room 9, pentagonal in shape, was mentioned in *Theophilus North*, a Thorton Wilder novel based in Newport. An upstairs suite combines a large living room and a bedroom. The six-unit Harbor House was recently renovated; each unit has a king-size bed, a Jacuzzi, and a private deck. For many repeat guests, the inn's antique and somewhat creaky charms, along with its fabulous views and private beach, convey the true essence of Newport. ♨ *13 double rooms with baths, 6 doubles share 1 bath, 2 suites, 18 seasonal doubles with baths. Restaurant (closed Mon.–Tues. Nov.– mid Apr.), private beach. $135–$325; Continental breakfast. AE, MC, V. 2-night minimum weekends.*

IVY LODGE 🐚
12 Clay St., 02840, tel. 401/849–6865

Just inside this elegant Queen Anne Victorian, designed by Stanford White, is an amazing sight: a 33-ft-high, Gothic-style oak-paneled entry with a three-story staircase and a dangling wrought-iron chandelier. Just off the foot of the staircase is a brick fireplace built in the shape of a Moorish arch. A welcoming fire burns here on chilly afternoons.

Ivy Lodge, which was built in 1886 for a prominent New York physician, has eight spacious guest rooms—all tastefully decorated with a combination of Victorian antiques and good-quality reproductions. Newporters and veteran innkeepers Maggie and Terry Moy live at Ivy Lodge. Their manner is low-key and gracious, their rates are reasonable, and they know how to make you very comfortable.

The Turret Room, decorated in peach and green, has a king-size bed and a private bath with a Victorian claw-foot tub. The Ivy Room has a queen-size four-poster bed with French-cut white linens, Waverly ivy wallpaper, and a private bath. A set of Herend dishes for the dining room has an ivy pattern.

The sumptuous breakfast served here might include such delicacies as smoked fish, homemade quiche, bread pudding, or fresh strawberries and popovers with whipped cream. A 20-ft-long mahogany table that seats 18 dominates the long dining room, with floor-to-ceiling bay windows at one end. The bright main-floor sitting room has floral wallpaper and wicker furniture; it's also invitingly full of books and magazines. The airy living room features pink-and-white-striped Art Deco sofas, thick carpeting, and a huge fireplace. The wraparound front porch with cushioned wicker chairs is popular with summer guests.

Although Ivy Lodge is neither as large nor as opulent as the fabled mansions on nearby Bellevue Avenue, it is every bit as gracious. △ *8 double rooms with baths. $100–$180; full breakfast. AE, MC, V. No smoking.*

SANFORD-COVELL VILLA MARINA 🐦
72 Washington St., 02840, tel. 401/847–0206, fax 401/848–5599

This elegant Eastlake-style home, with its spindlework detailing, was built in 1869 as a summer residence for Milton H. Sanford by architect William Ralph Emerson. In 1895 the house was sold to William Covell, and it is still owned by two of his descendants, Anne and Richard Cuvelier.

Inside the house elaborately carved wooden balconies open onto an entrance hall that soars 35 ft. The authenticity of this Gilded Age home is startling; in fact, from 1972 to 1980, the home was a museum run by the Society for the Protection of New England Antiquities. When the Culveliers reassumed the deed, a clause stipulated that nothing could be changed; so it is that a public coffeemaker sits on a table dating from the 1700s.

A few of the amazing features include black-walnut wainscoted walls, parquet floors in each room, original glass globes on bronze chandeliers, and walls decorated with original frescoes. Just beyond a gorgeous, heated, black-bottom pool, a private dock juts into Newport Harbor. △ *3 double rooms with baths, 3 doubles share bath. Heated saltwater pool. $75–$235; Continental breakfast, afternoon refreshments. No credit cards. 2-night minimum in summer.*

VICTORIAN LADIES 🐦
63 Memorial Blvd., 02840, tel. 401/849–9960

The location of the Victorian Ladies on busy Memorial Boulevard may, at first, give pause. But once you're inside, double-pane windows and air-conditioning muffle the street noise. In addition, the sumptuous furnishings and the friendly attention of hosts Don and Helene O'Neill fully compensate for any din that might slip through.

Don and Helene bought their home in 1985 after a B&B trip to California convinced them that they would enjoy being hosts at their own establishment. They purchased a fairly rundown home and carriage house built around 1840. The former occupants were elderly women who seemed to have stepped straight out of the Victorian era—thus the name. Thanks to his years of experience in restoration carpentry, Don was able to renovate the place himself.

The mansard exterior of the Victorian Ladies is now painted deep green and burgundy. Nine dormer windows are accented by scalloped wood shingles and curvaceous moldings. The main house and the carriage house are connected by a flower-filled latticed courtyard that serves as an outdoor breakfast area in the summer. Recent additions include a formal garden with vine-covered brick walls.

The living room, mauve and light blue, has a crystal chandelier, a cozy fireplace, floral wallpaper, several plump-pillowed couches, and many ornamental objects from the Far East. The adjoining dining room has more of a country feeling, with a Welsh dresser and a large English-pine table and sideboard, where ample traditional breakfasts of eggs and bacon or ham are served.

The rooms are furnished with an eclectic collection of antiques, reproductions, and modern pieces, that, through Helene's visual tastes, harmoniously coexist. Each room has a canopy, sleigh, or four-poster bed and colorful wallpaper. A favorite of many guests is the Honeymoon Suite. As in so many other rooms in the inn, the bed here is heaped with ruffled pillows handmade by Helene. Another guest room features children's lace dresses on the walls, set off by a black background with a rosebud print. A third has birdcage wallpaper, birdcages painted on cabinetry, and, of course, a Victorian-era birdcage. (Such details make this an inappropriate place for children.) ▲ *11 double rooms with baths. Air-conditioning, TV in rooms, free parking. $135–$185; full breakfast. MC, V. No smoking.*

OTHER CHOICES

Admiral Fitzroy Inn. 398 Thames St., 02840, tel. 401/848–8000 or 800/343–2863, fax 401/848–8006. 17 double rooms with baths. Air-conditioning, phone, TV, refrigerator, tea pot, hair dryer in rooms; elevator; free parking. $140–$195; full breakfast. AE, MC, V. 2-night minimum summer weekends, 3-night minimum holiday weekends and festivals.

The Inntowne. 6 Mary St., 02840, tel. 401/846–9200 or 800/457–7803, fax 401/846–1534. 26 double rooms with baths. Phone in rooms, kitchen facilities in some rooms, small patio off some rooms, 24-hr concierge, access to nearby health club. $95–$219; Continental breakfast. AE, MC, V. No no-smoking rooms available.

RESERVATIONS SERVICES

Anna's Victorian Connection (5 Fowler Ave., Newport 02840, tel. 401/849–2489 or 800/884–4288). **Bed and Breakfast Newport** (33 Russell Ave., Newport 02840, tel. 401/846–5408), **Bed and Breakfast of Rhode Island, Inc.** (Box 3291, Newport 02840, tel. 401/849–1298).

Coastal Rhode Island

THE RICHARDS ☙
144 Gibson Ave., Narragansett 02882, tel. 401/789–7746

This English manor–style home, built of granite quarried nearby, is a most unusual B&B. Joseph Peace Hazard, scion of a locally prominent industrialist family, reportedly built this fortresslike home in 1884 because of the property's excellent well water. He never lived in the house, and what exactly this transcendentalist baron and his guests did here is something of a mystery. Hazard had the words DRUID'S DREAM carved over the doorway. The owners of 11 years, Nancy and Steven Richards, will be happy to share what they know about the inn's intriguing history and the doorway's peculiar reference.

Meticulously restored and listed on the National Register of Historic Places, the Richards has a broodingly Gothic mystique that is almost the antithesis of a summer home. But the rooms are very comfortable, and the neighborhood is quiet (though construction crews have recently been putting up homes nearby). Each guest room is furnished with 19th-century English antiques and has a working fireplace, down comforters, and floral-upholstered or wicker couches and chairs. Nancy serves a breakfast of fresh fruit, strudel, cereal, coffee, and muffins, as well as such main courses as eggs Florentine and oven pancakes.

French windows look out onto a lush landscape, with a grand swamp oak the centerpiece of a handsome garden. On chilly afternoons you'll find the library fireplace ablaze. You can walk a nature trail to the rocky coast and then to sandy Narragansett Beach. Fine restaurants are also within walking distance.

Many guests spend an entire week, as Newport and Block Island are easy to reach from here. Though Nancy and Steven are welcoming, this is not a B&B for travelers who desire a great deal of personal attention; Nancy is quick to point out that this is a family home first, and a business second. ♣ *2 double rooms with baths, 2 doubles share bath, 1 2-bedroom suite. $60–$160; full breakfast. No credit cards. No smoking, 2-night minimum summer weekends, 3-night minimum holidays.*

SHELTER HARBOR INN 🐚
10 Wagner Rd., Westerly 02891, tel. 401/322–8883

This inn and large restaurant is an institution in South County. During the past 70 years, the 1810 farmhouse has been a commune, a country club with stables, a nursing home, and an inn. In 1912 the 200-acre oceanside property became an off-season music colony for Newport summer performers. More than a dozen streets surrounding the inn are still named for famous musicians.

When current owner Jim Dye took over the property 20 years ago, the inn had essentially declined to a boardinghouse. "Kicking the boarders out was the best thing I could do. They all ended up buying houses!" says owner Jim Dye, a self-described Wall Street exile who spent childhood summers in Westerly.

The lobby, library, and sunporch are decorated with such quirky antiques as an enormous Hoosier hutch and a Simplex wall clock. The guest rooms are furnished with a combination of Victorian antiques and reproduction pieces; bedspreads and curtains are in muted floral patterns.

Most of the rooms have working fireplaces; some have decks (the corner room, Number 9, is a particular favorite). It should be noted that on damp spring days the pervasive musty scent of ashes can make fireplaces disagreeable.

The surrounding 4 acres include a croquet lawn, paddle-tennis courts, two patios, and a swing set (children are welcome at the inn). Men's and women's locker rooms open onto a rooftop replete with a barbecue grill and a massive stainless-steel hot tub. A shuttle bus runs on the hour to the private beach, one of the best stretches of sand in the state. (If you want to go to the beach on check-out day, you're welcome to use the locker rooms.)

Breakfast is right off the restaurant's menu, which typically includes banana-walnut French toast, eggs Benedict, and smoked haddock served over johnnycakes (an Ocean State favorite).

A few older guests fondly recall the property as an equestrian camp. Essentially, that healthful, cheery summer-camp atmosphere perseveres. ♣ *23 double rooms with baths. Restaurant, bar, air-conditioning, TV and phone in rooms;*

paddle tennis; croquet. $102–$130; full breakfast. AE, D, MC, V. 2-night minimum weekends Memorial Day–Thanksgiving, 3-night minimum holidays.

STONE LEA 🖙
40 Newton Ave., Narragansett 02882, tel. 401/783–9546, fax 401/792–8237

Off Ocean Drive in a section called Millionaire's Mile is Stone Lea, a dignified shingle-covered house with lines of sight across Narragansett Bay to Newport, Jamestown, Tiverton, and Block Island. Situated a mile south of Narragansett, this classic house (circa 1884) was designed by the famous architectural firm of McKim, Mead, and White, which was also responsible for the Rhode Island Statehouse and Narragansett's most recognized buildings: the Coast Guard House, the Towers, and the Casino. Built primarily of Rhode Island granite, this B&B is as solid as it is beautiful.

Rotundas and bay windows protrude hither and yon. Inside you'll find big windows, lots of light, and such elaborate details as carved wood paneling in the main entrance hall, a grand-piano staircase that rises from the parquet floor of the large foyer, and a Dutch door with inch-thick beveled glass. Off the entryway is an ostentatiously large living room; bright and inviting, it has a sunporch.

Stone Lea functioned as a B&B for eight years prior to its 1995 purchase by current live-in owner and surgeon Guy Lancellotti, who is fond of putting the business's income back into the house. Recent upgrades include new mattresses and linens for all the rooms, restoration of all the wooden floors and wainscoting, and new Oriental rugs. Vivacious innkeeper Sara Incollingo serves a full breakfast in the well-appointed dining room.

A few guest rooms (the Block Island Room is one) have unbeatable views, but all have at least a glimpse of the water. The four larger rooms offer truly topnotch accommodations that are worth the extra money. Despite the amazing architecture, Stone Lea's most memorable feature is its broad lawn, at the end of which a shoulder of flat rock runs along the shore of Narragansett Bay. Guests can hike along this field of stone all the way to Scarboro Beach, a favorite of Rhode Island's sunbathers. Stone Lea is also within walking distance of restaurants and shops in the shore village of Narragansett Pier. ⚐ *7 double rooms with baths. Cable TV in common area. $100–$150; full breakfast. AE, MC, V. No smoking, 2-day minimum summer weekends, 3-night minimum holidays. Closed Thanksgiving and Dec. 25.*

WEEKAPAUG INN 🖙
25 Spring Ave., Weekapaug 02891, tel. 401/322–0301, fax 401/322–1016

At the end of curving Ninigret Avenue—past a line of gracious, vintage, beachfront homes—waits an enchanting inn where time seems to have stopped circa 1939. The Weekapaug Inn has been operated in summer by members of the Buffum family since 1899—with only one interruption: the hurricane of 1938. Even in the face of that catastrophe, the family acted quickly, rebuilding the destroyed inn from scratch several hundred yards from its former waterside site and reopening just one week late in the summer of 1939.

The building seems more a mansion than an inn, with a peaked roof, a stone foundation, and a huge wraparound porch. It was rebuilt to withstand a major hurricane (it has a steel understructure) and is on a peninsula in salty Quonochontaug Pond. There's a comfy tidiness about the furnishings throughout; the guest-room decor is cheerful though not particularly remarkable. Each room is big and has large windows with impressive views.

Many guests have been regulars here for years—some returning as many as 50 summers—although newcomers are made to feel just as welcome. "We like to see fresh faces here," comments caretaker Horst Taut. Standards in the restaurant are very high; a new menu every day offers from four to six entrées emphasizing seafood, and a full-time baker makes all the desserts, breads, and rolls. Thursday-night cookouts feature swordfish, steak, chicken, and seasonal vegetables.

The Weekapaug Inn is often described as a cruise ship on land or a summer camp—perhaps because it is an all-inclusive vacation spot with an American meal plan, card rooms, BYOB bars, lawn bowling, croquet, Ping-Pong, billiards, movies, and bingo nights. You also have access to a nearby golf course, a private beach, and tennis courts. Though many of its guests are middle-aged and older, the inn's children's program has made it a favorite of families, too. The full-time program director runs two daily sessions of special excursions and projects that make even the youngest guest feel welcome. △ *33 double rooms with baths, 21 singles with baths. Restaurant. $175–$185; AP. No credit cards. 3-night minimum weekends. Closed Labor Day–mid-June.*

OTHER CHOICES

Admiral Dewey Inn. 668 Matunuck Beach Rd., South Kingstown 02879, tel. 401/783–2090. 8 double rooms with baths, 2 doubles share bath. $80–$125; Continental breakfast. MC, V. No smoking.

Ocean House. 2 Bluff Ave., Watch Hill 02891, tel. 401/348–8161. 56 double rooms with baths, 3 singles with baths. Restaurant, lounge. $185–$230; breakfast, dinner. MC, V. 2-night minimum weekends, 3-night minimum holidays. Closed Labor Day–late June.

RESERVATIONS SERVICE

Bed and Breakfast of Rhode Island, Inc. (Box 3291, Newport 02840, tel. 401/849–1298).

Block Island

ATLANTIC INN ♥
High St. (Box 1788), 02807, tel. 401/466–5883 or 800/224–7422

When the Clinton family visited Block Island in the summer of 1997, the president and his host, Senator Jack Reed, chose the Atlantic Inn for dinner. Locals knew that this choice was a good one. Innkeeper Brad Marthens and his wife, Anne, bought the inn in 1994. The two had vacationed on the island for years. "We both love the ocean, so this place is perfect for us," says Brad, who, in addition to hiring a talented staff, has greatly improved the inn's offerings and services.

Since 1879 this long, white Victorian with a blue gambrel roof has bravely fronted the elements from a hilltop overlooking the ocean. Big windows, high ceilings, and a sweeping staircase make the atmosphere open and breezy. The inn is furnished with turn-of-the-century pieces, many of them golden oak, which make it seem austere. This is softened by the pastel colors that are used throughout and the many homey and unusual touches: Witness the oak phone booth, just off the lobby, and the common bathroom, which has framed clips from old advertising campaigns. Guest rooms are spacious—though not huge—and have oak and maple furnishings, most of which are original to the building.

And then there are the views. Isolated from the hubbub of the Old Harbor area, here you can perch on a hillside and contemplate the shape of the island or the sparkle of nearby ocean. The inn's remarkable location makes it a popular place for weddings; many shoulder-season weekends are booked with nuptial celebrations.

A buffet breakfast with fresh-baked goods is prepared each morning by the inn's pastry chef. The restaurant, which is open for dinner May through October, serves four-course, prix-fixe meals. The 6-acre grounds are carefully maintained and have large wildflower, herb, and vegetable gardens (the produce of which is used in the kitchen). You'll also find two tennis courts and a smooth green croquet lawn. △ *21 double rooms with baths. Restaurant, phone and fans in rooms, games, books. $115–$210; Continental breakfast. D, MC, V. No smoking, 2- or 3-night minimum weekends June–Aug. Closed Nov.–Mar.*

HOTEL MANISSES ☞
1 Spring St., 02807, tel. 401/466–2063 or 800/626–4773, fax 401/466–3162

If you were to stroll along Spring Street on a foggy night, your eye might be caught by a translucent glow in the sky. Continue down the street, and you'll discover the source: the magnificent brass chandelier—a beacon of welcome from a bygone era—suspended inside the cupola of the Manisses.

This 1870 Victorian inn has been restored with loving care and is now diligently maintained by its owners and operators—Joan and Justin Abrams, their daughter Rita Draper, and her husband, Steve. (The family also owns and operates the nearby 1661 Inn & Guest House; *see below.*) No expense was spared in the renovation and decoration, but what's perhaps more important, the Draper and Abrams families work hard to make you feel comfortable and pampered. Indeed, they have made attention to detail an art form; staff members dressed in ties or Victorian-era dresses are kept remarkably busy.

You can enjoy such unique offerings as afternoon wine and "nibblets" in the romantic parlor that overlooks the garden, coffee and tea available throughout the day, picnic baskets packed with lunch, guided tours of the island, and an animal farm with llamas and emus.

Furnishings were chosen with care. Many of the guest rooms, named after famous shipwrecks, are filled with intriguing knickknacks and unusual Victorian pieces, such as the many-leveled bureau in the Princess Augusta Room and an ivory toilet set on a bureau in another. (Note that because of all the antiques, this inn is not suitable for children.) Bedside decanters and bowls of candy are among the thoughtful touches, and some rooms have large hot tubs. The Manisses's restaurant, on the lower level, is considered one of Rhode Island's best and features vegetables grown in the inn's garden, local seafood, and homemade bread.

More economical accommodations are available down the road at Dodge Cottage. Although not as grand as accommodations at the Manisses, the cottage has a large common room and the cozy feel of a small B&B. A large breakfast is served at the 1661 Inn, a five-minute walk up the road. This buffet of eggs, sausage, cornbread, smoked bluefish, muffins, and much more is popular with guests and walk-ins alike. △ *17 double rooms with baths. Restaurant, phone and ceiling fan in rooms, whirlpool baths in some rooms, petting farm. $155–$260; buffet breakfast served at nearby inn. MC, V.*

1661 INN & GUEST HOUSE ☞

Spring St., 02807, tel. 401/466–2421, 401/466–2063, or 800/626–4773, fax 401/466–2858

If your island-vacation fantasy includes lounging in bed while gazing at swans in the marshes that overlook the blue Atlantic, consider booking a room at the 1661 Inn. Owners Joan and Justin Abrams and operators Rita and Steve Draper (*see* Hotel Manisses, *above*) are noted for their attention to detail. Even if your room doesn't face the water, you can loll on the inn's expansive deck or curl up in a chair on the gently sloping oceanside lawn; from both spots you'll enjoy the panorama of the water below.

In the front hallway a wall full of pictures of the inn taken by former guests attests to how special a stay here has been for many people. Although recent refurbishments reduced the number of guest rooms, those that remain have been enlarged and given luxurious appointments. Many rooms offer whirlpool baths, often accompanied by Victorian fainting couches that allow the whirlpool-induced glow to linger. Room decor reflects the innkeepers' attention to detail: floral wallpaper in one room matches the colors of the hand-painted tiles atop its antique bureau; another room has a collection of handmade wooden model ships; and a suite that faces the ocean has an antique canopy bed.

Breakfast is a splendid experience, particularly in summer, when it's served on the deck. The ample buffet may consist of fresh bluefish, corned-beef hash, Boston baked beans, sausage, Belgian waffles, roasted potatoes, French toast, scrambled eggs, hot and cold cereal, fruit juices, and fresh muffins. Afternoon cocktails are served down the street at the Hotel Manisses and include such hors d'oeuvres as bluefish pâté and superspicy nachos.

Adjacent to the inn is the Nicholas Ball Cottage, with smaller rooms and some shared baths. Though lodgings here are slightly more spartan, the prices are quite reasonable, and all the inn's amenities remain available. **△** *9 double rooms with baths in inn; 5 doubles with baths, 4 doubles share bath in guest house. Phone in rooms, 4 wheelchair-accessible rooms. $60–$325; full buffet breakfast. MC, V.*

OTHER CHOICES

Barrington Inn. Beach and Ocean Aves. (Box 397), 02807, tel. 401/466–5510, fax 401/466–5880. 6 double rooms with baths, 2 apartments. Ceiling fan in rooms, TV/VCR in common room. $105–$158; Continental breakfast. D, MC, V. No smoking. Closed Dec.–Mar.

Blue Dory Inn. Dodge St. (Box 488), 02807, tel. 401/466–5891 or 800/992–7290, fax 401/466–9910. 13 double rooms with baths, 3 suites, 4 cottages. Cable TV in lobby. $135–$350; Continental breakfast. AE, D, MC, V. No smoking, 2-night minimum weekends.

Rose Farm Inn. Roslyn Rd. (Box E), 02807, tel. 401/466–2034, fax 401/466–2021. 17 double rooms with baths, 2 doubles share bath. Cable TV in common room; refrigerator, ice machine available. $95–$179; Continental breakfast. AE, D, MC, V. No smoking, 3-night minimum July–Aug., 2-night minimum weekends June and Sept.–Oct.

Surf Hotel. Dodge St. (Box C), 02807, tel. 401/466–2241, fax 401/466–5686. 34 doubles and 1 single share 9 baths. Barbecue grill, beach towels, chairs, umbrellas, children's play area, picnic tables. $90–$100; Continental-plus breakfast. MC, V. 6-night minimum July–Aug. Closed Columbus Day–Memorial Day.

SOUTH CAROLINA

Myrtle Beach and the Grand Strand

CYPRESS INN ☞

16 Elm St., Conway 29528, tel. 843/248–8199 or 800/575–5307, fax 843/248–0329

This new inn in sleepy, old-fashioned Conway, about 20 minutes from Myrtle Beach, is a peaceful, soothing alternative to staying on the busy Strand. Built in 1997, the inn overlooks the Conway Marina on the Waccamaw River. It's clean and fresh, with shiny wood floors and spacious, airy public rooms. Yet resident innkeepers Jim and Carol Ruddick, who moved here from Atlanta, have also taken care to include the architectural details of an old house. The large public room downstairs, separated by a hall into a living room and a music room, has a fireplace and is decorated with the Ruddicks' finds from auction and estate sales. The breakfast room is sunny with many windows; guests help themselves to lemonade, tea, and juice from a small refrigerator. The long porch facing the marina is lined with rocking chairs and ferns; there are plenty of books and magazines about; stairways are hand-painted with birds and flowers of the region; and guest linens are luxurious. The place resounds with comfortable, unstuffy elegance.

Guest rooms are on the second and third floors, and each is different but has the same restful, well-thought-out style of old combined with new. Sinks and TV cabinets have been fashioned out of old armoires and buffets. Nearly all rooms have whirlpool baths and work spaces; three have gas fireplaces. The Carolina Room, decorated in soothing sage greens, has a fireplace, a rice bed, silk drapes, and a "waterfall" shower in the spacious bathroom. The Miss Marples Room, like an elegant old aunt's, with flowery wallpaper and red velvet, is filled with Agatha Christie novels.

You can stroll along the waterfront; borrow the bicycles and ride along streets lined with shady old oaks, historic houses, and churches; or walk a few yards to the riverboat *Kingston Lady,* which departs most afternoons for a lazy cruise down the black river. The more adventurous might want to rent their own boat from the marina.

The professionalism of the innkeepers combines the services of a small hotel with the personal attention of a B&B. The Ruddicks provide laundry service for guests, may of whom are business travelers. Breakfast is elaborate, with bacon and cheese puff pie, crab quiche, or Belgian waffles, all with fresh fruit and a basket of homemade breads and muffins. **⌂** *12 double rooms with baths. Air-conditioning, phone, cable TV and ceiling fan in rooms; bicycles. $95–$140; full breakfast, afternoon sherry and cookies. AE, D, MC, V. No.*

SEA VIEW INN 🐚
Myrtle Ave., Pawleys Island 29585, tel. 843/237–4253, fax 843/237–7909

On clean, lye-washed hardwood floors, you can pad barefoot back and forth, coming from the beach or the big, rocking chair–lined porch as the fresh air filters through starched white curtains and the sound of the surf and ease of long, languid days release your stress. This is the seaside as it was meant to be—unadulterated by air-conditioning, neon, and wall-to-wall carpeting. Built in the 1930s and rebuilt in the 1950s after being devastated by Hurricane Hazel, the Sea View is a no-frills, two-story beachside boardinghouse with long porches. There is also a six-room air-conditioned cottage on the marsh.

Page Oberlin, who once ran a large restaurant, took over as innkeeper about 25 years ago. A stay at her "barefoot paradise," though certainly not for everyone, is a special experience. Unless you're attending one of the semiannual painting workshops or wellness retreats, the time is yours—to read, swim, collect shells, walk on the beach, or just do nothing. This is life on Pawleys Island.

In the quiet, casual living room are comfortable sitting areas, a table for game-players, and a fire on cool days. Meals, which are included in the price of the rooms and are served family style in the oceanfront dining room, are the only scheduled events. The menu is diverse: grits, avocado soup, poached salmon, Cobb salad, pecan pie, oyster pie, and, on Mexican and Thai nights, enchiladas with green chilies, burritos, fried bananas. Day-trippers and picnic-lovers can opt for boxed lunches.

Each guest room has pickled-cypress walls and is simply furnished with a hand-painted dresser, a double bed and a twin covered with handmade bedspreads from Guatemala, and art from the spring workshop. Each room has a half-bath; showers are down the hall (and also outside for ocean swimmers). All the rooms have a view of the ocean or the marsh, and the design of the building guarantees a cross breeze. Your program for getting your life in order won't be disturbed here; the inn has a well-stocked library, the tube is nonexistent, and there's only one phone. Guests help themselves to rafts, chairs, umbrellas, and boogie boards. Sailing, golf, tennis, and arts-and-crafts shops are nearby; meditation and massage are available at the inn.

And you can always go ghost hunting among the moss-draped live oaks; you might encounter Alice, searching for her engagement ring in the marshes, or the Gray Man, who warns people about approaching storms. 🔔 *19 double rooms and 1 single share 6 showers. Ceiling fan in rooms. $184–$260; AP. No credit cards. 1-week minimum June–Aug. Closed Nov.–Apr.*

OTHER CHOICES

Chesterfield Inn. 700 N. Ocean Blvd. (Box 218), Myrtle Beach 29578, tel. 843/448–3177 or 800/392–3869, fax 843/626–4736. 57 double rooms with baths. Restaurant, air-conditioning, cable TV and phone in rooms; pool, shuffleboard, croquet. $74–$124 (breakfast not included); $112–$150. AE, D, MC, V. Closed Dec. 13–Feb. 13.

Mansfield Plantation. U.S. 701 N (Rte. 8, Box 590), Georgetown 29440, tel. 843/546–6961 or 800/355–3223. 8 double rooms with baths. Air-conditioning, VCR on request, video library, bicycles. $95; full breakfast, afternoon refreshments on request. No credit cards. No smoking.

Charleston and the
Low Country
◦◦◦✦◦◦◦

BATTERY CARRIAGE HOUSE INN ℘
20 South Battery, Charleston 29401, tel. 843/727–3100 or 800/775–5575,
fax 843/727–3130

Wander down the old carriageway that leads to this B&B, and you might think
you've wandered off to Europe. The walkway is bordered by a brick and stucco
wall that ends in an English-style garden with rose arbor and fountain. Breakfast is served here or in your room. Rooms are in the carriage house and on the
ground floor of the 1843 home (where owners Kat and Drayton Hastie live) that
looks out over Charleston's waterfront Battery. A glass-paneled sitting area has
a fireplace and board games. Rooms are intimate, each with a private entrance;
those on the top floor have high ceilings, several windows, garden views, and steam
showers. Dusky florals and warm colors blend with antiques, hand-painted desks,
and area rugs on wood floors. The suite is in the old cistern of the main house;
though not for everyone, its coved, adobelike ceiling and cavelike coolness create an escape from summer's heat. ▲ *10 double rooms with baths, 1 suite. Air-con-*
ditioning, cable TV, phone and robes in rooms, turndown service, complimentary
newspaper. $99–$225; Continental breakfast, evening wine and snacks. AE, D, MC,
V. No smoking, 2-night minimum weekends.

CUTHBERT HOUSE INN ℘
1203 Bay St., Beaufort 29902, tel. 843/521–1315 or 800/327–9275, fax 843/521–1314

From the front rooms of this grand, white, pillared 1790 home, long windows
and wide piazzas overlook the bay (across a street) through moss-draped trees.
This is how it feels to live in a grand old southern house—-amid detailed crown
and rope molding, original Federal fireplaces (one scratched with the signatures of Union soldiers), and tasteful antiques, on a section of a street called
General's Row. This is real but comfortable elegance. In the morning, awaken-
ing from your high, antique four-poster or rope bed, you might bathe in a cast-
iron soaking tub (one room has a shower but no tub), then walk out on one of
the nearby balconies to check out the weather. Owners and hosts Sharon and Gary
Groves, Florida natives who spent most of their career years in Washington,
D.C., live on the first floor; this inn, in Beaufort's historic district, is their way
of returning to the South.

The Groves have filled their B&B with 18th- and 19th-century heirlooms as
well as their own collection of American Empire and Eastlake Victorian antiques,
and Venetian reproductions. Rooms are large (most with 12-ft ceilings), elegant, and livable, with Oriental rugs on pine floors, commanding beds, dreamy
linens, quilts, and books.

Late afternoon, there are snacks and Gary's homemade cookies served in the
bay-front parlor or on the double-gazebo porch as the sun sets. Breakfast in the
lime sherbert–colored breakfast room will likely include Gary's homemade scones,
fresh juice and fruit, and eggs Benedict. ▲ *7 double rooms, 1 suite. Air-condi-*
tioning, cable TV, phone, robes and refrigerator with sodas in rooms; bicycles,
croquet, business services. $145–170; full breakfast, afternoon refreshments. AE,
D, MC, V.

EAST BAY BED & BREAKFAST ☜

301 East Bay St., Charleston 29401, tel. 843/722–4186, fax 843/720–8528

The Adam woodwork and dentil detailing throughout this Federal-style single house are incredible, accenting rooms, walls, doors, windows—even the porch. Built by a wealthy merchant in 1807, the mansion still has its separate kitchen house and slaves quarters, both of which now have two guest rooms upstairs and an open downstairs area including living room, dining room, kitchenette, and private garden.

The house was divided into several apartments when Carolyn Rivers, who is in the publishing business, bought it; she restored it and opened it as a B&B in the mid-'90s. Her bedroom and office are on the second floor; on your way up to a third-floor guest room, you're likely to find her doors slightly ajar. She's decorated and hand-picked most of the furniture in the house. In the bright yellow sitting room and black-and-white dining room, she's mixed antiques and reproductions with contemporary and African touches, including cream linen sofas and zebra prints. Colors and fabrics in guest rooms are cheerful yet refined; artwork is by Charleston artists.

The inn is off a busy street, but the piazza is cocooned by a palmetto-shaded walled garden that overlooks Charleston's port. A Continental breakfast of croissants and fruit is delivered to your room or is available on the porch. ♙ *6 double rooms with baths. Air-conditioning, cable TV, phone. $105–$185; Continental breakfast. MC, V. No smoking.*

HAYNE HOUSE BED AND BREAKFAST ☜

30 King St., Charleston 29401, tel. 843/577–2633, fax 843/577–5906

Stepping off a tranquil street lined with 18th- and 19th- century homes into the peaceful, lemon-color drawing room of this inn, you'll feel you've come home. In Charleston's prestigious South of Broad neighborhood, one block from the Battery, the Hayne House was built in 1755 by a Revolutionary War hero. Freshly painted and decorated, with a brick courtyard garden shaded by trees, the inn has the quirkiness of an old house but the easy, unintimidating style of Jane and Brian McGreevy, who purchased and reconfigured it in 1997 after moving from Atlanta with their three children. Rooms are dominated by heirlooms from both of their families—mostly Federal antiques. Two of the guest rooms are in the main portion of the house; the other four are in the kitchen house, with its narrow stairway and Colonial brickwork. Brian grew up in Charleston and worked with the Historic Charleston Foundation and Drayton Hall. He'll gladly point out the city's hidden charms and favorite restaurants.

Work by Charleston artists, books, family portraits, teacup collections, cotton sheets, gas fireplaces, and warm, bright colors bring rooms alive. Rooms in the kitchen house are truly historic, with leaning walls from the earthquake of 1886. The Plantation Suite has a sleigh bed and other furniture from Brian's family plantation; it also has a small sitting room. The Cypress Suite has a four-poster bed, sitting room with original fireplace, kitchen, whirlpool tub, and a private balcony nestled in the trees.

A breakfast of homemade breads, muffins, fruit, yogurt, and cheese-grits casserole or sausage-and-egg casserole is served in the formal dining room with linens, silver, and crystal. ♙ *4 double rooms with baths, 2 suites. Air-conditioning, turndown service with sherry, chocolates, robes; bicycles. $120–$295; full breakfast. MC, V.*

KINGS COURTYARD INN 🖙

198 King St., Charleston 29401, tel. 843/723–7000 or 800/845–6119,
fax 843/720–2608

It is easy to overlook the small doorway that leads into the shady courtyard of this European-style inn, a soothing oasis wedged between the city's best antiques shops and fashionable boutiques on King Street, one of Charleston's oldest shopping thoroughfares. Guests will quickly recognize the ambience, service, and respect for privacy that are characteristic here.

Built in 1853, the two structures that compose this Greek Revival inn have the appearance of being only one because of their exterior stucco, which was added after the great earthquake of 1886. Prior to the Civil War, plantation owners and shipping magnates stayed here when they did business in Charleston. The rooms are furnished with 18th-century reproductions, including French armoires and beds hung with hand-tied fishnet canopies, and decorated in elegant, traditional fabrics, with Oriental rugs accenting the original heart-pine floors. Two have pressed-tin ceilings, 14 have gas-burning fireplaces, and one has a private balcony. Most of the rooms open onto one of the two inner courtyards with fountains; the rest overlook King Street. A large whirlpool bath is the center of a rear garden area.

In a small formal room off the main courtyard, a fire burns in winter—complimentary wine and sherry are always available, as is brandy after dinner. Guests may have breakfast here, in one of the courtyards, the breakfast room, or their bedroom; a full meal is available and costs extra. Breakfast comes with a morning newspaper, and the nightly turndown service includes chocolates. ⚘ *37 double rooms with baths, 4 suites. Air-conditioning, cable TV and phone in rooms, VCR available, small meeting room, turndown service with chocolates; outdoor whirlpool bath. $175–$260; Continental breakfast. AE, D, DC, MC, V. Restricted smoking.*

LAUREL HILL PLANTATION 🖙

8913 N. Hwy. 17 (Box 190), McClellanville 29458, tel. 843/887–3708 or 888/887–3708

Down an unpaved, winding road off Highway 17, this inn almost effortlessly replaces the original 1850s plantation home that stood here until Hurricane Hugo demolished it in 1989. Built using the original floor plan of two large rooms on both sides of a wide hall, the home has wide plank pine floors. The outstanding feature, though, is the huge wraparound piazza and heated sunporch with magnificently unending views of the wildlife-studded creeks, salt marshes, and ocean of Cape Romain Wildlife Refuge. Guests idle the afternoon away here, on the dock, or in the nearby sleepy, shrimping village of McClellanville, which is about 45 minutes from Charleston and 30 minutes from Georgetown.

Jackie and Lee Morrison, who live on the first floor, have a longtime passion for this area; Lee's family has owned this property for generations. A relaxed mix of American primitive and Amish-style antiques, with lots of blue and red plaids and ginghams, decorates the rooms. Folk art and collections of depression-era glass and pitchers create a feeling of bygone days. Everywhere are sweet touches like vintage hand mirrors on dressing tables, extra pillows on the beds, piles of handmade quilts, and fresh mint for iced tea. Guest rooms make imaginative use of antique linens as shower curtains, window curtains, and canopies; three have antique queen-size beds and one has two beds of three-quarter size.

Guests help themselves to sodas, tea, beer, and wine. Afternoon refreshments might be homemade cheese dip with tomatoes from Lee's garden; the country breakfast, served on the porch or in the dining room around a big round table, is likely to be whole wheat pancakes with hot fruit compote and sausage, or artichoke strata with homemade breads and jam. △ *4 double rooms with baths. Ceiling fan, TV available on request; fishing, horseshoes. $95–$115; full breakfast, evening refreshments. AE, D, DC, MC, V. No smoking indoors.*

RHETT HOUSE INN ☞
1009 Craven St., Beaufort 29902, tel. 843/524–9030, fax 843/524–1310

This 1820 Greek Revival mansion in Beaufort's historic district was the home of Thomas Rhett, a rich planter, who summered here with his wife, Caroline Barnwell, and their children. The house exemplifies the rich and lavish lifestyle of prosperous southern planters prior to the Civil War—nowhere in the South was wealth flaunted more than in Beaufort. The three-story, square white building has black shutters and double-decker verandas on the second and third floors, supported by 14 fluted Doric columns. It stands on the edge of Craven Street, with a huge live oak dripping with Spanish moss directly in front and gardens to the side and the rear.

The mansion was looking somewhat sad when Steve and Marianne Harrison, executives in New York's garment industry, first spied it on a vacation in 1986. The Harrisons completely renovated the mansion and filled it with their own English and American antiques and art. Though elegant, the inn is warm and friendly with a French country-cottage look; guests feel comfortable in sweaters and tennis shoes, and boaters on the Intracoastal Waterway (only a block away) often drop in. Some rooms have private entrances. Famous guests have included Barbra Streisand and Nick Nolte (when they were filming *Prince of Tides*), Dennis Quaid, and Demi Moore.

Two rooms have working fireplaces, and the honeymoon suite has a private porch and a whirlpool bath. Amenities in the rooms include fresh flowers and miniature African violets, a CD player (there's a CD library in the sitting room), a full-length mirror, and four pillows.

The inn expanded in 1997, renovating another building across the street (which has been totally regutted and therefore hasn't the historic ambience of the main inn). The seven guest rooms offer the amenities and privacy of a small hotel, each with gas fireplace, whirlpool tub, honor bar, private entrance, and outdoor sitting area.

Guests can eat breakfast in the breakfast room, in the garden, on the porch, or in their room. Picnics can be arranged on request. △ *8 double rooms with baths, 1 suite in main house; 7 double rooms with baths in Carriage House. Air-conditioning, ceiling fan, cable TV, phone, and CD player in rooms, turndown service with robes; bicycles. $160–$250; full breakfast, afternoon tea and cookies, evening hors d'oeuvres. AE, MC, V. No smoking.*

TWO MEETING STREET ☞
2 Meeting St., Charleston 29401, tel. 843/723–7322

This Queen Anne Victorian, built in 1892, is one of the most beautiful houses in the city's historic district and is usually included in spring and fall house tours. You know this is a special place the minute you step through the iron gates onto a walk lined with flowers and shrubs. The landscaped gardens are manicured to perfection; the curved verandas, with their arched columns and balustrades, are freshly painted. The sparkle of the beveled glass and the polished brass on the heavy wooden door add to the welcome of the innkeeper's official greeting.

Its location, overlooking the Battery and the harbor, makes it convenient to all of Charleston's pleasures. In 1931, it was turned into an inn, and it eventually passed to Jean and Pete Spell. Together with their daughter, Karen Spell Shaw, the Spells have made the house a showplace, one of the city's most popular lodgings, and raised innkeeping to an art. All three are locals with insider's advice—Pete is a Citadel grad, and Jean is a licensed city guide who will enthusiastically help guests tailor a day of sightseeing around their interests. The Spells' fascination with Charleston and the Lowcountry is evident in the many books around the house.

You enter the foyer, a large open room with richly carved English oak paneling, stained-glass windows, and a heavy stairway over which hangs a huge crystal chandelier. The reception rooms are also paneled, and the house has nine stained-glass windows in all, two of them Tiffanys. The formal parlors, off the foyer, are furnished with Victorian reproduction love seats, 18th-century chairs, family heirlooms, and photos; the formal dining room has a dazzling crystal chandelier and highly polished silver. Guests can enjoy a firelit breakfast here in winter.

Each guest room has its own personality, and all are furnished with antique four-poster or canopy beds and Oriental rugs. The two honeymoon suites have working fireplaces and French doors that open to the outside, creating a feeling of privacy. The rooms on the first and second floors are the most sought after, but those on the third floor are just as appealing except that you must climb the stairs.

The staff members at Two Meeting Street go out of their way to make each stay memorable. Guests can enjoy afternoon tea with homemade cakes, Lowcountry sweets, cheese, and crackers. Breakfast is a treat, too, with fresh fruit salad and oversize "Texas" muffins. ♿ *9 double rooms with baths. Air-conditioning and TV in rooms. $175–$295; Continental breakfast, afternoon tea. No credit cards. No smoking, 2-night minimum weekends. Closed Dec. 24–26.*

WENTWORTH MANSION ⚑
149 Wentworth St., Charleston 29403, tel. 843/853–1886 or 888/466–1886, fax 843/723–8634

It's hard to believe this spectacular four-story brick mansion surrounded by 13,883 acres was once the private home of one family. Built around 1886 by cotton merchant and phosphate manufacturer Francis Silas Rodgers, the house eventually served as headquarters for an insurance company until the early 1990s. Opened as an inn in summer 1998, it's near the College of Charleston and about five blocks from shops and historic sites.

Amid hand-carved marble fireplaces, dark mahogany woodwork, Tiffany stained-glass windows, and Second Empire antiques (a few original to the house), guests enjoy complimentary afternoon tea, wine tastings, and evening cordials. The parlor has a carved plaster ceiling, marble mantel, and chandelier. Velvet drapes and fabrics in neutral shades of olive and gold accent the spacious guest rooms, each of which has at least one antique, a dramatic king bed, oversize bathroom with whirlpool, and sitting areas; most have gas fireplaces. The Grand Mansion Suite, originally the other half of the home's double parlors, has dramatic pocket doors between its huge sitting room and bedroom, both with a fireplace.

You can take your after-dinner cordial up a spiral staircase that leads to the mansion's cupola for a fantastic view of the city and the harbor. Breakfast is a buffet of fresh fruit, cereal, smoked salmon, bagels, muffins, and yogurt served on the sunporch. There is also a window-lined library, perfect for a quiet afternoon tea, which includes cheese, fruit, canapés, and sweets. Guests have only to stroll behind the inn to the carriage house for an elegant dinner at Circa 1886 Restaurant. ♨ *14 double rooms with baths, 7 suites. Restaurant, air-conditioning, cable TV and phone in rooms, turndown service with robes, lounge, meeting facilities, concierge. $275–$675; Continental breakfast, afternoon tea, evening cordials. AE, D, DC, MC, V. No smoking.*

OTHER CHOICES

Beaufort Inn. 809 Port Republic St., Beaufort 29902, tel. 843/521–9000, fax 843/521–9500. 11 double rooms with baths, 1 cottage. Restaurant, wine bar; air-conditioning, ceiling fan, TV, phone, refrigerator, and honor bar in rooms; small conference room. $125–$195; full breakfast, afternoon tea upon request. AE, D, MC, V. No smoking.

Craven Street Inn. 1103 Craven St., Beaufort 29902, tel. 888/522–0250, tel. and fax 843/522–1668. 4 double rooms, 3 suites, 1 cottage. Air-conditioning, ceiling fan, phone, cable TV, refrigerator in room. $95–$175; Continental breakfast. AE, MC, V. No smoking indoors.

Fulton Lane Inn. 202 King St., Charleston 29401, tel. 843/720–2600 or 800/720–2688, fax 843/720–2940. 22 double rooms with baths, 5 suites. Air-conditioning, cable TV, phone, refrigerator, and honor bar in rooms, turndown service. $165–$285; Continental breakfast. MC, V. No smoking.

Middleton Inn. Ashley River Rd., Charleston 29414, tel. 843/556–0500 or 800/543–4774. 52 double rooms with baths. Air-conditioning, TV, phone, and refrigerator in rooms, conference center; pool, bicycles, tennis, croquet, free admission to Middleton Place. $129–$149; full breakfast. AE, D, DC, MC, V. Restricted smoking.

Twenty-Seven State Street Bed & Breakfast. 27 State St., Charleston 29401, tel. 843/722–4243. 2 double rooms with baths, 3 suites for long-term visitors. Air-conditioning, ceiling fan, kitchenette, cable TV, and phone in rooms; bicycles. $85–$145; breakfast not included. No credit cards. No smoking.

RESERVATIONS SERVICES

Historic Charleston B & B (60 Broad St., Charleston 29401, tel. 843/722–6606 or 800/743–3583). **Southern Hospitality B&B Reservations** (110 Amelia Dr., Lexington 29464, tel. 843/356–6238 or 800/374–7422). **RSVP Reservation Service** (9489 Whitefield Ave., Box 49, Savannah, GA 31406, tel. 800/729–7787).

Thoroughbred Country and the Old Ninety Six

BELMONT INN 🦢
Court Sq., 104 E. Pickens St., Abbeville 29620, tel. 864/459–9625 or 888/251–2000

This three-story hotel, with its long, arched double veranda, planted on one corner of Court Square, has played a prominent role in the history of the town. Built in 1903 and called the Eureka, in its heyday it was the resort of famous statesmen, lawyers, and judges during court sessions and of drummers and vaudeville actors. The hotel went through hard times, closed in 1974, reopened in 1984, then closed again in a tattered state. Audrey and Alan Peterson reopened the inn in 1996 after giving it a major sprucing-up.

Since its rebirth, the Belmont has developed quite a following. Its guests like to combine a visit with an evening at the Opera House (theater packages include dinner and tours of the Burt-Stark house), following the example of stars like Jimmy Durante, Fanny Brice, Sarah Bernhardt, and Groucho Marx, who made overnight stops in Abbeville. The town calls itself the "birthplace and deathbed of the Confederacy," and there is a Confederate memorial in the town square.

Guest rooms have high ceilings and are furnished with Victorian reproductions, including four-poster beds and armoires; only rooms facing the town square have a noteworthy view. Though the heart-pine floors are original, the fireplaces are now only decorative. The John C. Calhoun Room opens onto the second-floor balcony that it shares with an adjacent room. The fancy Lafayette Room is accessorized completely in red and gold. The inn's original registration desk is now on the first floor; it and the two parlors upstairs have rich hunting colors and are furnished with Victorian reproductions, some period antiques, and wicker.

Timothy's restaurant, serving regional cuisine, offers dinner and Sunday brunch. Guests help themselves to a Continental buffet breakfast served here and may take it out to the veranda overlooking the square. Light fare is served in the Curtain Call Lounge on the basement level. The meeting rooms, also on this level, were originally used by traveling salesmen to display their merchandise. ⚠ *25 double rooms with baths. Restaurant, air-conditioning, cable TV and phone in rooms; lounge, parking. $69–$129; Continental breakfast, afternoon wine and cheese. AE, D, DC, MC, V. Restricted smoking.*

ROSEMARY HALL ☙
804 Carolina Ave., North Augusta 29841, tel. 803/278–6222 or 800/531–5578

This gem in North Augusta spares no possible elegance. Parlors have down-stuffed love seats, period antiques, and luxurious drapes; guest rooms have canopy beds, European pillows, antique linens, and rugs custom-made in India, Pakistan, and Romania. About 10 mi from Aiken and 3 mi from downtown Augusta, Georgia, Rosemary Hall is an opulent feast for the senses, with service to match. Completed in 1902, the antebellum-style inn has an L-shape veranda with 50-ft columns, intricate curly-pine paneling and ceilings, and a fireplace in all but one room.

Guests can enjoy smoked salmon, cheese, and crackers in the jewel-toned gentlemen's parlor or the elegant ladies' parlor. The Georgian Suite has a gorgeous rug woven with tassle images, a tassle-draped fireplace, and an enormous bathroom with a claw-foot tub. Other guest rooms have private verandas or whirlpool tubs. Across the street is Lookaway Hall, another magnificent, three-story mansion; both homes were built by the Jackson brothers, who flipped a coin to see who got which property. ⚠ *8 double rooms with baths. Air-conditioning, cable TV and phone in rooms, turndown service with robes, concierge. $75–$200; full breakfast, afternoon tea and cookies, evening hors d'oeuvres. AE, D, DC, MC, V. No smoking.*

VINTAGE INN ☙
1205 N. Main St., Abbeville 29620, tel. 800/890–7312 or 864/459–4784

This two-story Princess Anne home with wraparound veranda is a 15-minute walk from Abbeville's town square. Built in the 1870s, the building was falling apart when Gail and Jim Uldrick began renovating it in 1991. Originally the two Abbeville natives planned to sell the house, but it worked its charms and they now call it home. (Gail later discovered that her great-grandparents had once lived in the house.) Jim and the Uldricks' four sons meticulously refurbished the home, including the scarred pine floors, fireplaces, wide foyer, and double doors.

The inn sparkles now: Gail has decorated the three guest rooms upstairs with homey quilts, lace curtains, antique books, and sweet knickknacks. The upstairs sitting area has plenty of magazines and a collection of antique hats for guests to try on. Or they can pop in the kitchen for a chat with Gail at the long, antique pine table in front of the carved fireplace mantle. That Abbeville is a family-centered community is evident here: Gail's mom lives in the carriage house out back, all four sons live nearby, and a portrait of one daughter-in-law holds the place of honor in the pink parlor. ♙ *1 double room with bath, 2 double rooms share bath. Ceiling fan in rooms, refrigerator stocked with drinks in sitting area. $65–$125; full breakfast. AE. No smoking.*

WILLCOX INN 🖋

100 Colleton Ave., Aiken 29801, tel. and fax 803/649–1377 or tel. 800/368–1047, fax 803/643–0971

Were it not for the white paint on this three-story classic inn, you would hardly notice the building amid the trees and shrubbery in Aiken's historic district. But it's right there with the elaborate estates and horse farms belonging to the winter people, who come from everywhere each year for the riding, racing, and hunting.

Frederick Sugden Willcox, an Englishman, came to Aiken around 1891 with his Swedish wife, Elise, and soon started the inn. The Willcox family managed the inn until 1957; Jim Bargren, who owns several other inns, took over in 1994.

Second Empire and Colonial Revival in architectural style, the weatherboard inn has a front porch supported by six Doric columns, over which there is a balcony. The rosewood-paneled lobby has heart-pine floors, a stone fireplace at either end, and a smaller fireplace on the second landing; decorated in leather and hunting-color plaids, it's a grand and handsome room. The Polo Lounge, with dark paneling and leather chairs, is a perfect setting for the horsey set during racing season. The Pheasant Room Restaurant serves lunch, dinner, and Sunday brunch; the duck with raspberry sauce is wonderful. Guest rooms are large, with reproduction antiques, four-poster beds, and floral wallpapers. The Winston Churchill Suite has a separate sitting room, a private entrance, two fireplaces, and a porch. Room 106, on the back side, is cool and quiet; its large bathroom has a claw-foot tub. ♙ *24 double rooms with baths, 6 suites. Restaurant, air-conditioning, cable TV and phone in rooms, lounge, meeting room; free use of nearby health club. $90–$135; Continental breakfast. AE, D, DC, MC, V.*

OTHER CHOICES

Annie's Inn. U.S. 78 E (Box 300), Montmorenci 29839, tel. 803/649—6836, fax 803/642–6709. 5 double rooms with baths, 6 cottages. Ceiling fan, TV, phone in rooms. $65–$95; full breakfast. AE, D, DC, MC, V. Restricted smoking.

Brodie Residence. 422 York St. SE, Aiken 29801, tel. 803/648–1445. 2 double rooms share bath. Ceiling fan in rooms, turndown service with chocolates; pool, indoor hot tub, bicycles. $55; Continental breakfast, afternoon refreshments. No credit cards. No smoking.

Town & Country Inn. 2340 Sizemore Circle, Aiken 29803, tel. 803/642–0270, fax 803/642–1299. 5 double rooms with baths. Air-conditioning; pool. $65–$95; full breakfast, evening coffee and dessert. AE, D, MC, V. No smoking.

RESERVATIONS SERVICE

Southern Hospitality B&B Reservations (110 Amelia Dr., Lexington 29464, tel. 803/356–6238 or 800/374–7422).

SOUTH DAKOTA

Black Hills

RASPBERRY LACE BED AND BREAKFAST 🍃

12175 White Horse Rd., Custer 57730, tel. 605/574–4920

If you're on your way to the Crazy Horse Monument, you can't miss the Raspberry Lace Bed and Breakfast, tucked neatly in a nook along U.S. Highway 16 just 4 mi from the monument, between the Mickelson bicycle trail and one of the dozens of mountain streams that decorate the Black Hills roadways.

Raspberry Lace got its name from the raspberries that grow wild along the hillside trail behind the inn. The trail leads up the mountainside where visitors can get an unobstructed view of the daily work at Crazy Horse. Owners Roland and Loretta Daigle will gladly pack a picnic lunch for visitors who opt for this outing. Residents of the region since 1984, Roland and Loretta renovated this 1920s-era farmhouse for their own family with the intent of opening a bed-and-breakfast, which they did in 1997.

The house itself is very simple, but the Daigles have created a casual, homey retreat, perfect for a large family or multiple families traveling together. A semi-private entrance opens into a large common area with fireplace, a refrigerator, and microwave. Three rooms with queen beds have a casual, rustic decor.

Breakfast includes—what else—raspberry muffins or raspberry streusel served with an egg casserole and other fresh fruits and juices in season. Guests have a choice of dining with the Daigles in their airy dining room or of being served on the slate patio or the deck off their rooms. ⌂ *1 double room with bath, 2 doubles share bath. TV/VCR, stereo, fireplace in common room, hot tub. $65–$80; full breakfast. MC, V.*

VILLA THERESA BED AND BREAKFAST 🍃

801 Almond St., Hot Springs 57747, tel. 605/745–4633

The Old West charm of Villa Theresa Bed and Breakfast is what attracted Rick and Mary Jo Johnson to the inn as guests and resulted in their purchasing it in 1998. They haven't changed a thing, from the relaxing setting of the Poker Room, now used as a reading room since gambling is not legal here, to the elegant decor initiated by designer Marshall Fields in the 1920s.

The name Villa Theresa is a tribute to the wife of Fred Evans, founder of Evans Plunge, a swimming pool, sauna, hot tub, and health spa complex that is fed by natural hot springs and still this town's major attraction. The inn was a gentlemen's club until Evans turned it into a private residence in the 1920s.

The house has an 18-ft, intricately hand-painted green-and-peach floral ceiling, and some of the original furnishings are still part of this exquisitely decorated home. Each guest room, which varies in size, has its own theme: The Old West Room has an antique wire-framed bed, handmade comforter, and old-fashioned claw-foot tub; depictions of parrots and exotic flowers surround the Jacuzzi, and mosquito netting is draped around the bed in the Tropical Suite; a tepee encircles the bed in the American Indian Room, which also has authentic Sioux artwork and a Jacuzzi; the Music Room is for those with an interest in classical music; and the Royal Room, with the best view in the house, has elegant decor including a crystal chandelier and a brass shower rise. From the windows, your view takes you over the bluffs and to downtown Hot Springs. △ *7 double rooms with baths. Private entrances. $80–$149. D, MC, V.*

WILLOW SPRINGS CABINS 🐾
11515 Sheridan Lake Rd., Rapid City 57702, tel. 605/342–3665

These two simple cabins, on 160 acres of land that was originally a gold mine, are surrounded by the Black Hills National Forest, rich in native Ponderosa pine. The owners are Joyce and Russell Payton; Russell's grandparents homesteaded this area, a secluded spring-fed valley 11 mi southwest of Rapid City.

Although built in 1991 by Joyce and Russell, the Frontier Cabin (for adults only) seems older due to its pine exterior and tin roof. Inside, rustic western decorations include a woven Lakota dream catcher (a traditional Indian ornament used to filter bad dreams) above the bed's headboard, which Russell fashioned from the same wood as the cabin frame. Lamps with metal-cutout bison silhouettes hang from both sides of the headboard. The small bathroom has a clawfoot tub.

Willows Cabin, a log structure built for the Forest Service in the 1950s and later moved to the Payton place, is decorated with the Paytons' heirlooms—a dark wood-frame bed, entry bench, and Great-grandmother's wooden rocker. A more modern pull-out couch accommodates family stays. The log walls display Russell's mother's eyelet lace baptismal gown and large, ornately gilded framed photographs of his grandparents. The small bathroom off the main room has a shower, no bath.

A short walk from the cabins is the historic Flume Trail. If you have the time (and energy) you can walk the 6 mi to Sheridan Lake, enjoying the many varieties of wildflowers and wildlife along the way, or meander to a replica log cabin built alongside an abandoned railroad bed. Also nearby is an old-fashioned swimming hole near a creek for fishing.

A full breakfast of freshly ground gourmet coffee or tea, fresh fruit and juices, egg dishes or waffles, and homemade breads is served on your private porch, in bed, or in a basket to take to the creek. △ *2 cabins with baths. TV/VCR, cassette player, mini-refrigerator, microwave, coffeemakers, 2 outdoor hot tubs. $95–$120; full breakfast.*

OTHER CHOICES
Black Hills Hideaway. U.S. Hwy. 385, 7 mi south of Deadwood 57732, tel. 605/578–3054, fax 605/578–2028. 10 rooms with baths. TV/VCR and air-conditioning available, whirlpool baths, gas fireplaces, bicycles. $89–$169; full breakfast, afternoon snacks and beverages. MC, V.

Bunkhouse B & B. 14630 Lower Spring Creek Rd., Hermosa 57744, tel. 605/342–5462 or 888/756–5462. 1 room with bath, 2 rooms share bath. Air-conditioning, TV/VCR in recreation room, woodstove in family room, gift shop, nearby hiking and riding trails (bring your own horse). $55–$135; full breakfast. MC, V.

Carriage House. 721 West Blvd., Rapid City, SC 57701, tel. 605/343–6415 or 888/343–6418. 5 rooms with baths, whirlpool in 3 rooms, library and living room with TV/VCR and stereo. $89–$149; full breakfast. MC, V.

Custer Mansion. 35 Centennial Dr., Custer 57730, tel. 605/673–3333. 5 double rooms with baths. Whirlpool, TV in library. $55–$95; full breakfast. AE, MC, V.

Flying B Ranch B & B. R.R. 10 (Box 2640), Rapid City 57701, tel. 605/342–5324. 3 rooms with baths. Air-conditioning, TV/VCR, hot tub, fireplace, phone in rooms, TV and pool table in recreation room, pool. $125; full breakfast. D, MC, V.

Eastern South Dakota

ROSE STONE INN 🐦

504 E. 4th St., Dell Rapids, Custer 57022, tel. 605/428–3698, fax 605/428–3698.

Not all of the interesting sights of South Dakota are in the Black Hills, as visitors learn from conversation with Rick and Sharon Skinner, owners of the Rose Stone Inn. The couple grew up in the Black Hills but moved to the far eastern part of the state in 1991 after they visited and fell in love with the town of Dell Rapids, just 20 minutes north of Sioux Falls.

Now on the National Register of Historic Places, their inn has been welcoming guests since 1883 and, like much of the town, is built of red quartzite stone from local quarries. A massive front porch is decorated with a number of state, regional, and national flags, as well as wicker chairs and a table set ready for a checkers game.

Sharon has decorated the spacious lobby with dozens of live plants, family photos, heirloom quilts, and a talking bird. Rick made all of the stained-glass windows throughout the two-story building. But the true delight of the common area is when the Skinners' son Shane sits down to the piano and the windows rattle with the sounds of ragtime, jazz, and modern melodies.

Other entertainment for guests include an old-time movie theater across the street and the newly renovated Grand Opera House, just two blocks away. The Skinners are owners of the Fountain of the Opera, an ice cream and soda fountain in the lobby of the opera house. Guests receive complimentary coupons when attending a performance.

Family heirlooms and other turn-of-the-century furnishings generate a true warmth and homelike atmosphere, especially when Sharon shares the stories of numerous items. The Violet Room is one of her favorites, named for Sharon's mother and stenciled by her sister.

Breakfast is generous, complete with fruits and homemade rolls, individual quiches, and French toast and served in an elegant dining room on family china, just off the main lobby. Private dining is available for anniversaries and special occasions. ♣ *2 double rooms with baths, 6 doubles share bath. $50–$70; full breakfast. D, MC, V.*

OTHER CHOICES

Prairie House Manor. R.R. 2 (Box 61A), DeSmet 57231, tel. 800/297–2416.
5 double rooms with bath, 1 room with bath sleeps 6. $39–$109; full breakfast.
AE, MC, V. Closed Dec.–Apr.

TENNESSEE

East Tennessee

ADAMS EDGEWORTH INN ☙

Monteagle Assembly (Box 340), Monteagle 37356, tel. 931/924–4000, fax 931/924–3236

Adams Edgeworth Inn is atop the Cumberland Plateau inside a Victorian community nicknamed the Chautauqua of the South. It is a southern hotel in the grand, old-fashioned sense, with a wraparound porch and screen doors. Every summer, the Monteagle Assembly, the 96-acre community surrounding the inn, hosts an eight-week program of events that range from literary seminars to classical music concerts. Guests are free to wander the paths among 160 Victorian houses. Originally a boardinghouse, the 1896 inn was renovated and reopened in 1977, losing none of its authenticity. The entire compound is listed on the National Register of Historic Places.

Proprietors David and Wendy Adams are outgoing and articulate, both retired from prominent jobs in Atlanta. Wendy was fund-raising director for the opera and ballet, and David headed the research department at a brokerage firm. The Edgeworth art collection ranges from Old Master paintings to contemporary art picked up during the Adamses' travels, and its library boasts some 2,000 volumes.

A gentle quiet pervades the Edgeworth, where guests read, talk, or play board games. Rooms have 12-ft ceilings and a country cottage decor, with lots of chintz in warm colors. Some rooms have fireplaces and four-poster beds; others have twin brass beds. In warm weather, the porch is the perfect place to spend an evening in a rocking chair; in the afternoon, the hammocks are irresistible. Breakfast is served in a cozy dining room, where Wendy, who graduated from the Culinary Institute of America, elegantly presents five-course, candlelit dinners by reservation.

Nearby attractions include the University of the South at Sewanee, a small, well-respected school, and the trails of South Cumberland State Recreation Area. The Monteagle Winery produces a nice selection of sweet German wines.
🛆 *13 double rooms with baths, 1 suite. Air-conditioning, cable TV in 5 rooms, library, dining room, gift shop; pool, tennis courts on the Assembly grounds. $95–$195; full breakfast. AE, MC, V. No smoking, 2-night minimum weekends.*

BIG SPRING INN ☙

315 N. Main St., Greeneville 37745, tel. 423/638–2917

Walnut, maple, pecan, and magnolia trees shroud Big Spring Inn, a Greek Revival house built in 1905 as a wedding present. Since 1993, it has been owned by

Oregonians Nancy and Marshall Ricker, who were a manager of a speech pathology department and an architect, respectively.

The expansive front porch has white wicker furniture. Inside are English and American antiques and good reproductions, purchased from one of many nearby antiques stores. The 1790 Hepplewhite dining table seats 12 for breakfast. The Rickers' taste runs to Laura Ashley prints and accessories, which complement the oak floors; beveled, leaded-glass windows; and original chandeliers. Six chimneys punctuate the unusual roof line, and metal shingles produce a soothing rhythm in the rain. A favorite bedroom is the Felice Noell Austin Room, light and airy with Victorian Rose wallpaper and a white wrought-iron bed. Its spacious bath has original black and white tiles and a large tub. The Hassie Hacker Doughty Room, the original master bedroom, has a fireplace with mantel, large bay window, king-size antique brass bed, and oversize bathroom.

The Rickers are gracious yet unobtrusive hosts and provide many special touches. At 7 AM a tea cart appears on the second-floor landing. Rooms have robes, Caswell-Massey toiletries, and homemade cookies, and croquet and other lawn games are played in the well-kept yard.

The inn is in historic Greeneville, a New England–style village settled in 1783, and is a short walk from the burial site and birthplace of President Andrew Johnson. The village is close to the brilliant fall colors of the Cherokee National Forest and the Great Smoky Mountains; white-water rafting; the Dixon-Williams Mansion, a pre–Civil War showplace that housed troops from both sides; and storytelling in Jonesborough—but it's far from the crowds and mini traffic jams that plague Gatlinburg. *2 double rooms and 2 singles with baths, 1 suite, 1 carriage house for long-term stays. Air-conditioning, cable TV, and phone in rooms; pool. $70–$86; full breakfast. AE, MC, V. No smoking. Closed Nov.–Mar.*

BUCKHORN INN ❦
2140 Tudor Mtn. Rd., Gatlinburg 37738, tel. 423/436–4668, fax 423/436–5009

The lobby of the Buckhorn Inn, on a wooded hillside at the edge of Great Smoky Mountains National Park, commands a good view of the local peaks, and several of the rooms have views as well. Designed to blend in with its surroundings, the 1938 inn has a rustic flavor. It sits in the middle of a lush, 35-acre estate surrounded by pine trees; comfortable fireside chairs in the sitting and dining rooms invite guests to relax with a glass of wine and look out on Mt. LeConte, one of the highest peaks in the Smokies. A Steinway grand piano rests in one niche of the lobby, and a library dubbed the "hikers' corner" is in another spot. With its well-loved, shabby decor, this inn appeals to the old-money crowd.

Rooms are small, carpeted, and furnished with simple, understated grace. With the feel of a tree house, the most interesting bedroom is in the inn's original water tower, where bath facilities are on one level and the bedroom is above. On all but the warmest days, the scent of wood smoke lingers in the air. In the dining room, breakfast and a six-course gourmet dinner are served by reservation on small tables. Four cottages and two relatively spacious guest houses are on the grounds, but the cottages are a cut below the inn rooms. Each has a fireplace, screened-in porch, and good view.

This secluded inn has its own ½-mi nature trail and fishing pond. It's 1 mi from the entrance to the national park and about 6 mi northeast of Gatlinburg and its myriad activities. It is in the midst of some 70 shops, galleries, and eateries of the Great Smoky Mountains Arts and Crafts Community. *6 double rooms with baths, 4 cottages, 2 guest houses. Air-conditioning, cable TV in cottages. $105–*

$250; full breakfast. MC, V. Smoking in 2 cottages only, 2-night minimum holidays, weekends, and Oct.

INN AT BLACKBERRY FARM ℘
1471 W. Millers Cove Rd., Walland 37886, tel. 423/984–8166

What started as a private mountain estate, built in quiet Walland in the 1930s, has become a thriving inn that sets the standard for luxury among Tennessee B&Bs. Its 110 acres loll across the foothills of the Great Smokies, on green land full of blackberry brambles, two stocked ponds, trails, a fly-fishing stream, a cemetery, and a chapel, finally ending at the national park boundary.

A swarm of fresh-faced staff members in khaki uniforms attends each guest, whisking away cars, luggage, and every last care. Spacious common areas have an English country manor feel, thawed by American informality. Oriental rugs, English and French antiques, and handsome art are softened by overstuffed chairs in intimate groupings. Rooms continue the look, often with bright chintz or fireplaces, and always with feather beds and inspiring views. The Cotswold-style cottages are the crème de la crème, with wood-burning fireplaces, whirlpools, and loaded pantries. A flagstone veranda is a favorite place to breathe in the panorama.

But decor and land are only part of the story. Chef and inn director John Fleer, a Culinary Institute of America graduate, orchestrates a notable cuisine of such items as sweet tea–cured roast pork and mint-julep quail, served in a large dining room. Three gourmet meals a day are included in the room rate.

Owners Sandy and Kreis Beall bought the property in 1976 and reside in a renovated pre–Civil War farmhouse on the land. Sandy is CEO of Ruby Tuesday's; his wife, Kreis, devotes her time to Blackberry and is its chief decorator.

Should Adam or Eve deign to leave Paradise, Gatlinburg and Pigeon Forge are a half hour away, and the Great Smoky Mountains National Park is even closer. ⌂ *23 double rooms with baths, 16 suites, 3-bedroom cottage, 2-bedroom gatehouse. Air-conditioning, terry cloth robes, turndown service with chocolates; fireplaces, mini-refrigerators, whirlpools in some rooms; TV in game room; fly-fishing, trout and bass fishing, tennis, swimming, fitness facilities. $395–$1745; full gourmet dinner and breakfast, picnic lunch, 24-hour access to snacks and beverages. AE, D, MC, V. No smoking, 2-night minimum (3-night minimum during Oct.).*

OTHER CHOICES

Adams Hilborne. 801 Vine St., Chattanooga 37403, tel. 423/265–5000, fax 423/265–5555. 10 double rooms with baths. Restaurant. $100–$250; full breakfast. AE, MC, V. No smoking.

Blue Mountain Mist Country Inn. 1811 Pullen Rd., Sevierville 37862, tel. 423/428–2335 or 800/497–2335, fax 423/453–1720. 12 double rooms with baths, 5 cottages. Meal service for groups, cable TV/VCR in parlor. $98–$140; full breakfast, evening dessert. MC, V. No smoking, 2-night minimum holidays and Oct.

Hippensteal's Mountain View Inn. Grassy Branch Rd. (Box 707), Gatlinburg 37738, tel. 423/436–5761 or 800/527–8110, fax 423/436–8917. 9 double rooms with baths. Air-conditioning, ceiling fans, TV/VCR and phone jacks in rooms. $95–$130; full breakfast, evening dessert. AE, D, MC, V. No smoking. Closed Dec. 24–25.

Richmont Inn. 220 Winterberry La., Townsend 37882, tel. 423/448–6751. 10 double rooms with baths. Air-conditioning, robes, coffeemakers, hair dryers in rooms; gift shop, café, chapel, nature trail. $95–$200; full breakfast, evening dessert. No credit cards. No smoking.

Von-Bryan Inn. 2402 Hatcher Mountain Rd., Sevierville 37862, tel. 423/453–9832 or 800/633–1459, fax 423/428–8634. 5 double rooms with baths, 1 suite, 1 chalet. Air-conditioning, TV in living room. $90–$200; full breakfast. AE, D, MC, V. No smoking. 2-night minimum holidays and weekends and in chalet.

Middle Tennessee
◆◦◦◦◦◦◦◦◆

CHIGGER RIDGE ☙
1060 Hwy. 70 W (Box 349), Pegram 37143, tel. 615/952-4354

Don't be put off by the name. This secluded cedar-log home is as much a retreat as a bed-and-breakfast, sitting on 67 acres in woodsy Cheatham County, outside Nashville. Its 5 mi of trails meander through thick maples, hickories, and dogwoods, hidden valleys, and a 25-ft waterfall, which the wayfarer shares with wild turkey, deer, rabbits, and blackberry brambles.

Blond heart-pine floors, hand-chiseled cedar log walls, and skylights lend the airy main house, built in 1989, a rustic western chic. The roomy and casual B&B has modern couches and chairs with chunky American primitive antiques, such as a pie safe from the early 1800s. In the tall vaulted dining room, guests eat robust breakfasts, featuring such fare as two-layer egg soufflés with cheese sauce or hash brown casseroles, which proprietor Jane Crisp prepares on a reproduction wood-burning stove. A stone fireplace warms the two-story common room, whose balcony leads to two bedrooms.

The vaulted bedrooms have extra-plush carpets. One room's white iron bed frame is coupled with wicker furniture; another has a reproduction four-poster canopy brass bed. A three-bedroom, more sparsely furnished guest house sits on the hill and sleeps up to 10. Outside, there are wraparound decks and a large gazebo that holds 60.

Chigger Ridge is the name Jane Crisp and her husband, Doug O'Rear, affectionately gave the property after an ill-fated trek without insect repellent—which they now supply to guests. Jane is relaxed and unassuming, a semiretired attorney who had been on the hunt for a cabin in the woods after reading Thoreau's *Walden*. Doug works full time as a financial planner.

Nearby are Harpeth River with its fishing and canoeing excursions, the Narrows of Harpeth State Recreation Area, Natchez Trace Parkway, and Cheatham Wildlife Preserve. ⌂ *2 double rooms with baths, 1 3-bedroom guest house. Air-conditioning, phone in rooms, TV/VCR in common rooms. $85–$250; full breakfast. MC, V. No smoking.*

FALCON MANOR BED & BREAKFAST ☙
2645 Faulkner Springs Rd., McMinnville 37110, tel. 931/668–4444, fax 931/815–4444

McMinnville offers an out-of-the-way base at the center of the Nashville-Chattanooga-Knoxville triangle. Twenty-five miles east of I–24's Manchester Exit 111 or 33 mi south of I–40's Smithville exit is Falcon Manor, an historic Victorian mansion lovingly cared for by George and Charlien McGlothin. For nature lovers, Rock Island State Park is 10 mi away; Fall Creek Falls, 35 mi; Old Stone Fort, 25 mi; and Savage Gulf State Natural Area, 15 mi away.

The house was built in 1896 by entrepreneur Clay Faulkner for his wife, Mary. Faulkner had a woolen mill nearby and produced "gorilla pants," so labeled because their strength kept even a gorilla from tearing them apart. Strength is evident here, too, as the house sits on a 17-ft concrete foundation with walls three bricks thick. From 1946 to 1968, the property was used as a hospital and nursing home. Attempts to demolish it in 1968 were unsuccessful. George McGlothlin bought the house at auction in 1989 (sight unseen by Charlien), but by then, it required massive renovation. Charlien left her job at NASA and joined George in four years of restoration; they estimate they did 95 percent of the work themselves.

Guests will find rooms filled with massive Victoriana antiques. Red velvet settees and chairs, with marble-top tables, fill the common living room. Bedrooms have an almost overpowering amount of authenticity. What is called the Upstairs Suite has three bedrooms and one bathroom; two people can rent it for $105, four people for $170, and six people for $225. For group tours, George and Charlien dress in Victorian costumes.

Full breakfasts sometimes include New Orleans specialties like beignets. A Victorian Gift Shop offers stationery, potpourri, mugs, calendars, and a host of other items embellished with roses and other Victorian emblems. The carriage house has been converted into a restaurant with red walls, white medallion light fixtures, and a tile floor. ▲ *3 double rooms with baths, 1 3-bedroom suite. Cable TV in common areas, restaurant. $105; full breakfast. MC, V. No smoking.*

HACHLAND HILL DINING INN ☞
1601 Madison St., Clarksville 37043, tel. 931/647–4084, fax 931/552–3454

This inn is a treat for the traveler in search of a rustic evening beside a fireplace. Forty-five minutes north of Nashville in rural Clarksville, it is surrounded by an 80-acre park full of raccoon and deer. Trails wander into the woods, and guests wake up to the sound of birds.

Phila Hach is a worldly woman who was a flight attendant before founding the inn in 1955 with her late husband, Adolph Hach. She appears on local television shows and is the author of 14 cookbooks. The dinner menu is laden with fried chicken, Tennessee country ham, surprises like Moroccan leg of lamb, and a decadent plantation breakfast. Phila's specialty is catering large events; the grand ballroom seats 300.

Phila designed the inn after Federal-style Cape Cod homes, and on winter nights, soup bubbles in a pot dangling on a fireplace crane. The bedrooms are neat and comfortable, with historic touches: One has a spool bed with a wedding-ring quilt, and many furnishings are Early American. Some have Germanic touches, heirlooms from Phila's North Sea ancestors. The mantel keystone over the main fireplace comes from the long-since-demolished local tobacco exchange (Adolph was a tobacconist). A 150-year-old, 2,000-piece "postage-stamp" quilt hangs from a wall. The Hachs traveled widely, and items from their sojourns are in evidence: a Japanese print here, a Swiss vase there.

The 1790 House is a log cabin transformed into a dormitory space for those taking part in a wedding or reunion. Out back sits a pair of cabins, perfect for either romantic solitude or family lodging. Each cabin offers modern bathrooms and tranquillity, with non-ringing phones on which guests can make but not receive calls. The cabins are on a wide, shady terrace, where warm-weather cookouts are held, overlooking a wooded ravine. ▲ *7 double rooms with baths, 3 cabins. Air-conditioning, TV/VCR in 3 rooms, outgoing-only phone in rooms, office facilities. $75–$160. AE, MC, V. Closed Dec. 24–25.*

PEACOCK HILL COUNTRY INN ☞
6994 Giles Hill Rd., College Grove 37046, tel. 615/368–7727, 800/327–6663

Thirty-five peacocks bob among these hills, neck and neck with cows and horses, on the 650-acre working farm and inn in sleepy College Grove, south of Franklin. The restored 1850s sprawling farmhouse bears little witness to its age. It rises pristine and white from a hilltop garden of hydrangeas and sunflowers, two neighboring log cabins—a renovated smokehouse and grainery—recalling its rustic origins.

Original hand-hewn cedar logs make an impressive entry in the main house. Stone fireplaces tower in the common rooms branching off on either side. Overstuffed couches and chairs, in bright florals and plaids, lend the rooms a cheerful air. Well-placed antiques, such as a vegetable bin turned coffee table, coexist with modern-day luxuries. Rooms have king-size beds, temperature controls, and possibly the finest bathrooms in the state, with massive whirlpools and separate European showers.

In the two-story Grainery Suite, a red toile armchair faces a fireplace; upstairs is a cozy sitting room with a stocked kitchenette. Down the road, the McCall House, another restored mid-1800s farmhouse, has large rooms with stupendous bathrooms. In the Grand Suite, the standing shower is of Italian tile, with rain-shower fixtures overhead and on the sides.

The sunny dining room's fireside tables host full—but healthy—breakfasts like German pancakes, as well as gourmet dinners at extra cost, with two days' notice.

Walter and Anita Ogilvie returned home to their family property in College Grove from Indiana, after Walter retired from a career in banking. Walter manages their working farm and cattle ranch. They live in the converted carriage house out back, with their outgoing sheepdog, Abby.

Murfreesboro, 30 minutes away, and picturesque Franklin are havens for both antiques lovers and Civil War buffs. Nashville is an hour away. **⌂** *7 double rooms with baths, 1 suite, 2 cabins. Air-conditioning, terry cloth robes; TV in suite, cabins, den; fitness facilities. $125–$225; full breakfast, serve-yourself snacks and beverages. Dinners $20, box lunches $10, with 48 hours' notice. AE, D, MC, V. No smoking.*

SIMPLY SOUTHERN ☞
211 N. Tennessee Blvd., Murfreesboro 37130, tel. 615/896–4998

This stately, redbrick, 1907 four-square home rivals any in Murfreesboro's historic district. It sits on one of the town's main thoroughfares, right across from the endless lawn of Middle Tennessee State University's campus and the kindred architecture of the college president's house.

The myriad ways in which Simply Southern lives up to its name begin outside, on the wide, cushily furnished wraparound porch. A backyard patio has a slate tile path that leads to a small garden pond near flowering chives and other prolific herbs. Inside, 12-ft ceilings downstairs have thick poplar beams in the original extra-dark finish. Abundant Eastlake Victorian antiques and burgundy and green fabrics give the rooms a lush though tasteful atmosphere. Magnolia blossoms are the dining table's centerpiece.

Rooms are carpeted, formal, and floral, many with original fireplaces (now purely decorative) and all with antiques and private baths. Deep tubs, some claw-foot, retain old fixtures. The upstairs suite feels like a one-bedroom apartment, with its own sitting room and kitchenette. There are several common areas: two spacious parlors downstairs, one cozier area upstairs, and a large basement rec room with a pool table, vintage Coke machine, 1910 player piano, and karaoke.

Georgia and Carl Buckner are gracious hosts. They even provide a trunk full of stuffed bears on the landing, should anyone need a sleeping companion. They had planned for 15 years to find an old home and open a B&B, before they retired from being, respectively, a retailer and high school principal.

Simply Southern is a perfect destination for those visiting MTSU. Murfreesboro has the Stones River National Battlefield and other Civil War sites. Downtown Nashville is a 30-minute drive, as is the airport. ♨ *4 double rooms with baths, 1 suite. Air-conditioning, cable TV/VCR in some rooms and rec room. $80–$140; full breakfast. D, MC, V. No smoking.*

OTHER CHOICES

Blueberry Hill Bed and Breakfast. 4591 Peytonsville Rd., Franklin 37064, tel. 615/791–9947 or 800/400–4923 (PIN 7929). 2 double rooms with baths. Air-conditioning, TV/VCRs, terry cloth robes. $70–$80; full breakfast. D, MC, V. No smoking.

Inn at Evins Mill. 1535 Evins Mill Rd. (Box 606), Smithville 37166, tel. 615/597–2088, fax 615/597–2090. 14 double rooms with baths. Air-conditioning, TV in lodge's living room. $120–$170 including breakfast and dinner; $135–$200 including three meals; holiday weekends $155–$410 including 2 nights and 5 meals. AE, D, MC, V.

Old Cowan Plantation. 126 Old Boonshill Rd., Fayetteville 37334, tel. 931/433–0225. 2 double rooms with baths, 1 apartment. Air-conditioning, TV in common area. $48; Continental breakfast. No credit cards. No smoking.

RESERVATIONS SERVICE

Tennessee Bed & Breakfast Innkeepers Association (Box 120428, Nashville 37212, tel. 615/321–5482 or 800/820–8144).

West Tennessee
※❖※

BRIDGEWATER HOUSE ☞
7015 Raleigh LaGrange Rd., Cordova 38018, tel. 901/384–0080

This Greek Revival, redbrick converted schoolhouse, circa 1890, sits on what used to be a country road on the outskirts of Memphis but has since become a path through subdivisions. Here and there a thick patch of trees recalls a more peaceful era, and within one of these patches sits an unobtrusive sign, easy to miss, identifying the small bed-and-breakfast hidden behind the trees.

Inside the 2-acre lot, the city falls away. A wide slope of land nurtures old oaks and a vineyard. In the massive common room, 10-ft leaded-glass windows rise to 15-ft vaulted ceilings with hand-marbleized beams and moldings. Narcissus blooms on the coffee table. Colors of terra-cotta and sand warm the homelike couches and armchairs. The Red Oak Room contains a fin-de-siècle French bed of glossy burled maple. In the Blue Silk Room an antique trunk houses a Victorian doll collection.

Katherine and Steve Mistilis, both talkative and hospitable, pull out all the stops in pampering their guests: gourmet snacks such as miniature tarts and fine cheeses, turndown service with chocolates, terry cloth robes, Egyptian cotton linens, toiletries, and mineral water in the rooms. During candlelight breakfasts served on china, guests have the good fortune of sampling the Mistilises' creations, like Katherine's baked grapefruit meringue with Grand Marnier sauce or stuffed French toast with Cointreau.

Both Katherine and Steve are professional chefs. Katherine teaches culinary arts, caters, and does freelance food styling. Steve, who makes jams and preserves from the grapes and apples that grow on the property, is head chef at a well-regarded country club.

It takes about 20 minutes to get downtown, to Beale Street and other attractions. Shelby Farms, one of the largest city parks in the country, is practically next door. △ *2 double rooms with baths. Air-conditioning, terry cloth robes, turndown service with chocolates. $100; full breakfast, evening snacks and beverages. D, MC, V. No smoking.*

MAGNOLIA MANOR 🐚

418 N. Main St., Bolivar 38008, tel. 901/658–6700, fax 901/658–6700

Well off the beaten path, Magnolia Manor creates an imposing presence along Main Street in tiny Bolivar, a historic burg whose claim to fame is the oldest courthouse in West Tennessee. The B&B is one of two dozen or so antebellum homes in the neighborhood spared from Union torches during the Civil War; tours of the area can be arranged.

The 1849 Georgian Colonial-style house has 13-inch-thick walls, made of sun-dried red brick laid by slaves. It was constructed as a two-story symmetrical rectangle, with center halls upstairs and down separating the airy rooms.

Oil portraits of the four Union generals who occupied the house hang in the entry hall. Fourteen-foot ceilings, original sage-green silk wallpaper, heavy furnishings, and a lingering, musty scent bring the Old South to life. The downstairs suite is furnished opulently with early-Victorian, museum-quality pieces: a towering rosewood headboard, a rosewood gentleman's chair, and other pieces adorned with hand-carved roses. Upstairs are two double rooms and a spacious suite, which has a walnut-and-rosewood Victorian bed, shipped upriver by steamboat from New Orleans. Its shared bath has a claw-foot tub but no shower. All bedrooms have working fireplaces.

Elaine and Jim Cox, a reserved, polite couple, opened the inn in 1984 after visiting bed-and-breakfasts on a long trip through Europe. Elaine teaches cosmetology; Jim is a semi-retired hospital administrator. The Coxes stay busy with travel, decorating, cooking, and floral-arranging classes.

For history buffs, Bolivar makes for a pleasant day trip from Memphis, 90 minutes away. An hour away is Shiloh National Military Park. Also of interest are the nearby Pinson Mounds, where there is a Native American museum. Historians believe Hernando de Soto passed through the area on his epic search for the Mississippi River, a journey noted by various markers. △ *2 double rooms and 1 suite share 1½ baths; 1 full suite. Air-conditioning, cable TV on sunporch. $85–$95; full breakfast. No credit cards. No smoking.*

WHITE ELEPHANT B&B INN 🐚
304 Church St., Savannah 38372, tel. 901/925–6410

There's no overlooking the White Elephant, which is 10 mi from Shiloh National Park, on a peaceful street in tiny Savannah's historic district. White and tall, the circa 1901 Queen Anne Victorian home is lent curves by a wraparound porch, circular tower with conical roof, and Palladian attic windows in gables. Two white elephant statues pose on the walkway.

The 1½-acre lot is simply landscaped, dominated by sugar maples and oaks. Columns and pediments distinguish the porch entrance. Two front parlors on either side of the entrance hall have curved-glass bay windows; fireplaces with original tiles, mirrors, and full carved mantels; and natural woodwork. Despite the 12-ft ceilings, the parlors feel surprisingly cozy, full of newspapers, magazines, and Civil War publications. Throughout, comfortable furnishings mix Victorian antiques and reproductions.

Upstairs are three airy bedrooms, with transoms, queen-size beds, and private baths. The cinnamon-toned Poppy Room has a towering carved Victorian oak suit; the whitewashed Ivy Room's walls and fabrics have crisp ivy patterns. Both these rooms have claw-foot tubs.

Quiet, unpretentious owners Sharon and Ken Hansgen have an unusual story. The Californians discovered Savannah in 1991 while on a hunt for ancestral records. Two other discoveries—a "white elephant" for sale and nearby Shiloh—kept them here. Ken is more than just a Civil War buff. His tours of Shiloh have earned him a substantial following. He even dons a uniform for school groups.

Needless to say, the key word for nearby activities is "Shiloh." Savannah's genealogical library is of note, as are many antebellum homes, such as Cherry Mansion, yet another stop on Grant's extensive march. ♣ *3 double rooms with baths, 1 additional room may be rented in tandem with another double and share its bath, creating a suite. Air-conditioning, TV in parlor. $75–$95; full breakfast. No credit cards. No smoking.*

OTHER CHOICES

Bonne Terre Country Inn & Cafe. 4715 Church Rd. W, Nesbit, MS 38651, tel. 601/781–5100, fax 601/781–5466. 14 double rooms with baths. Air-conditioning, robes, in-room masseuse, pool. $135–$185; full breakfast. AE, D, DC, MC, V. No smoking.

Highland Place Bed & Breakfast. 519 N. Highland Ave., Jackson 38301, tel. 901/427–1472. 3 double rooms with baths, 1 suite. Air-conditioning, TV/VCR in living room. $85–$135; full breakfast. MC, V. No smoking.

RESERVATIONS SERVICES

Bed & Breakfast Memphis Reservation Service (Box 41621, Memphis 38174, tel. 901/327–6129). **Tennessee Bed & Breakfast Innkeepers Association** (Box 120428, Nashville 37212, tel. 615/321–5482 or 800/820–8144).

TEXAS

East Texas, Including Dallas and Fort Worth

CHARNWOOD HILL ☙

223 E. Charnwood St., Tyler 75701, tel. 903/597–3980, fax 903/592–6473

In the city that hosts the famed Texas Rose Festival, you can pay no greater compliment to a residence than to say that a Rose Queen lived there and that the Queen's Tea was held on the lawn. Tyler's Charnwood Hill, converted to a B&B in 1993, has housed not one but two queens: Margaret Hunt, daughter of the late oilman H. L. Hunt, was crowned in 1935; Jo Anne Miller received the honor in 1954.

As much as the yellow rose of Texas, the name Hunt is the stuff of Lone Star legend. And the Charnwood Hill estate, where the Hunt family lived before moving to Dallas in 1938, does not disappoint. Built in the 1860s by the headmaster of a school for girls, the three-story structure housed both a college and a hospital during the 19th century. The elegant, Greek Revival–influenced residence was bricked in 1901 by J. B. Mayfield, who raised a family here before selling the home to Hunt.

Hunt added his own touch to the home: a third-floor Art Deco suite constructed for daughters Margaret and Caroline. The suite's stark whites, barely-there pastels, and indirect lighting combine to stamp an indelible air of Great Gatsby–era privilege on the accommodation, and they contrast sharply with the frilly, floral guest bedrooms that dominate the first and second floors.

Male business travelers tend to favor the sprawling Millers' Trophy Room, named for H. C. Miller, who bought the house from Hunt. The blue-and-burgundy room has a full bar, gun cabinet, and bed that can be folded into the wall to make room for a small conference area.

Throughout the high-ceiling home, the furnishings are extravagant. The Walker family purchased the residence from the Millers in 1978, and in a four-year restoration, they have spared no expense to create a regal atmosphere, with crystal chandeliers, 100-year-old Oriental rugs, and antique pieces.

Common areas include a library and TV room, two second-floor balconies, and a screened swing porch. Guests enjoy a breakfast that might feature eggs Benedict or French toast in the formal dining room. And, more than 50 years after it served as the setting for Hunt's Queen's Tea, the west garden is as lovely as ever.

⌂ *5 double rooms with baths, 1 suite. TV/VCR in most rooms, phone in rooms, free airport transfers. $95–$270; full breakfast, complimentary beverages. AE, D, MC, V. No smoking indoors.*

EXCELSIOR HOUSE ☙
211 W. Austin St., Jefferson 75657, tel. 903/665–2513

The Excelsior House is the remarkably restored centerpiece of Jefferson, a town sometimes called the "Williamsburg of Texas." Built in the 1850s by riverboat captain William Perry, the historic hotel has remained in continuous operation since then, although by the middle of this century, the brick-and-timber structure had slowly deteriorated and was largely forgotten.

Its rebirth began in 1954, when Estella Fonville Peters purchased the inn and undertook its renovation. Opening the building to public tours, filling the drawing room with the music of noted orchestras, and hosting elaborate balls, she revived interest in the hotel—and, in the process, sowed the seeds of Jefferson's commercial future. The Jessie Allen Wise Garden Club bought the hotel when Peters died in 1961 and has maintained and operated the facility with care ever since. The club has also made significant improvements, such as adding bathrooms and tearing down walls between the tiny rooms once consigned to traveling salesmen.

With iron columns and a lacy ironwork gallery that lend flourish to the simple rectangular edifice, the Excelsior House looks like it came to the Wild West by way of New Orleans. The ballroom features a French chandelier, Oriental rugs, antique marble mantles, and a pair of period pianos. The dining room includes a glassed-in patio, where guests can enjoy a Plantation Breakfast of orange blossom muffins, country ham, scrambled eggs, and biscuits.

Each of the inn's 15 guest rooms and suites has a story to tell. Past guests have included William Vanderbilt and Oscar Wilde; both Ulysses S. Grant and Rutherford B. Hayes slept in what is now the Presidential Suite. Lady Bird Johnson was a frequent visitor and donated a good deal of the furniture in the room that bears her name. All the rooms are furnished with antiques, including marble-topped dressers, spool beds, and mahogany, cherry, and maple pieces.

Spurned railroad tycoon Jay Gould had predicted doom for Jefferson in the Excelsior House lobby in the 1870s, so it's fitting revenge that one of the hotel's most popular rooms is named after him. Across the street from the hotel, "Atalanta," Gould's decadently ornate private railroad car, is open to public tours.

⚓ *14 double rooms with baths, 1 suite. Air-conditioning, TV and phone in rooms. $65–$100; breakfast not included. AE, MC, V. No smoking.*

HOTEL ST. GERMAIN ☙
2516 Maple Ave., Dallas 75201, tel. 214/871–2516 or 800/683–2516, fax 214/871–0740

In a city known for glitziness, the Hotel St. Germain is perhaps the definitive lodging. Nestled amid some of Dallas's most exclusive restaurants and shops, the boutique hotel, opened in 1991, gives visitors the chance to indulge in the high life of a different time and place: 19th-century France.

A Victorian prairie mansion built in 1906 for a prominent Dallas financier and home for many decades to a variety of commercial ventures, the inn was purchased in 1989 by Claire Heymann. She set out to reclaim the structure's noble origins while paying tribute to her own French-Creole roots. You enter through a large entry hall embellished with crackle-back moldings and crystal chandeliers; from the moment you open the hotel's front doors, you're swept into a lavish, self-contained universe.

Heymann's secret is painstaking authenticity. A New Orleans native whose mother was an antiques dealer, she has been assembling French collectibles since her childhood. Her acquisitions are complemented by her knowledge of French design, developed through frequent trips abroad and study at the University of Paris.

The entry hall gives way to a pair of sitting rooms, a parlor, and a library, each housing its own treasures—such as the library's grand piano, bedecked with ancient, marbled candelabra. The dining room, which looks out onto a New Orleans–style walled courtyard with a fountain, is perhaps the most evocative of Gaul: The long table, draped in a burgundy damask tapestry, is topped by a rose-filled centerpiece that rests on a silver Alsatian platter; a mid-19th-century French basket chandelier hangs from the room's ceiling. Breakfast—which typically includes fresh fruit compote, croissants, quiche, and café au lait—is served on a rare, century-old set of Limoges china. Dinner, which could be lamb tenderloin or game hen, is served Friday and Saturday nights.

Upstairs, the seven spacious guest suites feature plush, canopied feather beds. All have wood-burning fireplaces, sitting rooms, and baths with soaking tubs or whirlpool baths. Although rates are prohibitive, and the hotel has a reputation for boarding the glitterati, Heymann promotes her inn as a place where common folk can come for that once-in-a-lifetime splurge. ⚓ *7 suites. Limited restaurant, air-conditioning, cable TV, VCRs available, phone and mini-refrigerator in rooms, robes, room service, concierge, valet parking, nightly turndown service, privileges at nearby fitness club. $245–$600; Continental breakfast. AE, DC, MC, V. No smoking.*

MCKAY HOUSE 🦜
306 Delta St., Jefferson 75657, tel. 903/665-7322 or 800/468-2627, fax 903/665-8551

In 1877, when Jefferson was a worldly river port, it was rocked by the brief visit of "Diamond Bessie"—the stage name of Annie Stone Moore Rothchild, a popular entertainer. While in town with her husband, a wealthy Cincinnati gambler named Abe Rothchild, the pair walked alone into a field. A gunshot was heard, and Abe returned alone, claiming his wife had shot herself by accident. After three trials over seven years, Rothchild was a free man, but the people of Jefferson never accepted the "not guilty" verdict.

One of the attorneys who successfully defended Rothchild was Hector McKay, the first of two generations of McKays who lived in this 1851 Greek Revival. In the early 1980s, the McKay House was purchased by Dallasites Tom and Peggy Taylor, who, through extensive renovations, transformed it into the city's most luxurious B&B.

The inn is furnished almost entirely with antiques, mostly Eastlake, many of them quite valuable. But this place is anything but stuffy. Innkeepers Roger and Lisa Cantrell know how to break the ice, from the funny period hats distributed for visitors to wear at breakfast to Victorian gowns and nightshirts provided in the rooms, and, in one room, his-and-hers claw-foot tubs that offer an opportunity for simultaneous scrub-downs. An ancient Packard pump organ is played to call guests to the hearty "Gentleman's Breakfast," which is served in period dress and may consist of honey-cured ham, cheese biscuits, and homemade pineapple zucchini bread and strawberry preserves. Afterward, guests can relax on the wide front porch, outfitted with a swing and white wicker chairs.

The guest rooms are individual in personality but uniform in elegance; each has such furnishings as a canopy bed and antique armoire. The two downstairs rooms have coal-burning fireplaces; the two upstairs suites feature a balcony, skylight, and his-and-hers tubs; and a downstairs suite includes two bedrooms, each with its own fireplace. But perhaps the most memorable rooms are the two set off from a central, dogtrot hall in the tin-roofed Victorian garden cottage located behind the main house. The Keeping Room, in particular, is amusingly authentic: A claw-foot tub sits exposed in a bay window, next to a transplanted outdoor privy, fully equipped with a lantern and a Sears Roebuck catalog. △ *3 double rooms with baths, 4 suites. Air-conditioning, cable TV and phone in all rooms, romantic and murder-mystery packages. $89–$155; full breakfast. AE, MC, V. Smoking on porches only, 2-night minimum holiday weekends.*

OTHER CHOICES

Inn on the River. 205 S.W. Barnard St., Glen Rose 76043, tel. 972/424–7119 or 800/575–2101, fax 972/424–9766. 19 double rooms with baths, 3 suites. Air-conditioning, pool. $115–$195; full breakfast. AE, D, MC, V. No smoking indoors.

Maison-Bayou. 300 Bayou St., Jefferson 75657, tel. 903/665–7600, fax 903/665–7100. 11 double rooms with baths. Air-conditioning, kitchen in some rooms, games rooms, flat-bottom boat with 1 cabin, fishing, horseback riding, paddle boat, nature trails, tandem bike. $79–$135; breakfast included with some rooms. MC, V. No smoking indoors.

Miss Molly's Bed & Breakfast. 109½ W. Exchange Ave., Fort Worth 76106, tel. 817/626–1522 or 800/99–MOLLY, fax 817/625–2723. 1 double room with bath, 7 doubles share 3 baths. Fans in rooms. $95–$170; Continental-plus breakfast. AE, D, DC, MC, V. No smoking.

1934 Bed and Breakfast. 322 College St., Grapevine 76051, tel. and fax 817/251–1934. 2 double rooms with baths, 1 suite. Air-conditioning, phones, TV in meeting room. $95–$115; full breakfast. AE, D, MC, V. No smoking.

Sanford House. 506 N. Center St., Arlington 76011, tel. 817/861–2129 or 877/205–4914. 8 double rooms with baths, 4 cottages. Air-conditioning, TV in some rooms, phones, pool, massages available. $150–$200; full breakfast. MC, V. No smoking.

Village Bed and Breakfast. Hwy. 155 N. (Box 928), Big Sandy 75755, tel. 903/636–4355 or 800/BB–ANNIE, fax 903/636–4744. 7 double rooms with baths, 5 doubles share 3 baths. Mini-refrigerator in rooms, TV in some rooms. $50–$115; Continental-plus breakfast. AE, D, MC, V. No smoking.

RESERVATIONS SERVICES

Bed and Breakfast Texas Style (4224 W. Red Bird La., Dallas 75237, tel. 972/298–8586 or 800/899–4538). **Book-A-Bed-Ahead** (Box 723, Jefferson 75657, tel. 903/665–3956 or 800/468–2627). **Jefferson Reservation Service** (Box A, Jefferson 75657, tel. 903/665–2592 or 800/833–6758).

San Antonio, Austin, and the Hill Country

AUSTIN STREET RETREAT ☙
231 W. Main St., Fredericksburg 78624, tel. 830/997–5612, fax 830/997–8282

Only a block from Main Street and minutes from Fredericksburg's shopping district, this B&B is actually a compound of five historic homes. Owned by a

Chicago couple and managed by a local reservation service, these stylish retreats have created a new standard for area properties. The luxurious whirlpool bath for two found in each structure is your tip-off that hedonistic luxuries are emphasized here.

From the outside, you might wonder how Annie's Cabin could be one of the top guest rooms in Fredericksburg, requiring reservations months in advance. The answer comes as soon as you walk in the room: over-the-top decadence, handcrafted for honeymooners. With smoky-rose-colored walls in the bedroom, the cabin is dominated by a king-size bed made from a fence reconfigured by a craftsman Cupid to resemble hearts and arrows; it's covered with a thick layer of linens, a tapestry duvet, and a sumptuous pile of pillows.

In Kristen's Cabin, a king-size iron bed overlooks a fireplace in the front bedroom. An Italian tapestry sofa and chair complete the look, and a painting of the owner's grandmother in her wedding dress lends a romantic air. Connected to the bedroom by a Saltillo-tile hallway is the bath, its focal point a whirlpool bath on a limestone pedestal. The bars on the windows are there because the room served as a cell in 1885 when the town jail burned. Outside, a private flagstone courtyard with a three-tiered fountain provides a quiet, private retreat.

Eli's Cabin is less frilly, starting with the cast-iron mantel saved from a Philadelphia mansion. A pencil-post bed, Mexican tin mirror, and a staghorn chandelier add a southwestern touch. This cabin also has a private courtyard with a double hammock.

The oldest structure of the five is Maria's Cabin, a log cabin built in 1867. Its two bedrooms preserve its historic flavor with plank floors, twig furniture, chinked log walls, and historic paintings, but they pamper visitors with extras the pioneers never enjoyed: two queen-size beds with down comforters and a whirlpool bath.

But none of the other getaways share the aged elegance of El Jefe (The Boss). Decorated in 1900s southwestern style, this two-story cottage has beamed ceilings and appointments that range from frayed sombreros to well-worn leather chairs to antique suitcases. Upstairs, the whirlpool bath overlooks the complex through French doors. ⌂ *4 1-bedroom cabins, 1 2-bedroom cabin. Airconditioning, phone, whirlpool bath, cable TV in 2 cabins, CD player in 2 cabins, fireplace in 4 cabins, coffee bar with microwave. $125; breakfast not included. D, MC, V. No smoking.*

INN ON THE CREEK 🐾
Box 858, Salado 76571, tel. 254/947–5554, fax 254/947–9198

Suzi Epps is a picky one. Ask her about most any bed-and-breakfast in Texas and she's been there—and found it lacking. That kind of perfectionism, along with Epps's experience as a professional architect, has helped turn the Inn on the Creek into a reason to stop in Salado, a little town 45 mi north of Austin known mostly for its well-preserved 19th-century Main Street.

Inn on the Creek is a collection of five houses, three of which were salvaged from condemnation and brought to a shady spot on Salado Creek from elsewhere in Texas; all were painstakingly restored by Suzi, along with her parents, Bob and Sue Whistler, and her husband, Lynn. The oldest of the houses, an 1892 woodframe Victorian imported from Cameron, is connected to another house by a covered wooden walkway to form the inn's main complex. The second building, a two-story, wood frame, includes a large dining room that on weekends opens for dinner as a full-service restaurant. The breakfasts served here tend toward the exotic, ranging from German puff pancakes to Italian frittatas.

The furnishings throughout the main complex are anything but exotic; they run toward the simpler, more understated pieces of the Victorian age. The rooms exude a quiet elegance, each furnished with Victorian antiques, family photographs, and antique dresser sets. White wrought iron and wicker fill the Tyler Room. In the Rose Room, a Victorian walnut bed is covered with a collection of antique pillowcases. The most impressive is the spacious, third-floor McKie Room, which has a king-size bed as well as a library nook with a daybed that overlooks the creek—the perfect spot for a lazy weekend afternoon.

Directly across the street is the Holland House, built circa 1880, and up the block the Reue House, a Civil War–era farmhouse with four guest rooms. Its highlight is the Kiowa Room, which has a bed made from a 300-year-old loom. Sally's Cottage, a tiny one-bedroom hideaway with an adjoining living room, rounds out the inn's facilities.

All the guest rooms at Inn on the Creek have private baths—some with a pair of vintage bloomers hanging from the wall. Evenings at the inn, and throughout Salado, are quiet. Most guests just sit on the back porch and listen to the cicadas sing on a warm summer evening. ♨ *18 double rooms with baths, 2 cottage suites. Limited restaurant, air-conditioning, cable TV, and phone in rooms; small refrigerator and coffeemaker in 13 rooms. $80–$145; full breakfast. AE, MC, V. No smoking indoors.*

OGÉ HOUSE ON THE RIVERWALK ☞

209 Washington St., San Antonio 78204, tel. 210/223–2353 or 800/242–2770, fax 210/226–5812

A classic plantation house built during the Greek Revival craze that spread across the South in the years before the Civil War, the Ogé (pronounced *Oh*-jhay) House is the crowning glory of San Antonio's historic King William neighborhood. Owners Patrick and Sharrie Magatagan have created an understated tribute to the antebellum South, complete with a veranda from which one can look out over the pecan-shaded estate. But it has all the modern amenities: From the registration desk to the in-room premium cable TV and the state-of-the-art telephone system, their inn has the ambience of a luxury hotel.

Built in 1857 by pioneer Texas ranger and cattle rancher Louis Ogé, the three-story manse sits on 1½ acres of landscaped lawns and gardens overlooking the Paseo del Rio. It had been a boardinghouse before the Magatagans purchased it in 1991 and set out to transform it into San Antonio's brightest B&B. Kitchenettes were turned into lovely vanities; walls were painted in creamy whites; bathrooms were overhauled; and pine floors were polished and draped with fine Oriental rugs.

Patrick, who had lived with San Antonio native Sharrie in Connecticut for eight years before returning to the Alamo City, fell in love with antiques while living in the Northeast and—ironically, in this antebellum southern mansion—purchased many of the furnishings for the inn there. Even one of the home's tributes to things Texan—a bullhorn sofa in an upstairs lounging area—was purchased "up nawth." Texas-theme furnishings are also found in the Bluebonnet Room, complete with a rolling-pin bed and a West Texas judge's desk. Otherwise, Early American Victorian furniture dominates the guest rooms and suites.

The house's second floor is the main floor, with an entryway, sitting room, library, kitchen, dining room, and two guest rooms. The first floor is an English basement, which houses a guest room and suite as well as the Magatagans' living quarters. The three third-floor suites are the most impressive: Each has access to the wide veranda or, in one case, a small private balcony.

Sharrie prepares the Continental breakfast, which may consist of scones, croissants, sweet rolls, popovers, and hot and cold cereals. It's served in the formal dining room or on the front veranda. ⌂ *9 double rooms with bath. Air-conditioning, cable TV, telephone, refrigerator, fireplace in 5 rooms. $145—205; full breakfast. AE, D, DC, MC, V. No smoking indoors, 2-night minimum weekends, 3-night minimum holidays.*

SETTLERS CROSSING 🌾
Settlers Crossing Rd. (Rte. 1, Box 315), Fredericksburg 78624, tel. 830/997–2722 or 800/874–1020, fax 830/997–3372

Ever wondered what it was like for German settlers on the American frontier in the 19th century? You and your clan can spend the weekend in your own "Little Haus on the Prairie" at Settlers Crossing, a 35-acre tract located in the rolling countryside between Luckenbach and Fredericksburg. Dotted by log cabins, mesquite trees, and friendly farm animals, this is easily the best family-oriented B&B in the Hill Country.

Of course, the German settlers didn't have access to a whirlpool bath—a feature of the luxurious Von Heinrich Home, one of four guest houses on the estate of hosts David and Judy Bland. The structures are close enough to one another to be convenient for groups or family reunions but far enough apart to allow for private getaways.

The Pioneer Homestead, a stone-and-log cabin original to the property, was constructed in the 1850s by the Kusenberger family, German immigrants who were among Fredericksburg's first settlers. The modern appliances in the full kitchen of the two-bedroom house are skillfully tucked away to preserve a feeling of authenticity. The most striking feature is a robin's-egg-blue stenciled ceiling, painted when the house was built. Also original to the grounds, the Baag Farm House was built in the 1920s as a wedding gift for a Kusenberger descendant. The simple, blue wood-frame house has a wood-burning stove and antique dining-room table that seats eight.

Outside the Indiana House, you may well encounter bleating sheep, grazing goats, and braying donkeys, who like to approach the split-rail fence surrounding the house. The log cabin was built in the Hoosier state in 1849 and transported to Settlers Common by the Blands. The mood of the living room is set by an antique camelback sofa; the high-ceiling master bedroom features a queen-size, four-poster bed with acorn finials. The hosts live in a nearby three-story house imported from Kentucky.

But the most remarkable guest home on the property is the Von Heinrich Home, a two-story German fachwerk cottage built in Pennsylvania in 1787. Inside is an outstanding collection of 19th-century folk art, including an antique horse sculpture and an old hooked rug over the fireplace. ⌂ *5 2-bedroom guest houses, 1 3-bedroom guest house, 1 1-bedroom guest house. Air-conditioning, TV/VCR, phone, fireplace or wood-burning stove in houses, full kitchen in 5 houses, whirlpool bath in 4 houses. $95–$135; Continental breakfast. AE, D, MC, V. No smoking.*

STAGE STOP RANCH ☜

Stage Stop Ranch, 100 Old Mail Route Road, Fischer 78623, tel. 830/935–4455
or 800/782–4378, fax 830/935–4445

From Wimberley to Blanco stretches a ridge of hills called the Devil's Backbone—an area often thought of as one of the most scenic in Texas. Right in the heart of this region is the Stage Stop Ranch, a combination B&B inn and guest ranch that's right on a former stagecoach trail.

"People get here and are uptight and by the next day they're relaxed and smiling and really seem to find themselves," explains Lee Caffey. Lee and husband Troy own and operate the Stage Stop Ranch together, coming to the B&B business after living all around the world as a navy family.

Many guests here relax with horseback rides on trails that follow parts of the old stage route, winding among tall oaks and alongside rock walls that predate the Civil War. "Riding uses nearly every muscle in the body," says Lee, who also recognizes the sport's psychological benefits. "Someone once said there's something about the outside of a horse that's good for the inside of man. It's very true." For after those long rides—or anytime for those not interested in riding—there are hot tubs for relaxing.

Days at Stage Stop begin with a full breakfast prepared by Lee in the country kitchen. A favorite dish is pecan praline French toast. Morning and afternoon activities are as busy or leisurely as guests choose, ranging from strolling quietly along the country road to horseshoe pitching to horseback riding. Wranglers are available to teach novices the basics so that anyone can participate in a ride along the trails that snake along the expansive property. For other visitors, a day's fun might include fishing for rainbow trout below the dam of nearby Canyon Lake or shopping for antiques in the community of Wimberley.

After a day of ranch fun, evenings at Stage Stop often feature a western theme as well. Live music, chuck-wagon suppers, campfire dinners and sing-alongs, hay rides, and other activities recall the cowboy heritage of this western ranch. △ *3 double rooms with bath, 13 cabins, 1 cottage. Air-conditioning in rooms, minirefrigerator in some rooms, 10 private hot tubs, bicycles for guest use, horseback riding, western outdoor activities. $85–$225; full breakfast. AE, D, MC, V. Smoking outdoors only, 2-night minimum holidays.*

OTHER CHOICES

Crystal River Inn. 326 W. Hopkins St., San Marcos 78666, tel. 512/396–3739, fax 512/353–3248. 7 double rooms with baths, 4 2-bedroom suites. Air-conditioning in rooms, TV in most rooms, mini-refrigerator and microwave in cottage. $70–$140; full breakfast. AE, D, DC, MC, V. No smoking, 2-day minimum most weekends.

Fredericksburg Bed and Brew. 245 E. Main St., Fredericksburg 78624, tel. 830/997–1646, fax 830/997–8026. 12 rooms with baths. Air-conditioning in rooms. $79–$89. MC, V. No smoking.

Page House. 1000 Leander Rd., Georgetown 78628, tel. 512/863–8979 or 800/828–7700. 6 double rooms with baths. Air-conditioning, TV in some rooms. $75–$95; full breakfast weekends, Continental breakfast weekdays. AE, D, DC, MC, V. No smoking, 2-night minimum holidays. Closed Mon.

Riverwalk Inn. 329 Old Guilbeau, San Antonio 78204, tel. 210/212–8300 or 800/254–4440, fax 210/229–9422. 11 double rooms with bath. Air-conditioning, cable TV and phones. $99–$155; full breakfast. AE, D, MC, V. Smoking outdoors only.

Woodburn House. 4401 Ave. D, Austin 78751, tel. 512/458–4335, fax 512/458–4339. 4 double rooms with baths. Desk, phone in rooms, TV/VCR in living room, exchange library. $68–$95; full breakfast. AE, MC, V. Smoking on porches only.

RESERVATIONS SERVICES

Bed and Breakfast Hosts of San Antonio (Box 831203, San Antonio 78283, tel. 210/824–8036). **Be My Guest Travel Services** (110 N. Milam, Fredericksburg 78624, tel. 830/997–7227). **Gastehaus Schmidt Reservation Service** (231 W. Main St., Fredericksburg 78624, tel. 830/997–5612).

West Texas

HOTEL GARZA HISTORIC INN AND CONFERENCE CENTER

302 E. Main St., Post 79356, tel. 806/495–3962

Innkeepers Janice and Jim Plummer are a busy pair. They left their respective jobs as legal secretary and radio executive in Lubbock to be self-employed and work together. The result is a completely restored historic property that is the only B&B in town.

Forty-five miles southwest of Lubbock, Post was founded as a utopian community by Charles Post, of Post Toasties fame. The cereal king had visions of a city where saloons were prohibited and residents were required to have three references before moving to town. The Hotel Garza, built in 1915 (after Post's death), had lesser ambitions. Post's version of a red-light district, the hotel was the kind of place that locals crossed the street to avoid.

But in 1992 the Plummers saw that the hotel, vacant beneath a heavy coat of West Texas dust, had potential. Post had recently undergone transformation as a federally designated "Main Street City," and the Plummers began their own renovation. Room by room, they refinished floors, repainted, and added baths to produce a two-story inn with still more rooms planned. Today's B&B combines elegant dining with clean, simple accommodations that reflect the mood of an earlier time. Lovely new gardens have been sculpted in the landscape; there's even a waterfall.

The expansive lobby, with more than a dozen antique tables and a corner sitting area, greets guests. Its wood floors were protected through the years by layers of linoleum and now gleam with a new finish. Above, the original pressed-tin ceiling has fresh white paint. Ceiling fans hum on warm afternoons, and chandeliers illuminate the room.

Like those in a western hotel in the area's earliest days, its guest rooms are off long hallways, now lined with antique benches. In the small, spartan rooms, many of the furnishings are original to the hotel. Most have an iron bed, antique dressers, and area rugs. Guests are free to enjoy the mezzanine-level library filled with a collection of first editions, along with popular titles, games, and a TV. Wainscoting and a stained-glass window recall the hotel's early days.

Early risers can head to the kitchen to brew a pot of coffee or wait for a plate of Janice's egg casserole, sausage, and homemade breads. On Friday and Saturday, the Plummers serve lunch to the public. On evenings when the neighboring Garza Theater hosts a production, the Hotel Garza also serves dinner. ⚐ *7 double rooms with baths, 4 doubles share 2 baths, 2 suites. Limited restaurant, air-conditioning, phone and cable TV in 3 rooms, TV in library, theater packages. $35–$95; full breakfast on weekends, Continental breakfast on weekdays. AE, MC, V. No smoking.*

OTHER CHOICES

Parkview House. 1311 S. Jefferson St., Amarillo 79101, tel. 806/373-9464. 3 double rooms with baths, 2 doubles share bath. Air-conditioning, phone hookup in rooms, cable TV in living room and kitchen, bicycles, hot tub. $65–$85; Continental breakfast. AE, MC, V. No smoking.

UTAH

Salt Lake City and Northern Utah

Anton Boxrud Bed and Breakfast. 57 S. 600 East St., Salt Lake City 84102, tel. 801/363–8035 or 800/524–5511, fax 435/596–1316. 3 double rooms with baths, 1 double and 1 single with shared baths, 2 suites. Down comforters, fresh flowers, robes, toiletries, whirlpool in 1 suite, fireplace and TV in common room, outdoor hot tub, gazebo, covered porch, business facilities. $74–$134; full breakfast and refreshments. AE, D, DC, MC, V. No smoking.

Brigham Street Inn. 1135 E. South Temple St., Salt Lake City 84102, tel. 801/364–4461 or 800/417–4461, fax 435/521–3201. 7 doubles with bath, 1 suite. Kitchen and whirlpool bath in 1 suite, fireplace in 4 rooms, breakfast room. $125–$185; Continental breakfast. AE, MC, V.

Inn on Center Street. 169 E. Center St., Logan 84321, 435/752–3443. 18 double rooms with baths. Down comforters and pillows, large screen TV/VCR, fireplace in 3 rooms, kitchenette in 1 room, whirlpool bath, hot tub, indoor pool, maid service. $110–$180; Continental breakfast. AE, MC, V. No smoking.

Snowberry Inn. 1315 N. Rte. 158 (Box 795), Eden 84310, tel. 801/745–2634. 5 double rooms with baths. Outdoor hot tub, exercise room, coin laundry. $95; full breakfast. AE, D, MC, V.

Southwestern Utah

THE BARD'S INN ☙

150 S. 100 West, Cedar City 84720, tel. 435/586–6612

Now pillars of the Utah Shakespearean Festival Guild in Cedar City, Jack and Audrey Whipple got hooked on the Bard during their first visit to town. Their 1900s-era golden shingle-and-brick bungalow reflects their passion for the playwright, from dolls in Elizabethan costumes to guest rooms named after the characters in Shakespeare's plays. Indeed, their knowledge about the festival, and the inn's location near three national parks, makes this a choice destination.

The well-traveled Whipples have acquired scores of unique antiques and decorations for their inn. Audrey designed and created the stained-glass panels—some reassembled from discarded church windows—seen throughout the house. A salvaged oak banister follows the slow curl of the stairway from an enclosed porch to the three upstairs guest rooms.

It is the unexpected touches—creamy crocheted gloves lying across a dropleaf desk in the upstairs sitting room, a Chinese checker board in a bathroom—that make this such a fascinating place to stay. Everything in the house seems to have a story; ask Audrey to tell you how she rescued the claw-foot stool from a sheep pasture in northern Idaho.

The Katharina Room has a turn-of-the-century high-back walnut bed with spring-colored linens, and a big braided runner on the floor; its small alcove hosts a twin walnut sleigh bed. Across the hall, the Olivia Room has cranberry carpeting, antique oak furnishings, and a collection of ceramic figures on an intricately carved wall shelf. A strawberry border trails around the ceiling of the Titania Room, and stained-glass circles are suspended in two windows. On the main floor is the sophisticated Mistress Ford suite, with a sunny private library. The Beatrice Suite, in the basement, is fitted with matching twin oak beds and a double bed. Thoughtful items in all the rooms include night-lights and plump pincushions bristling with needles and thread.

The inn has a refrigerator and sink for guest use and a small dining area with a festive collection of marbles centered on the table. Audrey's healthy but delicious breakfasts might include her home-baked Boston raisin bread, poppyseed rolls, almond-cherry zucchini bread, and Jack's personal favorite, made from an old recipe passed down verbally—dainty, frosted *colachis* filled with apricots. △ *3 double rooms with baths, 2 suites, 1 duplex cottage. Kitchenette in cottage and 1 suite, off-street parking. $75–$85; full breakfast. AE, MC, V. No smoking indoors. Closed Oct.–Apr. (can be opened by prior arrangement).*

GREENE GATE VILLAGE ☙
76 West Tabernacle St., St. George 84770, tel. 435/628–6999 or 800/350–6999

Diagonally across from the historic adobe Mormon Tabernacle, Greene Gate Village looks like a tiny pioneer settlement, and, in a way, it is. This unusual complex brings together seven pioneer-era structures—among them adobe homes, a rock granary, and spruced-up wooden cabins—moved from sites scattered across the St. George Valley. In most cases, an entire house can be rented, making this an excellent place to stay with family or a group of friends. The spacious interior yard is a perfect group common area, with its flower beds, tidy lawns, and postcard-pretty swimming pool.

Built in the mid-1800s and the only village structure original to this site, the tan-stucco Orson Pratt House sports a gingerbread-trimmed porch. The first-floor Shanna suite of rooms has brass and oak furniture and hand-quilted floral bedspreads. Next door, in the Lindsay Room, the paper-white cutwork shams and bedspread stand in crisp contrast to the royal blue carpet; photographs of Orson Pratt, a counselor to Brigham Young, hang over the fireplace. The bathroom is tiny, but there's a large Jacuzzi tub in a separate room.

Creaking wicker chairs sit on the rustic porch of the weathered two-room Tolley cabin, which looks out toward the swimming pool. Inside, where a family of 13 once lived, are two simply decorated rooms, each with a fireplace.

Village founders Mark and Barbara Greene had to reconstruct the two-bedroom Morris House, originally located several blocks away: On moving day, the axle on the house trailer broke, and the two-story home suddenly became a pile of shattered glass, adobe brick, and broken door and window frames.

Breakfast, served in the garden room of the Bentley House, usually includes omelets, bacon, sausage, juices, and either pecan waffles, homemade bread, or croissants. △ *Village: 3 double rooms, 2 triples, 5 quads, all with baths. Off-site: 1 double room and 1 quad with baths; Greene House complex includes house and carriage house, which sleeps 22 total. Phone, TV, kitchen in 5 rooms, fire-*

place in 6 rooms, whirlpool bath in 6 rooms, pool, walking tour, off-street park-
ing. $55–$125; full breakfast, 5-course dinners served Thurs.-Sat. by reserva-
tion. AE, DC, MC, V. No smoking, 2-night minimum for Greene House complex.

HARVEST HOUSE ☜
29 Canyon View Dr., Springdale 84767, tel. 435/772–3880

When native Bostonians Steve and Barbara Cooper first visited Zion Canyon, they
were determined to find a way to come back permanently. Barbara, a gourmet chef
and former co-owner of Boston's Harvest Catering Company, also wanted to be
able to use her culinary and decorating skills. Luckily for their guests, the Coop-
ers found the ways and means to bring their plans to pass.

Just off Springdale's main drag, Harvest House is a modern, two-story ranch-style
structure, built of mottled tan-and-brown brick and buttery stucco. Best of all,
practically every window in the house lets in a personal slice of Zion Canyon.

Shades of black and gray dominate in the living room, including a nubby char-
coal sofa and many black-and-white photographs; splashes of color come from
a collection of cups and saucers and brightly painted wooden animals romping
on the hearth. A stained-glass cactus-bloom set above the front door sends prisms
of light sparkling across the walls, and French doors lead to a flagstone patio.

The main-floor guest room sports lacy curtains on windows that have a view of
the cactus garden Steve created; blue-and-green linens look refreshing, and
Barbara's handmade paper collages accent the walls. Upstairs, one west-side room
is done in stylish pink and black, with a wicker chaise longue for reading or dreaming. A snug love seat highlights another room decorated in rose and ferny green.
Sunsets bathe both rooms in colorful light. The pastel-toned master bedroom
has a wide window looking out on the apple orchard next door, which attracts
deer each evening. On warm summer nights, the sound of the Virgin River is a soft
counterpoint to conversations on the private deck.

Breakfast at Harvest House is both festive and delicious. Colorful place settings and butter sculptures formed in a collection of Victorian-era pewter molds
are all part of the glamorous presentation of such entrées as poached eggs with
basil hollandaise or cheese blintzes with rivers of fresh fruit topping. Fresh muffins,
pastries or breads, and Steve's stout coffee help round out the morning meal.

△ *3 double rooms with baths, 1 triple with bath. Air-conditioning, TV/VCR,*
video library, wet bar in living room, outdoor hot tub, fish pond, off-street park-
ing. $75–$95; full breakfast, afternoon refreshments. D, MC, V. No smoking.

NINE GABLES INN ☜
106 W. 100 N, Kanab 84741, tel. 435/644–5079

Jeanne Bantlin was visiting her brother in Kanab when she and her husband,
Frank, discovered on an evening walk that the home they had been admiring
throughout their stay was suddenly for sale. The former US West Communications
employees promptly bought this 1890s, two-story ranch house and set about turning it into a bed-and-breakfast.

White stucco now covers the red sunbaked adobe brick, the building material
used for most of the houses in the area. A pert white picket fence encloses a
alive with myrtle and vinca and a vegetable garden twined with perennial blooms.

The completely remodeled living room has shining new hardwood floors that
reflect light from tall, narrow windows. Many of the furnishings in this room,
and throughout the inn, are family treasures. But by far the most inviting com-

mon area is the upstairs sitting room, with its large circle rug, ceiling fan, rocking chairs, surprisingly comfortable dignified courthouse bench, wood-burning stove, and Victrola with a cabinet full of board games.

A small, sunny guest room at the front of the house has textured gray carpet and matte white walls; a first-edition Zane Grey novel on the nightstand is a reminder that the author was a guest in this home while researching some of his books. In a medium-size room down the hall are a honey-colored oak-slatted bed and the most comfortable chair in the inn: a reupholstered horsehair rocker found in an old milk house.

The long, quiet bedroom at the back of the house features a curly-maple rolltop desk that invites letter writing; a firm bed covered with a blue-and-pink "Briar Rose"–patterned quilt; a framed crocheted collar and a colorful old Certificate of Baptism on the wall; and the trunk that carried Jeanne's grandfather's belongings when he emigrated from Norway.

Frank's breakfasts are served in what was once the front parlor; boasting the original bay window and a working fireplace, it's now a very pleasant dining room. Hot or cold cereal shares the board with pastries or muffins, juices, and fresh fruit. A summer treat to hope for is a bowl of huge raspberries from the backyard berry patch. ♣ *3 double rooms with baths. Air-conditioning and ceiling fan in rooms, TV in common area, off-street parking. $80; full breakfast. MC, V. No smoking. Closed Nov.–mid-May.*

O'TOOLE'S UNDER THE EAVES 🦢
980 Zion Park Blvd. (Box 29), Springdale 84767, tel. 435/772–3457

It's easy to see why construction of this two-story mock-Tudor cottage, begun in 1935, took five years: Under the Eaves is made of buff sandstone blocks cut from the walls of Zion Canyon. Fronted by a lovely flower-filled square porch, the inn is a pleasantly incongruous sight on Springdale's motel-lined main street.

Owners Rick and Michelle O'Toole bought the already established property in the spring of 1993. Their first step toward making the guest house their own was to plant favorite flowers in the small backyard, a delightful oasis where pecan, almond, and fruit trees blend with flourishing perennials, lilacs, and lavender.

The parlor and dining room are filled with cozy, worn antiques, and shelves are stocked with books and games. Beyond the kitchen lie two guest accommodations. The cheerful south room has a polished hardwood floor and crisp country linens. The small blue-and-white north room is decorated with a springy hand-loomed rug and a simple ladder-back chair. Both rooms are illuminated by antique light fixtures taken from the "upstairs rooms" of an old saloon in Pioche, Nevada.

A popular suite nestled "under the eaves" encompasses the entire second floor. Its kitchen and sitting area overlook the gardens, and additional windows face Zion Canyon. A claw-foot tub adds an element of fun to the bathroom.

A separate Garden Cottage holds three small rooms. Two have fanciful linens and stained-glass windows in their compact bathrooms. A mahogany sleigh bed is the focal point of the antiques-filled third room, set in the large, well-lighted basement. This room also boasts a whirlpool tub.

Guests can enjoy sunrise coffee service on the front porch of the main house and then eat family-style in the dining room. Breakfast highlights include fresh breads, egg-and-cheese casseroles with homemade salsa, and the occasional breakfast tostada with chilies and beans. ♣ *3 double rooms with baths, 2 dou-*

bles share bath, 1 suite. Air-conditioning, kitchenette in suite, off-street parking. $69–$125; full breakfast. D, MC, V. No smoking.

SEVEN WIVES INN ☙
217 N. 100 W, St. George 84770, tel. 435/628–3737 or 800/600–3737

In the heart of St. George's Historic District, two neighboring homes compose Seven Wives Inn, named for an ancestor of one of the owners, who indeed had seven wives. The larger two-story house, built in 1873, features a double-tier veranda and a wood-shingled roof projecting gables in three directions; its attic was the occasional hiding place of die-hard polygamists fleeing federal marshals after multiple marriages were outlawed in 1882. The adjacent President's House, a modified two-story Renaissance Revival cube built in 1883, often provided lodging for visiting presidents of the Mormon Church.

Innkeepers Jay and Donna Curtis are always keeping their eyes open for antiques to add to those collected in the parlors of both houses and throughout the guest rooms. Jon, a popular local artist, has pencil drawings and oil paintings hanging in the inn's common areas.

In the main house, the Lucinda Room is a study in pastels, with an elaborate antique brass bed; soft, gray hooked rugs; a rose-colored velvet sofa and chair; and a green French ceramic stove. Small children can be accommodated in a Murphy bed that descends from an antique armoire. The romantic, high-ceiling Melissa Room on the second floor has a lace minicanopy over the bed and a private balcony. The notorious attic room is brightened by a skylight and an Art Deco pewter chandelier; a high, floral-painted bed sits against a wall of exposed adobe brick.

The four rooms in the President's House are accessed by a steep, narrow staircase. The Caroline Room has dark green walls lightened by large windows and a kaleidoscopic "Nine Patch" quilt on the bed. Spring is eternal in the small Rachel Room, where the walls are papered with pastel tulips. The furnishings are white wicker, and floral swags arch over white wooden blinds. The Sarah Room is actually a three-room suite with a fireplace, but its most extraordinary feature is the model-T Ford whirlpool tub.

The high-ceiling dining room in the main house has tables set for two or four. In addition to homemade granola, breakfast choices might include German apple or apple pecan pancakes, bread pudding, sausage *en croûte* or bacon, eggs, and cheese in a nest of hash browns. ⌂ *12 double rooms with baths. TV, phone, fireplace in 4 rooms, private balcony in 5 rooms, pool, off-street parking. $60–$125; full breakfast. AE, D, DC, MC, V. No smoking.*

SKYRIDGE BED AND BREAKFAST ☙
Box 750220, Torrey 84775, tel. and fax 435/425–3222

SkyRidge Bed and Breakfast is near the western boundary of Capitol Reef National Park. The house's design echoes territorial style, and the exterior is an unusual greenish brown—close in color to blooming rice grass, one of the native plants that surround the inn.

Owners Karen Kesler and Sally Elliot relocated from Mendocino, California, in 1993 to design, build, and decorate SkyRidge. Above all, the women wanted a visual feast. Seventy-five windows bring the outside beauty in. Art furniture fashioned by Karen accents every room, and works by other local artists add visual interest and are available for purchase.

In the cozy living room, guests can relax around a central fireplace with a patterned facade made from more than 30 pounds of roofing nails. Built-in shelves are filled with books, from dog-eared Mother Goose to lush art tomes, and small pieces of African art. The walls here, as elsewhere in the inn, are hand-textured and sponge-painted neutral colors.

All of SkyRidge's guest rooms are comfortable and intriguing. On the first level, the Buffalo Berry Room mixes Oriental rugs with plump cactus-strewn pillows piled on the bed. Mannequin hands holding crystal doorknobs further the room's funky feel. Across the front porch, the Tumble Weed Suite has antique walnut furnishings.

Upstairs, in the large Sagebrush Room, cream and jewel-toned quilts accent two beds perched on gray Berber carpet. Seven windows look across a valley to aspen-covered slopes. The Pinyon Room has heavily textured walls, a pitched roof line, and an oddly appealing jumble of furniture including a matchstick four-poster bed, and an Art Deco floor lamp. A small hot tub is on an enclosed deck. From the high-back bed in the Juniper Room, a bay of six windows provides views of peaks and cliffs silhouetted against the sunrise.

In the main-floor dining room, seven tall, narrow windows share wall space with Mexican masks and a vivid canvas of a cactus in bloom. Sturdy wicker chairs provide comfortable seating for Sally's culinary specialties—croissant French toast, Mexican frittata with fresh tomatillo salsa, or apple spice pecan waffles—all accompanied by yogurt, granola, and fruit harvested from Capitol Reef National Park. *△ 5 double rooms with baths. Ceiling fan and individual heat control, TV/VCR, phone, hot tubs in 3 rooms, kitchenette in 1 suite, outdoor hot tub, video library, guest refrigerator, horseshoe pits, picnic area, barbecue, off-street parking, activity and trip planning. $92–$138; full breakfast and afternoon refreshments. MC, V. No smoking, 2-night minimum on holiday weekends.*

OTHER CHOICES

Blue House. 125 E. Main, Rockville 84763, tel. 435/772–3912. 2 double rooms with bath, 1 double and 1 quad share bath. TV in common area, trampoline, outdoor patio. $60–$65; full breakfast. MC, V. No smoking.

Bryce Point Bed and Breakfast. 61 N. 400 W (Box 96), Tropic 84776, tel. 435/679–8629. 5 double room with baths, 1 cottage. Ceiling fan, TV/VCR, gas fireplace in cottage, outdoor hot tub, barbecue, off-street parking. 70–$90; full breakfast. MC, V. No smoking. Closed mid-Nov.–mid-Feb.

Francisco Farm Bed & Breakfast. 51 Francisco La. (Box 3), Tropic 84776, tel. 435/679–8721 or 800/642–4136. 3 double rooms with baths. TVs, deck, kitchen, hot tub, off-street parking. $55–$70; full breakfast. No credit cards. No smoking.

Grandma Bess' Cottage. 291 W. 200 S (Box 640), Parowan 84761, tel. 435/477–8224. 3 double rooms share bath. Air-conditioning, TV in common area. $45; full breakfast. No credit cards. No smoking, no alcohol.

Morning Glory Inn. 25 Big Springs Rd., Springdale 84767, tel. 435/772–3301. 2 triple rooms with baths, 1 quad with bath, 1 3-person cottage. Hot tub in cottage; volleyball, basketball, and badminton courts; playground equipment; picnic area; off-street parking. $60–$85; full breakfast. MC, V. No smoking.

Paxman's House Bed & Breakfast. 170 N. 400 W, Cedar City 84720, tel. 435/586–3755. 3 double rooms with baths. TVs, off-street parking. $65; full breakfast. AE, MC, V. No smoking.

Smith House Bed and Breakfast. Hwy. 89, Box 106, Glendale 84729, tel./fax 435/648–2156 or 800/528–3558. 7 double rooms with baths. Separate entrances, breakfast porch, hot tub, laundry, off-street parking, antiques for sale. $44–$74; Continental breakfast. D, MC, V. No smoking. Closed Jan. 2–Mar. 30.

Snow Family Guest Ranch. 653 E. Hwy. 9 (Box 790190), Virgin 84779, tel. 435/635–2500 or 435/308–7669. 9 double rooms with baths. Big-screen TV, pool, outdoor hot tub, gazebo, garden, pond. $85–$150; full breakfast, afternoon refreshments. MC, V. No smoking.

Theater Bed & Breakfast. 118 S. 100 W, Cedar City 84720, tel. 435/586–0404. 1 double room with adjoining bath, 2 doubles share bath. Hot tub, exercise equipment, off-street parking, guest bicycles, ski storage, free airport shuttle. $65; full breakfast Mon.–Sat., Continental breakfast Sun. No credit cards. No smoking, no alcohol.

Zion House. 801 Zion Park Blvd. (Box 323), Springdale 84767, tel./fax 435/772–3281. 1 double room with bath, 2 doubles share bath, 1 suite (sleeps 4). Air-conditioning, kitchen, and private entrance in suite; TV/VCR in common room; off-street parking. $75–$110; full breakfast. No credit cards. No smoking.

Zion's Blue Star. 28 W. State Rte. 9, Virgin 84779, tel. 435/635–3830. 2 double rooms share bath, cottage. Air-conditioning, kitchen in cottage, TV in common room. $65; full breakfast. MC, V. No smoking. Closed Oct.–Mar.

RESERVATIONS SERVICES

There are no bed-and-breakfast reservation services in southwestern Utah. **Bed and Breakfast Inns of Utah, Inc.** (Box 3066, Park City 84060) and the **Utah Travel Council** (Council Hall/Capitol Hill, Salt Lake City 84114, tel. 435/538–1030 or 800/200–1160) both publish free directories.

Southeastern Utah

CASTLE VALLEY INN 🕊

CVSR Box 2602, Moab 84532, tel. 435/259–6012, fax 435/259–1501

Although it feels as though it's way out past nowhere, stunning Castle Valley is only about 20 mi from Moab; it's reached via S.R. 128, a designated Scenic Byway that winds along the Colorado River. A road marked by buildings ranging from a red rock–colored geodesic dome to a western movie set leads to the Castle Valley Inn, a wooden rambler home with a native-stone chimney and sparkling geodes set into the foundation.

When you arrive, you'll be surrounded by 360 degrees of ragged-topped cliffs—and a lot of silence. There is a tendency to want to linger outside in the 11-acre yard and orchard, and new innkeepers Robert Ryan and Hertha Wakefield have made this easy with balconies on bungalows, a large patio adjacent to the main house, lighted paths, and benches scattered about to take advantage of the vistas. A sheltered hot tub is magical at night.

The main-house guest rooms, some upstairs, some down, are decorated in a simple, contemporary southwestern style, with striking color combinations such as variegated shades of lavender and green. Each bathroom includes a hair dryer, robe, and shower-massage head in a stall artistically tiled. Three separate bungalows have private decks and porches. Baskets from Africa and a handcrafted chest decorate the Fremont Bungalow.

Breakfast, which might include green chili quiche, mango yogurt, muesli, and fresh-ground coffee, is served on the patio whenever possible. A sumptuous fixed-price dinner is offered five nights a week. ♧ *5 double rooms with baths, 3 double bungalows. Air-conditioning, hair dryer and robes in main-house rooms, kitchenette in bungalows; VCR, video library in common room; outdoor hot tub. $95–$155; full breakfast, afternoon refreshments. D, MC, V. No smoking indoors, 2-night minimum on weekends.*

THE GRIST MILL INN 🕏
64 S. 300 E (Box 156), Monticello 84535, tel. 435/587–2597 or 800/645–3762, fax 435/587–2580

There was a lot of head-shaking among Monticello locals when plans to gut a vacant mill and redesign and rebuild it were announced. Doubt changed to admiration by the time the project was completed back in 1988: More than 900 people showed up to tour the inn before its opening. Now a place worth staying in an otherwise passing-through kind of town, the Grist Mill Inn is also distinctive for its reasonable rates.

The portions of the huge three-story flour mill that were wooden clapboard when the mill was constructed in 1933 have been sheathed in light-gray aluminum siding. Bright-blue tin roofs top both sections of the structure. The entire renovation is documented in a photo album.

A multicolored firebrick hearth in the lobby sitting room is the focal point for a conversation area, with plush purple wing chairs and soft lamplight. If you look up you'll see the driveshaft for a grain sacker that sits a few feet away—one of the many original pieces of mill equipment left throughout the inn. Other lovely common areas include the second-floor Blue Goose TV room (named after an old saloon in town), which also has a pump organ. A bank of high, square windows in the third-floor library provides sufficient light to enjoy reading materials ranging from magazines, remodeling books, and contemporary novels to a complete collection of Hardy Boys and Nancy Drew mysteries.

The Corbin Room, named for the man who owned the first telephone company hereabouts, has phones everywhere; one wall and the ceiling are horizontally paneled with rosy stained wood, and an antique armoire holds a Murphy bed. The three-level Bailey Room has two sleeping areas and several antique sewing machines; the bathroom sink is in a treadle machine cabinet. Behind the inn a wooden railroad caboose holds a snug Victorian-style bedroom and a kitchen; its observation tower has a sitting room.

Breakfast is served in the dining room; you can see the Abajo Mountains through glass doors and windows. The morning specialties include country French toast stuffed with sweet peaches or served with a clove-tinged maple syrup, and scrambled eggs and cheese piled on cubed potatoes. ♧ *11 double rooms with baths. Cable TVs, outdoor hot tub, gazebo, gift shop, bookstore, old-time photo studio. $66–$92; full breakfast. D, MC, V. No smoking indoors.*

SUNFLOWER HILL 🕏
185 N. 300 E, Moab 84532, tel. 435/259–2974 or 800/MOABSUN, fax 435/259–3065

Once a bare adobe-brick farmhouse surrounded by nothing but crop land, Sunflower Hill was enlarged and renovated, and the crumbling adobe was fortified and covered with pale stucco. A separate cottage was added to the original late-19th-century structure, and the farm field became a spacious wooded lot with a hedge of white roses lining the split-log fence.

The main common area, which doubles as the dining room, is cheerful as innkeeper Gregg Stuvki. Mismatched antique chairs are pulled up to several small tables covered with blue-and-white-checked cloths; a century-old Austrian sideboard with dishes peeking through its heavy glass-pane doors sits between windows curtained in crisp white ruffles; and a tall umbrella stand and coat tree are topped with a bright-red hatbox. Across the hall, a small office area known as the Welcome Room contains copious information on the Moab area. An antique cash register is a reminder, perhaps, that this is where reservations are taken and accounts are settled.

The guest rooms are varied in size, but each has a distinctive character. In truth, there's not a bad choice among them. Accessed from the enclosed porch opposite the dining-room door, the Sun Porch Room has been fitted with floor-to-ceiling windows covered in vertical miniblinds for privacy. Up a step is a painted metal bed; a woven sunflower throw draped on a quilt stand echoes a ceiling border blooming with golden sunflowers. The Rose Room has stenciled roses twining along the walls, a graceful four-poster bed, and an antique dressing table. The blue-and-white Morning Glory Room has a private garden entrance with morning-glory vines growing around the door.

Across the yard, the Garden Cottage has a stenciled tulip border high on the sitting-room walls. A whimsical flower garden is painted on the wall of the sunny bedroom.

Sunflower Hill's breakfasts are a variety of sturdy homemade breads, fruity muffins, yogurt, honey granola, and lots of fresh fruit, or hot entrées such as fruit-filled pancakes, southwestern-style eggs, and whole-wheat waffles with tangy berry patch syrup. △ *9 double rooms with baths, 2 suites. Air-conditioning, TVs, outdoor hot tub, barbecue, laundry. $85–$155; full breakfast, afternoon refreshments. AE, D, MC, V. No smoking.*

OTHER CHOICES

Bankurz Hatt. 214 Farrer St., Green River 84525, tel. 435/564–3382. 2 double rooms with baths, 1 suite. Ceiling fans, outdoor hot tub, bicycles, off-street parking. $75–$125; full breakfast. AE, D, DC, MC, V. No smoking.

Bluff Bed and Breakfast. Box 158, Bluff 84512, tel. 435/672–2220. 2 double rooms with baths. TV in common area, off-street parking, hiking. $75; full breakfast. No credit cards. No smoking.

Desert Chalet. 1275 E. San Juan Dr., Moab 84532, tel. 435/259–5793 or 800/549–8504. 3 double rooms with baths, 2 triples with baths. Ceiling fans, TV/VCR, stereo in common area, outdoor hot tub, barbecue, kitchen, laundry, storage available, transportation and support vehicle service. $45–$75; Continental breakfast. MC, V. No smoking.

Grayson Country Inn. 118 E. 300 S, Blanding 84511, tel. 435/678–2388 or 800/365–0868. 7 double rooms with baths, 1 3-bedroom cottage. Air-conditioning, TVs, kitchen in cottage. $37–$57; full breakfast. AE, MC, V. No smoking.

Pack Creek Ranch Bed and Breakfast. LaSal Mountain Loop Rd. (Box 1270), Moab 84532, tel. 435/259–5505, fax 435/259–8879. 11 cabins. Kitchen in cabins, fireplace in 7 cabins, gift shop, masseuse, hot tub, sauna, pool, trail rides. $115–$150; full breakfast. AE, D, MC, V. Closed Nov.–Mar.

Valley of the Gods Bed and Breakfast. Box 310307, Mexican Hat 84531, tel. 970/749–1164 (cellular). 4 double rooms with baths. Raft trips, pack-horse or llama trips and archaeological tours available. $90; full breakfast. MC, V. No smoking.

RESERVATIONS SERVICES

There are no bed-and-breakfast reservation services in the area; write the statewide **Bed and Breakfast Inns of Utah, Inc.** (Box 3066, Park City 84060) or the **Utah Travel Council** (Council Hall/Capitol Hill, Salt Lake City 84114) for a free brochure.

VERMONT

Southeastern Vermont

GOVERNOR'S INN 🐦

86 Main St., Ludlow 05149, tel. 802/228–8830 or 800/468–3766

The atmosphere at this formal little retreat just 10 minutes from the Okemo Mountain ski area is high Victorian. Everything from the vest-pocket lobby, where afternoon tea is served, to the innkeepers' collection of antique teacups and chocolate pots evokes a turn-of-the-century elegance. As visitors learn during Deedy Marble's orientation tour, the governor in question is Vermont governor William Wallace Stickney, who in 1890 had the house built as a wedding present for his wife; the bride's and groom's portraits still hang near the faux-marble fireplace in the living room. These romantic beginnings haven't been forgotten by innkeepers Deedy and her husband, Charlie, who have created an appealing hideaway for honeymooners and couples celebrating anniversaries. The new third-floor suite is very private and has fantastic views of the mountains, a whirlpool tub, and an enormous floral daybed. Room 7 comes with a telescope for stargazing or watching skiers descend the slopes. The Marbles' thoughtful attention to detail is evident everywhere: the inn's wide-plank pine floors gleam; lace-trimmed floral-chintz duvets on the beds match the sheets, and terry cloth robes hang in the closets; arriving guests find glasses and miniature cordials in their rooms; and the inn's special chocolates appear every evening when the beds are turned down.

The hosts take as much pleasure in entertaining their guests as in providing a restful atmosphere. It was partly because they had become so proficient at orchestrating elaborate dinner parties for friends that they finally left management jobs in 1981 to open an inn. Before welcoming their first guests, however, they decided to hone their skills at Roger Verge's famed cooking school in the south of France. As a result of the Marbles' training (and their flair for presentation), the six-course dinners at the Governor's Inn border on the theatrical. Fresh-faced waitresses in floral skirts, white high-neck blouses, and mobcaps announce each course. Guests dine by candlelight with table settings of antique bone china and sterling silver and often linger over meals that might include hot wine broth, Cornish hens with cinnamon glaze and apple and pâté stuffing, and Edwardian cream with raspberry sauce. The award-winning apple pie is especially recommended. Charlie is in charge of breakfast, which often includes his signature rum-raisin French toast. ♨ *8 double rooms with baths, 1 suite. Restaurant (closed Mon.—Tues. and Apr.), air-conditioning, game room. $190–$240 MAP, afternoon tea; $130–$170 B&B. MC, V. No smoking, 2-night minimum weekends, 3–4 night minimum holidays and at Christmastime.*

INN AT SAWMILL FARM ☞

Rte. 100 (Box 367), West Dover 05356, tel. 802/464–8131 or 800/493–1133, fax 802/464–1130

Staying at this aristocratic inn in the Haystack Mountain–Mt. Snow ski region is like being a guest at the country home of a British lord whose family fortune is still intact. In 1968 architect Rodney Williams and his wife, Ione, an interior designer, bought a dairy farm that dated from 1897, but don't expect a rugged rural retreat. The decor here may be country, but it's the kind of country featured in glossy home-and-garden magazines: There's a polished copper milk tank used as a table base, a plaid carpet, a brick foyer decorated with a horse collar and farm tools, and chamber music piped into the low-ceiling reception area. The atmosphere is on the formal side—the owners prefer that men wear jackets in the public areas after 6 PM—and caters to a select clientele. Guests like to congregate around the huge fireplace in the living room in winter with their afternoon tea or stroll by one of the two ponds when it's warm.

Wallpaper in the guest rooms matches the bedspreads and upholstery; one room might be all soft pastels, another bright with vibrant hues. The carpet is thick enough to swallow high heels. The beds all have down comforters and might be decorated with a tiny lace pillow, or a wall might display a framed quilt sample. Some bathrooms have whirlpool tubs. The 10 rooms in the main building are somewhat smaller than the remaining rooms (some are suites), which have working fireplaces and are in buildings scattered throughout the 28-acre property.

The Williamses' son, Brill, presides as chef in the restaurant, which consists of two dining rooms. The first is a formal dining room with six tables, an antique sideboard, Early American portraits, Queen Anne furniture, and a baby grand piano. In the second, a greenhouselike area, simple whitewashed timber pillars contrast nicely with silver napkin rings. The wine list has won numerous awards and has more than 160 labels. The menu features such entrées as roasted semiboneless *poussin* with apple and sausage stuffing or rack of lamb for two with mint sauce. A breakfast specialty is shirred eggs with Vermont smoked ham and cheddar cheese. ⚭ *20 double rooms with baths. Restaurant, air-conditioning, TV in public area, tennis court, 2 trout ponds. $360–$470; MAP. AE, MC, V. No smoking, 2-night minimum weekends. Closed Apr.–mid-May.*

INN AT WEATHERSFIELD ☞

Rte. 106, Weathersfield 05151, tel. 802/263–9217 or 800/477–4828, fax 802/263–9219

In this rambling Colonial farmhouse, built in 1795, visitors are greeted in the entry by Terry and Mary Carter and by the smell of hot apple cider simmering in an iron kettle over an open hearth. The wide-plank floors, brick beehive oven, and candlelight lend authenticity to this keeping room. The Carters enhance the Early American feel by illuminating the common areas with candles—seven dozen tapers daily.

The 10 rooms and 2 suites are distinctly decorated with period antiques, and each is inspired by and named after a famous love story; one room even contains gifts Terry's grandmother received at her wedding. In the Twelve Oaks Room, swaths of lace over the bedstead form a canopy anchored by a bouquet of dried flowers. Wuthering Heights has yellow rag-roll-painted walls; a faux-marble fireplace; three skylights; and a private deck. A camelback trunk sits at the foot of a four-poster bed in one room; a stenciled Windsor chair and hardwood floors lend simple grace to another. Eight rooms have working fireplaces, and Colonial spareness doesn't preclude such modern comforts as electric blankets. Some bathrooms are small and have 1940s-style fixtures, though one of the suites does have a two-person whirlpool. The inn has several gathering areas, including a tavern, a formal parlor, and a lounge called the Prentis Room.

Dinner might include rack of lamb—with mustard, herbs, and raspberry sauce— or salmon Wellington. On the weekends there's often dinner music on the dining room's grand piano. At Sunday breakfast you are often treated to a poetry reading by Harold Groat, an eighth-generation Vermonter. ♠ *10 double rooms with baths, 2 suites. Restaurant, TV/VCR in game room, exercise equipment, sauna, pool table. $195–$225; MAP, afternoon tea. AE, D, DC, MC, V. No smoking, 2-night minimum most weekends, 3-night minimum holiday weekends.*

OLD TAVERN AT GRAFTON ☜
Rte. 121, Grafton 05146, tel. 802/843–2231 or 800/843–1801, fax 802/843–2245

White-columned porches wrap around both stories of the Old Tavern's main building, creating an impressive facade. The history here is even more impressive. It has been an inn almost continuously since it was built in 1801, and the old guest register bears signatures of such prominent visitors as Daniel Webster and Nathaniel Hawthorne. Yet the Old Tavern hardly shows its age. In 1963 the Windham Foundation began to buy and restore historic homes like this one in and around Grafton. Thanks to the foundation, you can now indulge in creative idleness amid perfectly preserved white-clapboard buildings. Why not stroll to the stream that flows through the center of town; linger on the Old Tavern's porch; take a horse-drawn carriage tour; or read the notices on the bulletin board at the general store?

The inn's main building has 14 rooms, the oldest just above the lobby. There are also 22 rooms in the restored Windham and Homestead houses across the street and 7 guest houses, all with full kitchens. Main-building guest rooms evoke New England's 18th-century frontier days. Each is decorated with country antiques; some have crocheted canopies or four-poster beds that could easily be as old as the inn itself. The newer rooms are generally sunnier and are decorated with bright pastels.

There's a well-stocked library off the main building's lobby, and the Phelps Barn in the back houses a comfortable tavern with authentic English pub furniture; you may want to stop by for afternoon tea. Both spots have brick fireplaces that invite you to linger long after dinner. Although breakfast is served in the solarium, there are also two dining rooms—one with Georgian furniture and oil portraits, the other with rustic paneling and low beams. Both serve inspired New England cuisine: grilled choice sirloin steeped in McNeill's stout and a blend of spices or fresh spinach and egg fettuccine tossed with bay scallops, shrimp, and littleneck clams in a lightly brandied Parmesan cream sauce. Some offerings use cheddar cheese made just down the road at the Grafton Village Cheese Factory.

The trail system at Grafton Ponds, the Tavern's Nordic ski and mountain-bike center, covers close to 2,000 acres. In winter skiing is guaranteed because of a state-of-the-art snow-making system. ♠ *36 double rooms with baths, 7 guest houses. Restaurant, lounge, TV in public area, game room, swimming pond, tennis courts, hiking, ice-skating, snowshoeing, tubing, cross-country skiing, mountain bikes. $125–$710; Continental breakfast. MC, V. Smoking only in Phelps Barn. Closed Apr.*

OTHER CHOICES

Deerhill Inn. Off Rte. 100, Valley View Rd. (Box 136), West Dover 05356, tel. 802/464–3100 or 800/993–3379, fax 802/464–5474. 13 double rooms with baths, 2 suites. Restaurant, TV/VCR in common area, pool. $95–$290; full breakfast. AE, MC, V. No smoking, 2-night minimum most weekends.

Four Columns. West St. (Box 278), Newfane 05345, tel. 802/365–7713 or 800/787–6633, fax 802/365–0022. 15 double rooms with baths. Restaurant, tavern, air-conditioning, TV in public area, phone and cassette player in rooms, pool, hiking trails, 2 trout ponds. $100–$205, full breakfast; $200–$325, MAP (mandatory during foliage season). AE, D, DC, MC, V. No smoking. Closed Dec. 24–25.

Juniper Hill Inn. Juniper Hill Rd. (R.R. 1, Box 79), Windsor 05089-9703, tel. 802/674–5273 or 800/359–2541, fax 802/674–2041. 16 double rooms with baths. Restaurant, TV in public area, ceiling fans, pool, hiking and cross-country ski trails nearby. $90–$170; full breakfast, afternoon refreshments. D, MC, V. No smoking. Closed Apr., 2 wks in Nov.

Kedron Valley Inn. Rte. 106, South Woodstock 05071, tel. 802/457–1473 or 800/ 836–1193, fax 802/457–4469. 26 double rooms with baths. Restaurant, lounge, TV in rooms, swimming pond. $120–$215; full breakfast. AE, D, MC, V. 2-night minimum weekends, mid-Sept.–late Oct. and Dec. 24–Jan. 1; 3-night minimum holiday weekends. Closed Apr.

Parker House. 16 Main St., Box 0780, Quechee 05059, tel. 802/295–6077. 7 double rooms with baths. Restaurant, air-conditioning in some rooms, TV in public area, golf, swimming, skiing nearby. $100–$125; full breakfast. AE, MC, V. 2-night minimum during foliage season, commencement weekends, Christmas, and other holidays.

Whetstone Inn. South Rd., Marlboro 05344, tel. 802/254–2500 or 877/254–2500. 8 double rooms with baths, 4 doubles share bath. Restaurant, kitchenettes in 3 rooms, swimming and skating pond. $65–$95; breakfast extra. No credit cards. No smoking in public areas, 3-night minimum holiday and festival weekends.

RESERVATIONS SERVICE

Vermont Centerpoint Reservation Service (Box 8513, Essex 05451, tel. 802/ 872–2745 or 800/449–2745).

Southwestern Vermont

BATTENKILL INN ☜

Rte. 100 (Box 948), Manchester Village 05254, tel. 802/362–4213 or 800/441–1628, fax 802/362–0975

The hearts carved into the outside trim were final touches on this architectural gem, which was built in 1840 as a wedding present; the rosebushes surrounding the grounds are a modern-day toast to that romance. Recently taken over by Laine and Yoshi Akiyama, who left careers with Disney Imagineering to begin an innkeeping adventure, this refurbished inn exudes all the elements you'd expect from a New England B&B.

Deep red wallpaper and dark green prints lure you into the dining and sitting rooms. Original wooden door and window frames, polished oak floors, and a grand curving walnut staircase all allow you to forgive the rather small bathrooms. Rooms in the rear have decks that look out toward a meadow and the Battenkill. The attentive hospitality and the breakfasts are fast becoming this inn's hallmarks. Raspberry and cream cheese–filled French toast is a favorite, and everything is made with low- or non-fat ingredients when possible. ♨ *11 double rooms with baths. Air-conditioning. $105–$155; full breakfast. MC, V. No smoking.*

BLUEBERRY HILL INN ☞
Rte. 32, Goshen 05733, tel. 802/247–6735 or 800/448–0707, fax 802/247–3983

If you're looking for a true escape affording total peace and quiet, you have found the perfect repose. Located in the Green Mountain National Forest and only accessible by dirt road, Blueberry Hill is an idyllic spot. The Colonial building is bordered by lush gardens, a stream, glorious blueberry bushes, and a pond with a wood-fired sauna on its bank. Many of the rooms have views of the surrounding mountains; all are furnished with antiques and quilts. Rooms in the back of the inn are entered by a brick walkway through a greenhouse of blooming plants. Three rooms have lofts that can accommodate additional guests; the Moosalamoo Room is in a private cottage and also has a loft and a small sitting room. The open kitchen is a gathering spot and always has a jar full of the inn's famous chocolate-chip cookies. Tony Clark, innkeeper for more than 20 years, often joins guests for cocktails by the living-room fireplace.

Blueberry Hill is probably best known for its ski touring center, which turns into a mountain-biking mecca in the summer. There are also 45 mi of marked hiking trails. Robert Frost lived in this area, and the inn is not far from a nature trail that has Frost quotations posted along the way. ♨ *7 double rooms with baths, 5 quadruples with baths. Restaurant, cross-country skiing, hiking, mountain biking, sauna. $95–$164 per person, MAP; B&B rates available. MC, V. No smoking.*

CORNUCOPIA ☞
Rte. 30 (Box 307), Dorset 05251, tel. 802/867–5751 or 800/566–5751

The Cornucopia has only a few guest rooms, and this enables innkeepers Linda and Bill Ley to truly pamper their guests. You are welcomed into this 1880 Colonial house with champagne; a wake-up tray with flowers and coffee or tea served in English bone china is available in the morning; and at night you'll find a chocolate-covered butter crunch on your pillow. All rooms have Crabtree & Evelyn toiletries, terry robes, and either down comforters or quilts; three rooms have fireplaces, and most have canopy or four-poster beds. The entire first floor is a comfortable public area decorated with antiques and several grandfather clocks; the solarium overlooks English country gardens. The private cottage in the backyard has a loft bedroom with skylights, a living room with a cathedral ceiling and a fireplace, a full kitchen, and a patio.

The gourmet candlelighted breakfast always includes fresh fruit and might be followed by maple-swirl French toast soufflé or pecan, sausage, and apple crepes. The inn is an easy stroll from the center of historic Dorset village, with its crisp white buildings and town green. ♨ *4 double rooms with baths, 1 cottage. Air-conditioning, phones. $115–$225; full breakfast, afternoon refreshments. AE, MC, V. No smoking.*

1811 HOUSE ☞
Rte. 7A (Box 39), Manchester 05254, tel. 802/362–1811 or 800/432–1811, fax 802/362–2443

Classic Colonial good looks and friendliness make the 1811 House the most enviable place to stay in town. The inn's handsome brown clapboard main building anchors the north end of Manchester Village, the charming alter ego of the outlet scene that is a mile north in Manchester Center. The contrast makes this inn that much more of a haven, where you could easily pass the day sinking into one of the common room's armchairs or strolling through the back lawns and gardens—if you ever leave your room at all, that is. Antiques, old portraits and horse paintings, and wide-plank floorboards give the place an irresistible English country house atmosphere.

Parts of the inn date from 1770, and it has been in operation as a hostelry since 1811—the only break in service was when Abraham Lincoln's granddaughter used it for a summer house. She was among the New York elite who spent their summers in Manchester at the turn of the last century. The inn and other buildings in the village still have that aristocratic air.

Most of the guest rooms are spacious and have writing tables; six rooms have working fireplaces. The three rooms that face the town green have wonderful old fixtures in their bathrooms. Among them, the Robinson Room has its own porch with mountain views and a marble-walled shower room, and the front-corner Mary Lincoln Isham Room has a bed with a canopy of white chenille and is decorated with floral wallpaper and matching drapes. The view of the lawns and distant hills from its porch is splendid. Bathrooms in the separate cottage's three rooms (which are good for families) are the most modern.

Owners Bruce and Marnie Duff have done much to refine the 1811 house; their antiques and decorative touches are particularly appealing. Marnie and her staff present full, rich, and very tasty breakfasts—with scones, eggs and bacon, and potatoes and mushrooms—and Marnie makes delicious monster cookies that you'll find on the bar every afternoon. Bruce is an expert on single-malt scotches, and his cozy, English pub–style bar has the largest selection of them in the state—53 varieties strong. The bar area has a dartboard and is open to nonguests evenings 5:30–8. In the kitchen you can help yourself to tea or coffee all day. For Thanksgiving and on occasional gourmet weekends, Marnie prepares elaborate dinners. ♠ *11 double rooms with baths, 3 cottage rooms. Bar, air-conditioning. $110–$200; full breakfast. AE, D, MC, V. No smoking, 2-night minimum weekends, holidays, and during foliage season. Closed Dec. 25.*

WEST MOUNTAIN INN ☞

River Rd. off Rte. 313, Arlington 05250, tel. 802/375–6516, fax 802/375–6553

This 1840s farmhouse, restored over the past 13 years, sits on 150 secluded acres. And everywhere you turn there are reminders of owners Wes and Mary Ann Carlson's idiosyncratic enthusiasms. Take the llama ranch on the property, which started as a hobby, or the small African violets in the guest rooms, which you can take home with you. A small pond is stocked with exotic goldfish, and squirrels feed outside the inn's windows. The Adirondack chairs on the front lawn are perfect for contemplating a spectacular view of the surrounding countryside, and in winter the sloping lawn practically cries for a sled.

Plush carpets, quilted bedspreads, fresh fruit in pottery bowls, trail maps, and copies of the books of local author Dorothy Canfield Fisher are among the luxurious guest-room touches. Rooms 2, 3, 4, and 5, in the front of the house, afford the same panorama as the front lawn (though there are almost no bad views in the place); the three small nooks of Room 11 resemble railroad sleeper berths and are perfect for children. A new children's room is brightly painted with life-size Disney characters and is fully stocked with games, stuffed animals, and a TV with a VCR. A spacious conference room has also been added with a cathedral ceiling, a fireplace, and a full kitchen.

You can gather in the library for happy hour; nibble on complimentary hors d'oeuvres, such as chicken fingers and fruit; and get acquainted with other guests before moving into the low-beamed, candlelighted paneled dining room for a six-course meal. The menu offers creative country cuisine with interesting little twists. Aunt Min's Swedish rye and other flavorful breads, as well as desserts, are made on the premises. Tables by the windows offer a splendid view of the mountains—a view that goes a long way toward promoting inner peace. ⚇ *15 double rooms with baths, 3 suites. Restaurant, bar, air-conditioning, TV and phones in public area, children's room, hiking and cross-country ski trails. $145–$244; MAP. AE, D, MC, V. No smoking, 2-night minimum weekends.*

OTHER CHOICES

Arlington Inn. Rte. 7A, Arlington 05250, tel. 802/375–6532 or 800/443–9442, fax 802/375–6534. 16 double rooms with baths, 3 suites. Restaurant (closed Mon., Dec. 24, Jan. 1), lounge, air-conditioning, TV/VCR in public area, tennis court. $70–$205, full breakfast. AE, D, DC, MC, V. No smoking, 2-night minimum most weekends.

Inn at Ormsby Hill. Rte. 7A (R.R. 2, Box 3264), Manchester Center 05255, tel. 802/362–1163 or 800/670–2841, fax 802/362–5176. 10 double rooms with baths. Air-conditioning, phone in rooms, TV in common area. $115–240; full breakfast, afternoon tea. D, MC, V. No smoking.

Molly Stark Inn. 1067 E. Main St., Bennington 05201, tel. 802/442–9631 or 800/356–3076, fax 802/442–5224. 4 double rooms with baths, 2 triples with baths, 1 cottage. Air-conditioning in some rooms, ceiling fan in rooms, TV in public area. $70–$145; full breakfast. AE, D, MC, V. No smoking, 2-night minimum weekends and holidays.

South Shire Inn. 124 Elm St., Bennington 05201, tel. 802/447–3839, fax 802/442–3547. 9 double rooms with baths. Air-conditioning, phone in rooms, whirlpool bath in some rooms, TV in public area and some rooms. $105–$180; full breakfast. AE, MC, V. No smoking, 3-night minimum fall weekends.

Wilburton Inn. River Rd., Manchester 05254, tel. 802/362–2500 or 800/648–4944, fax 802/362–1107. 34 double rooms with baths. Restaurant, air-conditioning, TV in lobby and some rooms, pool, 3 tennis courts. $155–$255; full breakfast, afternoon tea. AE, MC, V. No smoking, 2-night minimum holidays.

RESERVATIONS SERVICES

Bennington Area Chamber of Commerce (Veterans Memorial Dr., Bennington 05201, tel. 802/447–3311). **Chamber of Commerce–Manchester and the Mountains** (R.R. 2, Box 3451, Manchester Center 05255, tel. 802/362–2100 or 800/752–9199). **Vermont Centerpoint Reservation Service** (Box 8513, Essex 05451, tel. 802/872–2745 or 800/449–2745).

Northern Vermont

BEAVER POND FARM INN ☙

Golf Course Rd. (R.D. Box 306), Warren 05674, tel. 802/583–2861

A peaceful drive down a country lane lined with sugar maples brings you to this small, restored, 1840 farmhouse. Overlooking rolling meadows, a golf course, and, in winter, cross-country ski trails, the setting is very nearly perfect. Innkeepers Betty and Bob Hansen bought the house as a second home almost 20 years ago, and, realizing they had an idyllic, beautiful spot, they decided to turn it into an inn.

A full breakfast that may include orange-yogurt pancakes is served at an oblong walnut table; a low wooden buffet lines the wall and holds four generations of china. Dinner is also offered three nights a week; favorites are the goat cheese soufflé and chicken stuffed with roasted red peppers served with a scallion, plum, and wine sauce. Guest rooms are decorated simply, and all have down comforters and ample bathrooms. The focal point of the inn is the huge deck, where you can lounge about gazing at the mountains and meadows after, of course, having spent the day hiking or golfing or skiing—it's all just steps from the front door. **△** *4 double rooms with baths, 2 doubles share bath. Golf, hiking, ski trails nearby. $72–$104; full breakfast. MC, V. No smoking. Closed mid-Apr.–late May and early Nov.*

GREEN TRAILS INN ☞
Main St., Brookfield 05036, tel. 802/276–3412 or 800/243–3412

The two 1790 and 1830 farmhouses that form this inn are the focal point of a sleepy yet stubborn town that has voted several times to keep the village's dirt roads. On a 17-acre estate, the inn overlooks Sunset Lake and the longest floating bridge east of the Mississippi. Green Trails was started in the 1930s by Jessie Fisk, one of the first female professors at Rutgers University. Current innkeepers Mark and Sue Erwin maintain a relaxing atmosphere of quiet, comfortable country elegance.

A massive fieldstone fireplace dominates the living and dining area; the common rooms are filled with antique clocks, soothing music, and flowers. Guests rooms are simply furnished with quilts and a smattering of Early American antiques; one corner room in the 18th-century house is decorated with original wall stenciling and has a whirlpool. Meals represent home cooking at its best; rates always include a gourmet breakfast, and in the winter you can also request dinner. The Erwins maintain 30 km (19 mi) of cross-country ski trails, and snowshoeing, fishing, swimming, canoeing, hiking, and biking are all available nearby. You can also opt for a tranquil walk down a tree-shaded country road. **△** *8 double rooms with baths, 6 doubles share bath. Whirlpool bath in some rooms. $79–$130; full breakfast. D, MC, V. No smoking.*

INN AT MONTPELIER ☞
47 Main St., Montpelier 05602, tel. 802/223–2727, fax 802/223–0722

Until 1988 if you had wanted to stay in the state capital, you had your choice of large chain hotels or small motels. But then came Maureen and Bill Russell, who renovated a spacious, yellow, Federal brick house only a short walk from the center of town. Built in 1828, the inn was designed with the business traveler in mind, but the architectural details, the antique four-poster beds and Windsor chairs, and the piped-in classical music also attract visitors whose most pressing business is deciding how late to sleep (never a problem in the tranquil historic district).

The formal sitting room—with its large marble fireplace, cream-color woodwork, and tapestry-upholstered wing chairs—has a stately Federal feel to it, as if the original owners were about to glide down the polished staircase in rustling taffeta and black knee breeches. The wide, wraparound Colonial Revival porch, with its octagonal section, is especially conducive to relaxing and is one of the inn's most notable features.

Guest rooms in the frame building across the driveway are as elegant as (even slightly larger than) those in the main building. Each building has a small pantry where you can prepare coffee, store food, and/or grab a midnight snack. All rooms (some have fireplaces) are done in a mix of antique and reproduction furniture and rich floral decorator fabrics; the walls are often hung with original artwork, some of it by local artists. Maureen's Room has a sundeck; others have sitting rooms. The soft rose-color decor and the marble fireplace make the dining room a luxurious place for breakfast on fresh-baked goods. ▲ *19 double rooms with baths. Air-conditioning, TV, phone in rooms; meeting rooms. $99–$169; Continental breakfast. AE, D, DC, MC, V. No smoking.*

INN AT THE ROUND BARN FARM ✐

E. Warren Rd. (R.R. 1, Box 247), Waitsfield 05673, tel. 802/496–2276, fax 802/496–8832

Wedding parties have replaced cows in the big round barn here, but the Shaker-style building still dominates the farm's 85 acres of countryside. As the picture albums attest, the process of restoring the 1910 12-sided barn involved jacking up the entire structure and putting in a new foundation. The result is one of the 12 remaining round (at least, dodecahedral) barns in the state; it's used for summer concerts, weddings, and parties and is on the National Register of Historic Places.

It was the barn that first caught the Simkos' eye; they had owned a ski house in the Mad River valley for 15 years and had driven past it frequently. Looking for a place to retire from the family floral business, they bought the property in 1986. Although the Simkos have since semiretired from innkeeping as well, their daughter, AnneMarie, remains on hand as the wedding coordinator. Resident innkeepers Tim O'Brien and Tracy Caslin hail from Oregon and bring a youthful, entrepreneurial energy and flair to the place.

Guest rooms are in the 1810 farmhouse that overlooks several landscaped ponds and rolling acreage. Guest rooms are plush, with eyelet-trimmed sheets, new quilts on canopy or sleigh beds, Neutrogena toiletries, brass reading lamps, and floral drapes that match the wallpaper. The Richardson Room has low windows with mountain views, skylights, a canopy and headboard done with matching fabric, a gas fireplace, a large whirlpool tub, and a hand-painted mural. The equally luxurious Joslin Room also has a steam shower. Breakfast, served in a spacious room with exposed hand-hewn beams, might be French toast or cottage-cheese pancakes with a maple-raspberry syrup. Guests often gather by the fireplace in the cream-color library to discuss the day's activities—biking, hiking, canoeing, skiing, and the like—and to relax with a glass of sherry. ▲ *11 double rooms with baths. TV in public area; whirlpool bath, steam shower in some rooms; indoor lap pool. $135–$220; full breakfast. AE, MC, V. No smoking, 2-night minimum weekends.*

LAREAU FARM COUNTRY INN ✐

Rte. 100 (Box 563), Waitsfield 05673, tel. 802/496–4949 or 800/833–0766, fax 802/496–7979

Surrounded by 67 acres of pasture and woodland and just an amble away from the Mad River, this collection of old farm buildings appeals both to outdoor enthusiasts and those simply seeking a rejuvenating country retreat. There's lots of history here—the original settler is buried on the property—that innkeepers Susan and Dan Easley love to share. They also provide information on exploring the area: you can take a 1-mi stroll with the help of a detailed walking guide they've created.

Although the inn has been around since the late-18th century (the oldest part dates from 1790), the furnishings are an eclectic mix—Victorian sofas, Oriental rugs, handmade quilts. The effect is always country and always casual. The many-windowed dining room is the most inviting space. Here, you'll be served a family-style breakfast at one of four massive oak and cherry tables. Sitting on the covered porch in an Adirondack chair, staring at horses in pastures out back, is the epitome of peace. You can also explore the big jazz-recordings collection, swim in the river, take a horse or sleigh ride, and stroll through beautiful gardens. American Flatbread, the warm and lively restaurant in the barn next door, serves great pizza made using organic ingredients (open Friday and Saturday only). ▲ *11 double rooms with baths, 2 doubles share bath. TV in sitting room, whirlpool bath in 1 room, swimming, sleigh rides. $75–$125; full breakfast. MC, V. No smoking, 2-day minimum weekends.*

RABBIT HILL INN ☜

Rte. 18 (Box 55), Lower Waterford 05848, tel. 802/748–5168 or 800/76–BUNNY, fax 802/748–8342

Upon arriving here, you'll find that the door will swing open, and you'll be welcomed (often by name) into enough warmth to melt away the stress of even the most difficult journeys. The Rabbit Hill Inn, on 15 wooded acres, has been receiving guests since its days as a stagecoach stop on the Montréal–Portland route. Innkeepers Brian and Leslie Mulcahy are dedicated to upholding a long-standing tradition of gracious hospitality.

The Mulcahys' fondness for the gentility of days past is expressed in the formal, Federal-period parlor, where mulled cider from the fireplace crane is served on chilly afternoons. The low wooden beams and cozy warmth of the Irish pub next door create a comfortable contrast that's carried throughout the inn: Guest rooms are as stylistically different as they are consistently indulgent. The seven suites (the Mulcahys call them "fantasy chambers") have double whirlpool tubs and fireplaces; most contain a whimsical secret (a hidden door, perhaps) in their design. The Loft, with its 8-ft Palladian window and its king-size canopy bed, is one of the most requested. The abundant windows, Victrola, and working pump organ with period sheet music make the Music Chamber another favorite. Rooms toward the front of the inn have views of the Connecticut River and the White Mountains in New Hampshire; those in the Carriage House are smaller but more private.

In the elegant dining room, chef Russell Stannard prepares eclectic, regional cuisine that might include grilled sausage of Vermont pheasant with pistachios or smoked chicken and red-lentil dumplings nestled in red pepper linguine. Heart-healthful meals, reviewed by a dietician, are also offered. The bountiful country breakfast includes a buffet of home-baked coffee cakes and muffins, quiches, and fresh fruits. ▲ *15 double rooms with baths, 6 suites. Restaurant, pub, air-conditioning in most rooms, whirlpool bath in some rooms, TV in public area, walking and cross-country ski trails, canoes. $189–$289, MAP; B&B rates available. AE, MC, V. No smoking, 2-night minimum weekends, 3-night minimum holiday weekends. Closed 1st 2 wks in Apr. and 1st 2 wks in Nov.*

SWIFT HOUSE INN ☜

25 Stewart La., Middlebury 05753, tel. 802/388–9925, fax 802/388–9927

Christine and John Nelson didn't exactly intend to open an inn when they did; they were looking at inns with the idea of buying something in 10 years, after John retired from IBM's finance department. But on the way to the airport to return to New Jersey one day in 1985, they stopped by the big white Federal home set atop a sweeping expanse of lawn, and their decision was made. They've made the Swift House Inn one of the most elegant in the state. The Nelsons have since retired, but their daughter, Karla Nelson-Loura, is now the innkeeper.

The patrician air here is no coincidence; the inn was the private home of two of Middlebury's most prominent families: the Swifts, who built the oldest section of the house in 1814, and the Stewarts, one of whom married the grandson of the original owner and lived in the home until 1943. As a result of the long private ownership, elegant detailing has been well preserved. The richly ornamented cherry paneling and trim glow in the dining room, where the bright purple and green grape–clustered wallpaper is an exact reproduction of the pattern installed in 1905. Guest rooms are also luxurious. The Swift Room not only has a private porch but also retains the built-in, brass wall phone Mrs. Swift installed so she could—believe it or not—listen to church services. White-eyelet-trimmed sheets, gathered lace curtains, floral chintz draperies that match a wing chair, a fresh carnation in a bedside vase—the attention to detail gives the impression that this is still an affluent family's private home.

The carriage house was converted in 1990 and is recommended for families; the rooms are very spacious and have enormous bathrooms with whirlpool baths. One rooms has French doors that open onto a patio. Rooms in the gatehouse are closer to the road and therefore a bit noisier.

In the dining room an attentive staff serves an adventurous, seasonal menu that might include grilled citrus-marinated duck breast with roasted beet coulis or angel hair pasta with fresh mushrooms and marinara sauce. ♲ *21 double rooms with baths. Restaurant; air-conditioning, TV in most rooms, phone in rooms, sauna, steam room, meeting room. $90–$195; Continental breakfast. AE, D, DC, MC, V. No smoking.*

WILDFLOWER INN ☜
Darling Hill Rd., Lyndonville 05851, tel. 802/626–8310 or 800/627–8310, fax 802/626–3039

Nearly every room in one of the inn's four buildings gets a piece of the 500 acres of incredible views. Sitting atop a long ridge that affords panoramic vistas in every direction, this rambling complex of old buildings—which date from 1796—was a working dairy farm until innkeepers Mary and Jim O'Reilly bought it in 1985. Guest rooms in the restored Federal-style main house, as well as in the carriage houses, are decorated simply with both reproductions and contemporary furnishings; some have their own porch. The most spacious rooms are suites called the Meadows, situated in what used to be the blacksmith shop. The inn is family oriented in every respect, with a petting barn, planned children's activities, a children's room that even has dress-up clothes, and a kids' swimming pool. In winter the place quiets down and caters more to cross-country skiers. Meals feature hearty, country-style food, with homemade breads and vegetables from the garden. ♲ *10 double rooms with baths, 11 suites. Restaurant, game room, children's playroom, pool, hot tub, sauna, hiking and cross-country ski trails, pony and sleigh rides, skating, tennis court, batting cage, petting barn. $110–$250; full breakfast, afternoon tea. MC, V. 2-night minimum weekends.*

WILLARD STREET INN ☜
349 S. Willard St., Burlington 05401, tel. 802/651–8710 or 800/577–8712, fax 802/651–8714

In 1996 innkeepers Beverly and Gordon Watson purchased this home built for a state senator circa 1880. High in Burlington's historic hill section, this grand house incorporates elements of Queen Anne and Colonial Georgian styles. The stately foyer is paneled in cherry and leads to a formal sitting room with velvet drapes. The solarium has marble floors, myriad plants, and big velvet couches to relax on while you contemplate the views of Lake Champlain. Both rooms have pianos. Some guest rooms have views of the lake and canopy beds; all have antiques and down comforters.

After breakfast—perhaps of baked orange French toast in a triple sec glaze—in the dining room, you can stroll down the exterior marble staircase for a walk in the English gardens. The inn's off-site restaurant, Isabel's, is a short distance away on the waterfront. ♨ *7 double rooms with baths, 8 doubles share baths. Cable TV and phone in rooms. $75–$200; full breakfast, afternoon tea. AE, D, MC, V. No smoking.*

OTHER CHOICES

Black Lantern Inn. Rte. 118, Montgomery Village 05470, tel. 802/326–4507 or 800/255–8661, fax 802/326–4077. 10 double rooms with baths, 6 suites. Restaurant, bar, TV/VCR in some rooms, whirlpool bath in suites, cross-country skiing and hiking nearby. $85–$145, full breakfast. AE, D, MC, V. No smoking.

Fox Hall Inn. Rte. 16, Barton 05822, tel. 802/525–6930, fax 802/525–1185. 4 double rooms with baths, 4 doubles share 3 baths. Hiking and cross-country ski trails, canoes, paddleboat. $60–$90; full breakfast, afternoon snacks. MC, V. No smoking, 2-night minimum during foliage season.

Gables Inn. 1457 Mountain Rd., Stowe 05672, tel. 802/253–7730 or 800/422–5371, fax 802/253–8989. 17 double rooms with baths, 2 suites. Restaurant, air-conditioning in rooms, TV in some rooms and public area, hot tub, pool. $65–$200; full breakfast. AE, MC, V. No smoking.

Inn on the Common. On the common, Rte. 14, Craftsbury Common 05827, tel. 802/586–9619 or 800/521–2233, fax 802/586–2249. 16 double rooms with baths, 1 suite. TV/VCR in living room, pool, tennis court. $220–$280, MAP; $15 charge per pet. AE, MC, V. 2-day minimum during foliage season.

RESERVATIONS SERVICES

Stowe Area Association (Box 1230, Stowe 05672, tel. 800/247–8693). **Sugarbush Reservations** (tel. 800/537–8427). **Vermont Centerpoint Reservation Service** (Box 8513, Essex 05451, tel. 802/872–2745 or 800/449–2745).

VIRGINIA

Northern Virginia

ASHBY INN & RESTAURANT ☜
692 Federal St., Paris 20130, tel. 540/592–3900, fax 540/592–3781

West of Middleburg and Upperville along U.S. 50, the turnoff for minuscule Paris may surprise unwary motorists; half the travelers looking for this hamlet in a hollow below the road probably miss it completely and end up crossing Ashby Gap or the Shenandoah River. At the Ashby's restaurant, visitors are treated to some of rural Virginia's most sophisticated food, masterminded by innkeepers Roma and John Sherman. The menu changes seasonally; crab cakes, game-bird potpie, and venison prepared any number of ways reign as favorites. Dinner runs about $70 for two.

Perhaps the only danger in staying at the inn is that dinners leave many guests too blissfully comatose to appreciate their rooms. There are six in the main building and four in the adjacent former schoolhouse. Those in the main building are all furnished with a spareness that is a calming contrast to the rich food. Quilts, blanket chests, rag rugs, and the occasional cannonball bed set the country tone, though in every case, the views are the chief enhancement. As morning light shines through the windows, some guests may feast anew upon the garden, Blue Ridge foothills, lowing cows, and other pastoral delights. The coveted Fan Room has four skylights and a glorious fan window opening onto a balcony.

The four expansive rooms in the former one-room schoolhouse are top-of-the-line and excellent values. Each has a private porch that opens onto those splendid countryside views. The Glascock Room has deep red walls, a canopied four-poster bed, and an antique trunk with extra towels. Oriental rugs cover the many hardwood floors, though some are carpeted, and there are two sinks in each large bathroom. Two wing chairs facing the fireplace and a window seat are inviting places for curling up with a book.

Roma and John take a tag-team approach to serving and mingling with guests during breakfast, which usually consists of eggs cooked to order and muffins. Roma, an avid equestrian, left advertising for innkeeping. John, once a House Ways and Means Committee staffer and speechwriter, now tends the garden, where he grows seasonal herbs and vegetables for the restaurant. Between stints as the inn's maître d' he even hunts some of the fowl used in the restaurant's potpies. ♨ *8 double rooms with baths, 2 doubles with sinks share 1½ baths. Restaurant (closed for dinner Sun.–Tues., open for Sun. brunch), air-conditioning, TV, phone, and fireplaces in schoolhouse rooms. $100–$220; full breakfast. MC, V. No smoking in bedrooms. Closed Jan. 1, July 4, and Dec. 24–25.*

BAILIWICK INN 🍃
4023 Chain Bridge Rd., Fairfax 22030, tel. 703/691–2266 or 800/366–7666,
fax 703/934–2112

As visitors to the Bailiwick, Annette and Bob Bradley fell in love with the inn, and when it went on the market they spontaneously bought it. They've given the dining room a French-American flair but retained the Bailiwick's historic theme, befitting its location on one of the nation's oldest roads, across the street from the courthouse where George Washington's will is filed.

Each room in the 19th-century house honors a famous Virginian in portraits, accessories, and biographies. The window treatment and red-and-gold scheme in the Thomas Jefferson room mimic the decor of his bedroom in Monticello. The sumptuous Antonia Ford suite, named for a Confederate spy, has dormer windows, a Chippendale sitting room, and a bath with whirlpool tub. All rooms have plump feather beds and goose-down pillows.

There are two elegant parlors for lounging by the fire or taking afternoon tea. Guests staying here can head west to the countryside or hop the Metro going into the nation's capital. △ *13 double rooms with baths, 1 suite. Restaurant, air-conditioning, cable TV and phone in rooms, fireplace in parlors and 4 rooms, whirlpool bath in 2 rooms, turndown service. $140–$310; full breakfast, afternoon tea. AE, MC, V. No smoking indoors.*

INN AT LITTLE WASHINGTON 🍃
Middle and Main Sts., Washington 22747, tel. 540/675–3800, fax 540/675–3100

In 1978, in a village of 160 people an hour and a half west of Washington, D.C., master chef Patrick O'Connell and his partner, Reinhardt Lynch, opened a restaurant that grew into a legend, attracting guests from all over the world to these eastern foothills of the Blue Ridge. From the outside, the three-story white-frame building looks like any other quiet southern hotel; only the Chinese Chippendale balustrade on the second-floor porch suggests the decorative fantasy within. The garden, with crabapple trees, fountain, and fishpond, cries out to be used as a stage backdrop.

The rich interior of the inn is the work of British designer Joyce Conway-Evans, who has designed theatrical sets and rooms in English royal houses. The settees in the inn bear as many as 13 elegantly mismatched pillows each. One bedroom has a bed with a bold plaid spread, shaded by a floral-print half-canopy—and, amazingly, the mélange works. In the slate-floor dining room with William Morris wallpaper, a fabric-swathed ceiling makes guests feel like pashas romantically sequestered in a tent.

A room and a suite in the guest house across the street are good for two couples traveling together, but they lack the sumptuousness of the main building. At press time, the kitchen was being expanded and two junior suites were being added over it.

Chef O'Connell's food appears to cast a spell over those who sample it, as the abundant positive reviews testify. The menu, which changes nightly, makes compelling reading; the seven-course dinner costs $108 per person on Saturday, $98 Friday, and $88 Sunday and weekdays, not including wine and drinks. Some rare vintages rest in the 14,000-bottle cellar, representing more than 900 selections.

Breakfast, served overlooking the courtyard garden, is far above the usual Continental fare. Miniature pastries and muffins are tucked in a basket alongside tasty croissants; raspberries glisten in large goblets. Those not still sated from dinner can order, for $18, a full breakfast—a lobster omelet with rainbow salsa and a baked Irish oatmeal soufflé with rum-soaked currants.

Clearly the inn, with its staff of 50, is a place for indulgence, and anyone unwilling to succumb to it—both psychologically and financially—should opt for humbler digs. But the waiting list alone suggests there are plenty of hedonists out there. △ *9 double rooms with baths, 5 suites. Room service, air-conditioning and phones in rooms, fireplace in entrance lobby and 1 suite, robes, turndown service, whirlpool bath and separate double showers in suites, in-room safes, bicycles. $260–$720; Continental breakfast, afternoon tea. MC, V. No smoking in dining room. Closed Dec. 25 and Tues. except in May and Oct.*

L'AUBERGE PROVENÇALE ☜
Rte. 340 (Box 119), White Post 22663, tel. 540/837–1375 or 800/638–1702, fax 540/837–2004

Fourth-generation chef Alain Borel and his wife, Celeste, have brought the romance, personal touches, and fine dining of a French country inn to tiny White Post, an hour and a half west of the Beltway. This 1753 stone house is set on 8½ acres and is surrounded by rolling pastureland. Inside are the Borels' special accents: Alain's great-grandmother's copper pots in the dining room, provincial prints in the guest rooms, whimsical carved carousel animals, painted tiles, and art by Picasso, Buffet, and Dufy.

Don't fill up on the plate of fresh fruit, chocolate, and homemade cookies that welcomes you to your room; instead, save your appetite for the five-course prix-fixe dinner ($57). The menu changes monthly to take advantage of seasonal produce. In spring, it may include La Truite Shenandoa—Shenandoah mountain trout with sesame seed batter, fresh local Blue Ridge Morel mushrooms, tomato *concasse*, and tarragon. Celeste, who handles the wine, has assembled a 250-selection list, plus the captain's list, with rare vintages for the connoisseur. Breakfast in the sunny, bay-windowed, peach-colored dining room starts with a mix of tangerine and orange juice and is followed by such delicacies as fresh fruit, rich croissants, poached egg in phyllo cups, applewood smoked bacon, and house-cured smoked salmon.

If you ask, a bit of Borel magic can accompany you in the form of a picnic basket (tablecloth, fruit, cheese, sandwiches, salads, chocolates, and wine) to be savored in some nook along Skyline Drive or at one of the local wineries. Alain's particularity extends to his gardens, where he fusses over herbs and vegetables grown from seeds imported from France or one of the 54 fruit trees, including such exotics as Asian pears, persimmons, and kiwis.

Celeste is as deft a decorator as she is a wine selector. The four rooms in the new wing are furnished with the fabrics and colors of Provence, accented by hand-painted Spanish tiles; they have fireplaces and private entrances opening onto the gardens. Room 9, the Chambre des Amis, features a canopy bed, cheery yellow and blue prints, and windows facing two directions. For lazy hours with a book or for just views of the countryside, the large private deck off Room 7 in the main house is perfect. △ *8 double rooms with baths, 3 suites. Restaurant (closed Mon.–Tues.), air-conditioning, TV in suite, phone jacks in 3 rooms, fireplace in 6 rooms, living room, and dining room. $125–$275; full breakfast. AE, D, DC, MC, V. Inn closed Jan.*

RED FOX INN ℞

*2 East Washington St., Middleburg 20118, tel. 540/687–6301 or 800/223–1728,
fax 540/687–6053*

This former tavern, built by Joseph Chinn in 1728 on the estate of Lord Fairfax, became a popular frontier stopping point for westward-bound colonists and later helped Middleburg grow into its role as the center of Virginia fox-hunt country. It still holds the charm and much of the rustic appeal that attracted a young surveyor named George Washington for a stay some 250 years ago. Too bad for the nation's first president that he was unable to enjoy one of the many four-poster beds with lace canopy, air-conditioning, and other modern appointments available in every room. The original building, an impressive three-story field-stone structure in the middle of town, has just 6 rooms; the rest of the inn's 24 rooms are scattered in seven additional historic buildings over a two-block area.

During the Civil War, when the Red Fox Inn (formerly a frontier tavern, built in 1728 and known as the Ordinary) was known as the Beveridge House, it saw action as a Confederate headquarters and hospital. Confederate general Jeb Stuart held strategy sessions in the guest room named in his honor. In the main building, exposed wide-plank floors slope and creak a bit—lest guests forget the stories they could tell. Homemade chocolates and two bottles of complimentary wine—one red, one white, and both from local vineyards—greet guests in every room. Those in search of a romantic hideaway will enjoy the Belmont Suite (1½ blocks from the main building) with its two walls of pane-glass windows overlooking manicured shrubs and a garden area. There's even a grand piano in the Belmont's spacious living room.

The inn serves up country breakfasts (for an extra charge; Continental breakfast is included in rate), lunches, and dinners in the Red Fox Restaurant. You can't miss the restaurant—its greeting stand doubles as the lodging's registration area. ⌂ *13 double rooms with baths, 11 suites. Air-conditioning, phone in rooms, 6 fireplaces (gas or electric), robes. $135–$245; Continental breakfast. AE, D, DC, MC, V. Smoking in designated public areas only, 3 no-smoking rooms.*

OTHER CHOICES

Bleu Rock Inn. 12567 Lee Hwy., Washington 22747, tel. 540/987–3190 or 800/537–3652, fax 540/987–3193. 5 double rooms with baths. Restaurant, air-conditioning, fireplace in dining rooms and lounge. $109–$195; full breakfast. AE, D, DC, MC, V. No smoking. Closed Mon.–Tues. and Dec. 24–25.

Morrison House. 116 S. Alfred St., Alexandria 22314, tel. 703/838–8000 or 800/367–0800, fax 703/684–6283. 42 double rooms with baths, 3 suites. 2 restaurants, air-conditioning, cable TV and phone in rooms, robes, turndown service. $150–$295; Continental breakfast, seasonal afternoon tea. AE, DC, MC, V. Smoking on 1 floor and in the Grill only.

Norris House Inn. 108 Loudoun St. SW, Leesburg 20175, tel. 703/777–1806 or 800/644–1806, fax 703/771–8051. 6 double rooms share 3 baths. Air-conditioning, phone jacks in rooms, fireplace in 3 rooms, robes, turndown service. $75–$145; full breakfast, evening refreshments on weekends. AE, D, DC, MC, V. Smoking on veranda only, 2-night minimum weekends Apr.–Dec.

Richard Johnston Inn. 711 Caroline St., Fredericksburg 22401, tel. 540/899–7606. 6 double rooms with baths, 2 suites. Air-conditioning, cable TV in 3 rooms. $95–$145; Continental breakfast. AE, MC, V. No smoking.

Sycamore Hill. 110 Menefee Mountain La., Washington 22747, tel. 540/675–3046. 3 double rooms with baths. Air-conditioning, TV in living room and 1 room, fireplace in living room, turndown service. $115–$165; full breakfast, after-

noon refreshments. MC, V. No smoking indoors, 2-night minimum holiday and
May weekends and Oct.

RESERVATIONS SERVICES

Blue Ridge Bed & Breakfast Reservation Service (Rocks & Rills Farm,
Rte. 2, Box 3895, Berryville 22611, tel. 540/955–1246 or 800/296–1246).
Princely Bed & Breakfast Reservation Service (819 Prince St., Alexandria
22314, tel. 800/470–5588). For a copy of the **Bed and Breakfast Association of Virginia**'s directory, call the **Virginia Division of Tourism**'s B&B line
(tel. 800/262–1293). The **Virginia Tourism Corporation**'s Washington, D.C., office also operates a B&B and small-inn booking service (tel. 202/659–5523; 800/
934–9184 outside DC).

The Eastern Shore

CAPE CHARLES HOUSE 🐚
645 Tazewell Ave., Cape Charles 23310, tel. 757/331–4920, fax 757/331–4960

This 1912 Colonial Revival frame house, with its spacious wraparound front porch,
is one of Cape Charles's largest and most opulent inns. Innkeepers Carol and Bruce
Evans, who renovated the inn in 1994, quickly learned how to make their guests
feel pampered, from the soft classical music in the parlor to gourmet and heart-
healthy breakfasts. Carol credits a fellow innkeeper with persuading the Evanses
to move from Chesapeake to join the reawakening of what she calls "this jewel
of a town."

Rooms, named after prominent people in Cape Charles's history, are furnished
with antiques, unusual collectibles, and family items, such as furniture painted
by Carol's mother. The tiniest room is named after Alexander Cassatt, former
vice president of the local railroad and brother of artist Mary Cassatt, whose works
are featured here. The Julia Wilkins Room has a whirlpool and private balcony.

Carol is writing a cookbook of breakfast, lunch, and dinner specialties; she teaches
cooking classes and serves five-course dinners (about $100 per couple). **♦** *5 dou-
ble rooms with baths. Air-conditioning, cable TV in parlor, ceiling fan, whirlpool
tub in 1 room, beach chairs, bicycles. $80–$105; full breakfast, afternoon refreshments. AE, D, MC, V. Smoking on porch only.*

CHANNEL BASS INN 🐚
*6228 Church St., Chincoteague 23336, tel. 804/336–6148 or 800/221–5620,
fax 804/336–1342*

The Channel Bass Inn occupies one of Chincoteague's oldest buildings, a pale-
lemon structure built in the 1880s and added onto in the 1920s. The inn, just
off Main Street, got a face-lift in 1996 and is a more welcoming destination than
ever. It is under the command of David Wiedenheft and his wife, Barbara, who
also manage the successful Miss Molly's (*see below*), just a stone's throw away.

The six guest rooms, located on the second and third floors, are extremely large
and open onto airy seating areas. None of them share a common hall, so they
are all very quiet. Rooms and halls abound with original artwork. Ceramic tile
baths meet the expectations of formal decor set by the inn's neat peach-and-
green facade. One self-contained suite offers all the space more privacy-conscious

guests could seek, along with its own mini-refrigerator. The comfortable front sitting rooms downstairs make pleasant space for reading. ⌂ *5 double rooms with baths, 1 suite. Air-conditioning. $89–$175; full breakfast. No smoking, 2-night minimum weekends, 3-night minimum holidays, and 4-night minimum during Pony Penning.*

GARDEN AND THE SEA INN ☙

4188 Nelson Rd., New Church 23415, tel. 757/824–0672; 800/824–0672 outside VA

The Garden and the Sea Inn sits on a quiet lane near Route 13, the main thoroughfare along the Eastern Shore, in tiny New Church, just 1½ mi south of the Maryland border and 15 minutes from Chincoteague. The main house of the inn is composed of the 1802-built Bloxom's Tavern and its 1901 addition. A few years ago New Church's oldest farmhouse, dating from the mid-19th century, was moved onto the property. It's now the Garden House, with a parlor where guests can relax with sherry, apples, and brownies; an inviting wide porch; and three guest rooms.

In 1994 Sara and Tom Baker bought the inn because they wanted to be in business together. After looking at properties from Pennsylvania to Florida, the newly married couple visited this property, and Tom said, "Let's do it."

Although it has less of the feel of a little French inn than the previous owners imparted (mainly because of a more American slant on the menu), the Garden and the Sea is still a sophisticated, inviting place to stay. The decor mixes antique furnishings, French wicker, Oriental rugs, ballooning fabrics, Victorian moldings and detail, and bay windows. From the multicolored gingerbread trim on the wide front porch to the sunny, rose-hued dining room, it's exceptionally appealing. Guest rooms are spacious. In the main house, the Chantilly Room, with a wicker sleigh bed and painted dresser, and the Giverny Room, with floral prints and dark-green lacquered wrought-iron furniture, have large baths with double sinks and bidets. The large, private Champagne Room in the Garden House has a two-person whirlpool tub and shower and a wrought-iron canopy bed.

Tom, who has been the chef at top Washington hotels and the Williamsburg Inn, creates dinners featuring produce from local farms and fresh fish from nearby waters in menus that change every three weeks. There are two fixed-price menus, as well as à la carte choices (entrées run about $14–$21). Specialties include a sea scallop, shrimp, and oyster dish and Tom's outstanding soups. The mainly self-serve buffet breakfast, a bit of a letdown after the excellent dinner, is available in the dining room or—when weather permits—in the garden patio beside the lily pond and fountain. ⌂ *6 double rooms with baths. Restaurant, air-conditioning, ceiling fans, robes, whirlpool bath in 4 rooms. $75–$175; Continental breakfast, afternoon refreshments. AE, D, MC, V. Smoking on open porches only, 2-night minimum weekends. Closed Dec.–mid-Mar.*

INN AT POPLAR CORNER AND THE WATSON HOUSE ☙

4240 Main St. (Box 905), Chincoteague 23336, tel. 757/336–6115 or 800/336–6787, fax 757/336–5776

As more and more tourists discover Chincoteague, proprietors Tom and Jacque Derrickson are watching the path to the doors of their twin locations on Main Street become more well trod. Newly opened over the last six years, these structures, which sit astride the intersection with quiet Poplar Street, deceptively look as though they date from the same era. The Watson House, for architecture buffs, is the real McCoy (dating from the 1890s), but the more elaborately decorated Inn, inspired by a Victorian in Suffolk, Virginia, is of 1995 vintage. Guests at both benefit from the warm, attentive hospitality of Jacque and co-owner JoAnne Snead and the thoroughness of innkeeper Karen Mason.

The Watson House offers country Victorian furnishings and a claw-foot tub in the Bayview Room. The Inn at Poplar Corner features all Victorian decor, with oak and walnut head- and footboards and a private balcony in Room 1. Operation of the B&Bs is a shared responsibility for the Derricksons and co-owners JoAnne and husband David Snead. Tom and David are natives of the island and, over generous breakfasts and refreshments either at the long antique dining table or on the side porch, may be eager to share stories of growing up among the wild ponies. ▲ *10 double rooms with baths. Air-conditioning, whirlpool tub in 4 rooms, balcony in 1 room, beach chairs and towels, bicycles. $69–$149; full breakfast, afternoon refreshment. MC, V. Smoking on veranda only, 2-night minimum weekends, 3- or 4-night minimum some holiday weekends. Closed Dec.–Mar.*

OTHER CHOICES

Island Manor House. 4160 Main St., Chincoteague 23336, tel. 757/336–5436 or 800/852–1505, fax 757/336–1333. 6 double rooms with baths, 2 doubles share 1 bath. Air-conditioning, bicycles. $70–$130; full breakfast, afternoon tea. AE, MC, V. Smoking in courtyard only, 2-night minimum weekends, 3-night minimum holidays.

Miss Molly's Inn. 4141 Main St., Chincoteague 23336, tel. 757/336–6686 or 800/221–5620, fax 757/336–1342. 5 double rooms with baths, 2 doubles share 1 bath. Air-conditioning, clock radio in rooms, woodstove in dining room, beach equipment, bicycles. $69–$155; full breakfast, afternoon tea. D, MC, V. No smoking, 2-night minimum weekends, 3-night minimum holiday weekends. Closed Jan.–Mar. 15.

Nottingham Ridge. 28184 Nottingham Ridge La., Cape Charles 23310, tel. 757/331–1010. 3 double rooms with baths, 1 suite. Air-conditioning, TV/VCR in den and suite, beach. $85–$130; full breakfast, afternoon refreshments. No credit cards. No smoking.

Pickett's Harbor. 28288 Nottingham Ridge La., Cape Charles 23310, tel. 757/331–2212. 3 double rooms with baths, 2 doubles share 1 bath. Air-conditioning, TV/VCR in family room, fireplace in family and dining rooms, bicycles. $80–$130; full breakfast. No credit cards. Smoking on porch only, 2-night minimum holiday weekends.

Spinning Wheel Bed and Breakfast. 31 North St., Onancock 23417, tel. 757/787–7311, fax 757/787–8555. 5 double rooms with baths. Air-conditioning, wood-burning stove in living room, bicycles. $75–$95; full breakfast. D, MC, V. No smoking indoors. Closed Thanksgiving.–Apr.

RESERVATIONS SERVICES

Amanda's Bed & Breakfast Reservation Service (1428 Park Ave., Baltimore, MD 21217, tel. 410/225–0001). **Bed & Breakfast of Tidewater Virginia Reservation Service** (Box 568, Norfolk 23501, tel. 757/627–1983). For a copy of the **Bed and Breakfast Association of Virginia**'s directory, describing more than 100 establishments, call the **Virginia Division of Tourism**'s B&B line (tel. 800/262–1293).

Williamsburg and the Peninsula

EDGEWOOD ☞

4800 John Tyler Memorial Hwy., Charles City 23030, tel. 804/829–2962 or 800/296–3343

Says frothy innkeeper Dot Boulware in her liquid southern accent, "I have to tell you, I am a romantic." And so is Edgewood—three marriage proposals were made in one week here. But before she and her husband, Julian, bought Edgewood Plantation, on scenic Route 5 approximately half an hour from Colonial Williamsburg, in 1978, she didn't care a bit for Victoriana. Fortunately tastes change, and when she became the mistress of an 1849 Carpenter Gothic house, she began collecting Victorian antiques like a woman possessed.

Dot's eight-bedroom house, visible from Route 5, looks on the inside like Miss Havisham's dining room, minus the cobwebs. It is full to bursting with old dolls, antique corsets and lingerie, lace curtains and pillows, love seats, baby carriages, stuffed steamer trunks, mighty canopied beds, highboys, Confederate caps—the list goes on and on. At Christmastime she professionally decorates 18 trees and festoons the banister of the graceful three-story staircase with bows. Clearly, more is better at Dot Boulware's Edgewood.

In her hands, Victoriana is thoroughly feminine, even though in one chamber, the Civil War Room, she's tried to cater to the opposite sex, decorating with intimate details of men's 19th-century apparel. Large people of either sex will have a hard time moving freely in this wildly crowded bed-and-breakfast. Lizzie's Room, the favorite, has a king-size pencil-post canopy bed and a private bath with a double marble shower and claw-foot tub. The room enshrines the memory of a teenager who, Dot says, died of a broken heart when her beau failed to return from the Civil War. Prissy's Quarters, a large upstairs room in the main building, has a kitchen area.

Breakfast is served in the dining room by candlelight. The brick-walled, beam-ceilinged downstairs tavern is a cozy sitting area with a fireplace, backgammon board, TV, and popcorn machine. There are also fireplaces in the dining room, a kitchen, a tearoom, and three bedrooms. Outside there's an unrestored mill house dating from 1725, an antiques shop, gazebo, swimming pool, and formal 18th-century garden (which makes a delightful wedding setting). Edgewood is centrally located for touring the James River plantations. △ *6 double rooms with baths, 2 suites. Air-conditioning, TV/VCR in rooms, Jacuzzi in 1 room, satellite TV in downstairs tavern, tearoom, turndown service, pool. $125–$188; full breakfast, light afternoon refreshments. MC, V. Smoking on porch and patio only, 2-night minimum holiday weekends.*

LIBERTY ROSE ☞

1022 Jamestown Rd., Williamsburg 23185, tel. 757/253–1260 or 800/545–1825

Bed-and-breakfast keepers in Williamsburg are in something of a bind. Because all the historic buildings in town are owned by either the Williamsburg Foundation or the College of William and Mary, they can't offer travelers authentic Colonial accommodations. Some have Colonial-style decoration anyway, but others, like Sandi and Brad Hirz, owners of the Liberty Rose, have come up with different, imaginative solutions to the dilemma.

Sandi and Brad have a tremendously romantic story. They were just friends when Sandi decided to leave the West Coast to open a B&B in Williamsburg. Brad was helping Sandi house-hunt when they looked at a 1920s white clapboard and brick home a mile west of the restored district (on the road to Jamestown). Sandi bought it in five minutes. Then Brad started seriously courting her, but it was Sandi, and not the B&B, who inspired him. Now they run Williamsburg's most beguiling B&B, decorated à la nouvelle Victorian with turn-of-the-century touches.

Sandi, a former interior designer, has a special talent for fabrics and is responsible for the handsome tieback curtains, many-layered bed coverings, and plush canopies. The patterns are 19th-century reproductions. Brad has held up his end of the business by managing remodeling details. The bathrooms are particularly attractive: One has a floor taken from a plantation in Gloucester, a claw-foot tub, and an amazing freestanding, glass-sided shower. The sumptuous Suite Williamsburg has an elaborate carved-ball and claw-foot four-poster bed and a fireplace. (The parlor, too, has a fireplace.) Magnolia's Peach, upstairs, has a side room with a single twin feather bed. Each room has a TV with VCR and a collection of videos, and an amenities basket bulging with everything the traveler might need, from bandages to needle and thread. The furnishings are a fetching mix of 18th- and 19th-century reproductions and antiques. The latest romantic touch is two tree swings (one a two-seater) by the courtyard.

Liberty Rose sits on a densely wooded hilltop, and the lake on the William and Mary campus is within easy walking distance. A stroll at dusk may be hard to resist, since romance sets the tone here all year round. △ *1 double room with bath, 3 suites. Air-conditioning, phone and TV/VCR in rooms, turndown service. $135– $205; full breakfast, afternoon refreshments. AE, MC, V. No smoking indoors.*

NORTH BEND PLANTATION ☙
12200 Weyanoke Rd., Charles City 23030, tel. 804/829–5176 or 800/841–1479, fax 804/829–6828

Routinely, a stay at this Charles City County plantation begins with a tour of the house and grounds conducted by Ridgely Copland, a farmer's wife and a nurse (once named Virginia nurse of the year). Along the way Ridgely points out Union breastworks from 1864, wild asparagus, herds of deer, a swamp, and the wide James River. This is a well-maintained working farm, and the Coplands are salt-of-the-earth people striving to keep their 850 acres intact in the face of modern agricultural dilemmas.

North Bend, on the National Register of Historic Places and also a Virginia Historic Landmark, was built for Sarah Harrison, sister of William Henry Harrison, the ninth president, who died in office having served just one month. It's a fine example of the Academic Greek Revival style, a wide white-frame structure with a slender chimney at each corner. Built in 1819 with a classic two-over-two layout, large center hall, and Federal mantels and stair carvings, it was remodeled in 1853 according to Asher Benjamin designs. But beyond its architectural distinctions, North Bend is drenched in history. The Sheridan Room, the premier guest bedroom, represents both sides of the Civil War. It contains a walnut desk used by Union general Philip Sheridan, complete with his labels on the pigeonholes. A copy of his map was found in one of its drawers and is now laminated for guests' viewing. The room's tester bed belonged to Edmund Ruffin, the ardent Confederate who fired the first shot of the war at Ft. Sumter. The headboard is a reproduction; a Yankee cannonball in 1864 splintered its predecessor. The Federal Room has a new iron-and-brass bed.

Above all, though, at North Bend history means family. George Copland is the great-great-nephew of Sarah Harrison and the great-great-grandson of Edmund Ruffin. Family heirlooms are everywhere, as is the amazing collection of Civil War first editions, which make fascinating bedtime reading. There's an inviting upstairs wicker-furnished sunporch and a one-of-a-kind children's area with vintage toys. △ *4 double rooms with baths, 1 suite. Air-conditioning, TV in rooms, fireplace in 1 room, ceiling fans, robes, pool, tandem bicycles, croquet, horseshoes, badminton, volleyball. $115–$135; full breakfast, welcoming refreshments. MC, V. Smoking on porches only. Closed Thanksgiving and Dec. 25.*

OTHER CHOICES

Applewood. 605 Richmond Rd., Williamsburg 23185, tel. 757/229–0205 or 800/899–2753, fax 757/229–9405. 3 double rooms with baths, 1 suite. Air-conditioning, cable TV and fireplace in parlor. $90–$150. AE, MC, V. No smoking indoors, 2-night minimum holiday and special-event weekends.

Colonial Capital. 501 Richmond Rd., Williamsburg 23185, tel. 757/229–0233 or 800/776–0570, fax 757/253–7667. 4 double rooms with baths, 1 suite. Air-conditioning, cable TV/VCR in parlor and suite, turndown service, bicycles. $95–$150; full breakfast, welcoming drink. AE, D, MC, V. Smoking outside only, 2-night minimum during peak weekends.

Newport House. 710 S. Henry St., Williamsburg 23185, tel. 757/229–1775, fax 757/229–6408. 2 double rooms with baths. Air-conditioning, TV/VCR and videos in rooms, fireplace in living room. $140; full breakfast. No credit cards. No smoking indoors, 2-night minimum weekends and holidays.

War Hill Inn. 4560 Longhill Rd., Williamsburg 23188, tel. 757/565–0248 or 800/743–0248, fax 757/565–4550. 4 double rooms with baths, 1 cottage. Air-conditioning, cable TV in rooms, fireplace in parlor, whirlpool bath in cottage. $75–$120; full breakfast. MC, V. No smoking, 2-night minimum weekends.

RESERVATIONS SERVICES

Bensonhouse (2036 Monument Ave., Richmond 23220, tel. 804/353–6900). For a copy of the **Bed and Breakfast Association of Virginia**'s directory, describing more than 100 establishments, call the **Virginia Division of Tourism**'s B&B line (tel. 800/262–1293). The **Virginia Tourism Corporation**'s Washington, D.C., office also operates a B&B and small-inn booking service (tel. 202/659–5523; 800/934–9184 outside DC).

Piedmont
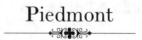

CLIFTON ✿

1296 Clifton Inn Dr., Charlottesville 22911, tel. 804/971–1800 or 888/971–1800, fax 804/971–7098

From the warm, paneled library and the comforter-covered beds to the sunny terrace and the languid lake, there are reasons aplenty to settle in here. One of the state's top inns, Clifton stands in quiet Shadwell, a small community in Charlottesville, near Jefferson's birthplace.

It's no wonder the inn is a National Historic Landmark: The handsome whiteframe, six-columned manse was once home to Thomas Mann Randolph, governor of Virginia, member of Congress, and husband of Thomas Jefferson's daughter,

Martha. It's now owned by a Washington attorney but ably administered by innkeeper Craig Hartman. As chef, Craig also oversees Clifton's wonderful meals (the applewood-smoked loin of veal with Vidalia-onion marmalade has lots of takers). Midweek dinners are $48; Saturday's five-course, prix-fixe dinners ($58) include entertainment.

There are guest rooms in the manor house, the carriage house, the livery, and Randolph's former law office. All have wood-burning fireplaces and antique or canopy beds. Six rooms have recently renovated large baths with multiple showerheads that grow vertically up the wall so no part of the body gets missed. French limestone floors were installed in all bathrooms. Some rooms have French windows, some have lake views, and there are plenty of antique bed-coverings. Rooms in the dependencies have a fresh, cottagelike feel, with whitewashed walls, bright floral prints, and lots of windows. Manor House rooms are bright and airy with touches of the original woodwork and design still intact to remind guests of the history that surrounds them. Suites in the carriage house have windows, shutters, and other artifacts from the home of the explorer Meriwether Lewis.

The grounds spread through 48 acres of woods. The 20-acre lake offers good fishing (the inn provides rods and tackle boxes) and lazy floats on inner tubes. Vines and slate stonework blend the swimming pool and heated spa tub into the bucolic setting. There's a clay tennis court, as well as croquet, volleyball, horseshoes, and badminton. For pure loafing, there are wooden chairs scattered across the lawns and a small gazebo. The extensive gardens are carefully tended: The estate grows its own flowers, lettuce, and herbs, many of which find their way into Craig's epicurean creations.

With fireplaces in common areas, Clifton offers a magical combination of elegance and hominess. It is rapidly gaining national attention for superbly attentive (but not hovering) guest service. A smiling staff member is always nearby, ready to assist guests with any needs they may have. A corner of the big butcher-block island in the kitchen is for guests, who often sit and chat with Craig as he cooks. A jar of cookies is always there, and sodas are in the refrigerator. Underneath the manor house is a newly installed wine cellar, complete with 220 varieties, and a formal tasting table. The tasting room, equipped with state-of-the art audiovisual equipment, can be used for small-group meetings. ♣ *7 double rooms with baths, 7 suites. Restaurant, air-conditioning, lake, pool, spa tub, tennis court. $150–$315; full breakfast, afternoon tea. MC, V. No smoking, 2-night minimum weekends.*

1817 HISTORIC BED & BREAKFAST ❦
1211 W. Main St., Charlottesville 22903, tel. 804/979–7353 or 800/730–7443, fax 804/979–7209

The 1817 Historic Bed & Breakfast is ideal for parents and alums visiting the University of Virginia, since the campus is just a block away. The Federal-style town house, built by James Dinsmore, one of Thomas Jefferson's craftsmen, was just the historic gem that interior designer Candace DeLoach was seeking when she came to the area in 1992. Raised in Savannah, with parents in the antiques business, Candace used her background in southern hospitality and decorating to create an eclectically furnished inn connected to her antiques shop.

Guest rooms include the room named for Miss Olive, a turn-of-the-century guest; another with a private marble bathroom and glassed-in shower; a small hall room (without windows), filled with Candace's grandmother's furniture; a white-paneled sleeping porch with two double white-metal beds; and a vast suite with yellow walls and a rose ceiling. The inn's small tearoom offers imaginative sandwiches, homemade soups, and Candace's prizewinning muffins. ♨ *4 double rooms with baths, 1 suite. Air-conditioning, cable TV in rooms, phone in 2 rooms and suite, tearoom, bicycles. $89–$199; Continental-plus breakfast, lemonade and tea on arrival. AE, MC, V. Smoking outdoors only, 2-night minimum on UVA-event weekends, 3-night minimum at graduation.*

HIGH MEADOWS AND MOUNTAIN SUNSET ☞

High Meadows La. (Rte. 4, Box 6), Scottsville 24590, tel. 804/286–2218 or 800/232–1832, fax 804/286–2124

High Meadows, which stands on 50 acres in Scottsville, is above all a bed-and-breakfast inn done by hand. The hands in question are those of Peter Shushka, a retired submariner, and his wife, Mary Jae Abbitt, a financial analyst.

In this unique B&B, Federal and late-Victorian architecture exist side by side, happily joined by a longitudinal hall. It wasn't always so. The Italianate front section was built in 1882 by C. B. Harris, who had intended to level the older house several paces behind it. But bearing in mind her growing family, his wife refused to give up the old place, built in 1830, and for a time a plank between the two was the tenuous connector that kept the marriage intact. Today High Meadows is on the National Register of Historic Places.

Peter and Mary Jae have decorated the place with great originality, keeping intact the stylistic integrity of each section. They've also used fabrics on the bed hangings and windows imaginatively. Fairview, in the 1880s portion, is the quintessential bride's room, with a fireplace, flowing bed drapery, a three-window alcove, and a claw-foot tub. The Scottsville suite, upstairs in the Federal section, has stenciled walls lined with antique stuffed animals, a fireplace, and rafters across the ceiling. A two-person whirlpool sits in the middle of the Music Room.

The Carriage House, also called Glenside, is a contemporary building of cedar, glass, and slate on the site of the original; this two-room suite has a kitchen, deck, and two-person outdoor hot tub. The property also includes the Mountain Sunset (named for its view), a 1910 Queen Anne manor house with two suites, two rooms, fireplaces, decks, and plenty of privacy.

Full country breakfasts may include strada (potato, cheese, and onion cooked together and served in a small bowl); Hungarian *bonitza*; or Amish pancakes. On Saturday, a six-course dinner is included in the room rate; during the week, dinner runs $20–$30 per person and includes wine. The inn has 5 acres of vineyards, which produce pinot noir grapes for its own private-label wine. ♨ *7 double rooms with baths, 7 suites. Air-conditioning, fireplace in 12 rooms and 2 common areas, robes, turndown service, whirlpool bath in 3 rooms. $84–$295; full breakfast, evening hors d'oeuvres and wine tasting Fri.–Sun. AE, D, MC, V. No smoking indoors, 2-night minimum all spring, fall, and holiday weekends. Closed Dec. 24–25.*

INN AT MEANDER PLANTATION ☞

U.S. Rte. 15 (Rte. 5, Box 460A), Locust Dale 22948, tel. 540/672–4912 or 800/385–4936, fax 540/672–0405

Even those already versed in the treasures of the Piedmont region may be guilty of a gasp when they visit the Inn at Meander Plantation, just off Route 15 about 10 mi north of Orange. The simple sign and whitewashed brick markers give little hint of the architectural jewel that comes into view at the top of the driveway. Located on an estate settled in 1727 by Joshua Fry, a map-making partner of Thomas Jefferson's father, the inn bears faithful testament to its Colonial origins, replete with slave quarters and summer kitchen.

Innkeepers Suzanne Thomas and Suzie Blanchard—both former newspaper people who, along with Blanchard's husband, Bob, run the establishment—offer a reliably warm welcome that has kept a host of visitors coming back regularly to this historic hilltop residence.

An ample parlor and dining area, an occasional low-slung hallway, and bedrooms notable for their high, roomy beds and large windows recall the days before electric light and central air, when natural assets had to be exploited. The series of outbuildings, including a stable, recalls the role that equestrian expertise has played in the area's history, both military and economic. The owners still keep horses on the property.

Another dependency, the summer kitchen, circa 1760s, separated from the main house by a shaded brick walkway decked out with an American boxwood hedge, features a two-story suite with a claw-foot tub and shower in the sunny bathroom upstairs. Here, as in any of the other spacious rooms, visitors can revel in the immense solitude the estate affords or contemplate the nearby attractions, a list of which the hosts provide at check-in. Located far beyond the reach of city lights and sounds, the inn has a wide back porch for those who want to savor the dusk, and brick paths for others who want to take the property's name at face value and wander off to enjoy the pristine view of the constellations. △ *3 double rooms with baths, 5 suite. Air-conditioning, fireplaces in 5 rooms and in living room of main building, TV in library piano, conference facilities, hiking, fishing, tubing, pony rides, stabling for horses, lawn games. $105–$195; full breakfast. No smoking.*

KESWICK HALL ☙
701 Club Dr., Keswick 22947, tel. 804/979–3440 or 800/274–5391, fax 804/977–4171

Visiting Keswick Hall is like spending a weekend with friends in the English countryside—that is, if those friends are very wealthy and live in a vast house with armies of antiques, plump chairs and couches, a butler to serve drinks, and a golf course in the backyard. Keswick sits on 600 acres in the wooded, rolling countryside east of Charlottesville. It's owned by Sir Bernard Ashley, who was married to the late Laura Ashley, so fabrics and furnishings from the company are used throughout. Tiny floral prints, though, do not dominate the place. Instead, fabrics, none of which are repeated, run the gamut from crisp stripes to elegant brocades. Sir Bernard's personal collection of antiques, century-old books, paintings, and silver-framed family photos gives the house the lived-in-for-generations look. An innkeeping colleague of Ashley's once said, somewhat in awe, that each interior door alone contains $1,000 worth of hardware.

Bedrooms are individually decorated in color schemes ranging from soft beige and white to crisp blues to cozy dark green. All have comfy chairs, couches, or cushioned window seats. Baths have extra touches, such as whirlpool tubs in six rooms, extra-long tubs in several others, heated towel racks, hair dryers, an abundance of thick towels, terry cloth robes, and dishes with cotton balls. Some rooms have private terraces with golf-course views, and several have decorative fireplaces.

Visitors want to loaf here, perhaps in front of a roaring fire on chilly days, lingering over coffee and the paper in the sunny morning room, having afternoon tea with delicate madeleines and scones in the yellow Crawford Lounge, or penning a letter at Sir Bernard's desk in the library. The all-red snooker room is the spot for predinner drinks and canapés and a late-night brandy, served by the friendly butler.

There's a full country breakfast with a wide range of choices in the Ashley room. Prix-fixe four- and five-course dinners are served there for $58.

Guests have access to the Keswick Club (a private facility with an Arnold Palmer–designed 18-hole golf course), fitness facilities, an indoor-outdoor pool, tennis courts, a croquet lawn, and a wood-paneled casual dining room. ♨ *45 double rooms with baths, 4 suites. Restaurants, air-conditioning, cable TV and phone in rooms, turndown service, conference facilities, tennis courts, golf course, massage, and fitness facility, bicycles, pool. $250–$595; full breakfast, afternoon tea. AE, DC, MC, V. No smoking in dining rooms.*

PROSPECT HILL ☞
2887 Poindexter Rd., Trevilians 23093, tel. 540/967–0844 or 800/277–0844, fax 540/967–0102

For elegance and luxury, Prospect Hill is one of Virginia's finest inns, lying just east of Charlottesville in the 14-square-mi Green Springs National Historic District. Built circa 1732, it's the oldest continuously occupied frame manor house in Virginia. But except for the obligatory dependencies and impressive boxwood hedges, Prospect Hill doesn't look like a plantation, because it was expanded in the Victorian era, when a columned facade and decorative cornices were added. The innkeepers have painted it lemony yellow.

Fresh flowers, a basket of fruit, and just-baked cookies welcome guests to their rooms. There are four nicely furnished rooms in the main house, but the big treat is the six refurbished dependencies. Sanco Pansy's cottage, 100 ft from the manor, has a sitting room and whirlpool tub for two. The carriage house, lit by four Palladian windows, offers views of ponies in the meadow nibbling the green Virginia turf. Surrounded by such *luxe, calme, et volupté,* it's strange to consider that in the last century, the dependencies were filled with hams, ice blocks, and livestock.

Dinner at the inn is a marvelous production, not so much for the cuisine (French-inspired and well above average) as for the ceremony. This begins with complimentary wine and cider a half hour before supper—outdoors in good weather. When the dinner bell rings, guests file in to hear the menu and an earnest grace recited by second-generation innkeeper Michael Sheehan, who recently took over after he and his father, Bill, had run the place together for years. Michael is also the chef and serves up excellent gourmet five-course dinners.

A hot breakfast arrives on a tray for guests wishing to stay ensconced in the dependencies. Some, however, crawl from the soothing whirlpool tub into the dining room. As splendid as the inn is, it hasn't become too smoothly professional. Even the most low-profile guest is liable to meet the gregarious innkeeper and appreciate the way his family has put its stamp on Prospect Hill.

Guests should get directions to the inn. It is several miles from Trevilians, the town where it receives mail. ♨ *5 double rooms with baths in manor, 5 doubles with baths and 3 suites in dependencies. Air-conditioning, fireplace in rooms, whirlpool in 8 rooms, clock radio in rooms, TV/VCR in meeting room, pool. $170–$345; MAP, dinner and breakfast; mid-week breakfast-only rates available. AE, D, DC, MC, V. 2-night minimum with Sat. stay. Closed Dec. 24–25.*

OTHER CHOICES

Holladay House. 155 W. Main St., Orange 22960, tel. 540/672–4893 or 800/358–4422, fax 540/672–3028. 4 double rooms with baths, 2 suites. Air-conditioning, cable TV in 3 rooms. $95–$195; full breakfast. AE, D, MC, V. No smoking, 2-night minimum weekends May, Oct.–Nov., and during graduations. Closed Thanksgiving, and Dec. 22–26.

Inn at Monticello. Hwy. 20 S, 1188 Scottsville Rd., Charlottesville 22902, tel. 804/979–3593, fax 804/296–1344. 5 double rooms with baths. Air-conditioning, fireplace in 2 rooms. $110–$140; full breakfast, afternoon refreshments. MC, V. No smoking, 2-night minimum some high-season weekends.

The Shadows. 14291 Constitution Hwy., Orange 22960, tel. 540/672–5057. 4 double rooms with baths, 2 cottage suites. Air-conditioning, gas-log fireplace in 1 cottage, turndown service. $80–$110; full breakfast, afternoon refreshments. MC, V. No smoking, 2-night minimum in May, some fall weekends, and holidays.

Silver Thatch Inn. 3001 Hollymead Dr., Charlottesville 22911, tel. 804/978–4686, fax 804/973–6156. 7 double rooms with baths. Restaurant, air-conditioning, clock radio in rooms, cable TV in bar. $115–$150; Continental breakfast. AE, DC, MC, V. No smoking, 2-night minimum weekends Apr.–mid-June and Sept.–mid-Nov. Closed Dec. 24–25.

Sleepy Hollow Farm. 16280 Blue Ridge Turnpike, Gordonsville 22942, tel. 540/832–5555 or 800/215–4804, fax 540/832–2515. 3 double rooms with baths, 1 2-bedroom suite, 1 cottage. Air-conditioning; TV in 3 rooms; kitchen, whirlpool, and fireplace in cottage; TV/VCR in sitting room; wood-burning stove in main house and 1 room; swimming pond; riding arranged. $65–$150; full breakfast, afternoon refreshments. MC, V. No smoking in dining room, 2-night minimum some weekends.

Tivoli. 9171 Tivoli Dr., Gordonsville 22942, tel. 540/832–2225 or 800/840–2225, fax 540/832–3691. 4 double rooms with baths. Phone in rooms, TV/VCR in reading room. $90–$125; full breakfast. D, MC, V. No smoking in rooms, 2-night minimum preferred on weekends.

200 South Street. 200 South St., Charlottesville 22902, tel. 804/979–0200 or 800/964–7008, fax 804/979–4403. 18 double rooms with baths, 2 suites. Air-conditioning, cable TV and phone in rooms, fireplace in 9 rooms, turndown service, whirlpool bath in 7 rooms. $105–$195; Continental breakfast, afternoon tea and wine. AE, DC, MC, V. No smoking in public rooms, 2-night minimum weekends Apr.–May and Sept.–Oct.

RESERVATIONS SERVICES

Guesthouses Bed & Breakfast, Inc. (Box 5737, Charlottesville 22905, tel. 804/979–7264) can arrange entrée to private houses that are otherwise closed to the public. For a copy of the **Bed and Breakfast Association of Virginia**'s directory, describing more than 100 establishments, call the **Virginia Division of Tourism**'s B&B line (tel. 800/262–1293). The **Virginia Tourism Corporation**'s Washington, D.C., office also operates a B&B and small-inn booking service (tel. 202/659–5523; 800/934–9184 outside DC).

The Blue Ridge/ Shenandoah Valley

JORDAN HOLLOW FARM INN ℱ

326 Hawksbill Park Rd., Stanley 22851, tel. 540/778–2285 or 888/418–7000,
fax 540/778–1759

As anyone who's traveled much in rural America knows, farms aren't always the idyllic-looking places about which city folk fantasize. However, this one comes close. Jordan Hollow Farm is situated on 150 acres in the middle of the scenic Shenandoah Valley at the base of the Blue Ridge range, with great views of the Massanutten Mountains. It is a restored Colonial working horse farm that has been given new life as a cozy, beautiful, and serene country inn. At the heart of the farm, amid maple trees, sits a 200-year-old farmhouse incorporating two hand-hewn log cabins and now known as the Farmhouse Restaurant.

Two of the proprietors, Gail Kyle and Betsy Anderson, run the place with a staff of 20. Guests can choose from the low-ceiling Farmhouse Room, 16 more in the Arbor View Lodge, and 4 upscale rooms in the Mare Meadow Lodge, which is built of hand-hewn logs. The last are carpeted and have fireplaces, quilts, cedar furniture, and whirlpool tubs. The old carriage house and corn crib have a new life as a gathering lounge known as the Great Room, whose antique couches and chairs, game tables, and a small library put guests at ease.

Half the guests here come to ride, half to savor the tranquillity. Every day, several equestrian groups (including beginners) leave the farm to wander over the foothills; youngsters go on pony rides. Guests can even bring their own horses; a stall is $15. Great hiking trails crisscross the property, and folks at the farm can direct guests to more trails in Shenandoah National Park or George Washington National Forest. Canoeing on the Shenandoah, caving, swimming, and golfing are also nearby.

The Farmhouse Restaurant has built a considerable reputation with locally grown ingredients. Chefs Julia Slye, an expert at regional American recipes, and Greg Scott ensure that Virginia wines and local microbrews remain staples of the menu. ⚓ *21 double rooms with baths. Restaurant, air-conditioning, cable TV in 8 rooms and Great Room, phones in rooms, fireplace in Great Room and 4 rooms, horseback riding. $110–$154. D, DC, MC, V. No smoking. 2-night minimum on holidays.*

TRILLIUM HOUSE ℱ

Wintergreen Dr., Wintergreen (Box 280, Nellysford), VA 22958, tel. 804/325–9126 or
800/325–9126 (reservations only), fax 804/325–1099

Guests from near and far alike have to hand it to Ed and Betty Dinwiddie. For the pair, building a bed-and-breakfast on the grounds of Wintergreen resort may have seemed the most natural thing in the world; after all, their family had vacationed there for years. But to skiers, refugees from the Blue Ridge Parkway, wildflower enthusiasts, and all-round mountain devotees, the idea was a stroke of genius. The fact that Trillium House lies across the road from the gargantuan sports complex, with its indoor pool, tennis courts, ski slopes, hiking trails, and golf course, should give prospective visitors a clue as to the activities available.

From Wintergreen's gate, a roller-coasterish road brings guests 3½ mi to the doorstep of Trillium House. The beige frame building fronted by a porch and a Palladian window, surrounded by trees and stylish condominiums owned by Wintergreen residents, was built in 1983. Entrance is through the Great Room, which is two stories high, near a staircase at the side leading to a loft library. The front sitting area has a wood-burning stove, above which hang several organ pipes; by the front door, a canister holds a collection of walking sticks. Breakfast is served in the dining rooms, with views of bird feeders and the backyard gazebo, and Friday and Saturday dinners (by reservation) are cooked by chef Ellen English, who formerly worked in one of Wintergreen's restaurants. The 12 guest rooms at Trillium House lie in two wings off the Great Room. Their architectural tone is slightly motelish, but decorative touches add some personality—here a quilt or a framed picture that could only have been created by one of the Dinwiddie brood, there a writing desk from the Homestead or a bed with a lace canopy.

The odds are that guests will spend most of their stay here pursuing varieties of R&R on the resort or ensconced in the Great Room, chatting with other guests or Ed and Betty, who manage to seem amazingly relaxed despite their demanding housekeeping duties. The single disappointment is that Trillium House doesn't have mountain views; those after such scenery will have to grab a stick and walk. △ *10 double rooms with baths, 2 suites. Air-conditioning, TV in rooms on request, phones in rooms, cable TV/VCR and movie collection in sitting room, turndown service. $95–$160; full breakfast. MC, V. No smoking, 2-night minimum weekends, 3-night minimum some holidays.*

OTHER CHOICES

Ashton Country House. 1205 Middlebrook Ave., Staunton 24401, tel. 540/885–7819 or 800/296–7819. 4 double rooms with baths, 1 suite. Air-conditioning, ceiling fan in rooms, fireplace in 4 guest rooms, dining and living room. $90–$125; full breakfast, afternoon refreshments. MC, V. No smoking indoors.

Belle Grae Inn. 515 W. Frederick St., Staunton 24401, tel. 540/886–5151, fax 540/886–6641. 9 double rooms with baths, 5 suites, 2 cottages. 2 restaurants, air-conditioning, cable TV and phone in 11 rooms, fireplace in 13 rooms and 3 common areas, turndown service, nearby health club. $85–$170; full breakfast. AE, MC, V. No smoking.

Chester House. 43 Chester St., Front Royal 22630, tel. 540/635–3937 or 800/621–0441 (reservations only), fax 540/636–8695. 5 double rooms with baths. Air-conditioning, ceiling fans, cable TV in lounges, fireplaces in 2 rooms and public rooms, robes, clock radios. $85–$180; Continental breakfast, afternoon refreshments. AE, MC, V. Smoking in TV lounge only, 2-night minimum some weekends.

Fassifern. Rte. 39 W (R.R. 5, Box 87), Lexington 24450, tel. 540/463–1013 or 800/782–1587. 5 double rooms with baths. Air-conditioning, ceiling fans, fireplace in living room. $84–$92; full breakfast. MC, V. No smoking. Closed Thanksgiving, Dec. 24–25, Dec. 31.

Fort Lewis Lodge. Rte. 625 (HCR3, Box 21A), Millboro 24460, tel. 540/925–2314, fax 540/925–2352. 8 double rooms with baths, 3 suites, 2 cabins. TV/VCR in game room, bicycles, hot tub. $145–$195; MAP. MC, V. No smoking in rooms. Closed mid-Oct.–Mar.

Inn at Gristmill Square. Rte. 619, Court House Hill Rd. (Box 359), Warm Springs 24484, tel. 540/839–2231, fax 540/839–5770. 16 double rooms with baths, 1 apartment. Restaurant, bar, air-conditioning, cable TV, phone and mini-refrigerator in rooms, fireplace in 8 rooms. $85–$140; Continental breakfast; MAP available. D, MC, V. Smoking in rooms and in the bar.

Inn at Narrow Passage. U.S. 11 S (Box 608), Woodstock 22664, tel. 540/459–8000 or 800/459–8002, fax 540/459–8001. 12 double rooms with baths. Air-conditioning, TV/VCR in sitting room, clock radios $95–$145; full breakfast, afternoon refreshments. D, MC, V. No smoking indoors, 2-night minimum in spring, fall, and holiday weekends. Closed Dec. 24–25.

Joshua Wilton House. 412 S. Main St., Harrisonburg 22801, tel. 540/434–4464 or 888/294–5866. 5 double rooms with baths. Restaurant, café, air-conditioning, phone in rooms, fireplace in 1 room. $95–$105; full breakfast. AE, D, DC, MC, V. Smoking in café bar and patio only, 2-night minimum some weekends. Closed Dec. 24–25.

Lavender Hill Farm. 1374 Big Spring Dr. (R.R. 1, Box 515), Lexington 24450, tel. 540/464–5877 or 800/446–4240. 2 double rooms with baths, 1 2-bedroom suite. Air-conditioning, ceiling fans, satellite TV/VCR in living room, horse boarding. $69–$115; full breakfast. MC, V. No smoking indoors, 2-night minimum on holidays, special-event weekends, and in May, Sept., and Oct.

Sampson Eagon Inn. 238 E. Beverley St., Staunton 24401, tel. 540/886–8200 or 800/597–9722. 3 double rooms with baths, 2 suites. Air-conditioning, cable TV/VCR and phone in rooms, fax, photocopying, turndown service. $94–$120; full breakfast, snacks and refreshments. AE, MC, V. No smoking indoors, 2-night minimum Apr.–Nov. and some holiday weekends.

Seven Hills Inn. 408 S. Main St., Lexington 24450, tel. 540/463–4715 or 888/845–3801, fax 540/463–6526. 6 double rooms with baths, 1 suite. Air-conditioning. $80–$125; full breakfast. AE, MC, V. No smoking in rooms, 2-night minimum some weekends.

Thornrose House. 531 Thornrose Ave., Staunton 24401, tel. 540/885–7026 or 800/861–4338. 5 double rooms with baths. Air-conditioning, cable TV in parlor, fireplace in dining room and parlor, turndown service, bicycles. $60–$80; full breakfast, afternoon refreshments. No credit cards. No smoking, 2-night minimum Oct. and May weekends.

RESERVATIONS SERVICES

Bed & Breakfasts of the Historic Shenandoah Valley (355 Orchard Dr., Mt. Jackson 22842-9753, tel. 540/477–2400 or 800/478–8714). **Virginia's Inns of the Shenandoah Valley** (Box 1387, Staunton 24401). For a copy of the **Bed and Breakfast Association of Virginia**'s directory, describing more than 100 establishments, call the **Virginia Division of Tourism**'s B&B line (tel. 800/262–1293). The **Virginia Tourism Corporation**'s Washington, D.C., office also operates a B&B and small-inn booking service (tel. 202/659–5523; 800/934–9184 outside DC).

WASHINGTON

Columbia River and Long Beach Peninsula

BIRCHFIELD MANOR ☞

2018 Birchfield Rd., Yakima 98901, tel. 509/452–1960 or 800/375–3420,
fax 509/452–2334

What is now Birchfield Manor, 2 mi outside Yakima, was once the headquarters of a sprawling, 15,000-acre sheep ranch. The scale of the property is considerably diminished these days, but the elegance of the 1910 manor house remains. If anything, things have improved at Birchfield with the arrival of chef and owner Will Masset.

Masset, who apprenticed in Switzerland, came with his wife, Sandy, and family to the Yakima Valley from Issaquah, where he taught classic cuisine. In addition to turning the ground floor into an award-winning restaurant, the Massets have greatly expanded the accommodations with a large guest cottage. Rooms in the new building have TVs and private-line telephones, and most have whirlpool tubs and private decks with panoramic views of the valley. There are fewer modern amenities in the original structure, but there's more old-house charm, with a sunporch in one room and corner bays in two others.

The Birchfield's dinner menu changes seasonally and may include king salmon in puff pastry, filet mignon, and rack of lamb; guests in the cottage can arrange to have dinner delivered to their room. The extensive wine list is particularly strong in wines of the Northwest. Breakfast involves a large country spread of quiche, meat and egg dishes, and fresh local fruit. The Massets have also turned the 1893 carriage house into a cigar lounge; with a refined interior and an array of wing chairs, it looks as though it were taken straight out of an exclusive private club. △ *11 double rooms with baths. TV and whirlpool bath in some rooms. Restaurant. $80–$175; full breakfast. AE, DC, MC, V. No smoking.*

SCANDINAVIAN GARDENS INN ☞

1610 California St., Long Beach 98631, tel. 360/642–8877 or 800/988–9277

When you enter the Scandinavian Gardens, innkeepers Rod and Marilyn Dakan will ask you to take off your shoes. It may have nothing to do with Scandinavian custom, but you can immediately see a practical reason—the white wool carpeting that covers the ground floor. The house is immaculate; there doesn't seem to be a single corner where even the most fastidious person wouldn't feel comfortable eating lutefisk off the floor.

The main common area, with its white carpet and blond-wood furnishings, is somewhat intimidating, but the colorful guest rooms easily compensate for it. On the main floor is the Icelandic Room, done in plums and greens, with an antique armoire and love seat and rosemaling on wall cabinet doors. The Danish Room, all blue and cinnamon tones, is decorated with hearts and nautical knickknacks. The Norwegian Room features greens and golds and a simple pine bed.

Upstairs, the teal and red Finnish Room offers such special touches as a skylight in the bath and an antique vanity. The main attraction here, however, is the Swedish Suite, done in soft pinks and light blues. The view is pedestrian—guests look out on the surrounding residential area—but inside there's a hot tub for two with an overhead skylight. The bedroom features a teak bed set, antique vanity, and a half-bath of its own.

Even if you haven't booked the honeymoon suite, you need not go without a hot soak: The recreation room offers a hot tub, sauna, and exercise equipment. You can also enjoy the games in the social room, which doubles as the dining area. Breakfast is a feast, including traditional creamed rice and fruit soup, granola, sorbet, pastries, and a hot entrée. ⌂ *4 double rooms with baths, 1 suite. Hot tub and mini-refrigerator in suite. Exercise room, hot tub, sauna, games room. $85–$140; full breakfast. D, MC, V. No smoking, 2-night minimum on holiday and local festival weekends.*

SHELBURNE INN ❦
4415 Pacific Way (Box 250), Seaview 98644, tel. 360/642–2442 or 800/466–1896, fax 360/642–8904

The Shelburne Inn, a green wood-frame building on the peninsula's main thoroughfare, is the oldest continuously run hotel in the state. Opened in 1896, the Craftsman-style inn joined to a late-Victorian building is owned by Laurie Anderson and David Campiche. David met Laurie—who had worked for a cruise line and traveled widely before settling here—when he helped pull her vehicle out of the sand.

The inn has a homey, country atmosphere. The lobby is somewhat cramped, with a seating area around a fireplace, a church altar as a check-in desk, a large oak breakfast table, and more. The original beaded-fir paneling, as well as large panels of Art Nouveau stained glass rescued from an old church in England, ise found throughout the inn. A new section, built in 1983, is quieter than the older sections, though the latter have been soundproofed and carpeted.

Fresh flowers, original artwork, and fine-art prints adorn the guest rooms, most of which have decks or balconies. Some rooms feature country pine furnishings, others mahogany or oak. Beds have either handmade quilts or hand-crocheted spreads. Some rooms are rather small, but the suites are spacious.

The Shelburne's breakfast is one of the top three, if not *the* best, in the state. David makes use of regional produce from wild mushrooms to local seafood, and Laurie does all the baking. You can choose from among five or six entrées, which may include an asparagus omelet or grilled oysters with salsa.

The highly regarded Shoalwater Restaurant, housed in the enclosed front porch, offers such elegant entrées as duck with dried cherry sauce. The wine list has more than 400 titles. The Heron and Beaver Pub serves light meals, along with the best concoctions from the Northwest's microbreweries. ⌂ *13 double rooms with baths, 2 suites. Restaurant, pub. $109–$179; full breakfast. AE, MC, V. No smoking, 2-night minimum on weekends and holidays.*

SOU'WESTER LODGE ☞
Beach Access Rd. (Box 102), Seaview 98644, tel. 360/642–2542

Just behind the sand dunes on the peninsula is this red-shingle, three-story inn. Make no mistake about it: The Sou'wester is not for everyone. Perhaps more than any other B&B in the state, it is an experience weighted as much by the unique character of the innkeepers as it is by the setting, a big old lodge built in 1892 as the country estate of Sen. Henry Winslow Corbett of Oregon.

Len and Miriam Atkins left their native South Africa in the early 1950s to work in Israel, then moved to Chicago to work with the late child psychologist Bruno Bettelheim. With the idea of establishing a treatment program on the West Coast for emotionally disturbed children, they spent six months in 1981 in a camper, scouting potential sites. Instead, they opted to help adults unwind from the stresses of daily life.

An unusual aspect of the Sou'wester is that it bills itself not as a B&B but as a B&MYODB (make your own darn breakfast), with kitchen access provided (but not food). Second- and third-story accommodations are suites with full kitchens and views of the Pacific. Guest rooms are furnished with the occasional antique but more often Salvation Army furniture, with marbleized linoleum floors; nicer touches are the handmade quilts or chenille bedspreads and artwork done by various artists while staying in that room.

Another slightly offbeat note that adds to the Sou'wester's charm is the collection of guest cabins and trailers scattered among the firs. The cabins are a bit more rustic than the guest rooms. Trailers feature handsome blond-wood interiors with lots of 1950s rounded corners. The Disoriented Express features an exterior mural of a train full of animal passengers. Tent and RV spots are also available. △ *3 double rooms share bath, 6 suites, 4 cabins, 15 trailers. Kitchens in suites, cabins, and trailers; cable TV on request in some units. $39–$119; no breakfast. D, MC, V. No smoking.*

TROUT LAKE COUNTRY INN ☞
15 Guler Rd., Trout Lake 98650, tel. 509/395–2898

In 1904, pioneers in the upper Trout Lake Valley built a large hall for community meetings. Since then the rustic western-style building, with its distinctive false front, has been everything from a post office to a bowling alley to a public bath house.

Whatever the incarnation, the building has always been the center of the small community of ranchers and farmers wedged up against the bulk of Mt. Adams about 25 mi north of the Columbia River. Since 1988, it has been a charming bed-and-breakfast run by Gil and Milly Martin. Besides catering to guests who may be on their way to a rigorous hike in the wilderness or a breezy drive around the northeast side of Mt. St. Helens, the Trout Lake Country Inn offers a restaurant, country store, soda fountain, dinner theater, and small video store for locals.

Straight past the soda fountain–cum–cash register–cum–registration desk lies the main hall. Across the stage up front is a hand-painted drop curtain emblazoned with "Trout Lake Art Players" in the style of old vaudeville acts. Gil writes his own plays, usually comedy revues or melodramas starring Milly.

Accommodations—two rooms upstairs and one in a nearby cabin—are simple and rustic. The pine walls are original, cut by a local mill at the turn of the century. The creekside cabin is a treat, built on top of the icehouse that once served the whole settlement. The cabin's deck provides perhaps the best view of Mt. Adams in the valley and is just above a swimming hole in the creek.

Served in the main hall, breakfast is a tasty collection of fresh fruit, huckleberry pancakes, and baked egg dishes. Besides the dinner theater, meals and snacks are also available to you from a small but diverse menu. ♨ *1 double room with bath, 1 suite, 1 cabin. Restaurant, soda fountain, dinner theater, gift shop. $55–$90; full breakfast. MC, V. No smoking.*

OTHER CHOICES

Bingen Haus. Box 818, Bingen 98605, tel. 509/493–4888, fax 509/493–2771. 6 double rooms share 2 baths. Hot tub. $65–$85; full breakfast. MC, V. No smoking.

Bradley House Bed & Breakfast. 61 Main St., Cathlamet 98612, tel. 360/795–3030 or 800/551–1691. 2 double rooms with baths, 2 doubles share bath. $75–$95; full breakfast, afternoon refreshments. MC, V. No smoking.

Borea's Bed & Breakfast Inn. 607 North Blvd., Long Beach 98631, tel. 360/642–8069 or 888/642–8069. 5 double rooms with baths. Whirlpool bath in 1 room. Private hot tub. $105–$135; full breakfast. AE, D, DC, MC, V. No smoking.

Caswell's on the Bay. 25204 Sandridge Rd., Ocean Park 98640, tel. 360/665–6535. 5 double rooms with baths. $95–$150; full breakfast, afternoon refreshments. D, DC, MC, V. No smoking.

Chick-a-Dee Inn at Ilwaco. 120 Williams St., Ilwaco 98624, tel. 360/642–8686 or 888/244–2523, fax 360/642–8642. 8 double rooms with baths, 1 suite. $76–$180; full breakfast. MC, V. No smoking, 2-night minimum for summer weekends and holidays.

Coast Watch Bed & Breakfast. Box 841, Ocean Park 98640, tel. 360/665–6774. 2 suites. $95; Continental-plus breakfast. MC, V. No smoking.

Farm Bed and Breakfast. 490 Sunnyside Rd., Trout Lake 98650, tel. 509/395–2488. 2 double rooms share bath. Robes in rooms. Bicycles, area tours. $70–$80; full breakfast, box lunches available. No credit cards. No smoking.

Flying L Ranch. 25 Flying L La., Glenwood 98619, tel. 509/364–3488 or 888/682–3267. 8 double rooms with baths, 2 doubles share 2 baths, 3 cabins. 2 common kitchens, bicycles, hot tub. $70–$110; full breakfast. AE, MC, V. No smoking.

Inn at White Salmon. 172 W. Jewett St., White Salmon 98672, tel. 509/493–2335 or 800/972–5226. 16 double rooms with baths. Air-conditioning, TV and phone in rooms. Hot tub. $99–$129; full breakfast. AE, D, DC, MC, V. No smoking in common rooms.

Kola House Bed & Breakfast. 211 Pearl Ave., Ilwaco 98624, tel. 360/642–2819. 4 double rooms with baths, 1 suite, 1 cabin. Fireplace and Finnish sauna in suite. $60–$75; full breakfast. MC, V. No smoking.

Land's End. Box 1199, Long Beach 98361, tel. 360/642–8268. 2 double rooms with baths. Cable TV in rooms. $95–$120; full breakfast. MC, V. No smoking.

Moby Dick Hotel and Oyster Farm. Sandridge Rd. (Box 82), Nahcotta 98637, tel. 360/665–4543, fax 360/665–6887. 1 double room with bath, 9 doubles share 5 baths. TV in common area. $75–$95; full breakfast. AE, MC, V. No smoking, 2-night minimum on summer weekends.

Sunnyside Inn. 800 E. Edison Ave., Sunnyside 98944, tel. 509/839–5557 or 800/221–4195, fax 509/839–5350. 9 double rooms with baths, 1 suite. Whirlpool bath in most rooms. $59–$89; full breakfast. AE, D, MC, V. No smoking.

Touch of Europe Bed and Breakfast Inn. 220 N. 16th Ave., Yakima 98902, tel. 509/454–9775 or 888/438–7073. 1 double room with bath, 2 doubles share bath. Library. $65–$110; full breakfast, lunch and dinner by arrangement. AE, MC, V. No smoking.

Wine Country Inn. 1106 Wine Country Rd., Prosser 99350, tel. 509/786–2855, fax 509/786–7414. 2 double rooms with bath, 2 doubles share bath. Restaurant. $65–75; full breakfast. AE, MC, V. No smoking.

RESERVATIONS SERVICES

Pacific Reservation Service (Box 46894, Seattle 98146, tel. 206/439–7677 or 800/684–2932). **Washington State Bed & Breakfast Guild** (Box 355-FD, 2442 N.W. Market St., Seattle 98107, tel. 800/647–2918).

Olympic Peninsula

ANN STARRETT MANSION ☞

744 Clay St., Port Townsend 98368, tel. 360/385–3205 or 800/321–0644, fax 360/385–2976

This improbably ornate Queen Anne in Port Townsend, painted in cream, teal, and rose, was built by George Starrett, a contractor, mortician, and sawmill owner, in 1889 at a cost of $6,000 as a wedding present for his wife, Ann. In 1996, it was awarded fourth place in the Great American Home Search sponsored by the National Trust for Historic Preservation.

You may find the almost museum quality of the mansion off-putting, but hosts Bob and Edel Sokol are low-key and friendly. Bob is a retired air force pilot and was navigator on *Air Force One* for President Jimmy Carter. Edel, a native of Germany, is an avid collector and baker.

The foyer—with a front desk handcrafted in Port Townsend when Washington was a territory—opens to a dramatic free-hung, three-tier spiral staircase of Honduran and African mahogany, English walnut, oak, and cherry. At the top is the eight-side tower dome, frescoed by George Chapman with allegorical figures of the four seasons and the four virtues. The dome was designed as a solar calendar: Sunlight coming through small dormer windows on the first days of each new season shines onto a ruby glass, causing a red beam to point toward the appropriate seasonal panel.

The Master Suite looks like a museum period room. Once the Starretts' master bedroom, it features Persian rugs, a Brussels tapestry tablecloth, an 1880 mahogany Eastlake bedroom suite, and a floral tapestry canopy that extends from the floor to the 12-ft ceiling. The Drawing Room has a little antique tin tub painted with cherubs and an 1860 Renaissance Revival mahogany bed. The contemporary Gable Suite offers a view of Puget Sound and the Cascades, as well as a two-person hot tub.

Breakfast, served in the elegant dining room, includes champagne, juice, New Orleans French toast stuffed with chocolate cream and berries and topped with a spirited berry sauce; homemade muffins, and German griddle cakes stuffed with apples and cinnamon. △ *8 double rooms with baths, 2 doubles share bath, 2 suites, 2 cottages. Hot soaking tub in 1 suite, whirlpool bath in 1 suite. $80–$185; full breakfast. AE, D, MC, V. No smoking, 2-night minimum on holiday and festival weekends.*

JAMES HOUSE ☞

1238 Washington St., Port Townsend 98368, tel. 360/385–1238 or 800/385–1238, fax 360/379–5551

The picture-perfect location—high atop a bluff, with sweeping views of Port Townsend's waterfront, the Cascade and Olympic mountains, and Puget Sound— is only one of the many striking features of the 1889 James House.

The gray wood-frame Queen Anne house, with gables, dormers, porches, and five redbrick chimneys, is one of Port Townsend's grandest Victorian accommodations. In an era when a large house could be built for $4,000, this one, with 8,000 square ft of living space, cost $10,000.

The entrance hallway, dominated by a hand-carved cherry staircase made from logs that came around Cape Horn, is a monument to fine woodworking. Like the two front parlors, the hall features original parquet floors in elaborate patterns of oak, walnut, and cherry. Breakfast is served in the large dining room or in the homey kitchen by the Great Majestic cookstove.

Years of restoration work preceded the house's 1973 opening as one of the first Northwest bed-and-breakfasts. It is furnished with period antiques (some original to the house), Oriental rugs, an antique player piano, and many beveled- and stained-glass windows. Four of the house's nine original fireplaces remain, with carved mantels and Minton tile framing.

Guest rooms are on three floors of the house and in the cottage out back. The house's master or bridal suite offers unsurpassed views, its own balcony, a sitting parlor, a fireplace, a private bath, and the original late-Victorian bed, armoire, and fainting couch. The cottage, which sleeps four, has lots of windows and a more contemporary feel.

Innkeeper Carol McGough, a health care professional, moved here from Boston in 1990. She enjoys tending the roses, daisies, geraniums, herbs, and other plants that spill out of the inn's gardens, as well as making potpourris for her guests. Breakfast includes fruit, scones or muffins, and soufflés or quiches, all made from fresh ingredients. ⚠ *7 double rooms with baths, 2 doubles with detached baths, 3 suites, 1 cottage, 1 bungalow. $75–$165; full breakfast. AE, MC, V. No smoking.*

MANOR FARM INN ☞

26069 Big Valley Rd. NE, Poulsbo 98370, tel. 360/779–4628, fax 360/779–4876

The Manor Farm Inn is an oasis of elegance and country charm just across Puget Sound from Seattle. Here, a classic 1886-vintage white clapboard farmhouse is the centerpiece of a 25-acre "gentleman's farm," complete with sheep, horses, donkeys, and other animals. Innkeeper Jill Hughes-Day, a former teacher, provides rods, flies, even floppy fishing hats for those who want to try their luck in the well-stocked trout pond. Bicycles, the best way to explore the inn's extensive grounds, are also available. (Jill prefers not to house families with children under 17.)

The interior of the Manor Farm Inn is filled with special touches. White walls, oatmeal-color carpets, rough-hewn beams, and wide, sunny windows give the spacious guest rooms a clean and soothing simplicity. French and English pine armoires, writing desks, and tables are arranged around the king-size beds, warmed by stylish comforters.

The large kitchen is another special feature at Manor Farm. A sonorous old brass bell summons you to the comfortable drawing room. The farm-style breakfast, which begins with warm scones and coffee delivered to each room, includes oatmeal, fresh eggs from the farm chickens, oven-roasted potatoes, bacon, and sausage. Be sure to save a slice or two of home-baked bread for the inn's friendly goats, Cinnamon and Nutmeg, who occupy a fenced pasture down by the trout pond. △ *7 double rooms with baths. Bicycles, croquet, fly-fishing, horseshoes. $100–$170; full breakfast. MC, V.*

OLD CONSULATE INN 🐚
313 Walker St., Port Townsend 98368, tel. 360/385–6753 or 800/300–6753, fax 360/385–2097

Another Port Townsend Queen Anne Victorian on the bluff overlooking the water—similar to the James House (*see above*)—this redbrick beauty comes complete with conical turret, dormers, an unusual sloping "wedding cake" porch with a bay-view swing, well-tended gardens, and lots of white Adirondack chairs for lounging. Also known as the F. W. Hastings House, the inn was built as a private home in 1889 by the son of the town's founder and served as the German consulate from 1908 to 1911.

The inn is owned by Rob and Joanna Jackson. Transplanted Californians, they fell in love with Port Townsend on their 25th anniversary, chucked their old jobs, and became innkeepers.

The oak-paneled front parlor features its original chandelier, with large bunches of green glass grapes, and a fireplace framed in Italian tile. A large sitting room is comfortable for reading and conversation, with a fireplace, Queen Anne sofas and chairs, a baby grand piano, a pump organ once owned by England's royal family, and a chinoiserie chest original to the house and inlaid with mother-of-pearl. In the evening, the Jacksons serve complimentary port and sherry by the fire, as well as tasty desserts, including Joanna's infamous hot bourbon bread pudding. A smaller anteroom off the dining room offers cable TV, a VCR, and lots of books. The doll, beer stein, and other collections displayed throughout the house can get a bit overwhelming.

Guest rooms on the second and third floors have a Victorian ambience, with floral wallpapers, custom-made comforters, dolls placed on bureaus, and a picture hat here and there on the walls. From the Tower Room there is a sweeping view of the bay. All suites have claw-foot tubs.

Joanna is a cookbook author and her breakfasts show it. They are leisurely seven-course affairs and usually include brandy baked apples topped with fresh brandied applesauce and cream; a Greek puffed-egg dish stuffed with goat cheese, sautéed bell peppers, and onions and topped with a lemon-cheese sauce; fresh biscuits; and a small fruit quick-bread laced with a matching cordial. △ *5 double rooms with baths, 3 suites. Air-conditioning in rooms. Billiards, hot tub. $96–$195; full breakfast, afternoon refreshments. AE, MC, V. No smoking.*

OTHER CHOICES

Annapurna Inn Massage and Retreat Center. 538 Adams St., Port Townsend 98368, tel. 360/385–2909 or 800/868–2662. 6 double rooms with baths. Sauna, steam room, massage and reflexology services, yoga instruction, accommodations for groups up to 18, conference facilities. $70–$110; full vegan breakfast. MC, V.
Domaine Madeleine. 146 Wildflower La. (8 mi east of town), Port Angeles 98362, tel. 360/457–4174, fax 360/457–3037. 3 double rooms with baths, 2 suites, 1 cottage. Fireplace, TV/VCR, CD player, and phone in rooms. Kitchen in cottage. Video library. $125–$175; full breakfast. AE, MC, V. No smoking.
Harbinger Inn. 1136 E. Bay Dr., Olympia 98507, tel. 360/754–0389. 5 double rooms with baths. $60–$125; full breakfast. AE, MC, V. No smoking.

Lake Crescent Lodge. 416 Lake Crescent Rd., Port Angeles 98362, tel. 360/928–3211. 47 double rooms with baths, 5 doubles in lodge share bath. Restaurant, lounge, gift shop, rowboats. $67–$170; breakfast and box lunches not included. AE, D, DC, MC, V. Closed late Oct.–late Apr.

Lake Quinault Lodge. S. Shore Rd. (Box 7), Quinault 98575, tel. 360/288–2900 or 800/562–6672, fax 800/288–2901. 89 double rooms with baths, 3 suites. Restaurant, no-smoking rooms, indoor pool and hot tub, sauna, pool tables, gift shop, fishing, hiking, boat rentals. $62–$250; breakfast not included. AE, MC, V. No smoking in dining rooms.

Lizzie's Victorian Bed & Breakfast. 731 Pierce St., Port Townsend 98368, tel. 360/385–4168 or 800/700–4168. 7 double rooms with baths. $70–$135; full breakfast. D, MC, V. No smoking, 2-night minimum on holiday and festival weekends.

Quimper Inn. 1306 Franklin St., Port Townsend 98368, tel. 360/385–1060 or 800/557–1060, fax 360/385–2688. 3 double rooms with baths, 2 doubles share bath. $75–$140; full breakfast. MC, V. No smoking.

Ravenscroft Inn. 533 Quincy St., Port Townsend 98368, tel. 360/385–2784 or 800/782–2691, fax 360/385–6724. 8 double rooms with baths, 2 suites. Fireplace in 3 rooms. $67–$175; full breakfast. AE, D, MC, V. No smoking, 2-night minimum on holiday and festival weekends.

Simone's Groveland Cottage. 4861 Sequim Dungeness Way, Dungeness 98382, tel. 360/683–3565 or 800/879–8859. 4 rooms with private baths. TV/VCR in rooms. $80–$110; full breakfast. AE, D, DC, MC, V. No smoking.

Swantown Inn. 1431 11th Ave. SE, Olympia 98501, tel. 360/ 753–9123. 3 double rooms with baths. $85–$115; full breakfast. V, MC. No smoking.

Tudor Inn. 1108 S. Oak St., Port Angeles 98362, tel. 360/452–3138, fax 360/457–9360. 5 double rooms with baths. $75–$120; full breakfast. MC, V. No smoking, 2-night minimum on summer weekends and holidays.

RESERVATIONS SERVICES

Pacific Reservation Service (Box 46894, Seattle 98146, tel. 206/439–7677 or 800/684–2932). **A Travelers Reservation Service** (14716 26th Ave. NE, Seattle 98155, tel. 206/364–5900).

Seattle and Environs

BACON MANSION/BROADWAY GUEST HOUSE 🐾
959 Broadway E (corner of Broadway E and E. Prospect), Seattle 98102, tel. 206/329–1864 or 800/240–1864, fax 206/860–9025

On a quiet tree-lined street in the Harvard-Belmont Historical District, only five minutes from downtown, the zestfully run Bacon Mansion/Broadway Guest House was a welcome addition to the Seattle bed-and-breakfast scene. Owners Daryl King and Tim Avenmarg-Stiles opened the doors of this huge, imposing 1909 Edwardian-style Tudor in February 1993.

The house had been operated as an inn for several years when King and Avenmarg-Stiles bought it; they added seven guest rooms to the original three, installed new bathrooms and furnishings, and in the process created an ambience of comfortable luxury. The inn's public areas are tasteful, with wool carpets in shades of rose, cream, and indigo laid over glossy hardwood floors. Headlining the decor of the main sitting room is a black concert grand piano adorned with a

Liberace-style candelabra. French doors overlook the garden courtyard, complete with fountain, out back. Flowers in every room make it feel like June all year around.

Guest rooms at the Bacon Mansion run the gamut from the floral motifs of the Garden Suite and the Iris Room to the more masculine confines of the Clipper Room and the Capitol Suite. The latter is the largest and most impressive of the in-house accommodations, with a pine four-poster bed, carved oak fireplace, wet bar, original tile bath (with two-person soaking tub), and a fine view of the Space Needle. There's also a nice view of Mt. Rainier from the Iris Room, on the top floor at the opposite end of the house.

Out back, past the fountain, is the two-story Carriage House. On the main floor is the spacious Carriage Suite with white plaster walls, forest-green carpeting, and a queen-size brass bed; on the second floor is the Carriage Loft, another, smaller suite. The full-size living-room hide-a-bed on the first floor makes this the best choice for families or other large groups. ♉ *6 double rooms with baths, 2 doubles share bath, 2 suites. Phone and TV in rooms. $74–$139; Continental breakfast. AE, D, MC, V. No smoking.*

BOMBAY HOUSE ☙
8490 Beck Rd. NE, Bainbridge Island 98110, tel. 206/842–3926 or 800/598–3926

In a quiet, rural setting just a 30-minute ferry ride from Seattle, Bombay House is a three-story Victorian mansion owned by Bunny Cameron, a former caterer, and her husband, Roger Kanchuk, who ran a business that served legal papers. The couple pulled up stakes in Anchorage, Alaska, looking for a better climate. One might question whether Puget Sound is an improvement, but in 1986, after scouring various western locations, Bunny and Roger landed on Bainbridge Island and bought the Bombay House.

The house, which has a widow's walk and wraparound porch, was built in 1907 by a master shipbuilder from Port Blakely (famous for its four-masted schooners built in the heyday of the tall ships). The entrance opens to a spacious, sunny living room with 10-ft-high ceilings and stained-glass windows. A century-old rock maple loom from Maine stands against one wall; a 1912 upright piano stands against another. One of the guest rooms on the main floor has a functioning old tin bathtub, and an open staircase leads up to the other guest rooms. The Captain State Room is a large, airy room decorated in forest green and white, with a wood-burning parlor stove, large bird's-eye maple bed, and clawfoot soaking tub with shower.

In the glass-enclosed breakfast area you can munch on Bunny's special fruit-bran muffins, quick breads, cakes, pastries, and homemade granola while you watch the large white ferries plying the waters of Rich Passage between Bainbridge Island and the Kitsap Peninsula.

The half-acre yard contains a rough cedar gazebo and informal gardens of roses, daisies, peonies, and lilies exploding with color.

A favorite activity on the 15-mi-long island is berry picking. If you haven't immediately consumed everything you've picked, you'll have an appetite for the fresh pasta dishes at Ruby's (4569 Lynnwood Center Rd., tel. 206/780–9303). ♉ *2 double rooms with baths, 2 doubles share bath, 1 suite. $59–$149; Continental-plus breakfast, complimentary beverages. AE, MC, V. No smoking.*

GASLIGHT INN ❦
1727 15th Ave., Seattle 98122, tel. 206/325–3654, fax 206/328–4803

The three-story, teal-color Gaslight Inn atop historic Capitol Hill was always a showplace. A developer built the Arts and Crafts foursquare–style home in 1906 to show prospective customers the kind of home they could build after they had bought their lot from him.

Owners Stephen Bennett and Trevor Logan bought the dilapidated building in 1980 and, after four years of painstaking restoration, opened it as a bed-and-breakfast. If you reject the excesses of Victorians, you will love the more austere aesthetic.

The inn, named for its original gaslight fixtures, also retains the original beveled and stained-glass windows on all three floors, oak millwork, graceful fluted columns, and oak-paneled wainscoting with egg and dart detailing. All the oak and the muted color schemes lend a warm feel to the inn, and large windows and unfussy furnishings—authentic Arts and Crafts, Mission, and Eastlake—give it a bright, clean look.

Each of the guest rooms is unique, with its own distinctive and well-executed decor; every one is equipped with remote-control TV and a small refrigerator. Some rooms have views of downtown, only a short bus ride away. Room 1 has a crisp, hardy appeal, with its ivory-and-blue mattress-ticking wallpaper and lots of wood. It features two Eastlake walnut chests and table, a walnut headboard, a hand-pieced quilt, and a bathroom with dark-stained wainscoting and a small Eastlake mirror. Despite dark taupe walls, Room 2 is warm and sunny, with white millwork, an elaborately carved golden oak bed and dresser, and an Arts and Crafts armoire. Another room is rustic, with a log bed made in the San Juan Islands and pine furniture. The five suites in the house next door, including a very spacious third-floor suite with kitchen, desk, fireplace, and expansive view of the Puget Sound, are elegant, comfortable, and particularly ideal if you're planning an extended stay.

Breakfast at the Gaslight is not a celebrated event, as is the case at other B&Bs. It's a strictly Continental affair of store-bought pastries, fresh fruit, coffee, and juice. △ *12 double rooms with baths, 4 doubles share baths, 7 suites. Fireplace in 1 room and 3 suites, cable TV and refrigerator in rooms. Pool. $68–$158; Continental-plus breakfast. AE, MC, V. 2-night minimum Memorial Day–Labor Day and on weekends.*

M.V. *CHALLENGER* ❦
1001 Fairview Ave. N (park at Yale St. Landing shopping center and marina), Seattle 98109, tel. 206/340–1201, fax 206/621–9208

In a city that's defined by water, what could be more appropriate than a stay on a tugboat? Doing the improbable, owner Jerry Brown, a real-estate appraiser from the Midwest, bought the 96-ft working tug, built in 1944 for the U.S. Army, renovated it, and opened the M.V. *Challenger* as a bed-and-breakfast. It's definitely not hyperbole to call it unique.

Moored on the south end of Lake Union, a small lake 10 blocks from the heart of Seattle and filled with sailboats, cruisers, and charter boats, the *Challenger* is not for the claustrophobic. Common areas inside the vessel are open and fairly spacious, but some cabins are very snug.

You are asked to remove your shoes as you enter the main salon, built over the former cargo hatch, now decorated in ivory, blue, and beige with wood trim, brass candlesticks, and nautical gauges. The aft-deck solarium, which affords panoramic views of the waterfront, can be opened to the sky on sunny days and, more typically, enclosed with canvas and vinyl for Seattle's fog and drizzle.

Staterooms, some no bigger than a walk-in closet, are papered with nautical maps. Two cabins have bunks, the others double or queen-size beds. All come equipped with radios and phones. The red-striped comforter and matching pillowcases and curtains, towels, and a small painted radiator, also in red, make the Captain's Cabin cozy and bright. If you've been assigned to the Master's Cabin, you might be tempted to take to your bed, from which you can observe the busy comings and goings on the lake.

Two new boats have been added to the *Challenger* fleet: A modern trawler with wooden boat charm and a newer power boat, which is more spacious but lacks the personality of the tug and trawler.

An extensive Continental breakfast, complete with cereals, pastries, fruits, juices, hot chocolate, coffee, and tea, is served in the main salon. ◬ *9 double rooms with baths, 3 doubles share bath, 1 suite. Phone and TV/VCR in rooms. $55–$275; Continental-plus breakfast. AE, MC, V. No smoking, no shoes indoors.*

WALL STREET INN 〰

2507 1st Ave., Seattle 98121, tel. 206/448–0125, fax 206/448–2406

The Wall Street Inn was originally built as a land base for the Sailors of the Pacific Union. Between voyages spanning 1952 to 1996, merchant marines lodged in the 500-square-ft studio apartments in Seattle's Belltown. This former rough-and-tumble waterfront neighborhood has been invigorated over the past 10 years and is now home to a thriving collection of nightclubs, boutiques, art studios, and some of the city's best restaurants.

While living in a Seattle suburb raising their three children, innkeepers Greg and Kirsten Waham always knew they wanted to own a B&B. And when they found this two-story 1950s apartment building on the market in 1996, they knew it was the place to start. They sold their home, converted two of the apartments into living quarters for their family, then got started renovating the rest of the building. Greg has owned and managed several restaurants and now spends his days running the inn, while Kirsten works at a local department store.

No two of the 20 guest rooms are alike. Seven of the rooms have glorious views of Elliott Bay and the Olympic Mountains, four have kitchenettes, and half of the rooms still have the original Murphy beds from the old sailor days (the other half have queen-size beds). The corner rooms are a bit larger, but all rooms have sitting areas, refrigerators, and that infectiously comfortable mix-and-match approach to furnishing commonly found in suburban homes. Each room has its own bathroom with either a tub or a shower, plus hair dryers, terry cloth robes, and slippers.

A breakfast of fruit, quiche, and fresh pastries from neighborhood bakeries is laid out in the reception area each morning. Guests are free to enjoy their coffee and morning paper in the leather chairs in front of the fireplace. When the weather permits, breakfast can be taken on the interior courtyard patio, where on some evenings Greg, Kirsten, and their children invite you to join them for barbecues. ◬ *20 double rooms with baths. Cable TV, phones, terry cloth robes, and slippers in rooms. $100–$135; Continental-plus breakfast, AE, MC, V. No smoking.*

OTHER CHOICES

Chambered Nautilus. 5005 22nd Ave. NE, Seattle 98105, tel. 206/522–2536 or 800/545–8459 or 800/545–8459, fax 206/545–8459. 6 double rooms with baths. TV in rooms (on request). $89–$119; full breakfast. AE, MC, V. No smoking, 2-night minimum on weekends mid-Apr.–mid-Oct., 3-night minimum on holiday weekends.

Hill House. 1113 E. John St., Seattle 98102, tel. 206/720–7161 or 800/720–7161, fax 206/323–0772. 1 double room with bath, 2 doubles share bath, 2 suites. TV, phone, and refrigerator in suites. Free parking. $90–$145; full breakfast. AE, D, MC, V. No smoking.

Inn at Harbor Steps. 1221 1st Ave., Seattle 98101, tel. 206/748–0973 or 888/728–8910, fax 206/682–6045. 20 double rooms with baths. Kitchenette, cable TV, and fireplace in rooms. Pool, hot tub, sauna, basketball, exercise room, coin laundry. $150–$200; full breakfast. AE, D, MC, V. No smoking.

Inn at the Market. 86 Pine St., Seattle 98101, tel. 206/443–3600 or 800/446–4484, fax 206/448–0631. 60 double rooms with baths, 10 suites. Room service, cable TV, robes in room, rooftop deck, access to athletic club, conference facilities. $150–$335; no breakfast, complimentary morning coffee. AE, D, DC, MC, V.

Roberta's Bed & Breakfast. 1147 16th Ave. E, Seattle 98112, tel. 206/329–3326, fax 206/324–2149. 3 double rooms with baths, 1 double with bath in hall, 1 suite. Phone in rooms. $90–$135; full breakfast. MC, V. No smoking.

Salisbury House. 750 16th Ave. E, Seattle 98112, tel. 206/328–8682, fax 206/720–1019. 4 double rooms with baths, 1 suite. Phone and TV in suite. $89–$140; full breakfast. AE, DC, MC, V. No smoking, 2-night minimum holiday and summer weekends.

Sorrento Hotel. 900 Madison St., Seattle 98104, tel. 206/622–6400 or 800/426–1265, fax 206/343–6159. 34 double rooms with baths, 42 suites. Air-conditioning, cable TV, and phone in rooms, fireplace in suite. Restaurant, bar, on-premises shiatsu masseur, concierge, access to health club, complimentary downtown limousine service. $210–$1,200; no breakfast. AE, D, DC, MC, V.

Villa Heidelberg. 4845 45th Ave. SW, Seattle 98116, tel. 206/938–3658 or 800/671–2942, fax 206/935–7077. 4 double rooms share 2 baths, 2 suites. Cable TV in rooms. Fireplace and phone in suite. $80–$120; full breakfast. AE, MC, V. No smoking.

RESERVATIONS SERVICES

Pacific Reservation Service (Box 46894, Seattle 98146, tel. 206/439–7677 or 800/684–2932). **Seattle B&B Association Hotline** (Box 31772, Seattle 98103, tel. 206/547–1020). **A Travelers Reservation Service** (14716 26th Ave. NE, Seattle 98155, tel. 206/364–5900). **Washington State Bed & Breakfast Guild** (2442 N.W. Market St., Box 355-FD, Seattle 98107, tel. 800/647–2918).

Whidbey Island

CLIFF HOUSE AND SEA CLIFF COTTAGE ☞
727 Windmill Dr., Freeland 98249, tel. 360/331–1566

High on a cliff above Admiralty Strait, on 400 ft of secluded waterfront, stand the Cliff House and Sea Cliff Cottage. Natural beauty and tranquillity led owner Peggy Moore to build her incredible home on Whidbey Island. The 1981 Cliff

House—a contemporary statement in glass, wood, and stone—has brought awards to its architect, Arne Bystrom, and is elegantly appointed in art and artifacts.

A large open kitchen and dining area stands on one side of a 30-ft glass atrium; a study and seating area is on the other side. The sunken living room has a fireplace and a sectional with a perimeter of tiny lights that make it appear to float at night. Floor-to-ceiling windows allow glorious views of Admiralty Strait, Puget Sound, and the Olympic Mountains.

Because guests share living and dining facilities, Peggy will only rent the two spacious loft bedrooms to acquainted parties. The larger room opens out over the living area. Amenities include a king-size feather bed, whirlpool bath, and two upholstered swivel chairs so guests can fully appreciate the sun setting over the mountains. The second bedroom overlooks the kitchen and dining area to the forest beyond. A skylight brightens the dark-blue tile bathroom. Comprehensive music and video libraries can keep you entertained on chilly evenings.

Sea Cliff Cottage is as romantic and cozy as Cliff House is airy and elegant. The porch has a bit of gingerbread among the driftwood railing, and Adirondack chairs. There's a country feel to the living room: whitewashed pine walls, pine armoire, wicker chairs and love seat, and a brick fireplace. Ralph Lauren linens on the bed and a cushioned window seat overlooking the trees and the water add to the comfort. There is also a fully equipped kitchenette and a dining area, as well as a bathroom. ♨ *2 double rooms with baths in house, 1 cottage. Kitchen and fireplace in cottage, hot tub with house. $165–$385; Continental breakfast. No credit cards. No smoking, 2-night minimum.*

COLONEL CROCKETT FARM ☙
1012 S. Fort Casey Rd., Coupeville 98239, tel. 360/678–3711

Col. Walter Crockett, a relative of Davy Crockett, built this house in 1855. It was derelict in 1984 when Robert and Beulah Whitlow found it; today the house is listed in the National Register of Historic Places. They spent 18 months and $235,000 transforming the old farmhouse into an inn, which stands amid 3 acres of lawn and flower gardens.

The Victorian cross-gabled structure has Doric pilasters on pedestals, lending an incongruous grandeur to the otherwise modest house. The entry hall and small solarium have stained- and leaded-glass windows and wicker furniture. The main public room is a well-stocked library with red oak paneling, a slate fireplace, an English brass rubbing, and a collection of bulldogs in an antique case. Furnishings include a mirror-back English settee and matching chairs, an upholstered Eastlake chair and matching rocker, and another hand-carved rocker.

The five guest rooms are individually decorated. The Crockett Room, the inn's bridal suite, is furnished with a four-poster canopy bed, a marble-top washstand, and a Belgian field desk; its extra-long tub has lion's-head paws. The Edwardian fainting couch in the sitting area is a particularly rare piece. The Alexander Room, with a tiger-maple bed and dresser, overlooks meadows, Crockett Lake, and Admiralty Bay.

The dining room has a fireplace, a view out to the iris gardens and Crockett Lake, and a telescope for guests' use. Small tables are surrounded by collections of antique porcelain plates; Royal Copenhagen, Wedgwood, and Belleek pieces; and gleaming English silver. Breakfast specialties include eggs California, fruit platters, and homemade muffins with seasonal ingredients. (Beulah may share some of her original recipes.)

The farm is on a major flyway, so many migrating birds stop over on Crockett Lake. It's also close to 9 mi of beach with public access and the Port Townsend ferry terminal. *5 double rooms with baths. $75–$105; full breakfast. MC, V. No smoking, 2-night minimum on holiday weekends.*

INN AT LANGLEY ☙
400 1st St. (Box 835), Langley 98260, tel. and fax 360/221–3033

This contemporary structure at the edge of the Langley business district is a contemplative melding of earth, sky, water, wood, and concrete. The two cedar-shake, Mission-style buildings—inspired by Frank Lloyd Wright—are surrounded by quiet gardens of herbs, berries, flowers, and fruit trees.

An archway leads to a long, rectangular reflecting pond, which connects with the Country Kitchen, a restaurant that serves Continental breakfast to guests and opens to the public for dinner on Friday and Saturday. A longer building with similar lines includes the office, 22 guest rooms, and two suites trailing down the bluff to the beach.

An Asian sense of space and understatement shapes the interior in neutral earth tones. The waterside wall in the common area is nearly all glass, affording a staggeringly beautiful view past the deck to Saratoga Passage, Camano Island, and the Cascade Mountains. The fireplace and maple, fir, cherry, and pine appointments meld with the outdoors.

The Country Kitchen might be a wealthy friend's dining room. You'll find no maître d' standing at an official podium, no coat check, and no cash register. A huge river-rock fireplace rises before you; tables for two line the walls unobtrusively. The restaurant, a veritable gallery of local crafts, has a locally made, Wright-inspired "great table" for 10 on the far side of the fireplace.

Steve and Sandy Nogal, the inn's managers, see stressed and exhausted guests arrive and watch with pleasure as they "unwind and blossom." Steve is the creative force behind the incredible dinners served each weekend. He builds menus around Whidbey Island foodstuffs, and has a ready group of suppliers that bring in salad greens, eggs, baby vegetables, jams and jellies, and freshly harvested mussels for his artful culinary presentations. *22 double rooms with baths, 2 suites. Phone with voice mail, TV/VCR, mini-refrigerator, whirlpool bath, and fireplace in rooms. Restaurant, conference facilities. $189–$279; Continental breakfast, dinner Fri. and Sat. AE, MC, V. No smoking, 2-night minimum on weekends.*

OTHER CHOICES

Anchorage Inn. 807 N. Main St., Coupeville 98239, tel. 360/678–5581. 6 double rooms with baths. Air-conditioning, cable TV in rooms. $75–$90; full breakfast. D, MC, V. No smoking.

Captain Whidbey Inn. 2072 W. Captain Whidbey Inn Rd., Coupeville 98239, tel. 360/678–4097 or 800/366–4097, fax 360/678–4110. 12 double rooms with baths, 10 doubles and 2 suites share 2 baths, 3 cottages and 4 cabins. Phone in some rooms, kitchen in cottages. Restaurant, bar, conference facilities. $95–$225; full breakfast. AE, D, DC, MC, V. 2-night minimum on weekends, 3-night minimum on holiday weekends.

Compass Rose Bed and Breakfast. 508 S. Main St., Coupeville 98239, tel. 360/678–5318 or 800/237–3881, fax 360/678–5318. 2 double rooms share bath and parlor. Phone, cable TV/VCR. $85; full breakfast, complimentary beverages. No credit cards. No smoking.

Country Cottage of Langley. 215 6th St., Langley 98260, tel. 360/221–8709 or 800/713–3860. 5 double rooms with baths. TV/VCR, CD player, down comforters, feather beds, coffeemaker, and refrigerator in rooms, fireplace in 2 rooms. Whirlpool bath, video library. $105–$169; full breakfast. AE, MC, V. No smoking, 2-night minimum on summer weekends and holidays.

Eagles Nest Inn. 4680 Saratoga Rd., Langley 98260, tel. and fax 360/221–5331. 4 double rooms with baths, cottage. Cable TV/VCR and stereo in rooms. Hot tub. $95–$235; full breakfast, complimentary beverages. D, MC, V. No smoking, 2-night minimum on weekends.

Fort Casey Inn. 1124 S. Engle Rd., Coupeville 98239, tel. 360/678–8792. 1 suite, 1 2-bedroom cottage, 8 2-bedroom units. Wood-burning stove and kitchen in most units. Bicycles. $75–$125; Continental breakfast. AE, MC, V. No smoking.

Guest House Cottages. 3366 S. Hwy. 525, Greenbank 98253, tel. 360/678–3115, fax 360/678–3115. 5 cottages and 1 cabin. TV/VCR, video library, whirlpool bath in units. Pool, exercise room, video library, hot tub. $160–$285; full breakfast. AE, D, MC, V. No smoking, 2-night minimum on weekends, 3-night minimum on holiday weekends.

Home by the Sea Cottages. 2388 E. Sunlight Beach Rd., Clinton 98236, tel. 360/321–2964, fax 360/321–4378. 1 suite, 2 cottages. Kitchen, phone, TV/VCR, sound system, whirlpool tub in units. $155–$175; Continental breakfast. MC, V. No smoking, 2-night minimum on weekends.

Inn at Penn Cove. 702 N. Main St. (Box 85), Coupeville 98239, tel. 360/678–8000 or 800/688–2683. 3 double rooms with baths, 2 doubles share bath, 1 suite. Fireplace in 3 rooms, whirlpool tub in suite. Cable TV/VCR in video library in Kineth House. $60–$125; full breakfast, complimentary beverages. AE, D, MC, V. No smoking.

Log Castle Bed & Breakfast. 4693 Saratoga Rd., Langley 98260, tel. 360/221–5483, fax 360/221–6249. 4 double rooms with baths. Woodstove in 2 rooms. Nature trail. $95–$120; full breakfast, afternoon refreshments. D, MC, V. No smoking, 2-night minimum on holiday weekends.

Lone Lake Cottage and Breakfast. 5206 S. Bayview Rd., Langley 98260, tel. 360/321–5325. 1 houseboat with detached bath, 1 suite, 2 cottages. Kitchen, TV/VCR, CD player, whirlpool tub in units. Video library, bicycles, canoes, paddleboat, rowboat, fishing gear. $140; Continental breakfast for 1st 2 days. No credit cards. No smoking, 2-night minimum on weekends.

Saratoga Inn. 201 Cascade Ave., Langley 98260, tel. 360/221–5801 or 800/698–2910, fax 360/221–5804. 15 double rooms with baths, carriage house. Phones, cable TV, fireplace in units. $110–$225; full breakfast, complimentary snacks and beverages. AE, D, MC, V. No smoking.

RESERVATIONS SERVICES

Pacific Bed & Breakfast Agency (Box 46894, Seattle 98146, tel. 206/439–7677 or 800/684–2932). **Washington State Bed & Breakfast Guild** (2442 N.W. Market St., Box 355–FD, Seattle 98107, tel. 800/647–2918). **Whidbey Island Bed & Breakfast Association** (Box 259, Langley 98260).

San Juan Islands

FRIDAY HARBOR HOUSE ☞
130 West St. (Box 1385), Friday Harbor 98250, tel. 360/378–8455, fax 360/378–8453

On a prominent bluff overlooking the marina in San Juan Channel stands the Friday Harbor House. The natural colors of the scenic setting are echoed in the guest rooms, and an array of textures gives them an outside-in feeling, as do the walls of glass opening on to decks and narrow step-out balconies. Local artwork is showcased throughout the inn, including driftwood benches handmade by innkeeper Jim Skoog.

Double-size whirlpool tubs and fireplaces set the stage for romantic interludes. Rooms are very spacious, averaging 550 square ft, and appointed with coffeemakers, mini-refrigerators, plush robes, and televisions. In all rooms you can enjoy the radiance of the fireplace while relaxing in the whirlpool tub. The inn is also very family friendly; kids under 17 stay free in their parents' room, and futons and cribs are readily available.

A generous breakfast buffet is offered downstairs in the dining room, with freshly baked pastries, granola, yogurt, bagels, seasonal fruit, and juice. Local produce and herbs, lamb, and seafood play a major role in the critically acclaimed culinary productions created each evening by local chef Laurie Paul. Outdoor dining is available in the summer. Reserve a spot for dinner well in advance. △
19 double rooms with baths, 1 suite. Fireplace, whirlpool tub, mini-refrigerator, phones, modem line, and TV/VCR in rooms. Restaurant, conference facilities. $150–$275; Continental-plus breakfast. No smoking, 2-night minimum July–Sept. and holidays.

INN AT SWIFTS BAY ☞
Port Stanley Rd. (Rte. 2, Box 3402), Lopez Island 98261, tel. 360/468–3636, fax 360/468-3637

Rob Aney and Mark Adcock first discovered the Inn at Swifts Bay in 1993 through a gift certificate that they received for being "best men" in their friend's wedding. They loved the place so much that they returned year after year until they found out the inn was for sale. They had always dreamed of owning a B&B but didn't know where or how, until this enchanting property presented itself to them.

A 1975 mock-Tudor building, 2 mi from the Lopez Island ferry landing, the inn is surrounded by rhododendrons, madronas, and firs amid 3 acres of woods, with another acre of beach a four-minute walk away. The inn's decor is sophisticated, but the rooms feel lived-in and loved. The sunny living room has large bay windows, a fireplace, a chintz sofa and chairs on an Oriental rug, and shelves of books. The den–music room behind the living room features a large brick fireplace, two Queen Anne upholstered wing chairs, a TV/VCR with more than 300 videotapes, and French doors that open onto the deck and the woods.

The individually decorated guest rooms are spacious and airy. Room 2 has hunter-green walls with cream accents, window swags of patterned fabric, an Arts and Crafts headboard on the queen-size bed, a gateleg desk, and a large dark-cherry mirror and chest. An attic suite has pale peach walls, a queen-size sleigh bed, and an English armoire and chest; three long, narrow skylights have been cut into the sloping ceiling; and there's a private entrance and small deck.

The raised dining room, pale yellow with hand-stenciled ivy around the ceiling, is the setting for breakfast, which might include hazelnut waffles with fresh island berries and crème fraîche or salmon dill blintzes. △ *2 double rooms with baths, 2 doubles share bath, 1 suite. Fireplace and mini-refrigerator in suite and 2 rooms, TV/VCR in den and suite. Video library, exercise room, hot tub. $95–$175; full breakfast. AE, D, MC, V. No smoking.*

ORCAS HOTEL 🐚
Box 155, Orcas 98280, tel. 360/376–4300 or 888/672–2792, fax 360/376–4399

On the hill overlooking the Orcas Island ferry landing sits a three-story red-roof Victorian with a wraparound porch and a white picket fence. The Orcas Hotel, a bustling seaside inn, was built between 1900 and 1904 by Canadian landowner William Sutherland. Today the hotel is listed on the National Register of Historic Places; even the flower gardens—drifts of daffodils, wisteria vines, irises, and roses—have been restored. The hostelry is managed by Craig and Linda Sanders and Brad Harlow—three active young people who, when they aren't bicycling, hiking, or playing volleyball or softball, are likely to be in the kitchen cooking gourmet meals.

The hotel has a colorful past. A bullet hole through a veranda post recalls the Prohibition-era escape of a bootlegger who foiled his pursuers by leaping to freedom over the porch railing. Some islanders claim that liquor was smuggled in by small boats and stored in the woodpile and the attic. During the hotel's restoration in 1985, loose planks were discovered in the attic, with enough space underneath to store dozens of bottles of booze.

The main floor features a bakery-espresso café, dining room, and parlor furnished with Queen Anne settees, marble-top tables, and Oriental rugs. The dining room (open to the public) overlooks the ferry landing as well as part of the garden. All public rooms have splendid harbor views and showcase works by Orcas artists.

Two romantic guest rooms at the front of the inn have French doors opening onto a wrought-iron-furnished sundeck with views of the waterfront. Both rooms feature fluffy feather beds and duvets and marble-top tables. Each has a large bathroom with a double whirlpool bath. △ *2 double rooms with baths, 2 doubles and 1 triple with ½ baths share 2 full baths, 5 doubles and 1 triple share 4 baths. Whirlpool bath in two rooms. Restaurant (June–Sept.), bakery, cocktail lounge, conference facilities, bicycle rentals. $69–$170; full breakfast. AE, D, MC, V. No smoking, 2-night minimum on holiday weekends.*

TURTLEBACK FARM INN 🐚
Crow Valley Rd. (Rte. 1, Box 650), Eastsound 98245, tel. 360/376–4914 or 800/376–4914, fax 360/376–5329

Bill and Susan Fletcher abandoned suburban life in the San Francisco Bay area (he was a real-estate broker, she a homemaker) for 80 acres of meadow, forest, and farmland on Orcas Island. Forest green with white trim, the renovated, Folk National–style farmhouse, a 10-minute drive from the Orcas Island ferry landing, stands in the shadow of Turtleback Mountain, with Mt. Constitution to the east.

The cream-color sitting room, with a beamed ceiling and peach-and-green accents, includes a Rumford fireplace, pilgrim-style trunk, cabbage-rose upholstered sofa, and a corner game table. The salmon-color dining room has fir wainscoting and five small oak tables.

The guest rooms are decorated with Cape May Collection wallpaper. All have reading lamps, comfortable seating, cream-colored muslin curtains, and meadow and forest views. The Meadow Room has a private deck overlooking the pasture. The light fixtures and crystal doorknobs in most rooms and the claw-foot tubs and bathroom mirrors were rescued from Seattle's old Savoy Hotel before it was razed, and the sinks and beveled-glass bathroom shelves above them come from Victoria's grand old Empress Hotel. The comforters on the beds are stuffed with wool batting from the Fletchers' own sheep. The Orchard House, a new cedar building appropriately set in the apple orchard, offers four luxurious rooms with king beds, fireplaces, claw-foot tubs, and private decks overlooking the valley.

If you are staying in the main house, breakfast is served in the dining room or, in nice weather, on the deck on tables set with bone china, silver, and linen. Guests staying in the Orchard House enjoy breakfast in the privacy of their room or deck. Breakfast brings fresh fruit and juice, homemade granola, and specialty hot dishes including an egg fritatta and breakfast pizza. If you want the recipes, you can buy Susan's cookbook. Full meal service is available by reservation for groups.
△ *11 double rooms with baths. Fireplace in 4 doubles. Walking paths. $80–$210; full breakfast, complimentary beverages. D, MC, V. No smoking, 2-night minimum on holidays and weekends Apr.–Oct.*

OTHER CHOICES

Chestnut Hill Inn. Box 213, Orcas 98280, tel. 360/376–5157, fax 360/376–5283. 4 double rooms with baths, 1 suite. Fireplace, robes, and slippers in rooms, TV/VCR in suite. Airport and ferry pickup. $145–$195; full breakfast. MC, V. No smoking.

Deer Harbor Inn. Deer Harbor Rd., Box 142, Deer Harbor 98243, tel. 360/376–4110, fax 360/376–2237. 8 double rooms with baths, 3 cottages. TV, fireplace, and hot tub in cottages. Restaurant. $99–$189; Continental-plus breakfast. AE, MC, V. No smoking.

Duffy House. 760 Pear Point Rd., Friday Harbor 98250, tel. 360/378–5604 or 800/972–2089, fax 360/378–6535. 5 double rooms with baths. Private beach. $90–$110; full breakfast. MC, V. No smoking, 2-night minimum on weekends July–Sept. and holidays.

Edenwild Inn. Box 271, Lopez Island 98261, tel. 360/468–3238, fax 360/468–4080. 8 double rooms with baths. Fireplace in suite. Conference facilities; ferry, seaplane, and airport pickup. $100–$155; full breakfast. AE, MC, V. No smoking.

Hillside House. 365 Carter Ave., Friday Harbor 98250, tel. 360/378–4730 or 800/232–4730, fax 360/378–4715. 7 double rooms with baths. Robes in rooms. TV and whirlpool tub in suite. $85–$165; full breakfast. AE, D, MC, V. No smoking.

Kangaroo House. N. Beach Rd., Box 334, Eastsound 98245, tel. 360/376–2175, 888/371–2175 fax 360/376–3604. 1 double room with bath, 3 doubles share 1½ baths, 1 suite. Robes in rooms. Games room, hot tub. $75–$125; full breakfast. AE, D, MC, V. No smoking.

Lopez Farm Cottages. Fisherman Bay Rd., Lopez 98261, tel. 360/468–3555, fax 360/468–3966. 4 cottages. Kitchenette and fireplace in cottages. Hot tub, ferry and airport pickup. $125; Continental breakfast. MC, V. No smoking.

MacKaye Harbor Inn. Rte. 1 (Box 1940), Lopez Island 98261, tel. 360/468–2253, fax 360/468–2393. 2 double rooms with baths, 2 doubles share 2½ baths, 2 suites, 1 carriage house. Kitchenette in suite. Kayak instruction and rental, mountain bikes, boat buoy, airport and ferry pickup. $99–$175; full breakfast. MC, V. No smoking, 2-night minimum July–Sept.

Mariella Inn & Cottages. 630 Turn Point Rd., Friday Harbor 98250, tel. 360/378–6868 or 800/700–7668, fax 360/378–6822. 8 double rooms with baths, 3 suites, 12 cottages. Kitchenette, fireplace, and whirlpool bath in some cottages.. Hot tub, volleyball court, tennis court, boat dock, private beach, bicycle rentals, sailing and cruise charters. $125–$375; Continental breakfast. AE, MC, V. No smoking, 2-night minimum June–Sept., 3-night minimum on holidays.

OldTrout Inn. Horseshoe Hwy., Rte. 1, Box 45A, Eastsound 98245, tel. 360/376–8282, fax 360/376–3626. 6 suites, 1 cottage. Robes in rooms; kitchenette and fireplace in suites; kitchenette, hot tub, and fireplace in cottage. Hot tub, canoe, ferry pickup. $125–$185; Continental-plus breakfast. D, MC, V. No smoking.

Olympic Lights. 4531-A Cattle Point Rd., Friday Harbor 98250, tel. 360/378–3186, fax 360/378–2097. 1 double room with bath, 4 doubles share 2 baths. Croquet, boccie, horseshoes. $75–$110; full breakfast. No credit cards. No smoking, 2-night minimum June–Sept. and on holiday weekends.

San Juan Inn. 50 Spring St. (Box 776), Friday Harbor 98250, tel. 360/378–2070 or 800/742–8210, fax 360/378–6437. 4 double rooms with baths, 5 doubles share 3 baths, 2 suites. Kitchen, TV/VCR, and hot tub in suites. $78–$220; Continental-plus breakfast. AE, D, MC, V. No smoking.

Sand Dollar Inn. Horseshoe Hwy. (Box 152), Olga 98279, tel. and fax 360/376–5696. 4 double rooms with baths. Guest refrigerator, rowboat. $90–$125; full breakfast. AE, MC, V. No smoking.

Spring Bay Inn. Obstruction Pass Park Rd. (Box 97), Olga 98279, tel. 360/376–5531, fax 360/376–2193. 5 double rooms with baths. Fireplace in rooms. Guest refrigerator, hot tub, barbecue, nature trails, kayak and hiking tours, binoculars. $175–$225; Continental breakfast and full brunch, dinner available. AE, D, MC, V. No smoking, 2-night minimum Apr.–Oct.

States Inn. 2039 W. Valley Rd., Friday Harbor 98250, tel. 360/378–6240, fax 360/378–6241. 8 double rooms with baths, 2 doubles share bath. Fireplace in 1 room. Bicycle storage, horseback riding, ferry and airport pickup/dropoff. $85–$125; full breakfast. MC, V. No smoking.

Trumpeter Inn. 420 Trumpeter Way, Friday Harbor 98250, tel. 360/378–3884 or 800/826–7926, fax 360/378–8235. 5 double rooms with baths. TV in den, games, hot tub, bicycle storage, ferry and airport pickup. $80–$125; full breakfast. AE, D, MC, V. No smoking.

Wharfside Bed & Breakfast. K-Dock, Slip 13, Port of Friday Harbor Marina (Box 1212), Friday Harbor 98250, tel. 360/378–5661. 2 double rooms share bath. Robes in rooms. Fishing gear, rowboat. $95; full breakfast. AE, MC, V. No smoking, 2-night minimum June–Sept. and holidays.

Windsong. 2 Deer Harbor Rd. (Box 32), Orcas 98280, tel. 360/376–2500 or 800/669–3948, fax 360/376–4453. 4 double rooms with baths. Robes, fireplace, and chocolates in rooms. Library, hot tub, barbecue, kayak storage, ferry and airport pickup. $115–$140; full breakfast. MC, V. No smoking.

RESERVATIONS SERVICES

Orcas Island Chamber of Commerce Inkeeper Hotline (tel. 360/376–8888). **Pacific Reservation Service** (Box 46894, Seattle 98146, tel. 206/439–7677 or 800/684–2932). **Washington State Bed & Breakfast Guild** (2442 N.W. Market St., Box 355-FD, Seattle 98107, tel. 800/647–2918).

Whatcom and Skagit Counties, Including Anacortes, Bellingham, and La Conner

CHANNEL HOUSE 🐚

2902 Oakes Ave., Anacortes 98221, tel. 360/293–9382 or 800/238–4353, fax 360/299–9208

Midway between downtown Anacortes and the ferry terminal is the Channel House, a 1902 shingled Craftsman bungalow with awe-inspiring views of Guemes Channel and the ferry landing, which can be seen from most rooms. Innkeepers Dennis and Patricia McIntyre tell guests all about the 2,500 acres of nearby forest and seven fresh-water lakes to explore, regularly scheduled whale-watching trips, and sea-kayak rentals all in the vicinity.

The dining room features lush potted plants that stand against dark blue-and-peach wallpaper, white wainscoting, and the original glazed terra-cotta tile floor with cobalt-blue borders. As you breakfast on the house specialty—French toast stuffed with cream cheese, pineapple, and pecans—you can watch the ferries plying Rosario Strait. Ten steps up are the living room, with exposed beams and a 10-ft-high ceiling, and a cozy study. Both rooms display porcelain dolls made by Dennis's mother from antique molds, complete with hand-painted features and hand-sewn costumes.

Each guest room has its own style, but all are spacious and light, with high ceilings, hardwood floors, and Oriental rugs. Grandma's Room is furnished with an antique four-poster bed with Laura Ashley bedding and a turn-of-the-century Eastlake-type oak dresser; the walls are covered with old family photos and little china collectibles. The more formal Canopy Room has a canopy bed covered with the same antique lace that dresses the window and an early 19th-century fainting couch upholstered in cream-color damask. The walls are covered with a cream and green striped paper with a floral border. In a separate cottage, the Victorian Rose room seems a perfect spot for reverie; its window seat is crowded with soft throw pillows, and the fireplace has cream tiles with hand-painted pink roses that are echoed in the pale-pink walls and ceiling border of roses against a black background. ♠ *4 double rooms with baths, 2 doubles with baths in cottage. Whirlpool bath and fireplace in cottage rooms. Hot tub. $79–$109; full breakfast. AE, D, MC, V. No smoking.*

LA CONNER CHANNEL LODGE AND COUNTRY INN 🐚

205 N. 1st St. and 107 S. 2nd St., La Conner 98257, tel. 360/466–1500 or 360/466–3101, fax 360/466–1525

A shingled, Northwest contemporary structure with rose-entwined lattice fences, the Channel Lodge is one of few waterside inns in the Puget Sound area. High-beamed ceilings add to the spacious country atmosphere of its sister facility, the Country Inn. Both are located a short walk from the many restaurants and boutiques lining the waterfront.

Twig furniture, bark bowls, hand-woven baskets, and dried and fresh flower arrangements bring the Northwest indoors to the Channel Lodge's lobby lounge. A towering stone fireplace and a cozy adjacent library help create a relaxed, homey mood. Weekend evenings, musicians entertain on the grand piano, behind which doors open onto a terraced stone deck leading down to the pier. You can occasionally hear tribal songs and drumming from a Native American gathering across the narrow waterway.

In the Channel Lodge's guest chambers, a marine motif reflects the inn's waterfront location. Extras abound: gas fireplaces, cushioned lounge chairs, coffeemakers, mini-refrigerators and cable TVs discretely hidden in cabinets, bedside chocolate truffles, soft terry cloth robes, and slate-tile bathrooms with two-person whirlpool tubs. Each of the rooms has a deck or balcony. The Captain's Suite, perfect for families, has a small second bedroom with twin beds, porthole windows, and a nautical door. Couples seeking romance and privacy might opt for the gatehouse with a whirlpool bath in the bedroom (but no view of the channel). Comfortable guest rooms, individual fireplaces, and an intimate library at the Country Inn carry travelers back in time to a quiet space. Simple furnishings complemented by earth-tone colors and fabrics add to the country atmosphere.

A Continental breakfast buffet with fruit, fresh-baked goods, and bowls of yogurt and granola is available at each inn. If you prefer, the congenial staff will deliver breakfast to your room. *68 double rooms with baths, 12 suites. Phone, cable TV, refrigerator in rooms. Moorage and charter boats available. $93–254; Continental breakfast, afternoon refreshments. AE, DC, MC, V. No smoking.*

MAJESTIC HOTEL ☜
419 Commercial Ave., Anacortes 98221, tel. 360/293–3355 or 800/588–4780, fax 360/293–5214

Dominating the historical district of Anacortes, the Majestic is one of the Northwest's premier small hotels.

Standing in the two-story lobby filled with 19th-century English leather sofas and wing chairs, an elegant brass chandelier, a white marble mantelpiece flanked by engaged columns, and copious flower arrangements, it's difficult to believe that this space was part of a meat market until 1954. Jeff and Virginia Wetmore, restaurant and inn developers from northern California, discovered this 1889 diamond in the rough. They spent six years stripping away everything except the original framework and restoring it, ultimately opening the Majestic in 1990. Two years later they added a charming English garden, an oasis of greenery and flowers where guests can relax over coffee or play with children.

The Wetmores take particular pride in the Rose & Crown Pub behind the lobby, which serves draft beers from local microbreweries and light meals amid 200-year-old English mahogany wainscoting, a backbar from a Victorian ice cream parlor, and beveled- and stained-glass doors from a London pub. Fancier environs enhance the fare in the Salmon Run, where compelling cuisine such as clams Bordelaise, swordfish, and salmon Caesar salad feature the freshest seasonal ingredients available in the area and a wine selection to match.

Each of the hotel's 23 guest rooms is individually custom-decorated and furnished with art and antiques from around the world. The Scottish Highland Room sports fishing rods, baskets, and old shotguns mounted on the walls, and there is a Scottish military chest from the 1880s. In the Asian Room the walls have been marbleized, and Japanese, Korean, and Chinese furniture and art are featured. An oak-paneled cupola grants a 360° view of Puget Sound, the marina, the San Juan Islands, and the Cascade and Olympic mountains. *23 double rooms with baths. Phone, cable TV, minibar, and refrigerator in rooms, VCR in most rooms. Restaurant, pub, conference facilities. $98–$225; Continental breakfast. AE, D, MC, V. Smoking on 2nd floor only.*

OTHER CHOICES

Albatross. 5708 Kingsway W, Anacortes 98221, tel. 360/293–0677 or 800/662–8864. 4 double rooms with baths. Guest phone, cable TV/VCR, library, ferry pickups on request. $85–$95; full breakfast. D, MC, V. No smoking.

Big Trees Bed & Breakfast. 4840 Fremont St., Bellingham 98226, tel. 360/647–2850 or 800/647–2850, fax 360/647–2850. 3 double rooms share 2 baths. TV/VCR, phone in rooms. Stereo in living room. $95–$115; full breakfast. MC, V. No smoking.

Hasty Pudding House. 1312 8th St., Anacortes 98221, tel. 360/293–5773 or 800/368–5588. 4 double rooms with baths. TV/VCR in 1 room. $75–$89; full breakfast. AE, D, MC, V. No smoking.

Hotel Planter. 715 1st St., La Conner 98257, tel. 360/466–4710 or 800/488–5409, fax 360/466–1320. 12 double rooms with baths. Phone, TV in rooms. Hot tub. $75–$120; no breakfast. AE, MC, V. No smoking.

North Garden Inn. 1014 N. Garden St., Bellingham 98225, tel. 360/671–7828 or 800/922–6414. 8 double rooms with baths, 2 double rooms share baths. $50–$99; full breakfast. MC, V. No smoking.

Ridgeway Farm. 14914 McLean Rd. (Box 475), La Conner 98257, tel. 360/428–8068 or 800/428–8068, fax 360/428–8880. 4 double rooms with baths, 2 doubles share bath and shower, cottage. Cable TV in lounge and cottage. $75–$155; full breakfast, evening desserts. D, MC, V. No smoking, 2-night minimum late Mar.–early Apr.

Schnauzer Crossing. 4421 Lakeway Dr., Bellingham 98226, tel. 360/733–0055 or 800/562–2808, fax 360/734–2808. 1 double room with bath, 1 suite, 1 cottage. CD player and phone in rooms, fireplace, cable TV/VCR, and whirlpool tub in suite and cottage. Hot tub. $120–$200; full breakfast, afternoon refreshments. MC, V. No smoking, 2-night minimum on weekends and holidays.

Shannon House. 2615 D Ave., Anacortes 98221, tel. 360/299–3876 or 800/828–1474, fax 360/299–8352. 1 double room with bath, 2 doubles share baths. $80–110; full breakfast. MC, V. No smoking.

South Bay Bed & Breakfast. 4095 S. Bay Dr., Lake Whatcom, Sedro Woolley 98284, tel. 360/595–2086. 5 double rooms with baths. CD player in rooms, fireplace in 4 rooms, whirlpool tubs in 3 rooms. Canoeing, kayaking, pedal-boating, fishing, mountain bikes. $125–150; full breakfast. MC, V. No smoking.

Storyville. 1880 Chilberg Rd., Mount Vernon 98273, tel. 360/466–3207 or 888/373–3207, fax 360/466–3066. 3 double rooms with baths, 2 double rooms share bath. TV/VCR, CDs player in rooms. $90–$125; full breakfast. MC, V. No smoking.

Stratford Manor Bed & Breakfast. 1416 Van Wyck Rd., Bellingham 98226, tel. 360/715–8441, fax 360/671–0840. 3 double rooms with baths. Fourth double room with bath available in summer. CD player, fireplace, whirlpool bath in rooms. Outdoor hot tub. $125–$175; full breakfast, snacks and refreshments. MC, V. No smoking.

White Swan Guest House. 15872 Moore Rd., Mt. Vernon 98273, tel. 360/445–6805. 3 double rooms share 2 baths, 1 cottage. Kitchen in cottage. $80–$150; Continental breakfast. MC, V. No smoking.

Wild Iris and the Heron Inn. 117 Maple Ave., La Conner 98257, tel. 360/466–4626. 32 double rooms with baths and suites. Phone, TV, clock radio in rooms, 2-person whirlpool tub in some suites. Hot tub. $75–$180; full breakfast. AE, MC, V. No smoking.

RESERVATIONS SERVICES

Bed & Breakfast Service (445 W. Lake Samish Dr., Bellingham 98226, tel. 360/733–8642). **Pacific Reservation Service** (Box 46894, Seattle 98146, tel. 206/439–7677 or 800/684–2932). **Washington State Bed & Breakfast Guild** (2442 N.W. Market St., Box 355-FD, Seattle 98107, tel. 800/647–2918).

Cascade Mountains and Foothills

MAZAMA COUNTRY INN ☞

42 Lost River Rd. (HCR 74/Box B9), Mazama 98833, tel. 509/996–2681 or, in WA, 800/843–7951, fax 509/996–2646

East of the North Cascades National Park, nestled in a valley laced with cross-country skiing trails, is this serenely rural, rustic mountain lodge. Owned by George Turner and Bill Pope, the Mazama is a sprawling 6,000-square-ft, two-story wood-sided building with a front entry of stone and log posts, dormer windows, and a brick-red roof set against a backdrop of pine trees and mountains.

The spacious dining and living room features a massive Russian stone fireplace, vaulted ceiling, peeled-log furniture, and floor-to-ceiling windows that look out at the valley floor and the mountains beyond. Watercolor landscapes by a local artist are displayed throughout.

Most guest rooms are comfortable, but certainly not opulent. Some of the rooms on the second floor have two levels, with a queen-size bed on the upper and a child-size bed tucked under the staircase. Four larger rooms have decks. Also available are six cabins (including one cabin that accommodates 12), ideal for families.

The inn attracts guests who want a mountain experience. In summer, the area offers mountain biking, hiking, horseback riding, river rafting, llama trekking, and fishing. In winter, the inn itself provides ski rentals and lessons and arranges for heli-skiing, inn-to-hut ski touring, and dog-sled riding. One of the hedonistic experiences you can enjoy after a day of cross-country skiing is slipping into the outdoor hot tub, surrounded by snowbanks, and gazing at the stars.

Winter breakfasts include hearty oatmeal, eggs, and fruit; in summer, the main dish might be a vegetarian omelet. Makings for sandwiches are set out after breakfast for you to fix your own brown-bag lunches. In winter, dinner is served family style. In summer, dinners are offered from the restaurant menu and may include baby-back ribs. ⌂ *14 double rooms with baths, 6 cabins. Kitchen in cabins. Restaurant, sauna, hot tub, bike rentals, gift shop. $60–$190; full breakfast (not included in summer), lunch and dinner included in winter. D, MC, V. No smoking, 2-night minimum and no meals in cabins.*

RUN OF THE RIVER INN ☞

9308 E. Leavenworth Rd. (Box 285), Leavenworth 98826, tel. 800/288–6491, fax 509/548–7547

On the Icicle River 1½ mi from Leavenworth, with a bird refuge on two sides, is this bed-and-breakfast in a classic log structure. It was built in 1979 to take advantage of extraordinary views of the river, Tumwater and Icicle canyons, and the towering Cascades.

A second story with cathedral ceilings was added by innkeepers Karen and Monty Turner, who moved here in 1987 from Las Vegas, where they both taught fifth grade. Karen still teaches, while Monty runs the inn and maintains his collection of classic and antique bicycles.

You have the entire wood-burning-stove–warmed living area downstairs to yourself because the Turners live in a small house adjacent to the inn. A guest sitting room is at the top of the circular staircase off the entryway; supported by hand-peeled logs fashioned by a local craftsman; the staircase is one of the inn's many hand-hewn log features custom-made for the Turners. Like the rest of the inn, the sitting room has an upscale country look, with handmade willow furniture and a stenciled pine dry sink. Beverages and fresh cookies are set out to make you feel at home.

Three upstairs bedrooms have high cathedral ceilings of pine, hand-hewn log furniture, and locally made hand-embroidered quilts on queen-size beds. Each room has a commanding view of the natural surroundings, along with an old fly rod, ski pole, or snowshoe on one wall as a reminder of the diversions the area offers.

The inn overlooks 70 acres of wetlands, including a small island in the river. The Turners' own landscaping includes a small pond with a log bench, a wildflower meadow with a few trails, and aspen and alpine fir trees.

In winter, the area affords the opportunity for sleigh rides and plenty of cross-country skiing and snowmobiling. Summer activities include hiking, white-water rafting, bicycling, horseback riding, fishing, golfing, and harvesting fruit at orchards.

The country breakfast may include yogurt with fruit or a fresh fruit plate, hash browns, cinnamon rolls, and a cheese and sausage strata. ⚑ *4 double rooms with baths, 2 suites. Cable TV in rooms. Hot tub, bicycles. $100–$155; full breakfast. AE, D, MC, V. No smoking, 2-night minimum on weekends and during festivals.*

SALISH LODGE ☙

6501 Railroad Ave. SE (Box 1109), Snoqualmie 98065, tel. 425/888–2556 or 800/826–6124, fax 425/888–2533

At the crest of Snoqualmie Falls is the lodge whose authentic Northwest look and dramatic site made it the choice for exterior shots of the Great Northern Hotel in the old TV series *Twin Peaks*. Rebuilt in 1988 to follow the style of the original roadway inn built here in 1916, with dormers, porches, and balconies, the lodge has a stunning new Japanese-style spa where you can relax in hydrotherapy pools and sauna and steam rooms or arrange for a facial or mud wrap.

Run with the professional flair of a small elegant hotel, the entire inn is decorated in a sophisticated Pacific Northwest theme, with warm woods, rusticated stone, and fabrics and wallpapers in rich shades. Northwest art and Native American crafts complement the decor.

The library is an inviting room, with a hardwood floor, hefty maple beams, and rows of maple bookshelves; tea and cookies are set out in the afternoon. Comfortable armchairs, a sofa, and a game table are arranged around the large stone fireplace. Although the lodge is used for meetings and the restaurant is open to the public, access to this room, as well as to the enclosed hydrotherapy and sauna rooms and fitness center, is restricted to overnight guests.

Guest rooms have stone fireplaces, minibars, natural wicker and Shaker-style furniture, either a balcony or a window seat, and goose-down comforters. All baths feature double whirlpool tubs, with French doors that open for fireplace viewing (candles are provided); each comes with thick, hooded terry cloth robes. The four corner suites all offer spectacular views of the waterfalls.

Lighted paths leading to the top of the falls make for romantic evening walks. Walking trails wend their way to the bottom of the falls, and bike paths connect with extensive country roads. A sports court (for pickleball, volleyball, and badminton) is across the road.

The dining room serves excellent regional cuisine. The country breakfast is legendary, with course upon course of oatmeal, eggs, bacon, trout, pancakes, hash browns, and fresh fruit. *△ 91 double rooms with baths, 4 suites. Air-conditioning, TV, phone, minibar, down comforters, terry cloth robes, whirlpool tub, and fireplace in rooms. Restaurant, lounge, VCR and video rentals, steam room, sauna, hydrotherapy pools, exercise room, 3 lighted courts for tennis and basketball, bicycles, professional spa services. $180–$575; breakfast not included. AE, D, DC, MC, V.*

SUN MOUNTAIN LODGE ☞

Patterson Lake Rd. (Box 1000), Winthrop 98862, tel. 509/996–2211 or 800/572–0493, fax 509/996–3133

Perched high on a mountaintop above the former gold-mining town of Winthrop, this grand resort offers panoramic vistas of the 3,000 acres of wilderness surrounding the resort, 500,000 acres of national forest, the North Cascades, and the Methow Valley below.

In keeping with its mountain setting, the lodge is constructed from massive timbers and local stone. Lobby sitting areas include hand-hewn furniture, stone floors, and large picture windows. The huge wrought-iron chandelier was created by a local artisan, as were most of the handsome, lodge-style fixtures.

Guest rooms feature hand-hewn birch furniture, original regional art, and, of course, fine views. The best vistas are from the Gardner and the Mt. Robinson wings, actually separate buildings adjacent to the lodge. All rooms in the wings are equipped with gas fireplaces, private decks, and wet bars. (Some main-lodge rooms also feature fireplaces and wet bars.) Housekeeping cabins, with brick fireplaces, are available on Patterson Lake, about a mile from the main lodge.

The restaurant is renowned for its superb cuisine, wines, and expansive views. Dinner might include smoked, autumn-run salmon or pork with cilantro and red chili butter.

An interpretive center offers nature activities, including slide shows and guided walks. Trail rides, riding lessons, hayrides, and cookouts are available; rowboats, sailboats, canoes, and mountain bikes are for hire. In winter, the lodge offers sleigh rides, ice skating, ski lessons, and cross-country skiing on the second-largest ski trail system in the United States. *△ 94 double rooms with baths, 8 suites, 13 cabins. Room service, phone in lodge rooms, wet bar and fireplace in wing rooms and some lodge rooms, kitchen in cabins. 2 restaurants, 2 heated pools, 3 hot tubs, spa, 2 tennis courts, exercise room, horseback riding, ice-skating rink, gift shop, athletic shop, meeting rooms, 2 playgrounds. $95–$270; breakfast extra. AE, MC, V. No smoking in main dining room.*

OTHER CHOICES

Abendblume Pension. 12570 Ranger Rd. (Box 981), Leavenworth 98826, tel. 509/548–4059 or 800/669–7634. 6 double rooms with baths. Down comforters and massages in rooms, wood-burning fireplace in 1 room, whirlpool bath in 1 room. Hot tub. $77–$159; full breakfast. AE, D, MC, V. No smoking.

Alexander's Country Inn. 37515 State Rd. 706 E, Ashford 98304, tel. 360/569–2300 or 800/654–7615, fax 360/569–2323. 8 double rooms with baths, 4 suites, 2 guest houses. Restaurant, hot tub. $95–$129; full breakfast. MC, V. No smoking.

All Seasons River Inn Bed & Breakfast. 8751 Icicle Rd. (Box 788), Leavenworth 98826, tel. 509/548–1425 or 800/254–0555. 3 double rooms with baths; 3 suites. Cable TV and air-conditioning in rooms. Whirlpool baths in 5 rooms. Bicycles, games room. $95–$145; full breakfast. MC, V. No smoking, 2-night minimum on weekends, festivals, holidays, and Dec.

Freestone Inn. 17798 Hwy. 20, Mazama 98833, tel. 800/639–3809. 17 double rooms with baths, 4 suites, 15 cabins, 2 lodges. Fireplace in all units. Nature walks, fly fishing, white-water rafting, ice-skating, cross-country skiing, horseback riding, mountain climbing. $115–$325; Continental-plus breakfast (complimentary for main inn guests only). AE, D, DC, MC, V. No smoking, minimum-length stay during holidays.

Haus Lorelei. 347 Division St., Leavenworth 98826, tel. 509/548–5726, 800/514–8868, fax 509/548–6548. 10 rooms with baths, guest house with 3 rooms. Hot tub, tennis court, basketball, hiking, cross-country skiing, billiards. $89–$99; full breakfast, afternoon tea and dessert. No credit cards. No smoking.

Haus Rohrbach Pension. 12882 Ranger Rd., Leavenworth 98826, tel. 509/548–7024 or 800/548–4477, fax 509/548–5038. 5 double rooms with baths, 2 doubles share bath, 3 suites. Air-conditioning. Hot tub, pool. $75–$160; full breakfast. AE, D, DC, MC, V. No smoking, 2-night minimum on weekends Sept.–mid-Mar. and on festival weekends.

Maple Valley Bed & Breakfast. 20020 S.E. 228th St., Maple Valley 98038, tel. 425/432–1409, fax 425/413–1459. 2 double rooms share bath. $75; full breakfast. No credit cards. No smoking.

Moore House Bed & Breakfast. 526 Marie Ave. (Box 629), South Cle Elum 98943, tel. 509/674–5939 or, in OR and WA, 800/228–9246. 3 double rooms with baths, 6 doubles share 2 baths, 3 suites. Mini-refrigerator, coffeemaker, and TV in suites. Hot tub. $50–$125; full breakfast, full meal service for groups by prior arrangement. AE, MC, V. No smoking, 2-night minimum on holiday weekends.

Mountain Home Lodge. Box 687, Leavenworth 98826, tel. 509/548–7077 or 800/414–2378, fax 509/548–5008. 10 double rooms with baths. Air-conditioning, pool, hot tub, tennis court. Summer $100–$330; full breakfast (lunch and dinner included in winter). D, MC, V. No smoking, 2-night minimum Dec.–Mar.

Mountain Meadows Inn Bed & Breakfast at Mt. Rainier. 28912 State Rte. 706 E, Ashford 98304, tel. 360/569–2788. 3 double rooms with baths, 1 suite, 2 housekeeping units in separate building. Access to sauna and hot tub. $75–$110; full breakfast. MC, V. No smoking.

Sleeping Lady. 7375 Icicle Rd., Leavenworth 98826, tel. 800/574–2123, fax 509/548–6312. 46 double rooms with baths, 2 cabins. Phone in rooms. $100 per person (includes 3 meals); full breakfast. AE, D, MC, V. No smoking.

RESERVATIONS SERVICES

Bedfinders Vacation Rentals (305 8th St., Leavenworth 98826, tel. 800/323–2920). **Pacific Reservation Service** (Box 46894, Seattle 98146, tel. 206/439–

7677 or 800/684–2932). **Washington State Bed & Breakfast Guild** (2442 N.W. Market St., Box 355-FD, Seattle 98107, tel. 800/647–2918).

Spokane and Environs, Including Coeur d'Alene

CLARK HOUSE ON HAYDEN LAKE 🐦
E. 4550 S. Hayden Lake Rd., Hayden Lake, ID 83835, tel. 208/772–3470 or 800/765–4593, fax 208/772–6899

If you visit the Clark House on Idaho's Hayden Lake, a 40-minute drive from Spokane, you will most likely be instantly caught up in the history and mystery surrounding the place. A reclusive mining millionaire, F. Lewis Clark had the home built as a copy of a summer palace of Kaiser Wilhelm II of Germany. With 33 rooms and 10 fireplaces, the building, whose construction began in 1895, wasn't completed until 1910. Clark and his wife, Winifred, lived in the house for four years; then he and all of his money disappeared mysteriously. Winifred waited patiently for her husband's return but was forced to sell off the land, furnishings, and eventually the house to pay back taxes.

In 1989 innkeeper Monty Danner and his son Mark bought and restored the mansion, now on the National Register of Historic Places, after it sat empty for 20 years. Monty and his partner, Rod Palmer, decorated the house in a masterful way; the result is a sumptuously comfortable country inn, set on a secluded 13-acre estate. In the long second-floor gallery, light filters through grand Palladian windows at both ends and murals brighten the walls. The walls of the smaller downstairs dining room are also covered by a mural, this time depicting the artist's interpretation of the house's history. The downstairs library offers a variety of diversions, including a scrapbook chronicling the disappearance of F. Lewis Clark.

The furnishings are both elegant and understated, and even the occasional spectacular decorative flourishes, such as the intricately carved walnut buffet crafted in Connecticut during the 1870s, blend in effortlessly with the overall scheme. Guest rooms are individually decorated and quietly luxurious. Mrs. Clark's Room, done in a tea-rose motif, has a white-and-gold-trimmed Louis XIV–style writing table and high chest. The F. Lewis Clark Room, with its canopied bed, and the Cedar Suite, done in burgundy and deep green, have a masculine Ralph Lauren look. The Hayden Lake Room, with cream and white brocade and natural wicker furniture, has the best view of the lake. French doors are in every room, some leading outdoors to deck and terrace areas, a lush lawn overlooking Hayden Lake, and a wildflower-filled garden. △ *10 double rooms with baths. TV (on request) and robes in rooms, fireplace in 4 rooms. Guest refrigerator, hot tub, conference facilities. $85–$200; full breakfast, 6-course gourmet dinner by reservation 5 nights a week, wine and beer available. AE, D, DC, MC, V. No smoking, 2-night minimum Memorial Day–Labor Day.*

THE PORTICO 🐦
502 S. Adams St., Ritzville 99169, tel. 509/659–0800

Travelers between Spokane and Seattle can pull off the freeway and find respite at the Portico, a beautifully restored historic landmark in an unlikely place— Ritzville, a farming town 60 mi southwest of Spokane. At first glance, there seems to be little to see or do here, but this unassuming little town is home to a 1937 Art Deco movie house, a nine-hole golf course, a bowling alley, and a park, which, coupled with Ritzville's clean, safe streets, evoke a simpler time.

The Portico, originally built in 1902, was the home of Nelson H. Greene, a prominent merchant, financier, and wheat broker. When the town burned down in 1889, Greene financed its reconstruction, encouraging the use of brick; hence the Portico's unusual mating of material—buff-color brick—and Queen Anne, Classical Revival, and Craftsman styles.

Innkeepers Bill and Mary Anne Phipps are passionate about architecture and period furnishings, and their attention to detail is evident. The parquet floor in the entrance hall bears a pattern of unstained dark and light oak, bordered with serpentine work in bird's-eye maple. The fireplace in the parlor is framed by oak spindle work supported by Ionic columns. Although the ceiling in the same room resembles pressed tin, it was actually produced by anaglyph, a process favored at the turn of the century for creating a design in relief.

There are two inviting guest rooms. The larger room is decorated with rich paisley wallpaper and mid- to late-19th-century English furniture. A carved walnut canopy bed is adorned with a two-tailed mermaid at its head and an angel protecting a child at its foot, both symbols of good luck. The other room is bright and cheerful, with a white wrought-iron bed topped with a quilt handmade by Mary Anne.

Breakfast is fresh and generous. In season, Mary Anne serves raspberries and blackberries fresh from her garden; homemade cinnamon rolls, delicious yeasty waffles, and homemade granola are often on the menu. ♙ *2 double rooms with baths. Air-conditioning, cable TV. $59–$74; full breakfast. AE, D, MC, V. No smoking.*

WAVERLY PLACE ❦
W. 709 Waverly Pl., Spokane 99205, tel. 509/328–1856, fax 509/326–7059

Waverly Place offers lodgings in a quiet old neighborhood just five minutes from downtown Spokane. The turreted Queen Anne house sits across the street from Corbin Park, whose 11½ acres encompass tennis courts, a running track, a baseball diamond, and a playground. Waverly Place, built in 1902, is one of several turn-of-the-century houses bordering the park; the neighborhood is listed on the state's Register of Historic Places.

Innkeepers Marge and Tammy Arndt are a mother-and-daughter team whose love for rambling Victorian houses led them to buy the building more than a decade ago. With distinctive late-Victorian pieces—many of them from Marge's mother-in-law's attic—they've created an environment in which the furnishings seem truly at home amid the graceful architecture of the house. Guests have exclusive use of two parlors, where the gleaming fir woodwork includes intricate beading around the mantelpiece and Grecian columns that separate the rooms. Most of the original light fixtures are intact, and Victorian lamps throughout the house sport fringed shades handmade by Tammy. Both women enjoy researching the house; in painting its exterior they consulted old photographs and the builder's grandson in order to remain faithful to the original look.

The guest rooms on the second floor are airy and comfortable, with queen-size reproduction beds and Oriental carpets and dhurrie rugs over shiny hardwood floors. The converted attic is a spacious, cheerful suite.

Breakfast, served in the dining room on Haviland china, reflects the innkeepers' Swedish heritage. Menus feature puffy Swedish pancakes with huckleberry sauce and almond-flavored pastries called *kringla*, as well as egg dishes, sausages, and fresh fruits and juices. △ *1 double room with bath, 2 double rooms share 2 baths, 1 3-room suite. Air-conditioning and robes in rooms. Pool, whirlpool tub. $75–$105; full breakfast. AE, D, MC, V. No smoking, 2-night minimum weekends in May and holiday weekends.*

OTHER CHOICES

Cricket on the Hearth Bed and Breakfast Inn. 1521 Lakeside Ave., Coeur d'Alene, ID 83814, tel. 208/664–6926. 3 double rooms with baths, 2 doubles share bath. Guest refrigerator. Hot tub, ski packages. $55–$85; full breakfast. No credit cards. No smoking.

Fotheringham House. 2128 W. 2nd Ave., Spokane 99204, tel. 509/838–1891, fax 509/838–1807. 1 double room with bath, 3 doubles share 2 baths. Robes in rooms. Guest refrigerator, tennis available. $75–$90; full breakfast, afternoon tea. D, MC, V. No smoking.

Gregory's McFarland House. 601 Foster Ave., Coeur d'Alene, ID 83814, tel. 208/667–1232. 5 double rooms with baths. Air-conditioning. $85–$125; full breakfast, afternoon refreshments, high tea (with 48 hrs' notice). MC, V. No smoking, 2-night minimum mid-May–mid-Oct., mid-Nov.–early Jan., and holidays.

Love's Victorian Bed and Breakfast. 31317 N. Cedar Rd., Deer Park 99006, tel. 509/276–6939. 2 double rooms with baths. Air-conditioning, robes in rooms, fireplace in one room. TV/VCR indoor hot tub, bicycles, cross-country skis. $85–$110; full breakfast, evening refreshments. MC, V. No smoking. Closed 1st weekend in Dec.

Marianna Stoltz House. 427 E. Indiana Ave., Spokane 99207, tel. 509/483–4316 or 800/978–6587, fax 509/483–67738. 2 double rooms with baths, 2 doubles share bath. Air-conditioning, cable TV in rooms. Bicycles. $65–$95; full breakfast, evening refreshments. AE, D, DC, MC, V. No smoking.

RESERVATIONS SERVICE

Spokane Bed & Breakfast Reservation Service (627 E. 25th Ave., Spokane 99203, tel. 509/624–3776).

The Palouse

GREEN GABLES INN 🐚
922 Bonsella St., Walla Walla 99362, tel. 509/525–5501

In a business where location is often everything, Green Gables Inn has everything. One block from the Whitman College campus, the Arts and Crafts–style mansion is in a picturesque historic district: Trees nearly a century old line the peaceful streets, and most of the homes in the area have been carefully restored.

Rowland H. Smith and Clarinda Green Smith, for whom the house was built in 1909, took the lead in developing the neighborhood. For nearly four decades after 1940, their place housed the nurses and offices of the Walla Walla General Hospital; it didn't return to being a private residence until 1978. Margaret Buchan and her husband, Jim, the sports editor at the local newspaper, bought the mansion in 1990 and converted it into a B&B and reception facility.

A broad porch, tucked under the overhanging eaves, sweeps across the front of the mansion and around one side, an ideal setting for relaxing on a warm afternoon, lemonade and book in hand. The Buchans filled the yard with flowering plants, bulbs, and shrubs. Inside the front vestibule, a large foyer is flanked by two sitting areas, both with fireplaces and one with a TV.

The five guest rooms, whose names are derived from Lucy Maud Montgomery's novel *Anne of Green Gables*, are on the second floor; the hallway between them is lined with floor-to-ceiling bookshelves, and a love seat tucked into a corner creates a cozy library. All of the rooms feature baths with claw-foot tubs. The only room with a fireplace, Idlewild, also has a private deck and a hot tub. Dryad's Bubble is sufficiently spacious to accommodate a reading area with an overstuffed chair and ottoman, a dresser and dressing table, and a king-size bed with striped comforter; French doors open to a small private balcony. The smallest room, Mayflowers, was once the maid's quarters; now the picture of Victorian femininity, with floral wallpaper, an antique quilt, and plenty of pillows with lace shams, it affords lots of privacy.

Margaret serves breakfast, which might include sausage quiche and seasonal fruit, in a formal dining room. An Arts and Crafts–style sideboard displaying her collection of china and serving pieces from the early 1900s runs the length of one wall. Children under 12 are welcome in the carriage house. ♨ *5 double rooms with baths, 2 suites. Fireplace in 1 room, kitchen in 1 suite. Cable TV. $75–$160; full breakfast. AE, D, MC, V. No smoking.*

PURPLE HOUSE BED AND BREAKFAST ☜
415 E. Clay St., Dayton 99328, tel. and fax 509/382-3159 or 800/486-2474

Although only a block off Highway 12—which is also the main street through Dayton—the Purple House Bed and Breakfast is quiet. Perhaps this is because Dayton isn't on the way to anywhere, and traffic is never too bad here. Owner Christine Williscroft spent 12 years remodeling and decorating the Queen Anne Italianate–style home, which is on the National Register of Historical Places. It was built in 1882 by a pioneer physician in what is now one of Dayton's oldest neighborhoods and was opened to guests in 1991.

A native of southern Germany, Christine brought European touches to her B&B. In the main-floor guest room, which she calls the luxurious master bedroom, French doors open to the patio and swimming pool that compose the entire backyard of the house. Christine's real passion, however, is for things Chinese. Her formal living room is filled with Chinese antiques and appointments: Oriental rugs, an antique screen, a wedding kimono, and a hutch. Two carved wooden temple dogs guard the room's grand piano, and two live shih tzus guard the house.

Privacy was a priority in the design of the guest rooms. The carriage-house suite has a freestanding fireplace, a kitchenette, and a sunken Japanese soaking tub. The master bedroom has a pink sunken tub, color-coordinated with the rest of the room, which includes a rose-print bedspread. Two accommodations upstairs share not only a bath with a marble shower, floor, sink, and counter but also a small sitting area and library at the top of the stairs. An antique oak sleigh bed and tasteful forest-green wallpaper make the smaller of the rooms feel snug. The other room, cheerful and sunny, faces the front yard and has a Victorian feel, with 19th-century mahogany antiques and matching chintz fabrics.

Strudel and huckleberry pancakes often turn up at breakfast along with local bacon or sausage. Christine is a thoughtful host: she packs picnic lunches for her guests, offers afternoon pastries and tea in the parlor, and will accommodate dining restrictions and requests. Dinner, served family style, is available at $25 per person for guests (minimum six people). A typical entrée might be Hungarian goulash, pork roast, or standing rib roast. ⌂ *1 double room with bath, 2 doubles share bath, 1 suite. Kitchen in suite, cable TV in common room. Pool May–Sept., ski equipment, bicycle storage. $85–$125; full breakfast, afternoon refreshments, picnic lunches, and dinner available. MC, V. No smoking.*

OTHER CHOICES

Country Bed & Breakfast. Rte. 2 (Box 666), Pullman 99163, tel. 509/334–4453, fax 509/332–5163. 1 queen room with bath, 2 doubles share bath, 2 suites. TV in den, TV/VCR in Playroom, hot tub. $50–$100 ($25 for additional beds in Playroom); Continental-plus breakfast, full breakfast and dinner by reservation. D, MC, V. No smoking; 2-night minimum stay during college-activity weekends.

Stone Creek Inn. 720 Bryant Ave., Walla Walla 99362, tel. 509/529–8120, fax 509/529–8120. 2 double rooms with baths, 2 doubles share bath. Fireplace in 2 rooms. Pool, hot tub, limousine service from Walla Walla airport. $95–$125; full breakfast. MC, V. No smoking.

WEST VIRGINIA

The Eastern Panhandle

EDGEWOOD MANOR ❧
Rte. 2 (Box 329), Bunker Hill 25413, tel. 304/229–9353, fax 304/229–9359

Gen. Elisha M. Boyd would not be disappointed if he returned today to the red-brick Federal house he built in 1839, especially if he arrived during one of Edgewood Manor's occasional Civil War cavalry reenactments. In the house, once temporary headquarters for Gen. Stonewall Jackson, he'd find an 1860 Austrian pianoforte, authentic Civil War paraphernalia, and a cabinet filled with American history books.

Sharon and John Feldt, she a teacher and he a lawyer, stumbled onto the vacant house while traveling to battle sites from Texas. They bought it on the spot in 1995, because it was just what Sharon and her mother, Birdie Lamkin, had envisioned for their inn. A gravel drive points to the white columned portico and house on 52 acres. Nearby, a fertile spring spews daily more than 4 million gallons of fresh water, supplying all of Berkeley County. Sharon's tasteful hand has touched each immense room, most with four-poster bed, simple lace curtains, and Oriental rugs. The Texas Room features the yellow rose, and the General James Pettigrew Room, like the rest of the house, carries a Civil War theme, with framed battle scenes and soldier paraphernalia.

Sharon's creative breakfasts of fresh breads, casseroles, and fruit dishes; afternoon teas; and murder mystery weekends have summoned guests both local and afar. ♙ *6 double rooms, 2 doubles share bath. Air-conditioning, fireplace in 3 guest rooms. $85–$145; full breakfast. AE, MC, V. No smoking.*

HILLBROOK ❧
Rte. 2 (Box 152), Charles Town 25414, tel. 304/725–4223 or 800/304–4223, fax 304/725–4455

Would Hillbrook, hidden along a country lane outside Charles Town, be such a special place without its innkeeper, Gretchen Carroll? One tends to think not, although the house itself is spectacularly eccentric, splayed in six stages along a hill, never more than one room wide or one room deep. The house has 13 sharply peaked gables, half-timbered white-stucco walls, and mullioned windows—the one in the living room has 360 panes. Ann Hathaway would feel right at home. Gretchen calls the style "Norman Tudor" and explains that during World War I a civil engineer by the name of Bamford fell in love with an inn in Normandy and determined to re-create it in the wilds of West Virginia. Erratically, he chose to start with two ancient log cabins. The logs and mortises of one of these are still apparent in the dining porch.

Gretchen was a foreign-service brat who grew up in the far corners of the world, including Turkey, Thailand, and the Ivory Coast; and Hillbrook is full of exotic curios and objets d'art. The living room holds pottery and a Senegalese fertility statue; in bedrooms you'll find Oriental rugs, an antique Vuitton steamer trunk, and a Thai spirit house. Richly patterned wallpaper, upholstery, and pillows; randomly angled ceilings; potted plants; and architectural cubbyholes complete the Hillbrook picture. The Cottage guest room, with its private entry overlooking an ancient springhouse (from which Hillbrook gets its water), has paisley-pattern wallpaper and a wood-burning stove backed with Italian tile. Locke's Nest overlooks the living room from 20 ft up and has brass double and single beds and a lavender bathtub. There is also now a Gatehouse available for small weddings and meetings.

The inn's seven-course dinners feature stuffed quail or grilled rosemary lamb chops; feta-cheese-and-pomegranate salad; and chocolate "decadence" cake. Breakfast specialties are sherried mushroom omelets, home-baked grilled fruitbreads, and a delightful "egg blossom" dish.

Bullskin Run Creek trickles away at the bottom of the Hillbrook lawn, the haunt of ducks, inn guests, and a cat named Princess Fuzzy Butt. There are, of course, attractions to visit in the surrounding area but nothing that would keep one away from idyllic Hillbrook for long. △ *6 double rooms with baths. Air-conditioning in rooms, fireplace in 2 rooms. $160–$300; full breakfast, high tea on Sun. Nov.– Apr. (Lunch $30, by reservation only; dinner $70). AE, D, MC, V. Dinner required with 1-night stay. No smoking in dining area.*

WASHINGTON HOUSE INN 🐚
216 S. George St., Charles Town 25414, tel. 304/725–7923 or 800/297–6957

Mel and Nina Vogel glided into the inn business in 1993; he was a software consultant, and she, born of restaurateur parents, an experienced flight attendant with Eastern Airlines. Pampering and personality come naturally to the duo, and they set out to transform the turreted 1899 Victorian into a plush but unpretentious spot. Nina, elected to the local city council in 1997, knows what travelers need and supplies it—from scented soaps and hard candies to tufted side chairs, Limoges china, and layers of handmade quilts. The grandnephew of the first U.S. president built the house, which is fitted with a breezy, wraparound front porch just right for lounging on its wicker chairs and flipping through the daily newspaper. Guest rooms comfort, several with fireplaces and Casablanca paddle ceiling fans, while every available public space is stuffed with knickknacks that command curiosity. Breakfast is served on the porch or in the genteel, oxblood-hued dining room. If the cinnamon French toast dripping with strawberry cream cheese won't do, then Nina might offer you a Mexican omelet, fruit cup, and array of muffins or an egg and sausage casserole. △ *6 double rooms with baths. Air-conditioning, fireplace in 2 public rooms. $75–$125; full breakfast. AE, D, MC, V. No smoking.*

OTHER CHOICES

Bavarian Inn and Restaurant. Shepherd Grade Rd., Rte. 480 (Rte. 1, Box 30), Shepherdstown 25443, tel. 304/876–2551, fax 304/876–9355. 73 double rooms with baths. Restaurant, TV and phone in rooms, fireplace and whirlpool tub in 26 rooms, private balconies, 3 conference rooms, pool, tennis courts, exercise room. $85–$165; breakfast extra. AE, D, DC, MC, V. No smoking in some areas and rooms, 2-night minimum holiday weekends.

Boydville. 601 S. Queen St., Martinsburg 25401, tel. 304/263–1448 or 202/626–2896. 6 double rooms with baths. Air-conditioning, fireplace in 2 rooms, fireplace and cable TV in common area. $100–$140; full breakfast. MC, V. No smoking, 2-night minimum Memorial Day weekend and Oct. weekends. Closed Mon.–Wed., except holiday weekends; Aug.; Dec. 20–30.

Country Inn. 207 S. Washington St., Berkeley Springs 25411, tel. 304/258–2210 or 800/822–6630, fax 304/258–3986. 66 double rooms with baths, 11 doubles share 4 baths, 5 suites. Restaurant, pub, room service, air-conditioning, cable TV in rooms, phone in annex rooms, spa, 2 conference rooms. $39–$136; breakfast extra. AE, D, DC, MC, V. No smoking in suites, 2-night minimum weekends May–Oct. and major holiday weekends.

The Mountains

CHEAT MOUNTAIN CLUB ☙

Red Run Rd., Cheat Bridge (11 mi south of Huttonsville) Box 28, Durbin 26264, tel. 304/456–4627, fax 304/456–3192

Standing 3,800 ft above sea level, on the shoulder of the colossal Cheat Mountain and surrounded by 9 of West Virginia's 10 highest peaks and the 901,000-acre Monongahela National Forest, the Cheat Mountain Club has a setting that will always be enough to make it special among inns. Lovers of the outdoors are sure to appreciate the changing seasons here, whether the lodge is buried in snow, blanketed with wild rhododendrons, or enveloped in a fog so thick that no one bothers to step outside the front door. The grounds include 188 acres, across which the trout-rich Shavers Fork River flows. From it a tracery of old logging roads spirals away into the mountains—one route leading 18 mi south to Bald Knob. Five miles of trails within the club's boundaries, along which shy black bears are often spied, are groomed for hiking, mountain biking, and cross-country skiing.

Until 1988 this paradise was privately owned, used as a retreat for the executives of a logging company. Later it was sold to a group of five West Virginia families who opened it to the public. Resident manager Cynthia Loebig brings a knowledge of the outdoors and three excellent meals that are included in the club's daily rate. Fly-fishing pro Frank Oliverio is called in to teach his delicate art to novices or share his knowledge of local streams with the more experienced.

The pine-paneled guest rooms on the lodge's second floor are functionally decorated and immaculately kept. Only one has a private bath, but the large, multiple shared bathrooms (one for women, another for men) are extremely comfortable and outfitted with tubs, showers, and piles of fresh linen; there's also a sink in each guest room. The third floor holds a dormitory-style room that can sleep extra kids. Downstairs is a large gathering hall scattered with Adirondack chairs, and a dining room with self-serve bar. There is almost always a crackling fire in both of the huge stone hearths. The room is full of topographical maps, magazines, and books and is a meeting place where guests enjoy predinner drinks. ⌂ *1 king-size room with bath; 7 doubles, 1 single, and dormitory (sleeps 6) share 2 multiple baths. Box lunches available, 2 meeting rooms, game room, fishing, mountain biking, cross-country skiing, canoeing, horseshoes, and snowshoes. $80–$150 per person; full breakfast, lunch, and dinner. MC, V. No smoking in rooms.*

GENERAL LEWIS INN ✸

301 E. Washington St., Lewisburg 24901, tel. 304/645–2600 or 800/628–4454,
fax 304/645–2600

This is a country hostel of perfect proportions (just 25 rooms), run by the Hock family since 1928. It lies in a shady residential section of Lewisburg, a National Register town with a historic academy, stone church, and Confederate cemetery. Down the street from the inn are pleasant shops selling West Virginia quilts, ladies' dresses, and antiques. You can see everything Lewisburg has to offer in an easy afternoon, leaving you lots of time to sit on the veranda at the General Lewis. Out front there's a restored carriage, which used to rumble over the James River and Kanawha Turnpike (now Route 60), and in the back garden is owner Mary Hock Morgan's large old dollhouse.

Mary's parents started the General Lewis in the original house, built in the early 1800s; the architect who designed the West Virginia governor's mansion in Charleston later supervised a 1920s addition to the building, which blends flawlessly with the older section. The Hocks were great antiques collectors, and the inn is full of their prizes, including farming implements and a nickelodeon that still plays "The Man in the Moon Has His Eyes on You." The front desk came from the Sweet Chalybeate Springs Hotel and was reputedly leaned on by Patrick Henry and Thomas Jefferson. In fact, the only non-antiques you'll come across are the chairs in the dining room.

Though the inn is ably managed by Nan Morgan, granddaughter of Randolph and Mary Hock, Mary Hock Morgan is usually around to show children where to find the checkers. She lived in the General Lewis until the age of 15 and is dedicated to keeping it retrogressive. The inn has some newfangled touches, such as central heat and air-conditioning with individual room controls. But Mary balks at refinishing the furniture; she wants guests to see where generations of hands have rubbed and polished the cannonball beds.

All the rooms on the first and second floors are different, and when unoccupied, the doors are left open so that guests might peek inside. Because the same rate can apply to rooms of radically varying size, guests might want to ask for the largest in any given category. But even if you wind up in a cozy chamber, you won't be disappointed. △ *23 double rooms with baths, 2 suites. Restaurant, room service during restaurant hrs, air-conditioning, cable TV, phone in rooms. $75–$112; breakfast not included. AE, D, MC, V. No smoking.*

GRACELAND INN ✸

100 Campus Dr., Davis & Elkins College, Elkins 26241, tel. 304/637–1600
or 800/624–3157, fax 304/637–1809

When Sen. Henry Gassaway Davis built this extravagant "summer retreat" in 1893, he named it for his fifth child, Grace. Its turreted, Queen Anne architecture blends native oak, cherry, and maple timbers with Tiffany glass and a broad, imposing stairway, lending a country elegance to the rustic castle, now an inn run by Davis & Elkins College and its students. After standing empty for two decades, the National Historic Landmark underwent a $2 million restoration and reopened in 1996. With sweeping views of the town below, it has a sitting room and nine huge guest rooms (one is octagonal and measures 600 square ft), lavishly decorated with reproductions and some period pieces. Eventually, 13 rooms will be renovated. A light breakfast greets guests, but a grander repast is dinner in the Mingo Room, featuring smoked salmon pâté, veal Oscar, and grilled duck breast. Grace would be pleased at her namesake's Renaissance. ♨ *5 double rooms with baths, 3 suites, 1 single with bath. Restaurant, phone in rooms, TV in public room, nearby conference center. $118–180; Continental breakfast. AE, D, DC, MC, V. No smoking.*

HUTTON HOUSE ☙

Rtes. 250 and 219 (Box 88), Huttonsville 26273, tel. 304/335–6701

Most of the guests at this inn overlooking the Tygart River valley have been here before. "Regulars" have fallen in love with this Queen Anne Victorian, just as Loretta Murray and Dean Ahern did while honeymooning in the area in 1987. The couple gave up their careers and moved from Philadelphia to undertake the meticulous restoration of the house, showcasing original oak woodwork, ornate windows, arched pocket doors, a winding staircase, and a three-story turret.

Guest rooms are decorated in different styles, from the Art Deco–style Waterfall Room with its veneer furniture to the brass bed and ice-cream-parlor table of the dormered Corrine's Room. The antiques-filled and formal parlor is a quiet place to read, but the recreation room with its bumper pool table, TV, and other games sees the most use.

Breakfast is a feast of fresh fruit, crème brûlée, maple-walnut and multigrain pancakes, cheese-filled French toast, and a variety of egg dishes. ♨ *6 double rooms with baths. TV in public room, parlor, recreation room. $75–$80; full breakfast. MC, V. No smoking.*

OTHER CHOICES

Henderson House and A Governor's Inn. A Governor's Inn, 76 E. Main St.; Henderson House, 29 Sedgewick St., Buckhannon, WV 26201, tel. 304/472–2516 or 800/CALLWVA, fax 304/472–1613. Henderson House: 3 double rooms with baths; air-conditioning. Governor's Inn: 6 double rooms, 3 with shared baths, 4 with air-conditioning; 1 suite with 2-person tub. TV in public room, board games. $59–$150; full breakfast. AE, MC, V. No smoking.

Warfield House. 318 Buffalo St., Elkins 26241, tel. 304/636–4555. 3 double rooms with baths, 2 doubles share bath. $65–$75; full breakfast. No credit cards. No smoking.

Woodcrest. Rte. 2, Box 520, Beckwith 25840, tel. 304/574–3870. 4 rooms with baths (5th room available but must share bath with another room), 4-bedroom cabin with 2 baths. Air-conditioning, TV room, library, room service, shelter by pond for picnics. $50–$70 (cabin: $100 for 4 people, $15 per additional person); full breakfast. AE, D, MC, V. No smoking. Closed Nov.–Mar.

WISCONSIN

Milwaukee and Southeast Wisconsin

ALLYN MANSION INN 🐚

511 E. Walworth Ave., Delavan 53115, tel. 414/728–9090

When Alexander Allyn, along with Milwaukee architect E. Townsend Mix, built this palatial mansion in 1885, his motto may well have been "If you've got it, flaunt it—and do it in good taste." Current owners Joe Johnson and Ron Markwell followed that dictum when restoring Allyn's home, which had spent decades as a furniture store and then a nursing home. The house, listed on the National Register of Historic Places, is considered Wisconsin's best-preserved example of the Queen Anne–Eastlake style.

The duo filled the mansion's 23 rooms with American antiques that, along with six original gasoliers, French walnut woodwork, parquet floors, and 10 Italian marble fireplaces—4 topped with grand Eastlake mirrors—create the very picture of late-19th-century elegance. The high, coved ceilings in each of the three parlors have been repainted with floral scrollwork, as in Allyn's day, following the designs uncovered during restoration. The front room glitters with gold French wallpaper, and green velvet portieres dangle from walnut rings over the doorway. Shutters on the tall windows shield from sunlight the room's stately grandfather clock, Victorian tufted-silk sofa, and matching chairs, and a cribbage board made from a walrus tusk stands ready on the marble coffee table. In another parlor is an 1890 Steinway grand piano, originally from a convent (and now the focus of the inn's musicales). The dining room displays English china from Chicago's 1893 Columbian Exposition. In the library, floor-to-ceiling bookshelves accommodate a collection of books about the Windy City.

The Empire Room is furnished completely in that period's antiques and dazzles guests with an 1830 tester bed with a slipper sofa at its foot, a mirror, fireplace clock, game table, curvy settee, and marble-topped table. In the Mary Elizabeth Room, guests can relax on the chaise longue before bedding down on the 9½-ft-tall full-tester. To retain the historical integrity of the mansion, new bathrooms have been added in a separate wing.

Enormous trees and colorful flower beds surround the house, and the grand porte cochere, a replica, will have you looking for carriages to drive up and complete the picture. **⚠** *8 double rooms share 7 baths. Air-conditioning. $90–$100, $60 single weekdays; full breakfast, evening refreshments. MC, V. No smoking.*

INN AT OLD TWELVE HUNDRED 🐚
806 W. Grand Ave., Port Washington 53074, tel. 414/268–1200, fax 414/284–6855

When Stephanie Bresette and her husband Ellie bought this magnificent Victorian home in 1990, they almost felt like they were the original owners. Built in 1890 by a wealthy local widower, it was purchased in 1920 by a Chicago bachelor. In 1945, it was acquired by a childless couple, who then sold it to the Bresettes. Because it had only a few owners—none of whom wanted to "modernize" it—the 6,000-square-ft home retains many original light fixtures, its original oak woodwork, lead and stained glass, and such period fixtures as pocket doors and quaint fireplaces.

Happily, Stephanie had an extensive antiques collection, which fit perfectly into the home. The parlor and living room are now furnished in shades of Victorian plum, rose, and cranberry, with velvet-upholstered wing chairs and matching sofa. Two of the home's many Oriental rugs cover the floors. The dining room, where Stephanie serves breakfast on cool days, has oak paneling and a beamed ceiling and is furnished with two antique oak sideboards and a china cabinet that houses Stephanie's collection of Waterford crystal and antique cut glass.

Upstairs, the original master suite has a private porch and is furnished with a king-size brass-and-iron bed. The sitting area has two comfy wing chairs facing a fireplace. Another suite has a four-season enclosed porch, complete with fireplace. That suite is furnished in a light and informal 1920s cottage style.

Stephanie and Ellie completely refurbished the third floor, which was unfinished when they purchased the home. They removed 6 tons of original plaster and created two luxury suites. While decked out with whirlpool baths, the rooms retain the character of the house because the Bresettes reused original woodwork and custom-ordered new woodwork to match the old. The two suites have cable TV and VCRs as well as fireplaces; one also has its own treetop-level porch.

The Inn's annex, just 50 ft from the main house, includes two suites and a double room. One suite has a whirlpool bath as well as an oversize shower with two showerheads. It is furnished with an antique walnut bed and matching dresser. The second suite has Oriental rugs and antique oak furniture. All three rooms in the annex have a refrigerator, microwave, and coffeemaker. △ *1 double room with bath, 6 suites. Air-conditioning, cable TV/VCR in suites, fireplace in rooms, whirlpool bath in 4 rooms, bathrobes, refrigerator for guests. $95–$175; Continental breakfast. AE, MC, V. No smoking.*

MANSARDS ON-THE-LAKE 🐚
827 Lake Ave., Racine 53403, tel. 414/632–1135

This Second Empire–style house, built in 1867, sports a green mansard roof and neat rows of dormers. The structure has been occupied by a string of colorful people: Its first owners were an inventor and his wife, a suffragist who worked as an editor; they were followed by a family of musicians and a circus acrobat whose wife, also a circus performer, did trick horseback riding. Today's owner is a retired Russian-language teacher who inherited the house and many of its furnishings from her mother.

The second and third floors and the rear wing are now self-contained suites, each with a living room, a bedroom, a bathroom, and a kitchen. The high-ceiling Polonaise Suite, on the second floor, is decorated with theatrical posters from Eastern Europe collected by the innkeeper during study tours. Its kitchen has a full-size refrigerator, stove, and microwave oven and is stocked with the makings for breakfast, including cheeses and the locally famous pretzel-shape pastry known as Danish Kringle. The dining area, though small, has a view of Lake Michigan and contains a lively display of Polish circus posters, cut paper, and framed embroidery. Still other theatrical posters, these for European productions of *Romeo and Juliet* and *The Student Prince*, hang in the bedroom. An old-fashioned metal ice-cream-parlor table and chairs sit beside the room's sunny bay windows. The crocheted bedspread was made by the innkeeper's mother, who sat in the very same wooden rocker you can relax in today. French doors open to a balcony with a lake view. The bathroom is "bigger than an airplane's," says the host—though not by much; it contains a tub and shower.

The third-floor Garret Suite has a Bohemian artist-in-residence ambience. Low dormer windows punctuate the sloped walls, and the living room is full of books and magazines. The white reproduction French provincial–style furnishings do little to enhance the room's charm—the living room's sectional sofa does even less. But a 1950s-style chrome dinette gives the kitchen lots of character, and its terrific view of the lake doesn't hurt, either. Here, too, the refrigerator is stocked with breakfast fixings. The Seascapes Suite, in the rear, has the best lake view and the best furnishings—a bright contemporary sofa and Colonial-reproduction bedroom set. The fourth suite is a two-room efficiency.

This inn is a good bet for guests who will be in town for longish stays. The backyard leads straight to Lake Michigan, and Racine's historic district is a stroll away.
    ▲ *4 suites. Air-conditioning, cable TV in suites. $65–$85; breakfast fixings stocked in kitchens. MC, V. No smoking.*

STAGECOACH INN ☜

W61 N. 520 Washington Ave., Cedarburg 53012, tel. 414/375–0208 or 888/375–0208, fax 414/375–6170

After careful restoration by historian Brook Brown and his wife, Liz, this compact Greek Revival limestone inn once again welcomes travelers, as it did when stagecoaches stopped in Cedarburg on their journey between Milwaukee and Green Bay in 1853, when the house was built. Restoring the corner pub was the Browns' first project. They uncovered the tin ceiling; set up a long, well-used wooden bar where the original had stood; refinished the rough plank floors; brought in some handsome tavern tables; and—in a place of honor behind the bar, next to the vintage silver cash register and grandmother clock—installed the original pub's wooden signpost depicting a fleet of white steeds. This is where the inn's guests gather for breakfast every morning and where, in the evenings, they congregate for draughts of Sprecher, a local root beer.

A prize wallflower bench from an old-time dance hall sits in the front-hall corridor, at the bottom of the steep, narrow cherry-wood staircase that leads to the guest rooms on the second and third floors. The rooms' sunny nooks and low dormers host a collection of rustic furniture, much of it 100-year-old pine. Braided rugs and Oriental carpets warm the rough pine floors.

One suite has an exposed limestone wall, an antique oak dresser, and a whirlpool bath. Another, one of three that overlook Cedarburg's beautifully preserved old main street, has a hand-stenciled frieze on the walls and a cherrywood country Victorian bed, wardrobe, and dresser. The walls of the third-floor rooms are also stenciled, and the furniture is antique pine; two rooms have whirlpool baths, and another has two sleigh beds and is brightened by a skylight. The only guest room on the ground floor is a suite. In it are an 1860 four-poster bed, a sturdy immigrant chest that still looks capable of transporting all your worldly possessions, and a well-worn Oriental carpet.

The 1847 frame house across the street now houses three of the Stagecoach's whirl-pool suites, all furnished with antiques. Guests return to the main building in the morning to join other guests for a breakfast of freshly ground coffee, juice, cereals, croissants, and homemade muffins. ♙ *6 double rooms with baths, 6 suites. Air-conditioning, cable TV in most rooms, phone in rooms on request, fireplace in 2 suites, whirlpool bath in suites, pub, chocolate shop. $75–$130; Continental breakfast, afternoon refreshments. AE, D, DC, MC, V. No smoking.*

WASHINGTON HOUSE INN 🐦

W62 N573 Washington Ave., Cedarburg 53012, tel. 414/375–3550 or 800/554–4717, fax 414/375–9422

This cream-colored brick Victorian building, built on Cedarburg's main street in 1886, is actually the second hostelry to stand on this site; the first was established in 1846. Jim Pape, who restored Cedarburg's Stone Hill Winery (and spearheaded the town's historic-preservation movement), took on the task of returning the Washington House to its former glory. The building had been used as offices and apartments since the 1920s, and nearly the only thing that hadn't been modernized or covered up was the lobby's parquet floor. After removing decades' worth of "improvements," Jim and his wife, Sandy, decided to leave many of the building's broad supporting beams and rough limestone walls exposed and set about filling guest rooms with regional period antiques.

Guest rooms are named after pillars of 19th-century Cedarburg society. The Frederich Hilgen Room, dressed in Bradbury & Bradbury wallpaper popular in the late 1800s, has a half-canopy bed draped with burgundy paisley print, a vintage marble-topped walnut table, and two reproduction wing chairs flanking the tall, narrow, shuttered windows. The bathroom is done in 1-inch-square white tiles and contains a marble sink and an antique dresser.

Dr. Friedrich Luening's Room is genteelly rustic, with its tall South Carolina pencil-post bed and its plank floor strewn with rag rugs. Patchwork quilts decorate the walls, and a fire-engine-red circular iron stairway from the old Pabst Brewery leads to the loft sitting area under the exposed-beam ceiling. Plants adorn the spalike adjoining room, and there's a modern fireplace and a decidedly 20th-century double whirlpool bath.

Windows in the dining room, on the ground floor, overlook Washington Avenue, the town's main thoroughfare. But even when the comings and goings abate, there's plenty to look at inside, with the pressed-tin ceiling, the farm tables, and the rustic Victorian chairs. On your way in or out, glance at the original hotel register on display in the spacious lobby.

The nearby Schroeder House, an 1880s stone home now converted to an inn annex, houses five rooms. Ask for the Gertrude Schroeder Room, which has a private entrance and sitting room. ♙ *34 double rooms with baths. Air-conditioning, phone, and cable TV in 29 rooms, whirlpool bath in 31 rooms, gas fireplace in 14 rooms, elevator, sauna. $69–$189; Continental breakfast, social hour with locally made wine and cheese. AE, D, DC, MC, V.*

OTHER CHOICES

Eagle Centre House. W370 S9590 Hwy. 67, Eagle 53119, tel. 414/363–4700. 5 double rooms with baths. Air-conditioning, radio in rooms, double whirl-pool bath in 2 rooms. $95–$145; full breakfast, evening refreshments, AE, MC, V. No.

Elizabethan Inn. 463 Wrigley Dr., Lake Geneva 53147, tel. 414/248–9131. 10 double rooms with baths. Air-conditioning, private pier. $99–$159; full breakfast. No credit cards. No smoking, 2-night minimum weekends and holidays.

Lawrence House. 403 S. Lake Shore Dr., Lake Geneva 53147, tel. 414/248–4684 or 800/530–2262, fax 414/248–3412. 5 double rooms with baths. Air-conditioning, cable TV, whirlpool baths, video library, wheelchair-accessible room. $140–$195; full breakfast, afternoon refreshments. AE, D, DC, MC, V. 2-night minimum weekends in summer.

Lazy Cloud Lodge. N2025 N. Lake Shore Dr., Fontana 53125, tel. 414/275–3322, fax 414/275–8340. 9 double rooms with baths. Air-conditioning, fireplace, and whirlpool bath in rooms. $135–$195; Continental breakfast. AE, MC, V.

Pederson Victorian Bed & Breakfast. 1782 Hwy. 120 N, Lake Geneva 53147, tel. 414/248–9110. 1 double room with bath, 3 doubles share bath. Air-conditioning, ceiling fans, hammocks and porch swing. $70–$80, $45 single weekdays Nov.–Apr.; full breakfast. MC, V. No smoking.

Roses. 429 S. Lake Shore Dr., Lake Geneva 53147, tel. 414/248–4344 or 888/ROSEBNB, fax 414/248–5766. 4 double rooms with baths. Air-conditioning, cable TV. $75–$105 Nov.–Apr., $95–$145 May–Oct; full breakfast. Smoking on 1st floor only.

Water's Edge. W4232 West End Rd., Lake Geneva 53147, tel. and fax 414/245–9845. 4 double rooms with baths, 1 suite, 2 2-bedroom apartments. Air-conditioning, cable TV, fireplace in 2 rooms, whirlpool bath in 1 room, private pier. $110–$145 (plus $10 per person in apartments); full breakfast. AE, MC, V. No smoking, 2-night minimum on summer weekends.

Madison and Environs

ARBOR HOUSE 🐦
3402 Monroe St., Madison 53711, tel. 608/238–2981, fax 608/238–1175

This handsome Greek Revival building began life in the 1830s as a one-room pioneer home. That original structure, the oldest residence in Madison, is preserved as the living room of the Arbor House. In 1854, an inn was attached to the front of the small house, which became a stagecoach stop on the route from Madison to the west. The building began to deteriorate after the stagecoach gave way to the railroad, but was saved in the 1940s when an art professor at the nearby University of Wisconsin purchased the historic structure and restored it, adding a rear wing that contained his studio.

The home has been a B&B since 1986, and today, thanks to careful restoration, the entire building retains its pioneer feel, with original pine-and-oak floors, stone fireplaces, and narrow hallways. But innkeepers Cathie and John Imes are not only preserving a venerable building. They're also developing an environmentally friendly B&B, with organic cotton sheets and towels, wool carpets and rugs, organic soaps and bath products, and water- and energy-saving plumbing and lighting—all while providing a quiet, luxurious retreat in the city.

The front rooms of the building, which served as the tavern in the 1850s, are now luxurious quarters called the Tap Room. Brass fixtures, a fish tank, and an old porthole window create a nautical theme, while a wet bar reminds guests of the room's original purpose. The antique brass bed in the Cozy Rose Room is made up with floral-patterned linens; one of the original stone fireplaces and a double whirlpool bath add to the relaxing, romantic mood. A view of the wooded yard and two skylights in the vaulted ceiling betray the origins of the top-floor suite called the Studio. Once the professor's atelier, it's now dominated by a brass bed with a lively southwestern-design quilt; there's a separate dressing room, and another skylight crowns the cedar-paneled whirlpool room.

The adjoining annex features a two-story great room with beamed ceiling of massive Douglas-fir timbers salvaged from a Sears building in Chicago. The annex's three rooms are furnished in comfortable style; one has a pine sleigh bed and plaid linens, another a four-poster bed with wildflower-patterned linens.

Breakfast is served either on an enclosed pine-paneled porch that overlooks the flower garden or in the Annex great room. △ *7 double rooms with baths, 1 suite. Air-conditioning, TV in 6 rooms, fireplace in 3 rooms, radio in rooms, refrigerator in 2 rooms, whirlpool bath in 5 rooms, cotton robes for guests, phone, TV, fax, and computer available in common room, badminton, bird-watching, bike path across street, bicycles, pond. $84–$195; Continental breakfast weekdays, full breakfast weekends, evening refreshments. AE, MC, V. No smoking, 2-night minimum on holidays and football-game weekends.*

COLLINS HOUSE ✿

704 E. Gorham St., Madison 53703, tel. 608/255–4230, fax 608/255–0830

This sturdy brick Prairie-style house, built for a lumber magnate in 1911, was divided into apartments, then used as an office building, and then abandoned. But it was on a prime corner lot in Madison's historic district, next to a small city park and overlooking Lake Mendota. So in 1985, Barb and Mike Pratzel bought it and dismantled its "modernizations," revealing ceilings with oak and mahogany beams, decorative leaded-glass windows, and the clean geometric lines of Prairie design. Then they polished the rare red-maple floors, filled the house with a collection of vintage Mission and Arts and Crafts furnishings that complement the exquisite woodwork, and opened it as a bed-and-breakfast.

In the living room, a hassock and armchairs are grouped in front of a fireplace bordered in large, unglazed, moss-green tiles, which are surrounded by a massive mahogany frame and mantel. The ceiling has beams, and an oak-leaf frieze is stenciled on the cream-colored walls; moldings are dark mahogany. Twin lead glass–fronted bookcases mark the entry to the library, whose frieze is in the Arts and Crafts style; inside, a plump upholstered armchair and sturdy rockers ring a well-worn Persian rug. Outside the library are three lakefront sunporches. Breakfast is served on one of the porches, where guests can watch the sailboats and crew teams and, in winter, ice skaters and ice fishermen. Barb and Mike, who also own a gourmet catering firm, often serve Swedish oatmeal pancakes in the morning.

The light and airy guest rooms upstairs have handmade quilts, soothing color schemes, and striking mission and Arts and Crafts furniture. The largest room affords views in two directions, over Lake Mendota and the capitol building's dome. A tea cart filled with begonias and an immense oak breakfront and matching secretary give the room, which stretches the entire width of the house, a turn-of-the-century feel. Another suite, created by removing a wall between two small bedrooms, has its own balcony facing Lake Mendota.

Collins House is only a short walk from the capitol, the university, State Street shops, a park on Lake Mendota, and Lake Monona. △ *2 double rooms with baths, 3 suites. Air-conditioning, TV in 1 room, TV/VCR in common room, phone in rooms, double whirlpool bath in 2 suites, whirlpool tub in 1 room, video film library. $85–$140; full breakfast. D, MC, V. No smoking.*

FARGO MANSION INN ☞

406 Mulberry St., Lake Mills (mailing address: 211 N. Main St., Lake Mills 53551),
tel. 920/648–3654

The Wells Fargo Company was doing rather well in 1890, so when E. J. Fargo bought himself this grand house, he made it even grander. To the already stately Queen Anne building, Fargo added a gabled third floor, the cupola atop the showpiece octagonal turret, and an elaborate, gabled porte cochere. Over the years, however, the house fell into disrepair and sat empty and condemned until it caught the eye of a developer who drove past it after making a wrong turn; Barry Luce decided then and there to buy it. He completely renovated it, and the house became an inn, furnished with antiques from the town's Opera Mall Antiques Center, which the developer and his partner, Tom Bolks, also operate.

The sunny, spacious living room, a popular spot for weddings, is a Victorian confection full of sculpted moldings and other architectural furbelows. The focal point is the fireplace of laurel wreath–patterned tiles framed by an ornately carved wood mantelpiece; the shelves above are crammed with figurines and antique clocks. The music room holds a huge Federal dining table, two matching side tables, and two movable cabinets. The everyday dining room, wainscoted in oak, is no less elaborate, from its mirrored Victorian buffet and sideboard to the Corinthian columns that frame the doorway to the adjoining solarium. The small library contains a Victorian pump organ, a sled filled with antique dolls and teddy bears, and a vintage toy ironing board.

Of the guest rooms upstairs, the Master Suite is the most popular because of its private balcony and its size—large enough to dwarf a bed with an 8-ft-tall headboard and to accommodate a teardrop chandelier and the plump velvet sofa by the white marble fireplace. A "secret" doorway, disguised as a bookcase, opens to reveal one of the inn's signature modern marble bathrooms; this one also has a whirlpool tub. The other rooms, of varying sizes, are decorated in late-Victorian style and filled with antiques.

On the house's double lot, lovely gardens of shrubbery and banks of daffodils have replaced the bear pit in which Mr. Fargo staged battles between bruins for the entertainment of his guests. **△** *5 double rooms with baths. Air-conditioning, TV in living room, Jacuzzi in 2 rooms, conference facilities. $84–$165; full breakfast. MC, V. No smoking.*

MANSION HILL INN ☞

424 N. Pinckney St., Madison 53703, tel. 608/255–3999 or 800/798–9070,
fax 608/255–2217

Considered by Madisonites to be the height of opulence when it was built in 1858, this ornately carved, sandstone Romanesque Revival mansion still upstages its neighbors in the historic district. Swagged with double tiers of delicate wrought-iron balconies, it would be more at home in New Orleans. Inside, a spiral staircase anchored by an immense, intricately carved newel post rises four stories from the jewel-box foyer to a turreted belvedere with sweeping views of the city. The tawny marble floor, flamboyant floral arrangements, elaborate gilt moldings, friezes, rich detailing, and three hand-carved Italian marble fireplaces create the atmosphere of a small European hotel and set the tone for the entire inn.

The small front parlor is arranged with conversational groupings of Rococo Revival–style furniture: settees upholstered in rose damask, side chairs with velvet ottomans. Guests can warm up at the elegant marble fireplace or sashay over to the Emerson square grand piano for a musical interlude. The carved walnut dining table, original to the mansion, holds plates and pitchers of refreshments and newspapers from near and far to which guests are welcome to help themselves.

Each of the guest rooms is individually and lavishly decorated, and most are embellished with ornate cornices and ceiling medallions and elegant, modern marble baths. In nine of the rooms, French doors open onto pleasant terraces. The Lillie Langtry Room has a white marble fireplace, a veranda, wallpaper hand-painted in neo-Grecian patterns, Renaissance Revival furniture, and a bed draped in lace. The room known as the Turkish Nook recalls the 1890s craze for things Asian: The wallpaper depicts a stylized lotus blossom design, and the bed, whose spread is a Near East–style tapestry, sits under a lacy sultan's tent. Velvet pouf ottomans complete the look. Rooms on the lower levels are smaller and not as elaborately decorated but have their own patios.

You can have breakfast delivered to your room on a silver tray, along with your choice of morning newspaper, or arrange to partake in the parlor. ⚠ *11 double rooms with baths. Air-conditioning, phone, TV, and stereo in rooms, fireplace in 4 rooms, 6 rooms with sitting areas, 9 rooms with terrace, whirlpool bath in 8 rooms; private wine cellar, teleconference facilities; 24-hr valet service and valet parking, access to health club. $100–$300 single, $20 additional person; Continental breakfast. AE, MC, V. No smoking.*

OTHER CHOICES

Cameo Rose. 1090 Severson Rd., Belleville 53508, tel. 608/424–6340. 4 double rooms with baths, 1 suite. Air-conditioning, TV/VCR in 2 rooms, fireplace in living room, ceiling fans, whirlpool bath in 1 room, hiking and cross-country ski trails. $79–$139; full breakfast, afternoon refreshments. MC, V. No smoking.

Canterbury Inn. 315 W. Gorham St., Madison 53703, tel. 608/258–8899 or 800/838–3850, fax 608/283–2541. 2 double rooms with baths, 4 suites. Air-conditioning, phone, TV, CD player, robes, and refrigerator in rooms, whirlpool bath in suites, VCR available, gift certificate for bookstore. $150–$260; Continental breakfast, evening refreshments. AE, MC, V. No smoking.

Jamieson House. 407 N. Franklin St., Poynette 53955, tel. 608/635–2277 or 608/635–4100, fax 608/635–2290. 11 double rooms with baths. Air-conditioning, TV and VCR in 4 rooms and in common area, fireplace in 3 rooms, double whirlpool bath in 5 rooms. $70–$150; full breakfast. AE, D, MC, V. No smoking.

Past and Present Inn. 2034 Main St., Cross Plains 53528, tel. 608/798–4441, fax 608/798–0642. 2 2-bedroom suites. Restaurant, air-conditioning, phone, whirlpool bath, and TV in suites, gift shop. $120–$150; full breakfast. MC, V. No smoking.

University Heights Bed and Breakfast. 1812 Van Hise Ave., Madison 53705, tel. 608/233–3340, fax 608/233–3255. 2 double rooms with baths, 2 suites. Air-conditioning, whirlpool bath in suites, TV in common area. $65–$150; full breakfast. AE, D, MC, V. No smoking.

Victoria-on-Main. 622 W. Main St., Whitewater 53190, tel. 414/473–8400. 1 double room with bath, 2 doubles share bath. Air-conditioning, TV in sitting room, kitchen available for guests' use. $48–$75; full breakfast. MC, V. No smoking.

Wisconsin River Valley

CRYSTAL RIVER INN 🐚
E1369 Rural Rd., Waupaca 54981, tel. 715/258–5333 or 800/236–5789

With its white clapboard walls and green shutters, Crystal River Inn is one of the first buildings visitors to Rural see as they turn off busy Highway 22. It is in perfect keeping with the history-rich heritage of its town. And it's quite a town: The entire community is listed on the National Register of Historic Places. Settled by New Englanders in the 1850s, the tiny hamlet has the white clapboard–green shutter look often found along the Eastern seaboard. Fortunately, Rural was bypassed by the railroad early on, and it has a preserved-in-amber air to it. The few dozen Rural residents work diligently to maintain the unique character of their town—and two of the hardest working are Lois and Gene Sorenson, owners of this inn.

They have furnished the inn with a tactful eye for its enduring appeal. The oldest part of the inn was built in 1853 by Andrew Potts, one of Rural's first settlers. Additions followed, the most recent being a sunroom and indoor gazebo built by the Sorensons to provide additional space to serve guests. An antique pressback rocker and wood-burning stove anchor the living room, while the sitting room has a picture window looking out on the Crystal River and the shaded backyard with its gazebo. An indoor gazebo is furnished with casual patio tables and chairs—not Victorian perhaps, but comfortable; guests gather here to eat breakfast, as well as play cards and board games. A nearby sunroom holds an antique feed chest Lois found in the barn.

The bedrooms are furnished in an eclectic mixture of country Victorian and contemporary styles. The Canopy Room has a four-poster bed Gene made from boards and pillars of the porch of a house about to be demolished. The Attic Room has a window seat overlooking the woods and an antique brass bed. Andrew's Room has an iron bed, behind which is hung a decorative filigreed gable peak from a 19th-century church. Helen's Summer Room features a tiny porch overlooking the river as well as a gas fireplace.

Many guests come to the inn to enjoy not only the town but the neighboring river, which winds through the community and is crossed by four bridges. The Crystal is popular for canoeing because it is cool, clear, fast, and shallow—if paddlers tip over, they just stand up and climb back into the canoe. Bicyclists also like the area because there's plenty of scenery and—even better—lots of lightly traveled paved roads. ♠ *5 double rooms with baths, 2 doubles share 1 bath. Air-conditioning, TV in common room, ceiling fans, double whirlpools in 2 rooms, fireplaces in 4 rooms. $65–$115; full breakfast, evening refreshments. MC, V. No smoking.*

DREAMS OF YESTERYEAR 🐚
1100 Brawley St., Stevens Point 54481, tel. 715/341–4525

Designed in 1901 by architect J. H. Jeffers (who was also the architect of the Wisconsin Pavilion for the 1904 St. Louis World's Fair), Dreams of Yesteryear was singled out from among its Victorian peers by Bonnie and Bill Maher, a couple determined to save the attractive, grand, old Queen Anne from destruction. Bonnie, an antiques collector, recognized the value and aesthetic potential in the oak woodwork, hardwood floors, leaded-glass windows, and footed tubs that remained in the house. She replaced a rotting roof with wooden shingles and restored the Queen Anne lines of "a chimney you could watch the sunset through." Then, with the major overhaul complete, she began "gathering" Victoriana. The voluptuously carved parlor sofa became theirs when a stranger telephoned to say, "Aunt Minerva just died at 93—could you use it?"

Today that sofa, along with a revolving library table discovered at a church bazaar, faces the fancy fireplace with its Victorian cascade decorations and surrounding tools. Sheet music for "Lola" sits on the vintage upright piano, alongside a 1904 phonograph that still has its wooden needles. Bonnie's lavish breakfasts, which feature local cranberry juice and pecan-stuffed French toast, are served on the inn's original dining room set.

Upstairs, it's hard to choose: Gerald's Room, done in French blue with a pineapple-post bed, is next to a tiny balcony; Isabella's Room, with an elaborately carved headboard, has an ivy-filled bay window and a cozy reading nook; Florence Myrna's Room, with gardenia wall coverings comes with its own deep-green ceramic-tiled bathroom lit by antique wall sconces; and the cozy Maid's Quarters offers telephone access and a desk, making it appealing to business travelers.

The two suites on the third floor each have a bedroom and sitting room. One is furnished with a white wrought-iron bed and has a whirlpool bath, while the other is done in brown wicker and has a black wrought-iron bed. ♗ *2 double rooms with baths, 2 doubles share bath, 2 suites. Air-conditioning, fan in rooms, whirlpool in 1 room, TV in suites and 1 room, fireplace in common room. $55–$129; full breakfast, afternoon refreshments. AE, D, MC, V. No smoking.*

HISTORIC BENNETT HOUSE ♗
825 Oak St., Wisconsin Dells 53965, tel. 608/254–2500

Historic Bennett House is a pleasant alternative to the many hotels and resorts in the Wisconsin Dells. A handsome 1863 Greek Revival mansion, the inn helps guests recall a gentler era. It was here that Civil War veteran Henry Hamilton Bennett became a pioneer photographer; his stop-action pictures, the first ever taken, are displayed today in the Smithsonian Museum. Gail and Richard Obermeyer, a former stage actress and a university communications professor, are running the inn in their retirement years. "We wanted the change of seasons. We'd visited relatives in the Dells and loved it." The couple knew exactly what they wanted: the intimate atmosphere of a European bed-and-breakfast and a "historic home with warmth and charm," Gail says.

First they found the perfect house, complete with a white picket fence, only a block from downtown and the Wisconsin River. Then they waited for it to come on the market—which it soon did.

Guests from as far away as Germany and South Korea have come to this casually elegant inn. Before dinner, visitors relax with a glass of wine on the floral-patterned sofa or in a pair of wing chairs drawn up to the white, wood-burning fireplace in the living room. Breakfast is served at the communal table in the other half of the long room, which has a walnut-toned china cabinet and buffet and, on cool days, an open fire. Here Gail brings out the house specialty, eggs Bennett, or another favorite, toast Bennett (a variation on stuffed French toast). There's also a small, cozy den with a TV and comfortable sofa.

The ground-floor suite has a bedroom with Eastlake furniture, a parlor furnished with a love seat, antique table and chairs, and a framed antique tapestry; there's also a VCR and video library. Upstairs, the English Room has the original black floors, a walnut canopy bed, and an antique armoire from Britain. It shares a bathroom with the snug Garden Room, fitted with a brass bed and wicker furniture.

The bathroom, with its gold fixtures, hand-painted Italian sinks, and claw-foot tub, is so seductive that some guests call it a therapeutic environment. ♙ *1 double room with bath, 1 suite. Air-conditioning, TV/VCR in suite and common room, fireplace in common rooms. $70–$95; full breakfast, evening refreshments. No credit cards. No smoking.*

ROSENBERRY INN ☙

511 Franklin St., Wausau 54401, tel. 715/842–5733

This 1908 Prairie schoolhouse built for Judge Rosenberry, in what is now Wausau's Andrew Warren Historic District, was divided into efficiency apartments back in the 1940s. Fortunately, two enthusiastic devotees came along and returned the old home to life as a B&B. By the time Fred and Laurie Schmidt bought the Rosenberry in 1995, it had a well-established reputation. The Schmidts haven't rested on the inn's laurels, however. They turned one of the downstairs rooms into a dining room for guests and another into a common room with TV. They painted and refurnished and generally improved the rooms and the historic feel of the Rosenberry House. They also own the DeVoe House across the street; it's the oldest home in the historic district, dating from 1868.

Today, each guest room in the Rosenberry House contains a tiny kitchen (a remnant of its efficiency apartment days), eating nook, bath, and rustic Victorian furnishings—patchwork quilts, wooden rockers, and braided rugs. The three first-floor bedrooms still have tiled working fireplaces; rooms with western exposure are the sunniest and most spacious.

An imposing staircase with a breathtaking stained-glass window on the landing leads to the second floor. Here, four rooms evoke a comfortable and Victorian setting. The Rosenberry Room, in the corner overlooking the street and gardens, has a bird's-eye maple bed, wicker armchairs, and a tiled fireplace. In one corner is a china cabinet showcasing a collection of antique tea sets. Decorations in other rooms include a calliope horse, a stenciled bed, and a wicker settee. The Schmidts have mixed antiques and contemporary furniture in pleasing combinations.

Across the street, the DeVoe House has been divided into two guest suites; both the downstairs and upstairs accommodations contain whirlpool tubs, fireplaces, and open-to-view kitchen appliances, all in one large room with partitions. Throughout the house are collections of antique hope chests, patchwork quilts, and, in the room under the rafters, a rope-suspended porch swing.

Both establishments on this quiet, almost aristocratic residential street have porches and gardens for relaxation. Fred serves breakfast on the spacious porch of the Rosenberry House in warm weather, and, in cooler days, in the dining room, accented with its antique lace tablecloth. Hustle and bustle aren't too far away: The inn is only a quick walk from downtown. ♙ *6 double rooms with baths, cottage has 2 double rooms with baths. Air-conditioning, fireplace in 4 rooms, TV in 5 rooms. $65–$135; full breakfast. AE, D, MC, V. No smoking.*

OTHER CHOICES

Bettinger House. 855 Wachter Ave., Hwy. 23, Plain 53577, tel. 608/546–2951. 2 double rooms with baths, 3 doubles share 2 baths. Air-conditioning, ceiling fan in 2 rooms. $50–$65; full breakfast. No credit cards. No smoking, 2-night minimum summer weekends.

Breese Waye. 816 MacFarlane Rd., Portage 53901, tel. 608/742–5281. 4 double rooms with baths. Air-conditioning, ceiling fans, TV/VCR in common room, fireplace in living room. $65–$75; full breakfast. No credit cards. No smoking.

Candlewick Inn. 700 W. Main St., Merrill 54452, tel. 715/536–7744 or 800/382–4376. 3 double rooms with baths, 2 rooms share bath. Air-conditioning, fireplace in 1 room and common rooms. $55–$95; full breakfast, afternoon refreshments. MC, V. No smoking.

Hill Street. 353 W. Hill St., Spring Green 53588, tel. 608/588–7751. 4 double rooms with baths, 1 triple with bath, 2 doubles share bath. Air-conditioning, ceiling fan in some rooms, TV in common room. $70–$80; full breakfast, evening refreshments. MC, V. No smoking, 2-day minimum weekends June–Oct.

Oakwood Lodge. 365 Lake St., Green Lake 54941, tel. and fax 920/294–6580 or 800/498–8087. 12 double rooms with baths. Ceiling fan in 10 rooms, whirlpool bath in 1 room, TV/VCR in parlor, private pier. $85–$120; full breakfast, coffee and snacks. MC, V. No smoking.

Parkview. 211 N. Park St., Reedsburg 53959, tel. 608/524–4333, fax 608/524–1172. 2 double rooms with baths, 2 doubles share bath. Air-conditioning, ceiling fan in rooms, fireplace in common room, refreshments on arrival. $65–$80; full breakfast. AE, MC, V. No smoking.

Pinehaven. E13083 Rte. 33, Baraboo 53913, tel. 608/356–3489. 4 double rooms with baths, 2-bedroom cottage with kitchen. Air-conditioning, candy in rooms, fireplace in common room, whirlpool in cottage; small private lake with paddleboat and rowboat. $79–$135; full breakfast (no breakfast in cottage). MC, V. No smoking.

Sherman House. 930 River Rd. (Box 397), Wisconsin Dells 53965, tel. 608/253–2721. 2 double rooms with baths, 1 suite. Air-conditioning, TV in common room. $55–$70; Continental breakfast. No credit cards.

Swallow's Nest. 141 Sarrington St. (Box 418), Lake Delton 53940, tel. 608/254–6900. 4 double rooms with baths. Air-conditioning, fireplace in common rooms, pool table, TV in common room. $75; full breakfast. MC, V. No smoking.

Ty-Bach. 3104 Simpson La., Lac du Flambeau 54538, tel. 715/588–7851. 2 double rooms with baths. TV/VCR in common area, swimming, boating, private pier, bikes, outdoor hot tub, hiking and cross-country ski trails. $65–$70; full breakfast. No credit cards. No smoking.

Victorian Swan on Water. 1716 Water St., Stevens Point 54481, tel. 715/345–0595 or 800/454–9886, fax 715/345–0569. 3 double rooms with baths, 1 suite. Air-conditioning, fireplace in parlor and in suite, whirlpool in suite. $60–$135; full breakfast. AE, D, MC, V. No smoking.

Hidden Valleys, Including La Crosse and Prairie du Chien

FRANKLIN VICTORIAN 🐦
220 E. Franklin Pl., Sparta 54656, tel. 608/269–3894 or 800/845–8767

W. G. Williamson, a prominent Sparta banker, personally inspected every piece of wood that went into the interior of this raspberry-red clapboard Victorian. His meticulous standards are evident the minute you cross the white-columned front porch. The floors are of glowing maple complemented by black ash and quarter-cut oak. Pocket doors of curly birch lead to a parlor with russet ceramic tiles, a beveled-glass window, and a double-manteled fireplace with fluted Corinthian columns—elegant reminders of the late 1800s, when Sparta, with its spas and mineral waters, was a hub of social activity.

Cordial innkeepers Jane and Lloyd Larson have integrated their family heirlooms into the house. In the dining room, which has an elaborate parquet floor with a "braided" border, is a built-in buffet with floor-to-ceiling glass doors showcasing china that's been in Jane's family for three generations. In the parlor is the Civil War–era miniature pump organ that belonged to Jane's grandfather. The portable instrument, which he played at funerals, keeps company with a boxy Victorian velvet sofa trimmed in mahogany and its honor guard of stuffed velvet chairs that belonged to Jane's great-grandparents. The intricate sunset-motif stained-glass window faces west, providing a vivid late-afternoon glow to the stairway landing.

Guests love the Wicker Room, with its white wrought-iron bed and wicker furnishings, which contrast with the dark blue floral-design wallpaper. Most requested, however, is the Master Bedroom, which has a grand titled fireplace with decorative columns, an immense oak headboard crafted by Lloyd Larson from the wall of a judge's chamber, and a tall highboy of bird's-eye maple that belonged to Jane's parents. Its bathroom, with tongue-and-groove wainscoting, still boasts the original marble-top sink.

Guests can enjoy a private chat in the upstairs sitting room or sit in rocking chairs and sip lemonade on the side or front porch. They overlook this corner lot in a quiet residential neighborhood, where the trees loom taller than dormers and turrets. ▲ *2 double rooms with baths, 2 doubles share bath. Air-conditioning, canoe rental, shuttle service for bikers and canoeists. $70–$95; full breakfast, early morning coffee. MC, V. No smoking.*

JONES HOUSE 🕏
215 Ridge St. (Box 130), Mineral Point 53565, tel. 608/987–2337

This regional showcase looks as grand as it did on the day it was built; oddly enough, it was hardly lived in. William Jones, once commissioner of the Bureau of Indian Affairs for President McKinley, erected the 16-room redbrick mansion in 1906 as a homecoming present to himself after his stint in Washington. He died soon after, and his will forbade its sale until the death of his wife and children. Although boarded up intact, a housekeeper faithfully dusted it twice a week until 1986, when June and Art Openshaw purchased it.

A grand, boxy staircase winds around one of the seven unusual fireplaces. The stairs rise from the foyer to a stained-glass skylight that casts patterns on the entry carpet. The mahogany-beamed dining room is graced by forest-green woodland scenes painted above the wainscoting. A green-tile fireplace warms guests during breakfast. Twin sideboards topped by graceful arches glint with beveled glass, and padded velvet window seats on either side of the fireplace overlook the broad side lawn. To complete the *après-la-chasse* feel, the hardwood floor is covered with moss-green carpet.

The Persian and floral-print rugs, dark patterned wallpapers, and brass lighting fixtures, all of which came with the house, create a decidedly masculine atmosphere. The small Ladies' Parlor overlooking the front walk, however, provides respite for the frill-deprived with its garlands of roses painted on high, pale walls.

In the Master Suite, a white tile fireplace, original needlepoint chairs, and a floral covering on the daybed in the suite's sitting room also bestow a more feminine air. A screen door leads to a porch-top balcony that overlooks the town. The adjacent front bedroom, with a view of the spreading side yard as well as the avenue, features another white tile fireplace and a Colonial-reproduction four-poster bed with pineapple finials on the posts. The Ivy Suite, which overlooks the hills to the north of town, has a green tile fireplace and a Colonial-reproduction four-poster; the smaller back bedroom, in contrast, has a country-antique look.

There are still traces of William Jones in the house: Outside the Master Suite stand the master's antique golf clubs; his leatherbound books still line the library's shelves; and his umbrella hangs on the door of the vestibule. ⚘ *1 double room with bath, 1 suite and 1 double share bath. No air-conditioning, fan in rooms, 7 fireplaces. $58–$88; full breakfast. No credit cards. No smoking.*

JUST-N-TRAILS ⚘
Rte. 1 (Box 274), Sparta 54656, tel. 608/269–4522 or 800/488–4521, fax 608/269–3280

Ask Don and Donna Justin why they added a bed-and-breakfast to their 213-acre working farm, and they just laugh, "We'd been doing it free for 15 years anyway for all the relatives." The accommodations are "all things to all people," claim the friendly, laid-back couple, who delight in welcoming guests. Their 50 head of Holstein cattle occasionally provide visitors with a rare late-night show (no cover charge)—the birth of a calf. An athlete's nirvana, their spread has 10 mi of groomed and mapped hiking and ski trails, six nearby cycling trails (the area calls itself "the bike capital of America"), and five rivers close at hand, where guests can fish or go canoeing. And then, of course, there's always the B&B's own "traditional agrarian fitness center"—decked out with pitchfork and hay bales.

The farm is also a romantic getaway spot, with three private cabins and Laura Ashley–decorated rooms upstairs in the farmhouse. The Granary Cottage has a front deck from which you can watch the sun sinking past the fields and wooded hills. The cabin decor includes a garden-gate queen-size bed, Amish bentwood rockers made by local craftsmen, and its own whirlpool bath. The beds are invitingly comfortable, with an abundance of pillows that make reading a pleasure.

The second log cabin, Little House on the Prairie, has a log bed, country-style furnishings, a fireplace, and a whirlpool bath in the loft under skylights. The Paul Bunyan, the two-bedroom cottage, is made of aspen logs from the farm's woodlots and is furnished with a log bed and other rustic pieces. It also has a double whirlpool bath and both a rear porch and a rear balcony from which to watch deer coming out of the nearby woods. All three cottages have kitchenettes, and the Paul Bunyan is accessible to wheelchair users.

Guests in the farmstead's bedrooms—such as the Green Room, with a green, pink, and white floral scheme and double bird's-eye maple bed and matching dresser—get the same nine-pillow treatment as those in the cabins. The morning wake-up call is a wren's warble or perhaps a moo, followed by Donna's hearty, farm-style breakfast, served up in the nearby lodge. There's also a microwave guests can use when the hungries hit, as sometimes happens after a ramble on the hills up to the farm pond and down again via the Bambi Trail—so named to reassure novice skiers. ⚘ *3 double rooms with baths, 1 suite, 2 1-bedroom cabins, 1 2-bedroom cabin. Air-conditioning, fireplace and whirlpool tub in cabins, hammock, picnic tables, hiking and cross-country ski trails, ski and snowshoe rentals, snow tubes available free. $80–$300; full breakfast. AE, D, MC, V. No smoking.*

MARTINDALE HOUSE ☞
237 S. 10th St., La Crosse 54601, tel. 608/782–4224

When Anita Philbrook opened the Martindale House in a quiet residential section of La Crosse, she was concerned that bed-and-breakfast establishments would prove to be "a fad, like the vitamin craze." But repeat guests—from as far away as England, Spain, and Scandinavia—have made her fears groundless. "I offer not just a bed, but an experience," Martindale's polished hostess maintains. Luckily, that experience includes a hearty Swedish breakfast served on the fifth-generation family china patterned in wedding-ring gold, which complements antique silver coffee spoons. This repast is served in the white, bright Scandinavian-style dining room, lined with a collection of traditional family portraits.

The imposing green-shuttered house, built in 1859, is a grand architectural mélange of Italianate cupola and Colonial clapboard, with a Victorian-style wrap-around porch to boot. Combating years of disrepair, Anita restored moldings and chandeliers discovered in the basement and returned them to their proper places; she also resurrected the iron fence, hidden in the carriage house. Then she replanted the entire garden.

Inside, the parlor is a historian's delight. The room contains a stately grandfather clock, an antique chess table, antique Oriental rugs on the blond-oak floors, floor-to-ceiling windows flanked by their original shutters, and a piano that's been in her husband's family for five generations.

The white staircase in the foyer leads to four bedrooms. The Martindale Room features an 1800 cannonball bed, a warming pan, a 1740 Queen Anne highboy, and quilts from the nearby Amish community. The French Room derives its name from the carved Louis XVI bed that came from a castle in Lyons; its other highlights are a 1640 campaign chest and an antique grandfather clock. The English Room offers a fireplace, a garden view, and a lace-canopied four-poster bed. This room has the advantage of a vast, soothing bathroom, dubbed the "rub-a-dub" by guests. The antique twin beds in the sunny Scandinavian Room came from a convent, and the Lapland dolls on display belonged to Anita's grandmother. Anita also renovated the 1860 carriage house into a two-story, three-room suite. The downstairs sitting room has a microwave, coffeemaker, and small refrigerator. The upstairs bedroom has an iron-and-brass bed and an antique Franklin stove, as well as a heart-shaped double whirlpool bath. ♠ _4 double rooms with baths, 1 suite. Air-conditioning, use of portable phones, several languages spoken. $89–$145; full breakfast, snack on arrival. MC, V. No smoking._

WESTBY HOUSE ☞
200 W. State St., Westby 54667, tel. 608/634–4112

Guests heading for Westby tend to book well in advance at this B&B during the merry month of May, for this is when this very Norwegian town is especially lively, thanks to the Syttendai Mai Festival. Year-round, however, the Old World Norskedalen Village, 6 mi away, attracts visitors. They arrive at a house that is archetypal Midwest American: Topped with an imposing Queen Anne witch's turret, the country manor–style abode was commissioned in the 1890s by a well-to-do Norwegian immigrant. Today, its fine oak woodwork, lighting fixtures, stained-glass accents, and imposing pillared fireplaces are still in place.

Upstairs, in an otherwise undistinguished hallway, the original dining-room buffet stands guard over a pair of spacious front bedrooms. The Tower Room has a small bathroom and a down quilt–covered brass bed set into an alcove of bay windows. The Fireplace Room has a brass bed, tiled fireplace, and a rocking chair; a TV helps to compensate for a lackluster view of storefronts just off the town's main street. The two rooms are connected by double doors and can be rented as a suite. The Anniversary Room is almost a suite, with reproduction wing chairs and a sofa forming a conversation group in its bay window. Its brass bed merits the handmade quilt and white eyelet comforter. The Greenbriar Room's caned chairs, rag rugs, marble-top washstand, and old-fashioned white iron bed, topped with another antique quilt, have the look of Grandma's house—comfortable but not fancy. △ *2 double rooms with baths, 4 doubles share 1½ baths. Air-conditioning, TV in 1 room, fireplace in common rooms. $60–$80; Continental breakfast weekdays, full breakfast weekends, refreshments on arrival. MC, V.*

OTHER CHOICES

Eckhart House. 220 E. Jefferson St., Viroqua 54665, tel. 608/637–3306, fax 608/637–6844. 3 double rooms with baths, 2 doubles share 1 bath. Air-conditioning, fireplace in common room, TV available, refrigerator and microwave. $55–$79; full breakfast, afternoon refreshments. AE, D, MC, V. No smoking.

Geiger House. 401 Denniston St., Cassville 53806, tel. 608/725–5419 or 800/725–5429, fax 608/725–5206. 3 double rooms share 2 baths. Air-conditioning, bikes, shuttle to river ferry. $60–$75; full breakfast, morning coffee, afternoon refreshments. AE, MC, V. No smoking.

Oak Hill Manor. 401 E. Main St., Albany 53502, tel. 608/862–1400, fax 608/862–1403. 4 double rooms with baths. Air-conditioning, TV/VCR in sitting room and parlor, fireplace in 1 room and common rooms, bikes. $65–$80; full breakfast, afternoon refreshments. MC, V. No smoking.

Parson's Inn. Rock School Rd., Glen Haven 53810, tel. 608/794–2491. 3 double rooms share bath, 1 suite. Air-conditioning, TV in common room. $50–$70 ($85 for 4 in suite); full breakfast, afternoon refreshments. No credit cards. No smoking.

Sugar River Inn. 304 S. Mills St., Albany 53502, tel. 608/862–1248. 2 double rooms with baths. Air-conditioning, fireplace in parlor, turndown service. $52–$62; full breakfast, wake-up coffee, afternoon refreshments. MC, V. No smoking.

Trillium. Rte. 2 E10596 Salem Ridge Rd., La Farge 54639, tel. 608/625–4492. 1 1-bedroom cottage, 1 3-bedroom cottage. No air-conditioning, fireplace and kitchen in cottages, tree house, hiking trails, picnic area with grill. $75–$85 double, $25 for each additional person over 12; full breakfast. No credit cards.

Victorian Garden. 1720 16th St., Monroe 53566, tel. 608/328–1720, fax 608/328–1722. 3 double rooms with baths, single room can be rented with one of the doubles. Air-conditioning, robes for guests, TV in sitting room. $75–$85; full breakfast, afternoon or evening refreshments. D, MC, V. No smoking.

Viroqua Heritage Inn. 220 E. Jefferson St., Viroqua 54665, tel. 608/637–3306. 2 double rooms with baths, 2 doubles share 1½ baths. Air-conditioning, phone in hall, TV in rooms, robes, refrigerator, and microwave available to guests. $50–$79; full breakfast. AE, D, MC, V. No smoking indoors.

Hiawatha Valley, Including Hudson, River Falls, and Stockholm

KNOLLWOOD HOUSE ☞
N. 8257 950th St., Knollwood Dr., River Falls 54022, tel. 715/425–1040 or 800/435–0628

The comfortable atmosphere of the two-story Knollwood House and the warm hospitality of owners Jim and Judy Tostrud quickly transform guests into friends. Built in 1886 with red bricks from a local factory, the house, set on 85 acres in the rolling Kinnickinnic River valley, draws people into its rich history. Jim has farmed the land for many years, as his father did before him, and Judy, a horticulturalist, fills the landscape with perennials and hydroponically grown plants. Inside, you'll appreciate the Tostruds' personal touches, displayed in the plants that grace the windowsills and the family heirlooms that furnish the rooms.

Christie Ann's Room is filled with Tostrud family memorabilia. The queen-size bed with carved head- and footboards and matching dresser belonged to Jim's parents. An Amish quilt covers the bed. The suite includes an unusually spacious bathroom with tub and shower. The Country Rose Room is decorated in forest green and mauve and is furnished with an antique oak four-poster bed and an armoire of similar vintage.

The Sherlock Wales Room, a smaller room with wainscoting and an antique brass bed, overlooks a garden and small goldfish pond below the window. The aptly named Garden Room, on the first floor, allows guests access to the plant-filled solarium, which has a hot tub, and to the Daybed Room, which indeed has a daybed—and a small enclosed porch. The Garden and Daybed rooms are usually rented as a suite.

The kitchen contains an antique cast-iron stove, a glazed pottery watercooler, and a farmhouse pie cabinet with screen doors to tempt the hungry. Judy prepares a down-home breakfast featuring muffins made with the strawberries and raspberries she grows herself. The meal is served either in the solarium or on the arbor-draped deck beside the swimming pool.

There is no lack of activities at Knollwood; just about everything you could want is right outside the door. Badminton, croquet, basketball, softball, shuffleboard, boccie, a swimming pool, an in-ground trampoline, and a 180-yard par-three golf drive are found within the 3½-acre yard. The more ambitious athlete can try the 2 mi of well-maintained hiking and cross-country ski trails on land owned by the Tostruds. Ready to assist hikers are the Tostruds' two llamas, Hustler and Rivera. ⚠ *2 double rooms with baths, 1 double and 1 suite share bath. Air-conditioning, fireplace in common room, ceiling fans, robes, hot tub, sauna, pool, hiking, cross-country ski trails. $95–$170; full breakfast. No credit cards. No smoking.*

OTTER CREEK INN ☞
2536 Hwy. 12, Eau Claire 54701, tel. 715/832–2945, fax 715/832–4607

The original house on this site was built in 1920, then enlarged in the 1960s and again in the 1980s. The additions were well done—it's impossible to tell the old from the new. In 1987, Shelley and Randy Hansen purchased the house and have run it as a B&B ever since. Approaching the inn up the wooded drive, visitors feel they are in the country. The truth is, busy Highway 12 is nearby, and the Eau Claire city limits are only a few yards away.

The house has a Tudor Revival look, with steep gables and half-timbered stucco on the upper story; a brick, stucco, and stone chimney add to the Tudor image. The country-manor feel is enhanced by the beautiful landscaping done by Shelley and Randy; the tidy flower beds on the 1-acre wooded lot are often abloom. At the rear of the house, guests enjoy a deck and a brick terrace. Here awaiting you is a relaxing swimming pool, at one end of which lies a flower-bedecked gazebo—just the place to enjoy an iced tea after a dip in the water.

Inside, the spacious two-story common area has two dark brown leather couches in front of a wood-burning stove, a favorite gathering place on winter evenings. Off in a corner, surrounded by large potted plants, is the cozy breakfast nook, but Shelley likes to serve breakfast poolside in warm weather. However, guests often prefer to have breakfast brought to their rooms; a selection of cheese omelets or waffles can be made the night before.

The six large guest rooms are furnished in country-Victorian style. The Palm Room, actually a two-room suite, features an antique-sleigh bed, a sitting room, and a bathroom that's so big Shelley has furnished it with a wicker chair and étagère. Most guests prefer serious quality time in the double whirlpool bath. The Gardenia Room, decorated in tones of mauve and cream, has white rustic French furniture. The Jasmine Room has an ornately carved antique bed and a sunken whirlpool bath set within a 9-ft-wide bay window. A mahogany canopy bed is the centerpiece of the Violet Room. The Rose Room features an iron-and-brass bed with an Eastlake dresser and matching chair and an antique Mission-style rocker. The Magnolia Room is furnished with Mission-style furniture and a canopy bed. ⚘ *5 double rooms with baths, 1 suite. Air-conditioning, TV, whirlpool bath in rooms, pool. $79–$159; full breakfast, afternoon refreshments. AE, D, DC, MC, V. No smoking.*

PHIPPS INN ☙
1005 3rd St., Hudson 54016, tel. 715/386–0800, fax 715/386–0509

This Queen Anne house has remained virtually untouched since its debut in 1884. From the octagonal tower under the witch's-cap roof to the wraparound veranda with scrolled friezes and pedimented gables, the house, which is on the National Register of Historic Places, is the showplace of the river town.

William Phipps, a prominent Hudson banker, politician, and philanthropist, moved here to serve as land commissioner for the railroad and certainly wasn't averse to living well. The interior of his former house is equipped with six fireplaces that are flamboyantly carved, guarded by Ionic columns, and set with Italian tiles. Ornate brass hardware, stained-glass windows, and parquet flooring in intricate geometric designs add to the got-it-flaunt-it look.

Innkeepers John and Cyndi Berglund bought the mansion intact but empty. This gave them the mandate of filling it with antiques from the St. Croix River valley, including an 1890s pump organ and Victorian sofas and chairs in the two parlors. In the music room, they've installed a snazzy 1920 baby grand piano; these days it's set with afternoon snacks. Guests linger over breakfast in the dining room, warmed by sun streaming through the stained-glass windows and by one of the fireplaces.

The Bridal Suite boasts a wicker canopy bed and wicker dresser, table and chairs, and a fireplace with Italian ceramic tile. The Master Suite has a canopied four-poster pine bed, another fireplace, and a large, climb-through window that leads to a private balcony. Victoria's Room, a more intimate hideaway done in a black-and-gold Victorian floral motif, is furnished with a brass bed and antique armoire; the Queen Anne's Room features hand-stenciled walls, a half-tester brass bed, and a gas fireplace that opens on both the bedroom and the adjoining whirlpool room. Guests can sit in the whirlpool bath and look out the windows on one side and enjoy the fireplace on the other.

Above all looms the third floor's grand ballroom. Once the site of the Phipps's elegant gatherings, it has been converted into the Willow Chamber, which is furnished with willow furniture, and the Peacock Chamber, with its antique walnut half-tester bed and redwood paneling. Guests will find Jacuzzis in every bathroom. **△** *6 double rooms with baths. Air-conditioning, fireplace in 5 rooms and in common rooms, whirlpool tub in 6 rooms; billiards room, bathrobes, picnics available with advance notice and at an extra charge. $99–$189; full breakfast, afternoon refreshments. AE, D, MC, V. No smoking.*

OTHER CHOICES

Arbor Inn. 434 N. Court St., Prescott 54021, tel. 715/262–4522. 3 double rooms with baths. Air-conditioning, TV/VCR in rooms, fireplace in 1 room and common area, whirlpool bath in 1 room, outdoor hot tub for 1 room, bikes. $105–$145; full breakfast. MC, V. No smoking.

Cedar Trails Guesthouse. E4761 County Road C, Menomonie 54751, tel. 715/664–8828. 2 double rooms with baths, 2 doubles share bath. Air-conditioning, TV in common room. $50–705; full breakfast. MC, V. No smoking.

The Creamery. 1 Creamery Rd. (Box 22), Downsville 54735, tel. 715/664–8354. 3 double rooms with baths, 1 suite. Restaurant (closed Mon.), air-conditioning, phone, TV, and whirlpool tub in rooms; fireplaces in common rooms, bar, lounge, restaurant. $100–$130; Continental breakfast. MC, V. No smoking in rooms. Closed Jan.–Mar.

Gallery House. 215 N. Main St., Alma 54610, tel. 608/685–4975. 3 double rooms with baths. Air-conditioning, ceiling fans. $70–$85; full breakfast. MC, V. No smoking.

Grapevine Inn. 702 Vine St., Hudson 54016, tel. 715/386–1989. 3 double rooms with baths. Air-conditioning, fireplace in 1 room, whirlpool bath in 1 room, pool. $89–$139; full breakfast, morning wake-up tray, afternoon refreshments. MC, V. No smoking.

Great River Bed & Breakfast. Rte. 35, Stockholm 54769, tel. 715/442–5656 or 800/657–4756. 1-bedroom farmhouse. Woodstove in bedroom and living room. $125; full breakfast. No credit cards. No smoking.

Harrisburg Inn. W3334 Rte. 35, Maiden Rock 54750, tel. 715/448–4500, fax 715/448–3908. 4 double rooms with baths, 2 rooms can be joined to make a suite. Air-conditioning, ceiling fans. $68–$98; full breakfast, afternoon refreshments. D, MC, V. Smoking on porches only. Closed Jan.–Feb.

Jefferson-Day House. 1109 3rd St., Hudson 54016, tel. 715/386–7111. 4 double rooms with baths, 1 suite. Air-conditioning, fireplace, double whirlpool bath in rooms. $99–$179; full breakfast, afternoon refreshments. MC, V. No smoking.

Pine Creek Lodge. N447 244th St., Stockholm 54769, tel. 715/448–3203. 3 double rooms with baths. Climate-controlled guest rooms, whirlpool bath in 1 room, steam room in 1 room; TV/VCR and CD player in common room; kitchen access, masseuse on call, hiking, cross-country skiing. $85–$120; full breakfast. MC, V. No smoking indoors.

Pleasant Lake B&B. 2238 60th Ave., Osceola 54020, tel. 715/294–2545 or 800/ 294–2545. 6 double rooms with baths, 1 suite. Air-conditioning, fireplace in 3 rooms, whirlpool bath in 5 rooms, TV/VCR in common room, lake access, canoe and paddleboat, evening bonfires. $80–$130; full breakfast. MC, V. No smoking.
Ryan House. W4375 U.S. Hwy. 10, Durand 54737, tel. 715/672–8563. 1 double room with bath, 2 doubles share bath. Fireplace and TV in common room. $40– $60; full breakfast, afternoon refreshments. MC, V. No smoking. Closed Jan.–Mar.
St. Croix River Inn. 305 River St., Osceola 54020, tel. 715/294–4248 or 800/ 645–8820. 2 double rooms with baths, 5 suites. Air-conditioning, TV in 1 room, TV/VCR in 2 rooms, fireplace in 2 rooms, stereo/cassette player and whirlpool bath in rooms, robes for guests, grill and picnic table for guest use. $85–$200; full breakfast, afternoon refreshments. AE, MC, V. Smoking in lobby and game room only.

Door County

EPHRAIM INN 🦢
Rte. 42 (Box 247), Ephraim 54211, tel. 920/854–4515 or 800/622–2193

In the picture of his son that inn owner Tim Christofferson carries in his wallet, another man is included—the Wal-Mart photographer who took the picture (yup, the camera timer allowed him to join the son in the photo). Tim just wanted to make sure he remembered the guy. That's the kind of good humor Tim exudes, and inn guests feel it from the time they walk in the door. A former McDonald's marketing executive, Tim had always wanted his own business; he and his wife, Nancy, moved to Door County in 1979 when they bought Wilson's Ice Cream Parlor, overlooking the harbor in Ephraim's charming historic district. Then, in 1985, the big white house next door, where the town doctor, Dr. Sneeberger, had lived and practiced for 40 years, went up for sale. Tim and Nancy bought it and built a large addition that turned it into a sprawling horseshoe-shaped inn with a center cupola. Much to the dismay of their sons, Tim and Nancy sold Wilson's in 1987 (it's still in operation) to concentrate on the inn.

The Christoffersons live in most of the old main house; all of the 17 guest bedrooms are in the new addition, where such modern essentials as soundproofing, air-conditioning, and private baths were easy to install. Each room has its own motif, often Shaker-inspired, it shows up on the room's wooden key tags, the painted symbol on its door, and the hand-stenciled border on its ceiling. Shaker-style peg rails around the walls hold such decorative touches as dried flowers, grapevine wreaths, straw hats, and even chairs. The furniture is a mix of reproductions and antiques revealing the couple's preference for the simple, clean lines of country furniture.

The large common room with its harbor view brings guests together around a large fireplace or in a well-stocked library nook. Full breakfasts, served in three small dining areas, may include homemade granola, fresh-baked pastries, and an Ephraim Inn omelet, a quichelike dish of baked eggs, cheese, and spices.

The shorefront location, a decided asset, gives the inn wonderful water views and puts guests within walking distance not only of Ephraim's historic sights but also of an unspoiled beach just around a curve of the road. Not much farther up the road are Peninsula State Park and its fine 18-hole golf course. ♨

17 double rooms with baths. Air-conditioning, TV in rooms, beach across street. $79–$145; full breakfast. MC, V. No smoking, 2-night minimum.

GRIFFIN INN 🐦
11976 Mink River Rd., Ellison Bay 54210, tel. 920/845–4306

Converted from a private house to a summer hotel in 1921, Griffin Inn is a classic country retreat, on 5 acres of rolling lawn shaded by maple trees. Long verandas with porch swings and a gazebo give guests plenty of places to sit and enjoy the breeze. Besides the main building, a Dutch Colonial–style house built in 1910, there are two cottages on the property, each with two guest units.

For innkeepers Paul Ennis and family, who recently purchased the Griffin from Jim and Laurie Roberts (who now own the Whistling Swan in Fish Creek; *see below*), it's a case of having come full circle. A brother and sister-in-law had managed the property in the mid-'70s. When Ennis decided to return to his northeastern Wisconsin roots from Maryland where he'd been living, his search for a business to run ended when he learned the familiar old inn was available.

Though the bedrooms are fairly small, they have been comfortably furnished with a collection of pieces reflecting the tastes of the inn's various owners throughout the years.

Common rooms include the dining room, a downstairs living room with a large fieldstone fireplace where guests gather for popcorn every night, and a small library where guests can curl up on a love seat with a good book.

The cottages, which are open from May through October, are a bit more rustic, with open-beam ceilings, rough cedar walls, and ceiling fans. Cottage guests can either pick up a breakfast basket each morning or make arrangements to join the main-house guests for the dazzling gourmet breakfast always prepared from scratch. Fresh fruit and baked goods (scones, muffins, and breads) are always on the menu, along with a changing selection of temptations such as baby Dutch pancakes topped with lemon butter and cherry sauce, stuffed blueberry French toast, and made-to-order omelets.

Only two blocks from downtown Ellison Bay, the inn is within walking distance of the waterfront. It sits on a well-traveled bike route, and the Peninsula Cross-Country Ski Trail runs through the backyard. Guests often play badminton or croquet on the inn grounds, a sight that conjures up images of the inn's venerable role as a summer retreat. ♨ *8 double rooms and 2 triples share 2½ baths; 4 cottages each sleep 4 people. Air-conditioning in inn, TV in cottages. $79–$86; full breakfast for inn guests; Continental breakfast with full-breakfast option for cottage guests. No credit cards. No smoking, 2-night minimum weekends, 3-night minimum holidays.*

WHISTLING SWAN 🐦
4192 Main St. (Box 193), Fish Creek 54212, tel. 920/868–3442 or 888/277–4289, fax 920/868–1783

A fixture on Fish Creek's Main Street since 1907, what is now the Whistling Swan was originally built in 1887 in Marinette—22 mi due west, more or less, across the waters of Green Bay. Dr. Herman Welcker, a legendary figure in the history of tourism in Door County, had the white-frame Victorian towed across the ice to its present location, where it became part of a resort complex that also included the current White Gull Inn (*see below*).

Now meticulously restored, the inn features such touches as floral prints, brass fixtures, and claw-foot tubs, recalling the romance of that bygone era. Guests will find fresh flowers on their nightstands, too, along with complimentary bottles of spring water. An expanded Continental breakfast is served on the sunny, glass-enclosed porch during clement seasons; come winter, full breakfast becomes the rule. Afternoon tea is served year-round.

While owners Jim and Laurie Roberts are newcomers to the Whistling Swan—they purchased the property in 1996—they're no strangers to innkeeping, after having owned and operated the nearby Griffin Inn (*see above*) for the previous 10 years. In addition to elegant accommodations, they offer sophisticated women's fashions in their boutique on the building's main level. It's one of the many upscale specialty shops that make the neighborhood one of the peninsula's toniest. ◬ *4 double rooms with baths, 1 deluxe queen room with bath, 2 suites. Air-conditioning, cable TV, phone in rooms. $99–$159; expanded Continental breakfast (full breakfast in winter). AE, D, MC, V. No smoking, 2-night minimum weekends, 3-night minimum holidays.*

WHITE GULL INN ☞
4225 Main St. (Box 160), Fish Creek 54212, tel. 920/868–3517, fax 920/868–2367

One of the oldest lodging establishments in Door County, the White Gull Inn was founded in 1896 by a Dr. Welcker as a lodging for wealthy German immigrants who came to Fish Creek by steamer. Its current owner and manager, Andy Coulson, is a former journalist. He was traveling in Australia when a friend contacted him about joining a group of investors seeking to buy the White Gull. Andy said yes—on the condition he could run the place. The other partners happily agreed. One of Andy's first managerial decisions was to hire a new housekeeper, Jan; five years later, wedding bells happily rang.

The Coulsons have worked hard to maintain the original feel of the white-frame inn, with its inviting front porches (upstairs and down), gleaming hardwood floors covered with braided rugs, and country-style antiques. The main entry is the focus of activity; it's here that guests watch television or gather around the large fieldstone fireplace. Besides overnight guests, crowds of people visit the inn's restaurant, famous throughout Door County for its traditional fish boils, on Wednesday, Friday, Saturday, and Sunday nights in summer (Wednesday and Saturday in winter). The restaurant serves three meals a day; breakfast may include eggs Benedict, hash browns, or buttermilk pancakes.

The inn is perfectly situated: To the left is Sunset Beach Park; to the right, the charming shops of Fish Creek and then Peninsula State Park. Accommodations are spread around a number of buildings. The main house has several guest rooms, each with a comfortable wrought-iron or carved-wood bed and each decorated with antiques, some of them once owned by Dr. Welcker himself. Behind the inn is the Cliffhouse, whose two suites have fireplaces and lush furnishings; the inn also owns three nearby cottages, which make wonderful little family vacation homes. ◬ *6 double rooms with baths, 3 suites, 5 cottages each sleep 2–8 people. Restaurant, air-conditioning, cable TV, complimentary coffee, and newspaper each morning in rooms. $102–$270; breakfast not included. AE, D, DC, MC, V. No smoking, 2-night minimum weekends, 3-night minimum holidays.*

OTHER CHOICES

Barbican Guest House. 132 N. 2nd Ave., Sturgeon Bay 54235, tel. 920/743–4854. 18 suites. Air-conditioning, cable TV/VCR, fireplace, whirlpool bath, stereo, and refrigerator in suites. $120–$175; Continental breakfast. MC, V. 2-night minimum weekends, 3-night minimum holidays.

Eagle Harbor Inn. 9914 Water St. (Box 558), Ephraim 54211, tel. 920/854–2121 or 800/324–5427, fax 920/854–2121. 9 double rooms with bath, 16 1-bedroom suites, 16 2-bedrooms suites. Air-conditioning, cable TV, whirlpool bath in 1 room and all suites, sauna, lap pool, fitness center. $89–$189; full breakfast for inn guests; breakfast available at additional charge for suite guests. MC, V. No smoking, 2-night minimum weekends, 3-night minimum holidays.

French Country Inn of Ephraim. 3052 Spruce La. (Box 129), Ephraim 54211, tel. and fax 920/854–4001. 2 double rooms with baths, 5 doubles share 2 baths; 1 2-bedroom cottage. Ceiling fans. $62–$94; cottage $495–$595 per week; Continental breakfast, evening refreshments. No credit cards. No smoking, 2-night minimum weekends, 3-night minimum holidays.

Harbor House Inn. 12666 Rte. 42, Gills Rock 54210, tel. 920/854–5196. 12 double rooms with baths, 2 cottages each sleep 4. Air-conditioning, TVs, sauna, hot tub; private beach, bicycle rentals. $49–$109; Continental breakfast. AE, MC, V. No smoking.

Inn at Cedar Crossing. 336 Louisiana St., Sturgeon Bay 54235, tel. 920/743–4200. 9 double rooms with baths. Restaurant, air-conditioning, whirlpool bath in 5 rooms. $95–$155; Continental breakfast. AE, D, MC, V. No smoking, 2-night minimum weekends, 3-night minimum holidays.

Inn on Maple. 414 Maple Dr., Sister Bay 54234, tel. 920/854–5107. 5 double rooms with baths, 2 singles with baths. Ceiling fans. $55–$75; full breakfast. MC, V. No smoking, 2-night minimum, 3-night minimum holidays.

Scofield House. 908 Michigan St. (Box 761), Sturgeon Bay 54235, tel. 920/743–7727 or 888/463–0204. 6 double rooms with baths. Air-conditioning, cable TV/VCR in 5 rooms, whirlpool bath in 5 rooms. $89–$190; full breakfast. No credit cards. No smoking, 2-night minimum, 3-night minimum holidays.

WYOMING
Jackson and Vicinity

NOWLIN CREEK INN ☜
660 E. Broadway (Box 2766), Jackson Hole 83001, tel. 307/733–0882 or 800/533–0882

If you ask who lives across the street from her B&B, Susan Nowlin replies "Nine thousand elk" without blinking an eye. The property fronts the National Elk Refuge, which partly explains why Susan and her husband, Mark, came up with the name for their new inn: Deep within the protected park lies Nowlin Creek, named to honor Mark's great-grandfather, the refuge's first superintendent. In fact, many aspects of Jackson Hole's past supply a kind of pleasing obbligato to this inn's distinctive character.

Near the entrance sits an antique wooden model of the town's central square. Throughout the rooms, vintage photographs depict Jackson Hole "before it had trees," as Susan puts it, when it was being settled and seeded by 1880s homesteaders. Out back on a broad patio, a huge cowboy-shape sign, which once pointed the way to a trading post on the town square, has been decked out in lights to provide funky illumination for the hot tub. Susan used to be an exhibition designer at the Smithsonian Institution in Washington, D.C., so it's easy to understand why this B&B has almost become a minimuseum of Jackson Hole history.

The inn—designed by Mark and Susan—is a two-story wood house with a lodgepole-pine railing and distinct echoes of Prairie School design. Susan has brought the outdoors into the living room by stenciling the unique rough-hewn fir floors with twining ivy borders. Windows are draped with curtains strung loosely on slender wrought-iron rods, also budding with leaves. The furnishings are sturdy and colorful: a supple teal leather sofa, end tables made by Susan and her daughters from weathered window frames, and a massive buffalo skull mounted on the wall.

Jackson Hole is the home for the nation's third-largest western-art market, and both Mark and Susan are active in the community as practicing artists (they also run a framing business). Throughout the rooms, Susan's drawings and handmade papers complement Audubon prints and etchings done by local artists, while Mark's sculptures adorn the grounds. They seem proudest of the trompe l'oeil wood-grained window casing Susan painted around several of the guest-room windows, which have even duped building contractors.

Above the landing, a beveled-glass window casts rainbows across the hall walls. In the pleasant dining area, breakfast may feature huevos rancheros, caramelized French toast served with sour cream and blueberries, or puffy Dutch pancakes with sautéed apples.

There are five spacious guest accommodations in the house: two downstairs and three up, each named for a regional lake. The Solitude Suite has a western motif with a lodgepole-pine bed, fireplace, and shadow boxes on the walls holding an array of miscellany from poker "death hands" to a collection of arrowheads. In the Goodwin Room, a mirror-top dresser matches the antique carved-oak high-back bed. Windows face toward Snow King Mountain's ski runs. The most interesting "room," however, might be the authentic sheepherder's wagon located behind the house, which guests may choose as their sleeping quarters in warm weather. There's also a guest cabin—an historic structure with two bedrooms that can comfortably sleep five in pine pole beds. It has a full kitchen, telephone, TV/VCR, and laundry facilities, but breakfast isn't included. △ *4 double rooms with baths, 1 suite, 1 2-bedroom cabin. Fireplace in 2 rooms and suite; kitchen, TV/VCR, telephone, and washer/dryer in cabin; outdoor library; hot tub; activities arranged. $105–$270; full breakfast (except for cabin). AE, MC, V.*

PAINTED PORCH ☞
Off Teton Village Rd. (Box 6955), Jackson Hole 83001, tel. 307/733–1981

A stay at this cherry-color farmhouse on a large wooded lot is a retreat into an atmosphere sparked with decorative whimsy, a reflection of hostess Martha MacEachern's warm and imaginative personality. Trompe l'oeil paintings, 1950s cowboy decor, and antique knickknacks are just some of the touches she uses to bring a smile to guests' faces.

A rustic-style flagstone hallway with lemon sponge-painted walls leads to the Garden Cottage Suite—one of two cheery and imaginative guest accommodations, each of which comes with its own porch and private entrance. Both bedroom and parlor positively bloom with artful combinations of Ralph Lauren fabrics in chambray, ticking stripes, and jewel-tone florals. The bedroom has a sage Berber carpet. Everywhere are clever trompe l'oeil–painted touches: a dresser whose drawers spill faux pearls, neckties, suspenders, and a delicate pocket-watch; a fool-the-eye coat rack near the door; faux flowers hanging from nails above the bed; and a painted chipmunk scurrying along the baseboard. The parlor window seat is plump with pillows beneath tab-top floral curtains on willow-branch rods—a relaxing spot from which to study the eye-filling vistas of the Grand Tetons.

Aficionados of "cow-camp" kitsch will want to stay in the Cowboy Room, with its covered-wagon lamps, bronco-shape sconces, "branded" wood furniture, and cowboy-and-Indian-pattern fabrics. Hidden within a peeled-log armoire are a TV and coffeemaker. Although the room is given a trendy spin, Gene Autry would feel right at home.

The smaller Cabin and Margaret's Room have their own charms. The Cabin has a dresser with a scene of a bear in a hammock, and special tile in the bathroom is also of bears. Margaret's Room has a blue ceiling dotted with clouds, white wicker furniture, and bright comforter and pillows.

Sharing the common areas—a tiny, square family room and a living room, with hardwood floors and a fireplace with a screen that's a silhouette of the house—Martha, her husband, Mark, and their grade-school-age son enjoy an easy rapport with guests. On any given morning, the breakfast table, positioned near a window seat filled with pillows, may be set with the MacEacherns' "bucking bronco" wedding china, with matching brown bandanna napkins. Martha's breakfasts are just as unusual, ranging from Grand Marnier French toast to her gingerbread pancakes, a fragrant recipe that once brought a moose to the kitchen window.

Guests may fish, ski at the nearby resort, enjoy the rest in a hammock, or catch some more worldly pleasures in Jackson, 8 mi distant. A word of warning: Don't head into town for a movie matinee when the cattle herds are being moved from their winter to summer pastures; there's no way you'll be on time. △ *3 double* *rooms with bath, 1 suite. Air-conditioning, TVs, coffeemakers, turndown service, ski storage. $110–$170; full breakfast. MC, V.*

TETON TREE HOUSE ☙
Heck of a Hill Rd. (Box 550), Wilson 83014, tel. 307/733–3233

A little bit of childhood fancy is mixed in with a lot of adult comfort at Teton Tree House, ¾ mi from Wilson. Without a doubt, a sense of quiet escape is palpable from the moment guests turn onto the steep, tree-lined road that leads to the parking area. From there, 95 steps climb gently through a forest of evergreens to the angular, multilevel wood home, with jutting balconies and wide, recessed windows.

Denny Becker and wife Chris designed and built this home for their family. It became a bed-and-breakfast when Denny, once a river guide, decided to try his hand at being a full-time host. When she isn't playing hostess, or being mom to their two daughters, Chris teaches at the local elementary school.

From the tree house's entry level, a spiral wood staircase curls gracefully up from the two-story Grand Room. Here, leather-covered earth-tone sofas and chairs have been gathered around an enormous stucco-and-brick fireplace fitted with a wood-burning stove. The white walls and neutral striped carpet are brightened by wood-framed windows, golden peeled-log support beams, and a collection of vivid scenic and wildlife photos. Fitted with a piano, games, and shelves full of books on varied topics, this room is an ideal place to while away part of an evening.

Guest rooms are on three of the house's four levels. Each bedroom is spacious and affords a forest or valley view through immaculate windows curtained, in some cases, only by leaves and branches. Private decks enhance the tree-house effect. However, there is plenty of luxury here: down comforters, silky cotton sheets, and bathroom baskets brimming with upscale soaps and lotions. In summer, bunches of wildflowers, such as paintbrush, arnica, and columbine, gathered from the hillside around the house, add delicate touches of color.

Denny himself made the long table where breakfast is served on glossy stoneware—handiwork of the potter down the road a ways. Cream of the West, a whole-grain, hot cereal, is always on the menu along with plenty of fresh fruit and surprises like strawberry juice, Amish friendship bread, whole-wheat pancakes, or deep-dish French toast.

Feeders hanging under the eaves guarantee birds at breakfast as well as the occasional snowshoe rabbit nibbling birdseed on the ground, and a few reckless squirrels who leap wildly from the house walls to raid the feeders. △ *6 double rooms with baths. Outdoor hot tub. $105–$160; full breakfast. MC, V.*

OTHER CHOICES
Inn at Buffalo Fork. Hwy. 26/287 (Box 311), Moran 83013, tel. 307/543–2010, fax 307/543–0935. 3 rooms with queen-size beds and baths, 1 room with 2 twin beds and bath, 1 king suite with bath. Outdoor hot tub, cross-country skiing, snowmobiling, fly fishing guide service, reservations service for area activities, horse boarding. $100–$165; full breakfast, snacks. MC, V.
Moose Meadows B&B. 1225 Green La. (Box 371), Wilson 83014, tel. 307/733–9510, fax 307/739–3053. 1 room with queen-size bed and two single beds with bath, 1 room with queen-size bed and bath, 1 room with queen-size bed and 2 single beds and 1 double room share 1 bath. TV, fireplace, and woodstove in living room; outdoor hot tub; ski packages. $65–$135; full breakfast, evening snacks. D, DC, MC, V.

Sassy Moose Inn. 3895 Miles Rd. at Tucker Ranch (HC 362), Jackson 83001, tel. 307/733–1277 or 800/356–1277, fax 307/739–0793. 5 double rooms with baths. Fireplace in 2 rooms, hot tub in 1 room. June–Sept. $85–$139; full breakfast, afternoon and evening light snacks. AE, D, MC, V.

Twin Trees, A Bed and Breakfast. 575 S. Willow St. (Box 7533), Jackson 83002, tel. 307/739–9737 or 800/728—7337, fax 307/734–1266. 3 double rooms with baths. Ski storage, outdoor hot tub, reservations service for area activities. $105–$115; full breakfast, afternoon snacks. AE, MC, V. No smoking.

Wildflower Inn. Shooting Star La. (Box 11000), Jackson 83002, tel. 307/733–4710, fax 307/739–0914. 5 double rooms with baths. TVs, alarm clocks, hot tub, pond, horses. $120–$170; full breakfast. MC, V.

Window on the Winds. 10151 Hwy. 191 (Box 996), Pinedale 82941, tel. 307/367–2600, fax 307/367–2395. 4 double rooms share 2 baths. Fireplace in common room, hot tub, horse boarding with advance notice. $60–$70; full breakfast, afternoon snacks, evening vegetarian meals with advance notice. MC, V.

Northern Wyoming

SPAHN'S BIG HORN MOUNTAIN B&B 🐾
70 Upper Hideaway La., off I—90 (Box 579), Big Horn 82833, tel. 307/674–8150

In the Rocky Mountains, 15 mi from Sheridan, Spahn's Big Horn Mountain B&B is on a pine-clustered hillside with 100-mi views spreading across a pastoral valley patterned, like a crazy quilt, with buck-rail fences.

Host Ron Spahn brings eclectic experience to his role as innkeeper. He has been a geologist, a coal miner, an attorney, and even a ranger at Yellowstone National Park. But occupation aside, it is his zest for the mountain lifestyle that makes him the consummate host in this setting. Ron, wife Bobbie, and their teenage son and daughter share equally in cooking and conversing.

According to Ron, an element of fantasy accompanies living in the mountains of the American West—a fantasy he intends to fulfill for his guests. Everything here—such as the solar-powered, hand-peeled log structures built by the Spahns themselves—is part of the rustic experience.

There are two guest rooms in the main house, a log lodge with three-story living room and multilevel decks under a ruddy metal roof. The bedrooms have tongue-and-groove woodwork and peeled-log beams; ruffled curtains contrast gently with the wooden walls. Both rooms have extremely comfortable lodgepole-pine beds.

On the hillside above the house, sheltered by evergreen trees, are two cabins. The Homestead Cabin, originally built by the Spahns as a family retreat, is compact but complete, with a tidy kitchen, wood-burning stove, living room, bedroom, and kid-size loft. The other cabin, dubbed the Eagle's Nest, is romantically furnished with white wicker, ruffled curtains, and colorful hand-stitched quilts.

Two evenings a week, Ron leads moose-photo safaris, which include a steak cookout, the promise of an unforgettable sunset, and wildlife aplenty—if not moose, then certainly deer, elk, and an abundance of birds. As for daytime activities on the mountain, the Spahns have plenty of suggestions and may even be persuaded to come along.

Breakfast is served family-style on the deck. As often as not, binoculars for wildlife-watching are set side-by-side with an array of condiments. In cooler weather, guests eat in the dining room under a ceiling beamed in a wagon-spoke pattern. Morning meals hark back to simplicity: pancakes, scrambled eggs and sausage, fresh fruit, and lots of good, hot coffee. ▲ *2 double rooms with baths, 2 cabins. Fireplace and piano in main house, recreation and tour packages with full meals extra. $65–$120; full breakfast. MC, V.*

OTHER CHOICES

Blue Barn. 304 Hwy. 335 (Box 416), Big Horn 82833, tel. and fax 307/672–2381. 3 double rooms with baths. Outdoor hot tub, horse boarding, guided hiking, fly-fishing and mountain-biking packages. $75–$90; full breakfast. MC, V.

Cheyenne River Ranch. 1031 Steinle Rd., Douglas 82633, tel. 307/358–2380. 2 double rooms share bath, 2 bunkhouse cabins. Pool, campfire meals, horseback trail riding, weeklong cattle drives in summer. 65–$75; full breakfast, lunches and dinners offered. No credit cards. 3-night minimum; weekly and family rates available.

Cloud Peak Inn. 590 N. Burritt Rd., Buffalo 82834, tel. 307/684–5794 or 800/715–5794, fax 307/684–7653. 3 double rooms with baths, 2 doubles share bath. TV, fireplace in common area, whirlpool tub, mountain-biking and photography tours available. June–Sept., $45–$75; full breakfast, lunch and dinner by arrangement (extra). AE, MC, V.

Parson's Pillow Bed and Breakfast. 1202 14th St., Cody 82414, tel. 307/587–2382 or 800/377–2348. 1 double room with bath, 3 rooms with queen-size bed and baths. TV in living room, piano. $50–$99; full breakfast, evening snacks and beverages. MC, V.

Southern Wyoming

FERRIS MANSION 🦜
607 W. Maple St., Rawlins 82301, tel. 307/324–3961

This three-story, multigabled Queen Anne–style mansion with encircling porch, bay windows, and conical-roofed tower was built in 1903 by Julia Ferris, the widow of a prominent Rawlins mining magnate. She lived in it until her death in 1931. During the 1940s the elegant house was divided into apartments, which, decade by decade, fell into disrepair. In 1979, when David and Janice Lubbers bought the mansion, it was a mishmash of shag carpeting, metallic wallpaper, and psychedelic-accented "crash pads." Although it seemed impossible, not to mention expensive, Janice was determined to restore and refurbish the house as a B&B.

By 1986, the Lubbers were renting just one bedroom. Today, the house reflects their labors of love, with four heirloom-filled guest rooms. The common areas gleam with polished woodwork and antique lamplight and with windows framed by wide lace curtains.

The bedrooms are on the second floor, up an oak staircase that had been removed and discarded before the Lubbers pieced it together, something like a jigsaw puzzle, and had it reinstalled.

In the Lavender Room, the bed—attractively covered in a spread made of antique handkerchiefs—fills the round tower bay window, set with stained-glass panels from a church in Minnesota. A fireplace is tiled in muted green. Above it a rectangular mirror tops the carved mantel. The Blue Room has rich paisley linens, and its window overlooks the tall porch roof. The Rose Room is shaded and subdued, with an ornate bed carved with flowers. In the Gold Room, a high shelf near the ceiling is filled with intriguing bric-a-brac. Each of the guest rooms has an electric mattress pad to warm the bed. On the landing between the rooms, women's hats add splashes of color and charm to the walls.

For sing-alongs and lovers of old-time music, the downstairs foyer holds a player grand piano and a collection of more than 100 piano rolls. A gingerbread arch separates the foyer from the formal parlor, where soft teal walls are enlivened by a red-velvet sofa and a pink-tile fireplace. Pocket doors open on to a bay-windowed side parlor furnished in white wicker. The side parlor and the adjacent bird's-eye maple–paneled library alternate as the inn's breakfast site.

Breakfast itself is a sampler's dream. There are always homemade breads—anything from wheat to orange–chocolate chip—that guests can warm up in a collection of antique toasters. Jars of orange marmalade and chokecherry jelly add colorful accents on the lace-draped table. There is granola with cream, plenty of fresh fruit, and the temptation of chewy caramel buns. △ *4 double rooms with baths. TV in rooms, fireplace in 2 rooms. $55–$65; Continental breakfast, D, MC, V.*

OTHER CHOICES

A. Drummond's Ranch B&B. 399 Happy Jack Rd., Cheyenne 82007, tel. and fax 307/634–6042. 1 room with queen-size bed, 1 double and 1 triple share bath, 1 suite. Phones, terry cloth robes; outdoor hot tub, fireplace, kitchen, and steam sauna in suite; horse boarding. $60–$150; full breakfast, evening desserts and beverages; dinner and trail lunches extra. MC, V.

Adventurers' Country B&B at Raven Cry Ranch. 3803 I–80 South Service Rd., Cheyenne 82001, tel. and fax 307/632–4087. 4 double rooms with baths, 1 3-room suite. Jet tub in suite. TV/VCR in common area, high-mountain horseback trips, special-event and seasonal packages. $60–$125; full breakfast, dinners and trail lunches extra. No credit cards.

Blackbird Inn. 1101 11th St., Wheatland 82201, tel. 307/322–4540. 4 double rooms share 2 baths, 1 suite. TV\VCR in common area, fireplace in library, bicycles. $45–$55; full breakfast in summer and on winter weekends, Continental breakfast on winter weekdays, afternoon snacks and beverages. No credit cards.

Porch Swing B&B. 712 E. 20th St., Cheyenne 82001, tel. and fax 307/778–7182. 1 double room with bath, 2 doubles share bath. TV\VCR in living room, woodstoves in dining room and enclosed porch. $42–$66; full breakfast, afternoon and evening snacks. MC, V.

Rainsford Inn. 219 E. 18th St., Cheyenne 82001, tel. 307/638–2337, fax 307/634–4506. 5 double rooms, 2 rooms share bath. Gas fireplace in 1 room. $65–$100; full breakfast. AE, D, DC, MC, V.

RESERVATIONS SERVICES

B&B Western Adventures (Box 20972, Billings, MT, tel. 406/259–7993). **Jackson Hole B&B Association** (Box 2766, Jackson Hole 83001, tel. 800/542–2632). **WHOA–Wyoming Homestate Outdoor Adventures** (1031 Steinle Rd., Douglas 82633, tel. 307/358–2380).

NOTES

NOTES

NOTES

NOTES

NOTES

NOTES

Looking for a different kind of vacation?

Fodor's makes it easy with a full line of guidebooks to suit
a variety of interests—from sports and adventure to romance
to family fun.

At bookstores everywhere.
www.fodors.com

Fodor's Travel Publications

Available at bookstores everywhere. For descriptions of all our titles and a key to Fodor's guidebook series, visit www.fodors.com/books

Gold Guides
U.S.

Alaska
Arizona
Boston
California
Cape Cod, Martha's Vineyard, Nantucket
The Carolinas & Georgia
Chicago
Colorado

Florida
Hawai'i
Las Vegas, Reno, Tahoe
Los Angeles
Maine, Vermont, New Hampshire
Maui & Lāna'i
Miami & the Keys
New England

New Orleans
New York City
Oregon
Pacific North Coast
Philadelphia & the Pennsylvania Dutch Country
The Rockies
San Diego
San Francisco

Santa Fe, Taos, Albuquerque
Seattle & Vancouver
The South
U.S. & British Virgin Islands
USA
Virginia & Maryland
Washington, D.C.

Foreign

Australia
Austria
The Bahamas
Belize & Guatemala
Bermuda
Canada
Cancún, Cozumel, Yucatán Peninsula
Caribbean
China
Costa Rica
Cuba
The Czech Republic & Slovakia
Denmark

Eastern & Central Europe
Europe
Florence, Tuscany & Umbria
France
Germany
Great Britain
Greece
Hong Kong
India
Ireland
Israel
Italy
Japan

London
Madrid & Barcelona
Mexico
Montréal & Québec City
Moscow, St. Petersburg, Kiev
The Netherlands, Belgium & Luxembourg
New Zealand
Norway
Nova Scotia, New Brunswick, Prince Edward Island
Paris
Portugal
Provence & the Riviera

Scandinavia
Scotland
Singapore
South Africa
South America
Southeast Asia
Spain
Sweden
Switzerland
Thailand
Toronto
Turkey
Vienna & the Danube Valley
Vietnam

Special-Interest Guides

Adventures to Imagine
Alaska Ports of Call
Ballpark Vacations
The Best Cruises
Caribbean Ports of Call
The Complete Guide to America's National Parks
Europe Ports of Call
Family Adventures
Fodor's Gay Guide to the USA

Fodor's How to Pack
Great American Learning Vacations
Great American Sports & Adventure Vacations
Great American Vacations
Great American Vacations for Travelers with Disabilities
Halliday's New Orleans Food Explorer

Healthy Escapes
Kodak Guide to Shooting Great Travel Pictures
National Parks and Seashores of the East
National Parks of the West
Nights to Imagine
Orlando Like a Pro
Rock & Roll Traveler Great Britain and Ireland

Rock & Roll Traveler USA
Sunday in San Francisco
Walt Disney World for Adults
Weekends in New York
Wendy Perrin's Secrets Every Smart Traveler Should Know
Worlds to Imagine

Fodor's Special Series

Fodor's Best Bed & Breakfasts

America
California
The Mid-Atlantic
New England
The Pacific Northwest
The South
The Southwest
The Upper Great Lakes

Compass American Guides

Alaska
Arizona
Boston
Chicago
Coastal California
Colorado
Florida
Hawai'i
Hollywood
Idaho
Las Vegas
Maine
Manhattan
Minnesota
Montana
New Mexico
New Orleans
Oregon
Pacific Northwest
San Francisco
Santa Fe
South Carolina
South Dakota
Southwest
Texas
Underwater Wonders of the National Parks
Utah
Virginia
Washington
Wine Country
Wisconsin
Wyoming

Citypacks

Amsterdam
Atlanta
Berlin
Boston
Chicago
Florence
Hong Kong
London
Los Angeles
Miami
Montréal
New York City
Paris

Prague
Rome
San Francisco
Sydney
Tokyo
Toronto
Venice
Washington, D.C.

Exploring Guides

Australia
Boston & New England
Britain
California
Canada
Caribbean
China
Costa Rica
Cuba
Egypt
Florence & Tuscany
Florida
France
Germany
Greek Islands
Hawai'i
India
Ireland
Israel
Italy
Japan
London
Mexico
Moscow & St. Petersburg
New York City
Paris
Portugal
Prague
Provence
Rome
San Francisco
Scotland
Singapore & Malaysia
South Africa
Spain
Thailand
Turkey
Venice
Vietnam

Flashmaps

Boston
New York
San Francisco
Washington, D.C.

Fodor's Cityguides

Boston
New York
San Francisco

Fodor's Gay Guides

Amsterdam
Los Angeles & Southern California
New York City
Pacific Northwest
San Francisco and the Bay Area
South Florida
USA

Karen Brown Guides

Austria
California
England B&Bs
England, Wales & Scotland
France B&Bs
France Inns
Germany
Ireland
Italy B&Bs
Italy Inns
Portugal
Spain
Switzerland

Languages for Travelers (Cassette & Phrasebook)

French
German
Italian
Spanish

Mobil Travel Guides

America's Best Hotels & Restaurants
Arizona
California and the West
Florida
Great Lakes
Major Cities
Mid-Atlantic
Northeast
Northwest and Great Plains
Southeast
Southern California
Southwest and South Central

Pocket Guides

Acapulco
Aruba
Atlanta
Barbados
Beijing
Berlin
Budapest
Dublin
Honolulu

Jamaica
London
Mexico City
New York City
Paris
Prague
Puerto Rico
Rome
San Francisco
Savannah & Charleston
Shanghai
Sydney
Washington, D.C.

Rivages Guides

Bed and Breakfasts of Character and Charm in France
Hotels and Country Inns of Character and Charm in France
Hotels and Country Inns of Character and Charm in Italy
Hotels of Character and Charm in Paris
Hotels of Character and Charm in Portugal
Hotels of Character and Charm in Spain
Wines & Vineyards of Character and Charm in France

Short Escapes

Britain
France
Near New York City
New England

Fodor's Sports

Golf Digest's Places to Play (USA)
Golf Digest's Places to Play in the Southeast
Golf Digest's Places to Play in the Southwest
Skiing USA
USA Today The Complete Four Sport Stadium Guide

Fodor's upCLOSE Guides

California
Europe
France
Great Britain
Ireland
Italy
London
Los Angeles
Mexico
New York City
Paris
San Francisco

WHEREVER YOU TRAVEL, *H*ELP IS NEVER FAR AWAY.

From planning your trip to

providing travel assistance along

the way, American Express®

Travel Service Offices are

always there to help

you do more.

do more AMERICAN EXPRESS
Travel

www.americanexpress.com/travel

American Express Travel Service Offices
are located throughout America.
For the office nearest you, call 1-800-AXP-3429.